1951

FOURTH SERIES

1957

Best AMERICAN Plays

EDITED WITH AN INTRODUCTION BY

John Gassner

Crown Publishers, Inc., NEW YORK

© 1958, BY CROWN PUBLISHERS, INC.

LIBRARY OF CONGRESS CATALOG CARD NUMBER: 57-12830

ISBN: 0-517-504367

NOTE: All plays contained in this volume are fully protected under the copyright laws of the United States of America, the British Empire, including the Dominion of Canada, and all other countries of the Copyright Union. Permission to reproduce, wholly or in part, must be obtained from the copyright owners or their agents.

PRINTED IN THE UNITED STATES OF AMERICA

20   19   18   17   16   15   14   13   12

In Memory of PHYLLIS ANDERSON

WHO LED A NEW GENERATION OF PLAYWRIGHTS TO THE STAGE

BUT WAS TAKEN AWAY FROM IT HERSELF

AND FROM HER MANY DEVOTED FRIENDS

ON NOVEMBER 28, 1956

CONTENTS

PREFACE

The well-known relentlessness of time imposes periodic obligations on an anthologist whose good and ill fortune it is to reckon with the flux of theatrical production. My last *Best Plays of the American Theatre* carried us into the 1951-1952 Broadway season, and the five-year inventory that has become customary in the Crown Publishers "best plays" venture, of which I am the editor, required a new volume at the close of the 1956-1957 season. Here it is, after a decent cooling-off period and an editorially convenient interval.

Best Plays of the Modern American Theatre: Fourth Series is actually the fifth volume in the series because the Crown compilations covering the quarter of a century since the 1930-1931 season are preceded by another anthology, the "Early Series." It contains plays staged during the preceding period of some fifteen seasons, designated as the "formative years" of the modern American drama. With the new volume, the Crown Publishers collection has now reached a formidable total of 96 plays. And as if this total were not large enough to impress the editor, if no one else, there is the recent tangential *20 Best European Plays on the American Stage* to be included in the reckoning. Since it presents not only translations but also adaptations by S. N. Behrman, Sidney Howard, and others, this volume boosts the total to over 100. The inescapable thought that the quantitative record is no measure of the qualitative one need not intimidate us. It need only chasten us.

As for our new volume, it is being presented with the usual apologies for inability to obtain some clearances. The complete text of O'Neill's posthumously produced *Long Day's Journey Into Night* was unavailable for reproduction and *The Diary of Anne Frank* was under litigation when this volume was being prepared. Both plays, it is hoped, will appear in the next "best plays" collection. Mr. John Patrick had private reasons for declining requests for his attractive dramatization of *The Teahouse of the August Moon*, and Mr. Clifford Odets had no final version of his piquant Noah play, *The Flowering Peach*, for publication. Other possible apologies would be supererogatory if they referred to matters of taste, and impudent if they concerned the plays for which my request for republication permission was granted.

Nor were these works intended to have their maximum effect outside the theatre, without the ministrations of their authors' collaborators, the actors. The private act of reading the text of a play must always be an act, if not indeed a *feat*, of the imagination. Nor is it my intention to conclude with any excuse, for the brief period under review has provided plays of considerable variety, range, and interest.

It has been possible to represent the work of the leading playwrights of the 1950's, Tennessee Williams, Arthur Miller, and William Inge, each of whom appears with *two* plays in the anthology, as well as the work of more recently arrived authors such as Robert Anderson and Michael Gazzo. And although the harvest from an earlier generation has been smaller than in previous periods, it has been possible to include plays by two of its most congenial survivors, Thornton Wilder and George S. Kaufman, and by its departed giant, Eugene O'Neill (whose latest play to appear on Broadway, *A Moon for the Misbegotten*, is included). It is a comfort, too, to be able to represent our late citizen-by-adoption, John Van Druten, with *I Am a Camera*, one of his most substantial plays. I have also found it possible to do justice to the veins of comedy assiduously worked by our playwrights, and the book contains such varied comic matter as *The Matchmaker*, *The Fourposter*, *The Solid Gold Cadillac*, *No Time for Sergeants*, *The Seven Year Itch* and, with some somber overtones from the heartstrings of Mr. Inge's talent, *Bus Stop*. All these were certified as entertaining pieces on the stage. And works of the period variously expressive of insight and reflection are present in even greater measure. A far from trivial theatre is represented by such dramas as *The Crucible*, *A View from the Bridge*, *Cat on a Hot Tin Roof*, *Picnic*, *Tea and Sympathy*, *The Rose Tattoo*, *A Moon for the Misbegotten*, *A Hatful of Rain*, *The Caine Mutiny Court-*

Martial, and *I Am a Camera.* If their substance or point of view is not invariably beyond criticism any more than their style or technique is, one thing is certain. The plays represent a theatre that has commanded interest and support at home and respect abroad. Added to the aforementioned comedies, they should provide an ample experience of contemporary American theatre. For the studious reader, besides, this volume provides some special features—the amplified version of *A View from the Bridge* now in use in our community and university theatres, and Mr. Williams' original last act for *Cat on a Hot Tin Roof,* added to the Broadway version.

As usual, I am indebted to my wife, Mollie Gassner, and to Crown Publishers and its editor, Herbert Michelman, for making this collection possible, as well as to the friendly publishers and authors of the individual plays.

JOHN GASSNER
March 1958

AND STILL IT MOVES

By JOHN GASSNER

At the beginning of the present decade the present viewer-with-alarm was moved to write a funereal essay entitled "Entropy in the Theatre." It seemed to him that, after the brief creative spurt between 1945 and 1949 that gave us Tennessee Williams and Arthur Miller, energy had started running downhill in American playwriting. Certainly there was little evidence of momentum or clear direction, and the first few seasons of the new decade verified my unflattering prognosis. But evidently there is much risk in short-term predictions about the American theatre, which according to reasonable expectations should be gasping out its life by now instead of enjoying better health than those giants of mass-communication, the motion pictures and television.

The evidence of renewed vitality accumulated gradually, and it was all the more surprising in view of the inflationary character of production costs in the professional theatre. It is possible to conclude, then, that the cumbersome old institution has resources of strength we are chronically inclined to underestimate. And no doubt the most valuable of these is an independence and integrity the mass-communication media conspicuously lack. Fundamentally unintimidated by the pressure of bigots, advertising sponsors, and the need to be all things to all men, women, and children, the professional stage continued to allow its playwrights to have their say or speak their piece. As a result, the theatre retained its appeal to a comparatively intelligent and independent clientele. And when the writer is not under constant pressure to curb his spirit, he is apt to at least deviate into passionate or lively writing. Provided he has "talent," of course. But, then, it is no small mystery how a writer can discover what he can do if he is hobbled from the start, as he is apt to be by censors and by the pragmatists

sitting in judgment over him in studios.

The latter are, of course, his *employers,* and only in the theatre does the dramatic writer have no employers. Nobody can draw up rules for him to obey, and he is able to leave the imprint of his personality upon his work; neither his success nor his failure is faceless. This independence, it is true, also allows him to be poor as well as free. Moreover, it is conceivable that all writers some of the time and some writers all of the time will prove foolish or even corrupt or "decadent" in the exercise of their prerogatives. These are the risks of license that liberty must take in an imperfect world and a transitional age. Clearly, the theatre takes these risks, while the mass-communication media do not, though there is this paradox to be noted: their neutralism is actually partisanship—it is propaganda for the commonplace.

It is in an atmosphere conducive to individuality and personal intensities that the theatre of the 1950's managed to gather momentum after an interval of declining vigor. And there is surely no better way of ascertaining whether or not this was the case than to review the work of some of the competent playwrights of the period.

It may not be cricket to write into our record O'Neill's plays, but it is undeniable that fine productions of several in the 1950's, beginning with José Quintero's revival of *The Iceman Cometh* (see *Best American Plays: Third Series*) at his Greenwich Village theatre, Circle-in-the-Square, are to be credited to the period. The same gifted director's production of *Long Day's Journey Into Night* in the 1956-57 season brought playwriting by the generation of the 1920's back to its all but vanished eminence. No other American play of the period, moreover, approached O'Neill's unique combination of insight and compassion, and I know of no other new dramatic work from other countries that approximated its unsophisticated but penetrating power. If the play was trans-

* For further comment on individual authors and plays the reader is referred to the introductions to the individual plays.

parently autobiographical, it was also more than the story of a greatly troubled family. It was a testament to the growth of tragic awareness on the part of America's foremost tragedian. Without O'Neill's sense of tragedy, our theatre would have remained largely trivial during the years when he was alive and well. The posthumous production of *Long Day's Journey Into Night*, written in 1940, made his tragic power no less apparent. But his art was at the same time more humane and persuasive than it had ever been before.

The appearance of *A Moon for the Misbegotten*, a somewhat later work the Theatre Guild had hoped to bring to Broadway in 1947, was not as warmly received. It surprised the public with O'Neill's curious tenderness for his grotesque figures, and drew the charge of sentimentality from some reviewers. These failed to distinguish the considerable difference there is between compassionate and false characterization. Nor was it possible to say that O'Neill had yielded to facile optimism; he was still tragedian enough not to let his pity for the characters relieve them from the doom of tragic isolation. It was chiefly a deficiency of finesse and an excess of labor that hobbled the production as a whole and taxed the patience of some of O'Neill's admirers. At the same time, it was still evident that this was no ordinary work; *A Moon for the Misbegotten* would be towering and weighty work in any man's theatre. There is a greatness in its very defects which it would be wrong to ignore anywhere, and especially in a book that includes some very light contrivances for the sake of balance and lacks, if through no fault of the anthologist, the unquestionably superior *Long Day's Journey Into Night*.

The O'Neill revival in the 1950's was an important feature of the period. There were weeks in the spring of 1957 when it was possible to see five of the deceased master's plays in Manhattan, if we count the musical version of *Anna Christie* given under the unedifying title of *New Girl in Town*. A frivolous theatre could have taken to the latter, but only a public accustomed to strenuous playgoing could be presented with *Long Day's Journey Into Night* and *A Moon for the Misbegotten*. That such a public existed at all was itself a tribute to O'Neill, whose influence on our theatre had started to make itself felt

more than thirty years before. He had taught American producers and playgoers to take a serious view of the drama while he was alive; and his sultry genius continued to teach them the same lesson after his death. It remains to be added that his last plays showed the playwright inclining toward the naturalism he had disavowed in the 1920's when he was writing expressionist pieces such as *The Emperor Jones*, *The Hairy Ape*, and *The Great God Brown*. And in returning to realistic technique he was a more typical American playwright than he would have liked to be. His power in such pieces as *The Iceman Cometh*, *Long Day's Journey Into Night*, and *A Moon for the Misbegotten* lay where his observation and conviction took him. He was not alone among serious playwrights in showing that naturalism did not have to be arid and might even be poetic.

If the American playgoer of this period was disposed to accept O'Neill's somber playwriting, however, some of the credit should also go to the younger playwrights. And among these, Tennessee Williams and Arthur Miller, who had invigorated our theatre in the 1940's, continued to startle or stimulate the playgoer. From Williams came *The Rose Tattoo* in 1951, *Camino Real* in 1953, and *Cat on a Hot Tin Roof* in 1955, each work a minor explosion in the theatre. And Miller contributed *The Crucible* in 1953 and *A View from the Bridge* in 1955 to the worthy enterprise of disturbing the equilibrium of the Broadway clientele.

The range of talent represented by *The Rose Tattoo* and *Cat on a Hot Tin Roof* in the present anthology is not the most remarkable fact about Tennessee Williams' playwriting. But it is significant nonetheless in indicating that his sympathies were not exclusively reserved for the greatly tormented and the hopelessly defeated. Neither Serafina delle Rose in the earlier drama nor Margaret, "Maggie the Cat," does anything but insistently, if naïvely, assert the life-spirit. I believe it is necessary to stress the "health" in these plays because it has been so fashionable both in commending and condemning the plays to stress the "disease" in them. And it is a gain, rather than a loss, in dramatic art that affirmation comes hard in the plays and health is something to be gained or defended with strenuous exertions. Williams continued to manifest a remarkable dramatic talent and to extend its range in the 1950's even if his power to disturb remained greater than his power or disposition to heal.

How are we to explain the impression of significance Williams was able to create with these plays? This was surely not the result of the "bigness" of the themes, the "social significance" of the issues, or the universality of the external, of even the *internal,* conflicts. He was least successful with *Camino Real,* the play that spelled out "Significance" in capital letters and courted it with literary allusions. The other plays Williams contributed to our period could be charged with sensationalism or clinicism, and were so charged; moreover, their action was decidedly private in being confined to a special and obsessed character such as Serafina or a special and obsessed family such as Brick's. The tempestuously romantic Serafina of *The Rose Tattoo* could be looked upon, or looked *down* upon, as an exotic female. She seemed to combine a Latin temperament with the disposition of a virago and the sexual ambitions of a strumpet. And a London *Times* reviewer felt compelled to protest that *Cat on a Hot Tin Roof* did not move him, that the characters behaved with so much ferocity that they "cease to resemble human beings."

Yet there could be little doubt that both *The Rose Tattoo* and *Cat on a Hot Tin Roof* were not only extraordinarily vivid works of the dramatic imagination but that they possessed an immediate impact that makes plays seem important. To acknowledge the pungency and colloquial poetry of the writing is not enough. Nor is it sufficient to take note of the author's dramaturgic skill and apparently instinctive theatricality. It is instructive only to observe how well he can vary the tension of his scenes, "build" toward climaxes, and maneuver revelations of plot or character. The decisive strength of these plays, to which resistance could be an act of both intelligence and taste and yet remain quite futile, lay in the author's sensibility. His fascination with human perversity is part of it, but so is his fascination with humanity's impassioned vitality. His characters do not want to die emotionally (or physically), and the struggles of a Serafina in *The Rose Tattoo* or a Big Daddy in *Cat on a Hot Tin Roof* reach proportions diffi-

cult to discount with our esthetic or moral reservations. The author's sensibility creates extraordinarily vital characters along with the nightmares to which they succumb. And this sensibility calls into play judgment and measure—that is, the detachment as well as attachment, the objectivity as well as sympathy, of art. What he has called "the timeless world of a play" in his prefatory article to *The Rose Tattoo* is the timeless world of art in which it is possible to achieve clarity and order. It is also the world in which it is possible to transcend triviality—one's own and other people's.

In *The Rose Tattoo* and especially in *Cat on a Hot Tin Roof* Williams endeavored less to escape triviality than to transcend it. To a degree that will be in dispute so long as judgment is subjective, he succeeded. He did not, of course, translate his matter into the idiom of classic art. He remained in part a naturalist, and the pungency of his work has been known to affront as well as to attract playgoers. *The Rose Tattoo* is bizarre in motivation, a trifle scandalous in behavior, and sometimes tatterdemalion in humor—delightfully so, I believe, in the case of the lovable clown who carries the ostentatious name of Alvaro Mangiacavallo. And *Cat on a Hot Tin Roof,* called an "enthralling" play by one British reviewer, was described by another as an "ugly" one; and if that description strikes me as less than apt, it must nevertheless be conceded that life in Big Daddy's plantation-home in the Mississippi Delta is not exactly inspiring either. Nor is the piquant dialogue of Serafina or the scabrous speech of the Delta patriarch calculated to gratify ears accustomed to dulcet seminary tones. But it is completely as a man of his own time and place that Tennessee Williams made himself a vital force in the theatre of the period.

It is also completely as a man of his own time and place that Arthur Miller demonstrated himself, during the same years, to be a realist of a different temper and intention. His sympathies and moral fibre were especially apparent in *The Crucible* and *A View from the Bridge.* Although Miller, too, entertained poetic ambitions and now and then realized them, his poetic achievement was less verbal than dramaturgic. He conceived and shaped a poetic drama mainly in prose when he gave *The Crucible* and, especially, *A View from the*

Bridge their dramatic contours. Miller remained, above all, a moralist in measuring individual and collective conduct by rigorous standards of right and wrong. Sufficiently aware of human weakness, he had a high regard for the heroic spirit and continued to look for it in his characters. He wrote under the influence of a tragic imagination, and, at the very least, it could be seen that Miller had tragic *intentions*. And if these seemed at times to force his dramatic action and to strain his language, they also augmented his social realism. He might have written problem plays, but instead wrote tragedies or approximations of tragedy. His concern with the issues of his day was certainly no secret. A social situation of the early 1950's was the spread of inquisition under the pressure of Communist aggression. It aroused the Ibsenite moralist in Miller (would that it had also found an ironist in him!), and it affected him both as a citizen and an imaginative writer. As citizen he clashed with a Congressional committee that interrogated him concerning Communist activities, and he carried his quarrel with Congress to the higher courts. As playwright, he turned to the American past and made the historic Salem witchcraft trials the subject of *The Crucible*, and he also made the act of informing against one's fellow men the crux of the wholly private tragedy of *A View from the Bridge*.

In both plays the core of interest, however, was a moral rather than political issue. The center of the conflict was the individual, and the question was whether he would maintain or lose his sense of right and wrong, his self-respect, his dignity as a human being. In both plays, the playwright endeavored to combine a time-conditioned situation with a timeless conflict and ethic, thereby making claims for his dramatic pieces as tragedy.

Although neither play duplicated the Broadway success of *Death of a Salesman* in 1949 or was as meritorious, Miller's new dramas increased the Broadway theatre's reputation and his own considerably. *The Crucible* had at first a mild reception in England, but *A View from the Bridge* brought 50,000 members to the New Watergate Theatre Club. In Paris, it was *The Crucible* that won the public; the play ran there for two years, and was subsequently filmed in an adaptation prepared by the then reigning arbiter of French letters, Jean-Paul Sartre. And ironically in the case of a work that was construed as a lesson for Americans beset by "McCarthyism," *The Crucible* was staged in Russia soon after the death of Stalin. The author, who had been under indictment since the summer of 1956 for contempt of Congress, could not be displeased to report this event in *The New York Times* of July 21, 1957: "I have heard," he wrote, "that very soon after Stalin died a production of *The Crucible* was suddenly put on in Leningrad, its lines edited and new ones inserted in order to drive home unmistakably its lesson for Russians—that political purges are monstrously evil." In Leningrad—and as Miller put it, "for a reason that no fancy of mine can grasp"—*The Crucible* was given the title of his first produced play, *The Man Who Had All the Luck!* But it must also be noted that *The Crucible* was presented earlier at Brussels in the spring of 1954, and that, by another twist of historical irony, Miller was refused a passport to attend the opening. For a writer whose ambitions made him seek the "timelessness" of tragic art, Miller was decidedly involved with his own times, and both his political and domestic fortunes were much in the news. But especially to the point here is the fact that his plays and his published views on the drama gave weight to the theatre of the period.

So did other playwrights when they impinged upon the consciousness of the public with individual works, even if they could not be said to have set a strong personal stamp upon the theatre. This was notably the case when the husband-and-wife writing team of Albert Hackett and Frances Goodrich dramatized Anne Frank's famous diary. The dramatization was produced in the fall of 1955 under the title of *The Diary of Anne Frank*. An ably executed and intensely moving work, the play made a powerful impression in New York in a production that will be most remembered for Joseph Schildkraut's compelling dignity in the part of Otto Frank, the father, and the radiance of Broadway's youngest star, Susan Strasberg, in the role of Anne Frank. As might have been expected, besides, European productions followed rapidly; they multiplied for years, and they had even greater impact than the Broadway presentation. *The Diary of Anne Frank* indeed became a cause rather than a play in many parts of Europe, and in Germany the story of the fifteen-year-old victim of German brutality had the additional force of a reminder of collective guilt and disgrace. "By February 1," wrote a correspondent of *The New York Times* from Bonn, *"Das Tagebuch von Anne Frank* had established itself as the outstanding dramatic hit of postwar Germany. Twenty-three municipal theatre companies were playing it in their repertory, including six in the Soviet zone. At least two dozen had scheduled it for the 1957-58 season." That such an appeal to human conscience should have come from the New York theatre did much to dignify it in the eyes of the Western European public on which the plays of O'Neill, Miller, and Williams were constantly making an impression. Unfortunately legal complications prevented the inclusion of *The Diary of Anne Frank* in the current anthology.

A strong impression was also created by the American stage with *The Teahouse of the August Moon,* an account of the occupation of a country by foreign troops, in this case the occupation of Okinawa by Americans. Many American plays dealt forcefully with man's inhumanity to man; this work had the opposite effect of showing man's humanity to man. Like the *Diary,* this play, too, was a dramatization of a book, but it succeeded with qualities of the theatre almost exclusively: with qualities of visual action and movement. It was a product of the theatrical imagination of John Patrick, who had given evidence of his powers of sympathy in his earlier war-play *The Hasty Heart.* He cultivated a fresh vein with his new work. It was a genial play, composed as a theatrical experience even if its political implications were evident, especially to Europeans sensitive to relations between occupying troops and "occupied" people. That a turn to the left in Okinawa should have jolted the optimistic assumptions upon which the play was built was an irony of history rather than a fault of the play. An allowable criticism that the second act was weak or that the American officers were cartoons, and they were, was of minor consequence on Broadway. It was a droll piece of theatre and a lightly satirical one, and it took a pleasantly romantic view of the Orient and its people. All this could endear a play about the problems of

an Army Occupation to a public that did not exact and was not being promised profound revelations.

Another play about a military occupation, *The Girl on the Via Flaminia,* was not in the least genial. It was a moving story of tragic relations between a naïve soldier and a proud but hungry girl during the American occupation of Rome. It was written by the poet and novelist Alfred Hayes with sympathetic observation, and it was staged by José Quintero. The production, though acclaimed by New York reviewers, was not a popular success, but it gave further distinction to the most vital of the so-called off-Broadway enterprises, Quintero's Circle-in-the-Square. Another provocative work stemming from World War II, Herman Wouk's *The Caine Mutiny Court-Martial,* had no difficulty in locating itself on Broadway and attracting a large following. The play, drawn from the author's Pulitzer Prize novel, was a remarkably taut drama except for its last scene, which gave the impression of contradicting the substance of the theme. As a straightforward trial-drama up to this point, the play, which its director Charles Laughton staged as a staccato conflict of characters and temperaments, left nothing to be desired except a consistent point of view. At the same time, *The Caine Mutiny Court-Martial* was not devoid of moral conflict and character revelation.

More historical in subject matter, and utilizing the past more clearly as a corrective of the present, was *Inherit the Wind* written by the previously little-known playwrights Jerome Lawrence and Robert E. Lee. The subject of the celebrated Scopes "monkey trial" in Dayton, Tennessee, provided the authors with an opportunity to dramatize a struggle for freedom of thought, to castigate bigotry, and to expose political opportunism. It cannot be imagined that they chose this historic conflict over the right to teach evolutionary theory in the schools without keeping one eye on the political weather in the United States. A work of no great literary distinction, it nevertheless gained some of the power of literature. The play acquired eloquence and apt phrasing, as well as strong conflict, from its semi-documentary character; there was an effect of rapid fire in the oratory and repartee of antagonists as redoubtable as Clarence Darrow and William Jennings Bryan. At the same time the authors, by modifying the circumstances and giving fictional names to the characters, allowed themselves freedom for condensing events and humanizing the conflict. It does not follow that theirs was the optimal way to treat the subject and utilize Darrow's memorable speeches; a technique of highlighting the conflict of ideas, possibly in the manner of Brecht, may well have proved more enlightening and compelling. But their procedure of combining intellectual and familiar emotional elements won the support of the general public. And the decisive scenes of the drama proved electrifying on a stage held by Paul Muni (briefly replaced by Melvyn Douglas) as Darrow and Ed Begley as Bryan. A more documentary approach could have been just as effective as the fictional one, or more so; but the period was unfavorable to a more intellectual approach to dramaturgy and the exigencies of Broadway stage production would have also been unfavorable to it.

Inherit the Wind achieved a different kind of excitement, the excitement of a knockdown fight in the vivid manner of a frontier political rumpus; and it was a fight that called for full-sized acting. As Walter Kerr exulted, Paul Muni had "one of those parts that actors have been known to hock their wives and children for." And the spirit of the whole was puffily broad and loud at its best, very much at home in the American theatre with its suggestion of an old-fashioned Fourth of July fracas down to its cartoon-like features. A playgoer would have been quite dense to miss the point of this revivification of an old skirmish for academic freedom. But the absence of solemnity in the proceedings and the vivacity of folk-drama in the treatment enabled *Inherit the Wind* to overcome Broadway's notable aversion to preachment.

In the main, however, the period's theatre revealed no great impulse to make much of history even in fictionalized form. One could indeed point to the persistence of *The Lost Colony* and other vivid outdoor pageant-plays of the South written by Paul Green and Kermit Hunter, and to the addition of new ventures in "symphonic drama" such as the former's somewhat anti-segregationist *Wilderness Road* produced at Berea, Kentucky. But these historical dramas were exclusively summer attractions and, to a degree, spectacles. A

historical piece on Broadway, *Small War on Murray Hill,* came from Robert Sherwood shortly before his death; but this romantic episode from the American Revolutionary War was a mild and inconsequential affair. Fired by his customary distaste for oppressors, Maxwell Anderson went back to classic Greece and the trial of Socrates in his prose drama *Barefoot in Athens*. But this protest against thought-control was more noteworthy for nobility of intention than for power of execution. Only Miller with *The Crucible* managed to overcome indifference to anything but the very recent past, and even Miller expressed disappointment over the fate of *The Crucible* on Broadway and the professional circuit. Nor was the recent past particularly favored. An intense drama about the brainwashing of American captives in Korea, *Time Limit!,* by Harry Denker and Ralph Berkey, failed to attract audiences despite favorable reviews.

Only the late John Van Druten's *I Am a Camera* attained some measure of success with an historical picture, which is what the production presented in dealing with life in Berlin on the eve of Hitler's rise to power. The picture was admirably vivid and disturbing, whether it drew attention to the futility of two expatriates from England or to the confused condition of Germany in 1930. Basing the play on Christopher Isherwood's *Berlin Stories,* John Van Druten developed a landscape of the soul on various levels of interest and placed in the foreground a disoriented, self-driven young Englishwoman. She became a vivid and exciting character-study when portrayed on the stage by the remarkable Julie Harris. Van Druten's style was virtually impeccable in the dramatization, and his Chekhovian fragmentation and atmospheric blending of elements was high-calibre artistry, weakened though it was for us by inconclusiveness. But it may be doubted that the popular success of *I Am a Camera* was assured by its virtue rather than by its defects, which caused the playgoer to concentrate more on the heroine's dissipation than on a central conflict of greater consequence. It seemed as if it was less history than the breathtakingly virtuoso performance of Julie Harris that floated the success of *I Am a Camera*.

Related playwriting that dealt with contemporary political and social situations fared poorly as a rule; the writers, although intelligent, faltered and the public, although friendly, lagged. This was the case with the ex-journalist George Tabori's intensely felt European pieces, *The Emperor's Clothes* and *Flight into Egypt*. It was less so with some treatments of the American scene such as Calder Willingham's astringent drama of life in a Southern military academy, *End as A Man*, based on the author's own novel of the same name, and Louis Peterson's *Take a Giant Step*, the attractive picture of a Negro lad's adolescence in New England. But *End as a Man*, for all its good scenewriting, ran to excess in concentrating on a congenital sadist; and *Take a Giant Step*, for all its freshness, suffered from desultory dramaturgy. And diffuseness vitiated Norman Rosten's moving drama of racial conflict in Africa, *Mister Johnson*.

The one sociological piece that did, Paul Osborn's *Point of No Return*, was based on John P. Marquand's novel and conformed to a familiar pattern of self-criticism that Mr. Marquand had long popularized. It was partly comedy of manners and partly "human interest" made especially appealing by Henry Fonda's portrait of a young tycoon who ruefully reviews his past before compromising with his future. It was hardly satire, and it was only faintly protest. It was, rather, the kind of protestation that intelligent, moderately successful Americans are wont to make while enjoying the fleshpots. It must be said, however, that Mr. Marquand was an expert in translating these protestations into fiction, and Mr. Osborn in translating them into drama. Provided one did not expect depth of conviction or penetration of analysis—and our playgoers did not while the play reviewing fraternity was complaisant—one could approve the effort. It provided the prosperous America of the early 1950's with a sobering but hardly shattering view of itself.

The only other flourishing play faintly suggestive of social drama was Joseph Hayes' well-managed melodrama *The Desperate Hours*, an account of crisis in a household captured by criminals. And, for all its moralistic as well as psychologic aspirations, *The Desperate Hours* was only an expert suspense thriller with a sober Sunday face. It was described by Woolcott Gibbs as "an almost perfect melodrama . . . containing just enough ethical reflection to give the simpler members of the audience a feeling that they are turning something weighty over in their minds . . ." Plainly, then, the period was not noteworthy for achievements in "social drama." And, for that matter, neither in "psychological drama." Neither type of play, long the mainstay of the realistic theatre, was any longer at the peak of its career either in the United States or abroad. The bloom had faded as a result of use and abuse, but above all in consequence of the lack of anything new to say. The law of diminishing returns had set in for Freud as well as Marx in the theatre, and to note this fact one does not have to be so overjoyed as to embrace the alternatives of old-fashioned action-drama uncontaminated by thought, protest or analysis. Boucicault is no substitute when Ibsen and Chekhov fail to sustain new playwriting, or when Strindberg and his psychoanalytical successors fail to do so.

Maxwell Anderson's popular dramatization about a child-murderess, *The Bad Seed*, was no more, as well as no less, than an expertly turned melodrama in which the "psychology" was good for an extra turn of plot discovery. Joseph Kramm's *The Shrike* was a study of feminine ruthlessness; it revolved around a woman who incarcerates her husband in a mental institution when he tries to rid himself of her. Brooks Atkinson considered it "a frightening piece of work," the Pulitzer Prize Committee approved the play in 1952, and sensitive psychiatrists protested against the author's description of psychiatric procedure in a hospital. But *The Shrike* was primarily contrived for excitement. Mr. Atkinson defined it best when he exclaimed, "Wonderful stuff and all theatre—like a grand guignol with a college education." And if it wasn't melodrama that eventuated from the interest in "personality problems," the results were apt to be desultory playwriting. Dramatic interest was diffused in the Dorothy Parker and Arnaud D'Usseau drama of distrait women, *Ladies of the Corridor*, or muddled, if now and then penetrative, in Jane Bowles' drama of a domineering mother and her dominated daughter, *In the Summer House*. A season or two later, too, Arthur Laurents came close to developing a remarkable play about a woman's effort to master an emotionally crippling neurosis by reliving her past. The talented author of *A Clearing in the Woods,* however, employed an expressionistic technique which produced confusion and diffusion as well as illumination. Only in Robert Anderson's *Tea and Sympathy,* indeed, did the psychological interest of the subject yield consistently exciting drama, and here success was the result of artful writing.

With his first appearance on Broadway, Robert Anderson proved himself a master-builder among the younger playwrights. And playwriting intelligence was important in handling the delicate theme of homosexuality in *Tea and Sympathy.* More, rather than less, artfulness was necessary, besides, precisely because the young protagonist was an inexperienced adolescent and because the accusation of homosexuality directed at him at a boy's boarding school was false. For some the falsity of the charge could seem like an evasion on the grounds that a psychological and social issue was thus avoided. For others, and obviously for the author himself, the calumny was the more challenging reality. And not only because accusations of homosexuality have had great vogue in contemporary society (they are a sort of passport to sophistication self-issued by an immature intelligentsia), but because the effect of calumny in this instance has much psychological consequence. Mr. Anderson, moreover, found new sources of dramatic interest in probing the chief accuser, the housemaster, as much as the accused, and in giving prominence to the latter's wife. Much of the dramatic action arose from her efforts to counter the ill effects of the accusation by overcoming the schoolboy's readiness to accept the verdict of his persecutors. This element of the dramatic action, which shifted it from clinical to normal interest, also enlarged the play. It became domestic drama, in the first instance, since it involved conflict between the suspicious schoolmaster and his sympathetic wife; and moral drama, in the second instance, since it involved the woman's defense of sensitivity against the drive for conformity in society. The play concluded with a well-managed yet unavoidably uncertain conclusion, here treated as conclusive. The good woman gave herself to the schoolboy in order to restore his all-but-destroyed confidence in his normality. And an extra twist of dramaturgy turned the tables on the boy's self-righteous persecutor, the housemaster

himself, when his wife exposed his strident masculinity as no more than a futile façade.

If an effective play was to be made of the material without deviating into the clinic, a more effective procedure than Mr. Anderson's would not be easily found anywhere. More than that, there could be little doubt that a fine intelligence had ranged our sympathies on the side where they have the greatest relevance; Mr. Anderson was concerned with the defense of the individual non-conformist against the obtuseness and complacency of the "adjusted" majority. Still, we must avoid making grandiose missionary claims for the play. Mr. Anderson wrote *Tea and Sympathy* out of experience, observation, and feeling, and with an intelligent attitude. He wrote as he felt and thought, and with an awareness of the dramatic medium. The author himself warned us against attributing a vast ambition to him when he wrote in *Theatre Arts* (March, 1958) that "Whenever a dramatic author is asked to discuss 'the mission of the playwright' there is a great temptation for him to become pretentious. Instead of being just a hard-working writer, he suddenly becomes a Man with a Mission."

There was no mission either in *A Hatful of Rain,* Michael V. Gazzo's drama of drug addiction. Nothing could be plainer than the author's picture of seemingly commonplace lives turning into an inferno for the principals, with some dope-pushers playing the role of the demons and their leader called "Mother" performing the part of the Prince of Darkness himself. And nothing could be more appalling than this direct realism that made one suffer virtually every moment in the theatre. Here was realism almost as an end in itself rather than as a means for saying what would have been too obvious to be stated —namely, that addiction to drugs was a state of damnation not only for the victim but for those who love him. It was the means rather than the end that really mattered in *A Hatful of Rain,* and the means included a series of experiences one might have desired to escape but could not easily forget. To expect the play to rise to the estate of tragedy would have been to look for an altogether different kind of composition than the author was apparently disposed to provide. There is no tragic experience in a swamp, there is only a great threshing about and floundering in it. The characters have no means of escape—that is a major point in the play. And tragic decision comes into the play only at the end when the wife decides to inform the police that her husband must be institutionalized. At this point, the dreary action is climaxed by an achievement of will on the part of the previously passive wife, and it is a painful decision that lifts a very ordinary woman above the commonplaceness of her seedy existence.

Alternating between character study and melodrama (and very original melodrama it was, thanks to the bizarre "Mother" and his odd associates), *A Hatful of Rain* maintained theatrical pressure on several levels of interest. It should have failed according to "literary" standards and also according to the standards predicated for "entertainment," since the subject was hardly an exhilarating one. Instead, Mr. Gazzo's play succeeded through the sheer compulsion of character reality, on the one hand, and theatricality, on the other. The action was a succession of explosions while the play nevertheless escaped sensationalism because of the naturalness, the patently matter-of-fact character of the writing in the central situation. The author of this terse and pulsing play was unmistakably a man of the theatre by instinct, temperament, and training (he was primarily a student of acting), even though he was evidently still only a journeyman dramatist. And the work proved again, as late as the 1950's, (as did also *Cat on a Hot Tin Roof* and Paddy Chaycvsky's *Middle of the Night*), how very much realism has retained its hold on the American theatre—this despite objections to realistic drama and efforts to go beyond it.

The efforts to go beyond realism would carry us, of course, into the field broadly designated as the "poetic" drama or theatre. Here, regrettably, the report must be meager because the achievement continued to be slight. It included an attempt by Clifford Odets to write philosophical folk-drama with his Noah play, *The Flowering Peach,* which had a rather undeservedly brief career. However, the author contributed to the abridgment of its public life with some diffuse dramaturgy and misty thought. An imaginative play possessed of colloquial poetry and rueful wisdom, *The Flowering Peach* was especially persuasive as a vehicle for the affecting comedian Menasha Skulnik. An account of the poetic efforts of the period would also have to give prominence to Tennessee Williams' unsuccessful symbolic drama *Camino Real.* It was the kind of play that could be evolved by a romantic poet out of his distress, on the one hand, and his trust in the power of spirit to defeat the world, the flesh, and the devil, on the other. And it was the kind of work that only a man of genius would be able to perpetrate or be likely to display. *Camino Real* was almost inevitably a failure, as was the same imaginative author's strongly symbolic *Orpheus Descending* a few years later. But even irritation with this attempt to write symbolic and imaginative drama could be tempered by wonder, perhaps even gratitude, that the attempt was made.

A more temperate kind of prose poetry was apparent in the successful N. Richard Nash comedy *The Rainmaker,* the play with which Geraldine Page made a great hit on Broadway. And many were disposed to rate this comedy highly; they liked its carefree young scamp, the self-proclaimed rainmaker, and enjoyed the imaginative turn of situation which shows the promised rain coming down just as he leaves the scene of his latest adventures after having also ended the drought in a girl's heart. Whether the play actually came up to the estimation of its admirers could be strongly questioned after discounting its folksy humor and its indulgence toward an agreeable charlatan as minor gratifications.

The record dwindles down to moderately supported "off-Broadway" productions. These included a lovely literary play based on the myth of Aurora and Tithonus, *Immortal Husband,* by the poet James Merrill, which won Tennessee Williams' commendation, and Robinson Jeffers' *The Cretan Woman,* a beautifully written version of Euripides' *Hippolytus.* Moreover, considering the cultural context of American drama, it would have to be noted that plays such as *Immortal Husband* and *The Cretan Woman* did not constitute poetic drama really intrinsic to the American theatre.

One must conclude that considerably greater satisfaction was experienced by the public in a less ambitious style of theatre which may be described as realism enriched by atmosphere and mood. And of this kind of playwriting, which might be called "poetic realism," there were a few examples—*The Time of the Cuckoo, Picnic,* and *Bus Stop*—that proved eminently attractive and won generous support.

During the period under review several plays qualified with considerable success for the modest category of somewhat poetic, somewhat sad, plays for which the term tragicomedy may be a trifle too formal. *The Rose Tattoo* could be included in this category but is too explosive to be associated with such pieces as Arthur Laurents' *The Time of the Cuckoo* and William Inge's *Picnic.* Perhaps the loveliest but also mildest of the three was *The Time of the Cuckoo,* the poignant romance of an American spinster in Venice, memorably played by Shirley Booth. Mr. Laurents treated the brief love affair of a career woman and an Italian shopkeeper with a lively understanding for national differences, as well as with a rueful sense of comedy. But it was out of the matter of the American Midwest that the theatre of the period derived two of its most attractive plays. William Inge, their author, had an authentic supply of character and mood, a wry realism, and a rueful sense of comedy to give the stage in *Picnic* and *Bus Stop.*

Picnic, which won for Inge both the Drama Critics Circle award and the Pulitzer Prize in 1953, firmly established the career upon which he was launched several years before with *Come Back, Little Sheba.* Louis Kronenberger's appreciation of *Picnic* was perhaps the most accurate brief description of its merits. He asserted (in *The Best Plays 1952-53*) that the author's "naturalistic round dance of frustrated, unfulfilled, life-hungry women catches something of the mischance and misbegottenness of life itself; imparts some of the pity born, in a writer, of the helplessness before the facts." And from this vantage point the conclusion of the Broadway version of the play seemed somewhat facile. The director, Mr. Joshua Logan, had sought an "upbeat" resolution for a "downbeat" play, and the author had complied with the request for an optimistic conclusion. The rewards in box-office terms were unmistakable, but the question remained whether the original conclusion, in which the heroine does not follow her lover, should have been sacrificed. Nevertheless, the main point of *Picnic* was con-cluded in effect *before* the ending. It was a play written in the minor key, modest in proportions, muted in feeling, yet also quietly vital like its reflective and mild-spoken but tenacious author. *Bus Stop* was a related play, yet different enough to free the author from the onus of repeating himself. In *Picnic* the even tenor of small-town life was interrupted by the arrival of a vital vagrant, an American semi-collegiate Peer Gynt; "tragical-comical" excitement broke out everywhere in the neighborhood. In *Bus Stop,* dramatic events and revelations of greater diversity were held together by an external, indeed arbitrary, situation; a snow storm marooned a busload of people whom chance had brought together. The play was a mixture of different elements, of farce edging over into pathos in the case of the young cowboy and his strenuously wooed girl, of norms of conduct and poignant abnormality in the case of an educated failure of a man. *Bus Stop* was lusty and sad, extravagant and sober, ordinary and extraordinary, deceptively banal in situation and curiously original in treatment.

William Inge himself appeared a deceptively simple writer. There were depths in him that were indicated in the action of his plays and suggested in their tone. The plays were obvious—and elusive. Unlike Williams and Miller, with whom he was beginning to be ranked in the 1950's after three successive victories on the rough terrain of Broadway, Inge was not the man to set off explosions. He was stirring and perturbing in a casual way—and in a singularly persuasive manner. He never sent comets blazing across the horizons of the theatre and he knew he didn't. He said of himself, in the April, 1954, issue of *Theatre Arts,* "I am moved to write a play only when I find, sometimes with a little shock to myself, that I have seen inside a person's heart. Then, with a little feeling of identification, I can begin." His significance as a playwright lay in the authentically Midwestern tone and measure of his writing. He was especially unique in seeming so ordinary, as ordinary as a Benton landscape and a prairie day. Robert Frost, with whom a kinship could be sensed without being pressed, had well defined the character of this poetic ordinariness in writing of the Oven Bird:

> The bird would cease and be as
> other birds

But that he knows in singing
   not to sing.
And like Frost's feathered singer, the question that William Inge has tended to frame is "what to make of a diminished thing."

With Inge's *Bus Stop*, however, we are also carried into the more familiar areas of Broadway entertainment, for *Bus Stop* is preponderantly a comedy. And comedy and farce are a profitable occupation in the theatrical emporium where the buyer wants to buy entertainment and the seller strives to sell it. The range of commodities remained large and it is the obligation of the present editor to reflect the trade as well as the art if he is to render a true report. Fortunately, moreover, the "trade" and the "art" are not necessarily disjunctive. They were not disjunctive in Jan de Hartog's chronicle-comedy of marriage *The Fourposter*, which was rich in light human observation, and in Thornton Wilder's delightful literary farce *The Matchmaker*. At the same time, George Axelrod's fabulously successful comedy *The Seven Year Itch* brought lively fantastication into the theatre; George S. Kaufman and Howard Teichmann made big business operations an occasion for expert farce; and Ira Levin, in dramatizing Mac Hyman's novel *No Time for Sergeants*, made the military life a springboard for genial extravaganza.

The Fourposter has delighted audiences for years; as a two-character play it is something of a *tour de force*, but it is managed with unforced and deft dramaturgy in scenes never too long for their content. It has afforded the pleasure of recognition for the middle-aged and of anticipation for the young. It promises no depths and yields none. It is a wise play, nonetheless, in taking the measure of male and female vanity in the interval between nubility and senescence; in not making that measure too large or strict for the little life and little world a sense of humor makes endurable. The irreverence of *No Time for Sergeants* had an almost fairytale quality of unreality, but its robust action and dialogue had nothing to do with fairy tales. If it recalled anything at all in the world of fable, it was the "tall tale" of the American frontier, something more modestly proportioned than, let us say, the Paul Bunyan saga but not unre-

lated to it. The irreverence of *The Solid Gold Cadillac* revived memories of the irreverent theatre of the 1920's in which co-author George S. Kaufman had been the prince of cheerful "debunkers." Memories of *Dulcy, Merton of the Movies, Beggar on Horseback,* and other Kaufman collaborations came to mind. We shouldn't call this comedy a satire—satire, Mr. Kaufman once explained, is what closes Saturday night. *The Solid Gold Cadillac* was intended for a long life. It was a lively entertainment compounded of familiar American figures and attitudes, and the entertainment also possessed a glow not so much its own as Josephine Hull's. Broadway, which has been consistently richer in winning personalities than in winning plays, suffered a severe loss when the last curtain came down for Josephine Hull, then seventy-one, on March 12, 1957.

Comedies of contemporary manners were many, while comedies with a period background, such as Liam O'Brien's play about the troubles of a Delaware freethinker in 1890, *The Remarkable Mr. Pennypacker,* were rare. There was romance enlivened with wild extravagance and spiced with wit in Carolyn Green's *Janus,* a vehicle for the delightful Margaret Sullavan; and there was satire in *Oh, Men! Oh, Women!*, Edward Chodorov's comedy about a young psychoanalyst's misadventures in love. There were also folksy comedies, such as Sylvia Regan's *The Fifth Season* and Theodore Reeves' *Wedding Breakfast,* that derived a substantial portion of their humor from informal New York life, as well as glossy "upper-class" comedies such as Samuel Taylor's *Sabrina Fair* set in the midst of North Shore Long Island "society." Broadway also had "folksiness" from other certified provinces, notably the South in the bizarre comedy Joseph Fields and Jerome Chodorov fabricated from Eudora Welty's story *The Ponder Heart.* A grotesque humor also animated the Sam and Bella Spewack free adaptation from the French, *My Three Angels,* which had its setting in French Guiana. And sophistication enlivened the Jerome Lawrence and Robert E. Lee dramatization of the Patrick Dennis novel *Auntie Mame,* set in Beekman Place, and the Joseph Fields dramatization of the Peter DeVries novel *The Tunnel of Love,* set in suburban Westport. In the last-mentioned, the art of exposé was also cultivated, though mildly, and it was employed by Jean Kerr and Eleanore Brooke with commendable incisiveness in *King of Hearts*, the portrait of an egotistical contemporary culture-hero—to wit, a comic-strip artist. And the theatre was host to a few malice-free excursions into humor, the most fanciful of which was Mary Chase's whimsical *Mrs. McThing*, a fresh entertainment which played havoc with a respectable home and kept Helen Hayes busy coping with witchcraft and a little fellow's inclinations to lead a life of delightful delinquency. And fantastication, with many a sideswipe at our planetary follies, was brisk and farcically effervescent in Gore Vidal's *Visit to a Small Planet*.

Beyond distillations of contemporary comic substance, only genius could carry the art of humor in a period acutely conscious of the present but only dimly aware of the past and rather dubious about any future. Genius of any complexion is proverbially rare, but it was available to the period in the case of Mr. Thornton Wilder, scholar, poet, and wit extraordinary to the world of the theatre. The laughter was lusty while the manner was philosophical when Mr. Wilder revamped *The Merchant of Yonkers*, his version of an old Austrian farce, and gave Broadway and the nation *The Matchmaker*. There are distillations of current comic matter in a more or less uncensored or unintimidated market. There are also some timeless comedies and timeless farces. *The Matchmaker* is one of the latter. The author compounded it of past manners, the pure childishness that clownage keeps in pay, a little stardust, and a sprinkling of miscellaneous wisdom. Although the humor could become arch, the author's gifts overcame most impediments to gratification in the field of literate farce. *The Matchmaker* was a miraculous combination of literature and theatrical hocus-pocus. To say more would be pretentious. It is possible to advert to the many talents of the author and to salute the geniality of his temperament, the buoyancy of his theatrical sense. But miracles however minor cannot be explained. It is not surprising therefore that it was impossible to find another play like *The Matchmaker* during the period under review.

If other miracles did seem to occur in the world of light entertainment, they did so only on the musical comedy stage, where

our superiority has remained unchallenged since *Oklahoma* was presented by the Theatre Guild in 1943. If it is not possible to report that the team of Rodgers and Hammerstein were able to equal their famous early successes, except to a degree with *The King and I*, which opened in the spring of 1951, there was compensation for the musical-comedy afficionados in the extraordinary vitality of *My Fair Lady* and in the more moderate attractions of such musicals as *Wonderful Town*, *The Most Happy Fella*, *The Golden Apple*, *The Pajama Game*. And had the production been supported, Broadway could have complimented itself on the Lillian Hellman adaptation of *Candide*, with lyrics by the poet Richard Wilbur and others and music by Leonard Bernstein, a work of sardonic vigor. Approaching opera, moreover, the indomitable Chandler Cowles introduced Gian-Carlo Menotti's weighty music drama *The Saint of Bleeker Street* to Broadway. It was a work bound to confuse judgment and make playgoing arduous; Broadway reviewers were impressed; indeed the reviews on this music drama about an ailing, saintly girl in New York's "little Italy" were rapturous, but the public maintained a discreet distance from the box-office.

And so ends our chronicle! What conclusions it leads to other than that the professional American theatre was important and unimportant, lively and laggard, fresh and stale, venturesome and timid, I do not know. All I know is that, despite dire predictions, the high and low enterprise of our professional stage was kept going. It even went better during the period, it appears, than commercial production in the theatrical capitals of other countries, with the possible exception of Paris. American theatrical enterprise as a whole, moreover, calls for one very important acknowledgment. It is that Broadway stage production in the early 1950's began to be increasingly supplemented by "off-Broadway" enterprise, the extent and success of which cannot be described and assessed here with any trace of justice. The enterprise was widespread in New York City, and when supplemented by "off-Broadway" productions in our community and university theatres would vastly outweigh Broadway's record of stage-production for the same period.

BEST AMERICAN PLAYS

Fourth Series—1951-1957

I AM A CAMERA

John van Druten

First presented by Gertrude Macy, in association with Walter
Starcke, at the Empire Theatre, New York, on Wednesday,
November 28, 1951, with the following cast:

CHRISTOPHER ISHERWOOD William Prince
FRÄULEIN SCHNEIDER Olga Fabian
FRITZ WENDEL Martin Brooks
SALLY BOWLES Julie Harris

NATALIA LANDAUER Marian Winters
CLIVE MORTIMER Edward Andrews
MRS. WATSON-COURTNEIDGE
Catherine Willard

The play is in three acts and seven scenes. The set, throughout, is a
room in Fräulein Schneider's flat in Berlin in 1930, before the rise of
the Hitler regime. The action covers about four months.

INTRODUCTION

WHEN John Van Druten died in his sleep in California on December 19, 1957, at the age of 56, the trade magazine *Variety* announced the sad news under the headline "Theatre Loses a Superb Craftsman." That was not the only reason for regret. Another was that the theatre lost one of its most civilized talents, for Van Druten possessed the inclination and ability to look at all humanity with refined understanding. Van Druten, who so often distinguished himself in the rarefied field of high comedy, was also capable of evoking the depth of the simple characters in *I Remember Mama,* the pathos of a troubled adolescent in *Young Woodley,* and the disorientations of rootless people in *I Am a Camera.*

Born in London in 1901, of an English mother and a Dutch father, and educated at London University where he took a Bachelor of Laws degree, Van Druten soon qualified as solicitor of the Supreme Court of Judicature in England. The theatre won his interest early, however, and he had a play, *The Return Half,* performed in London by student amateurs. He wrote *Young Woodley* while teaching English law and legal history at the University College of Wales. Although this study of a schoolboy's adolescent disturbances, barbed with criticism of British school-life, was banned in England, *Young Woodley* was produced with marked success in New York in 1925, and Broadway success led to a successful production in London three years later. Some thirty plays followed, mostly comedies of manners, such as *There's Always Juliet, Old Acquaintance, The Distaff Side,* and *The Voice of the Turtle.* Then the author turned to work of a deeper tone with *I Remember Mama, The Druid Circle,* and *I Am a Camera.*

Among the styles of drama that attracted him was the Chekhovian, which represented freedom from the requirements of the so-called well-made play technique. He expressed a strong regard for plays of character rather than plot, and the culmination of his efforts to write drama of character was *I Am a Camera.* In recording the confusions of a period and the dim strivings of his characters Van Druten could say with his hero Chris (Christopher Isherwood), "I am a camera with its shutter open . . ." Intrigued when someone called *I Am a Camera* a "mood play," the author proclaimed his indebtedness to Chekhov, noting that the latter's influence has been as important to playwrights as Ibsen's. And Van Druten's explanation is not only highly descriptive of *I Am a Camera* but of the style of playwriting with which the theatre has been trying to come to terms for half a century. "Ibsen," he said, "threw out the trimmings and concentrated rigidly on his dramatic purpose," whereas Chekhov "re-established the trimmings, but used them quite differently. They were no longer embroidery; they were the play. The play, its characters, and their detailed lives and thoughts were one single thing." Van Druten pointed out that "To many playwrights, this was a new door to freedom," and declared, "It was to me," claiming that he had never actually been "any good" in making plots. All of which does not necessarily vindicate *I Am a Camera* from charges of somewhat desultory and inconclusive playwriting. That was indeed the impression formed by reviewers from the production as a whole and from the disproportionate impact of Sally Bowles as a character and as a virtuoso role for Julie Harris. Perhaps greater balance in the production and in the play itself would have solved the difficult problems of domesticating Chekhov's method. Harold Clurman (in the *New Republic* of December 24, 1951) saw the center of the play in the theme that "Everybody is adrift." Mr. Clurman elaborated: "The fact that these people are basically 'nice,' that their sin lies in their lack of any moral anchor, that they are cut off from one another, from society and even from themselves—since the self hardly exists without the recognition of ties—makes the political violence outside them a result and a reflection of their inner disarray."

Van Druten, who visited the United States in the 1920's as a lecturer, became an American citizen in 1944, and in 1951 was made a member of our National Institute of Arts and Letters. He also worked on films in America and was frequently called upon to direct plays. In fact, he distinguished himself as a stage director no less than as a playwright. He directed all his own plays after 1941, and his direction of *I Am a Camera* was especially noteworthy. The play received the New York Drama Critics prize in 1952 and several of the actors, led by Julie Harris, won honors for their performance.

ACT ONE

SCENE ONE

SCENE: *The scene throughout is a room in* FRÄULEIN SCHNEIDER's *flat in Berlin around 1930.*

The bed is hidden, or partially so, behind curtains upstage. The door to the hall is in the right wall. Windows in the left wall.

The room is excessively German and middle-class. There is a tall, tiled stove with an angel on it. A washstand by the curtains, like a Gothic shrine. A best chair like a bishop's throne. Antlers make a kind of hatstand by the door. There is a small table for tea. A backless sofa, and an ottoman. A large table by the window piled with books, papers and notebooks. There are one or two good Medici prints on the walls, between heavy German engravings.

TIME: *A summer afternoon. When the curtain rises, the stage is dark except for a light on* CHRISTOPHER ISHERWOOD, *seated alone at the table. He is in his twenties, English and untidy. He wears flannel trousers, very dirty, and a shirt. (He wears this throughout the play. The only change will be in his tie.) He is writing and smoking. Then he stops and reads over what he has written.*

CHRIS (*reading aloud*). "In the last few days, there has been a lot of Nazi rioting in the streets, here in Berlin. They are getting bolder, more arrogant." (*He stops.*) No, that's all wrong. (*He crumples the page and throws it aside.*) That's not the right way to start. It's sheer journalism. I must explain who it is who is telling all this—a typical beachcomber of the big city. He comes to Berlin for the week end, stays on, runs out of money, starts giving English lessons. Now he sits in a rented room, waiting for something to happen—something that will help him understand what his life is all about. (*Rises, pouring beer into a glass.*) When Lord Tennyson wanted to write a poem, they say he used to put himself into a mystic trance by just repeating his own name. Alfred Tennyson. Christopher Isherwood. Christopher Isherwood. Christopher Isherwood. I like the sound of my name. "Alone among the writers of his generation, Christopher

Isherwood can be said to have achieved true greatness." Shut up, idiot. The only book I ever published got five reviews, all bad, and sold two hundred and thirty-three copies to date. And I haven't even started this new one, though I've been here six months already. (*Sits at the table again.*) Well, you're going to start now, this minute. You're not leaving this chair until you do. Write "Chapter One." (*Does so.*) Good. Now begin. Create something. Anything. (*He writes, then reads.*) "I am a camera, with its shutter open, quite passive. Some day all of this will have to be developed, printed, fixed." (*The lights come up on the room. There is a knock on the door.*) Who's that?

FRÄULEIN SCHNEIDER (*off*). It is I, Herr Issyvoo.

CHRIS. Come in, Fräulein.

(*She comes in. She is a large, bosomy, German woman. She carries a lace tea-cloth.*)

FRÄULEIN SCHNEIDER. I bring you this tea-cloth. When you are having a lady guest, you can trust Schneiderschen to make things elegant. Now, where do you want all of these things to go, Herr Issyvoo?

CHRIS. Oh, put them on the floor.

FRÄULEIN SCHNEIDER. But you cannot put things on the floor.

CHRIS. There are a lot of things there already.

FRÄULEIN SCHNEIDER. But they must not stay there, not if a lady is coming. It does not look good at all.

CHRIS. You'd better put them on the bed. She won't be looking at the bed.

FRÄULEIN SCHNEIDER. And how do you know that, Herr Issyvoo? A handsome young man like you?

CHRIS. Fräulein Schneider. I'm surprised at you.

FRÄULEIN SCHNEIDER (*with a big laugh*). Oh, Herr Issyvoo, I have been young, too. Young and saucy. (*Rather archly, she takes the things to the bed behind the curtains.*)

CHRIS. I suppose you had a great many admirers, Fräulein Schneider?

FRÄULEIN SCHNEIDER. Oh, I had dozens, Herr Issyvo. But only one Friend. (*She returns for more stuff.*) Eleven years we were together. Then he died. And it was after that that I became fat. The bosom, you know. It grew and it grew. I think it is still growing. And it is such a weight to carry about with you. It is like carrying a suitcase. *Two* suitcases. And it is sad that it should all have grown after he died. He was a man for bosoms. It would have made him so happy. And now it does no one any good. This young lady you are expecting—she is very attractive?

CHRIS. She is one of my pupils. She wanted to see where I lived. Though when I say she is one of my pupils, it isn't true. She's the only one I have left. The others have all gone away for the summer. Fräulein Schneider, I have got to have a talk with you.

FRÄULEIN SCHNEIDER. Ja, Herr Issyvoo?

CHRIS. I don't think I can go on living here.

FRÄULEIN SCHNEIDER. What? Oh, Herr Issyvoo, you are not going to leave me? Are you not comfortable here?

CHRIS. Yes, I am very comfortable. It's just that I can't afford it.

FRÄULEIN SCHNEIDER. Oh, that can wait.

CHRIS. No. It's been waiting too long. I haven't paid you for two months—not properly. I've got it here. (*Takes money from wallet.*) I was just wondering—that little room across the passage—just across the passage—that's not let.

FRÄULEIN SCHNEIDER. But it is so small, Herr Issyvoo. Why, I can hardly get into it myself. And what do I do with this room? With the summer coming on, I shall never find a tenant for it.

CHRIS. Oh, I'm sure you will. And until you do, why don't you live in it yourself, instead of the sitting room?

FRÄULEIN SCHNEIDER (*setting tea-cloth*). I like the sitting room. I can look onto the corner and see what's going on. And believe me, Herr Issyvoo, there is plenty. Those women—they are as old as I am—almost—and they stand there and whisper to all the men who pass by—Komm, Süsser. And believe me, Herr Issyvoo, they come. Sometimes I think I shall adopt that profession myself.

CHRIS. Can I rent the other room, Fräulein Schneider? What do you charge for it?

FRÄULEIN SCHNEIDER. I have charged twenty-eight marks when times were good.

CHRIS. I can't afford twenty-eight.

FRÄULEIN SCHNEIDER (*ruffling his hair*). Ach, du armer Junger. But of course you can rent it. I will not have you leave. You rent it for twenty marks.

CHRIS. You're very sweet, Fräulein Schneider.

FRÄULEIN SCHNEIDER. Sweet? Ja. Once I was sweet. Sweet as a sugar cake. Now I am sweet like a fat old bun. And soon you make a great deal of money with your stories that you are always writing, and you take this room again, and everyone is happy once more.

CHRIS. I'll buy you a fur coat.

FRÄULEIN SCHNEIDER. And then I become one of the ladies. Only I will not go up and down the street. I sit at my window in my fur coat and call out, "Komm, Süsser." Komm to the third floor. And then I open the coat a little—just a little—and what do you think I have on underneath? Nothing! I have nothing on underneath. (*Bell rings.*) Ach Gott, there is the bell. It will be your young lady.

CHRIS. You need not tell here that I am leaving this room.

FRÄULEIN SCHNEIDER (*on her way out*). But of course not, Herr Issyvoo. You can trust me perfectly. And I will bring you serviettes for your coffee. Most ladylike. Ladies appreciate these things. (*She goes out.* CHRIS *starts to tidy the room.*)

FRÄULEIN SCHNEIDER'S VOICE (*off*). Nein, nein, Herr Wendel. Sie können nicht hinein gehen. Herr Issyvoo erwartet heute eine Dame.

FRITZ'S VOICE. Aber ich muss mit ihm sprechen. Christopher. Christopher.

CHRIS (*going to door*). Fritz.

FRITZ'S VOICE. Fräulein Schneider says I cannot come in. She says you expect a lady.

CHRIS. Yes, I do. But that's all right. Come in, Fritz. (FRITZ *enters. Young and dark.* FRÄULEIN SCHNEIDER *stands behind*). Do you want some coffee? One of my pupils is coming.

FRITZ. But yes, I would like some coffee. *Black* coffee.

CHRIS. Will you make enough for three, Fräulein Schneider?

FRÄULEIN SCHNEIDER. You are too good, Herr Issyvoo. You entertain whoever comes. No matter whoever. (*She goes out.*)

FRITZ. I do not think your landlady likes me. And that is with me all right. Ultimately, I do not like her, too. In fact, I think the world is lousy.

CHRIS. Is business bad?

FRITZ. It is terrible. Lousy and terrible. Or I pull off a new deal in the next month, or I go as a gigolo.

CHRIS. Either—or. I'm sorry. That's just force of habit.

FRITZ. I am speaking a lousy English just now. Sally says maybe she will give me a few lessons.

CHRIS. Who is Sally?

FRITZ. She is a friend of mine. Eventually she is coming around here this afternoon. I want that you should know each other.

CHRIS. Is she a girl friend of yours?

FRITZ. Not yet. But she is wonderful, Chris.

CHRIS. Who is she? What does she do?

FRITZ. She is an actress. She sings at the Lady Windermere. Hot stuff, believe me. Ultimately she has a bit of French in her. Her mother was French.

CHRIS. I wonder what Natalia will think of her. Natalia Landauer is the pupil I am expecting.

FRITZ. Landauer? Of the big department store?

CHRIS. Her father owns it. It's the family business.

FRITZ. But they must be enormously wealthy.

CHRIS. Oh, yes, they're stinking rich.

FRITZ. And are you going to marry her?

CHRIS (*laughing*). Me? No, of course not.

FRITZ. Do you not want her?

CHRIS. Not a bit. Except as a pupil.

FRITZ. Then if I should meet her and perhaps make a pass after her, you would not mind?

CHRIS. But you haven't even seen her.

FRITZ. Why would that make a difference? I tell you, Chris, I need money. Maybe then her father will take a liking from me, and give me a job in the business. If I marry her, a partnership, perhaps.

CHRIS. What makes you think she'd have you?

FRITZ. All women will have me if I want them.

CHRIS. Not Sally, apparently.

FRITZ. Sally has been too busy. With other men. But one day she will be free, and then I will ultimately get my look in.

CHRIS (*teasing him*). Perhaps *you* won't be free. Perhaps you will be all tied up with Natalia.

FRITZ (*seriously*). Yes, business must come first, ultimately. I suppose she is a Jewess?

CHRIS. Oh, yes.

FRITZ. Well, there is always something. And you know, Chris, I am very broadminded. (*Bell rings.*)

CHRIS. That will be Natalia.

FRITZ. How do I look, Chris? How is my hair? (*He gets out a comb and mirror.*) Um Gotteswillen . . . a gray hair. No, that is too much. (*He pulls it out.*) 'You see, Chris dear, I must marry soon. You will help me to arrange the marriage settlement? (*Voices off.*)

SALLY'S VOICE. Herr Isherwood ist er zu Hause?

FRITZ. That is Sally. Chris, put on your coat.

CHRIS. Why?

FRITZ. She is a lady. Very elegant.

FRÄULEIN'S VOICE. He is not here. He is not to house.

SALLY'S VOICE. But he must be. He is expecting me. Isn't Herr Wendel here?

FRITZ (*going to the door while* CHRIS *gets his coat from the cupboard*). Sally— liebling . . .

SALLY'S VOICE. Fritz, darling. The old lady said there was nobody here.

FRITZ. Come in. (SALLY *comes in. She is young and attractive. She wears black silk with a small cape over her shoulders, and a page boy's cap stuck jauntily on one side of her head. Her fingernails are painted emerald green.* FRÄULEIN SCHNEIDER *stands again in the doorway.*) Sally, this is Christopher. Christopher, this is Sally. Sally Bowles.

CHRIS. How do you do?

SALLY. I'm terribly glad to meet you.

CHRIS. Make coffee for four, will you, Fräulein Schneider?

SALLY. Oh, not for me. I'm allergic to coffee. I come out in the most sinister spots if I drink it before dinner.

CHRIS (*to* FRÄULEIN SCHNEIDER). Just for three, then. (FRÄULEIN SCHNEIDER *goes.*)

SALLY. I always have Prairie Oysters for breakfast. Don't you adore them? Eggs with Worcester Sauce all sort of wooshed up together. I simply live on them. Actually, I suppose I couldn't have a whiskey and soda, could I? I'm simply dead.

CHRIS. I'm afraid I haven't got any whiskey.

SALLY. I thought you were English.

CHRIS. I am. But I'm also poor.

SALLY. Oh, so am I. Terribly poor. But I always have whiskey. I mean, I think one must. Do you have anything? I mean, anything besides coffee?

CHRIS. I think I've got a little spot of gin.

SALLY. Dear old Mother's ruin. Gin will be wonderful. (CHRIS *gets gin out of cupboard*.) Am I terribly late, Fritz darling?

FRITZ. No, you are beautifully on time.

SALLY. I thought I wasn't going to be able to come at all. I had a most frantic row with my landlady. Finally, I just said Pig, and swept out.

CHRIS. What would you like in this—or this in?

SALLY. Have you got anything?

CHRIS (*helplessly*). No, I don't think I have.

SALLY. Then I'll just have it straight.

CHRIS. I'm afraid it will have to be in a tooth glass.

SALLY. That will be wonderful. Give me one of your marvelous cigarettes, Fritz darling. Do you ever smoke any of Fritz's cigarettes? They're absolutely devastating. I'm sure they're full of opium, or something. They always make me feel terribly sensual.

CHRIS (*handing her the glass*). Here you are.

SALLY. Thank you so much. This looks wonderful. (*Sips it.*) Oh, it is. It's got an extraordinary taste. Like peppermint.

CHRIS. Oh, I'm afraid I can't have washed out the glass properly. That must be toothpaste. I'm so sorry.

SALLY. I think it is wonderful. Have some, Fritz. Taste it. Perhaps we can all make a fortune selling mint-flavored gin.

FRITZ (*tasting*). It is extremely interesting.

SALLY (*to* CHRIS). You have some, too.

CHRIS (*tasting*). It really isn't bad.

FRITZ. What for was your row with your landlady?

SALLY. Oh, it was absolutely awful. You should have heard the things she called me. I mean—well, I suppose in a way I may be a bit of a tart. . . . I mean, in a nice way—but one doesn't like to be called that. Just because I brought a man home with me last night. And, anyway, I'm terribly in love with him.

FRITZ. Anyone I know?

SALLY. You'll never guess. Klaus.

FRITZ. Klaus? Your accompanist, Klaus?

SALLY. Yes. He was always just like part of the piano to me. And then last night he was absolutely astonishing. Just like a faun, or something. He made me feel like a most marvelous nymph, miles away from anywhere, in the middle of the forest. And then the landlady came in and made the most boring remarks, so I simply can't go back. I shall have to find a new room. (*To* CHRIS) I don't suppose you know of any, do you?

CHRIS. A room?

SALLY. Something like this, perhaps. I suppose there aren't any more in this flat?

CHRIS. Well, there is this one.

FRITZ. Why, are you leaving?

CHRIS. I'm leaving this room. I can't afford it any more.

SALLY. Is it terribly expensive?

CHRIS. I pay fifty marks a month. That includes breakfast.

SALLY (*rising*). But that's nothing. I pay eighty for mine. This is very nice. (*She looks around.*) Is that your bed? Oh, I think that's sweet—all hidden away like that. (*She looks behind the curtains.*) Oh, that's where you keep things.

CHRIS (*laughing*). Only when I have visitors.

SALLY. You mean I could really have this? How soon?

CHRIS. As soon as you like. I've only got to move across the hall. It won't take me a minute. And I know Fräulein Schneider is very anxious to let it.

SALLY. What is she like? I mean, is she going to make trouble if I bring men home occasionally? I mean, it would only be very occasionally, because I do think one ought to go to the man's rooms, if one can. I mean, it doesn't look so much as if one was sort of expecting it. And men feel very keenly about that sort of thing. And it won't be men, anyway. It'll only be Klaus. I've decided to be absolutely faithful to him. I really have. She wouldn't mind that, would she, or would she?

CHRIS. If she can let the room, I'm sure she wouldn't mind anything.

SALLY. I say, am I shocking you, talking like this?

CHRIS. Not a bit. No one ever shocks me when they try to.

SALLY (*rather sharply*). Why do you say I'm trying to shock you?

CHRIS. I have an idea you like to try and

shock everyone. Why do you paint your fingernails green?

SALLY. I think it's pretty. Don't you?

CHRIS. Suppose you thought it was pretty to paint dirty pictures on them, would you do that, too?

SALLY. Yes. You know, that's rather a good idea. Not dirty pictures exactly, but sort of *stimulating* ones. I must get someone to do it for me. Is he really unshockable, Fritz, or is he just pretending?

FRITZ. Oh, no. Chris is quite unshockable. I have tried many times, but ultimately I cannot do it.

CHRIS. But—there is a young lady coming this afternoon who *is* shockable. So would you mind awfully being just a bit more careful what you say? She's one of my pupils, and I do rather need her.

SALLY. Oh, but darling, of course. I'll be terribly ladylike.

CHRIS. And don't let her know I'm going to move out of here, do you mind? She'd probably start cutting down on my terms.

SALLY. I won't breathe a word. (*Bell rings.*)

CHRIS. That must be her now.

SALLY. You'd better put the gin away.

CHRIS. Oh, yes, thanks.

SALLY. I'm afraid there isn't time for me to clean my nails. I'll try and keep my fists clenched.

NATALIA'S VOICE. Herr Isherwood?

FRÄULEIN SCHNEIDER'S VOICE. Ja, gnädiges Fräulein. Er erwartet Sie. Bitte sehr. (*She opens the door and ushers in* NATALIA.)

FRÄULEIN SCHNEIDER. Bitte. Hier ist die Dame die sie erwartet haben, Herr Issyvoo. (*She goes.* NATALIA *is about twenty-two— correctly dressed, very German, formal and decided.*)

CHRIS. Natalia. These are friends of mine. Miss Bowles, Fräulein Landauer, and Mr. Wendel. Fräulein Landauer.

FRITZ. Sehr erfreut, gnädiges Fräulein.

CHRIS. I think we'd better speak English. Fräulein Landauer speaks wonderful English.

FRITZ. I am charmed, dearest Miss. (NATALIA *shakes hands with Sally, noticing her nails.*)

SALLY (*concealing them*). How do you do?

NATALIA. I am well. I have just had a cold, but it is better now.

SALLY (*doing her best*). Oh, I'm so sorry. Colds are beastly things, aren't they? One's head gets all stopped up.

NATALIA. This was a cold in the chest. It was not in my head. All the plegm was here. (*She points to her chest.*)

SALLY. All the what?

NATALIA. The plegm that comes into the tubes.

CHRIS. Phlegm. You pronounce the "h."

NATALIA. Oh. Then why do you say phthisis—what the Lady of the Camellias had—and not pronounce the "h" there, too? (*A pause while she waits for an answer.*)

CHRIS. Well . . .

NATALIA. There must be a reason. You give it to me, please.

CHRIS. I don't know it. But you don't say p-tisis, either.

NATALIA. Then you should say "lem," and leave it right out as in thisis. I have leim in my chest. Is it not so? It is not an exact language, your English.

SALLY. What *is* phthisis?

NATALIA. It is consumption. From the lungs. They are consumed in phlegm.

SALLY. Do you mind not going on about it? I think I am going to be sick. (FRÄULEIN SCHNEIDER *enters with the coffee, and then returns with a cake-stand and paper napkins.*)

NATALIA. But why should it make you sick? You do not have it.

SALLY. All stories about illness make me want to throw up. I saw a movie about syphilis the other night that was too awful. I couldn't let a man touch me for almost a week. Is it true you can get it from kissing?

FRITZ. Oh, yes—and your King, Henry the Eighth, caught it from letting Cardinal Wolsey whisper to him.

NATALIA. That is not, I think, founded in fact. But kissing, most decidedly yes. And from towels. And cups. I hope these have been cleaned properly.

CHRIS (*flippantly*). Oh, yes. Fräulein Schneider always boils them every day.

SALLY. I mean, you can't ask every man to run and and have tests and things before you let him touch you. I mean, there isn't time, and he'd be off in a nip to someone much less particular. (NATALIA *freezes.* CHRIS *comes in hastily.*)

CHRIS. Natalia, let me give you some coffee.

SALLY (*rising*). Oh, Fräulein. Could I

have a talk with your landlady, Chris darling?

CHRIS. There's plenty of time.

SALLY. Oh, we'll talk outside. Won't we, Fräulein darling? We'll have secrets together. (*To* NATALIA) If you'll excuse me.

NATALIA. But most obligingly.

SALLY (*to* FRÄULEIN SCHNEIDER). Komm, liebes Fräulein, wir werden haben Geheimnesse zusammen. (*They go out together.*)

FRITZ (*to* NATALIA, *while* FRITZ *passes coffee*). You will allow me to pass you a cake, dearest Miss? They are jam tarts.

NATALIA. I thank you, no. I do not eat between meals. And Miss is not the correct way to address a lady in English. No sugar, neither. Just plain black coffee.

FRITZ. That, too, is how I like it. Black, black, black, like Othello.

NATALIA. You tell me, please, about Fräulein Bowles. She is a remarkable girl.

FRITZ. She is a night-club artist. Very talented.

NATALIA. Where does she perform?

FRITZ. At a club calling the Lady Windermere. You know perhaps the play from Oscar Villder, calling *Lady Windermere's Fan?*

NATALIA (*correcting him*). Called *Lady Windermere's Fan.* But of course I know it. I have read it, both in English and in German. I think it is better in German. But the club I do not know.

FRITZ. Would you let me take you to it one night, to hear Sally sing?

CHRIS. Do you think it is quite the right place for Fräulein Landauer?

NATALIA. But why not?

CHRIS. Oh, I don't know. I just thought . . .

NATALIA. You thought what, please?

CHRIS. I don't know, really.

NATALIA. You don't know. Then I cannot help you.

CHRIS. I thought it might be just a bit —Bohemian.

NATALIA. Then I must see it. I accept your invitation, my dear sir. When shall we go?

FRITZ. We could go tonight, if you are free.

NATALIA. I can be free. You will come and fetch me at a quarter to nine.

FRITZ. Oh, but it doesn't start until after midnight. Sally never goes on until one o'clock.

NATALIA. Then you fetch me please at a quarter to midnight. I will give you my address. You will come, too, Christopher, and we will be a party to hear your girl friend sing.

CHRIS. She is not my girl friend.

NATALIA. No? Then what is she, please?

CHRIS. She's—just a friend.

NATALIA. I see. And she is not a girl?

CHRIS. Yes, but . . .

NATALIA. Then why is she not a girl friend?

FRITZ. Girl friend means something more than a friend who is a girl, Fräulein.

NATALIA. So? What does it mean?

FRITZ. It means a sweetheart.

NATALIA. Ah, so. I did not know. Then I am not a girl friend of yours, Christopher?

CHRIS (*feebly*). Unfortunately—no . . .

NATALIA. You do not mean that, Christopher. You say it only to be polite.

FRITZ. He ought to mean it.

NATALIA (*ever so slightly coquettish*). You think, Herr Wendel?

FRITZ. I think very much.

NATALIA. And you too, are polite.

FRITZ. No, I am never polite. I am only sincere.

(SALLY *returns.*)

SALLY. It's all fixed up, Chris. The poor old thing was almost in tears of gratitude.

NATALIA. And why was she so grateful?

SALLY. Because I'm moving in here.

CHRIS (*hurriedly*). Sally! We are all coming to hear you sing tonight.

SALLY. Tonight? Oh, but, my dear, I shall be exhausted. I didn't sleep a wink last night.

NATALIA. You had rather I come some other evening?

SALLY. Oh, I expect it will be all right. Only don't let the proprietor bother you. He's quite a darling, really, but he takes dope quite a lot, and sometimes it doesn't agree with him. He pinches people. It doesn't mean anything.

NATALIA (*stiffly*). I think now that I must go.

FRITZ. Please, if I may accompany you?

NATALIA. My dear young man, I am not sixty years old, and I can go home unmolested all by myself.

CHRIS (*quoting*). Bin weder Fräulein, weder schön, kann ungeleitet nach Hause gehen.

SALLY. What is that?

NATALIA. It is from *Faust.*

CHRIS. It means, "I am not a virgin, and I am not beautiful, and I can go home alone."

FRITZ (*earnestly*). Oh, but that is not true. None of it is true. Not in this case.

SALLY (*eagerly*). You mean you think Fräulein Landauer *is* a virgin? How do you know?

NATALIA. You are filled with interesting curiosity, Fräulein Bowles, but I must pull myself away. I say good-by.

SALLY. Good-by.

NATALIA. Good-by, Christopher. I think I will talk to your landlady on my way out. I do not like these rooms, and she is charging you too much. (*She goes out with* FRITZ.)

SALLY (*after a moment*). I don't think that girl liked me very much, did she?

CHRIS. No, I don't think she really did.

SALLY. I'm sure I don't know why. I was doing my best. It won't make any difference to you, will it? To your lessons, I mean?

CHRIS. No, I don't think so. She's very broad-minded in an intellectual sort of way. She'll probably decide it's her duty to understand you.

SALLY. What on earth was Fritz up to? I can't think what got into him, dancing about like that. He isn't after her, is he?

CHRIS. She's very rich, you know. And Fritz is very broke.

SALLY. Do you think he'll get anywhere with her?

CHRIS. I've always understood from him that women find him attractive.

SALLY. I shouldn't think *she* would, with his going on like that. I should think his best way with a girl of that kind would be to make a pounce.

CHRIS. I can't imagine anyone pouncing on Natalia.

SALLY. No, dear. That's why it would be so effective.

CHRIS. I believe you're right. You know, that's quite wonderful of you, Sally.

SALLY. It seems very simple to me. Give me the rest of that gin, will you, Chris? There's just a little left. Then you won't have to pack the bottle.

CHRIS (*getting it*). Sure.

SALLY. And you're going to be right across the hall. I took a look at the room. It's not very nice. But you can use this any time you like, you know, and then if I'm low—or you are—we can just sob on each other's bosoms. I say, Fräulein Schneider's got a big one, hasn't she? Like an opera singer, or that woman in the music halls who can make hers jump. Can Fräulein Schneider do that?

CHRIS. We might train her.

SALLY (*looking at the paper on the table*). Chapter One. Are you writing a novel?

CHRIS. Starting one.

SALLY (*reading*). "I am a Camera, with its shutter open, quite passive." Do you mean this is a story written by a camera?

CHRIS (*laughing*). No, it's written by me. I'm the camera.

SALLY. How do you mean?

CHRIS. I'm the one who sees it all. I don't take part. I don't really even think. I just sort of photograph it. Ask questions, maybe. How long have you been in Germany?

SALLY. About two months.

CHRIS. And your mother is French. (*She looks blank.*) Fritz told me she was.

SALLY (*irritated*). Fritz is an idiot. He's always inventing things. Mother's a bit county, but she's an absolute darling. I simply worship her. I'm afraid Daddy's side of the family comes out in me. You'd love Daddy. He doesn't care a damn for anyone. It was he who said I could go to London and learn acting. You see, I couldn't bear school, so I got myself expelled.

CHRIS. How did you do that?

SALLY. I told the headmistress I was going to have a baby.

CHRIS. Oh, rot, Sally, you didn't.

SALLY. Yes, I did. So they got a doctor to examine me, and then when they found out there was nothing the matter they were most frightfully disappointed. And the headmistress said that a girl who could even think of anything so disgusting couldn't possibly be let stay on. So I went to London. And that's where things started happening.

CHRIS. What sort of things?

SALLY. Oh—things. I had a wonderful, voluptuous little room—with no chairs—that's how I used to seduce men. One of them told me I'd do better in Berlin. What do you think, Chris?

CHRIS. I think you're doing fine. I think you're wonderful, Sally.

SALLY. Do you, Chris dear? I think

you're wonderful, too. We're going to be real good friends, aren't we?

CHRIS (*rather slowly*). Do you know, I believe we are. Real good friends.

SALLY. You know, Chris, you were quite right about my wanting to shock people. I do, and I don't know why. I do think you were clever to notice it. And, Chris, there's one thing more. I'm not sure if you'll understand or not. I did tell Fritz my mother was French. I suppose I wanted to impress him.

CHRIS. What's so impressive about a French mother?

SALLY. I suppose it's like whores calling themselves French names to excite men. I'm a bit mad like that sometimes, Chris. You must be patient with me.

CHRIS. I will, Sally.

SALLY. And you'll swear on your honor not to tell Fritz? And if you do, I can cut your throat? (*Stands over him, mock-bullying him with a paper knife.*)

CHRIS. From ear to ear. Sally, was that all true just now, what you told me about your family?

SALLY. Yes, of course it was. Well, most of it. (*Puts paper knife down.*) Only, Chris, you mustn't ever ask me questions. If I want to tell you anything, I will. But I've got to be free.

CHRIS (*amused*). Very well, Sally.

SALLY. I've got to have a free soul. You know, I think I'm really rather a strange and extraordinary person, Chris.

CHRIS. So do I, Sally. (*Copying her tone*) Quite extraordinary. (*He starts to laugh. She joins in. Their laughter grows louder. She embraces him.*)

SALLY. Oh, Chris, you are awful. (*Releasing herself, she picks up her handbag and starts for the door.*) Look, darling, I must go. I'll be back in an hour with all my things, and you can help me unpack. So long, Chris.

CHRIS. So long, Sally. (*She leaves.*)

CHRIS. Well, I'd better start moving out of here. I bet Fräulein Schneider's pleased. Sally is just the kind of person she goes for. (*Takes two personal pictures from the wall and puts them on the table.*) How do I know that? How do I know what kind of a person Sally is? I suppose that's what's so fascinating about her. People who talk like that about themselves *ought* to be lying. But I don't believe she is. And yet she's that mysterious thing my family

calls a lady, too. (*Looks out of the window.*) Look at her. She's even flirting with the taxi-driver. And she knows I'm watching her. Oh, my God. (*He laughs.*) I've got to put that down right away. (*He sits at the desk and starts to write in a notebook.*) Let's make notes. How would you describe her? Sally Bowles was a girl of about . . . I wonder how old she is. Her face is young, but her hands look terribly old. And they were dirty, too. Dirty as a little girl's hands. (*He writes again.*) Sally's hands were like the old hands of a dirty little girl.

CURTAIN

SCENE TWO

TIME: *About three months later.*

SCENE: *The scene is very slightly changed. A few feminine touches. A doll or two. Some bottles and jars are spread out on the table. The Medici prints are missing, and a couple of other pictures, very sentimental, are in their places. A pair of silk stockings and a pair of panties on a hanger, drying. When the curtain rises,* FRÄULEIN SCHNEIDER *is tidying up the room. There is a knock on the door.*

FRÄULEIN SCHNEIDER. Ja, herein. (CHRIS *enters.*)

CHRIS. Oh, is Sally not here?

FRÄULEIN SCHNEIDER. No, Herr Issyvoo, she has gone out. And so late she was getting up. It's not as if she were working nights any more. I don't think she is well, Herr Issyvoo.

CHRIS. Do you know where she keeps my thermometer, Fräulein Schneider? I want to take my temperature.

FRÄULEIN SCHNEIDER. What, again?

CHRIS. I've got pains in my back. I think I've got a slipped disk.

FRÄULEIN SCHNEIDER. I thought it was your stomach.

CHRIS. That was yesterday.

FRÄULEIN SCHNEIDER (*feeling his head*). You have no temperature.

CHRIS. I'm not so sure. I'd like to see, if I can find the thermometer.

FRÄULEIN SCHNEIDER (*looking for it*). I saw her using it only yesterday to stir those Prairie Oysters with. Ah, here it is.

I think there is still a little egg on it, but it's on the case.

CHRIS. Thank you. (*He opens thermometer and shakes it down.*) Has the afternoon post come yet?

FRÄULEIN SCHNEIDER. It will be here soon now. There was nothing for her this morning. (CHRIS *puts the thermometer in his mouth.*) I begin to worry for Fräulein Sally. That friend Klaus of hers. Six weeks he has been away now in England and only one letter has he written. (*Bell rings.*) There is the bell. (*She goes to answer it.*)

FRITZ's VOICE. Ist Fräulein Bowles zu Hause?

FRÄULEIN SCHNEIDER. Nein, Herr Wendel. Aber Herr Issyvoo is da. In ihren Zimmer. Gehen Sie nur hinein. (FRITZ *enters.*)

FRITZ. Hello, Chris. Are you ill?

CHRIS. I don't know yet. Sit down.

FRITZ. What's the matter?

CHRIS. My legs don't seem to work properly.

FRITZ. That can be locomotor ataxia.

CHRIS. I know. That's what I'm afraid of. (FRITZ *sits beside him, and tests his knee for reflex action. The first time nothing happens. They both look worried.* FRITZ *tries again, and* CHRIS's *leg reacts.*)

FRITZ (*pushing* CHRIS's *leg away*). There is nothing the matter with you.

CHRIS (*removing the thermometer*). I think it's just over normal. (*Shakes thermometer down.*) I think I'll take some aspirin. How are you, Fritz? How's Natalia?

FRITZ. Christopher, I cannot get anywhere with that girl. I have spent money on her. Money I have not got. I meet her parents. I write her poems. Poems from Heinrich Heine, and always she recognizes them, and then she laughs at me. It is not even the money any more. But when she will not let me make love to her, it drives me ultimately mad. I kiss her, and it is like my aunt. And, Chris, she has a wonderful body, and it is untouched. By me or anybody.

CHRIS. Sally said you ought to pounce on her.

FRITZ. But no one could pounce on Natalia.

CHRIS. Sally said that's why it would be so effective. Knock her down, or something. Throw her on a couch and ravish her.

FRITZ. You do not mean that, Chris.

CHRIS. You don't seem to be doing any good the usual way. How do you ordinarily manage with women?

FRITZ. I have only to uncurl my little finger, and purr a little, and they come running. I think perhaps I try. I can after all do myself no harm. She is away now. I write to her every day. Now I will write no more. I wait for her to come home, and then I will pounce, and I will ravish, and I will snarl.

CHRIS. Good.

FRITZ. And what is with you, Chris? You still live in that dark, tiny prison of a room?

CHRIS. Oh, yes.

FRITZ. And can you get anyone else in the room at the same time?

CHRIS. Oh, yes. If they're fond of me.

FRITZ. Do you have any love-life now?

CHRIS. I have a little. Now and then.

FRITZ. And you will not talk about it. Not ever. You are so reti*c*ent. If Sally did not ultimately have a French mother, she would not talk about it, either.

CHRIS. A what? (*Remembering*) Oh . . . yes.

FRITZ. She is a strange girl. Half of her is so ultimately frank, and half is so sentimental. (*He takes a picture from the wall.*) This picture. She has it with her everywhere. It is called "The Kitten's Awakening." It is childish.

(SALLY *enters. She is rather smarter than when we last saw her—a new and rather unsuitable hat. She carries several packages. She looks tired.*)

SALLY. Oh, hello, Chris. Hello, Fritz.

FRITZ. Hello, Sally. We were just admiring your picture.

SALLY. Oh, "The Kitten's Awakening." I've had that ever since I was a child. It's a dead kitten waking up in Heaven—with angel kittens around. Chris makes awful fun of it. But I think it's rather sweet.

FRITZ. It is very sweet.

SALLY. Goodness, it's hot out, and it's late September already.

CHRIS. You are very dressy today.

SALLY. I am? Oh, this hat. Yes, it's new. (*She takes it off.*) Clive bought it for me. I don't like it much, but it cost so much money. Let's have a Prairie Oyster. Will you, Chris?

CHRIS. Not for me. I think they affect my legs.

SALLY. Fritz?

FRITZ. I would like to try one.

SALLY. I'll make them. Chris doesn't really know how. (*She starts to do so, getting the eggs and things from under the washstand, and mixing them in two tooth glasses.*)

FRITZ. And who is this Clive who gives you hats?

SALLY. He's an American. Chris and I met him a week ago at the Troika bar. We were both sitting alone, having a beer each because we were both so bloody miserable, and he was sitting next to us, and he ordered champagne for us all, and we didn't separate till four the next morning. And ever since then we've hardly been apart, have we, Chris?

CHRIS. He's so rich, we daren't let him out of our sight.

FRITZ. And he is here just on vacation?

CHRIS. He lives on vacation. I've never seen anyone drink so much. He's unhappy, he says. But I've never really found out why. Have you, Sally?

SALLY. Yes, dear. It's his wives. There have been four of them, and they none of them liked him. And, before that, it was his peculiar grandfathers. They both raised him six months each. One was a Baptist, and the other lived in Paris. So, no wonder it split him! He's sort of lost faith in everything, and I think Chris and I are putting it back, in bits. That's why I feel all right about letting Clive give us things. There's a dozen pairs of silk stockings in there, Chris. And absolutely gallons of Chanel 5. Oh, and some shirts for you. Some silk shirts.

CHRIS. Good God.

SALLY. The colors are a bit outrageous, but they're the best silk. Where's something to stir this with? Oh, this pen will do. (*She picks up a fountain pen and stirs the Oysters.*) There. (*She hands one over to* FRITZ, *who chokes over it. She gulps her own.*) Oh, that's marvelous. I feel better already. How are you, Fritz? You know, Natalia came to see me several times, as though she were doing District Visiting and I were a fallen woman or something. But she seems to have stopped.

FRITZ. She is away with her parents. She comes back next week, and then there is a surprise for her. Chris has told me your advice—that I should pounce on her—

and I am going to take it. (*He takes another sip of his drink.*)

SALLY. What's the matter? Don't you like your Prairie Oyster?

FRITZ. It is a little painful. You drink them all down at once?

SALLY. Yes, they're better that way. Especially when you are not feeling well. They sort of come back at you.

CHRIS. Aren't you feeling well, Sally?

SALLY. Not really.

FRITZ. You would like me to go?

SALLY. Fritz darling—would you mind terribly? I would like to lie down a bit.

FRITZ. But of course. With me there are no compliments. Sally, you lie down. Then you feel better. I go now. You take her to dinner, Chris, and cheer her up.

CHRIS. I'll try. Good-by, Fritz. (FRITZ *goes.*) Sally, are you really feeling ill? (*He gets her slippers, and helps her on with them.*)

SALLY. Not so much ill, as just wanting to get rid of him. Fritz is sweet. I mean, he's an old friend, but I thought if I had to go on being bright any longer that I'd die. I've got something to tell you, Chris.

CHRIS. What is it?

SALLY. Chris, I went to the doctor this afternoon, and—I'm going to have a baby.

CHRIS. Oh, my God!

SALLY. I've been afraid of it for a long time, only I wouldn't think about it. I kept pretending it wasn't true. Then yesterday I was sick, and then I fainted this morning. And that's what made me go.

CHRIS. Is it Klaus's child?

SALLY. Yes.

CHRIS. Does he know?

SALLY (*sharply*). No, he doesn't.

CHRIS. Well, you're going to tell him, aren't you?

SALLY. I don't know. Chris, I haven't heard from him for weeks and weeks. I wrote to him last week, the nicest letter I could, and he hasn't answered. Not a word. You didn't like him, did you?

CHRIS. I didn't really know him. I didn't think he was good enough for you.

SALLY. That's sweet of you.

CHRIS. But you're going to tell him this, now?

SALLY. No. Not if he doesn't write to me. It's awful, Chris. I do want to marry him, and have a family. But I can't beg him. And that's what it would be like. I mean, I mayn't be up to much, but I do have some pride.

CHRIS. Well, what then—if he doesn't write?

SALLY. I don't know. That's what scares me. It's silly, Chris . . . it happens to other girls. Almost all other girls. But I am scared. Do you suppose they all are, too?

(*A knock at the door.*)

FRÄULEIN SCHNEIDER'S VOICE. It is I, Fräulein Sally. The post is here.

CHRIS (*sotto voce*). She's been keeping an eye out for it.

SALLY. Come in.

FRÄULEIN SCHNEIDER (*entering*). There is a letter for you. The one you want. From England.

SALLY. Oh, thank you.

FRÄULEIN SCHNEIDER. Ja, Fräulein. (*She hands it to her, and waits.* SALLY *starts to undo her packages.* FRÄULEIN SCHNEIDER *gives up and goes out.* SALLY *waits for her to leave. Then she rips the letter open.* CHRIS *stands by. She reads it. Her face changes.*)

CHRIS. What's the matter?

SALLY. It's what I thought. He's throwing me over.

CHRIS. Oh, no.

SALLY. Right over. With a whole lot of stuff about how badly he's behaved to me. (*She hands* CHRIS *the first page. He reads it. She goes on with the second.*) Apparently there's someone else. An English girl. A Lady Gore-Eckersley. He says she is wonderful. She's a virgin. A Communist Virgin. (*She lays the letter down.*) Well, those are two things no one could ever say of *me.*

CHRIS (*going to her, putting his arms around her*). Oh, Sally, I'm sorry.

SALLY (*leaning against him*). It's silly, isn't it?

CHRIS. It is a kind of bloody letter.

SALLY. I'm afraid he's rather a bloody person, really. Oh, Chris, I am a lousy picker. Always the duds who'll do me in.

CHRIS. I won't, Sally.

SALLY. I know. I suppose that's why I haven't been interested in you that way.

CHRIS. Sally, you'll have to tell Klaus. He'll have to help you.

SALLY. He'd only run away. Leave no address. Besides, it's just as much my fault as his.

CHRIS. Well, what are you going to do?

SALLY. I knew this was going to happen. I can't have the baby, Chris. It's awful because I want to. But not unless I'm married, and can look after it.

CHRIS (*after a second*). I'll marry you, Sally.

SALLY. Oh, Chris, what good would that do? Klaus's child—and I'd be a rotten sort of mother. Just a betrayed whore.

CHRIS (*sharply*). Sally, for God's sake, stop calling yourself that. You know you're not.

SALLY (*bitterly*). Yes, I am. Just that. A whore who's fallen in love with a swine, because he's her type, and then got caught. That's all. Just a whore and a fool. (*She starts to cry.*)

CHRIS. Sally, stop crying.

SALLY. I've got to find someone.

CHRIS. Won't this doctor . . . ?

SALLY. No. He was quite shocked when I told him I wasn't married.

CHRIS. Then we'll get someone. Maybe we should ask Fräulein Schneider.

SALLY. Do you think *she'd* know anyone?

CHRIS. She knows just about everything, I've always thought. I'll call her. (*Opens door.*) Fräulein Schneider. Fräulein. Can you come in here? (*He comes back.*) It will be all right, Sally. I promise you. (FRÄULEIN SCHNEIDER *enters.*)

FRÄULEIN SCHNEIDER. You called for me, Herr Issyvoo?

CHRIS. Yes. We need your advice. Do you want to tell her, Sally?

SALLY (*her back to them*). No. You do it.

CHRIS. Well, you see, Fräulein Schneider, Sally is in a little bit of trouble . . .

FRÄULEIN SCHNEIDER. Ja?

CHRIS. She's going to have a baby.

FRÄULEIN SCHNEIDER. Um Gotteswillen.

CHRIS. So you see . . .

FRÄULEIN SCHNEIDER. But then this Herr Klaus, he will come back and marry her.

CHRIS. Well, you see, he isn't awfully anxious to. You see . . .

SALLY (*angrily*). It isn't that at all, Chris. You never can tell anything right. It's I who doesn't want him, Fräulein. I don't ever want to see him again.

FRÄULEIN SCHNEIDER. Ach, so . . .

CHRIS. So you see, we want to get—er—to get rid of the baby. The point is—do you know anyone?

FRÄULEIN SCHNEIDER. Yes, I do. There

was a young lady living here once, and she went to the doctor.

SALLY. For the same thing?

FRÄULEIN SCHNEIDER. Exactly the same thing.

SALLY. And was it all right?

FRÄULEIN SCHNEIDER. It was quite all right. I have his address and telephone number still. I kept it just in case it should ever happen again.

SALLY (*trying to be easy over it*). I suppose it happens quite often, really?

FRÄULEIN SCHNEIDER. It can always happen. It is just bad luck.

SALLY. I'm glad you know someone.

FRÄULEIN SCHNEIDER. He is rather expensive. It is a certificate he has to give that your health will not let you have the risk of childbirth. It costs money, that certificate.

SALLY. How much?

FRÄULEIN SCHNEIDER. For this other young lady, it was three hundred marks.

CHRIS. Three hundred!

FRÄULEIN SCHNEIDER. We could make it a little cheaper, I think, if we argued. Maybe two hundred and fifty.

CHRIS. That's still an awful lot.

SALLY. I know it is. But I've got to do it, Chris. I really have. You'd better ring up the doctor, Fräulein, and see if he can see us.

FRÄULEIN SCHNEIDER. You like that I come with you?

SALLY. Oh, would you? That would be marvelous. Where—where does he do it?

FRÄULEIN SCHNEIDER. There is a nursing home. You stay there two or three days, and then you come back here and rest. In maybe ten days, no more, it is all forgotten. I go telephone. (*She goes out, gaily.*)

SALLY. It's like a treat to *her*.

CHRIS. It'll be all right, Sally. I know it will. The other girl was all right.

SALLY. There's something so *degrading* about it, as well as dangerous. Oh, damn! Isn't it idiotic? All the men I've had—and there have been quite a lot—and this has to happen to me. It's awful, too, when you think about it—that there's something alive inside of you—that you can't have. That you mustn't have. It's like finding out that all the old rules are true, after all. But I've got to go through with it.

CHRIS. Sally, two hundred and fifty marks. And the home will probably cost

a bit of money, too. I've started making a little more now, too. If I can help you . . .

SALLY. Oh, Chris, you are an angel. I'll pay you back. I swear I will. And you know, I think maybe you had better come with us. We'll say you're the father. I think it looks better to have him along.

CHRIS. Yes, Sally, of course I'll come with you.

SALLY. Oh, Chris, I don't know what I'd do without you. (*He holds her. Bell rings.*) Oh, damn, there's the bell. If it's anyone for me, I'm not home. I won't see anyone. (*Opens the door, and goes down the passage.*) Fräulein Schneider, I'm not . . . Oh, hello, Clive.

CLIVE'S VOICE. Hello, there. I just thought I'd come and look you up.

SALLY (*returning*). Yes, of course. Come in. (CLIVE *enters. He is in his late thirties, large, American, blond and drunkish.*)

CLIVE. Well, hello, Chris, you son of a gun.

CHRIS. Hello, Clive.

CLIVE (*to* SALLY). I've never seen your place before. I thought I'd come and take a gander at it. I brought you these. (*He presents an enormous box of very expensive flowers.*)

SALLY. Oh, Clive, how wonderful of you. Look, Chris, from that terribly expensive shop on the Linden.

CHRIS. Goodness.

CLIVE. So this is where you live, eh? Just one room? Say, it's not very grand, is it? Can't you do better than this?

SALLY. I—er—I have in my time. This is just temporary.

CLIVE. Oh, sure. Sure.

CHRIS (*defensive*). What's the matter with it?

CLIVE. Well, it's not exactly *de luxe*, do you think?

CHRIS (*as before*). I think it's fine.

CLIVE. Oh, sure. Sure. I wasn't casting any slurs. I just thought maybe something a bit larger. More modern. But it's okay. Say, I bet your rooms are bigger.

SALLY. Oh, yes, they're much bigger. They're wonderful.

CLIVE. Where are they?

CHRIS. Just across the hall.

CLIVE. Mind if I take a look? (SALLY *starts to gesture wildly at* CHRIS *not to show his room.*)

CHRIS. Well—er—they're rather untidy just now.

CLIVE. That's all right with me. (SALLY *repeats her gesture.*)

CHRIS. There are some things lying around that—well, that I wouldn't want anyone to see.

CLIVE. Say, what are those?

CHRIS. Just some personal things.

CLIVE. Boy, that's what I'd like to look at.

CHRIS. I'm awfully sorry, but I don't think . . .

CLIVE. You mean, you've got someone in there?

CHRIS. Well, er . . .

CLIVE. Why don't you come right out and say it, feller? Don't beat about the bush. Go on back to her. I'll understand.

CHRIS (*again on a gesture from* SALLY). Well, she's—er—asleep just now.

CLIVE. And, boy, I bet she needs it. Well, say, now what have you got in the way of liquor?

SALLY. We've got some gin.

CHRIS. Not much.

SALLY. I'm afraid we're out of whiskey.

CLIVE. Say, you need some stores. I'll send you in a cellar. Now, look, what are we going to do? I've been all by myself all day, and it's driving me nuts. There's a place I've heard of out on the Wannsee. The Regina Palast Garten. I thought we might drive out there for dinner.

SALLY. The three of us.

CLIVE (*to* CHRIS). If you're free. (SALLY *nods at* CHRIS.)

CHRIS. Oh, yes, I'll be free.

CLIVE. Is that a good place?

CHRIS. I've always heard it was.

CLIVE. But you've never been there?

CHRIS. It's much too expensive for us.

CLIVE. Well, fine. Only is it *really* a good place? Can we have a good time there? The real McCoy?

SALLY. It's about the best place there is.

CLIVE. Oh, well, swell, then. That's great. That's the *real* thing. Well, shall we go?

SALLY. I can't go yet.

CLIVE. Why, what have you got on? (FRÄULEIN SCHNEIDER *enters.*)

FRÄULEIN SCHNEIDER. Fräulein Sally, can I speak to you a moment, please?

CLIVE. That's all right. You speak up. No secrets here. No secrets in front of Uncle Clive.

SALLY. Have you talked to the—to the man, Fräulein?

FRÄULEIN SCHNEIDER. He says he can see you right away.

SALLY. Oh—oh, thanks.

FRÄULEIN SCHNEIDER. It takes twenty minutes from here. I think maybe you should go now.

SALLY. Oh, yes, I will. You get your hat and coat, Fräulein, and I'll be ready.

FRÄULEIN SCHNEIDER. Ja, Fräulein. (*She goes.*)

CLIVE. What man is this?

SALLY. It's just a man about a job. A sort of audition.

CLIVE. I'll drive you there.

SALLY. I don't think you'd better. I mean, it's not a very big job, and it would look a little funny if I were to arrive in a Dusenberg car.

CLIVE. It would make them pay you more.

SALLY. Look, Clive, it's awfully sweet of you, but I think we'd better go by bus.

CLIVE. You take your landlady on auditions with you?

SALLY. Sometimes. She gives me confidence.

CLIVE. Well, then, Chris and I will go to the Adlon, and sit in the bar and wait for you. He can bring his girl along, if he wants to.

CHRIS. Oh, no, that's all right. But—I've got to go out, too.

CLIVE. Not with Sally?

CHRIS. No, but I have to go—and then come back here for just a minute. Why don't we all meet at the Adlon?

CLIVE. I'll send my car back here for you. Six o'clock?

SALLY. That would be wonderful. And thank you so much for these.

CLIVE. Well, good luck. I hope you get the job.

SALLY. I do, too. At least, I—I think I do.

CLIVE. We'll celebrate tonight, if you do. And if you don't, well, then, we'll tie a bun on anyway, just to forget it all. So either way, you can't lose. So long, Chris, you sexy old bastard. See you both later. (*He goes.*)

SALLY. Oh, Chris, I thought we were never going to get rid of him.

CHRIS. Yes, so did I. You know, he is an extraordinary man.

SALLY. But he's awfully sweet, really. Perhaps when this is over, I can devote myself to him. I've always thought I'd like to have a really rich man for a lover. I wouldn't want more than three thousand a year—pounds, I mean—and a flat and a decent car. Or maybe I could marry him, and then I might reform him. I could, you know, I really could.

CHRIS. Sally, do you really think you could reform anyone?

SALLY. Oh, Chris, don't. Don't pull me down again. I feel awful.

CHRIS. I'm sorry, Sally. And don't worry about reforming people. You're sweet. You really are.

SALLY. Thank you, Chris. Even if you don't mean it.

CHRIS. But I do. And now we'd better get going.

SALLY. Yes, I suppose so. (CHRIS *helps* SALLY *on with her shoes.*) I suppose we should put these flowers in water. They cost such a lot. I'll just put them in the bath for now. Then I'll see if Fräulein Schneider is ready, and come back for my hat. (*She goes to the door, and turns to* CHRIS.) Thank you for offering to marry me. (*She exits.*)

CHRIS (*her slippers in his hand*). And this is the kind of thing we used to make dirty jokes about at school. The facts of life. And here we go to prove they're not true, or that you can duck them. (*Drops the slippers.*) And then we'll get pounds and pounds spent on us for dinner. And drink too much. And try to believe that none of it matters anyway. (*Gets a cigarette from his pocket.*) And soon, as Fräulein Schneider said, we'll forget the whole thing. It'll seem like another of those nasty dreams. And we won't believe or remember a thing about it. Either of us. (*He starts to put the cigarette in his mouth. Then he stops, and looks at the door.*) Or will we?

CURTAIN

ACT TWO

SCENE ONE

SCENE: *About a week later.* CHRIS *is alone, sitting on the ottoman pasting photographs in an album. The sofa has been moved to the window and the table to the center of the room. The large chair has been placed at the right of the table. There is another chair to the left of the table.*

———

CHRIS. (*arranges some photographs, then stops*). This awful, obscene laziness. I ought to be flogged. Where has the time gone to? Jittering helplessly over the bad news in the papers, staring half-drunk at my reflection in the mirrors of bars, skimming crime-novels, hunting for sex. This place stinks of my failure. (SALLY *comes back into the room. She wears a robe and looks pale and ill.*)

CHRIS. Are you all right?

SALLY. Yes, I'm all right. Just. Goodness, if it takes all that effort, just to go across the hall. (*Passing behind* CHRIS, *she ruffles his hair.*) How's all your locomotor ataxia, Chris?

CHRIS. Oh, that's gone. I must have imagined it. (*Feeling his left side*) But, you know, I think I've got appendicitis.

SALLY (*settling down to a half-finished Solitaire*). If you have, you just die of it. Don't let them operate on you. You know, Chris, what I would really like would be some champagne. Some really cold champagne.

CHRIS. I'm afraid we haven't got any of that.

SALLY. Clive ought to have sent us whole baskets of it. I do think it was odd his disappearing like he did. Where do you think he went, Chris?

CHRIS. I wonder if he didn't go off on an opium jag.

SALLY. That's quite possible. I never thought of that. Oh dear, I've known a lot of opium fiends, and you never could really rely on them. And then what happens to my career?

CHRIS. Do you really think he's going to do anything about that?

SALLY. He says he's going to put up all the money for a show for me. All I've got to do now is find the show. And then find *him* again. But until he shows up we don't get any champagne, and I do want some. I want some terribly, now I've thought about it.

CHRIS. I'd buy you some, if I could, Sally. But you know we really are desperately broke.

SALLY. You know, Chris, in some ways now I wish I had had that kid. The last day or two, I've been sort of feeling what it would be like to be a mother. Do you know, last night I sat here for a long time by myself, and held this teddy-bear in my arms, and imagined it was my baby? I felt a most marvelous sort of shut-off feeling from all the rest of the world. I imagined how it would grow up, and how after I'd put it to bed at nights, I'd go out and make love to filthy old men to get money to pay for its clothes and food.

CHRIS. You mean, a baby would be your purpose in life?

SALLY. Yes, I wouldn't think of myself at all. Just it. It must be rather wonderful never to think of yourself, just of someone else. I suppose that's what people mean by religion. Do you think I could be a nun, Chris? I really rather think I could. All pale and pious, singing sort of faint and lovely hymns all day long.

CHRIS. I think you'd get tired of it. You'd better just marry and have a child.

SALLY. I feel as if I'd lost faith in men. Even you, Christopher, if you were to go out into the street now and be run over by a taxi . . . I should be sorry in a way, of course, but I shouldn't really care a damn.

CHRIS (*laughing*). Thank you, Sally.

SALLY (*moving to him*). I didn't mean that, of course, darling—at least, not personally. You mustn't mind what I say when I'm like this. I can see now why people say operations like that are wrong. They are. You know, the whole business of having children is all wrong. It's a most wonderful thing, and it ought to be the result of something very rare and special and sort of privileged, instead of just *that!* What are you grinning about?

CHRIS. Well, that's what it's supposed to be. The result of something rare and special. That's what *that's* supposed to be.

SALLY. Oh, goodness, is it? Yes, I suppose it *is* supposed to be. Oh, is *that* why people say it's wrong to do it when you're not married, or terribly deeply in love?

CHRIS. Yes, of course it is.

SALLY. Well, why didn't anyone ever *tell* me?

CHRIS. I expect they did, and you didn't believe them.

SALLY. Did *you* believe them when they told you?

CHRIS. No, Sally.

SALLY. But you think they're right?

CHRIS. I suppose I do.

SALLY. Then why can't we do things that we know are right?

CHRIS. I don't know, Sally. But it seems we can't. Do you really think you're going to stop having sex just because of this? Forever?

SALLY. No, I don't suppose I do.

CHRIS. I don't think we'll ever quite trust things, in the long run.

SALLY. I trust you, Chris. I'm terribly fond of you.

CHRIS. I'm fond of you too, Sally.

SALLY. And you're not in love with me, are you?

CHRIS. No, I'm not in love with you.

SALLY. I'm awfully glad. I wanted you to like me from the first minute we met. But I'm glad you're not in love with me. Somehow or other, I couldn't possibly be in love with you. . . . So, if you had been, everything would have spoiled. Hold my hand, Chris, and let's swear eternal friendship.

CHRIS (*taking her hand*). I swear eternal friendship.

SALLY. So do I. (*The bell rings.*) Oh dear, I wonder who that is. I hope it's no one for us. Chris, suppose it was Klaus?

CHRIS. What would you do?

SALLY. I'd be very good and noble about it. I wouldn't tell him anything—about the child, or anything. I'd just forgive him, beautifully. (FRÄULEIN SCHNEIDER *enters.*)

FRÄULEIN SCHNEIDER. It is Fräulein Landauer to see you, Fräulein. (NATALIA *enters.*)

CHRIS. Hello, Natalia.

NATALIA. Fräulein Bowles, I am but just back from the country and I have only just heard that you have not been well. So I have hurried in to see you.

SALLY. That's very nice of you.

NATALIA (*turning*). Oh, hello, Christopher.

CHRIS. Hello, Natalia.

NATALIA (*to* SALLY). I bring you these few flowers.

SALLY. Oh, thank you so much. Chris . . . (*He takes them.*)

NATALIA. What is, please, that has been the matter with you?

CHRIS (*quickly*). Oh, just a little ulcer, that's all. They had to cut it out.

NATALIA. Where was the ulcer?

SALLY. Inside.

NATALIA. But, of course, it was inside. Where, please, inside?

SALLY. I don't really know. In here, somewhere.

NATALIA. And who, please, was it who cut it out for you?

SALLY. The doctor.

NATALIA. But yes, it was the doctor. I did not think it was the sewing-lady. What doctor is it you go to?

SALLY. A doctor . . . (*She checks herself.*) I forget his name. What was it, Chris?

CHRIS. A Doctor—Mayer.

NATALIA. I do not know of him. All of my uncles are doctors. You should have gone to one of them. I will ask one of them to come and examine you.

SALLY. Oh, I'm quite all right again now. Would you like some coffee or anything?

NATALIA. Yes, I think that I would like some coffee.

SALLY. Will you get it, Chris?

NATALIA. And Christopher, if you could stay away for just a little while, it would be nice, too. I have something that I wish to say to Fräulein Bowles.

CHRIS. Yes, of course. (*He goes out.*)

NATALIA. Tell me, Fräulein, please, have you seen Fritz Wendel lately?

SALLY. No, I haven't.

NATALIA. I come back from the country two days before yesterday. He comes to call on me that evening. Fräulein, I think I have done you perhaps an injustice.

SALLY. Oh?

NATALIA. I have always think of you as a young lady who has no control of herself, and I have been disdainful of you therefrom. I am sorry. I do not think I quite understood.

SALLY. How do you mean?

NATALIA. I have think always that I have control of myself. Please, you will not laugh at me if I tell you something that is very personal to me?

SALLY. No, of course I won't.

NATALIA. I do not know of anyone else to whom I can go for some advice. Fräulein Bowles, Fritz Wendel has made love to me, and I have not taken him seriously, because it is all too formal, too discreet. Then, two nights before last, it is all changed. He throws aside his formality, and it is quite different. I have never known a man like that. And it has disturbed me. I cannot sleep for it. And that is not like me.

SALLY. But what am I supposed to tell you?

NATALIA. I wish to know, please, if I should marry him. My parents tell me no. They care for me. They think only of me, and they do not care for him. And he is not Jewish, and they wish that I should marry a Jewish man. I have always wished so, myself. Now I do not care. Only I think perhaps there is something of Herr Wendel's life that I do not know, that perhaps you do. And that therefore I should not marry him. You will tell me, please?

SALLY. Yes, I . . . I think perhaps there is.

NATALIA. What, please?

SALLY. I . . . I don't think I can tell you, exactly. But I don't really think he's your kind. I don't really think you ought to marry him—not if you ask me like that, point-blank.

NATALIA. I do not think so, too. But I think if I do not, that perhaps I will kill myself.

SALLY. Oh, no, you won't.

NATALIA. I do not think you know me. I do not think I know myself. (*She begins to cry.*)

SALLY. Oh, there's nothing to cry about. (NATALIA *goes on.*) Oh, don't. Please don't. You'll have me crying, too. I'm most frightfully weak still, and I cry over almost anything.

NATALIA (*still crying*). I am sorry. I did not know that love was like this. It is not what the poets have said. It is awful, and it is degrading.

SALLY. Yes, I know it. It is. It's absolutely awful when it really hits you. But you mustn't give in to it, really you mustn't. I know that sounds silly coming from me. But what do you think has been the matter with me? I was going to have a baby, and the chap let me down, and I had to get rid of it.

NATALIA (*turning, amazed*). Oh, I am sorry. I did not know.

SALLY. And marriage isn't going to make it any better if it's not the right man. And I really don't think Fritz is. For you.

NATALIA. You think, then, that I must be strong?

SALLY. Yes, I do.

NATALIA. I think so, too. But um Gotteswillen, what is there to *do* with one's life, all of a sudden?

SALLY. You could become a nun. Do they have Jewish nuns? (CHRIS *taps on the door.*)

CHRIS'S VOICE. The coffee is all ready.

NATALIA. You may come in now. (*She turns her back, and straightens her face.* CHRIS *comes in with coffee.*)

CHRIS. I only brought one cup. Sally doesn't take it, and I think I'm getting allergic to it, too.

NATALIA. You are very kind, but I do not think now that I have time. (*She turns.*) So, Christopher, we will start our lessons again now? I think now that I will perhaps take more. I will take two every day. You can manage that?

CHRIS. Yes, I can manage it. But that is an awful lot for you. It's an awful lot to do.

NATALIA. I need an awful lot to do. Good-by, Fräulein. I thank you, and I come again. (*She goes out, rather hurriedly.*)

CHRIS. What was all that about?

SALLY (*very nobly and remotely*). That was something personal. That poor girl is terribly unhappy.

CHRIS. What about?

SALLY (*as before*). This is something between women. (CHRIS *giggles.*) It is. I've given her some advice. Some very good advice.

CHRIS. You gave Fritz some advice, too.

SALLY. Oh, I did, didn't I? Oh, that was awful. Because it paid off. I'm never going to be funny and flippant again. I'm going to be dead serious, and take everyone's problems to heart. I am, Chris. I wish you wouldn't sit there, and snigger like that. You don't know how silly it makes you look.

(*Bell rings offstage.*)

CHRIS. I'm a bit on your nerves, aren't I, Sally?

SALLY. Yes, you are. Oh, it's not only you. It's everyone. I'm on my own nerves.

FRÄULEIN SCHNEIDER (*opening door*). Fräulein Sally, hier ist der Herr Americaner. Bitte, mein Herr. Bitte sehr.

(CLIVE *comes in. He carries a basket of champagne.*)

CLIVE. Well, hello, hello, hello there.

SALLY. Well, hello, Clive.

CHRIS. Hello. (*Handshakes are performed.*)

SALLY. We thought you'd forgotten all about us.

CLIVE. Oh, for God's sake, no. Say, I've only just heard you'd been sick. Why didn't you let me know?

SALLY. You weren't around.

CLIVE. What was the matter with you, anyway?

SALLY. I had an operation.

CLIVE. Oh gee, that's tough. How are you feeling now?

SALLY. Better. Much better. Now that I've seen you.

CLIVE. Well, that's fine. Feel like coming out to dinner tonight?

SALLY. I can't do that. It's all I can do to get to the bathroom.

CLIVE. Ah, come on. Do you good.

CHRIS. She can't, Clive. She really can't walk yet.

CLIVE. Oh, hell, anyone can walk if they want to.

CHRIS. No, she mustn't. Really.

CLIVE. Well, let's have dinner up here, then. All of us. I brought you some champagne.

SALLY. Oh, Clive, how wonderful of you. I was just saying to Chris that what I'd like best in the world would be some champagne.

CLIVE. Well, let's have it. It's still good and cold. I only just got it. Open it, will you, Chris, there's a good feller?

CHRIS. I'll just get another glass from my room. (*He goes out.*)

CLIVE. Well, let's take a look at you. Gee, you're a pale little lady. We'll have to pack you off some place to perk you up a bit. Where would you like to go?

SALLY. I don't really know, Clive. I think maybe I ought to stay here for my career.

CLIVE (*vaguely*). Your career?

SALLY. Yes, the theatre.

CLIVE. Oh, sure, sure.

SALLY. I mean, if I am going to do a play, we ought to start thinking and planning a bit quite soon.

CLIVE. Oh, plenty of time for that. Get you well first.

(CHRIS *returns with a tooth glass, and gets two more from the washstand.*)

SALLY. I'll be all right in a few days.

CLIVE. Get you really well.

SALLY. No, but Clive, I do think . . .

CLIVE. You leave that all to me. Leave that all to Uncle Clive. (*To* CHRIS) Say, are those the best glasses you can manage?

CHRIS. I think Fräulein Schneider may have some others.

SALLY. Don't bother, darling. All I want is champagne. Open it, won't you?

CHRIS. All right. (*He starts to do so.*)

SALLY. Where have you been, Clive?

CLIVE. Been?

SALLY. You've been away somewhere, haven't you?

CLIVE. Ah, just for a day or two.

SALLY. It's ten days.

CLIVE. Is it? Yeah, it may have been. I can never keep track of time when I'm on a bat. You know, this is a funny city. Driving here, just now, we ran right into a bit of shooting.

CHRIS. Shooting?

CLIVE. Seemed just like Chicago.

SALLY. Who was shooting at whom?

CLIVE. I don't know. Just shooting. Couple of people in the street, I guess. I thought I saw a fellow lying there, and a lot of people running in the opposite direction.

CHRIS. Where was this?

CLIVE. I don't know. Right in front of one of the big department stores. Birnbaum's, I think, where we bought you those fancy undies.

CHRIS. That's a Jewish store. That would be Nazi rioting, I imagine.

CLIVE. Say, who are these Nazis, anyway? I keep reading the word in the papers, when I look at them, and I never know who they are referring to. Are the Nazis the same as the Jews?

CHRIS. No—they're—well, they're more or less the opposite.

(*The champagne bottle is opened.*)

SALLY. Oh, that looks wonderful.

CLIVE. And there's a funeral going on to-day, too.

SALLY. Darling, isn't there always?

CLIVE. No, but this is the real thing. This is a real elegant funeral. It's been going on for over an hour. With banners and streamers, and God knows what all. I wonder who the guy was? He must have been a real swell.

CHRIS (*passing glasses*). He was an old liberal leader. They put him in prison once for trying to stop the war. So now everybody loves him.

SALLY. Oh, this is marvelous. Just what the doctor ordered. Let's drink to Clive. Our best friend.

CHRIS. To Clive. (*They drink.*)

CLIVE. Well, thank you both. I'll drink to the pair of you. Two real good playmates. (*He does so.*)

SALLY. You know, I think there's something almost sacred about champagne. The taste and the look of it. Like holy wine, or something. I think it's absolutely right that it's as expensive as it is. It makes one appreciate it more, like something really special. Like . . .

CHRIS. Like—*that!*

SALLY. Yes, exactly like *that.*

CLIVE. What's *that?*

SALLY (*vaguely noble*). Oh—love, and that sort of thing.

CLIVE. You know, kids, this is a pretty dreary sort of town. I've been here three weeks, and I'm getting kind of fed up with it.

SALLY (*alarmed*). You're not going away?

CLIVE. I was kinda thinking of it.

SALLY. Oh, no, Clive. You mustn't.

CLIVE (*suddenly*). What do you say we *all* go? All three of us.

CHRIS. But where?

CLIVE. Where would you like to go?

CHRIS (*as in a game*). Anywhere in the world?

CLIVE. Anywhere in the world.

CHRIS. I think I'd like to go to India.

SALLY. Oh no, it's all so terribly unsanitary. I want to go somewhere terrifically mysterious and sinister, and full of history. I'd like to go to Egypt.

CLIVE. We can do both. Say, what do you say—we take off from here as soon as Sally's well enough? Take the Orient Express.

SALLY. That's such a lovely name.

CLIVE. Take it as far as Athens. Then we can fly to Egypt. Then back to Marseilles. From there we can get a boat to South America. Then Tahiti. Singapore. Japan.

CHRIS. You know, you manage to say those names as though they were stations on the subway.

SALLY. Well, he's been to them all heaps of times, haven't you, Clive darling?

CLIVE. Sure. Sure, I have. But I'd kind of get a kick out of showing them to you two kids. And then we can end up in California.

CHRIS. You don't mean it, do you, Clive? Just take off and go—just like that?

SALLY. But of course, Chris. Why ever not? This is sheer absolute heaven.

CHRIS. And what happens to your stage career?

SALLY. Oh, that can wait. Or we can pick it up again in California. I'm sure

Clive knows all the movie magnates, don't you, Clive?

CLIVE. I know quite a few of them.

SALLY. I mean, you could get me on the films like that, if you wanted to?

CLIVE. Oh, I guess so. Well, what about it? When shall we take off? You won't need more than a week, will you? You can rest on the train.

SALLY. I can rest anywhere.

CLIVE. How's about a week from today?

SALLY. I think it would be marvelous.

CLIVE (*to* CHRIS). All right with you?

CHRIS (*sitting down, helplessly*). Yes, I —I guess so.

CLIVE. Okay, that's that, then. And, look, if we're going to have dinner up here, I'd better go get us a few things. What would you like? Some caviar, to start with?

SALLY. Oh, I'd adore that.

CLIVE. Then some soup. Some green turtle, maybe. And a partridge. With salad, of course. And I guess some of that chestnut ice cream with whipped cream all over it. And some fruit—some peaches.

SALLY. Get something for Fräulein Schneider.

CHRIS. Get her a pineapple. It's her idea of real luxury.

CLIVE. I think maybe we'd better get some new china, too, and some decent glasses.

CHRIS. Well, if we're going away next week . . .

CLIVE. Oh heck, you can present them to your landlady to make up for your rent. I'll go get them.

SALLY. Why don't you send your driver?

CLIVE. Heck no, this is kinda fun. Something to do. I'll be right back. I'll get some real good brandy, too—half a dozen bottles—and we'll make a real picnic of it. So long, kids. (*He goes out. A long silence.*)

SALLY. Isn't life extraordinary? Just when you think you've really touched bottom, something always turns up.

CHRIS. Do you think he means it?

SALLY. Yes, of course he does. You know, Chris, I really do adore him. I mean that. I really do.

CHRIS. I know. I've watched you doing it.

SALLY. You're looking all stunned. What's the matter?

CHRIS. I feel stunned. Doesn't it stun you when someone comes along and just whirls you right out of the whole flux of your life?

SALLY. No, dear, not a bit. Besides, my life hasn't got a flux. And I don't think yours has, either.

CHRIS. No, you're right, it hasn't.

SALLY. Well, then?

CHRIS. But what will become of us?

SALLY. We shall have a wonderful time.

CHRIS. And then?

SALLY. I don't know. Oh, stop bothering with it, Chris. You always spoil things so.

CHRIS. We shall never come back.

SALLY. I don't want to come back.

CHRIS. I suppose you'll marry him.

SALLY. Of course I will.

CHRIS. And I? What will I be?

SALLY. You'll be a sort of private secretary, or something.

CHRIS. Without any duties. You know, Sally, I can suddenly see myself ten years from now—in flannels and black-and-white shoes, pouring out drinks in the lounge of a Californian hotel. I'll be a bit glassy in the eyes, and a lot heavier round the jowls.

SALLY. You'll have to take a lot of exercise, that's all.

CHRIS (*going to the window*). You were both quite right. We've got nothing to do with these Germans down there—or the shooting, or the funeral, with the dead man in his coffin, or the words on the banners. You know, in a few days, we shall have forfeited all kinship with about ninety-nine per cent of the world's population. The men and women who earn their livings, and insure their lives, and are anxious about the future of their children.

SALLY. It's the only way to live. Isn't there something in the Bible about "Take no thought for the morrow"? That's exactly what it means.

CHRIS. I think in the Middle Ages, people must have felt like this when they believed they had sold themselves to the devil.

SALLY. Well, you needn't come, if you don't want to.

CHRIS. Oh no, I shall come. It's a funny feeling. Sort of exhilarating. Not really unpleasant. And yet, I'm sort of scared, too. If I do this, I'm lost. And yet I'm going to do it.

SALLY. Darling, is there any more in that bottle of champagne?

CHRIS. Sure.

SALLY (*pouring*). Chris, this is the end of one life, and the beginning of another. Two weeks from now, we'll probably be floating down the Nile, with the desert all round us in the moonlight, and all those marvelous sensual Arabs watching us from the tops of the pyramids. And then there'll be India. And a Maharajah will offer me my weight in diamonds if I'll spend one night in his harem.

CHRIS. You'd better put on some weight. Will you do it?

SALLY. Well, not unless he's one of the kind who looks like a sort of mixture of Valentino and Buddha. If you know what I mean.

CHRIS. Well, not exactly. What will I be doing all this time?

SALLY. Oh, you'll be looking simply marvelous and sexy in jodhpurs and an explorer's hat. And then there'll be feasts on volcanoes in the South Seas, and cocktails with Garbo. (*She pours more drinks.*) Chris, what is it they say in German when you're going on a journey, and they want to wish you luck?

CHRIS. Hals and Beinbruch.

SALLY. What does that mean?

CHRIS. Neck and leg-break. It's supposed to stop you having them.

SALLY. That's wonderful. (*Raising her glass*) Neck and leg-break, Chris.

CHRIS. Neck and leg-break.

(*They drink.*)

CURTAIN

SCENE TWO

SCENE: *Five days later. When the curtain rises,* CHRIS *is seated at the table finishing some coffee. There are one or two dress boxes lying around, and an open suitcase in front of the bed.*

FRÄULEIN SCHNEIDER *enters, carrying a large package.*

FRÄULEIN SCHNEIDER. Herr Issyvoo, there is a box for you from Landauer's store. I bring it in here, because the man has not come yet to repair the ceiling in your room. I think perhaps it is the news that has stopped him.

CHRIS. What news?

FRÄULEIN SCHNEIDER. They have closed the National Bank. I heard it this morning, and I couldn't believe it. I went down to see. And, Herr Issyvoo, it is true. The bank is closed at the corner of the Nollendorf Platz. There will be thousands ruined, I shouldn't wonder. Such times we live in! It was bad during the war. Then they promise us it will be better. And now it is almost worse again. It is the Jews. I know it is the Jews.

CHRIS. Fräulein Schneider, how can it be? You don't know what you are saying.

FRÄULEIN SCHNEIDER. They are too clever. And you buy things at Landauer's store. That is a Jewish store. What did you buy?

CHRIS (*opening the parcel*). I bought a suit. It's—it's a tropical suit. (*Then, with determination*) Fräulein Schneider, there is something that I have got to tell you. I should have told you before. Fräulein Sally and I are going away. We're going—well, right round the world. We're leaving on Thursday.

FRÄULEIN SCHNEIDER. *This* Thursday? The day after tomorrow?

CHRIS. Yes, I'm afraid so. We'll pay you till the end of the month, of course.

FRÄULEIN SCHNEIDER. But, Herr Issyvoo, this is dreadful. Both of you going away, and my other rooms empty, too. And now with the banks closing—what shall I do?

CHRIS. I'm terribly sorry, but there are other tenants. There must be.

FRÄULEIN SCHNEIDER. How shall I live? And you tell me now, at the last minute!

CHRIS. I know. I'm sorry, but—you can have all that new china and glass we have.

FRÄULEIN SCHNEIDER (*in an outburst*). Never, never did I think it would come to this. To live on other people—to become fond of them, as I have on you. To help Fräulein Sally, take her to the doctor—and then to have you walk out like this, as though I were nothing but a landlady to whom you can fling the rent.

CHRIS (*helplessly*). Fräulein Schneider, it's not that. . . .

FRÄULEIN SCHNEIDER. And now I am an old woman, and nobody will care what becomes of me. I can go drown myself in the Spree. (*She is crying now.* CHRIS *touches her.*)

CHRIS. Oh, please, Fräulein Schneider . . .

FRÄULEIN SCHNEIDER (*springing up*). No, do not touch me. It is the Judas touch.

(SALLY *comes in. She wears a new, light*

suit, carries another dress box. She is very gay.)

SALLY. What on earth's going on?

CHRIS. I've just broken it to Fräulein Schneider that we're leaving. I am afraid that she is rather upset.

FRÄULEIN SCHNEIDER. Upset? Yes, I am upset. You go off on a trip of the whole world. You can afford to do that. But me, I have had to wait for my money, because you were too hard up sometimes to pay me. And now you throw me the china and the glass as a tip. The china and the glass . . . I will throw them from the windows after your taxi as you go away. That is what I think from your china and your glass. And from you, too. (*She goes out.*)

SALLY. You're quite right, Chris. She *is* upset. What did you have to tell her for?

CHRIS. Well, I thought we had to. It's only two days now. You know, that was sort of awful what she said, about our being able to afford this trip.

SALLY. I don't see why.

CHRIS. It doesn't seem wrong to you—to let Clive pay it all?

SALLY. Well, we couldn't do it, if he didn't. And he *wants* to. I mean, we didn't *ask* for it. (*The bell rings.*)

CHRIS. I didn't feel that I could quite explain that to Fräulein Schneider.

SALLY. I've got an absolutely exquisite negligee. I must show it to you. (*She opens the box, and takes out a fluffy pink negligee.*) Look, isn't it simply marvelous?

CHRIS. But, Sally, what are you going to need that for?

SALLY. Darling, to lie around in.

CHRIS. Where?

SALLY. Anywhere. I expect we'll do lots of lying around.

FRÄULEIN SCHNEIDER (*quite grim now, announces*). Herr Wendel.

(FRITZ *enters.* FRÄULEIN SCHNEIDER *retires.*)

FRITZ. Well, then, hello, you.

SALLY. Hello. Look, Fritz, don't you think this is wonderful? (*She shows the negligee, jumping on the ottoman to do so.*)

FRITZ. But, yes. That is extremely seductive. It is for a part in the movies?

SALLY. No, it's to wear. We're going away, Fritz. Clive is taking us. All around the world. We're leaving on Thursday.

FRITZ. You say again, please.

CHRIS. We're going round the world.

FRITZ. The two of you. (*They nod.*) With Clive?

CHRIS. I know, Fritz. It doesn't sound likely. But he did ask us.

SALLY. Chris, do we have any of that champagne left?

CHRIS. Oh, yes, there are still about four bottles. You know he brought a dozen.

SALLY. Let's open one.

CHRIS (*getting it*). It isn't cold.

SALLY. That's all right. I'm terribly thirsty, and we've just got time before his car arrives to fetch us to lunch. (CHRIS *gets a bottle and glasses from the washstand.*) How are you, Fritz?

FRITZ. I am not good. I am not good at all.

SALLY. Oh, dear, what's the trouble now?

FRITZ. I would like to tell you. Can I, please?

SALLY. Yes, of course.

FRITZ. You remember, Chris, the advice you give me from Natalia. I attempt it. I think it goes well. And then I go again to see her, and she sends me a note. She will not see me, she will never see me again. (SALLY *turns away in embarrassment.*) I beg. I plead. I go again. At last she see me. She tell me it is all over. (CHRIS *opens the bottle and pours.*) And she shows me a note that her father has received.

SALLY. From whom?

FRITZ. It is not signed. But it say, Herr Landauer, beware. We are going to settle the score with all you dirty Jews. We give you twenty-four hours to leave Germany. If not, you are dead men.

CHRIS (*stopping pouring*). Good God! When was this?

FRITZ. This was last night. And she say that with that sort of thing she cannot think now from anything else, and I am to go away and never come back. And when I try to comfort her, and tell her that it is some silly schoolboy who writes it, she scream at me that I do not understand. That I am like all the others. That her father is worried sick, and her mother is falling all the time ohnmächtig . . .

SALLY. What is that?

CHRIS. Fainting.

FRITZ. Ja, she is falling fainting, and now will I go, please. Please. Please. Please. So I go.

SALLY (*embarrassed*). Well . . . Chris, isn't that champagne ready yet?

CHRIS (*roused*). Oh, yes.

SALLY. Well, let's have it. Here, Fritz. Here's how.

CHRIS. How.

FRITZ (*sadly*). How.

SALLY. Oh, this is wonderful. Even warm, it is wonderful.

CHRIS. What is Herr Landauer going to do?

SALLY. I should think he is going away, isn't he?

FRITZ. No, he will not go away. He wants that Natalia and her mother should go. And Natalia will not. I think her mother will go to Paris. But Natalia will stay by her father.

SALLY. If it was me, I'd fly like a bird. If I could afford it. And I'm sure they can. I mean, what is the point of staying, with that sort of thing going on?

FRITZ. I do not know. (*He drinks again, then suddenly flings his glass from him with a melodramatic gesture.*) Verfluchter Kerl! (*He buries his head in his hands.*)

SALLY. Fritz, what on earth's the matter?

CHRIS. What is it?

FRITZ. It is I. Please, can I tell you something else? Can I tell you both something?

SALLY. Yes, of course.

FRITZ. It is something I have never told anyone in my life before. But now I must make confession. I am a Jew.

SALLY (*quite unperturbed*). Well?

FRITZ. That does not surprise you?

SALLY. I sort of had an idea you were, especially when you made so much fuss about not being. And then I forgot all about it. But so what?

FRITZ. So what? I have lied and pretended. Even to Natalia I have lied.

CHRIS. If you were so keen on getting her, I should have thought that was the very thing to tell her.

SALLY. Her parents wanted her to marry a Jew.

FRITZ. I know. I know. She has told me that. And still I could not say it. I think I wanted it even more, that no one should ever know. Even now, I cannot be one from the Landauers, and have letters like that written to me. I am ashamed from myself, but it is so. And now I have told you, and now you know me for what I am. And it is not nice. It is not nice at all. (*A long pause.*) Well, you say something, please.

SALLY. Fritz, I think you are taking it all too seriously. I mean, it is your own business.

FRITZ. I do not think it is any more. But still I cannot speak.

(*Bell rings.*)

SALLY. That'll be the car. Clive's car. Quick, let's have another drop of champagne. Fritz?

FRITZ. No, I do not want any more.

SALLY. Come on, it'll do you good. Here . . . (*She offers him her glass. He pushes it away.*) Oh, well, have it your own way.

CHRIS (*touching* FRITZ). Fritz, I am terribly sorry. (FRÄULEIN SCHNEIDER *enters with a note. She gives it to* SALLY *and goes out again.*) I know it's not for me to give you any advice. I don't think I could, anyhow. But don't you think maybe you should tell Natalia that . . .

SALLY (*who has opened the note and read it*). But . . . but . . . (*She cannot speak.*)

CHRIS. What is it, Sally?

SALLY. Oh, it's nothing. Look, Fritz, we've got to go out to lunch . . .

CHRIS (*shocked*). But, Sally . . .

SALLY (*sharply*). Well, we have. And right away. Fritz, I'm not trying to get rid of you, but we do have to go.

FRITZ. Ja, Ja, of course.

SALLY. I'm most terribly sorry. And please, please come back. Come back soon.

FRITZ. But you are going away.

SALLY. Oh . . . yes . . . Well, come to-morrow.

FRITZ. I will see. Good-by, Sally. Good-by, Chris. I think maybe now I go pray a little. But in what church? I do not know. (*He goes out.*)

CHRIS. Really, Sally, that was a little cruel. Fritz really is in trouble . . .

SALLY. Yes, well, so are we. Real trouble. Read that. (*She hands him the note. He reads it.*)

CHRIS. Good God!

SALLY. Read it aloud, will you? I want to be sure I got it right.

CHRIS (*reading*). "Dear Sally and Chris, I can't stick this damned town any longer. I'm off to the States. Hoping to see you sometime. Clive. These are in case I forgot anything." (*He looks in the envelope.*) Three hundred marks. (*A long pause.*) Well!

SALLY. I should think you might be able to say something better than "well."

CHRIS. I said "well" when it happened. I can't think of anything else to say, now it isn't going to.

SALLY. Do you think it's true?

CHRIS. Do you want to call up the hotel and see? See if he's gone?

SALLY. You call. I don't want him to think I'm running after him.

CHRIS. I feel rather the same way.

SALLY. We could ask Fräulein Schneider to call. (*Opens door.*) Fräulein Schneider . . . Fräulein Schneider . . .

CHRIS. What are you going to tell her?

SALLY. Nothing. Just ask her to call.

CHRIS. And if he's gone . . . ?

SALLY. Well, we should have to tell her in the end. That just shows why you shouldn't have told her now.

(FRÄULEIN SCHNEIDER *enters.*)

FRÄULEIN SCHNEIDER. You called for me?

SALLY (*over-sweetly*). Yes, Schneiderschen. Will you be a liebling, and call the Adlon Hotel, and ask for Mr. Mortimer?

FRÄULEIN SCHNEIDER. You want to speak to him?

SALLY. No, I don't. I just want you to ask for him. And if he *is* there—well, say we'll be a little late for lunch. And then come and tell us. (FRÄULEIN SCHNEIDER *goes without a word.*)

CHRIS. You know he's gone, don't you?

SALLY. I suppose I do, really. But we've got to be sure. Do you think he did it on purpose? Just to get us all steamed up, and then let us down like this?

CHRIS. I think he just got fed up.

SALLY. And what about us?

CHRIS. I don't imagine he even remembered us—or not for more than a minute. I think that's the way he lives. And that he leaves every town and every set of acquaintances just that way.

SALLY. Easy come, easy go.

CHRIS. Yes.

SALLY. We were easy come, all right. But, Chris, don't you think it was outrageous? I mean, really outrageous?

CHRIS. Sally, I don't think we've got too much right to have an opinion anyway, about the whole thing.

SALLY. And what have we got out of it?

CHRIS. Not much. But it didn't last very long.

SALLY. I don't think we're much good as gold-diggers, are we, darling? (*They be-*

gin to laugh. FRÄULEIN SCHNEIDER *returns.*)

FRÄULEIN SCHNEIDER. Herr Mortimer has left, Fräulein. He has gone back to the United States.

SALLY. I see. Thank you.

CHRIS. And, Fräulein Schneider, we won't be going away—after all.

FRÄULEIN SCHNEIDER (*overjoyed*). Ah, Herr Issyvoo, you mean that?

CHRIS. Yes, I do.

FRÄULEIN SCHNEIDER. Oh, but that is good. That is wonderful. Neither of you? Not Fräulein Sally, either?

SALLY. No, neither of us.

FRÄULEIN SCHNEIDER. Then, that is a miracle! Oh, but I am happy. I am happy. (*She seizes* SALLY *by the waist, and starts to dance.*)

SALLY (*releasing herself*). Yes, I'm sure you're happy, Fräulein. But not now, please. I'd like you to leave us alone.

FRÄULEIN SCHNEIDER (*repentant*). But, of course. Forgive me, Fräulein Sally. I go now. (*She leaves.*)

CHRIS. Do you want to come out and have some lunch?

SALLY. I don't think I could eat any.

CHRIS. I don't, either.

SALLY. Well, there we are. We've got three hundred marks.

CHRIS. What are you going to do with them?

SALLY. We'll divide them.

CHRIS. No, you take them. They were sent to you.

SALLY. They were meant for both of us. Halves, Chris.

CHRIS. Well, thank you. (*She halves the money.*)

SALLY. I shall take this negligee back.

CHRIS. I'll take this suit back, too.

SALLY (*changing into mules and opening the jacket of her suit*). And we shall have to find some work. There was a man who wrote to me the other day about a job in Frankfurt. I never answered him, because I thought we'd be gone. I'll go and see him this afternoon. (*Starting to go through her address book.*) He's a horrible old man, and he's always trying to go to bed with me, but I've got to make some money, somehow—I suppose. I've got his address here somewhere.

CHRIS. I'll have to put my advertisement in the paper again. English lessons given.

SALLY (*finding something else*). Oh, and

there's this. Do you want to earn some money, Chris?

CHRIS. You know I do. I need to. (*Puts suit box on floor.*)

SALLY (*pouring champagne*). Well, there's a man who's starting a magazine. It's going to be terribly highbrow with lots of marvelous modern photographs— you know, girls' heads reflected upside down in inkpots. (*Passing drinks*) Here, Chris. It's silly to waste it. Well, he wanted me to write an article in the first number on the English girl. I forgot all about it, and I haven't an idea what to say, so why don't you do it for me? I'll give you the money.

CHRIS. That's fine. Thank you. But you must have part. How soon do you want it done?

SALLY. I should give it him in a day or two at the latest.

CHRIS. How long is it to be?

SALLY. Oh, I don't know. About *that* long. (*She gesticulates, then gets a book.*) Here's a dictionary, in case there are any words you can't spell.

CHRIS (*taking it, amused*). Good.

SALLY (*her arms around his neck*). Oh, Chris, I do like you. You're like a marvelous brother.

CHRIS. I feel the same thing. But, you know, Sally, we've been delivered from something. From the Devil. I know it's disappointing, in a way. . . . That's where the old plays and operas were wrong. . . . There ought to be a sort of disappointment chorus at the end. But it is another chance.

SALLY. Yes, I know. It couldn't have gone on forever. Clive wasn't the type. He'd have ditched us somewhere, and that would have been far worse.

CHRIS. It would have been worse still if he hadn't ditched us.

SALLY. He never meant to play straight with us. You're right. He was the Devil.

CHRIS. I didn't mean that. The Devil was in *us*. Sally, how about our trying to reform, and change our way of life a bit?

SALLY. What's wrong with our way of life?

CHRIS. Just about everything. Isn't it?

SALLY. I suppose so. Not getting any work. Not even trying to. That operation. The lies I've written Mother. The way I haven't written her at all for weeks now.

CHRIS. Me, too. Can't we reform, Sally?

SALLY. Yes, we can. I'll tell you something, Chris. Something I've just decided.

CHRIS. What's that?

SALLY. I'm sick of being a whore. I'm never going to look at another man with money, as long as I live. (*He laughs.*) What's funny about that?

CHRIS. Nothing. It's a beginning, anyway.

SALLY. What are *you* going to begin on?

CHRIS. I'm going to start work tomorrow morning.

SALLY (*carried away*). We're both going to begin. We're going to be good. Oh, Chris, isn't it wonderful?

CHRIS (*smiling*). Yes, Sally.

SALLY. We're going to be quite, quite different people. We're even going to look wonderful, too. People will turn around and stare at us in the street, because our eyes will be shining like diamonds.

CHRIS. Diamonds—without any rings under them.

SALLY (*very gaily*). And think how we'll feel in the mornings. Imagine what it will be like to wake up without coughing, or feeling even the least little bit sick.

CHRIS. We'll have appetites like wolves. Ravening wolves.

SALLY. Don't you suppose we ought to diet? Eat just nuts and things?

CHRIS. All right. And we'll give up smoking in bed . . .

SALLY. And drinking before breakfast.

CHRIS (*shocked*). Sally, do you?

SALLY. We must have a time-table. What time shall we get up?

CHRIS. Eight o'clock.

SALLY. Half-past seven.

CHRIS. All right.

SALLY. We shall take cold baths. You have yours first.

CHRIS. And do exercises.

SALLY. Then we'll have breakfast together, and talk German. Nothing but German.

CHRIS. Ja. Jawohl.

SALLY. Then we should study something. Do you think we could learn a useful trade?

CHRIS. We'll weave from eight-thirty to nine. And then spend an hour making small, hand-painted boxes.

SALLY (*laughing hard*). And then it'll be time for you to start your novel, while I practice Interpretive Dancing. You know, with shawls and things . . .

CHRIS. Sally, joking aside. You are serious about all this, aren't you?

SALLY. Of course I am. Terribly serious. (*She gets the address book.*) I'm going to start calling up everyone I know.

CHRIS. What for?

SALLY. To see what's going on. And then, one decent piece of luck . . .

CHRIS (*urgently*). Oh, no, Sally. That isn't what we need. A piece of good luck today—a piece of bad luck tomorrow—always at the mercy of *things* again . . .

SALLY. One *is*. That's life. It's all accident.

CHRIS (*as before*). Accidents are only the result of things one's done. Things that one is.

SALLY. Why, I could go to a party tonight, and I could meet the most wonderful man, who'd make all the difference to my whole life and my career . . . (*She breaks off, looking at him.*) What's the matter? Why do you look like that?

CHRIS (*slowly*). Sally, you weren't serious. You didn't mean a word of it.

SALLY. Yes, I did. I meant every word. I'm going to be quite different. But there's no reason why I shouldn't go out. I don't have to shut myself up in prison. That isn't what you want, is it?

CHRIS. No, Sally, of course not. But . . .

SALLY (*angrily*). Well, then, stop looking so disapproving. You're almost as bad as Mother. She never stopped nagging at me. That's why I had to lie to her. I always lie to people, or run away from them, if they won't accept me as I am.

CHRIS. I know you do, Sally.

SALLY (*putting on an act*). I think I'm really rather a strange and extraordinary person, Chris. (*Pause.*) What's the matter? You laughed at me the first time I told you that. Can't you laugh now? Come on. (*She starts to laugh, not too brightly. He starts a moment later, still more feebly. The laughter dies. She tries again—it fails. They move slowly away from each other.*)

CURTAIN

ACT THREE

SCENE ONE

SCENE: *Two days later. The room is untidy. A half-used coffee tray is on the table with a glass of brandy. The bed is unmade,* *and clothes are strewn around the room.* FRÄULEIN SCHNEIDER *is tidying up. There is a knock on the door.*

———

CHRIS's VOICE. Sally, may I come in?

FRÄULEIN SCHNEIDER. Come in, Herr Issyvoo. (CHRIS *comes in.*) Fräulein Sally is telephoning.

CHRIS. She's up very late.

FRÄULEIN SCHNEIDER. She was in very late last night.

CHRIS. I left a manuscript in here for her yesterday afternoon.

FRÄULEIN SCHNEIDER. She did not come back until almost six this morning. I think maybe she drank a little too much. Her clothes are all over the floor. And she had only half her coffee this morning, and some brandy too. It is not good so early. (SALLY *enters. She is wearing a robe, and looks hung-over.*)

SALLY. Oh, hello, Chris.

CHRIS. Hello, Sally.

SALLY. Leave all that stuff for now, Fräulein. I'm going to wear it. I'm going out quite soon. You can do the room then.

FRÄULEIN SCHNEIDER. Very good, Fräulein. (*She goes.*)

CHRIS. I haven't seen you for a day and a half.

SALLY. I know. I've missed you, Chris.

CHRIS. I've missed you, too. I say, you don't look too well this morning.

SALLY. I've got a terrible hangover.

CHRIS. What were you doing last night?

SALLY. I was out with some people. I've been out both nights. I've been an awful fool, Chris. But don't scold me, please.

CHRIS. What have you been up to?

SALLY. Oh, not *that*.

CHRIS. I wasn't thinking of that!

SALLY. But we never stopped going around. And then I got drunk and sentimental the first night, and I telephoned Mother in London.

CHRIS. Good God, what for?

SALLY. I suddenly felt like it. But we had the most awful connection, and I couldn't hear a word. And last night was worse. We went to the most boring places. Oh, Chris, I need someone to stop me. I really do. I wish I'd stayed home with you.

CHRIS. Well, thank you, Sally.

SALLY. But you're awfully nice to come back to.

CHRIS. You're nice to have come back. I say, that sounds like a popular song.

SALLY. Oh, it does. Maybe we could write it together and make a fortune. (*She improvises a tune.*) "You're awfully nice to come back to."

CHRIS (*doing the same*). "You're awfully nice to come back."

SALLY AND CHRIS (*singing together*). "You're awfully nice to come back to . . ."

SALLY (*her arms around him*). I do think we belong together. Much more than if we'd ever had an affair. That little quarrel we had didn't mean anything, did it?

CHRIS. I don't think two people can live as close as we do, and not have them.

SALLY. But it was that that sent me out on that idiotic binge.

CHRIS (*pause*). Did you read the article I left you?

SALLY. The what, dear?

CHRIS. My article.

SALLY (*vaguely*). Oh, yes, I—looked at it.

CHRIS. Well?

SALLY (*too brightly*). I'm terribly sorry, Chris. But it won't do.

CHRIS. Why, what's wrong with it?

SALLY. It's not nearly snappy enough.

CHRIS. Snappy?

SALLY. But it's all right, Christopher. I've got someone else to do it.

CHRIS. Oh? Who?

SALLY. Kurt Rosenthal. I called him this morning.

CHRIS. Who's he?

SALLY. Really, Chris, I thought you took an interest in the cinema. He's miles the best young scenario writer. He earns pots of money.

CHRIS. Then why's he doing this?

SALLY. As a favor to me. He said he'd dictate it while he's shaving, and send it round to the editor's flat.

CHRIS. Well, journalism isn't really in my line. But I think you might have let me know.

SALLY. I didn't think you'd want to be bothered.

CHRIS. And *he* would?

SALLY (*starting to dress*). He doesn't make such a fuss about writing as you do. He's writing a novel in his spare time. He's so terribly busy, he can only dictate it while he's having a bath.

CHRIS (*bitterly*). I bet that makes it wonderful.

SALLY. He read me the first few chap-ters. Honestly, I think it's the best novel I've ever read.

CHRIS. But that doesn't add up to very many, does it?

SALLY (*her tone sharpening, from his*). He's the kind of author I really admire. And he's not stuck up, either. Not like one of these young men who, because they've written one book, start talking about art, and imagining they're the most wonderful authors in the world.

CHRIS. Just who are you talking about, Sally?

SALLY (*brushing her hair*). Well, you do, Chris. You know you do. And it's silly to get jealous.

CHRIS (*angrily*). Jealous? Who's jealous?

SALLY. There's no need to get upset, either.

CHRIS (*furious*). I am not upset. You don't like my article. All right, you needn't go on about it. I can't think why I expected you to, with that snappy little bird-brain of yours. Or your rich, successful friends either, from whom you seem to have got all this stuff about me.

SALLY (*equally angry*). Would you like to know what my friends said about you?

CHRIS. No, I wouldn't.

SALLY. Well, I'll tell you. They said you were ruining me. That I'd lost all my sparkle and my effervescence. And that it was all due to you. I've let you eat me up, just sitting here, pouring myself into you.

CHRIS. Oh, is that what you've been doing?

SALLY. It's all you want. You're like a vampire. If you don't have someone around you, you sit about in bars waiting to devour someone.

CHRIS. Your friends said that?

SALLY. My friends are a lot better than the tatty people you run around with. All your friends seem to be interested in, is just flopping into bed.

CHRIS. And since when have you had anything against bed?

SALLY. I haven't anything. So long as it leads somewhere.

CHRIS. You mean not just for the fun of it.

SALLY. That's disgusting. That's like ani-mals. But, you know, Chris, I'll tell you something. I've outgrown you.

CHRIS (*turns to her*). You've *what*?

SALLY. I've gone beyond you. I'd better move away from here.

CHRIS. All right. When?

SALLY. The sooner the better, I should think.

CHRIS. That's fine with me.

SALLY. Good.

CHRIS. So, this is the end for us?

SALLY. Yes. If you want it that way. We'll probably bump into each other somewhere, sometime, I expect.

CHRIS. Well, call me sometime, and ask me around for a cocktail.

SALLY (*pausing*). I never know whether you're being serious, or not.

CHRIS. Try it and find out, if your friends will spare you the time.

SALLY (*throwing it at him*). You know, you make me sick. Good-by, Chris.

CHRIS (*alone*). What a little bitch she is! Well, I've always known that from the start. No, that's not true. I've flattered myself she was fond of me. Nothing would please me better than to see her whipped. Really whipped. Not that I care a curse what she thinks of my article . . . Well, not much. My literary conceit is proof against anything she could say. It's her criticism of myself. The awful, sexual flair women have for taking the stuffing out of men. It's no good telling myself that Sally had the vocabulary and mind of a twelve-year-old schoolgirl. . . . I mismanaged our interview, right from the beginning. I should have been wonderful, convincing, fatherly, mature. I made the one fatal mistake. I let her see I was jealous. Vulgarly jealous. I feel prickly all over with shame. Friends, indeed! Well, I certainly won't see her again, after all this. Never. Never! (SALLY *returns, very shattered.*)

SALLY. Chris, something awful's happened. Guess who I met in the street, right outside. I met Mother.

CHRIS. Whose mother?

SALLY. Mine.

CHRIS. I thought you said she was in London.

SALLY. She was. But that call of mine upset her. I suppose I did sound a bit drunk. Anyway, she jumped to conclusions, and into an aeroplane. Chris, you're going to have to do something for me. I've been writing her now and then . . . I mean, they do send me money from time to time. I've never had the nerve to tell you, but I sort of gave her to understand—when I first moved in here—that we were engaged.

CHRIS. That who was engaged?

SALLY. You and I. To be married.

CHRIS. Sally, you didn't!

SALLY. Well, I needed someone who sounded like a good, steady influence—and you were the best I could think of. She's in the sitting-room. I told her this place was all untidy, but she'll be in in a minute. Oh, and her name isn't Mrs. Bowles. It's Mrs. Watson-Courtneidge. That's my real name. Only you can't imagine the Germans pronouncing it.

CHRIS. And I'm supposed to stand by and pretend? Oh, no, Sally.

SALLY. Chris, you've got to. You owe it to me.

CHRIS. For what? For letting me eat you up? I'm sorry. And I'm going to my room.

SALLY (*getting in his way*). If you don't, I'll tell her the most awful things about you.

CHRIS. I'm afraid I don't care. Tell her what you like.

SALLY (*pleading*). Chris, you can't do this to me.

CHRIS. After the things you just said to me? That I made you sick.

SALLY. That was just an expression.

CHRIS. No, Sally. We're through. Quite through.

SALLY. Well, we still can be, after she goes home. Only, help me keep her happy. Don't believe everything I said at first about Mother. She isn't easy. Please, darling. Please! (*Her arms are around his neck. He struggles to disengage himself. Then* MRS. WATSON-COURTNEIDGE *comes in. She is a middle-aged English lady, in tweeds. She carries a coat.*)

MRS. WATSON-COURTNEIDGE (*catching sight of the embrace*). Excuse me.

SALLY (*extricating herself*). Oh . . .

MRS. WATSON-COURTNEIDGE. I hope this is Mr. Isherwood.

SALLY. Yes. Christopher.

MRS. WATSON-COURTNEIDGE. I'm Mother.

CHRIS. I imagined that.

MRS. WATSON-COURTNEIDGE. Well—don't I deserve a kiss, too?

CHRIS (*as* SALLY *looks pleadingly at him*). Oh—yes, of course. (*A kiss is performed.*)

MRS. WATSON-COURTNEIDGE. You're not a bit like I imagined you.

CHRIS. Oh, really. How did you imagine me?

MRS. WATSON-COURTNEIDGE. Oh, quite

different. So this is your room, Sally. Yes, I can see why you said it was untidy.

SALLY. I got up very late this morning. Fräulein Schneider hasn't really had time to do it.

MRS. WATSON-COURTNEIDGE. I don't imagine she does it very well at the best of times. I've just been having a little talk with her. I can't say I like her very much. And why does she sleep in the sitting-room?

CHRIS. So that she can watch the corner.

MRS. WATSON-COURTNEIDGE. And what happens on the corner?

CHRIS. Oh—*that*!

SALLY. Chris!

MRS. WATSON-COURTNEIDGE. I beg your pardon?

CHRIS (*vaguely*). This and that.

MRS. WATSON-COURTNEIDGE. I should think she'd be much better occupied, looking after . . . (*Dusting the table with her fingers*) that and this! (*She picks up the brandy glass.*) Sally, you haven't been drinking brandy, I hope.

SALLY. That's Chris's glass.

MRS. WATSON-COURTNEIDGE. On *your* breakfast tray? Where do *you* live, Mr. Isherwood?

CHRIS. Just across the hall.

MRS. WATSON-COURTNEIDGE (*dryly*). How convenient!

SALLY. What do you mean by that, Mother?

MRS. WATSON-COURTNEIDGE. Sally, dear, I'm not asking for details. There are things one doesn't choose to know. But tell me, you two, when are you getting married?

SALLY. I don't know, Mother. We're happy as—we are. Aren't we, Chris?

CHRIS (*grimly*). Just as we are.

MRS. WATSON-COURTNEIDGE. I can well believe it. But sooner or later, these things have to be—well, shall we say, tidied up. There are some questions I would like to ask you, Mr. Isherwood.

CHRIS. Yes?

MRS. WATSON-COURTNEIDGE. I've read your book.

CHRIS. Oh, really?

MRS. WATSON-COURTNEIDGE. After Sally wrote me the title, I got it from the library—with a good deal of trouble. It's an odd book. Was it a success?

CHRIS. No. Not really.

MRS. WATSON-COURTNEIDGE. That doesn't altogether surprise me. I take it you don't live on your writing?

CHRIS. No. Hardly. (*Warningly*) Sally!

MRS. WATSON-COURTNEIDGE. What do you live on?

CHRIS. I teach English.

MRS. WATSON-COURTNEIDGE. And is that sufficient?

CHRIS. I get by.

MRS. WATSON-COURTNEIDGE. Can two get by?

CHRIS. I'm inclined to doubt it. (*As before, but more so*) Sally!

MRS. WATSON-COURTNEIDGE. Well that is not my concern. That will be Sally's father's.

CHRIS (*getting no response from SALLY*). Well, now if you'll excuse me, Sally . . .

MRS. WATSON-COURTNEIDGE. Are you not lunching with us?

SALLY. Yes, of course he is.

CHRIS. Sally, I can't.

SALLY. Yes, you can. You were lunching with me.

CHRIS. Look, I think there's something we ought to clear up.

SALLY. *No!*

MRS. WATSON-COURTNEIDGE. What is that? (*Silence a moment. Then* CHRIS *gives way.*)

CHRIS. I haven't got any decent clothes.

SALLY. You've got your blue suit.

CHRIS. It's almost in rags by daylight.

MRS. WATSON-COURTNEIDGE. My dear Mr. Isherwood, it's not your clothes we want, it's your company. I know all about your background. Anything you wear will be all right, so long as it is clean.

CHRIS. Well, that's part of the point.

SALLY (*pushing him out*). Go and change, Chris. We'll wait here for you.

CHRIS (*after a look at her*). I won't be a minute. (*He goes.*)

MRS. WATSON-COURTNEIDGE. He's an odd young man, Sally.

SALLY. Oh, I don't know, Mother.

MRS. WATSON-COURTNEIDGE. Tell me, that strange telephone call of yours—how much was Mr. Isherwood involved in it?

SALLY. Involved?

MRS. WATSON-COURTNEIDGE. Had you had a few too many cocktails because of some —well—little quarrel with him?

SALLY. Oh, no, Mother. Chris and I never quarrel.

MRS. WATSON-COURTNEIDGE. Well, in any case, I think you two have been together quite enough for the moment. You had better move into the hotel with me.

SALLY (*protesting*). No, Mother, I . . .

MRS. WATSON-COURTNEIDGE. Sally, don't answer back. You always answer back. I've begun to realize that things are a little more complicated than I had imagined. Hasn't Mr. Isherwood suggested any date for your wedding?

SALLY. No, Mother, I don't think he has.

MRS. WATSON-COURTNEIDGE. I'm not suggesting he will let you down. He's a gentleman. That's one comfort. But . . .

SALLY (*urgently*). Mother, you've got entirely the wrong idea about Chris and me. We aren't . . .

MRS. WATSON-COURTNEIDGE (*interrupting her*). Sally, that is something you might have had to say to your grandmother. You don't have to say it to me.

SALLY. But, Mother . . .

MRS. WATSON-COURTNEIDGE (*as before*). Mother's quite broad-minded.

SALLY (*giving way*). Well, all right, but don't rush him. Don't try and force him, or anything.

MRS. WATSON-COURTNEIDGE. Trust Mother! I see you still have that picture. You had that in the nursery. "The Kitten's Awakening." I'm glad you still have that. The old things are still the best, after all, aren't they?

SALLY (*subdued*). Yes, Mother.

MRS. WATSON-COURTNEIDGE (*embracing her*). We must get you back to them.

CURTAIN

SCENE TWO

SCENE: *The same. Afternoon. About three days later.*

AT RISE: FRITZ *is on stage.* FRÄULEIN SCHNEIDER *is setting a tray of coffee for him. The old pictures are back on the walls. The room is again as in Scene I.*

FRÄULEIN SCHNEIDER. He is always back around this time, Herr Wendel. You cannot have to wait long.

FRITZ. I am glad that Christopher could move back into this room again. Will he stay on here?

FRÄULEIN SCHNEIDER. Oh, I hope. He is doing better now. Starting new lessons. It is true they are almost all to the Jews, but

even so there is at least some good that comes from them that way. (FRITZ *does not answer.*) Is it true, Herr Wendel, that they will take the money away from the Jews, and drive them all out?

FRITZ. I have no idea.

FRÄULEIN SCHNEIDER. It would be a good thing. Do you not agree with me?

FRITZ. I don't really know.

FRÄULEIN SCHNEIDER. But you must know, Herr Wendel. That is what the speakers all say. Everyone must know, and everyone must agree and only then can Germany be saved. (*Voices heard off stage.*)

CHRIS'S VOICE. Go right in there, Natalia. Are you sure you're all right?

NATALIA'S VOICE. Oh, yes, I thank you. I am all right.

CHRIS'S VOICE. And then come to my room. It's the old room. (*He comes in. He is a little more messed up than usual.*) Oh, hello, Fritz. I didn't know you were here. (FRÄULEIN SCHNEIDER *goes out.*)

FRITZ. Was that Natalia's voice I heard outside?

CHRIS. Yes, she's gone to the bathroom. I must wash my hands.

FRITZ. What is the matter?

CHRIS. There was a bit of trouble. (*He pours water into the basin.*)

FRITZ. But what is it all about?

CHRIS (*washing his hands*). I was walking with Natalia after her lesson. We ran into a bunch of toughs. Nazis, of course. They were holding a street meeting. And Natalia insisted on joining in.

FRITZ. Joining in?

CHRIS. Yes, she got quite fierce. She made a speech. She was almost like Joan of Arc. I was quite astonished.

FRITZ. She is wonderful, that girl.

CHRIS. And she was hit in the face with a stone.

FRITZ. Um Gotteswillen.

CHRIS. It wasn't serious. At least, I don't think it was. I wanted her to go to a doctor, but she wouldn't. I think she is a bit shaken, that's all. And this place was nearer than her home. I brought her here.

FRITZ. It is better perhaps if your landlady does not see her.

CHRIS. Why?

FRITZ. She is not very partial to the Jews, your landlady.

CHRIS. Yes, I know. But she doesn't know what she is talking about.

FRITZ. She knows as much as most people.

CHRIS. And that is the tragedy. (CHRIS *takes a series of Band-Aids, and starts to put them on his hands rather excessively.*)

FRITZ. What is with your hands? Were you in it too?

CHRIS. Well, after Natalia started, I couldn't really keep out of it. Trying to get her away.

FRITZ. Natalia should not stay here.

CHRIS. She'll stay as long as her father stays.

FRITZ. She would go if she married.

CHRIS. I doubt that.

FRITZ (*urgently*). But she ought to go! Christopher, I know now I am in love with Natalia. I have not seen her, but I am in love with her. (NATALIA *enters. There is a small scar, newly washed, on her face.*)

NATALIA. So, Christopher, I think now . . . (*She sees* FRITZ, *and stops*) Oh, Fritz.

FRITZ. Ja, Natalia.

NATALIA. Christopher did not tell me you were here.

FRITZ. He did not know.

CHRIS. Let me give you some brandy, Natalia.

NATALIA. I do not think so.

CHRIS. Yes, but I do think so. You need something. And it's quite good brandy. It's part of—quite a good loot. I'm going to have some.

FRITZ (*to* NATALIA). Please, may I see your face?

NATALIA (*turning*). There is nothing there.

FRITZ (*kneeling*). I would like to see, please. It is clean? You have washed it? You have washed it thoroughly?

NATALIA. I have washed it thoroughly.

CHRIS. Would you like to put a Band-Aid on it?

NATALIA. On my face?

CHRIS. I think you should. You can get blood poisoning.

NATALIA. And a bandage will help that?

CHRIS. I have some iodine. I can put that on for you.

NATALIA. Not on my face, I thank you.

FRITZ. You let me put one of these on. Just a very small one. Like so. (*He holds one up.*)

NATALIA (*touched, but unwilling to show it*). I can put it on myself.

FRITZ. I know, but let me do it, please.

You drink your brandy, and let me do it. (*He starts to do so.*)

CHRIS (*looking at his hands*). You know, I wonder if I shouldn't take these Band-Aids off, and put on some iodine. I could get gangrene.

NATALIA. No, Christopher, you could not.

CHRIS. You never know. Then they amputate your hands. And you can't write or type any more. (*He tears off the Band-Aids and paints on iodine.*)

FRITZ (*finishing his job*). There (*He seems to feel a little faint.*) Now I take some brandy. (*He and* NATALIA *gulp some, hastily.*)

NATALIA. And now I think I go home.

FRITZ. You let me take you, please.

NATALIA. My dear young man, I . . .

FRITZ (*finishing for her*). I am not yet sixty years old, and I can go home unmolested.

NATALIA. I prefer that I go alone.

FRITZ. I would like that you let me take you.

NATALIA. And if we run into another of these street riots?

FRITZ. I would still like to take you. (CHRIS *raises his head. The two men exchange glances.* FRITZ *nods very gently.*) I tell it now.

CHRIS. Let him take you, Natalia. I would feel better.

NATALIA. Very well. I see you tomorrow, Christopher. At the usual hour.

CHRIS. Yes, of course. Good-by, Natalia. I admired you very much this afternoon.

FRITZ. I, too.

NATALIA. I cannot see why. Come. (*She goes out with* FRITZ.)

(CHRIS *looks after them, then picks up the Band-Aids and the iodine, and resumes his painting.*)

CHRIS. It doesn't look too good. (*He splashes on some more iodine.*)

(FRÄULEIN SCHNEIDER *comes in.*)

FRÄULEIN SCHNEIDER. I take the coffee tray. What is with your hands, Herr Issyvoo?

CHRIS. I think they may be poisoned.

FRÄULEIN SCHNEIDER. But how did you come to hurt them?

CHRIS. It was in a street riot.

FRÄULEIN SCHNEIDER. An anti-Jewish riot?

CHRIS. Yes.

FRÄULEIN SCHNEIDER. And you were attacking the Jews.

CHRIS. No, I was doing the other thing. I was defending them.

FRÄULEIN SCHNEIDER. But that is not right, Herr Issyvoo. The Jews are at the bottom of all the trouble.

CHRIS (*sharply*). Fräulein Schneider, I think I've heard enough of that this afternoon. Let's not talk about it any more.

FRÄULEIN SCHNEIDER. But that is wrong, Herr Issyvoo. We must all talk about it. That is what the speakers say. Germany must come first.

CHRIS (*turning angrily*). And what does that mean? How can any country come first that does things like this? Suppose I push this in your face (*He thrusts his fist near her face, and she retreats.*) because Germany must come first—and I'm strong enough to do it, and to hurt you? What does that prove?

FRÄULEIN SCHNEIDER. But, Herr Issyvoo . . .

CHRIS. I've always been fond of you. Now I'm ashamed of you. And everything you say is horrible and dangerous and abominable. And now please go away.

FRÄULEIN SCHNEIDER (*angrily*). You will see, Herr Issyvoo. You will see. (*Bell rings.*)

CHRIS. I know that talking like this makes me almost as bad as you. Or perhaps worse. Because I've got intelligence—I hope—and you've just been listening to things. Now go and answer the bell. (*She goes. He cries out in exasperation to himself.*) God, what is one supposed to do? (*He examines his hands again.*) I wonder if I've broken anything. It feels awfully loose. (*He flexes his thumb.*) Ought that to move like that, or oughtn't it? (SALLY *comes in. She wears the coat her mother was carrying in the previous scene.*)

SALLY. Hello, Chris.

CHRIS. Well, fancy seeing you again, without your mother. (MRS. WATSON-COURTNEIDGE *comes in.*) Oh, hello, Mrs. Watson-Courtneidge!

MRS. WATSON-COURTNEIDGE. Good afternoon, Christopher.

CHRIS. And how are things with you two?

MRS. WATSON-COURTNEIDGE. They're very well. Sally has been making me very happy.

CHRIS. I see you've dressed her up in your clothes.

SALLY (*defensively*). What's wrong with that? Mother's got very good taste.

CHRIS. But it's hardly *your* taste, is it?

MRS. WATSON-COURTNEIDGE (*lifting the glass*). Brandy again?

CHRIS (*defiantly*). Yes.

MRS. WATSON-COURTNEIDGE. I see. What's the matter with your hands?

CHRIS. I hurt them. I was in a fight.

SALLY. Good gracious, you! What was the fight about?

CHRIS. Jews.

MRS. WATSON-COURTNEIDGE. Why were you fighting about *them*?

CHRIS. I don't like seeing people being pushed around. (*To* SALLY.) Or made to pretend they're what they're not.

MRS. WATSON-COURTNEIDGE. Oh, I see. Well, now, Christopher, there's something I want to tell you. I'm taking Sally home.

CHRIS. Oh? And what do *you* say about that, Sally?

SALLY. Mother's quite right, Chris. She really is. I ought to go home. To my past, and my roots and things. They're very important to a girl.

CHRIS. Sally, don't. Don't let her!

SALLY. Let her what?

CHRIS. You're disappearing, right in front of my eyes.

MRS. WATSON-COURTNEIDGE. I hope the girl you knew *is* disappearing. I want you to come, too, Christopher. Then you can meet Sally's father, and, if he approves of you, he will find you a job of some sort. Then you can be married from our house at the end of next month. That will give me time to arrange Sally's trousseau.

CHRIS. Look, Sally, haven't you told your mother yet?

SALLY (*miserably*). No, not yet.

MRS. WATSON-COURTNEIDGE. Told me what?

CHRIS. Sally, I think you should.

SALLY (*desperately*). No, Chris, not now.

CHRIS. Yes, now. Mrs. Courtneidge, there's something I have to tell you. Sally and I are no longer engaged. She sent me a note this morning, to break it off.

MRS. WATSON-COURTNEIDGE. Sally, you never told me.

SALLY (*very relieved*). I wanted to speak to Chris first.

MRS. WATSON-COURTNEIDGE. This is all a little sudden.

CHRIS. I don't think it's very sudden, really. We had a sort of quarrel the morning you arrived, and we never really made it up since.

MRS. WATSON-COURTNEIDGE. I thought you never quarreled.

CHRIS. Who said that?

MRS. WATSON-COURTNEIDGE. Sally did. Are you sure about this, Sally?

SALLY. Well, yes, Mother, as a matter of fact, I am. I don't think Chris and I are really suited to each other.

MRS. WATSON-COURTNEIDGE. Neither do I. But I didn't expect you to realize it. Well, this alters everything. I will not expect *you* to come back to England, Christopher.

CHRIS. Good.

MRS. WATSON-COURTNEIDGE. But I'm very glad that Sally has been able to see the truth for herself. I was afraid that she had changed almost too much. That *you* had changed her.

SALLY (*to* CHRIS). See?

MRS. WATSON-COURTNEIDGE (*to* SALLY). Now you'll come back and settle down again, and quite soon all of this will be forgotten. I'm sure it will seem like a rather bitter experience, but one gets over everything in the right surroundings.

SALLY (*subdued again*). Yes, Mother.

MRS. WATSON-COURTNEIDGE. She has been very good about you, Christopher. She has continued to deny everything that I am absolutely sure has taken place. I think that shows a very fine character.

CHRIS. No doubt that was due to *your* influence.

MRS. WATSON-COURTNEIDGE. Perhaps you'll forgive me if I say a few things to you, Christopher. I think someone should say them, and Sally's father isn't here to do so. Perhaps that's lucky for you. He's not a patient man, and he adores Sally. I know he'd think that anyone who'd harmed her richly deserved a sound horse-whipping.

CHRIS. Now, listen, Mrs. Courtneidge . . .

MRS. WATSON-COURTNEIDGE. I have no intention of listening to you, Mr. Isherwood. Sally has done quite enough of that, already. She's a very sweet, simple girl, but she's too easily influenced.

CHRIS (*with meaning*). Yes, I know.

MRS. WATSON-COURTNEIDGE. Perhaps you think I'm a simple woman, too. Perhaps you think I haven't noticed that, while you've dragged me to the opera and all the museums, you have never introduced me to a single one of your friends. I can well imagine why.

CHRIS. Look, do we have to go into all this?

MRS. WATSON-COURTNEIDGE (*sharply*). Yes, I think we do. It's people like you who are ruining the world. Unprincipled drifters who call themselves authors, never write a word, and then vote Labor on the slightest provocation. No wonder we're headed for socialism. You live in foreign countries, and you let yourself get involved in obscure political issues that are no concern of yours . . .

SALLY (*suddenly*). Yes, they are.

MRS. WATSON-COURTNEIDGE (*surprised*). Sally!

SALLY. Some sort of principles are, and I'm very glad to see he has some, and that there is something he is willing to fight for, instead of just sitting around.

CHRIS. Now, Sally, wait a minute . . .

SALLY. I know. I've told you a lot of the same things, myself. But I don't like to hear Mother say them. Certainly not to you. You don't know Chris, Mother. You don't understand him. He's a very fine person. He's been wonderful to me. He has. He's done a lot for me, and he's tried to do more. And he's an artist. Well—potentially. All artists need time. He's going to write a wonderful book one day, that'll sell millions of copies—or a lot of short stories all about Germany or something—which will tell the world wonderful things about life and people and everything—and then you'll feel very silly for the things you've just said.

MRS. WATSON-COURTNEIDGE. I thought you'd just broken off your engagement.

SALLY. Yes, I have. But I'm not going to stand here and let you nag at him like that. He doesn't chase around after horrible, influential people, and I bet he wouldn't take a job from Father if he offered him one. He's got too much pride. And character. It just wants—working up, that's all. And now let's go.

MRS. WATSON-COURTNEIDGE (*staggered*). Well . . . I'll say good-by, Christopher. We shall be leaving tomorrow, or the next day. I don't imagine that we'll meet again. And I would prefer that you and Sally did not see each other again, either. Shall we go, Sally?

SALLY. Yes, Mother.

(*They leave,* SALLY *refusing to look back at* CHRIS.)

CHRIS. Well. Really! (*He goes to the table, and the brandy bottle, then stops.*) No, I won't. I *will* have some principles!

CURTAIN

SCENE THREE

TIME: *Three days later. Evening.*

SCENE: *A large trunk is open in the middle of the floor.* CHRIS *is putting things into it and sorting others from the closet.*

CHRIS. Where did I ever get all these things? This shirt—I can't possibly have bought it. No, I didn't of course. I remember. It was at that party at the Lithuanian sculptor's, where a whole bottle of crème de menthe got spilled over mine. These are Clive's silk ones. I don't suppose I'll ever wear them, but you never know. This pair of drawers. No, really, they're too far gone. Out! (*He throws them away. Enter* SALLY. *She is dressed as in the first scene.*)

SALLY. Chris!

CHRIS. Sally! I thought you'd gone. I thought you'd gone home.

SALLY. No. Mother left this morning.

CHRIS. And you're not going?

SALLY. Not home. Oh, Chris, it was ghastly getting rid of Mother. But I knew I had to, after that scene here.

CHRIS. How did you do it?

SALLY (*giggling*). I did something awful. I got a friend in London to send her an anonymous telegram telling her Daddy was having an affair. That sent her off in a mad whirl. But Daddy will forgive me. Besides, it's probably true—and I don't blame him. I told Mother I'd follow her when I got some business settled. And something will turn up to stop it. It always does, for me. I'm all right, Chris. I'm back again.

CHRIS (*smiling*). Yes. I can see you are.

SALLY. Is there anything to drink?

CHRIS. There's just a little gin, that's all.

SALLY. I'd love a little gin. In a tooth glass. Flavored with peppermint. Where are you off to?

CHRIS. I *am* going home.

SALLY. When?

CHRIS. Tomorrow night. I'm going to

Fritz and Natalia's wedding in the afternoon.

SALLY. Wedding? How did that happen?

CHRIS. Fritz told Natalia about himself, and that did it. And now he doesn't have to pretend any more. Come with me, Sally. They'd love to see you.

SALLY. Oh, I'd like to, but I won't be here.

CHRIS. Where will you be?

SALLY. I'm leaving for the Riviera tonight.

CHRIS. With whom?

SALLY. For a picture.

CHRIS. Well, fine. Is it a good part?

SALLY. I don't really know. I expect so. You haven't got a drink, Chris. Have a drop of this. Make it a loving cup. (*He takes a sip.*) Why are you going away, Chris?

CHRIS. Because I'll never write as long as I'm here. And I've got to write. It's the only thing I give a damn about. I don't regret the time I've spent here. I wouldn't have missed a single hangover of it. But now I've got to put it all down—what I think about it. And live by it, too, if I can. Thank you for the idea about that book, Sally. The short stories. I think maybe that will work out.

SALLY. Oh, I hope so. I do want you to be good, Chris.

CHRIS. I am going to try, Sally. Now, tell me about you and this job that you don't seem to know anything about. Or care about. Who's the man, Sally?

SALLY. Man?

CHRIS. Oh, come off it.

SALLY (*giggling a little*). Well, there is a man. He's wonderful, Chris. He really is.

CHRIS. Where did you meet him?

SALLY. Two days ago. Just after we left here. He saw us in the street. . . . Mother and me, I mean—and our eyes met—his and mine, I mean—and he sort of followed us. To a tea shop, where he sat and gazed at me. And back to the hotel. And at the restaurant. He had the table next to us, and he kept sort of hitching his foot around my chair. And he passed me a note in the fruit-basket. Only Mother got it by mistake. But it was in German. I told her it was from a movie agent. And I went over and talked to him, and he *was!* Then we met later. He's quite marvelous, Chris. He's got a long, black beard. Well, not really long. I've never been kissed by a beard before. I thought it would be awful. But it isn't. It's quite exciting. Only he doesn't speak much German. He's a Yugoslavian. That's why I don't know much about the picture. But I'm sure it will be all right. He'll write in something. And now I've got to run.

CHRIS. Oh, Sally, *must* you? Must you go on like this? Why don't you go home, too? Come back with me. I mean it, Sally. My family'll give me some money if I'm home. Or I'll get a job. I'll see that you're all right.

SALLY. It wouldn't be any good, Chris. I'd run away from you, too. The moment anything attractive came along. It's all right for you. You're a writer. You really are. I'm not even an actress, really. I'd love to see my name in lights, but even if I had a first-night tomorrow, if something exciting turned up, I'd go after it. I can't help it. That's me. I'm sentimental enough to hope that one day I'll meet the perfect man, and marry him and have an enormous family and be happy, but until then—well, that's how I am. You know that really, don't you?

CHRIS. Yes, Sally, I'm afraid I do.

SALLY. Afraid? Oh, Chris, am I too awful—for *me*, I mean?

CHRIS. No, Sally. I'm very fond of you.

SALLY. I do hope you are. Because I am of you. Was it true about eternal friendship that we swore?

CHRIS. Yes, of course it was. Really true. Tell me, do you have an address?

SALLY. No, I don't. But I'll write. I really will. Postcards and everything. And you write to me. Of course, you'll be writing all sorts of things—books and things—that I can read. Will you dedicate one to me?

CHRIS. The very first one.

SALLY. Oh, good. Perhaps that'll be my only claim to fame. Well—good-by for now, Chris. Neck and leg-break.

CHRIS. Neck and leg-break. (*They go into each other's arms.*)

SALLY (*starts to go, then turns to* CHRIS). I do love you. (*She goes, swiftly.*)

CHRIS (*stares after her, for a moment*). I love you too, Sally. And it's so damned stupid that that's not enough to keep two people together. (*He starts to move toward the window. The lights begin to dim.*) The camera's taken all its pictures, and now it's going away to develop them. I wonder how Sally will look when I've developed her? I haven't got an end for her yet, but there probably isn't one. She'll just go on and on, as she always has—somewhere. (*He looks out of the window.*) There she goes now. Into the photograph. She's just going around the corner. (*He watches as the curtain starts to fall.*) Don't forget those postcards, Sally.

CURTAIN

CAT ON A HOT TIN ROOF

Tennessee Williams

First presented by the Playwrights' Company at the Morosco Theatre,
New York, on March 24, 1955, with the following cast:

LACEY   Maxwell Glanville

SOOKEY   Musa Williams

MARGARET   Barbara Bel Geddes

BRICK   Ben Gazzara

MAE   Madeleine Sherwood

COOPER   Pat Hingle

BIG MAMA   Mildred Dunnock

DIXIE   Pauline Hahn

BUSTER   Darryl Richard

SONNY   Seth Edwards

TRIXIE   Janice Dunn

BIG DADDY   Burl Ives

REVEREND TOOKER   Fred Stewart

DOCTOR BAUGH   R. G. Armstrong

DAISY   Eva Vaughan Smith

BRIGHTIE   Brownie McGhee

SMALL   Sonny Terry

INTRODUCTION

Cat on a Hot Tin Roof was one of its author's greatest Broadway successes, although it fared poorly in Chicago, where the critical reception was largely unfavorable. The British production had to be "private" because of the Lord Chamberlain's ban on the subject of homosexuality and on the salty speech of "Big Daddy." In London, the play was presented by the New Watergate Theatre Club with the gifted American actress Kim Stanley playing Margaret, the frustrated but indomitable wife of the dissolute and disturbed Brick. In London, the reception was "mixed," and doubt was expressed by one critic that the violence of the work added up to anything of consequence. However, the London production was bound to have a different effect from that experienced by the New York playgoer. Londoners saw the third act as originally written and evidently still preferred by Tennessee Williams, for which reason it is reproduced in this book along with the act as modified for the Broadway presentation at the urging of its strong-minded stage-director, Elia Kazan. The last-mentioned version provides a more positive conclusion and brings back "Big Daddy," who is surely one of the contemporary theatre's most exciting personalities. But since both versions are given here, it is possible to let the interested reader arrive at his own preference.

One point that should perhaps be stressed is that *Cat on a Hot Tin Roof* lives on the stage not exclusively as the drama of Brick, Margaret, and Big Daddy, but also as the tragicomedy of the other characters who, together with the three principals, constitute as vivid a family unit as any produced by an American playwright, with the possible exception of O'Neill's *Long Day's Journey Into Night* and Clifford Odets' memorable *Awake and Sing!* The play is there to be experienced as a whole rather than merely as Brick's psychological problem. And as a family drama it is a mélange at once comic and distressing. If the characters remain hopelessly separated, that too is an aspect of the little world in which Brick is isolated by his suffering. Technical boldness in the author's use of monologues and of tangential nearly unrelated speeches is also distinctive.

Less persuasive is the point of the play as a whole, the rationale and justification, which the fervor of the performance and the theatrical virtuosity of Mr. Kazan may have made a question of little importance on Broadway but which is of no small consequence to criticism of the play, especially in the printed text. The present editor has made an effort to answer that question without being able to arrive at a conclusion. Perhaps there is really no answer except some forced, exegetical one he is not prepared to understand, or the ambiguous "answer" that emerged from the Broadway production —namely, the saving power of "the Truth," hard and unpleasant though it be for individuals to ascertain it. It would seem that the racy dialogue and harsh details of the work actually conceal more than they reveal, although it does not at all follow that the author was trying to hide anything from his public and critics. Nor did he appear on any podium to offer them a revelation that he then proceeded to falsify. Mr. Williams has not pretended to transmit messages; nor has he concealed his own uncertainties and ambivalences for the purpose of appearing wiser, purer, or nobler than the rest of mankind. (He has thus far claimed only the distinction of being an artist, and it is a claim few will be disposed to deny him.) It is to the flux and eruption of the drama rather than to its direction that it is possible to respond with the greatest approbation.

A good technical point offered in the *Times Literary Supplement* of February 10, 1956, has particular relevance to the above opinion. The reviewer claims that "the concentration of power in the central duologue [between Brick and his father] . . . is so intense that the rest of the play is bound to suffer . . . There remains only the comparably unimportant question whether 'Maggie the Cat' shall repossess her spiritually moribund husband and snatch thereby the coveted inheritance." The English reviewer, however, adds that "Most readers, and probably most playgoers, will feel that it was well worth spoiling the story for the sake of the unbalancing episode." To this view a Broadway playgoer's remonstrance could have been that, in performance, or at least in Barbara Bel Geddes' performance, "Maggie the Cat" keeps the latter part of the play afloat with her own buoyancy. After witnessing the production sustained by the performances of Barbara Bel Geddes, Burl Ives, Ben Gazzara, and Mildred Dunnock, Brooks Atkinson rendered a majority verdict in declaring *Cat on a Hot Tin Roof* simply "stunning drama."

ACT ONE

NOTES FOR THE DESIGNER

The set is the bed-sitting-room of a plantation home in the Mississippi Delta. It is along an upstairs gallery which probably runs around the entire house; it has two pairs of very wide doors opening onto the gallery, showing white balustrades against a fair summer sky that fades into dusk and night during the course of the play, which occupies precisely the time of its performance, excepting, of course, the fifteen minutes of intermission.

Perhaps the style of the room is not what you would expect in the home of the Delta's biggest cotton-planter. It is Victorian with a touch of the Far East. It hasn't changed much since it was occupied by the original owners of the place, Jack Straw and Peter Ochello, a pair of old bachelors who shared this room all their lives together. In other words, the room must evoke some ghosts; it is gently and poetically haunted by a relationship that must have involved a tenderness which was uncommon. This may be irrelevant or unnecessary, but I once saw a reproduction of a faded photograph of the verandah of Robert Louis Stevenson's home on that Samoan Island where he spent his last years, and there was a quality of tender light on weathered wood, such as porch furniture made of bamboo and wicker, exposed to tropical suns and tropical rains, which came to mind when I thought about the set for this play, bringing also to mind the grace and comfort of light, the reassurance it gives, on a late and fair afternoon in summer, the way that no matter what, even dread of death, is gently touched and soothed by it. For the set is the background for a play that deals with human extremities of emotion, and it needs that softness behind it.

The bathroom door, showing only pale-blue tile and silver towel racks, is in one side wall; the hall door in the opposite wall. Two articles of furniture need mention: a big double bed which staging should make a functional part of the set as often as suitable, the surface of which should be slightly raked to make figures on it seen more easily; and against the wall space between the two huge double doors upstage: a monumental monstrosity peculiar to our times, a *huge* console combination of radio-phonograph (Hi-Fi with three speakers) TV set *and* liquor cabinet, bearing and containing many glasses and bottles, all in one piece, which is a composition of muted silver tones, and the opalescent tones of reflecting glass, a chromatic link, this thing, between the sepia (tawny gold) tones of the interior and the cool (white and blue) tones of the gallery and sky. This piece of furniture (?!), this monument, is a very complete and compact little shrine to virtually all the comforts and illusions behind which we hide from such things as the characters in the play are faced with. . . .

The set should be far less realistic than I have so far implied in this description of it. I think the walls below the ceiling should dissolve mysteriously into air; the set should be roofed by the sky; stars and moon suggested by traces of milky pallor, as if they were observed through a telescope lens out of focus.

Anything else I can think of? Oh, yes, fanlights (transoms shaped like an open glass fan) above all the doors in the set, with panes of blue and amber, and above all, the designer should take as many pains to give the actors room to move about freely (to show their restlessness, their passion for breaking out) as if it were a set for a ballet.

An evening in summer. The action is continuous, with two intermissions.

At the rise of the curtain someone is taking a shower in the bathroom, the door of which is half open. A pretty young woman, with anxious lines in her face, enters the bedroom and crosses to the bathroom door.

MARGARET (*shouting above roar of water*). One of those no-neck monsters hit me with a hot buttered biscuit so I have t' change! (MARGARET's *voice is both rapid and drawling. In her long speeches she has the vocal tricks of a priest delivering a liturgical chant, the lines are almost sung, always continuing a little beyond her breath so she has to gasp for another. Sometimes she intersperses the lines with a little wordless singing, such as "Da-da-daaaa!"*)

(*Water turns off and* BRICK *calls out to her, but is still unseen. A tone of politely feigned interest, masking indifference, or worse, is characteristic of his speech with* MARGARET.)

BRICK. What'd you say, Maggie? Water was on s' loud I couldn't hearya. . . .

MARGARET. Well, I!—just remarked that! —one of th' no-neck monsters messed up m' lovely lace dress so I got t'—cha-a-ange. . . . (*She opens and kicks shut drawers of the dresser.*)

BRICK. Why d'ya call Gooper's kiddies no-neck monsters?

MARGARET. Because they've got no necks! Isn't that a good enough reason?

BRICK. Don't they have any necks?

MARGARET. None visible. Their fat little heads are set on their fat little bodies without a bit of connection.

BRICK. That's too bad.

MARGARET. Yes, it's too bad because you can't wring their necks if they've got no necks to wring! Isn't that right, honey? (*She steps out of her dress, stands in a slip of ivory satin and lace.*) Yep, they're no-neck monsters, all no-neck people are monsters . . . (*Children shriek downstairs.*) Hear them? Hear them screaming? I don't know where their voice-boxes are located since they don't have necks. I tell you I got so nervous at that table tonight I thought I would throw back my head and utter a scream you could hear across the Arkansas border an' parts of Louisiana an' Tennessee. I said to your charming sister-in-law, Mae, honey, couldn't you feed those precious little things at a separate table with an oilcloth cover? They make such a mess an' the lace cloth looks *so* pretty! She made enormous eyes at me and said, "Ohhh, noooooo! On Big Daddy's birthday? Why, he would never forgive me!" Well, I want you to know, Big Daddy hadn't been at the table two minutes with those five no-neck monsters slobbering and drooling over their food before he threw down his fork an' shouted, "Fo' God's sake, Gooper, why don't you put them pigs at a trough in th' kitchen?"—Well, I swear, I simply could have di-ieed!

Think of it, Brick, they've got five of them and number six is coming. They've brought the whole bunch down here like animals to display at a county fair. Why, they have those children doin' tricks all the time! "Junior, show Big Daddy how you do this, show Big Daddy how you do that, say your little piece fo' Big Daddy, Sister. Show your dimples, Sugar. Brother, show Big Daddy how you stand on your head!"—It goes on all the time, along with constant little remarks and innuendos about the fact that you and I have not produced any children, are totally childless and therefore totally useless!—Of course it's comical but it's also disgusting since it's so obvious what they're up to!

BRICK (*without interest*). What are they up to, Maggie?

MARGARET. Why, you know what they're up to!

BRICK (*appearing*). No, I don't know what they're up to. (*He stands there in the bathroom doorway drying his hair with a towel and hanging onto the towel rack because one ankle is broken, plastered and bound. He is still slim and firm as a boy. His liquor hasn't started tearing him down outside. He has the additional charm of that cool air of detachment that people have who have given up the struggle. But now and then, when disturbed, something flashes behind it, like lighting in a fair sky, which shows that at some deeper level he is far from peaceful. Perhaps in a stronger light he would show some signs of deliquescence, but the fading, still warm, light from the gallery treats him gently.*)

MARGARET. I'll tell you what they're up to, boy of mine!—They're up to cutting you out of your father's estate, and—(*She freezes momentarily before her next remark. Her voice drops as if it were somehow a personally embarrassing admission.*) —Now we know that Big Daddy's dyin' of—cancer. . . . (*There are voices on the lawn below: long-drawn calls across distance.* MARGARET *raises her lovely bare arms and powders her armpits with a light sigh. She adjusts the angle of a magnifying mirror to straighten an eyelash, then rises fretfully saying:*) There's so much light in the room it—

BRICK (*softly but sharply*). Do we?

MARGARET. Do we what?

BRICK. Know Big Daddy's dyin' of cancer?

MARGARET. Got the report today.

BRICK. Oh . . .

MARGARET (*letting down bamboo blinds which cast long, gold-fretted shadows over the room*). Yep, got th' report just now . . . it didn't surprise me, Baby. . . . (*Her voice has range, and music; sometimes it drops low as a boy's and you have a sudden image of her playing boys' games as a child.*) I recognized the symptoms soon's we got here last spring and I'm willin' to bet you that Brother Man and his wife were pretty sure of it, too. That more than likely explains why their usual summer migration to the coolness of the Great Smokies was passed up this summer in favor of—hustlin' down here ev'ry whip-stitch with their whole screamin' tribe! And why so many allusions have been made to Rainbow Hill lately. You know what Rainbow Hill is? Place that's famous for treatin' alcoholics an' dope fiends in the movies!

BRICK. I'm not in the movies.

MARGARET. No, and you don't take dope. Otherwise you're a perfect candidate for Rainbow Hill, Baby, and that's where they aim to ship you—over my dead body! Yep, over my dead body they'll ship you there, but nothing would please them better. Then Brother Man could get a-hold of the purse strings and dole out remittances to us, maybe get power-of-attorney and sign checks for us and cut off our credit wherever, whenever he wanted! Son-of-a-bitch!—How'd you like that, Baby?—Well, you've been doin' just about ev'rything in your power to bring it about, you've just been doin' ev'rything you can think of to aid and abet them in this scheme of theirs! Quittin' work, devoting yourself to the occupation of drinkin'!—Breakin' your ankle last night on the high school athletic field: doin' what? Jumpin' hurdles? At two or three in the morning? Just fantastic! Got in the paper. *Clarksdale Register* carried a nice little item about it, human interest story about a well-known former athlete stagin' a one-man track meet on the Glorious Hill High School athletic field last night, but was slightly out of condition and didn't clear the first hurdle! Brother Man Gooper claims he exercised his influence t' keep it from goin' out over AP or UP or every goddam "P."

But, Brick? You still have one big advantage!

(*During the above swift flood of words,* BRICK *has reclined with contrapuntal leisure on the snowy surface of the bed and has rolled over carefully on his side or belly.*)

BRICK (*wryly*). Did you *say* something, Maggie?

MARGARET. Big Daddy dotes on you, honey. And he can't stand Brother Man and Brother Man's wife, that monster of fertility, Mae; she's downright odious to him! Know how I know? By little expressions that flicker over his face when that woman is holding fo'th on one of her choice topics such as—how she refused twilight sleep!—when the twins were delivered! Because she feels motherhood's an experience that a woman ought to experience fully!—in order to fully appreciate the wonder and beauty of it! HAH! (*This loud "HAH!" is accompanied by a violent action such as slamming a drawer shut.*) —and how she made Brother Man come in an' stand beside her in the delivery room so he would not miss out on the "wonder and beauty" of it either!—producin' those no-neck monsters. . . . (*A speech of this kind would be antipathetic from almost anybody but* MARGARET; *she makes it oddly funny, because her eyes constantly twinkle and her voice shakes with laughter which is basically indulgent.*)—Big Daddy shares my attitude toward those two! As for me, well—I give him a laugh now and then and he tolerates me. In fact!—I sometimes suspect that Big Daddy harbors a little unconscious "lech" fo' me. . . .

BRICK. What makes you think that Big Daddy has a lech for you, Maggie?

MARGARET. Way he always drops his eyes down my body when I'm talkin' to him, drops his eyes to my boobs an' licks his old chops! Ha ha!

BRICK. That kind of talk is disgusting.

MARGARET. Did anyone ever tell you that you're an ass-aching Puritan, Brick?

I think it's mighty fine that the ole fellow, on the doorstep of death, still takes in my shape with what I think is deserved appreciation!

And you wanta know something else? Big Daddy didn't know how many little Maes and Goopers had been produced! "How many kids have you got?" he asked at the table, just like Brother Man and his wife were new acquaintances to him! Big Mama said he was jokin', but that old boy wasn't jokin', Lord, no!

And when they infawmed him that they had five already and were turning out number six!—the news seemed to come as a sort of unpleasant surprise . . . (*Children yell below.*) Scream, monsters! (*Turns to* BRICK *with a sudden, gay, charming smile which fades as she notices that he is not looking at her but into fad-*

ing gold space with a troubled expression.)

(*It is constant rejection that makes her humor "bitchy."*) Yes, you should of been at that supper-table, Baby. (*Whenever she calls him "baby" the word is a soft caress.*) Y'know, Big Daddy, bless his ole sweet soul, he's the dearest ole thing in the world, but he does hunch over his food as if he preferred not to notice anything else. Well, Mae an' Gooper were side by side at the table, direckly across from Big Daddy, watchin' his face like hawks while they jawed an' jabbered about the cuteness an' brilliance of th' no-neck monsters! (*She giggles with a hand fluttering at her throat and her breast and her long throat arched.*)

(*She comes downstage and recreates the scene with voice and gesture.*) And the no-neck monsters were ranged around the table, some in high chairs and some on th' *Books of Knowledge,* all in fancy little paper caps in honor of Big Daddy's birthday, and all through dinner, well, I want you to know that Brother Man an' his partner never once, for one moment, stopped exchanging pokes an' pinches an' kicks an' signs an' signals!—Why, they were like a couple of cardsharps fleecing a sucker.—Even Big Mama, bless her ole sweet soul, she isn't th' quickest an' brightest thing in the world, she finally noticed, at last, an' said to Gooper, "Gooper, what are you an' Mae makin' all these signs at each other about?"—I swear t' goodness, I nearly choked on my chicken! (MARGARET, *back at the dressing-table, still doesn't see* BRICK. *He is watching her with a look that is not quite definable.— Amused? shocked? contemptuous?—part of those and part of something else.*) Y'know—your brother Gooper still cherishes the illusion he took a giant step up on the social ladder when he married Miss Mae Flynn of the Memphis Flynns. (MARGARET *moves about the room as she talks, stops before the mirror, moves on.*) But I have a piece of Spanish news for Gooper. The Flynns never had a thing in this world but money and they lost that, they were nothing at all but fairly successful climbers. Of course, Mae Flynn came out in Memphis eight years before I made my debut in Nashville, but I had friends at Ward-Belmont who came from Memphis and they used to come to see me and I used to go to see them for Christmas and spring vacations, and so I know who rates an' who doesn't rate in Memphis society. Why, y'know ole Papa Flynn, he barely escaped doing time in the Federal pen for shady manipulations on th' stock market when his chain stores crashed, and as for Mae having been a cotton carnival queen, as they remind us so often, lest we forget, well, that's one honor that I don't envy her for!—Sit on a brass throne on a tacky float an' ride down Main Street, smilin', bowin', and blowin' kisses to all the trash on the street—(*She picks out a pair of jeweled sandals and rushes to the dressing-table.*) Why, year before last, when Susan McPheeters was singled out fo' that honor, y'know what happened to her? Y'know what happened to poor little Susie McPheeters?

BRICK (*absently*). No. What happened to little Susie McPheeters?

MARGARET. Somebody spit tobacco juice in her face.

BRICK (*dreamily*). Somebody spit tobacco juice in her face?

MARGARET. That's right, some old drunk leaned out of a window in the Hotel Gayoso and yelled, "Hey, Queen, hey, hey, there, Queenie!" Poor Susie looked up and flashed him a radiant smile and he shot out a squirt of tobacco juice right in poor Susie's face.

BRICK. Well, what d'you know about that.

MARGARET (*gaily*). What do I know about it? I was there, I saw it!

BRICK (*absently*). Must have been kind of funny.

MARGARET. Susie didn't think so. Had hysterics. Screamed like a banshee. They had to stop th' parade an' remove her from her throne an' go on with—(*She catches sight of him in the mirror, gasps slightly, wheels about to face him. Count ten.*)— Why are you looking at me like that?

BRICK (*whistling softly, now*). Like what, Maggie?

MARGARET (*intensely, fearfully*). The way y' were lookin' at me just now, befo' I caught your eye in the mirror and you started t' whistle! I don't know how t' describe it but it froze my blood!—I've caught you lookin' at me like that so often lately. What are you thinkin' of when you look at me like that?

BRICK. I wasn't conscious of lookin' at you, Maggie.

MARGARET. Well, I was conscious of it! What were you thinkin'?

BRICK. I don't remember thinking of anything, Maggie.

MARGARET. Don't you think I know that—? Don't you—?—Think I know that—?

BRICK (*coolly*). Know *what*, Maggie?

MARGARET (*struggling for expression*). That I've gone through this—*hideous!*—*transformation*, become—*hard! Frantic!* (*Then she adds, almost tenderly:*)—*cruel!!* That's what you've been observing in me lately. How could y' help but observe it? That's all right. I'm not—thin-skinned any more, can't afford t' be thin-skinned any more. (*She is now recovering her power.*) —But Brick? Brick?

BRICK. Did you say something?

MARGARET. I was goin' t' say something: that I get—lonely. Very!

BRICK. Ev'rybody gets that . . .

MARGARET. Living with someone you love can be lonelier—than living entirely *alone!*—if the one that y' love doesn't love you. . . . (*There is a pause.* BRICK *hobbles downstage and asks, without looking at her.*)

BRICK. Would you like to live alone, Maggie?

(*Another pause: then—after she has caught a quick, hurt breath:*)

MARGARET. *No!—God!—I wouldn't!* (*Another gasping breath. She forcibly controls what must have been an impulse to cry out. We see her deliberately, very forcibly, going all the way back to the world in which you can talk about ordinary matters.*) Did you have a nice shower?

BRICK. Uh-huh.

MARGARET. Was the water cool?

BRICK. No.

MARGARET. But it made y' feel fresh, huh?

BRICK. Fresher. . . .

MARGARET. I know something would make y' feel *much* fresher!

BRICK. What?

MARGARET. An alcohol rub. Or cologne, a rub with cologne!

BRICK. That's good after a workout but I haven't been workin' out, Maggie.

MARGARET. You've kept in good shape, though.

BRICK (*indifferently*). You think so, Maggie?

MARGARET. I always thought drinkin' men lost their looks, but I was plainly mistaken.

BRICK (*wryly*). Why, thanks, Maggie.

MARGARET. You're the only drinkin' man I know that it never seems t' put fat on.

BRICK. I'm gettin' softer, Maggie.

MARGARET. Well, sooner or later it's bound to soften you up. It was just beginning to soften up Skipper when—(*She stops short.*) I'm sorry. I never could keep my fingers off a sore—I wish you *would* lose your looks. If you did it would make the martyrdom of Saint Maggie a little more bearable. But no such goddam luck. I actually believe you've gotten better looking since you've gone on the bottle. Yeah, a person who didn't know you would think you'd never had a tense nerve in your body or a strained muscle. (*There are sounds of croquet on the lawn below: the click of mallets, light voices, near and distant.*) Of course, you always had that detached quality as if you were playing a game without much concern over whether you won or lost, and now that you've lost the game, not lost but just quit playing, you have that rare sort of charm that usually only happens in very old or hopelessly sick people, the charm of the defeated.— You look so cool, so cool, so enviably cool. (*Music is heard.*) They're playing croquet. The moon has appeared and it's white, just beginning to turn a little bit yellow. . . .

You were a wonderful lover. . . .

Such a wonderful person to go to bed with, and I think mostly because you were really indifferent to it. Isn't that right? Never had any anxiety about it, did it naturally, easily, slowly, with absolute confidence and perfect calm, more like opening a door for a lady or seating her at a table than giving expression to any longing for her. Your indifference made you wonderful at lovemaking—*strange?*—but true. . . .

You know, if I thought you would never, never, *never* make love to me again —I would go downstairs to the kitchen and pick out the longest and sharpest knife I could find and stick it straight into my heart, I swear that I would!

But one thing I don't have is the charm of the defeated, my hat is still in the ring, and I am determined to win! (*There is the sound of croquet mallets hitting croquet balls.*)—What is the victory of a cat on a hot tin roof?—I wish I knew. . . .

Just staying on it, I guess, as long as she can. . . . (*More croquet sounds.*) Later tonight I'm going to tell you I love you an' maybe by that time you'll be drunk enough to believe me. Yes, they're playing croquet. . . .

Big Daddy is dying of cancer. . . .

What were you thinking of when I caught you looking at me like that? Were you thinking of Skipper? (BRICK *takes up his crutch, rises.*) Oh, excuse me, forgive me, but laws of silence don't work! No, laws of silence don't work. . . . (BRICK *crosses to the bar, takes a quick drink, and rubs his head with a towel.*) Laws of silence don't work. . . .

When something is festering in your memory or your imagination, laws of silence don't work, it's just like shutting a door and locking it on a house on fire in hope of forgetting that the house is burning. But not facing a fire doesn't put it out. Silence about a thing just magnifies it. It grows and festers in silence, becomes malignant. . . . Get dressed, Brick.

(*He drops his crutch.*)

BRICK. I've dropped my crutch. (*He has stopped rubbing his hair dry but still stands hanging onto the towel rack in a white towel-cloth robe.*)

MARGARET. Lean on me.

BRICK. No, just give me my crutch.

MARGARET. Lean on my shoulder.

BRICK. *I don't want to lean on your shoulder, I want my crutch!* (*This is spoken like sudden lightning.*) Are you going to give me my crutch or do I have to get down on my knees on the floor and—

MARGARET. *Here, here, take it, take it!* (*She has thrust the crutch at him.*)

BRICK (*hobbling out*). Thanks . . .

MARGARET. We mustn't scream at each other, the walls in this house have ears. . . . (*He hobbles directly to liquor cabinet to get a new drink.*)—but that's the first time I've heard you raise your voice in a long time, Brick. A crack in the wall?—Of composure?

—I think that's a good sign. . . .

A sign of nerves in a player on the defensive!

(BRICK *turns and smiles at her coolly over his fresh drink.*)

BRICK. It just hasn't happened yet, Maggie.

MARGARET. What?

BRICK. The click I get in my head when I've had enough of this stuff to make me peaceful. . . . Will you do me a favor?

MARGARET. Maybe I will. What favor?

BRICK. Just, just keep your voice down!

MARGARET (*in a hoarse whisper*). I'll do you that favor, I'll speak in a whisper, if not shut up completely, if *you* will do *me* a favor and make that drink your last one till after the party.

BRICK. What party?

MARGARET. Big Daddy's birthday party.

BRICK. Is this Big Daddy's birthday?

MARGARET. You know this is Big Daddy's birthday!

BRICK. No, I don't, I forgot it.

MARGARET. Well, I remembered it for you. . . .

(*They are both speaking as breathlessly as a pair of kids after a fight, drawing deep exhausted breaths and looking at each other with faraway eyes, shaking and panting together as if they had broken apart from a violent struggle.*)

BRICK. Good for you, Maggie.

MARGARET. You just have to scribble a few lines on this card.

BRICK. You scribble something, Maggie.

MARGARET. It's got to be your handwriting; it's your present, I've given him my present; it's got to be your handwriting!

(*The tension between them is building again, the voices becoming shrill once more.*)

BRICK. I didn't get him a present.

MARGARET. I got one for you.

BRICK. All right. You write the card, then.

MARGARET. And have him know you didn't remember his birthday?

BRICK. I didn't remember his birthday.

MARGARET. You don't have to prove you didn't!

BRICK. I don't want to fool him about it.

MARGARET. Just write "Love, Brick!" for God's—

BRICK. No.

MARGARET. You've *got* to!

BRICK. I don't have to do anything I don't want to do. You keep forgetting the conditions on which I agreed to stay on living with you.

MARGARET (*out before she knows it*).

I'm not living with you. We occupy the same cage.

BRICK. You've got to remember the conditions agreed on.

MARGARET. They're impossible conditions!

BRICK. Then why don't you—?

MARGARET. HUSH! Who is out there? Is somebody at the door?

(*There are footsteps in hall.*)

MAE (*outside*). May I enter a moment?

MARGARET. Oh, *you!* Sure. Come in, Mae. (MAE *enters bearing aloft the bow of a young lady's archery set.*)

MAE. Brick, is this thing yours?

MARGARET. Why, Sister Woman—that's my Diana Trophy. Won it at the intercollegiate archery contest on the Ole Miss campus.

MAE. It's a mighty dangerous thing to leave exposed round a house full of nawmal rid-blooded children attracted t'weapons.

MARGARET. "Nawmal rid-blooded children attracted t'weapons" ought t'be taught to keep their hands off things that don't belong to them.

MAE. Maggie, honey, if you had children of your own you'd know how funny that is. Will you please lock this up and put the key out of reach?

MARGARET. Sister Woman, nobody is plotting the destruction of your kiddies. —Brick and I still have our special archers' license. We're goin' deer-huntin' on Moon Lake as soon as the season starts. I love to run with dogs through chilly woods, run, run leap over obstructions—(*She goes into the closet carrying the bow.*)

MAE. How's the injured ankle, Brick?

BRICK. Doesn't hurt. Just itches.

MAE. Oh, my! Brick—Brick, you should've been downstairs after supper! Kiddies put on a show. Polly played the piano, Buster an' Sonny drums, an' then they turned out the lights an' Dixie an' Trixie puhfawmed a toe dance in fairy costume with *spahkluhs!* Big Daddy just beamed! He just beamed!

MARGARET (*from the closet with a sharp laugh*). Oh, I bet. It breaks my heart that we missed it! (*She reenters.*) But Mae? Why did y' give dawgs' names to all your kiddies?

MAE. *Dogs'* names?

(MARGARET *has made this observation as she goes to raise the bamboo blinds, since the sunset glare has diminished. In crossing she winks at* BRICK.)

MARGARET (*sweetly*). Dixie, Trixie, Buster, Sonny, Polly!—Sounds like four dogs and a parrot . . . animal act in a circus!

MAE. Maggie? (MARGARET *turns with a smile.*) Why are you so catty?

MARGARET. Cause I'm a cat! But why can't *you* take a joke, Sister Woman?

MAE. Nothin' pleases me more than a joke that's funny. You know the real names of our kiddies. Buster's real name is Robert. Sonny's real name is Saunders. Trixie's real name is Marlene and Dixie's —(*Someone downstairs calls for her. "Hey, Mae!"—She rushes to door, saying.*) Intermission is over!

MARGARET (*as* MAE *closes door*). I wonder what Dixie's real name is?

BRICK. Maggie, being catty doesn't help things any . . .

MARGARET. I know! WHY!—Am I so catty?—Cause I'm consumed with envy an' eaten up with longing?—Brick, I've laid out your beautiful Shantung silk suit from Rome and one of your monogrammed silk shirts. I'll put your cuff-links in it, those lovely star sapphires I get you to wear so rarely. . . .

BRICK. I can't get trousers on over this plaster cast.

MARGARET. Yes, you can, I'll help you.

BRICK. I'm not going to get dressed, Maggie.

MARGARET. Will you just put on a pair of white silk pajamas?

BRICK. Yes, I'll do that, Maggie.

MARGARET. *Thank* you, thank you so *much!*

BRICK. Don't mention it.

MARGARET. *Oh, Brick!* How long does it have t' go on? This punishment? Haven't I done time enough, haven't I served my term, can't I apply for a— pardon?

BRICK. Maggie, you're spoiling my liquor. Lately your voice always sounds like you'd been running upstairs to warn somebody that the house was on fire!

MARGARET. Well, no wonder, no wonder. Y'know what I feel like, Brick? (*Children's and grownups' voices are blended, below, in a loud but uncertain rendition of "My Wild Irish Rose."*) I feel all the time like a cat on a hot tin roof!

BRICK. Then jump off the roof, jump off

it, cats can jump off roofs and land on their four feet uninjured!

MARGARET. Oh, yes!

BRICK. Do it!—fo' God's sake, do it . . .

MARGARET. Do what?

BRICK. Take a lover!

MARGARET. I can't see a man but you! Even with my eyes closed, I just see you! Why don't you get ugly, Brick, why don't you please get fat or ugly or something so I could stand it? (*She rushes to hall door, opens it, listens.*) The concert is still going on! Bravo, no-necks, bravo! (*She slams and locks door fiercely.*)

BRICK. What did you lock the door for?

MARGARET. To give us a little privacy for a while.

BRICK. You know better, Maggie.

MARGARET. No, I don't know better. . . . (*She rushes to gallery doors, draws the rose-silk drapes across them.*)

BRICK. Don't make a fool of yourself.

MARGARET. I don't mind makin' a fool of myself over you!

BRICK. I mind, Maggie. I feel embarrassed for you.

MARGARET. Feel embarrassed! But don't continue my torture. I can't live on and on under these circumstances.

BRICK. You agreed to—

MARGARET. I know but—

BRICK. —Accept that condition!

MARGARET. *I CAN'T! CAN'T! CAN'T!* (*She seizes his shoulder.*)

BRICK. Let go! (*He breaks away from her and seizes the small boudoir chair and raises it like a lion-tamer facing a big circus cat.*

(*Count five. She stares at him with her fist pressed to her mouth, then bursts into shrill, almost hysterical laughter. He remains grave for a moment, then grins and puts the chair down.* BIG MAMA *calls through closed door.*)

BIG MAMA. Son? Son? Son?

BRICK. What is it, Big Mama?

BIG MAMA (*outside*). Oh, son! We got the most wonderful news about Big Daddy. I just had t' run up an' tell you right this—(*She rattles the knob.*)— What's this door doin', locked, faw? You all think there's robbers in the house?

MARGARET. Big Mama, Brick is dressin', he's not dressed yet.

BIG MAMA. That's all right, it won't be the first time I've seen Brick not dressed. Come on, open this door!

(MARGARET, *with a grimace, goes to unlock and open the hall door, as* BRICK *hobbles rapidly to the bathroom and kicks the door shut.* BIG MAMA *has disappeared from the hall.*)

MARGARET. Big Mama?

(BIG MAMA *appears through the opposite gallery doors behind* MARGARET, *huffing and puffing like an old bulldog. She is a short, stout woman; her sixty years and 170 pounds have left her somewhat breathless most of the time; she's always tensed like a boxer, or rather, a Japanese wrestler. Her "family" was maybe a little superior to* BIG DADDY'S, *but not much. She wears a black or silver lace dress and at least half a million in flashy gems. She is very sincere.*)

BIG MAMA (*loudly, startling* MARGARET). Here—I come through Gooper's and Mae's gall'ry door. Where's Brick? *Brick*—Hurry on out of there, son, I just have a second and want to give you the news about Big Daddy.—I hate locked doors in a house. . . .

MARGARET (*with affected lightness*). I've noticed you do, Big Mama, but people have got to have *some* moments of privacy, don't they?

BIG MAMA. No, ma'am, not in *my* house. (*Without pause*) Whacha took off you' dress faw? I thought that little lace dress was so sweet on yuh, honey.

MARGARET. I thought it looked sweet on me, too, but one of m' cute little table-partners used it for a napkin so—!

BIG MAMA (*picking up stockings on floor*). What?

MARGARET. You know, Big Mama, Mae and Gooper's so touchy about those children—thanks, Big Mama . . . (BIG MAMA *has thrust the picked-up stockings in* MARGARET'S *hand with a grunt.*)—that you just don't dare to suggest there's any room for improvement in their—

BIG MAMA. Brick, hurry out!—Shoot, Maggie, you just don't like children.

MARGARET. I do SO like children! Adore them!—well brought up!

BIG MAMA (*gentle—loving*). Well, why don't you have some and bring them up well, then, instead of all the time pickin' on Gooper's an' Mae's?

GOOPER (*shouting up the stairs*). Hey, hey, Big Mama, Betsy an' Hugh got to go, waitin' t' tell yuh g'by!

BIG MAMA. Tell 'em to hold their hawses,

I'll be right down in a jiffy! (*She turns to the bathroom door and calls out.*) Son? Can you hear me in there? (*There is a muffled answer.*) We just got the full report from the laboratory at the Ochsner Clinic, completely negative, son, ev'rything negative, right on down the line! Nothin' a-tall's wrong with him but some little functional thing called a spastic colon. Can you hear me, son?

MARGARET. He can hear you, Big Mama.

BIG MAMA. Then why don't he say something? God Almighty, a piece of news like that should make him shout. It made *me* shout, I can tell you. I shouted and sobbed and fell right down on my knees!—Look! (*She pulls up her skirt.*) See the bruises where I hit my kneecaps? Took both doctors to haul me back on my feet! (*She laughs—she always laughs like hell at herself.*) Big Daddy was furious with me! But ain't that wonderful news? (*Facing bathroom again, she continues:*) After all the anxiety we been through to git a report like that on Big Daddy's birthday? Big Daddy tried to hide how much of a load that news took off his mind, but didn't fool *me*. He was mighty close to crying about it *himself!* (*Good-bys are shouted downstairs, and she rushes to door.*) Hold those people down there, don't let them go!—Now, git dressed, we're all comin' up to this room fo' Big Daddy's birthday party because of your ankle.—How's his ankle, Maggie?

MARGARET. Well, he broke it, Big Mama.

BIG MAMA. I know he broke it. (*A phone is ringing in hall. A Negro voice answers: "Mistuh Polly's res'dence."*) I mean does it hurt him much still.

MARGARET. I'm afraid I can't give you that information, Big Mama. You'll have to ask Brick if it hurts much still or not.

SOOKEY (*in the hall*). It's Memphis, Mizz Polly, it's Miss Sally in Memphis.

BIG MAMA. Awright, Sookey. (*BIG MAMA rushes into the hall and is heard shouting on the phone.*) Hello, Miss Sally. How are you, Miss Sally?—Yes, well, I was just gonna call you about it. Shoot!—(*She raises her voice to a bellow.*) Miss Sally? Don't ever call me from the Gayoso Lobby, too much talk goes on in that hotel lobby, no wonder you can't hear me! Now listen, Miss Sally. They's nothin' serious wrong with Big Daddy. We got the report just now, they's nothin' wrong but a thing called a—spastic! SPASTIC!—colon . . . (*She appears at the hall door and calls to* MARGARET.)—Maggie, come out here and talk to that fool on the phone. I'm shouted breathless!

MARGARET (*goes out and is heard sweetly at phone*). Miss Sally? This is Brick's wife, Maggie. So nice to hear your voice. Can you hear *mine?* Well, *good!*—Big Mama just wanted you to know that they've got the report from the Ochsner Clinic and what Big Daddy has is a spastic colon. Yes. Spastic colon, Miss Sally. That's right, spastic colon. *G'by, Miss Sally, hope I'll see you real soon!* (*Hangs up a little before Miss Sally was probably ready to terminate the talk. She returns through the hall door.*) She heard me perfectly. I've discovered with deaf people the thing to do is not shout at them but just enunciate clearly. My rich old Aunt Cornelia was deaf as the dead but I could make her hear me just by sayin' each word slowly, distinctly, close to her ear. I read her the *Commercial Appeal* ev'ry night, read her the classified ads in it, even, she never missed a word of it. But was she a mean ole thing! Know what I got when she died? Her unexpired subscriptions to five magazines and the Book-of-the-Month Club and a LIBRARY full of ev'ry dull book ever written! All else went to her hellcat of a sister . . . meaner than she was, even!

(*BIG MAMA has been straightening things up in the room during this speech.*)

BIG MAMA (*closing closet door on discarded clothes*). Miss Sally sure is a case! Big Daddy says she's always got her hand out fo' something. He's not mistaken. That poor ole thing always has her hand out fo' somethin'. I don't think Big Daddy gives her as much as he should. (*Somebody shouts for her downstairs and she shouts.*) I'm comin'! (*She starts out. At the hall door, turns and jerks a forefinger, first toward the bathroom door, then toward the liquor cabinet, meaning: "Has Brick been drinking?"* MARGARET *pretends not to understand, cocks her head and raises her brows as if the pantomimic performance was completely mystifying to her.* BIG MAMA *rushes back to* MARGARET.)*Shoot! Stop playin' so dumb!*—I mean has he been drinkin' that stuff much yet?

MARGARET (*with a little laugh*). Oh! I think he had a highball after supper.

BIG MAMA. Don't laugh about it!—some single men stop drinkin' when they git married and others start! Brick never touched liquor before he—!

MARGARET (*crying out*). *THAT'S NOT FAIR!*

BIG MAMA. Fair or not fair I want to ask you a question, one question: D'you make Brick happy in bed?

MARGARET. Why don't you ask if he makes *me* happy in bed?

BIG MAMA. Because I know that—

MARGARET. *It works both ways!*

BIG MAMA. Something's not right! You're childless and my son drinks! (*Someone has called her downstairs and she has rushed to the door on the line above. She turns at the door and points at the bed.*) —When a marriage goes on the rocks, the rocks are *there*, right *there!*

MARGARET. *That's*—(BIG MAMA *has swept out of the room and slammed the door.*) —not—*fair . . .*

(MARGARET *is alone, completely alone, and she feels it. She draws in, hunches her shoulders, raises her arms with fists clenched, shuts her eyes tight as a child about to be stabbed with a vaccination needle. When she opens her eyes again, what she sees is the long oval mirror and she rushes straight to it, stares into it with a grimace and says: "Who are you?"— Then she crouches a little and answers herself in a different voice which is high, thin, mocking: "I am Maggie the Cat!"— Straightens quickly as bathroom door opens a little and* BRICK *calls out to her.*)

BRICK. Has Big Mama gone?

MARGARET. She's gone. (*He opens the bathroom door and hobbles out, with his liquor glass now empty, straight to the liquor cabinet. He is whistling softly.* MARGARET'S *head pivots on her long, slender throat to watch him. She raises a hand uncertainly to the base of her throat, as if it was difficult for her to swallow, before she speaks.*) You know, our sex life didn't just peter out in the usual way, it was cut off short, long before the natural time for it to, and it's going to revive again, just as sudden as that. I'm confident of it. That's what I'm keeping myself attractive for. For the time when you'll see me again like other men see me. Yes, like other men see me. They still see me, Brick, and they like what they see. Uh-huh. Some of them would give their—

Look, Brick! (*She stands before the long oval mirror, touches her breast and then her hips with her two hands.*) How high my body stays on me!—Nothing has fallen on me—not a fraction. . . . (*Her voice is soft and trembling: a pleading child's. At this moment as he turns to glance at her— a look which is like a player passing a ball to another player, third down and goal to go—she has to capture the audience in a grip so tight that she can hold it till the first intermission without any lapse of attention.*) Other men still want me. My face looks strained, sometimes, but I've kept my figure as well as you've kept yours, and men admire it. I still turn heads on the street. Why, last week in Memphis everywhere that I went men's eyes burned holes in my clothes, at the country club and in restaurants and department stores, there wasn't a man I met or walked by that didn't just eat me up with his eyes and turn around when I passed him and look back at me. Why, at Alice's party for her New York cousins, the best lookin' man in the crowd—followed me upstairs and tried to force his way in the powder room with me, followed me to the door and tried to force his way in!

BRICK. Why didn't you let him, Maggie?

MARGARET. Because I'm not that common, for one thing. Not that I wasn't almost tempted to. You like to know who it was? It was Sonny Boy Maxwell, that's who!

BRICK. Oh, yeah, Sonny Boy Maxwell, he was a good end-runner but had a little injury to his back and had to quit.

MARGARET. He has no injury now and has no wife and still has a lech for me!

BRICK. I see no reason to lock him out of a powder room in that case.

MARGARET. And have someone catch me at it? I'm not that stupid. Oh, I might sometime cheat on you with someone, since you're so insultingly eager to have me do it!—But if I do, you can be damned sure it will be in a place and a time where no one but me and the man could possibly know. Because I'm not going to give you any excuse to divorce me for being unfaithful or anything else. . . .

BRICK. Maggie, I wouldn't divorce you for being unfaithful or anything else. Don't you know that? Hell. I'd be relieved to know that you'd found yourself a lover.

MARGARET. Well, I'm taking no chances.

No, I'd rather stay on this hot tin roof.

BRICK. A hot tin roof's 'n uncomfo'table place t' stay on. . . . (*He starts to whistle softly.*)

MARGARET (*through his whistle*). Yeah, but I can stay on it just as long as I have to.

BRICK. You could leave me, Maggie. (*He resumes whistle. She wheels about to glare at him.*)

MARGARET. *Don't want to and will not!* Besides if I did, you don't have a cent to pay for it but what you get from Big Daddy and he's dying of cancer! (*For the first time a realization of* BIG DADDY's *doom seems to penetrate to* BRICK's *consciousness, visibly, and he looks at* MARGARET.)

BRICK. Big Mama just said he *wasn't*, that the report was okay.

MARGARET. That's what she thinks because she got the same story that they gave Big Daddy. And was just as taken in by it as he was, poor ole things. . . .

But tonight they're going to tell her the truth about it. When Big Daddy goes to bed, they're going to tell her that he is dying of cancer. (*She slams the dresser drawer.*)—It's malignant and it's terminal.

BRICK. Does Big Daddy know it?

MARGARET. Hell, do they *ever* know it? Nobody says, "You're dying." You have to fool them. They have to fool *themselves*.

BRICK. Why?

MARGARET. *Why?* Because human beings dream of life everlasting, that's the reason! But most of them want it on earth and not in heaven. (*He gives a short, hard laugh at her touch of humor.*) Well. . . . (*She touches up her mascara.*) That's how it is, anyhow. . . . (*She looks about.*) Where did I put down my cigarette? Don't want to burn up the home-place, at least not with Mae and Gooper and their five monsters in it! (*She has found it and sucks at it greedily. Blows out smoke and continues.*) So this is Big Daddy's last birthday. And Mae and Gooper, they know it, oh, *they* know it, all right. They got the first information from the Ochsner Clinic. That's why they rushed down here with their no-neck monsters. Because. Do you know something? Big Daddy's made no will? Big Daddy's never made out any will in his life, and so this campaign's afoot to impress him, forcibly as possible, with the fact that you drink and I've borne no children!

(*He continues to stare at her a moment, then mutters something sharp but not audible and hobbles rather rapidly out onto the long gallery in the fading, much faded, gold light.*)

MARGARET (*continuing her liturgical chant*). Y'know, I'm fond of Big Daddy, I am genuinely fond of that old man, I really *am*, you know. . . .

BRICK (*faintly, vaguely*). Yes, I know you are. . . .

MARGARET. I've always sort of admired him in spite of his coarseness, his four-letter words and so forth. Because Big Daddy *is* what he *is*, and he makes no bones about it. He hasn't turned gentleman farmer, he's still a Mississippi red neck, as much of a red neck as he must have been when he was just overseer here on the old Jack Straw and Peter Ochello place. But he got hold of it an' built it into th' biggest an' finest plantation in the Delta.—I've always *liked* Big Daddy. . . . (*She crosses to the proscenium.*) Well, this is Big Daddy's last birthday. I'm sorry about it. But I'm facing the facts. It takes money to take care of a drinker and that's the office that I've been elected to lately.

BRICK. You don't have to take care of me.

MARGARET. Yes, I do. Two people in the same boat have got to take care of each other. At least you want money to buy more Echo Spring when this supply is exhausted, or will you be satisfied with a ten-cent beer?

Mae an' Gooper are plannin' to freeze us out of Big Daddy's estate because you drink and I'm childless. But we can defeat that plan. We're *going* to defeat that plan!

Brick, y'know, I've been so God damn disgustingly poor all my life!—That's the *truth*, Brick!

BRICK. I'm not sayin' it isn't.

MARGARET. Always had to suck up to people I couldn't stand because they had money and I was poor as Job's turkey. You don't know what that's like. Well, I'll tell you, it's like you would feel a thousand miles away from Echo Spring!—And had to get back to it on that broken ankle . . . without a crutch!

That's how it feels to be as poor as Job's turkey and have to suck up to relatives that you hated because they had money and all you had was a bunch of hand-me-down clothes and a few old moldy three per cent government bonds. My daddy loved his liquor, he fell in love with his liquor the way you've fallen in love with Echo Spring!—And my poor mama, having to maintain some semblance of social position, to keep appearances up, on an income of one hundred and fifty dollars a month on those old government bonds!

When I came out, the year that I made my debut, I had just two evening dresses! One Mother made me from a pattern in *Vogue,* the other a hand-me-down from a snotty rich cousin I hated!

—The dress that I married you in was my grandmother's weddin' gown. . . .

So that's why I'm like a cat on a hot tin roof!

(BRICK *is still on the gallery. Someone below calls up to him in a warm Negro voice, "Hiya, Mistuh Brick, how yuh feelin'?" Brick raises his liquor glass as if that answered the question.*)

MARGARET. You can be young without money but you can't be old without it. You've got to be old *with* money because to be old without it is just too awful, you've got to be one or the other, either *young* or *with money,* you can't be old and *without* it.—That's the *truth,* Brick. . . . (BRICK *whistles softly, vaguely.*) Well, now I'm dressed, I'm all dressed, there's nothing else for me to do. (*Forlornly, almost fearfully.*) I'm dressed, all dressed, nothing else for me to do.... (*She moves about restlessly, aimlessly, and speaks, as if to herself.*) I know when I made my mistake.— What am I—? Oh!—my bracelets.... (*She starts working a collection of bracelets over her hands onto her wrists, about six on each, as she talks.*) I've thought a whole lot about it and now I know when I made my mistake. Yes, I made my mistake when I told you the truth about that thing with Skipper. Never should have confessed it, a fatal error, tellin' you about that thing with Skipper.

BRICK. Maggie, shut up about Skipper. I mean it, Maggie; you got to shut up about Skipper.

MARGARET. You ought to understand that Skipper and I—

BRICK. You don't think I'm serious, Maggie? You're fooled by the fact that I am saying this quiet? Look, Maggie. What you're doing is a dangerous thing to do. You're—you're—you're—foolin'

with something that—nobody ought to fool with.

MARGARET. This time I'm going to finish what I have to say to you. Skipper and I made love, if love you could call it, because it made both of us feel a little bit closer to you. You see, you son of a bitch, you asked too much of people, of me, of him, of all the unlucky poor damned sons of bitches that happen to love you, and there was a whole pack of them, yes, there was a pack of them besides me and Skipper, you asked too goddam much of people that loved you, you—superior creature!—you godlike being!—And so we made love to each other to dream it was you, both of us! Yes, yes, yes! Truth, truth! What's so awful about it? I like it, I think the truth is— yeah! I shouldn't have told you. . . .

BRICK (*holding his head unnaturally still and uptilted a bit*). It was Skipper that told me about it. Not you, Maggie.

MARGARET. I told you!

BRICK. After he told me!

MARGARET. What does it matter who—?

(BRICK *turns suddenly out upon the gallery and calls.*)

BRICK. Little girl! Hey, little girl!

LITTLE GIRL (*at a distance*). What, Uncle Brick?

BRICK. Tell the folks to come up!—Bring everybody upstairs!

MARGARET. I can't stop myself! I'd go on telling you this in front of them all, if I had to!

BRICK. Little girl! Go on, go on, will you? Do what I told you, call them!

MARGARET. Because it's got to be told and you, you!—you never let me! (*She sobs, then controls herself, and continues almost calmly.*) It was one of those beautiful, ideal things they tell about in the Greek legends, it couldn't be anything else, you being you, and that's what made it so sad, that's what made it so awful, because it was love that never could be carried through to anything satisfying or even talked about plainly. Brick, I tell you, you got to believe me, Brick, I *do* understand all about it! I—I think it was—*noble!* Can't you tell I'm sincere when I say I respect it? My only point, the only point that I'm making, is life has got to be allowed to continue even after the *dream* of life is—all—over. . . . (BRICK *is without his crutch. Leaning on furniture, he crosses to pick it up as she continues as if possessed by a will outside her-*

self.) Why I remember when we double-dated at college, Gladys Fitzgerald and I and you and Skipper, it was more like a date between you and Skipper. Gladys and I were just sort of tagging along as if it was necessary to chaperone you!—to make a good public impression—

BRICK (*turns to face her, half lifting his crutch*). Maggie, you want me to hit you with this crutch? Don't you know I could kill you with this crutch?

MARGARET. Good Lord, man, d' you think I'd care if you did?

BRICK. One man has one great good true thing in his life. One great good thing which is true!—I had friendship with Skipper.—You are naming it dirty!

MARGARET. I'm not naming it dirty! I am naming it clean.

BRICK. Not love with you, Maggie, but friendship with Skipper was that one great true thing, and you are naming it dirty!

MARGARET. Then you haven't been listenin', not understood what I'm saying! I'm naming it so damn clean that it killed poor Skipper!—You two had something that had to be kept on ice, yes, incorruptible, yes!—and death was the only icebox where you could keep it. . . .

BRICK. I married you, Maggie. Why would I marry you, Maggie, if I was—?

MARGARET. Brick, don't brain me yet, let me finish!—I know, believe me I know, that it was only Skipper that harbored even any *unconscious* desire for anything not perfectly pure between you two!— Now let me skip a little. You married me early that summer we graduated out of Ole Miss, and we were happy, weren't we, we were blissful, yes, hit heaven together ev'ry time that we loved! But that fall you an' Skipper turned down wonderful offers of jobs in order to keep on bein' football heroes—pro-football heroes. You organized the Dixie Stars that fall, so you could keep on bein' team-mates forever! But somethin' was not right with it!—*Me included!* —between you. Skipper began hittin' the bottle . . . you got a spinal injury— couldn't play the Thanksgivin' game in Chicago, watched it on TV from a traction bed in Toledo. I joined Skipper. The Dixie Stars lost because poor Skipper was drunk. We drank together that night all night in the bar of the Blackstone and when cold day was comin' up over the Lake an' we were comin' out drunk to take a dizzy look at it, I said, "SKIPPER! STOP LOVIN' MY HUSBAND OR TELL HIM HE'S GOT TO LET YOU ADMIT IT TO HIM!"—one way or another!

HE SLAPPED ME HARD ON THE MOUTH!—then turned and ran without stopping once, I am sure, all the way back into his room at the Blackstone. . . .

—When I came to his room that night, with a little scratch like a shy little mouse at his door, he made that pitiful, ineffectual little attempt to prove that what I had said wasn't true. . . . (BRICK *strikes at her with crutch, a blow that shatters the gemlike lamp on the table.*)—In this way, I destroyed him, by telling him truth that he and his world which he was born and raised in, yours and his world, had told him could not be told?

—From then on Skipper was nothing at all but a receptacle for liquor and drugs. . . .

—*Who shot cock-robin? I with my—* (*She throws back her head with tight-shut eyes.*)—*merciful arrow!* (BRICK *strikes at her; misses.*) Missed me!—Sorry,—I'm not tryin' to whitewash my behavior, Christ, no! Brick, I'm not good. I don't know why people have to pretend to be good, nobody's good. The rich or the well-to-do can afford to respect moral patterns, conventional moral patterns, but I could never afford to, yeah, but—I'm honest! Give me credit for just that, will you *please*?—Born poor, raised poor, expect to die poor unless I manage to get us something out of what Big Daddy leaves when he dies of cancer! But Brick?!—*Skipper is dead! I'm alive!* Maggie the cat is—(BRICK *hops awkwardly forward and strikes at her again with his crutch.*)—*alive! I am alive, alive! I am* . . . (*He hurls the crutch at her, across the bed she took refuge behind, and pitches forward on the floor as she completes her speech.*)—*alive!* (*A little girl,* DIXIE, *bursts into the room, wearing an Indian war bonnet and firing a cap pistol at* MARGARET *and shouting: "Bang, bang, bang!" Laughter downstairs floats through the open hall door.* MARGARET *had crouched gasping to bed at child's entrance. She now rises and says with cool fury:*) Little girl, your mother or someone should teach you— (*Gasping*)—to knock at a door before you come into a room. Otherwise people might think that you—lack—good breeding. . . .

DIXIE. Yanh, yanh, yanh, what is Uncle Brick doin' on th' floor?

BRICK. I tried to kill your Aunt Maggie, but I failed—and I fell. Little girl, give me my crutch so I can get up off th' floor.

MARGARET. Yes, give your uncle his crutch, he's a cripple, honey, he broke his ankle last night jumping hurdles on the high school athletic field!

DIXIE. What were you jumping hurdles for, Uncle Brick?

BRICK. Because I used to jump them, and people like to do what they used to do, even after they've stopped being able to do it. . . .

MARGARET. That's right, that's your answer, now go away, little girl. (DIXIE *fires cap pistol at* MARGARET *three times.*) *Stop, you stop that, monster! You little no-neck monster!* (*She seizes the cap pistol and hurls it through gallery doors.*)

DIXIE (*with a precocious instinct for the cruelest thing*). You're *jealous!*—You're just jealous because you can't have babies! (*She sticks out her tongue at* MARGARET *as she sashays past her with her stomach struck out, to the gallery.* MARGARET *slams the gallery doors and leans panting against them. There is a pause.* BRICK *has replaced his spilt drink and sits, faraway, on the great four-poster bed.*)

MARGARET. You see?—they gloat over us being childless, even in front of their five little no-neck monsters! (*Pause. Voices on the stairs.*) Brick?—I've been to a doctor in Memphis, a—a gynecologist. . . . I've been completely examined, and there is no reason why we can't have a child whenever we want one. And this is my time by the calendar to conceive. Are you listening to me? Are you? Are you LISTENING TO ME!

BRICK. Yes. I hear you, Maggie. (*His attention returns to her inflamed face.*)—how in hell on earth do you imagine—that you're going to have a child by a man that can't stand you?

MARGARET. That's a problem that I will have to work out. (*She wheels about to face the hall door.*) Here they come!

(*The lights dim.*)

CURTAIN

ACT TWO

There is no lapse of time. MARGARET *and* BRICK *are in the same positions they held at the end of Act I.*

———

MARGARET (*at door*). Here they come!

(BIG DADDY *appears first, a tall man with a fierce, anxious look, moving carefully not to betray his weakness even, or especially, to himself.*)

BIG DADDY. Well, Brick.

BRICK. Hello, Big Daddy.—Congratulations!

BIG DADDY. —Crap. . . .

(*Some of the people are approaching through the hall, others along the gallery: voices from both directions.* GOOPER *and* REVEREND TOOKER *become visible outside gallery doors, and their voices come in clearly. They pause outside as* GOOPER *lights a cigar.*)

REVEREND TOOKER (*vivaciously*). Oh, but St. Paul's in Grenada has three memorial windows, and the latest one is a Tiffany stained-glass window that cost twenty-five hundred dollars, a picture of Christ the Good Shepherd with a Lamb in His arms.

GOOPER. Who give that window, Preach?

REVEREND TOOKER. Clyde Fletcher's widow. Also presented St. Paul's with a baptismal font.

GOOPER. Y'know what somebody ought t' give your church is a *coolin'* system, Preach.

REVEREND TOOKER. Yes, siree, Bob! And y'know what Gus Hamma's family gave in his memory to the church at Two Rivers? A complete new stone parish-house with a basketball court in the basement and a—

BIG DADDY (*uttering a loud barking laugh which is far from truly mirthful*). Hey, Preach! What's all this talk about memorials, Preach? Y' think somebody's about t' kick off around here? 'S that it?

(*Startled by this interjection,* REVEREND TOOKER *decides to laugh at the question almost as loud as he can. How he would answer the question we'll never know, as he's spared that embarrassment by the voice of* GOOPER's *wife,* MAE, *rising high and clear as she appears with* "DOC" BAUGH, *the family doctor, through the hall door.*)

MAE (*almost religiously*).—Let's see now, they've had their *tyyy*-phoid shots, and their tetanus shots, their diphtheria shots and their hepatitis shots and their polio shots, they got *those* shots every month from May through September, and—

Gooper? Hey! Gooper!—What all have the kiddies been shot faw?

MARGARET (*overlapping a bit*). Turn on the Hi-Fi, Brick! Let's have some music t' start off th' party with!

(*The talk becomes so general that the room sounds like a great aviary of chattering birds. Only* BRICK *remains unengaged, leaning upon the liquor cabinet with his faraway smile, an ice cube in a paper napkin with which he now and then rubs his forehead. He doesn't respond to* MARGARET'S *command. She bounds forward and stoops over the instrument panel of the console.*)

GOOPER. We gave 'em that thing for a third anniversary present, got three speakers in it. (*The room is suddenly blasted by the climax of a Wagnerian opera or a Beethoven symphony.*)

BIG DADDY. *Turn that damn thing off!*

(*Almost instant silence, almost instantly broken by the shouting charge of* BIG MAMA, *entering through hall door like a charging rhino.*)

BIG MAMA. *Wha's my Brick, wha's mah precious baby!!*

BIG DADDY. *Sorry! Turn it back on!*

(*Everyone laughs very loud.* BIG DADDY *is famous for his jokes at* BIG MAMA'S *expense, and nobody laughs louder at these jokes than* BIG MAMA *herself, though some times they're pretty cruel and* BIG MAMA *has to pick up or fuss with something to cover the hurt that the loud laugh doesn't quite cover.*

(*On this occasion, a happy occasion because the dread in her heart has also been lifted by the false report on* BIG DADDY'S *condition, she giggles, grotesquely, coyly, in* BIG DADDY'S *direction and bears down upon* BRICK, *all very quick and alive.*)

BIG MAMA. Here he is, here's my precious baby! What's that you've got in your hand? You put that liquor down, son, your hand was made fo' holdin' somethin' better than that!

GOOPER. Look at Brick put it down!

(*BRICK has obeyed* BIG MAMA *by draining the glass and handing it to her. Again everyone laughs, some high, some low.*)

BIG MAMA. Oh, you bad boy, you, you're my bad little boy. Give Big Mama a kiss, you bad boy, you!—Look at him shy away, will you? Brick never liked bein' kissed or made a fuss over, I guess because he's always had too much of it!

Son, you turn that thing off! (BRICK *has switched on the TV set.*) I can't stand TV, radio was bad enough but TV has gone it one better, I mean—(*Plops wheezing in chair*)—one worse, ha ha! Now what'm I sittin' down here faw? I want t' sit next to my sweetheart on the sofa, hold hands with him and love him up a little! (BIG MAMA *has on a black and white figured chiffon. The large irregular patterns, like the markings of some massive animal, the luster of her great diamonds and many pearls, the brilliants set in the silver frames of her glasses, her riotous voice, booming laugh, have dominated the room since she entered.* BIG DADDY *has been regarding her with a steady grimace of chronic annoyance. Still louder.*) Preacher, Preacher, hey, Preach! Give me you' hand an' help me up from this chair!

REVEREND TOOKER. None of your tricks, Big Mama!

BIG MAMA. What tricks? You give me you' hand so I can get up an'—(REVEREND TOOKER *extends her his hand. She grabs it and pulls him into her lap with a shrill laugh that spans an octave in two notes.*) Ever seen a preacher in a fat lady's lap? Hey, hey, folks! Ever seen a preacher in a fat lady's lap? (BIG MAMA *is notorious throughout the Delta for this sort of inelegant horseplay.* MARGARET *looks on with indulgent humor, sipping Dubonnet "on the rocks" and watching* BRICK, *but* MAE *and* GOOPER *exchange signs of humorless anxiety over these antics, the sort of behavior which* MAE *thinks may account for their failure to quite get in with the smartest young married set in Memphis, despite all. One of the Negroes,* LACEY *or* SOOKEY, *peeks in, cackling. They are waiting for a sign to bring in the cake and champagne. But* BIG DADDY'S *not amused. He doesn't understand why, in spite of the infinite mental relief he's received from the doctor's report, he still has these same old fox teeth in his guts.* "*This spastic thing sure is something,*" *he says to himself, but aloud he roars at* BIG MAMA:)

BIG DADDY. *BIG MAMA, WILL YOU QUIT HORSIN'?*—You're too old an' too fat fo' that sort of crazy kid stuff an' besides a woman with your blood-pressure —she had two hundred last spring!—is riskin' a stroke when you mess around like that. . . .

BIG MAMA. *Here comes Big Daddy's birthday!*

(*Negroes in white jackets enter with an enormous birthday cake ablaze with candles and carrying buckets of champagne with satin ribbons about the bottle necks.*

(MAE *and* GOOPER *strike up song, and everybody, including the Negroes and children, joins in. Only Brick remains aloof.*)

EVERYONE.
Happy birthday to you.
Happy birthday to you.
Happy birthday, Big Daddy—
(*Some sing: "Dear, Big Daddy!"*)
Happy birthday to you.
(*Some sing: "How old are you?"*)

(MAE *has come down center and is organizing her children like a chorus. She gives them a barely audible: "One, two, three!" and they are off in the new tune.*)

CHILDREN.
Skinamarinka—dinka—dink
Skinamarinka—do
We love you.
Skinamarinka—dinka—dink
Skinamarinka—do.

(*All together, they turn to* BIG DADDY.)
Big Daddy, you!

(*They turn back front, like a musical comedy chorus.*)
We love you in the morning;
We love you in the night.
We love you when we're with you.
And we love you out of sight.
Skinamarinka—dinka—dink
Skinamarinka—do.

(MAE *turns to* BIG MAMA.)
Big Mama, too!

(BIG MAMA *bursts into tears. The Negroes leave.*)

BIG DADDY. Now Ida, what the hell is the matter with you?

MAE. She's just so happy.

BIG MAMA. I'm just so happy, Big Daddy, I have to cry or something. (*Sudden and loud in the hush:*) Brick, do you know the wonderful news that Doc Baugh got from the clinic about Big Daddy? Big Daddy's one hundred per cent!

MARGARET. Isn't that wonderful?

BIG MAMA. He's just one hundred per cent. Passed the examination with flying colors. Now that we know there's nothing wrong with Big Daddy but a spastic colon, I can tell you something. I was worried sick, half out of my mind, for fear that Big Daddy might have a thing like—

(MARGARET *cuts through this speech, jumping up and exclaiming shrilly:*)

MARGARET. Brick, honey, aren't you going to give Big Daddy his birthday present? (*Passing by him, she snatches his liquor glass from him. She picks up a fancily wrapped package.*) Here it is, Big Daddy, this is from Brick!

BIG MAMA. This is the biggest birthday Big Daddy's ever had, a hundred presents and bushels of telegrams from—

MAE (*at same time*). What is it, Brick?

GOOPER. I bet 500 to 50 that Brick don't know what it is.

BIG MAMA. The fun of presents is not knowing what they are till you open the package. Open your present, Big Daddy.

BIG DADDY. Open it you'self. I want to ask Brick somethin! Come here, Brick.

MARGARET. Big Daddy's callin' you, Brick. (*She is opening the package.*)

BRICK. Tell Big Daddy I'm crippled.

BIG DADDY. I see you're crippled. I want to know how you got crippled.

MARGARET (*making diversionary tactics*). Oh, look, oh, look, why, it's a cashmere robe! (*She holds the robe up for all to see.*)

MAE. You sound surprised, Maggie.

MARGARET. I never saw one before.

MAE. That's funny.—Hah!

MARGARET (*turning on her fiercely, with a brilliant smile*). Why is it funny? All my family ever had was family—and luxuries such as cashmere robes still surprise me!

BIG DADDY (*ominously*). Quiet!

MAE (*heedless in her fury*). I don't see how you could be so surprised when you bought it yourself at Loewenstein's in Memphis last Saturday. You know how I know?

BIG DADDY. I said, Quiet!

MAE. —I know because the salesgirl that sold it to you waited on me and said, Oh, Mrs. Pollitt, your sister-in-law just bought a cashmere robe for your husband's father!

MARGARET. Sister Woman! Your talents are wasted as a housewife and mother, you really ought to be with the FBI or—

BIG DADDY. QUIET!

(REVEREND TOOKER'S *reflexes are slower than the others'. He finishes a sentence after the bellow.*)

REVEREND TOOKER (*to* DOC BAUGH). —the Stork and the Reaper are running neck and neck! (*He starts to laugh gaily when he notices the silence and* BIG DADDY's *glare. His laugh dies falsely.*)

BIG DADDY. Preacher, I hope I'm not butting in on more talk about memorial stained-glass windows, am I, Preacher? (REVEREND TOOKER *laughs feebly, then coughs dryly in the embarrassed silence.*) Preacher?

BIG MAMA. Now, Big Daddy, don't you pick on Preacher!

BIG DADDY (*raising his voice*). You ever hear that expression all hawk and no spit? You bring that expression to mind with that little dry cough of yours, all hawk an' no spit. . . .

(*The pause is broken only by a short startled laugh from* MARGARET, *the only one there who is conscious of and amused by the grotesque.*)

MAE (*raising her arms and jangling her bracelets*). I wonder if the mosquitoes are active tonight?

BIG DADDY. What's that, Little Mama? Did you make some remark?

MAE. Yes, I said I wondered if the mosquitoes would eat us alive if we went out on the gallery for a while.

BIG DADDY. Well, if they do, I'll have your bones pulverized for fertilizer!

BIG MAMA (*quickly*). Last week we had an airplane spraying the place and I think it done some good, at least I haven't had a—

BIG DADDY (*cutting her speech*). Brick, they tell me, if what they tell me is true, that you done some jumping last night on the high school athletic field?

BIG MAMA. Brick, Big Daddy is talking to you, son.

BRICK (*smiling vaguely over his drink*). What was that, Big Daddy?

BIG DADDY. They said you done some jumping on the high school track field last night.

BRICK. That's what they told me, too.

BIG DADDY. Was it jumping or humping that you were doing out there? What were you doing out there at three A.M., layin' a woman on that cinder track?

BIG MAMA. Big Daddy, you are off the sick-list, now, and I'm not going to excuse you for talkin' so—

BIG DADDY. Quiet!

BIG MAMA. —*nasty* in front of Preacher and—

BIG DADDY. QUIET!—I ast you, Brick, if you was cuttin' you'self a piece o' poontang last night on that cinder track? I thought maybe you were chasin' poontang on that track an' tripped over something in the heat of the chase—'sthat it?

(GOOPER *laughs, loud and false, others nervously following suit.* BIG MAMA *stamps her foot, and purses her lips, crossing to* MAE *and whispering something to her as* BRICK *meets his father's hard, intent, grinning stare with a slow, vague smile that he offers all situations from behind the screen of his liquor.*)

BRICK. No, sir, I don't think so. . . .

MAE (*at the same time, sweetly*). Reverend Tooker, let's you and I take a stroll on the widow's walk. (*She and the preacher go out on the gallery as* BIG DADDY *says:*)

BIG DADDY. Then what the hell were you doing out there at three o'clock in the morning?

BRICK. Jumping the hurdles, Big Daddy, runnin' and jumpin' the hurdles, but those high hurdles have gotten too high for me, now.

BIG DADDY. Cause you was drunk?

BRICK (*his vague smile fading a little*). Sober I wouldn't have tried to jump the *low* ones. . . .

BIG MAMA (*quickly*). Big Daddy, blow out the candles on your birthday cake!

MARGARET (*at the same time*). I want to propose a toast to Big Daddy Pollitt on his sixty-fifth birthday, the biggest cotton-planter in—

BIG DADDY (*bellowing with fury and disgust*). *I told you to stop it, now stop it, quit this—!*

BIG MAMA (*coming in front of* BIG DADDY *with the cake*). Big Daddy, I will not allow you to talk that way, not even on your birthday, I—

BIG DADDY. I'll talk like I want to on my birthday, Ida, or any other goddam day of the year and anybody here that don't like it knows what they can do!

BIG MAMA. You don't mean that!

BIG DADDY. What makes you think I don't mean it?

(*Meanwhile various discreet signals have been exchanged and* GOOPER *has also gone out on the gallery.*)

BIG MAMA. I just know you don't mean it.

BIG DADDY. You don't know a goddam thing and you never did!

BIG MAMA. Big Daddy, you don't mean that.

BIG DADDY. Oh, yes, I do, oh, yes, I do, I mean it! I put up with a whole lot of crap around here because I thought I was dying. And you thought I was dying and you started taking over, well, you can stop taking over now, Ida, because I'm not gonna die, you can just stop now this business of taking over because you're not taking over because I'm not dying, I went through the laboratory and the goddam exploratory operation and there's nothing wrong with me but a spastic colon. And I'm not dying of cancer which you thought I was dying of. Ain't that so? Didn't you think that I was dying of cancer, Ida? (*Almost everybody is out on the gallery but the two old people glaring at each other across the blazing cake.* BIG MAMA's *chest heaves and she presses a fat fist to her mouth.* BIG DADDY *continues, hoarsely.*) Ain't that so, Ida? Didn't you have an idea I was dying of cancer and now you could take control of this place and everything on it? I got that impression, I seemed to get that impression. Your loud voice everywhere, your fat old body butting in here and there!

BIG MAMA. Hush! The Preacher!

BIG DADDY. Rut the goddam preacher! (BIG MAMA *gasps loudly and sits down on the sofa which is almost too small for her.*) Did you hear what I said? I said rut the goddam preacher!

(*Somebody closes the gallery doors from outside just as there is a burst of fireworks and excited cries from the children.*)

BIG MAMA. I never seen you act like this before and I can't think what's got in you!

BIG DADDY. I went through all that laboratory and operation and all just so I would know if you or me was boss here! Well, now it turns out that I am and you ain't—and that's my birthday present—and my cake and champagne!—because for three years now you been gradually taking over. Bossing. Talking. Sashaying your fat old body around the place I made! I made this place! I was overseer on it! I was the overseer on the old Straw and Ochello plantation. I quit school at ten! I quit school at ten years old and went to work like a nigger in the fields. And I rose to be overseer of the Straw and Ochello plantation. And old Straw died and I was Ochello's partner and the place got bigger and bigger and bigger and bigger and bigger! I did all that myself with no goddam help from you, and now you think you're just about to take over. Well, I am just about to tell you that you are not just about to take over, you are not just about to take over a God damn thing. Is that clear to you, Ida? Is that very plain to you, now? Is that understood completely? I been through the laboratory from A to Z. I've had the goddam exploratory operation, and nothing is wrong with me but a spastic colon—made spastic, I guess, by *disgust!* By all the goddam lies and liars that I have had to put up with, and all the goddam hypocrisy that I lived with all these forty years that we been livin' together!

Hey! Ida!! Blow out the candles on the birthday cake! Purse up your lips and draw a deep breath and blow out the goddam candles on the cake!

BIG MAMA. Oh, Big Daddy, oh, oh, oh, Big Daddy!

BIG DADDY. What's the matter with you?

BIG MAMA. *In all these years you never believed that I loved you??*

BIG DADDY. Huh?

BIG MAMA. *And I did, I did so much, I did love you!*—I even loved your hate and your hardness, Big Daddy! (*She sobs and rushes awkwardly out onto the gallery.*)

BIG DADDY (*to himself*). *Wouldn't it be funny if that was true.* . . . (*A pause is followed by a burst of light in the sky from the fireworks.*) BRICK! HEY, BRICK! (*He stands over his blazing birthday cake. After some moments,* BRICK *hobbles in on his crutch, holding his glass.* MARGARET *follows him with a bright, anxious smile.*) I didn't call you, Maggie. I called Brick.

MARGARET. I'm just delivering him to you.

(*She kisses* BRICK *on the mouth which he immediately wipes with the back of his hand. She flies girlishly back out.* BRICK *and his father are alone.*)

BIG DADDY. Why did you do that?

BRICK. Do what, Big Daddy?

BIG DADDY. Wipe her kiss off your mouth like she'd spit on you.

BRICK. I don't know. I wasn't conscious of it.

BIG DADDY. That woman of yours has a better shape on her than Gooper's but somehow or other they got the same look about them.

BRICK. What sort of look is that, Big Daddy?

BIG DADDY. I don't know how to describe it but it's the same look.

BRICK. They don't look peaceful, do they?

BIG DADDY. No, they sure in hell don't.

BRICK. They look nervous as cats?

BIG DADDY. That's right, they look nervous as cats.

BRICK. Nervous as a couple of cats on a hot tin roof?

BIG DADDY. That's right, boy, they look like a couple of cats on a hot tin roof. It's funny that you and Gooper being so different would pick out the same type of woman.

BRICK. Both of us married into society, Big Daddy.

BIG DADDY. Crap . . . I wonder what gives them both that look?

BRICK. Well. They're sittin' in the middle of a big piece of land, Big Daddy, twenty-eight thousand acres is a pretty big piece of land and so they're squaring off on it, each determined to knock off a bigger piece of it than the other whenever you let it go.

BIG DADDY. I got a surprise for those women. I'm not gonna let it go for a long time yet if that's what they're waiting for.

BRICK. That's right, Big Daddy. You just sit tight and let them scratch each other's eyes out. . . .

BIG DADDY. You bet your life I'm going to sit tight on it and let those sons of bitches scratch their eyes out, ha ha ha. . . .

But Gooper's wife's a good breeder, you got to admit she's fertile. Hell, at supper tonight she had them all at the table and they had to put a couple of extra leafs in the table to make room for them, she's got five head of them, now, and another one's comin'.

BRICK. Yep, number six is comin'. . . .

BIG DADDY. Brick, you know, I swear to God, I don't know the way it happens?

BRICK. The way what happens, Big Daddy?

BIG DADDY. You git you a piece of land, by hook or crook, an' things start growin' on it, things accumulate on it, and the first thing you know it's completely out of hand, completely out of hand!

BRICK. Well, they say nature hates a vacuum, Big Daddy.

BIG DADDY. That's what they say, but sometimes I think that a vacuum is a hell of a lot better than some of the stuff that nature replaces it with.

Is someone out there by that door?

BRICK. Yep.

BIG DADDY. Who? (*He has lowered his voice.*)

BRICK. Someone int'rested in what we say to each other.

BIG DADDY. Gooper?—*GOOPER!* (*After a discreet pause,* MAE *appears in the gallery door.*)

MAE. Did you call Gooper, Big Daddy?

BIG DADDY. Aw, it was you.

MAE. Do you want Gooper, Big Daddy?

BIG DADDY. No, and I don't want you. I want some privacy here, while I'm having a confidential talk with my son Brick. Now it's too hot in here to close them doors, but if I have to close those rutten doors in order to have a private talk with my son Brick, just let me know and I'll close 'em. Because I hate eavesdroppers, I don't like any kind of sneakin' an' spyin'.

MAE. Why, Big Daddy—

BIG DADDY. You stood on the wrong side of the moon, it threw your shadow!

MAE. I was just—

BIG DADDY. You was just nothing but *spyin'* an' you *know* it!

MAE (*begins to sniff and sob*). Oh, Big Daddy, you're so unkind for some reason to those that really love you!

BIG DADDY. Shut up, shut up, shut up! I'm going to move you and Gooper out of that room next to this! It's none of your goddam business what goes on in here at night between Brick an' Maggie. You listen at night like a couple of rutten peek-hole spies and go and give a report on what you hear to Big Mama an' she comes to me and says they say such and such and so and so about what they heard goin' on between Brick an' Maggie, and Jesus, it makes me sick. I'm goin' to move you an' Gooper out of that room, I can't stand sneakin' an' spyin', it makes me sick. . . .

(MAE *throws her head and rolls her eyes heavenward and extends her arms as if invoking God's pity for this unjust martyrdom; then she presses a handkerchief to her nose and flies from the room with a loud swish of skirts.*)

BRICK (*now at the liquor cabinet*). They listen, do they?

BIG DADDY. Yeah. They listen and give reports to Big Mamma on what goes on in here between you and Maggie. They say that—(*He stops as if embarrassed.*)—You won't sleep with her, that you sleep on the sofa. Is that true or not true? If you don't like Maggie, get rid of Maggie!—What are you doin' there now?

BRICK. Fresh'nin' up my drink.

BIG DADDY. Son, you know you got a real liquor problem?

BRICK. Yes, sir, yes, I know.

BIG DADDY. Is that why you quit sports-announcing, because of this liquor problem?

BRICK. Yes, sir, yes, sir, I guess so. (*He smiles vaguely and amiably at his father across his replenished drink.*)

BIG DADDY. Son, don't guess about it, it's too important.

BRICK (*vaguely*). Yes, sir.

BIG DADDY. And listen to me, don't look at the damn chandelier. . . . (*Pause.* BIG DADDY'S *voice is husky.*)—Somethin' else we picked up at th' big fire-sale in Europe. (*Another pause.*) Life is important. There's nothing else to hold onto. A man that drinks is throwing his life away. Don't do it, hold onto your life. There's nothing else to hold onto. . . .

Sit down over here so we don't have to raise our voices, the walls have ears in this place.

BRICK (*hobbling over to sit on the sofa beside him*). All right, Big Daddy.

BIG DADDY. Quit!—how'd that come about? Some disappointment?

BRICK. I don't know. Do you?

BIG DADDY. I'm askin' you, God damn it! How in hell would I know if you don't?

BRICK. I just got out there and found that I had a mouth full of cotton. I was always two or three beats behind what was goin' on on the field and so I—

BIG DADDY. Quit!

BRICK (*amiably*). Yes, quit.

BIG DADDY. Son?

BRICK. Huh?

BIG DADDY (*inhales loudly and deeply from his cigar; then bends suddenly a little forward, exhaling loudly and raising a hand to his forehead*).—Whew!—ha ha!—I took in too much smoke, it made me a little light-headed. . . . (*The mantel clock chimes.*) Why is it so damn hard for people to talk?

BRICK. Yeah. . . . (*The clock goes on sweetly chiming till it has completed the stroke of ten.*)—Nice peaceful-soundin' clock, I like to hear it all night. . . . (*He slides low and comfortable on the sofa;* BIG DADDY *sits up straight and rigid with some unspoken anxiety. All his gestures are tense and jerky as he talks. He wheezes and pants and sniffs through his nervous speech, glancing quickly, shyly, from time to time, at his son.*)

BIG DADDY. We got that clock the summer we wint to Europe, me an' Big Mama on that damn Cook's Tour, never had such an awful time in my life, I'm tellin' you, son, those gooks over there, they gouge your eyeballs out in their grand hotels. And Big Mama bought more stuff than you could haul in a couple of boxcars, that's no crap. Everywhere she wint on this whirlwind tour, she bought, bought, bought. Why, half that stuff she bought is still crated up in the cellar, under water last spring! (*He laughs.*) That Europe is nothin' on earth but a great big auction, that's all it is, that bunch of old worn-out places, it's just a big fire-sale, the whole rutten thing, an' Big Mama wint wild in it, why, you couldn't hold that woman with a mule's harness! Bought, bought, bought!—lucky I'm a rich man, yes siree, Bob, an' half that stuff is mildewin' in th' basement. It's lucky I'm a rich man, it sure is lucky, well, I'm a rich man, Brick, yep, I'm a mighty rich man. (*His eyes light up for a moment.*) Y'know how much I'm worth? Guess, Brick! Guess how much I'm worth! (BRICK *smiles vaguely over his drink.*) Close on ten million in cash an' blue chip stocks, outside, mind you, of twenty-eight thousand acres of the richest land this side of the valley Nile! (*A puff and crackle and the night sky blooms with an eerie greenish glow. Children shriek on the gallery.*) But a man can't buy his life with it, he can't buy back his life with it when his life has been spent, that's one thing not offered in the Europe fire-sale or in the American markets or any markets on earth, a man can't buy his life with it, he can't buy back his life when his life is finished. . . .

That's a sobering thought, a very sobering thought, and that's a thought that I was turning over in my head, over and over and over—until today. . . .

I'm wiser and sadder, Brick, for this experience which I just gone through. They's one thing else that I remember in Europe.

BRICK. What is that, Big Daddy?

BIG DADDY. The hills around Barcelona in the country of Spain and the children running over those bare hills in their bare skins beggin' like starvin' dogs with howls and screeches, and how fat the priests are on the streets of Barcelona, so many of them and so fat and so pleasant, ha ha!—Y'know I could feed that country? I got money enough to feed that goddam country, but the human animal is a selfish beast and I don't reckon the money I passed out there to those howling children in the hills around Barcelona would more than upholster one of the chairs in this room, I mean pay to put a new cover on this chair!

Hell, I threw them money like you'd scatter feed corn for chickens, I threw money at them jut to get rid of them long enough to climb back into th' car and—drive away. . . .

And then in Morocco, them Arabs, why, prostitution begins at four or five, that's no exaggeration, why, I remember one day in Marrakech, that old walled Arab city, I set on a broken-down wall to have a cigar, it was fearful hot there and this Arab woman stood in the road and looked at me till I was embarrassed, she stood stock still in the dusty hot road and looked at me till I was embarrassed. But listen to this. She had a naked child with her, a little naked girl with her, barely able to toddle, and after a while she set this child on the ground and give her a push and whispered something to her.

This child come toward me, barely able t' walk, come toddling up to me and—

Jesus, it makes you sick t' remember a thing like this! It stuck out its hand and tried to unbutton my trousers!

That child was not yet five! Can you believe me? Or do you think that I am making this up? I wint back to the hotel and said to Big Mama, Git packed! We're clearing out of this country. . . .

BRICK. Big Daddy, you're on a talkin' jag tonight.

BIG DADDY (*ignoring this remark*). Yes, sir, that's how it is, the human animal is a beast that dies but the fact that he's dying don't give him pity for others, no, sir, it—Did you say something?

BRICK. Yes.

BIG DADDY. What?

BRICK. Hand me over that crutch so I can get up.

BIG DADDY. Where you goin'?

BRICK. I'm takin' a little short trip to Echo Spring.

BIG DADDY. To where?

BRICK. Liquor cabinet. . . .

BIG DADDY. Yes, sir, boy— (*He hands* BRICK *the crutch.*)—the human animal is a beast that dies and if he's got money he buys and buys and buys and I think the reason he buys everything he can buy is that in the back of his mind he has the crazy hope that one of his purchases will be life everlasting!—Which it never can be. . . . The human animal is a beast that—

BRICK (*at the liquor cabinet*). Big Daddy, you sure are shootin' th' breeze here tonight.

(*There is a pause and voices are heard outside.*)

BIG DADDY. I been quiet here lately, spoke not a word, just sat and stared into space. I had something heavy weighing on my mind but tonight that load was took off me. That's why I'm talking.—The sky looks diff'rent to me. . . .

BRICK. You know what I like to hear most?

BIG DADDY. What?

BRICK. Solid quiet. Perfect unbroken quiet.

BIG DADDY. Why?

BRICK. Because it's more peaceful.

BIG DADDY. Man, you'll hear a lot of that in the grave. (*He chuckles agreeably.*)

BRICK. Are you through talkin' to me?

BIG DADDY. Why are you so anxious to shut me up?

BRICK. Well, sir, ever so often you say to me, Brick, I want to have a talk with you, but when we talk, it never materializes. Nothing is said. You sit in a chair and gas about this and that and I look like I listen. I try to look like I listen, but I don't listen, not much. Communication is—awful hard between people an'—somehow between you and me, it just don't—

BIG DADDY. Have you ever been scared? I mean have you ever felt downright terror of something? (*He gets up.*) Just one moment. I'm going to close these doors. . . .

(*He closes doors on gallery as if he were going to tell an important secret.*)

BRICK. What?

BIG DADDY. Brick?

BRICK. Huh?

BIG DADDY. Son, I thought I had it!

BRICK. Had what? Had what, Big Daddy?

BIG DADDY. Cancer!

BRICK. Oh . . .

BIG DADDY. I thought the old man made out of bones had laid his cold and heavy hand on my shoulder!

BRICK. Well, Big Daddy, you kept a tight mouth about it.

BIG DADDY. A pig squeals. A man keeps a tight mouth about it, in spite of a man not having a pig's advantage.

BRICK. What advantage is that?

BIG DADDY. Ignorance—of mortality—is a comfort. A man don't have that comfort, he's the only living thing that conceives of death, that knows what it is. The others go without knowing which is the way that anything living should go, go without knowing, without any knowledge of it, and yet a pig squeals, but a man sometimes, he can keep a tight mouth about it. Sometimes he—(*There is a deep, smoldering ferocity in the old man.*)—can keep a tight mouth about it. I wonder if—

BRICK. What, Big Daddy?

BIG DADDY. A whiskey highball would injure this spastic condition?

BRICK. No, sir, it might do it good.

BIG DADDY (*grins suddenly, wolfishly*). Jesus, I can't tell you! The sky is open! Christ, it's open again! It's open, boy, it's open!

(BRICK *looks down at his drink.*)

BRICK. You feel better, Big Daddy?

BIG DADDY. Better? Hell! I can breathe!—All of my life I been like a doubled up fist. . . . (*He pours a drink.*)—Poundin', smashin', drivin'!—now I'm going to loosen these doubled up hands and touch things *easy* with them. . . . (*He spreads his hands as if caressing the air.*) You know what I'm contemplating?

BRICK (*vaguely*). No, sir. What are you contemplating?

BIG DADDY. Ha ha!—*Pleasure!*—pleasure with *women!* (BRICK's *smile fades a little but lingers.*) Brick, this stuff burns me!—

—Yes, boy. I'll tell you something that you might not guess. I still have desire for women and this is my sixty-fifth birthday.

BRICK. I think that's mighty remarkable, Big Daddy.

BIG DADDY. Remarkable?

BRICK. *Admirable,* Big Daddy.

BIG DADDY You're damn right it is, remarkable and admirable both. I realize now that I never had me enough. I let many chances slip by because of scruples about it, scruples, convention—crap. . . . All that stuff is bull, bull, bull!—It took the shadow of death to make me see it. Now that shadow's lifted, I'm going to cut loose and have, what is it they call it, have me a—ball!

BRICK. A ball, huh?

BIG DADDY. That's right, a ball, a ball! Hell!—I slept with Big Mama till, let's see, five years ago, till I was sixty and she was fifty-eight, and never even liked her, never did!

(*The phone has been ringing down the hall.* BIG MAMA *enters, exclaiming:*)

BIG MAMA. Don't you men hear that phone ring? I heard it way out on the gall'ry.

BIG DADDY. There's five rooms off this front gall'ry that you could go through. Why do you go through this one? (BIG MAMA *makes a playful face as she bustles out the hall door.*) Hunh!—Why, when Big Mama goes out of a room, I can't remember what that woman looks like, but when Big Mama comes back into the room, boy, then I see what she looks like, and I wish I didn't! (*Bends over laughing at his joke till it hurts his guts and he straightens with a grimace. The laugh subsides to a chuckle as he puts the liquor glass a little distrustfully down on the table.* BRICK *has risen and hobbled to the gallery doors.*) Hey! Where you goin'?

BRICK. Out for a breather.

BIG DADDY. Not yet you ain't. Stay here till this talk is finished, young fellow.

BRICK. I thought it was finished, Big Daddy.

BIG DADDY. It ain't even begun.

BRICK. My mistake. Excuse me. I just wanted to feel that river breeze.

BIG DADDY. Turn on the ceiling fan and set back down in that chair.

(BIG MAMA's *voice rises, carrying down the hall.*)

BIG MAMA. Miss Sally, you're a case! You're a caution, Miss Sally. Why didn't you give me a chance to explain it to you?

BIG DADDY. Jesus, she's talking to my old maid sister again.

BIG MAMA. Well, good-by, now, Miss Sally. You come down real soon, Big Daddy's dying to see you! Yaisss, good-by, Miss Sally. . . . (*She hangs up and bellows with mirth.* BIG DADDY *groans and covers his ears as she approaches. Bursting in:*) Big Daddy, that was Miss Sally callin' from Memphis again! You know what she done, Big Daddy? She called her doctor in Memphis to git him to tell her what that spastic thing is! Ha-*HAAAA!*—And called back to tell me how relieved she was that —Hey! Let me in! (BIG DADDY *has been holding the door half-closed against her.*)

BIG DADDY. Naw I ain't. I told you not to come and go through this room. You just back out and go through those five other rooms.

BIG MAMA. Big Daddy? Big Daddy? Oh, Big Daddy!—You didn't mean those things you said to me, did you? (*He shuts door firmly against her but she still calls.*) Sweetheart? Sweetheart? Big Daddy? You didn't mean those awful things you said to me?—I know you didn't. I know you didn't means those things in your heart. . . . (*The childlike voice fades with a sob and her heavy footsteps retreat down the hall.* BRICK *has risen once more on his crutches and starts for the gallery again.*)

BIG DADDY. All I ask of that woman is that she leave me alone. But she can't admit to herself that she makes me sick. That comes of having slept with her too many years. Should of quit much sooner but that old woman she never got enough of it— and I was good in bed . . . I never should of wasted so much of it on her. . . . They say you got just so many and each one is numbered. Well, I got a few left in me, a few, and I'm going to pick me a good one to spend 'em on! I'm going to pick me a choice one, I don't care how much she costs, I'll smother her in—minks! Ha! ha! I'll strip her naked and smother her in minks and choke her with diamonds! Ha ha! I'll strip her naked and choke her with diamonds and smother her with minks and hump her from hell to breakfast. *Ha aha ha ha ha!*

MAE (*gaily at door*). Who's that laughin' in there?

GOOPER. Is Big Daddy laughin' in there?

BIG DADDY. Crap!—them two—*drips.* . . . (*He goes over and touches* BRICK's *shoul-*

der.) Yes, son. Brick, boy.—I'm—*happy!* I'm happy, son, I'm happy! (*He chokes a little and bites his under lip, pressing his head quickly, shyly against his son's head and then, coughing with embarrassment, goes uncertainly back to the table where he set down the glass. He drinks and makes a grimace as it burns his guts.* BRICK *sighs and rises with effort.*) What makes you so restless? Have you got ants in your britches?

BRICK. Yes, sir . . .

BIG DADDY. Why?

BRICK. —Something—hasn't—happened. . . .

BIG DADDY. Yeah? What is that!

BRICK (*sadly*). —the click. . . .

BIG DADDY. Did you say click?

BRICK. Yes, click.

BIG DADDY. What click?

BRICK. A click that I get in my head that makes me peaceful.

BIG DADDY. I sure in hell don't know what you're talking about, but it disturbs me.

BRICK. It's just a mechanical thing.

BIG DADDY. What is a mechanical thing?

BRICK. This click that I get in my head that makes me peaceful. I got to drink till I get it. It's just a mechanical thing, something like a—like a—like a—

BIG DADDY. Like a—

BRICK. Switch clicking off in my head, turning the hot light off and the cool night on and—(*He looks up, smiling sadly.*)— all of a sudden there's—peace!

BIG DADDY (*whistles long and soft with astonishment; he goes back to* BRICK *and clasps his son's two shoulders*). Jesus! I didn't know it had gotten that bad with you. Why, boy, you're—*alcoholic!*

BRICK. That's the truth, Big Daddy. I'm alcoholic.

BIG DADDY. This shows how I—let things go!

BRICK. I have to hear that little click in my head that makes me peaceful. Usually I hear it sooner than this, sometimes as early as—noon, but—today it's—dilatory. . . . —I just haven't got the right level of alcohol in my bloodstream yet! (*This last statement is made with energy as he freshens his drink.*)

BIG DADDY. Uh—huh. Expecting death made me blind. I didn't have no idea that a son of mine was turning into a drunkard under my nose.

BRICK (*gently*). Well, now you do, Big Daddy, the news has penetrated.

BIG DADDY. UH-huh, yes, now I do, the news has—penetrated. . . .

BRICK. And so if you'll excuse me—

BIG DADDY. No, I won't excuse you.

BRICK. —I'd better sit by myself till I hear that click in my head, it's just a mechanical thing but it don't happen except when I'm alone or talking to no one. . . .

BIG DADDY. You got a long, long time to sit still, boy, and talk to no one, but now you're talkin' to me. At least I'm talking to you. And you set there and listen until I tell you the conversation is over!

BRICK. But this talk is like all the others we've ever had together in our lives! It's nowhere, nowhere!—it's—it's *painful*, Big Daddy. . . .

BIG DADDY. All right, then let it be painful, but don't you move from that chair!—I'm going to remove that crutch. . . . (*He seizes the crutch and tosses it across room.*)

BRICK. I can hop on one foot, and if I fall, I can crawl!

BIG DADDY. If you ain't careful you're gonna crawl off this plantation and then, by Jesus, you'll have to hustle your drinks along Skid Row!

BRICK. That'll come, Big Daddy.

BIG DADDY. Naw, it won't. You're my son and I'm going to straighten you out; now that *I'm* straightened out, I'm going to straighten out you!

BRICK. Yeah?

BIG DADDY. Today the report come in from Ochsner Clinic. Y'know what they told me? (*His face glows with triumph.*) The only thing that they could detect with all the instruments of science in that great hospital is a little spastic condition of the colon! And nerves torn to pieces by all that worry about it. (*A little girl bursts into room with a sparkler clutched in each fist, hops and shrieks like a monkey gone mad and rushes back out again as BIG DADDY strikes at her. Silence. The two men stare at each other. A woman laughs gaily outside.*) I want you to know I breathed a sigh of relief almost as powerful as the Vicksburg tornado!

BRICK. You weren't ready to go?

BIG DADDY. GO WHERE?—crap. . . .

—When you are gone from here, boy, you are long gone and no where! The human machine is not no different from the animal machine or the fish machine or the bird machine or the reptile machine or the insect machine! It's just a whole God damn lot more complicated and consequently more trouble to keep together. Yep. I thought I had it. The earth shook under my foot, the sky come down like the black lid of a kettle and I couldn't breathe!—Today!!—that lid was lifted, I drew my first free breath in—how many years?—*God—three.* . . . (*There is laughter outside, running footsteps, the soft, plushy sound and light of exploding rockets. BRICK stares at him soberly for a long moment; then makes a sort of startled sound in his nostrils and springs up on one foot and hops across the room to grab his crutch, swinging on the furniture for support. He gets the crutch and flees as if in horror for the gallery. His father seizes him by the sleeve of his white silk pajamas.*) Stay here, you son of a bitch!—till I say go!

BRICK. I can't.

BIG DADDY. You sure in hell will, God damn it.

BRICK. No, I can't. We talk, you talk, in —circles! We get nowhere, nowhere! It's always the same, you say you want to talk to me and don't have a ruttin' thing to say to me!

BIG DADDY. Nothin' to say when I'm tellin' you I'm going to live when I thought I was dying?!

BRICK. Oh—*that*—Is that what you have to say to me?

BIG DADDY. Why, you son of a bitch! Ain't that, ain't that—*important?!*

BRICK. Well, you said that, that's said, and now I—

BIG DADDY. Now you set back down.

BRICK. You're all balled up, you—

BIG DADDY. I ain't balled up!

BRICK. You are, you're all balled up!

BIG DADDY. Don't tell me what I am, you drunken whelp! I'm going to tear this coat sleeve off if you don't set down!

BRICK. Big Daddy—

BIG DADDY. Do what I tell you! I'm the boss here, now! I want you to know I'm back in the driver's seat now! (*BIG MAMA rushes in, clutching her great heaving bosom.*) What in hell do you want in here, Big Mama?

BIG MAMA. Oh, Big Daddy! Why are you shouting like that? I just cain't *stainnnnnnnd*—it. . . .

BIG DADDY (*raising the back of his hand above his head*). GIT!—outa here.

(*She rushes back out, sobbing.*)

BRICK (*softly, sadly*). Christ. . . .

BIG DADDY (*fiercely*). Yeah! Christ!—is right . . . (BRICK *breaks loose and hobbles toward the gallery.* BIG DADDY *jerks his crutch from under* BRICK *so he steps with the injured ankle. He utters a hissing cry of anguish, clutches a chair and pulls it over on top of him on the floor.*) Son of a —tub of—hog fat. . . .

BRICK. Big Daddy! Give me my crutch. (BIG DADDY *throws the crutch out of reach.*) Give me that crutch, Big Daddy.

BIG DADDY. Why do you drink?

BRICK. Don't know, give me my crutch!

BIG DADDY. You better think why you drink or give up drinking!

BRICK. Will you please give me my crutch so I can get up off this floor?

BIG DADDY. First you answer my question. Why do you drink? Why are you throwing your life away, boy, like somethin' disgusting you picked up on the street?

BRICK (*getting onto his knees*). Big Daddy, I'm in pain, I stepped on that foot.

BIG DADDY. Good! I'm glad you're not too numb with the liquor in you to feel some pain!

BRICK. You—spilled my—drink . . .

BIG DADDY. I'll make a bargain with you. You tell me why you drink and I'll hand you one. I'll pour you the liquor myself and hand it to you.

BRICK. Why do I drink?

BIG DADDY. Yea! Why?

BRICK. Give me a drink and I'll tell you.

BIG DADDY. Tell me first!

BRICK. I'll tell you in one word.

BIG DADDY. What word?

BRICK. DISGUST! (*The clock chimes softly, sweetly.* BIG DADDY *gives it a short, outraged glance.*) Now how about that drink?

BIG DADDY. What are you disgusted with? You got to tell me that, first. Otherwise being disgusted don't make no sense!

BRICK. Give me my crutch.

BIG DADDY. You heard me, you got to tell me what I asked you first.

BRICK. I told you, I said to kill my disgust!

BIG DADDY. DISGUST WITH WHAT!

BRICK. You strike a hard bargain.

BIG DADDY. What are you disgusted with? —an' I'll pass you the liquor.

BRICK. I can hop on one foot, and if I fall, I can crawl.

BIG DADDY. You want liquor that bad?

BRICK (*dragging himself up, clinging to bedstead*). Yeah, I want it that bad.

BIG DADDY. If I give you a drink, will you tell me what it is you're disgusted with, Brick?

BRICK. Yes, sir, I will try to. (*The old man pours him a drink and solemnly passes it to him. There is silence as* BRICK *drinks.*) Have you ever heard the word "mendacity"?

BIG DADDY. Sure. Mendacity is one of them five dollar words that cheap politicians throw back and forth at each other.

BRICK. You know what it means?

BIG DADDY. Don't it mean lying and liars?

BRICK. Yes, sir, lying and liars.

BIG DADDY. Has someone been lying to you?

CHILDREN (*chanting in chorus offstage*). We want Big Dad-dee! We want Big Dad-dee!

(GOOPER *appears in the gallery door.*)

GOOPER. Big Daddy, the kiddies are shouting for you out there.

BIG DADDY (*fiercely*). Keep out, Gooper!

GOOPER. 'Scuse *me!*

(BIG DADDY *slams the doors after* GOOPER.)

BIG DADDY. Who's been lying to you, has Margaret been lying to you, has your wife been lying to you about something, Brick?

BRICK. Not her. That wouldn't matter.

BIG DADDY. Then who's been lying to you, and what about?

BRICK. No one single person and no one lie. . . .

BIG DADDY. Then what, what then, for Christ's sake?

BRICK. —The whole, the whole—thing. . . .

BIG DADDY. Why are you rubbing your head? You got a headache?

BRICK. No, I'm tryin' to—

BIG DADDY. —Concentrate, but you can't because your brain's all soaked with liquor, is that the trouble? Wet brain! (*He snatches the glass from* BRICK's *hand.*) What do you know about this mendacity thing? Hell! I could write a book on it! Don't you know that? I could write a book on it and still not cover the subject? Well, I could, I could write a goddam book on it and still not cover the subject anywhere near enough!!—Think of all the lies I got to put up with!—Pretenses! Ain't that mendacity? Having to pretend stuff you don't think or feel or have any idea of? Having for instance to act like I care for Big Mama!—I haven't been able to stand the sight, sound, or smell of that woman for forty years now!—even when I *laid* her!—regular as a piston. . . .

Pretend to love that son of a bitch of a Gooper and his wife Mae and those five same screechers out there like parrots in a jungle? Jesus! Can't stand to look at 'em!

Church!—it bores the Bejesus out of me but I go!—I go an' sit there and listen to the fool preacher!

Clubs!—Elks! Masons! Rotary!—*crap!* (*A spasm of pain makes him clutch his belly. He sinks into a chair and his voice is softer and hoarser.*) You I *do* like for some reason, did always have some kind of real feeling for—affection—respect—yes, always. . . .

You and being a success as a planter is all I ever had any devotion to in my whole life!—and that's the truth. . . . I don't know why, but it is!

I've lived with mendacity!—Why can't *you* live with it? Hell, you *got* to live with it, there's nothing *else* to *live* with except mendacity, is there?

BRICK. Yes, sir. Yes, sir there is something else that you can live with!

BIG DADDY. What?

BRICK (*lifting his glass*). This!—Liquor. . . .

BIG DADDY. That's not living, that's dodging away from life.

BRICK. I want to dodge away from it.

BIG DADDY. Then why don't you kill yourself, man?

BRICK. I like to drink. . . .

BIG DADDY. Oh, God, I can't talk to you. . . .

BRICK. I'm sorry, Big Daddy.

BIG DADDY. Not as sorry as I am. I'll tell you something. A little while back when I thought my number was up—(*This speech should have torrential pace and fury.*)—before I found out it was just this—spastic—colon. I thought about you. Should I or should I not, if the jig was up, give you this place when I go—since I hate Gooper an' Mae an' know that they hate me, and since all five same monkeys are little Maes an' Goopers.—And I thought, No!—Then I thought, Yes!—I couldn't make up my mind. I hate Gooper and his five same

monkeys and that bitch Mae! Why should I turn over twenty-eight thousand acres of the richest land this side of the valley Nile to not my kind?—But why in hell, on the other hand, Brick—should I subsidize a goddam fool on the bottle?—Liked or not liked, well, maybe even—*loved!*—Why should I do that?—Subsidize worthless behavior? Rot? Corruption?

BRICK (*smiling*). I understand.

BIG DADDY. Well, if you do, you're smarter than I am, God damn it, because I don't understand. And this I will tell you frankly. I didn't make up my mind at all on that question and still to this day I ain't made out no will!—Well, now I don't *have* to. The pressure is gone. I can just wait and see if you pull yourself together or if you don't.

BRICK. That's right, Big Daddy.

BIG DADDY. You sound like you thought I was kidding.

BRICK (*rising*). No, sir, I know you're not kidding.

BIG DADDY. But you don't care—?

BRICK (*hobbling toward the gallery door*). No, sir, I don't care. . . . Now how about taking a look at your birthday fireworks and getting some of that cool breeze off the river? (*He stands in the gallery doorway as the night sky turns pink and green and gold with successive flashes of light.*)

BIG DADDY. WAIT—Brick. . . . (*His voice drops. Suddenly there is something shy, almost tender, in his restraining gesture.*) Don't let's—leave it like this, like them other talks we've had, we've always —talked around things, we've—just talked around things for some rutten reason, I don't know what, it's always like something was left not spoken, something avoided because neither of us was honest enough with the—other. . . .

BRICK. I never lied to you, Big Daddy.

BIG DADDY. Did I ever to *you?*

BRICK. No, sir. . . .

BIG DADDY. Then there is at least two people that never lied to each other.

BRICK. But we've never *talked* to each other.

BIG DADDY. We can *now*.

BRICK. Big Daddy, there don't seem to be anything much to say.

BIG DADDY. You say that you drink to kill your disgust with lying.

BRICK. You said to give you a reason.

BIG DADDY. Is liquor the only thing that'll kill this disgust?

BRICK. Now. Yes.

BIG DADDY. But not once, huh?

BRICK. Not when I was still young an' believing. A drinking man's someone who wants to forget he isn't still young an' believing.

BIG DADDY. Believing what?

BRICK. Believing. . . .

BIG DADDY. Believing *what*?

BRICK (*stubbornly evasive*). Believing.
. . .

BIG DADDY. I don't know what the hell you mean by believing and I don't think you know what you mean by believing, but if you still got sports in your blood, go back to sports announcing and—

BRICK. Sit in a glass box watching games I can't play? Describing what I can't' do while players do it? Sweating out their disgust and confusion in contests I'm not fit for? Drinkin' a coke, half bourbon, so I can stand it? That's no goddam good any more, no help—time just outran me, Big Daddy—got there first . . .

BIG DADDY. I think you're passing the buck.

BRICK. You know many drinkin' men?

BIG DADDY (*with a slight, charming smile*). I have known a fair number of that species.

BRICK. Could any of them tell you why he drank?

BIG DADDY. Yep, you're passin' the buck to things like time and disgust with "mendacity" and—crap!—if you got to use that kind of language about a thing, it's ninety-proof bull, and I'm not buying any.

BRICK. I had to give you a reason to get a drink!

BIG DADDY. You started drinkin' when your friend Skipper died.

(*Silence for five beats. Then Brick makes a startled movement, reaching for his crutch.*)

BRICK. What are you suggesting?

BIG DADDY. I'm suggesting nothing. (*The shuffle and clop of* BRICK's *rapid hobble away from his father's steady, grave attention.*)—But Gooper an' Mae suggested that there was something not right exactly in your—

BRICK (*stopping short downstage as if backed to a wall*). "Not right?"

BIG DADDY. Not, well, exactly *normal* in your friendship with—

BRICK. They suggested that, too? I thought that was Maggie's suggestion. (BRICK's *detachment is at last broken through. His heart is accelerated; his fore-head sweat-beaded; his breath becomes more rapid and his voice hoarse. The thing they're discussing, timidly and painfully on the side of* BIG DADDY, *fiercely, violently on* BRICK's *side, is the inadmissible thing that Skipper died to disavow between them. The fact that if it existed it had to be dis-avowed to "keep face" in the world they lived in, may be at the heart of the "men-dacity" that* BRICK *drinks to kill his dis-gust with. It may be the root of his col-lapse. Or maybe it is only a single mani-festation of it, not even the most important. The bird that I hope to catch in the net of this play is not the solution of one man's psychological problem. I'm trying to catch the true quality of experience in a group of people, that cloudy, flickering, evanescent —fiercely charged!—interplay of live hu-man beings in the thundercloud of a com-mon crisis. Some mystery should be left in the revelation of character in a play, just as a great deal of mystery is always left in the revelation of character in life, even in one's own character to himself. This does not absolve the playwright of his duty to ob-serve and probe as clearly and deeply as he legitimately can: but it should steer him away from "pat" conclusions, facile defini-tions which make a play just a play, not a snare for the truth of human experience. The following scene should be played with great concentration, with most of the power leashed but palpable in what is left unspoken.*) Who else's suggestion is it, is it *yours*? How many others thought that Skipper and I were—

BIG DADDY (*gently*). Now, hold on, hold on a minute, son.—I knocked around in my time.

BRICK. What's that got to do with—

BIG DADDY. I said 'Hold on!'—I bummed, I bummed this country till I was—

BRICK. Whose suggestion, who else's sug-gestion is it?

BIG DADDY. Slept in hobo jungles and railroad Y's and flophouses in all cities be-fore I—

BRICK. Oh, *you* think so, too, you call me your son and a queer. Oh! Maybe that's why you put Maggie and me in this room that was Jack Straw's and Peter Ochello's, in which that pair of old sisters slept in a double bed where both of 'em died!

BIG DADDY. *Now just don't go throwing rocks at*—(*Suddenly* REVEREND TOOKER *appears in the gallery doors, his head slightly, playfully, fatuously cocked, with a practised clergyman's smile, sincere as a bird-call blown on a hunter's whistle, the living embodiment of the pious, conventional lie.* BIG DADDY *gasps a little at this perfectly timed, but incongruous, apparition.*)—What're you lookin' for, Preacher?

REVEREND TOOKER. The gentleman's lavatory, ha ha!—heh, heh . . .

BIG DADDY (*with strained courtesy*).—Go back out and walk down to the other end of the gallery, Reverend Tooker, and use the bathroom connected with my bedroom, and if you can't find it, ask them where it is!

REVEREND TOOKER. Ah, thanks. (*He goes out with a deprecatory chuckle.*)

BIG DADDY. It's hard to talk in this place . . .

BRICK. Son of a—!

BIG DADDY (*leaving a lot unspoken*).—I seen all things and understood a lot of them, till 1910. Christ, the year that—I had worn my shoes through, hocked my—I hopped off a yellow dog freight car half a mile down the road, slept in a wagon of cotton outside the gin—Jack Straw an' Peter Ochello took me in. Hired me to manage this place which grew into this one.—When Jack Straw died—why, old Peter Ochello quit eatin' like a dog does when its master's dead, and died, too!

BRICK. Christ!

BIG DADDY. I'm just saying I understand such—

BRICK (*violently*). Skipper is dead. I have not quit eating!

BIG DADDY. No, but you started drinking. (BRICK *wheels on his crutch and hurls his glass across the room shouting.*)

BRICK. YOU THINK SO, TOO?

BIG DADDY. Shhh! (*Footsteps run on the gallery. There are women's calls.* BIG DADDY *goes toward the door.*) Go way!—Just broke a glass. . . .

(BRICK *is transformed, as if a quiet mountain blew suddenly up in volcanic flame.*)

BRICK. You think so, too? You think so, too? You think me an' Skipper did, did, did!—sodomy!—together?

BIG DADDY. Hold—!

BRICK. That what you—

BIG DADDY. —*ON*—a minute!

BRICK. You think we did dirty things between us, Skipper an'—

BIG DADDY. Why are you shouting like that? Why are you—

BRICK. —Me, is that what you think of Skipper, is that—

BIG DADDY. —so excited? I don't think nothing. I don't know nothing. I'm simply telling you what—

BRICK. You think that Skipper and me were a pair of dirty old men?

BIG DADDY. Now that's—

BRICK. Straw? Ochello? A couple of—

BIG DADDY. Now just—

BRICK. —ducking sissies? Queers? Is that what you—

BIG DADDY. Shhh.

BRICK. —think? (*He loses his balance and pitches to his knees without noticing the pain. He grabs the bed and drags himself up.*)

BIG DADDY. Jesus!—Whew. . . . Grab my hand!

BRICK. Naw, I don't want your hand. . . .

BIG DADDY. Well, I want yours. Git up! (*He draws him up, keeps an arm about him with concern and affection.*) You broken out in a sweat! You're panting like you'd run a race with—

BRICK (*freeing himself from his father's hold*). Big Daddy, you shock me, Big Daddy, you, you—*shock* me! Talkin' so—(*He turns away from his father.*) —casually!—about a—thing like that . . .

—Don't you know how people *feel* about things like that? How, how *disgusted* they are by things like that? Why, at Ole Miss when it was discovered a pledge to our fraternity, Skipper's and mine, did a, *attempted* to do a, unnatural thing with—

We not only dropped him like a hot rock!—We told him to git off the campus, and he did, he got!—All the way to— (*He halts, breathless.*)

BIG DADDY. —Where?

BRICK. —North Africa, last I heard!

BIG DADDY. Well, I have come back from further away than that, I have just now returned from the other side of the moon, death's country, son, and I'm not easy to shock by anything here. (*He comes downstage and faces out.*) Always, anyhow, lived with too much space around me to be infected by ideas of other people. One thing you can grow on a big place more important than cotton!—is *tolerance!*—I grown it. (*He returns toward* BRICK.)

BRICK. Why can't exceptional friendship, *real, real, deep, deep friendship!* between two men be respected as something clean and decent without being thought of as—

BIG DADDY. It can, it is, for God's sake.

BRICK. —*Fairies.* . . . (*In his utterance of this word, we gauge the wide and profound reach of the conventional mores he got from the world that crowned him with early laurel.*)

BIG DADDY. I told Mae an' Gooper—

BRICK. Frig Mae and Gooper, frig all dirty lies and liars!—Skipper and me had a clean, true thing between us!—had a clean friendship, practically all our lives, till Maggie got the idea you're talking about. Normal? No!—It was too rare to be normal, any true thing between two people is too rare to be normal. Oh, once in a while he put his hand on my shoulder or I'd put mine on his, oh, maybe even, when we were touring the country in pro-football an' shared hotel-rooms we'd reach across the space between the two beds and shake hands to say good-night, yeah, one or two times we—

BIG DADDY. Brick, nobody thinks that that's not normal!

BRICK. Well, they're mistaken, it was! It was a pure an' true thing an' that's not normal.

(*They both stare straight at each other for a long moment. The tension breaks and both turn away as if tired.*)

BIG DADDY. Yeah, it's—hard t'—talk. . . .

BRICK. All right, then, let's—let it go. . . .

BIG DADDY. Why did Skipper crack up? Why have you?

(BRICK *looks back at his father again. He has already decided, without knowing that he has made this decision, that he is going to tell his father that he is dying of cancer. Only this could even the score between them: one inadmissible thing in return for another.*)

BRICK (*ominously*). All right. You're asking for it, Big Daddy. We're finally going to have that real true talk you wanted. It's too late to stop it, now, we got to carry it through and cover every subject. (*He hobbles back to the liquor cabinet.*) Uh-huh. (*He opens the ice bucket and picks up the silver tongs with slow admiration of their frosty brightness.*) Maggie declares that Skipper and I went into pro-football after we left "Ole Miss" because we were scared to grow up . . . (*He moves downstage with the shuffle and clop of a cripple on a crutch. As* MARGARET *did when her speech became "recitative," he looks out into the house, commanding its attention by his direct, concentrated gaze—a broken, "tragically elegant" figure telling simply as much as he knows of "the Truth."*) —Wanted to—keep on tossing—those long, long!—high, high!—passes that —couldn't be intercepted except by time, the aerial attack that made us famous! And so we did, we did, we kept it up for one season, that aerial attack, we held it high!—Yeah, but—

—that summer, Maggie, she laid the law down to me, said, Now or never, and so I married Maggie. . . .

BIG DADDY. How was Maggie in bed?

BRICK (*wryly*). Great! the greatest! (BIG DADDY *nods as if he thought so.*) She went on the road that fall with the Dixie Stars. Oh, she made a great show of being the world's best sport. She wore a—wore a— tall bearskin cap! A shako, they call it, a dyed moleskin coat, a moleskin coat dyed red!—Cut up crazy! Rented hotel ball-rooms for victory celebrations, wouldn't cancel them when it—turned out—defeat. . . .

MAGGIE THE CAT! Ha ha! (BIG DADDY *nods.*)—But Skipper, he had some fever which came back on him which doctors couldn't explain and I got that injury —turned out to be just a shadow on the X-ray plate—and a touch of bursitis. . . . I lay in a hospital bed, watched our games on TV, saw Maggie on the bench next to Skipper when he was hauled out of a game for stumbles, fumbles!—Burned me up the way she hung on his arm!—Y'know, I think that Maggie had always felt sort of left out because she and me never got any closer together than two people just get in bed, which is not much closer than two cats on a—fence humping. . . .

So! She took this time to work on poor dumb Skipper. He was a less than average student at Ole Miss, you know that, don't you?!—Poured in his mind the dirty, false idea that what we were, him and me, was a frustrated case of that ole pair of sisters that lived in this room, Jack Straw and Peter Ochello!—He, poor Skipper, went to bed with Maggie to prove it wasn't true, and when it didn't work out, he thought it *was* true!—Skipper broke in two like a rotten stick—nobody ever turned so fast to a lush—or died of it so quick. . . .

—Now are you satisfied?

(BIG DADDY *has listened to this story, dividing the grain from the chaff. Now he looks at his son.*)

BIG DADDY. Are *you* satisfied?

BRICK. With what?

BIG DADDY. That half-ass story!

BRICK. What's half-ass about it?

BIG DADDY. Something's left out of that story. What did you leave out?

(*The phone has started ringing in the hall. As if it reminded him of something,* BRICK *glances suddenly toward the sound and says.*)

BRICK. Yes!—I left out a long-distance call which I had from Skipper, in which he made a drunken confession to me and on which I hung up!—last time we spoke to each other in our lives. . . .

(*Muted ring stops as someone answers phone in a soft, indistinct voice in hall.*)

BIG DADDY. You hung up?

BRICK. Hung up. Jesus! Well—

BIG DADDY. Anyhow now!—we have tracked down the lie with which you're disgusted and which you are drinking to kill your disgust with, Brick. You been passing the buck. This disgust with mendacity is disgust with yourself.

You!—dug the grave of your friend and kicked him in it!—before you'd face truth with him!

BRICK. *His* truth, not *mine!*

BIG DADDY. His truth, okay! But you wouldn't face it with him!

BRICK. Who *can* face truth? Can *you?*

BIG DADDY. Now don't start passin' the rotten buck again, boy!

BRICK. *How about these birthday congratulations, these many, many happy returns of the day, when ev'rybody but you knows there won't be any!* (*Whoever has answered the hall phone lets out a high, shrill laugh; the voice becomes audible saying:* "no, no, you got it all wrong! Upside down! Are you crazy?"

(BRICK *suddenly catches his breath as he realizes that he has made a shocking disclosure. He hobbles a few paces, then freezes, and without looking at his father's shocked face, says:*) Let's, let's—go out, now, and—(BIG DADDY *moves suddenly for-*

ward and grabs hold of the boy's crutch like it was a weapon for which they were fighting for possession.)

BIG DADDY. Oh, no, no! No one's going out! What did you start to say?

BRICK. I don't remember.

BIG DADDY. "Many happy returns when they know there won't be any"?

BRICK. Aw, hell, Big Daddy, forget it. Come on out on the gallery and look at the fireworks they're shooting off for your birthday. . . .

BIG DADDY. First you finish that remark you were makin' before you cut off. "Many happy returns when they know there won't be any"?—Ain't that what you just said?

BRICK. Look, now. I can get around without that crutch if I have to but it would be a lot easier on the furniture an' glassware if I didn't have to go swinging along like Tarzan of th'—

BIG DADDY. FINISH! WHAT YOU WAS SAYIN'!

(*An eerie green glow shows in sky behind him.*)

BRICK (*sucking the ice in his glass, speech becoming thick*). Leave th' place to Gooper and Mae an' their five little same little monkeys. All I want is—

BIG DADDY. "LEAVE TH' PLACE," did you say?

BRICK (*vaguely*). All twenty-eight thousand acres of the richest land this side of the valley Nile.

BIG DADDY. Who said I was "leaving the place" to Gooper or anybody? This is my sixty-fifth birthday! I got fifteen years or twenty years left in me! I'll outlive *you!* I'll bury you an' have to pay for your coffin!

BRICK. Sure. Many happy returns. Now let's go watch the fireworks, come on, let's—

BIG DADDY. Lying, have they been lying? About the report from th'—clinic? Did they, did they—find something?—*Cancer.* Maybe?

BRICK. Mendacity is a system that we live in. Liquor is one way out an' death's the other. . . . (*He takes the crutch from* BIG DADDY's *loose grip and swings out on the gallery leaving the doors open.*

(*A song, "Pick a Bale of Cotton," is heard.*)

MAE (*appearing in door*). Oh, Big Daddy, the field-hands are singin' fo' you!

BIG DADDY (*shouting hoarsely*). BRICK! BRICK!

MAE. He's outside drinkin', Big Daddy.

BIG DADDY. *BRICK!*

(MAE *retreats, awed by the passion of his voice. Children call* BRICK *in tones mocking* BIG DADDY. *His face crumbles like broken yellow plaster about to fall into dust.*

(*There is a glow in the sky.* BRICK *swings back through the doors, slowly, gravely, quite soberly.*)

BRICK. I'm sorry, Big Daddy. My head don't work any more and it's hard for me to understand how anybody could care if he lived or died or was dying or cared about anything but whether or not there was liquor left in the bottle and so I said what I said without thinking. In some ways I'm no better than the others, in some ways worse because I'm less alive. Maybe it's being alive that makes them lie, and being almost *not* alive makes me sort of accidentally truthful—I don't know but—anyway—we've been friends . . . And being friends is telling each other the truth. . . . (*There is a pause.*) You told *me!* I told *you!*

(*A child rushes into the room and grabs a fistful of firecrackers and runs out again.*)

CHILD (*screaming*). Bang, bang, bang, bang, bang, bang, bang, bang, bang!

BIG DADDY (*slowly and passionately*). CHRIST — DAMN — ALL — LYING SONS OF—LYING BITCHES! (*He straightens at last and crosses to the inside door. At the door he turns and looks back as if he had some desperate question he couldn't put into words. Then he nods reflectively and says in a hoarse voice.*) Yes, all liars, all liars, all lying dying liars! (*This is said slowly, slowly, with a fierce revulsion. He goes on out.*) —Lying! Dying! Liars! (*His voice dies out. There is the sound of a child being slapped. It rushes, hideously bawling, through room and out the hall door.*)

(BRICK *remains motionless as the lights dim out and the curtain falls.*)

CURTAIN

ACT THREE

There is no lapse of time. MAE *enters with* REVEREND TOOKER.

MAE. Where is Big Daddy! Big Daddy?

BIG MAMA (*entering*). Too much smell of burnt fireworks makes me feel a little bit sick at my stomach.—Where is Big Daddy?

MAE. That's what I want to know, where has Big Daddy gone?

BIG MAMA. He must have turned in, I reckon he went to baid. . . .

(GOOPER *enters.*)

GOOPER. Where is Big Daddy?

MAE. We don't know where he is!

BIG MAMA. I reckon he's gone to baid.

GOOPER. Well, then, now we can talk.

BIG MAMA. What *is* this talk, *what* talk?

(MARGARET *appears on gallery, talking to* DR. BAUGH.)

MARGARET (*musically*). My family freed their slaves ten years before abolition, my great-great-grandfather gave his slaves their freedom five years before the war between the States started!

MAE. Oh, for God's sake! Maggie's climbed back up in her family tree!

MARGARET (*sweetly*). What, Mae?—Oh, where's Big Daddy?!

(*The pace must be very quick. Great Southern animation.*)

BIG MAMA (*addressing them all*). I think Big Daddy was just worn out. He loves his family, he loves to have them around him, but it's a strain on his nerves. He wasn't himself tonight, Big Daddy wasn't himself, I could tell he was all worked up.

REVEREND TOOKER. I think he's remarkable.

BIG MAMA. Yaiss! Just remarkable. Did you all notice the food he ate at that table? Did you all notice the supper he put away? Why, he ate like a hawss!

GOOPER. I hope he doesn't regret it.

BIG MAMA. Why, that man—ate a huge piece of cawn-bread with molasses on it! Helped himself twice to hoppin' john.

MARGARET. Big Daddy loves hoppin' john.—We had a real country dinner.

BIG MAMA (*overlapping* MARGARET). Yais, he simply adores it! An' candied yams? That man put away enough food at that table to stuff a nigger *field*-hand!

GOOPER (*with grim relish*). I hope he don't have to pay for it later on. . . .

BIG MAMA (*fiercely*). What's *that,* Gooper?

MAE. Gooper says he hopes Big Daddy doesn't suffer tonight.

BIG MAMA. Oh, shoot, Gooper says,

Gooper says! Why should Big Daddy suffer for satisfying a normal appetite? There's nothin' wrong with that man but nerves, he's sound as a dollar! And now he knows he is an' that's why he ate such a supper. He had a big load off his mind, knowin' he wasn't doomed t'—what he thought he was doomed to. . . .

MARGARET (*sadly and sweetly*). Bless his old sweet soul. . . .

BIG MAMA (*vaguely*). Yais, bless his heart, where's Brick?

MAE. Outside.

GOOPER. —Drinkin' . . .

BIG MAMA. I know he's drinkin'. You all don't have to keep tellin' *me* Brick is drinkin'. Cain't I see he's drinkin' without you continually tellin' me that boy's drinkin'?

MARGARET. Good for you, Big Mama! (*She applauds.*)

BIG MAMA. Other people *drink* and *have* drunk an' will *drink*, as long as they make that stuff an' put it in bottles.

MARGARET. That's the truth. I never trusted a man that didn't drink.

MAE. Gooper never drinks. Don't you trust Gooper?

MARGARET. Why, Gooper don't you drink? If I'd known you didn't drink, I wouldn't of made that remark—

BIG MAMA. *Brick?*

MARGARET. —at least not in your presence. (*She laughs sweetly.*)

BIG MAMA. *Brick!*

MARGARET. He's still on the gall'ry. I'll go bring him in so we can talk.

BIG MAMA (*worriedly*). I don't know what this mysterious family conference is about. (*Awkward silence. BIG MAMA looks from face to face, then belches slightly and mutters, "Excuse me. . . ." She opens an ornamental fan suspended about her throat, a black lace fan to go with her black lace gown and fans her wilting corsage, sniffing nervously and looking from face to face in the uncomfortable silence as MARGARET calls "Brick?" and BRICK sings to the moon on the gallery.*) I don't know what's wrong here, you all have such long faces! Open that door on the hall and let some air circulate through here, will you please, Gooper?

MAE. I think we'd better leave that door closed, Big Mama, till after the talk.

BIG MAMA. Reveren' Tooker, will *you* please open that door?!

REVEREND TOOKER. I sure will, Big Mama.

MAE. I just didn't think we ought t' take any chance of Big Daddy hearin' a word of this discussion.

BIG MAMA. *I swan!* Nothing's going to be said in Big Daddy's house that he cain't hear if he wants to!

GOOPER. Well, Big Mama, it's—(MAE *gives him a quick, hard poke to shut him up. He glares at her fiercely as she circles before him like a burlesque ballerina, raising her skinny bare arms over her head, jangling her bracelets, exclaiming.*)

MAE. *A breeze! A breeze!*

REVEREND TOOKER. I think this house is the coolest house in the Delta.—Did you all know that Halsey Banks' widow put air-conditioning units in the church and rectory at Friar's Point in memory of Halsey?

(*General conversation has resumed; everybody is chatting so that the stage sounds like a big bird-cage.*)

GOOPER. Too bad nobody cools your church off for you. I bet you sweat in that pulpit these hot Sundays, Reverend Tooker.

REVEREND TOOKER. Yes, my vestments are drenched.

MAE (*at the same time to* DR. BAUGH). You think those vitamin B_{12} injections are what they're cracked up t' be, Doc Baugh?

DOCTOR BAUGH. Well, if you want to be stuck with something I guess they're as good to be stuck with as anything else.

BIG MAMA (*at gallery door*). Maggie, Maggie, aren't you comin' with Brick?

MAE (*suddenly and loudly, creating a silence*). I have a strange feeling, I have a peculiar feeling!

BIG MAMA (*turning from gallery*). What feeling?

MAE. That Brick said somethin' he shouldn't of said t' Big Daddy.

BIG MAMA. Now what on earth could Brick of said t' Big Daddy that he shouldn't say?

GOOPER. Big Mama, there's somethin'—

MAE. NOW, WAIT! (*She rushes up to* BIG MAMA *and gives her a quick hug and kiss.* BIG MAMA *pushes her impatiently off as the* REVEREND TOOKER'S *voice rises serenely in a little pocket of silence.*)

REVEREND TOOKER. Yes, last Sunday the gold in my chasuble faded into th' purple. . . .

GOOPER. Reveren' you must of been preachin' hell's fire last Sunday! (*He guffaws at this witticism but the* REVEREND *is not sincerely amused. At the same time* BIG MAMA *has crossed over to* DR. BAUGH *and is saying to him:*)

BIG MAMA (*her breathless voice rising high-pitched above the others*). In my day they had what they call the Keeley cure for heavy drinkers. But now I understand they just take some kind of tablets, they call them "Annie Bust" tablets. But *Brick* don't need to take *nothin'.*

(BRICK *appears in gallery doors with* MARGARET *behind him.*)

BIG MAMA (*unaware of his presence behind her*). That boy is just broken up over Skipper's death. You know how poor Skipper died. They gave him a big, big dose of that sodium amytal stuff at his home and then they called the ambulance and give him another big, big dose of it at the hospital and that and all of the alcohol in his system fo' months an' months an' months just proved too much for his heart. . . . I'm scared of needles! I'm more scared of a needle than the knife. . . . I think more people have been needled out of this world than—(*She stops short and wheels about.*) OH!—here's Brick! My precious baby—(*She turns upon* BRICK *with short, fat arms extended, at the same time uttering a loud, short sob, which is both comic and touching.* BRICK *smiles and bows slightly, making a burlesque gesture of gallantry for* MAGGIE *to pass before him into the room. Then he hobbles on his crutch directly to the liquor cabinet and there is absolute silence, with everybody looking at* BRICK *as everybody has always looked at* BRICK *when he spoke or moved or appeared. One by one he drops ice cubes in his glass, then suddenly, but not quickly, looks back over his shoulder with a wry, charming smile, and says.*)

BRICK. I'm sorry! Anyone else?

BIG MAMA (*sadly*). No, son. I *wish* you wouldn't!

BRICK. I wish I didn't have to, Big Mama, but I'm still waiting for that click in my head which makes it all smooth out!

BIG MAMA. Aw, Brick, you—BREAK MY HEART!

MARGARET (*at the same time*). Brick, go sit with Big Mama!

BIG MAMA. I just cain't *staiiiiiiii-nnnnnd* —it. . . . (*She sobs.*)

MAE. Now that we're all assembled—

GOOPER. We kin talk. . . .

BIG MAMA. Breaks my heart. . . .

MARGARET. Sit with Big Mama, Brick, and hold her hand. (BIG MAMA *sniffs very loudly three times, almost like three drum beats in the pocket of silence.*)

BRICK. You do that, Maggie. I'm a restless cripple. I got to stay on my crutch. (BRICK *hobbles to the gallery door; leans there as if waiting.*

(MAE *sits beside* BIG MAMA, *while* GOOPER *moves in front and sits on the end of the couch, facing her.* REVEREND TOOKER *moves nervously into the space between them; on the other side,* DR. BAUGH *stands looking at nothing in particular and lights a cigar.* MARGARET *turns away.*)

BIG MAMA. Why're you all *surroundin'* me—like this? Why're you all starin' at me like this an' makin' signs at each other?

(REVEREND TOOKER *steps back startled.*)

MAE. Calm yourself, Big Mama.

BIG MAMA. Calm you'self, *you'self*, Sister Woman. How could I calm myself with everyone starin' at me as if big drops of blood had broken out on m'face? What's this all about, Annh! What?

(GOOPER *coughs and takes a center position.*)

GOOPER. Now, Doc Baugh.

MAE. Doc Baugh?

BRICK (*suddenly*). SHHH!—(*Then he grins and chuckles and shakes his head regretfully.*)—Naw!—that wasn't th' click.

GOOPER. Brick, shut up or stay out there on the gallery with your liquor! We got to talk about a serious matter. Big Mama wants to know the complete truth about the report we got today from the Ochsner Clinic.

MAE (*eagerly*). —on Big Daddy's condition!

GOOPER. Yais, on Big Daddy's condition, we got to face it.

DOCTOR BAUGH. Well. . . .

BIG MAMA (*terrified, rising*). Is there? Something? Something that I? Don't—Know? (*In these few words, this startled, very soft, question,* BIG MAMA *reviews the history of her forty-five years with* BIG DADDY, *her great, almost embarrassingly true-hearted and simple-minded devotion to* BIG DADDY, *who must have had something* BRICK *has, who made himself loved so much by the "simple expedient" of not loving enough to disturb his charming de-*

tachment, also once coupled, like BRICK's, *with virile beauty.* BIG MAMA *has a dignity at this moment: she almost stops being fat.*)

DOCTOR BAUGH (*after a pause, uncomfortably*). Yes?—Well—

BIG MAMA. *I!!!—want to—knowwwwww ww.* . . . (*Immediately she thrusts her fist to her mouth as if to deny that statement. Then, for some curious reason, she snatches the withered corsage from her breast and hurls it on the floor and steps on it with her short, fat feet.*)—*Somebody must be lyin'!—I want to know!*

MAE. Sit down, Big Mama, sit down on this sofa.

MARGARET (*quickly*). Brick, go sit with Big Mama.

BIG MAMA. *What is it, what is it?*

DOCTOR BAUGH. I never have seen a more thorough examination than Big Daddy Pollitt was given in all my experience with the Ochsner Clinic.

GOOPER. It's one of the best in the country.

MAE. It's *THE* best in the country—bar *none!* (*For some reason she gives* GOOPER *a violent poke as she goes past him. He slaps at her hand without removing his eyes from his mother's face.*)

DOCTOR BAUGH. Of course they were ninety-nine and nine-tenths percent sure before they even started.

BIG MAMA. Sure of what, sure of what, sure of—*what?—what!* (*She catches her breath in a startled sob.* MAE *kisses her quickly. She thrusts* MAE *fiercely away from her, staring at the doctor.*)

MAE. Mommy, be a brave girl!

BRICK (*in the doorway, softly*). "By the light, by the light, Of the sil-ve-ry mo-ooo-n . . ."

GOOPER. Shut up!—Brick.

BRICK.—Sorry. . . . (*He wanders out on the gallery.*)

DOCTOR BAUGH. But now, you see, Big Mama, they cut a piece off this growth, a specimen of the tissue and—

BIG MAMA. Growth? You told Big Daddy—

DOCTOR BAUGH. Now wait.

BIG MAMA (*fiercely*). You told me and Big Daddy there wasn't a thing wrong with him but—

MAE. Big Mama, they always—

GOOPER. Let Doc Baugh talk, will yuh?

BIG MAMA. —little spastic condition of— (*Her breath gives out in a sob.*)

DOCTOR BAUGH. Yes, that's what we told Big Daddy. But we had this bit of tissue run through the laboratory and I'm sorry to say the test was positive on it. It's—well —malignant. . . .

(*Pause.*)

BIG MAMA. —Cancer?! Cancer?!

(DR. BAUGH *nods gravely.* BIG MAMA *gives a long gasping cry.*)

MAE *and* GOOPER. Now now, now, Big Mama, you had to know. . . .

BIG MAMA. *WHY DIDN'T THEY CUT IT OUT OF HIM? HANH? HANH?*

DOCTOR BAUGH. Involved too much, Big Mama, too many organs affected.

MAE. Big Mama, the liver's affected and so's the kidneys, both! It's gone way past what they call a—

GOOPER. A surgical risk.

MAE. —Uh-huh. . . .

(BIG MAMA *draws a breath like a dying gasp.*)

REVEREND TOOKER. Tch, tch, tch, tch, tch!

DOCTOR BAUGH. Yes, it's gone past the knife.

MAE. *That's why he's turned yellow, Mommy!*

BIG MAMA. *Git away from me, git away from me, Mae!* (*She rises abruptly.*) *I want Brick! Where's Brick? Where is my only son?*

MAE. Mama! Did she say *"only* son"?

GOOPER. What does that make *me?*

MAE. A sober responsible man with five precious children!—*Six!*

BIG MAMA. I want Brick to tell me! Brick! Brick!

MARGARET (*rising from her reflections in a corner*). Brick was so upset he went back out.

BIG MAMA. *Brick!*

MARGARET. Mama, let *me* tell you!

BIG MAMA. No, no, leave me alone, you're not my blood!

GOOPER. *Mama, I'm your son!* Listen to *me!*

MAE. Gooper's your son, Mama, he's your first-born!

BIG MAMA. Gooper never liked Daddy.

MAE (*as if terribly shocked*). *That's not TRUE!*

(*There is a pause. The minister coughs and rises.*)

REVEREND TOOKER (*to* MAE). I think I'd better slip away at this point.

MAE (*sweetly and sadly*). Yes, Doctor Tooker, you go.

REVEREND TOOKER (*discreetly*). Good night, good night, everybody, and God bless you all . . . on this place. . . . (*He slips out.*)

DOCTOR BAUGH. That man is a good man but lacking in tact. Talking about people giving memorial windows—if he mentioned one memorial window, he must have spoke of a dozen, and saying how awful it was when somebody died intestate, the legal wrangles, and so forth.

(MAE *coughs, and points at* BIG MAMA.)

DOCTOR BAUGH. Well, Big Mama. . . . (*He sighs.*)

BIG MAMA. It's all a mistake, I know it's just a bad dream.

DOCTOR BAUGH. We're gonna keep Big Daddy as comfortable as we can.

BIG MAMA. Yes, it's just a bad dream, that's all it is, it's just an awful dream.

GOOPER. In my opinion Big Daddy is having some pain but won't admit that he has it.

BIG MAMA. Just a dream, a bad dream.

DOCTOR BAUGH. That's what lots of them do, they think if they don't admit they're having the pain they can sort of escape the fact of it.

GOOPER (*with relish*). Yes, they get sly about it, they get real sly about it.

MAE. Gooper and I think—

GOOPER. Shut up, Mae!—Big Daddy ought to be started on morphine.

BIG MAMA. Nobody's going to give Big Daddy morphine.

DOCTOR BAUGH. Now, Big Mama, when that pain strikes it's going to strike mighty hard and Big Daddy's going to need the needle to bear it.

BIG MAMA. I tell you, nobody's going to give him morphine.

MAE. Big Mama, you don't want to see Big Daddy suffer, you know you—

(GOOPER *standing beside her gives her a savage poke.*)

DOCTOR BAUGH (*placing a package on the table*). I'm leaving this stuff here, so if there's a sudden attack you all won't have to send out for it.

MAE. I know how to give a hypo.

GOOPER. Mae took a course in nursing during the war.

MARGARET. Somehow I don't think Big Daddy would want Mae to give him a hypo.

MAE. You think he'd want *you* to do it? (DR. BAUGH *rises.*)

GOOPER. Doctor Baugh is goin'.

DOCTOR BAUGH. Yes, I got to be goin'. Well, keep your chin up, Big Mama.

GOOPER (*with jocularity*). She's gonna keep *both* chins up, aren't you Big Mama? (BIG MAMA *sobs.*) Now stop that, Big Mama.

MAE. Sit down with me, Big Mama.

GOOPER (*at door with* DR. BAUGH). Well, Doc, we sure do appreciate all you done. I'm telling you, we're surely obligated to you for—

(DR. BAUGH *has gone out without a glance at him.*)

GOOPER. —I guess that doctor has got a lot on his mind but it wouldn't hurt him to act a little more human. . . . (BIG MAMA *sobs.*) Now be a brave girl, Mommy.

BIG MAMA. It's not true, I know that it's just not true!

GOOPER. Mama, those tests are infallible!

BIG MAMA. Why are you so determined to see your father daid?

MAE. Big Mama!

MARGARET (*gently*). I know what Big Mama means.

MAE (*fiercely*). Oh, do you?

MARGARET (*quietly and very sadly*). Yes, I think I do.

MAE. For a newcomer in the family you sure do show a lot of understanding.

MARGARET. Understanding is needed on this place.

MAE. I guess you must have needed a lot of it in your family, Maggie, with your father's liquor problem and now you've got Brick with his!

MARGARET. Brick does not have a liquor problem at all. Brick is devoted to Big Daddy. This thing is a terrible strain on him.

BIG MAMA. Brick is Big Daddy's boy, but he drinks too much and it worries me and Big Daddy, and, Margaret, you've got to cooperate with us, you've got to cooperate with Big Daddy and me in getting Brick straightened out. Because it will break Big Daddy's heart if Brick don't pull himself together and take hold of things.

MAE. Take hold of *what* things, Big Mama?

BIG MAMA. The place.

(*There is a quick violent look between* MAE *and* GOOPER.)

GOOPER. Big Mama, you've had a shock.

MAE. Yais, we've all had a shock, but . . .

GOOPER. Let's be realistic—

MAE. —Big Daddy would never, would *never,* be foolish enough to—

GOOPER. —put this place in irresponsible hands!

BIG MAMA. Big Daddy ain't going to leave the place in anybody's hands; Big Daddy is *not* going to die. I want you to get that in your heads, all of you!

MAE. Mommy, Mommy, Big Mama, we're just as hopeful an' optimistic as you are about Big Daddy's prospects, we have faith in *prayer*—but nevertheless there are certain matters that have to be discussed an' dealt with, because otherwise—

GOOPER. Eventualities have to be considered and now's the time. . . . Mae, will you please get my briefcase out of our room?

MAE. Yes, honey. (*She rises and goes out through the hall door.*)

GOOPER (*standing over* BIG MAMA). Now Big Mom. What you said just now was not at all true and you know it. I've always loved Big Daddy in my own quiet way. I never made a show of it, and I know that Big Daddy has always been fond of me in a quiet way, too, and he never made a show of it neither.

(MAE *returns with* GOOPER's *briefcase.*)

MAE. Here's your briefcase, Gooper, honey.

GOOPER (*handing the briefcase back to her*). Thank you. . . . Of ca'use, my relationship with Big Daddy is different from Brick's.

MAE. You're eight years older'n Brick an' always had t'carry a bigger load of th' responsibilities than Brick ever had t'carry. He never carried a thing in his life but a football or a highball.

GOOPER. Mae, will y' let me talk, please?

MAE. Yes, honey.

GOOPER. Now, a twenty-eight thousand acre plantation's a mighty big thing t'run.

MAE. Almost singlehanded.

(MARGARET *has gone out onto the gallery, and can be heard calling softly to* BRICK.)

BIG MAMA. You never had to run this place! What are you talking about? As if Big Daddy was dead and in his grave, you had to run it? Why, you just helped him out with a few business details and had

your law practice at the same time in Memphis!

MAE. Oh, Mommy, Mommy, Big Mommy! Let's be fair! Why, Gooper has given himself body and soul to keeping this place up for the past five years since Big Daddy's health started failing. Gooper won't say it, Gooper never thought of it as a duty, he just did it. And what did Brick do? Brick kept living in his past glory at college! Still a football player at twenty-seven!

MARGARET (*returning alone*). Who are you talking about, now? Brick? A football player? He isn't a football player and you know it. Brick is a sport's announcer on TV and one of the best-known ones in the country!

MAE. I'm talking about what he was.

MARGARET. Well, I wish you would just stop talking about my husband.

GOOPER. I've got a right to discuss my brother with other members of MY OWN family which don't include *you.* Why don't you go out there and drink with Brick?

MARGARET. I've never seen such malice toward a brother.

GOOPER. How about his for me? Why, he can't stand to be in the same room with me!

MARGARET. This is a deliberate campaign of vilification for the most disgusting and sordid reason on earth, and I know what it is! It's *avarice, avarice, greed, greed!*

BIG MAMA. *Oh, I'll scream! I'll scream in a moment unless this stops!*

(GOOPER *has stalked up to* MARGARET *with clenched fists at his sides as if he would strike her.* MAE *distorts her face again into a hideous grimace behind* MARGARET's *back.*)

MARGARET. We only remain on the place because of Big Mom and Big Daddy. If it is true what they say about Big Daddy we are going to leave here just as soon as it's over. Not a moment later.

BIG MAMA (*sobs*). Margaret. Child. Come here. Sit next to Big Mama.

MARGARET. Precious Mommy. I'm sorry, I'm so sorry, I—! (*She bends her long graceful neck to press her forehead to* BIG MAMA's *bulging shoulder under its black chiffon.*)

GOOPER. How beautiful, how touching this display of devotion!

MAE. Do you know why she's childless?

She's childless because that big beautiful athlete husband of hers won't go to bed with her!

GOOPER. You jest won't let me do this in a nice way, will yah? Aw right—Mae and I have five kids with another one coming! I don't give a goddam if Big Daddy likes me or don't like me or did or never did or will or will never! I'm just appealing to a sense of common decency and fair play. I'll tell you the truth. I've resented Big Daddy's partiality to Brick ever since Brick was born, and the way I've been treated like I was just barely good enough to spit on and sometimes not even good enough for that. Big Daddy is dying of cancer, and it's spread all through him and it's attacked all his vital organs including the kidneys and right now he is sinking into uremia, and you all know what uremia is, it's poisoning of the whole system due to the failure of the body to eliminate its poisons.

MARGARET (*to herself, downstage, hissingly*). Poisons, poisons! Venomous thoughts and words! In hearts and minds!—That's poisons!

GOOPER (*overlapping her*). I am asking for a square deal, and I expect to get one. But if I don't get one, if there's any peculiar shenanigans going on around here behind my back, or before me, well, I'm not a corporation lawyer for nothing, I know how to protect my own interests.—*OH! A late arrival!*

(BRICK *enters from the gallery with a tranquil, blurred smile, carrying an empty glass with him.*)

MAE. Behold the conquering hero comes!

GOOPER. The fabulous Brick Pollitt! Remember him?—Who could forget him!

MAE. He looks like he's been injured in a game!

GOOPER. Yep, I'm afraid you'll have to warm the bench at the Sugar Bowl this year, Brick! (MAE *laughs shrilly.*) Or was it the Rose Bowl that he made that famous run in?

MAE. The punch bowl, honey. It was in the punch bowl, the cut-glass punch bowl!

GOOPER. Oh, that's right, I'm getting the bowls mixed up!

MARGARET. Why don't you stop venting your malice and envy on a sick boy?

BIG MAMA. *Now you two hush, I mean it, hush, all of you, hush!*

GOOPER. All right, Big Mama. A family crisis brings out the best and the worst in every member of it.

MAE. *That's* the truth.

MARGARET. *Amen!*

BIG MAMA. *I said, hush!* I won't tolerate any more catty talk in my house.

(MAE *gives* GOOPER *a sign indicating briefcase.* BRICK's *smile has grown both brighter and vaguer. As he prepares a drink, he sings softly.*)

BRICK.
Show me the way to go home,
I'm tired and I wanta go to bed,
I had a little drink about an hour ago—

GOOPER (*at the same time*). Big Mama, you know it's necessary for me t'go back to Memphis in th' mornin' t'represent the Parker estate in a lawsuit.

(MAE *sits on the bed and arranges papers she has taken from the briefcase.*)

BRICK (*continuing the song*).
Wherever I may roam,
On land or sea or foam.

BIG MAMA. Is it, Gooper?

MAE. Yaiss.

GOOPER. That's why I'm forced to—to bring up a problem that—

MAE. Somethin' that's too important t' be put off!

GOOPER. If Brick was sober, he ought to be in on this.

MARGARET. Brick is present; we're here.

GOOPER. Well, good. I will now give you this outline my partner, Tom Bullitt, an' me have drawn up—a sort of dummy—trusteeship.

MARGARET. Oh, that's it! You'll be in charge an' dole out remittances, will you?

GOOPER. This we did as soon as we got the report on Big Daddy from th' Ochsner Laboratories. We did this thing, I mean we drew up this dummy outline with the advice and assistance of the Chairman of the Boa'd of Directors of th' Southern Plantahs Bank and Trust Company in Memphis, C. C. Bellowes, a man who handles estates for all th' prominent fam'lies in West Tennessee and th' Delta.

BIG MAMA. Gooper?

GOOPER (*crouching in front of* BIG MAMA). Now this is not—not final, or anything like it. This is just a preliminary outline. But it does provide a basis—a design—a—possible, feasible—*plan!*

MARGARET. Yes. I'll bet.

MAE. It's a plan to protect the biggest

estate in the Delta from irresponsibility an'—

BIG MAMA. Now you listen to me, all of you, you listen here! They's not goin' to be any more catty talk in my house! And Gooper, you put that away before I grab it out your hand and tear it right up! I don't know what the hell's in it, and I don't want to know what the hell's in it. I'm talkin' in Big Daddy's language now; I'm his *wife,* not his *widow,* I'm still his *wife!* And I'm talkin' to you in his language an'—

GOOPER. Big Mama, what I have here is—

MAE. Gooper explained that it's just a plan. . . .

BIG MAMA. I don't care what you got there. Just put it back where it came from, an' don't let me see it again, not even the outside of the envelope of it! Is that understood? Basis! Plan! Preliminary! Design! I say—what is it Big Daddy always says when he's disgusted?

BRICK (*from the bar*). Big Daddy says "crap" when he's disgusted.

BIG MAMA (*rising*). That's right— *CRAP!* I say *CRAP* too, like Big Daddy!

MAE. Coarse language doesn't seem called for in this—

GOOPER. Somethin' in me is *deeply outraged* by hearin' you talk like this.

BIG MAMA. *Nobody's goin' to take nothin'!*—till Big Daddy lets go of it, and maybe, just possibly, not—not even then! No, not even then!

BRICK.
*You can always hear me singin' this song,
Show me the way to go home.*

BIG MAMA. Tonight Brick looks like he used to look when he was a little boy, just like he did when he played wild games and used to come home all sweaty and pink-cheeked and sleepy, with his—red curls shining. . . . (*She comes over to him and runs her fat shaky hand through his hair. He draws aside as he does from all physical contact and continues the song in a whisper, opening the ice bucket and dropping in the ice cubes one by one as if he were mixing some important chemical formula.*)

BIG MAMA (*continuing*). Time goes by so fast. Nothin' can outrun it. Death commences too early—almost before you're half-acquainted with life—you meet with the other. . . .

Oh, you know we just got to love each other an' stay together, all of us, just as close as we can, especially now that such a *black* thing has come and moved into this place without invitation. (*Awkwardly embracing* BRICK, *she presses her head to his shoulder.*

(GOOPER *has been returning papers to* MAE *who has restored them to briefcase with an air of severely tried patience.*)

GOOPER. Big Mama? Big Mama? (*He stands behind her, tense with sibling envy.*)

BIG MAMA (*oblivious of* GOOPER). Brick, you hear me, don't you?

MARGARET. Brick hears you, Big Mama, he understands what you're saying.

BIG MAMA. Oh, Brick, son of Big Daddy! Big Daddy does so love you! Y'know what would be his fondest dream come true? If before he passed on, if Big Daddy has to pass on, you gave him a child of yours, a grandson as much like his son as his son is like Big Daddy!

MAE (*zipping briefcase shut: an incongruous sound*). Such a pity that Maggie an' Brick can't oblige!

MARGARET (*suddenly and quietly but forcefully*). Everybody listen. (*She crosses to the center of the room, holding her hands rigidly together.*)

MAE. Listen to what, Maggie?

MARGARET. I have an announcement to make.

GOOPER. A sports announcement, Maggie?

MARGARET. Brick and I are going to— *have a child!*

(BIG MAMA *catches her breath in a loud gasp.*)

(*Pause.* BIG MAMA *rises.*)

BIG MAMA. Maggie! Brick! This is too good to believe!

MAE. That's right, too good to believe.

BIG MAMA. Oh, my, my! This is Big Daddy's dream, his dream come true! I'm going to tell him right now before he—

MARGARET. We'll tell him in the morning. Don't disturb him now.

BIG MAMA. I want to tell him before he goes to sleep, I'm going to tell him his dream's come true this minute! And Brick! A child will make you pull yourself together and quit this drinking! (*She seizes the glass from his hand.*) The responsibilities of a father will—(*Her face contorts and she makes an excited gesture; bursting into sobs, she rushes out, crying.*) I'm

going to tell Big Daddy right this minute!
(*Her voice fades out down the hall.*)

(BRICK *shrugs slightly and drops an ice cube into another glass.* MARGARET *crosses quickly to his side, saying something under her breath, and she pours the liquor for him, staring up almost fiercely into his face.*)

BRICK (*coolly*). Thank you, Maggie, that's a nice big shot.

(MAE *has joined* GOOPER *and she gives him a fierce poke, making a low hissing sound and a grimace of fury.*)

GOOPER (*pushing her aside*). Brick, could you possibly spare me one small shot of that liquor?

BRICK. Why, help yourself, Gooper boy.

GOOPER. I will.

MAE (*shrilly*). Of course we know that this is—

GOOPER. *Be still, Mae!*

MAE. I won't be still! I know she's made this up!

GOOPER. God damn it, I said to shut up!

MARGARET. Gracious! I didn't know that my little announcement was going to provoke such a storm!

MAE. *That* woman isn't *pregnant!*

GOOPER. Who said she was?

MAE. *She* did.

GOOPER. The doctor didn't. Doc Baugh didn't.

MARGARET. I haven't gone to Doc Baugh.

GOOPER. Then who'd you go to, Maggie?

MARGARET. One of the best gynecologists in the South.

GOOPER. Uh huh, uh huh!—I see. . . . (*He takes out pencil and notebook.*)—May we have his name, please?

MARGARET. No, you may not, Mister Prosecuting Attorney!

MAE. He doesn't have any name, he doesn't exist!

MARGARET. Oh, he exists all right, and so does my child, Brick's baby!

MAE. You can't conceive a child by a man that won't sleep with you unless you think you're—

(BRICK *has turned on the phonograph. A scat song cuts* MAE's *speech.*)

GOOPER. *Turn that off!*

MAE. We know it's a lie because we hear you in here; he won't sleep with you, we hear you! So don't imagine you're going to put a trick over on us, to fool a dying man with a—

(*A long drawn cry of agony and rage fills the house.* MARGARET *turns phonograph down to a whisper. The cry is repeated.*)

MAE (*awed*). Did you hear that, Gooper, did you hear that?

GOOPER. Sounds like the pain has struck.

MAE. Go see, Gooper!

GOOPER. Come along and leave these love birds together in their nest!

(*He goes out first.* MAE *follows but turns at the door, contorting her face and hissing at* MARGARET.)

MAE. *Liar!* (*She slams the door.*)

(MARGARET *exhales with relief and moves a little unsteadily to catch hold of* BRICK's *arm.*)

MARGARET. Thank you for—keeping still . . .

BRICK. OK, Maggie.

MARGARET. It was gallant of you to save my face!

BRICK. —It hasn't happened yet.

MARGARET. What?

BRICK. The click. . . .

MARGARET. —the click in your head that makes you peaceful, honey?

BRICK. Uh-huh. It hasn't happened. . . . I've got to make it happen before I can sleep. . . .

MARGARET. —I—know what you—mean. . . .

BRICK. Give me that pillow in the big chair, Maggie.

MARGARET. I'll put it on the bed for you.

BRICK. No, put it on the sofa, where I sleep.

MARGARET. Not tonight, Brick.

BRICK. I want it on the sofa. That's where I sleep. (*He has hobbled to the liquor cabinet. He now pours down three shots in quick succession and stands waiting, silent. All at once he turns with a smile and says.*) There!

MARGARET. What?

BRICK. The *click.* . . . (*His gratitude seems almost infinite as he hobbles out on the gallery with a drink. We hear his crutch as he swings out of sight. Then, at some distance, he begins singing to himself a peaceful song.*)

(MARGARET *holds the big pillow forlornly as if it were her only companion, for a few moments, then throws it on the bed. She rushes to the liquor cabinet, gathers all the bottles in her arms, turns about undecidedly, then runs out of the room with them, leaving the door ajar on the dim yellow hall.* BRICK *is heard hobbling back along the gallery, singing his peaceful song. He comes back in, sees the pillow on the bed, laughs lightly, sadly, picks it up. He has it under his arm as* MARGARET *returns to the room.* MARGARET *softly shuts the door and leans against it, smiling softly at* BRICK.)

MARGARET. Brick, I used to think that you were stronger than me and I didn't want to be overpowered by you. But now, since you've taken to liquor—you know what?—I guess it's bad, but now I'm stronger than you and I can love you more truly!

Don't move that pillow. I'll move it right back if you do!—Brick? (*She turns out all the lamps but a single rose-silk-shaded one by the bed.*) I really have been to a doctor and I know what to do and— Brick?—this is my time by the calendar to conceive!

BRICK. Yes, I understand, Maggie. But how are you going to conceive a child by a man in love with his liquor?

MARGARET. By locking his liquor up and making him satisfy my desire before I un-lock it!

BRICK. Is that what you've done, Maggie?

MARGARET. Look and see. That cabinet's mighty empty compared to before!

BRICK. Well, I'll be a son of a—(*He reaches for his crutch but she beats him to it and rushes out on the gallery, hurls the crutch over the rail and comes back in, panting.*

(*There are running footsteps.* BIG MAMA *bursts into the room, her face all awry, gasping, stammering.*)

BIG MAMA. Oh, my God, oh, my God, oh, my God, where is it?

MARGARET. Is this what you want, Big Mama? (MARGARET *hands her the package left by the doctor.*)

BIG MAMA. I can't bear it, oh, God! Oh, Brick! Brick, baby! (*She rushes at him. He averts his face from her sobbing kisses.* MARGARET *watches with a tight smile.*) My son, Big Daddy's boy! Little Father! (*The groaning cry is heard again. She runs out, sobbing.*)

MARGARET. And so tonight we're going to make the lie true, and when that's done, I'll bring the liquor back here and we'll get drunk together, here, tonight, in this place that death has come into. . . . What do you say?

BRICK. I don't say anything. I guess there's nothing to say.

MARGARET. Oh, you weak people, you weak, beautiful people!—who give up.— What you want is someone to—(*She turns out the rose-silk lamp.*)—take hold of you —Gently, gently, with love! And—(*The curtain begins to fall slowly.*) I do love you, Brick, I do!

BRICK (*smiling with charming sadness*) Wouldn't it be funny if that was true?

THE CURTAIN COMES DOWN

NOTE OF EXPLANATION

Some day when time permits I would like to write a piece about the influence its dangers and its values, of a powerful and highly imaginative director upon the development of a play, before and during production. It does have dangers, but it has them only if the playwright is excessively malleable or submissive, or the direc tor is excessively insistent on ideas or in terpretations of his own. Elia Kazan and I have enjoyed the advantages and avoided the dangers of this highly explosive re lationship because of the deepest mutual respect for each other's creative function we have worked together three times with a phenomenal absence of friction between us and each occasion has increased the trust.

If you don't want a director's influence on your play, there are two ways to avoid it, and neither is good. One way is to ar rive at an absolutely final draft of your play before you let your director see it then hand it to him saying, Here it is, take it or leave it! The other way is to select a director who is content to put your play on the stage precisely as you conceived it with no ideas of his own. I said neither is a good way, and I meant it. No living playwright, that I can think of, hasn't something valuable to learn about his own work from a director so keenly perceptive as Elia Kazan. It so happened that in the case of *Streetcar*, Kazan was given a script that was completely finished. In the case of *Cat*, he was shown the first typed version of the play, and he was excited by it, but he had definite reservations about it which were concentrated in the third act. The gist of his reservations can be listed as three points: one, he felt that Big Daddy was too vivid and important a character to disappear from the play except as an off-stage cry after the second act curtain; two, he felt that the character of Brick should undergo some apparent mutation as a result of the virtual vivisection that he undergoes in his interview with his father in Act Two. Three, he felt that the character of Margaret, while he understood that I sympathized with her and liked her myself, should be, if possible, more clearly sympathetic to an audience.

It was only the third of these suggestions that I embraced wholeheartedly from the outset, because it so happened that Maggie the Cat had become steadily more charming to me as I worked on her characterization. I didn't want Big Daddy to reappear in Act Three and I felt that the moral paralysis of Brick was a root thing in his tragedy, and to show a dramatic progression would obscure the meaning of that tragedy in him and because I don't believe that a conversation, however revelatory, ever effects so immediate a change in the heart or even conduct of a person in Brick's state of spiritual disrepair.

However, I wanted Kazan to direct the play, and though these suggestions were not made in the form of an ultimatum, I was fearful that I would lose his interest if I didn't re-examine the script from his point of view. I did. And you will find included in this published script the new third act that resulted from his creative influence on the play. The reception of the playing-script has more than justified, in my opinion, the adjustments made to that influence. A failure reaches fewer people, and touches fewer, than does a play that succeeds.

It may be that *Cat* number one would have done just as well, or nearly, as *Cat* number two; it's an interesting question. At any rate, with the publication of both third acts in this volume, the reader can, if he wishes, make up his own mind about it.

TENNESSEE WILLIAMS

ACT THREE

AS PLAYED IN NEW YORK PRODUCTION

BIG DADDY *is seen leaving as at the end of* ACT II.

———

BIG DADDY (*shouts, as he goes out DR on gallery*). ALL—LYIN'—DYIN'—LIARS! LIARS! LIARS!
(*After* BIG DADDY *has gone,* MARGARET *enters from DR on gallery, into room through DS door. She X to* BRICK *at LC.*)
MARGARET. Brick, what in the name of God was goin' on in this room?
(DIXIE *and* TRIXIE *rush through the room from the hall, L to gallery R, brandishing cap pistols, which they fire repeatedly, as they shout: "Bang! Bang! Bang!"* MAE *appears from DR gallery entrance, and turns the children back UL, along gallery. At the same moment,* GOOPER, REVEREND TOOKER *and* DR. BAUGH *enter from L in the hall.*)
MAE. Dixie! You quit that! Gooper, will y'please git these kiddies t'baid? Right now?
(GOOPER *and* REVEREND TOOKER *X along upper gallery.* DR. BAUGH *holds, UC, near hall door.* REVEREND TOOKER *X to* MAE *near section of gallery just outside doors, R.*)
GOOPER (*urging the children along*). Mae—you seen Big Mama?
MAE. Not yet.
(DIXIE *and* TRIXIE *vanish through hall, L.*)
REVEREND TOOKER (*to* MAE). Those kiddies are so full of vitality. I think I'll have to be startin' back to town.
(MARGARET *turns to watch and listen.*)
MAE. Not yet, Preacher. You know we regard you as a member of this fam'ly, one of our closest an' dearest, so you just got t'be with us when Doc Baugh gives Big Mama th' actual truth about th' report from th' clinic. (*Calls through door.*) Has Big Daddy gone to bed, Brick?
(GOOPER *has gone out DR at the beginning of the exchange between* MAE *and* REVEREND TOOKER.)
MARGARET (*replying to* MAE). Yes, he's gone to bed. (*To* BRICK.) Why'd Big Daddy shout "liars"?
GOOPER (*off DR*). Mae!
(MAE *exits DR.* REVEREND TOOKER *drifts along upper gallery.*)

BRICK. I didn't lie to Big Daddy. I've lied to nobody, nobody but myself, just lied to myself. The time has come to put me in Rainbow Hill, put me in Rainbow Hill, Maggie, I ought to go there.

MARGARET. Over my dead body! (BRICK *starts R. She holds him.*) Where do you think you're goin'?

(MAE *enters from DR on gallery, X to* REVEREND TOOKER, *who comes to meet her.*)

BRICK (*X below to C*). Out for some air, I want air—

GOOPER (*entering from DR to* MAE, *on gallery*). Now, where is that old lady?

MAE. Cantcha find her, Gooper?

(REVEREND TOOKER *goes out DR.*)

GOOPER (*X to* DOC *above hall door*). She's avoidin' this talk.

MAE. I think she senses somethin'.

GOOPER (*calls off L*). Sookey! Go find Big Mama an' tell her Doc Baugh an' the Preacher've got to go soon.

MAE. Don't let Big Daddy hear yuh! (*Brings* DR. BAUGH *to R on gallery.*)

REVEREND TOOKER (*off DR, calls*). Big Mama.

SOOKEY and DAISY (*running from L to R in lawn, calling*). Miss Ida! Miss Ida! (*They go out UR.*)

GOOPER (*calling off upper gallery*). Lacey, you look downstairs for Big Mama!

MARGARET. Brick, they're going to tell Big Mama the truth now, an' she needs you!

(REVEREND TOOKER *appears in lawn area, UR, X C.*)

DOCTOR BAUGH (*to* MAE, *on R gallery*). This is going to be painful.

MAE. Painful things can't always be avoided.

DOCTOR BAUGH. That's what I've noticed about 'em, Sister Woman.

REVEREND TOOKER (*on lawn, points off R*). I see Big Mama! (*Hurries off L. and reappears shortly in hall.*)

GOOPER (*hurrying into hall*). She's gone round the gall'ry to Big Daddy's room. Hey, Mama! (*Off.*) Hey, Big Mama! Come here!

MAE (*calls*). Hush, Gooper! Don't holler, go to her!

GOOPER and REVEREND TOOKER *now appear together in hall.* BIG MAMA *runs in from DR, carrying a glass of milk. She X past* DR. BAUGH *to* MAE, *on R gallery.* DR. BAUGH *turns away.*)

BIG MAMA. Here I am! What d'you all want with me?

GOOPER (*steps toward* BIG MAMA). Big Mama, I told you we got to have this talk.

BIG MAMA. What talk you talkin' about? I saw the light go on in Big Daddy's bedroom an' took him his glass of milk, an' he just shut the shutters right in my face. (*Steps into room through R door.*) When old couples have been together as long as me an' Big Daddy, they, they get irritable with each other just from too much—devotion! Isn't that so? (*X below wicker seat to RC area.*)

MARGARET (*X to* BIG MAMA, *embracing her*). Yes, of course it's so.

(BRICK *starts out UC through hall, but sees* GOOPER *and* REVEREND TOOKER *entering, so he hobbles through C out DS door and onto gallery.*)

BIG MAMA. I think Big Daddy was just worn out. He loves his fam'ly. He loves to have 'em around him, but it's a strain on his nerves. He wasn't himself tonight, Brick— (*XC toward* BRICK. BRICK *passes her on his way out, DS.*) Big Daddy wasn't himself, I could tell he was all worked up.

REVEREND TOOKER (*USC*). I think he's remarkable.

BIG MAMA. Yaiss! Just remarkable. (*Faces US, turns, X to bar, puts down glass of milk.*) Did you notice all the food he ate at that table? (*XR a bit.*) Why he ate like a hawss!

GOOPER (*USC*). I hope he don't regret it.

BIG MAMA (*turns US toward* GOOPER). What! Why that man ate a huge piece of cawn bread with molasses on it! Helped himself twice to hoppin' john!

MARGARET (*X to* BIG MAMA). Big Daddy loves hoppin' john. We had a real country dinner.

BIG MAMA. Yais, he simply adores it! An' candied yams. Son— (*X to DS door, looking out at* BRICK. MARGARET *X above* BIG MAMA *to her L.*) That man put away enough food at that table to stuff a fieldhand.

GOOPER. I hope he don't have to pay for it later on.

BIG MAMA (*turns US*). What's that, Gooper?

MAE. Gooper says he hopes Big Daddy doesn't suffer tonight.

BIG MAMA (*turns to* MARGARET, *DC*).

Oh, shoot, Gooper says, Gooper says! Why should Big Daddy suffer for satisfyin' a nawmal appetite? There's nothin' wrong with that man but nerves; he's sound as a dollar! An' now he knows he is, an' that's why he ate such a supper. He had a big load off his mind, knowin' he wasn't doomed to—what—he thought he was—doomed t'— (*She wavers.*)

(MARGARET *puts her arms around* BIG MAMA.)

GOOPER (*urging* MAE *forward*). MAE!

(MAE *runs forward below wicker seat. She stands below* BIG MAMA, MARGARET *above* BIG MAMA. *They help her to the wicker seat.* BIG MAMA *sits.* MARGARET *sits above her.* MAE *stands behind her.*)

MARGARET. Bless his ole sweet soul.

BIG MAMA. Yes—bless his heart.

BRICK (*DS on gallery, looking out front*). Hello, moon, I envy you, you cool son of a bitch.

BIG MAMA. I want Brick!

MARGARET. He just stepped out for some fresh air.

BIG MAMA. Honey! I want Brick!

MAE. Bring li'l Brother in here so we cin talk. (MARGARET *rises, X through DS door to* BRICK *on gallery.*)

BRICK (*to the moon*). I envy you—you cool son of a bitch.

MARGARET Brick, what're you doin' out here on the gall'ry, Baby?

BRICK. Admirin' an' complimentin' th' man in the moon.

(MAE *X to* DR. BAUGH *on R gallery.* REVEREND TOOKER *and* GOOPER *move R UC, looking at* BIG MAMA.)

MARGARET (*to* BRICK). Come in, Baby. They're gettin' ready to tell Big Mama the truth.

BRICK. I can't witness that thing in there.

MAE. Doc Baugh, d'you think those vitamin B$_{12}$ injections are all they're cracked up t'be? (*Enters room to upper side, behind wicker seat.*)

DOCTOR BAUGH (*X to below wicker seat*). Well, I guess they're as good t'be stuck with as anything else. (*Looks at watch; X through to LC.*)

MARGARET (*to* BRICK). Big Mama needs you!

BRICK. I can't witness that thing in there!

BIG MAMA. What's wrong here? You all have such long faces, you sit here waitin' for somethin' like a bomb—to go off.

GOOPER. We're waitin' for Brick an' Maggie to come in for this talk.

MARGARET (*X above* BRICK, *to his R*). Brother Man an' Mae have got a trick up their sleeves, an' if you don't go in there t'help Big Mama, y'know what I'm goin' to do—?

BIG MAMA. Talk. Whispers! Whispers! (*Looks out DR.*) Brick! . . .

MARGARET (*answering* BIG MAMA's *call*). Comin', Big Mama! (*To* BRICK:) I'm goin' to take every dam' bottle on this place an' pitch it off th' levee into th' river!

BIG MAMA. Never had this sort of atmosphere here before.

MAE (*sits above* BIG MAMA *on wicker seat*). Before what, Big Mama?

BIG MAMA. This occasion. What's Brick an' Maggie doin' out there now?

GOOPER (*X DC, looks out*). They seem to be havin' some little altercation.

(BRICK *X toward DS step.* MAGGIE *moves R above him to portal DR.* REVEREND TOOKER *joins* DR. BAUGH, *LC.*)

BIG MAMA (*taking a pill from pill box on chain at her wrist*). Give me a little somethin' to wash this tablet down with. Smell of burnt fireworks always makes me sick.

(MAE *X to bar to pour glass of water.* DR. BAUGH *joins her.* GOOPER X *to* REVEREND TOOKER, *LC.*)

BRICK (*to* MAGGIE). You're a live cat, aren't you?

MARGARET. You're dam' right I am!

BIG MAMA. Gooper, will y'please open that hall door—an' let some air circulate in this stiflin' room?

(GOOPER *starts US, but is restrained by* MAE *who X through C with glass of water.* GOOPER *turns to men DLC.*)

MAE (*X to* BIG MAMA *with water, sits above her*). Big Mama, I think we ought to keep that door closed till after we talk.

BIG MAMA. I swan! (*Drinks water. Washes down pill.*)

MAE. I just don't think we ought to take any chance of Big Daddy hearin' a word of this discussion.

BIG MAMA (*hands glass to* MAE). What discussion of what? Maggie! Brick! Nothin' is goin' to be said in th' house of Big Daddy Pollitt that he can't hear if he wants to!

(MAE *rises, X to bar, puts down glass, joins* GOOPER *and the two men, LC.*)

BRICK. How long are you goin' to stand behind me, Maggie?

MARGARET. Forever, if necessary.

(BRICK *X US to R gallery door.*)

BIG MAMA. Brick!

(MAE *rises, looks out DS, sits.*)

GOOPER. That boy's gone t'pieces—he's just gone t'pieces.

DOCTOR BAUGH. Y'know, in my day they used to have somethin' they called the Keeley cure for drinkers.

BIG MAMA. Shoot!

DOCTOR BAUGH. But nowadays, I understand they take some kind of tablets that kill their taste for the stuff.

GOOPER (*turns to* DR. BAUGH). Call 'em anti-bust tablets.

BIG MAMA. Brick don't need to take nothin'. That boy is just broken up over Skipper's death. You know how poor Skipper died. They gave him a big, big dose of that sodium amytal stuff at his home an' then they called the ambulance an' give him another big, big dose of it at th' hospital an' that an' all the alcohol in his system fo' months an' months just proved too much for his heart an' his heart quit beatin'. I'm scared of needles! I'm more scared of a needle than th' knife—

(BRICK *has entered the room to behind the wicker seat. He rests his hand on* BIG MAMA's *head.* GOOPER *has moved a bit URC, facing* BIG MAMA.)

BIG MAMA. Oh! Here's Brick! My precious baby!

(DR. BAUGH *X to bar, puts down drink.* BRICK *X below* BIG MAMA *through C to bar.*)

BRICK. Take it, Gooper!

MAE (*rising*). What?

BRICKER. Gooper knows what. Take it, Gooper!

(MAE *turns to* GOOPER *URC.* DR. BAUGH *X to* REVEREND TOOKER. MARGARET, *who has followed* BRICK *US on R gallery before he entered the room, now enters room, to behind wicker seat.*)

BIG MAMA (*to* BRICK). You just break my heart.

BRICK (*at bar*). Sorry—anyone else?

MARGARET. Brick, sit with Big Mama an' hold her hand while we talk.

BRICK. You do that, Maggie. I'm a restless cripple. I got to stay on my crutch.

(MAE *sits above* BIG MAMA. GOOPER *moves in front, below, and sits on couch, facing* BIG MAMA. REVEREND TOOKER *closes in to*

RC. DR. BAUGH *XDC, faces upstage, smoking cigar.* MARGARET *turns away to R doors.*)

BIG MAMA. Why're you all *surroundin'* me?—like this? Why're you all starin' at me like this an' makin' signs at each other? (BRICK *hobbles out hall door and X along R gallery.*) I don't need nobody to hold my hand. Are you all crazy? Since when did Big Daddy or me need anybody—?

(REVEREND TOOKER *moves behind wicker seat.*)

MAE. Calm yourself, Big Mama.

BIG MAMA. Calm you'self *you'self,* Sister Woman! How could I calm myself with everyone starin' at me as if big drops of blood had broken out on m'face? What's this all about Annh! What?

GOOPER. Doc Baugh— (MAE *rises.*) Sit down, Mae— (MAE *sits.*)—Big Mama wants to know the complete truth about th' report we got today from the Ochsner Clinic!

(DR. BAUGH *buttons his coat, faces group at RC.*)

BIG MAMA. Is there somethin'—somethin' that I don't know?

DOCTOR BAUGH. Yes—well . . .

BIG MAMA (*rises*). I—want to—knowwwwww! (*X to* DR BAUGH.) Somebody must be lyin'! *I want to know!*

(MAE, GOOPER, REVEREND TOOKER *surround* BIG MAMA.)

MAE. Sit down, Big Mama, sit down on this sofa!

(BRICK *has passed* MARGARET *Xing DR on gallery.*)

MARGARET. Brick! Brick!

BIG MAMA. *What is it, what is it?* (BIG MAMA *drives* DR. BAUGH *a bit DLC. Others follow, surrounding* BIG MAMA.)

DOCTOR BAUGH. I never have seen a more thorough examination than Big Daddy Pollitt was given in all my experience at the Ochsner Clinic.

GOOPER. It's one of th' best in th' country.

MAE. It's *THE* best in th' country—bar none!

DOCTOR BAUGH. Of course they were ninety-nine and nine-tenths per cent certain before they even started.

BIG MAMA. Sure of what, sure of what, sure of what—*what!?*

MAE. Now, Mommy, be a brave girl!

BRICK (*on DR gallery, covers his ears,*

sings). "By the light, by the light, of the silvery moon!"

GOOPER (*breaks DR. Calls out to* BRICK). Shut up, Brick! (*Returns to group LC.*)

BRICK. Sorry . . . (*Continues singing.*)

DOCTOR BAUGH. But now, you see, Big Mama, they cut a piece off this growth, a specimen of the tissue, an'—

BIG MAMA. Growth? You told Big Daddy—

DOCTOR BAUGH. Now, wait—

BIG MAMA. You told me an' Big Daddy there wasn't a thing wrong with him but—

MAE. Big Mama, they always—

GOOPER. Let Doc Baugh talk, will yuh?

BIG MAMA. —little spastic condition of—

REVEREND TOOKER (*throughout all this*). Shh! Shh! Shh!

(BIG MAMA *breaks UC, they all follow.*)

DOCTOR BAUGH. Yes, that's what we told Big Daddy. But we had this bit of tissue run through the laboratory an' I'm sorry t'say the test was positive on it. It's malignant.

(*Pause.*)

BIG MAMA. *Cancer! Cancer!*

MAE. Now now, Mommy—

GOOPER (*at the same time*). You had to know, Big Mama.

BIG MAMA. *Why didn't they cut it out of him? Hanh? Hannh?*

DOCTOR BAUGH. Involved too much, Big Mama, too many organs affected.

MAE. Big Mama, the liver's affected, an' so's the kidneys, both. It's gone way past what they call a—

GOOPER. —a surgical risk.

(BIG MAMA *gasps.*)

REVEREND TOOKER. Tch, tch, tch.

DOCTOR BAUGH. Yes, it's gone past the knife.

MAE. That's why he's turned yellow!

(BRICK *stops singing, turns away UR on gallery.*)

BIG MAMA (*pushes* MAE *DS*). Git away from me, git away from me, Mae! (*XDSR*) I want Brick! Where's Brick! *Where's my only son?*

MAE (*a step after* BIG MAMA). Mama! Did she say "only" son?

GOOPER (*following* BIG MAMA). What does that make me?

MAE (*above* GOOPER). A sober responsible man with five precious children—*six!*

BIG MAMA. I want Brick! Brick! Brick!

MARGARET (*a step to* BIG MAMA *above couch*). Mama, let *me* tell you.

BIG MAMA (*pushing her aside*). No, no, leave me alone, you're not my blood! (*She rushes onto the DS gallery.*)

GOOPER (*X to* BIG MAMA *on gallery*). Mama! I'm your son! Listen to me!

MAE. Gooper's your son, Mama, he's your first-born!

BIG MAMA. Gooper never liked Daddy!

MAE. That's not true!

REVEREND TOOKER (*UC*). I think I'd better slip away at this point. Good night, good night everybody, and God bless you all—on this place. (*Goes out through hall.*)

DOCTOR BAUGH (*XDR to above DS door*). Well, Big Mama—

BIG MAMA (*leaning against* GOOPER, *on lower gallery*). It's all a mistake, I know it's just a bad dream.

DOCTOR BAUGH. We're gonna keep Big Daddy as comfortable as we can.

BIG MAMA. Yes, it's just a bad dream, that's all it is, it's just an awful dream.

GOOPER. In my opinion Big Daddy is havin' some pain but won't admit that he has it.

BIG MAMA. Just a dream, a bad dream.

DOCTOR BAUGH. That's what lots of 'em do, they think if they don't admit they're havin' the pain they can sort of escape th' fact of it.

(BRICK *X US on R gallery.* MARGARET *watches him from R doors.*)

GOOPER. Yes, they get sly about it, get real sly about it.

MAE (*X to R of* DR. BAUGH). Gooper an' I think—

GOOPER. Shut up, Mae—Big Mama, I really do think Big Daddy should be started on morphine.

BIG MAMA (*pulling away from* GOOPER). Nobody's goin't to give Big Daddy morphine!

DOCTOR BAUGH. Now, Big Mama, when that pain strikes it's goin' to strike mighty hard an' Big Daddy's goin' t'need the needle to bear it.

BIG MAMA (*X to* DR. BAUGH). I tell you, nobody's goin' to give him morphine!

MAE. Big Mama, you don't want to see Big Daddy suffer, y'know y'—

DOCTOR BAUGH (*X to bar*). Well, I'm leavin' this stuff here (*Puts packet of morphine, etc., on bar.*) so if there's a sudden attack you won't have to send out for it. (BIG MAMA *hurries to L side bar.*)

MAE (*X C, below* DR. BAUGH). I know how to give a hypo.

BIG MAMA. Nobody's goin' to give Big Daddy morphine!

GOOPER (*X C*). Mae took a course in nursin' durin' th' war.

MARGARET. Somehow I don't think Big Daddy would want Mae t'give him a hypo.

MAE (*to* MARGARET). You think he'd want *you* to do it?

DOCTOR BAUGH. Well—

GOOPER. Well, Doc Baugh is goin'—

DOCTOR BAUGH. Yes, I got to be goin'. Well, keep your chin up, Big Mama. (*X to hall.*)

GOOPER (*as he and* MAE *follow* DR. BAUGH *into the hall*). She's goin' to keep her ole chin up, aren't you, Big Mama? (*They go out L.*) Well, Doc, we sure do appreciate all you've done. I'm telling you, we're obligated—

BIG MAMA. Margaret! (*XRC.*)

MARGARET (*meeting* BIG MAMA *in front of wicker seat*). I'm right here, Big Mama.

BIG MAMA. Margaret, you've got to cooperate with me an' Big Daddy to straighten Brick out now—

GOOPER (*off L, returning with* MAE). I guess that Doctor has got a lot on his mind, but it wouldn't hurt him to act a little more human—

BIG MAMA. —because it'll break Big Daddy's heart if Brick don't pull himself together an' take hold of things here.

(BRICK *XDSR on gallery.*)

MAE (*UC, overhearing*). Take hold of what things, Big Mama?

BIG MAMA (*sits in wicker chair,* MARGARET *standing behind chair*). The place.

GOOPER (*UC*). Big Mama, you've had a shock.

MAE (*X with* GOOPER *to* BIG MAMA). Yais, we've all had a shock, but—

GOOPER. Let's be realistic—

MAE. Big Daddy would not, would *never,* be foolish enough to—

GOOPER. —put this place in irresponsible hands!

BIG MAMA. Big Daddy ain't goin' t'put th' place in anybody's hands, Big Daddy is *not* goin' t'die! I want you to git that into your haids, all of you!

(MAE *sits above* BIG MAMA, MARGARET *turns R to door,* GOOPER *X L C a bit.*)

MAE. Mommy, Mommy, Big Mama,

we're just as hopeful an' optimistic as you are about Big Daddy's prospects, we have faith in prayer—but nevertheless there are certain matters that have to be discussed an' dealt with, because otherwise—

GOOPER. Mae, will y'please get my briefcase out of our room?

MAE. Yes, honey. (*Rises, goes out through hall L.*)

MARGARET (*X to* BRICK *on DS gallery*). Hear them in there? (*X back to R gallery door.*)

GOOPER (*stands above* BIG MAMA. *Leaning over her*). Big Mama, what you said just now was not at all true, an' you know it. I've always loved Big Daddy in my own quiet way. I never made a show of it. I know that Big Daddy has always been fond of me in a quiet way, too.

(MARGARET *drifts UR on gallery.* MAE *returns, X to* GOOPER'S *L with briefcase.*)

MAE. Here's your briefcase, Gooper, honey. (*Hands it to him.*)

GOOPER (*hands briefcase back to* MAE). Thank you. Of ca'use, my relationship with Big Daddy is different from Brick's.

MAE. You're eight years older'n Brick an' always had t'carry a bigger load of th' responsibilities than Brick ever had t'carry; he never carried a thing in his life but a football or a highball.

GOOPER. Mae, will y'let me talk, please?

MAE. Yes, honey.

GOOPER. Now, a twenty-eight thousand acre plantation's a mighty big thing t'run.

MAE. Almost single-handed!

BIG MAMA. You never had t'run this place, Brother Man, what're you talkin' about, as if Big Daddy was dead an' in his grave, you had to run it? Why, you just had t'help him out with a few business details an' had your law practice at the same time in Memphis.

MAE. Oh, Mommy, Mommy, Mommy! Let's be fair! Why, Gooper has given himself body an' soul t'keepin' this place up fo' the past five years since Big Daddy's health started fallin'. Gooper won't say it, Gooper never thought of it as a duty, he just did it. An' what did Brick do? Brick kep' livin' in his past glory at college!

(GOOPER *places a restraining hand on* MAE's *leg;* MARGARET *drifts DS in gallery.*)

GOOPER. Still a football player at twenty-seven!

MARGARET (*bursts into UR door*). Who are you talkin' about now? Brick? A football player? He isn't a football player an' you know it! Brick is a sports announcer on TV an' one of the best-known ones in the country!

MAE (*breaks UC*). I'm talkin' about what he was!

MARGARET (*X to above lower gallery door*). Well, I wish you would just stop talkin' about my husband!

GOOPER (*X to above* MARGARET). Listen, Margaret, I've got a right to discuss my own brother with other members of my own fam'ly, which don't include *you!* (*Pokes finger at her; she slaps his finger away.*) Now, why don't you go on out there an' drink with Brick?

MARGARET. I've never seen such malice toward a brother.

GOOPER. How about his for me? Why he can't stand to be in the same room with me!

BRICK (*on lower gallery*). That's the truth!

MARGARET. This is a deliberate campaign of vilification for the most disgusting and sordid reason on earth, and I know what it is! *It's avarice, avarice, greed, greed!*

BIG MAMA. Oh, I'll scream, I will scream in a moment unless this stops! Margaret, child, come here, sit next to Big Mama.

MARGARET (*X to* BIG MAMA, *sits above her*). Precious Mommy. (GOOPER *X to bar.*)

MAE. How beautiful, how touchin' this display of devotion! Do you know why she's childless? She's childless because that big, beautiful athlete husband of hers won't go to bed with her, that's why! (*X to L of bed, looks at* GOOPER.)

GOOPER. You jest won't let me do this the nice way, will yuh? Aw right—(*X to above wicker seat.*) I don't give a goddam if Big Daddy likes me or don't like me or did or never did or will or will never! I'm just appealin' to a sense of common decency an' fair play! I'm tellin' you th' truth—(*X DS through lower door to* BRICK *on DR gallery.*) I've resented Big Daddy's partiality to Brick ever since th' goddam day you were born, son, an' th' way I've been treated, like I was just barely good enough to spit on, an' sometimes not even good enough for that. (*X back through room to above wicker seat.*) Big Daddy is dyin' of cancer an' it's spread all through him an' it's attacked all his vital organs includin' the kidneys an' right now he is sinkin' into uremia, an' you all know what uremia is, it's poisonin' of the whole system due to th' failure of th' body to eliminate its poisons.

MARGARET. Poisons, poisons, venomous thoughts and words! In hearts and minds! That's poisons!

GOOPER. I'm askin' for a square deal an' by God I expect to get one. But if I don't get one, if there's any peculiar shenanigans goin' on around here behind my back, well I'm not a corporation lawyer for nothin! (*XDS toward lower gallery door, on apex.*) I know how to protect my own interests. (*Rumble of distant thunder.*)

BRICK (*entering the room through DS door*). Storm comin' up.

GOOPER. Oh, a late arrival!

MAE (*X through C to below bar, LCO*). Behold, the conquerin' hero comes!

GOOPER (*X through C to bar, following* BRICK, *imitating his limp*). The fabulous Brick Pollitt! Remember him? Who could forget him?

MAE. He looks like he's been injured in a game!

GOOPER. Yep, I'm afraid you'll have to warm th' bench at the Sugar Bowl this year, Brick! Or was it the Rose Bowl that he made his famous run in. (*Another rumble of thunder, sound of wind rising.*)

MAE (*X to L of* BRICK, *who has reached the bar*). The punch bowl, honey, it was the punch bowl, the cut-glass punch bowl!

GOOPER. That's right! I'm always gettin' the boy's *bowls* mixed up! (*Pats* BRICK *on the butt.*)

MARGARET (*rushes at* GOOPER, *striking him*). Stop that! You stop that!

(*Thunder.* MAE *X toward* MARGARET *from L. of* GOOPER, *flails at* MARGARET; GOOPER *keeps the women apart.* LACEY *runs through the US lawn area in a raincoat.*)

DAISY and SOOKEY (*off UL*). Storm! Storm comin! Storm! Storm!

LACEY (*running out UR*). Brightie, close them shutters!

GOOPER (*X onto R gallery, calls after* LACEY). Lacey, put the top up on my Cadillac, will yuh?

LACEY (*off R*). Yes, sur, Mistah Pollitt!

GOOPER (*X to above* BIG MAMA). Big Mama, you know it's goin' to be necessary for me t'go back to Memphis in th' mornin' t'represent the Parker estate in a lawsuit.

(MAE *sits on L side bed, arranges papers she removes from brief case.*)

BIG MAMA. Is it, Gooper?

MAE. Yaiss.

GOOPER. That's why I'm forced to—to bring up a problem that—

MAE. Somethin' that's too important t' be put off!

GOOPER. If Brick was sober, he ought to be in on this. I think he ought to be present when I present this plan.

MARGARET (*UC*). Brick is present, we're present!

GOOPER. Well, good. I will now give you this outline my partner, Tom Bullit, an' me have drawn up—a sort of dummy—trusteeship!

MARGARET. Oh, that's it! You'll be in charge an' dole out remittances, will you?

GOOPER. This we did as soon as we got the report on Big Daddy from th' Ochsner Laboratories. We did this thing, I mean we drew up this dummy outline with the advice and assistance of the Chairman of the Boa'd of Directors of th' Southern Plantuhs Bank and Trust Company in Memphis, C. C. Bellowes, a man who handles estates for all th' prominent fam'lies in West Tennessee and th' Delta!

BIG MAMA. Gooper?

GOOPER (*X behind seat to below* BIG MAMA). Now this is not—not final, or anything like it, this is just a preliminary outline. But it does provide a—basis—a design —a—possible, feasible—*plan*! (*He waves papers* MAE *has thrust into his hand, US.*)

MARGARET (*XDL*). Yes, I'll bet it's a plan! (*Thunder rolls. Interior lighting dims.*)

MAE. It's a plan to protect the biggest estate in the Delta from irresponsibility an'—

BIG MAMA. Now you listen to me, all of you, you listen here! They's not goin' to be no more catty talk in my house! And Gooper, you put that away before I grab it out of your hand and tear it right up! I don't know what the hell's in it, and I don't want to know what the hell's in it. I'm talkin' in Big Daddy's language now, I'm his *wife*, not his *widow*, I'm still his *wife*! And I'm talkin' to you in his language an'—

GOOPER. Big Mama, what I have here is—

MAE. Gooper explained that it's just a plan . . .

BIG MAMA. I don't care what you got there, just put it back where it come from an' don't let me see it again, not even the outside of the envelope of it! Is that understood? Basis! Plan! Preliminary! Design!—I say—what is it that Big Daddy always says when he's disgusted? (*Storm clouds race across sky.*)

BRICK (*from bar*). Big Daddy says "crap" when he is disgusted.

BIG MAMA (*rising*). That's right— CRAPPPP! I say CRAP too, like Big Daddy!

(*Thunder rolls.*)

MAE. Coarse language don't seem called for in this—

GOOPER. Somethin' in me is *deeply outraged* by this.

BIG MAMA. *Nobody's goin' to do nothin'!* till Big Daddy lets go of it, and maybe just possibly not—not even then! No, not even then!

(*Thunder clap. Glass crash, off L. Off UR, children commence crying. Many storm sounds, L and R: barnyard animals in terror, papers crackling, shutters rattling.* SOOKEY *and* DAISY *hurry from L to R in lawn area. Inexplicably,* DAISY *hits together two leather pillows. They cry, "Storm! Storm!"* SOOKEY *waves a piece of wrapping paper to cover lawn furniture.* MAE *exits to hall and upper gallery. Strange man runs across lawn, R to L. Thunder rolls repeatedly.*)

MAE. Sookey, hurry up an' git that po'ch fu'niture covahed; want th' paint to come off? (*Starts DR on gallery.* GOOPER *runs through hall to R gallery.*)

GOOPER (*yells to* LACEY, *who appears from R*). Lacey, put mah car away!

LACEY. Cain't, Mistah Pollitt, you got the keys! (*Exit US.*)

GOOPER. Naw, you got 'em, man. (*Exit DR. Reappears UR, calls to* MAE.) Where th' keys to th' car, honey? (*Runs C.*)

MAE (*DR on gallery*). You got 'em in your pocket! (*Exit DR.* GOOPER *exits UR. Dog howls.* DAISY *and* SOOKEY *sing off UR to comfort children.* MAE *is heard placating the children. Storm fades away. During the storm,* MARGARET *X and sits on couch, DR.* BIG MAMA *X DC.*)

BIG MAMA. BRICK! Come here, Brick, I need you.

(*Thunder distantly. Children whimper, off L* MAE *consoles them.* BRICK *X to R of* BIG MAMA.)

BIG MAMA. Tonight Brick looks like he used to look when he was a little boy just like he did when he played wild games in the orchard back of the house and used to come home when I hollered myself hoarse for him! all—sweaty—and pink-cheeked —an' sleepy with his curls shinin'— (*Thunder distantly. Children whimper, off L.* MAE *consoles them. Dog howls, off.*) Time goes by so fast. Nothin' can outrun it. Death commences too early—almost before you're half-acquainted with life—you meet with the other. Oh, you know we just got to love each other, an' stay together all of us just as close as we can, specially now that such a *black* thing has come and moved into this place without invitation. (*Dog howls, off.*) Oh, Brick, son of Big Daddy, Big Daddy does so love you. Y'know what would be his fondest dream come true? If before he passed on, if Big Daddy has to pass on . . . (*Dog howls, off.*) You give him a child of yours, a grandson as much like his son as his son is like Big Daddy. . . .

MARGARET. I know that's Big Daddy's dream.

BIG MAMA. That's his dream.

BIG DADDY (*off DR on gallery*). Looks like the wind was takin' liberties with this place.

(LACEY *appears UL, X to UC in lawn area;* BRIGHTIE *and* SMALL *appear UR on lawn.* BIG DADDY *X onto the UR gallery.*)

LACEY. Evenin', Mr. Pollitt.

BRIGHTIE *and* SMALL. Evenin', Cap'n. Hello, Cap'n.

MARGARET (*X to R door*). Big Daddy's on the gall'ry.

BIG DADDY. Stawm crossed th' river, Lacey?

LACEY. Gone to Arkansas, Cap'n.

(BIG MAMA *has turned toward the hall door at the sound of* BIG DADDY's *voice on the gallery. Now she X's DSR and out the DS door onto the gallery.*)

BIG MAMA. I can't stay here. He'll see somethin' in my eyes.

BIG DADDY (*on upper gallery, to the boys*). Stawm done any damage around here?

BRIGHTIE. Took the po'ch off ole Aunt Crawley's house.

BIG DADDY. Ole Aunt Crawley should of been settin' on it. It's time fo' th' wind to blow that ole girl away! (*Field-hands laugh, exit, UR.* BIG DADDY *enters room,*

UC, *hall door.*) Can I come in? (*Puts his cigar in ash tray on bar.* MAE *and* GOOPER *hurry along the upper gallery and stand behind* BIG DADDY *in hall door.*)

MARGARET. Did the storm wake you up, Big Daddy?

BIG DADDY. Which stawm are you talkin' about—th' one outside or th' hullaballoo in here? (GOOPER *squeezes past* BIG DADDY.)

GOOPER (*X toward bed, where legal papers are strewn*). 'Scuse me, sir . . . (MAE *tries to squeeze past* BIG DADDY *to join* GOOPER, *but* BIG DADDY *puts his arm firmly around her.*)

BIG DADDY. I heard some mighty loud talk. Sounded like somethin' important was bein' discussed. What was the pow-wow about?

MAE (*flustered*). Why—nothin', Big Daddy . . .

BIG DADDY (*XDLC, taking* MAE *with him*). What is that pregnant-lookin' envelope you're puttin' back in your brief-case, Gooper?

GOOPER (*at foot of bed, caught, as he stuffs papers into envelope*). That? Nothin', suh—nothin' much of anythin' at all . . .

BIG DADDY. Nothin'? It looks like a whole lot of nothing! (*Turns US to group.*) You all know th' story about th' young married couple—

GOOPER. Yes, sir!

BIG DADDY. Hello, Brick—

BRICK. Hello, Big Daddy.

(*The group is arranged in a semi-circle above* BIG DADDY, MARGARET *at the extreme R, then* MAE *and* GOOPER, *then* BIG MAMA, *with* BRICK *at L.*)

BIG DADDY. Young married couple took Junior out to th' zoo one Sunday, inspected all of God's creatures in their cages, with satisfaction.

GOOPER. Satisfaction.

BIG DADDY (*XUSC, face front*). This afternoon was a warm afternoon in spring an' that ole elephant had somethin' else on his mind which was bigger'n peanuts. You know this story, Brick? (GOOPER *nods.*)

BRICK. No, sir, I don't know it.

BIG DADDY. Y'see, in th' cage adjoinin' they was a young female elephant in heat!

BIG MAMA (*at* BIG DADDY's *shoulder*). Oh, Big Daddy!

BIG DADDY. What's the matter, preacher's gone, ain't he? All right. That female elephant in the next cage was permeatin' the atmosphere about her with a powerful and excitin' odor of female fertility! Huh! Ain't that a nice way to put it, Brick?

BRICK. Yes, sir, nothin' wrong with it.

BIG DADDY. Brick says the's nothin' wrong with it!

BIG MAMA. Oh, Big Daddy!

BIG DADDY (*XDSC*). So this ole bull elephant still had a couple of fornications left in him. He reared back his trunk an' got a whiff of that elephant lady next door! —began to paw at the dirt in his cage an' butt his head against the separatin' partition and, first thing y'know, there was a conspicuous change in his *profile*—very *conspicuous!* Ain't I tellin' this story in decent language, Brick?

BRICK. Yes, sir, too ruttin' decent!

BIG DADDY. So, the little boy pointed at it and said, "What's that?" His Mam said, "Oh, that's—nothin'!"—His Papa said, "She's spoiled!"

(*Field-hands sing off R, featuring* SOOKEY: *"I Just Can't Stay Here by Myself," through following scene.* BIG DADDY *X to* BRICK *at L.*)

BIG DADDY. You didn't laugh at that story, Brick.

(BIG MAMA *X DRC crying.* MARGARET *goes to her.* MAE *and* GOOPER *hold URC.*)

BRICK. No, sir, I didn't laugh at that story.

(*On the lower gallery,* BIG MAMA *sobs.* BIG DADDY *looks toward her.*)

BIG DADDY. What's wrong with that long, thin woman over there, loaded with diamonds? Hey, what's-your-name, what's the matter with you?

MARGARET (*X toward* BIG DADDY). She had a slight dizzy spell, Big Daddy.

BIG DADDY (*ULC*). You better watch that, Big Mama. A stroke is a bad way to go.

MARGARET (*X to* BIG DADDY *at C*). Oh, Brick, Big Daddy has on your birthday present to him, Brick, he has on your cashmere robe, the softest material I have ever felt.

BIG DADDY. Yeah, this is my soft birthday, Maggie. . . . Not my gold or my silver birthday, but my soft birthday, everything's got to be soft for Big Daddy on this soft birthday.

(MAGGIE *kneels before* BIG DADDY *C. As* GOOPER *and* MAE *speak,* BIG MAMA *X USRC in front of them, hushing them with a gesture.*)

GOOPER. Maggie, I hate to make such a crude observation, but there is somethin' a little indecent about your—

MAE. Like a slow-motion football tackle—

MARGARET. Big Daddy's got on his Chinese slippers that I gave him, Brick. Big Daddy, I haven't given you my big present yet, but now I will, now's the time for me to present it to you! I have an announcement to make!

MAE. What? What kind of announcement?

GOOPER. A sports announcement, Maggie?

MARGARET. Announcement of life beginning! A child is coming, sired by Brick, and out of Maggie the Cat! I have Brick's child in my body, an' that's my birthday present to Big Daddy on this birthday! (BIG DADDY *looks at* BRICK *who X behind* BIG DADDY *to DS portal, L.*)

BIG DADDY. Get up, girl, get up off your knees, girl. (BIG DADDY *helps* MARGARET *rise. He X above her, to her R, bites off the end of a fresh cigar, taken from his bathrobe pocket, as he studies* MARGARET.) *Uh-huh, this girl has life in her body, that's no lie!*

BIG MAMA. BIG DADDY'S DREAM COME TRUE!

BRICK. *JESUS!*

BIG DADDY (*X R below wicker seat*). Gooper, I want my lawyer in the mornin'.

BRICK. Where are you goin', Big Daddy?

BIG DADDY. Son, I'm goin' up on the roof to the belvedere on th' roof to look over my kingdom before I give up my kingdom —twenty-eight thousand acres of th' richest land this side of the Valley Nile! (*Exit through R doors, and DR on gallery.*)

BIG MAMA (*following*). Sweetheart, sweetheart, sweetheart—can I come with you? (*Exits DR.* MARGARET *is DSC in mirror area.*)

GOOPER (*X to bar*). Brick, could you possibly spare me one small shot of that liquor?

BRICK (*DLC*). Why, help yourself, Gooper boy.

GOOPER. I will.

MAE (*X forward*). Of course we know that this is a lie!

GOOPER (*drinks*). Be still, Mae!

MAE (*X to* GOOPER *at bar*). I won't be still! I know she's made this up!

GOOPER. God damn it, I said to shut up!

MAE. That woman isn't pregnant!

GOOPER. Who said she was?

MAE. She did!

GOOPER. The doctor didn't. Doc Baugh didn't.

MARGARET (*X R to above couch*). I haven't gone to Doc Baugh.

GOOPER (*X through to L of* MARGARET). Then who'd you go to, Maggie? (*Offstage song finishes.*)

MARGARET. One of the best gynecologists in the South.

GOOPER. Uh-huh, I see—(*Foot on end of couch, trapping* MARGARET.) May we have his name please?

MARGARET. No, you may not, Mister—Prosecutin' Attorney!

MAE (*X to R of* MARGARET, *above*). He doesn't have any name, he doesn't exist!

MARGARET. He does so exist, and so does my baby, Brick's baby!

MAE. You can't conceive a child by a man that won't sleep with you unless you think you're—(*Forces* MARGARET *onto couch, turns away C.* BRICK *starts C for* MAE.) He drinks all the time to be able to tolerate you! Sleeps on the sofa to keep out of contact with you!

GOOPER (*X above* MARGARET, *who lies face down on couch*). Don't try to kid us, Margaret—

MAE (*X to bed, L side, rumpling pillows*). How can you conceive a child by a man that won't sleep with you? How can you conceive? How can you? How can you!

GOOPER (*sharply*). *MAE!*

BRICK (*X below* MAE *to her R, takes hold of her*). Mae, Sister Woman, how d'you know that I don't sleep with Maggie?

MAE. We occupy the next room an' th' wall between isn't soundproof.

BRICK. Oh . . .

MAE. We hear the nightly pleadin' and the nightly refusal. So don't imagine you're goin' t'put a trick over on us, to fool a dyin' man with—a—

BRICK. Mae, Sister Woman, not everybody makes much noise about love. Oh, I know some people are huffers an' puffers, but others are silent lovers.

GOOPER (*behind seat, R*). This talk is pointless, completely.

BRICK. How d'y'know that we're not silent lovers? Even if y'got a peep-hole drilled in the wall, how can y'tell if sometime when Gooper's got business in Memphis an' you're playin' scrabble at the country club with other ex-queens of cotton,

Maggie and I don't come to some temporary agreement? How do you know that—? (*He X above wicker seat to above R end couch.*)

MAE. Brick, I never thought that you would stoop to her level, I just never dreamed that you would stoop to her level.

GOOPER. I don't think Brick will stoop to her level.

BRICK (*sits R of* MARGARET *on couch*). What is your level? Tell me your level so I can sink or rise to it. (*Rises.*) You heard what Big Daddy said. This girl has life in her body.

MAE. That is a lie!

BRICK. No, truth is something desperate, an' she's got it. Believe me, it's somethin' desperate, an' she's got it. (*X below seat to below bar.*) An' now if you will stop actin' as if Brick Pollitt was dead an' buried, invisible, not heard, an' go on back to your peep-hole in the wall—I'm drunk, and sleepy—not as alive as Maggie, but still alive. . . . (*Pours drink, drinks.*)

GOOPER (*picks up briefcase from R foot of bed*). Come on, Mae. We'll leave these love birds together in their nest.

MAE. Yeah, nest of lice! Liars!

GOOPER. Mae—Mae, you jes' go on back to our room—

MAE. Liars! (*Exits through hall.*)

GOOPER (*DR above* MARGARET). We're jest goin' to wait an' see. Time will tell. (*X to R of bar.*) Yes, sir, little brother, we're just goin' to wait an' see! (*Exit, hall. The clock strikes twelve.*

(MAGGIE *and* BRICK *exchange a look. He drinks deeply, puts his glass on the bar. Gradually, his expression changes. He utters a sharp exhalation. The exhalation is echoed by the singers, off UR, who commence vocalizing with "Gimme a Cool Drink of Water Fo' I Die," and continue till end of act.*)

MARGARET (*as she hears* BRICK's *exhalation*). The click?

(BRICK *looks toward the singers, happily, almost gratefully. He XR to bed, picks up his pillow, and starts toward head of couch, DR, Xing wicker seat.* MARGARET *seizes the pillow from his grasp, rises, stands facing C, holding the pillow close.* BRICK *watches her with growing admiration. She moves quickly USC, throwing pillow onto bed. She X to bar.* BRICK *counters below wicker seat, watching her.* MARGARET *grabs all the bottles from the bar. She goes into hall, pitches the bottles, one after the other, off the platform into the UL lawn area. Bottles break, off L.* MARGARET *reenters the room, stands UC, facing* BRICK.) Echo Spring has gone dry, and no one but me could drive you to town for more.

BRICK. Lacey will get me—

MARGARET. Lacey's been told not to!

BRICK. I could drive—

MARGARET. And you lost your driver's license! I'd phone ahead and have you stopped on the highway before you got halfway to Ruby Lightfoot's gin mill. I told a lie to Big Daddy, but we can make that lie come true. And then I'll bring you liquor, and we'll get drunk together, here, tonight, in this place that death has come into! What do you say? What do you say, baby?

BRICK (*X to L side bed*). I admire you, Maggie.

(BRICK *sits on edge of bed. He looks up at the overhead light, then at* MARGARET. *She reaches for the light, turns it out; then she kneels quickly beside* BRICK *at foot of bed.*)

MARGARET. Oh, you weak, beautiful people who give up with such grace. What you need is someone to take hold of you—gently, with love, and hand your life back to you, like something gold you let go of—and I can! I'm determined to do it—and nothing's more determined than a cat on a tin roof—is there? Is there, baby? (*She touches his cheek, gently.*)

CURTAIN

THE ROSE TATTOO

Tennessee Williams

First presented by Cheryl Crawford at the Martin Beck Theatre in
New York, on February 3, 1951, with the following cast:

SALVATORE Salvatore Mineo	TERESA Nancy Franklin
VIVI Judy Ratner	FATHER DE LEO Robert Carricart
BRUNO Salvatore Taormina	A DOCTOR Andrew Duggan
ASSUNTA Ludmilla Toretzka	MISS YORK Dorrit Kelton
ROSA DELLE ROSE Phyllis Love	FLORA Jane Hoffman
SERAFINA DELLE ROSE Maureen Stapleton	BESSIE Florence Sundstrom
ESTELLE HOHENGARTEN Sonia Sorel	JACK HUNTER Don Murray
THE STREGA Daisy Belmore	THE SALESMAN Eddie Hyans
GIUSEPPINA Rossana San Marco	ALVARO MANGIACAVALLO Eli Wallach
PEPPINA Augusta Merighi	A MAN David Stewart
VIOLETTA Vivian Nathan	ANOTHER MAN Martin Balsam
MARIELLA Penny Santon	

ACT ONE. SCENE 1: Evening. SCENE 2: Almost morning, the next
day. SCENE 3: Noon of that day. SCENE 4: A late spring morning,
three years later. SCENE 5: Immediately following. SCENE 6:
Two hours later that day.

ACT TWO. SCENE 1: Two hours later that day.

ACT THREE. SCENE 1: Evening of the same day. SCENE 2: Just
before dawn of the next day. SCENE 3: Morning.

INTRODUCTION

The Rose Tattoo, a less formidable play than *Cat on a Hot Tin Roof*, which followed it, or *A Streetcar Named Desire*, which preceded it, was among other things Tennessee Williams' answer to critics who thought he could draw only faded women of the South and was responsive only to the poetry of decay in Dixieland. Attracted to vitality as much as to its loss, Mr. Williams had early developed a regard for Latin characters; and their exuberant way of life had charms for him that competed for his attention with the female neurotics of the Southern aristocracy. The result of this attraction was one of his most vivid heroines, Serafina, and the bizarre drama he compounded with her had humor and tenderness and some frenetic quasi-heroic pathos. The play enjoyed success on Broadway, although it was judged as a distinctly smaller achievement than *Streetcar*, and subsequently attracted considerable attention in Europe even before becoming a motion picture utilizing Anna Magnani's tempestuous talents. The stage work had its European premiere in the fall of 1952 at the Thalia-Theater in Hamburg, Germany, and was greeted with enthusiasm in the production staged by Leo Mittler. One Hamburg newspaper, which commended the "naiveté," "wildness" or passion, and "lovableness" of *The Rose Tattoo*, supplied an apt description in calling it a "tragicomedy."

Williams, who already possessed an international reputation by then, was believed to have enlarged it with *The Rose Tattoo*, an opinion that exceeded most expectations entertained in New York. But it is possible that Broadway saw less than there was in the play just as Europe may have seen too much in it. While writing a racy work on the surface, its author came close to primal matters. Like D. H. Lawrence, he suggested a mystical connection between sexuality and religiosity or instinctive, ritualistic relation to the universe. Of Serafina the director-critic Harold Clurman remarked that she was "tempestuously emotional, but also innocent, childlike and almost wise." Her sexual drive, he added, "has no petty sensuosity but burns like a sacred flame; licentiousness shocks her like a blasphemy."

In New York, the most weighty opinion in favor of the play was Brooks Atkinson's, who described it in the Sunday *Times* as a "segment of human life torn out of the universe and put on the stage intact—observed and recorded by an artist and not forced into any pattern." And Mr. Atkinson noted a quality of lyricism in the speech and dramaturgy that could not be overlooked without giving *The Rose Tattoo* less than its due: "Behind the fury and uproar of the characters are the eyes, ears, and mind of a lyric dramatist who has brought into the theatre a new freedom of style. Out of the lives of some simple human beings Mr. Williams has composed a song of earth." Certainly the author, attached to prototypes of his Sicilian characters and invigorated by their vivacity, had not stinted on the abundance and bustle of the life of impulse.

AUTHOR'S PRODUCTION NOTES

*The locale of the play is a village pop-
ulated mostly by Sicilians somewhere along
the Gulf Coast between New Orleans and
Mobile. The time is the present.*

*As the curtain rises we hear a Sicilian
folk-singer with a guitar. He is singing.
At each major division of the play this
song is resumed and it is completed at the
final curtain.*

*The first lighting is extremely romantic.
We see a frame cottage, in a rather poor
state of repair, with a palm tree leaning
dreamily over one end of it and a flimsy
little entrance porch, with spindling pillars, sagging steps and broken rails, at the
other end. The setting seems almost tropical, for, in addition to the palm trees, there
are tall canes with feathery fronds and a
fairly thick growth of pampas grass. These
are growing on the slope of an embankment along which runs a highway, which
is not visible, but the cars passing on it can
occasionally be heard. The house has a
rear door which cannot be seen. The facing wall of the cottage is either a trans-
parency that lifts for the interior scenes, or
is cut away to reveal the interior.*

*The romantic first lighting is that of late
dusk, the sky a delicate blue with an opalescent shimmer more like water than air.
Delicate points of light appear and disappear like lights reflected in a twilight harbor. The curtain rises well above the low
tin roof of the cottage.*

*We see an interior that is as colorful as a
booth at a carnival. There are many religious articles and pictures of ruby and gilt,
the brass cage of a gaudy parrot, a large
bowl of goldfish, cutglass decanters and
vases, rose-patterned wallpaper and a rose-
colored carpet; everything is exclamatory
in its brightness like the projection of a
woman's heart passionately in love. There
is a small shrine against the wall between
the rooms, consisting of a prie-dieu and a
little statue of the Madonna in a starry
blue robe and gold crown. Before this
burns always a vigil light in its ruby glass
cup. Our purpose is to show these gaudy,
childlike mysteries with sentiment and
humor in equal measure, without ridicule
and with respect for the religious yearn-
ings they symbolize.*

An outdoor sign indicates that SERAFINA,
whose home the cottage is, does "SEWING."

*The interior furnishings give evidence of
this vocation. The most salient feature is
a collection of dressmaker's dummies.
There are at least seven of these life-size
mannequins, in various shapes and attitudes. (They will have to be made especially for the play as their purpose is not
realistic. They have pliable joints so that
their positions can be changed. Their arms
terminate at the wrist. In all their attitudes
there is an air of drama, somewhat like the
poses of declamatory actresses of the old
school.) Principal among them are a
widow and a bride who face each other in
violent attitudes, as though having a shrill
argument, in the parlor. The widow's costume is complete from black-veiled hat to
black slippers. The bride's featureless head
wears a chaplet of orange blossoms from
which is depended a flowing veil of white
marquisette, and her net gown is trimmed
in white satin—lustrous, immaculate.*

*Most of the dummies and sewing equip-
ment are confined to the dining room
which is also* SERAFINA's *work room. In
that room there is a tall cupboard on top
of which are several dusty bottles of im-
ported Sicilian Spumanti.*

ACT ONE

SCENE ONE

*It is the hour that the Italians call
"prima sera," the beginning of dusk. Between the house and the palm tree burns
the female star with an almost emerald
luster.*

*The mothers of the neighborhood are
beginning to call their children home to
supper, in voices near and distant, urgent
and tender, like the variable notes of wind
and water. There are three children:*
BRUNO, SALVATORE, *and* VIVI, *ranged in
front of the house, one with a red paper
kite, one with a hoop, and the little girl
with a doll dressed as a clown. They are in
attitudes of momentary repose, all looking
up at something—a bird or a plane passing
over—as the mothers' voices call them.*

BRUNO. The white flags are flying at the
Coast Guard station.

SALVATORE. That means fair weather.

VIVI. I love fair weather.

GIUSEPPINA. Vivi! Vieni mangiare!

PEPPINA. Salvatore! Come home!

VIOLETTA. Bruno! Come home to supper!
(*The calls are repeated tenderly, musically.*

(*The interior of the house begins to be visible.* SERAFINA DELLE ROSE *is seen on the parlor sofa, waiting for her husband* ROSARIO'S *return. Between the curtains is a table set lovingly for supper; there is wine in a silver ice-bucket and a great bowl of roses.*

(SERAFINA *looks like a plump little Italian opera singer in the role of Madame Butterfly. Her black hair is done in a high pompadour that glitters like wet coal. A rose is held in place by glittering jet hairpins. Her voluptuous figure is sheathed in pale rose silk. On her feet are dainty slippers with glittering buckles and French heels. It is apparent from the way she sits, with such plump dignity, that she is wearing a tight girdle. She sits very erect, in an attitude of forced composure, her ankles daintily crossed and her plump little hands holding a yellow paper fan on which is painted a rose. Jewels gleam on her fingers, her wrists and her ears and about her throat. Expectancy shines in her eyes. For a few moments she seems to be posing for a picture.*

(ROSA DELLE ROSE *appears at the side of the house, near the palm tree.* ROSA, *the daughter of the house, is a young girl of twelve. She is pretty and vivacious, and has about her a particular intensity in every gesture.*)

SERAFINA. Rosa, where are you?

ROSA. Here, Mama.

SERAFINA. What are you doing, cara?

ROSA. I've caught twelve lightning bugs.

(*The cracked voice of* ASSUNTA *is heard approaching.*)

SERAFINA. I hear Assunta! Assunta!

(ASSUNTA *appears and goes into the house,* ROSA *following her in.* ASSUNTA *is an old woman in a gray shawl, bearing a basket of herbs, for she is a fattuchiere, a woman who practices a simple sort of medicine. As she enters the children scatter.*)

ASSUNTA. Vengo, vengo. Buona sera. Buona sera. There is something wild in the air, no wind but everything's moving.

SERAFINA. I don't see nothing moving and neither do you.

ASSUNTA. Nothing is moving so you can see it moving, but everything is moving, and I can hear the star-noises. Hear them? Hear the star-noises?

SERAFINA. Naw, them ain't the star-noises. They're termites, eating the house up. What are you peddling, old woman, in those little white bags?

ASSUNTA. Powder, wonderful powder. You drop a pinch of it in your husband's coffee.

SERAFINA. What is it good for?

ASSUNTA. What is a husband good for! I make it out of the dry blood of a goat.

SERAFINA. Davero!

ASSUNTA. Wonderful stuff! But be sure you put it in his coffee at supper, not in his breakfast coffee.

SERAFINA. My husband don't need no powder!

ASSUNTA. Excuse me, Baronessa. Maybe he needs the opposite kind of a powder, I got that, too.

SERAFINA. Naw, naw, *no* kind of powder at all, old woman. (*She lifts her head with a proud smile.*)

(*Outside the sound of a truck is heard approaching up on the highway.*)

ROSA (*joyfully*). Papa's truck!

(*They stand listening for a moment, but the truck goes by without stopping.*)

SERAFINA (*to* ASSUNTA). That wasn't him. It wasn't no 10-ton truck. It didn't rattle the shutters! Assunta, Assunta, undo a couple of hooks, the dress is tight on me!

ASSUNTA. Is it true what I told you?

SERAFINA. Yes, it is true, but nobody needed to tell me. Assunta, I'll tell you something which maybe you won't believe.

ASSUNTA. It is impossible to tell me anything that I don't believe.

SERAFINA. Va bene! Senti, Assunta!—I knew that I had conceived on the very night of conception! (*There is a phrase of music as she says this.*)

ASSUNTA. Ahhhh?

SERAFINA. Senti! That night I woke up with a burning pain on me, here, on my left breast! A pain like a needle, quick, quick, hot little stitches. I turned on the light, I uncovered my breast!—On it I saw the rose tattoo of my husband!

ASSUNTA. Rosario's tattoo?

SERAFINA. On me, on my breast, his tattoo! And when I saw it I knew that I had conceived . . .

(SERAFINA *throws her head back, smiling proudly, and opens her paper fan.* ASSUNTA *stares at her gravely, then rises and hands her basket to* SERAFINA.)

ASSUNTA. Ecco! *You* sell the powders! (*She starts toward the door.*)

SERAFINA. You don't believe that I saw it?

ASSUNTA (*stopping*). Did Rosario see it?

SERAFINA. I screamed. But when he woke up, it was gone. It only lasted a moment. But I *did* see it, and I *did* know, when I seen it, that I had conceived, that in my body another rose was growing!

ASSUNTA. Did he believe that you saw it?

SERAFINA. No. He laughed.—He laughed and I cried . . .

ASSUNTA. And he took you into his arms, and you stopped crying!

SERAFINA. Si!

ASSUNTA. Serafina, for you everything has got to be different. A sign, a miracle, a wonder of some kind. You speak to Our Lady. You say that She answers your questions. She nods or shakes Her head at you. Look, Serafina, underneath Our Lady you have a candle. The wind through the shutters makes the candle flicker. The shadows move. Our Lady seems to be nodding!

SERAFINA. She gives me signs.

ASSUNTA. Only to you? Because you are most important? The wife of a barone? Serafina! In Sicily they called his uncle a baron, but in Sicily everybody's a baron that owns a piece of land and a separate house for the goats!

SERAFINA. They said to his uncle "Voscenza!" and they kissed their hands to him! (*She kisses the back of her hand repeatedly, with vehemence.*)

ASSUNTA. His uncle in Sicily!—Si—But *here* what's he do? Drives a truck of bananas?

SERAFINA (*blurting out*). No! *Not* bananas!

ASSUNTA. Not bananas?

SERAFINA. Stai zitta (*She makes a warning gesture.*)—No—Vieni qui, Assunta! (*She beckons her mysteriously.* ASSUNTA *approaches.*)

ASSUNTA. Cosa dici?

SERAFINA. On top of the truck is bananas! But underneath—something else!

ASSUNTA. Che altre cose?

SERAFINA. Whatever it is that the Brothers Romano want hauled out of the state, he hauls it for them, underneath the bananas! (*She nods her head importantly.*) And money, he gets so much it spills from his pockets! Soon I don't have to make dresses!

ASSUNTA (*turning away*). Soon I think you will have to make a black veil!

SERAFINO. Tonight is the last time he does it! Tomorrow he quits hauling stuff for the Brothers Romano! He pays for the 10-ton truck and works for himself. We live with dignity in America, then! Own truck! Own house! And in the house will be everything electric! Stove—deep-freeze—*tutto!*—But tonight, stay with me . . . I can't swallow my heart!—Not till I hear the truck stop in front of the house and his key in the lock of the door!—When I call him, and him shouting back, *"Si, sono qui!"* In his hair, Assunta, he has—oil of roses. And when I wake up at night—the air, the dark room's—full of—roses. . . . Each time is the first time with him. Time doesn't pass. . . .

(ASSUNTA *picks up a small clock on the cupboard and holds it to her ear.*)

ASSUNTA. Tick, tick, tick, tick.—You say the clock is a liar.

SERAFINA. No, the clock is a fool. I don't listen to it. My clock is my heart and my heart don't say tick-tick, it says love-love! And now I have two hearts in me, both of them saying love-love!

(*A truck is heard approaching, then passes.* SERAFINA *drops her fan.* ASSUNTA *opens a bottle of Spumanti with a loud pop.* SERAFINA *cries out.*)

ASSUNTA. Stai tranquilla! Calmati! (*She pours her a glass of wine.*) Drink this wine and before the glass is empty he'll be in your arms!

SERAFINA. I can't—swallow my heart!

ASSUNTA. A woman must not have a heart that is too big to swallow! (*She crosses to the door.*)

SERAFINA. Stay with me!

ASSUNTA. I have to visit a woman who drank rat poison because of a heart too big for her to swallow.

(ASSUNTA *leaves.* SERAFINA *returns indolently to the sofa. She lifts her hands to her great swelling breasts and murmurs aloud:*)

SERAFINA. Oh, it's so wonderful, having *two* lives in the body, not *one* but two! (*Her hands slide down to her belly, luxuriously.*) I am heavy with life, I am big, big, big with life! (*She picks up a bowl of roses and goes into the back room.*)

(ESTELLE HOHENGARTEN *appears in front of the house. She is a thin blonde woman in a dress of Egyptian design, and her blonde hair has an unnatural gloss in the clear, greenish dusk.* ROSA *appears from behind the house, calling out:)*

ROSA. Twenty lightning bugs, Mama!

ESTELLE. Little girl? Little girl?

ROSA *(resentfully).* Are you talking to me? *(There is a pause.)*

ESTELLE. Come here. *(She looks* ROSA *over curiously.)* You're a twig off the old rose-bush.—Is the lady that does the sewing in the house?

ROSA. Mama's at home.

ESTELLE. I'd like to see her.

ROSA. Mama?

SERAFINA. Dimi?

ROSA. There's a lady to see you.

SERAFINA. Oh. Tell her to wait in the parlor. *(*ESTELLE *enters and stares curiously about. She picks up a small framed picture on the cupboard. She is looking at it as* SERAFINA *enters with a bowl of roses.* SERAFINA *speaks sharply.)* That is my husband's picture.

ESTELLE. Oh!—I thought it was Valentino.—With a mustache.

SERAFINA *(putting the bowl down on the table).* You want something?

ESTELLE. Yes. I heard you do sewing.

SERAFINA. Yes, I do sewing.

ESTELLE. How fast can you make a shirt for me?

SERAFINA. That all depends. *(She takes the picture from* ESTELLE *and puts it back on the cupboard.)*

ESTELLE. I got the piece of silk with me. I want it made into a shirt for a man I'm in love with. Tomorrow's the anniversary of the day we met. . . . *(She unwraps a piece of rose-colored silk which she holds up like a banner.)*

SERAFINA *(involuntarily).* Che bella stoffa!—Oh, that would be wonderful stuff for a lady's blouse or for a pair of pyjamas!

ESTELLE. I want a man's shirt made with it.

SERAFINA. Silk this color for a shirt for a *man?*

ESTELLE. This man is wild like a Gypsy.

SERAFINA. A woman should not encourage a man to be wild.

ESTELLE. A man that's wild is hard for a woman to hold, huh? But if he was tame—would the woman want to hold him? Huh?

SERAFINA. I am a married woman in business. I don't know nothing about wild

men and wild women and I don't have much time—so . . .

ESTELLE. I'll pay you twice what you ask me.

(Outside there is the sound of the goat bleating and the jingle of its harness; then the crash of wood splintering.)

ROSA *(suddenly appearing at the door).* Mama, the black goat is loose! *(She runs down the steps and stands watching the goat.* SERAFINA *crosses to the door.)*

THE STREGA *(in the distance).* Hyeh, Billy, hyeh, hyeh, Billy!

ESTELLE. I'll pay you three times the price that you ask me for it.

SERAFINA *(shouting).* Watch the goat! Don't let him get in our yard! *(To* ESTELLE*)*—if I ask you five dollars?

ESTELLE. I will pay you fifteen. Make it twenty; money is not the object. But it's got to be ready tomorrow.

SERAFINA. Tomorrow?

ESTELLE. Twenty-five dollars! *(*SERAFINA *nods slowly with a stunned look.* ESTELLE *smiles.)* I've got the measurements with me.

SERAFINA. Pin the measurements and your name on the silk and the shirt will be ready tomorrow.

ESTELLE. My name is Estelle Hohengarten.

(A little boy races excitedly into the yard.)

THE BOY. Rosa, Rosa, the black goat's in your yard!

ROSA *(calling).* Mama, the goat's in the yard!

SERAFINA *(furiously, forgetting her visitor).* Il becco della strega!—Scusi! *(She runs out onto the porch.)* Catch him, catch him before he gets at the vines!

*(*ROSA *dances gleefully.* THE STREGA *runs into the yard. She has a mop of wild gray hair and is holding her black skirts up from her bare hairy legs. The sound of the goat's bleating and the jingling of his harness is heard in the windy blue dusk.*

*(*SERAFINA *descends the porch steps. The high-heeled slippers, the tight silk skirt and the dignity of a baronessa make the descent a little gingerly. Arrived in the yard, she directs the goat-chase imperiously with her yellow paper fan, pointing this way and that, exclaiming in Italian.*

(She fans herself rapidly and crosses back of the house. The goat evidently makes a sudden charge. Screaming, SERA-

FINA *rushes back to the front of the house, all out of breath, the glittering pompadour beginning to tumble down over her forehead.*)

SERAFINA. Rosa! You go in the house! Don't look at the Strega!

(*Alone in the parlor,* ESTELLE *takes the picture of* ROSARIO. *Impetuously, she thrusts it in her purse and runs from the house, just as* SERAFINA *returns to the front yard.*)

ROSA (*refusing to move*). Why do you call her a witch?

(SERAFINA *seizes her daughter's arm and propels her into the house.*)

SERAFINA. She has a white eye and every finger is crooked. (*She pulls* ROSA'S *arm.*)

ROSA. She has a cataract, Mama, and her fingers are crooked because she has rheumatism!

SERAFINA. Malocchio—the evil eye—*that's* what she's got! And her fingers are crooked because she shook hands with the devil. Go in the house and wash your face with salt water and throw the salt water away! *Go in! Quickly!* She's coming!

(*The boy utters a cry of triumph.*

(SERAFINA *crosses abruptly to the porch. At the same moment the boy runs triumphantly around the house leading the captured goat by its bell harness. It is a middle-sized black goat with great yellow eyes.* THE STREGA *runs behind with the broken rope. As the grotesque little procession runs before her*—THE STREGA, *the goat and the children*—SERAFINA *cries out shrilly. She crouches over and covers her face.* THE STREGA *looks back at her with a derisive cackle.*)

SERAFINA. Malocchio! Malocchio!

(*Shielding her face with one hand,* SERAFINA *makes the sign of the horns with the other to ward off the evil eye. And the scene dims out.*)

SCENE TWO

It is just before dawn the next day. FATHER DE LEO, *a priest, and several blackshawled women, including* ASSUNTA, *are standing outside the house. The interior of the house is very dim.*

GIUSEPPINA. There is a light in the house.
PEPPINA. I hear the sewing machine!
VIOLETTA. There's Serafina! She's working. She's holding up a piece of rose-

colored silk.

ASSUNTA. She hears our voices.

VIOLETTA. She's dropped the silk to the floor and she's . . .

GIUSEPPINA. Holding her throat! I think she . . .

PEPPINA. Who's going to tell her?

VIOLETTA. Father De Leo will tell her.

FATHER DE LEO. I think a woman should tell her. I think Assunta must tell her that Rosario is dead.

ASSUNTA. It will not be necessary to tell her. She will know when she sees us.

(*It grows lighter inside the house.* SERAFINA *is standing in a frozen attitude with her hand clutching her throat and her eyes staring fearfully toward the sound of voices.*)

ASSUNTA. I think she already knows what we have come to tell her!

FATHER DE LEO. Andiamo, Signore! We must go to the door.

(*They climb the porch steps.* ASSUNTA *opens the door.*)

SERAFINA (*gasping*). Don't speak!

(*She retreats from the group, stumbling blindly backwards among the dressmaker's dummies. With a gasp she turns and runs out the back door. In a few moments we see her staggering about outside near the palm tree. She comes down in front of the house, and stares blindly off into the distance.*)

SERAFINA (*wildly*). Don't speak!

(*The voices of the women begin keening in the house.* ASSUNTA *comes out and approaches* SERAFINA *with her arms extended.* SERAFINA *slumps to her knees, whispering hoarsely:* "Don't speak!" ASSUNTA *envelopes her in the gray shawl of pity as the scene dims out.*)

SCENE THREE

It is noon of the same day. ASSUNTA *is removing a funeral wreath on the door of the house. A* DOCTOR *and* FATHER DE LEO *are on the porch.*

THE DOCTOR. She's lost the baby. (ASSUNTA *utters a low moan of pity and crosses herself.*) Serafina's a very strong woman and that won't kill her. But she is trying not to breathe. She's got to be watched and not allowed out of the bed. (*He removes a hypodermic and a small package from his bag and hands them to* ASSUNTA.)—This is morphia. In the arm with the needle if she screams or struggles to get up again.

ASSUNTA. Capisco!

FATHER DE LEO. One thing I want to make plain. The body of Rosario must not be burned.

THE DOCTOR. Have you seen the "body of Rosario?"

FATHER DE LEO. Yes, I have seen his body.

THE DOCTOR. Wouldn't you say it was burned?

FATHER DE LEO. Of course the body was burned. When he was shot at the wheel of the truck, it crashed and caught fire. But deliberate cremation is not the same thing. It's an abomination in the sight of God.

THE DOCTOR. Abominations are something I don't know about.

FATHER DE LEO. The Church has set down certain laws.

THE DOCTOR. But the instructions of a widow have to be carried out.

FATHER DE LEO. Don't you know why she wants the body cremated? So she can keep the ashes here in the house.

THE DOCTOR. Well, why not, if that's any comfort to her?

FATHER DE LEO. Pagan idolatry is what I call it!

THE DOCTOR. Father De Leo, you love your people but you don't understand them. They find God in each other. And when they lose each other, they lose God and they're lost. And it's hard to help them—Who is that woman?

(ESTELLE HOHENGARTEN *has appeared before the house. She is black-veiled, and bearing a bouquet of roses.*)

ESTELLE. I am Estelle Hohengarten.

(*Instantly there is a great hubbub in the house. The women mourners flock out to the porch, whispering and gesticulating excitedly.*)

FATHER DE LEO. What have you come here for?

ESTELLE. To say good-by to the body.

FATHER DE LEO. The casket is closed; the body cannot be seen. And you must never come here. The widow knows nothing about you. Nothing at all.

GIUSEPPINA. *We* know about you!

PEPPINA. Va via! Sporcacciona!

VIOLETTA. Puttana!

MARIELLA. Assassina!

TERESA. You sent him to the Romanos.

FATHER DE LEO. Shhh!

(*Suddenly the women swarm down the steps like a cloud of attacking birds, all crying out in Sicilian.* ESTELLE *crouches and bows her head defensively before their savage assault. The bouquet of roses is snatched from her black-gloved hands and she is flailed with them about the head and shoulders. The thorns catch her veil and tear it away from her head. She covers her white sobbing face with her hands.*)

FATHER DE LEO. Ferme! Ferme! Signore, fermate vi nel nome di Dio!—Have a little respect!

(*The women fall back from* ESTELLE, *who huddles weeping on the walk.*)

ESTELLE. See him, see him, just see him. . . .

FATHER DE LEO. The body is crushed and burned. Nobody can see it. Now go away and don't ever come here again, Estelle Hohengarten!

THE WOMEN (*in both languages, wildly*). Va via, va via, go way.

(ROSA *comes around the house.* ESTELLE *turns and retreats. One of the mourners spits and kicks at the tangled veil and roses.* FATHER DE LEO *leaves. The others return inside, except* ROSA.

(*After a few moments the child goes over to the roses. She picks them up and carefully untangles the veil from the thorns.*

(*She sits on the sagging steps and puts the black veil over her head. Then for the first time she begins to weep, wildly, histrionically. The little boy appears and gazes at her, momentarily impressed by her performance. Then he picks up a rubber ball and begins to bounce it.*

(ROSA *is outraged. She jumps up, tears off the veil and runs to the little boy, giving him a sound smack and snatching the ball away from him.*)

ROSA. Go home! My papa is dead!

(*The scene dims out, as the music is heard again.*)

SCENE FOUR

A June day, three years later. It is morning and the light is bright. A group of local mothers are storming SERAFINA'S *house, indignant over her delay in delivering the graduation dresses for their daughters. Most of the women are chattering continually in Sicilian, racing about the house and banging the doors and shutters. The scene moves swiftly and violently until the moment when* ROSA *finally comes out in her graduation dress.*

———

GIUSEPPINA. Serafina! Serafina delle Rose!

PEPPINA. Maybe if you call her "Baronessa" she will answer the door. (*With a mocking laugh*) Call her "Baronessa" and kiss your hand to her when she opens the door.

GIUSEPPINA (*tauntingly*). Baronessa! (*She kisses her hand toward the door.*)

VIOLETTA. When did she promise your dress?

PEPPINA. All week she say, "Domani—domani—domani." But yestiddy I told her . . .

VIOLETTA. Yeah?

PEPPINA. Oh yeah. I says to her, "Serafina, domani's the high school graduation. I got to try the dress on my daughter *today*." "Domani," she says, "Sicuro! Sicuro! Sicuro!" So I start to go away. Then I hear a voice call, "Signora! Signora!" So I turn round and I see Serafina's daughter at the window.

VIOLETTA. Rosa?

PEPPINA. Yeah, Rosa. An' you know how?

VIOLETTA. How?

PEPPINA. *Naked!* Nuda, nuda! (*She crosses herself and repeats a prayer.*) In nominis padri et figlio et spiritus sancti. Aaahh!

VIOLETTA. What did she do?

PEPPINA. Do? She say, "Signora! Please, you call this numero and ask for Jack and tell Jack my clothes are lock up so I can't get out from the house." Then Serafina come and she grab-a the girl by the hair and she pull her way from the window and she slam the shutters right in my face!

GIUSEPPINA. Whatsa the matter the daughter?

VIOLETTA. Who is this boy? Where did she meet him?

PEPPINA. Boy! What boy? He's a sailor. (*At the word "sailor" the women say "Ahhh!"*) She met him at the high school dance and somebody tell Serafina. That's why she lock up the girl's clothes so she can't leave the house. She can't even go to the high school to take the examinations. Imagine!

VIOLETTA. Peppina, this time *you* go to the door, yeah?

PEPPINA. Oh yeah, I go. Now I'm getting nervous. (*The women all crowd to the door.*) Sera-feee-na!

VIOLETTA. Louder, louder!

PEPPINA. Apri la porta! Come on, come on!

THE WOMEN (*together*). Yeah, apri la porta! . . . Come on, hurry up! . . . Open up!

GIUSEPPINA. I go get-a police.

VIOLETTA. Whatsa matta? You want more trouble?

GIUSEPPINA. Listen, I pay in advance five dollars and get no dress. Now what she wear, my daughter, to graduate in? A couple of towels and a rose in the hair? (*There is a noise inside: a shout and running footsteps.*)

THE WOMEN. Something is going on in the house! I hear someone! Don't I? Don't you?

(*A scream and running footsteps are heard. The front door opens and* SERAFINA *staggers out onto the porch. She is wearing a soiled pink slip and her hair is wild.*)

SERAFINA. Aiuto! Aiuto! (*She plunges back into the house.*)

(*Miss Yorke, a spinsterish high school teacher, walks quickly up to the house. The Sicilian women, now all chattering at once like a cloud of birds, sweep about her as she approaches.*)

MISS YORKE. You ladies know I don't understand Italian! So, please. . . .

(*She goes directly into the house. There are more outcries inside.* THE STREGA *comes and stands at the edge of the yard, cackling derisively.*)

THE STREGA (*calling back to someone*). The Wops are at it again!—She got the daughter lock up naked in there all week. Ho, ho, ho! She lock up all week—naked —shouting out the window tell people to call a number and give a message to Jack. Ho, ho, ho! I guess she's in trouble already, and only fifteen!—They ain't civilized, these Sicilians. In the old country they live in caves in the hills and the country's run by bandits. Ho, ho, ho! More of them coming over on the boats all the time.

(*The door is thrown open again and* SERAFINA *reappears on the porch. She is acting wildly, as if demented.*)

SERAFINA (*gasping in a hoarse whisper*). She cut her wrist, my daughter, she cut her wrist! (*She runs out into the yard.*) Aiiii-eeee! Aiutatemi, aiutatemi! Call the dottore! (ASSUNTA *rushes up to* SERAFINA *and supports her as she is about to fall to her knees in the yard.*) Get the knife away from her! Get the knife, please! Get the knife away from—she cut her wrist with—Madonna! Madonna mia . . .

ASSUNTA. Smettila, smettila, Serafina.

MISS YORKE (*coming out of the back room*). Mrs. Delle Rose, your daughter has not cut her wrist. Now come back into the house.

SERAFINA (*panting*). Che dice, che dice? Che cosa? Che cosa dice?

MISS YORKE. Your daughter's all right. Come back into the house. And you ladies please go away!

ASSUNTA. Vieni, Serafina. Andiamo a casa. (*She supports the heavy, sagging bulk of* SERAFINA *to the steps. As they climb the steps one of the Sicilian mothers advances from the whispering group.*)

GIUSEPPINA (*boldly*). Serafina, we don't go away until we get our dresses.

PEPPINA. The graduation begins and the girls ain't dressed.

(SERAFINA's *reply to this ill-timed request is a long, animal howl of misery as she is supported into the house.* MISS YORKE *follows and firmly closes the door upon the women, who then go around back of the house. The interior of the house is lighted up.*)

MISS YORKE (*to* SERAFINA). No, no, no, she's not bleeding. Rosa? Rosa, come here and show your mother that you are not bleeding to death.

(ROSA *appears silently and sullenly between the curtains that separate the two rooms. She has a small white handkerchief tied around one wrist.* SERAFINA *points at the wrist and cries out: "Aiieee!"*)

MISS YORKE (*severely*). Now *stop* that, Mrs. Delle Rose!

(SERAFINA *rushes to* ROSA, *who thrusts her roughly away.*)

ROSA. Lasciami stare, Mama!—I'm so ashamed I could die. This is the way she goes around all the time. She hasn't put on clothes since my father was killed. For three years she sits at the sewing machine and never puts a dress on or goes out of the house, and now she has locked my clothes up so *I* can't go out. She wants me to be like her, a freak of the neighborhood, the way she is! Next time, next time, I

won't cut my wrist but my throat! I don't want to live locked up with a bottle of ashes! (*She points to the shrine.*)

ASSUNTA. Figlia, figlia, figlia, non devi parlare cosi!

MISS YORKE. Mrs. Delle Rose, please give me the key to the closet so that your daughter can dress for the graduation!

SERAFINA (*surrendering the key*). Ecco la—chiave . . . (ROSA *snatches the key and runs back through the curtains.*)

MISS YORKE. Now why did you lock her clothes up, Mrs. Delle Rose?

SERAFINA. The wrist is still bleeding!

MISS YORKE. No, the wrist is not bleeding. It's just a skin cut, a scratch. But the child is exhausted from all this excitement and hasn't eaten a thing in two or three days.

ROSA (*running into the dining room*). Four days! I only asked her one favor. Not to let me go out but to let Jack come to the house so she could meet him!—Then she locked my clothes up!

MISS YORKE. Your daughter missed her final examinations at the high school, but her grades have been so good that she will be allowed to graduate with her class and take the examinations later.—You understand me, Mrs. Delle Rose!

(ROSA *goes into the back of the house.*)

SERAFINA (*standing at the curtains*). See the way she looks at me? I've got a wild thing in the house, and her wrist is still bleeding!

MISS YORKE. Let's not have any more outbursts of emotion!

SERAFINA. Outbursts of—you make me sick! Sick! Sick at my stomach you make me! Your school, you make all this trouble! You give-a this dance where she gets mixed up with a sailor.

MISS YORKE. You are talking about the Hunter girl's brother, a sailor named Jack, who attended the dance with his sister?

SERAFINA. "Attended with sister!"—Attended with *sister!*—My daughter, she's nobody's sister!

(ROSA *comes out of the back room. She is radiantly beautiful in her graduation gown.*)

ROSA. Don't listen to her, don't pay any attention to her, Miss Yorke.—I'm ready to go to the high school.

SERAFINA (*stunned by her daughter's beauty, and speaking with a wheedling tone and gestures, as she crouches a little*).

O tesoro, tesoro! Vieni qua, Rosa, cara!—
Come here and kiss Mama one minute!—
Don't go like that, now!

ROSA. Lasciami stare!

(*She rushes out on the porch.* SERAFINA *gazes after her with arms slowly drooping from their imploring gesture and jaw dropping open in a look of almost comic desolation.*)

SERAFINA. Ho solo te, solo te—in questo mondo!

MISS YORKE. Now, now, Mrs. Delle Rose, no more excitement, please!

SERAFINA (*suddenly plunging after them in a burst of fury*). Senti, senti, per favore!

ROSA. Don't you dare come out on the street like that!—*Mama!*

(*She crouches and covers her face in shame, as* SERAFINA *heedlessly plunges out into the front yard in her shocking deshabille, making wild gestures.*)

SERAFINA. You give this dance where she gets mixed up with a sailor. What do you think you want to do at this high school? (*In weeping despair,* ROSA *runs to the porch.*) How high is this high school? Listen, how high is this high school? Look, look, look, I will show you! It's high as the horse's dirt out there in the street! (SERAFINA *points violently out in front of the house.*) Si! 'Sta fetentissima scuola! Scuola maledetta!

(ROSA *cries out and rushes over to the palm tree, leaning against it, with tears of mortification.*)

MISS YORKE. Mrs. Delle Rose, you are talking and behaving extremely badly. I don't understand how a woman that acts like you could have such a sweet and refined young girl for a daughter!—You don't deserve it!—Really . . . (*She crosses to the palm tree.*)

SERAFINA. Oh, you want me to talk refined to you? Then do me one thing! Stop ruining the girls at the high school!

(*As* SERAFINA *paces about, she swings her hips in the exaggeratedly belligerent style of a parading matador.*)

ASSUNTA. Piantala, Serafina! Andiamo a casa!

SERAFINA. No, no, I ain't through talking to this here teacher!

ASSUNTA. Serafina, look at yourself, you're not dressed!

SERAFINA. I'm dressed okay; I'm not naked! (*She glares savagely at the teacher by the palm tree. The Sicilian mothers return to the front yard.*)

ASSUNTA. Serafina, cara? Andiamo a casa, adesso!—Basta! Basta!

SERAFINA. Aspetta!

ROSA. I'm so ashamed I could die, I'm so ashamed. Oh, you don't know, Miss Yorke, the way that we live. She never puts on a dress; she stays all the time in that dirty old pink slip!—And talks to my father's ashes like he was living.

SERAFINA. Teacher! Teacher, senti! What do you think you want to do at this high school? Sentite! per favore! You give this dance! What kind of a spring dance is it? Answer this question, please, for me! What kind of a spring dance is it? She meet this boy there who don't even go to no high school. What kind of a boy? Guardate! *A sailor that wears a gold earring!* That kind of a boy is the kind of boy she meets there!—That's why I lock her clothes up so she can't go back to the high school! (*Suddenly to* ASSUNTA) She cut her wrist! It's still bleeding! (*She strikes her forehead three times with her fist.*)

ROSA. Mama, you look disgusting! (*She rushes away.*)

(MISS YORKE *rushes after her.* SERAFINA *shades her eyes with one hand to watch them departing down the street in the brilliant spring light.*)

SERAFINA. Did you hear what my daughter said to me?—"You look—disgusting." —She calls me . . .

ASSUNTA. Now, Serafina, we must go in the house. (*She leads her gently to the porch of the little house.*)

SERAFINA (*proudly*). How pretty she look, my daughter, in the white dress, like a bride! (*To all*) Excuse me! Excuse me, please! Go away! Get out of my yard!

GIUSEPPINA (*taking the bull by the horns*). No, we ain't going to go without the dresses!

ASSUNTA. Give the ladies the dresses so the girls can get dressed for the graduation.

SERAFINA. That one there, she only paid for the goods. I charge for the work.

GIUSEPPINA. Ecco! I got the money!

THE WOMEN. We *got* the money!

SERAFINA. The names are pinned on the dresses. Go in and get them. (*She turns to* ASSUNTA.) Did you hear what my daughter called me? She called me "disgusting!"

(SERAFINA *enters the house, slamming*

*the door. After a moment the mothers
come out, cradling the white voile dresses
tenderly in their arms, murmuring "ca-
rino!" and "bellissimo!"*

*(As they disappear the inside light is
brought up and we see* SERAFINA *standing
before a glazed mirror, looking at herself
and repeating the daughter's word.)*

SERAFINA. Disgusting!

*(The music is briefly resumed to mark
a division.)*

SCENE FIVE

Immediately following. SERAFINA'S *movements gather momentum. She snatches a
long-neglected girdle out of a bureau
drawer and holds it experimentally about
her waist. She shakes her head doubtfully,
drops the girdle and suddenly snatches the
$8.98 hat off the millinery dummy and
plants it on her head. She turns around
distractedly, not remembering where the
mirror is. She gasps with astonishment
when she catches sight of herself, snatches
the hat off and hastily restores it to the
blank head of the dummy. She makes another confused revolution or two, then
gasps with fresh inspiration and snatches
a girlish frock off a dummy—an Alice
blue gown with daisies crocheted on it.
The dress sticks on the dummy.* SERAFINA
*mutters savagely in Sicilian. She finally
overcomes this difficulty but in her exas-
perations she knocks the dummy over. She
throws off the robe and steps hopefully
into the gown. But she discovers it won't
fit over her hips. She seizes the girdle
again; then hurls it angrily away. The parrot calls to her; she yells angrily back at
the parrot: "Zitto!"*

*In the distance the high school band
starts playing.* SERAFINA *gets panicky that
she will miss the graduation ceremonies,
and hammers her forehead with her fist,
sobbing a little. She wriggles despairingly
out of the blue dress and runs out back in
her rayon slip as* FLORA *and* BESSIE *appear
outside the house.* FLORA *and* BESSIE *are
two female clowns of middle years and
juvenile temperament.* FLORA *is tall and
angular;* BESSIE *is rather stubby. They are
dressed for a gala.* FLORA *runs up the steps
and bangs at the cottage door.*

BESSIE. I fail to understand why it's so
important to pick up a polka-dot blouse
when it's likely to make us miss the twelve
o'clock train.

FLORA. Serafina! Serafina!

BESSIE. We only got fifteen minutes to
get to the depot and I'll get faint on the
train if I don't have m' coffee . . .

FLORA. Git a coke on th' train, Bessie.

BESSIE. Git nothing on the train if we
don't git the train!

*(*SERAFINA *runs back out of the bedroom, quite breathless, in a purple silk
dress. As she passes the millinery dummy
she snatches the hat off again and plants it
back on her head.)*

SERAFINA. Wrist-watch! Wrist-watch!
Where'd I put th' wrist-watch? *(She hears*
FLORA *shouting and banging and rushes to
the door.)*

BESSIE. Try the door if it ain't open.

FLORA *(pushing in)*. Just tell me, is it
ready or not?

SERAFINA. Oh! You. Don't bother me.
I'm late for the graduation of my daughter and now I can't find her graduation
present.

FLORA. You got plenty of time.

SERAFINA. Don't you hear the band playing?

FLORA. They're just warming up. Now,
Serafina, where is my blouse?

SERAFINA. Blouse? Not ready! I had to
make fourteen graduation dresses!

FLORA. A promise is a promise and an
excuse is just an excuse!

SERAFINA. I got to get to the high school!

FLORA. I got to get to the depot in that
blouse!

BESSIE. We're going to the American
Legion parade in New Orleans.

FLORA. There, there, there, there it is!
(She grabs the blouse from the machine.)
Get started, woman, stitch them bandanas
together! If you don't do it, I'm a-gonna
report you to the Chamber of Commerce
and git your license revoked!

SERAFINA *(anxiously)*. What license you
talking about? I got no license!

FLORA. You hear that, Bessie? *She hasn't
got no license!*

BESSIE. *She ain't even got a license?*

SERAFINA *(crosses quickly to the machine)*. I—I'll stitch them together! But if
you make me late to my daughter's graduation, I'll make you sorry some way . . .

*(She works with furious rapidity. A
train whistle is heard.)*

BESSIE (*wildly and striking* FLORA *with her purse*). Train's pullin' out! Oh, God, you made us miss it!

FLORA. Bessie, you know there's another at 12:45!

BESSIE. It's the selfish—principle of it that makes me sick! (*She walks rapidly up and down.*)

FLORA. Set down, Bessie. Don't wear out your feet before we git to th' city . . .

BESSIE. Molly tole me the town was full of excitement. They're dropping paper sacks full of water out of hotel windows.

FLORA. Which hotel are they dropping paper sacks out of?

BESSIE. What a fool question! The Monteleone Hotel.

FLORA. That's an old-fashioned hotel.

BESSIE. It might be old-fashioned but you'd be surprised at some of the modern, up-to-date things that go on there.

FLORA. I heard, I heard that the Legionnaires caught a girl on Canal Street! They tore the clothes off her and sent her home in a taxi!

BESSIE. I double dog dare anybody to try that on me!

FLORA. You? Huh! You never need any assistance gittin' undressed!

SERAFINA (*ominously*). You two ladies watch how you talk in there. This here is a Catholic house. You are sitting in the same room with Our Lady and with the blessed ashes of my husband!

FLORA (*wildly*). Well, ex-cuse *me!* (*She whispers maliciously to* BESSIE.) It sure is a pleasant surprise to see you wearing a dress, Serafina, but the surprise would be twice as pleasant if it was more the right size. (*To* BESSIE, *loudly*) She used to have a sweet figure, a little plump but attractive, but setting there at that sewing machine for three years in a kimona and not stepping out of the house has naturally given her hips!

SERAFINA. If I didn't have hips I would be a very uncomfortable woman when I set down.

(*The parrot squawks.* SERAFINA *imitates its squawk.*)

FLORA. Polly want a cracker?

SERAFINA. No. He don't want a cracker! What is she doing over there at that window?

BESSIE. Some Legionnaires are on the highway!

FLORA. A Legionnaire? No kidding?

(*She springs up and joins her girl friend at the window. They both laugh fatuously, bobbing their heads out the window.*)

BESSIE. He's looking this way; yell something!

FLORA (*leaning out the window*). Mademoiselle from Armentieres, parley-voo!

BESSIE (*chiming in rapturously*). Mademoiselle from Armentieres, parley-voo!

A VOICE OUTSIDE (*gallantly returning the salute*). Mademoiselle from Armentieres, hadn't been kissed for forty years!

BOTH GIRLS (*together; very gaily*). Hinky-dinky parley-voooo!

(*They laugh and applaud at the window. The Legionnaires are heard laughing. A car horn is heard as the Legionnaires drive away.* SERAFINA *springs up and rushes over to the window, jerks them away from it and slams the shutters in their faces.*)

SERAFINA (*furiously*). I told you wimmen that you was not in a honky-tonk! Now take your blouse and git out! Get out on the streets where you kind a wimmen belong.—This is the house of Rosario delle Rose and those are his ashes in that marble urn and I won't have—unproper things going on here or dirty talk neither!

FLORA. Who's talking dirty?

BESSIE. What a helluva nerve.

FLORA. I want you to listen!

SERAFINA. You are, you are, dirty talk, all the time men, men, men! You men-crazy things, you!

FLORA. Sour grapes—sour grapes is your trouble! You're wild with envy!

BESSIE. Isn't she green with jealousy? Huh!

SERAFINA (*suddenly and religiously*). When I think of men I think about my husband. My husband was a Sicilian. We had love together every night of the week, we never skipped one, from the night we was married till the night he was killed in his fruit truck on the road there! (*She catches her breath in a sob*) And maybe that is the reason I'm not man-crazy and don't like hearing the talk of women that are. But I am interested, now, in the happiness of my daughter who's graduating this morning out of high school. And now I'm going to be late, the band is playing! And I have lost her wrist watch!—her graduation present! (*She whirls about distractedly.*)

BESSIE. Flora, let's go!—The hell with

that goddam blouse!

FLORA. Oh, no, just wait a minute! I don't accept insults from no one!

SERAFINA. Go on, go on to New Orleans, you two man-crazy things, you! And pick up a man on Canal Street but not in my house, at my window, in front of my dead husband's ashes! (*The high school band is playing a martial air in the distance.* SERAFINA's *chest is heaving violently; she touches her heart and momentarily seems to forget that she must go.*) I am not at all interested, I am not interested in men getting fat and bald in soldier-boy play suits, tearing clothes off girls on Canal Street and dropping paper sacks out of hotel windows. I'm just not interested in that sort of man-crazy business. I remember my husband with a body like a young boy and hair on his head as thick and black as mine is and skin on him smooth and sweet as a yellow rose petal.

FLORA. Oh, a *rose,* was he?

SERAFINA. Yes, yes, a rose, a rose!

FLORA. Yes, a rose of a Wop!—of a gangster!—shot smuggling dope under a load of bananas!

BESSIE. Flora, Flora, let's go!

SERAFINA. My folks was peasants, contadini, but he—he come from *land*-owners! *Signorile,* my husband!—At night I sit here and I'm satisfied to remember, because I had the best.—Not the third best and not the second best, but the *first* best, the *only* best!—So now I stay here and am satisfied now to remember, . . .

BESSIE. Come on, come out! To the depot!

FLORA. Just wait, I wanta hear this, it's too good to miss!

SERAFINA. I count up the nights I held him all night in my arms, and I can tell you how many. Each night for twelve years. Four thousand—three hundred—and eighty. The number of nights I held him all night in my arms. Sometimes I didn't sleep, just held him all night in my arms. And I am satisfied with it. I grieve for him. Yes, my pillow at night's never dry— but I'm satisfied to remember. And I would feel cheap and degraded and not fit to live with my daughter or under the roof with the urn of his blessed ashes, those— ashes of a rose—if after that memory, after knowing that man, I went to some middle-aged man, not young, not full of young passion, but getting a pot belly on him and losing his hair and smelling of sweat and liquor—and trying to fool myself that *that* was love-making! I *know* what love-making was. And I'm satisfied just to remember . . . (*She is panting as though she had run upstairs.*) Go on, you do it, you go on the streets and let them drop their sacks of dirty water on you!—I'm satisfied to remember the love of a man that was mine—*only mine!* Never touched by the hand of *nobody! Nobody* but *me!*— Just me! (*She gasps and runs out to the porch. The sun floods her figure. It seems to astonish her. She finds herself sobbing. She digs in her purse for her handkerchief.*)

FLORA (*crossing to the open door*). Never touched by nobody?

SERAFINA (*with fierce pride*). Never nobody but me!

FLORA. *I* know somebody that could a tale unfold! And not so far from here neither. Not no further than the Square Roof is, that place on Esplanade!

BESSIE. Estelle Hohengarten!

FLORA. Estelle Hohengarten!—the blackjack dealer from Texas!

BESSIE. Get into your blouse and let's go.

FLORA. Everybody's known it but Serafina. I'm just telling the facts that come out at the inquest while she was in bed with her eyes shut tight and the sheet pulled over her head like a female ostrich! Tie this damn thing on me! It was a romance, not just a fly-by-night thing, but a steady affair that went on for more than a year.

(SERAFINA *has been standing on the porch with the door open behind her. She is in the full glare of the sun. She appears to have been struck senseless by the words shouted inside. She turns slowly about. We see that her dress is unfastened down the back, the pink slip showing. She reaches out gropingly with one hand and finds the porch column which she clings to while the terrible words strike constantly deeper. The high school band continues as a merciless counterpoint.*)

BESSIE. Leave her in ignorance. Ignorance is bliss.

FLORA. He had a rose tattoo on his chest, the stuck-up thing, and Estelle was so gone on him she went down to Bourbon Street and had one put on her. (SERAFINA *comes onto the porch and* FLORA *turns to her, viciously.*) Yeah, a rose tattoo on her chest same as the Wop's!

SERAFINA (*very softly*). Liar . . . (*She comes inside; the word seems to give her strength.*)

BESSIE (*nervously*). Flora, let's go, let's go!

SERAFINA (*in a terrible voice*). Liar!—*Lie-arrrrr!*

(*She slams the wooden door shut with a violence that shakes the walls.*)

BESSIE (*shocked into terror*). Let's get outa here, Flora!

FLORA. Let her howl her head off. I don't care.

(SERAFINA *has snatched up a broom.*)

BESSIE. What's she up to?

FLORA. I don't care what she's up to!

BESSIE. I'm a-scared of these Wops.

FLORA. I'm not afraid of nobody!

BESSIE. She's gonna hit you.

FLORA. She'd better not hit me!

(*But both of the clowns are in retreat to the door.* SERAFINA *suddenly rushes at them with the broom. She flails* FLORA *about the hips and shoulders.* BESSIE *gets out. But* FLORA *is trapped in a corner. A table is turned over.* BESSIE, *outside, screams for the police and cries: "Murder! Murder!" The high school band is playing* The Stars and Stripes Forever. FLORA *breaks wildly past the flailing broom and escapes out of the house. She also takes up the cry for help.* SERAFINA *follows them out. She is flailing the brilliant noon air with the broom. The two women run off, screaming.*)

FLORA (*calling back*). I'm going to have her arrested! Police, police! I'm going to have you arrested!

SERAFINA. *Have* me arrested, *have* me, you dirt, you devil, you *liar!* Li-i-arr!

(*She comes back inside the house and leans on the work table for a moment, panting heavily. Then she rushes back to the door, slams it and bolts it. Then she rushes to the windows, slams the shutters and fastens them. The house is now dark except for the vigil light in the ruby glass cup before the Madonna, and the delicate beams admitted through the shutter slats.*)

SERAFINA (*in a crazed manner*). Have me—have me—arrested—dirty slut—bitch—liar! (*She moves about helplessly, not knowing what to do with her big, stricken body. Panting for breath, she repeats the word "liar" monotonously and helplessly as she thrashes about. It is necessary for her, vitally necessary for her, to believe that the woman's story is a malicious invention. But the words of it stick in her mind and she mumbles them aloud as she thrashes crazily around the small confines of the parlor.*) Woman—Estelle—(*The sound of band music is heard.*) Band, band, already—started.—Going to miss—graduation. Oh! (*She retreats toward the Madonna.*) Estelle, Estelle Hohengarten?—"A shirt for a man I'm in love with! This man—is—wild like a gypsy."—Oh, oh, Lady—The—rose-colored—silk. (*She starts toward the dining room, then draws back in terror.*) No, no, no, no, no! I don't remember! It wasn't that name, I don't remember the name! (*The band music grows louder.*) High school—graduation—late! I'll be—late for it.—Oh, Lady, give me a—*sign!* (*She cocks her head toward the statue in a fearful listening attitude.*) Che? Che dice, Signora? Oh, Lady! Give me a sign!

(*The scene dims out.*)

SCENE SIX

It is two hours later. The interior of the house is in complete darkness except for the vigil light. With the shutters closed, the interior is so dark that we do not know SERAFINA *is present. All that we see clearly is the starry blue robe of Our Lady above the flickering candle of the ruby glass cup. After a few moments we hear* SERAFINA'S *voice, very softly, in the weak, breathless tone of a person near death.*

SERAFINA (*very softly*). Oh, Lady, give me a sign . . .

(*Gay, laughing voices are heard outside the house.* ROSA *and* JACK *appear, bearing roses and gifts. They are shouting back to others in a car.*)

JACK. Where do we go for the picnic?

A GIRL'S VOICE (*from the highway*). We're going in three sailboats to Diamond Key.

A MAN'S VOICE. Be at Municipal Pier in half an hour.

ROSA. Pick us up here! (*She races up the steps.*) Oh, the door's locked! Mama's gone *out!* There's a key in that bird bath.

(JACK *opens the door. The parlor lights up faintly as they enter.*)

JACK. It's dark in here.

ROSA. Yes, Mama's gone out!

JACK. How do you know she's out?

ROSA. The door was locked and all the shutters are closed! Put down those roses.

JACK. Where shall I . . .

ROSA. Somewhere, anywhere!—Come here! (*He approaches her rather diffidently.*) I want to teach you a little Dago word. The word is "bacio."

JACK. What does this word mean?

ROSA. This and this and this! (*She rains kisses upon him till he forcibly removes her face from his.*) Just think. A week ago Friday—I didn't know boys existed!—Did you know girls existed before the dance?

JACK. Yes, I knew they existed . . .

ROSA (*holding him*). Do you remember what you said to me on the dance floor? "Honey, you're dancing too close"?

JACK. Well, it was—hot in the Gym and the—floor was crowded.

ROSA. When my girl friend was teaching me how to dance, I asked her, "How do you know which way the boy's going to move?" And she said, "You've got to feel how he's going to move with your body!" I said, "How do you feel with your body?" And she said, "By pressing up close!"— That's why I pressed up close! I didn't realize that I was—Ha, ha! Now you're blushing! Don't go *away*!—And a few minutes later you said to me, "Gee, you're beautiful!" I said, "Excuse me," and ran to the ladies' room. Do you know why? To look at myself in the mirror! And I saw that I was! For the first time in my life I was beautiful! You'd made me beautiful when you *said* that I was!

JACK (*humbly*). You *are* beautiful, Rosa! So much, I . . .

ROSA. *You've* changed, *too.* You've stopped laughing and joking. Why have you gotten so old and serious, Jack?

JACK. Well, honey, you're sort of . . .

ROSA. What am I "sort of"?

JACK (*finding the exact word*). Wild! (*She laughs. He seizes the bandaged wrist.*) I didn't know nothing like this was going to happen.

ROSA. Oh, that, that's nothing! I'll take the handkerchief off and you can forget it.

JACK. How could you do a thing like that over me? I'm—nothing!

ROSA. Everybody is nothing until you love them!

JACK. Give me that handkerchief. I want to show it to my shipmates. I'll say, "This is the blood of a beautiful girl who cut her wrist with a knife because she loved me!"

ROSA. Don't be so pleased with yourself. It's mostly Mercurochrome!

SERAFINA (*violently, from the dark room adjoining*). Stai zitta!—Cretina!

(ROSA *and* JACK *draw abruptly apart.*)

JACK (*fearfully*). I knew somebody was here!

ROSA (*sweetly and delicately*). Mama? Are you in there, Mama?

SERAFINA. No, no, no, I'm not, I'm dead and buried!

ROSA. Yes, Mama's in there!

JACK. Well, I—better go and—wait outside for a—while . . .

ROSA. You stay right here!—Mama?— Jack is with me.—Are you dressed up nicely? (*There is no response.*) Why's it so dark in here?—Jack, open the shutters!—I want to introduce you to my mother . . .

JACK. Hadn't I better go and . . .

ROSA. No. Open the shutters!

(*The shutters are opened and* ROSA *draws apart the curtains between the two rooms. Sunlight floods the scene.* SERAFINA *is revealed slumped in a chair at her work table in the dining room near the Singer sewing machine. She is grotesquely surrounded by the dummies, as though she had been holding a silent conference with them. Her appearance, in slovenly deshabille, is both comic and shocking.*)

ROSA (*terribly embarrassed*). Mama, Mama, you said you were dressed up pretty! Jack, stay out for a minute! What's happened, Mama?

(JACK *remains in the parlor.* ROSA *pulls the curtains, snatches a robe and flings it over* SERAFINA. *She brushes* SERAFINA's *hair back from her sweat-gleaming face, rubs her face with a handkerchief and dusts it with powder.* SERAFINA *submits to this cosmetic enterprise with a dazed look.*)

ROSA (*gesturing vertically*). Su, su, su, su, su, su, su, su, su!

(SERAFINA *sits up slightly in her chair, but she is still looking stupefied.* ROSA *returns to the parlor and opens the curtains again.*)

ROSA. Come in, Jack! Mama is ready to meet you!

(ROSA *trembles with eagerness as* JACK *advances nervously from the parlor. But before he enters* SERAFINA *collapses again into her slumped position, with a low moan.*)

ROSA (*violently*). Mama, Mama, su, Mama! (SERAFINA *sits half erect.*) She didn't sleep good last night.—Mama, this is Jack Hunter!

JACK. Hello, Mrs. Delle Rose. It sure is a pleasure to meet you.

(*There is a pause.* SERAFINA *stares indifferently at the boy.*)

ROSA. Mama, Mama, say something!

JACK. Maybe your Mama wants me to . . . (*He makes an awkward gesture toward the door.*)

ROSA. No, no, Mama's just tired. Mama makes dresses; she made a whole lot of dresses for the graduation! How many, Mama, how many graduation dresses did you have to make?

SERAFINA (*dully*). Fa niente . . .

JACK. I was hoping to see you at the graduation, Mrs. Delle Rose.

ROSA. I guess that Mama was too worn out to go.

SERAFINA. Rosa, shut the front door, shut it and lock it. There was a—policeman . . . (*There is a pause.*) What?—What?

JACK. My sister was graduating. My mother was there and my aunt was there —a whole bunch of cousins—I was hoping that you could—all—get together . . .

ROSA. Jack brought you some flowers.

JACK. I hope you are partial to roses as much as I am. (*He hands her the bouquet. She takes them absently.*)

ROSA. Mama, say something, say something simple like "Thanks."

SERAFINA. Thanks.

ROSA. Jack, tell Mama about the graduation; describe it to her.

JACK. My mother said it was just like fairyland.

ROSA. Tell her what the boys wore!

JACK. What did—what did they wear?

ROSA. Oh, you know what they wore. They wore blue coats and white pants and each one had a carnation! And there were three couples that did an old-fashioned dance, a minuet, Mother, to Mendelssohn's *Spring Song!* Wasn't it lovely, Jack? But one girl slipped; she wasn't used to long dresses! She slipped and fell on her—ho, ho! Wasn't it funny, Jack, wasn't it, wasn't it, Jack?

JACK (*worriedly*). I think that your Mama . . .

ROSA. Oh, my prize, my prize, I have forgotten my prize!

JACK. Where is it?

ROSA. You set them down by the sewing sign when you looked for the key.

JACK. Aw, excuse me, I'll get them. (*He goes out through the parlor.* ROSA *runs to her mother and kneels by her chair.*)

ROSA (*in a terrified whisper*). Mama, something has happened! What has happened, Mama? Can't you tell me, Mama? Is it because of this morning? Look. I took the bandage off, it was only a scratch! So, Mama, forget it! Think it was just a bad dream that never happened! Oh, Mama! (*She gives her several quick kisses on the forehead.* JACK *returns with two big books tied in white satin ribbon.*)

JACK. Here they are.

ROSA. Look what I got, Mama.

SERAFINA (*dully*). What?

ROSA. The Digest of Knowledge!

JACK. Everything's in them, from Abracadabra to Zoo! My sister was jealous. She just got a diploma!

SERAFINA (*rousing a bit*). Diploma, where is it? Didn't you get no diploma?

ROSA. Si, si, Mama! Eccolo! Guarda, guarda! (*She holds up the diploma tied in ribbon.*)

SERAFINA. Va bene.—Put it in the drawer with your father's clothes.

JACK. Mrs. Delle Rose, you should be very, very proud of your daughter. She stood in front of the crowd and recited a poem.

ROSA. Yes, I did. Oh, I was so excited!

JACK. And Mrs. Delle Rose, your daughter, Rosa, was so pretty when she walked on the stage—that people went "Ooooooooooo!"—like that! Y'know what I mean? They all went—"Ooooooooooo!" Like a—like a—*wind* had—blown over! Because your daughter, Rosa, was so—*lovely* looking! (*He has crouched over to deliver this description close to* SERAFINA *to deliver this description close to her face. Now he straightens up and smiles proudly at* ROSA.) How does it feel to be the mother of the prettiest girl in the world?

ROSA (*suddenly bursting into pure delight*). Ha, ha ha, ha, ha, ha! (*She throws her head back in rapture.*)

SERAFINA (*rousing*). Hush!

ROSA. Ha, ha, ha, ha, ha, ha, ha, ha, ha, ha! (*She cannot control her ecstatic laughter. She presses her hand to her mouth but the laughter still bubbles out.*)

SERAFINA (*suddenly rising in anger*). Pazza, pazza, pazza! Finiscila! Basta, via!

(ROSA *whirls around to hide her convulsions of joy. To* JACK:) Put the prize books in the parlor, and shut the front door; there was a policeman come here because of—some trouble . . .

(JACK *takes the books.*)

ROSA. Mama, I've never seen you like this! What will Jack think, Mama?

SERAFINA. Why do I care what Jack thinks?—You wild, wild crazy thing, you—with the eyes of your—father . . .

JACK (*returning*). Yes, ma'am, Mrs. Delle Rose, you certainly got a right to be very proud of your daughter.

SERAFINA (*after a pause*). I am proud of the—memory of her—father.—He was a baron . . . (ROSA *takes* JACK'S *arm.*) And who are *you?* What are you?—per piacere!

ROSA. Mama, I just introduced him; his name is Jack Hunter.

SERAFINA. Hunt-er?

JACK. Yes, ma'am, Hunter. Jack Hunter.

SERAFINA. What are you hunting?—Jack?

ROSA. Mama!

SERAFINA. What all of 'em are hunting? To have a good time, and the Devil cares who pays for it? I'm sick of men, I'm almost as sick of men as I am of wimmen.—Rosa, get out while I talk to this boy!

ROSA. I didn't bring Jack here to be insulted!

JACK. Go on, honey, and let your Mama talk to me. I think your Mama has just got a slight wrong—impression . . .

SERAFINA (*ominously*). Yes, I got an impression!

ROSA. I'll get dressed! Oh, Mama, don't spoil it for me!—the happiest day of my life! (*She goes into the back of the house.*)

JACK (*after an awkward pause*). Mrs. Delle Rose . . .

SERAFINA (*correcting his pronunciation*). Delle Rose!

JACK. Mrs. Delle Rose, I'm sorry about all this. Believe me, Mrs. Delle Rose, the last thing I had in mind was getting mixed up in a family situation. I come home after three months to sea, I docked at New Orleans, and come here to see my folks. My sister was going to a high school dance. She took me with her, and I met your daughter.

SERAFINA. What did you do?

JACK. At the high school dance? We danced! My sister had told me that Rose had a very strict mother and wasn't allowed to go on dates with boys so when it was over, I said, "I'm sorry you're not allowed to go out." And she said, "Oh! What gave you the idea I *wasn't!*" So then I thought my sister had made a mistake and I made a date with her for the next night.

SERAFINA. What did you do the next night?

JACK. The next night we went to the movies.

SERAFINA. And what did you do—that night?

JACK. At the movies? We ate a bag of popcorn and watched the movie!

SERAFINA. She come home midnight and said she had been with a girl-friend studying "civics."

JACK. Whatever story she told you, it ain't my fault!

SERAFINA. And the night after that?

JACK. Last Tuesday? We went roller skating!

SERAFINA. And afterwards?

JACK. After the skating? We went to a drug store and had an ice cream soda!

SERAFINA. Alone?

JACK. At the drug store? No. It was crowded. And the skating rink was full of people skating!

SERAFINA. You mean that you haven't been alone with my Rosa?

JACK. Alone or not alone, what's the point of that question? I still don't see the point of it.

SERAFINA. We are Sicilians. We don't leave the girls with the boys they're not engaged to!

JACK. Mrs. Delle Rose, this is the United States.

SERAFINA. But we are Sicilians, and we are not cold-blooded.—My girl is a *virgin!* She *is*—or she *was*—I would like to know—*which!*

JACK. Mrs. Delle Rose! I got to tell you something. You might not believe it. It is a hard thing to say. But I am—*also* a—*virgin* . . .

SERAFINA. *What? No.* I do not believe it.

JACK. Well, it's true, though. This is the first time—I . . .

SERAFINA. First time you *what?*

JACK. The first time I really wanted to . . .

SERAFINA. Wanted to what?

JACK. Make—love . . .

SERAFINA. You? A sailor?

JACK (*sighing deeply*). Yes, ma'am. I had opportunities to!—But I—always thought of my mother . . . I always asked myself, would she or would she not —think—this or that person was—decent!

SERAFINA. But with my daughter, my Rosa, your mother tells you *okay?*—go ahead, son!

JACK. Mrs. Delle Rose! (*With embarrassment*)—Mrs. Delle Rose, I . . .

SERAFINA. Two weeks ago I was slapping her hands for scratching mosquito bites. She rode a bicycle to school. Now all at once—I've got a wild thing in the house. She says she's in love. And you? Do you say *you're* in love?

JACK (*solemnly*). Yes, ma'am, I do, I'm in love!—very much . . .

SERAFINA. Bambini, tutti due, bambini! (*ROSE comes out, dressed for the picnic.*)

ROSA. I'm ready for Diamond Key!

SERAFINA. Go out on the porch. Diamond Key!

ROSA (*with a sarcastic curtsy*). Yes, Mama!

SERAFINA. What are you? Catholic?

JACK. Me? Yes, ma'am, Catholic.

SERAFINA. You don't look Catholic to me!

ROSA (*shouting, from the door*). Oh, God, Mama, how do Catholics look? How do they look different from anyone else?

SERAFINA. Stay out till I call you! (*ROSA crosses to the bird bath and prays.* SERAFINA *turns to* JACK.) Turn around, will you?

JACK. Do what, ma'am?

SERAFINA. I said, *turn around!* (*JACK awkwardly turns around.*) Why do they make them Navy pants so tight?

ROSA (*listening in the yard*). Oh, my God . . .

JACK (*flushing*). That's a question you'll have to ask the Navy, Mrs. Delle Rose.

SERAFINA. And that gold earring, what's the gold earring for?

ROSA (*yelling from the door*). For crossing the equator, Mama; he crossed it three times. He was initiated into the court of Neptune and gets to wear a gold earring! He's a shellback!

(*SERAFINA springs up and crosses to slam the porch door.* ROSA *runs despairingly around the side of the house and leans, exhausted with closed eyes, against the trunk of a palm tree.* THE STREGA *creeps into the yard, listening.*)

SERAFINA. You see what I got. A wild thing in the house!

JACK. Mrs. Delle Rose, I guess that Sicilians are very emotional people . . .

SERAFINA. I want nobody to take advantage of that!

JACK. You got the wrong idea about me, Mrs. Delle Rose.

SERAFINA. I know what men want—not to eat popcorn with girls or to slide on ice! And boys are the same, only younger. —Come here. Come here!

(*ROSA hears her mother's passionate voice. She rushes from the palm tree to the back door and pounds on it with both fists.*)

ROSA. Mama! Mama! Let me in the door, Jack!

JACK. Mrs. Delle Rose, your daughter is calling you.

SERAFINA. Let her call!—Come here. (*She crosses to the shrine of Our Lady.*) Come here!

(*Despairing of the back door,* ROSA *rushes around to the front. A few moments later she pushes open the shutters of the window in the wall and climbs half in.* JACK *crosses apprehensively to* SERAFINA *before the Madonna.*)

SERAFINA. You said you're Catholic, ain't you?

JACK. Yes, ma'am.

SERAFINA. Then kneel down in front of Our Lady!

JACK. Do—do what, did you say?

SERAFINA. I said to get down on your knees in front of Our Lady!

(*ROSA groans despairingly in the window.* JACK *kneels awkwardly upon the hassock.*)

ROSA. Mama, Mama, *now* what? !

(*SERAFINA rushes to the window, pushes* ROSA *out and slams the shutters.*)

SERAFINA (*returning to* JACK). Now say after me what I say!

JACK. Yes, ma'am.

(*ROSA pushes the shutters open again.*)

SERAFINA. I promise the Holy Mother that I will respect the innocence of the daughter of . . .

ROSA (*in anguish*). Ma-maaa!

SERAFINA. Get back out of that window! Well? Are you gonna say it?

JACK. Yes, ma'am. What was it, again?

SERAFINA. I promise the Holy Mother . . .

JACK. I promise the Holy Mother . . .

SERAFINA. As I hope to be saved by the

Blessed Blood of Jesus . . .

JACK. As I hope to be saved by the . . .

SERAFINA. Blessed Blood of . . .

JACK. Jesus . . .

SERAFINA. That I will respect the innocence of the daughter, Rosa, of Rosario delle Rose.

JACK. That I will respect the innocence —of—Rosa . . .

SERAFINA. Cross yourself! (*He crosses himself.*) Now get up, get up, get up! I am satisfied now . . .

(ROSA *jumps through the window and rushes to* SERAFINA *with arms outflung and wild cries of joy.*)

SERAFINA. Let me go, let me breathe! (*Outside* THE STREGA *cackles derisively.*)

ROSA. Oh, wonderful Mama, don't breathe! Oh, Jack! *Kiss* Mama! *Kiss Mama!* Mama please kiss Jack!

SERAFINA. Kiss? Me? No, no, no, no! Kiss my *hand* . . .

(*She offers her hand, shyly, and* JACK *kisses it with a loud smack.* ROSA *seizes the wine bottle.*)

ROSA. Mama, get some wine glasses!

(SERAFINA *goes for the glasses, and* ROSA *suddenly turns to* JACK. *Out of her mother's sight, she passionately grabs hold of his hand and presses it, first to her throat, then to her lips and finally to her breast.* JACK *snatches his hand away as* SERAFINA *returns with the glasses.* VOICES *are heard calling from the highway.*)

VOICES OUTSIDE. Ro-osa! — Ro-osa! — Ro-osa!

(*A car horn is heard blowing.*)

SERAFINA. Oh, I forgot the graduation present.

(*She crouches down before the bureau and removes a fancily wrapped package from its bottom drawer. The car horn is honking, and the voices are calling.*)

ROSA. They're calling for us! *Coming!* Jack! (*She flies out the door, calling back to her mother.*) G'by, Mama!

JACK (*following* ROSA). Good-by, Mrs. Delle Rose!

SERAFINA (*vaguely*). It's a Bulova wrist watch with seventeen jewels in it . . . (*She realizes that she is alone.*) Rosa! (*She goes to the door, still holding out the present. Outside the car motor roars, and the voices shout as the car goes off.* SERAFINA *stumbles outside, shielding her eyes with one hand, extending the gift with the other.*) Rosa, Rosa, your present!

Regalo, regalo—tesoro!

(*But the car has started off, with a medley of voices shouting farewells, which fade quickly out of hearing.* SERAFINA *turns about vaguely in the confusing sunlight and gropes for the door. There is a derisive cackle from the witch next door.* SERAFINA *absently opens the package and removes the little gold watch. She winds it and then holds it against her ear. She shakes it and holds it again to her ear. Then she holds it away from her and glares at it fiercely.*)

SERAFINA (*pounding her chest three times*). Tick—tick—tick! (*She goes to the Madonna and faces it.*) Speak to me, Lady! Oh, Lady, give me a sign!

(*The scene dims out.*)

ACT TWO

It is two hours later the same day.

SERAFINA *comes out onto the porch, barefooted, wearing a rayon slip. Great shadows have appeared beneath her eyes; her face and throat gleam with sweat. There are dark stains of wine on the rayon slip. It is difficult for her to stand, yet she cannot sit still. She makes a sick moaning sound in her throat almost continually.*

A hot wind rattles the cane-brake. VIVI, *the little girl, comes up to the porch to stare at* SERAFINA *as at a strange beast in a cage.* VIVI *is chewing a licorice stick which stains her mouth and her fingers. She stands chewing and staring.* SERAFINA *evades her stare. She wearily drags a broken gray wicker chair down off the porch, all the way out in front of the house, and sags heavily into it. It sits awry on a broken leg.*

VIVI *sneaks toward her.* SERAFINA *lurches about to face her angrily. The child giggles and scampers back to the porch.*

SERAFINA (*sinking back into the chair*). Oh, Lady, Lady, Lady, give me a—sign . . . (*She looks up at the white glare of the sky.*)

(FATHER DE LEO *approaches the house.* SERAFINA *crouches low in the chair to escape his attention. He knocks at the door. Receiving no answer, he looks out into the yard, sees her, and approaches her chair. He comes close to address her with a gentle severity.*)

FATHER DE LEO. Buon giorno, Serafina.

SERAFINA (*faintly, with a sort of disgust*). Giorno . . .

FATHER DE LEO. I'm surprised to see you sitting outdoors like this. What is that thing you're wearing?—I think it's an undergarment!—It's hanging off one shoulder, and your head, Serafina, looks as if you had stuck it in a bucket of oil. Oh, I see now why the other ladies of the neighborhood aren't taking their afternoon naps! They find it more entertaining to sit on the porches and watch the spectacle you are putting on for them!—Are you listening to me?—I must tell you that the change in your appearance and behavior since Rosario's death is shocking—shocking! A woman can be dignified in her grief but when it's carried too far it becomes a sort of self-indulgence. Oh, I knew this was going to happen when you broke the Church law and had your husband cremated! (SERAFINA *lurches up from the chair and shuffles back to the porch.* FATHER DE LEO *follows her.*)—Set up a little idolatrous shrine in your house and give worship to a bottle of ashes. (*She sinks down upon the steps.*)—Are you listening to me?

(*Two women have appeared on the embankment and descend toward the house.* SERAFINA *lurches heavily up to meet them, like a weary bull turning to face another attack.*)

SERAFINA. You ladies, what you want? I don't do sewing! Look, I quit doing sewing. (*She pulls down the* "SEWING" *sign and hurls it away.*) Now you got places to go, you ladies, go places! Don't hang around front of my house!

FATHER DE LEO. The ladies want to be friendly.

SERAFINA. Naw, they don't come to be friendly. They think they know something that Serafina don't know; they think I got *these* on my head! (*She holds her fingers like horns at either side of her forehead.*) Well, I ain't got them! (*She goes padding back out in front of the house.* FATHER DE LEO *follows.*)

FATHER DE LEO. You called me this morning in distress over something.

SERAFINA. I called you this morning but now it is afternoon.

FATHER DE LEO. I had to christen the grandson of the Mayor.

SERAFINA. The Mayor's important people, not Serafina!

FATHER DE LEO. You don't come to confession.

SERAFINA (*starting back toward the porch*). No, I don't come, I don't go, I—Ohhh! (*She pulls up one foot and hops on the other.*)

FATHER DE LEO. You stepped on something?

SERAFINA (*dropping down on the steps*). No, no, no, no, no, I don't step on—noth'n . . .

FATHER DE LEO. Come in the house. We'll wash it with antiseptic. (*She lurches up and limps back toward the house.*) Walking barefooted you will get it infected.

SERAFINA. Fa niente . . .

(*At the top of the embankment a little boy runs out with a red kite and flourishes it in the air with rigid gestures, as though he were giving a distant signal.* SERAFINA *shades her eyes with a palm to watch the kite, and then, as though its motions conveyed a shocking message, she utters a startled soft cry and staggers back to the porch. She leans against a pillar, running her hand rapidly and repeatedly through her hair.* FATHER DE LEO *approaches her again, somewhat timidly.*)

FATHER DE LEO. Serafina?

SERAFINA. Che, che, che cosa vuole?

FATHER DE LEO. I am thirsty. Will you go in the house and get me some water?

SERAFINA. Go in. Get you some water. The faucet is working.—I can't go in the house.

FATHER DE LEO. Why can't you go in the house?

SERAFINA. The house has a tin roof on it. I got to breathe.

FATHER DE LEO. You can breathe in the house.

SERAFINA. No, I can't breathe in the house. The house has a tin roof on it and I . . .

(THE STREGA *has been creeping through the cane-brake pretending to search for a chicken.*)

THE STREGA. Chick, chick, chick, chick, chick? (*She crouches to peer under the house.*)

SERAFINA. What's that? Is that the . . . ? Yes, the Strega! (*She picks up a flower pot containing a dead plant and crosses the yard.*) Strega! Strega! (THE STREGA *looks up, retreating a little.*) Yes, you, I mean you! You ain't look for no chick! Getta hell out of my yard! (THE STREGA *retreats, viciously muttering, back into the cane-brake.* SERAFINA *makes the protective sign of the horns with her fingers. The goat bleats.*)

FATHER DE LEO. You have no friends, Serafina.

SERAFINA. I don't want friends.

FATHER DE LEO. You are still a young woman. Eligible for—loving and—bearing again! I remember you dressed in pale blue silk at Mass one Easter morning, yes, like a lady wearing a—piece of the—weather! Oh, how proudly you walked, *too* proudly!—But now you crouch and shuffle about barefooted; you live like a convict, dressed in the rags of a convict. You have no companions; women you don't mix with. You . . .

SERAFINA. No, I don't mix with them women. (*Glaring at the women on the embankment*) The dummies I got in my house, I mix with them better because they don't make up no lies—What kind of women are them? (*Mimicking fiercely*) "Eee, Papa, eeee, baby, eee, me, me, me! At thirty years old they got no more use for the letto matrimoniale, no. The big bed goes to the basement! They get little beds from Sears Roebuck and sleep on their bellies!

FATHER DE LEO. Attenzione!

SERAFINA. They make the life without glory. Instead of the heart they got the deep-freeze in the house. The men, they don't feel no glory, not in the house with them women; they go to the bars, fight in them, get drunk, get fat, put horns on the women because the women don't give them the love which is glory.—I did, I give him the glory. To me the big bed was beautiful like a religion. Now I lie on it with dreams, with memories only! But it is still beautiful to me and I don't believe that the man in my heart gave me horns! (*The women whisper.*) What, what are they saying? Does ev'rybody know something that I don't know?—No, all I want is a sign, a sign from Our Lady, to tell me the lies is a lie! And then I . . . (*The women laugh on the embankment.* SERAFINA *starts fiercely toward them. They scatter.*) Squeak, squeak, squawk, squawk! Hens—like water thrown on them! (*There is the sound of mocking laughter.*)

FATHER DE LEO. People are laughing at you on all the porches.

SERAFINA. I'm laughing, too. Listen to me, I'm laughing! (*She breaks into loud, false laughter, first from the porch, then from the foot of the embankment, then crossing in front of the house.*) Ha, ha, ha, ha, ha, ha, ha! Now ev'rybody is laughing. Ha, ha, ha, ha, ha, ha!

FATHER DE LEO. Zitta ora!—Think of your daughter.

SERAFINA (*understanding the word "daughter"*). You, *you* think of my daughter! Today you give out the diplomas, today at the high school you give out the prizes, diplomas! You give to my daughter a set of books call the Digest of Knowledge! What does she know? How to be cheap already?—Oh, yes, that is what to learn, how to be cheap and to cheat!—You know what they do at this high school? They ruin the girls there! They give the spring dance because the girls are man-crazy. And there at that dance my daughter goes with a sailor that has in his ear a gold ring! And pants so tight that a woman ought not to look at him! This morning, this morning she cuts with a knife her wrist if I don't let her go!—Now all of them gone to some island, they call it a picnic, all of them, gone in a—boat!

FATHER DE LEO. There *was* a school picnic, chaperoned by the teachers.

SERAFINA. Oh, lo so, lo so! The man-crazy old-maid teachers!—They all run wild on the island!

FATHER DE LEO. Serafina delle Rose! (*He picks up the chair by the back and hauls it to the porch when she starts to resume her seat.*)—I *command* you to go in the house.

SERAFINA. Go in the house? I will. I will go in the house if you will answer one question.—Will you answer one question?

FATHER DE LEO. I will if I know the answer.

SERAFINA. Aw, you know the answer!—You used to hear the confessions of my husband. (*She turns to face the priest.*)

FATHER DE LEO. Yes, I heard his confessions . . .

SERAFINA (*with difficulty*). Did he ever speak to you of a *woman*?

(*A child cries out and races across in front of the house.* FATHER DE LEO *picks up his panama hat.* SERAFINA *paces slowly toward him. He starts away from the house.*)

SERAFINA (*rushing after him*). Aspettate! Aspettate un momento!

FATHER DE LEO (*fearfully, not looking at her*). Che volete.

SERAFINA. Rispondetemi! (*She strikes her breast.*) Did he speak of a woman to you?

FATHER DE LEO. You know better than to ask me such a question. I don't break the Church laws. The secrets of the confessional are sacred to me. (*He walks away.*)

SERAFINA (*pursuing and clutching his arm*). I got to know. You could tell me.

FATHER DE LEO. Let go of me, Serafina!

SERAFINA. Not till you tell me, Father. Father, you tell me, please tell me! Or I will go mad! (*In a fierce whisper*) I will go back in the house and smash the urn with the ashes—if you don't tell me! I will go mad with the doubt in my heart and I will smash the urn and scatter the ashes—of my husband's body!

FATHER DE LEO. What could I tell you? If you would not believe the known facts about him . . .

SERAFINA. Known facts, who knows the known facts?

(*The neighbor women have heard the argument and begin to crowd around, muttering in shocked whispers at SERAFINA's lack of respect.*)

FATHER DE LEO (*frightened*). Lasciatemi, lasciatemi stare—Oh, Serafina, I am too old for this—please!—Everybody is . . .

SERAFINA (*in a fierce, hissing whisper*). Nobody knew my rose of the world but me and now they can lie because the rose ain't living. They want the rose ashes scattered because I had too much glory. They don't want glory like *that* in nobody's heart. They want—mouse-squeaking!—known facts.—Who knows the known facts? You—padres—wear black because of the fact that the facts are known by nobody!

FATHER DE LEO. Oh, Serafina! There are people watching!

SERAFINA. Let them watch something. That will be a change for them.—It's been a long time I wanted to break out like this and now I . . .

FATHER DE LEO. I am too old a man; I am not strong enough. I am sixty-seven years old! Must I call for help, now?

SERAFINA. Yes, call! Call for help, but I won't let you go till you tell me!

FATHER DE LEO. You're not a respectable woman.

SERAFINA. No, I'm not a respectable; I'm a woman.

FATHER DE LEO. No, you are not a woman. You are an animal!

SERAFINA. Si, si, animale! Sono animale! Animale. Tell them all, shout it all to them, up and down the whole block! The widow Delle Rose is not respectable, she is not even a woman, she is an animal! She is attacking the priest! She will tear the black suit off him unless he tells her the whores in this town are lying to her!

(*The neighbor women have been drawing closer as the argument progresses, and now they come to* FATHER DE LEO's *rescue and assist him to get away from* SERAFINA, *who is on the point of attacking him bodily. He cries out, "Officer! Officer!" but the women drag* SERAFINA *from him and lead him away with comforting murmurs.*)

SERAFINA (*striking her wrists together*). Yes, it's me, it's me!! Lock me up, lock me, lock me up! Or I will—*smash!*—the marble . . . (*She throws her head far back and presses her fists to her eyes. Then she rushes crazily to the steps and falls across them.*)

ASSUNTA. Serafina! Figlia! Figlia! Andiamo a casa!

SERAFINA. Leave me alone, old woman.

(*She returns slowly to the porch steps and sinks down on them, sitting like a tired man, her knees spread apart and her head cupped in her hands. The children steal back around the house. A little boy shoots a bean-shooter at her. She starts up with a cry. The children scatter, shrieking. She sinks back down on the steps, then leans back, staring up at the sky, her body rocking.*)

SERAFINA. Oh, Lady, Lady, Lady, give me a sign!

(*As if in mocking answer, a novelty salesman appears and approaches the porch. He is a fat man in a seersucker suit and a straw hat with a yellow, red and purple band. His face is beet-red and great moons of sweat have soaked through the armpits of his jacket. His shirt is lavender, and his tie, pale blue with great yellow polka dots, is a butterfly bow. His entrance is accompanied by a brief, satiric strain of music.*)

THE SALESMAN. Good afternoon, lady. (*She looks up slowly.* THE SALESMAN *talks sweetly, as if reciting a prayer.*) I got a little novelty here which I am offering to just a few lucky people at what we call an introductory price. Know what I mean? Not a regular price but a price which is less than what it costs to manufacture the article, a price we are making for the sake of introducing the product in the Gulf Coast territory. Lady, this thing here that I'm droppin' right in youah lap is bigger than television; it's going to revolutionize the domestic life of America.—Now I don't do house to house canvassing. I sell directly to merchants but when I stopped over there to have my car serviced, I seen you taking the air on the steps and I thought I would just drop over and . . .

(*There is the sound of a big truck stopping on the highway, and a man's voice,* ALVARO's, *is heard shouting.*)

ALVARO. Hey! Hey, you road hog!

THE SALESMAN (*taking a sample out of his bag*). Now, lady, this little article has a deceptive appearance. First of all, I want you to notice how *compact* it is. It takes up no more space than . . .

(ALVARO *comes down from the embankment. He is about twenty-five years old, dark and very good-looking. He is one of those Mediterranean types that resemble glossy young bulls. He is short in stature, has a massively sculptural torso and bluish-black curls. His face and manner are clownish; he has a charming awkwardness. There is a startling, improvised air about him, he frequently seems surprised at his own speeches and actions, as though he had not at all anticipated them. At the moment when we first hear his voice the sound of a timpani begins, at first very pianissimo, but building up as he approaches, till it reaches a vibrant climax with his appearance to* SERAFINA *beside the house.*)

ALVARO. Hey.

THE SALESMAN (*without glancing at him*). Hay is for horses!—Now, madam, you see what happens when I press this button?

(*The article explodes in* SERAFINA's *face. She slaps it away with an angry cry. At the same time* ALVARO *advances, trembling with rage, to the porch steps. He is sweating and stammering with pent-up fury at a world of frustrations which are temporarily localized in the gross figure of this salesman.*)

ALVARO. Hey, you! Come here! What the hell's the idea, back there at that curve? You make me drive off the highway!

THE SALESMAN (*to* SERAFINA). Excuse m[e] for just one minute. (*He wheels menac[?]ingly about to face* ALVARO.) Is something giving you gas pains, Maccaroni?

ALVARO. My name is not Maccaroni.

THE SALESMAN. All right. Spaghetti.

ALVARO (*almost sobbing with passion*) I am not maccaroni. I am not spaghetti[.] I am a human being that drives a truck of bananas. I drive a truck of bananas for the Southern Fruit Company for a living not to play cowboys and Indians on n[o] highway with a rotten road hog. You go[t] a 4-lane highway between Pass Christia[n] and here. I give you the sign to pass me[.] You tail me and give me the horn. You yell "Wop" at me and "Dago." "Mov[e] over, Wop, move over, Dago." Then a[t] the goddam curve, you go pass me an[d] make me drive off the highway and yel[l] back "Son of a bitch of a Dago!" I don'[t] like that, no, no! And I am glad you stop[ped] here. Take the cigar from your mouth take out the cigar!

THE SALESMAN. Take it out for m[e] greaseball.

ALVARO. If I take it out I will push i[t] down your throat. I got three dependents If I fight, I get fired, but I will fight an[d] get fired. Take out the cigar!

(*Spectators begin to gather at the edge of the scene.* SERAFINA *stares at the truck driver, her eyes like a somnambule's. Al[l] at once she utters a low cry and seem[s] about to fall.*)

ALVARO. Take out the cigar, take out take out the cigar!

(*He snatches the cigar from* THE SALES[-]MAN's *mouth and* THE SALESMAN *brings hi[s] knee up violently into* ALVARO's *groin. Bending double and retching with pain* ALVARO *staggers over to the porch.*)

THE SALESMAN (*shouting, as he goes off*) I got your license number, Maccaroni! [I] know your boss!

ALVARO (*howling*). Drop dead! (*He suddenly staggers up the steps.*) Lady, lady, I got to go in the house!

(*As soon as he enters, he bursts into rending sobs, leaning against a wall and shaking convulsively. The spectators outside laugh as they scatter.* SERAFINA *slowly enters the house. The screen door rasps loudly on its rusty springs as she lets it swing gradually shut behind her, her eyes remaining fixed with a look of stupefied wonder upon the sobbing figure of the*

*ruck driver. We must understand her pro-
found unconscious response to this sudden
contact with distress as acute as her own.
There is a long pause as the door makes its
whining, catlike noise swinging shut by
degrees.*)

SERAFINA. Somebody's—in my house?
(*Finally, in a hoarse, tremulous whisper*)
What are you—doing in here? Why have
you—come in my house?

ALVARO. Oh, lady—leave me alone!—
Please—now!

SERAFINA. You—got no business—in
here . . .

ALVARO. I got to cry after a fight. I'm
sorry, lady. I . . . (*The sobs still shake
him. He leans on a dummy.*)

SERAFINA. Don't lean on my dummy. Sit
down if you can't stand up.—What is the
matter with you?

ALVARO. I always cry after a fight. But
I don't want people to see me. It's not like
a man. (*There is a long pause; SERAFINA's
attitude seems to warm toward a man.*)

SERAFINA. A man is not no different
from no one else . . . (*All at once her
face puckers up, and for the first time in
the play SERAFINA begins to weep, at first
soundlessly, then audibly. Soon she is sobbing as loudly as ALVARO. She speaks between sobs.*)—I always cry—when somebody else is crying . . .

ALVARO. No, no, lady, *don't* cry! Why
should *you* cry? I will stop. I will stop
in a minute. This is not like a man. I am
ashame of myself. I will stop now; please,
lady . . .

(*Still crouching a little with pain, a
hand clasped to his abdomen, ALVARO turns
away from the wall. He blows his nose between two fingers. SERAFINA picks up a
scrap of white voile and gives it to him to
wipe his fingers.*)

SERAFINA. Your jacket is torn.

ALVARO (*sobbing*). My company jacket
is torn?

SERAFINA. Yes . . .

ALVARO. Where is it torn?

SERAFINA (*sobbing*). Down the—back.

ALVARO. Oh, Dio!

SERAFINA. Take it off. I will sew it up
for you. I do—sewing.

ALVARO. Oh, Dio! (*Sobbing*) I got three
dependents! (*He holds up three fingers
and shakes them violently at SERAFINA.*)

SERAFINA. Give me—give me your
jacket.

ALVARO. He took down my license number!

SERAFINA. People are always taking down
license numbers and telephone numbers
and numbers that don't mean nothing—
all them numbers . . .

ALVARO. Three, three dependents! Not
citizens, even! No relief checks, no nothing!
(*SERAFINA sobs.*) He is going to complain
to the boss.

SERAFINA. I wanted to cry all day.

ALVARO. He said he would fire me if I
don't stop fighting!

SERAFINA. Stop crying so I can stop crying.

ALVARO. I am a sissy. Excuse me. I am
ashame.

SERAFINA. Don't be ashame of nothing,
the world is too crazy for people to be
ashame in it. I'm not ashame and I had
two fights on the street and my daughter
called me "disgusting." I got to sew this
by hand; the machine is broke in a fight
with two women.

ALVARO. That's what—they call a cat
fight . . . (*He blows his nose.*)

SERAFINA. Open the shutters, please, for
me. I can't see to work. (*She has crossed
to her work table. He goes over to the
window. As he opens the shutters, the
light falls across his fine torso, the under-
shirt clinging wetly to his dark olive skin.
SERAFINA is struck and murmurs: "Ohhh
. . . " There is the sound of music.*)

ALVARO. What, lady?

SERAFINA (*in a strange voice*). The light
on the body was like a man that lived
here . . .

ALVARO. Che dice?

SERAFINA. Niente.—Ma com'è strano!—
Lei è Napoletano? (*She is threading a
needle.*)

ALVARO. Io sono Siciliano! (*SERAFINA
sticks her finger with her needle and cries
out.*) Che fa?

SERAFINA. I—stuck myself with the—
needle!—You had—better wash up . . .

ALVARO. Dov'è il gabinetto?

SERAFINA (*almost inaudibly*). Dietro.
(*She points vaguely back.*)

ALVARO. Con permesso! (*He moves past
her. As he does so, she picks up a pair of
broken spectacles on the work table. Holding them up by the single remaining side
piece, like a lorgnette, she inspects his passing figure with an air of stupefaction. As
he goes out, he says:*) A kick like that can

have serious consequences! (*He goes into the back of the house.*)

SERAFINA (*after a pause*). Madonna Santa!—*My husband's body,* with the head of a *clown!* (*She crosses to the Madonna.*) O Lady, O Lady! (*She makes an imploring gesture.*) Speak to me!—What are you saying?—Please, Lady, I can't hear you. Is it a sign? Is it a sign of something? What does it mean? Oh, *speak to me,* Lady!—Everything is too strange!

(*She gives up the useless entreaty to the impassive statue. Then she rushes to the cupboard, clambers up on a chair and seizes a bottle of wine from the top shelf. But she finds it impossible to descend from the chair. Clasping the dusty bottle to her breast, she crouches there, helplessly whimpering like a child, as* ALVARO *comes back in.*)

ALVARO. Ciao!

SERAFINA. I can't get up.

ALVARO. You mean you can't get down?

SERAFINA. I mean I—can't get down . . .

ALVARO. Con permesso, Signora! (*He lifts her down from the chair.*)

SERAFINA. Grazie.

ALVARO. I am ashame of what happen. Crying is not like a man. Did anyone see me?

SERAFINA. Nobody saw you but me. To me it don't matter.

ALVARO. You are simpatica, molto!—It was not just the fight that makes me break down. I was like this all today! (*He shakes his clenched fists in the air.*)

SERAFINA. You and—me, too!—What was the trouble today?

ALVARO. My name is Mangiacavallo which means "Eat-a-horse." It's a comical name, I know. Maybe two thousand and seventy years ago one of my grandfathers got so hungry that he ate up a horse! That ain't my fault. Well, today at the Southern Fruit Company I find on the pay envelope not "Mangiacavallo" but "EAT A HORSE" in big print! Ha, ha, ha, very funny!—I open the pay envelope! In it I find a notice.—The wages have been *garnishee!* You know what garnishee is? (SERAFINA *nods gravely.*) Garnishee!—Eat a horse!—Road hog!—All in one day is too much! I go crazy, I boil, I cry, and I am ashame but I am not able to help it!—Even a Wop truck driver's a human being! And human beings must cry . . .

SERAFINA. Yes, they must cry. I couldn't cry all day but now I have cried and I am feeling much better.—I will sew up the jacket . . .

ALVARO (*licking his lips*). What is that in your hand? A bottle of vino?

SERAFINA. This is Spumanti. It comes from the house of the family of my husband. The Delle Rose! A very great family. I was a peasant, but I married a baron!—No, I still don't believe it! I married a baron when I didn't have shoes!

ALVARO. Excuse me for asking—but where is the Baron now? (SERAFINA *points gravely to the marble urn.*) Where did you say?

SERAFINA. Them're his ashes in that marble urn.

ALVARO. Ma! Scusatemi! Scusatemi! (*Crossing himself*)—I hope he is resting in peace.

SERAFINA. It's him you remind me of—when you opened the shutters. Not the face but the body.—Please get me some ice from the icebox in the kitchen. I had a—very bad day . . .

ALVARO. Oh, ice! Yes—ice—I'll get some . . . (*As he goes out, she looks again through the broken spectacles at him.*)

SERAFINA. *Non posso crederlo!*—A clown of a face like that with my husband's body!

(*There is the sound of ice being chopped in the kitchen. She inserts a corkscrew in the bottle but her efforts to open it are clumsily unsuccessful.* ALVARO *returns with a little bowl of ice. He sets it down so hard on the table that a piece flies out. He scrambles after it, retrieves it and wipes it off on his sweaty undershirt.*)

SERAFINA. I think the floor would be cleaner!

ALVARO. Scusatemi!—I wash it again?

SERAFINA. Fa niente!

ALVARO. I am a—clean!—I . . .

SERAFINA. Fa niente, niente!—The bottle should be in the ice but the next best thing is to pour the wine over the bottle.

ALVARO. You mean over the ice?

SERAFINA. I mean over the . . .

ALVARO. Let me open the bottle. Your hands are not used to rough work. (*She surrenders the bottle to him and regards him through the broken spectacles again.*)

SERAFINA. These little bits of white voile on the floor are not from a snowstorm. I been making voile dresses for high school graduation.—One for my daughter and for thirteen other girls—All of the work I'm not sure didn't kill me!

ALVARO. The wine will make you feel better.

(*There is a youthful cry from outside.*)

SERAFINA. There is a wild bunch of boys and girls in this town. In Sicily the boys would dance with the boys because a girl and a boy could not dance together unless they was going to be married. But here they run wild on islands!—boys, girls, man-crazy teachers . . .

ALVARO. Ecco! (*The cork comes off with a loud pop.* SERAFINA *cries out and staggers against the table. He laughs. She laughs with him, helplessly, unable to stop, unable to catch her breath.*)—I like a woman that laughs with all her heart.

SERAFINA. And a woman that cries with her heart?

ALVARO. I like everything that a woman does with her heart.

(*Both are suddenly embarrassed and their laughter dies out.* SERAFINA *smooths down her rayon slip. He hands her a glass of the sparkling wine with ice in it. She murmurs "Grazie."*)

(*Unconsciously the injured finger is lifted again to her lip and she wanders away from the table with the glass held shakily.*)

ALVARO (*continuing nervously.*) I see you had a bad day.

SERAFINA. Sono così—stanca . . .

ALVARO (*suddenly springing to the window and shouting*). Hey, you kids, git down off that truck! Keep your hands off them bananas! (*At the words "truck" and "bananas"* SERAFINA *gasps again and spills some wine on her slip.*) Little buggers!—Scusatemi . . .

SERAFINA. You haul—you haul bananas?

ALVARO. Si, Signora.

SERAFINA. Is it a 10-ton truck?

ALVARO. An 8-ton truck.

SERAFINA. My husband hauled bananas in a 10-ton truck.

ALVARO. Well, he was a baron.

SERAFINA. Do you haul just bananas?

ALVARO. Just bananas. What else would I haul?

SERAFINA. My husband hauled bananas, but underneath the bananas was something else. He was—wild like a—Gypsy. —"Wild—like a—Gypsy?" Who said that?—I hate to start to remember, and then not remember . . .

(*The dialogue between them is full of odd hesitations, broken sentences and tentative gestures. Both are nervously exhausted after their respective ordeals. Their fumbling communication has a curious intimacy and sweetness, like the meeting of two lonely children for the first time. It is oddly luxurious to them both, luxurious as the first cool wind of evening after a scorching day.* SERAFINA *idly picks up a little Sicilian souvenir card from a table.*)

SERAFINA. The priest was against it.

ALVARO. What was the priest against?

SERAFINA. Me keeping the ashes. It was against the Church law. But I had to have something and that was all I could have.

ALVARO. I don't see nothing wrong with it.

SERAFINA. You don't?

ALVARO. No! Niente!—The body would've decayed, but ashes always stay clean.

SERAFINA (*eagerly*). Si, si, bodies decay, but ashes always stay clean! Come here. I show you this picture—my wedding. (*She removes a picture tenderly from the wall.*) Here's me a bride of fourteen, and this—this—this— (*drumming the picture with her finger and turning her face to* ALVARO *with great lustrous eyes*) My husband! (*There is a pause. He takes the picture from her hand and holds it first close to his eyes, then far back, then again close with suspirations of appropriate awe.*) Annnh?—Annnh?—Che dice!

ALVARO (*slowly, with great emphasis*). Che bell' uomo! Che bell' uomo!

SERAFINA (*replacing the picture*). A rose of a man. On his chest he had the tattoo of a rose. (*Then, quite suddenly*)—Do you believe strange things, or do you doubt them?

ALVARO. If strange things didn't happen, I wouldn't be here. You wouldn't be here. We wouldn't be talking together.

SERAFINA. Davvero! I'll tell you something about the tattoo of my husband. My husband, he had this rose tattoo on his chest. One night I woke up with a burning pain on me here. I turn on the light. I looked at my naked breast and on it I see the rose tattoo of my husband, on me, on *my* breast, *his* tattoo.

ALVARO. Strano!

SERAFINA. And that was the night that—I got to speak frankly to tell you . . .

ALVARO. Speak frankly! We're grown-up people.

SERAFINA. That was the night I conceived my son—the little boy that was lost when I lost my husband . . .

ALVARO. Che cosa—strana!—Would you be willing to show me the rose tattoo?

SERAFINA. Oh, it's gone now, it only lasted a moment. But I did see it. I saw it clearly.—Do you believe me?

ALVARO. Lo credo!

SERAFINA. I don't know why I told you. But I like what you said. That bodies decay but ashes always stay clean—immacolate!—But, you know, there are some people that want to make everything dirty. Two of them kind of people come in the house today and told me a terrible lie in front of the ashes.—So awful a lie that if I thought it was true—I would smash the urn—and throw the ashes away! (*She hurls her glass suddenly to the floor.*) Smash it, *smash it like that!*

ALVARO. Ma!—Baronessa!

(SERAFINA *seizes a broom and sweeps the fragments of glass away.*)

SERAFINA. And take this broom and sweep them out the back door like so much trash!

ALVARO (*impressed by her violence and a little awed*). What lie did they tell you?

SERAFINA. No, no, no! I don't want to talk about it! (*She throws down the broom.*) I just want to forget it; it wasn't true, it was false, false, false!—as the hearts of the bitches that told it . . .

ALVARO. Yes. I would forget anything that makes you unhappy.

SERAFINA. The memory of a love don't make you unhappy unless you believe a lie that makes it dirty. I don't believe in the lie. The ashes are clean. The memory of the rose in my heart is perfect!—your glass is weeping . . .

ALVARO. *Your* glass is weeping too.

(*While she fills his glass, he moves about the room, looking here and there. She follows him. Each time he picks up an article for inspection she gently takes it from him and examines it herself with fresh interest.*)

ALVARO. Cozy little homelike place you got here.

SERAFINA. Oh, it's—molto modesto.—You got a nice place too?

ALVARO. I got a place with three dependents in it.

SERAFINA. What—dependents?

ALVARO (*counting them on his fingers*). One old maid sister, one feeble-minded grandmother, one lush of a pop that's no worth the powder it takes to blow him to hell.—They got the parchesi habit. They play the game of parchesi, morning, night, noon. Passing a bucket of beer around the table . . .

ALVARO. Oh, yes. And the numbers habit. This spring the old maid sister gets female trouble—mostly mental, I think—she turns the housekeeping over to the feeble-minded grandmother, a very sweet old lady who don't think it is necessary to pay the grocery bill so long as there's money to play the numbers. She plays the numbers. She has a perfect system except it don't ever work. And the grocery bill goes up, up, up, up!—so high you can't even see it! —Today the Ideal Grocery Company garnishees my wages . . . There, now! I've told you my life . . . (*The parrot squawks. He goes over to the cage.*) Hello, Polly, how's tricks?

SERAFINA. The name ain't Polly. It ain't a she; it's a he.

ALVARO. How can you tell with all them tail feathers? (*He sticks his finger in the cage, pokes at the parrot and gets bitten.*) Owww!

SERAFINA (*vicariously*). Ouuu . . . (AL-VARO *sticks his injured finger in his mouth.* SERAFINA *puts her corresponding finger in her mouth. He crosses to the telephone.*) I told you watch out.—What are you calling, a doctor?

ALVARO. I am calling my boss in Biloxi to explain why I'm late.

SERAFINA. The call to Biloxi is a ten-cent call.

ALVARO. Don't worry about it.

SERAFINA. I'm not worried about it. You will pay it.

ALVARO. You got a sensible attitude toward life . . . Give me the Southern Fruit Company in Biloxi—seven-eight-seven!

SERAFINA. You are a bachelor. With three dependents? (*She glances below his belt.*)

ALVARO. I'll tell you my hopes and dreams!

SERAFINA. Who? Me?

ALVARO. I am hoping to meet some sensible older lady. Maybe a lady a little bit older than me.—I don't care if she's a little too plump or not such a stylish dresser! (SERAFINA *self-consciously pulls up a dan-*

gling strap.) The important thing in a lady is understanding. Good sense. And I want her to have a well-furnished house and a profitable little business of some kind . . . (*He looks about him significantly.*)

SERAFINA. And such a lady, with a well-furnished house and business, what does she want with a man with three dependents with the parchesi and the beer habit, playing the numbers!

ALVARO. Love and affection!—in a world that is lonely—and cold!

SERAFINA. It might be lonely but I would not say "cold" on this particular day!

ALVARO. Love and affection is what I got to offer on hot or cold days in this lonely old world and is what I am looking for. I got nothing else. Mangiacavallo has nothing. In fact, he is the grandson of the village idiot of Ribera!

SERAFINA (*uneasily*). I see you like to make—jokes!

ALVARO. No, no joke!—Davvero!—He chased my grandmother in a flooded rice field. She slip on a wet rock.—Ecco! Here I am.

SERAFINA. You ought to be more respectful.

ALVARO. What have I got to respect? The rock my grandmother slips on?

SERAFINA. Yourself at least! Don't you work for a living?

ALVARO. If I *don't* work for a living I would respect myself *more*. Baronessa, I am a healthy young man, existing without no love life. I look at the magazine pictures. Them girls in the advertisement —you know what I mean? A little bitty thing here? A little bitty thing there?

(*He touches two portions of his anatomy. The latter portion embarrasses* SERAFINA, *who quietly announces:*)

SERAFINA. The call is ten cents for three minutes. Is the line busy?

ALVARO. Not the line, but the boss.

SERAFINA. And the charge for the call goes higher. That ain't the phone of a millionaire you're using!

ALVARO. I think you talk a poor mouth. (*He picks up the piggy bank and shakes it.*) This pig sounds well-fed to me.

SERAFINA. Dimes and quarters.

ALVARO. Dimes and quarters're better than nickles and dimes. (SERAFINA *rises severely and removes the piggy bank from his grasp.*) Ha, ha, ha! You think I'm a

bank robber?

SERAFINA. I think you are maleducto! Just get your boss on the phone or hang the phone up.

ALVARO. What, what! Mr. Siccardi? How tricks at the Southern Fruit Comp'ny this hot afternoon? Ha, ha, ha!—Mangiacavallo!—What? You got the complaint already? Sentite, per favore! This road hog was—Mr. Siccardi? (*He jiggles the hook; then slowly hangs up.*) A man with three dependents!—out of a job . . . (*There is a pause.*)

SERAFINA. Well, you better ask the operator the charges.

ALVARO. Oofla! A man with three dependents—out of a job!

SERAFINA. I can't see to work no more. I got a suggestion to make. Open the bottom drawer of that there bureau and you will find a shirt in white tissue paper and you can wear that one while I am fixing this. And call for it later. (*He crosses to the bureau.*)—It was made for somebody that never called for it. (*He removes the package.*) Is there a name pinned to it?

ALVARO. Yes, it's . . .

SERAFINA (*fiercely, but with no physical movement*). Don't tell me the name! Throw it away, out the window!

ALVARO. Perchè?

SERAFINA. Throw it, throw it away!

ALVARO (*crumpling the paper and throwing it through the window*). Ecco fatto! (*There is a distant cry of children as he unwraps the package and holds up the rose silk shirt, exclaiming in Latin delight at the luxury of it.*) Colore di rose! Seta! Seta pura!—Oh, this shirt is too good for Mangiacavallo! Everything here is too good for Mangiacavallo!

SERAFINA. Nothing's too good for a man if the man is good.

ALVARO. The grandson of a village idiot is not that good.

SERAFINA. No matter whose grandson you are, put it on; you are welcome to wear it.

ALVARO (*slipping voluptuously into the shirt*). Sssssss!

SERAFINA. How does it feel, the silk, on you?

ALVARO. It feels like a girl's hands on me! (*There is a pause, while he shows her the whiteness of his teeth.*)

SERAFINA (*holding up her broken spectacles*). It will make you less trouble.

ALVARO. There is nothing more beautiful than a gift between people!—Now you are smiling!—You like me a little bit better?

SERAFINA (*slowly and tenderly*). You know what they should of done when you was a baby? They should of put tape on your ears to hold them back so when you grow up they wouldn't stick out like the wings of a little kewpie! (*She touches his ear, a very slight touch, betraying too much of her heart. Both laugh a little and she turns away, embarrassed.*)

(*Outside the goat bleats and there is the sound of splintering timber. One of the children races into the front yard, crying out.*)

SALVATORE. Mizz' Dell' Rose! The black goat's in your yard!

SERAFINA. Il becco della strega!

(SERAFINA *dashes to the window, throws the shutters violently open and leans way out. This time, she almost feels relief in this distraction. The interlude of the goat chase has a quality of crazed exaltation. Outside is heard the wild bleating of the goat and the jingling of his harness.*)

SERAFINA. Miei pomodori! Guarda i miei pomodori!

THE STREGA (*entering the front yard with a broken length of rope, calling out*). Heyeh, Billy! Heyeh. Heyeh, Billy!

SERAFINA (*making the sign of horns with her fingers*). There is the Strega! She lets the goat in my yard to eat my tomatoes! (*Backing from the window*) She has the eye; she has the malocchio, and so does the goat! The goat has the evil eye, too. He got in my yard the night that I lost Rosario and my boy! Madonna, Madonna mia! Get that goat out of my yard! (*She retreats to the Madonna, making the sign of the horns with her fingers, while the goat chase continues outside.*)

ALVARO. Now take it easy; I will catch the black goat and give him a kick that he will never forget!

(ALVARO *runs out the front door and joins in the chase. The little boy is clapping together a pair of tin pan lids which sound like cymbals. The effect is weird and beautiful with the wild cries of the children and the goat's bleating.* SERAFINA *remains anxiously half way between the shutters and the protecting Madonna. She gives a furious imitation of the bleating goat, contorting her face with loathing. It is the fury of woman at the desire she suf-fers. At last the goat is captured.*)

BRUNO. Got him, got him, got him!

ALVARO. Vieni presto, Diavolo!

(ALVARO *appears around the side of the house with a tight hold on the broken rope around the goat's neck. The boy follows behind, gleefully clapping the tin lids together, and further back follows* THE STREGA, *holding her broken length of rope, her gray hair hanging into her face and her black skirts caught up in one hand, revealing bare feet and hairy legs.* SERA-FINA *comes out on the porch as the gro-tesque little procession passes before it, and she raises her hand with the fingers mak-ing horns as the goat and* THE STREGA *pass her.* ALVARO *turns the goat over to* THE STREGA *and comes panting back to the house.*)

ALVARO. Niente paura!—I got to go now. —You have been troppo gentile, Mrs. . . .

SERAFINA. I am the widow of the Baron Delle Rose.—Excuse the way I'm—not dressed . . . (*He keeps hold of her hand as he stands on the porch steps. She continues very shyly, panting a little.*) I am not always like this.—Sometimes I fix my-self up!—When my husband was living, when my husband comes home, when he was living—I had a clean dress on! And sometimes even, I—put a rose in my hair . . .

ALVARO. A rose in your hair would be pretty!

SERAFINA. But for a widow—it ain't the time of roses . . .

(*The sound of music is heard, of a man-dolin playing.*)

ALVARO. Naw, you make a mistake! It's always for everybody the time of roses! The rose is the heart of the world like the heart is the—heart of the—body! But you, Baronessa—you know what I think you have done?

SERAFINA. What—what have I—done?

ALVARO. You have put your heart in the marble urn with the ashes. (*Now singing is heard along with the music, which con-tinues to the end of the scene.*) And if in a storm sometime, or sometime when a 10-ton truck goes down the highway—the marble urn was to *break!* (*He suddenly points up at the sky.*) Look! Look, Bar-onessa!

SERAFINA (*startled*). Look? Look? I don't see!

ALVARO. I was pointing at your heart,

broken out of the urn and away from the ashes!—*Rondinella felice!* (*He makes an airy gesture toward the fading sky.*)

SERAFINA. Oh! (*He whistles like a bird and makes graceful winglike motions with his hands.*) Buffone, buffone—piantatela! I take you serious—then you make it a joke . . . (*She smiles involuntarily at his antics.*)

ALVARO. When can I bring the shirt back?

SERAFINA. When do you pass by again?

ALVARO. I will pass by tonight after supper. Volete?

SERAFINA. Then look at the window tonight. If the shutters are open and there is a light in the window, you can stop by for your—jacket—but if the shutters are closed, you better not stop because my Rosa will be home. Rosa's my daughter. She has gone to a picnic—maybe—home early—but you know how picnics are. They—wait for the moon to—start singing. —Not that there's nothing wrong in two grown-up people having a quiet conversation!—but Rosa's fifteen—I got to be careful to set her a perfect example.

ALVARO. I will look at the window.—I will look at the win-doow! (*He imitates a bird flying off with gay whistles.*)

SERAFINA. Buffone!

ALVARO (*shouting from outside*). Hey, you little buggers, climb down off that truck! Lay offa them bananas!

(*His truck is heard starting and pulling away.* SERAFINA *stands motionless on the porch, searching the sky with her eyes.*)

SERAFINA. Rosario, forgive me! Forgive me for thinking the awful lie could be true!

(*The light in the house dims out. A little boy races into the yard holding triumphantly aloft a great golden bunch of bananas. A little girl pursues him with shrill cries. He eludes her. They dash around the house. The light fades and the curtain falls.*)

ACT THREE

SCENE ONE

It is the evening of the same day. The neighborhood children are playing games around the house. One of them is counting by fives to a hundred, calling out the numbers, as he leans against the palm tree.

SERAFINA *is in the parlor, sitting on the sofa. She is seated stiffly and formally, wearing a gown that she has not worn since the death of her husband, and with a rose in her hair. It becomes obvious from her movements that she is wearing a girdle that constricts her unendurably.*

There is the sound of a truck approaching up on the highway. SERAFINA *rises to an odd, crouching position. But the truck passes by without stopping. The girdle is becoming quite intolerable to* SERAFINA *and she decides to take it off, going behind the sofa to do so. With much grunting, she has gotten it down as far as her knees, when there is the sound outside of another truck approaching. This time the truck stops up on the highway, with a sound of screeching brakes. She realizes that* ALVARO *is coming, and her efforts to get out of the girdle, which is now pinioning her legs, become frantic. She hobbles from behind the sofa as* ALVARO *appears in front of the house.*

———

ALVARO (*gaily*). Rondinella felice! I will look at win-dooooo! Signora delle Rose!

(SERAFINA'S *response to this salutation is a groan of anguish. She hobbles and totters desperately to the curtains between the rooms and reaches them just in time to hide herself as* ALVARO *comes into the parlor from the porch through the screen door. He is carrying a package and a candy box.*)

ALVARO. C'è nessuno?

SERAFINA (*at first inaudibly*). Si, si, sono qui. (*Then loudly and hoarsely, as she finally gets the girdle off her legs*). Si, si, sono qui! (*To cover her embarrassment, she busies herself with fixing wine glasses on a tray.*)

ALVARO. I hear the rattle of glasses! Let me help you! (*He goes eagerly through the curtain but stops short, astonished.*)

SERAFINA. Is—something the—matter?

ALVARO. I didn't expect to see you looking so pretty! You are a *young* little widow!

SERAFINA. You are—fix yourself up . . .

ALVARO. I been to The Ideal Barber's! I got the whole works!

SERAFINA (*faintly, retreating from him a little*). You got—rose oil—in your hair . . .

ALVARO. Olio di rose! You like the smell of it? (*Outside there is a wild, distant cry of children, and inside a pause.* SERAFINA *shakes her head slowly with the infinite wound of a recollection.*)—You—*don't*—like—the smell of it? Oh, then I wash the smell *out,* I go and . . . (*He starts toward the back. She raises her hand to stop him.*)

SERAFINA. No, no, no, fa—niente.—I *like* the smell of it . . .

(*A little boy races into the yard, ducks some invisible missile, sticks out his tongue and yells: "Yahhhhh!" Then he dashes behind the house.*)

SERAFINA. Shall we—set down in the parlor?

ALVARO. I guess that's better than standing up in the dining room. (*He enters formally.*)—Shall we set down on the sofa?

SERAFINA. You take the sofa. I will set down on this chair.

ALVARO (*disappointed*). You don't like to set on a sofa?

SERAFINA. I lean back too far on that sofa. I like a straight back behind me . . .

ALVARO. That chair looks not comfortable to me.

SERAFINA. This chair is a comfortable chair.

ALVARO. But it's more easy to talk with two on a sofa!

SERAFINA. I talk just as good on a chair as I talk on a sofa . . . (*There is a pause.* ALVARO *nervously hitches his shoulder.*) Why do you hitch your shoulders like that?

ALVARO. Oh that!—That's a—nervous—habit . . .

SERAFINA. I thought maybe the suit don't fit you good . . .

ALVARO. I bought this suit to get married in four years ago.

SERAFINA. But didn't get married?

ALVARO. I give her, the girl, a zircon instead of a diamond. She had it examined. The door was slammed in my face.

SERAFINA. I think that maybe I'd do the same thing myself.

ALVARO. Buy the zircon?

SERAFINA. No, slam the door.

ALVARO. Her eyes were not sincere looking. You've got sincere looking eyes. Give me your hand so I can tell your fortune! (*She pushes her chair back from him.*) I see two men in your life. One very handsome. One not handsome. His ears are too big but not as big as his heart! He has three dependents.—In fact he has four dependents! Ha, ha, ha!

SERAFINA. What is the fourth dependent?

ALVARO. The one that every man's got, his biggest expense, worst troublemaker and chief liability! Ha, ha, ha!

SERAFINA. I hope you are not talking vulgar. (*She rises and turns her back to him. Then she discovers the candy box.*) What's that fancy red box?

ALVARO. A present I bought for a nervous but nice little lady!

SERAFINA. Chocolates? Grazie! Grazie! But I'm too fat.

ALVARO. You are not fat, you are just pleasing and plump. (*He reaches way over to pinch the creamy flesh of her upper arm.*)

SERAFINA. No, please. Don't make me nervous. If I get nervous again I will start to cry . . .

ALVARO. Let's talk about something to take your mind off your troubles. You say you got a young daughter?

SERAFINA (*in a choked voice*). Yes. I got a young daughter. Her name is Rosa.

ALVARO. Rosa, Rosa! She's pretty?

SERAFINA. She has the eyes of her father, and his wild, stubborn blood! Today was the day of her graduation from high school. She looked so pretty in a white voile dress with a great big bunch of—roses . . .

ALVARO. Not no prettier than her Mama, I bet—with that rose in your hair!

SERAFINA. She's only fifteen.

ALVARO. Fifteen?

SERAFINA (*smoothing her blue silk lap with a hesitant hand*). Yes, only fifteen . . .

SERAFINA. She met a sailor.

ALVARO. Oh, Dio! No wonder you seem to be nervous.

SERAFINA. I didn't want to let her go out with this sailor. He had a gold ring in his ear.

ALVARO. Madonna Santa!

SERAFINA. This morning she cut her wrist—not much but enough to bleed—with a kitchen knife!

ALVARO. Tch, tch! A very wild girl!

SERAFINA. I had to give in and let her bring him to see me. He said he was Catholic. I made him kneel down in front of Our Lady there and give Her his promise that he would respect the innocence of my Rosa!—But how do I know that he was a Catholic, *really*?

ALVARO (*taking her hand*). Poor little worried lady! But you got to face facts. Sooner or later the innocence of your daughter cannot be respected.—Did he—have a—tattoo?

SERAFINA (*startled*). Did who have—what?

ALVARO. The sailor friend of your daughter, did he have a tattoo?

SERAFINA. Why do you ask me that?

ALVARO. Just because most sailors have a tattoo.

SERAFINA. How do I know if he had a tattoo or not!

ALVARO. *I* got a tattoo!

SERAFINA. *You* got a tattoo?

ALVARO. Si, si, veramente!

SERAFINA. What kind of tattoo you got?

ALVARO. What kind you think?

SERAFINA. Oh, I think—you have got—a South Sea girl without clothes on . . .

ALVARO. No South Sea girl.

SERAFINA. Well, maybe a big red heart with MAMA written across it.

ALVARO. Wrong again, Baronessa.

(*He takes off his tie and slowly unbuttons his shirt, gazing at her with an intensely warm smile. He divides the unbuttoned shirt, turning toward her his bare chest. She utters a gasp and rises.*)

SERAFINA. No, no, no!—Not a rose! (*She says it as if she were evading her feelings.*)

ALVARO. Si, si, una rosa!

SERAFINA. I—don't feel good! The air is . . .

ALVARO. Che fate, che fate, che dite?

SERAFINA. The house has a tin roof on it!—The air is—I got to go outside the house to breathe! Scu-scusatemi! (*She goes out onto the porch and clings to one of the spindling porch columns for support, breathing hoarsely with a hand to her throat. He comes out slowly.*)

ALVARO (*gently*). I didn't mean to surprise you!—Mi dispiace molto!

SERAFINA (*with enforced calm*). Don't talk about it! Anybody could have a rose tattoo.—It don't mean nothing.—You know how a tin roof is. It catches the heat all day and it don't cool off until—midnight . . .

ALVARO. No, no, not until midnight. (*She makes a faint laughing sound, is quite breathless and leans her forehead against the porch column. He places his fingers delicately against the small of her back.*) It make it hot in the bedroom—so

that you got to sleep without nothing on you . . .

SERAFINA. No, you—can't stand the covers . . .

ALVARO. You can't even stand a—*nightgown!* (*His fingers press her back.*)

SERAFINA. Please. There is a strega next door; she's always watching!

ALVARO. It's been so long since I felt the soft touch of a woman! (*She gasps loudly and turns to the door.*) Where are you going?

SERAFINA. I'm going back in the house! (*She enters the parlor again, still with forced calm.*)

ALVARO. (*following her inside*). Now, now, what is the matter?

SERAFINA. I got a feeling like I have—forgotten something.

ALVARO. What?

SERAFINA. I can't remember.

ALVARO. It couldn't be nothing important if you can't remember. Let's open the chocolate box and have some candy.

SERAFINA (*eager for any distraction*). Yes! Yes, open the box!

(ALVARO *places a chocolate in her hand. She stares at it blankly.*)

ALVARO. Eat it, eat the chocolate. If you don't eat it, it will melt in your hand and make your fingers all gooey!

SERAFINA. Please, I . . .

ALVARO. Eat it!

SERAFINA (*weakly and gagging*). I can't, I can't, I would choke! Here, you eat it.

ALVARO. Put it in my mouth! (*She puts the chocolate in his mouth.*) Now, look. Your fingers are gooey!

SERAFINA. Oh!—I better go wash them! (*She rises unsteadily. He seizes her hands and licks her fingers.*)

ALVARO. Mmmm! Mmmmm! Good, very good!

SERAFINA. Stop that, stop that, stop that! That—ain't—nice . . .

ALVARO. I'll lick off the chocolate for you.

SERAFINA. No, no, no!—I am the mother of a fifteen-year-old girl!

ALVARO. You're as old as your arteries, Baronessa. Now set back down. The fingers are now white as snow!

SERAFINA. You don't—understand—how I feel . . .

ALVARO. You don't understand how I feel.

SERAFINA (*doubtfully*). How do you—feel? (*In answer, he stretches the palms of his hands out toward her as if she were a fireplace in a freezing-cold room.*)—What does—*that*—mean?

ALVARO. The night is warm but I feel like my hands are—freezing!

SERAFINA. Bad—circulation . . .

ALVARO. No, too *much* circulation! (AL-VARO *becomes tremulously pleading, shuffling forward a little, slightly crouched like a beggar.*) Across the room I feel the sweet warmth of a lady!

SERAFINA (*retreating, doubtfully*). Oh, you talk a sweet mouth. I think you talk a sweet mouth to fool a woman.

ALVARO. No, no, I know that's what warms the world, that is what makes it the summer! (*He seizes the hand she holds defensively before her and presses it to his own breast in a crushing grip.*) Without it, the rose—the rose would not grow on the bush; the fruit would not grow on the tree!

SERAFINA. I know, and the truck—the truck would not haul the bananas! But, Mr. Mangiacavallo, that is my hand, not a sponge. I got bones in it. Bones break!

ALVARO. Scusatemi, Baronessa! (*He returns her hand to her with a bow.*) For me it is winter, because I don't have in my life the sweet warmth of a lady. I live with my hands in my pockets! (*He stuffs his hands violently into his pants' pockets, then jerks them out again. A small cellophane-wrapped disk falls on the floor, escaping his notice, but not* SERAFINA's.)— You don't like the poetry!—How can a man talk to you?

SERAFINA (*ominously*). I like the poetry good. Is that a piece of the poetry that you dropped out of your pocket? (*He looks down.*)—No, no, right by your foot!

ALVARO (*aghast as he realizes what it is that she has seen*). Oh, that's—that's nothing! (*He kicks it under the sofa.*)

SERAFINA (*fiercely*). You talk a sweet mouth about women. Then drop such a thing from your pocket?—Va via, vigliacco! (*She marches grandly out of the room, pulling the curtains together behind her. He hangs his head despairingly between his hands. Then he approaches the curtains timidly.*)

ALVARO (*in a small voice*). Baronessa?

SERAFINA. Pick up what you dropped on the floor and go to the Square Roof with it. Buona notte!

ALVARO. Baronessa! (*He parts the curtains and peeks through them.*)

SERAFINA. I told you good night. Here is no casa privata. Io, non sono puttana!

ALVARO. Understanding is—very—necessary!

SERAFINA. I understand plenty. You think you got a good thing, a thing that is cheap!

ALVARO. You make a mistake, Baronessa! (*He comes in and drops to his knees beside her, pressing his cheek to her flank. He speaks rhapsodically.*) So soft is a lady! So, so, so, so soft—is a lady!

SERAFINA. Andate via, sporcaccione, andate a casa! Lasciatemi! Lasciatemi stare!

(*She springs up and runs into the parlor. He pursues. The chase is grotesquely violent and comic. A floor lamp is overturned. She seizes the chocolate box and threatens to slam it into his face if he continues toward her. He drops to his knees, crouched way over, and pounds the floor with his fists, sobbing.*)

ALVARO. Everything in my life turns out like this!

SERAFINA. Git up, git up, git up!—you village idiot's grandson! There is people watching you through that window, the—strega next door . . . (*He rises, slowly.*) And where is the shirt that I loaned you? (*He shuffles abjectly across the room, then hands her a neatly wrapped package.*)

ALVARO. My sister wrapped it up for you. —My sister was very happy I met this *nice* lady!

SERAFINA. Maybe she thinks I will pay the grocery bill while she plays the numbers!

ALVARO. She don't think nothing like that. She is an old maid, my sister. She wants—nephews—nieces . . .

SERAFINA. You tell her for me I don't give nephews and nieces!

(ALVARO *hitches his shoulders violently in his embarrassment and shuffles over to where he had left his hat. He blows the dust off it and rubs the crown on his sleeve.* SERAFINA *presses a knuckle to her lips as she watches his awkward gestures. She is a little abashed by his humility. She speaks next with the great dignity of a widow whose respectability has stood the test.*)

SERAFINA. Now, Mr. Mangiacavallo, please tell me the truth about something. *When* did you get the tattoo put on your chest?

ALVARO (*shyly and sadly, looking down*

at his hat). I got it tonight—after supper . . .

SERAFINA. That's what I thought. You had it put on because I told you about my husband's tattoo.

ALVARO. I wanted to be—close to you . . . to make you—happy . . .

SERAFINA. *Tell it to the marines!* (*He puts on his hat with an apologetic gesture*). You got the tattoo and the chocolate box after supper, and then you come here to fool me!

ALVARO. I got the chocolate box a long time ago.

SERAFINA. How long ago? If that is not too much a personal question!

ALVARO. I got it the night the door was slammed in my face by the girl that I give —the zircon . . .

SERAFINA. Let that be a lesson. Don't try to fool women. You are not smart enough! —Now take the shirt back. You can keep it.

ALVARO. Huh?

SERAFINA. Keep it. I don't want it back.

ALVARO. You just now said that you did.

SERAFINA. It's a man's shirt, ain't it?

ALVARO. You just now accused me of trying to steal it off you.

SERAFINA. Well, you been making me nervous!

ALVARO. Is it my fault you been a widow too long?

SERAFINA. You make a mistake!

ALVARO. *You* make a mistake!

SERAFINA. Both of us make a mistake! (*There is a pause. They both sigh profoundly.*)

ALVARO. We should of have been friends, but I think we meet the wrong day.— Suppose I go out and come in the door again and we start all over?

SERAFINA. No, I think it's no use. The day was wrong to begin with, because of two women. Two women, they told me today that my husband had put on my head the nanny-goat's horns!

ALVARO. How is it possible to put horns on a widow?

SERAFINA. That was before! They told me my husband was having a steady affair with a woman at the Square Roof. What was the name on the shirt, on the slip of paper? Do you remember the name?

ALVARO. You told me to . . .

SERAFINA. Tell me! Do you remember?

ALVARO. I remember the name because I know the woman. The name was Estelle Hohengarten.

SERAFINA. Take me there! Take me to the Square Roof!—Wait, wait!

(*She plunges into the dining room, snatches a knife out of the sideboard drawer and thrusts it in her purse. Then she rushes back, with the blade of the knife protruding from the purse.*)

ALVARO (*noticing the knife*). They—got a cover charge there . . .

SERAFINA. I will charge them a cover! Take me there now, this minute!

ALVARO. The fun don't start till midnight.

SERAFINA. I will start the fun sooner.

ALVARO. The floor show commences at midnight.

SERAFINA. I will commence it! (*She rushes to the phone.*) Yellow Cab, please, Yellow Cab. I want to go to the Square Roof out of my house! Yes, you come to my house and take me to the Square Roof right this minute! My number is— what is my number? Oh my God, what is my number?—64 is my number on Front Street! Subito, subito—quick!

(*The goat bleats outside.*)

ALVARO. Baronessa, the knife's sticking out of your purse. (*He grabs the purse.*) What do you want with this weapon?

SERAFINA. To cut the lying tongue out of a woman's mouth! Saying she has on her breast the tattoo of my husband because he had put on me the horns of a goat! I cut the heart out of that woman, she cut the heart out of me!

ALVARO. Nobody's going to cut the heart out of nobody!

(*A car is heard outside, and* SERAFINA *rushes to the porch.*)

SERAFINA (*shouting*). Hey, Yellow Cab, Yellow Cab, Yellow—Cab . . . (*The car passes by without stopping. With a sick moan she wanders into the yard. He follows her with a glass of wine.*)—Something hurts—in my heart . . .

ALVARO (*leading her gently back to the house*). Baronessa, drink this wine on the porch and keep your eyes on that star. (*He leads her to a porch pillar and places the glass in her trembling hand. She is now submissive.*) You know the name of that star? That star is Venus. She is the only female star in the sky. Who put her up there? Mr. Siccardi, the transportation

manager of the Southern Fruit Company?
No. She was put there by God. (*He enters
the house and removes the knife from her
purse.*) And yet there's some people· that
don't believe in nothing. (*He picks up the
telephone.*) Esplanade 9-7-0.

SERAFINA. What are you doing?

ALVARO. Drink that wine and I'll settle
this whole problem for you. (*On the
telephone*) I want to speak to the blackjack dealer, please, Miss Estelle Hohengarten . . .

SERAFINA. Don't talk to that woman,
she'll lie!

ALVARO. Not Estelle Hohengarten. She
deals a straight game of cards—Estelle?
This is Mangiacavallo. I got a question
to ask you which is a personal question.
It has to do with a very good-looking
truckdriver, not living now but once on
a time thought to have been a very well-
known character at the Square Roof. His
name was . . . (*He turns questioningly
to the door where* SERAFINA *is standing.*)
What was his name, Baronessa?

SERAFINA (*hardly breathing*). Rosario
delle Rose!

ALVARO. Rosario delle Rose was the
name. (*There is a pause.*)—E vero?—
Mah! Che peccato . . .

(SERAFINA *drops her glass and springs
into the parlor with a savage outcry. She
snatches the phone from* ALVARO *and
screams into it.*)

SERAFINA (*wildly*). This is the wife
that's speaking! What do you know of
my husband, what is the lie?

(*A strident voice sounds over the wire.*)

THE VOICE (*loud and clear*). Don't you
remember? I brought you the rose-colored silk to make him a shirt. You said,
"For a man?" and I said, "Yes, for a
man that's wild like a Gypsy!" But if
you think I'm a liar, come here and let
me show you his rose tattooed on my
chest!

(SERAFINA *holds the phone away from
her as though it had burst into flame.
Then, with a terrible cry, she hurls it to
the floor. She staggers dizzily toward the
Madonna.* ALVARO *seizes her arm and
pushes her gently onto the sofa.*)

ALVARO. Piano, piano, Baronessa! This
will be gone, this will pass in a moment.
(*He puts a pillow behind her, then replaces the telephone.*)

SERAFINA (*staggering up from the sofa*).

The room's—going round . . .

ALVARO. You ought to stay lying down
a little while longer. I know, I know
what you need! A towel with some ice
in it to put on your forehead—Baronessa.
—You stay right there while I fix it! (*He
goes into the kitchen, and calls back.*)
Tòrno subito, Baronessa!

(*The little boy runs into the yard. He
leans against the bending trunk of the
palm, counting loudly.*)

THE LITTLE BOY. Five, ten, fifteen, twenty, twenty-five, thirty . . .

(*There is the sound of ice being chopped
in the kitchen.*)

SERAFINA. Dove siete, dove siete?

ALVARO. In cucina!—Ghiaccio . . .

SERAFINA. Venite qui!

ALVARO. Subito, subito . . .

SERAFINA (*turning to the shrine, with
fists knotted*). Non voglio, non voglio
farlo!

(*But she crosses slowly, compulsively
toward the shrine, with a trembling arm
stretched out.*)

THE LITTLE BOY. Seventy-five, eighty,
eighty-five, ninety, ninety-five, one hundred! (*Then, wildly*) *Ready or not you
shall be caught!*

(*At this cry,* SERAFINA *seizes the marble
urn and hurls it violently into the furthest
corner of the room. Then, instantly, she
covers her face. Outside the mothers are
heard calling their children home. Their
voices are tender as music, fading in and
out. The children appear slowly at the
side of the house, exhausted from their
wild play.*)

GIUSEPPINA. Vivi! Vi-vi!

PEPPINA. Salvatore!

VIOLETTA. Bruno! Come home, come
home!

(*The children scatter.* ALVARO *comes in
with the ice-pick.*)

ALVARO. I broke the point of the ice-
pick.

SERAFINA (*removing her hands from her
face*). *I don't want ice* . . . (*She looks
about her, seeming to gather a fierce
strength in her body. Her voice is hoarse,
her body trembling with violence, eyes narrow and flashing, her fists clenched.*) Now
I show you how wild and strong like a
man a woman can be! (*She crosses to the
screen door, opens it and shouts.*) Buona
notte, Mr. Mangiacavallo!

ALVARO. You—you make me go *home*,

now?

SERAFINA. No, no; senti, cretino! (*In a strident whisper*) You make out like you are going. You drive the truck out of sight where the witch can't see it. Then you come back and I leave the back door open for you to come in. Now, tell me good-by so all the neighbors can hear you! (*She shouts.*) Arrivederci!

ALVARO. Ha, ha! Capish! (*He shouts too.*) Arrivederci! (*He runs to the foot of the embankment steps.*)

SERAFINA (*still more loudly*). Buona notte!

ALVARO. Buona notte, Baronessa!

SERAFINA (*in a choked voice*). Give them my love; give everybody—my love . . . Arrivederci!

ALVARO. Ciao!

(ALVARO *scrambles on down the steps and goes off.* SERAFINA *comes down into the yard. The goat bleats. She mutters savagely to herself.*)

SERAFINA. Sono una bestia, una bestia feroce!

(*She crosses quickly around to the back of the house. As she disappears, the truck is heard driving off; the lights sweep across the house.* SERAFINA *comes in through the back door. She is moving with great violence, gasping and panting. She rushes up to the Madonna and addresses her passionately with explosive gestures, leaning over so that her face is level with the statue's.*)

SERAFINA. Ora, ascolta, Signora! You hold in the cup of your hand this little house and you smash it! You break this little house like the shell of a bird in your hand, because you have hate Serafina?— Serafina that *loved* you!—No, no, no, you don't speak! I don't believe in you, Lady! You're just a poor little doll with the paint peeling off, and now I blow out the light and I forget you the way you forget Serafina! (*She blows out the vigil light.*) Ecco —fatto!

(*But now she is suddenly frightened: the vehemence and boldness have run out. She gasps a little and backs away from the shrine, her eyes rolling apprehensively this way and that. The parrot squawks at her. The goat bleats. The night is full of sinister noises, harsh bird cries, the sudden flapping of wings in the cane-brake, a distant shriek of Negro laughter.* SERAFINA *retreats to the window and opens the shutters wider to admit the moonlight. She*

stands panting by the window with a fist pressed to her mouth. In the back of the house a door slams open. SERAFINA *catches her breath and moves as though for protection behind the dummy of the bride.* ALVARO *enters through the back door, calling out softly and hoarsely, with great excitement.*)

ALVARO. Dove? Dove sei, cara?

SERAFINA (*faintly*). Sono qui . . .

ALVARO. You have turn out the light!

SERAFINA. The moon is enough . . . (*He advances toward her. His white teeth glitter as he grins.* SERAFINA *retreats a few steps from him. She speaks tremulously, making an awkward gesture toward the sofa.*) Now we can go on with our—conversation . . . (*She catches her breath sharply.*)

(*The curtain comes down.*)

SCENE TWO

It is just before daybreak of the next day. ROSA *and* JACK *appear at the top of the embankment steps.*

ROSA. I thought they would never leave. (*She comes down the steps and out in front of the house, then calls back to him.*) Let's go down there.

(*He obeys hesitatingly. Both are very grave. The scene is played as close as possible to the audience. She sits very straight. He stands behind her with his hands on her shoulders.*)

ROSA (*leaning her head back against him*). This was the happiest day of my life, and this is the saddest night . . .

(*He crouches in front of her.*)

SERAFINA (*from inside the house*). Aaaaaahhhhhhhh!

JACK (*springing up, startled*). What's that?

ROSA (*resentfully*). Oh! That's Mama dreaming about my father.

JACK. I—feel like a—*heel!* I feel like a rotten heel!

ROSA. Why?

JACK. That promise I made your mother.

ROSA. I hate her for it.

JACK. Honey—Rosa, she—wanted to protect you.

(*There is a long-drawn cry from the back of the house: "Ohhhh—Rosario!"*)

ROSA. She wanted me not to have what

she's dreaming about . . .

JACK. Naw, naw, honey, she—wanted to —protect you . . .

(*The cry from within is repeated softly.*)

ROSA. Listen to her making love in her sleep! Is that what she wants *me* to do, just—*dream* about it?

JACK (*humbly*). She knows that her Rosa *is* a rose. And she wants her rose to have someone—better than *me* . . .

ROSA. *Better* than—*you!* (*She speaks as if the possibility were too preposterous to think of.*)

JACK. You see me through—rose-colored —glasses . . .

ROSA. I see you with love!

JACK. Yes, but your Mama sees me with —common sense . . . (SERAFINA *cries out again.*) I got to be going! (*She keeps a tight hold on him. A rooster crows.*) Honey, it's so late the roosters are crowing!

ROSA. They're fools, they're fools, it's early!

JACK. Honey, on that island I almost forgot my promise. Almost, but not quite. Do you understand, honey?

ROSA. Forget the promise!

JACK. I made it on my knees in front of Our Lady. I've got to leave now, honey.

ROSA (*clasping him fiercely*). You'd have to break my arms to!

JACK. Rosa, Rosa! You want to drive me crazy?

ROSA. I want you not to remember.

JACK. You're a very young girl! Fifteen —fifteen is too young!

ROSA. Caro, caro, carissimo!

JACK. You got to save some of those feelings for when you're grown up!

ROSA. Carissimo!

JACK. Hold some of it back until you're grown!

ROSA. I have been grown for two years!

JACK. No, no, that ain't what I . . .

ROSA. Grown enough to be married, and have a—baby!

JACK (*springing up*). Oh, good—Lord! (*He circles around, pounding his palm repeatedly with his fist and champing his teeth together with a grimace. Suddenly he speaks.*) I got to be going!

ROSA. You want me to scream? (*He groans and turns away from her to resume his desperate circle.* ROSA *is blocking the way with her body.*)—I know, I know! You don't want me! (*Jack groans through*

his gritting teeth.) No, no, you don't want me . . .

JACK. Now you listen to me! You almost got into trouble today on that island! You almost did, but not quite!—But it didn't quite happen and no harm is done and you can just—forget it . . .

ROSA. It is the only thing in my life that I want to remember!—When are you going back to New Orleans?

JACK. Tomorrow.

ROSA. When does your—ship sail?

JACK. Tomorrow.

ROSA. Where to?

JACK. Guatemala.

SERAFINA (*from the house*). Aahh!

ROSA. Is that a long trip?

JACK. After Guatemala, Buenos Aires. After Buenos Aires, Rio. Then around the Straits of Magellan and back up the west coast of South America, putting in at three ports before we dock at San Francisco.

ROSA. I don't think I will—ever see you again . . .

JACK. The ship won't sink!

ROSA (*faintly and forlornly*). No, but— I think it could just happen once, and if it don't happen that time, it never can— later . . . (*A rooster crows. They face each other sadly and quietly.*) You don't need to be very old to understand how it works out. One time, one time, only once, it could be—God!—to remember.—Other times? Yes—they'd be something.—But only once, God—to remember . . . (*With a little sigh she crosses to pick up his white cap and hand it gravely to him.*)—I'm sorry to you it didn't—mean—that much . . .

JACK (*taking the cap and hurling it to the ground*). Look! Look at my knuckles? You know how them scabs got there? They got there because I banged my knuckles that hard on the deck of the sailboat!

ROSA. Because it—didn't quite happen? (JACK *jerks his head up and down in grotesquely violent assent to her question.* ROSA *picks up his cap and returns it to him again.*)—Because of the promise to Mama! I'll never forgive her . . . (*There is a pause.*) What time in the afternoon must you be on the boat?

JACK. Why?

ROSA. Just tell me what time.

JACK. Five!—Why?

ROSA. What will you be doing till five?

JACK. Well, I could be a goddam liar and tell you I was going to—pick me a hatful of daisies in—Audubon Park.—Is that what you want me to tell you?

ROSA. No, tell me the truth.

JACK. All right, I'll tell you the truth. I'm going to check in at some flea-bag hotel on North Rampart Street. Then I'm going to get loaded! And then I'm going to get . . . (*He doesn't complete the sentence but she understands him. She places the hat more becomingly on his blond head.*)

ROSA. Do me a little favor. (*Her hand slides down to his cheek and then to his mouth.*) Before you get loaded and before you—before you—

JACK. Huh?

ROSA. Look in the waiting room·at the Greyhound bus station, please. At twelve o'clock, noon!

JACK. Why?

ROSA. You might find me there, waiting for you . . .

JACK. What—what good would that do?

ROSA. I never been to a hotel but I know they have numbers on doors and some-times—numbers are—lucky.—Aren't they? —Sometimes?—Lucky?

JACK. You want to buy me a ten-year stretch in the brig?

ROSA. I want you to give me that little gold ring on your ear to put on my finger. —I want to give you my heart to keep forever! And ever! And ever! (*Slowly and with a barely audible sigh she leans her face against him.*) Look for me! I will be there!

JACK (*breathlessly*). In all of my life, I never felt nothing so sweet as the feel of your little warm body in my arms . . .

(*He breaks away and runs toward the road. From the foot of the steps he glares fiercely back at her like a tiger through the bars of a cage. She clings to the two porch pillars, her body leaning way out.*)

ROSA. Look for me! I will be there!

(*JACK runs away from the house. ROSA returns inside. Listlessly she removes her dress and falls on the couch in her slip, kicking off her shoes. Then she begins to cry, as one cries only once in a lifetime, and the scene dims out.*)

SCENE THREE

The time is three hours later.

We see first the exterior view of the small frame building against a night sky which is like the starry blue robe of Our Lady. It is growing slightly paler.

The faint light discloses ROSA asleep on the couch. The covers are thrown back for it has been a warm night, and on the con-cave surface of the white cloth, which is like the dimly lustrous hollow of a shell, is the body of the sleeping girl which is clad only in a sheer white slip.

A cock crows. A gentle wind stirs the white curtains inward and the tendrils of vine at the windows, and the sky lightens enough to distinguish the purple trumpets of the morning glory against the very dim blue of the sky in which the planet Venus remains still undimmed.

In the back of the cottage someone is heard coughing hoarsely and groaning in the way a man does who has drunk very heavily the night before. Bedsprings creak as a heavy figure rises. Light spills dimly through the curtains, now closed, between the two front rooms.

There are heavy, padding footsteps and ALVARO comes stumbling rapidly into the dining room with the last bottle of Spu-manti in the crook of an arm, his eyes barely open, legs rubbery, saying, "Wuh-wuh-wuh-wuh-wuh-wuh . . ." like the breathing of an old dog. The scene should be played with the pantomimic lightness, almost fantasy, of an early Chaplin comedy. He is wearing only his trousers and his chest is bare. As he enters he col-lides with the widow dummy, staggers back, pats her inflated bosom in a timid, apologetic way, remarking:

ALVARO. Scusami, Signora, I am the grandson of the village idiot of Ribera!

(*ALVARO backs into the table and is pro-pelled by the impact all the way to the curtained entrance to the parlor. He draws the curtains apart and hangs onto them, peering into the room. Seeing the sleeping girl, he blinks several times, suddenly makes a snoring sound in his nostrils and waves one hand violently in front of his eyes as if to dispel a vision. Outside the goat utters a long "Baaaaaaaaaa!" As if in response, ALVARO whispers, in the same basso key, "Che bella!" The first vowel of "bella" is enormously prolonged like the "baaa" of the goat. On his rub-bery legs he shuffles forward a few steps*

*and leans over to peer more intently at the
vision. The goat bleats again.* ALVARO *whispers more loudly:* "Che bel-*la!" He drains
the Spumanti, then staggers to his knees,
the empty bottle rolling over the floor. He
crawls on his knees to the foot of the bed,
then leans against it like a child peering
into a candy shop window, repeating:* "Che
bel-*la, che* bel-*la!" with antiphonal responses from the goat outside. Slowly,
with tremendous effort, as if it were the
sheer side of a precipice, he clambers upon
the couch and crouches over the sleeping
girl in a leap-frog position, saying* "Che
bel-*la!" quite loudly, this time, in a tone
of innocently joyous surprise. All at once*
ROSA *wakens. She screams, even before she
is quite awake, and springs from the couch
so violently that* ALVARO *topples over to the
floor.*

(SERAFINA *cries out almost instantly after*
ROSA. *She lunges through the dining room
in her torn and disordered nightgown. At
the sight of the man crouched by the couch
a momentary stupefaction turns into a
burst of savage fury. She flies at him like
a great bird, tearing and clawing at his
stupefied figure. With one arm* ALVARO
*wards off her blows, plunging to the floor
and crawling into the dining room. She
seizes a broom with which she flails him
about the head, buttocks and shoulders
while he scrambles awkwardly away. The
assault is nearly wordless. Each time she
strikes at him she hisses:* "Sporcaccione!"
He continually groans: "Dough, dough,
dough!" *At last he catches hold of the
widow dummy which he holds as a shield
before him while he entreats the two
women.*)

ALVARO. Senti, Baronessa! Signorina! I
didn't know what I was doin', I was
dreamin', I was just dreamin'! I got turn
around in the house; I got all twisted! I
thought that you was your Mama!—Sono
ubriaco! Per favore!

ROSA (*seizing the broom*). That's enough,
Mama!

SERAFINA (*rushing to the phone*). Police!

ROSA (*seizing the phone*). No, no, no,
no, no, no!—You want everybody to know?

SERAFINA (*weakly*). Know?—Know
what, cara?

ROSA. Just give him his clothes, now,
Mama, and let him get out! (*She is clutching a bedsheet about herself.*)

ALVARO. Signorina—young lady! I swear

I was *dreaming!*

SERAFINA. Don't speak to my daughter!
(*Then, turning to* ROSA)—Who is this
man? How did this man get here?

ROSA (*coldly*). Mama, don't say any
more. Just give him his clothes in the bedroom so he can get out!

ALVARO (*still crouching*). I am so sorry,
so sorry! I don't remember a thing but
that I was dreaming!

SERAFINA (*shoving him toward the back
of the room with her broom*). Go on, go
get your clothes on, you—idiot's grandson,
you!—Svelto, svelto, piu svelto! (ALVARO
*continues his apologetic mumbling in the
back room.*) Don't talk to me, don't say
nothing! Or I will kill you!

(*A few moments later* ALVARO *rushes
around the side of the house, his clothes
half buttoned and his shirttails out.*)

ALVARO. But, Baronessa, I love you! (*A
tea kettle sails over his head from behind
the house.* THE STREGA *bursts into laughter. Despairingly* ALVARO, *tucking his shirttails in and shaking his head.*) Baronessa,
Baronessa, I love you!

(*As* ALVARO *runs off,* THE STREGA *is heard
cackling:*)

THE STREGA'S VOICE. The Wops are at it
again. Had a truckdriver in the house all
night!

(ROSA *is feverishly dressing. From the
bureau she has snatched a shimmering
white satin slip, disappearing for a moment behind a screen to put it on as* SERAFINA *comes padding sheepishly back into
the room, her nightgown now covered by a
black rayon kimona sprinkled with poppies, her voice tremulous with fear, shame
and apology.*)

ROSA (*behind the screen*). Has the man
gone?

SERAFINA. That—man?

ROSA. Yes, "that man!"

SERAFINA (*inventing desperately*). I don't
know how he got in. Maybe the back door
was open.

ROSA. Oh, yes, maybe it was!

SERAFINA. Maybe he—climbed in a window . . .

ROSA. Or fell down the chimney, maybe!
(*She comes from behind the screen, wearing the white bridal slip.*)

SERAFINA. Why you put on the white
things I save for your wedding?

ROSA. Because I want to. That's a good
enough reason. (*She combs her hair sav-*

agely.)

SERAFINA. I want you to understand about that man. That was a man that— that was—that was a man that . . .

ROSA. You can't think of a lie?

SERAFINA. He was a—truckdriver, cara. He got in a fight, he was chase by—policemen!

ROSA. They chased him into your bedroom?

SERAFINA. I took pity on him, I give him first aid, I let him sleep on the floor. He give me his promise—he . . .

ROSA. Did he kneel in front of Our Lady? Did he promise that he would respect your innocence?

SERAFINA. Oh, cara, cara! (*Abandoning all pretense*) He was Sicilian; he had rose oil in his hair and the rose tattoo of your father. In the dark room I couldn't see his clown face. I closed my eyes and dreamed that he was your father! I closed my eyes! I dreamed that he was your father . . .

ROSA. Basta, basta, non voglio sentire piu niente! The only thing worse than a liar is a liar that's also a hyprocrite!

SERAFINA. Senti, per favore! (ROSA *wheels about from the mirror and fixes her mother with a long and withering stare.* SERAFINA *cringes before it.*) Don't look at me like that with the eyes of your father! (*She shields her face as from a terrible glare.*)

ROSA. Yes, I am looking at you with the eyes of my father. I see you the way *he* saw you. (*She runs to the table and seizes the piggy bank.*) Like this, this pig! (SERAFINA *utters a long, shuddering cry like a cry of childbirth.*) I need five dollars. I'll take it out of this! (ROSA *smashes the piggy bank to the floor and rakes some coins into her purse.* SERAFINA *stoops to the floor. There is the sound of a train whistle.* ROSA *is now fully dressed, but she hesitates, a little ashamed of her cruelty— but only a little.* SERAFINA *cannot meet her daughter's eyes. At last the girl speaks.*)

SERAFINA. How beautiful—is my daughter! Go to the boy!

ROSA (*as if she might be about to apologize*). Mama? He didn't touch me—he just said—"Che bella!"

(SERAFINA *turns slowly, shamefully, to face her. She is like a peasant in the presence of a young princess.* ROSA *stares at her a moment longer, then suddenly catches her breath and runs out of the house. As the girl leaves,* SERAFINA *calls:*)

SERAFINA. Rosa, Rosa, the—wrist watch! (SERAFINA *snatches up the little gift box and runs out onto the porch with it. She starts to call her daughter again, holding the gift out toward her, but her breath fails her.*) Rosa, Rosa, the—wrist watch . . . (*Her arms fall to her side. She turns, the gift still ungiven. Senselessly, absently, she holds the watch to her ear again. She shakes it a little, then utters a faint, startled laugh.*)

(ASSUNTA *appears beside the house and walks directly in, as though* SERAFINA *had called her.*)

SERAFINA. Assunta, the urn is broken. The ashes are spilt on the floor and I can't touch them.

(ASSUNTA *stops to pick up the pieces of the shattered urn.* SERAFINA *has crossed to the shrine and relights the candle before the Madonna.*)

ASSUNTA. There are no ashes.

SERAFINA. Where—where are they? Where have the ashes gone?

ASSUNTA (*crossing to the shrine*). The wind has blown them away.

(ASSUNTA *places what remains of the broken urn in* SERAFINA'S *hands.* SERAFINA *turns it tenderly in her hands and then replaces it on the top of the prie-dieu before the Madonna.*)

SERAFINA. A man, when he burns, leaves only a handful of ashes. No woman can hold him. The wind must blow him away.

(ALVARO'S *voice is heard, calling from the top of the highway embankment.*)

ALVARO'S VOICE. Rondinella felice!

(*The nieighborhood women hear* ALVARO *calling, and there is a burst of mocking laughter from some of them. Then they all converge on the house from different directions and gather before the porch.*)

PEPPINA. Serafina delle Rose!

GIUSEPPINA. Baronessa! Baronessa delle Rose!

PEPPINA. There is a man on the road without the shirt!

GIUSEPPINA (*with delight*). Si, si! Senza camicia!

PEPPINA. All he got on his chest is a rose tattoo! (*To the women*) She lock up his shirt so he can't go to the high school?

(*The women shriek with laughter. In the house* SERAFINA *snatches up the package containing the silk shirt, while* ASsunta *closes the shutters of the parlor windows.*)

serafina. Un momento! (*She tears the paper off the shirt and rushes out onto the porch, holding the shirt above her head defiantly.*) Ecco la camicia!

(*With a soft cry,* serafina *drops the shirt, which is immediately snatched up by* peppina. *At this point the music begins again, with a crash of percussion, and continues to the end of the play.* peppina *flourishes the shirt in the air like a banner and tosses it to* giuseppina, *who is now on the embankment.* giuseppina *tosses it on to* mariella, *and she in her turn to* violetta, *who is above her, so that the brilliantly colored shirt moves in a zig-zag course through the pampas grass to the very top of the embankment, like a streak of flame shooting up a dry hill. The women call out as they pass the shirt along:*)

peppina. Guardate questa camicia! Coloro di rose!

mariella (*shouting up to* alvaro). Corragio, signor!

giuseppina. Avanti, avanti, signor!

violetta (*at the top of the embankment, giving the shirt a final flourish above her*). Corragio, corragio! The Baronessa is waiting!

(*Bursts of laughter are mingled with the cries of the women. Then they sweep away like a flock of screaming birds, and* serafina *is left upon the porch, her eyes closed, a hand clasped to her breast. In the meanwhile, inside the house,* assunta *has poured out a glass of wine. Now she comes to the porch, offering the wine to* serafina *and murmuring:*)

assunta. Stai tranquilla.

serafina (*breathlessly*). Assunta, I'll tell you something that maybe you won't believe.

assunta (*with tender humor*). It is impossible to tell me anything that I don't believe.

serafina. Just now I felt on my breast the burning again of the rose. I know what it means. It means that I have conceived! (*She lifts the glass to her lips for a moment and then returns it to* assunta.) Two lives again in the body! Two, two lives again, two!

alvaro's voice (*nearer now, and sweetly urgent*). Rondinella felice!

(alvaro *is not visible on the embankment but* serafina *begins to move slowly toward his voice.*)

assunta. Dove vai, Serafina?

serafina (*shouting now, to* alvaro). Vengo, vengo, amore!

(*She starts up the embankment toward* alvaro *and the curtain falls as the music rises with her in great glissandi of sound.*)

A MOON FOR THE MISBEGOTTEN

Eugene O'Neill

First presented on Broadway by Carmen Capalbo and Stanley Chase
at the Bijou Theatre on May 2, 1957, with the following cast:

JOSIE HOGAN	Wendy Hiller	JAMES TYRONE, JR.	Franchot Tone
MIKE HOGAN	Glenn Cannon	T. STEDMAN HARDER	William Woodson
PHIL HOGAN	Cyril Cusack		

ACT ONE: The farmhouse. Around noon. Early September, 1923.

ACT TWO: The same, but with the interior of sitting room
revealed—11 o'clock that night.

ACT THREE: The same as Act One. No time elapses between
Acts Two and Three.

ACT FOUR: The same—Dawn of the following morning.

FOREWORD TO THE FIRST EDITION

A Moon for the Misbegotten is published herewith with no revisions or deletions. It is
an exact reproduction of the original manuscript which I delivered to Random House,
Inc., on completing the play in 1943.

It has never been presented on the New York stage nor are there outstanding rights or
plans for its production. Since I cannot presently give it the attention required for
appropriate presentation, I have decided to make it available in book form.
April, 1952   E. O'N.

INTRODUCTION

EUGENE GLADSTONE O'NEILL, born in New York on October 16, 1888, died at the age of 65 in Boston on November 27, 1953, after having been stricken with a form of palsy known as Parkinson's Disease about six years before. His death concluded a triumphant career that had temporarily ended by the middle of the 1930's when he was acknowledged the foremost American playwright and was the nonchalant possessor of three Pulitzer Prizes and the Nobel Prize, a distinction only one American had won before him. Death, however, produced only a brief hiatus in that career, for it was resumed posthumously by the publication and production of new plays written in his later years.

For a long time he had been working on an immense cycle of plays, most of which remained in so unfinished a state that he destroyed them in 1953, shortly before his death. One manuscript spared by the author and Mrs. O'Neill, *A Touch of the Poet,* has since been published by the Yale University Press and produced in Sweden at the Royal Dramatic Theatre (in April, 1957). A New York production is scheduled for the fall of 1958. Another play belonging to the cycle, entitled *More Stately Mansions,* was discovered in the spring of 1957 by Dr. Karl Ragnar Gierow, the director of the Royal Dramatic Theatre of Stockholm and producer of *Long Day's Journey Into Night.*

Setting aside his Cyclopean project for a nine-play history of the rise and fall of a New England family, for which he had once chosen the significant title *A Tale of Possessors Self-Dispossessed,* O'Neill in 1939 first wrote a remarkable long drama of disillusionment, *The Iceman Cometh.* It was presented on Broadway by the Theatre Guild in 1946, then more successfully staged by José Quintero at his Greenwich Village Circle-in-the-Square theatre in 1956. In 1940, O'Neill next composed the autobiographical play *Long Day's Journey Into Night,* which he kept from both playgoers and readers during his lifetime. When Mrs. O'Neill decided that there was no longer any reason to keep the play from the public, *Long Day's Journey Into Night* was published by the Yale University Press in 1956. It was staged on February 10 of the same year in Sweden and then with resounding success on Broadway, by Mr. Quintero, on November 27. A third play, *A Moon for the Misbegotten,* was written several years later, in 1943.* In requiring an exceptionally tall young actress for the part of the heroine Josie, the author posed a difficult casting problem for the Theatre Guild, the sponsoring management, which withdrew the play after an unsatisfactory mid-Western tryout in 1947. Ten years later, Carmen Capalbo and Stanley Chase, the venturesome producers of the Brecht-Weill *Threepenny Opera* and other off-beat works, gave *A Moon for the Misbegotten* its first Broadway showing after prevailing upon Wendy Hiller to play the part of Josie Hogan, O'Neill's slatternly virago, virgin, and *magna mater.*

Thinking of the author in general, but making a special reference to *A Moon for the Misbegotten,* the eminent critic Joseph Wood Krutch declared in *Theatre Arts* magazine (October, 1954) that "if you value at too high a rate mere deftness of construction and smoothness of dialogue, you are bound to underestimate him . . ." That is the danger to which many have been prone in assessing this drama. It is not necessary, however, to claim superiority for this play in the O'Neill canon to acknowledge its right to represent the higher reaches of the theatre of the 1950's. Mr. Krutch said of the author's work as a whole, "the faults are not fatal," and the play supports the conclusion of the critic: "A score of recent American writers know how to avoid his [O'Neill's] crudities. Not one can produce the impact which his sincerity produces." *A Moon for the Misbegotten* was O'Neill's last finished work, and in it he once more concerned himself lengthily and intensely with the themes of alienation and self-destructiveness that evoked his tragic plots and morose humor.

---

* From the same period of O'Neill's second spurt of playwriting, there has also survived a long one-acter, *Hughie,* written about 1940. A "comedy" about a hotel night-clerk and a touring vaudeville actor who is afraid to go to bed, the play was intended to be one of a series of one-acters entitled *By Way of Obit.* Since the plan was abandoned, *Hughie* is said to be the only one-act piece written by O'Neill after 1919, when he turned out three pieces (*Exorcism, The Trumpet,* and *Honor among the Bradleys*), which remained both unproduced and unpublished. *Hughie* has been scheduled for a premiere in Sweden, at the Royal Dramatic Theatre of Stockholm, in December, 1958, or January, 1959. Shortly thereafter the play will have its first production in English at the Circle-in-the-Square.

SCENE OF THE PLAY

The play takes place in Connecticut at the home of tenant farmer, Phil Hogan, between the hours of noon on a day in early September, 1923, and sunrise of the following day.

The house is not, to speak mildly, a fine example of New England architecture, placed so perfectly in its setting that it appears a harmonious part of the landscape, rooted in the earth. It has been moved to its present site, and looks it. An old box-like, clapboarded affair, with a shingled roof and brick chimney, it is propped up about two feet above ground by layers of timber blocks. There are two windows on the lower floor of this side of the house which faces front, and one window on the floor above. These windows have no shutters, curtains or shades. Each has at least one pane missing, a square of cardboard taking its place. The house had once been painted a repulsive yellow with brown trim, but the walls now are a blackened and weathered gray, flaked with streaks and splotches of dim lemon. Just around the left corner of the house, a flight of steps leads to the front door.

To make matters worse, a one-story, one-room addition has been tacked on at right. About twelve feet long by six high, this room, which is JOSIE HOGAN's bedroom, is evidently home-made. Its walls and sloping roof are covered with tar paper, faded to dark gray. Close to where it joins the house, there is a door with a flight of three unpainted steps leading to the ground. At right of door is a small window.

From these steps there is a footpath going around an old pear tree, at right-rear, through a field of hay stubble to a patch of woods. The same path also extends left to join a dirt road which leads up from the county highway (about a hundred yards off left) to the front door of the house, and thence back through a scraggly orchard of apple trees to the barn. Close to the house, under the window next to JOSIE's bedroom, there is a big boulder with a flat top.

ACT ONE

SCENE: *As described. It is just before noon. The day is clear and hot.*

The door of JOSIE's *bedroom opens and she comes out on the steps, bending to avoid bumping her head.*

JOSIE *is twenty-eight. She is so oversize for a woman that she is almost a freak— five feet eleven in her stockings and weighs around one hundred and eighty. Her sloping shoulders are broad, her chest deep with large, firm breasts, her waist wide but slender by contrast with her hips and thighs. She has long smooth arms, immensely strong, although no muscles show. The same is true of her legs.*

She is more powerful than any but an exceptionally strong man, able to do the manual labor of two ordinary men. But there is no mannish quality about her. She is all woman.

The map of Ireland is stamped on her face, with its long upper lip and small nose, thick black eyebrows, black hair as coarse as a horse's mane, freckled, sunburned fair skin, high cheekbones and heavy jaw. It is not a pretty face, but her large dark-blue eyes give it a note of beauty, and her smile, revealing even white teeth, gives it charm.

She wears a cheap, sleeveless, blue cotton dress. Her feet are bare, the soles earth-stained and tough as leather.

She comes down the steps and goes left to the corner of the house and peers around it toward the barn. Then she moves swiftly to the right of the house and looks back.

JOSIE. Ah, thank God. (*She goes back toward the steps as her brother,* MIKE, *appears hurrying up from right-rear.*)

(MIKE HOGAN *is twenty, about four inches shorter than his sister. He is sturdily built, but seems almost puny compared to her. He has a common Irish face, its expression sullen, or slyly cunning, or primly self-righteous. He never forgets that he is a good Catholic, faithful to all the observances, and so is one of the élite of Almighty God in a world of damned sinners composed of Protestants and bad Catholics. In brief,* MIKE *is a New England Irish Catholic Puritan, Grade B, and an extremely irritating youth to have around.*

(MIKE *wears dirty overalls, a sweat-stained brown shirt. He carries a pitchfork.*)

JOSIE. Bad luck to you for a slowpoke. Didn't I tell you half-past eleven?

MIKE. How could I sneak here sooner

with him peeking round the corner of the barn to catch me if I took a minute's rest, the way he always does? I had to wait till he went to the pigpen. (*He adds viciously*) Where he belongs, the old hog! (JOSIE's *right arm strikes with surprising swiftness and her big hand lands on the side of his jaw. She means it to be only a slap, but his head jerks back and he stumbles, dropping the pitchfork, and pleads cringingly.*) Don't hit me, Josie! Don't, now!

JOSIE (*quietly*). Then keep your tongue off him. He's my father, too, and I like him, if you don't.

MIKE (*out of her reach—sullenly*). You're two of a kind, and a bad kind.

JOSIE (*good-naturedly*). I'm proud of it. And I didn't hit you, or you'd be flat on the ground. It was only a love tap to waken your wits, so you'll use them. If he catches you running away, he'll beat you half to death. Get your bag now. I've packed it. It's inside the door of my room with your coat laid over it. Hurry now, while I see what he's doing. (*She moves quickly to peer around the corner of the house at left. He goes up the steps into her room and returns carrying an old coat and a cheap bulging satchel. She comes back.*) There's no sight of him. (MIKE *drops the satchel on the ground while he puts on the coat.*) I put everything in the bag. You can change to your Sunday suit in the can at the station or in the train, and don't forget to wash your face. I know you want to look your best when our brother, Thomas, sees you on his doorstep. (*Her tone becomes derisively amused.*) And him way up in the world, a noble sergeant of the Bridgeport police. Maybe he'll get you on the force. It'd suit you. I can see you leading drunks to the lockup while you give them a lecture on temperance. Or if Thomas can't get you a job, he'll pass you along to our brother, John, the noble barkeep in Meriden. He'll teach you the trade. You'll make a nice one, who'll never steal from the till, or drink, and who'll tell customers they've had enough and better go home just when they're beginning to feel happy. (*She sighs regretfully.*) Ah, well, Mike, you was born a priest's pet, and there's no help for it.

MIKE. That's right! Make fun of me again, because I want to be decent.

JOSIE. You're worse than decent. You're

virtuous.

MIKE. Well, that's a thing nobody can say about— (*He stops, a bit ashamed, but mostly afraid to finish.*)

JOSIE (*amused*). About me? No, and what's more, they don't. (*She smiles mockingly.*) I know what a trial it's been to you, Mike, having a sister who's the scandal of the neighborhood.

MIKE. It's you that's saying it, not me. I don't want to part with hard feelings. And I'll keep on praying for you.

JOSIE (*roughly*). Och! To hell with your prayers!

MIKE (*stiffly*). I'm going. (*He picks up his bag.*)

JOSIE (*her manner softening*). Wait. (*She comes to him.*) Don't mind my rough tongue, Mike. I'm sorry to see you go, but it's the best thing for you. That's why I'm helping you, the same as I helped Thomas and John. You can't stand up to the Old Man any more than Thomas or John could, and the old divil would always keep you a slave. I wish you all the luck in the world, Mike. I know you'll get on—and God bless you. (*Her voice has softened, and she blinks back tears. She kisses him—then fumbling in the pocket of her dress, pulls out a little roll of one-dollar bills and presses it in his hand.*) Here's a little present over your fare. I took it from his little green bag, and won't he be wild when he finds out! But I can handle him.

MIKE (*enviously*). You can. You're the only one. (*Gratefully moved for a second*) Thank you, Josie. You've a kind heart. (*Then virtuously*) But I don't like taking stolen money.

JOSIE. Don't be a bigger jackass than you are already. Tell your conscience it's a bit of the wages he's never given you.

MIKE. That's true, Josie. It's rightfully mine. (*He shoves the money into his pocket.*)

JOSIE. Get along now, so you won't miss the trolley. And don't forget to get off the train at Bridgeport. Give my love to Thomas and John. No, never mind. They've not written me in years. Give them a boot in the tail for me.

MIKE. That's nice talk for a woman. You've a tongue as dirty as the Old Man's.

JOSIE (*impatiently*). Don't start preaching, like you love to, or you'll never go.

MIKE. You're as bad as he is, almost. It's his influence made you what you are, and him always scheming how he'll cheat people, selling them a broken-down nag or a sick cow or pig that he's doctored up to look good for a day or two. It's no better than stealing, and you help him.

JOSIE. I do. Sure, it's grand fun.

MIKE. You ought to marry and have a home of your own away from this shanty and stop your shameless ways with men. (*He adds, not without moral satisfaction*) Though it'd be hard to find a decent man who'd have you now.

JOSIE. I don't want a decent man, thank you. They're no fun. They're all sticks like you. And I wouldn't marry the best man on earth and be tied down to him alone.

MIKE (*with a cunning leer*). Not even Jim Tyrone, I suppose? (*She stares at him.*) You'd like being tied to money, I know that, and he'll be rich when his mother's estate is settled. (*Sarcastically*) I suppose you've never thought of that? Don't tell me! I've watched you making sheep's eyes at him.

JOSIE (*contemptuously*). So I'm leading Jim on to propose, am I?

MIKE. I know it's crazy, but maybe you're hoping if you got hold of him alone when he's mad drunk— Anyway, talk all you please to put me off, I'll bet my last penny you've cooked up some scheme to hook him, and the Old Man put you up to it. Maybe he thinks if he caught you with Jim and had witnesses to prove it, and his shotgun to scare him—

JOSIE (*controlling her anger*). You're full of bright thoughts. I wouldn't strain my brains any more, if I was you.

MIKE. Well, I wouldn't put it past the Old Man to try any trick. And I wouldn't put it past you, God forgive you. You've never cared about your virtue, or what man you went out with. You've always been brazen as brass and proud of your disgrace. You can't deny that, Josie.

JOSIE. I don't. (*Then ominously*) You'd better shut up now. I've been holding my temper, because we're saying good-by. (*She stands up.*) But I'm losing patience.

MIKE (*hastily*). Wait till I finish and you won't be mad at me. I was going to say I wish you luck with your scheming, for once. I hate Jim Tyrone's guts, with his quotin' Latin and his high-toned Jesuit College education, putting on airs as if he was too good to wipe his shoes on me, when he's nothing but a drunken bum

who never done a tap of work in his life, except acting on the stage while his father was alive to get him the jobs. (*Vindictively*) I'll pray you'll find a way to nab him, Josie, and skin him out of his last nickel!

JOSIE (*makes a threatening move toward him*). One more word out of you—(*Then contemptuously*) You're a dirty tick and it'd serve you right if I let you stay gabbing until father came and beat you to a jelly, but I won't. I'm too anxious to be rid of you. (*Roughly*) Get out of here, now! Do you think he'll stay all day with the pigs, you gabbing fool? (*She goes left to peer around the corner of the house—with real alarm.*) There he is, coming up to the barn. (MIKE *grabs the satchel, terrified. He slinks swiftly around the corner and disappears along the path to the woods, right-rear. She keeps watching her father and does not notice* MIKE's *departure.*) He's looking toward the meadow. He sees you're not working. He's running down there. He'll come here next. You'd better run for your life! (*She turns and sees he's gone—contemptuously*) I might have known. I'll bet you're a mile away by now, you rabbit! (*She peeks around the corner again—with amused admiration*) Look at my poor old father pelt. He's as spry on his stumpy legs as a yearling— and as full of rage as a nest of wasps! (*She laughs and comes back to look along the path to the woods.*) Well, that's the last of you, Mike, and good riddance. It was the little boy you used to be that I had to mother, and not you, I stole the money for. (*This dismisses him. She sighs.*) Well, himself will be here in a minute. I'd better be ready. (*She reaches in her bedroom corner by the door and takes out a sawed-off broom handle.*) Not that I need it, but it saves his pride. (*She sits on the steps with the broom handle propped against the steps near her right hand. A moment later, her father,* PHIL HOGAN, *comes running up from left-rear and charges around the corner of the house, his arms pumping up and down, his fists clenched, his face full of fighting fury.*)

(HOGAN *is fifty-five, about five feet six. He has a thick neck, lumpy, sloping shoulders, a barrel-like trunk, stumpy legs, and big feet. His arms are short and muscular, with large hairy hands. His head is round with thinning sandy hair. His face is fat with a snub nose, long upper lip, big mouth, and little blue eyes with bleached lashes and eyebrows that remind one of a white pig's. He wears heavy brogans, filthy overalls, and a dirty short-sleeved under-shirt. Arms and face are sunburned and freckled. On his head is an old wide-brimmed hat of coarse straw that would look more becoming on a horse. His voice is high-pitched with a pronounced brogue.*)

HOGAN (*stops as he turns the corner and sees her—furiously*). Where is he? Is he hiding in the house? I'll wipe the floors with him, the lazy bastard! (*Turning his anger against her*) Haven't you a tongue in your head, you great slut you?

JOSIE (*with provoking calm*). Don't be calling me names, you bad-tempered old hornet, or maybe I'll lose my temper, too.

HOGAN. To hell with your temper, you overgrown cow!

JOSIE. I'd rather be a cow than an ugly little buck goat. You'd better sit down and cool off. Old men shouldn't run around raging in the noon sun. You'll get sun-stroke.

HOGAN. To hell with sunstroke! Have you seen him?

JOSIE. Have I seen who?

HOGAN. Mike! Who else would I be after, the Pope? He was in the meadow, but the minute I turned my back he sneaked off. (*He sees the pitchfork.*) There's his pitchfork! Will you stop your lying!

JOSIE. I haven't said I didn't see him.

HOGAN. Then don't try to help him hide from me, or— Where is he?

JOSIE. Where you'll never find him.

HOGAN. We'll soon see! I'll bet he's in your room under the bed, the cowardly lump! (*He moves toward the steps.*)

JOSIE. He's not. He's gone like Thomas and John before him to escape your slave-driving.

HOGAN (*stares at her incredulously*). You mean he's run off to make his own way in the world?

JOSIE. He has. So make up your mind to it, and sit down.

HOGAN (*baffled, sits on the boulder and takes off his hat to scratch his head—with a faint trace of grudging respect*). I'd never dream he had that much spunk. (*His temper rising again*) And I know damned well he hadn't, not without you to give him the guts and help him, like the great soft fool you are!

JOSIE. Now don't start raging again, Father.

HOGAN (*seething*). You've stolen my satchel to give him, I suppose, like you did before for Thomas and John?

JOSIE. It was my satchel, too. Didn't I help you in the trade for the horse, when you got the Crowleys to throw in the satchel for good measure? I was up all night fixing that nag's forelegs so his knees wouldn't buckle together till after the Crowleys had him a day or two.

HOGAN (*forgets his anger to grin remi-niscently*). You've a wonderful way with animals, God bless you. And do you re-member the two Crowleys came back to give me a beating, and I licked them both?

JOSIE (*with calculating flattery*). You did. You're a wonderful fighter. Sure, you could give Jack Dempsey himself a run for his money.

HOGAN (*with sharp suspicion*). I could, but don't try to change the subject and fill me with blarney.

JOSIE. All right. I'll tell the truth then. They were getting the best of you till I ran out and knocked one of them tail over tin cup against the pigpen.

HOGAN (*outraged*). You're a liar! They was begging for mercy before you came. (*Furiously*) You thief, you! You stole my fine satchel for that lump! And I'll bet that's not all. I'll bet, like when Thomas and John sneaked off, you—(*He rises from the boulder threateningly.*) Listen, Josie, if you found where I hid my little green bag, and stole my money to give to that lousy altar boy, I'll—

JOSIE (*rises from the steps with the broom handle in her right hand*). Well, I did. So now what'll you do? Don't be threatening me. You know I'll beat better sense in your skull if you lay a finger on me.

HOGAN. I never yet laid hands on a woman—not when I was sober—but if it wasn't for that club—(*Bitterly*) A fine curse God put on me when he gave me a daughter as big and strong as a bull, and as vicious and disrespectful. (*Suddenly his eyes twinkle and he grins admiringly.*) Be God, look at you standing there with the club! If you ain't the damnedest daugh-ter in Connecticut, who is? (*He chuckles and sits on the boulder again.*)

JOSIE (*laughs and sits on the steps, put-ting the club away*). And if you ain't the damnedest father in Connecticut, who is?

HOGAN (*takes a clay pipe and plug of tobacco and knife from his pocket. He cuts the plug and stuffs his pipe—without rancor*). How much did you steal, Josie?

JOSIE. Six dollars only.

HOGAN. *Only!* Well, God grant someone with wits will see that dopey gander at the depot and sell him the railroad for the six. (*Grumbling*) It isn't the money I mind, Josie—

JOSIE. I know. Sure, what do you care for money? You'd give your last penny to the first beggar you met—if he had a shotgun pointed at your heart!

HOGAN. Don't be teasing. You know what I mean. It's the thought of that pious lump having my money that maddens me. I wouldn't put it past him to drop it in the collection plate next Sunday, he's that big a jackass.

JOSIE. I knew when you'd calmed down you'd think it worth six dollars to see the last of him.

HOGAN (*finishes filling his pipe*). Well, maybe I do. To tell the truth, I never liked him. (*He strikes a match on the seat of his overalls and lights his pipe.*) And I never liked Thomas and John, either.

JOSIE (*amused*). You've the same bad luck in sons I have in brothers.

HOGAN (*puffs ruminatively*). They all take after your mother's family. She was the only one in it had spirit, God rest her soul. The rest of them was a pious lousy lot. They wouldn't dare put food in their mouths before they said grace for it. They was too busy preaching temperance to have time for a drink. They spent so much time confessing their sins, they had no chance to do any sinning. (*He spits disgustedly.*) The scum of the earth! Thank God, you're like me and your mother.

JOSIE. I don't know if I should thank God for being like you. Sure, everyone says you're a wicked old tick, as crooked as a corkscrew.

HOGAN. I know. They're an envious lot, God forgive them. (*They both chuckle. He pulls on his pipe reflectively.*) You didn't get much thanks from Mike, I'll wager, for your help.

JOSIE. Oh, he thanked me kindly. And then he started to preach about my sins—and yours.

HOGAN. Oho, did he? (*Exploding*) For the love of God, why didn't you hold him till I could give him one good kick for a father's parting blessing!

JOSIE. I near gave him one myself.

HOGAN. When I think your poor mother was killed bringing that crummy calf into life! (*Vindictively*) I've never set foot in a church since, and never will. (*A pause. He speaks with a surprising sad gentleness.*) A sweet woman. Do you remember her, Josie? You were only a little thing when she died.

JOSIE. I remember her well. (*With a teasing smile which is half sad*) She was the one could put you in your place when you'd come home drunk and want to tear down the house for the fun of it.

HOGAN (*with admiring appreciation*). Yes, she could do it, God bless her. I only raised my hand to her once—just a slap because she told me to stop singing, it was after daylight. The next moment I was on the floor thinking a mule had kicked me. (*He chuckles.*) Since you've grown up, I've had the same trouble. There's no liberty in my own home.

JOSIE. That's lucky—or there wouldn't be any home.

HOGAN (*after a pause of puffing on his pipe*). What did that donkey, Mike, preach to you about?

JOSIE. Oh, the same as ever—that I'm the scandal of the countryside, carrying on with men without a marriage license.

HOGAN (*gives her a strange, embarrassed glance and then looks away. He does not look at her during the following dialogue. His manner is casual*). Hell roast his soul for saying it. But it's true enough.

JOSIE (*defiantly*). It is, and what of it? I don't care a damn for the scandal.

HOGAN. No. You do as you please and to hell with everyone.

JOSIE. Yes, and that goes for you, too, if you are my father. So don't you start preaching too.

HOGAN. Me, preach? Sure, the divil would die laughing. Don't bring me into it. I learned long since to let you go your own way because there's no controlling you.

JOSIE. I do my work and I earn my keep and I've a right to be free.

HOGAN. You have. I've never denied it.

JOSIE. No. You've never. I've often wondered why a man that likes fights as much as you didn't grab at the excuse of my disgrace to beat the lights out of the men.

HOGAN. Wouldn't I look a great fool, when everyone knows any man who tried to make free with you, and you not willing, would be carried off to the hospital? Anyway, I wouldn't want to fight an army. You've had too many sweethearts.

JOSIE (*with a proud toss of her head—boastfully*). That's because I soon get tired of any man and give him his walking papers.

HOGAN. I'm afraid you were born to be a terrible wanton woman. But to tell the truth, I'm well satisfied you're what you are, though I shouldn't say it, because if you was the decent kind, you'd have married some fool long ago, and I'd have lost your company and your help on the farm.

JOSIE (*with a trace of bitterness*). Leave it to you to think of your own interest.

HOGAN (*puffs on his pipe*). What else did my beautiful son, Mike, say to you?

JOSIE. Oh, he was full of stupid gab, as usual. He gave me good advice—

HOGAN (*grimly*). That was kind of him. It must have been good—

JOSIE. I ought to marry and settle down —if I could find a decent man who'd have me, which he was sure I couldn't.

HOGAN (*beginning to boil*). I tell you, Josie, it's going to be the saddest memory of my life I didn't get one last swipe at him!

JOSIE. So the only hope, he thought, was for me to catch some indecent man, who'd have money coming to him I could steal.

HOGAN (*gives her a quick, probing side glance—casually*). He meant Jim Tyrone?

JOSIE. He did. And the dirty tick accused you and me of making up a foxy scheme to trap Jim. I'm to get him alone when he's crazy drunk and lead him on to marry me. (*She adds in a hard, scornful tone*) As if that would ever work. Sure, all the pretty little tarts on Broadway, New York, must have had a try at that, and much good it did them.

HOGAN (*again with a quick side glance—casually*). They must have, surely. But that's in the city where he's suspicious. You never can tell what he mightn't do here in the country, where he's innocent, with a moon in the sky to fill him with poetry and a quart of bad hootch inside of him.

JOSIE (*turns on him angrily*). Are you taking Mike's scheme seriously, you old goat?

HOGAN. I'm not. I only thought you wanted my opinion. (*She regards him suspiciously, but his face is blank, as if he hadn't a thought beyond enjoying his pipe.*)

JOSIE (*turning away*). And if that didn't work, Mike said maybe we had a scheme that I'd get Jim in bed with me and you'd come with witnesses and a shotgun, and catch him there.

HOGAN. Faith, me darlin' son never learnt that from his prayer book! He must have improved his mind on the sly.

JOSIE. The dirty tick!

HOGAN. Don't call him a tick. I don't like ticks but I'll say this for them, I never picked one off me yet was a hypocrite.

JOSIE. Him daring to accuse us of planning a rotten trick like that on Jim!

HOGAN (*as if he misunderstood her meaning*). Yes, it's as old as the hills. Everyone's heard of it. But it still works now and again, I'm told, and sometimes an old trick is best because it's so ancient no one would suspect you'd try it.

JOSIE (*staring at him resentfully*). That's enough out of you, Father. I never can tell to this day, when you put that dead mug on you, whether you're joking or not, but I don't want to hear any more—

HOGAN (*mildly*). I thought you wanted my honest opinion on the merits of Mike's suggestion.

JOSIE. Och, shut up, will you? I know you're only trying to make game of me. You like Jim and you'd never play a dirty trick on him, not even if I was willing.

HOGAN. No—not unless I found he was playing one on me.

JOSIE. Which he'd never.

HOGAN. No, I wouldn't think it, but my motto in life is never trust anyone too far, not even myself.

JOSIE. You've reason for the last. I've often suspected you sneak out of bed in the night to pick your own pockets.

HOGAN. I wouldn't call it a dirty trick on him to get you for a wife.

JOSIE (*exasperatedly*). God save us, are you off on that again?

HOGAN. Well, you've put marriage in my head and I can't help considering the merits of the case, as they say. Sure, you're two of a kind, both great disgraces. That would help make a happy marriage because neither of you could look down on the other.

JOSIE. Jim mightn't think so.

HOGAN. You mean he'd think he was marrying beneath his station? He'd be a damned fool if he had that notion, for his Old Man who'd worked up from nothing to be rich and famous didn't give a damn about station. Didn't I often see him working on his grounds in clothes I wouldn't put on a scarecrow, not caring who saw him? (*With admiring affection*) God rest him, he was a true Irish gentleman.

JOSIE. He was, and didn't you swindle him, and make me help you at it? I remember when I was a slip of a girl, and you'd get a letter saying his agent told him you were a year behind in the rent, and he'd be damned if he'd stand for it, and he was coming here to settle the matter. You'd make me dress up, with my hair brushed and a ribbon in it, and leave me to soften his heart before he saw you. So I'd skip down the path to meet him, and make him a courtesy, and hold on to his hand, and bat my eyes at him and lead him in the house, and offer him a drink of the good whiskey you didn't keep for company, and gape at him and tell him he was the handsomest man in the world, and the fierce expression he'd put on for you would go away.

HOGAN (*chuckles*). You did it wonderful. You should have gone on the stage.

JOSIE (*dryly*). Yes, that's what he'd tell me, and he'd reach in his pocket and take out a half dollar, and ask me if you hadn't put me up to it. So I'd say yes, you had.

HOGAN (*sadly*). I never knew you were such a black traitor, and you only a child.

JOSIE. And then you'd come and before he could get a word out of him, you'd tell him you'd vacate the premises unless he lowered the rent and painted the house.

HOGAN. Be God, that used to stop him in his tracks.

JOSIE. It didn't stop him from saying you were the damnedest crook ever came out of Ireland.

HOGAN. He said it with admiration. And we'd start drinking and telling stories, and singing songs, and by the time he left we were both too busy cursing England to worry over the rent. (*He grins affectionately.*) Oh, he was a great man entirely.

JOSIE. He was. He always saw through your tricks.

HOGAN. Didn't I know he would? Sure, all I wanted was to give him the fun of seeing through them so he couldn't be hard-hearted. That was the real trick.

JOSIE (*stares at him*). You old divil, you've always a trick hidden behind your tricks, so no one can tell at times what you're after.

HOGAN. Don't be so suspicious. Sure, I'd never try to fool you. You know me too well. But we've gone off the track. It's Jim we're discussing, not his father. I was telling you I could see the merit in your marrying him.

JOSIE (*exasperatedly*). Och, a cow must have kicked you in the head this morning.

HOGAN. I'd never give it a thought if I didn't know you had a soft spot in your heart for him.

JOSIE (*resentfully*). Well, I haven't! I like him, if that's what you mean, but it's only to talk to, because he's educated and quiet-spoken and has politeness even when he's drunkest, and doesn't roar around cursing and singing, like some I could name.

HOGAN. If you could see the light in your eyes when he blarneys you—

JOSIE (*roughly*). The light in me foot! (*Scornfully*) I'm in love with him, you'll be saying next!

HOGAN (*ignores this*). And another merit of the case is, he likes you.

JOSIE. Because he keeps dropping in here lately? Sure, it's only when he gets sick of the drunks at the Inn, and it's more to joke with you than see me.

HOGAN. It's your happiness I'm considering when I recommend your using your wits to catch him, if you can.

JOSIE (*jeeringly*). If!

HOGAN. Who knows? With all the sweethearts you've had, you must have a catching way with men.

JOSIE (*boastfully*). Maybe I have. But that doesn't mean—

HOGAN. If you got him alone tonight—there'll be a beautiful moon to fill him with poetry and loneliness, and—

JOSIE. That's one of Mike's dirty schemes.

HOGAN. Mike be damned! Sure, that's every woman's scheme since the world was created. Without it there'd be no population. (*Persuasively*) There'd be no harm trying it, anyway.

JOSIE. And no use, either. (*Bitterly*) Och, Father, don't play the jackass with me. You know, and I know, I'm an ugly overgrown lump of a woman, and the men that want me are no better than stupid bulls. Jim can have all the pretty, painted little Broadway girls he wants—and dancers on the stage, too—when he comes into his estate. That's the kind he likes.

HOGAN. I notice he's never married one. Maybe he'd like a fine strong handsome figure of a woman for a change, with beautiful eyes and hair and teeth and a smile.

JOSIE (*pleased, but jeering*). Thank you kindly for your compliments. Now I know a cow kicked you in the head.

HOGAN. If you think Jim hasn't been taking in your fine points, you're a fool.

JOSIE. You mean you've noticed him? (*Suddenly furious*) Stop your lying!

HOGAN. Don't fly in a temper. All I'm saying is, there may be a chance in it to better yourself.

JOSIE (*scornfully*). Better myself by being tied down to a man who's drunk every night of his life? No, thank you!

HOGAN. Sure, you're strong enough to reform him. A taste of that club you've got, when he came home to you paralyzed, and in a few weeks you'd have him a dirty prohibitionist.

JOSIE (*seriously*). It's true, if I was his wife, I'd cure him of drinking himself to death, if I had to kill him. (*Then angrily*) Och, I'm sick of your crazy gab, Father! Leave me alone!

HOGAN. Well, let's put it another way. Don't tell me you couldn't learn to love the estate he'll come into.

JOSIE (*resentfully*). Ah, I've been waiting for that. That's what Mike said, again. Now we've come to the truth behind all your blather of my liking him or him liking me. (*Her manner changing—defiantly*) All right, then. Of course I'd love the money. Who wouldn't? And why shouldn't I get my hands on it, if I could? He's bound to be swindled out of it, anyway. He'll go back to the Broadway he thinks is heaven, and by the time the pretty little tarts, and the barroom sponges and racetrack touts and gamblers are through with him he'll be picked clean. I'm no saint, God knows, but I'm decent and deserving compared to those scum.

HOGAN (*eagerly*). Be God, now you're using your wits. And where there's a will there's a way. You and me have never been

beat when we put our brains together. I'll keep thinking it over, and you do the same.

JOSIE (*with illogical anger*). Well, I won't! And you keep your mad scheming to yourself. I won't listen to it.

HOGAN (*as if he were angry, too*). All right. The divil take you. It's all you'll hear from me. (*He pauses—then with great seriousness, turning toward her*) Except one thing—(*As she starts to shut him up—sharply*) I'm serious, and you'd better listen, because it's about this farm, which is home to us.

JOSIE (*surprised, stares at him*). What about the farm?

HOGAN. Don't forget, if we have lived on it twenty years, we're only tenants and we could be thrown out on our necks any time. (*Quickly*) Mind you, I don't say Jim would ever do it, rent or no rent, or let the executors do it, even if they wanted, which they don't, knowing they'd never find another tenant.

JOSIE. What's worrying you, then?

HOGAN. This. I've been afraid lately the minute the estate is out of probate, Jim will sell the farm.

JOSIE (*exasperatedly*). Of course he will! Hasn't he told us and promised you can buy it on easy time payments at the small price you offered?

HOGAN. Jim promises whatever you like when he's full of whiskey. He might forget a promise as easy when he's drunk enough.

JOSIE (*indignantly*). He'd never! And who'd want it except us? No one ever has in all the years—

HOGAN. Someone has lately. The agent got an offer last month, Jim told me, bigger than mine.

JOSIE. Och, Jim loves to try and get your goat. He was kidding you.

HOGAN. He wasn't. I can tell. He said he told the agent to tell whoever it was the place wasn't for sale.

JOSIE. Of course he did. Did he say who'd made the offer?

HOGAN. He didn't know. It came through a real-estate man who wouldn't tell who his client was. I've been trying to guess, but I can't think of anyone crazy enough unless it'd be some damn fool of a millionaire buying up land to make a great estate for himself, like our beautiful neighbor, Harder, the Standard Oil thief, did years ago. (*He adds with bitter fervency*) May he roast in hell and his Limey superintendent with him!

JOSIE. Amen to that. (*Then scornfully*) This land for an estate? And if there was an offer, Jim's refused it, and that ends it. He wouldn't listen to any offer, after he's given his word to us.

HOGAN. Did I say he would—when he's in his right mind? What I'm afraid of is, he might be led into it sometime when he has one of his sneering bitter drunks on and talks like a Broadway crook himself, saying money is the only thing in the world, and everything and anyone can be bought if the price is big enough. You've heard him.

JOSIE. I have. But he doesn't fool me at all. He only acts like he's hard and shameless to get back at life when it's tormenting him—and who doesn't? (*He gives her a quick, curious side glance which she doesn't notice.*)

HOGAN. Or take the other kind of queer drunk he gets on sometimes when, without any reason you can see, he'll suddenly turn strange, and look sad, and stare at nothing as if he was mourning over some ghost inside him, and—

JOSIE. I think I know what comes over him when he's like that. It's the memory of his mother comes back and his grief for her death. (*Pityingly*) Poor Jim.

HOGAN (*ignoring this*). And whiskey seems to have no effect on him, like water off a duck's back. He'll keep acting natural enough, and you'd swear he wasn't bad at all, but the next day you find his brain was so paralyzed he don't remember a thing until you remind him. He's done a lot of mad things, when he was that way, he was sorry for after.

JOSIE (*scornfully*). What drunk hasn't? But he'd never— (*Resentfully*) I won't have you suspecting Jim without any cause, d'you hear me!

HOGAN. I don't suspect him. All I've said is, when a man gets as queer drunk as Jim, he doesn't know himself what he mightn't do, and we'd be damned fools if we didn't fear the possibility, however small it is, and do all we can to guard against it.

JOSIE. There's no possibility! And how could we guard against it, if there was?

HOGAN. Well, you can put yourself out to be extra nice to him, for one thing.

JOSIE. How nice is extra nice?

HOGAN. You ought to know. But here's one tip. I've noticed when you talk rough and brazen like you do to other men, he may grin like they do, as if he enjoyed it, but he don't. So watch your tongue.

JOSIE (*with a defiant toss of her head*). I'll talk as I please, and if he don't like it he can lump it! (*Scornfully*) I'm to pretend I'm a pure virgin, I suppose? That would fool him, wouldn't it, and him hearing all about me from the men at the Inn? (*She gets to her feet, abruptly changing the subject.*) We're wasting the day, blathering. (*Then her face hardening*) If he ever went back on his word, no matter how drunk he was, I'd be with you in any scheme you made against him, no matter how dirty. (*Hastily*) But it's all your nonsense. I'd never believe it. (*She comes and picks up the pitchfork.*) I'll go to the meadow and finish Mike's work. You needn't fear you'll miss his help on the farm.

HOGAN. A hell of a help! A weak lazy back and the appetite of a drove of starving pigs! (*As she turns to go—suddenly bellicose*) Leaving me, are you? When it's dinner time? Where's my dinner, you lazy cow?

JOSIE. There's stew on the stove, you bad-tempered runt. Go in and help yourself. I'm not hungry. Your gab has bothered my mind. I need hard work in the sun to clear it. (*She starts to go off toward rear-right.*)

HOGAN (*glancing down the road, off left-front*). You'd better wait. There's a caller coming to the gate—and if I'm not mistaken, it's the light of your eyes himself.

JOSIE (*angrily*). Shut up! (*She stares off —her face softens and grows pitying.*) Look at him when he thinks no one is watching, with his eyes on the ground. Like a dead man walking slow behind his own coffin. (*Then roughly*) Faith, he must have a hangover. He sees us now. Look at the bluff he puts up, straightening himself and grinning. (*Resentfully*) I don't want to meet him. Let him make jokes with you and play the old game about a drink you both think is such fun. That's all he comes for, anyway. (*She starts off again.*)

HOGAN. Are you running away from him? Sure, you must be afraid you're in love. (JOSIE *halts instantly and turns back defiantly. He goes on.*) Go in the house now, and wash your face, and tidy your dress, and give a touch to your hair. You want to look decent for him.

JOSIE (*angrily*). I'll go in the house, but only to see the stew ain't burned, for I suppose you'll have the foxiness to ask him to have a bite to eat to keep in his good graces.

HOGAN. Why shouldn't I ask him? I know damned well he has no appetite this early in the day, but only a thirst.

JOSIE. Och, you make me sick, you sly miser! (*She goes in through her bedroom, slamming the door behind her.* HOGAN *refills his pipe, pretending he doesn't notice* TYRONE *approaching, his eyes bright with droll expectation.* JIM TYRONE *enters along the road from the highway, left.*)

(TYRONE *is in his early forties, around five feet nine, broad-shouldered and deep-chested. His naturally fine physique has become soft and soggy from dissipation, but his face is still good-looking despite its unhealthy puffiness and the bags under the eyes. He has thinning dark hair, parted and brushed back to cover a bald spot. His eyes are brown, the whites congested and yellowish. His nose, big and aquiline, gives his face a certain Mephistophelian quality which is accentuated by his habitually cynical expression. But when he smiles without sneering, he still has the ghost of a former youthful, irresponsible Irish charm—that of the beguiling ne'er-do-well, sentimental and romantic. It is his humor and charm which have kept him attractive to women, and popular with men as a drinking companion. He is dressed in an expensive dark-brown suit, tight-fitting and drawn in at the waist, dark-brown made-to-order shoes and silk socks, a white silk shirt, silk handkerchief in breast pocket, a dark tie. This get-up suggests that he follows a style set by well-groomed Broadway gamblers who would like to be mistaken for Wall Street brokers.*

(*He has had enough pick-me-ups to recover from morning-after nausea and steady his nerves. During the following dialogue, he and* HOGAN *are like players at an old familiar game where each knows the other's moves, but which still amuses them.*)

TYRONE (*approaches and stands regarding* HOGAN *with sardonic relish.* HOGAN *scratches a match on the seat of his over-* alls *and lights his pipe, pretending not to see him.* TYRONE *recites with feeling*). "Fortunate senex, ergo tua, rura manebunt, et tibi magna satis, quamvis lapis omnia nudus."

HOGAN (*mutters*). It's the landlord again, and my shotgun not handy. (*He looks up at* TYRONE.) Is it Mass you're saying, Jim? That was Latin. I know it by ear. What the hell—insult does it mean?

TYRONE. Translated very freely into Irish English, something like this. (*He imitates* HOGAN's *brogue*) "Ain't you the lucky old bastard to have this beautiful farm, if it is full of nude rocks."

HOGAN. I like that part about the rocks. If cows could eat them this place would make a grand dairy farm. (*He spits.*) It's easy to see you've a fine college education. It must be a big help to you, conversing with whores and barkeeps.

TYRONE. Yes, a very valuable worldly asset. I was once offered a job as office boy—until they discovered I wasn't qualified because I had no Bachelor of Arts diploma. There had been a slight misunderstanding just before I was to graduate.

HOGAN. Between you and the Fathers? I'll wager!

TYRONE. I made a bet with another Senior I could get a tart from the Haymarket to visit me, introduce her to the Jebs as my sister—and get away with it.

HOGAN. But you didn't?

TYRONE. Almost. It was a memorable day in the halls of learning. All the students were wise and I had them rolling in the aisles as I showed Sister around the grounds, accompanied by one of the Jebs. He was a bit suspicious at first, but Dutch Maisie—her professional name—had no make-up on, and was dressed in black, and had eaten a pound of Sen-Sen to kill the gin on her breath, and seemed such a devout girl that he forgot his suspicions. (*He pauses.*) Yes, all would have been well, but she was a mischievous minx, and had her own ideas of improving on my joke. When she was saying good-by to Father Fuller, she added innocently: "Christ, Father, it's nice and quiet out here away from the damned Sixth Avenue El. I wish to hell I could stay here!" (*Dryly*) But she didn't, and neither did I.

HOGAN (*chuckles delightedly*). I'll bet you didn't! God bless Dutch Maisie! I'd like to have known her.

TYRONE (*sits down on the steps—with a change of manner*). Well, how's the Duke of Donegal this fine day?

HOGAN. Never better.

TYRONE. Slaving and toiling as usual, I see.

HOGAN. Hasn't a poor man a right to his noon rest without being sneered at by his rich landlord?

TYRONE. "Rich" is good. I would be, if you'd pay up your back rent.

HOGAN. You ought to pay me, instead, for occupying this rockpile, miscalled a farm. (*His eyes twinkling*) But I have fine reports to give you of a promising harvest. The milkweed and the thistles is in thriving condition, and I never saw the poison ivy so bounteous and beautiful. (TYRONE *laughs. Without their noticing,* JOSIE *appears in the doorway behind* TYRONE. *She has tidied up and arranged her hair. She smiles down at* JIM, *her face softening, pleased to hear him laugh.*)

TYRONE. You win. Where did Josie go, Phil? I saw her here—

HOGAN. She ran in the house to make herself beautiful for you.

JOSIE (*breaks in roughly*). You're a liar. (*To* TYRONE, *her manner one of bold, free-and-easy familiarity*) Hello, Jim.

TYRONE (*starts to stand up*). Hello, Josie.

JOSIE (*puts a hand on his shoulder and pushes him down*). Don't get up. Sure, you know I'm no lady. (*She sits on the top step—banteringly*) How's my fine Jim this beautiful day? You don't look so bad. You must have stopped at the Inn for an eye-opener—or ten of them.

TYRONE. I've felt worse. (*He looks up at her sardonically.*) And how's my Virgin Queen of Ireland?

JOSIE. Yours, is it? Since when? And don't be miscalling me a virgin. You'll ruin my reputation, if you spread that lie about me. (*She laughs.* TYRONE *is staring at her. She goes on quickly.*) How is it you're around so early? I thought you never got up till afternoon.

TYRONE. Couldn't sleep. One of those heebie-jeebie nights when the booze keeps you awake instead of— (*He catches her giving him a pitying look—irritably*) But what of it!

JOSIE. Maybe you had no woman in bed with you, for a change. It's a terrible thing to break the habit of years.

TYRONE (*shrugs his shoulders*). Maybe.

JOSIE. What's the matter with the tarts in town, they let you do it? I'll bet the ones you know on Broadway, New York, wouldn't neglect their business.

TYRONE (*pretends to yawn boredly*). Maybe not. (*Then irritably*) Cut out the kidding, Josie. It's too early.

HOGAN (*who has been taking everything in without seeming to*). I told you not to annoy the gentleman with your rough tongue.

JOSIE. Sure I thought I was doing my duty as hostess making him feel at home.

TYRONE (*stares at her again*). Why all the interest lately in the ladies of the profession, Josie?

JOSIE. Oh, I've been considering joining their union. It's easier living than farming, I'm sure. (*Then resentfully*) You think I'd starve at it, don't you, because your fancy is for dainty dolls of women? But other men like—

TYRONE (*with sudden revulsion*). For God's sake, cut out that kind of talk, Josie! It sounds like hell.

JOSIE (*stares at him startledly—then resentfully*). Oh, it does, does it? (*Forcing a scornful smile*) I'm shocking you, I suppose? (HOGAN *is watching them both, not missing anything in their faces, while he seems intent on his pipe.*)

TYRONE (*looking a bit sheepish and annoyed at himself for his interest—shrugs his shoulders*). No. Hardly. Forget it. (*He smiles kiddingly.*) Anyway, who told you I fall for the dainty dolls? That's all a thing of the past. I like them tall and strong and voluptuous, now, with beautiful big breasts. (*She blushes and looks confused and is furious with herself for doing so.*)

HOGAN. There you are, Josie, darlin'. Sure he couldn't speak fairer than that.

JOSIE (*recovers herself*). He couldn't indeed. (*She pats* TYRONE's *head—playfully.*) You're a terrible blarneying liar, Jim, but thank you just the same. (TYRONE *turns his attention to* HOGAN. *He winks at* JOSIE *and begins in an exaggeratedly casual manner.*)

TYRONE. I don't blame you, Mr. Hogan, for taking it easy on such a blazing hot day.

HOGAN (*doesn't look at him. His eyes twinkle*). Hot, did you say? I find it cool, meself. Take off your coat if you're hot,

Mister Tyrone.

TYRONE. One of the most stifling days I've ever known. Isn't it, Josie?

JOSIE (*smiling*). Terrible. I know you must be perishing.

HOGAN. I wouldn't call it a damned bit stifling.

TYRONE. It parches the membranes in your throat.

HOGAN. The what? Never mind. I can't have them, for my throat isn't parched at all. If yours is, Mister Tyrone, there's a well full of water at the back.

TYRONE. Water? That's something people wash with, isn't it? I mean, some people.

HOGAN. So I've heard. But, like you, I find it hard to believe. It's a dirty habit. They must be foreigners.

TYRONE. As I was saying, my throat is parched after the long dusty walk I took just for the pleasure of being your guest.

HOGAN. I don't remember inviting you, and the road is hard macadam with divil a spec of dust, and it's less than a quarter mile from the Inn here.

TYRONE. I didn't have a drink at the Inn. I was waiting until I arrived here, knowing that you—

HOGAN. Knowing I'd what?

TYRONE. Your reputation as a generous host—

HOGAN. The world must be full of liars. So you didn't have a drink at the Inn? Then it must be the air itself smells of whiskey today, although I didn't notice it before you came. You've gone on the water-wagon, I suppose? Well, that's fine, and I ask pardon for misjudging you.

TYRONE. I've wanted to go on the wagon for the past twenty-five years, but the doctors have strictly forbidden it. It would be fatal—with my weak heart.

HOGAN. So you've a weak heart? Well, well, and me thinking all along it was your head. I'm glad you told me. I was just going to offer you a drink, but whiskey is the worst thing—

TYRONE. The Docs say it's a matter of life and death. I must have a stimulant— one big drink, at least, whenever I strain my heart walking in the hot sun.

HOGAN. Walk back to the Inn, then, and give it a good strain, so you can buy yourself two big drinks.

JOSIE (*laughing*). Ain't you the fools, playing that old game between you, and both of you pleased as punch!

TYRONE (*gives up with a laugh*). Hasn't he ever been known to loosen up, Josie?

JOSIE. You ought to know. If you need a drink you'll have to buy it from him or die of thirst.

TYRONE. Well, I'll bet this is one time he's going to treat.

HOGAN. Be God, I'll take that bet!

TYRONE. After you've heard the news I've got for you, you'll be so delighted you won't be able to drag out the old bottle quick enough.

HOGAN. I'll have to be insanely delighted.

JOSIE (*full of curiosity*). Shut up, Father. What news, Jim?

TYRONE. I have it off the grapevine that a certain exalted personage will drop in on you before long.

HOGAN. It's the sheriff again. I know by the pleased look on your mug.

TYRONE. Not this time. (*He pauses tantalizingly*)

JOSIE. Bad luck to you, can't you tell us who?

TYRONE. A more eminent grafter than the sheriff— (*Sneeringly*) A leading aristocrat in our Land of the Free and Get-Rich-Quick, whose boots are licked by one and all—one of the Kings of our Republic by Divine Right of Inherited Swag. In short, I refer to your good neighbor, T. Stedman Harder, Standard Oil's sappiest child, whom I know you both love so dearly. (*There is a pause after this announcement. HOGAN and JOSIE stiffen, and their eyes begin to glitter. But they can't believe their luck at first.*)

HOGAN (*in an ominous whisper*). Did you say Harder is coming to call on us, Jim?

JOSIE. It's too good to be true.

TYRONE (*watching them with amusement*). No kidding. The great Mr. Harder intends to stop here on his way back to lunch from a horseback ride.

JOSIE. How do you know?

TYRONE. Simpson told me. I ran into him at the Inn.

HOGAN. That English scum of a superintendent!

TYRONE. He was laughing himself sick. He said he suggested the idea to Harder— told him you'd be overwhelmed with awe if he deigned to interview you in person.

HOGAN. Overwhelmed isn't the word. Is it, Josie?

JOSIE. It isn't indeed, Father.

TYRONE. For once in his life, Simpson is cheering for you. He doesn't like his boss. In fact, he asked me to tell you he hopes you kill him.

HOGAN (*disdainfully*). To hell with the Limey's good wishes. I'd like both of them to call together.

JOSIE. Ah, well, we can't have everything. (*To* TYRONE) What's the reason Mr. Harder decided to notice poor, humble scum the like of us?

TYRONE (*grinning*). That's right, Josie. Be humble. He'll expect you to know your place.

HOGAN. Will he now? Well, well. (*With a great happy sigh*) This is going to be a beautiful day entirely.

JOSIE. But what's Harder's reason, Jim?

TYRONE. Well, it seems he has an ice pond on his estate.

HOGAN. Oho! So that's it!

TYRONE. Yes, That's it. Harder likes to keep up the good old manorial customs. He clings to his ice pond. And your pig-pen isn't far from his ice pond.

HOGAN. A nice little stroll for the pigs, that's all.

TYRONE. And somehow Harder's fence in that vicinity has a habit of breaking down.

HOGAN. Fences are queer things. You can't depend on them.

TYRONE. Simpson says he's had it repaired a dozen times, but each time on the following night it gets broken down again.

JOSIE. What a strange thing! It must be the bad fairies. I can't imagine who else could have done it. Can you, Father?

HOGAN. I can't surely.

TYRONE. Well, Simpson can. He knows you did it and he told his master so.

HOGAN (*disdainfully*). Master is the word. Sure, the English can't live unless they have a lord's backside to kiss, the dirty slaves.

TYRONE. The result of those breaks in the fence is that your pigs stroll—as you so gracefully put it—stroll through to wallow happily along the shores of the ice pond.

HOGAN. Well, why not? Sure, they're fine ambitious American-born pigs and they don't miss any opportunities. They're like Harder's father who made the money for him.

TYRONE. I agree, but for some strange reason Harder doesn't look forward to the taste of pig in next summer's ice water.

HOGAN. He must be delicate. Remember he's delicate, Josie, and leave your club in the house. (*He bursts into joyful menacing laughter.*) Oh, be God and be Christ in the mountains! I've pined to have a quiet word with Mr. Harder for years, watching him ride past in his big shiny automobile with his snoot in the air, and being tormented always by the complaints of his Limey superintendent. Oh, won't I welcome him!

JOSIE. Won't *we,* you mean. Sure, I love him as much as you.

HOGAN. I'd kiss you, Jim, for this beautiful news, if you wasn't so damned ugly. Maybe Josie'll do it for me. She has a stronger stomach.

JOSIE. I will! He's earned it. (*She pulls* TYRONE's *head back and laughingly kisses him on the lips. Her expression changes. She looks startled and confused, stirred and at the same time frightened. She forces a scornful laugh.*) Och, there's no spirit in you! It's like kissing a corpse.

TYRONE (*gives her a strange surprised look—mockingly*). Yes? (*Turning to* HOGAN) Well, how about that drink, Phil? I'll leave it to Josie if drinks aren't on the house.

HOGAN. *I* won't leave it to Josie. She's prejudiced, being in love.

JOSIE (*angrily*). Shut up, you old liar! (*Then guiltily, forcing a laugh*) Don't talk nonsense to sneak out of treating Jim.

HOGAN (*sighing*). All right, Josie. Go get the bottle and one small glass, or he'll never stop nagging me. I can turn my back, so the sight of him drinking free won't break my heart. (JOSIE *gets up, laughing, and goes in the house.* HOGAN *peers at the road off left.*) On his way back to lunch, you said? Then it's time— (*Fervently*) O Holy Joseph, don't let the bastard change his mind!

TYRONE (*beginning to have qualms*). Listen, Phil. Don't get too enthusiastic. He has a big drag around here, and he'll have you pinched, sure as hell, if you beat him up.

HOGAN. Och, I'm no fool. (JOSIE *comes out with a bottle and a tumbler.*) Will you listen to this, Josie. He's warning me not to give Harder a beating—as if I'd dirty my hands on the scum.

JOSIE. As if we'd need to. Sure, all we want is a quiet chat with him.

HOGAN. That's all. As neighbor to neighbor.

JOSIE (*hands* TYRONE *the bottle and tumbler*). Here you are, Jim. Don't stint yourself.

HOGAN (*mournfully*). A fine daughter! I tell you a small glass and you give him a bucket! (*As* TYRONE *pours a big drink, grinning at him, he turns away with a comic shudder.*) That's a fifty-dollar drink, at least.

TYRONE. Here's luck, Phil.

HOGAN. I hope you drown. (TYRONE *drinks and makes a wry face.*)

TYRONE. The best chicken medicine I've ever tasted.

HOGAN. That's gratitude for you! Here, pass me the bottle. A drink will warm up my welcome for His Majesty. (*He takes an enormous swig from the bottle.*)

JOSIE (*looking off left*). There's two horseback riders on the county road now.

HOGAN. Praise be to God! It's him and a groom. (*He sets the bottle on top of the boulder.*)

JOSIE. That's McCabe. An old sweetheart of mine. (*She glances at* TYRONE *provokingly—then suddenly worried and protective*) You get in the house, Jim. If Harder sees you here, he'll lay the whole blame on you.

TYRONE. Nix, Josie. You don't think I'm going to miss this, do you?

JOSIE. You can sit inside by my window and take in everything. Come on, now, don't be stubborn with me. (*She puts her hands under his arms and lifts him to his feet as easily as if he was a child—banteringly*) Go into my beautiful bedroom. It's a nice place for you.

TYRONE (*kiddingly*). Just what I've been thinking for some time, Josie.

JOSIE (*boldly*). Sure, you've never given me a sign of it. Come up tonight and we'll spoon in the moonlight and you can tell me your thoughts.

TYRONE. That's a date. Remember, now.

JOSIE. It's you who'll forget. Get inside now, before it's too late. (*She gives him a shove inside and closes the door.*)

HOGAN (*has been watching the visitor approach*). He's dismounting—as graceful as a scarecrow, and his poor horse longing to give him a kick. Look at Mac grinning at us. Sit down, Josie. (*She sits on the*

steps, he on the boulder.*) Pretend you don't notice him. (T. STEDMAN HARDER *appears at left. They act as if they didn't see him.* HOGAN *knocks out his pipe on the palm of his hand.*)

(HARDER *is in his late thirties but looks younger because his face is unmarked by worry, ambition, or any of the common hazards of life. No matter how long he lives, his four undergraduate years will always be for him the most significant in his life, and the moment of his highest achievement the time he was tapped for an exclusive Senior Society at the Ivy university to which his father had given millions. Since that day he has felt no need for further aspiring, no urge to do anything except settle down on his estate and live the life of a country gentleman, mildly interested in saddle horses and sport models of foreign automobiles. He is not the blatantly silly, playboy heir to millions whose antics make newspaper headlines. He doesn't drink much except when he attends his class reunion every spring—the most exciting episode of each year for him. He doesn't give wild parties, doesn't chase after musical-comedy cuties, is a mildly contented husband and father of three children. A not unpleasant man, affable, good-looking in an ordinary way, sunburnt and healthy, beginning to take on fat, he is simply immature, naturally lethargic, a bit stupid. Coddled from birth, everything arranged and made easy for him, deferred to because of his wealth, he usually has the self-confident attitude of acknowledged superiority, but assumes a supercilious, insecure air when dealing with people beyond his ken. He is dressed in a beautifully tailored English tweed coat and whipcord riding breeches, immaculately polished English riding boots with spurs, and carries a riding crop in his hand.*

(*It would be hard to find anyone more ill-equipped for combat with the* HOGANS. *He has never come in contact with anyone like them. To make matters easier for them he is deliberate in his speech, slow on the uptake, and has no sense of humor. The experienced strategy of the* HOGANS *in verbal battle is to take the offensive at once and never let an opponent get set to hit back. Also, they use a beautifully co-ordinated, bewildering change of pace, switching suddenly from jarring shouts to low, confidential vituperation. And they exag-*

gerate their Irish brogues to confuse an enemy still further.)

HARDER (walks toward HOGAN—stiffly). Good morning. I want to see the man who runs this farm.

HOGAN (surveys him deliberately, his little pig eyes gleaming with malice). You do, do you? Well, you've seen him. So run along now and play with your horse, and don't bother me. (He turns to JOSIE, who is staring at HARDER, much to his discomfiture, as if she had discovered a cockroach in her soup.) D'you see what I see, Josie? Be God, you'll have to give that damned cat of yours a spanking for bringing it to our doorstep.

HARDER (determined to be authoritative and command respect—curtly). Are you Hogan?

HOGAN (insultingly). I am Mister Philip Hogan—to a gentleman.

JOSIE (glares at HARDER). Where's your manners, you spindle-shanked jockey? Were you brought up in a stable?

HARDER (does not fight with ladies, and especially not with this lady—ignoring her). My name is Harder. (He obviously expects them to be immediately impressed and apologetic.)

HOGAN (contemptuously). Who asked you your name, me little man?

JOSIE. Sure, who in the world cares who the hell you are?

HOGAN. But if you want to play politeness, we'll play with you. Let me introduce you to my daughter, Harder—Miss Josephine Hogan.

JOSIE (petulantly). I don't want to meet him, Father. I don't like his silly sheep's face, and I've no use for jockeys, anyway. I'll wager he's no damned good to a woman. (From inside her bedroom comes a burst of laughter. This revelation of an unseen audience startles HARDER. He begins to look extremely unsure of himself.)

HOGAN. I don't think he's a jockey. It's only the funny pants he's wearing. I'll bet if you asked his horse, you'd find he's no cowboy either. (To HARDER, jeeringly) Come, tell us the truth, me honey. Don't you kiss your horse each time you mount and beg him, please don't throw me today, darlin', and I'll give you an extra bucket of oats. (He bursts into an extravagant roar of laughter, slapping his thigh, and JOSIE guffaws with him, while they watch the disconcerting effect of this theatrical mirth on HARDER.)

HARDER (beginning to lose his temper). Listen to me, Hogan! I didn't come here— (He is going to add "to listen to your damned jokes" or something like that, but HOGAN silences him.)

HOGAN (shouts). What? What's that you said? (He stares at the dumbfounded HARDER with droll amazement, as if he couldn't believe his ears.) You didn't come here? (He turns to JOSIE—in a whisper) Did you hear that, Josie? (He takes off his hat and scratches his head in comic bewilderment.) Well, that's a puzzle, surely. How d'you suppose he got here?

JOSIE. Maybe the stork brought him, bad luck to it for a dirty bird. (Again TYRONE's laughter is heard from the bedroom.)

HARDER (so off balance now he can only repeat angrily). I said I didn't come here—

HOGAN (shouts). Wait! Wait, now! (Threateningly) We've had enough of that. Say it a third time and I'll send my daughter to telephone the asylum.

HARDER (forgetting he's a gentleman). Damn you, I'm the one who's had enough—!

JOSIE (shouts). Hold your dirty tongue! I'll have no foul language in my presence.

HOGAN. Och, don't mind him, Josie. He's said he isn't here, anyway, so we won't talk to him behind his back. (He regards HARDER with pitying contempt.) Sure, ain't you the poor crazy creature? Do you want us to believe you're your own ghost?

HARDER (notices the bottle on the boulder for the first time—tries to be contemptuously tolerant and even to smile with condescending disdain). Ah! I understand now. You're drunk. I'll come back sometime when you're sober—or send Simpson — (He turns away, glad of an excuse to escape.)

JOSIE (jumps up and advances on him menacingly). No, you don't! You'll apologize first for insulting a lady—insinuating I'm drunk this early in the day—or I'll knock some good breeding in you!

HARDER (actually frightened now). I—I said nothing about you—

HOGAN (gets up to come between them). Aisy now, Josie. He didn't mean it. He don't know what he means, the poor loon. (To HARDER—pityingly) Run home, that's a good lad, before your keeper misses you.

HARDER (hastily). Good day. (He turns eagerly toward left but suddenly HOGAN *grabs his shoulder and spins him around—then shifts his grip to the lapel of* HARDER's *coat.*)

HOGAN (*grimly*). Wait now, me Honey Boy. I'll have a word with you, if you plaze. I'm beginning to read some sense into this. You mentioned that English bastard, Simpson. I know who you are now.

HARDER (*outraged*). Take your hands off me, you drunken fool. (*He raises his riding crop.*)

JOSIE (*grabs it and tears it from his hand with one powerful twist—fiercely*). Would you strike my poor infirm old father, you coward, you!

HARDER (*calling for help*). McCabe!

HOGAN. Don't think McCabe will hear you, if you blew Gabriel's horn. He knows I or Josie can lick him with one hand. (*Sharply*) Josie! Stand between us and the gate. (JOSIE *takes her stand where the path meets the road. She turns her back for a moment, shaking with suppressed laughter, and waves her hand at* MC CABE *and turns back.* HOGAN *releases his hold on* HARDER's *coat.*) There now. Don't try running away or my daughter will knock you senseless. (*He goes on grimly before* HARDER *can speak.*) You're the blackguard of a millionaire that owns the estate next to ours, ain't you? I've been meaning to call on you, for I've a bone to pick with you, you bloody tyrant! But I couldn't bring myself to set foot on land bought with Standard Oil money that was stolen from the poor it ground in the dust beneath its dirty heel—land that's watered with the tears of starving widows and orphans—(*He abruptly switches from this eloquence to a matter-of-fact tone.*) But never mind that, now. I won't waste words trying to reform a born crook. (*Fiercely, shoving his dirty unshaven face almost into* HARDER's) What I want to know is, what the hell d'you mean by your contemptible trick of breaking down your fence to entice my poor pigs to take their death in your ice pond? (*There is a shout of laughter from* JOSIE's *bedroom, and* JOSIE *doubles up and holds her sides.* HARDER *is so flabbergasted by this mad accusation he cannot even sputter. But* HOGAN *acts as if he'd denied it—savagely*) Don't lie, now! None of your damned Standard Oil excuses, or be Jaysus, I'll break you in half! Haven't I mended that fence

morning after morning, and seen the footprints where you had sneaked up in the night to pull it down again. How many times have I mended that fence, Josie?

JOSIE. If it's once, it's a hundred, Father.

HOGAN. Listen, me little millionaire! I'm a peaceful, mild man that believes in live and let live, and as long as the neighboring scum leave me alone, I'll let them alone, but when it comes to standing by and seeing my poor pigs murthered one by one—! Josie! How many pigs is it caught their death of cold in his damned ice pond and died of pneumonia?

JOSIE. Ten of them, Father. And ten more died of cholera after drinking the dirty water in it.

HOGAN. All prize pigs, too! I was offered two hundred dollars apiece for them. Twenty pigs at two hundred, that's four thousand. And a thousand to cure the sick and cover funeral expenses for the dead. Call it four thousand you owe me. (*Furiously*) And you'll pay it, or I'll sue you, so help me Christ! I'll drag you in every court in the land! I'll paste your ugly mug on the front page of every newspaper as a pig-murdering tyrant! Before I'm through with you, you'll think you're the King of England at an Irish wake! (*With a quick change of pace to a wheedling confidential tone*) Tell me now, if it isn't a secret, whatever made you take such a savage grudge against pigs? Sure, it isn't reasonable for a Standard Oil man to hate hogs.

HARDER (*manages to get in three sputtering words*). I've had enough—!

HOGAN (*with a grin*). Be God, I believe you! (*Switching to fierceness and grabbing his lapel again*) Look out, now! Keep your place and be soft-spoken to your betters! You're not in your shiny automobile now with your funny nose cocked so you won't smell the poor people. (*He gives him a shake.*) And let me warn you! I have to put up with a lot of pests on this heap of boulders some joker once called a farm. There's a cruel skinflint of a landlord who swindles me out of my last drop of whiskey, and there's poison ivy, and ticks and potato bugs, and there's snakes and skunks! But, be God, I draw the line somewhere, and I'll be damned if I'll stand for a Standard Oil man trespassing! So will you kindly get the hell out of here before I plant a kick on your backside that'll land you in the Atlantic Ocean! (*He gives*

HARDER *a shove*.) Beat it now! (HARDER *tries to make some sort of disdainfully dignified exit. But he has to get by* JOSIE.)

JOSIE (*leers at him idiotically*). Sure, you wouldn't go without a word of good-by to me, would you, darlin'? Don't scorn me just because you have on your jockey's pants. (*In a hoarse whisper*) Meet me tonight, as usual, down by the pigpen. (HARDER's *retreat becomes a rout. He disappears on left, but a second later his voice, trembling with anger, is heard calling back threateningly*.)

HARDER. If you dare touch that fence again, I'll put this matter in the hands of the police!

HOGAN (*shouts derisively*). And I'll put it in my lawyer's hands and in the newspapers! (*He doubles up with glee*.) Look at him fling himself on his nag and spur the poor beast! And look at McCabe behind him! He can hardly stay in the saddle for laughing! (*He slaps his thigh*.) O Jaysus, this is a great day for the poor and oppressed! I'll do no more work! I'll go down to the Inn and spend money and get drunk as Moses!

JOSIE. Small blame to you. You deserve it. But you'll have your dinner first, to give you a foundation. Come on, now. (*They turn back toward the house. From inside another burst of laughter from* TYRONE *is heard*. JOSIE *smiles*.) Listen to Jim still in stitches. It's good to hear him laugh as if he meant it. (TYRONE *appears in the doorway of her bedroom*.)

TYRONE. O God, my sides are sore. (*They all laugh together. He joins them at the left corner of the house*.)

JOSIE. It's dinner time. Will you have a bite to eat with us, Jim? I'll boil you some eggs.

HOGAN. Och, why do you have to mention eggs? Don't you know it's the one thing he might eat? Well, no matter. Anything goes today. (*He gets the bottle of whiskey*.) Come in, Jim. We'll have a drink while Josie's fixing the grub. (*They start to go in the front door,* HOGAN *in the lead*.)

TYRONE (*suddenly—with sardonic amusement*). Wait a minute. Let us pause to take a look at this very valuable property. Don't you notice the change, Phil? Every boulder on the place has turned to solid gold.

HOGAN. What the hell—? You didn't get the D.T.'s from my whiskey, I know that.

TYRONE. No D.T.'s about it. This farm has suddenly become a gold mine. You know that offer I told you about? Well, the agent did a little detective work and he discovered it came from Harder. He doesn't want the damned place but he dislikes you as a neighbor and he thinks the best way to get rid of you would be to become your landlord.

HOGAN. The sneaking skunk! I'm sorry I didn't give him that kick.

TYRONE. Yes. So am I. That would have made the place even more valuable. But as it is, you did nobly. I expect him to double or triple his first offer. In fact, I'll bet the sky is the limit now.

HOGAN (*gives* JOSIE *a meaningful look*). I see your point! But we're not worrying you'd ever forget your promise to us for any price.

TYRONE. Promise? What promise? You know what Kipling wrote: (*Paraphrasing the "Rhyme of the Three Sealers"*) There's never a promise of God or man goes north of ten thousand bucks.

HOGAN. D'you hear him, Josie? We can't trust him.

JOSIE. Och, you know he's kidding.

HOGAN. I don't! I'm becoming suspicious.

TYRONE (*a trace of bitterness beneath his amused tone*). That's wise dope, Phil. Trust and be a sucker. If I were you, I'd be seriously worried. I've always wanted to own a gold mine—so I could sell it.

JOSIE (*bursts out*). Will you shut up your rotten Broadway blather!

TYRONE (*stares at her in surprise*). Why so serious and indignant, Josie? You just told your unworthy Old Man I was kidding. (*To* HOGAN) At last, I've got you by the ears, Phil. We must have a serious chat about when you're going to pay that back rent.

HOGAN (*groans*). A landlord who's a blackmailer! Holy God, what next! (JOSIE *is smiling with relief now*.)

TYRONE. And you, Josie, please remember when I keep that moonlight date tonight I expect you to be very sweet to me.

JOSIE (*with a bold air*). Sure, you don't have to blackmail me. I'd be that to you, anyway.

HOGAN. Are you laying plots in my presence to seduce my only daughter? (*Then philosophically*) Well, what can I do? I'll be drunk at the Inn, so how could I prevent it? (*He goes up the steps*.) Let's eat, for the love of God. I'm starving. (*He disappears inside the house.*)

JOSIE (*with an awkward playful gesture, takes* TYRONE *by the hand*). Come along, Jim.

TYRONE (*smiles kiddingly*). Afraid you'll lose me? Swell chance! (*His eyes fix on her breasts—with genuine feeling*) You have the most beautiful breasts in the world, do you know it, Josie?

JOSIE (*pleased—shyly*). I don't—but I'm happy if you think— (*Then quickly*) But I've no time now to listen to your kidding, with my mad old father waiting for his dinner. So come on. (*She tugs at his hand and he follows her up the steps. Her manner changes to worried solicitude.*) Promise me you'll eat something, Jim. You've got to eat. You can't go on the way you are, drinking and never eating, hardly. You're killing yourself.

TYRONE (*sardonically*). That's right. Mother me, Josie, I love it.

JOSIE (*bullyingly*). I will, then. You need one to take care of you. (*They disappear inside the house.*)

CURTAIN

ACT TWO

SCENE: *The same, with the wall of the living room removed.*

It is a clear warm moonlight night, around eleven o'clock.

JOSIE *is sitting on the steps before the front door. She has changed to her Sunday best, a cheap dark-blue dress, black stockings and shoes. Her hair is carefully arranged, and by way of adornment a white flower is pinned on her bosom. She is hunched up, elbows on knees, her chin in her hands. There is an expression on her face we have not seen before, a look of sadness and loneliness and humiliation.*

She sighs and gets slowly to her feet, her body stiff from sitting long in the same position. She goes into the living room, fumbles around for the box of matches, and lights a kerosene lamp on the table.

The living room is small, low-ceilinged, with faded, fly-specked wallpaper, a floor of bare boards. It is cluttered up with furniture that looks as if it had been picked up at a fire sale. There is a table at center, a disreputable old Morris chair beside it; two ugly sideboards, one at left, the other at right-rear; a porch rocking-chair, painted green, with a hole in its cane bottom; a bureau against the rear wall, with two chairs on either side of a door to the kitchen. On the bureau is an alarm clock which shows the time to be five past eleven. At right-front is the door to JOSIE's bedroom.

———

JOSIE (*looks at the clock—dully*). Five past eleven, and he said he'd be here around nine. (*Suddenly in a burst of humiliated anger, she tears off the flower pinned to her bosom and throws it in the corner.*) To hell with you, Jim Tyrone! (*From down the road, the quiet of the night is shattered by a burst of melancholy song. It is unmistakably* HOGAN's *voice wailing an old Irish lament at the top of his lungs.* JOSIE *starts—then frowns irritably.*) What's bringing him home an hour before the Inn closes? He must be more paralyzed than ever I've known him. (*She listens to the singing—grimly*) Ah, here you come, do you, as full as a tick! I'll give you a welcome, if you start cutting up! I'm in no mood to put up with you. (*She goes into her bedroom and returns with her broomstick club. Outside the singing grows louder as* HOGAN *approaches the house. He only remembers one verse of the song and he has been repeating it.*)

HOGAN.
Oh the praties they grow small
Over here, over here,
Oh, the praties they grow small
Over here.
Oh the praties they grow small
And we dig them in the fall
And we eat them skins and all
Over here, over here.

(*He enters left-front, weaving and lurching a bit. But he is not as drunk as he appears. Or rather, he is one of those people who can drink an enormous amount and be absolutely plastered when they want to be for their own pleasure, but at the same time are able to pull themselves together when they wish and be cunningly clear-headed. Just now, he is letting himself go and getting great satisfaction from it. He pauses and bellows belligerently at the house.*) Hurroo! Down with all tyrants, male and female! To hell with

England, and God damn Standard Oil!

JOSIE (*shouts back*). Shut up your noise, you crazy old billy goat!

HOGAN (*hurt and mournful*). A sweet daughter and a sweet welcome home in the dead of night. (*Beginning to boil*) Old goat! There's respect for you! (*Angrily— starting for the front door*) Crazy billy goat, is it? Be God, I'll learn you manners! (*He pounds on the door with his fist.*) Open the door! Open this door, I'm saying, before I drive a fist through it, or kick it into flinders! (*He gives it a kick.*)

JOSIE. It's not locked, you drunken old loon! Open it yourself!

HOGAN (*turns the knob and stamps in*). Drunken old loon, am I? Is that the way to address your father?

JOSIE. No. It's too damned good for him.

HOGAN. It's time I taught you a lesson. Be Jaysus, I'll take you over my knee and spank your tail, if you are as big as a cow! (*He makes a lunge to grab her.*)

JOSIE. Would you, though! Take that, then! (*She raps him smartly, but lightly, on his bald spot with the end of her broom handle.*)

HOGAN (*with an exaggerated howl of pain*). Ow! (*His anger evaporates and he rubs the top of his head ruefully—with bitter complaint*) God forgive you, it's a great shame to me I've raised a daughter so cowardly she has to use a club.

JOSIE (*puts her club on the table— grimly*). Now I've no club.

HOGAN (*evades the challenge*). I never thought I'd see the day when a daughter of mine would be such a coward as to threaten her old father when he's helpless drunk and can't hit back. (*He slumps down on the Morris chair.*)

JOSIE. Ah, that's better. Now that little game is over. (*Then angrily*) Listen to me, Father. I have no patience left, so get up from that chair, and go in your room, and go to bed, or I'll take you by the scruff of your neck and the seat of your pants and throw you in and lock the door on you! I mean it, now! (*On the verge of angry tears*) I've had all I can bear this night, and I want some peace and sleep, and not to listen to an old lush!

HOGAN (*appears drunker, his head wagging, his voice thick, his talk rambling*). That's right. Fight with me. My own daughter has no feelings or sympathy. As if I hadn't enough after what's happened tonight.

JOSIE (*with angry disgust*). Och, don't try— (*Then curiously*) What's happened? I thought something must be queer, you coming home before the Inn closed, but then I thought maybe for once you'd drunk all you could hold. (*Scathingly*) And, God pity you, if you ain't that full, you're damned close to it.

HOGAN. Go on. Make fun of me. Old lush! You wouldn't feel so comical, if— (*He stops, mumbling to himself.*)

JOSIE. If what?

HOGAN. Never mind. Never mind. I didn't come home to fight, but seek comfort in your company. And if I was singing coming along the road, it was only because there's times you have to sing to keep from crying.

JOSIE. I can see you crying!

HOGAN. You will. And you'll see yourself crying, too, when— (*He stops again and mumbles to himself.*)

JOSIE. When what? (*Exasperatedly*) Will you stop your whiskey drooling and talk plain?

HOGAN (*thickly*). No matter. No matter. Leave me alone.

JOSIE (*angrily*). That's good advice. To hell with you! I know your game. Nothing at all has happened. All you want is to keep me up listening to your guff. Go to your room, I'm saying, before—

HOGAN. I won't. I couldn't sleep with my thoughts tormented the way they are. I'll stay here in this chair, and you go to your room and let me be.

JOSIE (*snorts*). And have you singing again in a minute and smashing the furniture—

HOGAN. Sing, is it! Are you making fun again? I'd give a keen of sorrow or howl at the moon like an old mangy hound in his sadness if I knew how, but I don't. So rest aisy. You won't hear a sound from me. Go on and snore like a pig to your heart's content. (*He mourns drunkenly*) A fine daughter! I'd get more comfort from strangers.

JOSIE. Och, for God's sake, dry up! You'll sit in the dark then. I won't leave the lamp lit for you to tip over and burn down the house. (*She reaches out to turn down the lamp.*)

HOGAN (*thickly*). Let it burn to the ground. A hell of a lot I care if it burns.

JOSIE (*in the act of turning down the lamp, stops and stares at him, puzzled and uneasy*). I never heard you talk that way before, no matter how drunk you were. (*He mumbles. Her tone becomes persuasive.*) What's happened to you, Father?

HOGAN (*bitterly*). Ah it's "Father" now, is it, not old billy goat? Well, thank God for small favors. (*With heavy sarcasm*) Oh, nothing's happened to me at all, at all. A trifle, only. I wouldn't waste your time mentioning it, or keep you up when you want sleep so bad.

JOSIE (*angrily*). Och, you old loon, I'm sick of you. Sleep it off till you get some sense. (*She reaches for the lamp again.*)

HOGAN. Sleep it off? We'll see if you'll sleep it off when you know— (*He lapses into drunken mumbling.*)

JOSIE (*again stares at him*). Know what, Father?

HOGAN (*mumbles*). The son of a bitch!

JOSIE (*trying a light tone*). Sure, there's a lot of those in the neighborhood. Which one do you mean? Is Harder on your mind again?

HOGAN (*thickly*). He's one and a prize one, but I don't mean him. I'll say this for Harder, you know what to expect from him. He's no wolf in sheep's clothing, nor a treacherous snake in the grass who stabs you in the back with a knife—

JOSIE (*apprehensive now—forces a joke*). Sure, if you've found a snake who can stab you with a knife, you'd better join the circus with him and make a pile of money.

HOGAN (*bitterly*). Make jokes, God forgive you! You'll soon laugh from the wrong end of your mouth! (*He mumbles*) Pretending he's our friend! The lying bastard!

JOSIE (*bristles resentfully*). Is it Jim Tyrone you're calling hard names?

HOGAN. That's right. Defend him, you big soft fool! Faith, you're a prize dunce! You've had a good taste of believing his word, waiting hours for him dressed up in your best like a poor sheep without pride or spirit—

JOSIE (*stung*). Shut up! I was calling him a lying bastard myself before you came, and saying I'd never speak to him again. And I knew all along he'd never remember to keep his date after he got drunk.

HOGAN. He's not so drunk he forgot to attend to business.

JOSIE (*as if she hadn't heard—defiantly*). I'd have stayed up anyway a beautiful night like this to enjoy the moonlight, if there wasn't a Jim Tyrone in the world.

HOGAN (*with heavy sarcasm*). In your best shoes and stockings? Well, well. Sure, the moon must feel flattered by your attentions.

JOSIE (*furiously*). You won't feel flattered if I knock you tail over tin cup out of that chair! And stop your whiskey gabble about Jim. I see what you're driving at with your dark hints and curses, and if you think I'll believe—(*With forced assurance*) Sure, I know what's happened as well as if I'd been there. Jim saw you'd got drunker than usual and you were an easy mark for a joke, and he's made a goat of you!

HOGAN (*bitterly*). Goat, again! (*He struggles from his chair and stands swaying unsteadily—with offended dignity*) All right, I won't say another word. There's no use telling the truth to a bad-tempered woman in love.

JOSIE. Love be damned! I hate him now!

HOGAN. Be Christ, you have me stumped. A great proud slut who's played games with half the men around here, and now you act like a numbskull virgin that can't believe a man would tell her a lie!

JOSIE (*threateningly*). If you're going to your room, you'd better go quick!

HOGAN (*fixes his eyes on the door at rear —with dignity*). That's where I'm going, yes—to talk to meself so I'll know someone with brains is listening. Good night to you, Miss Hogan. (*He starts—swerves left— tries to correct this and lurches right and bumps against her, clutching the supporting arm she stretches out.*)

JOSIE. God help you, if you try to go upstairs now, you'll end up in the cellar.

HOGAN (*hanging on to her arm and shoulder—maudlinly affectionate now*). You're right. Don't listen to me. I'm wrong to bother you. You've had sorrow enough this night. Have a good sleep, while you can, Josie, darlin'—and good night and God bless you. (*He tries to kiss her, but she wards him off and steers him back to the chair.*)

JOSIE. Sit down before you split in pieces on the floor and I have to get the wheelbarrow to collect you. (*She dumps him in the chair where he sprawls limply, his chin on his chest.*)

HOGAN (*mumbles dully*). It's too late. It's all settled. We're helpless, entirely.

JOSIE (*really worried now*). How is it all settled? If you're helpless, I'm not. (*Then as he doesn't reply—scornfully*) It's the first time I ever heard you admit you were licked. And it's the first time I ever saw you so paralyzed you couldn't shake the whiskey from your brains and get your head clear when you wanted. Sure, that's always been your pride—and now look at you, the stupid object you are, mumbling and drooling!

HOGAN (*struggles up in his chair—angrily*). Shut up your insults! Be God, I can get my head clear if I like! (*He shakes his head violently.*) There! It's clear. I can tell you each thing that happened tonight as clear as if I'd not taken a drop, if you'll listen and not keep calling me a liar.

JOSIE. I'll listen, now I see you have hold of your wits.

HOGAN. All right, then. I'll begin at the beginning when him and me left here, and you gave him a sweet smile, and rolled your big beautiful cow's eyes at him, and wiggled your backside, and stuck out your beautiful breasts you know he admires, and said in a sick sheep's voice. "Don't forget our moonlight date, Jim."

JOSIE (*with suppressed fury*). You're a —! I never—! You old—!

HOGAN. And he said: "You bet I won't forget, Josie."

JOSIE. The lying crook!

HOGAN (*his voice begins to sink into a dejected monotone*). We went to the Inn and started drinking whiskey. And I got drunk.

JOSIE (*exasperatedly*). I guessed that! And Jim got drunk, too. And then what?

HOGAN (*dully*). Who knows how drunk he got? He had one of his queer fits when you can't tell. He's the way I told you about this morning, when he talks like a Broadway crook, who'd sell his soul for a price, and there's a sneering divil in him, and he loves to pick out the weakness in people and say cruel, funny things that flay the hide off them, or play cruel jokes on them. (*With sudden rage*) God's curse on him, I'll wager he's laughing to himself this minute, thinking it's the cutest joke in the world, the fools he's made of us. You in particular. Be God, I had my suspicions, at least, but your head was stuffed with mush and love, and you wouldn't—

JOSIE (*furiously*). You'll tell that lie about my love once too often! And I'll play a joke on him yet that'll make him sorry he—

HOGAN (*sunk in drunken defeatism again*). It's too late. You shouldn't have let him get away from you to the Inn. You should have kept him here. Then maybe, if you'd got him drunk enough you could have—(*His head nodding, his eyes blinking—thickly*) But it's no good talking now—no good at all—no good—

JOSIE (*gives him a shake*). Keep hold of your wits or I'll give you a cuff on both ears! Will you stop blathering like an old woman and tell me plainly what he's done!

HOGAN. He's agreed to sell the farm, that's what! Simpson came to the Inn to see him with a new offer from Harder. Ten thousand, cash.

JOSIE (*overwhelmed*). Ten thousand! Sure, three is all it's worth at most. And two was what you offered that Jim promised—

HOGAN. What's money to Harder? After what we did to him, all he wants is revenge. And here's where he's foxy. Simpson must have put him up to it knowing how Jim hates it here living on a small allowance, and he longs to go back to Broadway and his whores. Jim won't have to wait for his half of the cash till the estate's settled. Harder offers to give him five thousand cash as a loan against the estate the second the sale is made. Jim can take the next train to New York.

JOSIE (*tensely, on the verge of tears*). And Jim accepted? I don't believe it!

HOGAN. Don't then. Be God, you'll believe it tomorrow! Harder proposed that he meet with Jim and the executors in the morning and settle it, and Jim promised Simpson he would.

JOSIE (*desperately*). Maybe he'll get so drunk he'll never remember—

HOGAN. He won't. Harder's coming in his automobile to pick him up and make sure of him. Anyway don't think because he forgot you were waiting—in the moonlight, eating your heart out, that he'd ever miss a date with five thousand dollars, and all the pretty whores of Broadway he can buy with it.

JOSIE (*distractedly*). Will you shut up! (*Angrily*) And where were you when all this happened? Couldn't you do anything to stop it, you old loon?

HOGAN. I couldn't. Simpson came and sat at the table with us—

JOSIE. And you let him!

HOGAN. Jim invited him. Anyway, I wanted to find out what trick he had up his sleeve, and what Jim would do. When it was all over, I got up and took a swipe at Simpson, but I missed him. (*With drunken sadness*) I was too drunk—too drunk—too drunk— I missed him, God forgive me! (*His chin sinks on his chest and his eyes shut.*)

JOSIE (*shakes him*). If you don't keep awake, be God, I won't miss you!

HOGAN. I was going to take a swipe at Jim, too, but I couldn't do it. My heart was too broken with sorrow. I'd come to love him like a son—a real son of my heart!—to take the place of that jackass, Mike, and me two other jackasses.

JOSIE (*her face hard and bitter*). I think now Mike was the only one in this house with sense.

HOGAN. I was too drowned in sorrow by his betraying me—and you he'd pretended to like so much. So I only called him a dirty lying skunk of a treacherous bastard, and I turned my back on him and left the Inn, and I made myself sing on the road so he'd hear, and they'd all hear in the Inn, to show them I didn't care a damn.

JOSIE (*scathingly*). Sure, wasn't you the hero! A hell of a lot of good—

HOGAN. Ah, well, I suppose the temptation was too great. He's weak, with one foot in the grave from whiskey. Maybe we shouldn't blame him.

JOSIE (*her eyes flashing*). Not blame him? Well, I blame him, God damn him! Are you making excuses for him, you old fool!

HOGAN. I'm not. He's a dirty snake! But I was thinking how do I know what I wouldn't do for five thousand cash, and how do you know what you wouldn't do?

JOSIE. Nothing could make me betray him! (*Her face grows hard and bitter.*) Or it couldn't before. There's nothing I wouldn't do now. (HOGAN *suddenly begins to chuckle.*) Do you think I'm lying? Just give me a chance—

HOGAN. I remembered something. (*He laughs drunkenly.*) Be Christ, Josie, for all his Broadway wisdom about women, you've made a prize damned fool of him and that's some satisfaction!

JOSIE (*bewildered*). How'd you mean?

HOGAN. You'll never believe it. Neither did I, but he kept on until, be God, I saw he really meant it.

JOSIE. Meant what?

HOGAN. It was after he'd turned queer—early in the night before Simpson came. He started talking about you, as if you was on his mind, worrying him—and before he finished I take my oath I began to hope you could really work Mike's first scheme on him, if you got him alone in the moonlight, because all his gab was about his great admiration for you.

JOSIE. Och! The liar!

HOGAN. He said you had great beauty in you that no one appreciated but him.

JOSIE (*shakenly*). You're lying.

HOGAN. Great strength you had, and great pride, he said—and great goodness, no less! But here's where you've made a prize jackass of him, like I said. (*With a drunken leer*) Listen now, darlin', and don't drop dead with amazement. (*He leans toward her and whispers.*) He believes you're a virgin! (JOSIE *stiffens as if she'd been insulted.* HOGAN *goes on.*) He does, so help me! He means it, the poor dunce! He thinks you're a poor innocent virgin! He thinks it's all boasting and pretending you've done about being a slut. (*He chuckles.*) A virgin, no less! You!

JOSIE (*furiously*). Stop saying it! Boasting and pretending, am I? The dirty liar!

HOGAN. Faith, you don't have to tell me. (*Then he looks at her in drunken surprise —thickly*) Are you taking it as an insult? Why the hell don't you laugh? Be God, you ought to see what a stupid sheep that makes him.

JOSIE (*forces a laugh*). I do see it.

HOGAN (*chuckling drunkenly*). Oh, be God, I've just remembered another thing, Josie. I know why he didn't keep his date with you. It wasn't that he'd forgot. He remembered well enough, for he talked about it—

JOSIE. You mean he deliberately, knowing I'd be waiting—(*Fiercely*) God damn him!

HOGAN. He as much as told me his reason, though he wouldn't come out with it plain, me being your father. His conscience was tormenting him. He's going to leave you alone and not see you again—for your sake, because he loves you! (*He chuckles.*)

JOSIE (*looks stricken and bewildered—*

her voice trembling). Loves me? You're making it up.

HOGAN. I'm not. I know it sounds crazy but—

JOSIE. What did he mean, for my sake?

HOGAN. Can't you see? You're a pure virgin to him, but all the same there's things besides your beautiful soul he feels drawn to, like your beautiful hair and eyes, and—

JOSIE (*strickenly*). Och, don't, Father! You know I'm only a big—

HOGAN (*as if she hadn't spoken*). So he'll keep away from temptation because he can't trust himself, and it'd be a sin on his conscience if he was to seduce you. (*He laughs drunkenly.*) Oh, be God! If that ain't rich!

JOSIE (*her voice trembles*). So that was his reason—(*Then angrily*) So he thinks all he has to do is crook a finger and I'll fall for him, does he, the vain Broadway crook!

HOGAN (*chuckling*). Be Jaysus, it was the maddest thing in the world, him gabbing like a soft loon about you—and there at the bar in plain sight was two of the men you've been out with, the gardener at Smith's and Regan, the chauffeur for Driggs, having a drink together!

JOSIE (*with a twitching smile*). It must have been mad, surely. I wish I'd been there to laugh up my sleeve. (*Angry*) But what's all his crazy lying blather got to do with him betraying us and selling the place?

HOGAN (*at once hopelessly dejected again*). Nothing at all. I only thought you'd like to know you'd had that much revenge.

JOSIE. A hell of a revenge! I'll have a better one than that on him—or I'll try to! I'm not like you, owning up I'm beaten and crying wurra-wurra like a coward and getting hopeless drunk! (*She gives him a shake.*) Get your wits about you and answer me this: Did Simpson get him to sign a paper?

HOGAN. No, but what good is that? In the morning he'll sign all they shove in front of him.

JOSIE. It's this good. It means we still have a chance. Or I have.

HOGAN. What chance? Are you going to beg him to take pity on us?

JOSIE. I'll see him in hell first! There's another chance, and a good one. But I'll

need your help—(*Angrily*) And look at you, your brains drowned in whiskey, so I can't depend on you!

HOGAN (*rousing himself*). You can, if there's any chance. Be God, I'll make myself as sober as a judge for you in the wink of an eye! (*Then dejectedly*) But what can you do now, darlin'? You haven't even got him here. He's down at the Inn sitting alone, drinking and dreaming of the little whores he'll be with tomorrow night on Broadway.

JOSIE. I'll get him here! I'll humble my pride and go down to the Inn for him! And if he doesn't want to come I've a way to make him. I'll raise a scene and pretend I'm in a rage because he forgot his date. I'll disgrace him till he'll be glad to come with me to shut me up. I know his weakness, and it's his vanity about his women. If I was a dainty, pretty tart he'd be proud I'd raise a rumpus about him. But when it's a big, ugly hulk like me—(*She falters and forces herself to go on.*) If he ever was tempted to want me, he'd be ashamed of it. That's the truth behind the lies he told you of his conscience and his fear he might ruin me, God damn him!

HOGAN. No, he meant it, Josie. But never mind that now. Let's say you've got him here. Then what will you do?

JOSIE. I told you this morning if he ever broke his promise to us I'd do anything and not mind how crooked it was. And I will! Your part in it is to come at sunrise with witnesses and catch us in—(*She falters.*)

HOGAN. In bed, is it? Then it's Mike's second scheme you're thinking about?

JOSIE. I told you I didn't care how dirty a trick—(*With a hard bitter laugh*) The dirtier the better now!

HOGAN. But how'll you get him in bed, with all his honorable scruples, thinking you're a virgin? But I'm forgetting he stayed away because he was afraid he'd be tempted. So maybe—

JOSIE (*tensely*). For the love of God, don't harp on his lies. He won't be tempted at all. But I'll get him so drunk he'll fall asleep and I'll carry him in and put him in bed—

HOGAN. Be God, that's the way! But you'll have to get a pile of whiskey down him. You'll never do it unless you're more sociable and stop looking at him, the way you do, whenever he takes a drink, as if you was praying Almighty God to forgive a poor drunkard. You've got to encourage him. The best way would be for you to drink with him. It would put him at his ease and unsuspecting, and it'd give you courage, too, so you'd act bold for a change instead of giving him brazen talk he's tired of hearing, while you act shy as a mouse.

JOSIE (*gives her father a bitter, resentful look*). You're full of sly advice all of a sudden, ain't you? You dirty little tick!

HOGAN (*angrily*). Didn't you tell me to get hold of my wits? Be God, if you want me drunk, I've only to let go. That'd suit me. I want to forget my sorrow, and I've no faith in your scheme because you'll be too full of scruples. Like the drinking. You're such a virtuous teetotaller—

JOSIE. I've told you I'd do anything now! (*Then confusedly*) All I meant was, it's not right, a father to tell his daughter how to—(*Then angrily*) I don't need your advice. Haven't I had every man I want around here?

HOGAN. Ah, thank God, that sounds natural! Be God, I thought you'd started playing virgin with me just because that Broadway sucker thinks you're one.

JOSIE (*furiously*). Shut up! I'm not playing anything. And don't worry I can't do my part of the trick.

HOGAN. That's the talk! But let me get it all clear. I come at sunrise with my witnesses, and you've forgot to lock your door, and we walk in, and there's the two of you in bed, and I raise the roof and threaten him if he don't marry you—

JOSIE. Marry him? After what he's done to us? I wouldn't marry him now if he was the last man on earth! All we want is a paper signed by him with witnesses that he'll sell the farm to you for the price you offered, and not to Harder.

HOGAN. Well, that's justice, but that's all it is. I thought you wanted to make him pay for his black treachery against us, the dirty bastard!

JOSIE. I do want! (*She again gives him a bitter resentful glance.*) It's the estate money you're thinking of, isn't it? Leave it to you! (*Hastily*) Well, so am I! I'd like to get my hooks on it! (*With a hard, brazen air*) Be God, if I'm to play whore, I deserve my pay! We'll make him sign a paper he owes me ten thousand dollars the minute the estate is settled. (*She laughs.*)

How's that? I'll bet none of his tarts on Broadway ever got a thousandth part of that out of him, no matter how dainty and pretty! (*Laughing again*) And here's what'll be the greatest joke to teach him a lesson. He'll pay it for nothing! I'll get him in bed but I'll never let him—

HOGAN (*with delighted admiration*). Och, by Jaysus, Josie, that's the best yet! (*He slaps his thigh enthusiastically.*) Oh, that'll teach him to double-cross his friends! That'll show him two can play at tricks! And him believing you so innocent! Be God, you'll make him the prize sucker of the world! Won't I roar inside me when I see his face in the morning! (*He bursts into coarse laughter.*)

JOSIE (*again with illogical resentment*). Stop laughing! You're letting yourself be drunk again. (*Then with a hard, business-like air*) We've done enough talking. Let's start—

HOGAN. Wait, now. There's another thing. Just what do you want me to threaten him with when I catch you? That we'll sue him for outraging your virtue? Sure, his lawyer would have all your old flames in the witness box, till the jury would think you'd been faithful to the male inhabitants of America. So what threat—I can't think of any he wouldn't laugh at.

JOSIE (*tensely*). Well, I can! Do I have to tell you his weakness again? It's his vanity about women, and his Broadway pride he's so wise no woman could fool him. It's the disgrace to his vanity—being caught with the likes of me—(*Falteringly, but forcing herself to go on*) My mug beside his in all the newspapers—the New York papers, too—he'll see the whole of Broadway splitting their sides laughing at him—and he'll give anything to keep us quiet, I tell you. He will! I know him! So don't worry—(*She ends up on the verge of bitter humiliated tears.*)

HOGAN (*without looking at her—enthusiastic again*). Be God, you're right!

JOSIE (*gives him a bitter glance—fiercely*). Then get the hell out of that chair and let's start it! (*He gets up. She surveys him resentfully.*) You're steady on your pins, ain't you, you scheming old thief, now there's the smell of money around! (*Quickly*) Well, I'm glad. I know I can depend on you now. You'll walk down to the Inn with me and hide outside until you see me come out with him. Then you can sneak in the Inn yourself and pick the witnesses to stay up with you. But mind you don't get drunk again, and let them get too drunk.

HOGAN. I won't, I take my oath! (*He pats her on the shoulder approvingly.*) Be God, you've got the proud, fighting spirit in you that never says die, and you make me ashamed of my weakness. You're that eager now, be damned if I don't almost think you're glad of the excuse!

JOSIE (*stiffens*). Excuse for what, you old—

HOGAN. To show him no man can get the best of you—what else?—like you showed all the others.

JOSIE. I'll show him to his sorrow! (*Then abruptly, starting for the screen door at left*) Come on. We've no time to waste. (*But when she gets to the door, she appears suddenly hesitant and timid—hurriedly*) Wait. I'd better give a look at myself in the mirror. (*In a brazen tone*) Sure, those in my trade have to look their best! (*She hurries back across the room into her bedroom and closes the door.* HOGAN *stares after her. Abruptly he ceases to look like a drunk who, by an effort, is keeping himself half-sober. He is a man who has been drinking a lot but is still clear-headed and has complete control of himself.*)

HOGAN (*watches the crack under* JOSIE's *door and speaks half-aloud to himself, shaking his head pityingly*). A look in the mirror and she's forgot to light her lamp! (*Remorsefully*) God forgive me, it's bitter medicine. But it's the only way I can see that has a chance now. (JOSIE's *door opens. At once, he is as he was. She comes out, a fixed smile on her lips, her head high, her face set defiantly. But she has evidently been crying.*)

JOSIE (*brazenly*). There, now. Don't I look ten thousand dollars' worth to any drunk?

HOGAN. You look a million, darlin'!

JOSIE (*goes to the screen door and pushes it open with the manner of one who has burned all bridges*). Come along, then. (*She goes out. He follows close on her heels. She stops abruptly on the first step—startledly*) Look! There's someone on the road—

HOGAN (*pushes past her down the steps —peering off left-front—as if aloud to himself, in dismay*). Be God, it's him! I never thought—

JOSIE (*as if aloud to herself*). So he didn't forget—

HOGAN (*quickly*). Well, it proves he can't keep away from you, and that'll make it easier for you—(*Then furiously*) Oh, the dirty, double-crossing bastard! The nerve of him! Coming to call on you, after making you wait for hours, thinking you don't know what he's done to us this night, and it'll be a fine cruel joke to blarney you in the moonlight, and you trusting him like a poor sheep, and never suspecting—

JOSIE (*stung*). Shut up! I'll teach him who's the joker! I'll let him go on as if you hadn't told me what he's done—

HOGAN. Yes, don't let him suspect it, or you wouldn't fool him. He'd know you were after revenge. But he can see me here now. I can't sneak away or he'd be suspicious. We've got to think of a new scheme quick to get me away—

JOSIE (*quickly*). I know how. Pretend you're as drunk as when you came. Make him believe you're so drunk you don't remember what he's done, so he can't suspect you told me.

HOGAN. I will. Be God, Josie, damned if I don't think he's so queer drunk himself he don't remember, or he'd never come here.

JOSIE. The drunker he is the better! (*Lowering her voice—quickly*) He's turned in the gate where he can hear us. Pretend we're fighting and I'm driving you off till you're sober. Say you won't be back tonight. It'll make him sure he'll have the night alone with me. You start the fight.

HOGAN (*becomes at once very drunk. He shouts*). Put me out of my own home, will you, you undutiful slut!

JOSIE. Celebration or not, I'll have no drunks cursing and singing all night. Go back to the Inn.

HOGAN. I will! I'll get a room and two bottles and stay drunk as long as I please!

JOSIE. Don't come back till you've slept it off, or I'll wipe the floor with you! (TY-RONE *enters, left-front. He does not appear to be drunk—that is, he shows none of the usual symptoms. He seems much the same as in Act One. The only perceptible change is that his eyes have a peculiar fixed, glazed look, and there is a certain vague quality in his manner and speech, as if he were a bit hazy and absent-minded.*)

TYRONE (*dryly*). Just in time for the Big Bout. Or is this the final round?

HOGAN (*whirls on him unsteadily*). Who the hell—(*Peering at him*) Oh, it's you, is it?

TYRONE. What was the big idea, Phil, leaving me flat?

HOGAN. Leave you flat? Be Jaysus, that reminds me I owe you a swipe on the jaw for something. What was it? Be God, I'm too drunk to remember. But here it is, anyway. (*He turns loose a round-house swing that misses* TYRONE *by a couple of feet, and reels away.* TYRONE *regards him with vague surprise.*)

JOSIE. Stop it, you damned old fool, and get out of here!

HOGAN. Taking his side against your poor old father, are you? A hell of a daughter! (*He draws himself up with drunken dignity.*) Don't expect me home tonight, Miss Hogan, or tomorrow either, maybe. You can take your bad temper out on your sweetheart here. (*He starts off down the road, left-front, with a last word over his shoulder.*) Bad luck to you both. (*He disappears. A moment later he begins to bawl his mournful Irish song.*) "Oh, the praties they grow small, Over here, over here," etc. (*During a part of the following scene the song continues to be heard at intervals, receding as he gets farther off on his way to the Inn.*)

JOSIE. Well, thank God. That's good riddance. (*She comes to* TYRONE, *who stands staring after* HOGAN *with a puzzled look.*)

TYRONE. I've never seen him that stinko before. Must have got him all of a sudden. He didn't seem so lit up at the Inn, but I guess I wasn't paying much attention.

JOSIE (*forcing a playful air*). I should think, if you were a real gentleman, you'd be apologizing to me, not thinking of him. Don't you know you're two hours and a half late? I oughtn't to speak to you, if I had any pride.

TYRONE (*stares at her curiously*). You've got too damn much pride, Josie. That's the trouble.

JOSIE. And just what do you mean by that, Jim?

TYRONE (*shrugs his shoulders*). Nothing. Forget it. I do apologize, Josie. I'm damned sorry. Haven't any excuse. Can't think up a lie. (*Staring at her curiously again*) Or, now I think of it, I had a damned good honorable excuse, but—(*He shrugs.*) Nuts. Forget it.

JOSIE. Holy Joseph, you're full of riddles tonight. Well, I don't need excuses. I forgive you, anyway, now you're here. (*She takes his hand—playfully*) Come on now and we'll sit on my bedroom steps and be romantic in the moonlight, like we planned to. (*She leads him there. He goes along in an automatic way, as if only half-conscious of what he is doing. She sits on the top step and pulls him down on the step beneath her. A pause. He stares vaguely at nothing. She bends to give him an uneasy appraising glance.*)

TYRONE (*suddenly, begins to talk mechanically*). Had to get out of the damned Inn. I was going batty alone there. The old heebie-jeebies. So I came to you. (*He pauses—then adds with strange, wondering sincerity*) I've really begun to love you a lot, Josie.

JOSIE (*blurts out bitterly*). Yes, you've proved that tonight, haven't you? (*Hurriedly regaining her playful tone*) But never mind. I said I'd forgive you for being so late. So go on about love. I'm all ears.

TYRONE (*as if he hadn't listened*). I thought you'd have given me up and gone to bed. I remember I had some nutty idea I'd get in bed with you—just to lie with my head on your breast.

JOSIE (*moved in spite of herself—but keeps her bold, playful tone*). Well, maybe I'll let you—(*Hurriedly*) Later on, I mean. The night's young yet, and we'll have it all to ourselves. (*Boldly again*) But here's for a starter. (*She puts her arms around him and draws him back till his head is on her breast.*) There, now.

TYRONE (*relaxes—simply and gratefully*). Thanks, Josie. (*He closes his eyes. For a moment, she forgets everything and stares down at his face with a passionate, possessive tenderness. A pause. From far off on the road to the Inn,* HOGAN's *mournful song drifts back through the moonlight quiet: "Oh, the praties they grow small, Over here, over here."* TYRONE *rouses himself and straightens up. He acts embarrassed, as if he felt he'd been making a fool of himself—mockingly*) Hark, Hark, the Donegal lark! "Thou wast not born for death, immortal bird." Can't Phil sing anything but that damned dirge, Josie?

(*She doesn't reply. He goes on hazily.*) Still, it seems to belong tonight—in the moonlight—or in my mind—(*He quotes*) "Now more than ever seems it rich to die, To cease upon the midnight with no pain, In such an ecstasy!" (*He has recited this with deep feeling. Now he sneers.*) Good God! Ode to Phil the Irish Nightingale! I must have the D.T.'s.

JOSIE (*her face grown bitter*). Maybe it's only your bad conscience.

TYRONE (*starts guiltily and turns to stare into her face—suspiciously*). What put that in your head? Conscience about what?

JOSIE (*quickly*). How would I know, if you don't? (*Forcing a playful tone*) For the sin of wanting to be in bed with me. Maybe that's it.

TYRONE (*with strange relief*). Oh. (*A bit shamefacedly*) Forget that stuff, Josie. I was half nutty.

JOSIE (*bitterly*). Och, for the love of God, don't apologize as if you was ashamed of— (*She catches herself.*)

TYRONE (*with a quick glance at her face*). All right. I certainly won't apologize—if you're not kicking. I was afraid I might have shocked your modesty.

JOSIE (*roughly*). My modesty? Be God, I didn't know I had any left.

TYRONE (*draws away from her—irritably*). Nix, Josie. Lay off that line, for tonight at least. (*He adds slowly*) I'd like tonight to be different.

JOSIE. Different from what? (*He doesn't answer. She forces a light tone.*) All right. I'll be as different as you please.

TYRONE (*simply*). Thanks, Josie. Just be yourself. (*Again as if he were ashamed, or afraid he had revealed some weakness—off-handedly*) This being out in the moonlight instead of the lousy Inn isn't a bad bet, at that. I don't know why I hang out in that dump, except I'm even more bored in the so-called good hotels in this hick town.

JOSIE (*trying to examine his face without his knowing*). Well, you'll be back on Broadway soon now, won't you?

TYRONE. I hope so.

JOSIE. Then you'll have all the pretty little tarts to comfort you when you get your sorrowful spell on.

TYRONE. Oh, to hell with the rough stuff, Josie! You promised you'd can it tonight.

JOSIE (*tensely*). You're a fine one to talk of promises!

TYRONE (*vaguely surprised by her tone*). What's the matter? Still sore at me for being late?

JOSIE (*quickly*). I'm not. I was teasing you. To prove there's no hard feelings, how would you like a drink? But I needn't ask. (*She gets up.*) I'll get a bottle of his best.

TYRONE (*mechanically*). Fine. Maybe that will have some kick. The booze at the Inn didn't work tonight.

JOSIE. Well, this'll work. (*She starts to go into her bedroom. He sits hunched up on the step, staring at nothing. She pauses in the doorway to glance back. The hard, calculating expression on her face softens. For a second she stares at him, bewildered by her conflicting feelings. Then she goes inside, leaving the door open. She opens the door from her room to the lighted living room, and is seen going to the kitchen on the way to the cellar. She has left the door from the living room to her bedroom open and the light reveals a section of the bedroom framed in the doorway behind* TYRONE. *The foot of the bed which occupies most of the room can be seen, and that is all except that the walls are unpainted pine boards.* TYRONE *continues to stare at nothing, but becomes restless. His hands and mouth twitch.*)

TYRONE (*suddenly, with intense hatred*). You rotten bastard! (*He springs to his feet —fumbles in his pockets for cigarettes— strikes a match which lights up his face, on which there is now an expression of miserable guilt. His hand is trembling so violently he cannot light the cigarette.*)

CURTAIN

ACT THREE

SCENE: *The living-room wall has been replaced and all we see now of its lighted interior is through the two windows. Otherwise, everything is the same, and this Act follows the preceding without any lapse of time.* TYRONE *is still trying with shaking hands to get his cigarette lighted. Finally he succeeds, and takes a deep inhale, and starts pacing back and forth a few steps, as if in a cell of his own thought. He swears defensively.* God damn it. You'll be crying in your beer in a minute.

(*He begins to sing sneeringly half under his breath a snatch from an old sob song, popular in the Nineties*)

"And baby's cries can't waken her
In the baggage coach ahead."

(*His sneer changes to a look of stricken guilt and grief.*) Christ! (*He seems about to break down and sob but he fights this back.*) Cut it out, you drunken fool! (*JOSIE can be seen through the windows, returning from the kitchen. He turns with a look of relief and escape.*) Thank God! (*He sits on the boulder and waits. JOSIE stops by the table in the living room to turn down the lamp until only a dim light remains. She has a quart of whiskey under her arm, two tumblers, and a pitcher of water. She goes through her bedroom and appears in the outer doorway. TYRONE gets up*) Ah! At last the old booze! (*He relieves her of the pitcher and tumblers as she comes down the steps.*)

JOSIE (*with a fixed smile*). You'd think I'd been gone years. You didn't seem so perishing for a drink.

TYRONE (*in his usual, easy, kidding way*). It's you I was perishing for. I've been dying of loneliness—

JOSIE. You'll die of lying some day. But I'm glad you're alive again. I thought when I left you really were dying on me.

TYRONE. No such luck.

JOSIE. Och, don't talk like that. Come have a drink. We'll use the boulder for a table and I'll be barkeep. (*He puts the pitcher and tumblers on the boulder and she uncorks the bottle. She takes a quick glance at his face—startledly*) What's come over you, Jim? You look as if you've seen a ghost.

TYRONE (*looks away—dryly*). I have. My own. He's punk company.

JOSIE. Yes, it's the worst ghost of all, your own. Don't I know? But this will keep it in its place. (*She pours a tumbler half full of whiskey and hands it to him.*) Here. But wait till I join you. (*She pours the other tumbler half full.*)

TYRONE (*surprised*). Hello! I thought you never touched it.

JOSIE (*glibly*). I have on occasion. And this is one. I don't want to be left out altogether from celebrating our victory over Harder. (*She gives him a sharp bitter glance. Meeting his eyes, which are regarding her with puzzled wonder, she forces a laugh.*) Don't look at me as if I

was up to some game. A drink or two will make me better company, and help me enjoy the moon and the night with you. Here's luck. (*She touches his glass with hers.*)

TYRONE (*shrugs his shoulders*). All right. Here's luck. (*They drink. She gags and sputters. He pours water in her glass. She drinks it. He puts his glass and the pitcher back on the boulder. He keeps staring at her with a puzzled frown.*)

JOSIE. Some of it went down the wrong way.

TYRONE. So I see. That'll teach you to pour out baths instead of drinks.

JOSIE. It's the first time I ever heard you complain a drink was too big.

TYRONE. Yours was too big.

JOSIE. I'm my father's daughter. I've a strong head. So don't worry I'll pass out and you'll have to put me to bed. (*She gives a little bold laugh.*) Sure, that's a beautiful notion. I'll have to pretend I'm—

TYRONE (*irritably*). Nix on the raw stuff, Josie. Remember you said—

JOSIE (*resentment in her kidding*). I'd be different? That's right. I'm forgetting it's your pleasure to have me pretend I'm an innocent virgin tonight.

TYRONE (*in a strange tone that is almost threatening*). If you don't look out, I'll call you on that bluff, Josie. (*He stares at her with a deliberate sensualist's look that undresses her.*) I'd like to. You know that, don't you?

JOSIE (*boldly*). I don't at all. You're the one who's bluffing.

TYRONE (*grabs her in his arms—with genuine passion*). Josie! (*Then as suddenly he lets her go.*) Nix. Let's cut it out. (*He turns away. Her face betrays the confused conflict within her of fright, passion, happiness, and bitter resentment. He goes on with an abrupt change of tone.*) How about another drink? That's honest-to-God old bonded Bourbon. How the devil did Phil get hold of it?

JOSIE. Tom Lombardo, the bootlegger, gave him a case for letting him hide a truckload in our barn when the agents were after him. He stole it from a warehouse on faked permits. (*She pours out drinks as she speaks, a half tumblerful for him, a small one for herself.*) Here you are. (*She gives him his drink—smiles at him coquettishly, beginning to show the effect of her big drink by her increasingly bold manner.*) Let's sit down where the moon will be in our eyes and we'll see romance. (*She takes his arm and leads him to her bedroom steps. She sits on the top step, pulling him down beside her but on the one below. She raises her glass*) Here's hoping before the night's out you'll have more courage and kiss me at least.

TYRONE (*frowns—then kiddingly*). That's a promise. Here's how. (*He drains his tumbler. She drinks half of hers. He puts his glass on the ground beside him. A pause. She tries to read his face without his noticing. He seems to be lapsing again into vague preoccupation.*)

JOSIE. Now don't sink back half-dead-and-alive in dreams the way you were before.

TYRONE (*quickly*). I'm not. I had a good final dose of heebie-jeebies when you were in the house. That's all for tonight. (*He adds a bit maudlinly, his two big drinks beginning to affect him*) Let the dead past bury its dead.

JOSIE. That's the talk. There's only to-night, and the moon, and us—and the bonded Bourbon. Have another drink, and don't wait for me.

TYRONE. Not now, thanks. They're com-ing too fast. (*He gives her a curious, cyni-cally amused look.*) Trying to get me soused, Josie?

JOSIE (*starts—quickly*). I'm not. Only to get you feeling happy, so you'll forget all sadness.

TYRONE (*kiddingly*). I might forget all my honorable intentions, too. So look out.

JOSIE. I'll look forward to it—and I hope that's another promise, like the kiss you owe me. If you're suspicious I'm trying to get you soused—well, here goes. (*She drinks what is left in her glass.*) There, now. I must be scheming to get myself soused, too.

TYRONE. Maybe you are.

JOSIE (*resentfully*). If I was, it'd be to make you feel at home. Don't all the pretty little Broadway tarts get soused with you?

TYRONE (*irritably*). There you go again with that old line!

JOSIE. All right, I won't! (*Forcing a laugh*) I must be eaten up with jealousy for them, that's it.

TYRONE. You needn't be. They don't be-long.

JOSIE. And I do?

TYRONE. Yes. You do.

JOSIE. For tonight only, you mean?

TYRONE. We've agreed there is only to-night—and it's to be different from any past night—for both of us.

JOSIE (*in a forced, kidding tone*). I hope it will be. I'll try to control my envy for your Broadway flames. I suppose it's be-cause I have a picture of them in my mind as small and dainty and pretty—

TYRONE. They're just gold-digging tramps.

JOSIE (*as if he hadn't spoken*). While I'm only a big, rough, ugly cow of a woman.

TYRONE. Shut up! You're beautiful.

JOSIE (*jeeringly, but her voice trembles*). God pity the blind!

TYRONE. You're beautiful to me.

JOSIE. It must be the Bourbon—

TYRONE. You're real and healthy and clean and fine and warm and strong and kind—

JOSIE. I have a beautiful soul, you mean?

TYRONE. Well, I don't know much about ladies' souls—(*He takes her hand.*) But I do know you're beautiful. (*He kisses her hand.*) And I love you a lot—in my fashion.

JOSIE (*stammers*). Jim—(*Hastily forcing her playful tone*) Sure, you're full of fine compliments all of a sudden, and I ought to show you how pleased I am. (*She pulls his head back and kisses him on the lips —a quick, shy kiss.*) That's for my beauti-ful soul.

TYRONE (*the kiss arouses his physical de-sire. He pulls her head down and stares into her eyes*). You have a beautiful strong body, too, Josie—and beautiful eyes and hair, and a beautiful smile and beautiful warm breasts. (*He kisses her on the lips. She pulls back frightenedly for a second —then returns his kiss. Suddenly he breaks away—in a tone of guilty irritation*) Nix! Nix! Don't be a fool, Josie. Don't let me pull that stuff.

JOSIE (*triumphant for a second*). You meant it! I know you meant it! (*Then with resentful bitterness—roughly*) Be God, you're right I'm a damned fool to let you make me forget you're the greatest liar in the world! (*Quickly*) I mean, the greatest kidder. And now, how about another drink?

TYRONE (*staring at nothing—vaguely*). You don't get me, Josie. You don't know —and I hope you never will know—

JOSIE (*blurts out bitterly*). Maybe I know more than you think.

TYRONE (*as if she hadn't spoken*). There's always the aftermath that poisons you. I don't want you to be poisoned—

JOSIE. Maybe you know what you're talking about—

TYRONE. And I don't want to be poisoned myself—not again—not with you. (*He pauses—slowly*) There have been too many nights—and dawns. This must be different. I want—(*His voice trails off into silence.*)

JOSIE (*trying to read his face—uneasily*). Don't get in one of your queer spells, now. (*She gives his shoulder a shake—forcing a light tone.*) Sure, I don't think you know what you want. Except another drink. I'm sure you want that. And I want one, too.

TYRONE (*recovering himself*). Fine! Grand idea. (*He gets up and brings the bottle from the boulder. He picks up his tumbler and pours a big drink. She is holding out her tumbler but he ignores it.*)

JOSIE. You're not polite, pouring your own first.

TYRONE. I said a drink was a grand idea —for me. Not for you. You skip this one.

JOSIE (*resentfully*). Oh, I do, do I? Are you giving me orders?

TYRONE. Yes. Take a big drink of moonlight instead.

JOSIE (*angrily*). You'll pour me a drink, if you please, Jim Tyrone, or—

TYRONE (*stares at her—then shrugs his shoulders*). All right, if you want to take it that way, Josie. It's your funeral. (*He pours a drink into her tumbler.*)

JOSIE (*ashamed but defiant—stiffly*). Thank you kindly. (*She raises her glass— mockingly*) Here's to tonight. (TYRONE *is staring at her, a strange bitter disgust in his eyes. Suddenly he slaps at her hand, knocking the glass to the ground.*)

TYRONE (*his voice hard with repulsion*). I've slept with drunken tramps on too many nights!

JOSIE (*stares at him, too startled and bewildered to be angry. Her voice trembles with surprising meekness*). All right, Jim, if you don't want me to—

TYRONE (*now looks as bewildered by his action as she does*). I'm sorry, Josie. Don't know what the drink got into me. (*He picks up her glass.*) Here. I'll pour you another.

JOSIE (*still meek*). No, thank you. I'll skip this one. (*She puts the glass on the ground.*) But you drink up.

TYRONE. Thanks. (*He gulps down his drink. Mechanically, as if he didn't know what he was doing, he pours another. Suddenly he blurts out with guilty loathing*) That fat blonde pig on the train—I got her drunk! That's why—(*He stops guiltily.*)

JOSIE (*uneasily*). What are you talking about? What train?

TYRONE. No train. Don't mind me. (*He gulps down the drink and pours another with the same strange air of acting unconsciously.*) Maybe I'll tell you—later, when I'm— That'll cure you—for all time! (*Abruptly he realizes what he is saying. He gives the characteristic shrug of shoulders—cynically*) Nuts! The Brooklyn boys are talking again. I guess I'm more stewed than I thought—in the center of the old bean, at least. (*Dully*) I better beat it back to the Inn and go to bed and stop bothering you, Josie.

JOSIE (*bullyingly—and pityingly*). Well, you won't, not if I have to hold you. Come on now, bring your drink and sit down like you were before. (*He does so. She pats his cheek—forcing a playful air.*) That's a good boy. And I won't take any more whiskey. I've all the effect from it I want already. Everything is far away and doesn't matter—except the moon and its dreams, and I'm part of the dreams— and you are, too. (*She adds with a rueful little laugh*) I keep forgetting the thing I've got to remember. I keep hoping it's a lie, even though I know I'm a damned fool.

TYRONE (*hazily*). Damned fool about what?

JOSIE. Never mind. (*Forcing a laugh*) I've just had a thought. If my poor old father had seen you knocking his prize whiskey on the ground—Holy Joseph, he'd have had three paralytic strokes!

TYRONE (*grins*). Yes, I can picture him. (*He pauses—with amused affection*) But that's all a fake. He loves to play tightwad, but the people he likes know better. He'd give them his shirt. He's a grand old scout, Josie. (*A bit maudlin*) The only real friend I've got left—except you. I love his guts.

JOSIE (*tensely—sickened by his hypocrisy*). Och, for the love of God—!

TYRONE (*shrugs his shoulders*). Yes, I

suppose that does sound like moaning-at-the-bar stuff. But I mean it.

JOSIE. Do you? Well, I know my father's virtues without you telling me.

TYRONE. You ought to appreciate him because he worships the ground you walk on—and he knows you a lot better than you think. (*He turns to smile at her teasingly.*) As well as I do—almost.

JOSIE (*defensively*). That's not saying much. Maybe I can guess what you think you know—(*Forcing a contemptuous laugh*) If it's that, God pity you, you're a terrible fool.

TYRONE (*teasingly*). If it's what? I haven't said anything.

JOSIE. You'd better not, or I'll die laughing at you. (*She changes the subject abruptly.*) Why don't you drink up? It makes me nervous watching you hold it as if you didn't know it was there.

TYRONE. I didn't, at that. (*He drinks.*)

JOSIE. And have another.

TYRONE (*a bit drunkenly*). Will a whore go to a picnic? Real bonded Bourbon. That's my dish. (*He goes to the boulder for the bottle. He is as steady on his feet as if he were completely sober.*)

JOSIE (*in a light tone*). Bring the bottle back so it'll be handy and you won't have to leave me. I miss you.

TYRONE (*comes back with the bottle. He smiles at her cynically*). Still trying to get me soused, Josie?

JOSIE. I'm not such a fool—with your capacity.

TYRONE. You better watch your step. It might work—and then think of how disgusted you'd feel, with me lying beside you, probably snoring, as you watched the dawn come. You don't know—

JOSIE (*defiantly*). The hell I don't! Isn't that the way I've felt with every one of them, after?

TYRONE (*as if he hadn't heard—bitterly*). But take it from me, I know. I've seen too God-damned many dawns creeping grayly over too many dirty windows.

JOSIE (*ignores this—boldly*). But it might be different with you. Love could make it different. And I've been head over heels in love ever since you said you loved my beautiful soul. (*Again he doesn't seem to have heard—resentfully*) Don't stand there like a loon, mourning over the past. Why don't you pour yourself a drink and sit down?

TYRONE (*looks at the bottle and tumbler in his hands, as if he'd forgotten them—mechanically*). Sure thing. Real bonded Bourbon. I ought to know. If I had a dollar for every drink of it I had before Prohibition, I'd hire our dear bully, Harder, for a valet. (*JOSIE stiffens and her face hardens.* TYRONE *pours a drink and sets the bottle on the ground. He looks up suddenly into her eyes—warningly*) You'd better remember I said you had beautiful eyes and hair—and breasts.

JOSIE. I remember you did. (*She tries to be calculatingly enticing.*) So sit down and I'll let you lay your head—

TYRONE. No. If you won't watch your step, I've got to. (*He sits down but doesn't lean back.*) And don't let me get away with pretending I'm so soused I don't know what I'm doing. I always know. Or part of me does. That's the trouble. (*He pauses—then bursts out in a strange threatening tone.*) You better look out, Josie. She was tickled to death to get me pie-eyed. Ha! an idea she could roll me, I guess. She wasn't so tickled about it—later on.

JOSIE. What she? (*He doesn't reply. She forces a light tone.*) I hope you don't think I'm scheming to roll you.

TYRONE (*vaguely*). What? (*Coming to—indignantly*) Of course not. What are you talking about? For God's sake, you're not a tart.

JOSIE (*roughly*). No, I'm a fool. I'm always giving it away.

TYRONE (*angrily*). That lousy bluff again, eh? You're a liar! For Christ sake, quit the smut stuff, can't you!

JOSIE (*stung*). Listen to me, Jim! Drunk or not, don't you talk that way to me or—

TYRONE. How about your not talking the old smut stuff to me? You promised you'd be yourself. (*Pauses—vaguely*) You don't get it, Josie. You see, she was one of the smuttiest talking pigs I've ever listened to.

JOSIE. What she? Do you mean the blonde on the train?

TYRONE (*starts—sharply*). Train? Who told you—? (*Quickly*) Oh— that's right —I did say—(*Vaguely*) What blonde? What's the difference? Coming back from the Coast. It was long ago. But it seems like tonight. There is no present or future —only the past happening over and over again—now. You can't get away from it. (*Abruptly*) Nuts! To hell with that crap.

JOSIE. You came back from the Coast about a year ago after—(*She checks herself.*)

TYRONE (*dully*). Yes. After Mama's death. (*Quickly*) But I've been to the Coast a lot of times during my career as a third-rate ham. I don't remember which time—or anything much—except I was pie-eyed in a drawing room the whole four days. (*Abruptly*) What were we talking about before? What a grand guy Phil is. You ought to be glad you've got him for a father. Mine was an old bastard.

JOSIE. He wasn't! He was one of the finest, kindest gentlemen ever lived.

TYRONE (*sneeringly*). Outside the family, sure. Inside, he was a lousy tightwad bastard.

JOSIE (*repelled*). You ought to be ashamed!

TYRONE. To speak ill of the dead? Nuts! He can't hear, and he knows I hated him, anyway—as much as he hated me. I'm glad he's dead. So is he. Or he ought to be. Everyone ought to be, if they have any sense. Out of a bum racket. At peace. (*He shrugs his shoulders.*) Nuts! What of it?

JOSIE (*tensely*). Don't Jim. I hate you when you talk like that. (*Forcing a light tone*) Do you want to spoil our beautiful moonlight night? And don't be telling me of your old flames, on trains or not. I'm too jealous.

TYRONE (*with a shudder of disgust*). Of that pig? (*He drinks his whiskey as if to wash a bad taste from his mouth—then takes one of her hands in both of his—simply*) You're a fool to be jealous of anyone. You're the only woman I care a damn about.

JOSIE (*deeply stirred, in spite of herself —her voice trembling*). Jim, don't—(*Forcing a tense little laugh*) All right, I'll try and believe that—for tonight.

TYRONE (*simply*). Thanks, Josie. (*A pause. He speaks in a tone of random curiosity.*) Why did you say a while ago I'd be leaving for New York soon?

JOSIE (*stiffens—her face hardening*). Well, I was right, wasn't I? (*Unconsciously she tries to pull her hand away.*)

TYRONE. Why are you pulling your hand away?

JOSIE (*stops*). Was I? (*Forcing a smile*) I suppose because it seems crazy for you to hold my big ugly paw so tenderly. But you're welcome to it, if you like.

TYRONE. I do like. It's strong and kind and warm—like you. (*He kisses it.*)

JOSIE (*tensely*). Och, for the love of God—! (*She jerks her hand away—then hastily forces a joking tone.*) Wasting kisses on my hand! Sure, even the moon is laughing at us.

TYRONE. Nuts for the moon! I'd rather have one light on Broadway than all the moons since Rameses was a pup. (*He takes cigarettes from his pocket and lights one.*)

JOSIE (*her eyes searching his face, lighted up by the match*). You'll be taking a train back to your dear old Broadway tomorrow night, won't you?

TYRONE (*still holding the burning match, stares at her in surprise*). Tomorrow night? Where did you get that?

JOSIE. A little bird told me.

TYRONE (*blows out the match in a cloud of smoke*). You'd better give that bird the bird. By the end of the week, is the right dope. Phil got his dates mixed.

JOSIE (*quickly*). He didn't tell me. He was too drunk to remember anything.

TYRONE. He was sober when I told him. I called up the executors when we reached the Inn after leaving here. They said the estate would be out of probate within a few days. I told Phil the glad tidings and bought drinks for all and sundry. There was quite a celebration. Funny, Phil wouldn't remember that.

JOSIE (*bewildered—not knowing what to believe*). It is—funny.

TYRONE (*shrugs his shoulders*). Well, he's stewed to the ears. That always explains anything. (*Then strangely*) Only sometimes it doesn't.

JOSIE. No—sometimes it doesn't.

TYRONE (*goes on without real interest, talking to keep from thinking*). Phil certainly has a prize bun on tonight. He never took a punch at me before. And that drivel he talked about owing me one— What got into his head, I wonder.

JOSIE (*tensely*). How would I know, if you don't?

TYRONE. Well, I don't. Not unless—I remember I did try to get his goat. Simpson sat down with us. Harder sent him to see me. You remember after Harder left here I said the joke was on you, that you'd made this place a gold mine. I was kidding, but I had the right dope. What do you think he told Simpson to offer? Ten grand! On the level, Josie.

JOSIE (*tense*). So you accepted?

TYRONE. I told Simpson to tell Harder I did. I decided the best way to fix him was to let him think he'd got away with it, and then when he comes tomorrow morning to drive me to the executor's office, I'll tell him what he can do with himself, his bankroll, and tin oil tanks.

JOSIE (*knows he is telling the truth—so relieved she can only stammer stupidly*). So that's—the truth of it.

TYRONE (*smiles*). Of course, I did it to kid Phil, too. He was right there, listening. But I know I didn't fool him.

JOSIE (*weakly*). Maybe you did fool him, for once. But I don't know.

TYRONE. And that's why he took a swing at me? (*He laughs, but there is a forced note to it.*) Well, if so, it's one hell of a joke on him. (*His tone becomes hurt and bitter.*) All the same, I'll be good and sore, Josie. I promised this place wouldn't be sold except to him. What the hell does he think I am? He ought to know I wouldn't double-cross you and him for ten million!

JOSIE (*giving away at last to her relief and joy*). Don't I know! Oh, Jim, darling! (*She hugs him passionately and kisses him on the lips.*) I knew you'd never—I told him—(*She kisses him again.*) Oh, Jim, I love you.

TYRONE (*again with a strange, simple gratitude*). Thanks, Josie. I mean, for not believing I'm a rotten louse. Everyone else believes it—including myself—for a damned good reason. (*Abruptly changing the subject*) I'm a fool to let this stuff about Phil get under my skin, but— Why, I remember telling him tonight I'd even written my brother and got his okay on selling the farm to him. And Phil thanked me. He seemed touched and grateful. You wouldn't think he'd forget that.

JOSIE (*her face hard and bitter*). I wouldn't, indeed. There's a lot of things he'll have to explain when he comes at sun —(*Hastily*) When he comes back. (*She pauses—then bursts out*) The damned old schemer, I'll teach him to—(*Again checking herself*) to act like a fool.

TYRONE (*smiles*). You'll get out the old club, eh? What a bluff you are, Josie. (*Teasingly*) You and your lovers, Messalina—when you've never—

JOSIE (*with a faint spark of her old defiance*). You're a liar.

TYRONE. "Pride is the sin by which the angels fell." Are you going to keep that up—with me?

JOSIE (*feebly*). You think I've never because no one would—because I'm a great ugly cow—

TYRONE (*gently*). Nuts! You could have had any one of them. You kidded them till you were sure they wanted you. That was all you wanted. And then you slapped them groggy when they tried for more. But you had to keep convincing yourself—

JOSIE (*tormentedly*). Don't, Jim.

TYRONE. You can take the truth, Josie—from me. Because you and I belong to the same club. We can kid the world but we can't fool ourselves, like most people, no matter what we do—nor escape ourselves no matter where we run away. Whether it's the bottom of a bottle, or a South Sea Island, we'd find our own ghosts there waiting to greet us—"sleepless with pale commemorative eyes," as Rossetti wrote. (*He sneers to himself.*) The old poetic bull, eh? Crap! (*Reverting to a teasing tone*) You don't ask how I saw through your bluff, Josie. You pretend too much. And so do the guys. I've listened to them at the Inn. They all lie to each other. No one wants to admit all he got was a slap in the puss, when he thinks a lot of other guys made it. You can't blame them. And they know you don't give a damn how they lie. So—

JOSIE. For the love of God, Jim! Don't!

TYRONE. Phil is wise to you, of course, but although he knew I knew, he would never admit it until tonight.

JOSIE (*startled—vindictively*). So he admitted it, did he? Wait till I get hold of him!

TYRONE. He'll never admit it to you. He's afraid of hurting you.

JOSIE. He is, is he? Well—(*Almost hysterically*) For the love of God, can't you shut up about him!

TYRONE (*glances up at her, surprised—then shrugs his shoulders*). Oh, all right. I wanted to clear things up, that's all—for Phil's sake as well as yours. You have a hell of a license to be sore. He's the one who ought to be. Don't you realize what a lousy position you've put him in with your brazen-trollop act?

JOSIE (*tensely*). No. He doesn't care, except to use me in his scheming. He—

TYRONE. Don't be a damned fool. Of course he cares. And so do I. (*He turns and pulls her head down and kisses her on the lips.*) I care, Josie. I love you.

JOSIE (*with pitiful longing*). Do you, Jim? Do you? (*She forces a trembling smile—faintly*) Then I'll confess the truth to you. I've been a crazy fool. I am a virgin. (*She begins to sob with a strange forlorn shame and humiliation.*) And now you'll never—and I want you to—now more than ever—because I love you more than ever, after what's happened—(*Suddenly she kisses him with fierce passion.*) But you will! I'll make you! To hell with your honorable scruples! I know you want me! I couldn't believe that until tonight—but now I know. It's in your kisses! (*She kisses him again—with passionate tenderness.*) Oh, you great fool! As if I gave a damn what happened after! I'll have had tonight and your love to remember for the rest of my days! (*She kisses him again.*) Oh, Jim darling, haven't you said yourself there's only tonight? (*She whispers tenderly.*) Come. Come with me. (*She gets to her feet, pulling at his arm—with a little self-mocking laugh.*) But I'll have to make you leave before sunrise. I mustn't forget that.

TYRONE (*a strange change has come over his face. He looks her over now with a sneering cynical lust. He speaks thickly as if he was suddenly very drunk*). Sure thing, Kiddo. What the hell else do you suppose I came for? I've been kidding myself. (*He steps up beside her and puts his arm around her and presses his body to hers.*) You're the goods, Kid. I've wanted you all along. Love, nuts! I'll show you what love is. I know what you want, Bright Eyes. (*She is staring at him now with a look of frightened horror. He kisses her roughly*). Come on, Baby Doll, let's hit the hay. (*He pushes her back in the doorway.*)

JOSIE (*strickenly*). Jim! Don't! (*She pulls his arms away so violently that he staggers back and would fall down the steps if she didn't grab his arm in time. As it is he goes down on one knee. She is on the verge of collapse herself—brokenly*) Jim! I'm not a whore.

TYRONE (*remains on one knee—confusedly, as if he didn't know what had happened*). What the hell? Was I trying to rape you, Josie? Forget it. I'm drunk—not

responsible. (*He gets to his feet, staggering a bit, and steps down to the ground.*)

JOSIE (*covering her face with her hands*). Oh, Jim! (*She sobs.*)

TYRONE (*with vague pity*). Don't cry. No harm done. You stopped me, didn't you? (*She continues to sob. He mutters vaguely, as if talking to himself.*) Must have drawn a blank for a while. Nuts! Cut out the faking. I knew what I was doing. (*Slowly, staring before him*) But it's funny. I *was* seeing things. That's the truth, Josie. For a moment I thought you were that blonde pig—(*Hastily*) The old heebie-jeebies. Hair of the dog. (*He gropes around for the bottle and his glass.*) I'll have another shot—

JOSIE (*takes her hands from her face—fiercely*). Pour the whole bottle down your throat, if you like! Only stop talking! (*She covers her face with her hands and sobs again.*)

TYRONE (*stares at her with a hurt and sad expression—dully*). Can't forgive me, eh? You ought to. You ought to thank me for letting you see—(*He pauses, as if waiting for her to say something but she remains silent. He shrugs his shoulders, pours out a big drink mechanically.*) Well, here's how. (*He drinks and puts the bottle and glass on the ground—dully*) That was a nightcap. Our moonlight romance seems to be a flop, Josie. I guess I'd better go.

JOSIE (*dully*). Yes. You'd better go. Good night.

TYRONE. Not good night. Good-by.

JOSIE (*lifts her head*). Good-by?

TYRONE. Yes. I won't see you again before I leave for New York. I was a damned fool to come tonight. I hoped— But you don't get it. How could you? So what's the good—(*He shrugs his shoulders hopelessly and turns toward the road.*)

JOSIE. Jim!

TYRONE (*turning back—bitter accusation in his tone now*). Whore? Who said you were a whore? But I warned you, didn't I, if you kept on— Why did you have to act like one, asking me to come to bed? That wasn't what I came here for. And you promised tonight would be different. Why the hell did you promise that, if all you wanted was what all the others want, if that's all love means to you? (*Then guiltily*) Oh, Christ, I don't mean that, Josie. I know how you feel, and if I could give you happiness— But it wouldn't work.

You don't know me. I'd poison it for myself and for you. I've poisoned it already, haven't I, but it would be a million times worse after— No matter how I tried not to, I'd make it like all the other nights —for you, too. You'd lie awake and watch the dawn come with disgust, with nausea retching your memory, and the wine of passion poets blab about, a sour aftertaste in your mouth of Dago red ink! (*He gives a sneering laugh.*)

JOSIE (*distractedly*). Oh, Jim, don't! Please don't!

TYRONE. You'd hate me and yourself— not for a day or two but for the rest of your life. (*With a perverse, jeering note of vindictive boastfulness in his tone*) Believe me, Kid, when I poison them, they stay poisoned!

JOSIE (*with dull bitterness*). Good-by, Jim.

TYRONE (*miserably hurt and sad for a second—appealingly*). Josie—(*Gives the characteristic shrug of his shoulders—simply*) Good-by. (*He turns toward the road —bitterly*) I'll find it hard to forgive, too. I came here asking for love—just for this one night, because I thought you loved me. (*Dully*) Nuts. To hell with it. (*He starts away.*)

JOSIE (*watches him for a second, fighting the love that, in spite of her, responds to his appeal—then she springs up and runs to him—with fierce, possessive, maternal tenderness*). Come here to me, you great fool, and stop your silly blather. There's nothing to hate you for. There's nothing to forgive. Sure, I was only trying to give you happiness, because I love you. I'm sorry I was so stupid and didn't see— But I see now, and you'll find I have all the love you need. (*She gives him a hug and kisses him. There is passion in her kiss but it is a tender, protective maternal passion, which he responds to with an instant grateful yielding.*)

TYRONE (*simply*). Thanks, Josie. You're beautiful. I love you. I knew you'd understand.

JOSIE. Of course I do. Come, now. (*She leads him back, her arm around his waist.*)

TYRONE. I didn't want to leave you. You know that.

JOSIE. Indeed I know it. Come now. We'll sit down. (*She sits on the top step and pulls him down on the step below her.*) That's it—with my arm around you. Now

lay your head on my breast—the way you said you wanted to do—(*He lets his head fall back on her breast. She hugs him— gently*) There, now. Forget all about my being a fool and forgive—(*Her voice trembles—but she goes on determinedly.*) Forgive my selfishness, thinking only of myself. Sure, if there's one thing I owe you tonight, after all my lying and scheming, it's to give you the love you need, and it'll be my pride and my joy—(*Forcing a trembling echo of her playful tone*) It's easy enough, too, for I have all kinds of love for you—and maybe this is the greatest of all—because it costs so much. (*She pauses, looking down at his face. He has closed his eyes and his haggard, dissipated face looks like a pale mask in the moonlight— at peace as a death mask is at peace. She becomes frightened.*) Jim! Don't look like that!

TYRONE (*opens his eyes—vaguely*). Like what?

JOSIE (*quickly*). It's the moonlight. It makes you look so pale, and with your eyes closed—

TYRONE (*simply*). You mean I looked dead?

JOSIE. No! As if you'd fallen asleep.

TYRONE (*speaks in a tired, empty tone, as if he felt he ought to explain something to her—something which no longer interests him*). Listen, and I'll tell you a little story, Josie. All my life I had just one dream. From the time I was a kid, I loved racehorses. I thought they were the most beautiful things in the world. I liked to gamble, too. So the big dream was that some day I'd have enough dough to play a cagey system of betting on favorites, and follow the horses south in the winter, and come back north with them in the spring, and be at the track every day. It seemed that would be the ideal life—for me. (*He pauses.*)

JOSIE. Well, you'll be able to do it.

TYRONE. No. I won't be able to do it, Josie. That's the joke. I gave it a try-out before I came up here. I borrowed some money on my share of the estate, and started going to tracks. But it didn't work. I played my system, but I found I didn't care if I won or lost. The horses were beautiful, but I found myself saying to myself, what of it? Their beauty didn't mean anything. I found that every day I was glad when the last race was over, and I could go back to the hotel—and the bottle in my room. (*He pauses, staring into the moonlight with vacant eyes.*)

JOSIE (*uneasily*). Why did you tell me this?

TYRONE (*in the same listless monotone*). You said I looked dead. Well, I am.

JOSIE. You're not! (*She hugs him protectively.*) Don't talk like that!

TYRONE. Ever since Mama died.

JOSIE (*deeply moved—pityingly*). I know. I've felt all along it was that sorrow was making you—(*She pauses—gently*) Maybe if you talked about your grief for her, it would help you. I think it must be all choked up inside you, killing you.

TYRONE (*in a strange warning tone*). You'd better look out, Josie.

JOSIE. Why?

TYRONE (*quickly, forcing his cynical smile*). I might develop a crying jag, and sob on your beautiful breast.

JOSIE (*gently*). You can sob all you like.

TYRONE. Don't encourage me. You'd be sorry. (*A deep conflict shows in his expression and tone. He is driven to go on in spite of himself.*) But if you're such a glutton for punishment— After all, I said I'd tell you later, didn't I?

JOSIE (*puzzled*). You said you'd tell me about the blonde on the train.

TYRONE. She's part of it. I lied about that. (*He pauses—then blurts out sneeringly*) You won't believe it could have happened. Or if you did believe, you couldn't understand or forgive—(*Quickly*) But you might. You're the one person who might. Because you really love me. And because you're the only woman I've ever met who understands the lousy rotten things a man can do when he's crazy drunk, and draws a blank—especially when he's nutty with grief to start with.

JOSIE (*hugging him tenderly*). Of course I'll understand, Jim, darling.

TYRONE (*stares into the moonlight—hauntedly*). But I didn't draw a blank. I tried to. I drank enough to knock out ten men. But it didn't work. I knew what I was doing. (*He pauses—dully*) No, I can't tell you, Josie. You'd loathe my guts, and I couldn't blame you.

JOSIE. No! I'll love you no matter what—

TYRONE (*with strange triumphant harshness*). All right! Remember that's a promise! (*He pauses—starts to speak—pauses again.*)

JOSIE (*pityingly*). Maybe you'd better not—if it will make you suffer.

TYRONE. Trying to welch now, eh? It's too late. You've got me started. Suffer? Christ, I ought to suffer! (*He pauses. Then he closes his eyes. It is as if he had to hide from sight before he can begin. He makes his face expressionless. His voice becomes impersonal and objective, as though what he told concerned some man he had known, but had nothing to do with him. This is the only way he can start telling the story.*) When Mama died, I'd been on the wagon for nearly two years. Not even a glass of beer. Honestly. And I know I would have stayed on. For her sake. She had no one but me. The Old Man was dead. My brother had married—had a kid—had his own life to live. She'd lost him. She had only me to attend to things for her and take care of her. She'd always hated my drinking. So I quit. It made me happy to do it. For her. Because she was all I had, all I cared about. Because I loved her. (*He pauses.*) No one would believe that now, who knew— But I did.

JOSIE (*gently*). I know how much you loved her.

TYRONE. We went out to the Coast to see about selling a piece of property the Old Man had bought there years ago. And one day she suddenly became ill. Got rapidly worse. Went into a coma. Brain tumor. The docs said, no hope. Might never come out of coma. I went crazy. Couldn't face losing her. The old booze yen got me. I got drunk and stayed drunk. And I began hoping she'd never come out of the coma, and see I was drinking again. That was my excuse, too—that she'd never know. And she never did. (*He pauses—then sneeringly*) Nix! Kidding myself again. I know damned well just before she died she recognized me. She saw I was drunk. Then she closed her eyes so she couldn't see, and was glad to die! (*He opens his eyes and stares into the moonlight as if he saw this deathbed scene before him.*)

JOSIE (*soothingly*). Ssshh. You only imagine that because you feel guilty about drinking.

TYRONE (*as if he hadn't heard, closes his eyes again*). After that, I kept so drunk I did draw a blank most of the time, but I went through the necessary motions and no one guessed how drunk—(*He pauses.*)

But there are things I can never forget— the undertakers, and her body in a coffin with her face made up. I couldn't hardly recognize her. She looked young and pretty like someone I remembered meeting long ago. Practically a stranger. To whom I was a stranger. Cold and indifferent. Not worried about me any more. Free at last. Free from worry. From pain. From me. I stood looking down at her, and something happened to me. I found I couldn't feel anything. I knew I ought to be heart-broken but I couldn't feel anything. I seemed dead, too. I knew I ought to cry. Even a crying jag would look better than just standing there. But I couldn't cry. I cursed to myself, "You dirty bastard, it's Mama. You loved her, and now she's dead. She's gone away from you forever. Never, never again—" But it had no effect. All I did was try to explain to myself, "She's dead. What does she care now if I cry or not, or what I do? It doesn't matter a damn to her. She's happy to be where I can't hurt her ever again. She's rid of me at last. For God's sake, can't you leave her alone even now? For God's sake, can't you let her rest in peace?" (*He pauses—then sneeringly*) But there were several people around and I knew they expected me to show something. Once a ham, always a ham! So I put on an act. I flopped on my knees and hid my face in my hands and faked some sobs and cried, "Mama! Mama! My dear mother!" But all the time I kept saying to myself, "You lousy ham! You God-damned lousy ham! Christ, in a minute you'll start singing 'Mother Ma-cree'!" (*He opens his eyes and gives a tortured, sneering laugh, staring into the moonlight.*)

JOSIE (*horrified, but still deeply pitying*). Jim! Don't! It's past. You've punished yourself. And you were drunk. You didn't mean—

TYRONE (*again closes his eyes*). I had to bring her body East to be buried beside the Old Man. I took a drawing room and hid in it with a case of booze. She was in her coffin in the baggage car. No matter how drunk I got, I couldn't forget that for a minute. I found I couldn't stay alone in the drawing room. It became haunted. I was going crazy. I had to go out and wander up and down the train looking for company. I made such a public nuisance of myself that the conductor threat-ened if I didn't quit, he'd keep me locked in the drawing room. But I'd spotted one passenger who was used to drunks and could pretend to like them, if there was enough dough in it. She had parlor house written all over her—a blonde pig who looked more like a whore than twenty-five whores, with a face like an overgrown doll's and a come-on smile as cold as a polar bear's feet. I bribed the porter to take a message to her and that night she sneaked into my drawing room. She was bound for New York, too. So every night —for fifty bucks a night—(*He opens his eyes and now he stares torturedly through the moonlight into the drawing room.*)

JOSIE (*her face full of revulsion—stammers*). Oh, how could you! (*Instinctively she draws away, taking her arms from around him.*)

TYRONE. How could I? I don't know. But I did. I suppose I had some mad idea she could make me forget—what was in the baggage car ahead.

JOSIE. Don't. (*She draws back again so he has to raise his head from her breast. He doesn't seem to notice this.*)

TYRONE. No, it couldn't have been that. Because I didn't seem to want to forget. It was like some plot I had to carry out. The blonde—she didn't matter. She was only something that belonged in the plot. It was as if I wanted revenge—because I'd been left alone—because I knew I was lost, with-out any hope left—that all I could do would be drink myself to death, because no one was left who could help me. (*His face hardens and a look of cruel vindic-tiveness comes into it—with a strange hor-rible satisfaction in his tone*) No, I didn't forget even in that pig's arms! I remem-bered the last two lines of a lousy tear-jerker song I'd heard when I was a kid kept singing over and over in my brain.

"And baby's cries can't waken her
In the baggage coach ahead."

JOSIE (*distractedly*). Jim!

TYRONE. I couldn't stop it singing. I didn't want to stop it!

JOSIE. Jim! For the love of God. I don't want to hear!

TYRONE (*after a pause—dully*). Well, that's all—except I was too drunk to go to her funeral.

JOSIE. Oh! (*She has drawn away from him as far as she can without getting up. He becomes aware of this for the first time and turns slowly to stare at her.*)

TYRONE (*dully*). Don't want to touch me now, eh? (*He shrugs his shoulders mechanically.*) Sorry. I'm a damned fool. I shouldn't have told you.

JOSIE (*her horror ebbing as her love and protective compassion returns—moves nearer him—haltingly*). Don't, Jim. Don't say—I don't want to touch you. It's—a lie. (*She puts a hand on his shoulder.*)

TYRONE (*as if she hadn't spoken—with hopeless longing*). Wish I could believe in the spiritualists' bunk. If I could tell her it was because I missed her so much and couldn't forgive her for leaving me—

JOSIE. Jim! For the love of God—!

TYRONE (*unheeding*). She'd understand and forgive me, don't you think? She always did. She was simple and kind and pure of heart. She was beautiful. You're like her deep in your heart. That's why I told you. I thought—(*Abruptly his expression becomes sneering and cynical—harshly*) My mistake. Nuts! Forget it. Time I got a move on. I don't like your damned moon, Josie. It's an ad for the past. (*He recites mockingly*)

"It is the very error of the moon:
  She comes more nearer earth than she
    was wont,
  And makes men mad."

(*He moves.*) I'll grab the last trolley for town. There'll be a speak open, and some drunk laughing. I need a laugh. (*He starts to get up.*)

JOSIE (*throws her arms around him and pulls him back—tensely*). No! you won't go! I won't let you! (*She hugs him close—gently*) I understand now, Jim, darling, and I'm proud you came to me as the one in the world you know loves you enough to understand and forgive—and I do forgive!

TYRONE (*lets his head fall back on her breast—simply*). Thanks, Josie. I knew you—

JOSIE. As *she* forgives, do you hear me! As *she* loves and understands and forgives!

TYRONE (*simply*). Yes, I know she—(*His voice breaks.*)

JOSIE (*bends over him with a brooding maternal tenderness*). That's right. Do what you came for, my darling. It isn't drunken laugher in a speakeasy you want to hear at all, but the sound of yourself crying your heart's repentance against her breast. (*His face is convulsed. He hides it*

on her breast and sobs rackingly. She hugs him more tightly and speaks softly, staring into the moonlight.*) *She* hears. I feel her in the moonlight, her soul wrapped in it like a silver mantle, and I know she understands and forgives me, too, and her blessing lies on me. (*A pause. His sobs begin to stop exhaustedly. She looks down at him again and speaks soothingly as she would to a child.*) There. There, now. (*He stops. She goes on in a gentle, bullying tone.*) You're a fine one, wanting to leave me when the night I promised I'd give you has just begun, our night that'll be different from all the others, with a dawn that won't creep over dirty windowpanes but will wake in the sky like a promise of God's peace in the soul's dark sadness. (*She smiles a little amused smile.*) Will you listen to me, Jim! I must be a poet. Who would have guessed it? Sure, love is a wonderful mad inspiration! (*A pause. She looks down. His eyes are closed. His face against her breast looks pale and haggard in the moonlight. Calm with the drained, exhausted peace of death. For a second she is frightened. Then she realizes and whispers softly*) Asleep. (*In a tender crooning tone like a lullaby*) That's right. Sleep in peace, my darling. (*Then with sudden anguished longing*) Oh, Jim, Jim, maybe my love could still save you, if you could want it enough! (*She shakes her head.*) No. That can never be. (*Her eyes leave his face to stare up at the sky. She looks weary and stricken and sad. She forces a defensive, self-derisive smile.*) God forgive me, it's a fine end to all my scheming, to sit here with the dead hugged to my breast, and the silly mug of the moon grinning down, enjoying the joke!

CURTAIN

ACT FOUR

SCENE: *Same as Act Three. It is dawn. The faint streaks of color, heralding the sunrise, appear in the eastern sky at left.*

JOSIE *sits in the same position on the steps, as if she had not moved, her arms around* TYRONE. *He is still asleep, his head on her breast. His face has the same exhausted, death-like repose.* JOSIE'S *face is set in an expression of numbed, resigned sadness. Her body sags tiredly. In spite of her strength, holding herself like this for hours, for fear of waking him, is becoming too much for her.*

The two make a strangely tragic picture in the wan dawn light—this big sorrowful woman hugging a haggard-faced, middle-aged drunkard against her breast, as if he were a sick child.

HOGAN *appears at left-rear, coming from the barn. He approaches the corner of the house stealthily on tiptoe. Wisps of hay stick to his clothes and his face is swollen and sleepy, but his little pig's eyes are sharply wide awake and sober. He peeks around the corner, and takes in the two on the steps. His eyes fix·on* JOSIE's *face in a long, probing stare.*

———

JOSIE *(speaks in a low grim tone).* Stop hiding, Father. I heard you sneak up. *(He comes guiltily around the corner. She keeps her voice low, but her tone is commanding.)* Come here, and be quiet about it. *(He obeys meekly, coming as far as the boulder silently, his eyes searching her face, his expression becoming guilty and miserable at what he sees. She goes on in the same tone, without looking at him.)* Talk low, now. I don't want him wakened— *(She adds strangely)* Not until the dawn has beauty in it.

HOGAN *(worriedly).* What? *(He decides it's better for the present to ask no questions. His eyes fall on* TYRONE's *face. In spite of himself, he is startled—in an awed, almost frightened whisper)* Be God, he looks dead!

JOSIE *(strangely).* Why wouldn't he? He is.

HOGAN. Is?

JOSIE. Don't be a fool. Can't you see him breathing? Dead asleep, I mean. Don't stand there gawking. Sit down. *(He sits meekly on the boulder. His face betrays a guilty dread of what is coming. There is a pause in which she doesn't look at him but he keeps glancing at her, growing visibly more uneasy. She speaks bitterly.)* Where's your witnesses?

HOGAN *(guiltily).* Witnesses? *(Then forcing an amused grin)* Oh, be God, if that ain't a joke on me! Sure, I got so blind drunk at the Inn I forgot all about our scheme and came home and went to sleep in the hayloft.

JOSIE *(her expression harder and more bitter).* You're a liar.

HOGAN. I'm not. I just woke up. Look at the hay sticking to me. That's proof.

JOSIE. I'm not thinking of that, and well you know it. *(With bitter voice)* So you just woke up—did you?—and then came sneaking here to see if the scheme behind your scheme had worked!

HOGAN *(guiltily).* I don't know what you mean.

JOSIE. Don't lie any more, Father. This time, you've told one too many. *(He starts to defend himself but the look on her face makes him think better of it and he remains uneasily silent. A pause.)*

HOGAN *(finally has to blurt out).* Sure, if I'd brought the witnesses, there's nothing for them to witness that—

JOSIE. No. You're right, there. There's nothing. Nothing at all. *(She smiles strangely.)* Except a great miracle they'd never believe, or you either.

HOGAN. What miracle?

JOSIE. A virgin who bears a dead child in the night, and the dawn finds her still a virgin. If that isn't a miracle, what is?

HOGAN *(uneasily).* Stop talking so queer. You give me the shivers. *(He attempts a joking tone.)* Is it you who's the virgin? Faith, that *would* be a miracle, no less! *(He forces a chuckle.)*

JOSIE. I told you to stop lying, Father.

HOGAN. What lie? *(He stops and watches her face worriedly. She is silent, as if she were not aware of him now. Her eyes are fixed on the wanton sky.)*

JOSIE *(as if to herself).* It'll be beautiful soon, and I can wake him.

HOGAN *(can't retain his anxiety any longer).* Josie, darlin'! For the love of God, can't you tell me what happened to you?

JOSIE *(her face hard and bitter again).* I've told you once. Nothing.

HOGAN. Nothing? If you could see the sadness in your face—

JOSIE. What woman doesn't sorrow for the man she loved who has died? But there's pride in my heart, too.

HOGAN *(tormentedly).* Will you stop talking as if you'd gone mad in the night! *(Raising his voice—with revengeful anger)* Listen to me! If Jim Tyrone has done anything to bring you sorrow— *(*TYRONE *stirs in his sleep and moans, pressing his face against her breast as if for protection. She looks down at him and hugs him close.)*

JOSIE *(croons softly).* There, there, my

darling. Rest in peace a while longer. (*Turns on her father angrily and whispers*) Didn't I tell you to speak low and not wake him! (*She pauses—then quietly*) He did nothing to bring me sorrow. It was my mistake. I thought there was still hope. I didn't know he'd died already— that it was a damned soul coming to me in the moonlight, to confess and be forgiven and find peace for a night—

HOGAN. Josie! Will you stop!

JOSIE (*after a pause—dully*). He'd never do anything to hurt me. You know it. (*Self-mockingly*) Sure, hasn't he told me I'm beautiful to him and he loves me—in his fashion. (*Then matter-of-factly*) All that happened was that he got drunk and he had one of his crazy notions he wanted to sleep the way he is, and I let him sleep. (*With forced roughness*) And, be God, the night's over. I'm half dead with tiredness and sleepiness. It's that you see in my face, not sorrow.

HOGAN. Don't try to fool me, Josie. I—

JOSIE (*her face hard and bitter—grimly*). Fool you, is it? It's you who made a fool of me with your lies, thinking you'd use me to get your dirty greasy paws on the money he'll have!

HOGAN. No! I swear by all the saints—

JOSIE. You'd swear on a Bible while you were stealing it! (*Grimly*) Listen to me, Father. I didn't call you here to answer questions about what's none of your business. I called you here to tell you I've seen through all the lies you told last night to get me to— (*As he starts to speak*) Shut up! I'll do the talking now. You weren't drunk. You were only putting it on as part of your scheme—

HOGAN (*quietly*). I wasn't drunk, no. I admit that, Josie. But I'd had slews of drinks and they were in my head or I'd never have the crazy dreams—

JOSIE (*with biting scorn*). Dreams, is it? The only dream you've ever had, or will have, is of yourself counting a fistful of dirty money, and divil a care of how you got it, or who you robbed or made suffer!

HOGAN (*winces—pleadingly*). Josie!

JOSIE. Shut up. (*Scathingly*) I'm sure you've made up a whole new set of lies and excuses. You're that cunning and clever, but you can save your breath. They wouldn't fool me now. I've been fooled once too often. (*He gives her a frightened

look, as if something he had dreaded has happened. She goes on, grimly accusing.*) You lied about Jim selling the farm. You knew he was kidding. You knew the estate would be out of probate in a few days, and he'd go back to Broadway, and you had to do something quick or you'd lose the last chance of getting your greedy hooks on his money.

HOGAN (*miserably*). No. It wasn't that, Josie.

JOSIE. You saw how hurt and angry I was because he'd kept me waiting here, and you used that. You knew I loved him and wanted him and you used that. You used all you knew about me— Oh, you did it clever! You ought to be proud! You worked it so it was me who did all the dirty scheming— You knew I'd find out from Jim you'd lied about the farm, but not before your lie had done its work— made me go after him, get him drunk, get drunk myself so I could be shameless— and when the truth did come out, wouldn't it make me love him all the more and be more shameless and willing? Don't tell me you didn't count on that, and you such a clever schemer! And if he once had me, knowing I was a virgin, didn't you count on his honor and remorse, and his loving me in his fashion, to make him offer to marry me? Sure, why wouldn't he, you thought. It wouldn't hold him. He'd go back to Broadway just the same and never see me again. But there'd be money in it, and when he'd finished killing himself, I'd be his legal widow and get what's left.

HOGAN (*miserably*). No! It wasn't that.

JOSIE. But what's the good of talking? It's all over. I've only one more word for you, Father, and it's this: I'm leaving you today, like my brothers left. You can live alone and work alone your cunning schemes on yourself.

HOGAN (*after a pause—slowly*). I knew you'd be bitter against me, Josie, but I took the chance you'd be so happy you wouldn't care how—

JOSIE (*as if she hadn't heard, looking at the eastern sky which is now glowing with color*). Thank God, it's beautiful. It's time. (*To* HOGAN) Go in the house and stay there till he's gone. I don't want you around to start some new scheme. (*He looks miserable, starts to speak, thinks better of it, and meekly tiptoes past her up the *steps and goes in, closing the door quietly after him. She looks down at* TYRONE. *Her face softens with a maternal tenderness—sadly*) I hate to bring you back to life, Jim, darling. If you could have died in your sleep, that's what you would have liked, isn't it? (*She gives him a gentle shake.*) Wake up, Jim. (*He moans in his sleep and presses more closely against her. She stares at his face.*) Dear God, let him remember that one thing and forget the rest. That will be enough for me. (*She gives him a more vigorous shake.*) Jim! Wake up, do you hear? It's time.

TYRONE (*half wakens without opening his eyes—mutters*). What the hell? (*Dimly conscious of a woman's body—cynically*) Again, eh? Same old stuff. Who the hell are you, sweetheart? (*Irritably*) What's the big idea, waking me up? What time is it?

JOSIE. It's dawn.

TYRONE (*still without opening his eyes*). Dawn? (*He quotes drowsily*)

"But I was desolate and sick of an old passion,
  When I awoke and found the dawn was gray."

(*Then with a sneer*) They're all gray. Go to sleep, Kid—and let me sleep. (*He falls asleep again.*)

JOSIE (*tensely*). This one isn't gray, Jim. It's different from all the others— (*She sees he is asleep—bitterly*) He'll have forgotten. He'll never notice. And I'm the whore on the train to him now, not— (*Suddenly she pushes him away from her and shakes him roughly.*) Will you wake up, for God's sake! I've had all I can bear—

TYRONE (*still half asleep*). Hey! Cut out the rough stuff, Kid. What? (*Awake now, blinking his eyes—with dazed surprise*) Josie.

JOSIE (*still bitter*). That's who, and none of your damned tarts! (*She pushes him.*) Get up now, so you won't fall asleep again. (*He does so with difficulty, still in a sleepy daze, his body stiff and cramped. She conquers her bitter resentment and puts on her old free-and-easy kidding tone with him, but all the time waiting to see how much he will remember.*) You're stiff and cramped, and no wonder. I'm worse from holding you, if that's any comfort. (*She stretches and rubs her numbed arms,*

groaning comically.) Holy Joseph, I'm a wreck entirely. I'll never be the same. (*Giving him a quick glance*) You look as if you'd drawn a blank and were wondering how you got here. I'll bet you don't remember a thing.

TYRONE (*moving his arms and legs gingerly—sleepily*). I don't know. Wait till I'm sure I'm still alive.

JOSIE. You need an eye-opener. (*She picks up the bottle and glass and pours him a drink.*) Here you are.

TYRONE (*takes the glass mechanically*). Thanks, Josie. (*He goes and sits on the boulder, holding the drink as if he had no interest in it.*)

JOSIE (*watching him*). Drink up or you'll be asleep again.

TYRONE. No, I'm awake now, Josie. Funny. Don't seem to want a drink. Oh, I've got a head all right. But no heebie-jeebies—yet.

JOSIE. That's fine. It must be a pleasant change—

TYRONE. It is. I've got a nice, dreamy peaceful hangover for once—as if I'd had a sound sleep without nightmares.

JOSIE. So you did. Divil a nightmare. I ought to know. Wasn't I holding you and keeping them away?

TYRONE. You mean you— (*Suddenly*) Wait a minute. I remember now I was sitting alone at a table in the Inn, and I suddenly had a crazy notion I'd come up here and sleep with my head on your— So that's why I woke up in your arms. (*Shamefacedly*) And you let me get away with it. You're a nut, Josie.

JOSIE. Oh, I didn't mind.

TYRONE. You must have seen how blotto I was, didn't you?

JOSIE. I did. You were as full as a tick.

TYRONE. Then why didn't you give me the bum's rush?

JOSIE. Why would I? I was glad to humor you.

TYRONE. For God's sake, how long was I cramped on you like that?

JOSIE. Oh, a few hours, only.

TYRONE. God, I'm sorry Josie, but it's your own fault for letting me—

JOSIE. Och, don't be apologizing. I was glad of the excuse to stay awake and enjoy the beauty of the moon.

TYRONE. Yes, I can remember what a beautiful night it was.

JOSIE. Can you? I'm glad of that, Jim. You seemed to enjoy it the while we were sitting here together before you fell alseep.

TYRONE. How long a while was that?

JOSIE. Not long. Less than an hour, anyway.

TYRONE. I suppose I bored the hell out of you with a lot of drunken drivel.

JOSIE. Not a lot, no. But some. You were full of blarney, saying how beautiful I was to you.

TYRONE (earnestly). That wasn't drivel, Josie. You were. You are. You always will be.

JOSIE. You're a wonder, Jim. Nothing can stop you, can it? Even me in the light of dawn, looking like something you'd put in the field to scare the crows from the corn. You'll kid at the Day of Judgment.

TYRONE (impatiently). You know damned well it isn't kidding. You're not a fool. You can tell.

JOSIE (kiddingly). All right, then, I'm beautiful and you love me—in your fashion.

TYRONE. "In my fashion," eh? Was I reciting poetry to you? That must have been hard to take.

JOSIE. It wasn't. I liked it. It was all about beautiful nights and the romance of the moon.

TYRONE. Well, there was some excuse for that, anyway. It sure was a beautiful night. I'll never forget it.

JOSIE. I'm glad, Jim.

TYRONE. What other bunk did I pull on you—or I mean, did old John Barleycorn pull?

JOSIE. Not much. You were mostly quiet and sad—in a kind of daze, as if the moon was in your wits as well as whiskey.

TYRONE. I remember I was having a grand time at the Inn, celebrating with Phil, and then suddenly, for no reason, all the fun went out of it, and I was more melancholy than ten Hamlets. (He pauses.) Hope I didn't tell you the sad story of my life and weep on your bosom, Josie.

JOSIE. You didn't. The one thing you talked a lot about was that you wanted the night with me to be different from all the other nights you'd spent with women.

TYRONE (with revulsion). God, don't make me think of those tramps now! (Then with deep, grateful feeling) It sure was different, Josie. I may not remember much, but I know how different it was from the way I feel now. None of my usual morning-after stuff—the damned sick remorse that makes you wish you'd died in your sleep so you wouldn't have to face the rotten things you're afraid you said and did the night before, when you were so drunk you didn't know what you were doing.

JOSIE. There's nothing you said or did last night for you to regret. You can take my word for it.

TYRONE (as if he hadn't heard—slowly). It's hard to describe how I feel. It's a new one on me. Sort of at peace with myself and this lousy life—as if all my sins had been forgiven— (He becomes self-conscious—cynically) Nuts with that sin bunk, but you know what I mean.

JOSIE (tensely). I do, and I'm happy you feel that way, Jim. (A pause. She goes on.) You talked about how you'd watched too many dawns come creeping grayly over dirty windowpanes, with some tart snoring beside you—

TYRONE (winces). Have a heart. Don't remind me of that now, Josie. Don't spoil this dawn! (A pause. She watches him tensely. He turns slowly to face the east, where the sky is now glowing with all the colors of an exceptionally beautiful sunrise. He stares, drawing a deep breath. He is profoundly moved but immediately becomes self-conscious and tries to sneer it off—cynically) God seems to be putting on quite a display. I like Belasco better. Rise of curtain, Act-Four stuff. (Her face has fallen into lines of bitter hurt, but he adds quickly and angrily) God damn it! Why do I have to pull that lousy stuff? (With genuine deep feeling) God, it's beautiful, Josie! I—I'll never forget it—here with you.

JOSIE (her face clearing—simply). I'm glad, Jim. I was hoping you'd feel beauty in it—by way of a token.

TYRONE (watching the sunrise—mechanically). Token of what?

JOSIE. Oh, I don't know. Token to me that—never mind. I forget what I meant. (Abruptly changing the subject) Don't think I woke you just to admire the sunrise. You're on a farm, not Broadway, and it's time for me to start work, not go to bed. (She gets to her feet and stretches.

There is a growing strain behind her free-and-easy manner.) And that's a hint, Jim. I can't stay entertaining you. So go back to the Inn, that's a good boy. I know you'll understand the reason, and not think I'm tired of your company. (*She forces a smile.*)

TYRONE (*gets up*). Of course, I understand. (*He pauses—then blurts out guiltily*) One more question. You're sure I didn't get out of order last night—and try to make you, or anything like that.

JOSIE. You didn't. You kidded back when I kidded you, the way we always do. That's all.

TYRONE. Thank God for that. I'd never forgive myself if—I wouldn't have asked you except I've pulled some pretty rotten stuff when I was drawing a blank. (*He becomes conscious of the forgotten drink he has in his hand.*) Well, I might as well drink this. The bar at the Inn won't be open for hours. (*He drinks—then looks pleasantly surprised.*) I'll be damned! That isn't Phil's rotgut. That's real, honest-to-God bonded Bourbon. Where— (*This clicks in his mind and suddenly he remembers everything and* JOSIE *sees that he does. The look of guilt and shame and anguish settles over his face. Instinctively he throws the glass away, his first reaction one of loathing for the drink which brought back memory. He feels* JOSIE *staring at him and fights desperately to control his voice and expression.*) Real Bourbon. I remember now you said a bootlegger gave it to Phil. Well, I'll run along and let you do your work. See you later, Josie. (*He turns toward the road.*)

JOSIE (*strickenly*). No! Don't, Jim! Don't go like that! You won't see me later. You'll never see me again now, and I know that's best for us both, but I can't bear to have you ashamed you wanted my love to comfort your sorrow—when I'm so proud I could give it. (*Pleadingly*) I hoped, for your sake, you wouldn't remember, but now you do, I want you to remember my love for you gave you peace for a while.

TYRONE (*stares at her, fighting with himself. He stammers defensively*). I don't know what you're talking about. I don't remember—

JOSIE (*sadly*). All right, Jim. Neither do I then. Good-by, and God bless you. (*She turns as if to go up the steps into the house.*)

TYRONE (*stammers*). Wait, Josie! (*Coming to her*) I'm a liar! I'm a louse! Forgive me, Josie. I do remember! I'm glad I remember! I'll never forget your love! (*He kisses her on the lips.*) Never! (*Kissing her again*) Never, do you hear! I'll always love you, Josie. (*He kisses her again.*) Good-by—and God bless you! (*He turns away and walks quickly down the road off left without looking back. She stands, watching him go, for a moment, then she puts her hands over her face, her head bent, and sobs.* HOGAN *comes out of her room and stands on top of the steps. He looks after* TYRONE *and his face is hard with bitter anger.*)

JOSIE (*sensing his presence, stops crying and lifts her head—dully*). I'll get your breakfast in a minute, Father.

HOGAN. To hell with my breakfast! I'm not a pig that has no other thought but eating! (*Then pleadingly*) Listen, darlin'. All you said about my lying and scheming, and what I hoped would happen, is true. But it wasn't his money, Josie. I did see it was the last chance—the only one left to bring the two of you to stop your damned pretending, and face the truth that you loved each other. I wanted you to find happiness—by hook or crook, one way or another, what did I care how? I wanted to save him, and I hoped he'd see that only your love could— It was his talk of the beauty he saw in you that made me hope— And I knew he'd never go to bed with you even if you'd let him unless he married you. And if I gave a thought to his money at all, that was the least of it, and why shouldn't I want to have you live in ease and comfort for a change, like you deserve, instead of in this shanty on a lousy farm, slaving for me? (*He pauses—miserably*) Can't you believe that's the truth, Josie, and not feel so bitter against me?

JOSIE (*her eyes still following* TYRONE—*gently*). I know it's the truth, Father. I'm not bitter now. Don't be afraid I'm going to leave you. I only said it to punish you for a while.

HOGAN (*with humble gratitude*). Thank God for that, darlin'.

JOSIE (*forces a teasing smile and a little of her old manner*). A ginger-haired, crooked old goat like you to be playing Cupid!

HOGAN (*his face lights up joyfully. He is almost himself again—ruefully*). You had me punished, that's sure. I was thinking after you'd gone I'd drown myself in Harder's ice pond. There was this consolation in it, I knew that the bastard would never look at a piece of ice again without remembering me. (*She doesn't hear this. Her thoughts are on the receding figure of* TYRONE *again.* HOGAN *looks at her sad face worriedly—gently*) Don't, darlin'. Don't be hurting yourself. (*Then as she still doesn't hear, he puts on his old, fuming irascible tone.*) Are you going to moon at the sunrise forever, and me with the sides of my stomach knocking together?

JOSIE (*gently*). Don't worry about me, Father. It's over now. I'm not hurt. I'm only sad for him.

HOGAN. For him? (*He bursts out in a fit of smoldering rage.*) May the blackest curse from the pit of hell—

JOSIE (*with an anguished cry*). Don't, Father! I love him!

HOGAN (*subsides, but his face looks sorrowful and old—dully*). I didn't mean it. I know whatever happened he meant no harm to you. It was life I was cursing— (*With a trace of his natural manner*) And, be God, that's a waste of breath, if it does deserve it. (*Then as she remains silent—miserably*) Or maybe I was cursing myself for a damned old scheming fool, like I ought to.

JOSIE (*turns to him, forcing a teasing smile*). Look out. I might say Amen to that. (*Gently*) Don't be sad, Father. I'm all right—and I'm well content here with you. (*Forcing her teasing manner again*) Sure, living with you has spoilt me for any other man, anyway. There'd never be the same fun or excitement.

HOGAN (*plays up to this—in his fuming manner*). There'll be excitement if I don't get my breakfast soon, but it won't be fun, I'm warning you!

JOSIE (*forcing her usual reaction to his threats*). Och, don't be threatening me, you bad-tempered old tick. Let's go in the house and I'll get your damned breakfast.

HOGAN. Now you're talking. (*He goes in the house through her room. She follows him as far as the door—then turns for a last look down the road.*)

JOSIE (*her face sad, tender and pitying—gently*). May you have your wish and die in your sleep soon, Jim, darling. May you rest forever in forgiveness and peace. (*She turns slowly and goes into the house.*)

CURTAIN

A HATFUL OF RAIN

Michael V. Gazzo

First presented by Jay Julien at the Lyceum Theatre, New York, on November 9, 1955, with the following cast:

JOHN POPE, SR. Frank Silvera

JOHNNY POPE Ben Gazzara

CELIA POPE Shelley Winters

MOTHER Henry Silva

APPLES Paul Richards

CHUCH Harry Guardino

POLO POPE Anthony Franciosa

MAN Steve Gravers

PUTSKI Christine White

The action takes place in a remodeled apartment on New York's Lower East Side.

ACT ONE. SCENE I: Early evening. SCENE II: Very late that night.

ACT TWO. SCENE I: Early the next morning. SCENE II: A few hours later. SCENE III: Early the same evening.

ACT THREE. Several hours later.

INTRODUCTION

MICHAEL VINCENTE GAZZO was voted the year's most promising new playwright when *A Hatful of Rain* opened on Broadway. But by then he was not altogether a neophyte in the theatre or a novice in non-theatrical life. Born in 1923, in Hillside, New Jersey, he knocked about considerably in his youth. He was an Air Force cadet in World War II until an accident ended that career. He held many odd jobs including that of a shoe-shine boy in Miami, where Walter Winchell became one of his customers and gave him some help. He later returned to the Air Force as a mechanic. Subsequently, he gave himself up to serious theatre study, enrolling as a student of acting, directing, and play-writing at the Dramatic Workshop of the famous refugee German director, Erwin Piscator, now back in Western Germany. Several years later, Mr. Gazzo joined Lee Strasberg's Actors' Studio with every intention of becoming an actor—and wound up as a playwright when the sketches he wrote for the purpose of acting out scenes became the basis of *A Hatful of Rain*.

By genesis an actor's play, *A Hatful of Rain* remained one to the end, as anyone could tell from watching Shelley Winters, Ben Gazzara, Anthony Franciosa and Frank Silvera in the cast. The last-mentioned actor's role of the dope-pusher called "Mother" is an unforgettable example of vivid playing elements. Henry Hewes reported in *The Saturday Review's* drama column that the play "grew in Actors' Studio, where actors' needs are put first . . . Whatever works for the actors has been nurtured. Whatever doesn't has been trimmed to a minimum." Brooks Atkinson noted in his Sunday *Times* article (December 4, 1955) that "if the play and performance seem like a single work, it is doubtless because author and cast have worked together intimately." And Mr. Atkinson noted further that "if the play is not primarily a sensational exposé of clandestine evil, it is because the actors are interested in human beings," which is exactly the kind of compliment that the directors, students, and graduates of the Actors' Studio like to hear.

ACT ONE

SCENE ONE

A tenement apartment on New York's Lower East Side. To our left we see a small kitchen, and to our right a combination living room-bedroom. There are two doors in the kitchen—one leading to the hallway, left, and the other, in the rear wall, leading to a bedroom. Looking through the living-room windows, we see the worn brick of the building next door and—beyond the fire-escape railing, which is just outside—distant window lights that outline a suspension bridge, marred only by the occasional suggestion of rooftops with jutting black chimneys.

It is only because of what is seen from these windows that we can place the apartment in the Lower East Side. Within the apartment itself there is everywhere the suggestion of a ceaseless effort to transform bedraggled rooms into rooms of comfort and taste. All the woodwork—formerly coated with twenty coats of paint—has been scraped, cleaned, stained and varnished. The windows have been refurbished; cases have been built beneath them, and they are spotlessly clean, as are the shades and draw curtains. Though the sink-and-tub combination is outdated in design, plywood has been used to cover up the intricacies of old-fashioned piping. Between the kitchen and bedroom, a partition of shelving has been built, and on each shelf are flowerpots, some of glass, others of copper, containing green plants. There is a sense of life.

In the kitchen, we see a cupboard, its paint removed, a table and four chairs. The chairs are old—picked up from one of the antique shops along Third Avenue. The table is solid and of heavy wood, something that might have been picked up from a farmer along a Jersey road.

In the living room, we see an armchair in a corner and a bed against the side wall. There is an unusual and startling use of color in the room; the bedspread is particularly lively, and all the objects in the room are colorful. Homemade bookcases made of wood planks and bricks line another wall.

The hallway, off the kitchen, is clearly in contrast to the apartment. Its walls are a drab brown and, off it, we see a suggestion of a stairway, leading to the roof, the railing of painted iron. Overhead there is a dim light, covered with a dusty and cracked skylight.

When the curtain rises, we hear the sound of rain. In the kitchen area, at the table, are JOHNNY *and his* FATHER. *The meal is almost at an end.*

———

FATHER (*moves away from the table, toward an umbrella which he picks up and works with difficulty, opening it and closing it*). I almost missed the plane up because of this umbrella . . . it's made of Japanese silk, the handle is ivory . . . and it was designed in Germany . . . and they make the damn things in Peru. This guy down in Palm Beach who sold me the thing . . . Anyway, I kept looking at my watch. He wouldn't tell me how much it was . . . I thought he was crazy until he told me the price. Twenty-seven dollars for an umbrella . . . Seven minutes from plane time he tells me the price . . .

JOHNNY (*calls off to* CELIA, *who is in* POLO's *room*). Honey! What's the trouble in there?

CELIA (*stands in the doorway*). I can't get Polo's windows closed. . . .

FATHER. Polo? That's Polo's room?

CELIA. Johnny . . . ? I can't close his windows and his bed is going to float out here any minute. The dampness has them jammed. . . .

FATHER. I thought you and Johnny slept in there—and Polo slept out here.

CELIA. That room isn't big enough for two people. Johnny and I tried to sleep in there but—

FATHER. What are you going to call him?

CELIA. Her. Not him. Her.

FATHER. I was counting on a grandson.

CELIA. Well, you'll have to settle for a granddaughter.

FATHER. Wow! Whew . . . That's strong coffee. Turkish?

CELIA. No, it's not Turkish. It's just plain ordinary everyday coffee.

JOHNNY. What did you put in that pot?

CELIA. I don't understand it. Last night I put nine tablespoons of coffee in the pot and it came out like weak tea.

JOHNNY. Which pot? You know you got four pots and they're all different sizes . . .

CELIA. Well, I didn't ask for all those pots.

JOHNNY. If you'd just put three of those

pots away—

CELIA. It's a curse, that's all. For as long as I could remember I could never make coffee . . .

JOHNNY. They gave her four pots . . . one of those showers when we got married.

CELIA. And you went out and bought one too—so never mind.

JOHNNY. How did I know that all your girl friends were coffee-pot happy. There were only six girls at the shower, and four of them show up with a coffee pot.

CELIA. This morning I had a headache— and I wanted to have my coffee, and I dropped an Alka Seltzer in my coffee. I thought for a minute the house was going to blow up . . .

FATHER. Sorry, honey, I didn't mean to knock your coffee.

CELIA. It's not you, Pop. I was late for work this morning . . . I had to go to the doctor's on my lunch hour—and I took a bus on the way back . . . and the bus had to wait ten minutes at an intersection while a parade passed by . . .

JOHNNY. Honey, you're behaving like a woman.

CELIA. Darling, if you'll just take a good look at me, you'll confirm the fact that I am a woman.

FATHER. What's this your wife writes me, you're not going to school any more . . .

JOHNNY. I'm going to start again soon, Pop. Working days and school nights, I—

FATHER. I don't want you to think that I'm pushing you, but I was down there feeling good about the fact that you got the government picking up the bill with that G.I. Rights thing . . . How long will it take you to finish, I mean if you started soon again . . . ?

CELIA. Another two years and he'll have his degree . . . Excuse me, Pop, I've got some ironing to do for work.

FATHER. Working in a machine shop, being a toolmaker, that must help you with engineering studies, huh?

JOHNNY. I'm a machinist, Pop. I'm not a toolmaker . . .

FATHER. You lost two years in the Army, another damn year laying in a hospital bed, now that's a big chunk of time—so look to the clock, Johnny.

JOHNNY. I was going to write and tell you myself about my not going to school

any more, but I didn't want to worry you—

FATHER. You don't have any pains, I mean, you're all cured.

JOHNNY. Yeh, I'm all cured . . .

FATHER. Sometimes things like that act up . . . you know, guys with rheumatism, their teeth start to hurt when it rains. I'm just asking you . . .

JOHNNY. I'm all right, Pop.

FATHER. I was proud of you, Johnny. I told everybody down the Club . . . how you laid in a cave for thirteen days. I showed them that picture you took at the hospital . . . I told them all—how you went down to ninety pounds. How you kept your mouth shut, no matter what they did to you.

JOHNNY. Aw, come on now, Pop— there's nothing to be proud of.

CELIA. You'd think it was something to be ashamed of.

JOHNNY. Can we just forget about it . . . ?

FATHER. Well, I couldn't have held out— and I don't think there are many men who could. And I'm proud of you, kid!

JOHNNY. All right, Pop, you're proud of me.

CELIA. He tore up all the newspaper clippings. . . .

JOHNNY. Honey, will you please forget it?

FATHER. It's really coming down . . . every time I think of having to get on that plane tomorrow my stomach starts doing flip flops. . . . We got a glass wall they just put in, the sun comes in and from behind the bar you can see the water. Exclusive, private, only for the big wheels. Corporation lawyers, senators, department-store heads and a few judges thrown in. It was a good job. Well, maybe I can get it back.

JOHNNY. You mean you quit your job?

FATHER. What do you think I was shouting about before. Your brother wrote me a hundred times. Pop, I've got twenty-five hundred stashed away. Any time you want it, it's yours. I put money down on the option, and I started the renovations. The carpenters have been working there for a week, and I got the plumbers fixing the pipes. . . .

CELIA. Can you get your job back?

FATHER. I wish you could see this new place. It's all good hard wood, the dining room's got heavy beams two feet thick, and there's a long oak bar.

CELIA. You could have wired Polo and confirmed the loan before you put any money down . . . certainly before you got men in to go to work.

FATHER. It's not the first time his brother's disappointed me, and look what he's doing now. A bouncer. He calls that place a cocktail lounge? That's no cocktail lounge. I've been in chippie joints in my time, it's more like a cat house. Excuse me, honey, I mean whore house.

JOHNNY. You could have made a two-dollar phone call.

FATHER. For what? Seven months ago when I thought I was going to buy that bar on the Bay, he sent me a check for twenty-five hundred bucks. The deal fell through, and I sent the money back to him. . . . That was seven lousy months ago! The bank never promised me a loan! My son promised me. Now he tells me the money is gone! Gone where? Where did it go?

JOHNNY. Now look, Pop, I know Polo as well as I know myself. If he had the money he'd give it to you.

FATHER. I don't want to be here when he gets back.

JOHNNY. You're not going to hold a grudge against him.

CELIA. I'm going to talk to Polo when he comes home.

JOHNNY. Pop, how about some wine?

FATHER. O.K., let's have some wine. Hey, that looks like homemade red.

CELIA. Yes, I buy it from a grocer in the neighborhood.

JOHNNY. He makes it in the cellar. The grocery store is just a front.

FATHER. Hey Johnny, remember the farm we used to have. Remember how we used to hitch those big bay horses to the trees and tear them up by the roots so's we could plant. Look at my hands . . . mixing pink ladies and daiquiris. It's embarrassing.

JOHNNY. What's embarrassing?

FATHER. I have to get a manicure twice a week.

CELIA. I can't imagine Johnny on a farm. He's got a face like the city.

FATHER. Yeh, well, he'd pick tomatoes until he'd fall on his face—walk right under the horse's belly, right, Johnny?

JOHNNY. Right, Pop.

FATHER. I was thinking about getting a farm while you were in the Army, Johnny. Every once in a while now, I feel a funny thing in the air. People look lost to me. All I see is movement. Trains, boats, planes. Look at an oak tree, it doesn't move so that you can notice it. I was thinking about a farm again. I just had the feeling that the time had come to stop . . . and really add up what counts. Maybe look back and see if we didn't pass something by.

CELIA. That's a lovely thought . . .

FATHER. Ah . . . It's all talk. When you come right down to it. Nothing is right. Nothing is wrong. Nobody's for, and nobody's against. Something happened somewhere along the line!

JOHNNY. Happened to who, Pop? I don't follow you . . .

FATHER. Happened to us, the people.

CELIA. Well, what happened to us?

FATHER. This is the age of the vacuum. The people—they don't believe any more.

CELIA. You know there's a joke now about *"they."* It's said that when you find out who *they* are, you don't need a psychiatrist any more.

FATHER. Now look, young lady—before psychiatrists struck oil, the bartenders did their job. There's no better place to feel the pulse of the nation.

CELIA. I hope the Senate and the rest of the legislators aren't making a survey of the bars.

JOHNNY. Honey, you're getting red in the face.

CELIA. I've heard this before—the age of the vacuum, everybody's waiting—and no one believes. It's been said enough in the last few years. What's the sense of having a child? Another war may come. Look out for the white light when you hear the siren . . . every time I hear this kind of talk my blood boils. . . .

FATHER. You have to be young to get excited. There's an old Italian saying—

CELIA. I'm not interested in old Italian sayings. Just what do you believe in?

FATHER. What do you suggest I believe in? I'm sorry, I'm trying to take you seriously—

CELIA. You have two sons! You have a grandchild coming—some day Polo will have a wife and there'll be more children.

FATHER. Oh Hell, there will always be children.

CELIA. No, there will not! Because people don't believe in staying married any more. If you can't be happy together, why stay together? Johnny has been back two years, and there hasn't been a married couple in this house for over two years. They're all divorced or separated, and they've excused themselves, and granted one another pardons. No, there will not always be children. Not if people go around talking about the age of the vacuum as if it were an indestructible fact.

JOHNNY. Honey! Calm down, you're going to get the neighbors in here.

CELIA. The neighbors should know that too . . . And I don't want to apologize for anything I've said.

(*The hall lights brighten slightly. A figure scurries down the fire escape. Two men appear in the hallway.*)

FATHER. She's all woman, Johnny—all woman. You know, you look just like Johnny's mother did. That light hair, and—

CELIA. I thought she had dark hair, in the pictures Johnny showed me, she—

FATHER. Sure, she had dark hair, but you look just like her.

(*Another figure has scurried down the fire escape. The three men whisper in the hallway; then the figure scurries up the fire escape again. The tall silhouetted man,* MOTHER, *raps him playfully with the umbrella as he goes up. The smaller figure,* APPLES, *knocks gently at the door.*)

JOHNNY (*opens the door*). Hi!

CELIA. Well, tell them to come in, Johnny. Don't have them standing out in the hall.

JOHNNY. Come on in . . .

(MOTHER *and* APPLES *appear and take a few steps into the doorway.* MOTHER *is tall, sleekly dressed and wears a pair of dark glasses.* APPLES, *at his side, has on a dirty raincoat. Both are wet.*)

MOTHER (*looking at shoes*). Our feet are wet, Johnny. We just want to see you for a minute.

JOHNNY. This is my wife—and this is my father.

FATHER. How do you do?

CELIA. I'm sorry I didn't get your names?

FATHER. Take off your glasses and stay a while.

APPLES. I got your floor all dirty. Maybe I'd better wait out in the hall.

MOTHER. Yeh, wait out in the hall. Could you step out for a few minutes, Johnny. Nice meeting you—

(*They both go out and stand out in the hallway, closing the door after them.* JOHNNY *walks to closet, gets out jacket.*)

CELIA. Who are they?

JOHNNY (*smiling*). They're a couple of guys I play poker with. They probably want to borrow a few bucks. . . .

CELIA. I don't care about the floor, tell them to come in.

JOHNNY. Why don't you get the album out and show the old man the pictures you were talking about? I'll be right back. . . .

CELIA. Put your coat on. It's damp.

(JOHNNY *goes out. Lights dim in apartment area and come up in the hallway.*)

JOHNNY. Look, Mother, everything went wrong. I called the clubhouse, I called Ginnino's, I've been trying to get you all day long.

APPLES. Every junkey in the city has been trying to call us. Right, Mother?

MOTHER. That's right. They picked up Alby this afternoon.

APPLES. We been walking in the shadows all day long. We can't stay in one place more than ten minutes.

MOTHER. The lid is all over the city.

APPLES. This is no three-day affair. They're hitting this city like a hurricane. In a week the city's going to be dry.

JOHNNY. I'm thin, Mother.

MOTHER. I'm no doctor, I'm a businessman.

APPLES. You got it for free in the hospital, Johnny, but Mother's no charity ward.

MOTHER. You got it?

JOHNNY. No.

MOTHER. You ain't even got a hunk of it?

JOHNNY. Where can I get it? All of a sudden you start to close in on me. That kind of money isn't easy to get.

(*The third figure,* CHUCH, *comes slowly down the ladder and hangs over* JOHNNY's *head; in the darkness he could pass for an ape.*)

MOTHER. What have you been trying to get us for then?

JOHNNY. My old man came in tonight. He's going to be here for a few days. I wanted you to give me enough to hold me over, until he gets on his plane. As soon as he goes, I'll try to get the money I owe you.

APPLES. How you going to pay? Two

dollars a week for the next five years?

MOTHER. You'll get it by tomorrow morning! Every penny of it . . .

JOHNNY. Oh, Mother, you must be crazy. Where am I going to get seven hundred dollars by tomorrow morning?

APPLES. Your wife must have something for a rainy day. . . . Huh?

JOHNNY. What do you expect me to do! Go to my wife and say—

MOTHER. Chuchie! (*Instantly* CHUCH's *arm comes down and wraps itself around* JOHNNY, *holding him pressed against the fire-escape ladder.*) Now you listen to me, you junkey bastard! I don't care how many jokes you told me, or how long I know you. I'd never press you, if they didn't press me. Your eyes can rattle out of your head. Just good faith . . . five hundred, and I'll carry you for the rest. Let him go, Chuchie. . . .

(CHUCH *lets his arm loose.*)

JOHNNY. What am I going to do for the next few days . . . ?

MOTHER. Riddle arm, that's your problem. (MOTHER *takes a small packet out of his pocket. He holds it up.*) Here. Feel it? Give me the weight minus the paper. And what do you have? Not even an ounce . . . one lousy spoon of morphine, and I put my life on the block every time I put it in my pocket. How many times did I bring it to you? They'll give me ten years for carrying that.

JOHNNY. Thanks, Mother. I'll pay you tomorrow.

MOTHER. Look! You need forty dollars a day now. You can't make it working. I don't care how you make it—push the stuff, steal . . .

APPLES (*handing* JOHNNY *a gun*). Here.

JOHNNY. You guys must be crazy. I don't want that.

APPLES. Keep it. It's not loaded.

JOHNNY. No!

MOTHER. Leave it lay on the floor, Apples. Gimme back that packet, Johnny!

JOHNNY. Look, I walked around all day long trying to—(*Suddenly* MOTHER *kicks* JOHNNY *in the groin*) Sshhhh . . . for. Quiet. My old man's here. . . .

CHUCH. His old man's here, Mother . . . his old man's here. Give him a break, willya. Can't you see he's going to curdle?

MOTHER (*taking packet*). His old man's here, and mine's dead. You go over the roof—and we'll meet you by Ginnino's.

CHUCH. Okay.

MOTHER. Five hundred . . . tomorrow morning, Johnny. (MOTHER *and* APPLES *walk out.*)

CHUCH. Johnny, you all right? Look, Johnny, he's not kidding. It's a shame what they did to Willy DeCarlo this afternoon. He didn't even owe as much as you do. He's no good: Mother . . . he'll do everything but kill you. Be a good guy, pick it up—It's not even loaded.

JOHNNY. Chuchie . . . You got anything at all.

CHUCH. No.

JOHNNY. Even half . . .

CHUCH. I ain't got enough for myself.

JOHNNY. When you tried to kick it, and you couldn't stand it—you called me, and I gave you my last drop.

CHUCH. All right. You come by my house later. And, Johnny, don't say nothing about my dog. I mean if the ole lady says anything, just change the subject. My dog fell out the window last night . . .

JOHNNY. All right, Chuch.

CHUCH. He died, Johnny. Right in my arms.

(CHUCH *scurries up the ladder.* JOHNNY *bends down, picks up the gun and puts it in his jacket pocket. The lights dim in the hallway and come up in the apartment area.*)

FATHER. It wasn't a big farm but you could eat and live off it. A cosmetic factory squeezed me on the mortgage. I built that barn and I was the last one to go. Johnny's mother died a short time after and the kid went to live with his Aunt Grace—No, Polo went to live with his Aunt Grace; Johnny went to live with his Uncle Louis. (JOHNNY *has entered.*) What did those characters want?

CELIA. I don't like those men . . .

JOHNNY. They're only a couple of guys I play poker with.

FATHER. Who ever heard of seeing people out in the hall? There's a room right here . . .

JOHNNY. Now, what in the world's the trouble—You've never seen them before.

CELIA. I've seen them with that Willy DeCarlo standing on a corner. And I never liked him coming up here either . . . and you never know where he's looking. He just stares in space.

JOHNNY. You don't see him coming around here any more.

CELIA. How much money did you lose?

JOHNNY. Couple of bucks.

CELIA. Should I try to make some more coffee . . . ?

FATHER. No, not for me, thanks. I'd better get back to the hotel. Oh—I brought a package in. What happened to it?

CELIA. I think I put it with your coat.

FATHER. When your brother comes in, don't say anything to him, Johnny. It's all water under the bridge. I bought a half a dozen Oxford shirts down there . . . they're all brand-new . . . I figured you and your brother could wear them. Put four of them in your drawer and give him two.

JOHNNY. Here, honey, put three in Polo's drawer . . .

FATHER. Keep four of them for yourself.

CELIA. You come early for dinner tomorrow night . . . and you come over for breakfast too. . . .

FATHER. I'll get a couple of box seats for the ball game, Johnny.

JOHNNY. He's got a back like a gorilla . . . he dumped Benny Leonard once . . . Isn't that right, Pop?

FATHER. Yeh, and I swam the English Channel both ways.

CELIA. Watch your step, Pop. (*Goes out and starts down the stairs with* FATHER.)

FATHER. See you in the morning, kid.

JOHNNY. Good night, Pop.

FATHER. Heh, Johnny . . . and if I drop my hat crossing the street . . .

JOHNNY. Oh . . . don't bend down to pick it up.

FATHER (*like an old vaudevillian*). Why not?

JOHNNY. You'll get an assful of taxicab bumpers . . .

(*The* FATHER *goes.*)

FATHER (*off*). That's an old standing gag we used to have.

(*We hear their voices trail off.* JOHNNY *moves to his jacket, takes out the gun, looks about the room and goes to a drawer to hide the gun. He walks to the kitchen, starts to roll up his sleeves without thinking—catches himself and rolls them down. As he begins to remove objects from the table, he notices the shirts his* FATHER *left and throws them into* POLO's *room. For a split second, he stops moving; he throws his head back, blinks his eyes and shakes his head as if to ward off sleep. He goes to the sink and throws water on his face;* then he again begins to clear the table, as CELIA *enters.*)

CELIA. There's no hot water, is there? Aren't we speaking to one another? The clock has stopped again? I guess we're not speaking to one another. Thanks for clearing the table. The cream belongs in the icebox.

JOHNNY. The refrigerator . . .

CELIA. Johnny, I'm sorry about this morning. It's silly, I don't even know what it was that I said now.

JOHNNY. You said I was useless . . . Something like that.

CELIA. Why should you be afraid to tell me that you lost a job? I felt like a fool when I called . . . your boss must have thought I was a fool, too . . . out of work three days and I have to find out by accident. . .

JOHNNY. I ruined a day's work. A whole day's work just botched . . . I don't know how I did it.

CELIA. Ruining a day's work—losing a job is no reason to go into hiding!

JOHNNY. Honey, I didn't lose that job— I was thrown out. I put fifteen shafts into the lathe that day and I undercut every one by twenty lousy thousandths of an inch. It's the fourth job I've lost in six months.

CELIA. All right—but this isn't 1929— so you lost four jobs.

JOHNNY. Where do these go?

CELIA. The top shelf.

JOHNNY. Don't start shouting now . . .

CELIA. I haven't even raised my voice . . .

JOHNNY. I know when you're shouting even when you don't raise your voice.

CELIA. Well, they go on the top shelf. The dishes go on the top shelf. The cream belongs in the ice—refrigerator. Your shoes are to be found in the closet . . . your shirts and shorts are in the bottom drawer. And we live at 967 Rivington Street! Let's not do the dishes. Can't we sit down in the front room. Let's just for once, sit down and talk. Come on, put that down.

JOHNNY. All right. Where do you want to sit? Where do I sit?

CELIA. Can we try to talk . . .

JOHNNY. I thought everything was decided. Do you leave, or do I leave?

CELIA. I thought we had more to talk about than that.

JOHNNY. Well, go ahead, I'm listening.

CELIA. You'll have to do more than listen.

JOHNNY. I can't talk. I just can't seem to talk to people any more.

CELIA. I'm not people. I'm your wife. I married you to live with you. I married you to have your child in me.

JOHNNY. Look, do we have to sit down like we're holding a class. Well—?

CELIA. Well, what about her? Is she rich? Is she pretty?

JOHNNY. I've told you I haven't even shaken hands with another woman since we've been married. And that's four years.

CELIA. One year, Johnny—that's all the marriage we ever had. The first year. I never said this before, I think I'm ashamed of it . . . but there were many times while you were gone, that I just wanted to be near a man. Sometimes I thought I'd go crazy. I just wanted to go out and watch people dance, I never went anywhere, I waited for you . . .

JOHNNY. I didn't go anywhere either. They told me where to go.

CELIA. I can understand how you might . . . Maybe I haven't given you what you want . . . or need. All right—who is she? Why do you have to lie to me?

JOHNNY. I'm not lying.

CELIA. You must think I've been stupid all these months . . . I thought that if I let you go and not say anything . . . I kept saying to myself, you love me and only me . . .

JOHNNY. I love you, and only you.

CELIA. God, I would like to know where you are! I waited for you and you never came home . . . I was here when you left, while you were gone, and I'm here now. Johnny, I spend more time with your brother than I do with you. Polo and I are together every night of the week. He never mentions you and neither do I. We just pretend that you don't exist . . . being lonely at night is nothing new, but last night I was lonely in a different way. I almost threw myself in Polo's arms.

JOHNNY. What are you talking about?

CELIA. We can't go on living like this any more. Not the three of us in one house. . . . Johnny, we used to talk all night long and wake up bleary-eyed. But it didn't matter because we were together. Don't you remember?

JOHNNY. All week-end long too . . . that week-end we spent at the Point. We didn't sleep from Friday to Sunday. . . .

CELIA. And that poor house detective—

he thought we weren't married.

JOHNNY. I told you to get out of the sun and you got sunburned.

CELIA. And I told you we shouldn't go out on the rocks . . . You hobbled around for a week with a stubbed toe.

JOHNNY. And you walked around for a week with that white stuff on your nose— you looked like a clown.

CELIA. The old man who climbed out to where we were, and caught us kissing.

JOHNNY. Caught us kissing . . . ? He must have been watching us for five minutes.

CELIA. Well, that's all we were doing.

JOHNNY. You're not remembering that day. . . .

CELIA. I remember that day most of all. . . . It was your week-end, before you went away. All I wanted to do was hold you and never let you go.

JOHNNY. You cried at the train station.

CELIA. I know. But I didn't know where you were going and how long you'd be gone. You cried too. . . .

JOHNNY. No, I didn't.

CELIA. I saw you through the window of the train, just as it was pulling out. You were smiling, but you were crying.

JOHNNY. Well—for crissake—you looked like a kid who lost her rag doll . . .

CELIA. And—we weren't just kissing. The old man saw us—

JOHNNY. Playing. The old man saw us playing.

CELIA. Playing . . . well, that's a new word for—Johnny, please love me.

JOHNNY. Love you? I love you more than I can say. Sometimes at night, when you sleep I walk the streets like I'm looking for something, and yet I know all the while what I want is sleeping. It's like I walk the streets looking for you . . . and you're right here.

CELIA. What's the matter?

JOHNNY. Nothing . . .

CELIA. I didn't mean to offend you by touching you . . .

JOHNNY. I'm sorry . . .

CELIA. Were you with her today . . . ?

JOHNNY. Never mind where I was today.

CELIA. Oh, yes, I'm going to mind . . . You walk the streets at night, you go out any time you want and come home any time you want. A day isn't just a day. It's no longer your day or my day—a day belongs to us both. All right, you didn't work today, you'll get another job, but what was today? What was your day? Did you take her to a movie or—

JOHNNY. This morning you said that the marriage was a bust, that we were on the rocks . . . After you left . . . Did you ever feel like you were going crazy? Ever since I knew the old man was coming up . . . I just can't stop remembering things . . . like all night long I've been hearing that whistle . . . The old man used to whistle like that when he used to call us . . . I was supposed to come right home from school, but I played marbles. Maybe every half-hour he'd whistle . . . I'd be on my knees in the schoolyard, with my immie glove on—you take a woman's gloves and you cut off the fingers . . . so your fingers are free and your knuckles don't bleed in the wintertime . . . and I just kept on playing and the whistle got madder and madder. It starts to get dark and I'd get worried but I wouldn't go home until I won all the marbles . . . and he'd be up on that porch whistling away. I'd cross myself at the door . . . there was a grandmother I had who taught me to cross myself to protect myself from lightning . . . I'd open the door and go in . . . hold up the chamois bag of marbles and I'd say, hey, Pop, I won! Wham! Pow! . . . I'd wind up in the corner saying, Pop, I didn't hear you. I didn't hear you . . .

CELIA. What did you do today? You didn't play marbles today, did you? You weren't home all day because I called here five times if I called once . . .

JOHNNY. I'm trying to tell you what I did today . . .

CELIA. You're trying to avoid telling me what you did today.

JOHNNY. I took a train see . . . then I took a bus . . . I went to look at the house I was born in. It's only an hour away . . . but in fifteen years, I've never gone anywhere near that house . . . or that town! I had to go back . . . I can't explain the feeling, but I was ten years old when I left there . . . The way I looked around, they must have thought I was crazy . . . because I kept staring at the old house— I was going to knock at the door and ask the people if I could just look around . . . and then I went to that Saybrook school where I used to hear the old man whistle . . . and those orange fire escapes . . .

and ivy still climbing up the walls. Then I took the bus and the train, and I went to meet the old man's plane . . . and we came here.

CELIA. You came here. Not home . . . but here.

JOHNNY. I mean home.

CELIA. You said here . . .

JOHNNY. All right, here, not home. You know, I've lived in a lot of places since I left that town. There was always a table, some cups and some windows . . . and somebody was the boss, somebody to tell you what to do and what not to do, always somebody to slap you down, pep you up, or tell you to use will power . . . there was always a bed. What do I know about a home?

CELIA. Johnny? Johnny! Do you want to run away from here . . . ?

JOHNNY. I want to live here.

CELIA. With me . . .

JOHNNY. Honey, there is no other woman. Look, baby—you don't know how much I need you, how much I love you, sometimes I want to bury myself in you . . .

CELIA. Well, do. . . .

JOHNNY. Honey—Honey, I've got to go out tonight . . . but, I'm . . . I love you . . .

CELIA. The rain's stopped. I think I'd better open the windows . . . everything's so damp in here.

(We hear rollicking, happy laughter in the hallway, and POLO's voice.)

POLO (off). Hey, boy, hey, Johnny, the walls are crooked.

JOHNNY. Hold on to those walls.

CELIA. Help him before he falls down the stairs.

(JOHNNY goes out. POLO appears, hanging on JOHNNY's arm and shoulder. He is quite drunk.)

POLO. Hey, come on . . . we're all going dancing. Hey, Celia, come on, we're all going dancing. The floors are crooked, Johnny.

CELIA. You ought to be ashamed of yourself.

POLO. I'm so drunk I couldn't walk a chalk line.

JOHNNY. Hold on. Let's see if we can get over to that chair.

POLO. I don't know what that would prove . . . if I could walk a chalk line. Leave me alone, Johnny, I'm all right.

Come on, lemme alone . . .

JOHNNY. Come on, let's get those clothes off.

POLO. Hey, Johnny, who you going to vote for Miss Rheingold of 1955?

JOHNNY. I haven't made my mind up yet.

POLO. I voted twenty-three times for Miss Woods . . . You think she cares, Johnny? She doesn't care.

CELIA. Here . . . drink this.

POLO. Oh, no, honey—I don't want any of that coffee. I'm not *that* drunk. Hey, hey . . . handle those shoes with care. They're Florsheim shoes . . . Hey, hey . . . le's get some good music on . . . hey, Johnny . . . take it easy with that shirt. That's an Arrow shirt. Hey, Celia, le's get some good music on.

CELIA. You get your clothes off and get to bed.

POLO. Aw come on, don't be a party pooper! Hey, Celia, you know there's a lady lives up there by the second-floor fire escape. . . . Every day, she hangs out her clothes—right, Popo . . . Dopo, Mopo. She dreamt she washed her windows in her Maidenform bra. . . . (*Growl*) Rub-a-dub, dub, three men in her tub . . . blow you March sonofabitchin winds blow. . . .

CELIA. I think we should undress you and put you to bed.

POLO. Oh, no, no . . . You're not undressing me. I'm ashamed. I got a big appendix scar. We all got scars. Johnny's got scars all the way down his back, huh? Johnny was fourteen days in a cave . . . all the way down his back. Celia, meet my brother . . . my guests are his guests . . . but his guests aren't my guests. Celia, Johnny's got a heart like a snake.

JOHNNY. All right, you said enough.

POLO. If I ever catch those sonsabitches around here again, Johnny, I'll tear their heads off.

JOHNNY. Shut up. Why don't you shut up?

POLO. I shut up. I'm shut up. I'm like you, Johnny . . . all you ever gave was your rank, your name and your serial number . . . I don't tell the old man.

JOHNNY. Let's forget the old man and get to bed.

POLO. That's right, Johnny. Let's forget the old man . . . let's forget everybody. We don't need anybody. I got . . . Flor-

sheim shoes . . . Paris belt . . . hey, where's my Paris belt . . . ? Thanks, Celia . . . You're an angel in disguise.

CELIA. Good night, Polo.

POLO. Don't worry about me. I got everything I need . . . except a Bond suit. I dreamt I fell asleep in my Bond suit.

(JOHNNY *leads him off; then comes back.*)

JOHNNY. Just a little high, that's all—like Christmas, once a year.

CELIA. I'd better put this on him. He'll freeze to death. (*The moment she goes into the room,* JOHNNY *goes to the drawer, takes out the gun and puts it in his pocket.* CELIA *stops in the doorway.*) Where are you going?

JOHNNY. Out, I'm going out, I'll take a walk for myself. Oh, no, leave your coat where it is. I don't want you coming with me . . .

CELIA. Why not . . . ?

JOHNNY. 'Cause, I just want to think . . .

CELIA. I won't even talk, I'll just hold on to your arm.

JOHNNY. You *can't* come with me . . . I'll be back.

CELIA. When? Tell me when so I can wait. Tonight, and—tomorrow, at dawn . . . Noon . . . When?

JOHNNY. Don't be mad, willya?

CELIA. Oh, no, no, no. I won't be mad. Do you know that I fell so in love with you all over again tonight? I wanted you. Do you understand what it means to want someone!

JOHNNY. Look, all the things you said tonight about trying—

CELIA. Trying? I've tried . . . if they gave out medals for trying I'd sink right through this floor. And every week, every day you keep slipping away—Why don't you look around you? You worked on the woodwork like a beaver, you built everything . . . but—nothing here belongs to you. This is yours . . . I'm yours . . . Go on tell her she's welcome to you . . .

JOHNNY. It's not another woman. Will you get that out of your mind . . . get it out, I love you . . . and believe me it's not another woman!

CELIA. Then what is it . . . ? This is the last time you'll ever do this to me.

JOHNNY. I'm sorry.

CELIA. Don't stand with one hand on the doorknob like that. You look like Mickey

Rooney leaving Boy's Town forever . . .

(JOHNNY *goes out, closing the door sharply behind him. He walks down the hall; at the end of it he stops.* CELIA *has walked away from the door. For a moment, they start to walk toward the door and each other—but they both stop.* JOHNNY *goes down the stairs.*)

THE LIGHTS DIM OUT

SCENE TWO

It is about two o'clock in the morning. The lights are dim. In the darkness we see the city beyond—glowing. There is the sound of a dog barking in the distance. The door to POLO'S *room opens, and, in the lighted doorway, we see* POLO *standing in shorts. He moves to the sink shakily and begins throwing water down his throat. . . . The lights are flicked on.*

CELIA. Don't do that, Polo! You'll give yourself a stomach cramp.

POLO. I got no choice . . . stomach cramp or I'll die of thirst . . . Where's my pants . . . who robbed my pants? Hey Johnny, where did you put my pants?

CELIA. Johnny went out.

POLO. You're mad at me too, huh?

CELIA. You ought to be ashamed of yourself. Your father was hurt . . . you almost took the doors off the hinges slamming it.

POLO. He was hurt, huh? His boy Johnny was here so he shouldn't feel so bad. Nobody said I was a bum, huh? All right, I never graduated high school . . . What's that make me, a bum?

CELIA. You're jealous . . .

POLO. Why should I be jealous? It's always been the same. It's not only him . . . it's all my damn relatives. As long as I can remember, always laughing at me . . .

CELIA. You don't like your father very much, do you? Why didn't you lend your father the money? He said you promised . . . he said that—

POLO. I know what he said—what I said . . . The money's gone. It flew south with the birds. I bet it on one of Ali Khan's horses—gone is gone, any kid knows that. Gone doesn't come back.

CELIA. I only asked a simple question, Polo.

POLO. I'm glad you didn't ask a difficult one. I don't like my father, huh? He comes over to that nightly circus I work in, he tells me it's a joint. People don't come in there to drink, that's what he says—that's bright on his part. There's thirteen whores leaning on the bar and he tells me people don't come in there to drink.

CELIA. What's the matter with you, Polo? I've never seen you like this before.

POLO. I'm drunk, that's all.

CELIA. I can see that you're drunk.

POLO. Well, can't a guy drink just because he likes to drink? Do you have to have a reason to drink?

CELIA. You don't like Johnny any more, do you? Why does he have a heart like a snake?

POLO. You're starting to sound like the 47th Precinct. Why? What? Who?

CELIA. Sometimes I get the feeling that you hate your brother . . .

POLO. I'll tell you one thing, I used to hate him . . . When I was a kid . . . Johnny kept getting adopted, nobody ever adopted me. *And I wanted to get adopted.* They'd line us up, and he'd get picked— then he'd run away and come back to the home the old man put us in . . . and I used to think to myself . . . just let me get adopted once and I'll stay. I used to hate him every time he left—and every time he came back. He'd say the same goddamn thing . . . We gotta stick together, Polo . . . we're the only family we got.

CELIA. Johnny never told me that . . .

POLO. Johnny never told you a lot of things. What I mean is . . . it's not a nice thing to say about the old man, is it?

CELIA. Polo, I want you to tell me what the matter is!

POLO. Why don't you ask your husband Johnny what's the matter with him and leave me alone?

CELIA. Everybody wants to be left alone. We're getting to be a house full of Garbos.

POLO. Just leave me alone . . .

CELIA. Just like Johnny. If I closed my eyes, I'd think you were Johnny.

POLO. You ask the old man who I am, he'll tell you. I'm Polo, the no-good sonofabitch. He'll never forget anything. I threw a lemon at a passing car once . . . and hit the driver in the head. I set fire to a barn once . . . and I never graduated high school. No, I'm not Johnny, he's my brother and he's a sonofabitch. That son-ofabitch is going to kill me.

(CELIA *throws a glass of water in* POLO's *face.*)

CELIA. I'm sorry I did that.

POLO. It's a sign of the times . . . a sign of the times. All the king's men, and all the king's horses . . . Oh, what's the difference. (*He goes into his room.*)

CELIA. Polo? Polo? Will you come out and talk to me.

POLO. No!

CELIA. Polo, please, I'm lonely.

(POLO *comes out.*)

CELIA. There's some muffins from to-night's supper. Would you like one?

POLO. No.

CELIA. Well, I'm going to have one.

POLO. I'll have one too. How's the job . . . ?

CELIA. Johnny got fired.

POLO. I know Johnny got fired. I was asking about your job.

CELIA. Well, why didn't you come and tell me that, Polo?

POLO. Honey, I'm not a personnel man-ager, I'm just a boarder.

CELIA. You're a bouncer in a cat house . . .

POLO. Who said that?

CELIA. Your father . . .

POLO. There must have been a full moon last night . . . boy, they showed up last night, mean, ugly and out of their minds . . . That slap-happy bouncer I work with, if he'd just learn to try to talk these bums out of the place—he's always grabbing somebody by the seat of their pants, and we're off. You know that sonofabitchin bouncer is six foot three and, as God is my witness, honey, every time hell breaks loose I'm in there getting the hell kicked out of me and that big bastard is up against the wall cheering me on! Atta boy, Polo! Atta boy! You got him going. Who have I got going? Who? I'll be punchy before Christmas.

CELIA. You're too light to be a bouncer, Polo. Why don't you quit?

POLO. Quit? Where can I make a hun-dred and twenty-five dollars a week? Where? Well, you can't beat it. You come into the world poor and you go out owing money. . . .

CELIA. You can say that again. . . .

POLO. You come into the world poor, and . . .

CELIA. All right, smarty, forget it. . . . . The Union Metal Company of America . . . that's where you should work, Polo. At least there's a little excitement at your job . . . Do you know that when I started working in the carpeted air-conditioned desert I could take dictation at the rate of 120 words a minute? I could type ninety words . . . Today I was sitting at my desk, pretending to be busy. I have papers in all the drawers. I keep shuffling them from drawer to drawer. I break pencils and sharpen them. Mr. Wagner called me in his office today and I bustled in with my steno pad and . . . you know what he called me in for? He wanted to know. Was I happy? Was Union Metals treating me right? I've been there five years come Ash Wednesday . . . and every **six** months they call you in and ask you the same thing. . . . Are you happy?

POLO. Why don't you quit?

CELIA. Nobody ever quits Union Metals . . . and no one ever gets fired. A bonus on Christmas, a turkey on Thanksgiving, long holiday week-ends. They've insured Johnny and I against sickness, and the plague, everything for the employees . . . boat rides, picnics, sick leave, a triple-savings interest, the vacations keep getting longer, we have a doctor, a nurse, and a cafeteria, four coffee breaks a day, if it gets too hot they send you home, and if it rains it's perfectly all right if you're late . . . and it's the dullest job in the whole world.

POLO. Honey . . . you know what? You've got a real problem there.

CELIA. I don't know whether to laugh or cry. . . .

POLO. Why?

CELIA. I got another raise today. . . .

POLO. Boy, I wish I didn't know right from wrong . . .

CELIA. What?

POLO. Nothing. . . .

CELIA. Polo, I've been wanting to talk to you every night this week.

POLO. We've been here every night this week . . . That's all we've done is talked.

CELIA. You're not listening to me, Polo. I've always liked you and Johnny thinks the world of you, but . . . but . . . I'm afraid you'll have to find a different place to live. . . . Maybe you could take a room somewhere in the neighborhod and still come over to dinner.

POLO. I could, huh? And what about

breakfast . . . ?

CELIA. You could come over for breakfast too . . . And I could do your shirts and everything but you'll have to find a different place to live.

POLO. I can do my own shirts . . . Why do I have to move?

CELIA. I know how you feel about me and it's embarrassing.

POLO. Love shouldn't be embarrassing.

CELIA. It's not really embarrassing, but I don't think the three of us can live together any more. I want you out of this house tomorrow. Tomorrow night—after dinner, your father gets his plane. I want you to leave.

POLO. Why?

CELIA. Because I don't want to take any chances.

POLO. What chances?

CELIA. Polo, let's not be children. You do know the difference between right and wrong and so do I. Tomorrow . . . I don't want you to go, but you have to. . . .

POLO. Tomorrow, for crissakes, even Simon Legree gave Little Eva two weeks' notice.

CELIA. I'm going to bed.

POLO. Yeh, go to bed. You're tired. Lay your head down on the pillow and close your eyes. If you want me to go, I'll go, but tonight I'll be in the room next to yours . . . I'll say I love you, but you won't be able to hear me because you'll be asleep. Maybe I'll sing you a lullaby.

CELIA. Polo, why are you doing this? Why now? We've been together so many nights and you've never been like this . . . . Why?

POLO. I'm drunk, that's the prize excuse for anything. I'm drunk and I don't know what I'm saying or doing. I could never say anything if I was sober . . . Celia?

CELIA. What?

POLO. Look, you know how I feel about you. How do you feel about me?

CELIA. I don't know.

POLO. Let's feel and find out.

CELIA. Please . . . don't.

POLO. Why didn't you slap me! I'll bet I could kiss you again and you wouldn't raise your hand.

CELIA. Why don't you? Go ahead, don't stop . . . pick me up in your arms and carry me to your brother's bed; I'm going to have a baby, Polo, so I might be a little heavy.

POLO. I'm sorry, but I love you. I didn't ask to. I didn't want to, but I do.

CELIA. Johnny . . . please go to bed.

POLO. I'm not Johnny, I'm Polo. . . .

CURTAIN

ACT TWO

SCENE ONE

It is about eight o'clock the following morning. CELIA *is in the kitchen and* POLO *in his bedroom.*

———

CELIA. Polo, your coffee's poured. Polo? Are you up?

POLO. I'm up.

CELIA. On your feet? I've called you three times.

POLO. All right. (*A moment later* POLO *appears in the doorway. He is wearing pajamas that are three sizes too big for him.*) Good morning.

CELIA. Good morning . . . Those pajamas? They're big enough for two people.

(*Rolling up his sleeve.*)

POLO. Christmas present. My relatives.

CELIA. They're absolutely precious. . . . I'm sorry, Polo, but they're hysterical.

POLO. Honey, what do you put in this coffee?

CELIA. Coffee and water and don't kid me about my coffee.

POLO. Well, for crissakes, do you know it has to boil?

CELIA. Give it back. I'll let it boil.

CELIA. See that Johnny gets these things for supper. I think you *should* come to supper and apologize to your father.

POLO. Since when do you have to apologize because you don't have money. If it's all the same to you I'll stop in Nedicks. They're running a special this week, two skinless franks and all the orange juice you can drink.

CELIA. You'll come to supper tonight.

POLO. Who said so?

CELIA. I said so.

POLO. I'll come to supper tonight. Boy, you're really going this morning. Did you have a long talk with God last night? You're like a new washing machine—pa ta-poom, pa ta-poom.

CELIA. You know what? You're blushing. Is your head killing you?

POLO. It isn't bleeding, is it?

CELIA. You're red as a beet.

POLO. I said an awful lot last night. I'm sorry. . . . I'm not sorry, I just think I should say I'm sorry. Just roll the sleeve up. Don't sit in my lap.

CELIA. I wasn't going to sit in your lap, Polo. What's so funny?

POLO. Nothing. I'm just so tired I'm silly. Did you ever get that tired? I'm so tired that nothing matters. I think if you dropped dead right now I'd laugh.

CELIA. That's sweet.

POLO. Where is Johnny?

CELIA. I don't know.

POLO. Well, where is he? Isn't that any of your business? I'll tell you the truth, sometimes . . . you just get me sick. He's your husband, isn't he? He hasn't been home all night . . . that happens two, three times a week. Honest it's been like living in a nut house.

CELIA. Polo! Johnny never asked me whether it would be all right if you came here and lived with us. He said you needed a home and brought you here.

POLO. I'm getting out. When I get good and ready and not before. I paid my rent this week.

CELIA. All right.

POLO. You see, you're like a dishrag. I thought I had to get out tonight—you didn't want to take any chances. Why don't you stand up on your feet!

CELIA. I've been standing on my feet all night long, Polo.

POLO. I must be going out of my mind. I could of sworn that I heard you come to my door . . . like a mirage, you want something and you see it . . . even when it's not there.

CELIA. Would you ask Johnny to take the laundry out when he comes in?

POLO. I'll take it out.

CELIA. Let Johnny do it.

POLO. All right! I'll let Johnny do it!

CELIA. There's no need to shout at me, Polo!

POLO. No, huh . . . You don't think so. For six months I kept my peace . . . You had your life to live and I let you live it, but I'm so in love with you . . . that I don't know what to do. But I'm just so fed up watching you being thrown away— What'll I do, go to Alaska—join the Foreign Legion? All right, I love you and

I'll get out of here as soon as I can. Now leave me alone! And if my sleeves roll down, just keep your hands off me. . . . I'll roll them up myself.

CELIA. Now you shut up!

POLO. Boy, that's getting to be a habit with you.

CELIA. I don't need you to tell me what I've been doing or what I haven't been doing.

POLO. Then you tell me. Why don't you ask—where he is? Where has he been? What has he been doing? How do you stand it day in and day out. Don't you want to know where your kid's going to live. You're going to have a baby, how do you live a life turning your back on what's been happening? You tell me.

CELIA. Because I don't love Johnny.

POLO. That's not true.

CELIA. It is—I don't love him.

POLO. All right.

CELIA. He hasn't even so much as held my hands in months. When he comes home at night, when he comes home, I pretend I'm sleeping . . . you'd think he'd touch my back, or kiss me good night. He wouldn't know the difference if he found Santa Claus in bed. He doesn't talk, he's always going . . . I'm having a baby, his baby and he never mentions the child or anything about it. Like anyone else . . . I need. Love, children . . . a home. He used to be like you . . . but he's not any more, and it's too late . . . it's too late.

POLO. We're all nice people. . . . Come on, now, stop crying.

CELIA. I can't tell him.

POLO. Why not?

CELIA. I don't know. I don't even know who he is. He's a stranger . . . I never married that person. . . . I thought he was so full of love. I don't know what it is . . . but it doesn't matter any more because I don't love him, and I can't tell him that.

POLO. Listen, are you sure? Maybe you're —maybe you just want to get even, show him something.

CELIA. Last night—and it wasn't a mirage, Polo—That was me at your door.

POLO. But you couldn't come in the door —and I couldn't open it.

CELIA. You take the laundry out.

POLO. Do you think I could . . . just put my arms around you? Do you think it would be all right?

CELIA. I think so.

POLO. When will you tell him?

CELIA. Tonight. You'll be here tonight?

POLO. Yes.

CELIA. Have the laundry bleached and dried.

POLO. All right.

CELIA. I don't want to go to work.

POLO. You'd better.

CELIA. I think I'd better. When he comes home, make him take a bath and put on his flannel pajamas.

THE LIGHTS DIM OUT

SCENE TWO

It is about ten in the morning. As the lights dim up, JOHNNY *is seen coming down the fire escape. Halfway down, he slips; panicked, he grabs the railing and stops his fall. He steadies himself and then climbs down to the hall. He opens the door and enters the kitchen. The door to* POLO's *room is ajar.*

JOHNNY. Polo! Hi!

POLO. Welcome home.

JOHNNY. Celia go to work?

POLO. It's ten o'clock in the morning. She starts at nine . . . she's not here, so figure it out for yourself.

JOHNNY. The old man wanted you to have those shirts. How do they fit?

POLO. I haven't put it on yet.

JOHNNY. I was out all night.

POLO. No kidding. Your wife wants you to get these things for supper.

JOHNNY. Where you going?

POLO. I' m going to take the laundry out. . . .

JOHNNY. You know what's happening . . .

POLO. I read the papers. Where you been?

JOHNNY. All over.

POLO. Where's all over?

JOHNNY. All over . . . Harlem, Lower East Side . . . everybody's disappeared.

POLO. It'll all blow over in a few weeks. . . .

JOHNNY. No. No. . . . they dropped the net, Polo . . . they're starting to tie the knot. Every pusher in the city's vanished. . . . Look, Polo. . . . I was lucky. I met Ginnino. I told him to hold some for me

. . . I have to get to him in fifteen minutes.

POLO. Who fixed you last night?

JOHNNY. Chuchie . . . I stopped over his place. He gave me half of his . . . enough to carry me through the night . . . but I'm thin now, Polo.

POLO. I told you yesterday, Johnny, the cupboard's bare. I'm out of the box and that's all there is to it. If I inherited the Chrysler building right now I wouldn't give you another dime. Try to understand that.

JOHNNY. Don't start lecturing me now. All I need is twenty bucks—and he won't do business on credit.

POLO. Take the kitchen set down and sell it to the Salvation Army. This linoleum isn't in bad shape. If you sell it at night in the dark, maybe you can get a few bucks for it. . . .

JOHNNY. Polo, you know I never sold a thing out of this house and I never will.

POLO. Try to listen, Johnny, try to hear me. I felt great refusing the old man that twenty-five hundred because I know the money went to a good cause. . . . It's only something he wanted all his life. You were right in the middle when he shouted, "Where? Where did it go?"

JOHNNY. Yeh, I was right in the middle. And I almost said, "Here!" It went here. (*thrusting his arm forward.*)

POLO. You went through that twenty-five hundred like grease through a tin horn. . . . I'm afraid to park my car out front . . . you might steal it some night.

JOHNNY. I'm quitting tomorrow. Tomorrow I'm quitting. . . .

POLO. It's been tomorrow for months, Johnny, the calendar never moves.

JOHNNY. Polo! This is the last time I'll ask you . . . I need twenty bucks. . . .

POLO. Twenty bucks, twice a day.

JOHNNY. Where am I gonna get it?

POLO. Get yourself a black felt hat, cut holes in it for eyes, and go down in the men's room of the subway like Apples does and clobber some poor bastard over the head. . . .

JOHNNY. The answer is no?

POLO. You look tired. . . .

JOHNNY. Here. . . . (*Tosses gun on bed.*) I almost used it four times last night . . . I picked dark streets and I waited. Four times . . . and they were set-ups. An old guy . . . must have been eighty years old . . . all alone. A guy and his girl, a young kid coming home from a dance drunk . . . some woman. Four times I left the doorway—I was on top of them . . . They weren't even afraid of me. I asked for a match, which way Fifty-sixth Street was . . . and would you give me a light please. Dust—that's all. Tired feet, tired eyes, and jammed up log tight.

POLO. Where did you get this . . . ?

JOHNNY. The lousy bastards told me it wasn't loaded. I'm into them for seven or eight hundred . . . on top of your twenty-five hundred cash. They want their money today . . . They'll be coming for me.

POLO. What do you mean?

JOHNNY. What do you think I mean?

POLO. It's not going to be Mother and Apples alone . . . they know I'm here, they'll bring company. Put those shoes on and let's get out of here.

JOHNNY. No more running, Polo. I'm through running. I can't run any more. If they don't get me today, they'll get me to-morrow.

POLO. You saw what happened to Willy DeCarlo . . .

JOHNNY. I'm not running away from them . . . and that's that! I'm going to stay right here. . . .

POLO. You're crazy, you're going crazy!

JOHNNY. I'm not moving. . . .

POLO. I haven't got seven or eight hundred dollars, Johnny . . . there's nothing I can do.

JOHNNY. Take the laundry out . . . and go to a movie or something.

POLO. What are you going to do?

JOHNNY. I'm going to wait for them . . .

POLO. You going to fight back . . . ?

JOHNNY. Well, I'm not going to stand still while they beat the hell out of me. . . .

POLO. You can't win . . . they'll kick your ribs in.

(FATHER *knocks and enters.*)

JOHNNY. Hi ya, Pop, you're up early . . .

FATHER. Good morning, Johnny—

POLO. Good morning, Pop. . . . I said good morning, Pop . . .

FATHER. Good morning.

POLO. I'm sorry about last night—

FATHER. How's the boy, Johnny . . . ?

POLO. I'm sorry about not getting to din-ner last night . . . Pop, I got looped. Come on, Pop, how about shaking hands and turning over a new leaf . . .

FATHER. I made a long-distance call to Palm Beach this morning trying to get the carpenter . . . and the plumber but I can't. They're putting in eight hours to-day, maybe copper tubing behind the bar . . .

JOHNNY. Have you had your breakfast—maybe I can whip you up a few scrambled. . . .

FATHER. I'll bet I could throw dollar bills out that window all morning long and there wouldn't be enough on the sidewalk to pay off the money I'm losing today. . . .

JOHNNY. We got an electric orange-juice squeezer—how about if I squeeze up some juice . . .

FATHER. I'm renovating a building I'll never be able to buy . . .

POLO. I'm sorry, Pop. I said I was sorry and I mean it.

FATHER. You said a lot of other things.

POLO. Let's shake hands on it, what do you say?

JOHNNY. The kid's got his hand out waiting for yours. . . .

POLO. I'd like to go to that ball game with you, Pop. Today's my day off . . .

FATHER. You made a jackass out of me! They'll laugh at me down there. I tell all my friends about you kids . . .

JOHNNY. Take the laundry out . . .

POLO. For crissakes, Pop, I haven't got the money. I'm not holding out on you.

JOHNNY. Take the laundry out!

POLO. I don't want to take it out.

JOHNNY. Take it out.

POLO. All right, Johnny. (*He goes out.*)

FATHER. A good rain cleans the streets . . . huh?

JOHNNY. You're up early, Pop.

FATHER. I didn't get much sleep. I was wondering about something, Johnny. Is today your day off? I mean, how can you take in the ball game if you're working?

JOHNNY. I'm not working.

FATHER. You say you and your wife are getting along . . . ?

JOHNNY. Yeh . . .

FATHER. Last night, when I went back to the hotel, I kept thinking about what your wife said, about believing. About what do I believe in. She's right, I got you kids to believe in. Like I come up here—you got a wife, a little home, a kid on the way, you're making a home for your brother. You did a good job of bringing yourself up . . . but what the hell's your brother doing? Holing up in some dame's apartment? Twenty-five hundred is a—

JOHNNY. I don't know. . . .

FATHER. You talk in awful short phrases, Johnny. . . .

JOHNNY. I'm not too used to talking to you, Pop.

FATHER. That's right, we don't talk very much, do we?

JOHNNY. No. . . .

FATHER. I like the letters you write me, Johnny . . . Life plays funny tricks on people. Hello and Good-by . . . and nothing in between, but I like the letters you write me.

JOHNNY. I'm glad you do, Pop.

FATHER. You take this believing thing—after your mother died, I used to read to you and your brother . . . Hi Diddle Diddle, the Cat and the Fiddle, Easter Bunny, Santa Claus and all that crap. You'd believe everything. I'd tell Polo Santa Claus was coming, and he'd look at me like I was out of my mind. You understand what I mean . . . ?

JOHNNY. I'm trying to, Pop. . . .

FATHER. Well, some people can talk, they have all the words. There are some things I feel that I don't have the words for. Maybe you're a little bit like me because you don't seem to be able to talk to me. . . .

JOHNNY. I always wanted to talk to you, Pop, but it's like you never wanted to talk to me, like you were afraid . . .

FATHER. What I want to say is that I care what happens to you. . . .

JOHNNY. Thanks. . . .

FATHER. And I love you—that's the thing, see?

JOHNNY. You what?

FATHER. You heard me the first time. Don't make me say it again.

JOHNNY. I feel the same way, Pop—

FATHER. How's that?

JOHNNY. You know what I mean—Polo, you and me, we're all kinda—Pop, willya do something for me. I never asked you for anything. When the kid comes back, tell him it's all water under the bridge. . . . Oh. . . .

FATHER. What's the matter?

JOHNNY. Headache . . .

FATHER. You wouldn't know anything about what happened to that money. Or would you? He doesn't pay a hundred dollars a week board here, does he?

JOHNNY. I'm asking you for something now. When Polo comes—

FATHER. That's the difference between you and Polo, you never asked me for anything.

JOHNNY. He never asked you for anything either, Pop.

FATHER. Yeh, but the way he looked at me sometimes—Maybe I never gave you much either.

JOHNNY. You gave me a coat once!

FATHER. A coat?

JOHNNY. Yeh, you came to the home, and you took me out to a department store—and you let me pick out a coat. And then you took me to a restaurant and made the guy give me some wine. . . .

FATHER. Your brother doesn't gamble, does he?

JOHNNY. No. . . .

FATHER. I always kinda thought that you and your brother and I had a special thing. I thought we were just kinda three men . . . Your brother did a lot of shouting last night.

JOHNNY. Pop, you did a little shouting yourself last night.

FATHER. I lived with my father until I was twenty-two years old, and I never raised my voice above a whisper . . .

JOHNNY. He lived with his father for nine years. What did you expect, Little Lord Fauntleroy.

FATHER. I expect the same thing I get from you. You don't go around crying like a kid in a crib. I like the letters you write me—'cause they're a man's letter. Dammit, you had a tough life but you made the best of it. Ever since he left home . . .

JOHNNY. He didn't leave home. He was sent away. Every time he gets a letter from you, he goes into his room and reads it. He's got a box of them in there. . . .

FATHER. Yeh . . . ?

JOHNNY. Yeh.

FATHER. Well, how would I know that!

JOHNNY. He's missed you for a long time, Pop. You shipped him out to uncles and aunts . . .

FATHER. And what was I doing? Gambling, drinking, laying on my can in Bermuda. I don't know anything about him. . . .

JOHNNY. Well, when he comes in, you ask him about that time in the orphan home when he wet the bed, and they made him stand on a staircase all day long with the wet sheet over his head . . .

FATHER. I shipped him—What was I supposed to do, buy a house, work nights, wash clothes during the day? Uncles and aunts, thank God he had them . . .

JOHNNY. All right, Pop . . .

FATHER. A man has only two hands.

JOHNNY. All right, Pop . . .

FATHER. And don't go around all-right-ing me. When I came yesterday, I had a funny feeling. Right now I got it again. You're not glad to see me, are you?

JOHNNY. Pop, I don't want to talk about it.

FATHER. You're not glad to see me, are you?

JOHNNY. Nobody's blaming you for anything. . . .

FATHER. You both always had a roof over your heads.

JOHNNY. Yeh, but when we woke up we didn't know what roof we were under.

FATHER. Waking up in a hotel room is no fun . . .

JOHNNY. Nobody's blaming you. When you stand in the snow your feet get cold—if you fall in the water and you can't swim, you drown. We call you Pop, and you call us Son, but it never was . . .

FATHER. You're a pretty cold-hearted cookie, Johnny.

JOHNNY. I don't save your letters . . . and I never saved my money to try to help you out. Don't come around knocking Polo to me . . . because he's my brother.

FATHER. And I'm not your father?

JOHNNY. Don't put words in my mouth . . .

FATHER. What the hell's the matter with you—all the things you say? What are you —the lawyer in the case . . . !

JOHNNY. I know you, Pop—either you clam up, or you start to push . . .

FATHER. As I listen to you, it sounds like I don't even know you. . . .

JOHNNY. Don't start to steam!

FATHER. I don't even know you!

JOHNNY. All right, you don't even know me.

FATHER. I don't even know you!

JOHNNY. How the hell could you know me? The last time I saw you I was in the hospital. You came to see me for three days. Before that . . . I saw you for two days, when I graduated school. How the hell could you know me? When you came to the hospital . . . you said, Jesus, it must have been rough, kid but it's all over . . . that's all you had to say . . . we shook hands, like two big men.

FATHER. If you felt that was wrong, why didn't you tell me.

JOHNNY. Tell you what? All I remember is laying there and smiling, thinking the old man's come to take me home.

FATHER. I live in a hotel, Johnny!

JOHNNY. Two big days. Six lousy visiting hours, and you run out. I was so glad to see you. . . .

FATHER. Your wife was there to take you home.

JOHNNY. I knew my wife for one year. I've known you for twenty-seven. Twenty-seven years. Your son! My boy Johnny. I didn't even know who she was.

(POLO *enters.*)

FATHER. That's a helluva thing to tell me —you didn't know who your wife was. You're not gonna blame me, are you? What's the matter with your brother?

POLO. Come on, Johnny, sit down. Sit down, will you.

JOHNNY. No, no, come on, let me stand up. I'd like to tell you right now what's standing in front of you . . . and it's not your Johnny boy.

POLO. No, Johnny, don't!

JOHNNY. I told you about the Sergeant, Polo. I told you all about that sonofabitchin Sergeant.

POLO. Come on, Pop, take a walk.

(JOHNNY *is not only disturbed by the pent-up emotion, but the narcotic's absence is beginning to become physically apparent.*)

JOHNNY. Tell him what they give you, Polo, tell him. He walked out, like the Sergeant ran out . . . The nurse came, and the doctor . . . They roll up your sleeve —one—then two—then another. You know what I'm talking about? Your son's trying to tell you something. . . .

FATHER. What have you been doing—hitting cheap gin?

POLO. You'd better go, Pop.

JOHNNY. And you come around here talking about an oak tree.

FATHER. Don't shake your finger in my face . . .

JOHNNY. I'm trying to tell you something, old man. . . .

POLO. Johnny, lay off . . .

FATHER. Are we still going to have supper tonight?

JOHNNY. Sure, we're going to have supper tonight. Why not?

FATHER. Why don't you meet me at the hotel in an hour or so? We'll go up and see the ball game.

POLO. Johnny and I will both be there. . . .

FATHER. You better see that he gets to bed. Make him get some sleep. (*The* FATHER *moves into the hallway.* POLO *follows him.*)

POLO. He's not feeling good, Pop. He doesn't mean—

FATHER. He means it, Polo.

JOHNNY. Okay, Sergeant. It's okay. Every man for himself. It's okay, Sarge. I got your number.

POLO (*off*). I'll see you in an hour. . . . (*Returning*) Come, Johnny, on your feet and walk around. Come on, get up. Take your shirt off, you're starting to sweat.

JOHNNY. Close the window, it's cold.

POLO. Johnny, I'm going to turn you in. (*Moves to phone.*) Johnny? Tell me to pick it up. Nobody will hate you, tell me to pick it up, will you?

JOHNNY. Tomorrow. Don't touch that . . . don't touch it, Sarge. Look, we'll get out of here alive.

POLO. Johnny! Johnny. This is Polo.

JOHNNY. The Sergeant—where's the Sergeant?

POLO. He's not here.

JOHNNY. You don't know what it is to need something, Sergeant. All alone in a cave and not a crumb in the whole cave.

POLO. Johnny, get up!

JOHNNY. You're not going to leave me, Sergeant.

POLO. No, Johnny. I'm not going to leave you. Come on get up. Now slow, go slow, Johnny.

JOHNNY. I'm all right, I'm all right. You go to sleep, Sarge. I'll watch for you. . . . Twenty dollars, that's all I need. Twenty dollars and I'll be the night watchman. . . . Twenty dollars, Sarge. I'll go to the desk myself. I'll turn myself in. (POLO *is at the phone.*) What are you doing with that? What are you taking my goddamn shoes for? You leave me something to eat, 'ya hear! (JOHNNY *grabs the phone.*) What are you taking my shoes for?

POLO. Johnny, give me the phone.

JOHNNY. You're not going to leave me, Sergeant, are you? Don't leave me, all I need is twenty lousy bucks.

POLO. Twenty bucks twice a day.

JOHNNY. Leave me something to eat, you hear? Go ahead, run! Run! Run and leave me alone, you sonofabitch. I can't move but you run, run and leave me here to die by myself, you sonofabitch.

POLO. Johnny!

JOHNNY. Sssssshhhh. Quiet. Be quiet. Here they come, run for it, run for it. Oh God, here they come. Hit it! Hit it! (*He cowers on the bed.*)

POLO. For the love of God, Johnny, it's Polo. . . . It's your brother. It's Polo. . . . Polo!

JOHNNY. Hit me, go ahead. Hit me. I don't have to tell you anything. There was nobody here with me. Nobody. Corporal John Pope, 122036617. Name, rank, serial number. I don't know who took my shoes.

(MOTHER *and* APPLES *appear.*)

POLO. Come on, will you snap out of it. Mother, do something for him. I'll make good for it.

MOTHER. I'd like to laugh, but I can't. The pocket's in trouble.

JOHNNY. Go ahead, beat me. I'm bleeding, but beat me. You sonsabitches—go ahead! Watch my back—will you watch my back—beat me, 1220—122036617—John Pope.

POLO. Give him something to quiet him down. I'll make good for it.

APPLES. He must think you're the Chase National Bank, Mother. We don't wake up and find our money in a rain barrel.

POLO. On my word of honor, I'll pay you tomorrow.

MOTHER. All eight hundred. You got enough to cover this trip.

POLO. I swore if it killed me I wasn't going to put another nickel into that arm!

JOHNNY. Don't hit me—will you watch my back. I didn't have a gun. I don't know who took my shoes.

POLO. Take it. You're the Mother of them all. Go ahead, count it.

APPLES. Mother's got a Horn and Hardart mentality. Nickels and dimes, right, Mother. Right?

MOTHER. I'll tell you what I'm going to do. I'll set him straight for twelve bucks. . . . We'll give him back his spine. Then we're going to work him over.

POLO. You'll get yours someday, Mother. I'll see that you get paid in full someday.

JOHNNY. 122036617! That's all I have to tell you. Nobody with me . . . that's all.

MOTHER (*picking up* JOHNNY). Just take it easy, Corporal—the General's here.

JOHNNY. (*as he is carried out by* MOTHER). Watch my back. . . . Watch my back.

APPLES. Old Mother's got some sense of humor—the General's here. You shouldn't treat Mother like a smell. You know the British Government's been sending tax collectors into the bush for years . . . trying to get them pygmy bastards to pay up their back taxes. That's right. Flies don't have brains . . . and pygmies don't have money, but they got goats. They got to pay their back taxes with goats . . . you understand. Flies don't have brains, but he's got brains.

(MOTHER *has returned.*)

MOTHER. You don't need a car in the city, no place to park.

APPLES. Allus getting parkin' tickets . . .

MOTHER. You got your keys . . . ?

POLO. Yeh.

MOTHER. You got your pink slip?

POLO. Yeh.

MOTHER. You get to the nearest used-car lot and sell that car! I want eight hundred dollars. We'll be back tonight. We don't get that money—we put your brother in the hospital with Willy DeCarlo. . . . Maybe we send you along too. Let's move it!

(*He and* APPLES *leave.*)

JOHNNY (*comes into the kitchen*). Where'd they go?

POLO. Are you all right?

JOHNNY. I'm all right. Polo—

POLO. Johnny— The shopping list is on the table, Johnny. I got something to do before I meet the old man. Do you want us to pick you up . . . go to the game with us?

JOHNNY. No, I think I'd better stay here.

POLO. I'll see you at supper.

JOHNNY. Polo . . . I have to tell her, but what can I say? I don't know what the hell's happening to me . . . that's the trouble . . . yesterday, I went all the way over to that Summittown . . . and I stand there like an idiot looking at the house. It's all gone, what the hell am I looking for? I trust you, Polo—how can I tell her?

POLO. Tell her, Johnny, just tell her.

JOHNNY. What'll I say for crissakes?

POLO. Just say . . . uh . . . I'm a junkey. That's what you are, isn't it, Johnny?

THE LIGHTS DIM OUT

SCENE THREE

It is early the same evening. As the lights fade in, we hear faintly the music of a street carousel and the eager, happy voices of children in the street below. Odd fragments of the phrases, "Ma, Ma, I wanna go again. . . ." JOHNNY, *wearing a neatly pressed shirt, is in the kitchen, spreading a tablecloth. He moves to the sink, and, as he turns around, we see that he has a bouquet of flowers; he sets them on the table. As he hears* CELIA *approach, he moves hurriedly into* POLO'S *room, leaving the door ajar.* CELIA *enters.*

CELIA. Polo.

JOHNNY (*from within*). Yeh.

CELIA. Did Johnny go to the game?

JOHNNY (*still inside*). Yeh.

CELIA. The flowers are beautiful. What smells so good? What are you doing in there? The kids are riding the carousel. The old horse looks like he wants to go home and sleep. (JOHNNY *sneaks up behind her and puts his hand over her eyes.*) What are you doing? A surprise . . . what's the surprise?

JOHNNY. Me.

CELIA. I thought you were going to the game with your father.

JOHNNY. Let's go down and ride the carousel.

CELIA. I've got to get things ready. Did Polo go to the game?

JOHNNY. Yeh. Come on, let's go down and take one ride on it.

CELIA. We'd break the horses.

JOHNNY. How was your day?

CELIA. What?

JOHNNY. I said, how was your day?

CELIA. Like any other day. Why?

JOHNNY. Why? I thought you said that a day wasn't just a day.

CELIA. Oh. I'll have to make a salad.

JOHNNY. It's in the icebox.

CELIA. I'll have to make the dressing.

JOHNNY. It's in the blue cup. I've looked for the shoe polish all day and I can't find it. Where do you hide it?

CELIA. The cabinet . . . under the sink. You did the floors.

JOHNNY. I swished a mop around. I took all my clothes to the cleaners, and I fixed that clock.

CELIA. You didn't look for a job today, did you?

JOHNNY. No, I didn't have time.

CELIA. I didn't mean anything. I was just curious . . . that's all.

JOHNNY. Yeh. You want to sit in a tub of hot water . . . I'll rub your back with alcohol.

CELIA. What is this? Flowers, the floors mopped, meat in the oven, shining your shoes—what's the occasion? I mean, what's all this for?

JOHNNY. Don't you like the flowers?

CELIA. Of course, I like the flowers. I didn't expect to find you home, flowers and the floor mopped.

JOHNNY. You just said that.

CELIA. Said what?

JOHNNY. Flowers and the floor mopped, you said that twice.

CELIA. All right, supposing I did say that twice, what difference does it make!

JOHNNY. No difference, I wasn't criticizing you, I was just—

CELIA. Can we forget it, Johnny, please?

JOHNNY. Forget what?

CELIA. That I said something twice!

JOHNNY. What is it? I was out last night again, is that it?

CELIA. No.

JOHNNY. How many more guesses do I get?

CELIA. It's over.

JOHNNY. What's over? What are you talking about?

CELIA. We've tried.

JOHNNY. I'm behind the times. I thought it was just going to begin. What you said yesterday, that I never came home . . . all the things you said, I've been thinking about them.

CELIA. I'll leave tonight.

JOHNNY. Is it because I lost my job?

CELIA. It's not the job, Johnny.

JOHNNY. What is it?

CELIA. I don't love you.

JOHNNY. And we snap our fingers and that's that?

CELIA. That's the way it is.

JOHNNY. I don't like this talk. Everything's so cold. What is this, a formal dance or something?

CELIA. Johnny, I refuse to get emotional. . . . I just refuse. My mind is made up. It's not easy, but it's something that has to be done. Now I refuse to get emotional. I'm

not going to blame you for anything and I don't want to be blamed for anything. We have to concede that the marriage has failed, not you, not I . . . but we have. I refuse to get emotional. Nothing will be settled by emotion.

JOHNNY. A day isn't just a day, that's what you said. It's not my day or your day. It's not just you and I now.

CELIA. If I understand you correctly, you are talking about the baby?

JOHNNY. Yeh, you understand me correctly.

CELIA. It's amazing, honestly.

JOHNNY. What's amazing? What?

CELIA. For four months I've been waiting for you to say something, one word, one syllable about the baby.

JOHNNY. Today isn't yesterday . . . things can change, you know?

CELIA. Johnny. I don't want to talk any more because I don't want to get emotional.

JOHNNY. I'm home! Do you understand that? I'm home now! I haven't been but I am now. Here! I bought this today. (*Gives package to her.*)

CELIA. What is it?

JOHNNY. You said it was going to be a girl, didn't you? Five dresses, one for every day of the week . . . that's another thing I did today.

CELIA. Where did you get the money?

JOHNNY. We don't need electric orange-juice squeezers. I can squeeze oranges with my hands.

CELIA. Well, thank you, Johnny. Thank you very much.

JOHNNY. Look, it's my turn to cry, to beg . . . you reached out your hand and I turned my back, you've looked at me and I've closed my eyes. You're not listening to me. Please listen to me. . . . Please.

CELIA. I'm listening.

JOHNNY. All right, you don't love me any more. There was something in me worthwhile loving. You must have loved me for some reason! What was the reason? Celia? Celia? I haven't even used your name. I say baby . . . and I say honey . . . but now I'm saying Celia. Celia. I love you.

CELIA. Oh, Johnny, please. Please stop . . . please.

JOHNNY. I know I've been deaf, dumb and blind but please don't do to me what I did to you. Something happened to me. It's something that's hard to understand.

Honey, I don't know whether I'm laughing or crying, but, Celia, you don't have to love me . . . not for a long time. You just don't even have to bother . . .

CELIA. Oh . . . oh . . . oh . . . Do you want to feel something? Johnny, give me your hand . . . Lightly, do you feel it . . . (*She has taken* JOHNNY's *hand and put it gently over her stomach*) You see?

JOHNNY. Oh—Wow! Holy cats . . . I felt it move. I swear I felt it move. Let me feel that again. I don't feel anything. What happened?

CELIA. Nothing happened. It doesn't move all day long. Just every once in a while.

JOHNNY. Well, let me know the next time you think it's going to move.

CELIA. I will.

JOHNNY. That's a real miracle, you know. Heh . . .

CELIA. Hold me, Johnny. Please . . . hold me.

JOHNNY. Oh, you're going to see some changes . . . I've been making plans all day. I've been like a kid waiting for you to come home. I kept looking at the clock.

CELIA. I don't have a handkerchief.

JOHNNY. You're not going to leave me? Are you? Tell me?

CELIA. No, Johnny, I'm gonna get an apron.

(POLO *comes in.*)

POLO. The old man's down in Garrity's. He wants to buy you a drink.

JOHNNY. Is he sore?

POLO. He says he wants bygones to be bygones.

JOHNNY. You got a little windburn. Who won the game?

POLO. Who played?

JOHNNY. What's eating you?

POLO. The old man. He thinks I still have that money . . . on the way home he started talking it up again. Gone where? You didn't buy a new car, what do you pay—five hundred dollars a week board. This time he's using the happy-time-U.S.A. approach.

JOHNNY. I'll go down and talk to him.

CELIA. I want you to forget this morning, Polo.

POLO. All right.

JOHNNY. What are you two talking about?

CELIA. Nothing that concerns you, Johnny.

POLO. It's forgotten. Did you tell her, Johnny? Did you tell her?

CELIA. Now what are you two talking about?

JOHNNY. Nothing that concerns you, honey.

POLO. The old man will wait a minute.

JOHNNY. Not now, Polo. I'll take care of it. I give you my word, but not now.

POLO. Johnny, I'm going away. I don't know where. I'd like to leave tonight . . . but I can't.

JOHNNY. Let the old man get on his plane and go back to Palm Beach. He doesn't have to know anything.

CELIA. Know what?

POLO. I'm not leaving her with you, Johnny.

JOHNNY. Will you leave us alone for a minute.

CELIA. Johnny! What's the matter!

POLO. I'll stay, Johnny. I've been part of it.

JOHNNY. Look, Celia—now it's nothing to get excited about. (*From off, we hear the* FATHER's *whistle.*) Will you just sit down for a minute. Polo had the money that the old man wanted, but I took it all.

CELIA. What do you mean?

JOHNNY. Look, honey, I'm . . . the thing is, I . . . I'll go down with the old man. He's whistling.

POLO. Tell her, will you please tell her.

CELIA. What is it?

JOHNNY. Get out of my way, Polo . . . you hear me. Get out of my way!

POLO. I'm not in your way. Go ahead, run.

JOHNNY. Honey, my father's whistling. Will you get away from that door. Let me out.

CELIA. Johnny, you can tell me . . . you can tell me anything. What have you done?

FATHER (*off*). Heh, Johnny . . .

POLO. Nobody's going to hate you, Johnny.

FATHER (*off*). Heh, Johnny boy . . .

JOHNNY. Honey, I'm hooked . . . I'm a junkey . . . I take dope. I'm hooked.

CELIA. You're what?

JOHNNY. I'm hooked!

CELIA. That's silly.

JOHNNY. No, it's not silly. I need it, two times . . . every day . . . and it costs money.

CELIA. It's all right. Whatever it is, it's

all right. It's all right.

JOHNNY. Don't say anything to the old man.

CELIA. We'll call a doctor.

JOHNNY. Not until the old man goes. He doesn't have to know.

CELIA. Johnny, it doesn't matter. There's nothing to be ashamed of, it's all right, everything's going to be all right.

(FATHER *comes in.*)

FATHER. Where the hell were you? I been downstairs whistling my brains out.

JOHNNY. I didn't hear you, Pop.

FATHER. Didn't hear you, Pop . . . do you know these bums of mine . . . these bums . . . ?

CELIA. They're not bums.

FATHER. These bums. I spent more time on the back porch whistling. I'd get all the cats and the dogs in the neighborhood . . . but no Johnny, not Polo . . . isn't that right, Johnny?

POLO. That's right, Pop.

FATHER. Got a towel for me, honey? (*Moving off into the john; out of sight.*) Did Johnny ever tell you about the time he was a kid I came home and found him digging up the backyard? I asked him what the hell are you doin? Workin', daddy . . . me workin' . . . I told him the only way you get money in your pockets is to work. He'd dig a hole, and then look in the pockets, dig another hole and in the pockets, and no money . . . Johnny was convinced . . . Work and you make money. One day I came home and it was raining . . . and there's the little bum there digging away . . . he had his hat laying alongside a big empty hole . . . and finally I convinced him not to believe what I told him in the first place, then . . . he bends down and picks up his hat— and the water goes running all over him . . . he worked and worked and all he got was a hatful of rain.

CELIA. I was on time for work today.

POLO. You were?

CELIA. Yes, I was.

POLO. Good!

FATHER. There's no napkins on the table. (*Coming out of the john*) What's everybody so quiet about . . . ?

CELIA. Pass me the pepper and salt . . . please, Polo.

FATHER. Let me have that salt after you.

JOHNNY. How about you, Polo, you want some salt too?

POLO. It needs it.

JOHNNY. I thought I put salt in.

CELIA. We're putting it in now. It doesn' matter.

FATHER. The soup's flat as Kelsey's.

CELIA. Johnny cooked that soup.

FATHER. Let's not start the Trojan wa over a bowl of soup.

JOHNNY. How'd you like the ball game Pop?

FATHER. When that Snider steps up t the plate . . . he looks like he owns th ball park. How about you, Johnny—do yo get out and see a ball game?

JOHNNY. No, Pop, I don't . . .

FATHER. You ought to—get out in the air Fresh air—it's good for you. What th . . . ? What is this, the last supper? Wha did I do now? Well, go ahead, you guy . . . Did I say something wrong?

JOHNNY. No—we're all a little tired that's all . . .

FATHER. Talking in short phrases again? Johnny? All right, yes, Pop, no, Pop—

POLO. It's your imagination . . .

CELIA. Can we just pretend that we are—

FATHER. Will you let me say what I wan to say! Now look—last night you gave m a working over, right, Polo? And toda you really laced into me. Did you see m walking around with my tail between m legs? You didn't come through with th money you promised me. We're eating her now—we're all together, now for crissake let's have a song or something. Let's get few laughs . . .

JOHNNY. I'm a junkey, Pop . . .

CELIA. Johnny's sick . . .

FATHER. You don't know what you'r talking about . . .

POLO. He knows what he's talking abou . . .

FATHER. You mean you take . . . dope? That's a junkey, isn't it?

JOHNNY. That's it.

FATHER. You've known about this, Polo? POLO. All the time . . .

FATHER. Well, where do you get it . . I mean, how?

POLO. Let's forget it.

FATHER. I'm asking your brother a ques tion. I'm not asking you for orders . . .

(CELIA *moves off into the living room.*) POLO. I'm giving you one—shut up!

FATHER. Don't say "shut up" to me.

POLO. Keep your hat on.

FATHER. What do you mean, "keep m

hat on?"

JOHNNY. Geez, I'm not so hungry. (*Calls to* CELIA) Honey, why don't you sit down and try to eat . . .

CELIA. I was looking for lipstick on your shirts.

FATHER. All the time you knew it . . . ? How long is all the time?

JOHNNY. I've been hooked . . . this time, seven months . . .

FATHER. This time? There was another time . . . ?

JOHNNY. Yeh . . . for a few months after I came out of the hospital, but I told Polo, and he helped me. I kicked it . . .

FATHER. You kicked it . . .

JOHNNY. Yeh, I kicked it . . . I got off the habit.

CELIA. Johnny, please! Don't start getting touchy!

JOHNNY. Well, go to a public library and read up on it! What do you expect me to do, sit here and—

FATHER. Look, I'm going to find out now whose fault this is and who's to blame. And you knew about it, so you talk.

POLO. I don't know whose fault it is. . . .

CELIA. What difference does it make who's to blame. Maybe it's my fault?

FATHER. You're his wife! What do you know about this? You been sleeping in the same bed with him and you don't even know you been sleeping with a dope addict!

POLO. Pop, will you shut up.

CELIA. I haven't been sleeping with a dope addict. We've just been sharing the bed for—

FATHER. For crissakes, it's disgusting. You sit down to dinner and your kid turns out to be a—

JOHNNY. Will you lay off.

CELIA. Why don't you tell me?

JOHNNY. I told you.

FATHER. I can't understand how a boy like you—

JOHNNY. Will you be quiet! And don't turn your back on me like I'm dead . . . I know what I am.

FATHER. What are you?

JOHNNY. I'm a *junkey!*

FATHER. I ought to beat the hell out of you!

POLO. Pop, the kid is trying . . .

FATHER. How could you sit at that table . . . ?

POLO (*between* JOHNNY *and the enraged* FATHER). Lay off him . . . come on now . . .

FATHER. Mind your own business!

CELIA. Please, please . . .

JOHNNY. I'm asking you to be quiet, Pop, I'm not begging . . . Be quiet!

FATHER. Polo, get out of my way . . .

JOHNNY. You raise that hand to me and I'll—

FATHER. Polo, get out of my way—

POLO. He told you, Pop . . .

JOHNNY. I'm trying to tell you something, Pop . . .

POLO. He told you—and telling you hasn't changed anything. He's still a junkey . . . For crissakes he's sick . . . don't you understand that he's sick . . . ?

JOHNNY. I'm not . . . I'm not . . . Oh, what the hell's the use. (*He rushes out.*)

FATHER. Johnny, come back here . . . ! Come back! Come back!

CELIA. Johnny . . . Johnny—oh, Johnny, I'm afraid.

POLO. He'll come back . . .

FATHER. He ran away.

POLO. I'll go out and find him.

CELIA. No, Polo. Don't leave me. Stay right here. Just let me sit for a minute. Something is wrong . . .

POLO. The baby?

CELIA. Polo? I think you'd better call a cab . . . Something is going wrong inside of me. I'm afraid to move. . . .

POLO. Get her coat, Pop. (POLO *runs downstairs.*)

CELIA. He'll come back. He's got to come back . . .

FATHER. Put your arms around me. (*He picks her up.*) Just hold tight . . .

POLO. Taxi! Yo . . . Yo . . . taxi . . . heh, taxi!

(*The* FATHER *moves with* CELIA *toward the door.*)

FATHER. Shhhhh . . . shhhhh. . . .

CURTAIN

ACT THREE

When the curtain rises, there are no lights in the apartment area. We see the glow of the skylight. In the distance we hear MOTHER *and* APPLES *laughing hysterically as they climb up the stairs. Their laughter suggests that they are having dif-*

ficulty in climbing the stairs, probably falling against the wall in hysterics. Finally they appear, their laughter subsiding somewhat. CHUCH *lags behind.* MOTHER *and* APPLES *walk directly to the door but* CHUCH *starts up the ladder.* MOTHER *turns and calls to him as he knocks on the door.*

MOTHER. Where you going, dummy? Come here . . .

CHUCH. I tole ya I'm not hittin' Johnny.

MOTHER (*calling*). Heh, Johnny . . . it's your old Mother.

CHUCH. You said I don't have to hit him . . .

MOTHER (*knocking*). Will you shut up . . . !

APPLES. He ain't home.

CHUCH. Come on, let's go.

MOTHER. Cross the roof . . . come in the fire escape, Chuchie . . . and open the door.

CHUCH. All right. . . . (*He scurries up the fire escape.*)

APPLES. You gonna sweat him out? Huh, Mother . . . ?

MOTHER. We gonna sweat him out.

APPLES. You know what I like about you, Mother?

MOTHER. What do you like about me?

APPLES. I'm gonna tell you what I like about you.

MOTHER. What?

APPLES. No matter what the band plays . . . you hear your own music.

MOTHER. That stuff was a hundred per cent pure. Man, I feel like King Kong ridin' a cloud . . . (MOTHER *opens the door and they both enter.*)

CHUCH (*coming from the other side*). That door was open there all the time!

MOTHER. Chuch, I goofed. What are you doing?

CHUCH. I'm sitting down.

MOTHER. I know you're sitting down. Go down to the car and keep an eye on that whacky broad . . .

CHUCH. Make Apples go down. I don't want to go near that whacky broad. She's always trying to grab me . . .

MOTHER. Well, let her grab you, but keep an eye on her . . .

CHUCH. I always get the short end . . . (CHUCH *goes out. The phone rings,* APPLES *picks it up.*)

APPLES. Hold on a minute, willya . . . It's Ginnino . . . No, nothing happened.

No, I'm not laughin' at you, Mother's startin' to float. Yeh . . . huh, yeh. Man, we almost got arrested four times today, and the day's not over yet. Mother's floatin' away, and he ain't coming back. . . .

MOTHER. Lay down the red carpet for our man.

APPLES. Heh, little Jim . . . Mother and me and that whacky broad, the one with all the money. We're going up to Connecticut . . . Her family went to Europe. She's out in the car now . . . with no clothes on. They raided the hotel she's at . . . and she had to run . . . she got no clothes on. Man, are you crazy? She got a coat on . . .

PUTSKI (*enters hurriedly,* CHUCH *following her*). Don't touch me . . . He tried to touch me . . . I was sitting lighting a cigarette and he grabbed the inside of my leg and I won't stand for it. After all, it's my car.

CHUCH. I didn't try to touch her. She grabbed me. . . .

PUTSKI. I don't want to go down to the car . . . I'll just sit here like the Queen Mother and not say a word.

APPLES. Where's your place in Connecticut . . . ?

PUTSKI. Just outside of Greenwich . . . and it's not my place, it's Lester's place, Lester's the man Mummy married since Daddy disappeared. . . .

APPLES. There's five bathrooms in the house. One for everybody . . . No, man, we're looking to collect some money. Right, Mother.

MOTHER. Right. Money or the lumps.

APPLES. Little Jim wants to know if we pick him up on the way.

MOTHER. He's with us.

APPLES. As soon as we can, man . . . sit tight and hold right . . . right? And there you go, Jim!

MOTHER. What time is it, Apples . . . ?

APPLES. My clock says eleven o'clock . . .

MOTHER. That's a nice clock you got there . . .

APPLES. I mean watcht. I allus say clock . . .

MOTHER. Yeh, an you *allus* say *axt.* It's *ask* with a K, not axt, you silly bastard . . .

APPLES. Wait a minute, teacher. I'll ring the bell and get the rest of the kids in. . . .

(*Everything becomes unusually silent for a good minute.* PUTSKI *is back in a*

chair, staring dreamily at the ceiling. APPLES
hums, "like a saxophone"; MOTHER *stands
doing absolutely nothing. Only* CHUCH
*looks about wondering why a silence has
descended . . . all being addicted and under the influence of drugs, their sense of
time becomes peculiar, not noticeable to
themselves, but to an onlooker they appear
to be either in slow motion or hopped.
There is a sense of a vacuum . . . and
then, coming from nowhere a sense of
chaos and speed.* MOTHER *sits, takes out a
book and reads as though he were in the
public library.)*

CHUCH. What are we doin'?

APPLES. We're waitin' . . .

CHUCH. What are we waitin' for?

APPLES. The money—we're waitin' for
the money.

CHUCH. Oh. . . .

PUTSKI. I can't stand people who feel a
compulsion to talk endlessly . . .

APPLES. What are you reading? You're
allus readin' . . . He allus reading, Chuch.
You remember what happened to Crazy
Stanley.

CHUCH. Yeh . . . Crazy Stanley was
allus readin'. I saw him flip. He never read
comic books. Always readin' about the
planets, rocket ships.

APPLES. You hear that, Mother?

MOTHER. Yeh . . .

APPLES. Keep on readin'. Just keep on
readin' . . .

MOTHER. You ever thought about com-
mitting suicide, Apples?

APPLES. No, man, I'm young yet. I'm
only nineteen . . .

CHUCH. Will you guys shut up!

APPLES. You know something, Chuch?
You ugly.

MOTHER. Apples is right, Chuch. You're
ugly . . .

APPLES. You can't help it if you're ugly,
Chuch. Mother's ugly too, but it doesn't
bother him. . . .

MOTHER. You know something, Apples,
you're getting disrespectful just because
we're friends, and you know something
else, you'd better have eyes in the back of
your head when you start getting disrespectful. . . .

APPLES. Take it easy, Brother Mother.

MOTHER. Don't butter me, Apples. Get
your hands out of your pockets. And don't
turn your back because I'll punch you right
in the back.

CHUCH. Go ahead, kill each other. Go
ahead. There's seven million people in this
city, and we have to fight each other. Go
ahead, I don't know whose side I'm going
to be on, start punching I'll pick a side.

MOTHER. Chuch, do yourself a favor.

CHUCH. Mother, do me a favor? Just do
me a favor. Don't start puttin' ideas in my
head.

APPLES. Take it easy, Chuch, we ain't
gonna steal nothin'. We're going to Connecticut . . .

CHUCH. He sees an ole lady pushin' a
baby carriage around at night collecting
newspapers . . . an' a bell goes off. Some
people got water on the knee, and he's got
hermits on the brain. . . .

MOTHER. What are you talking about,
Chuch?

CHUCH. You told me I can't keep chasin'
the tiger's tail. I got to lock horns if I
want to get my fix! You told me where she
kept the money . . . out of the frying pan
and into the gold-plated casserole. I could
sleep tight if I had a bundle of thousands
under my pillow . . . huh?

MOTHER. We're gonna go to Connecticut.
They got an A.S.P.C.A. in Connecticut.

CHUCH. Go by the A.S.P.C.A.? The cops
come two hours after he died . . . and
then the A.S.P.C.A. truck come too. The
cop says the dog is dead. He died in my
arms and he tells me the dog is dead. . . .
I says to the guy from the A.S.P.C.A.—
What'll I do with him? Throw him in
the garbage, he says, we don't take the
dead ones . . . that's for the sanitation department.

MOTHER. Huh, Chuchie Duchie . . .
you can buy a cocker spaniel for ten bucks
. . . !

CHUCH. Three dollars, and sixteen cents
. . . three dollars and sixteen cents! That's
all. . . . God punished me. (JOHNNY
bursts in the door. A MAN *slides down the
ladder and plants himself in the hallway.)*

MAN. Back up, Johnny . . . back up like
a mule.

CHUCH. I killed the old lady, Johnny. I
didn't mean to kill her. He wouldn't give
me no more credit. Three dollars and sixteen cents!

MOTHER. You got the eight hundred
. . . ?

JOHNNY. Where's my wife . . . ?

MOTHER. Button up your buttons, honey,
we're getting out of here. . . .

CHUCH. Johnny, you look bad. . . .

JOHNNY. I'll be all right. . . .

CHUCH. Yeh, sure, but three dollars and sixteen cents. I didn't mean to do it. (*Goes off, mumbling.*)

MOTHER. Button 'em up.

PUTSKI. I had the most wonderful dream. . . .

MOTHER. Get her down to the car. I'll take care of Johnny. . . .

PUTSKI. I'm not moving until it's perfectly understood that everyone will have their own room . . . and there'll be no going from one room to another . . . I hope no one here had any ideas about me . . . because they're completely mistaken. . . .

APPLES. Come on, nobody's got any ideas about you. . . .

MOTHER. Get her down to the car. . . .

PUTSKI (*going out*). It has to be perfectly understood that the run of the premises are yours—you can eat until your hearts are content . . . but there'll be no fooling around, no voyages from one room to another. Hey, who's that guy?

MOTHER. Come here, Junkey—I'm not going to hurt you. I'm not greedy. Come here, I want to give you something . . . honest. You're sick, Junkey . . . can you see me way over here? I'm smiling.

JOHNNY. You'll get your eight hundred . . . every lousy cent of it.

MOTHER. Your word is your bond, my man—you know how to use that thing you've got in your hand—Hey, can you see me over here? Look, pure white—a free ride on the midnight carousel, tax free, on the house.

JOHNNY. I'm through!

MOTHER. No more trying to get the things you wanted all your life . . . and you fly, Johnny, like a bird.

JOHNNY. I'm through, Mother, I'm quitting.

(POLO *enters.*)

POLO. Heh, Mother . . . There's eight hundred . . . Count it downstairs, will you?

MOTHER. He'll crawl . . . (*He goes out.*)

JOHNNY. Where's Celia . . . ?

POLO. She'll be here . . .

JOHNNY. Did you put the old man on his plane . . . ?

POLO. Where you going?

JOHNNY. I'm a half-hour from hell, Polo. I'm going up to the St. Nicholas and get myself a room. I'm going to kick it. . . .

POLO. I was in that room with you once before, Johnny . . .

JOHNNY. I lock myself up for three days . . . and I won't touch a thing. When I come out, I'll be straight again . . .

POLO. You won't last a day in that room . . .

JOHNNY. Come with me. You come with me . . . you watch me. You can keep me locked up for three days . . . That's all it takes, Polo. Three lousy days . . .

POLO. Johnny, I can't watch you go through that again . . .

JOHNNY. I did it once before— and I'll do it again.

POLO. Listen, Johnny—I held you down on that bed for three days! Maybe you can go through that hell again, but I can't watch you again . . . Johnny, sit down, willya . . . ?

JOHNNY. Polo, my time's running out . . .

POLO. Listen to me . . . Celia almost lost the baby. She's all right . . . take it easy. We left her at the doctor's . . . He wanted her to lay down for an hour. She knows you don't have to run any more . . .

JOHNNY. She's all right . . . ? Don't lie to me, Polo . . .

POLO. I just called the doctor's—she's on her way home.

JOHNNY. And the old man . . . ?

POLO. I told him I paid for it, Johnny —in the doctor's office. And I left him sitting there . . . saying, no, no, no, no, Polo, you couldn't do that to your brother . . .

JOHNNY. They'll be coming here . . .

POLO. You couldn't walk one block.

JOHNNY. Polo, I got to get out of here. I can't let them see me like this . . . Polo, I'm quitting, don't you believe me?

POLO. For the first time, I do. I know you can do it . . .

JOHNNY. Then for the last time, Polo, help me. Get a cab. Get me out of here. Polo, I don't want them to see me!

POLO. All right, Johnny, I'll go with you. I'll do what I have to do.

JOHNNY. It's starting, Polo . . . it's starting. Oh God . . .

FATHER (*knocks on door*). Polo? Polo? Open the door . . .

POLO. Go in the back room and be quiet . . .

(JOHNNY *goes into the bedroom.*)

FATHER. Polo . . . !

POLO (*going to door*). I'm sorry, Pop, . . .

FATHER. Did you find him? Did you find your brother Johnny?

POLO. No, Pop—did you go to all the places I told you to go?

FATHER. Nobody's seen him . . .

POLO. Celia'll be right home—I called her.

FATHER. It's a good thing that was a false alarm, Polo.

POLO. She's all right. She's on her way home.

FATHER. Where are you going?

POLO. Pop, your plane leaves in an hour.

FATHER. Planes fly every day. Where you going? You want to get out of here now, huh? That's all you want. Three thousand dollars' worth of poison in your brother's arm and you paid for it!

POLO. Twenty-five hundred.

FATHER. That was the right thing to do? Help your brother kill himself. You have an alibi . . . What have you got to say for yourself?

POLO. Nothing.

FATHER. What have you got to say to me?

POLO. Get on your plane and go back to Palm Beach where everything is nice and quiet. Come on, Pop—I want you to get out of here.

FATHER. Get away from that bag, and don't call me Pop. Let's just be two men talking. Talk to me like I'm your brother. You'll get out of here, maybe not on your own two feet, but you'll get out of here.

POLO. Take it easy, Pop.

FATHER. I'm getting red in the face, huh? Maybe I'd better sit down. I'm not as young as I used to be. I'm soft, not hard enough for you.

POLO. Now, look, Pop, you don't know what you're doing.

FATHER. Where's your brother? You're not your brother's keeper. Are you going to shut up on me again? You're forgetting I'm your father!

POLO. Well, for crissakes look at you. You don't even know what's happened and you're trying to put the blame somewhere.

FATHER. My son, if you knew how ashamed I was to admit that you're my son. Am I a child? Are you my father? You know what I'm going to do . . . ?

You remember once how Pete the big bay horse kicked me and put me in the hospital . . . and when I came out I turned that bastard loose in the barn and locked the doors . . . that ungrateful sonofabitch that I slept in the straw with when he was sick. I fought that horse with my bare hands . . . and you and Johnny were up in the hayloft, yelling, "Look out, Pop . . . that horse is going to kill you!" I'm going to beat you, Polo! And you can punch back, like he kicked back. You fight back. Take your coat off.

POLO. No, I'm not going to take my coat off. You couldn't hurt me any more if you killed me. Listen. You were two thousand miles away but I was here. You told me a hundred times in every letter you ever wrote that I should fall on my hands and knees and light twenty candles a day because my brother had taken me in.

FATHER. You couldn't write to me and tell me?

POLO. Write to you and tell you what? That your favorite son was a goddamned junkey. You going to swing. Swing! Take your failures out on me . . . and when you finish I'm going to tell you where your son is . . . I took care of him . . . I'm my brother's keeper more than you know. (*The* FATHER *swings and hits* POLO *soundly across the face with an open hand.*) You poor old man. What are you hitting me for? What have I done? You walk around with your head in the clouds. Why don't you stand still for a minute and try to find something out?

FATHER. Dope? Junkey? And you paid for it?

(*The kitchen door opens and* CELIA *enters.*)

CELIA. Johnny—Johnny—Where's Johnny?

POLO. He's not here. We looked all over, we couldn't find him. Isn't that right, Pop?

CELIA. I don't know who his friends are, Polo. You'd know that. There were two men here last night. What were their names?

FATHER. I don't know. One of them had on glasses.

POLO. Are you all right?

CELIA. I won't be all right until I see Johnny.

FATHER. He knows where he is . . .

POLO. What did the doctor say?

CELIA. My baby is all right.

POLO. This isn't the place to be. All you have to do is get out of here for a few—

CELIA. I live here and I'm staying here. I'm all right and I won't scream or cry, but are you all right, Polo? Are you?

POLO. You're going to miss your plane, Pop.

FATHER. I told you before, planes fly every day.

CELIA. Where is my husband?

POLO. He's waiting for me. He asked me to keep you and the old man away from him. Don't push me. He'd die of shame if you saw him now, and you'd get sick. I'll be running out in the street looking for a taxi again. I tell you, I know what I'm doing.

CELIA. You don't know what you're doing and don't know what you've done, Polo. I just keep thinking that you hate him—that you hate your brother!

POLO. You know I love him . . .

CELIA. You just don't love. When you love you have to be responsible to what you love.

POLO. He'll help himself—he wants to quit.

CELIA. He'll never do it by himself and you *know* that.

POLO. I don't know that.

CELIA. Polo, don't turn your back, you can look at me. I know you meant well, and that you mean well now, but I talked to my doctor, Polo, there is little any of us can do . . . There is little that all the doctors in the world can do right now but try to help him, and you *know* that. There's a slight chance . . . only a slight one—and don't tell me that you've been feeding him money all this time and that you don't know. You're afraid to admit that. . . .

POLO. Don't you see, as long as he gets it, he's all right. You'd never know he was any different.

CELIA. Polo! You're not two little kids huddled in a dark room any more. I should be angry at you, but I'm not.

POLO. I'm not afraid of anything . . . and I didn't do any wrong. When you have your baby—and if you can imagine for one minute your child writhing in *pain*—and all you have to do is reach out and hand—

CELIA. I'd reach out and stop its crying . . . I'd give it anything it needed but I wouldn't stop there, I'd try to find out what caused the pain—I love your brother Johnny, I have faith in that love. He is a perfect human being, and I'm proud of him, not ashamed of him, and I don't pity him, and I'm not afraid of him . . . and the more I see you now, the more I realize that your love is irresponsible. Now you tell me where he is, Polo, or I'll call the police and have them find him . . .

FATHER. You'd call the police, you're so proud of him . . .

CELIA. I'm not a member of your vacuum age, Mr. Pope. And I'm sorry I cannot regard you as his father at this moment; unfortunately you are just another man . . .

FATHER. No. No police. We'll get a doctor . . .

CELIA. They'd only have to call the police. Isn't that right, Polo?

FATHER. But we can take care of him together. I don't have to go back to Palm Beach, I can get a good job up here. We can all take care of him together. You don't have to call the police . . .

CELIA. There's a place in Kentucky that takes care of people like Johnny.

FATHER. What people like Johnny? Who do you think you're talking about? There's nothing wrong with him! What the hell—people drink, don't they? So he takes a little something once in a while, what are you running to the police for . . . ?

JOHNNY (*off*). Polo! (*Comes in.*) Get them out of here, get them out of here. I don't want them to see me like this.

FATHER. Johnny . . .

JOHNNY. Pop. Watch over me—watch over me. Don't let them come near me again. Don't let me go, willya, Pop.

FATHER. For crissakes, Polo, he's dying. He's freezing—what do we do?

POLO. Hold on, for the love of God, hold on. We're all here . . .

FATHER. Easy, Johnny, easy . . . Polo, what do I do?

POLO. Rock him—rock him like a baby in your arms. Hold him, hold him tight and never let him go. Rock him, you rock him, Pop, I rocked him long enough, you watch over him!

JOHNNY. Celia, Celia, Celia. I didn't want you to see this. I didn't want anybody to see this.

CELIA. Well, we've seen it, Johnny, and we can't just make believe we didn't, can we?

JOHNNY. Pop, I'm sorry about all that . . . all that—you know. Next time I open my mouth . . . you just haul off and give me a belt.

FATHER. Okay, kid.

JOHNNY. Pop, will you please go; I want to be alone with my wife.

FATHER. Yeh—You want to walk me over to the hotel, Polo?

POLO. Yeh, come on . . . (POLO *starts to leave.*)

FATHER. Good night, honey . . . (*Goes out.*)

CELIA. Good night, Pop. Come over for breakfast, please.

POLO (*from the doorway*). You'll be all right, Johnny. (*He leaves with* FATHER.)

JOHNNY. Hey—Pop—hey—if you drop your hat crossing the—Celia, I'm sorry, you don't know how sorry I am . . .

CELIA. I don't care how sorry you are, Johnny. I want to call the police and I want you to go into a hospital. I'm going to call them, no matter what you say, darling. We can't live like this, can we? You can live or die . . .

JOHNNY. I'm all right. It's so unbelievable. To know everything that's right. Thou shalt not kill or walk on the grass; I've been taught everything good . . . Make the phone call . . .

CELIA. Give me the police . . . I'd like to report a drug addict. My husband. Yes, he's here now. Would you send over whoever you send in a case like this—and try to hurry, please. Thank you. Mrs. Celia Pope, 967 Rivington Street . . . fourth flight up. And would you hurry, please . . . Thank you.

CURTAIN

PICNIC

William Inge

First presented by The Theatre Guild and Joshua Logan
at the Music Box Theatre, New York City,
on February 19, 1953, with the following cast:

HELEN POTTS   Ruth McDevitt

HAL CARTER   Ralph Meeker

MILLIE OWENS   Kim Stanley

BOMBER   Morris Miller

MADGE OWENS   Janice Rule

FLO OWENS   Peggy Conklin

ROSEMARY SYDNEY   Eileen Heckart

ALAN SEYMOUR   Paul Newman

IRMA KRONKITE   Reta Shaw

CHRISTINE SCHOENWALDER   Elizabeth Wilson

HOWARD BEVANS   Arthur O'Connell

The action of the play takes place in a small Kansas town in the yard shared by Flo Owens and Helen Potts.

ACT ONE. Early morning, Labor Day.

ACT TWO. Late the same afternoon.

ACT THREE. SCENE I: Very early the following morning. SCENE II: A few hours later.

INTRODUCTION

Picnic was William Inge's second play to reach Broadway, the first having been his deeply moving *Come Back, Little Sheba** in which Shirley Booth and Sidney Blackmer gave memorable performances. Born in Independence, Kansas, in 1913, he had come to playwriting *via* an academic and journalistic career which failed to afford him the opportunities for self-expression he needed. He taught at Stephens College in Columbia, Missouri, for a time, as a colleague of the celebrated actress Maude Adams in her years of retirement from the stage, and he later gave a playwriting course at Washington University, St. Louis, while holding the position of drama, film, and music critic on the St. Louis *Star-Times*. The late Margo Jones produced at her little Dallas Theatre his first work, *Farther Off from Heaven,* a play that already revealed the direction of his talents. *Come Back, Little Sheba,* a drama well summarized by Mr. Inge when he quoted Thoreau's remark that "the mass of men lead lives of quiet desperation," was produced by the Theatre Guild in association with the late Phyllis Anderson, who was one of the first persons on Broadway to evince interest in him. And it was the success of this production that smoothed his way to the much greater popular success of *Picnic,* for which he had the support of Joshua Logan's directorial powers.

Picnic, originally titled *Front Porch,* owed its essential quality to the author's concern with the conflict between character and environment, the one variously vulnerable and the other extremely oppressive, and all the more so for not being malign and so failing to inspire the excitement of rebellion. As the author told us in the April, 1953, issue of *Theatre Arts* magazine, the first draft began, characteristically for him, "with a scene of women sitting on a front porch at the close of a summer day." *Picnic* is a pathetic pastoral from the start. It constitutes "lyric realism in the sound 1920 tradition of the prairie novelists," as Harold Clurman put it. "Everything Mr. Inge's characters participate in is small and isolated," commented Brooks Atkinson. But it was generally conceded that these little people had large claims upon the author's sympathies.

It would be interesting to be able to supply the pre-Broadway original ending of *Picnic,* since there has been some question as to the value of the conclusion in the Broadway version. Unfortunately, the first ending is still in a state of revision at this time. A conscientious artist, Mr. Inge is still making revisions in a play that won the Pulitzer Prize and other awards, that had a long run in the professional theatre, and that was also filmed successfully. Originally, the young heroine did not follow her lover, a roving Peer Gynt character, when he left town, and the stalemate of small-town life was not broken.

* See *Best American Plays: Third Series.*

ACT ONE

The action of the play is laid on the porches and in the yards of two small houses that sit close beside each other in a small Kansas town. The house at the right belongs to MRS. FLORA OWENS, *a widow lady of about forty who lives there with her two young daughters,* MADGE *and* MILLIE. *The audience sees only a section of the house, from the doorstep and the front door extending to the back door, a porch lining all of the house that we see.*

The house at the left is inhabited by MRS. HELEN POTTS, *another but older widow lady who lives with her aged and invalid mother. Just the back of her house is visible, with steps leading up to the back door. Down farther is a woodshed, attached to the house by the roof. The space between woodshed and house forms a narrow passageway leading to the rest of* MRS. POTTS' *property. The yard between the houses is used interchangeably by members of both houses for visiting and relaxation.*

Both houses are humble dwellings built with no other pretension than to provide comfortable shelter for their occupants. The ladies cannot always afford to keep their houses painted, but they work hard to maintain a tidy appearance, keeping the yards clean, watching the flower beds, supplying colorful slip covers for the porch furniture.

Behind the houses is a stretch of picket fence with a gateway leading from the sidewalk into the yard between the houses. Beyond the fence, in the distance, is the panorama of a typical small Midwestern town, including a grain elevator, a railway station, a great silo and a church steeple, all blessed from above by a high sky of innocent blue.

The curtain rises on an empty, sunlit stage. It is early morning in late summer, Labor Day, and autumn has just begun to edge the green landscape with a rim of brown. Dew is still on the landscape and mist rises from the earth in the distance. MRS. POTTS *appears on her back porch, at left. She is a merry, dumpy little woman close to sixty. She comes down the steps and stands before the woodshed, waiting for* HAL CARTER *to follow.* HAL *comes out carrying a basket of trash on his shoulder, an exceedingly handsome, husky youth dressed in T-shirt, dungarees and cowboy boots. In a past era he would have been called a vagabond, but* HAL *today is usually referred to as a bum.* MRS. POTTS *speaks to him.*

———

MRS. POTTS. You just had a big breakfast. Wouldn't you like to rest a while before you go to work?

HAL (*managing to sound cheerful*). Work's good for my digestion, Mam.

MRS. POTTS. Now, stop being embarrassed because you asked for breakfast.

HAL. I never did it before.

MRS. POTTS. What's the difference? We all have misfortune part of the time.

HAL. Seems to me, Mam, like I have it lots of the time.

(*Then they laugh together.* MRS. POTTS *leads him off through the passageway. In a moment,* MILLIE OWENS *bursts out of the kitchen door of the house, right. She is a wiry kid of sixteen, boisterous and assertive, but likeable when one begins to understand that she is trying to disguise her basic shyness. Her secret habit is to come outside after breakfast and enjoy her morning cigarette where her mother will not see her. She is just lighting up when* BOMBER, *the newsboy, appears at the back gate and slings a paper noisily against the house. This gives* MILLIE *a chance to assail him.*)

MILLIE. Hey, Crazy, wanta knock the house down?

BOMBER (*a tough kid about* MILLIE'S *age*). I don't hear you.

MILLIE. If you ever break a window, you'll hear me.

BOMBER. Go back to bed.

MILLIE. Go blow your nose.

BOMBER (*with a look at the upper window of the house which presumably marks* MADGE'S *room*). Go back to bed and tell your pretty sister to come out. It's no fun lookin' at you. (MILLIE *ignores him.* BOMBER *doesn't intend to let her.*) I'm talking to *you*, Goonface!

MILLIE (*jumping to her feet and tearing into* BOMBER *with flying fists*). You take that back, you ornery bastard. You take that back.

BOMBER (*laughing, easily warding off her blows*). Listen to Goonface! She cusses just like a man.

MILLIE (*goes after him with doubled fists*). I'll kill you, you ornery bastard! I'll kill you!

BOMBER (*dodging her fists*). Lookit Mrs. Tar-zan! Lookit Mrs. Tar-zan!

(MADGE *comes out of the back door. She is an unusually beautiful girl of eighteen, who seems to take her beauty very much for granted. She wears sandals and a simple wash dress. She has just shampooed her hair and is now scrubbing her head with a towel.*)

MADGE. Who's making so much noise?

BOMBER (*with a shy grin*). Hi, Madge!

MADGE. Hi, Bomber.

BOMBER. I hope I didn't wake you, Madge, or bother you or anything.

MADGE. Nothing bothers me.

BOMBER (*warming up*). Hey, Madge, a bunch of us guys are chippin' in on a hot-rod—radio and everything. I get it every Friday night.

MADGE. I'm not one of those girls that jump in a hot-rod every time you boys turn a corner and honk. If a boy wants a date with me, he can come to the door like a gentleman and ask if I'm in.

MILLIE. Alan Seymour sends her flowers every time they go out.

BOMBER (*to* MADGE). I can't send you flowers, Baby—but I can *send* you!

MILLIE. Listen to him braggin'.

BOMBER (*persisting*). Lemme pick you up some night after Seymour brings you home.

MADGE (*a trifle haughty*). That wouldn't be fair to Alan. We go steady.

MILLIE. Don't you know what "steady" means, stupid?

BOMBER. I seen you riding around in his Cadillac like you was a duchess. Why do good-looking girls have to be so stuck on themselves?

MADGE (*jumps up, furious*). I'm not stuck on myself! You take that back, Bomber Gutzel!

BOMBER (*still persisting*). Lemme pick you up some night! Please! (MADGE *walks away to evade him but* BOMBER *is close behind her.*) We'll get some cans of beer and go down to the river road and listen to music on the radio.

(HAL CARTER *has come on from right and put a rake in the woodshed. He observes the scene between* MADGE *and* BOMBER.)

MILLIE (*laughing at* BOMBER). Wouldn't that be romantic!

BOMBER (*grabbing* MADGE's *arm*). C'mon, Madge give a guy a break!

HAL (*to* BOMBER). On your way, lover boy!

BOMBER (*turning*). Who're *you*?

HAL. What's that matter? I'm bigger'n you are.

(BOMBER *looks at* HAL, *feels a little inadequate, and starts off.*)

MILLIE (*calling after* BOMBER). Go peddle your papers! (*Gives* BOMBER *a raspberry as he disappears with papers.*)

HAL (*to* MILLIE). Got a smoke, kid? (MILLIE *gives* HAL *a cigarette, wondering who he is.*) Thanks, kid.

MILLIE. You workin' for Mrs. Potts?

HAL. Doin' a few jobs in the yard.

MILLIE. She give you breakfast?

HAL (*embarrassed about it*). Yah.

MADGE. Millie! Mind your business.

HAL (*turning to* MADGE, *his face lighting*). Hi.

MADGE. Hi.

(MADGE *and* HAL *stand looking at each other, awkward and self-conscious.* FLO, *the mother, comes out almost immediately, as though she had sensed* HAL's *presence.* FLO *carries a sewing basket in one arm and a party dress over the other. She is a rather impatient little woman who has worked hard for ten years or more to serve as both father and mother to her girls. One must feel that underneath a certain hardness in her character there is a deep love and concern for the girls. She regards* HAL *suspiciously.*)

FLO. Young man, this is *my* house. Is there something you want?

HAL. Just loafin', Mam.

FLO. This is a busy day for us. We have no time to loaf.

(*There is a quick glance between* HAL *and* FLO, *as though each sized up the other as a potential threat.*)

HAL. You the mother?

FLO. Yes. You better run along now.

HAL. Like you say, Lady. It's your house. (*With a shrug of the shoulders, he saunters off stage.*)

FLO. Has Helen Potts taken in another tramp?

MADGE. I don't see why he's a tramp just because Mrs. Potts gave him breakfast.

FLO. I'm going to speak to her about the way she takes in every Tom, Dick and Harry!

MADGE. He wasn't doing any harm.

FLO. I bet he'd like to. (*Sits on the porch and begins sewing on party dress. To*

MADGE) Have you called Alan this morning?

MADGE. I haven't had time.

MILLIE. He's coming by pretty soon to take us swimming.

FLO (*to* MADGE). Tell him they're expecting a big crowd at the park this evening, so he'd better use his father's influence at the City Hall to reserve a table. Oh, and tell him to get one down by the river, close to a Dutch oven.

MADGE. He'll think I'm being bossy.

FLO. Alan is the kind of man who doesn't mind if a woman's bossy.

(*A train whistle in the distance.* MADGE *listens.*)

MADGE. Whenever I hear that train coming to town, I always get a little feeling of excitement—in here. (*Hugging her stomach.*)

MILLIE. Whenever I hear it, I tell myself I'm going to get on it some day and go to New York.

FLO. That train just goes as far as Tulsa.

MILLIE. In Tulsa I could catch another train.

MADGE. I always wonder, maybe some wonderful person is getting off here, just by accident, and he'll come into the dime store for something and see me behind the counter, and he'll study me very strangely and then decide I'm just the person they're looking for in Washington for an important job in the Espionage Department. (*She is carried away.*) Or maybe he wants me for some great medical experiment that'll save the whole human race.

FLO. Things like that don't happen in dime stores. (*Changing the subject*) Millie, would you take the milk inside?

MILLIE (*as she exits into kitchen with milk*). Awwww.

FLO (*after a moment*). Did you and Alan have a good time on your date last night?

MADGE. Uh-huh.

FLO. What'd you do?

MADGE. We went over to his house and he played some of his classical records.

FLO (*after a pause*). Then what'd you do?

MADGE. Drove over to Cherryvale and had some barbecue.

FLO (*a hard question to ask*). Madge, does Alan ever—make love?

MADGE. When we drive over to Cherryvale we always park the car by the river and get real romantic.

FLO. Do you let him kiss you? After all, you've been going together all summer.

MADGE. Of course I let him.

FLO. Does he ever want to go beyond kissing?

MADGE (*embarrassed*). Mom!

FLO. I'm your mother, for heaven's sake! These things have to be talked about. Does he?

MADGE. Well—yes.

FLO. Does Alan get mad if you—won't?

MADGE. No.

FLO (*to herself, puzzled*). He doesn't . . .

MADGE. Alan's not like *most* boys. He doesn't wanta do anything he'd be sorry for.

FLO. Do *you* like it when he kisses you?

MADGE. Yes.

FLO. You don't sound very enthusiastic.

MADGE. What do you expect me to do—pass out every time Alan puts his arm around me?

FLO. No, you don't have to pass out. (*Gives* MADGE *the dress she has been sewing on.*) Here. Hold this dress up in front of you. (*She continues.*) It'd be awfully nice to be married to Alan. You'd live in comfort the rest of your life, with charge accounts at all the stores, automobiles and trips. You'd be invited by all his friends to parties in their homes and at the Country Club.

MADGE (*a confession*). Mom, I don't feel right with those people.

FLO. Why not? You're as good as they are.

MADGE. I know, Mom, but all of Alan's friends talk about college and trips to Europe. I feel left out.

FLO. You'll get over those feelings in time. Alan will be going back to school in a few weeks. You better get busy.

MADGE. Busy what?

FLO. A pretty girl doesn't have long—just a few years. Then she's the equal of kings and she can walk out of a shanty like this and live in a palace with a doting husband who'll spend his life making her happy.

MADGE (*to herself*). I know.

FLO. Because once, *once* she was young and pretty. If she loses her chance then, she might as well throw all her prettiness away. (*Giving* MADGE *the dress.*)

MADGE (*holding the dress before her as*

FLO *checks length*). I'm only eighteen.

FLO. And next summer you'll be nineteen, and then twenty and then twentyone, and then the years'll start going by so fast you'll lose count of them. First thing you know, you'll be forty, still selling candy at the dime store.

MADGE. You don't have to get morbid.

MILLIE (*comes out with sketch book, sees* MADGE *holding dress before her*). Everyone around here gets to dress up and go places except me.

MADGE. Alan said he'd try to find you a date for the picnic tonight.

MILLIE. I don't want Alan asking any of these crazy boys in town to take me anywhere.

MADGE. Beggars can't be choosers!

MILLIE. You shut up.

FLO. Madge, that was mean. There'll be dancing at the pavilion tonight. Millie should have a date, too.

MADGE. If she wants a date, why doesn't she dress up and act decent?

MILLIE. Cause I'm gonna dress and act the way I want to, and if you don't like it you know what you can do!

MADGE. Always complaining because she doesn't have any friends, but she smells so bad people don't want to be near her!

FLO. Girls, don't fight.

MILLIE (*ignoring* FLO). La-de-da! Madge is the pretty one—but she's so dumb they almost had to burn the schoolhouse down to get *her* out of it! (*She mimics* MADGE.)

MADGE. That's not so!

MILLIE. Oh, isn't it? You never would have graduated if it hadn't been for Jumpin' Jeeter.

FLO (*trying at least to keep up with the scrap*). Who's Jumpin' Jeeter?

MILLIE. Teaches history. Kids call him Jumpin' Jeeter cause he's so *jumpy* with all the pretty girls in his classes. He was flunking Madge till she went in his room and cried, and said . . . (*Resorting again to mimicry*) "I just don't know what I'll do if I don't pass history!"

MADGE. Mom, she's making that up.

MILLIE. Like fun I am! You couldn't even pass Miss Sydney's course in shorthand and you have to work in the dime store!

MADGE (*the girls know each other's most sensitive spots*). You *are* a goon!

FLO (*giving up*). Oh, girls!

MILLIE (*furious*). Madge, you slut! You take that back or I'll kill you! (*She goes after* MADGE, *who screams and runs on the porch*.)

FLO. Girls! What will the neighbors say!

(MILLIE *gets hold of* MADGE's *hair and yanks.* FLO *has to intercede.*)

MILLIE. No one can call me goon and get by with it!

FLO. You called her worse names!

MILLIE. It doesn't hurt what names I call her! She's pretty, so names don't bother her at all! She's pretty, so nothing else matters. (*She storms inside.*)

FLO. Poor Millie!

MADGE (*raging at the injustice*). All I ever hear is "poor Millie," and poor Millie won herself a scholarship for four whole years of college!

FLO. A girl like Millie can need confidence in other ways.

(*This quiets* MADGE. *There is silence.*)

MADGE (*subdued*). Mom, do you love Millie more than me?

FLO. Of course not!

MADGE. Sometimes you act like you did.

FLO (*with warmth, trying to effect an understanding*). You were the first born. Your father thought the sun rose and set in you. He used to carry you on his shoulder for all the neighborhood to see. But things were different when Millie came.

MADGE. How?

FLO (*with misgivings*). They were just —different. Your father wasn't home much. The night Millie was born he was with a bunch of his wild friends at the road house.

MADGE. I loved Dad.

FLO (*a little bitterly*). Oh, everyone loved your father.

MADGE. Did you?

FLO (*after a long pause of summing up*). Some women are humiliated to love a man.

MADGE. Why?

FLO (*thinking as she speaks*). Because— a woman is weak to begin with, I suppose, and sometimes—her love for him makes her feel—almost helpless. And maybe she fights him—'cause her love makes her seem so dependent.

(*There is another pause.* MADGE *ruminates.*)

MADGE. Mom, what good is it to be pretty?

FLO. What a question!

MADGE. I mean it.

FLO. Well—pretty things are rare in this life.

MADGE. But what good are they?

FLO. Well—pretty things—like flowers and sunsets and rubies—and pretty girls, too—they're like billboards telling us life is good.

MADGE. But where do *I* come in?

FLO. What do you mean?

MADGE. Maybe I get tired being looked at.

FLO. Madge!

MADGE. Well, maybe I do!

FLO. Don't talk so selfish!

MADGE. I don't care if I *am* selfish. It's no good just being pretty. It's no good!

HAL (*comes running on from passageway*). Mam, is it all right if I start a fire?

FLO (*jumps to see* HAL). What?

HAL. The nice lady, she said it's a hot enough day already and maybe you'd object.

FLO (*matter-of-factly*). I guess we can stand it.

HAL. Thank you, Mam.

(HAL *runs off.*)

FLO (*looking after him*). He just moves right in whether you want him to or not!

MADGE. I knew you wouldn't like him when I first saw him.

FLO. Do *you?*

MADGE. I don't like him or dislike him. I just wonder what he's like.

(ROSEMARY SYDNEY *makes a sudden, somewhat cavalier entrance out of the front door. She is a roomer, probably as old as* FLO *but would never admit it. Her hair is plastered to her head with wave-set and she wears a flowered kimono.*)

ROSEMARY. Anyone mind if an old-maid schoolteacher joins their company?

FLO. Sit down, Rosemary.

ROSEMARY. Mail come yet?

FLO. No mail today. It's Labor Day.

ROSEMARY. I forgot. I thought I might be gettin' a letter from that man I met at the high-school picnic last spring. (*A bawdy laugh*) Been wantin' to marry me ever since. A nice fellow and a peck of fun, but I don't have time for any of 'em when they start gettin' serious on me.

FLO. You schoolteachers are mighty independent!

(MILLIE *wanders out of kitchen, reading a book.*)

ROSEMARY. Shoot! I lived this long without a man. I don't see what's to keep me from getting *on* without one.

FLO. What about Howard?

ROSEMARY. Howard's just a friend-boy —not a boy friend. (MADGE *and* MILLIE *giggle at this.* ROSEMARY *sniffs the air.*) I smell smoke.

FLO. Helen Potts is having her leaves burned. Smells kind of good, doesn't it?

ROSEMARY (*seeing* HAL *off stage*). Who's the young man?

FLO. Just another no-good Helen Potts took in.

ROSEMARY (*very concerned*). Mrs. Owens, he's working over there with his shirt off. I don't think that's right in the presence of ladies.

FLO (*as* MILLIE *runs to look*). Get away from there, Millie!

MILLIE (*returning to doorstep*). Gee whiz! I go swimming every day and the boys don't have on half as much as he does now.

FLO. Swimming's different!

MILLIE. Madge, can I use your manicure set, just for kicks?

MADGE. If you promise not to get it messy.

(MILLIE *picks up the set and begins to experiment.*)

FLO (*looking off at* HAL). Look at him showing off!

ROSEMARY (*turning away with propriety*). Who does he think is interested? (*She continues to massage her face.*)

FLO (*to* ROSEMARY). What's that you're rubbing in?

ROSEMARY. Ponsella Three-Way Tissue Cream. Makes a good base for your make-up.

FLO. There was an article in *The Reader's Digest* about some woman who got skin poisoning from using all those face creams.

ROSEMARY. Harriett Bristol—she's the American history teacher—she got ahold of some of that beauty clay last winter and it darn near took her skin off. All we girls thought she had leprosy! (*She manages one more glance back at* HAL.)

MILLIE (*laboring over her manicure*). Madge, how do you do your right hand?

MADGE. If you were nicer to people, maybe people would do something nice for *you* some time.

ROSEMARY. You got a beau, Millie?

MILLIE. No!

ROSEMARY. You can't kid me! Girls don't paint their fingernails unless they think some boy is gonna take notice.

FLO. Madge, will you try this dress on now, dear? (MADGE *goes inside with her dress.*)

MRS. POTTS (*appears on her back porch, carrying a bundle of wet laundry*). Flo!

FLO (*calling back, a noise like an owl*). Hoooo!

MRS. POTTS. Are you going to be using the clothesline this morning?

FLO. I don't think so.

MRS. POTTS' MOTHER (*an aged and quivering voice that still retains its command, issuing from the upper window of the house, left*). Helen! Helen!

MRS. POTTS (*calling back*). I'm hanging out the clothes, Mama. I'll be right back. (*She goes busily off stage through the passageway.*)

FLO (*confidentially to* ROSEMARY). Poor Helen! She told me sometimes she has to get up *three* times a night to take her mother to the bathroom.

ROSEMARY. Why doesn't she put her in an old ladies' home?

FLO. None of 'em will take her. She's too mean.

ROSEMARY. She must be mean—if that story is true.

FLO. It *is* true! Helen and the Potts boy ran off and got married. Helen's mother caught her that very day and had the marriage annulled!

ROSEMARY (*with a shaking of her head*). She's Mrs. Potts in name only.

FLO. Sometimes I think she keeps the boy's name just to defy the old lady.

(ALAN's *car is heard approaching. It stops and the car door slams.*)

MILLIE (*putting down her book*). Hi, Alan! (*Jumps up, starts inside.*) Oh, boy! I'm gonna get my suit!

FLO (*calling after* MILLIE). See if Madge is decent. (ALAN *comes on downstage, right.*) Good morning, Alan!

ALAN. Morning, Mrs. Owens . . . Miss Sydney.

(ROSEMARY *doesn't bother to speak, usually affecting indifference to men.*)

MRS. POTTS (*coming back on from the passageway*). Have you girls seen the handsome young man I've got working for me?

ROSEMARY. I think it's a disgrace, his parading around, naked as an Indian.

MRS. POTTS (*protectingly*). I *told* him to take his shirt off.

FLO. Helen Potts, I wish you'd stop taking in all sorts of riffraff!

MRS. POTTS. He isn't riffraff. He's been to several colleges.

FLO. College—and he begs for breakfast!

MRS. POTTS. He's working for his breakfast! Alan, he said he knew you at the university.

ALAN (*with no idea whom she's talking about*). Who?

MILLIE (*coming out the front door*). We going swimming, Alan?

ALAN. You bet.

FLO. Alan, why don't you go up and see Madge? Just call from the bottom of the stairs.

ALAN (*goes inside, calling*). Hey, Delilah!

FLO (*seeing that* MILLIE *is about to follow* ALAN *inside*). Millie!

(MILLIE *gets the idea that* MADGE *and* ALAN *are to be left alone. She sulks.*)

ROSEMARY (*to* FLO, *confidentially*). Do you think Alan's going to marry Madge?

FLO (*she's usually a very truthful woman*). I hadn't thought much about it.

MRS. POTTS (*after a moment, drying her neck with handkerchief*). It's so hot and still this time of year. When it gets this way I'd welcome a good strong wind.

FLO. I'd rather wipe my brow than get blown away.

MRS. POTTS (*looking off at* HAL, *full of admiration*). Look at him lift that big old washtub like it was so much tissue paper!

MRS. POTTS' MOTHER (*off stage, again*). Helen! Helen!

MRS. POTTS (*patient but firm*). I'm visiting Flo, Mama. You're all right. You don't need me.

FLO. What did you feed him?

MRS. POTTS. Biscuits.

FLO. You went to all that trouble?

MRS. POTTS. He was *so* hungry. I gave him ham and eggs and all the hot coffee he could drink. Then he saw a piece of cherry pie in the icebox and he wanted that, too!

ROSEMARY (*laughs bawdily*). Sounds to me like Mrs. Potts had herself a new boy friend!

MRS. POTTS (*rising, feeling injured*). I don't think that's very funny.

FLO. Helen, come on. Sit down.

ROSEMARY. Shoot, Mrs. Potts, I'm just a tease.

FLO. Sit down, Helen.

MRS. POTTS (*still touchy*). I *could* sit on my own porch, but I hate for the neighbors to see me there all alone.

(MADGE *and* ALAN *come out together,* MADGE *in her new dress. They march out hand in hand in a mock ceremony as though they were marching down the aisle.*)

ROSEMARY (*consolingly*). Mrs. Potts, if I said anything to offend you . . .

FLO (*signals* ROSEMARY *to be quiet, points to* MADGE *and* ALAN). Bride and groom! Look, everybody! Bride and groom! (*To* MADGE.) How does it feel, Madge? (*Laughs at her unconscious joke.*) I mean the dress.

MADGE (*crossing to her mother*). I love it, Mom, except it's a little tight in places.

MRS. POTTS (*all eyes of admiration*). Isn't Madge the pretty one!

ALAN (*turning to* MILLIE). What are you reading, Millie?

MILLIE. *The Ballad of the Sad Café* by Carson McCullers. It's wonderful!

ROSEMARY (*shocked*). Good Lord, Mrs. Owens, you let your daughter read filthy books like that?

FLO. Filthy?

ROSEMARY. Everyone in it is some sort of degenerate!

MILLIE. That's not so!

ROSEMARY. The D.A.R.'s had it banned from the public library.

MRS. POTTS (*eliminating herself from the argument*). I don't read much.

FLO. Millie, give me that book!

MILLIE (*tenaciously*). No!

ALAN. Mrs. Owens, I don't wanta interfere, but that book is on the reading list at college. For the course in the modern novel.

FLO. Oh, dear! What's a person to believe?

(MILLIE *takes the book from* FLO. ALAN's *word about such matters is apparently final.*)

ROSEMARY. Well, those college professors don't have any morals!

(MILLIE *and* ALAN *shake hands.*)

FLO. Where Millie comes by her tastes, I'll never know.

MADGE (*as* FLO *inspects her dress*). Some of the pictures she has over her bed *scare* me.

MILLIE. Those pictures are by Picasso, and he's a great artist.

MADGE. A woman with seven eyes. Very pretty.

MILLIE (*delivering her ultimatum*). Pictures don't have to be *pretty*!

(*A sudden explosion from* MRS. POTTS' *backyard. The women are startled.*)

FLO. Helen!

MRS. POTTS (*jumping up, alarmed*). I'll go see what it is.

FLO. Stay here! He must have had a gun!

VOICE OFF STAGE. Helen! Helen!

FLO (*grabbing* MRS. POTTS' *arm*). Don't go over there, Helen! Your mother's old. She has to go so soon anyway!

MRS. POTTS (*running off stage*). Pshaw! I'm not afraid.

ALAN (*looking off at* HAL). Who did that guy say he was?

(*No one hears* ALAN.)

MRS. POTTS (*coming back and facing* FLO). I was a bad girl.

FLO. What *is* it, Helen?

MRS. POTTS. I threw the *new* bottle of cleaning fluid into the trash.

FLO. You're the limit! Come on, Madge, let's finish that dress.

(FLO *and* MADGE *go into the house.* ROSEMARY *looks at her watch and then goes into the house also.*)

MRS. POTTS. Come help me, Millie. The young man ran into the clothesline.

(*She and* MILLIE *hurry off stage.* ALAN *stands alone, trying to identify* HAL *who comes on from* MRS. POTTS'. HAL *is barechested now, wearing his T-shirt wrapped about his neck.* ALAN *finally recognizes him and is overjoyed at seeing him.*)

ALAN. Where did *you* come from?

HAL (*loud and hearty*). Kid!

ALAN. Hal Carter!

HAL. I was comin' over to see you a little later.

ALAN (*recalling some intimate roughhouse greeting from their college days*). How's the old outboard motor?

HAL (*with the eagerness of starting a game*). Want a ride?

ALAN (*springing to* HAL, *clasping his legs around* HAL's *waist, hanging by one hand wrapped about* HAL's *neck, as though riding some sort of imagined machine*). Gassed up? (*With his fingers, he twists* HAL's *nose as if it were a starter.* HAL *makes the sputtering noise of an outboard motor and swings* ALAN *about the stage,* ALAN *holding on like a bronco-buster. They laugh uproariously together.*) Ahoy, brothers! Who's winkin', blinkin', and stinkin'? (ALAN *drops to the ground, both of them still laughing uproariously with the recall of carefree, college days.*)

HAL. That used to wake the whole damn fraternity!

ALAN. The last time I saw you, you were on your way to Hollywood to become a movie hero.

HAL (*with a shrug of his shoulder*). Oh, that!

ALAN. What do you mean, "Oh that"? Isn't that what I loaned you the hundred bucks for?

HAL. Sure, Seymour.

ALAN. Well, what happened?

HAL (*he'd rather the subject had not been brought up*). Things just didn't work out.

ALAN. I tried to warn you, Hal. Every year some talent scout promised screen tests to all the athletes.

HAL. Oh, I got the test okay! I was about to have a big career. They were gonna call me Brush Carter. How d'ya like that?

ALAN. Yeah?

HAL. Yah! They took a lotta pictures of me with my shirt off. Real rugged. Then they dressed me up like the Foreign Legion. Then they put me in a pair of tights —and they gave me a big hat with a plume, and had me makin' with the sword play. (*Pantomimes a duel.*) Touché, mug! (*Returning the sword to its scabbard.*) It was real crazy!

ALAN (*a little skeptical*). Did they give you any lines to read?

HAL. Yah, that part went okay. It was my teeth.

ALAN. Your teeth?

HAL. Yah! Out there, you gotta have a certain kind of teeth or they can't use you. Don't ask me why. This babe said they'd have to pull all my teeth and give me new ones, so naturally . . .

ALAN. Wait a minute. What babe?

HAL. The babe that got me the test. She wasn't a babe exactly. She was kinda beat up—but not bad. (*He sees* ALAN's *critical eye.*) Jesus, Seymour, a guy's gotta get along somehow.

ALAN. Uh-huh. What are you doing here?

HAL (*a little hurt*). Aren't you glad to see me?

ALAN. Sure, but fill me in.

HAL. Well—after I left Hollywood I took a job on a ranch in Nevada. You'da been proud of me, Seymour. In bed every night at ten, up every morning at six. No liquor—no babes. I saved up two hundred bucks!

ALAN (*holding out a hand*). Oh! I'll take half.

HAL. Gee, Seymour, I wish I had it, but I got rolled.

ALAN. Rolled? *You?*

HAL (*he looks to see that no one can overhear*). Yeah, I was gonna hitchhike to Texas to get in a big oil deal. I got as far as Phoenix when two babes pull up in this big yellow convertible. And one of these dames slams on the brakes and hollers, "Get in, stud!" So I got in. Seymour, it was crazy. They had a shakerful of martinis right there in the car!

MRS. POTTS (*appears on her porch, followed by* MILLIE. MRS. POTTS *carries a cake*). Oh, talking over old times? Millie helped me ice the cake.

HAL. Any more work, Mam?

MRS. POTTS. No. I feel I've been more than paid for the breakfast.

HAL. 'Spose there's any place I could wash up?

MILLIE. We got a shower in the basement. Come on, I'll show you.

ALAN (*holding* HAL). He'll be there in a minute. (MRS. POTTS *and* MILLIE *exit into the* OWENS *house.*) Okay, so they had a shakerful of martinis!

HAL. And one of these babes was smokin' the weed!

ALAN (*with vicarious excitement*). Nothing like that ever happens to me! Go on!

HAL. Seymour, you wouldn't believe it, the things those two babes started doin' to me.

ALAN. Were they good-looking?

HAL. What do you care?

ALAN. Makes the story more interesting. Tell me what happened.

HAL. Well, you know *me,* Seymour. I'm an agreeable guy.

ALAN. Sure.

HAL. So when they parked in front of this tourist cabin, I said, "Okay, girls, if I gotta pay for the ride, this is the easiest way I know." (*He shrugs.*) But, gee, they musta thought I was Superman.

ALAN. You mean—*both* of them?

HAL. Sure.

ALAN. Golly!

HAL. Then I said, "Okay, girls, the party's over—let's get goin'." Then this dame on the weed, she sticks a gun in my back. She says, "This party's goin' on till *we* say it's over, Buck!" You'da thought she was Humphrey Bogart!

ALAN. Then what happened?

HAL. Finally I passed out! And when I woke up, the dames was gone and so was my two hundred bucks! I went to the police and they wouldn't believe me—they said my whole story was wishful thinking! How d'ya like *that!*

ALAN (*thinking it over*). Mmmm.

HAL. Women are gettin' desperate, Seymour.

ALAN. *Are* they?

HAL. Well, that did it. Jesus, Seymour, what's a poor bastard like me ever gonna do?

ALAN. You don't sound like you had such a hard time.

HAL. I got thinking of you, Seymour, at school—how you always had things under control.

ALAN. Me?

HAL. Yah. Never cut classes—understood the lectures—took notes! (ALAN *laughs*.) What's so funny?

ALAN. The hero of the campus, and he envied me!

HAL. Yah! Big hero, between the goal posts. You're the only guy in the whole fraternity ever treated me like a human being.

ALAN (*with feeling for* HAL). I know.

HAL. Those other snob bastards always watchin' to see which fork I used.

ALAN. You've got an inferiority complex. You imagined those things.

HAL. In a pig's eye!

ALAN (*delicately*). What do you hear about your father?

HAL (*grave*). It finally happened . . . before I left for Hollywood.

ALAN. What?

HAL (*with a solemn hurt*). He went on his last bender. The police scraped him up off the sidewalk. He died in jail.

ALAN (*moved*). Gee, I'm sorry to hear that, Hal.

HAL. The old lady wouldn't even come across with the dough for the funeral. They had to bury him in Pauper's Row.

ALAN. What happened to the filling station?

HAL. He left it to me in his will, but the old lady was gonna have him declared insane so she could take over. I let her have it. Who cares?

ALAN (*rather depressed by* HAL's *story*). Gee, Hal, I just can't believe people really do things like that.

HAL. Don't let *my* stories cloud up your rosy glasses.

ALAN. Why didn't you come to see me, when you got to town?

HAL. I didn't want to walk into your palatial mansion lookin' like a bum. I wanted to get some breakfast in my belly and pick up a little change.

ALAN. That wouldn't have made any difference.

HAL. I was hoping maybe you and your old man, between you, might fix me up with a job.

ALAN. What kind of a job, Hal?

HAL. What kinda jobs you got?

ALAN. What kind of job did you have in mind?

HAL (*this is his favorite fantasy*). Oh, something in a nice office where I can wear a tie and have a sweet little secretary and talk over the telephone about enterprises and things. (*As* ALAN *walks away skeptically*) I've always had a feeling, if I just had the chance, I could set the world on fire.

ALAN. Lots of guys have that feeling, Hal.

HAL (*with some desperation*). I gotta get some place in this world, Seymour. I *got* to.

ALAN (*with a hand on* HAL's *shoulder*). Take it easy.

HAL. This is a free country, and I got just as much rights as the next fellow. Why can't I get along?

ALAN. Don't worry, Hal. I'll help you out as much as I can. (MRS. POTTS *comes out the* OWENS' *back door.*) Sinclair is hiring new men, aren't they, Mrs. Potts?

MRS. POTTS. Yes, Alan. Carey Hamilton needs a hundred new men for the pipeline.

HAL (*had dared to hope for more*). Pipeline?

ALAN. If you wanta be president of the company, Hal, I guess you'll just have to work hard and be patient.

HAL (*clenching his fists together, so eager is he for patience*). Yah. That's something I gotta learn. Patience! (*He hurries inside the* OWENS' *back door now.*)

MRS. POTTS. I feel sorry for young men today.

ROSEMARY (*coming out the front door, very proud of the new outfit she is wearing, a fall suit and an elaborate hat*). Is this a private party I'm crashin'?

MRS. POTTS (*with some awe of ROSEMARY's finery*). My, you're dressed up!

ROSEMARY. 'S my new fall outfit. Got it in Kansas City. Paid twenty-two-fifty for the hat.

MRS. POTTS. You schoolteachers do have nice things.

ROSEMARY. And don't have to ask anybody when we wanta get 'em, either.

FLO (*coming out back door with MADGE*). Be here for lunch today, Rosemary?

ROSEMARY. No. There's a welcome-home party down at the hotel. Lunch and bridge for the new girls on the faculty.

MADGE. Mom, can't I go swimming, too?

FLO. Who'll fix lunch? I've got a million things to do.

MADGE. It wouldn't kill Millie if she ever did any cooking.

FLO. No, but it might kill the rest of us. (*Now we hear the voices of IRMA KRONKITE and CHRISTINE SCHOENWALDER, who are coming by for ROSEMARY. They think it playful to call from a distance.*)

IRMA. Rosemary! Let's get going, girl. (*As they come into sight, IRMA turns to CHRISTINE.*) You'll love Rosemary Sydney. She's a peck of fun! Says the craziest things.

ROSEMARY (*with playful suspiciousness*). What're you saying about me, Irma Kronkite? (*They run to hug each other like eager sisters who had not met in a decade.*)

IRMA. Rosemary Sydney!

ROSEMARY. Irma Kronkite! How was your vacation?

IRMA. I worked like a slave. But I had fun, too. I don't care if I *never* get that Masters. I'm not going to be a slave *all* my life.

CHRISTINE (*shyly*). She's been telling me about all the wicked times she had in New York—and *not* at Teachers College, if I may add.

IRMA (*to ROSEMARY*). Kid, this is Christine Schoenwalder, taking Mabel Fremont's place in Feminine Hygiene. (*ROSEMARY and CHRISTINE shake hands.*) Been a hot summer, Mrs. Owens?

FLO. The worst I can remember.

MRS. POTTS (*as ROSEMARY brings CHRISTINE up on porch*). Delighted to know you, Christine. Welcome back, Irma.

IRMA. Are you working now, Madge?

MADGE. Yes.

FLO (*taking over for MADGE*). Yes, Madge has been working downtown this summer—just to keep busy. (*Now HAL and MILLIE burst out the kitchen door, engaged in a noisy and furious mock fistfight. HAL is still bare-chested, his T-shirt still around his neck, and the sight of him is something of a shock to the ladies.*) Why, when did he . . .

ALAN (*seizing HAL for an introduction*). Mrs. Owens, this is my friend, Hal Carter. Hal is a fraternity brother.

MRS. POTTS (*nudging FLO*). What did I tell you, Flo?

FLO (*stunned*). Fraternity brother! Really? (*Making the best of it.*) Any friend of Alan's is a friend of ours. (*She offers HAL her hand.*)

HAL. Glad to make your acquaintance, Mam.

ALAN (*embarrassed for him*). Hal, don't you have a shirt?

HAL. It's all sweaty, Seymour. (*ALAN nudges him. HAL realizes he has said the wrong thing and reluctantly puts on the T-shirt.*)

ROSEMARY (*collecting IRMA and CHRISTINE*). Girls, we better get a hustle on.

CHRISTINE (*to IRMA*). Tell them about what happened in New York, kid.

IRMA (*the center of attention*). I went to the Stork Club!

ROSEMARY. How did *you* get to the Stork Club?

IRMA. See, there was this fellow in my Educational Statistics class . . .

ROSEMARY (*continuing the joke*). I *knew* there was a *man* in it.

IRMA. Now, girl! It was nothing serious. He was just a good sport, that's all. We made a bet that the one who made the lowest grade on the *final* had to take the other to the Stork Club—and *I* lost! (*The teachers go off noisily laughing, as FLO and MRS. POTTS watch them.*)

ALAN (*calling to HAL, at back of stage playing with MILLIE*). Wanta go swimming, Hal? I've got extra trunks in the car.

HAL. Why not?

MRS. POTTS (*in a private voice*). Flo, let's ask the young man on the picnic.

He'd be a date for Millie.

FLO. That's right, but . . .

MRS. POTTS (*taking it upon herself*). Young man, Flo and I are having a picnic for the young people. You come, too, and be an escort for Millie.

HAL. Picnic?

MRS. POTTS. Yes.

HAL. I don't think it's right, me bargin' in this way.

MRS. POTTS. Nonsense. A picnic's no fun without lots and lots of young people.

ALAN (*bringing* HAL *down center*). Hal, I want you to meet Madge.

MADGE. Oh, we've met already. That is, we *saw* each other.

HAL. Yah, we saw each other.

ALAN (*to* MADGE). Hal sees every pretty girl.

MADGE (*pretending to protest*). Alan.

ALAN. Well, you're the prettiest girl in town, aren't you? (*To* HAL.) The Chamber of Commerce voted her Queen of Neewollah last year.

HAL. I don't dig.

MILLIE. She was Queen of Neewollah. Neewollah is Halloween spelled backwards.

MRS. POTTS (*joining in*). Every year they have a big coronation ceremony in Memorial Hall, with all kinds of artistic singing and dancing.

MILLIE. Madge had to sit through the whole ceremony till they put a crown on her head.

HAL (*impressed*). Yah?

MADGE. I got awfully tired.

MILLIE. The Kansas City *Star* ran color pictures in their Sunday magazine.

MADGE. Everyone expected me to get real conceited, but I didn't.

HAL. You didn't?

MILLIE. It'd be pretty hard to get conceited about *those* pictures.

MADGE (*humorously*). The color got blurred and my mouth was printed right in the middle of my forehead.

HAL (*sympathetic*). Gee, that's too bad.

MADGE (*philosophically*). Things like that are bound to happen.

MILLIE (*to* HAL). I'll race you to the car.

HAL (*starting off with* MILLIE). Isn't your sister goin' with us?

MILLIE. Madge has to cook lunch.

HAL. Do you mean *she cooks?*

MILLIE. Sure! Madge cooks and sews and does all those things that women do.

(*They race off,* MILLIE *getting a head start through the gate and* HAL *scaling the fence to get ahead of her.*)

FLO (*in a concerned voice*). Alan!

ALAN. Yes?

FLO. How did a boy like him get into college?

ALAN. On a football scholarship. He made a spectacular record in a little high school down in Arkansas.

FLO. But a fraternity! Don't those boys have a little more . . . breeding?

ALAN. I guess they're *supposed* to, but fraternities like to pledge big athletes—for the publicity. And Hal could have been All-American . . .

MRS. POTTS (*delighted*). All-American!

ALAN. . . . if he'd only studied.

FLO. But how did the other boys feel about him?

ALAN (*reluctantly*). They didn't like him, Mrs. Owens. They were pretty rough on him. Every time he came into a room, the other fellows seemed to *bristle.* I didn't like him either, at first. Then we shared a room and I got to know him better. Hal's really a nice guy. About the best friend I ever had.

FLO (*more to the point*). Is he wild?

ALAN. Oh—not really. He just . . .

FLO. Does he drink?

ALAN. A little. (*Trying to minimize*) Mrs. Owens, Hal pays attention to me. I'll see he behaves.

FLO. I wouldn't want anything to happen to Millie.

MADGE. Millie can take care of herself. You pamper her.

FLO. Maybe I do. Come on, Helen. (*As she and* MRS. POTTS *go in through the back door.*) Oh, dear, why can't things be simple?

ALAN (*after* FLO *and* MRS. POTTS *leave*). Madge, I'm sorry I have to go back to school this fall. It's Dad's idea.

MADGE. I thought it was.

ALAN. Really, Madge, Dad likes you very much. I'm sure he does. (*But* ALAN *himself doesn't sound convinced.*)

MADGE. Well—he's always very polite.

ALAN. I'll miss you, Madge.

MADGE. There'll be lots of pretty girls at college.

ALAN. Honestly, Madge, my entire four years I never found a girl I liked.

MADGE. I don't believe that.

ALAN. It's true. They're all so affected, if

you wanted a date with them you had to call them a month in advance.

MADGE. Really?

ALAN. Madge, it's hard to say, but I honestly never believed that a girl like you could care for me.

MADGE (*touched*). Alan . . .

ALAN. I—I hope you do care for me, Madge. (*He kisses her.*)

HAL (*comes back on stage somewhat apologetically. He is worried about something and tries to get* ALAN's *attention*). Hey, Seymour . . .

ALAN (*annoyed*). What's the matter, Hal? Can't you stand to see anyone else kiss a pretty girl?

HAL. What the hell, Seymour!

ALAN (*an excuse to be angry*). Hal, will you watch your language!

MADGE. Alan! It's all right.

HAL. I'm sorry. (*Beckons* ALAN *to him.*)

ALAN (*crossing to him*). What's the trouble?

(MADGE *walks away, sensing that* HAL *wants to talk privately.*)

HAL. Look, Seymour, I—I never been on a picnic.

ALAN. What're you talking about? Everybody's been on a picnic.

HAL. Not me. When I was a kid, I was too busy shooting craps or stealing milk bottles.

ALAN. Well, there's a first time for everything.

HAL. I wasn't brought up proper like *you*. I won't know how to act around all these *women*.

ALAN. Women aren't anything new in *your* life.

HAL. But these are—*nice* women. What if I say the wrong word or maybe my stomach growls? I feel *funny*.

ALAN. You're a psycho!

HAL. OK, but if I do anything wrong, you gotta try to overlook it. (*He runs off stage.* ALAN *laughs. Then* ALAN *returns to* MADGE.)

ALAN. We'll be by about five, Madge.

MADGE. OK.

ALAN (*beside her, tenderly*). Madge, after we have supper tonight maybe you and I can get away from the others and take a boat out on the river.

MADGE. All right, Alan.

ALAN. I want to see if you look *real* in the moonlight.

MADGE. Alan! Don't say that!

ALAN. Why? I don't care if you're real or not. You're the prettiest girl I ever saw.

MADGE. Just the same, I'm real. (*As* ALAN *starts to kiss her, the noise of an automobile horn is heard.*)

HAL (*hollering lustily from off stage*). Hey, Seymour—get the lead outa your pants!

(ALAN *goes off, irritated.* MADGE *watches them as they drive away. She waves to them.*)

FLO (*inside*). Madge! Come on inside now.

MADGE. All right, Mom.

(*As she starts in, there is a train whistle in the distance.* MADGE *hears it and stands listening.*)

CURTAIN

ACT TWO

It is late afternoon, the same day. The sun is beginning to set and fills the atmosphere with radiant orange. When the curtain goes up, MILLIE *is on the porch alone. She has permitted herself to "dress up" and wears a becoming, feminine dress in which she cannot help feeling a little strange. She is quite attractive. Piano music can be heard off stage, somewhere past* MRS. POTTS' *house, and* MILLIE *stands listening to it for a moment. Then she begins to sway to the music and in a moment is dancing, a strange, impromptu dance over the porch and yard. The music stops suddenly and* MILLIE's *mood is broken. She rushes upstage and calls off, left.*

MILLIE. Don't quit now, Ernie! (*She cannot hear* ERNIE's *reply.*) Huh? (MADGE *enters from kitchen.* MILLIE *turns to* MADGE.) Ernie's waiting for the rest of the band to practice. They're going to play out at the park tonight.

MADGE (*crossing to center and sitting on chair*). I don't know why you couldn't have helped us in the kitchen.

MILLIE (*lightly, giving her version of the sophisticated belle*). I had to dress for the ball.

MADGE. I had to make the potato salad and stuff the eggs and make three dozen bread-and-butter sandwiches.

MILLIE (*in a very affected accent*). I had to bathe—and dust my limbs with powder

—and slip into my frock . . .

MADGE. Did you clean out the bathtub?

MILLIE. Yes, I cleaned out the bathtub. (*She becomes very self-conscious.*) Madge, how do I look? Now tell me the truth.

MADGE. You look very pretty.

MILLIE. I feel sorta funny.

MADGE. You can have the dress if you want it.

MILLIE. Thanks. (*A pause.*) Madge, how do you talk to boys?

MADGE. Why, you just talk, silly.

MILLIE. How d'ya think of things to say?

MADGE. I don't know. You just say whatever comes into your head.

MILLIE. Supposing nothing ever comes into my head?

MADGE. You talked with him all right this morning.

MILLIE. But now I've got a *date* with him, and it's *different!*

MADGE. You're crazy.

MILLIE. I think he's a big show-off. You should have seen him this morning on the high diving board. He did real graceful swan dives, and a two and a half gainer, and a back flip—and kids stood around clapping. He just ate it up.

MADGE (*her mind elsewhere*). I think I'll paint my toenails tonight and wear sandals.

MILLIE. And he was braggin' all afternoon how he used to be a deep-sea diver off Catalina Island.

MADGE. Honest?

MILLIE. And he says he used to make hundreds of dollars doin' parachute jumps out of a balloon. Do you believe it?

MADGE. I don't see why not.

MILLIE. You never hear Alan bragging that way.

MADGE. Alan never jumped out of a balloon.

MILLIE. Madge, I think he's girl crazy.

MADGE. You think every boy you see is something horrible.

MILLIE. Alan took us into the Hi Ho for Cokes and there was a gang of girls in the back booth—Juanita Badger and her gang. (MADGE *groans at hearing this name.*) When they saw him, they started giggling and tee-heeing and saying all sorts of crazy things. Then Juanita Badger comes up to me and whispers, "He's the cutest thing I ever saw." Is he, Madge?

MADGE (*not willing to go overboard*). I certainly wouldn't say he was "the cutest thing I ever *saw.*"

MILLIE. Juanita Badger's an old floozy. She sits in the back row at the movie so the guys that come in will see her and sit with her. One time she and Rubberneck Krauss were asked by the management to leave—and they weren't just kissin', either.

MADGE (*proudly*). I never even speak to Juanita Badger.

MILLIE. Madge, do you think he'll like me?

MADGE. Why ask me all these questions? You're supposed to be the smart one.

MILLIE. I don't really care. I just wonder.

FLO (*coming out of kitchen*). Now I tell myself I've got two beautiful daughters.

MILLIE (*embarrassed*). Be quiet, Mom!

FLO. Doesn't Millie look pretty, Madge?

MADGE. When she isn't picking her nose.

FLO. Madge! (*To* MILLIE) She doesn't want anyone to be pretty but her.

MILLIE. You're just saying I'm pretty because you're my mom. People we love are always pretty, but people who're pretty to begin with, everybody loves *them.*

FLO. Run over and show Helen Potts how nice you look.

MILLIE (*in a wild parody of herself*). Here comes Millie Owens, the great beauty of all time! Be prepared to swoon when you see her! (*She climbs up over the side of* MRS. POTTS' *porch and disappears.*)

FLO (*sits on chair on porch*). Whatever possessed me to let Helen Potts ask that young hoodlum to take Millie on the picnic?

MADGE. Hal?

FLO. Yes, Hal, or whatever his name is. He left every towel in the bathroom black as dirt. He left the seat up, too.

MADGE. It's not going to hurt anyone just to be nice to him.

FLO. If there's any drinking tonight, you put a stop to it.

MADGE. I'm not going to be a wet blanket.

FLO. If the boys feel they have to have a few drinks, there's nothing you can do about it, but you can keep Millie from taking any.

MADGE. She wouldn't pay any attention to me.

FLO (*changing the subject*). You better be getting dressed. And don't spend the whole evening admiring yourself in the mirror.

MADGE. Mom, don't make fun of me.

FLO. You shouldn't object to being kidded if it's well meant.

MADGE. It seems like—when I'm looking in the mirror that's the only way I can prove to myself I'm alive.

FLO. Madge! You puzzle me.

(*The three schoolteachers come on, downstage right, making a rather tired return from their festivity. After their high-spirited exit in Act One, their present mood seems glum, as though they had expected from the homecoming some fulfillment that had not been realized.*)

IRMA. We've brought home your wayward girl, Mrs. Owens!

FLO (*turning from* MADGE). Hello, girls! Have a nice party?

IRMA. It wasn't a real party. Each girl paid for her own lunch. Then we played bridge all afternoon. (*Confidentially to* ROSEMARY) I get tired playing bridge.

FLO. Food's good at the hotel, isn't it?

IRMA. Not very. But they serve it to you nice, with honest-to-goodness napkins. Lord, I hate paper napkins!

CHRISTINE. I had a French-fried pork chop and it was mostly fat. What'd you girls have?

ROSEMARY. I had the stuffed peppers.

IRMA. I had the Southern-fried chicken.

CHRISTINE. Linda Sue Breckenridge had pot roast of veal and there was only one little hunk of meat in it. All we girls at her table made her call the waiter and complain.

ROSEMARY. Well, I should hope so!

IRMA. Good for you! (*There is a pause.*) I thought by this time someone might have noticed my new dress.

ROSEMARY. I was going to say something, kid, and then I . . . uh . . .

IRMA. Remember that satin-back crepe I had last year?

ROSEMARY. Don't tell me!

IRMA. Mama remodeled it for me while I was at Columbia. I feel like I had a brand-new outfit. (*Smarting*) But nobody said anything all afternoon!

CHRISTINE. It's—chic.

IRMA (*this soothes* IRMA *a bit and she beams. But now there is an awkward pause wherein no one can think of any more to say*). Well—we better run along, Christine. Rosemary has a date. (*To* ROSEMARY) We'll come by for you in the morning. Don't be late. (*She goes upstage and waits at the gate for* CHRISTINE.)

CHRISTINE (*crossing to* ROSEMARY). Girl, I want to tell you, in one afternoon I feel I've known you my whole life.

ROSEMARY (*with assurance of devotion*). I look upon you as an old friend already.

CHRISTINE (*overjoyed*). Aw . . .

ROSEMARY (AS CHRISTINE *and* IRMA *go off*). Good-by, girls!

FLO (*to* ROSEMARY). What time's Howard coming by?

ROSEMARY. Any minute now.

MADGE. Mom, is there any hot water?

FLO. You'll have to see.

MADGE (*crosses to door, then turns to* ROSEMARY). Miss Sydney, would you mind terribly if I used some of your Shalimar?

ROSEMARY. Help yourself!

MADGE. Thanks. (*She goes inside.*)

ROSEMARY. Madge thinks too much about the boys, Mrs. Owens.

FLO (*disbelieving*). Madge?

(*The conversation is stopped by the excited entrance of* MRS. POTTS *from her house. She is followed by* MILLIE *who carries another cake.*)

MRS. POTTS. It's a *miracle*, that's what it is! I never knew Millie could look so pretty. It's just like a movie I saw once with Betty Grable—or was it Lana Turner? Anyway, she played the part of a secretary to some very important business man. She wore glasses and did her hair real plain and men didn't pay any attention to her at all. Then one day she took off her glasses and her boss wanted to marry her right away! Now all the boys are going to fall in love with Millie!

ROSEMARY. Millie have a date tonight?

FLO. Yes, I'm sorry to say.

MRS. POTTS. Why, Flo!

ROSEMARY. Who is he, Millie? Tell your Aunt Rosemary.

MILLIE. Hal.

ROSEMARY. Who?

FLO. The young man over at Helen's turned out to be a friend of Alan's.

ROSEMARY. Oh, *him!*

(MILLIE *exits into kitchen.*)

FLO. Helen, have you gone to the trouble of baking another cake?

MRS. POTTS. An old lady like me, if she wants any attention from the young men on a picnic, all she can do is bake a cake!

FLO (*rather reproving*). Helen Potts!

MRS. POTTS. I feel sort of excited, Flo. I think we plan picnics just to give ourselves an excuse—to let something thrilling happen in our lives.

FLO. Such as what?

MRS. POTTS. I don't know.

MADGE (*bursting out the door*). Mom, Millie makes me furious! Every time she takes a bath, she fills the whole tub. There isn't any hot water at all.

FLO. You should have thought of it earlier.

ROSEMARY (*hears* HOWARD's *car drive up and stop*). It's him! It's him!

MRS. POTTS. Who? Oh, it's Howard. Hello, Howard!

ROSEMARY (*sitting down again*). If he's been drinking, I'm not going out with him.

HOWARD (*as he comes on through gate*). Howdy, ladies. (HOWARD *is a small, thin man, rapidly approaching middle age. A small-town businessman, he wears a permanent smile of greeting which, most of the time, is pretty sincere.*)

FLO. Hello, Howard.

HOWARD. You sure look nice, Rosemary.

ROSEMARY (*her tone of voice must tell a man she is independent of him*). Seems to me you might have left your coat on.

HOWARD. Still too darn hot, even if it is September. Good evening Madge.

MADGE. Hi, Howard.

FLO. How are things over in Cherryvale, Howard?

HOWARD. Good business. Back to school and everybody buying.

FLO. When business is good, it's good for everyone.

MILLIE (*comes out of kitchen, stands shyly behind* HOWARD). Hi, Howard!

HOWARD (*turning around, making a discovery*). Hey, Millie's a good-lookin' kid. I never realized it before.

MILLIE (*crossing to* FLO, *apprehensive*). Mom, what time did the fellows say they'd be here?

FLO. At five-thirty. You've asked me a dozen times. (*There is a sound of approaching automobiles, and* FLO *looks off stage, right.*) Alan's brought *both* cars!

(MILLIE *runs into the house.*)

MRS. POTTS. Some day *you'll* be riding around in that big Cadillac, Lady-bug.

ALAN (*coming on from right*). Everyone ready?

FLO. Come sit down, Alan.

ROSEMARY (*like a champion hostess*). The more the merrier!

ALAN. I brought both cars. I thought we'd let Hal and Millie bring the baskets out in the Ford. Hal's parking it now. (*To* MADGE, *who is sitting up on* MRS. POTTS' *porch railing.*) Hello, Beautiful!

MADGE. Hello, Alan!

ALAN (*calling off stage*). Come on, Hal.

FLO. Is he a careful driver, Alan?

(*The question does not get answered.* HAL *comes running on, tugging uncomfortably at the shoulders of his jacket and hollering in a voice that once filled the locker rooms.*)

HAL. Hey, Seymour! Hey, I'm a big man, Seymour. I'm a lot huskier than you are. I can't wear your jacket.

ALAN. Then take it off.

MRS. POTTS. Yes. I like to see a man comfortable.

HAL (*with a broad smile of total confidence*). I never could wear another fellow's clothes. See, I'm pretty big through the shoulders. (*He demonstrates the fact.*) I should have all my clothes tailor-made. (*He now swings his arms in appreciation of their new freedom.* MRS. POTTS *is admiring, the other women speculative.*)

ALAN (*wanting to get over the formalities*). Hey—uh—Hercules, you've met Mrs. Owens . . .

HAL. Sure!

(FLO *nods at him.*)

ALAN. . . . and I believe you met Mrs. Potts this morning.

HAL (*throwing his arms around her*). Oh, she's my best girl!

MRS. POTTS (*giggling like a girl*). I baked a Lady Baltimore cake!

HAL (*expansively, as though making an announcement of public interest*). This little lady, she took pity on me when I was practically starving. I ran into some hard luck when I was travelin'. Some characters robbed me of every cent I had.

ALAN (*interrupting*). And—er—this is Rosemary Sydney, Hal. Miss Sydney teaches shorthand and typing in the local high school.

ROSEMARY (*offering her hand*). Yes, I'm an old-maid schoolteacher.

HAL (*with unnecessary earnestness*). I have every respect for schoolteachers, Mam. It's a lotta hard work and not much pay.

(ROSEMARY *cannot decide whether or not this is a compliment.*)

ALAN. And this is Howard Bevans, Hal. Mr. Bevans is a friend of Miss Sydney.

HOWARD (*as they shake hands*). I run a little shop over in Cherryvale. Notions, novelties and school supplies. You and Alan drive over some time and get acquainted.

(MILLIE *enters and stands on the porch, pretending to be nonchalant and at ease.*)

HAL (*to* HOWARD, *earnestly*). Sir, we'll come over as soon as we can fit it into our schedule. (*He spies* MILLIE.) Hey kid! (*He does an elaborate imitation of a swan dive and lands beside her on the porch.*) You got a little more tan today, didn't you? (*He turns to the others.*) You folks shoulda seen Millie this morning. She did a fine jack-knife off the high diving board!

MILLIE (*breaking away, sitting on steps*). Cut it out!

HAL. What'sa matter, kid? Think I'm snowin' you under? (*Back to the whole group*) I wouldn't admit this to many people, but she does a jack-knife almost as good as me! (*Realizes that this sounds bragging so goes on to explain.*) You see, I was diving champion on the West Coast, so I know what I'm talking about! (*He laughs to reassure himself and sits beside* MILLIE *on doorstep.*)

FLO (*after a moment*). Madge, you should be getting dressed.

ALAN. Go on upstairs and get beautiful for us.

MADGE. Mom, can I wear my new dress?

FLO. No. I made you that dress to save for dances this fall.

(*The attention returns now to* HAL, *and* MADGE *continues to sit, unnoticed, watching him.*)

ROSEMARY (TO HAL). Where'd you get those boots?

HAL. I guess maybe I should apologize for the way I look. But you see, those characters I told you about made off with all my clothes, too.

MRS. POTTS. What a pity!

HAL. You see, I didn't want you folks to think you were associatin' with a bum. (*He laughs uncomfortably.*)

MRS. POTTS (*intuitively, she says what is needed to save his ego*). Clothes don't make the man.

HAL. That's what I tell myself, Mam.

FLO. Is your mother taken care of, Helen?

MRS. POTTS. Yes, Flo. I've got a baby sitter for her. (*All laugh.*)

FLO. Then let's start packing the baskets.

(*She goes into kitchen.* MRS. POTTS *starts after her, but* HAL's *story holds her and she sits down again.*)

HAL (*continuing his explanation to* ROSEMARY). See, Mam, my old man left me these boots when he died.

ROSEMARY (*impishly*). That all he left you—just a pair of boots?

HAL. He said, "Son, the man of the house needs a pair of boots 'cause he's gotta do a lot of kickin'.

Your wages all are spent.

The landlord wants his rent.

You go to your woman for solace,

And she fills you fulla torment."

(HAL *smiles and explains proudly*) That's a little poem he made up. He says, "Son, there'll be times when the only thing you got to be proud of is the fact you're a man. So wear your boots so people can hear you comin', and keep your fists doubled up so they'll know you mean business when you get there." (*He laughs.*) My old man, he was a corker!

ALAN (*laughing*). Hal's always so shy of people before he meets them. Then you can't keep him still!

(*Suddenly* HAL's *eye catches* MADGE, *perched on* MRS. POTTS' *porch.*)

HAL. Hi!

MADGE. Hi!

(*Now they both look away from each other, a little guiltily.*)

HOWARD. What line of business you in, Son?

HAL (*he begins to expand with importance*). I'm about to enter the oil business, sir. (*He sits on the chair, center stage.*)

HOWARD. Oh!

HAL. You see, while my old man was no aristocratic millionaire or anything, he had some very important friends who were very big men—in their own way. One of them wanted me to take a position with this oil company down in Texas, but . . .

ALAN (*matter-of-factly*). Dad and I have found a place for Hal on the pipeline.

HAL. Gee, Seymour, I think you oughta let *me* tell the story.

ALAN (*knowing he might as well let* HAL *go on*). Sorry, Hal.

HAL (*with devout earnestness to all*). You see, I've decided to start in from the very bottom, 'cause that way I'll learn things lots better—even if I don't make much money for a while.

MRS. POTTS (*comes through again*).

Money isn't everything.

HAL. That's what I tell myself, Mam. Money isn't everything. I've learned that much. And I sure do appreciate Alan and his old . . . (*Thinks a moment and substitutes* father *for* man.) *father* . . . giving me this opportunity.

MRS. POTTS. I think that's wonderful. (*She has every faith in him.*)

HOWARD. It's a good business town. A young man can go far.

HAL. Sir! I intend to go *far*.

ROSEMARY (*her two-bits' worth*). A young man, coming to town, he's gotta be a good mixer.

MRS. POTTS. Wouldn't it be nice if he could join the Country Club and play golf?

ALAN. He won't be able to afford that.

ROSEMARY. The bowling team's a rowdy gang.

MRS. POTTS. And there's a young men's Bible class at the Baptist Church.

(HAL's *head has been spinning with these plans for his future. Now he reassures them.*)

HAL. Oh, I'm gonna join clubs and go to church and do all those things.

FLO (*coming out of the kitchen*). Madge! Are you still here?

MADGE (*running across to the front door of her own house*). If everyone will pardon me, I'll get dressed. (*She goes inside.*)

FLO. It's about time.

ALAN (*calling after* MADGE). Hurry it up, will you, Delilah?

MILLIE. You oughta see the way Madge primps. She uses about six kinds of face cream and dusts herself all over with powder, and rubs perfume underneath her ears to make her real mysterious. It takes her half an hour just to get her lipstick on. She won't be ready for hours.

FLO. Come on, Helen. Alan, we'll need a man to help us chip the ice and put the baskets in the car.

(MRS. POTTS *goes inside.*)

HAL (*generously*). I'll help you, Mam.

FLO (*she simply cannot accept him*). No, thank you. Alan won't mind.

ALAN (*to Hal as he leaves*). Mind your manners, Hal. (*He and* FLO *start in.*)

MILLIE (*uncertain how to proceed with* HAL *on her own, she runs to* FLO). Mom!

FLO. Millie, show the young man your drawings.

MILLIE (*to* HAL). Wanta see my art?

HAL. You mean to tell me you can draw pictures?

MILLIE (*gets her sketch book and shows it to* HAL. FLO *and* ALAN *go inside*). That's Mrs. Potts.

HAL (*impressed*). Looks just like her.

MILLIE. I just love Mrs. Potts. When I go to heaven, I expect everyone to be just like her.

HAL. Hey, kid, wanta draw me?

MILLIE. Well, I'll try.

HAL. I had a job as a model once. (*Strikes a pose.*) How's this? (MILLIE *shakes her head.*) Here's another. (*Sits on stump in another pose.*) Okay?

MILLIE. Why don't you just try to look natural?

HAL. Gee, that's hard. (*But he shakes himself into a natural pose finally.* MILLIE *starts sketching him.* ROSEMARY *and* HOWARD *sit together on the doorstep. The sun now is beginning to set, filling the stage with an orange glow that seems almost aflame.*)

ROSEMARY (*grabs* HOWARD's *arm*). Look at that sunset, Howard!

HOWARD. Pretty, isn't it?

ROSEMARY. That's the most flaming sunset I ever did see.

HOWARD. If you painted it in a picture, no one'd believe you.

ROSEMARY. It's like the daytime didn't want to end, isn't it?

HOWARD (*not fully aware of what she means*). Oh—I don't know.

ROSEMARY. Like the daytime didn't wanta end, like it was gonna put up a big scrap and maybe set the world on fire—to keep the nighttime from creepin' on.

HOWARD. Rosemary . . . you're a poet.

HAL (*as* MILLIE *sketches him he begins to relax and reflect on his life*). You know, there comes a time in every man's life when he's gotta settle down. A little town like this, this is the place to settle down in, where people are easygoin' and sincere.

ROSEMARY. No, Howard, I don't think there ought to be any drinking, while Millie's here.

HAL (*turns at the mention of drink*). What's that?

ROSEMARY. We were just talkin'.

HAL. (*back to* MILLIE). What'd you do this afternoon, kid?

MILLIE. Read a book.

HAL (*impressed*). You mean, you read a *whole* book in one afternoon?

MILLIE. Sure. Hold still.

HAL. I'm a son of a gun. What was it about?

MILLIE. There wasn't much story. It's just the way you feel when you read it—kind of warm inside and sad and amused—all at the same time.

HAL. Yeah—sure. (*After a moment*) I wish I had more time to read books. (*Proudly*) That's what I'm gonna do when I settle down. I'm gonna read all the better books—and listen to all the better music. A man owes it to himself. (MILLIE *continues sketching.*) I used to go with a girl who read books. She joined the Book-of-the-Month Club and they had her readin' books all the time! She wouldn't any more finish one book than they'd send her another!

ROSEMARY (*as* HOWARD *walks off*). Howard, where you goin'?

HOWARD. I'll be right back, Honey.

(ROSEMARY *follows him to gate and watches him while he is off stage.*)

HAL (*as* MILLIE *hands him the sketch*). Is that *me*? (*Admiring it*) I sure do admire people who are artistic. Can I keep it?

MILLIE (*shyly*). I write poetry, too. I've written poems I've never shown to a living soul.

HAL. Kid, I think you must be some sort of a genius.

ROSEMARY (*calling off to* HOWARD). Howard, leave that bottle right where it is!

HAL (*jumps at the word* bottle). Did she say "bottle"?

ROSEMARY (*coming down to* HAL). He's been down to the hotel, buying bootleg whiskey off those good-for-nothing porters!

HOWARD (*coming back, holding out a bottle*). Young man, maybe you'd like a swig of this.

HAL. Hot damn! (*He takes a drink.*)

ROSEMARY. Howard, put that away.

HOWARD. Millie's not gonna be shocked if she sees someone take a drink. Are you, Millie?

MILLIE. Gosh, no!

ROSEMARY. What if someone'd come by and tell the School Board? I'd lose my job quick as you can say Jack Robinson.

HOWARD. Who's gonna see you, Honey? Everyone in town's at the park, havin' a picnic.

ROSEMARY. I don't care. Liquor's against the law in this state, and a person oughta abide by the law. (*To* HAL) Isn't that what you say, young fellow?

HAL (*eager to agree*). Oh, sure! A person oughta abide by the law.

HOWARD. Here, Honey, have one.

ROSEMARY. No, Howard, I'm not gonna touch a drop.

HOWARD. Come on, Honey, have one little drink just for *me*.

ROSEMARY (*beginning to melt*). Howard, you oughta be ashamed of yourself.

HOWARD (*innocent*). I don't see why.

ROSEMARY. I guess I know why you want me to take a drink.

HOWARD. Now, Honey, that's not so. I just think you should have a good time like the rest of us. (*To* HAL) Schoolteachers gotta right to live. Isn't that what you say, young fella?

HAL. Sure, schoolteachers got a right to live.

ROSEMARY (*taking the bottle*). Now, Millie, don't you tell any of the kids at school.

MILLIE. What do you take me for?

ROSEMARY (*Looking around her*). Anyone coming?

HOWARD. Coast is clear.

ROSEMARY (*takes a hearty drink, and makes a lugubrious face*). Whew! I want some water!

HOWARD. Millie, why don't you run in the house and get us some?

ROSEMARY. Mrs. Owens'd suspect something. I'll get a drink from the hydrant! (*She runs off to* MRS. POTTS' *yard.*)

HOWARD. Millie, my girl, I'd like to offer *you* one, but I s'pose your old lady'd raise Ned.

MILLIE. What Mom don't know won't hurt her! (*She reaches for the bottle.*)

HAL (*grabs the bottle first*). No, kid. You lay off the stuff! (*He takes another drink.*)

ROSEMARY (*calling from off stage*). Howard, come help me! I see a snake!

HOWARD. You go, Millie. She don't see no snake. (MILLIE *goes off. As* HAL *takes another drink, he sees a light go on in* MADGE's *window.* HOWARD *follows* HAL's *gaze.*) Look at her there, powdering her arms. You know, every time I come over here I look forward just to seein' her. I tell myself, "Bevans, old boy, you can look at that all you want, but you couldn't touch it with a ten-foot pole."

HAL (*with some awe of her*). She's the

kind of girl a guy's gotta *respect*.

HOWARD. Look at her, putting lipstick on that cute kisser. Seems to me, when the good Lord made a girl as pretty as she is, he did it for a reason, and it's about time she found out what that reason is. (*He gets an idea.*) Look, son, if you're agonizin', I know a couple of girls down at the hotel.

HAL. Thanks, but I've given up that sorta thing.

HOWARD. I think that's a very fine attitude.

HAL. Besides, I never had to pay for it.

ROSEMARY (*entering, followed by MILLIE*). Lord, I thought I was going to faint!

MILLIE (*laughing at ROSEMARY's excitability*). It was just a piece of garden hose.

ROSEMARY (*regarding the two men suspiciously*). What're you two talking about?

HOWARD. Talkin' about the weather, Honey. Talkin' about the weather.

ROSEMARY. I bet.

MILLIE (*seeing MADGE in the window*). Hey, Madge, why don't you charge admission?

(MADGE's *curtains close.*)

ROSEMARY. Shoot! When I was a girl I was just as good-looking as she is!

HOWARD. Of course you were, Honey.

ROSEMARY (*taking the bottle*). I had boys callin' me all the time. But if my father had ever caught me showing off in front of the window he'd have tanned me with a razor strap. (*Takes a drink.*) Cause I was brought up strict by a God-fearing man. (*Takes another.*)

MILLIE (*music has started in the background*). Hey, hit it, Ernie! (*Explaining to HAL*) It's Ernie Higgins and his Happiness Boys. They play at all the dances around here.

ROSEMARY (*beginning to sway rapturously*). Lord, I like that music! Come dance with me, Howard.

HOWARD. Honey, I'm no good at dancin'.

ROSEMARY. That's just what you menfolks tell yourselves to get out of it. (*Turns to MILLIE.*) Come dance with me, Millie! (*She pulls MILLIE up onto the porch and they push the chairs out of the way.*)

MILLIE. I gotta lead! I gotta lead.

(ROSEMARY *and* MILLIE *dance together in a trim, automatic way that keeps time to the music but little else. Both women seem to show a little arrogance in dancing to-*gether, as though boasting to the men of their independence. Their rhythm is accurate but uninspired.* HOWARD *and* HAL *watch, laughing.*)

HOWARD. S'posin' Hal and I did that.

ROSEMARY. Go ahead for all I care. (HOWARD *turns to* HAL *and, laughing, they start dancing together,* HAL *giving his own version of a coy female.* ROSEMARY *is irritated by this.*) Stop it!

HOWARD. I thought we were doin' very nicely.

(ROSEMARY *grabs* HOWARD *and pulls him up on the porch.*)

HAL. Come and dance with me, Millie!

MILLIE. Well—I never danced with boys. I always have to lead.

HAL. Just relax and do the steps I do. Come on and try. (*They dance together but* MILLIE *has an awkward feeling of uncertainty that shows in her dancing.* HOWARD, *dancing with* ROSEMARY, *has been cutting up.*)

ROSEMARY. Quit clowning, Howard, and dance with me.

HOWARD. Honey, you don't get any fun out of dancing with *me*.

ROSEMARY. The band's playin'. You gotta dance with *someone*. (*They resume an uncertain toddle.*)

MILLIE (*to* HAL). Am I too bad?

HAL. Naw! You just need a little practice.

ROSEMARY. (*while dancing*). Lord, I love to dance. At school, kids all called me the Dancin' Fool. Went somewhere dancin' every night!

MRS. POTTS (*coming out of kitchen, she sits and watches the dancers.* FLO *and* ALAN *appear and stand in doorway watching.*) I can't stay in the kitchen while there's dancing!

HAL (*stops the dancing to deliver the needed instructions*). Now look, kid, you gotta remember *I'm* the *man,* and you gotta do the steps *I* do.

MILLIE. I keep wantin' to do the steps I make up myself.

HAL. The man's gotta take the lead, kid, as long as he's able. (*They resume dancing.*)

MRS. POTTS. You're doing fine, Millie!

MILLIE (*as she is whirled around*). I feel like Rita Hayworth!

(FLO *and* ALAN *go into the house.*)

ROSEMARY (*her youth returns in reverie*). One night I went dancin' at a big Valentine party. I danced so hard I swooned! That's when they called me the Dancin' Fool.

HAL (*stops dancing for a moment*). I'll show you a new step, kid. I learned this in L. A. Try it. (*He nimbly executes a somewhat more intricate step.*)

MRS. POTTS. Isn't he graceful?

MILLIE. Gee, that looks hard.

HAL. Takes a little time. Give it a try! (MILLIE *tries to do it, but it is too much for her.*)

MILLIE (*giving up*). I'm sorry, I just can't seem to get it.

HAL. Watch close, kid. If you learn this step you'll be the sharpest kid in town. See? (*He continues his demonstration.*)

MILLIE (*observing but baffled*). Yah— but . . .

HAL. Real loose, see? You give it a little of this—and give it a little of that. (*He snaps his fingers, keeping a nimble, sensitive response to the rhythm.*)

MILLIE. Gee, I wish *I* could do that.

(*Now the music changes to a slower, more sensuous rhythm.* HAL· *and* MILLIE *stop dancing and listen.*)

ROSEMARY (*who has been watching* HAL *enviously*). That's the way to dance, Howard! That's the way.

(HAL *begins to dance to the slower rhythm and* MILLIE *tries to follow him. Now* MADGE *comes out the front door, wearing her new dress. Although the dress is indeed "too fussy" for a picnic, she is ravishing. She stands watching* HAL *and* MILLIE.)

HOWARD (*drifting from* ROSEMARY). You sure look pretty, Madge.

MADGE. Thank you, Howard.

HOWARD. Would you like a little dance? (*She accepts and they dance together on the porch.* ROSEMARY *is dancing by herself on the porch, upstage, and does not notice them.*)

MRS. POTTS (*seeing* MADGE *and* HOWARD *dancing*). More dancers! We've turned the backyard into a ballroom!

ROSEMARY (*snatching* HOWARD *from* MADGE). Thought you couldn't dance.

(MADGE *goes down into the yard and watches* HAL *and* MILLIE.)

MRS. POTTS (*to* MADGE). The young man is teaching Millie a new step.

MADGE. Oh, that's fun. I've been trying to teach it to Alan. (*She tries the step herself and does it as well as* HAL.)

MRS. POTTS. Look, everyone! Madge does it, too!

HAL (*turns around and sees* MADGE *dancing*). Hey! (*Some distance apart, snapping their fingers to the rhythm, their bodies respond without touching. Then they dance slowly toward each other and* HAL *takes her in his arms. The dance has something of the nature of a primitive rite that would mate the two young people. The others watch rather solemnly.*)

MRS. POTTS (*finally*). It's like they were *made* to dance together, isn't it?

(*This remark breaks the spell.* MILLIE *moves to* MRS. POTTS' *steps and sits quietly in the background, beginning to inspect the bottle of whiskey.*)

ROSEMARY (*impatiently to* HOWARD). Can't *you* dance that way?

HOWARD. Golly, Honey, I'm a businessman.

ROSEMARY (*dances by herself, kicking her legs in the air.* MILLIE *takes an occasional drink from the whiskey bottle during the following scene, unobserved by the others*). I danced so hard one night, I swooned! Right in the center of the ballroom!

HOWARD (*amused and observing*). Rosemary's got pretty legs, hasn't she?

ROSEMARY (*this strikes her as hilarious*). That's just like you men, can't talk about anything but women's legs.

HOWARD (*a little offended to be misinterpreted*). I just noticed they had a nice shape.

ROSEMARY (*laughing uproariously*). How would you like it if we women went around talkin' 'bout *your* legs all the time?

HOWARD (*ready to be a sport, stands and lifts his trousers to his knees*). All right! There's *my* legs if you wanta talk about them.

ROSEMARY (*she explodes with laughter*). Never saw anything so ugly. Men's big hairy legs! (ROSEMARY *goes over to* HAL, *yanking him from* MADGE *possessively.*) Young man, let's see your legs.

HAL (*not knowing what to make of his seizure*). Huh?

ROSEMARY. We passed a new rule here tonight. Every man here's gotta show his legs.

HAL. Mam, I got on boots.

HOWARD. Let the young man alone, Rosemary. He's dancin' with Madge.

ROSEMARY. Now it's his turn to dance

with *me*. (*To* HAL) I may be an old-maid schoolteacher, but *I* can keep up with you. Ride 'em cowboy! (*A little tight, stimulated by* HAL's *physical presence, she abandons convention and grabs* HAL *closely to her, plastering a cheek next to his and holding her hips fast against him. One can sense that* HAL *is embarrassed and repelled.*)

HAL (*wanting to object*). Mam, I . . .

ROSEMARY. I used to have a boy friend was a cowboy. Met him in Colorado when I went out there to get over a case of flu. He was in love with me, 'cause I was an older woman and had some sense. Took me up in the mountains one night and made love. Wanted me to marry him right there on the mountain top. Said God'd be our preacher, the moon our best man. Ever hear such talk?

HAL (*trying to get away*). Mam, I'd like another li'l drink now.

ROSEMARY (*jerking him closer to her*). Dance with me, young man. Dance with me. I can keep up with you. You know what? You remind me of one of those ancient statues. There was one in the school library until last year. He was a Roman gladiator. All he had on was a shield. (*She gives a bawdy laugh.*) A shield over his arm. That was all he had on. All we girls felt insulted, havin' to walk past that statue every time we went to the library. We got up a petition and made the principal do something about it. (*She laughs hilariously during her narration.*) You know what he did? He got the school janitor to fix things right. He got a chisel and made that statue decent. (*Another bawdy laugh.*) Lord, those ancient people were depraved.

HAL (*he seldom has been made so uncomfortable*). Mam, I guess I just don't feel like dancin'.

ROSEMARY (*sobering from her story, grabs for* HAL, *catching him by the shirt*). Where you goin'?

HAL. Mam, I . . .

ROSEMARY (*commanding him imploringly*.) Dance with me, young man. Dance with me.

HAL. I . . . I . . . (*He pulls loose from her grasp but her hand, still clutching, tears off a strip of his shirt as he gets away.* HOWARD *intervenes.*)

HOWARD. He wants to dance with Madge,

Rosemary. Let 'em alone. They're young people.

ROSEMARY (*in a hollow voice*). Young? What do you mean, they're *young*?

MILLIE (*a sick groan from the background*). Oh, I'm sick.

MRS. POTTS. Millie!

MILLIE. I wanna die. (*All eyes are on* MILLIE *now as she runs over to the kitchen door.*)

MADGE. Millie!

HOWARD. What'd the little Dickens do? Get herself tight?

HAL. Take it easy, kid.

ROSEMARY (*she has problems of her own. She gropes blindly across the stage, suffering what has been a deep humiliation*). I suppose that's something wonderful— they're *young*.

MADGE (*going to* MILLIE). Let's go inside, Millie.

MILLIE (*turning on* MADGE *viciously*). I *hate* you!

MADGE (*hurt*). Millie!

MILLIE (*sobbing*). Madge is the pretty one— Madge is the pretty one. (MILLIE *dashes inside the kitchen door,* MRS. POTTS *behind her.*)

MADGE (*to herself*). What did she have to do that for?

HOWARD (*examining the bottle*). She must have had several good snifters.

ROSEMARY (*pointing a finger at* HAL. *She has found vengeance*). It's all *his* fault, Howard.

HOWARD. Now, Honey . . .

ROSEMARY (*to* HAL, *defiantly and accusingly*). Millie was your date. You shoulda been looking after her. But you were too busy making eyes at Madge.

HOWARD. Honey . . .

ROSEMARY. And you're no better than he is, Madge. You should be ashamed.

FLO (*flies out on the porch in a fury*). Who fed whiskey to my Millie?

ROSEMARY (*pointing fanatically at* HAL), He did, Mrs. Owens! It's all his fault!

(FLO *glares at* HAL.)

HOWARD (*trying to straighten things out*). Mrs. Owens, it was this way . . .

FLO. My Millie is too young to be drinking whiskey!

ROSEMARY. Oh, he'd have fed her whiskey and taken his pleasure with the child and then skidaddled!

HOWARD (*trying to bring them to reason*). Now listen, everyone. Let's . . .

ROSEMARY. I know what I'm doing, Howard! And I don't need any advice from *you*. (*Back at* HAL) You been stomping around here in those boots like you owned the place, thinking every woman you saw was gonna fall madly in love. But here's one woman didn't pay you any mind.

HOWARD. The boy hasn't done anything, Mrs. Owens!

ROSEMARY (*facing* HAL, *drawing closer with each accusation*). Aristocratic millionaire, my foot! You wouldn't know an aristocratic millionaire if he spit on you. Braggin' about your father, and I bet he wasn't any better'n you are.

(HAL *is as though paralyzed.* HOWARD *still tries to reason with* FLO.)

HOWARD. None of us saw Millie drink the whiskey.

ROSEMARY (*closer to* HAL). You think just cause you're a man, you can walk in here and make off with whatever you like. You think just cause you're young you can push other people aside and not pay them any mind. You think just cause you're strong you can show your muscles and nobody'll know what a pitiful specimen you are. But you won't stay young forever, didja ever thinka that? What'll become of you then? You'll end your life in the gutter and it'll serve you right, 'cause the gutter's where you came from and the gutter's where you belong. (*She has thrust her face into* HAL's *and is spitting her final words at him before* HOWARD *finally grabs her, almost as though to protect her from herself, and holds her arms at her sides, pulling her away.*)

HOWARD. Rosemary, shut your damn mouth.

(HAL *withdraws to the far edge of the porch, no one paying any attention to him now, his reaction to the attack still a mystery.*)

MRS. POTTS (*comes out of kitchen*). Millie's going to be perfectly all right, Flo. Alan held her head and let her be sick. She's going to be perfectly all right now.

FLO (*a general announcement, clear and firm*). I want it understood by everyone that there's to be no more drinking on this picnic.

HOWARD. It was all my fault, Mrs. Owens. My fault.

(ALAN *escorts a sober* MILLIE *out on the porch.*)

MRS. POTTS. Here's Millie now, good as new. And we're all going on the picnic and forget it.

ALAN (*quick to accuse* HAL). Hal, what's happened?

(HAL *does not respond.*)

FLO (*to* ALAN). Millie will come with us, Alan.

ALAN. Sure, Mrs. Owens. Hal, I told you not to drink!

(HAL *is still silent.*)

FLO. Madge, why did you wear your new dress?

MADGE (*as though mystified at herself*). I don't know. I just put it on.

FLO. Go upstairs and change, this minute. I mean it! You come later with Rosemary and Howard!

(MADGE *runs inside.*)

MRS. POTTS. Let's hurry. All the tables will be taken.

ALAN. Mr. Bevans, tell Madge I'll see her out there. Hal, the baskets are all in the Ford. Get goin'.

(HAL *doesn't move.* ALAN *hurries off.*)

FLO. Millie, darling, are you feeling better? (FLO *and* MILLIE *go off through alley, right.*)

MRS. POTTS (*to* HAL). Young man, you can follow us and find the way. (MRS. POTTS *follows the others off. We hear the Cadillac drive off.* HAL *is sitting silent and beaten on the edge of the porch.* HOWARD *and* ROSEMARY *are on the lawn by* MRS. POTTS' *house.*)

HOWARD. He's just a boy, Rosemary. You talked awful.

ROSEMARY. What made me do it, Howard? What made me act that way?

HOWARD. You gotta remember, men have feelings, too—same as women. (*To* HAL) Don't pay any attention to her, young man. She didn't mean a thing.

ROSEMARY (*has gone up to the gate*). I don't want to go on the picnic, Howard. This is my last night of vacation and I want to have a good time.

HOWARD. We'll go for a ride, Honey.

ROSEMARY. I want to drive into the sunset, Howard! I want to drive into the sunset! (*She runs off toward the car,* HOWARD *following.* HOWARD's *car drives away.* HAL *sits on the porch, defeated.* MADGE *soon comes out in another dress. She comes out very quietly and he makes no recognition of her presence. She sits on a bench on the porch and finally speaks in a soft voice.*)

MADGE. You're a wonderful dancer . . .

HAL (*hardly audible*). Thanks.

MADGE. . . . and I can tell a lot about a boy by dancing with him. Some boys, even though they're very smart, or very successful in some other way, when they take a girl in their arms to dance, they're sort of awkward and a girl feels sort of uncomfortable.

HAL (*he keeps his head down, his face in his hands*). Yah.

MADGE. But when you took me in your arms—to dance—I had the most relaxed feeling, that you knew what you were doing, and I could follow every step of the way.

HAL. Look, Baby, I'm in a pretty bad mood. (*He stands suddenly and walks away from her, his hands thrust into his pockets. He is uncomfortable to be near her, for he is trembling with insult and rage.*)

MADGE. You mustn't pay any attention to Miss Sydney. (HAL *is silent.*) Women like her make me mad at the whole female sex.

HAL. Look, Baby, why don't you beat it?

MADGE (*she is aware of the depth of his feelings*). What's the matter?

HAL (*gives up and begins to shudder, his shoulders heaving as he fights to keep from bawling*). What's the use, Baby? I'm a bum. She saw through me like a God-damn X-ray machine. There's no place in the world for a guy like me.

MADGE. There's got to be.

HAL (*with self-derision*). Yah?

MADGE. Of course. You're young, and—you're very entertaining. I mean—you say all sorts of witty things, and I just loved listening to you talk. And you're strong and—you're very good-looking. I bet Miss Sydney thought so, too, or she wouldn't have said those things.

HAL. Look, Baby, lemme level with you. When I was fourteen, I spent a year in the reform school. How ya like that?

MADGE. Honest?

HAL. Yah!

MADGE. What for?

HAL. For stealin' another guy's motor-cycle. Yah! I *stole* it. I stole it 'cause I wanted to get on the damn thing and go so far away, so fast, that no one'd ever catch up with me.

MADGE. I think—lots of boys feel that way at times.

HAL. Then my old lady went to the authorities. (*He mimics his "old lady."*) "I've done everything I can with the boy. I can't do anything more." So off I go to the God-damn reform school.

MADGE (*with all the feeling she has*) Gee!

HAL. Finally some welfare league hauls me out and the old lady's sorry to see me back. Yah! she's got herself a new boy friend and I'm in the way.

MADGE. It's awful when parents don't get along.

HAL. I never told that to another soul, not even Seymour.

MADGE (*at a loss*). I—I wish there was something I could say—or *do.*

HAL. Well—that's the Hal Carter story, but no one's ever gonna make a movie of it.

MADGE (*to herself*). Most people would be awfully shocked.

HAL (*looking at her, then turning away cynically*). There you are, Baby. If you wanta faint—or get sick—or run in the house and lock the doors—go ahead. I ain't stoppin' you. (*There is a silence. Then* MADGE, *suddenly and impulsively, takes his face in her hands and kisses him. Then she returns her hands to her lap and feels embarrassed.* HAL *looks at her in amazement.*) Baby! What'd you do?

MADGE. I . . . I'm proud you told me.

HAL (*with humble appreciation*). Baby!

MADGE. I . . . I get so tired of being told I'm pretty.

HAL (*folding her in his arms caressingly*). Baby, Baby, Baby.

MADGE (*resisting him, jumping to her feet*). Don't. We have to go. We have all the baskets in our car and they'll be waiting. (HAL *gets up and walks slowly to her, their eyes fastened and* MADGE *feeling a little thrill of excitement as he draws nearer.*) Really—we have to be going. (HAL *takes her in his arms and kisses her passionately. Then* MADGE *utters his name in a voice of resignation.*) Hal!

HAL. Just be quiet, Baby.

MADGE. Really . . . We have to go. They'll be waiting.

HAL (*picking her up in his arms and starting off. His voice is deep and firm*). We're not goin' on no God-damn picnic.

CURTAIN

ACT THREE

Scene One

It is after midnight. A great harvest moon shines in the sky, a deep, murky blue. The moon is swollen and full and casts a pale light on the scene below. Soon we hear HOWARD's *Chevrolet chugging to a stop by the house, then* HOWARD *and* ROSEMARY *come on,* ROSEMARY *first. Wearily, a groggy depression having set in, she makes her way to the doorstep and drops there, sitting limp. She seems preoccupied at first and her responses to* HOWARD *are mere grunts.*

———

HOWARD. Here we are, Honey. Right back where we started from.

ROSEMARY (*her mind elsewhere*). Uhh.

HOWARD. You were awful nice to me tonight, Rosemary.

ROSEMARY. Uhh.

HOWARD. Do you think Mrs. Owens suspects anything?

ROSEMARY. I don't care if she does.

HOWARD. A businessman's gotta be careful of talk. And after all, you're a schoolteacher. (*Fumbling to get away*) Well, I better be gettin' back to Cherryvale. I gotta open up the store in the morning. Good night, Rosemary.

ROSEMARY. Uhh.

HOWARD (*he pecks at her cheek with a kiss*). Good night. Maybe I should say, good morning. (*He starts off.*)

ROSEMARY (*just coming to*). Where you goin', Howard?

HOWARD. Honey, I gotta get home.

ROSEMARY. You can't go off without me.

HOWARD. Honey, talk sense.

ROSEMARY. You can't go off without me. Not after tonight. *That's* sense.

HOWARD (*a little nervous*). Honey, be reasonable.

ROSEMARY. Take me with you.

HOWARD. What'd people say?

ROSEMARY (*almost vicious*). To *hell* with what people'd say!

HOWARD (*shocked*). Honey!

ROSEMARY. What'd people say if I thumbed my nose at them? What'd people say if I walked down the street and showed 'em my pink panties? What do I care what people say?

HOWARD. Honey, you're not yourself tonight.

ROSEMARY. Yes, I am. I'm more myself than I ever was. Take me with you, Howard. If you don't I don't know what I'll do with myself. I mean it.

HOWARD. Now look, Honey, you better go upstairs and get some sleep. You gotta start school in the morning. We'll talk all this over Saturday.

ROSEMARY. Maybe you won't be back Saturday. Maybe you won't be back ever again.

HOWARD. Rosemary, you know better than that.

ROSEMARY. Then what's the next thing in store for me? To be nice to the next man, then the next—till there's no one left to care whether I'm nice to him or not. Till I'm ready for the grave and don't have anyone to take me there.

HOWARD (*in an attempt to be consoling*). Now, Rosemary!

ROSEMARY. You can't let that happen to me, Howard. I won't let you.

HOWARD. I don't understand. When we first started going together you were the best sport I ever saw, always good for a laugh.

ROSEMARY (*in a hollow voice*). I can't laugh any more.

HOWARD. We'll talk it over Saturday.

ROSEMARY. We'll talk it over *now*.

HOWARD (*squirming*). Well—Honey—I . . .

ROSEMARY. You said you were gonna marry me, Howard. You said when I got back from my vacation, you'd be waitin' with the preacher.

HOWARD. Honey, I've had an awful busy summer and . . .

ROSEMARY. Where's the preacher, Howard? Where is he?

HOWARD (*walking away from her*). Honey, I'm forty-two years old. A person forms certain ways of livin', then one day it's too late to change.

ROSEMARY (*grabbing his arm and holding him*). Come back here, Howard. I'm no spring chicken either. Maybe I'm a little older than you think *I* am. I've formed my ways too. But they can be changed. They *gotta* be changed. It's no good livin' like this, in rented rooms, meetin' a bunch of old maids for supper every night, then comin' back home alone.

HOWARD. *I* know how it is, Rosemary. My life's no bed of roses either.

ROSEMARY. Then why don't you do something about it?

HOWARD. I figure—there's some bad things about every life.

ROSEMARY. There's too much bad about mine. Each year, I keep tellin' myself, is the last. Something'll happen. Then nothing ever does—except I get a little crazier all the time.

HOWARD (*hopelessly*). Well . . .

ROSEMARY. A *well's* a hole in the ground, Howard. Be careful you don't fall in.

HOWARD. I wasn't trying to be funny.

ROSEMARY. . . . and all this time you just been leadin' me on.

HOWARD (*defensive*). Rosemary, that's not *so!* I've not been leading you *on.*

ROSEMARY. I'd like to know what else you call it.

HOWARD. Well—can't we talk about it Saturday? I'm dead tired and I got a busy week ahead, and . . .

ROSEMARY (*she grips him by the arm and looks straight into his eyes*). You gotta marry me, Howard.

HOWARD (*tortured*). Well—Honey, I can't marry you *now.*

ROSEMARY. You can be over here in the morning.

HOWARD. Sometimes you're unreasonable.

ROSEMARY. You gotta marry me.

HOWARD. What'll you do about your job?

ROSEMARY. Alvah Jackson can take my place till they get someone new from the agency.

HOWARD. I'll have to pay Fred Jenkins to take care of the store for a few days.

ROSEMARY. Then get him.

HOWARD. Well . . .

ROSEMARY. I'll be waitin' for you in the morning, Howard.

HOWARD (*after a few moments' troubled thought*). No.

ROSEMARY (*a muffled cry*). Howard!

HOWARD. I'm not gonna marry anyone that says, "You gotta marry me, Howard." I'm not gonna. (*He is silent.* ROSEMARY *weeps pathetic tears. Slowly* HOWARD *reconsiders.*) If a woman wants me to marry her—she can at least say "please."

ROSEMARY (*beaten and humble*). *Please* marry me, Howard.

HOWARD. Well—you got to give me time to think it over.

ROSEMARY (*desperate*). Oh, God! Please marry me, Howard. Please . . . (*She sinks to her knees.*) Please . . . please . . .

HOWARD (*embarrassed by her suffering*

humility). Rosemary . . . I . . . I gotta have some time to think it over. You go to bed now and get some rest. I'll drive over in the morning and maybe we can talk it over before you go to school. I . . .

ROSEMARY. You're not just tryin' to get out of it, Howard?

HOWARD. I'll be over in the morning, Honey.

ROSEMARY. Honest?

HOWARD. Yah. I gotta go to the courthouse anyway. We'll talk it over then.

ROSEMARY. Oh, God, please marry me, Howard. Please.

HOWARD (*trying to get away*). Go to bed, Honey. I'll see you in the morning.

ROSEMARY. Please, Howard!

HOWARD. I'll see you in the morning. Good night, Rosemary. (*Starting off.*)

ROSEMARY (*in a meek voice*). Please!

HOWARD. Good night, Rosemary.

ROSEMARY (*after he is gone*). Please. (ROSEMARY *stands alone on the doorstep. We hear the sound of* HOWARD's *car start up and drive off, chugging away in the distance.* ROSEMARY *is drained of energy. She pulls herself together and goes into the house. The stage is empty for several moments. Then* MADGE *runs on from the back, right. Her face is in her hands. She is sobbing.* HAL *follows fast behind. He reaches her just as she gets to the door, and grabs her by the wrist. She resists him furiously.*)

HAL. Baby . . . you're not sorry, are you? (*There is a silence.* MADGE *sobs.*)

MADGE. Let me go.

HAL. Please, Baby. If I thought I'd done anything to make you unhappy, I . . . I'd almost wanta die.

MADGE. I . . . I'm so ashamed.

HAL. Don't say that, Baby.

MADGE. I didn't even know what was happening, and then . . . all of a sudden, it seems like my whole life was changed.

HAL (*with bitter self-disparagement*). I oughta be taken out and hung. I'm just a no-good bum. That schoolteacher was right. I oughta be in the gutter.

MADGE. Don't talk that way.

HAL. Times like this, I hate myself, Baby.

MADGE. I guess . . . it's no more your fault than mine.

HAL. Sometimes I do pretty impulsive things. (MADGE *starts inside.*) Will I see you tomorrow?

MADGE. I don't know.

HAL. Gee, I almost forgot. I start a new job tomorrow.

MADGE. I have to be at the dime store at nine.

HAL. What time you through?

HAL. Maybe I could see you then, huh? Maybe I could come by and . . .

MADGE. I've got a date with Alan—if he'll still speak to me.

HAL (*a new pain*). Jesus, I'd forgot all about Seymour.

MADGE. So had I.

HAL. I can't go back to his house. What'll I do?

MADGE. Maybe Mrs. Potts could . . .

HAL. I'll take the car back to where we were, stretch out in the front seat and get a little sleep. (*He thinks a moment.*) Baby, how you gonna handle your old lady?

MADGE (*with a slight tremor*). I . . . I don't know.

HAL (*in a funk again*). Jesus, I oughta be shot at sunrise.

MADGE. I . . . I'll think of something to tell her.

HAL (*awkward*). Well—good night.

MADGE. Good night. (*She starts again.*)

HAL. Baby—would you kiss me good night . . . maybe? Just one more time.

MADGE. I don't think I better.

HAL. Please!

MADGE. It . . . It'd just start things all over again. Things I better forget.

HAL. Pretty please!

MADGE. Promise not to hold me?

HAL. I'll keep my hands to my side. Swear to God!

MADGE. Well . . . (*Slowly she goes toward him, takes his face in her hands and kisses him. The kiss lasts.* HAL's *hands become nervous and finally find their way around her. Their passion is revived. Then* MADGE *utters a little shriek, tears herself away from* HAL *and runs into the house, sobbing.*) Don't. You *promised.* I never wanta see you again. I might as well be dead. (*She runs inside the front door, leaving* HAL *behind to despise himself. He beats his fists together, kicks the earth with his heel, and starts off, hating the day he was born.*)

CURTAIN

SCENE TWO

It is very early the next morning. MILLIE *sits on the doorstep smoking a cigarette. She wears a fresh wash dress in honor of the first day of school.* FLO *breaks out of the front door. She is a frantic woman.* MILLIE *puts out her cigarette quickly.* FLO *has not even taken the time to dress. She wears an old robe over her nightdress. She speaks to* MILLIE.

———

FLO. Were you awake when Madge got in?

MILLIE. No.

FLO. Did she say anything to you this morning?

MILLIE. No.

FLO. Dear God! I couldn't get two words out of her last night, she was crying so hard. Now she's got the door locked.

MILLIE. I bet I know what happened.

FLO (*sharply*). You don't know anything, Millie Owens. And if anyone says anything to you, you just . . . (*Now she sniffs the air.*) Have you been smoking?

MRS. POTTS (*coming down the back-steps*). Did Madge tell you what happened?

FLO. The next time you take in tramps, Helen Potts, I'll thank you to keep them on your side of the yard.

MRS. POTTS. Is Madge all right?

FLO. Of course she's all right. She got out of the car and left that hoodlum alone. That's what she did.

MRS. POTTS. Have you heard from Alan?

FLO. He said he'd be over this morning.

MRS. POTTS. Where's the young man?

FLO. I know where he should be! He should be in the penitentiary, and that's where he's going if he shows up around here again!

ROSEMARY (*sticking her head out front door*). Has anyone seen Howard?

FLO (*surprised*). Howard? Why, no, Rosemary!

ROSEMARY (*nervous and uncertain*). He said he might be over this morning. Mrs. Owens, I'm storing my summer clothes in the attic. Could someone help me?

FLO. We're busy, Rosemary.

MRS. POTTS. I'll help you, Rosemary. (*She looks at* FLO, *then goes up on porch.*)

ROSEMARY. Thanks, Mrs. Potts. (*Goes inside.*)

FLO (*to* MRS. POTTS). She's been running around like a chicken with its head off all morning. Something's *up!* (MRS. POTTS *goes inside.* FLO *turns to* MILLIE.) You keep watch for Alan. (FLO *goes inside. Now we hear the morning voices of* IRMA *and* CHRISTINE, *coming by for* ROSEMARY.)

IRMA. Girl, I hope Rosemary is ready. I promised the principal that I'd be there early to help with registration.

CHRISTINE. How do I look, Irma?

IRMA. It's a cute dress. Let me fix it in the back. (IRMA *adjusts the hang of the dress as* CHRISTINE *stands patiently.*)

CHRISTINE. I think a teacher should dress up the first day of school, to give the students a good first impression.

IRMA (*going up on the porch*). Good morning, Millie!

MILLIE. Hi.

IRMA. Is Rosemary ready?

MILLIE. Go on up if you want to.

CHRISTINE. We missed seeing Madge on the picnic last night.

MILLIE. So did a lot of other people.

IRMA (*gives* CHRISTINE *a significant look*). Come on, Christine. I bet we have to get that sleepy girl out of bed. (*They go inside front door.* BOMBER *rides on, gets off his bicycle, throws a paper on* MRS. POTTS' *steps, then on* FLO's *back porch. Then he climbs up on* MRS. POTTS' *porch so he can look across into* MADGE's *room.*)

BOMBER. Hey, Madge! Wanta go dancin'? Let me be next, Madge!

MILLIE. You shut up, Crazy.

BOMBER. My brother seen 'em parked under the bridge. Alan Seymour was lookin' for 'em all over town. She always put on a lot of airs, but I knew she liked guys. (*He sees* ALAN *approaching from beyond the* OWEN's *house, and leaves quickly.*)

MILLIE. Some day I'm really gonna kill that ornery bastard. (*She turns and sees* ALAN.)

ALAN. Could I see Madge?

MILLIE. I'll call her, Alan. (*Calls up to* MADGE's *window.*) Madge! Alan's here! (*Back to* ALAN) She prob'ly has to dress.

ALAN. I'll wait.

MILLIE (*she sits on the stump and turns to him very shyly*). I . . . I always liked you, Alan. Didn't you know it?

ALAN (*with some surprise*). Like me?

MILLIE (*nods her head*). It's awfully hard to show someone you like them, isn't it?

ALAN (*with just a little bitterness*). It's easy for *some* people.

MILLIE. It makes you feel like such a

sap. I don't know why.

ALAN (*rather touched*). I . . . I'm glad you like me, Millie.

MILLIE (*one can sense her loneliness*). I don't expect you to do anything about it. I just wanted to tell you.

(HOWARD *comes bustling on through the gate, very upset. He addresses* MILLIE.)

HOWARD. Could I see Rosemary?

MILLIE. My gosh, Howard, what are you doing here?

HOWARD. I think she's expecting me.

MILLIE. You better holler at the bottom of the stairs—(HOWARD *is about to go in the door, but turns back at this.*) all the others are up there, too.

HOWARD (*he looks very grave*). The others?

MILLIE. Mrs. Potts and Miss Kronkite and Miss Schoenwalder.

HOWARD. Golly, I gotta see her alone.

ROSEMARY (*calling from inside*). Howard! (*Inside, to all the women*) It's Howard! He's here!

HOWARD (*knowing he is stuck*). Golly!

(*We hear a joyful bable of women's voices from inside.* HOWARD *gives one last pitiful look at* MILLIE, *then goes in.* MILLIE *follows him in and* ALAN *is left alone in the yard. After a moment,* MADGE *comes out the kitchen door. She wears a simple dress, and her whole being appears chastened. She is inscrutable in her expression.*)

MADGE. Hello, Alan.

ALAN (*very moved by seeing her*). Madge!

MADGE. I'm sorry about last night.

ALAN. Madge, whatever happened—it wasn't your fault. I know what Hal's like when he's drinking. But I've got Hal taken care of now! He won't be bothering you again!

MADGE. Honest?

ALAN. At school I spent half my life getting him out of jams. I knew he'd had a few tough breaks, and I always tried to be sorry for the guy. But this is the thanks I get.

MADGE (*still noncommittal*). Where is he now?

ALAN. Don't worry about Hal! I'll take it on myself now to offer you his official good-by!

MADGE (*one still cannot decipher her feelings*). Is he gone?

FLO (*running out kitchen door. She is dressed now*). Alan, I didn't know you were here!

(*Now we hear shouts from inside the house.* MILLIE *comes out, throwing rice over her shoulder at all the others, who are laughing and shouting so that we only hear bits of the following.*)

MRS. POTTS. Here comes the bride! Here comes the bride!

IRMA. May all your troubles be little ones!

CHRISTINE. You're getting a wonderful girl, Howard Bevans!

IRMA. Rosemary is getting a fine man!

CHRISTINE. They don't come any better'n Rosemary!

MRS. POTTS. Be happy!

IRMA. May all your troubles be little ones!

MRS. POTTS. Be happy forever and ever!

(*Now they are all out on the porch and we see that* HOWARD *carries two suitcases. His face has an expression of complete confusion.* ROSEMARY *wears a fussy going-away outfit.*)

IRMA (*to* ROSEMARY). Girl, are you wearing something old?

ROSEMARY. An old pair of nylons but they're as good as new.

CHRISTINE. And that's a brand-new outfit she's got on. Rosemary, are you wearing something blue? I don't see it!

ROSEMARY (*daringly*). And you're not gonna! (*They all laugh, and* ROSEMARY *begins a personal inventory.*) Something borrowed! I don't have anything to borrow!

(*Now we see* HAL's *head appear from the edge of the woodshed. He watches for a moment when he can be sure of not being observed, then darts into the shed.*)

FLO. Madge, you give Rosemary something to borrow. It'll mean good luck for you. Go on, Madge! (*She takes* ALAN's *arm and pulls him toward the steps with her.*) Rosemary, Madge has something for you to borrow!

MADGE (*crossing to the group by steps*). You can borrow my handkerchief, Miss Sydney.

ROSEMARY. Thank you, Madge. (*She takes the handkerchief.*) Isn't Madge pretty, girls?

IRMA AND CHRISTINE. Oh, yes! Yes, indeed!

(MADGE *turns and leaves the group, going toward* MRS. POTTS' *house.*)

ROSEMARY (*during the above*). She's modest! A girl as pretty as Madge can sail through life without a care! (ALAN *turns from the group to join* MADGE. FLO *then turns and crosses toward* MADGE. ROSEMARY *follows* FLO.) Mrs. Owens, I left my hot-water bottle in the closet and my curlers are in the bathroom. You and the girls can have them. I stored the rest of my things in the attic. Howard and I'll come and get 'em after we settle down. Cherryvale's not so far away. We can be good friends, same as before.

(HAL *sticks his head through woodshed door and catches* MADGE's *eye.* MADGE *is startled.*)

FLO. I hate to mention it now, Rosemary, but you didn't give us much notice. Do you know anyone I could rent the room to?

IRMA (*to* ROSEMARY). Didn't you tell her about Linda Sue Breckenridge?

ROSEMARY. Oh, yes! Linda Sue Breckenridge—she's the sewing teacher!

IRMA (*a positive affirmation to them all*). And she's a darling girl!

ROSEMARY. She and Mrs. Bendix had a fight. Mrs. Bendix wanted to charge her twenty cents for her orange juice in the morning and none of us girls ever paid more'n fifteen. Did we, girls?

IRMA AND CHRISTINE (*in staunch support*). No! Never! I certainly never did!

ROSEMARY. Irma, you tell Linda Sue to get in touch with Mrs. Owens.

IRMA. I'll do that very thing.

FLO. Thank you, Rosemary.

HOWARD. Rosemary, we still got to pick up the license . . .

ROSEMARY (*to* IRMA *and* CHRISTINE, *all of them blubbering*). Good-by, girls! We've had some awfully jolly times together!

(IRMA, CHRSTINE *and* ROSEMARY *embrace.*)

HOWARD (*a little restless*). Come on, Honey!

(ALAN *takes the suitcases from* HOWARD.)

HOWARD (*to* ALAN). A man's gotta settle down some time.

ALAN. Of course.

HOWARD. And folks'd rather do business with a married man!

ROSEMARY (*to* MADGE *and* ALAN). I hope both of you are going to be as happy as Howard and I will be. (*Turns to* MRS. POTTS.) You've been a wonderful friend, Mrs. Potts!

MRS. POTTS. I wish you all sorts of happiness, Rosemary.

ROSEMARY. Good-by, Millie. You're going to be a famous author some day and I'll be proud I knew you.

MILLIE. Thanks, Miss Sydney.

HOWARD (*to* ROSEMARY). All set?

ROSEMARY. All set and rarin' to go! (*A sudden thought.*) Where we goin'?

HOWARD (*after an awkward pause*). Well . . . I got a cousin who runs a tourist camp in the Ozarks. He and his wife could put us up for free.

ROSEMARY. Oh, I love the Ozarks! (*She grabs* HOWARD's *arm and pulls him off stage.* ALAN *carries the suitcase off stage.* IRMA, CHRISTINE, MRS. POTTS *and* MILLIE *follow them, all throwing rice and calling after them.*)

ALL (*as they go off*). The Ozarks are lovely this time of year!

Be happy!

May all your troubles be little ones!

You're getting a wonderful girl!

You're getting a wonderful man!

FLO (*alone with* MADGE). Madge, what happened last night? You haven't told me a word.

MADGE. Let me alone, Mom.

ROSEMARY (*off stage*). Mrs. Owens, aren't you going to tell us good-by?

FLO (*exasperated*). Oh, dear! I've been saying good-by to her all morning.

ALAN (*appearing in gateway*). Mrs. Owens, Miss Sydney wants to give you her house keys.

MRS. POTTS (*behind* ALAN). Come on, Flo!

FLO (*hurrying off*). I'm coming. I'm coming. (*She follows* ALAN *and* MRS. POTTS *to join the noisy shivaree in the background. Now* HAL *appears from the woodshed. His clothes are drenched and cling plastered to his body. He is barefoot and there is blood on his T-shirt. He stands before* MADGE.)

HAL. Baby!

MADGE (*backing from him*). You shouldn't have come here.

HAL. Look, Baby, I'm in a jam.

MADGE. Serves you right.

HAL. Seymour's old man put the cops on my tail. Accused me of stealin' the car. I had to knock one of the bastards cold and swim the river to get away. If they ever catch up with me, it'll be too bad.

MADGE (*things are in a different light now*). You were born to get in trouble.

HAL. Baby, I just *had* to say good-by.

MADGE (*still not giving away her feelings*). Where you going?

HAL. The freight train's by pretty soon. I'll hop a ride. I done it lotsa times before.

MADGE. What're you gonna do?

HAL. I got some friends in Tulsa. I can always get a job hoppin' bells at the Hotel Mayo. Jesus, I hate to say good-by.

MADGE (*not knowing what her precise feelings are*). Well . . . I don't know what else there is to do.

HAL. Are you still mad, Baby?

MADGE. I . . . I never knew a boy like you.

(*The shivaree is quieting down now, and* HOWARD *and* ROSEMARY *can be heard driving off as the others call.* FLO *returns, stopping in the gateway, seeing* HAL.)

FLO. Madge!

(*Now* ALAN *comes running on.*)

ALAN (*incensed*). Hal, what're you doing here?

(MRS. POTTS *and* MILLIE *come on, followed by* IRMA *and* CHRISTINE.)

MRS. POTTS. It's the young man!

HAL. Look, Seymour, I didn't swipe your lousy car. Get that straight!

ALAN. You better get out of town if you know what's good for you.

HAL. I'll go when I'm ready.

MRS. POTTS. Go? I thought you were going to stay here and settle down.

HAL. No'm. I'm not gonna settle down.

ALAN (*tearing into* HAL *savagely*). You'll go *now*. What do you take me for?

HAL (*holding* ALAN *off, not wanting a fight*). Look, Kid, I don't wanta fight with you. You're the only friend I ever had.

ALAN. We're not friends any more. I'm not scared of you. (ALAN *plows into* HAL, *but* HAL *is far beyond him in strength and physical alertness. He fastens* ALAN's *arms quickly behind him and brings him to the ground.* IRMA *and* CHRISTINE *watch excitedly from the gateway.* MRS. POTTS *is apprehensive.* ALAN *cries out in pain.*) Let me go, you God-damn tramp! Let me go!

FLO (*to* HAL). Take your hands off him, this minute.

(*But* ALAN *has to admit he is mastered.* HAL *releases him and* ALAN *retires to* MRS. POTTS' *back doorstep, sitting there, holding his hands over his face, feeling the deepest humiliation. A train whistle is heard in the distance.* HAL *hurries to* MADGE's *side.*)

HAL (*to* MADGE). Baby, aren't you gonna say good-by?

FLO (*to* IRMA *and* CHRISTINE). You better run along, girls. This is no side show we're running. (*They depart in a huff.*)

MADGE (*keeping her head down, not wanting to look at* HAL) . . . Good-by . . .

HAL. Please don't be mad, Baby. You were sittin' there beside me lookin' so pretty, sayin' all those sweet things, and I . . . I thought you liked me, too, Baby. Honest I did.

MADGE. It's all right. I'm not mad.

HAL. Thanks. Thanks a lot.

FLO (*like a barking terrier*). Young man, if you don't leave here this second, I'm going to call the police and have you put where you belong.

(MADGE *and* HAL *do not even hear.*)

MADGE. *And I . . . I did like you* . . . the first time I saw you.

FLO (*incensed*). Madge!

HAL (*beaming*). Honest? (MADGE *nods.*) I kinda thought you did. (*All has been worth it now for* HAL. MILLIE *watches skeptically from doorstep.* MRS. POTTS *looks lovingly from the back.* FLO *at times concerns herself with* ALAN, *then with trying to get rid of* HAL.)

FLO. *Madge,* I want you inside the house this minute.

(MADGE *doesn't move.*)

HAL. Look, Baby, I never said it before. I never could. It made me feel like such a freak, but I . . .

MADGE. What?

HAL. I'm nuts about you, Baby, I mean it.

MADGE. You make love to lots of girls . . .

HAL. A few.

MADGE. . . . just like you made love to me last night.

HAL. Not like last night, Baby. Last night was . . . (*Gropes for the word*) *inspired.*

MADGE. Honest?

HAL. The way you sat there, knowin' just how I felt. The way you held my hand and talked.

MADGE. I couldn't stand to hear Miss Sydney treat you that way. After all, you're a man.

HAL. And you're a woman, Baby, whether you know it or not. You're a real, live woman.

(*A police siren is heard stirring up the distance.* FLO, MRS. POTTS *and* MILLIE *are alarmed.*)

MILLIE. Hey, it's the cops.

MRS. POTTS. I'll know how to take care of them. (MRS. POTTS *hurries off, right,* MILLIE *watching.* HAL *and* MADGE *have not moved. They stand looking into each other's eyes. Then* HAL *speaks.*)

HAL. Do—do you love me?

MADGE (*tears forming in her eyes*). What good is it if I do?

HAL. I'm a poor bastard, Baby. I've gotta claim the things in this life that're mine. Kiss me good-by. (*He grabs her and kisses her.*) Come with me, Baby. They gimme a room in the basement of the hotel. It's kinda crummy but we could share it till we found something better.

FLO (*outraged*). Madge! Are you out of your senses?

MADGE. I couldn't.

(*The train whistles in the distance.*)

FLO. Young man, you'd better get on that train as fast as you can.

HAL (*to* MADGE). When you hear that train pull outa town and know I'm on it, your little heart's gonna be busted, cause you love me, God damn it! You love me, you love me, you love me. (*He stamps one final kiss on her lips, then runs off to catch his train.* MADGE *falls in a heap when he releases her.* FLO *is quick to console* MADGE.)

FLO. Get up, girl.

MADGE. Oh, Mom!

FLO. Why did this have to happen to you?

MADGE. I *do* love him! I *do!*

FLO. Hush, girl. Hush. The neighbors are on their porches, watching.

MADGE. I never knew what the feeling was. Why didn't someone tell me?

MILLIE (*peering off at the back*). He made it. He got on the train.

MADGE (*a cry of deep regret*). Now I'll never see him again.

FLO. Madge, believe me, that's for the best.

MADGE. Why? Why?

FLO. At least you didn't marry him.

MADGE (*a wail of anguish*). Oh, Mom, what can you do with the love you feel? Where is there you can take it?

FLO (*beaten and defeated*). I . . . I never found out.

(MADGE *goes into the house, crying.* MRS. POTTS *returns, carrying* HAL's *boots. She puts them on the porch.*)

MRS. POTTS. The police found these on the river bank.

ALAN (*on* MRS. POTTS' *steps, rises*). Girls have always liked Hal. Months after he'd left the fraternity, they still called. "Is Hal there?" "Does anyone know where Hal's gone?" Their voices always sounded so forlorn.

FLO. Alan, come to dinner tonight. I'm having sweet-potato pie and all the things you like.

ALAN. I'll be gone, Mrs. Owens.

FLO. Gone?

ALAN. Dad's been wanting me to take him up to Michigan on a fishing trip. I've been stalling him, but now I . . .

FLO. You'll be back before you go to school, won't you?

ALAN. I'll be back Christmas, Mrs. Owens.

FLO. Christmas! Alan, go inside and say good-by to Madge!

ALAN (*recalling his past love*). Madge is beautiful. It made me feel so proud—just to *look* at her—and tell myself she's mine.

FLO. See her one more time, Alan!

ALAN (*his mind is made up*). No! I'll be home Christmas. I'll run over then and —say hello. (*He runs off.*)

FLO (*a cry of loss*). Alan!

MRS. POTTS (*consolingly*). He'll be back, Flo. He'll be back.

MILLIE (*waving good-by*). Good-by Alan!

FLO (*getting life started again*). You better get ready for school, Millie.

MILLIE (*going to doorstep, rather sad*). Gee, I almost forgot. (*She goes inside.* FLO *turns to* MRS. POTTS.)

FLO. You—you liked the young man, didn't you, Helen? Admit it.

MRS. POTTS. Yes, I did.

FLO (*belittlingly*). Hmm.

MRS. POTTS. With just Mama and me in the house, I'd got so used to things as they were, everything so prim, occasionally a hairpin on the floor, the geranium in the window, the smell of Mama's medicines . . .

FLO. I'll keep things as they are in *my* house, thank you.

MRS. POTTS. Not when a man is there, Flo. He walked through the door and suddenly everything was different. He clomped through the tiny rooms like he was still in the great outdoors, he talked in a booming voice that shook the ceiling. Everything he did reminded me there was a man in the house, and it seemed good.

FLO (*skeptically*). Did it?

MRS. POTTS. And that reminded *me* . . . I'm a woman, and that seemed good, too.

(*Now* MILLIE *comes swaggering out the front door, carrying her schoolbooks.*)

MILLIE (*disparagingly*). Madge is in love with that crazy guy. She's in there crying her eyes out.

FLO. Mind your business and go to school.

MILLIE. I'm never gonna fall in love. Not me.

MRS. POTTS. Wait till you're a little older before you say that, Millie-girl.

MILLIE. I'm old enough already. Madge can *stay* in this jerkwater town and marry some ornery guy and raise a lot of dirty kids. When I graduate from college I'm going to New York, and write novels that'll shock people right out of their senses.

MRS. POTTS. You're a talented girl, Millie.

MILLIE (*victoriously*). I'll be so great and famous—I'll never have to fall in love.

A BOY'S VOICE (*from off stage, heckling* MILLIE). Hey, Goongirl!

MILLIE (*spotting him in the distance*). It's Poopdeck McCullough. He thinks he's so smart.

BOY'S VOICE. Hey Goongirl! Come kiss me. I wanna be sick.

MILLIE (*her anger aroused*). If he thinks he can get by with that, he's crazy. (*She finds a stick with which to chastise her offender.*)

FLO. Millie! Millie! You're a grown girl now.

(MILLIE *thinks better of it, drops the stick and starts off.*)

MILLIE. See you this evening. (*She goes off.*)

FLO (*wanting reassurance*). Alan *will* be back, don't you think so, Helen?

MRS. POTTS. Of course he'll be back, Flo. He'll be back at Christmas time and take her to the dance at the Country Club, and they'll get married and live happily ever after.

FLO. I hope so.

(*Suddenly* MADGE *comes out the front door. She wears a hat and carries a small cardboard suitcase. There is a look of firm decision on her face. She walks straight to the gateway.*)

FLO (*stunned*). Madge!

MADGE. I'm going to Tulsa, Mom.

MRS. POTTS (*to herself*). For heaven sake!

MADGE. Please don't get mad. I'm not doing it to be spiteful.

FLO (*holding her head*). As I live and breathe!

MADGE. I know how you feel, but I don't know what else to do.

FLO (*anxiously*). Now look, Madge, Alan's coming back Christmas. He'll take you to the dance at the Club. I'll make another new dress for you, and . . .

MADGE. I'm going, Mom.

FLO (*frantic*). Madge! Listen to what I've got to say . . .

MADGE. My bus leaves in a few minutes.

FLO. He's no good. He'll never be able to support you. When he does have a job, he'll spend all his money on booze. After a while, there'll be other women.

MADGE. I've thought of all those things.

MRS. POTTS. You don't love someone cause he's perfect, Flo.

FLO. Oh, God!

BOY's VOICE (*in the distance*). Hey, Madge! Hey Beautiful! You're the one for me!

MRS. POTTS. Who are those boys?

MADGE. Some of the gang, in their hot-rod. (*Kisses* MRS. POTTS.) Good-by, Mrs. Potts, I'll miss you almost as much as Mom.

FLO (*tugging at* MADGE, *trying to take the suitcase from her*). Madge, now listen to me. I can't let you . . .

MADGE. It's no use, Mom. I'm going. Don't worry. I've got ten dollars I was saving for a pair of pumps, and I saw ads in the Tulsa *World*. There's lots of jobs as waitresses. Tell Millie good-by for me, Mom. Tell her I never meant it all those time I said I hated her.

FLO (*wailing*). Madge . . . Madge . . .

MADGE. Tell her I've always been very proud to have such a smart sister. (*She runs off now,* FLO *still tugging at her, then giving up and standing by the gatepost, watching* MADGE *in the distance.*)

FLO. Helen, could I stop her?

MRS. POTTS. Could anyone have stopped you, Flo? (FLO *gives* MRS. POTTS *a look of realization.*)

BOY's VOICE. Hey Madge! You're the one for me!

FLO (*still watching* MADGE *in the distance*). She's so young. There are so many things I meant to tell her, and never got around to it.

MRS. POTTS. Let her learn them for herself, Flo.

MRS. POTTS' MOTHER. Helen! Helen!

MRS. POTTS. Be patient, Mama. (*Starts up the stairs to her back porch.* FLO *still stands in the gateway, watching in the distance.*)

CURTAIN

BUS STOP

William Inge

First presented by Robert Whitehead and
Roger L. Stevens at the Music Box Theatre, New York,
March 2, 1955, with the following cast:

ELMA DUCKWORTH	Phyllis Love	DR. GERALD LYMAN	Anthony Ross
GRACE HOYLARD	Elaine Stritch	CARL	Patrick McVey
WILL MASTERS	Lou Polan	VIRGIL BLESSING	Crahan Denton
CHERIE	Kim Stanley	BO DECKER	Albert Salmi

The action of the play takes place in a street-corner restaurant in a small town about thirty miles west of Kansas City.

ACT I. A night in early March. 1:00 A.M.

ACT II. A few minutes later.

ACT III. Early morning. About 5:00 A.M.

INTRODUCTION

Bus Stop, aside from being a work of depth in several of its scenes, is an entertainment—very nearly a theatrical showpiece—with its bizarre affair of the loud cowboy and the distrait night-club singer. Inge had not let himself go that far in theatricality in his earlier plays *Come Back Little Sheba* and *Picnic.* But he was not actually being out of character or out of his metier in *Bus Stop,* for "theatre," much of it quite uproarious, was not remote for one who, despite his two university degrees, could declare, "I sort of based my life on the theatre." And indeed he had been "a juvenile monologuist, an actor in high school and college plays, a trouper in tent shows, in stock, and on the radio." (*The New York Times,* March 22, 1953.) But comic theatricality was only one level of interest in *Bus Stop.* What would usually be overfamiliar—I have in mind such stock figures as a roistering cowboy, a Western sheriff, a hearty truckdriver, and an alcoholic derelict who can quote Shakespeare—possessed much freshness in Mr. Inge's treatment, which mingled the comic element with implications of the "tears in things." In Harold Clurman's noteworthy staging of the play, the balance between the moods of the work was altogether evident.

As a result there were reviewers in town prepared to vow, with Brooks Atkinson, that "having written a wonderful play two years ago [*Picnic*], William Inge has now written a better one." It was characteristic of this playwright's career, indeed, that somebody was always seeing evidences of progress in it, whether or not "progress" had much to do with the individual quality of each new play. And in the fall of 1957 he found a veritable chorus of reviewers ready to proclaim that the low-keyed work that followed *Bus Stop* about a year and a half later, *The Dark at the Top of the Stairs* (already bespoken for the next *Best American Plays* volume) was the best to date, a work of "size" in spite of the smallness of the characters in it.

ACT ONE

The entire play is set inside a street-corner restaurant in a small Kansas town about thirty miles west of Kansas City. The restaurant serves also as an occasional rest stop for the bus lines in the area. It is a dingy establishment with few modern improvements: scenic calendars and pretty-girl posters decorate the soiled walls, and illumination comes from two badly shaded light bulbs that hang on dangling cords from the ceiling; there are several quartet tables with chairs, for dining; at far L. is the counter with six stools before it, running the depth of the setting; behind the counter are the usual restaurant equipment and paraphernalia (coffee percolator, dishes, glasses, hot-plate, sink, electric refrigerator, etc.); on top of the counter are several large plates of doughnuts, sweet rolls, etc., under glass covers. Three sugar bowls and a few dishes. At the far R., close to the outside entrance-door, are a magazine stand and a rack of shelves piled with paper-back novels and books. At back C. is an old-fashioned Franklin stove. At the back R. is a great window that provides a view of the local scenery. Against the rear wall, beneath the window, are two long benches meant for waiting passengers. At the back L. is the rear door, close to the upper end of the counter. Above this door is a dim hand-painted sign, "Rest Rooms in the Rear." U. S. in the L. wall is the door to Grace's apartment. A closet below that door.

It is one A. M. on a night in early March and a near blizzard is raging outside. Through the window we can see the sweeping wind and flying snow. Inside, by comparison, the scene is warm and cozy, the Franklin stove radiating all the heat of which it is capable. Two young women, in uniforms that have lost their starched freshness, are employed behind the counter. ELMA is a big-eyed girl still in high school. GRACE is a more seasoned character in her thirties or early forties. A bus is expected soon and they are checking, somewhat lackadaisically, the supplies. Outside, the powerful, reckless wind comes and goes, blasting against everything in its path, seeming to shake the very foundation of the little restaurant building; then subsiding, leaving a period of uncertain stillness. When the curtain goes up, ELMA stands far

R., *looking out the large plate-glass window, awed by the fury of the elements.* GRACE *is at the telephone, an old-fashioned wall phone behind counter* U. L.

ELMA (U. R., *drying a glass*). Listen to that wind. March is coming in like a lion. (GRACE *jiggles the receiver on the telephone with no results.*) Grace, you should come over here and look out, to see the way the wind is blowing things all over town.

GRACE. Now I wonder why I can't get th' operator.

ELMA. I bet the bus'll be late.

GRACE (*finally hanging up*). I bet it won't. The roads are O.K. as far as here. It's ahead they're havin' trouble. I can't even get the operator. She must have more calls than she can handle. (*Crosses* D. L. *behind counter, clears dishes from* D. S. *end of counter.*)

ELMA (*still looking out the window*). I bet the bus doesn't *have* many passengers.

GRACE. Prob'ly not. But we gotta stay open even if there's only *one*. (*Takes dishes to sink.*)

ELMA. I shouldn't think anyone would take a trip tonight unless he absolutely *had* to.

GRACE. Are your folks gonna worry, Elma?

ELMA. No—Daddy said, before I left home, he bet this'd happen.

GRACE. Well, you better come back here and help me. The bus'll be here any minute and we gotta have things ready.

ELMA (*leaving the window, following* GRACE). Nights like this, I'm glad I have a home to go to.

GRACE (*washing and drying*). Well, I got a home to go to, but there ain't anyone in it.

ELMA (*puts tops on three sugar bowls on counter*). Where's your husband now, Grace?

GRACE. How should I know?

ELMA (*crosses* R. *with two sugars*). Don't you miss him?

GRACE. No!

ELMA (*puts sugars on tables*). If he came walking in now, wouldn't you be glad to see him?

GRACE. You ask more questions.

ELMA. I'm just curious about things, Grace.

GRACE. Well, kids your age *are*. I don't know. I'd be happy to see him, I guess, if I knew he wasn't gonna stay very long.

ELMA (*crosses back to* U. S. *end of counter*). Don't you get lonesome, Grace, when you're not working down here?

GRACE. Sure I do. If I didn't have this restaurant to keep me busy, I'd prob'ly go nuts. Sometimes, at night, after I empty the garbage and lock the doors and turn out the lights, I get kind of a sick feelin', 'cause I sure don't look forward to walkin' up those stairs and lettin' myself into an empty apartment.

ELMA. Gee, if you feel that way, why don't you write your husband and tell him to come back?

GRACE (*thinks a moment, leans on* D. S. *end of counter*). 'Cause I got just as lonesome when he was here. He wasn't much company, 'cept when we were makin' love. But makin' love is *one* thing, and bein' lonesome is another. The resta the time, me and Barton was usually fightin'.

ELMA (U. *of* GRACE). I guess my folks get along pretty well. I mean . . . they really seem to like each other.

GRACE. Oh, I know *all* married people aren't like Barton and I. Not all! (*Goes to* U. L. *telephone again.* ELMA *goes to sink, dries glasses which she puts* D. S. *on counter.*) Now, maybe I can get the operator. (*Jiggles receiver.*) Quiet as a tomb. (*Hangs up.*)

ELMA. I *like* working here with you, Grace.

GRACE. Do you, honey? I'm glad, 'cause I sure don't know what I'd do without ya. Week-ends especially.

ELMA. You know, I dreaded the job at first.

GRACE (*kidding her*). Why? Thought you wouldn't have time for all your boy friends? (ELMA *looks a little sour.* GRACE *gets rag from sink, wipes counter.*) Maybe you'd have more boy friends if you didn't make such good grades. Boys feel kind of embarrassed if they feel a girl is smarter than they are.

ELMA. What should I do? Flunk my courses?

GRACE (*puts rag on sink*). I should say not. You're a good kid and ya got good sense. I wish someone coulda reasoned with *me* when I was your age. But I was a headstrong brat, had to have my own way. I had my own way all right, and here I am now, a grass widow runnin' a restaurant, and I'll prob'ly die in this little town and they'll bury me out by the back-house.

(WILL, *the sheriff, comes in the front door, wind and snow flying through the door with him. He is a huge, saturnine man, well over six feet, who has a thick black beard and a scar on his forehead. He wears a battered black hat, clumsy overshoes, and a heavy mackinaw. He looks somewhat forbidding.*)

WILL (*on entering*). You girls been able to use your phone?

GRACE. No, Will. The operator don't answer.

WILL. That means *all* the lines are down. 'Bout time fer the Topeka bus, ain't it?

GRACE. Due now.

WILL. You're gonna have to hold 'em here, don't know how long. The highway's blocked 'tween here and Topeka. May be all night gettin' it cleared.

GRACE. I was afraid a that.

WILL. They got the highway gang workin' on it now and the telephone company's tryin' to get the lines back up. March is comin' in like a lion, all right.

GRACE. Yah.

WILL (*taking off his mackinaw, hanging it, going to the fire to warm his hands*). The station house's *cold*. Got any fresh coffee?

GRACE (*goes to coffee urn*). It just went through, Will. Fresh as ya could want it.

WILL (*goes to counter*). A storm like this makes me mad. (GRACE *laughs at his remark and gives him a cup of coffee.*) It *does*. It makes me mad. It's just like all the elements had lost their reason.

GRACE (*stands behind counter near* WILL). Nothin' you can do about a wind like *that*.

WILL. Maybe it's just 'cause I'm a sheriff, but I like to see things in order.

GRACE. Let the wind blow! I just pray to God to leave a roof over my head. That's about all a person *can* do.

(*The sound of the bus is heard outside, its great motor coming to a stop.*)

WILL. Here it is.

GRACE. Better fill some water glasses, Elma. (ELMA *gets water pitcher, fills glasses.*) Remember, the doughnuts are left over from yesterday but it'll be all right to serve 'em. We got everything for sandwiches but *cheese*. We got no cheese.

WILL. You *never* got cheese, Grace. (*Rises, crosses* R.)

GRACE (U. S. *of counter*). I guess I'm

kinda self-centered, Will. I don't care for cheese m'self, so I never think t' order it for someone else.

ELMA. Gee, I'm glad I'm not traveling on the bus tonight.

GRACE. I wonder who's drivin' tonight. This is Carl's night, isn't it?

ELMA. I think so.

GRACE. Yes it is. (*Obviously the idea of* CARL *pleases her. She nudges* ELMA *confidentially.*) Remember, honey, *I* always serve Carl.

ELMA. Sure, Grace.

(*The front door swings open, some of the snow flying inside, and* CHERIE, *a young blonde girl of about twenty, enters as though driven. She wears no hat, and her hair, despite one brilliant bobby pin, blows wild about her face. She is pretty in a fragile, girlish way. She runs immediately to the counter to solicit the attention of* GRACE *and* ELMA. *She lugs along an enormous straw suitcase that is worn and battered. Her clothes, considering her situations, are absurd: a skimpy jacket of tarnished metal cloth edged with not luxuriant fur, a dress of sequins and net, and gilded sandals that expose brightly enameled toes. Also, her make-up has been applied under the influence of having seen too many movies. Her lipstick creates a voluptuous pair of lips that aren't her own, and her eyebrows also form a somewhat arbitrary line. But despite all these defects, her prettiness still is apparent, and she has the appeal of a tender little bird. Her origin is the Ozarks and her speech is Southern.*)

CHERIE (*anxious, direct*). Is there some place I kin hide?

GRACE (*taken aback*). What?

CHERIE. There's a *man* on that bus . . . I wanna *hide*.

GRACE (*stumped*). Well, gee . . . I dunno.

CHERIE (*seeing the sign above the rear door* U. L., *starting for it*). I'll hide in the powder room. If a tall, lanky cowboy comes in here, you kin just tell him I disappeared.

GRACE (*her voice stopping* CHERIE *at the door*). Hey, you can't hide out there. It's cold. You'll freeze your . . .

CHERIE (*having opened the door, seeing it is an outside toilet*). Oh! It's outside.

GRACE. This is just a country town.

CHERIE (*starting again*). I kin stand any-thing fer twenty minutes.

GRACE (*stopping her again*). I got news for ya. The bus may be here all night.

CHERIE (*turning*). What?

GRACE. The highway's blocked. You're gonna have to stay here till it's cleared.

CHERIE (*shutting the door, coming to counter, lugging her suitcase. She is about to cry*). Criminey! What am I gonna do?

GRACE (*comes from behind counter, gets coat and goes to front door*). I better go out and tell Carl 'bout the delay. (*Goes out front door.*)

CHERIE (*dropping to a stool at the counter*). What am I gonna do? What am I ever gonna do?

ELMA (*in a friendly way*). There's a little hotel down the street.

CHERIE. What ya take me for? A millionaire?

WILL (*coming to* CHERIE *with a professional interest*). What's the trouble, Miss?

CHERIE (*looking at* WILL *suspiciously*). You a p'liceman? (*Rises, a step* L.)

WILL. I'm the local sheriff.

ELMA (C. *behind counter. Feeling some endorsement is called for*). But everyone likes him. Really!

CHERIE. Well . . . I ain't askin' t' have no one arrested.

WILL. Who says I'm gonna arrest anyone? What's your trouble?

CHERIE. I . . . I need protection.

WILL. What from?

CHERIE. There's a man after me. He's a cowboy.

WILL (*looking around*). Where is he?

CHERIE. He's on the bus asleep, him and his buddy. I jumped off the bus the very second it stopped, to make my getaway. But there ain't no place to *get* away to. And he'll be in here purty soon. You just *gotta* make him lemme alone.

WILL. Ya meet him on the bus?

CHERIE. No. I met him in Kansas City. I work at the Blue Dragon night club there, down by the stockyards. *He* come there with the annual rodeo, and him and the resta the cowboys was at the night club ev'ry night. Ev'ry night there was a big fight. The boss says he ain't gonna let the cowboys in when they come back next year.

WILL (C.). Then he followed ya on the bus?

CHERIE. He *put* me on the bus. I'm bein' abducted.

WILL. Abducted! But you took time to pack a suitcase!

CHERIE. I was goin' somewhere else, tryin' to get away from him, but he picked me up and carried me to the bus and put me on it. I din have nothin' to say about it at all.

WILL. Where's he plan on takin' ya?

CHERIE. Says he's got a ranch up in Montana. He says we're gonna git married soon as we get there.

WILL. And yor against it?

CHERIE. I don't wanta go up to some God-forsaken ranch in Montana.

WILL. Well, if this cowboy's really takin' ya against yor will, I s'pose I'll have to stop him from it.

CHERIE. You just don't know this cowboy. He's mean.

WILL. I reckon I kin handle him. You relax now. I'll be around mosta the night. If there's any trouble, I'll put a stop to it.

ELMA. You're safe with Will here. Will is very respected around here. He's never lost a fight.

WILL. What're ya talkin' about, Elma? Of course I've lost a fight . . . once.

ELMA. Grace always said you were *invincible.*

WILL. There ain't no one that's . . . *invincible.* A man's gotta learn that, the sooner the better. A good fighter has gotta know what it is to *get* licked. Thass what makes the diff'rence 'tween a fighter and a *bully.* (*Goes* U. R., *gets magazine from rack and sits on bench by window.*)

CHERIE (*shuddering*). There's gonna be trouble. I kin feel it in my bones.

(*Enter* DR. GERALD LYMAN, *a man of medium height, about fifty, with a ruddy, boyish face that smilingly defies the facts of his rather scholarly glasses and iron-gray hair. He wears an old tweed suit of good quality underneath a worn Burberry. His clothes are mussed, and he wears no hat, probably having left it somewhere; for he has been drinking and is, at present, very jubilant. He looks over the restaurant approvingly.*)

DR. LYMAN. Ah! "This castle hath a pleasant seat."

CHERIE (D. L. *end of counter. To* ELMA). Could I hide my suitcase behind the counter, so's he won't see it when he comes in? I ain't gonna say anything to him at all 'bout not goin' on to Montana with him. I'm just gonna let 'im think I'm goin' 'til the bus pulls out and he finds I ain't on it. Thaas th' only thing I know t' do. (*Crosses to stove.*)

ELMA (*taking the suitcase and putting it behind counter,* U. R. *end*). Oh, you needn't worry with Will here.

CHERIE. Think so? (*She studies* WILL.) Looks kinda like Moses, don't he? (*Crosses to counter, sits on stool* D. L.)

ELMA. He *is* a very religious man. Would you believe it? He's a deacon in the Congregational Church.

CHERIE (*just because she happens to think of it*). My folks was Holy Rollers. Will ya gimme a cup of coffee, please? Lotsa cream. (ELMA *draws a cup of coffee for her. Then* CARL, *the bus driver, comes in, followed by* GRACE. CARL *is a hefty man, loud and hearty, who looks very natty in his uniform.*)

WILL (*calling to him from across the room*). Howdy, Carl! You bring this wind? (CHERIE *drinks her coffee.*)

CARL (*hollering back*). No! It brought *me!* (*This greeting probably has passed between them a dozen times, but they still relish it as new.*)

GRACE (*slaps* CARL *on shoulder*). Aren't you the comedian? (*Takes off coat, puts it in closet and crosses to counter.*)

CARL. The wind is doin' ninety miles an hour. The bus is doin' twenty. What's *your* guess about the roads, Will?

WILL (*rises, moves* c). They got the highway gang out. It may take a few hours.

CARL. Telephone lines down, too?

WILL. Yah. But they're workin' on 'em. (DR. LYMAN, *having got his extremities warmed at the fire, seeks* CARL *privately to make certain clarifications.*)

DR. LYMAN. Driver, it seems to me we are still in the state of Kansas. Is that right?

CARL. What do ya mean, still? You been in the state of Kansas about a half hour.

DR. LYMAN. But I don't understand. I was told, when I left Kansas City, that I would be across the state line immediately. And now I find . . .

CARL (*eying* DR. LYMAN *suspiciously*). You was kinda anxious to get across that state line, too, wasn't you, Jack?

DR. LYMAN (*startled*). Why . . . what ever do you mean?

CARL. Nothin'. Anyway, you're across the line now. In case you didn't know it,

Kansas City is in *Missouri.*

DR. LYMAN. Are you joking?

CARL. There's a Kansas City, Kansas, too, but *you* got on in Kansas City, Missouri. That's the trouble with you Easterners. You don't know anything about any of the country west of the Hudson River.

DR. LYMAN. Come, come now. Don't scold.

GRACE (*as* CARL *gets out of his heavy coat*). Carl, let me hang up your coat fer ya, while you get warm at the stove. (*She hangs up his coat as he moves to stove.* DR. LYMAN's *eyes brighten when he sees* ELMA, *and he bows before her like a cavalier.*)

DR. LYMAN. "Nymph in thy orisons, be all my sins remembered!" (*Moves* D. L. *to counter.*)

ELMA (*smiling*). I'm sorry your bus is held up.

DR. LYMAN. Oohh! Is that a nice way to greet me?

ELMA (*confused*). I mean . . . (GRACE *is* U. C. *near* CARL L. *of stove.*)

DR. LYMAN. After my loving greeting, all you can think of to say is, "I'm sorry your bus is held up." (*Sits on stool at counter.*) Well, I'm not. I would much rather sit here looking into the innocent blue of your eyes than continue riding on that monotonous bus. (GRACE *gets coffee, takes it to* CARL.)

ELMA. Don't you have to get somewhere? (WILL *gets magazine, drifts to bench by window.*)

DR. LYMAN. I have a ticket in my pocket to Denver, but I don't have to get there. I never have to get *anywhere.* I travel around from one town to another just to prove to myself that I'm *free.*

ELMA. The bus probably won't get into Denver for another day.

DR. LYMAN. Ah, well! What is our next stop?

ELMA. Topeka.

DR. LYMAN. Topeka? Oh, yes! that's where the famous hospital is, isn't it?

ELMA. The Menninger Clinic? Yes, it's a very famous place. Lots of movie stars go there for nervous breakdowns and things.

DR. LYMAN (*wryly*). Does the town offer anything else in the way of diversion?

ELMA. It's the capital of Kansas. It's almost as big as Kansas City. They have a university and a museum, and sometimes symphony concerts and plays. I go over there every Sunday to visit my married sister.

DR. LYMAN. Aren't there any Indian tribes around here that have war dances?

ELMA (*laughing*). No, silly! We're very civilized.

DR. LYMAN. I'll make my own judgment about that. Meanwhile, you may fix me a double shot of rye whiskey . . . on the rocks. (*Rises, moves* R.)

ELMA (*leans on counter*). I'm sorry, sir. We don't sell drinks.

DR. LYMAN. You don't sell drinks?

ELMA. Not intoxicating drinks. No, sir.

DR. LYMAN. Alas!

ELMA. We have fresh coffee, homemade pies and cakes, all kinds of sandwiches . . .

DR. LYMAN. No, my girl. You're not going to sober me up with your dainties. I am prepared for such emergencies. (*Draws a pint bottle of whiskey from his overcoat pocket.*) You may give me a bottle of your finest lemon soda. (ELMA *gets bottle of lemon soda from refrigerator.*)

ELMA (*whispering*). You'd better not let Will see you do that. You're not supposed to.

DR. LYMAN. Who is *he,* the sheriff?

ELMA. Yes. Lots of people do spike their drinks here and we never say anything, but Will would have to make you stop if *he* saw you.

DR. LYMAN. I shall be *most* cautious. I promise. (*She sets the bottle of soda before him as he smiles at her benignly. He pours some soda in a glass, then some whiskey, and ambles over to a table, far* R., *sitting down with his drink before him.* WILL *rises, moves over to* CARL, *who's at the end of the counter chiding* GRACE, *where the two of them have been standing, talking in very personal voices that can't be overheard.*)

WILL. I sure don't envy ya, Carl, drivin' in weather like this. (GRACE *crosses behind counter.*)

CARL (*making it sound like a personal observation*). Yah! March is comin' in like a *lion.*

WILL. This all the passengers ya got?

CARL. There's a coupla crazy cowboys rolled up in the back seat, asleep. I thought I woke 'em, but I guess I didn't.

WILL. Shouldn't you go out and do it now?

CARL. I'd jest as soon they stayed where they're at. One of 'em's a real troublemaker. You know the kind, first time off a ranch and wild as a bronco. He's been on the make fer this li'l blonde down here . . . (*Indicates* CHERIE.)

WILL. She was tellin' me.

CARL. I've had a good mind to put him off the bus, the way he's been actin'. I say, there's a time and place for ev'rything.

WILL. That bus may get snowbound purty soon.

CARL. I'll go wake 'em in a minute, Will. Just lemme have a li'l *time* here. (WILL *sizes up the situation as* CARL *returns his attention to* GRACE, *then* WILL *picks up a copy of the Kansas City Star, sitting down close to the fire to read.* CARL *leans over counter.*) Ya know what, Grace? This is the first time you and I ever had more'n twenty minutes t'gether.

GRACE (*coyly*). So what?

CARL. Oh, I dunno. I'll prob'ly be here mosta the night. It'd sure be nice to have a nice li'l apartment to go to, some place to sit and listen to the radio, with a good-lookin' woman . . . somethin' like you . . . to talk with . . . maybe have a few beers.

GRACE. That wouldn't be a hint or anything, would it?

CARL (*faking innocence*). Why? Do you have an apartment like that, Grace?

GRACE. Yes, I do. But I never told *you* about it. Did that ornery Dobson fella tell you I had an apartment over the restaurant?

CARL (*in a query*). Dobson? Dobson? I can't seem to remember anyone named Dobson. (ELMA *is washing, drying dishes behind counter.*)

GRACE. You know him better'n *I* do. He comes through twice a week with the Southwest Bus. He told me you and him meet in Topeka sometimes and paint the town.

CARL. Dobson? Oh, yah, I know Dobson. Vern Dobson. A prince of a fella.

GRACE. Well, if he's been gabbin' to you about my apartment, I can tell ya he's oney been up there *once,* when he come in here with his hand cut, and I took him up there to bandage it. Now that's the oney time he was ever up there. On my word of honor.

CARL. Oh, Vern Dobson speaks very highly of you, Grace. Very highly.

GRACE. Well . . . he better. Now, what ya gonna have?

CARL (*sits on stool at counter*). Make it a ham and cheese on rye.

GRACE. I'm sorry, Carl. We got no cheese.

CARL. What happened? Did the mice get it?

GRACE. None of your wise remarks.

CARL. O.K. Make it a ham on rye, then.

GRACE (*at breadbox*). I'm sorry, Carl, but we got no rye, either.

DR. LYMAN (*chiming in, from his table*). I can vouch for that, sir. I just asked for rye, myself, and was refused. (ELMA, *at stove, watches.*)

CARL (*turns*). Look, Mister, don't ya think ya oughta lay off that stuff till ya get home and meet the missus?

DR. LYMAN. The *missus,* did you say? (*He laughs.*) I have no missus, sir. I'm *free.* I can travel the universe, with no one to await my arrival anywhere.

CARL (*sits on stool at counter. To* GRACE, *bidding for a little sympathy*). That's all I ever get on my bus, drunks and hoodlums. (DR. LYMAN *signals* ELMA *for more soda.*)

GRACE. How's fer whole-wheat, Carl?

CARL. O.K. Make it whole-wheat. (ELMA *gets soda from refrigerator, takes it to* DR. LYMAN.)

DR. LYMAN (*to* ELMA, *as she brings him more soda*). Yes, I am free. My third and last wife deserted me several years ago . . . for a ballplayer. (*He chuckles as though it were all a big absurdity.*)

ELMA (*starts back to counter, stops. A little astounded*). Your *third?* (GRACE *makes sandwich, gives it and coffee to* CARL, *stands behind counter talking to him as he eats.*)

DR. LYMAN (ELMA *sits at his table*). Yes, my third! Getting married is a careless habit I've fallen into. Sometime, really, I *must* give it all up. Oh, but she was pretty! Blonde, like the young lady over there. (*He indicates* CHERIE.) And Southern, too, or pretended to be. However, she was kinder than the others when we parted. She didn't care about money. All she wanted was to find new marital bliss with her ballplayer, so I never had to pay her alimony . . . as if I could. (*He chuckles, sighs and recalls another.*) My second wife was a different type entirely. But she was very pretty, too. I have always exercised the most excellent taste, if not the best judgment. She was a student of mine, when I was teaching at an eastern university. Alas! she sued me for divorce on the grounds that I was incontinent and always drunk. (ELMA *rises, starts* L.) I didn't have a chance to resign from that position. (*Still he manages to chuckle about it.*)

CHERIE (*from the counter*). Hey! how much are them doughnuts? (*She is counting the coins in her purse.*)

ELMA (*leaving* DR. LYMAN, *hurrying back to counter*). I'll make you a special price, two for a nickel.

CHERIE. O.K.

DR. LYMAN (*musingly he begins to recite as though for his own enjoyment:*)

"That time of year thou may'st in me
    behold
When yellow leaves, or none, or few,
    do hang
Upon those boughs ——"

CHERIE (*she shivers,* ELMA *hands her doughnuts on a plate,* CHERIE *gives* ELMA *money and crosses to stove*). I never was so cold in my life.

ELMA. Do you honestly work in a night club?

CHERIE (*brightening with this recognition*). Sure! I'm a *chanteuse*. I call m'self *Cherie.*

ELMA. That's French, isn't it?

CHERIE. I dunno. I jest seen the name once and it kinda appealed t' me.

ELMA. It's French. It means "dear one." Is that all the name you use?

CHERIE (*sits at a table*). Sure. Thass all the name ya need. Like Hildegarde. She's a *chanteuse,* too.

ELMA (*crosses to* CHERIE *with coffee*). *Chanteuse* means singer.

CHERIE. How come *you* know so much? (GRACE *sits at counter with* CARL.)

ELMA. I'm taking French in high school.

CHERIE. Oh! (*A reflective pause.*) I never got as far as high school. See, I was the oldest girl left in the fam'ly after my sister Violet ran away. I had two more sisters, both younger'n me, and five brothers, most of 'em older. Was they mean! Anyway, I had to quit school when I was twelve, to stay home and take care a the house and do the cookin'. I'm a real good cook. Honest!

ELMA (*sits* L. *of* CHERIE *at table*). Did you *study* singing?

CHERIE (*shaking her head*). Huh-uh. Jest picked it up listenin' to the radio, seein' movies, tryin' to put over my songs as good as them people did.

ELMA. How did you get started in the night club?

CHERIE. I won a amateur contest. Down in Joplin, Missouri. I won the second prize there . . . a coupla boys won *first* prize . . . they juggled milk bottles ... . I don't think that's fair, do you? To make an artistic performer compete with jugglers and knife-throwers and people like that?

ELMA. No, I don't.

CHERIE. Anyway, second prize was good enough to get me to Kanz City t'enter the contest there. It was a real *big* contest and I didn't win any prize at all, but it got me the job at the Blue Dragon.

ELMA. Is that where you're from, Joplin? (DR. LYMAN *is reading a book.*)

CHERIE (*with an acceptance of nature's catastrophes*). No. Joplin's a *big* town. I lived 'bout a hundred miles from there, in River Gulch, a li'l town in the Ozarks. I lived there till the floods come, three years ago this spring and washed us all away.

ELMA. Gee, that's too bad.

CHERIE. I dunno where any a my folks are now, 'cept my baby sister Nan. We all just separated when the floods come and I took Nan into Joplin with me. She got a job as a waitress and I went to work in Liggett's drug store, 'til the amateur contest opened.

ELMA. It must be fun working in a night club.

CHERIE (*a fleeting look of disillusionment comes over her face*). Well . . . it ain't all roses.

CARL (*leaving* GRACE *for the moment, crosses to* WILL, *gets his coat*). You gonna be here a while, Will?

WILL. I reckon. (ELMA *rises, crosses to below counter.*)

CARL. I'm gonna send them cowboys in here now, and leave *you* to look after 'em.

WILL. I'll do my best.

CARL. Tell ya somethin' else, Will. (CARL *looks at* DR. LYMAN *cautiously, as though he didn't want to be overheard by him, then moves very closely to* WILL *and whispers something in his ear.* WILL *looks very surprised.*)

WILL. I'll be jiggered.

CARL. So, ya better keep an eye on *him,* too. (*Starts off.*)

WILL. Ain't you comin' back, Carl?

CARL (*obviously he is faking, and a look between him and* GRACE *tells us something is up between them. He winks at her and stretches*). To tell the truth, Will, I git so darn *stiff,* sittin' at the wheel all day, I thought I'd go out fer a long walk.

WILL. In this blizzard? You gone crazy? (ELMA *is doing dishes behind the counter.*)

CARL. No. That's just the kinda fella I am, Will. I like to go fer long walks in rain and snow. Freshens a fella up. Sometimes I walk fer hours. (GRACE *clears dishes from counter.*)

WILL. Ya do?

CARL. Yah. Fer hours. That's just the kinda fella I am. (*He saunters out* R. *now, whistling to show his nonchalance.*)

WILL (*rises, crosses* L. *to counter. To* GRACE). Imagine! Goin' out fer a walk, a night like this.

GRACE. Well, it's really very good for one, Will. It really is.

CHERIE (*crosses* L. *to counter carrying coffee and doughnuts, sits on stool and leans over counter to talk to* ELMA *privately*). He said he was gonna wake him up. Then he'll be in here pretty soon. You won't let on I said anything 'bout him, will ya? (WILL *sits near stove, reads newspaper.*)

ELMA. No. Cross my heart.

(DR. LYMAN *is suddenly reminded of another poem, which he begins to recite in full voice as he rises.*)

DR. LYMAN.

"Shall I compare thee to a Summer's day?

Thou art more lovely and more temperate:

Rough winds do shake the darling buds of May,

And Summer's lease hath all too short a date."

ELMA (*still behind counter, she hears* DR. LYMAN, *smiles fondly, and calls to him across room*). Why, that's one of my favorite sonnets.

DR. LYMAN. It is! Do *you* read Shakespeare? (GRACE *crosses to* DR. LYMAN's *table, which she clears, taking dishes back to counter.* DR. LYMAN *is at counter.*)

ELMA. I studied him at school, in English class. I loved the sonnets. I memorized some of them myself.

DR. LYMAN (*sits on stool*). I used to know them *all*, by heart. And many of the plays I could recite in their entirety. I often did, for the entertainment and the annoyance of my friends. (*He and* ELMA *laugh together.*)

ELMA. Last fall I memorized the Balcony Scene from *Romeo and Juliet.* A boy in class played Romeo and we presented it for convocation one day.

DR. LYMAN. Ah! I wish I had been there to see. (CHERIE *feels called upon to explain her own position in regard to Shakespeare, as* ELMA *resumes work behind counter.* GRACE *crosses to sink, washes dishes.*)

CHERIE. Where I went to school, we din read no Shakespeare 'til the ninth grade. In the ninth grade everyone read *Julius Caesar.* I oney got as far as the eighth. I seen Marlon Brando in the movie, though. I sure do like that Marlon Brando.

DR. LYMAN (*now that* CHERIE *has called attention to herself*). Madam, where is thy Lochinvar?

CHERIE (*giggling*). I don't understand anything you say, but I just love the way you say it.

DR. LYMAN. And *I* . . . understand *every*thing I say . . . but privately despise the way I say it.

CHERIE (*giggling*). That's so cute. (*A memory returns.*) I had a very nice friend once that recited poetry.

DR. LYMAN (*with spoofing seriousness*). Whatever could have happened to him?

CHERIE. I dunno. He left town. His name was Mr. Everett Brubaker. He sold second-hand cars at the corner of Eighth and Wyandotte. He had a lovely Pontiac car-with-the-top-down. He talked nice, but I guess he really wasn't any nicer'n any of the others.

DR. LYMAN. The others?

CHERIE. Well . . . ya meet quite a few men in the place I worked at, the Blue Dragon night club, out by the stockyards. Ever hear of it?

DR. LYMAN. No, and I deeply regret the fact.

CHERIE. You're just sayin' that. An educated man like you, you wouldn't have no use fer the Blue Dragon.

DR. LYMAN (*with a dubious look*). I wouldn't?

(*The front door swings open again and the two cowboys,* BO DECKER *and* VIRGIL BLESSING, *enter.* VIRGIL *enters first, crosses* U. L. C. BO *stands inside door* R., *looks around.* CHERIE *moves* D. L. *Their appearance now is rumpledly picturesque and they both could pass, at first glance, for outlaws.* BO *is in his early twenties, is tall and slim and good looking in an outdoors way. Now he is very unkempt. He wears faded jeans that cling to his legs like shed-*

ding skin; his boots, worn under his jeans, are scuffed and dusty; and the Stetson on the back of his head is worn and tattered. Over a faded denim shirt he wears a shiny horsehide jacket, and around his neck is tied a bandana. VIRGIL *is a man in his forties who seems to regard* BO *in an almost parental way. A big man, corpulent and slow moving, he seems almost an adjunct of* BO. *Dressed similarly to* BO, *perhaps a trifle more tidy, he carries a guitar in a case and keeps a bag of Bull Durham in his shirt pocket, out of which he rolls frequent cigarettes. Both men are still trying to wake up from their snooze, but* BO *is quick to recognize* CHERIE. *Neither cowboy has thought to shut the door behind them and the others begin to shiver.*)

BO (*in a full voice accustomed to speaking in an open field*). Hey! Why din anyone wake us up? Virg 'n I mighta froze out there.

GRACE. Hey! Shut the door.

BO (*calling across the room*). Cherry! how come you get off the bus, 'thout lettin' me know? That any way to treat the man you're gonna marry?

WILL (*lifting his eyes from the paper*). Shut the door, cowboy! (BO *doesn't even hear* WILL, *but strides across the room to* CHERIE, *who is huddled over the counter as though hoping he might overlook her.* VIRGIL, *still rubbing sleep out of his eyes, drifts near the stove.*)

BO. Thass no way to treat a fella, Cherry, to slip off the bus like ya wanted to get rid of him, maybe. And come in here and eat by yourself. I thought we'd have a li'l snack t'*gether*. Sometimes I don't understand you, Cherry.

CHERIE. Fer the hunderth time, my name ain't *Cherry*.

BO. I cain't say it the way you do. What's wrong with Cherry?

CHERIE. It's kinda embarrassin'.

WILL (*in a firmer, louder voice*). Cowboy, will you have the decency to shut that door! (VIRGIL *now responds immediately, crosses* R. *and quickly closes the door as* BO *turns to* WILL.)

BO (*there is nothing to call him for the moment but insolent as he crosses* U. R. C. *to* WILL). Why, what's the matter with you, Mister? You afraid of a little fresh air? (WILL *glowers but* BO *is not fazed.*) Why, man, ya oughta breathe real deep and git yor lungs full of it. Thass the

trouble with you city people. You git *soft*. (WILL *rises, comes* L. *of* BO.)

VIRGIL (*whispering*). He's the sheriff, Bo.

BO (*in full voice, for* WILL's *benefit*). S'posin' he *is* the sheriff! What's that matter t' *me*? That don't give him the right t' insult my manners, does it? No man ever had to tell *me* what t' do, did he, Virge? Did he?

VIRGIL. No. No. But there allus comes a time, Bo, when . . . (VIRGIL *puts his guitar down*, BO *puts his hat on top of it.*)

BO (*ignoring* VIRGIL, *speaking out for the benefit of all*). My name's Bo Decker. I'm twenty-one years old and own me m'own ranch up in Timber Hill, Montana, where I got a herd a fine Hereford cattle and a dozen horses, and the finest sheep and hogs and chickens anywhere in the country. And I jest come back from a rodeo where I won 'bout ev'ry prize there *was*, din I, Virge? (*Joshingly, he elbows* VIRGIL *in the ribs.* WILL *drifts* D. S., *looking at* BO.) Yap, I'm the prize bronco-buster, 'n steerroper, 'n bull-dogger, anywhere 'round. I won 'em all. And what's more, had my picture taken by *Life* magazine. (*Confronting* WILL.) So I'd appreciate your talkin' to me with a little respect in yor voice, Mister, and not go hollerin' orders to me from across the room like I was some no-count servant. (WILL *is flabbergasted.*)

CHERIE (*privately to* ELMA). Did ya ever see anybody like him?

WILL (*finally finds his voice and uses it, after a struggle with himself to sound just and impartial*). You was the last one in, cowboy, and you left the door open. You shoulda closed it, I don't care *who* y'are. That's all I'm saying.

BO. Door's closed now. What ya arguin' 'bout? (*Leaving a hushed and somewhat awed audience,* BO *strides over to the counter and drops to a stool.*) Seems like we're gonna be here a while, Virge. How's fer some grub? (WILL *turns* U. C.)

VIRGIL (*remaining by magazine counter*). Not yet, Bo. I'm chewin' t'backy. (*Takes off coat and hat.*)

BO (*slapping a thigh*). Thass ole Virge for ya. Allus happy long's he's got a wad a t'backy in his mouth. Wall, I'm gonna have me a li'l snack. (*To* ELMA.) Miss, gimme 'bout three hamburgers.

ELMA Three? How do you want them? (WILL *crosses to stove, watches* BO.)

BO. I want 'em *raw*. (CHERIE *makes a sick face*. DR. LYMAN *quietly withdraws, taking his drink over to the window*.)

ELMA. Honest?

BO. It's the only way t'eat 'em, raw, with a thick slice a onion and some pickalili.

ELMA (*hesitant*). Well . . . if you're sure you're not joking.

BO (*his voice holding* ELMA *on her way to refrigerator*). Jest a minute, Miss. That ain't all. I'd also like me some ham and eggs . . . and some potaty salad . . . and a piece a pie. I ain't so pertikler what *kinda* pie it is, so long as it's got that murang on top of it. (GRACE *gives hamburger and eggs to* ELMA.)

ELMA. We have lemon and choc'late. They both have meringue. (VIRGIL *crosses* U. S., *sits near stove*. GRACE *crosses* U. R., *sits on bench*.)

BO (*thinking it over*). Lemon'n choc'late. I like 'em both. I dunno which I'd ruther have. (*Ponders a moment*.) I'll have 'em *both*, Miss. (CHERIE *makes another sick face*.)

ELMA. Both?

BO. Yep! 'N set a quart a milk beside me. I'm still a growin' boy. (ELMA *starts preparations as* BO *turns to* CHERIE.) Travelin' allus picks up my appetite. That all you havin', jest a measly doughnut?

CHERIE. I ain't hungry.

BO. Why not?

CHERIE. I jest ain't.

BO. Ya oughta be.

CHERIE. Well—I ain't!

BO. Wait til! I get ya up to the Susie-Q. I'll fatten ya up. I bet in two weeks time, ya won't recognize yorself. (*Now he puts a bearlike arm around her, drawing her close to him for a snuggle, kissing her on the cheek*.) But doggone, I *love* ya, Cherry, jest the way ya are. Yor about the cutest li'l piece I ever did see. And man! when I walked into that night club place and hear you singin' my favorite song, standin' before that orkester lookin' like a angel, I told myself then and there, she's fer *me*. I ain't gonna leave this place without her. And now I got ya, ain't I, Cherry?

CHERIE (*trying to avoid his embrace*). Bo . . . there's people here . . . they're lookin' . . . (*And she's right. They are*.)

BO. What if they are? It's no crime to show a li'l affection, is it? 'Specially, when we're gonna git married. It's no crime I ever heard of. (*He squeezes her harder now and forces a loud, smacking kiss on the lips*. CHERIE *twists loose of him and turns away*.)

CHERIE. Bo! fer cryin' out loud, lemme be! (*Breaks away* R.)

BO (*following her, grabs her shoulders*). Cherry, thass no way to talk to yor husband.

CHERIE (*breaks away* R. C.). That's all ya done since we left Kanz City, is maul me. (*Sits at table*.)

BO. Oh, is zat so? (*This is a deep-cutting insult*.) Wall, I certainly ain't one to *pester* any woman with my affections. I never had to *beg* no woman to make love to me. (*Calling over his shoulder to* VIRGIL.) Did I, Virge? I never had to coax no woman to make love to me, *did* I?

VIRGIL (*in a voice that sounds more and more restrained*). No . . . no . . .

BO (*still in full voice*). No! Ev'rywhere I go, I got all the wimmin I want, don't I, Virge? I gotta fight 'em to keep 'em off me, don't I, Virge? (VIRGIL *is saved from having to make a response as* ELMA *presents* BO *with his hamburgers*.)

ELMA. Here are the hamburgers. The ham and eggs will take a little longer.

BO (*sits at counter, eats*). O.K. These'll gimme a start. (GRACE *rubs her forehead with a feigned expression of pain*.)

GRACE (*rises, crosses* L. *to* U. S. *end of counter*). Elma, honey, I got the darndest headache.

ELMA. I'm sorry, Grace.

GRACE. Can you look after things, a while?

ELMA. Sure.

GRACE. 'Cause the only thing for me to do is go upstairs and lie down a while. That's the only thing gonna do me any good at all. (*Starts* U. L.)

WILL (*from his chair*). What's the matter, Grace?

GRACE (*at the rear door*). I got a headache, Will, that's just drivin' me *wild*.

WILL. That so? (GRACE *goes out rear door*.)

DR. LYMAN (*crosses to* U. S. *end of counter*. *To* ELMA). You are now the Mistress of the Inn.

ELMA. You haven't told me anything about your first wife.

DR. LYMAN (*to* D. S. *end of counter*). Now, how could I have omitted her?

ELMA. What was *she* like? (BO *eats, peeks at* CHERIE *now and then*.)

DR. LYMAN (*still in the highest of spirits*). Oh . . . she was the loveliest of them all. I do believe she was. We had such an idyllic honeymoon together, a golden month of sunshine and romance, in Bermuda. (*Sits on stool.* ELMA *leans on counter.*) She sued me for divorce later, on the grounds of mental cruelty, and persuaded the judge that she should have my house and my motor-car, and an alimony that I still find it difficult to pay, for she never chose to marry again. She found that for all she wanted out of marriage, she didn't have to marry. (*He chuckles.*) Ah, but perhaps I am being unkind. (ELMA *is a little mystified by the humor with which he always tells of his difficulties.* BO *now leans over the counter and interrupts.*)

BO. Miss, was you waitin' fer me to lay them eggs?

ELMA (*hurrying to stove*). Oh, I'm sorry. They're ready now. (BO *jumps up, grabs a plate and glides over the counter for* ELMA *to serve him from the stove.*)

BO. Them hamburgers was just a *horse d'oovrey*. (*He grins with appreciation of this word.* ELMA *fills his plate.*) Thank ya, Miss. (*He starts back for the stool but trips over* CHERIE's *suitcase on the way.*) Daggone! (*He looks down to see what has stopped him.* CHERIE *holds a rigid silence.* BO *brings his face slowly up, looking at* CHERIE *suspiciously. Puts plate of eggs on counter.*) Cherry! (*She says nothing. He crosses slowly toward her.*) Cherry, what'd ya wanta bring yor suitcase in here fer? (*She still says nothing.*) Cherry, I'm askin' ya a civil question. What'd ya bring yor suitcase in fer? *Tell* me? (WILL *rises.*)

CHERIE (*frightened, rises*). I . . . I . . . now don't you come near me, Bo. (*Backs* R.)

BO (*crosses, shaking* CHERIE *by the shoulders*). Tell me! What's yor suitcase doin' there b'hind the counter? What were ya tryin' to do, *fool* me? Was you plannin' to git away from me? That what you been sittin' here plannin' t'do?

CHERIE (*finding it hard to speak while he is shaking her*). Bo . . . lemme be . . . take your hands off me, Bo Decker.

BO. Tell me, Cherry. Tell me. (*Now* WILL *intercedes, coming up to* BO, *laying a hand on his shoulder.*)

WILL. Leave the little lady alone, cowboy.

BO (*turning on* WILL *fiercely.* CHERIE *backs* R.). Mister, ya got no right interferin' 'tween me and my feeancy.

WILL. Mebbe she's yor feeancy and maybe she ain't. Anyway, ya ain't gonna abuse her while *I'm* here. Unnerstand?

BO. *Abuse* her?

WILL (*to* CHERIE). I think you better tell him now, Miss, jest how you feel about things. (BO *looks at* CHERIE *with puzzled wonder.*)

CHERIE (*finding it impossible to say*). I . . . I . . .

BO. What's this critter tryin' to say, Cherry?

CHERIE. Well . . . I . . .

WILL. You better tell him, Miss.

CHERIE. Now, Bo, don't git mad.

BO. I'll git mad if I feel like it. What you two got planned?

CHERIE. Bo, I don't wanta go up to Montana and marry ya.

BO. Ya do, too.

CHERIE. I do not!

BO (*crosses* L. *a few steps*). Anyways, you'll come to like it in time. I *promised* ya would. Now we been through all that b'fore. (WILL *sits on stool at counter.*)

CHERIE. But, Bo . . . I ain't goin'.

BO (*a loud blast of protest*). *What?* (CHERIE *runs* U. L.)

CHERIE. I ain't goin'. The sheriff here said he'd help me. He ain't gonna let you take me any farther. I'm stayin' here and take the next bus back to Kanz City.

BO (*crosses* U. L. *Grubbing her by the shoulders to reassure himself of her*). You ain't gonna do nothin' of the kind.

CHERIE. Yes, I am, Bo. You gotta b'lieve me. I ain't goin' with ya. That's final.

BO (*in a most personal voice, baffled*). But, Cherry . . . we was *familiar* with each other.

CHERIE. That don't mean ya gotta *marry* me.

BO (*shocked at her, steps back*). Why . . . I oughta take you across my knee and blister yer li'l bottom.

CHERIE (*more frightened, runs* D. L.). Don't you touch me.

BO (*to* WILL, *crosses* L. *a step*). You cain't pay no tension to what she says, Mister. Womenfolk don't know their own minds. Never did. (CHERIE *runs* R. *near door,* BO *follows.*)

CHERIE. Don't you come near me!

BO (*crosses* R. *to* CHERIE). Yor gonna follow me back to Timber Hill and marry up. You just think you wouldn't like it now 'cause ya never been there and the whole idea's kinda strange. But you'll get over them feelin's. In no time at all, you're gonna be happy as a mudhen. I ain't takin' *no* fer an answer. By God, yor comin' along. (*He grabs her forcefully to him, as* WILL *interferes again, pulling the two apart.*)

WILL. You're not takin' her with ya if she don't wanta go. Can't you get that through your skull? Now leave her be. (BO *stands looking at* WILL *with sullen hatred.* CHERIE *trembles and backs* R. VIRGIL *stands far* R. *looking apprehensive.*)

BO (*confronts* WILL *threateningly*). This ain't no bizness of yors.

WILL. It's *my* business when the little lady comes t'me wantin' protection.

BO. Is that right, Cherry? (*She steps back, as he steps toward her.*) Did you go to the sheriff askin' fer pertection?

CHERIE (*meekly, backs away another step*). . . . yes, I guess I did.

BO (*bellowing out again*). Why? What'd ya need pertection for . . . from a man that wants to *marry* ya?

CHERIE (*shuddering*). . . . 'cause . . .

BO (*bellowing angrily*). 'Cause *why?* I said I *loved* ya, din I?

CHERIE (*about to cry*). I know ya did.

BO (*confronting* WILL *with a feeling of angry unjustness*). See there? I told her I loved her and I wanta marry her. And with a world fulla crazy people goin' 'round killin' each other, *you* ain't got nothin' better t'do than stand here tryin' to keep me from it. (*Turns away* R.)

WILL. Yor overlookin' jest one thing, cowboy.

BO (*with gruff impatience*). Yor so *smart.* Tell me what I'm overlookin'.

WILL. Yor overlookin' the simple but important fack that the little lady don't love *you.* (BO *now is trapped into silence. He can say nothing, and no one can tell that* WILL *has named a fact that* BO *did not intend to face.* VIRGIL *watches him alertly. He can tell that* BO *is angry enough to attack* WILL *and is about to.* VIRGIL *hurries to* BO's *side, holding his arms as though to restrain him.* DR. LYMAN *rises,* ELMA *starts* U. L. *for* GRACE, *then stops.*)

VIRGIL (*pacifyingly, pulls* BO R.). Now, Bo. Take it easy, Bo. Don't blow your lid. He's the sheriff, Bo. Hold yor temper.

BO (*to* VIRGIL). That polecat bastard!

He said she din love me.

VIRGIL (*trying to draw him away from the scene over to* R.). Pay no 'tention, Bo. Come on over here and sit down. Ya gotta think things over, Bo.

BO (*twisting loose from* VIRGIL's *hold, walks* D. L.). Lemme be, Virge.

WILL. Ask the li'l lady, if ya don't b'lieve *me.* Ask her if she loves ya.

BO. I won't ask her nothin' of the kind.

WILL. All right then, take my word for it.

BO. I wouldn't take yor word for a cloudy day. I'm tellin' ya, she loves me. And *I* oughta know. (*Starts toward* CHERIE. VIRGIL *goes* R. CHERIE *flees to the counter, sobbing.*)

WILL (*stops* BO). Wall . . . she ain't gettin' back on the bus with ya. We'll leave it at that. So you better take my advice and sit down with yor friend there, and have a quiet game a pinochle till the bus gets on its way and takes you with it.

VIRGIL. Do like he tells ya, Bo. I think mebbe ya got the li'l lady all wrong, anyway. (*Near a table* R.)

BO (*a defender of womanhood*). Don't you say nothin' against her, Virge.

VIRGIL. I *ain't* sayin' nothin' *against* her. I jest see no reason why you should marry a gal that says she don't love ya. That's all. And I kinda doubt she's as good a gal as you think she is. Now come on over here and sit down. (*Sits at table.*)

BO (*turns restlessly from* VIRGIL). I don't feel like sittin'. (*Instead, he paces up to the big window, standing there looking out, his back to the audience.* WILL *gets coat and hat.*)

ELMA (*from behind counter, to* VIRGIL). What shall I do with the ham and eggs?

VIRGIL. Just put 'em on the stove and keep 'em warm, Miss. He'll have 'em a li'l later. (*She puts plate on hot plate.*)

WILL (*to* CHERIE). I don't think you'll be bothered any more, Miss. If y'are, my station's right across the road. You kin holler. (DR. LYMAN *returns to counter, sits.*)

CHERIE (*dabbing at her eyes*). Thank you very much, I'm sure.

WILL. Are you gonna be all right, Elma?

ELMA (*surprised at the question*). Why, yes, Will! (WILL *just looks at* DR. LYMAN *who, we can tell, is made to feel a little uncomfortable.*)

WILL. I'll look in a little later.

ELMA. O.K., Will. (WILL *goes to the*

front door, takes a final look at BO, *then goes out.*)

DR. LYMAN. I don't know why, but . . . I always seem to relax more easily . . . when a sheriff leaves the room. (*He chuckles bravely.* CHERIE *drifts to* D. L. *end of counter, sits on stool.*)

ELMA. I think it's awfully unfair that people dislike Will just because he's a sheriff.

DR. LYMAN. But you see, my dear, he stands as a symbol of authority, the most dreaded figure of our time. Policemen, teachers, lawyers, judges, doctors, and I suppose, even tax collectors . . . we take it for granted that they are going to punish us for something we didn't do . . . or did do.

ELMA. But you said you were a teacher once.

DR. LYMAN. But not a successful one. I could never stay in one place very long at a time. And I hated having anyone *over* me, like deans and presidents and department heads. I never was a man who could take *orders* . . . from *anyone* . . . without feeling resentment. Right or wrong, I have always insisted on having my own way. (*Pours a drink.* BO *walks slowly down from his corner retreat, seeking* VIRGIL, *who is taking his guitar out of its case.* BO *speaks hesitantly in a low voice.*)

BO. What am I gonna do, Virge?

VIRGIL. Bo, ya just gotta quit dependin' on me so much. I don't know what to tell ya to do, except to sit down and be peaceful.

BO. I—I can't be peaceful. (*Moves* L.)

VIRGIL. All right then, pace around like a panther and be miserable.

BO (*to himself. Turns* R.). I—I jest can't believe it!

VIRGIL. *What* can't ya believe?

BO (*now he becomes embarrassed. Crosses* D. R.). Oh . . . nothin'.

VIRGIL. If ya got anything on your chest, Bo, it's best to get it off.

BO (*sits at table by* VIRGIL). Well, I . . . I just never realized . . . a gal might not . . . love me.

CURTAIN

ACT TWO

Only a few minutes have elapsed since the close of ACT I. *Our characters now are patiently trying to pass the time as best they can.* VIRGIL *has taken out his guitar and, after tuning it, begun to play a soft, melancholy cowboy ballad as he sits at the same table. He keeps his music an almost unnoticeable part of the background.* BO *lingers in the corner up* R., *a picture of troubled dejection.* CHERIE *has found a movie magazine which she sits at one of the tables and reads.* DR. LYMAN *continues sitting at the bar, sipping his drink and courting* ELMA, *although* ELMA *does not realize she is being courted. She is immensely entertained by him. She sits on a stool behind counter.*

ELMA. . . . and where else did you teach?

DR. LYMAN. My last position was at one of those revolting little progressive colleges in the East, where they offer a curriculum of what they call *functional* education. Educators, I am sure, have despaired of ever teaching students *anything*, so they have decided the second-best thing to do is to *understand* them. (BO *sits on bench by window.*) Every day there would be a meeting of everyone on the entire faculty, with whom the students ever came into any contact, from the President down to the chambermaids, and we would put our collective heads together to try to figure out why little Jane or little Mary was not getting out of her classes what she *should*. The suggestion that perhaps she wasn't studying was too simple, and if you implied that she simply did not have the brains for a college education, you were being undemocratic.

ELMA. You must have disapproved of that college.

DR. LYMAN. My dear girl, I have disapproved of my entire life.

ELMA. Really?

DR. LYMAN. Yes, but I suppose I couldn't resist living it over again. (*There is a touch of sadness about him now.*)

ELMA. Did you resign from that position?

DR. LYMAN. One day I decided I had had enough. I walked blithely into the Dean's office and said, "Sir! I graduated *Magna Cum Laude* from the University of Chicago, I studied at Oxford on a Rhodes Scholarship, and returned to take my Ph.D. at Harvard, receiving it with highest honors. I think I have the right to expect my students to try to understand *me*."

ELMA (*very amused*). What did he say?

DR. LYMAN. Oh, I didn't wait for a response. I walked out of the door and went to the railroad station, where I got a ticket for the farthest place I could think of, which happened to be Las Vegas. And I have been traveling ever since. It's a merry way to go to pot. (*He chuckles.*)

ELMA. I had thought *I* might teach one day, but you don't make it sound very attractive.

DR. LYMAN. Ah, suit yourself. Don't let me influence you one way or the other. (ELMA *smiles and* DR. LYMAN *gives in to the sudden compulsion of clasping her hand.*) You're a lovely young girl.

ELMA (*very surprised*). Why . . . thank you, Dr. Lyman.

DR. LYMAN (*clears his throat and makes a fresh approach*). Did you tell me you plan to go to Topeka tomorrow?

ELMA (*looking at clock. Removes hand*). You mean *today*. Yes. I have a ticket to hear the Kansas City Symphony. They come to Topeka every year to give a concert.

DR. LYMAN (*feeling his way*). You say . . . you stay with your sister there?

ELMA (*rises*). Yes, then I take an early morning bus back here, in time for school Monday. Then after school, I come here to work for Grace.

DR. LYMAN (*obviously he is angling for something*). Didn't you say there was a university in Topeka?

ELMA. Yes. Washburn University.

DR. LYMAN. Washburn University—of course! You know, it just occurs to me that I should stop there to check some references on a piece of research I'm engaged on.

ELMA. Oh, I've been to Washburn library lots of times.

DR. LYMAN. You have? (*He shows some cunning, but obviously* ELMA *does not see it.*) Perhaps you would take me there!

ELMA (*hesitant*). Well, I . . .

DR. LYMAN. I'll arrive in Topeka before you do, then meet your bus . . .

ELMA. If you really want me to.

DR. LYMAN. You can take me to the library, then perhaps we could have dinner together, and perhaps you would permit me to take you to the symphony.

ELMA (*overjoyed*). Are you serious?

DR. LYMAN. Why, of course I'm serious.

Why do you ask?

ELMA. I don't know. Usually, older people are too busy to take notice of kids. I'd just love to.

DR. LYMAN. Then I may depend on it that I have an engagement?

ELMA. Yes. Oh, that'll be lots of fun. I can't wait.

DR. LYMAN. But, my dear . . . let's not tell anyone of our plans, shall we? (CHERIE *rises, crosses* R *and puts magazine back in rack.* BO *rises, expectant.* CHERIE *stands near door, watching* VIRGIL.)

ELMA. Why not?

DR. LYMAN. You see . . . I have been married, and I am somewhat older than you, though perhaps not quite as old as you might take me to be . . . anyway, people might not understand.

ELMA. Oh!

DR. LYMAN. So let's keep our plans to ourselves. Promise?

ELMA. O.K. If you think best.

DR. LYMAN (*rises. Pats her hand. Crosses* R. *to book rack, looks at books.* ELMA *sits, knits.*) I think it best. (VIRGIL *has finished playing a ballad and* CHERIE *applauds.*)

CHERIE. That was real purty, Virgil.

VIRGIL. Thank ya, Miss. (*From his corner,* BO *has seen the moment's intimacy between them. He winces.* CHERIE *goes over to the counter and speaks to* ELMA.)

CHERIE. Isn't there some other way of me gettin' back to Kanz City?

ELMA. I'm sorry. The bus comes through here from Topeka, and it can't get through, either, until the road's cleared.

CHERIE. I was jest gettin' sorta restless. (*She sits at center table and lights a cigarette. Suddenly, the front door swings open and* WILL *appears carrying a thermos jug.*)

WILL (*crossing to counter*). Elma, fill this up for me, like a good girl.

ELMA. Sure, Will. (*Takes thermos from him and starts to fill it at urn.*)

WILL. I'm goin' down the highway a bit to see how the men are gettin' on. Thought they'd enjoy some hot coffee.

ELMA. Good idea, Will.

WILL (*with a look around*). Everyone behavin'?

ELMA. Of course.

WILL (*puzzled*). Grace not down yet?

ELMA. No.

WILL. I didn't see Carl any place outside. Suppose somethin' coulda happened to him?

ELMA. I wouldn't worry about him, Will.

WILL. I s'pose he can take care of himself. (ELMA *hands him thermos.*) Thank you, Elma. (*He pays her, then starts back out, saying for the benefit primarily of* BO *and* DR. LYMAN.) Oh, Elma. If anyone should be wantin' me, I won't be gone very long. (*He looks around to make sure everyone has heard him, then goes out front door.* BO *has heard and seen him, and suddenly turns from his corner and comes angrily down to* VIRGIL. DR. LYMAN *drifts to window and sits.*)

BO. That dang sheriff! If it wasn't fer *him,* I'd git Cherry now and . . . I . . .

VIRGIL. Where would ya take her, Bo?

BO. There's a justice a the peace down the street. You can see his sign from the window.

VIRGIL. Bo, ya cain't *force* a gal to marry ya. Ya jest cain't do it. That sheriff's a stern man and he'd shoot ya in a minute if he saw it was his duty. Now why don't ya go over to the counter and have yourself a drink . . . like the perfessor?

BO. I never did drink and I ain't gonna let no woman drive me to it.

VIRGIL. Ya don't drink. Ya don't smoke or chew. Ya oughta have *some* bad habits to rely on when things with women go wrong. (BO *thinks for a moment then sits opposite* VIRGIL.)

BO. Virge. I hate to sound like some pitiable weaklin' of a man, but there's been times the last few months, I been so lonesome, I . . . I jest didn't know what t'do with m'self.

VIRGIL. It's no disgrace to feel that way, Bo.

BO. How 'bout you, Virge? Don't you ever git lonesome, too?

VIRGIL. A long time ago, I gave up romancin' and decided I was just gonna take bein' lonesome for granted.

BO. I wish I could do that, but I cain't. (*They now sit in silence.* CHERIE, *at the counter, lifts her damp eyes to* ELMA, *seeking a confidante.*)

CHERIE. Mebbe I'm a sap.

ELMA. Why do you say that?

CHERIE. I dunno why I *don't* go off to Montana and marry him. I might be a lot better off'n I am now.

ELMA. He says he *loves* you.

CHERIE. He dunno what love is.

ELMA. What makes you say that?

CHERIE. All he wants is a girl to throw his arms around and hug and kiss, that's all. The resta the time, he don't even know I exist.

ELMA. What made you decide to marry him in the first place?

CHERIE (*giving* ELMA *a wise look*). Ya ain't very experienced, are ya?

ELMA. I guess not.

CHERIE. I never *did* decide to marry him. Everything was goin' fine till he brought up *that* subjeck. Bo come in one night when I was singin' "That Old Black Magic." It's one a my best numbers. And he liked it so much, he jumped up on a chair and yelled like a Indian, and put his fingers in his mouth and whistled like a steam engine. Natur'ly, it made me feel good. Most a the customers at the Blue Dragon was too drunk to pay any attention to my songs.

ELMA. And you liked him?

CHERIE. Well . . . I thought he was awful *cute.* (*She shows a mischievous smile.*)

ELMA. I think he looks a little like Burt Lancaster, don't you?

CHERIE. Mebbe. Anyway . . . I'd never seen a cowboy before. Oh, I'd seen 'em in movies, a course, but never in the *flesh* . . . Anyway, he's so darn healthy lookin', I don't mind admittin', I was attracted, right from the start.

ELMA. You were?

CHERIE. But it was only what ya might call a *sexual* attraction.

ELMA. Oh!

CHERIE. The very next mornin', he wakes up and hollers, "Yippee! We're gittin' married." (BO *rises, walks* L. VIRGIL *pulls him down to sit.*) I honestly thought he was crazy. But when I tried to reason with him, he wouldn't listen to a word. He stayed by my side all day long, like a shadow. At night, a course, he had to go back to the rodeo, but he was back to the Blue Dragon as soon as the rodeo was over, in time fer the midnight show. If any other fella claimed t'have a date with me, Bo'd beat him up.

ELMA. And you never told him you'd marry him?

CHERIE. No! He kep tellin' me all week, he and Virge'd be by the night the rodeo ended, and they'd pick me up and we'd all start back to Montana t'gether. I knew that if I was around the Blue Dragon that night, that's what'd happen. So I decided to beat it. One a the other girls at the Blue

Dragon lived on a farm 'cross the river in Kansas. She said I could stay with her. So I went to the Blue Dragon last night and just sang fer the first show. Then I told 'em I was quittin' . . . I'd been wantin' to find another job anyway . . . and I picked up my share of the kitty . . . but darn it, I had to go and tell 'em I was takin' the midnight bus. They had to go and tell Bo, a course, when he come in a li'l after eleven. He paid 'em five dollars to find out. So I went down to the bus station and hadn't even got my ticket, when here come Bo and Virge. (BO *rises, walks slowly to window.*) He jest steps up to the ticket window and says, "Three tickets to Montana!" I din know what to say. Then he dragged me onto the bus and I been on it ever since. And somewhere deep down inside me, I gotta funny feelin' I'm gonna end up in Montana. (*She sits now in troubled contemplation as* ELMA *resumes her work. On the other side of the stage,* BO *comes* D. S., *straddles a chair after a period of gestation, begins to question* VIRGIL.)

BO. Tell me somethin', Virge. We been t'gether since my folks died, and I allus wondered if mebbe I din spoil yer chances a settlin' down.

VIRGIL (*laughs*). No, you never, Bo. I used to tell myself ya did, but I just wanted an excuse.

BO. But you been lookin' after me since I was ten.

VIRGIL. I coulda married up, too.

BO. Was ya ever in love?

VIRGIL. Oncet. B'fore I went to work on your daddy's ranch.

BO. What happened?

VIRGIL. Nuthin'.

BO. Ya ask her to marry ya?

VIRGIL. Nope.

BO. Why not?

VIRGIL. Well . . . there comes a time in every fella's life, Bo, when he's gotta give up his own ways . . .

BO. How ya mean?

VIRGIL. Well, I was allus kinda uncomfortable around this gal, 'cause she was sweet and kinda refined. I was allus scared I'd say or do somethin' wrong.

BO. I know how ya mean.

VIRGIL. It was cowardly of me, I s'pose, but ev'ry time I'd get back from courtin' her, and come back to the bunkhouse where my buddies was sittin' around talk-

in', or playin' cards, or listenin' to music, I'd jest relax and feel m'self so much at home, I din wanta give it up.

BO. Yah! Gals can scare a fella.

VIRGIL. Now I'm kinda ashamed.

BO. Y'are?

VIRGIL. Yes I am, Bo. A fella can't live his whole life dependin' on buddies. (BO *takes another reflective pause, then asks directly.*)

BO. Why don't she like me, Virge?

VIRGIL (*hesitant*). Well . . .

BO. Tell me the truth.

VIRGIL. Mebbe ya don't go about it right.

BO. What do I do wrong?

VIRGIL. Sometimes ya sound a li'l bullheaded and mean.

BO. I do?

VIRGIL. Yah.

BO. How's a fella s'posed to act?

VIRGIL. I'm no authority, Bo, but it seems t'me you should be a little more gallant.

BO. Gall—? Gallant? I'm as gallant as I know how to be. You hear the way Hank and Orville talk at the ranch, when they get back from sojournin' in town, 'bout their women.

VIRGIL. They like to brag, Bo. Ya cain't b'lieve ev'rything Hank and Orville say.

BO. Is there any reason a gal wouldn't go fer *me,* soon as she would fer Hank or Orville?

VIRGIL. They're a li'l older'n you. They learned a li'l more. They can be *gallant* with gals . . . when they *wanta* be.

BO. I ain't gonna *pertend*.

VIRGIL. I cain't blame ya.

BO. But a gal *oughta* like me. I kin read and write, I'm kinda tidy, and I got good manners, don't I?

VIRGIL. I'm no judge, Bo. I'm used to ya.

BO. And I'm tall and strong. Ain't that what girls like? And if I do say so, m'self, I'm purty good lookin'.

VIRGIL. Yah.

BO. When I get spruced up, I'm just as good lookin' a fella as a gal might hope to see.

VIRGIL. I know ya are, Bo.

BO (*suddenly seized with anger at the injustice of it all. Jumps up, crosses* U. S.). Then hellfire and damnation! Why don't she go back to the ranch with me? (*His hands in his hip pockets, he begins pacing, returning to his corner like a panther, where he stands with his back to the others, watching the snow fly outside the win-*

dow.)

ELMA (*having observed* BO's *disquiet*). Gee, if you only loved him!

CHERIE. That'd solve ev'rything, wouldn't it? But I don't. So I jest can't see m'self goin' to some God-forsaken ranch in Montana where I'd never see no one but him and a lotta cows.

ELMA. No. If you don't love him, it'd be awfully lonely.

CHERIE. I dunno why I keep expectin' m'self to fall in love with someone, but I do.

ELMA (*sits on stool by* CHERIE). I know *I* expect to, some day.

CHERIE. I'm beginnin' to seriously wonder if there *is* the kinda love I have in mind.

ELMA. What's that?

CHERIE. Well . . . I dunno. I'm oney nineteen, but I been goin' with guys since I was fourteen.

ELMA (*astounded*). Honest?

CHERIE. Honey, I almost married a cousin a mine when I was fourteen, but Pappy wouldn't have it.

ELMA. I never heard of anyone marrying so young.

CHERIE. Down in the Ozarks, we don't waste much time. Anyway, I'm awful glad I never married my cousin Malcolm, 'cause he turned out real bad, like Pappy predicted. But I sure was crazy 'bout him at the time. And I been losin' my head 'bout some guy ever since. But Bo's the first one wanted to marry me, since Cousin Malcolm. And natur'ly, I'd like to get married and raise a fam'ly and all them things but . . .

ELMA. But you've *never* been in love?

CHERIE. Mebbe I have and din know it. Thass what I mean. Mebbe I don't know what love is. Mebbe I'm expectin' it t'be somethin' it ain't. I jest feel that, regardless how crazy ya are 'bout some guy, ya gotta feel . . . and it's hard to put into words, but . . . ya gotta feel he *respects* ya. Yah, thass what I mean.

ELMA (*not impudent*). I should think so.

CHERIE. I want a guy I can look up to and respect, but I don't want one that'll browbeat me. And I want a guy who can be sweet to me but I don't wanta be treated like a baby. I . . . I just gotta feel that . . . whoever I marry . . . has some real regard for me, apart from all the lovin' and sex. Know what I mean?

ELMA (*busily digesting all this*). I think so. What are you going to do when you get back to Kansas City?

CHERIE. I dunno.—There's a hillbilly program on one a the radio stations there. I might git a job on it. If I don't, I'll prob'ly git me a job in Liggett's or Walgreen's. Then after a while, I'll prob'ly marry some guy, whether I think I love him or not. Who'm *I* to keep insistin' I should fall in love? You hear all about love when yor a kid and jest take it for granted that such a thing really exists. Maybe ya have to find out fer yorself it don't. Maybe everyone's afraid to tell ya.

ELMA (*glum*). Maybe you're right . . . but I hope not.

CHERIE (*after squirming a little on the stool*). Gee, I hate to go out to that cold powder room, but I guess I better not put it off any longer. (CHERIE *hurries out the rear door as* DR. LYMAN *sits again at the counter, having returned from the bookshelves in time to overhear the last of* CHERIE'S *conversation. He muses for a few moments, gloomily, then speaks to* ELMA *out of his unconscious reflections.*)

DR. LYMAN. How defiantly we pursue love, like it was an inheritance due, that we had to wrangle about with angry relatives in order to get our share.

ELMA. You shouldn't complain. You've had three wives.

DR. LYMAN. Don't shame me. I loved them all . . . with passion. (*An afterthought*) At least I *thought* I did . . . for a while. (*He still chuckles about it as though it were a great irony.*)

ELMA. I'm sorry if I sounded sarcastic, Dr. Lyman. I didn't mean to be.

DR. LYMAN. Don't apologize. I'm too egotistical ever to take offense at anything people *say*. (*Pours drink.*)

ELMA. You're not egotistical at all.

DR. LYMAN. Oh, believe me. The greatest egos are those which are too egotistical to show just how egotistical they are.

ELMA. I'm sort of idealistic about things. I like to think that people fall in love and stay that way, forever and ever.

DR. LYMAN. Maybe we have lost the ability. Maybe Man has passed the stage in his evolution wherein love is possible. Maybe life will continue to become so terrifyingly complex that man's anxiety about his mere survival will render him too miserly to give of himself in any true relation.

ELMA. You're talking over my head. *Any*one can fall in love, I always thought . . . and . . .

DR. LYMAN. But two people, *really* in love, must give up something of themselves.

ELMA (*trying to follow*). Yes.

DR. LYMAN. That is the gift that men are afraid to make. Sometimes they keep it in their bosoms forever, where it withers and dies. Then they never know love, only its facsimiles, which they seek over and over again in meaningless repetition.

ELMA (*a little depressed*). Gee! How did we get onto this subject?

DR. LYMAN (*laughs heartily with sudden release, grabbing* ELMA's *hand*). Ah, my dear! Pay no attention to me, for whether there is such a thing as love, we can always . . . (*Lifts his drink.*) . . . pretend there is. Let us talk instead of our forthcoming trip to Topeka. Will you wear your prettiest dress?

ELMA. Of course. If it turns out to be a nice day, I'll wear a new dress Mother got me for spring. It's a soft rose color with a little lace collar.

DR. LYMAN. Ah, you'll look lovely, *lovely.* I know you will. I hope it doesn't embarrass you for me to speak these endearments . . .

ELMA. No . . . it doesn't embarrass me.

DR. LYMAN. I'm glad. Just think of me as a fatherly old fool, will you? And not be troubled if I take such rapturous delight in your sweetness, and youth, and innocence? For these are qualities I seek to warm my heart as I seek a fire to warm my hands.

ELMA. Now I *am* kind of embarrassed. I don't know what to say.

DR. LYMAN. Then say nothing, or nudge *me* and I'll talk endlessly about the most trivial matters. (*They laugh together as* CHERIE *comes back in, shivering.*)

CHERIE (*crosses to stove*). Brrr, it's cold. Virgil, I wish you'd play us another song. I think we all need somethin' to cheer us up. (ELMA *crosses* D. S., *around counter.*)

VIRGIL. I'll make a deal with ya. I'll play if you'll sing.

ELMA (*a bright idea comes to her*). Let's have a floor show! (*Her suggestion comes as a surprise and there is silence while all consider it.*) Everyone here can do something! (*Crosses* L.)

DR. LYMAN. A brilliant idea, straight from Chaucer. You must read Juliet for me.

ELMA (*not hearing* DR. LYMAN, *running to* VIRGIL). Will you play for us, Virgil? (CHERIE *runs* L. *behind counter, gets suitcase, takes it* U. L. *and looks for costume.*)

VIRGIL. I don't play opery music or jitterbug.

ELMA (*turning to* BO). Will you take part? (*Stubbornly,* BO *just turns the other way.*) Please! It won't be fun unless we all do something.

VIRGIL (*rises, crosses* L. *to* R. *of* BO). G'wan, Bo.

BO. I never was no play-actor, Miss.

VIRGIL. Ya kin say the Gettysburg Address.

BO (*gruffly*). I ain't gonna say it now.

VIRGIL. Then why don't ya do your rope tricks? Yer rope's out on the bus. I could get it for ya easy enough.

ELMA. Oh, please! Rope tricks would be lots of fun.

BO (*emphatically*). No! I ain't gonna get up before a lotta strangers and make a fool a m'self.

VIRGIL (*to* ELMA). I guess he means it, Miss.

ELMA. Shucks! (*Crosses* D. L. *to behind counter.*)

VIRGIL (*quietly to* BO). I don't see why ya couldn't a co-operated a little, Bo.

BO (*rises, stands at window facing* U. S.). I got too much on my mind to worry about doin' stunts.

ELMA (*to* CHERIE). You'll sing a song for us, won't you, Cherie?

CHERIE. I will fer a piece a pie and another cup a coffee.

ELMA. Sure. (CHERIE *hurries to* VIRGIL.)

CHERIE. Virgil, kin you play for me?

VIRGIL. You start me out and I think I can pick out the chords. (CHERIE *sits by his side as they work out their number together.* ELMA *hurries to* DR. LYMAN.)

ELMA. And you'll read poetry for us, won't you? (BO *walks* D. R.)

DR. LYMAN (*already assuming his character*). Why, I intend to play Romeo opposite your Juliet.

ELMA. Gee, I don't know if I can remember the lines.

DR. LYMAN (*handing her a volume he has taken off the shelves*). Sometimes one can find Shakespeare on these shelves among the many lurid novels of juvenile delinquents. Here it is, *Four Tragedies of*

Shakespeare, with my compliments. (*They begin to go over the scene together as* BO, *resentful of the closeness between* CHERIE *and* VIRGIL, *goes to them belligerently.*)

BO (*to* CHERIE). Thass *my* seat.

ELMA (*taking book from* DR. LYMAN). If I read it over a few times, it'll come back. Do you know the Balcony Scene?

CHERIE (*jumping to her feet*). You kin have it. (*Hurries to* ELMA, *at counter.*)

DR. LYMAN. My dear, I know the entire play by heart. I can recite it backwards. (ELMA *comes from behind counter to sit on stool.* DR. LYMAN *sits by her.*)

CHERIE (*to* ELMA). I got a costume with me. Where can I change?

ELMA. Behind the counter. There's a mirror over the sink. (CHERIE *darts behind the counter, digging into her suitcase.*)

BO (*to* VIRGIL). She shines up to *you* like a kitten to milk. (*Sits at* VIRGIL's *table.*)

ELMA. Gee, costumes and everything. (*She resumes her study with* DR. LYMAN.)

VIRGIL (*trying to make a joke of it*). Kin *I* help it if I'm so darn attractive to women? (*Unfortunately* BO *cannot take this as a joke, as* VIRGIL *intended.* VIRGIL *perceives he is deeply hurt.*) Shucks, Bo, it don't mean nothin'.

BO. Maybe it don't mean nothin' to *you.*

VIRGIL. She was bein' nice to me 'cause I was playin' my guitar, Bo. Guitar music's kinda tender and girls seem to like it.

BO. Tender?

VIRGIL. Yah, Bo! Girls like things t' be *tender.*

BO. They do!

VIRGIL. Sure they do, Bo.

BO. A fella gets "tender," then someone comes along and makes a sap outa him.

VIRGIL. Sometimes, Bo, but not always. You just gotta take a chance.

BO. Well . . . I allus tried t' be a *decent* sorta fella, but I don't know if I'm *tender.*

VIRGIL. I think ya are, Bo. You know how ya feel about deer-huntin'. Ya never could do it. Ya couldn't any more *shoot* one a them sweet li'l deers with the sad eyes than ya could jump into boilin' oil.

BO. Are you makin' fun of me?

VIRGIL (*impatient with him*). No, I'm not makin' fun of ya, Bo. I'm just tryin' to show ya that *you* got a tender side to your nature, same as anyone else.

BO. I s'pose I do.

VIRGIL. A course ya do.

BO (*with a sudden feeling of injustice*). Then how come Cherry don't come over and talk sweet to *me,* like she does to *you?*

VIRGIL. Ya *got* a tender side, Bo, but ya don't know how to *show* it.

BO (*weighing the verdict*). I don't!

VIRGIL. No, ya just don't know how.

BO. How does a person go about showin' his tender side, Virge?

VIRGIL. Well . . . I dunno as I can tell ya. (ELMA *comes over to them ready to start the show.*)

ELMA. Will you go first, Virgil?

VIRGIL. It's all right by me.

ELMA. O.K. Then I'll act as Master of the Ceremonies. (*Center-stage, to her audience*) Ladies and gentlemen! Grace's Diner tonight presents its gala floor show of celebrated artists from all over the world! (VIRGIL *plays an introductory chord.*) The first number on our show tonight is that musical cowboy, Mr. Virgil—(*She pauses and* VIRGIL *supplies her with his last name.*)—Virgil Blessing, who will entertain you with his guitar. (*Applause.* ELMA *retires to the back of the room where she sits on bench.* DR. LYMAN *crosses to sit by her.* VIRGIL *begins to play. During his playing,* BO *is drawn over to the counter where he tries to further himself with* CHERIE, *who is behind the counter, dressing.*)

BO (*at* U. S. *end of counter. Innocently*). I think you got me all wrong, Cherry.

CHERIE. Don't you come back here. (*He turns around, goes front of counter.*) I'm dressing.

BO. Cherry . . . I think you misjudged me.

CHERIE. Be quiet. (*Pops up.*) The show's started.

BO (*leans on counter*). Cherry, I'm really a very *tender* person. You jest don't know. I'm so tenderhearted I don't go deer-huntin'. 'Cause I jest couldn't kill them "sweet li'l deers with the sad eyes." Ask Virge.

CHERIE. I ain't int'rested. (*Ducks down.*)

BO. Ya ain't?

CHERIE. No. And furthermore I think you're a louse fer comin' over here and talkin' while yor friend is tryin' to play the guitar.

BO. Ya talk like ya thought more a Virge than ya do a me.

CHERIE. Would ya go away and lemme

alone?

BO (*a final resort*). Cherry, did I tell ya 'bout my color-television set with the twenty-four-inch screen?

CHERIE. One million times! Now go 'way. (ELMA *begins to make a shushing noise to quiet* BO. *Finally* BO *dejectedly returns to the other side of the room, where* VIRGIL *is just finishing his number.* BO *sits down at a table in the midst of* VIRGIL'S *applause.*)

(*Together*)

CHERIE. That was wonderful, Virge! ⎫
DR. LYMAN. Brilliant!   ⎬
ELMA. Swell! Play us another!   ⎭

VIRGIL. No more just now. I'm ready to see the rest of ya do somethin'.

BO (*to* VIRGIL). A lot *she* cares how tender I am!

ELMA (*coming forth again as Master of Ceremonies*). That was swell, Virgil. (*Turns back to* DR. LYMAN.) Are you ready?

DR. LYMAN (*preening himself, rises*). I consider myself so.

ELMA (*taking the book to* VIRGIL). Will you be our prompter?

VIRGIL. It's kinda funny writin', but I'll try.

ELMA (*back to* DR. LYMAN *above table*). Gee, what'll we use for a balcony?

DR. LYMAN. That offers a problem. (*Together they consider whether to use the counter for* ELMA *to stand on or one of the tables.*)

BO (*to* VIRGIL). What is it these folks are gonna do, Virge?

VIRGIL. *Romeo and Juliet* . . . by Shakespeare! (*Puts guitar down.*)

BO. Shakespeare!

VIRGIL. This Romeo was a great lover, Bo. Watch him and pick up a few pointers. (CHERIE *comes running out from behind the counter now, a dressing gown over her costume, and she sits at one of the tables.*)

CHERIE. I'm ready.

BO (*reading some of the lines from* VIRGIL'S *book*). "But soft . . . what light through . . . yonder window breaks? It is the East . . . and Juliet is the sun . . . Arise, fair . . ." (*He has got this far only with difficulty, stumbling over most of the words.* VIRGIL *takes the book away from him now.*)

VIRGIL. Shh, Bo! (ELMA *comes forth to introduce the act as* DR. LYMAN *clears the counter.*)

ELMA (*crosses to* C.). Ladies and gentlemen! you are about to witness a playing of the balcony scene from *Romeo and Juliet*. Dr. Gerald Lyman will portray the part of Romeo, and I'll play Juliet. My name is Elma Duckworth. The scene is the orchard of the Capulets' house in Verona, Italy. (DR. LYMAN *takes a quick drink.*) This counter is supposed to be a balcony. (DR. LYMAN *helps her onto the counter where she stands, waiting for him to begin.*) O.K.? (DR. LYMAN *takes a quick reassuring drink from his bottle, then tucks it in his pocket, and comes forward in the great Romantic tradition. He is enjoying himself tremendously. The performance proves to be pure ham, but there is pathos in the fact that he does not seem to be aware of how bad he is. He is a thoroughly selfish performer, too, who reads all his speeches as though they were grand soliloquies, regarding his Juliet as a prop.*)

DR. LYMAN.
   "He jests at scars, that never felt a
      wound.
   But soft! what light through yonder
      window breaks?
   It is the east, and Juliet is the sun!
(*He tries to continue, but* ELMA, *unmindful of cues and eager to begin her performance, reads her lines with compulsion.*)
   Arise . . . fair sun, and . . . kill the
      envious. . . ."

ELMA (*at same time as* DR. LYMAN).
   "O Romeo, Romeo! wherefore art
      thou, Romeo?
   Deny thy father, and refuse thy name:
   Or if thou wilt not, be but sworn my
      love,
   And I'll no longer be a Capulet."

DR. LYMAN.
   "She speaks, yet she says nothing:
      what of that?
   Her eye discourses; I will answer it.
   I am too bold—"

BO (*to* VIRGIL). Bold? He's drunk.

VIRGIL. Ssssh!

DR. LYMAN.
   ". . . 'tis not to me she speaks:
   Two of the fairest stars in all the
      heaven,
   Having some business, do entreat her
      eyes
   To twinkle in their spheres till they
      return."

ELMA.

"Ay, me!"

DR. LYMAN.

"O! speak again, bright angel; thou
art

As glorious to this night, being o'er
·my head

As is a winged messenger of heaven

Unto the white-upturned . . ."

(DR. LYMAN *continues with this speech,
even though* BO *talks over him.*)

BO. I don't understand all them words,
Virge.

VIRGE. It's *Romeo and Juliet,* for God's
sake. Now will you shut up?

DR. LYMAN (*continuing uninterrupted*).
". . . wondering eyes

Of mortals, that fall back to gaze on
him

When he bestrides the lazy-pacing
clouds,

And sails upon the bosom of the air."

(*He is getting weary but he is not yet
ready to give up.*)

ELMA.

"'Tis but thy name that is my enemy;

Thou art thyself though, not a Montague.

What's a Montague? it is not hand,
nor foot,

Nor arm, nor face, or any other part

Belonging to a man. O! be some other
name:

What's——"

DR. LYMAN (*interrupts. Beginning to
falter now. Leans on back of chair*).

"I take thee at thy word.

Call me but love, and . . . I'll be new
baptiz'd;

Henceforth . . . I never . . . will be
Romeo."

(*It is as though he were finding suddenly
a personal meaning in the lines.*)

ELMA.

"What man art thou, that, thus be-
screen'd in night,

So stumblest on my counsel?"

DR. LYMAN (*beginning to feel that he
cannot continue*).

"By a name
I know not how to tell thee . . .
who I am:

My name, dear saint, is . . . is *hateful* to myself."

(*He stops here. For several moments there
is a wondering silence.* ELMA *signals* VIR-
GIL.)

VIRGIL (*prompting*). "Because it is an
enemy to thee."

DR. LYMAN (*leaving the scene of action,
repeating the line dumbly, making his
way stumblingly back to the counter*).

"My name . . . is hateful . . . to myself . . ."

(ELMA *hurries to* DR. LYMAN's *side.* VIRGIL
grabs hold of BO, *pulls him back to the
floor and shames him.*)

ELMA. Dr. Lyman, what's the matter?

DR. LYMAN. My dear . . . let us not
continue this meaningless little act!

ELMA. Did I do something wrong?

DR. LYMAN. You couldn't possibly do
anything wrong . . . if you tried.

ELMA. I can try to say the lines differently.

DR. LYMAN. Don't. Don't. Just tell your
audience that Romeo suddenly is fraught
with remorse. (*He drops to a stool,* ELMA
*remaining by him a few moments, uncer-
tainly.* BO *turns to* VIRGIL.)

BO. Virge, if thass the way to make love
. . . I'm gonna give up.

ELMA (*crosses R. to* VIRGIL). I'm afraid
he isn't feeling well.

VIRGIL (*to* ELMA). I tried to prompt him.

ELMA (*to herself*). Well, we've only got
one more number. (*Crosses to* CHERIE.)
Are you ready?

CHERIE (*rises*). Sure.

ELMA (*crosses R. above table*). Ladies
and gentlemen, our next number is Mademoiselle Cherie, the international *chanteuse,* direct from the Blue Dragon night
club in Kansas City, *Cherie!* (*All applaud
as* CHERIE *comes forth,* VIRGIL *playing an
introduction for her.* BO *puts his finger
through his teeth and whistles for her.*
CHERIE *hands her robe to* VIRGIL. ELMA
clears central table, CHERIE *climbs up on
it.*)

CHERIE (*whispering to* ELMA). Remember, I don't allow no table service during
my numbers.

ELMA. O. K. (*She crosses to counter, sits
on* D. S. *stool. In the background now, we
can observe that* DR. LYMAN *is drinking
heavily from the bottle in his overcoat
pocket.* CHERIE *gets up on one of the tables
and begins singing her song with a chord
accompaniment from* VIRGIL. *Her rendition of the song is a most dramatic one,
that would seem to have been created from*
CHERIE's *observations of numerous torch-
singers. But she has appeal, and if she is*

funny, she doesn't seem to know it. Anyway, she rekindles BO's *most fervent love, which he cannot help expressing during her performance.*)

BO (*about the middle of the song*). Ain't she beautiful, Virge?

VIRGIL (*trying to keep his mind on his playing*). Shh, Bo!

BO. I'm gonna git her, Virge.

VIRGIL. Ssshh!

BO (*pause. He pays no attention to anyone*). I made up my mind. I told myself I was gonna git me a gal. Thass the only reason I entered that rodeo, and I ain't takin' no fer an answer.

VIRGIL. Bo, will you hush up and lemme be!

BO. Anything I ever wanted in this life, I went out and got and I ain't gonna stop now. I'm gonna git her. (*The song ends now and* CHERIE *is enraged. She jumps down from her table and while her audience applauds, she goes straight to* BO *and slaps him stingingly on the face.*)

CHERIE. You ain't got the manners God gave a monkey.

BO (*stunned*). Cherry!

CHERIE. . . . and if I was a man, I'd beat the livin' daylights out of ya, and thass what some man's gonna do some day, and when it happens, I hope I'm there to *see*. (*She flounces back to her dressing room and crouches down behind counter, as* BO *gapes. By this time* DR. LYMAN *has drunk himself almost to insensibility, and we see him weaving back and forth on his stool, mumbling almost incoherently.*)

DR. LYMAN. "Romeo . . . Romeo . . . wherefore art thou? Wherefore art thou . . . Romeo?" (*He laughs like a loon, falls off the stool and collapses on the floor.* ELMA *and* VIRGIL *rush to him.* BO *remains rooted, glaring at* CHERIE *with puzzled hurt.*)

ELMA (*deeply concerned*). Dr. Lyman! Dr. Lyman!

VIRGIL. The man's in a purty bad way. Let's get him on the bench. (ELMA *and* VIRGIL *manage to get* DR. LYMAN *to his feet as* BO *glides across the room, scales the counter in a leap and takes* CHERIE *in his arms.*)

BO. I was tellin' Virge I love ya. Ya got no right to come over and slap me.

CHERIE (*twisting*). Lemme be.

BO (*picking her up*). We're goin' down and wake up the justice of the peace and

you're gonna marry me t'night.

CHERIE (*as he takes her in his arms and transports her to the door, just as* ELMA *and* VIRGIL *are helping* DR. LYMAN *onto the bench*). Help! Virgil, help!

BO. Shut up! I'll make ya a good husband. Ya won't never have nothin' to be sorry about.

CHERIE (*as she is carried to the door*). Help! Sheriff! Help me, someone! Help me! (*The action is now like that of a two-ringed circus for* ELMA *and* VIRGIL, *whose attention suddenly is diverted from the plight of* DR. LYMAN *to the much noisier plight of* CHERIE. BO *gets her, kicking and protesting, as far as the front door when it suddenly opens and* BO *finds himself confronted by* WILL *who leaves the door open.*)

WILL. Put her down, cowboy!

BO (*trying to forge ahead*). Git outta my way.

WILL (*shoving* BO *back as* CHERIE *manages to jump loose from his arms and runs* L. *behind counter*). Yor gonna do as I say.

BO. I ain't gonna have no one interferin' in my ways. (*He makes an immediate lunge at* WILL, *which* WILL *is prepared for, coming up with a fist that sends* BO *back reeling.*)

VIRGIL (*hurrying to* BO's *side*). Bo, ya cain't do this, Bo. Ya cain't pick a fight with the sheriff.

BO (*slowly getting back to his feet*). By God, Mister, there ain't no man ever got the best a me, and there ain't no man ever gonna.

WILL. I'm ready and willin' to try, cowboy. Come on. (BO *lunges at him again.* WILL *steps aside and lets* BO *send his blow into the empty doorway as he propels himself through it, outside. Then* WILL *follows him out, where the fight continues.* VIRGIL *immediately follows them, as* ELMA *and* CHERIE *hurry to the window to watch.*)

CHERIE. I knowed this was gonna happen. I knowed it all along.

ELMA. Gee! I'd better call Grace. (*Starts for the rear door but* GRACE *comes through it before she gets there.* GRACE *happens to be wearing a dressing gown.*)

GRACE. Hey, what the hell's goin' on?

ELMA. Oh, Grace, they're fighting. Honest! It all happened so suddenly, I . . .

GRACE (*hurrying to* R. *of window.* ELMA *stands* L. *of window*). Let's see.

CHERIE (*leaving the window, not want-*

ing to see any more, going to a chair by one of the tables). Gee, I never wanted to cause so much trouble t'anyone.

GRACE. Wow! Looks like Will's gettin' the best of him.

ELMA (*at the window, frightened by what she sees*). Oh!

GRACE. Yap, I'll put my money on Will Masters *any* time. Will's got it up here. (*Points to her head.*) Lookit that cowboy. He's green. He just swings out wild.

ELMA (*leaving the window.* CHERIE *sits in chair by table*). I . . . I don't want to watch any more.

GRACE (*a real fight fan, she reports from the window*). God, I love a good fight. C'mon, Will—c'mon, Will—give him the old uppercut. That'll do it every time. Oh, oh, what'd I tell you, the cowboy's down. Will's puttin' handcuffs on him now. (CHERIE *sobs softly.* ELMA *goes to her.*)

ELMA. Will'll give him first aid. He always does.

CHERIE. Well . . . you gotta admit. He had it comin'.

GRACE (*leaving the window now*). I'm glad they got it settled outside. (*Looks around to see if anything needs to be straightened up.*) Remember the last time there was a fight in here, I had to put in a new window. (*She goes out rear door, and we become aware once more of* DR. LYMAN, *who gets up from the bench and weaves his way* c.)

DR. LYMAN. It takes strong men and women to *love* . . . (*About to fall, he grabs the back of a chair for support.*) People strong enough inside themselves to love . . . without humiliation. (*He sighs heavily and looks about him with blurred eyes.*) People big enough to *grow* with their love and live inside a whole, wide new dimension. People brave enough to bear the responsibility of *being* loved and not fear it as a burden. (*He sighs again and looks about him wearily.*) I . . . I never had the generosity to love, to give my own most private self to another, for I was *weak*. I thought the gift would somehow lessen me. Me! (*He laughs wildly and starts for the rear door.*) Romeo! Romeo! I am disgusting! (ELMA *hurries after him, stopping at the door.*)

ELMA. Dr. Lyman! Dr. Lyman!

DR. LYMAN. Don't bother, dear girl. Don't ever bother with a foolish old man like me.

ELMA. You're not a foolish old man. I like you more than anyone I've ever known.

DR. LYMAN. I'm flattered, my dear, and pleased, but you're young. In a few years, you will turn . . . from a girl into a woman; a kind, thoughtful, loving, intelligent woman . . . who could only pity me. For I'm a child, a drunken, unruly child, and I've nothing in my heart for a true woman. (GRACE *returns through rear door in time to observe the rest of the scene. She is dressed now.*)

ELMA. Let me get you something to make you feel better.

DR. LYMAN. No . . . no . . . I shall seek the icy comfort of the rest room (*He rushes out the rear door.* CHERIE *gets her robe, puts it on.*)

GRACE (*feeling concern for* ELMA). Elma, honey, what's the matter? What was he sayin' to you, Elma? (*Goes to her and they have a quiet talk between themselves as the action continues.* GRACE *is quite motherly at these times. Now* VIRGIL *comes hurrying through the front door, going to* CHERIE.)

VIRGIL. Miss, would ya help us? The sheriff says if you don't hold charges against Bo, he'll let him out to get back on the bus, if it ever goes.

CHERIE. So he can come back here and start maulin' me again? (GRACE *pours glass of water, gives it to* ELMA.)

VIRGIL. He won't do that no more, Miss. I promise.

CHERIE. *You promise!* How 'bout him?

VIRGIL. I think you can trust him now.

CHERIE. Thass what I thought before. Nothin' doin'. (*Starts* L.) He grabs ahold of a woman and kisses her . . . like he was Napoleon.

VIRGIL (*coming very close to speak as intimately as possible*). Miss . . . if he was to know I told ya this, he'd never forgive me, but . . . yor the first woman he ever made love to at all.

CHERIE. Hah! I sure don't b'lieve that.

VIRGIL. It's true, Miss. He's allus been as shy as a rabbit.

CHERIE (*in simple amazement*). My God! (*Sits on chair at table.*)

GRACE (*to* ELMA). Just take my advice and don't meet him in Topeka or anywhere else.

ELMA. I won't, Grace, but honest! I don't think he meant any harm. He just drinks a little too much. (DR. LYMAN *returns now through the rear door.* ELMA *hurries to him.*) Dr. Lyman, are you all right?

DR. LYMAN (*on his way to the bench*). I'm an old man, my dear. I feel very weary. (*He stretches out on the bench, lying on his stomach. He goes almost immediately to sleep.* ELMA *finds an old jacket and spreads it over his shoulders like a blanket. There is a long silence.* ELMA *sits by* DR. LYMAN *attentively.* CHERIE *is very preoccupied.*)

GRACE. Let him sleep it off. It's all you can do. (*Now* CARL *comes in the rear door. There is a look of impatient disgust on his face, as though he had just witnessed some revolting insult. He casts a suspicious look at* DR. LYMAN, *now oblivious to everything, and turns to* GRACE.)

CARL. Grace, fer Christ sake! who puked all over the backhouse?

GRACE. Oh, God! (DR. LYMAN *snores serenely.*)

CHERIE (*jumps up suddenly and grabs* VIRGIL's *jacket off hook*). Come on, Virge. Let's go.

VIRGIL (*enthused*). I'm awful glad you're gonna help him, Miss.

CHERIE. But if you're tellin' me a fib just to get him out of jail, I'll never forgive ya.

VIRGIL. It's no fib, Miss. You're the first gal he ever made love to at all.

CHERIE. Well, I sure ain't never had that honor before. (*They hurry out front door together.*)

CURTAIN

ACT THREE

By this time, it is early morning, about five o'clock. The storm has cleared, and outside the window we see the slow dawning, creeping above the distant hills, revealing a landscape all in peaceful white. BO, CHERIE *and* VIRGIL *are back now from the sheriff's office.* BO *has returned to his corner, where he sits as before, with his back to the others, his head low. We can detect, if we study him, that one eye is blackened and one of his hands is bandaged.* VIRGIL *sits close to him on arm of bench, like an attendant.* DR. LYMAN *is still asleep on the bench, snoring loudly.* CHERIE *tries to sleep at one of the tables.* ELMA *is clearing the tables and sweeping. The only animated people right now are* CARL *and*

GRACE. CARL *is at the telephone trying to get the operator, and* GRACE *is behind the counter.*

CARL (*after jiggling the receiver*). Still dead. (*He hangs up.*)

GRACE (*yawns*). I'll be glad when you all get out and I can go to bed. I'm tired.

CARL (*returning to counter, he sounds a trifle insinuating*). Had enough a me, baby? (GRACE *gives him a look, warning him not to let* ELMA *overhear.*) I'm kinda glad the highway was blocked tonight.

GRACE (*coquettishly*). Y'are?

CARL. Gave us a chance to become kinda acquainted, din it?

GRACE. Kinda!

CARL. Just pullin' in here three times a week, then pullin' out again in twenty minutes, I . . . I allus left . . . just wonderin' what you was like, Grace.

GRACE. I always wondered about *you*, too, Carl!

CARL. Ya did?

GRACE. Yah. But ya needn't go blabbing anything to the other drivers. (ELMA *sweeps* U. S. *and toward front door* R.)

CARL (*his honor offended*). Why, what makes ya think I'd . . . ?

GRACE. Shoot! I know how you men talk when ya get t'gether. Worse'n women.

CARL. Well, not *me*, Grace.

GRACE. I certainly don't want the other drivers on this route, some of 'em especially, gettin' the idea I'm gonna serve 'em any more'n what they order over the counter.

CARL. Sure. I get ya. (*It occurs to him to feel flattered.*) But ya . . . ya kinda *liked* me . . . din ya, Grace?

GRACE (*coquettish again*). Maybe I did.

CARL (*trying to get more of a commitment out of her*). Yah? Yah?

GRACE. Know what I first liked about ya, Carl? It was your hands. (*She takes one of his hands and plays with it.*) I like a man with big hands.

CARL. You got *everything*, baby. (*For just a moment, one senses the animal heat in their fleeting attraction. Now* WILL *comes stalking in through the front door, a man who is completely relaxed with the authority he posseses. He speaks to* GRACE.)

WILL (*crosses* L. *to* R. *of* CARL). One of the highway trucks just stopped by. They say it won't be very long now. (ELMA *crosses* D. R. *to sweep near* CHERIE.)

GRACE. I hope so.

WILL (*with a look around*). Everything peaceful?

GRACE. Yes, Will.

WILL (*he studies* BO *for a moment, then goes to him*). Cowboy, if yor holdin' any grudges against *me*, I think ya oughta ask yourself what you'd'a done in my *place*. I couldn't let ya carry off the li'l lady when she din wanta go, could I? (BO *has no answer. He just avoids* WILL's *eyes. But* WILL *is determined to get an answer.*) Could I? (GRACE *leans on counter.*)

BO. I don't feel like talkin', Mister.

WILL. Well, I couldn't. And I think you might also remember that this li'l lady . . . (CHERIE *begins to stir.*) if she wanted to . . . could press charges and get you sent to the penitentiary for violation of the Mann Act.

BO. The *what* act?

WILL. The Mann Act. You took a woman over the state line against her will.

VIRGIL. That'd be a serious charge, Bo.

BO (*stands facing* WILL). I loved her. (VIRGIL *crosses* D. R. *near door.*)

WILL. That don't make any difference.

BO. A man's gotta right to the things he loves.

WILL. Not unless he deserves 'em, cowboy.

BO. I'm a hard-workin' man, I own me my own ranch, I got six thousand dollars in the bank.

WILL. A man don't deserve the things he loves, unless he kin be a little humble about gettin' 'em.

BO (*comes* D. R., *sits at chair* R. *of* C. *table*). I ain't gonna get down on my knees and *beg*. (VIRGIL *crosses* D. S. L. *of* R. *table.*)

WILL. Bein' humble ain't the same thing as bein' *wretched*. (BO *doesn't understand.*) I had to learn that once, too, cowboy. I wasn't quite as old as you. I stole horses instead of women because you could *sell* horses. One day, I stole a horse off the wrong man, the Rev. Hezekiah Pearson. I never thought I'd get mine from any preacher, but he was very fair. Gave me every chance to put myself clear. But I wouldn't admit the horse was his. Finally, he did what he had to do. He threshed me to within a inch of my life. I never forgot. 'Cause it was the first time in my life, I had to admit I was wrong. I was miserable. Finally, after a few days, I decided the only thing to do was to admit to the man how I felt. Then I felt different about the whole thing. I joined his church, and we was bosom pals till he died a few years ago. (*He turns to* VIRGIL.) Has he done what I asked him to?

VIRGIL. Not yet, sheriff. (*Sits at a table.*)

WILL (*to* BO). Why should ya be so scared?

BO. Who says I'm scared?

WILL. Ya gimme yor word, didn't ya?

BO (*somewhat resentful*). I'm gonna do it, if ya'll jest gimme time.

WILL. But I warn ya, it ain't gonna do no good unless you really mean it. (ELMA *is* R. *with dust pan.*)

BO. I'll mean it.

WILL. All right then. Go ahead. (WILL *crosses* U. C. *Slowly, reluctantly,* BO *gets to his feet and awkwardly, like a guilty boy, makes his way over to the counter to* GRACE. CARL *crosses to stove.*)

BO. Miss, I . . . I wanna apologize.

GRACE. What for?

BO. Fer causin' such a commotion.

GRACE. Ya needn't apologize to *me*, cowboy. I like a good fight. You're welcome at Grace's Diner *any* time. I mean *any* time.

BO (*with an appreciative grin*). Thanks. (*Now he goes to* ELMA U. R.) I musta acted like a hoodlum. I apologize.

ELMA (*steps* L. *to him*). Oh, that's all right.

BO. Thank ya, Miss.

ELMA (*crosses* L., *empties dust pan in can under sink*). I'm awfully sorry we never got to see your rope tricks. (*Puts broom and dust pan away, sits on stool.*)

BO. They ain't much. (*Pointing to the sleeping* DR. LYMAN.) Have I gotta wake up the perfessor t'apologize t'him? (CARL *drifts toward counter.*)

WILL. You can overlook the perfessor. (*He nods toward* CHERIE, *whom* BO *dreads to confront, most of all. He starts toward her but doesn't get very far.*)

BO. I cain't do it. (*Turns* U. C. VIRGIL *rises.*)

VIRGIL (*disappointed*). Aw, Bo!

BO. I jest cain't do it.

WILL (*crosses* D. L. *a few steps*). Why not?

BO. She'd have no respeck for me now. She saw me beat.

WILL (*crosses to him*). You gave me your promise. You owe that girl an apology, whether you got beat or not, and you're going to say it to her or I'm not lettin' you back on the bus. (BO *is in a dilemma. He wipes his brow.*)

VIRGIL. G'wan, Bo. G'wan. (*Steps* U. L.)

BO. Well . . . I . . . I'll try. (*He makes his way to her tortuously and finally gets out her name.*) Cherry!

CHERIE (*rises*). Yah?

BO. Cherry . . . it wasn't right a me to treat ya the way I did, draggin' ya onto the bus, tryin' to make ya marry me whether ya wanted to or not. Ya think ya could ever forgive me?

CHERIE (*after some consideration*). I guess I been treated worse in my life.

BO (*taking out his wallet*). Cherry . . . I *got* ya here and I think I oughta get ya back in good style. So . . . take this. (*He hands her a bill.*)

CHERIE. Did the sheriff make you do this?

BO (*angrily*). No, by God! He din say nothin' 'bout my givin' ya money.

WILL (*crosses* D. L. *of* CHERIE's *table*). That's *his* idea, Miss. But I think it's a good one.

CHERIE. Ya don't have to gimme this much, Bo.

BO. I want ya to have it.

CHERIE. Thanks. I can sure use it.

BO. And I . . . I wish ya good luck, Cherry . . . Honest I do.

CHERIE. I wish you the same, Bo.

BO. Well . . . I guess I said ev'rything that's to be said, so . . . so long.

CHERIE (*in a tiny voice*). So long. (*Awkward and embarrassed now,* BO *returns to his corner, and* CHERIE *sits back down at the table, full of wistful wonder.*)

WILL. Now that wasn't so bad, was it, son?

BO. I'd ruther break in wild horses than have to do it again. (WILL *laughs heartily, then strolls over to the counter in a seemingly casual way.*)

WILL. How's your headache, Grace?

GRACE. Huh?

WILL. A while back, you said you had a headache.

GRACE. Oh, I feel fine now, Will.

WILL (*he looks at* CARL). You have a nice walk, Carl?

CARL. Yah. Sure.

WILL. Well, I think ya better go upstairs 'cause someone took your overshoes and left 'em outside the door to Grace's apartment. (WILL *laughs long and heartily,*

and ELMA *cannot suppress a grin.* CARL *looks at his feet and realizes his oversight.* GRACE *is indignant.*)

GRACE. Nosy old snoop!

WILL. I'll have me a cup of coffee, Grace, and one a these sweet rolls. (*He selects a roll from the glass dish on counter, sits on a stool.* GRACE *motions* ELMA *to get* WILL *coffee, which she does.*)

VIRGIL. Come on over to the counter now, Bo, and have a bite a breakfast.

BO. I ain't hungry, Virge.

VIRGIL. Maybe a cup a coffee? (GRACE *sits on stool behind counter.*)

BO. I couldn't get it down.

VIRGIL. Now what's the matter, Bo? Ya oughta feel purty good. The sheriff let ya go and . . .

BO. I might as well a stayed in the jail.

VIRGIL. Now, what kinda talk is that? The bus'll be leavin' purty soon and we'll be back at the ranch in a coupla days.

BO. I don't care if I never see that dang ranch again.

VIRGIL. Why, Bo, you worked half yor life earnin' the money to build it up.

BO. It's the lonesomest damn place I ever did see.

VIRGIL. Well . . . I never thought so.

BO. It'll be like goin' back to a graveyard.

VIRGIL. Bo . . . I heard Hank and Orville talkin' 'bout the new school marm, lives over to the Stebbins'. They say she's a looker.

BO. I ain't int'rested in no school marm.

VIRGIL. Give yourself time, Bo. Yor young. You'll find lotsa gals, gals that'll love *you*, too.

BO. I want Cherry. (*And for the first time we observe he is capable of tears.*)

VIRGIL (*with a futile shrug of his shoulders*). Aw—Bo——

BO (*dismissing him*). Go git yorself somethin' t'eat, Virge. (BO *remains in isolated gloom as* VIRGIL *makes his slow way to the counter. Suddenly the telephone rings.* GRACE *jumps to answer it.* ELMA *gives* VIRGIL *coffee. He sits on stool to drink it.*)

GRACE. My God! the lines are up. (*Into the telephone*) Grace's Diner! (*Pause.*) It is? (*Pause.*) O.K. I'll tell him. (*Hangs up and turns to* CARL.) Road's cleared now but you're gonna have to put on your chains 'cause the road's awful slick.

CARL. God damn! (*Gets up and hustles into his overcoat, going* C. *to make his announcement*). Road's clear, folks! Bus'll be ready to leave as soon as I get the chains on. That'll take about twenty minutes . . . (*Stops and looks back at them.*) . . . unless someone wants to help me. (*Goes out front door.* WILL *gets up from the counter.*)

WILL. I'll help ya, Carl. (*He goes out front door.* CHERIE *makes her way over to* BO.)

CHERIE. Bo?

BO. Yah?

CHERIE. I just wanted to tell ya somethin', Bo. It's kinda personal and kinda embarrassin', too, but . . . I ain't the kinda gal you thought I was. (ELMA *and* GRACE *are busy clearing counter.*)

BO. What ya mean, Cherry?

CHERIE. Well, I guess some people'd say I led a real wicked life. I guess I have.

BO. What ya tryin' to tell me?

CHERIE. Well . . . I figgered since ya found me at the Blue Dragon, ya just took it fer granted I'd had other boy friends 'fore you.

BO. Ya had?

CHERIE. Yes, Bo. Quite a few.

BO. Virge'd told me that, but I wouldn't b'lieve him.

CHERIE. Well, it's true. So ya see . . . I ain't the kinda gal ya want at all. (BO *is noncommittal.* CHERIE *slips back to her table.* ELMA *makes her way to the bench to rouse* DR. LYMAN.)

ELMA. Dr. Lyman! Dr. Lyman! (*He comes to with a jump, staring out wildly about him.*)

DR. LYMAN. Where am I? (*Recognizing* ELMA.) Oh, it's *you.* (*A great smile appears. Rises.*) Dear girl. What a sweet awakening!

ELMA. How do you feel?

DR. LYMAN. That's not a polite question. How long have I been asleep here?

ELMA. Oh—a couple of hours. (GRACE *sits on stool.*)

DR. LYMAN. Sometimes Nature blesses me with a total blackout. I seem to remember absolutely nothing after we started our performance. How were we?

ELMA. Marvelous.

DR. LYMAN. Oh, I'm glad. Now I'll have a cup of that coffee you were trying to force on me last night.

ELMA. All right. (*Crosses to* U. S. *end of counter.*) Can I fix you something to eat?

DR. LYMAN. No. Nothing to eat. (*He makes a face of repugnance.*)

ELMA. Oh, Dr. Lyman, you *must* eat something. Really.

DR. LYMAN. *Must* I?

ELMA. Oh, yes! Please!

DR. LYMAN. Very well, for your sweet sake, I'll have a couple of three-minute eggs, and some toast and orange juice. But I'm doing this for you, mind you. Just for you. (ELMA *slips behind the counter to begin his breakfast, as* VIRGIL *gets up from the counter and goes to* BO. DR. LYMAN *slowly crosses to counter and sits on stool.*)

VIRGIL. I'll go help the driver with his chains, Bo. You stay here and take care a that hand. (*He goes out front door.* BO *finds his way again to* CHERIE. GRACE *is working behind counter with* ELMA.)

BO. Cherry . . . would I be molestin' ya if I said somethin'?

CHERIE (*rises as* BO *crosses to her*). No . . .

BO. Well . . . since you brought the subject up, you *are* the first gal I ever had anything to do with. (*There is a silence.*) By God! I never thought I'd hear m'self sayin' that, but I said it.

CHERIE. I never woulda guessed it, Bo.

BO. Ya see . . . I'd lived all my life on a ranch . . . and I guess I din know much about women . . . 'cause they're *diff'rent* from men.

CHERIE. Well, natur'ly.

BO. Every time I got around one . . . I began to feel kinda scared . . . and I din know how t'act. It was aggravatin'.

CHERIE. Ya wasn't scared with *me,* Bo.

BO. When I come into that night club place, you was singin' . . . and you smiled at me while you was singin', and winked at me a coupla times. Remember?

CHERIE. Yah. I remember.

BO. Well, I guess I'm kinda green, but . . . no gal ever done that to me before, so I thought you was singin' yor songs just fer *me.*

CHERIE. Ya did kinda attrack me, Bo . . .

BO. Anyway, you was so purty, and ya seemed so kinda warm-hearted and sweet. I . . . I felt like I *could* love ya . . . and I did.

CHERIE. Bo—ya think you really did love me?

BO. Why, Cherry! I couldn't be *familiar* . . . with a gal I din love. (CHERIE *is brought almost to tears. Neither she nor* BO *can find any more words for the moment, and drift away from each other back to their respective places. At the counter*

DR. LYMAN *eats his breakfast, which* ELMA *has served him.* CARL *comes back in front door, followed by* VIRGIL *and* WILL. CARL *has got his overshoes on now. He comes* C. *again to make an announcement.*)

CARL. Bus headed west! All aboard! Next stop, Topeka! (*He rejoins* GRACE *at the counter and, taking a pencil from his pocket, begins making out his report.* WILL *speaks to* BO.)

WILL. How ya feelin' now, cowboy?

BO. I ain't the happiest critter that was ever born.

WILL. Just 'cause ya ain't happy now don't mean ya ain't gonna be happy t'morrow. Feel like shakin' hands now, cowboy?

BO (*hesitant*). Well . . .

VIRGIL. Go on, Bo. He's only trying to be friends.

BO (*offering his hand, still somewhat reluctantly*). I don't mind. (*They shake.*)

WILL. I just want you to remember there's no hard feelin's. So long.

BO. S'long.

WILL. I'm goin' home now, Grace. See you Monday.

GRACE. S'long, Will.

CARL. Thanks for helpin' me, Will. I'll be pullin' out, soon as I make out the reports.

WILL (*stops at the door and gives a final word to* CHERIE). Montana's not a bad place, Miss. (*He goes out front door.*)

VIRGIL. Nice fella, Bo.

BO (*concentrating on* CHERIE). Maybe I'll think so some day.

VIRGIL. Well, maybe we better be boardin' the bus, Bo. (*Without even hearing* VIRGIL, BO *makes his way suddenly over to* CHERIE.)

BO. Cherry!

CHERIE. Hi, Bo!

BO. Cherry, I promised not to molest ya, but if you was to give yor permission, it'd be all right. I . . . I'd like to kiss ya g'by.

CHERIE. Ya would? (BO *nods.*) I'd like ya to kiss me, Bo. I really would. (*A wide grin cracks open his face and he becomes all hoodlum boy again, about to take her in his arms roughly as he did before, but she stops him.*) Bo! I think this time when ya kiss me, it oughta be diff'rent.

BO (*not sure what she means*). Oh! (*He looks around at* VIRGIL *who turns quickly away, as though admitting his inability to advise his buddy.* BO *then takes her in his arms cautiously, as though holding a pre-*cious object that was still a little strange to him.*)

BO. Golly! When ya kiss someone fer serious, it's kinda scarey, ain't it?

CHERIE. Yah! It is. (*Anyway, he kisses her, long and tenderly.*)

GRACE (*at the counter*). It don't look like he was molestin' her now. (BO, *after the kiss is ended, is dazed. Uncertain of his feelings, he stampedes across the room to* VIRGIL, *drawing him to the bench where the two men can confer. The action continues with* DR. LYMAN, *at the counter, having his breakfast.*)

DR. LYMAN. I could tell you with all honesty that this was the most delicious breakfast I've ever eaten, but it wouldn't be much of a compliment because I have eaten very few breakfasts. (*They laugh together.*)

ELMA. It's my favorite meal. (*Turns to the refrigerator as he brings bottle out secretly and spikes his coffee.*)

DR. LYMAN (*when* ELMA *returns*). Dear girl, let us give up our little spree, shall we? You don't want to go traipsing over the streets of the State's capital with an old reprobate like me.

ELMA. Whatever you say.

DR. LYMAN. I shall continue my way to Denver. I'm sure it's best.

ELMA. Anyway, I've certainly enjoyed knowing you.

DR. LYMAN. Thank you. Ah! sometimes it is so gratifying to feel that one is doing the "right" thing, I wonder that I don't choose to always.

ELMA. What do you mean?

DR. LYMAN. Oh, I was just rambling. You know, perhaps while I am in the vicinity of Topeka, I should drop in at that hospital and seek some advice.

ELMA. Sometimes their patients come in here. They look perfectly all right to me.

DR. LYMAN. Friends have been hinting for quite a while that I should get psychoanalyzed. (*He chuckles.*) I don't know if they had my best interests at heart or their own.

ELMA. Golly. I don't see anything the matter with you.

DR. LYMAN (*a little sadly*). No. Young people never do. (*Now with a return of high spirits*) However, I don't think I care to be psychoanalyzed. I rather cherish myself as I am. (*The cavalier again, he takes her hand.*) Good-by, my dear! You were the loveliest Juliet since Miss Jane Cowl. (*Kisses her hand gallantly, then goes for his coat.* ELMA *comes from behind counter and follows him.*)

ELMA. Thank you, Dr. Lyman. I feel it's been an honor to know you. You're the smartest man I've ever met.

LYMAN. The smartest?

ELMA. Really you are.

DR. LYMAN. Oh, yes, I'm terribly smart. Wouldn't it have been nice . . . to be intelligent? (*He chuckles, blows a kiss to her, then hurries out the front door.* ELMA *lingers behind, watching him get on the bus.*)

CARL (*to* GRACE). Hey, know what I heard about the perfessor? The detective at the bus terminal in Kanz City is a buddy a mine. He pointed out the perfessor to me before he got on the bus. Know what he said? He said the p'lice in Kanz City picked the perfessor up for *loiterin'* round the schools.

GRACE (*appalled*). Honest?

CARL. Then they checked his record and found he'd been in trouble several times, for gettin' involved with young girls.

GRACE. My God! Did you tell Will?

CARL. Sure, I told him. They ain't *got* anything on the perfessor now, so there's nothin' Will could do. (ELMA *makes her way back to the counter now and hears the rest of what* CARL *has to say.*) What gets *me* is why does he call hisself a doctor? Is he some kinda phony?

ELMA (*going behind counter*). No, Carl. He's a Doctor of Philosophy.

CARL. What's that?

ELMA. It's the very highest degree there is, for scholarship.

GRACE. Ya'd think he'd have philosophy enough to keep outa trouble. (ELMA *resumes her work behind the counter now.*)

CARL (*to* GRACE). Sorry to see me go, baby?

GRACE. No . . . I told ya, I'm tired.

CARL (*good-naturedly*). Ya know, sometimes I get to thinkin', what the hell good is marriage, where ya have to put up with the same broad every day, and lookit her in the morning, and try to get along with her when she's got a bad disposition. This way suits me fine.

GRACE. I got no complaints, either. Incidentally, are you married, Carl?

CARL. Now, who said I was married, Grace? Who said it? You just tell me and I'll fix him.

GRACE. Relax! Relax! See ya day after tomorrow. (*She winks at him.*)

CARL (*winks back*). You might get surprised . . . what can happen in twenty minutes. (*Slaps* GRACE *on the buttocks as a gesture of farewell.*) All aboard! (*He hustles out the front door as* BO *hurries to* CHERIE. ELMA *and* GRACE *work behind counter.*)

GRACE (*to herself*). He still never said whether he was married.

BO. Cherry?

CHERIE (*a little expectantly*). Yah?

BO. I been talkin' with my buddy, and he thinks I'm virgin enough fer the two of us.

CHERIE (*snickers, very amused*). Honest? Did Virgil say that?

BO. Yah . . . and I like ya like ya are, Cherry. So I don't care how ya got that way.

CHERIE (*deeply touched*). Oh, God, thass the sweetest, tenderest thing that was ever said to me.

BO (*feeling awkward*). Cherry . . . it's awful hard for a fella, after he's been turned down once, to git up enough guts to try again . . .

CHERIE. Ya don't need guts, Bo.

BO (*not quite sure what she means*). I don't?

CHERIE. It's the last thing in the world ya need.

BO. Well . . . anyway, I jest don't have none now, so I'll . . . just have to say what I feel in my heart.

CHERIE. Yah?

BO. I still wish you was goin' back to the ranch with me, more'n anything I know.

CHERIE. Ya do?

BO. Yah. I do.

CHERIE. Why, I'd go anywhere in the world with ya now, Bo. Anywhere at all.

BO. Ya would? Ya would? (*They have a fast embrace. All look.*)

GRACE (*nudging* ELMA). I knew this was gonna happen all the time.

ELMA. Gee, I didn't. (*Now* BO *and* CHERIE *break apart, both running to opposite sides of the room.* BO *to tell* VIRGIL; CHERIE, ELMA. VIRGIL *rises.*)

BO. Hear that, Virge? Yahoo! We're gettin' married after all. Cherry's goin' back with me.

CHERIE (*at counter*). Ain't it wonderful when someone so awful turns out t'be so nice? We're gettin' married. I'm goin' to Montana. (CARL *sticks his head through the door and calls impatiently.* CHERIE *gets suitcase from behind counter, and jacket.*)

CARL. Hey! All aboard, fer Christ's sake! (*He goes out front door.* BO *grabs* VIRGIL *now by the arm.* CHERIE *goes to him, puts suitcase down.*)

BO. C'mon, Virge, y'old raccoon!

VIRGIL (*demurring*). Now look, Bo . . . listen t'me for a second.

BO (*who can't listen to anything in his high revelry. One arm is around* CHERIE, *the other tugs at* VIRGIL). C'mon! Doggone it, we wasted enough time. Let's git goin'.

VIRGIL (*pulls away*). Listen, Bo. Now be quiet jest a minute. You gotta hear me, Bo. You don't need me no more. I ain't goin'.

BO (*not believing his ears*). You ain't *what?*

VIRGIL. I . . . I ain't goin' with ya, Bo.

BO (*flabbergasted*). Well, what ya know about that?

VIRGIL. It's best I don't, Bo.

BO. Jest one blame catastrophe after another.

VIRGIL. I . . . I got another job in mind, Bo. Where the feed's mighty good, and I'll be lookin' after the cattle. I meant to tell ya 'bout it 'fore this.

BO. Virge, I can't b'lieve you'd leave yor old sidekick. Yor jokin', man.

VIRGIL. No . . . I ain't jokin', Bo. I ain't.

BO. Well, I'll be a . . .

CHERIE. Virgil—I wish you'd come. I liked *you* . . . 'fore I ever liked Bo.

BO. Ya *know* Cherry likes ya, Virge. It jest don't make sense, yor not comin'.

VIRGIL. Well . . . I'm doin' the right thing. I know I am.

BO. Who's gonna look after the cattle?

VIRGIL. Hank. Every bit as good as *I* ever was.

BO (*very disheartened*). Aw, Virge, I dunno why ya have to pull a stunt like this.

VIRGIL. You better hurry, Bo. That driver's not gonna wait all day.

BO (*starting to pull* VIRGIL, *to drag him away just as he tried once with* CHERIE). Daggone it, yor my buddy, and I ain't gonna let ya go. Yor goin' *with* Cherry and me 'cause we want ya . . .

VIRGIL (*it's getting very hard for him to control his feelings*). No . . . No . . . lemme be, Bo . . .

CHERIE (*holding* BO *back*). Bo . . . ya can't do it that way . . . ya jest can't . . .

if he don't wanta go, ya can't make him . . .

BO. But, Cherry, there ain't a reason in the world he shouldn't go. It's plumb crazy.

CHERIE. Well, sometimes people have their *own* reasons, Bo.

BO. Oh? (*He reconsiders.*) Well, I just hate to think of gettin' along without old Virge.

VIRGIL (*laughing*). In a couple weeks . . . ya'll never miss me.

BO (*disheartened*). Aw, Virge!

VIRGIL. Get along with ya now.

CHERIE. Virgil—(*Brightly.*) will ya come and visit us, Virgil?

VIRGIL. I'll be up in the summer.

BO. Where ya gonna be, Virge?

VIRGIL. I'll write ya th' address. Don't have time to give it to ya now. Nice place. Mighty nice. Now hurry and get on your bus. (CARL *honks the horn off* R.)

BO (*managing a quick embrace*). So long, old boy. So long!

VIRGIL. 'By, Bo! G'by! (*Now, to stave off any tears,* BO *grabs* CHERIE'*s hand.*)

BO. C'mon, Cherry. Let's make it fast. (*Before they are out the door, a thought occurs to* BO. *He stops, takes off his leather jacket and helps* CHERIE *into it. He has been gallant. Then he picks up her suitcase and they go out the front door, calling their farewells behind them.*)

CHERIE. 'By—'by—'by, everyone! 'By! (VIRGIL *stands at the door, waving goodby.* ELMA *runs to window. His eyes look a little moist. In a moment, the bus's motor is heard to start up. Then the bus leaves.*)

GRACE (*from behind counter*). Mister, we gotta close this place up now, if Elma and me're gonna get any rest. We won't be open again till eight o'clock when the day girl comes on. The next bus through is to Albuquerque, at eight forty-five. (ELMA *returns to counter.*)

VIRGIL. Albuquerque? I guess that's as good a place as any. (*He remains by the front entrance, looking out on the frosty morning.* ELMA *and* GRACE *continue their work behind the counter.*)

ELMA. Poor Dr. Lyman!

GRACE. Say, did you hear what Carl told me about that guy?

ELMA. No. What was it, Grace?

GRACE. Well, according to Carl, they run him outa Kanz City.

ELMA. I don't believe it.

GRACE. Honey, Carl got it straight from the detective at the bus terminal.

ELMA (*afraid to ask*). What . . . did Dr. Lyman do?

GRACE. Well, lots of old fogies like him just can't let young girls alone. (*A wondering look comes over* ELMA's *face.*) So, it's a good thing you didn't meet him in Topeka.

ELMA. Do you think . . . he wanted to make *love,* to *me?*

GRACE. I don't think he meant to play hopscotch.

ELMA (*very moved*). Gee!

GRACE. Next time any guy comes in here and starts gettin' fresh, you come tell your Aunt Grace. (VIRGIL *is seated on chair by a table.*)

ELMA. I guess I'm kinda stupid.

GRACE (ELMA *is at* C.). Everyone has gotta learn. (*Looking into refrigerator*) Now Monday, for sure, I gotta order some cheese.

ELMA. I'll remind you.

GRACE (*coming to* ELMA, *apologetically*). Elma, honey?

ELMA. Yes?

GRACE. I could kill Will Masters for sayin' anything about me and Carl. I didn't want you to know.

ELMA. I don't see why I shouldn't know, Grace. I don't wanta be a baby forever.

GRACE. Of course you don't. But still, you're a kid, and I don't wanta set no examples or anything. Do you think you can overlook it and not think bad of me?

ELMA. Sure, Grace.

GRACE. 'Cause I'm a restless sort of woman, and every once in a while, I gotta have me a man, just to keep m'self from gettin' grouchy. (ELMA *goes behind counter.*)

ELMA. It's not my business, Grace. (*She stops a moment to consider herself in the mirror, rather pleased.*) Just think, he wanted to make love to *me.*

GRACE. Now don't start gettin' stuck on yourself.

ELMA. I'm not, Grace. But it's nice to know that someone *can* feel that way.

GRACE. You're not gonna have any trouble. Just wait'll you get to college and start meeting all those cute *boys.* (GRACE *seems to savor this.*)

ELMA. All right. I'll wait.

GRACE (*takes apron off*). You can run along now, honey. All I gotta do is empty the garbage.

ELMA (*getting her coat from closet behind counter*). O.K.

GRACE. G'night!

ELMA (*coming from behind counter, slipping into her coat*). Good night, Grace. See you Monday. (*Passing* VIRGIL) It was very nice knowing you, Virgil, and I just loved your music.

VIRGIL. Thank you, Miss. G'night. (ELMA *goes out front door.*)

GRACE. We're closing now, Mister.

VIRGIL (*coming* C.). Any place warm I could stay till eight o'clock?

GRACE. Now that the p'lice station's closed, I don't know where you could go, unless ya wanted to take a chance of wakin' up the man that runs the hotel.

VIRGIL. No—I wouldn't wanta be any trouble.

GRACE. There'll be a bus to Kanz City in a few minutes. I'll put the sign out and they'll stop.

VIRGIL. No, thanks. No point a goin' back there.

GRACE. Then I'm sorry, Mister, but you're just left out in the cold. (*She carries a can of garbage out the rear door leaving* VIRGIL *for the moment alone.*)

VIRGIL (*to himself*). Well . . . that's what happens to some people. (*Quietly, he picks up his guitar and goes out.* GRACE *comes back in, locks back door, snaps wall switch, then yawns and stretches, then sees that the front door is locked. The sun outside is just high enough now to bring a dim light into the restaurant.* GRACE *stops at the rear door and casts her eyes tiredly over the establishment. One senses her aloneness. She sighs, then goes out the door. A cold sweep of morning wind whistles over the countryside. The curtain comes down on an empty stage.*)

TEA AND SYMPATHY

Robert Anderson

This is for
PHYLLIS
whose spirit is everywhere
in this play and in my life.

First presented by the Playwrights' Company, in association
with Mary K. Frank, at the Ethel Barrymore Theatre,
New York, on September 30, 1953, with the following cast:

LAURA REYNOLDS Deborah Kerr
LILLY SEARS Florida Friebus
TOM LEE John Kerr
DAVID HARRIS Richard Midgley
RALPH Alan Sues
AL Dick York

STEVE Arthur Steuer
BILL REYNOLDS Leif Erickson
PHIL Richard Franchot
HERBERT LEE John McGovern
PAUL Yale Wexler

In June, 1954, the principal roles were assumed by Joan Fontaine and Anthony Perkins.

ACT ONE. A dormitory in a boys' school in New England. Late
afternoon of a day early in June.

ACT TWO. SCENE I: Two days later. SCENE II: Eight-thirty Saturday
night.

ACT THREE. The next afternoon.

INTRODUCTION

ROBERT ANDERSON was thirty-six when *Tea and Sympathy* had its triumphant premiere on Broadway in the early fall of 1953, and the impression he made on his producers, The Playwrights Company, resulted in their making him a member of their distinguished organization. Born in New York in 1917, Mr. Anderson received his secondary schooling at Phillips Exeter and took a bachelor's and a master's degree at Harvard in 1939 and 1940. While at Harvard he met the late Phyllis Anderson, to whose memory this book is affectionately dedicated. She headed a dramatic department at the Erskine School for girls and found it necessary to draw young Harvard men into her productions. Robert Anderson was one of them; he became her husband and she became his inspiration. She had an extraordinary talent for discovering talent and watching over it. She became play editor for the Theatre Guild and, in the last years of her lamentably brief life, was head of the play department of the powerful show-business agency, M.C.A.

Mr. Anderson abandoned a teaching career for a theatrical one. But World War II had broken out and before long he had an intermediate career as a naval officer which terminated only when the war did. But he managed to write his first play, *Come Marching Home,* while in the service, submitted it to a National Theatre Conference play contest for servicemen, and won first prize with it in 1944. The piece was produced by the University of Iowa Theatre Department in 1945. This work along with two other manuscripts also won for the author a Playwriting Fellowship from the National Theatre Conference, an organization made up of leaders of the educational theatre, and then subsidized by the Rockefeller Foundation. *Love Revisited,* a later play, was tried out at the Westport Country Playhouse in the summer of 1950, and *All Summer Long,* later seen on Broadway, was very successfully presented in Washington, D.C., in 1953, by the capital's distinguished Arena Theatre.

Tea and Sympathy, which opened its tryout tour in Hartford, Conn., got a rousing reception in New York and became the first hit of the 1953-1954 season. John Kerr, the son of June Walker, achieved stardom in the role of the misunderstood young student, and the British film star Deborah Kerr was launched upon a successful career on the American stage. Success came to *Tea and Sympathy* a second time when it was staged on April 26, 1957, in London's West End at the Comedy Theatre by the flourishing New Watergate Theatre Club. A "Club" production was needed when the Lord Chamberlain forbade a "public" performance because of the subject matter, and Mr. Anderson joined the ranks of other distinguished American playwrights whose plays proved too strong for the Lord Chamberlain's office.

In view of the argument that developed over the degree to which the author had compounded his play as an artifice, Mr. Anderson's recollection of some of the origins of his play in the September, 1954, issue of *Theatre Arts* can be instructive: He recalled a walk down the Avenue of the Americas with his wife and a friend who declared "that she was living in a theatrical boardinghouse where the landlady had the girls down for *tea and sympathy."* He remembered a trip in 1947 to Phillips Exeter, and a visit to his first-year dormitory, "where I had been miserable and which I now found quite transformed, with a semi-private living room for the young boys presided over by a charming woman who told me that many tears were shed in that room by the younger boys." And he recalled reading Thoreau's *Walden* and marking a passage in it he considers more pertinent than the clinical question of homosexuality. The Thoreau passage reads: "If a man does not keep pace with his companions, perhaps it is because he hears a different drummer. Let him step to the music which he hears, however measured or far away." It would have been a good epigraph for the published play, even if it should not be construed as a capsule definition of the total meaning any more than the fine statement in the play that persons should give each other something more than conventional "tea and sympathy."

ACT ONE

The scene is a small old Colonial house which is now being used as a dormitory in a boys' school in New England.

On the ground floor at stage right we see the housemaster's study. To stage left is a hall and stairway which leads up to the boys' rooms. At a half-level on stage left is one of the boys' rooms.

The housemaster's study is a warm and friendly room, rather on the dark side, but when the lamps are lighted, there are cheerful pools of light. There is a fireplace in the back wall, bookcases, and upstage right double doors leading to another part of the house. Since there is no common room for the eight boys in this house, there is considerable leniency in letting the boys use the study whenever the door is left ajar.

The boys' bedroom is small, containing a bed, a chair and a bureau. It was meant to be Spartan, but the present occupant has given it a few touches to make it a little more homelike: an Indian print on the bed, India print curtains for the dormer windows. There is a phonograph on the ledge of the window. The door to the room is presumed to lead to the sitting room which the roommates share. There is a door from the sitting room which leads to the stair landing. Thus, to get to the bedroom from the stairs, a person must go through the sitting room.

As the curtain rises, it is late afternoon of a day early in June. No lamps have been lighted yet so the study is in a sort of twilight.

Upstairs in his room, TOM LEE *is sitting on his bed playing the guitar and singing softly and casually, the plaintive song, "The Joys of Love" . . .* TOM *is going on eighteen.*

He is young and a little gangling, but intense. He is wearing faded khaki trousers, a white shirt open at the neck and white tennis sneakers.

Seated in the study listening to the singing are LAURA REYNOLDS *and* LILLY SEARS. LAURA *is a lovely, sensitive woman in her mid to late twenties. Her essence is gentleness. She is compassionate and tender. She is wearing a cashmere sweater and a wool skirt. As she listens to* TOM's *singing, she is sewing on what is obviously a period costume.*

LILLY *is in her late thirties, and in contrast to the simple effectiveness of* LAURA's *clothes, she is dressed a little too flashily for her surroundings. . . . It would be in good taste on East 57th Street, but not in a small New England town. . . . A smart suit and hat and a fur piece. As she listens to* TOM *singing, she plays with the martini glass in her hand.*

———

TOM (*singing*).
    The joys of love
    Are but a moment long . . .
    The pains of love
    Endure forever . . .
(*When he has finished, he strums on over the same melody very casually, and hums to it intermittently.*)

LILLY (*while* TOM *is singing*). Tom Lee?

LAURA. Yes.

LILLY. Doesn't he have an afternoon class?

LAURA. No. He's the only one in the house that doesn't.

LILLY (*when* TOM *has finished the song*). Do you know what he's thinking of?

LAURA (*bites off a thread and looks up*). What do you mean?

LILLY. What all the boys in this school are thinking about. Not only now in the spring, but all the time . . . Sex! (*She wags her head a little wisely, and smiles.*)

LAURA. Lilly, you just like to shock people.

LILLY. Four hundred boys from the ages of thirteen to nineteen. That's the age, Laura. (*Restless, getting up*) Doesn't it give you the willies sometimes, having all these boys around?

LAURA. Of course not. I never think of it that way.

LILLY. Harry tells me they put saltpeter in their food to quiet them down. But the way they look at you, I can't believe it.

LAURA. At me?

LILLY. At any woman worth looking at. When I first came here ten years ago, I didn't think I could stand it. Now I love it. I love watching them look and suffer.

LAURA. Lilly.

LILLY. This is your first spring here, Laura. You wait.

LAURA. They're just boys.

LILLY. The authorities say the ages from thirteen to nineteen . . .

LAURA. Lilly, honestly!

LILLY. You sound as though you were in

the grave. How old are you?

LAURA (*smiling*). Over twenty-one.

LILLY. They come here ignorant as all get out about women and then spend the next four years exchanging misinformation. They're so cute, and so damned intense. (*She shudders again.*)

LAURA. Most of them seem very casual to me.

LILLY. That's just an air they put on. This is the age Romeo should be played. You'd believe him! So intense! These kids would die for love, or almost anything else. Harry says all their themes end in death.

LAURA. That's boys.

LILLY. Failure; death! Dishonor; death! Lose their girls; death! It's gruesome.

LAURA. But rather touching too, don't you think?

LILLY. You won't tell your husband the way I was talking?

LAURA. Of course not.

LILLY. Though I don't know why I should care. All the boys talk about me. They have me in and out of bed with every single master in the school—and some married ones, too.

LAURA (*kidding her*). Maybe I'd better listen to them.

LILLY. Oh, never with your husband, of course.

LAURA. Thanks.

LILLY. Even before he met you, Bill never gave me a second glance. He was all the time organizing teams, planning Mountain Club outings.

LAURA. Bill's good at that sort of thing; he likes it.

LILLY. And you? (LAURA *looks up at* LILLY *and smiles.*) Not a very co-operative witness, are you? I know, mind my own business. But watch out he doesn't drag his usual quota of boys to the lodge in Maine this summer.

LAURA. I've got my own plans for him. (*She picks up some vacation folders.*)

LILLY. Oh really? What?

LAURA. "Come to Canada" . . . I want to get him off on a trip alone.

LILLY. I don't blame you.

LAURA (*reflecting*). Of course I'd really like to go back to Italy. We had a good time there last summer. It was wonderful then. You should have seen Bill.

LILLY. Look, honey, you married Bill last year on his sabbatical leave, and abroad to boot. Teachers on sabbatical leave abroad are like men in uniform during the war. They never look so good again.

LAURA. Bill looks all right to me.

LILLY. Did Bill ever tell you about the party we gave him before his sabbatical?

LAURA. Yes. I have a souvenir from it. (*She is wearing a rather large Woolworth's diamond ring on a gold chain around her neck . . . She now pulls it out from her sweater.*)

LILLY. I never thought he'd use that Five-and-Dime engagement ring we gave him that night. Even though we gave him an awful ribbing, we all expected him to come back a bachelor.

LAURA. You make it sound as though you kidded him into marrying.

LILLY. Oh, no, honey, it wasn't that.

LAURA (*with meaning*). No, it wasn't. (LAURA *laughs at* LILLY.)

LILLY. Well, I've got to go. You know, Bill could have married any number of the right kind of girls around here. But I knew it would take more than the right kind of girl to get Bill to marry. It would take something special. And you're something special.

LAURA. How should I take that?

LILLY. As a compliment. Thanks for the drink. Don't tell Harry I had one when you see him at dinner.

LAURA. We won't be over to the hall. I've laid in a sort of feast for tonight.

LILLY. Celebrating something?

LAURA. No, just an impulse.

LILLY. Well, don't tell Harry anyway.

LAURA. You'd better stop talking the way you've been talking, or I won't have to tell him.

LILLY. Now, look, honey, don't you start going puritan on me. You're the only one in this school I can shoot my mouth off to, so don't change, baby. Don't change.

LAURA. I won't.

LILLY. Some day I'm going to wheedle out of you all the juicy stories you must have from when you were in the theater.

LAURA. Lilly, you would make the most hardened chorus girl blush.

LILLY (*pleased*). Really?

LAURA. Really.

LILLY. That's the sweetest thing you've said to me in days. Good-by. (*She goes out the door, and a moment later we hear the outside door close.*)

LAURA (*sits for a moment, listening to* TOM's *rather plaintive whistling. She rises and looks at the Canada vacation literature on the desk, and then, looking at her watch, goes to the door, opens it, and calls up the stairway*). Tom . . . Oh, Tom.

(*The moment* TOM *hears his name, he jumps from the bed, and goes through the sitting room, and appears on the stairs.*)

TOM. Yes?

LAURA (*she is very friendly with him, comradely*). If it won't spoil your supper, come on down for a cup of tea.

(TOM *goes back into his room and brushes his hair, then he comes on down the stairs, and enters the study. He enters this room as though it were something rare and special. This is where* LAURA *lives.*)

LAURA (*has gone out to the other part of the house. Comes to doorway for a moment pouring cream from bottle to pitcher*). I've just about finished your costume for the play, and we can have a fitting.

TOM. Sure. That'd be great. Do you want the door open or shut?

LAURA (*goes off again*). It doesn't make any difference. (TOM *shuts the door. He is deeply in love with this woman, though he knows nothing can come of it. It is a sort of delayed puppy love. It is very touching and very intense. They are easy with each other, casual, though he is always trying in thinly veiled ways to tell her he loves her.* LAURA *enters with tea tray and sees him closing the door. She puts tray on table.*) Perhaps you'd better leave it ajar, so that if some of the other boys get out of class early, they can come in too.

TOM (*is disappointed*). Oh, sure.

LAURA (*goes off for the plate of cookies, but pauses long enough to watch* TOM *open the door the merest crack. She is amused. In a moment, she re-enters with a plate of cookies.*) Help yourself.

TOM. Thanks. (*He takes a cookie, and then sits on the floor, near her chair.*)

LAURA. Are the boys warm enough in the rooms? They shut down the heat so early this spring, I guess they didn't expect this little chill.

TOM. We're fine. But this is nice. (*He indicates low fire in fireplace.*)

LAURA (*goes back to her sewing*). I heard you singing.

TOM. I'm sorry if it bothered you.

LAURA. It was very nice.

TOM. If it ever bothers you, just bang on the radiator.

LAURA. What was the name of the song? It's lovely.

TOM. It's an old French song . . . "The Joys of Love" . . . (*He speaks the lyric.*)

> The joys of love
> Are but a moment long,
> The pain of love
> Endures forever.

LAURA. And is that true? (TOM *shrugs his shoulders.*) You sang as though you knew all about the pains of love.

TOM. And you don't think I do?

LAURA. Well . . .

TOM. You're right.

LAURA. Only the joys.

TOM. Neither, really.

(*Teapot whistles off stage.*)

LAURA. Then you're a fake. Listening to you, one would think you knew everything there was to know. (*Rises and goes to next room for tea.*) Anyway, I don't believe it. A boy like you.

TOM. It's true.

LAURA (*off stage*). Aren't you bringing someone to the dance after the play Saturday?

TOM. Yes.

LAURA. Well, there.

TOM. You.

LAURA (*reappears in doorway with teapot*). Me?

TOM. Yes, you're going to be a hostess, aren't you?

LAURA. Yes, of course, but . . .

TOM. As a member of the committee, I'm taking you. All the committee drew lots . . .

LAURA. And you lost.

TOM. I won.

LAURA (*a little embarrassed by this*). Oh. My husband could have taken me. (*She sits down again in her chair.*)

TOM. He's not going to be in town. Don't you remember, Mountain Climbing Club has its final outing this week end.

LAURA. Oh, yes, of course. I'd forgotten.

TOM. He's out a lot on that kind of thing, isn't he? (LAURA *ignores his probing.*) I hope you're not sorry that I'm to be your escort.

LAURA. Why, I'll be honored.

TOM. I'm supposed to find out tactfully and without your knowing it what color dress you'll be wearing.

LAURA. Why?

TOM. The committee will send you a corsage.

LAURA. Oh, how nice. Well, I don't have much to choose from, I guess my yellow.

TOM. The boy who's in charge of getting the flowers thinks a corsage should be something like a funeral decoration. So I'm taking personal charge of getting yours.

LAURA. Thank you.

TOM. You must have gotten lots of flowers when you were acting in the theater.

LAURA. Oh, now and then. Nothing spectacular.

TOM. I can't understand how a person would give up the theater to come and live in a school . . . I'm sorry. I mean, I'm glad you did, but, well . . .

LAURA. If you knew the statistics on unemployed actors, you might understand. Anyway, I was never any great shakes at it.

TOM. I can't believe that.

LAURA. Then take my word for it.

TOM (*after a moment, looking into the fire, pretending to be casual, but actually touching on his love for* LAURA). Did you ever do any of Shaw's plays?

LAURA. Yes.

TOM. We got an assignment to read any Shaw play we wanted. I picked *Candida*.

LAURA. Because it was the shortest?

TOM (*laughs*). No . . . because it sounded like the one I'd like the best, one I could understand. Did you ever play Candida?

LAURA. In stock—a very small stock company, way up in Northern Vermont.

TOM. Do you think she did right to send Marchbanks away?

LAURA. Well, Shaw made it seem right. Don't you think?

TOM (*really talking about himself*). That Marchbanks sure sounded off a lot. I could never sound off like that, even if I loved a woman the way he did. She could have made him seem awfully small if she'd wanted to.

LAURA. Well, I guess she wasn't that kind of woman. Now stand up. Let's see if this fits. (*She rises with dress in her hand.*)

TOM (*gets up*). My Dad's going to hit the roof when he hears I'm playing another girl.

LAURA. I think you're a good sport not

to mind. Besides, it's a good part. Lady Teazle in *The School For Scandal.*

TOM (*puts on top of dress*). It all started when I did Lady Macbeth last year. You weren't here yet for that. Lucky you.

LAURA. I hear it was very good.

TOM. You should have read a letter I got from my father. They printed a picture of me in the *Alumni Bulletin,* in costume. He was plenty peeved about it.

LAURA. He shouldn't have been.

TOM. He wrote me saying he might be up here today on Alumni Fund business. If he comes over here, and you see him, don't tell him about this.

LAURA. I won't . . . What about your mother? Did she come up for the play? (*She helps him button the dress.*)

TOM. I don't see my mother. Didn't you know? (*He starts to roll up pants legs.*)

LAURA. Why no. I didn't.

TOM. She and my father are divorced.

LAURA. I'm sorry.

TOM. You need'nt be. They aren't. I was supposed to hold them together. That was how I happened to come into the world. I didn't work. That's a terrible thing, you know, to make a flop of the first job you've got in life.

LAURA. Don't you ever see her?

TOM. Not since I was five. I was with her till five, and then my father took me away. All I remember about my mother is that she was always telling me to go outside and bounce a ball.

LAURA (*handing him skirt of the dress*). You must have done something before Lady Macbeth. When did you play that character named Grace?

TOM (*stiffens*). I never played anyone called Grace.

LAURA. But I hear the boys sometimes calling you Grace. I thought . . . (*She notices that he's uncomfortable.*) I'm sorry. Have I said something terrible?

TOM. No.

LAURA. But I have. I'm sorry.

TOM. It's all right. But it's a long story. Last year over at the movies, they did a revival of Grace Moore in *One Night of Love.* I'd seen the revival before the picture came. And I guess I oversold it, or something. But she was wonderful! . . . Anyway, some of the guys started calling me Grace. It was my own fault, I guess.

LAURA. Nicknames can be terrible. I remember at one time I was called "Beany."

I can't remember why, now, but I remember it made me mad. (*She adjusts the dress a little.*) Hold still a moment. We'll have to let this out around here. (*She indicates the bosom.*) What size do you want to be?

TOM (*he is embarrassed, but rather nicely, not obviously and farcically. In his embarrassment he looks at* LAURA's *bosom, then quickly away.*) I don't know. Whatever you think.

LAURA (*she indicates he is to stand on a small wooden footstool*). I should think you would have invited some girl up to see you act, and then take her to the dance.

TOM (*gets on stool*). There's nobody I could ask.

LAURA (*working on hem of dress*). What do you mean?

TOM. I don't know any girls, really.

LAURA. Oh, certainly back home . . .

TOM. Last ten years I haven't been home, I mean really home. Summers my father packs me off to camps, and the rest of the time I've been at boarding schools.

LAURA. What about Christmas vacation, and Easter?

TOM. My father gets a raft of tickets to plays and concerts, and sends me and my aunt.

LAURA. I see.

TOM. So I mean it when I say I don't know any girls.

LAURA. Your roommate, Al, knows a lot of girls. Why not ask him to fix you up with a blind date?

TOM. I don't know . . . I can't even dance. I'm telling you this so you won't expect anything of me Saturday night.

LAURA. We'll sit out and talk.

TOM. Okay.

LAURA. Or I could teach you how to dance. It's quite simple.

TOM (*flustered*). You?

LAURA. Why not?

TOM. I mean, isn't a person supposed to go to some sort of dancing class or something? (*He gets down from footstool.*)

LAURA. Not necessarily. Look, I'll show you how simple it is. (*She assumes the dancing position.*) Hold your left hand out this way, and put your right hand around my—(*She stops, as she sees him looking at her.*) Oh, now you're kidding me. A boy your age and you don't know how to dance.

TOM. I'm not kidding you.

LAURA. Well, then, come on. I had to teach my husband. Put your arm around me. (*She raises her arms.*)

TOM (*looks at her a moment, afraid to touch this woman he loves. Then to pass it off*). We better put it off. We'd look kind of silly, both of us in skirts.

LAURA. All right. Take it off, then. No, wait a minute. Just let me stand off and take a look . . . (*She walks around him.*) You're going to make a very lovely girl.

TOM. Thank you, ma'am . . .

(*He kids a curtsy, like a girl, and starts out of his costume.* MR. HARRIS, *a good-looking young master, comes in the hallway and starts up to Tom's room. On the landing, he knocks on Tom's door.*)

LAURA. I wonder who that is?

TOM. All the other fellows have late afternoon classes.

LAURA (*opens the door wider, and looks up the stairs*). Yes? Oh, David.

HARRIS (*turns and looks down the stairs*). Oh, hello, Laura.

LAURA. I just was wondering who was coming in.

(TOM *proceeds to get out of the costume.*)

HARRIS. I want to see Tom Lee.

LAURA. He's down here. I'm making his costume for the play.

HARRIS. I wonder if I could see him for a moment?

LAURA. Why yes, of course. Tom, Mr. Harris would like to see you. Do you want to use our study, David? I can go into the living room.

HARRIS. No, thanks. I'll wait for him in his room. Will you ask him to come up? (*He opens the door and goes in.*)

LAURA (*is puzzled at his intensity, the urgency in his voice. Comes back in the study*). Tom, Mr. Harris would like to see you in your room. He's gone along.

TOM. That's funny.

LAURA. Wait a minute . . . take this up with you, try it on in front of your mirror . . . see if you can move in it . . . (*She hands him skirt of costume.*) When Mr. Harris is through, bring the costume back.

TOM (*anxious over what* HARRIS *wants to see him about*). Yeah, sure. (*He starts out, then stops and picks up a cookie. He looks at her lovingly.*) Thanks for tea.

LAURA. You're welcome.

(TOM *goes to the door as* LAURA *turns to the desk. He stands in the door a moment and looks at her back, then he turns and shuts the door and heads upstairs.* HARRIS *has come into TOM's bedroom, and is standing there nervously clenching and unclenching his hands.*)

TOM (*off stage, presumably in the study he shares with his roommate*). Mr. Harris?

(LAURA *wanders off into the other part of the house after looking for a moment at the Canada vacation material on the desk.*)

HARRIS. I'm in here.

TOM (*comes in a little hesitantly*). Oh. Hello, sir.

(HARRIS *closes the door to the bedroom.* TOM *regards this action with some nervousness.*)

HARRIS. Well?

TOM (*has dumped some clothes from a chair to his bed. Offers chair to* HARRIS). Sir?

HARRIS. What did you tell the Dean?

TOM. What do you mean, Mr. Harris?

HARRIS. What did you tell the Dean?

TOM. When? What are you talking about, sir?

HARRIS. Didn't the Dean call you in?

TOM. No. Why should he?

HARRIS. He didn't call you in and ask you about last Saturday afternoon?

TOM. Why should he? I didn't do anything wrong.

HARRIS. About being with me?

TOM. I'm allowed to leave town for the day in the company of a master.

HARRIS. I don't believe you. You must have said something.

TOM. About what?

HARRIS. About you and me going down to the dunes and swimming.

TOM. Why should I tell him about that?

HARRIS (*threatening*). Why didn't you keep your mouth shut?

TOM. About what? What, for God's sake?

HARRIS. I never touched you, did I?

TOM. What do you mean, touch me?

HARRIS. Did you say to the Dean I touched you?

TOM (*turning away from* HARRIS). I don't know what you're talking about.

HARRIS. Here's what I'm talking about. The Dean's had me on the carpet all afternoon. I probably won't be reappointed next year . . . and all because I took you swimming down off the dunes on Saturday.

TOM. Why should he have you on the carpet for that?

HARRIS. You can't imagine, I suppose.

TOM. What did you do wrong?

HARRIS. Nothing! Nothing, unless you made it seem like something, wrong, did you?

TOM. I told you I didn't see the Dean.

HARRIS. You will. He'll call for you. Bunch of gossiping old busy-bodies! Well . . . (*He starts for the door, stops, turns around and softens. He comes back to the puzzled* TOM.) I'm sorry . . . It probably wasn't your fault. It was my fault. I should have been more . . . discreet . . . Goodby. Good luck with your music.

(TOM *hasn't understood. He doesn't know what to say. He makes a helpless gesture with his hands.* HARRIS *goes into the other room on his way out. Three boys, about seventeen, come in from the downstairs hall door and start up the stairs. They're carrying books. All are wearing sport jackets, khaki or flannel trousers, white or saddle rubber-soled shoes.*)

AL. I don't believe a word of it.

RALPH (*he is large and a loud-mouthed bully*). I'm telling you the guys saw them down at the dunes.

AL (*he is TOM's roommate, an athlete*). So what?

RALPH. They were bare-assed.

AL. Shut up, will you? You want Mrs. Reynolds to hear you?

RALPH. Okay. You watch and see. Harris'll get bounced, and I'm gonna lock my room at night as long as Tom is living in this house.

AL. Oh, dry up!

RALPH. Jeeze, you're his roommate and you're not worried.

HARRIS (*comes out the door and starts down the stairs*). Hello. (*He goes down stairs and out.*)

AL. Sir.

RALPH. Do you believe me now? You aren't safe. Believe me.

STEVE (*he is small,* RALPH's *appreciative audience. He comes in the front door*). Hey, Al, can I come and watch Mrs. Morrison nurse her kid?

RALPH. You're the loudest-mouthed bastard I ever heard. You want to give it away.

STEVE. It's time. How about it, Al?

AL (*grudgingly*). Come on.

(TOM *hears them coming, and moves to*

bolt his door, but STEVE *and* RALPH *break in before he gets to the door. He watches them from the doorway.* STEVE *rushes to bed and throws himself across it, looking out window next to bed.* RALPH *settles down next to him.*)

AL (*to* TOM *as he comes in*). Hi. These horny bastards.

STEVE. Al, bring the glasses.

(AL *goes into sitting room.*)

RALPH. Some day she's going to wean that little bastard and spoil all our fun.

STEVE. Imagine sitting in a window . . .

TOM (*has been watching this with growing annoyance*). Will you guys get out of here?

RALPH (*notices* TOM *for the first time*). What's the matter with you, Grace?

TOM. This is my damned room.

RALPH. Gracie's getting private all of a sudden.

TOM. I don't want a lot of Peeping Toms lying on my bed watching a . . . a . . .

STEVE. You want it all for yourself, don't you?

RALPH. Or aren't you interested in women?

AL (*comes back in with field glasses*). Shut up! (*Looks out window, then realizes* TOM *is watching him. Embarrassed.*) These horny bastards.

STEVE (*looking*). Jeeze!

RALPH (*a bully, riding down on* TOM). I thought you were going to play ball with us Saturday.

TOM. I didn't feel like it.

RALPH. What *did* you feel like doing, huh?

AL. Will you shut up?

STEVE. Hey, lookit. (*Grabs glasses from* AL. AL *leaves room.*)

TOM (*climbing over* STEVE *and* RALPH *and trying to pull the shade*). I told you to get out. I told you last time . . .

RALPH (*grabbing hold of* TOM, *and holding him down*). Be still, boy, or she'll see, and you'll spoil everything.

TOM. Horny bastard. Get out of here.

RALPH. Who are you calling a horny bastard? (*He grabs hold of* TOM *more forcefully, and slaps him a couple of times across the face, not trying to hurt him, but just to humiliate him.* STEVE *gets in a few pokes and in a moment, it's not in fun, but verging on the serious.*) You don't mean that now, boy, do you . . . Do you, Grace! (*He slaps him again.*)

AL (*hearing the scuffle, comes in and hauls* RALPH *and* STEVE *off* TOM). Come on, come on, break it up. Clear out. (*He has them both standing up now,* TOM *still on the bed.*)

RALPH. I just don't like that son of a bitch calling me a horny bastard. Maybe if it was Dr. Morrison instead of Mrs. Morrison, he'd be more interested. Hey, wouldn't you, Grace? (*He tries to stick his face in front of* TOM, *but* AL *holds him back.*)

AL. Come on, lay off the guy, will you? Go on. Get ready for supper.

(*He herds them out during this. When they have left the room,* TOM *gets up and goes to bureau and gets a handkerchief. He has a bloody nose. He lies down on the bed, his head tilted back to stop the blood.*)

AL (*in doorway*). You all right?

TOM. Yeah.

(RALPH *and* STEVE *go up the stairway singing in raucous voices, "One Night of Love." The downstairs outside door opens, and* BILL REYNOLDS *enters the hall with a student,* PHIL. BILL *is* LAURA'S *husband. He is large and strong with a tendency to be gruff. He's wearing gray flannel trousers, a tweed jacket, a blue button-down shirt. He is around forty.*)

BILL. Okay, boy, we'll look forward to— (*He notices* RALPH *still singing. He goes to bend in the stairs and calls.*) Hey, Ralph . . . Ralph!

RALPH (*stops singing up out of sight*). You calling me, Mr. Reynolds, sir?

BILL. Yeah. Keep it down to a shout, will you?

RALPH. Oh, *yes, sir.* Sorry, I didn't know I was disturbing you, Mr. Reynolds.

BILL (*comes back and talks with* PHIL *at the bend in the stairway*). Phil, you come on up to the lodge around . . . Let's see . . . We'll open the lodge around July first, so plan to come up say, July third, and stay for two weeks. Okay?

PHIL. That'll be swell, sir.

BILL. Frank Hoctor's coming then. You get along with Frank, don't you? He's a regular guy.

PHIL. Oh, sure.

BILL. The float's all gone to pieces. We can make that your project to fix it up. Okay?

PHIL. Thanks a lot, Mr. Reynolds. (*He goes on up the stairs.*)

BILL. See you. (*He comes in and crosses to phone and starts to call.*)

LAURA (*off stage*). Tom?

(BILL *looks around in the direction of the voice, but says nothing.*)

LAURA (*comes on*). Oh, Bill. Tom·was down trying on his costume. I thought . . . You're early.

BILL. Yes. I want to catch the Dean be-before he leaves his office. (LAURA *goes up to him to be kissed, but he's too intent on the phone, and she compromises by kissing his cheek.*) Hello, this is Mr. Reynolds. Is the Dean still in his office?

LAURA. What's the matter, Bill?

BILL. Nothing very pretty. Oh? How long ago? All right. Thanks. I'll give him a couple of minutes, then I'll call his home. (*Hangs up.*) Well, they finally caught up with Harris. (*He goes into the next room to take off his jacket.*)

LAURA. What do you mean, "caught up" with him?

BILL (*off stage*). You're going to hear it anyhow . . . so . . . last Saturday they caught him down in the dunes, naked.

LAURA (*crosses to close door to hall*). What's wrong with that?

BILL (*enters and crosses to fireplace and starts to go through letters propped there. He has taken off his jacket*). He wasn't alone.

LAURA. Oh.

BILL. He was lying there naked in the dunes, and one of the students was lying there naked too. Just to talk about it is disgusting.

LAURA. I see.

BILL. I guess you'll admit that's something.

LAURA. I can't see that it's necessarily conclusive.

BILL. With a man like Harris, it's conclusive enough. (*Then casually*) The student with him was—

LAURA (*interrupting*). I'm not sure I care to know.

BILL. I'm afraid you're going to have to know sooner or later, Laura. It was Tom Lee.

(TOM *rises from bed, grabs a towel and goes out up the stairs.* LAURA *just looks at* BILL *and frowns.*)

BILL. Some of the boys down on the Varsity Club outing came on them . . . or at least saw them . . . And Fin Hadley saw them too, and he apparently used his

brains for once and spoke to the Dean.

LAURA. And?

BILL. He's had Harris on the ·carpet this afternoon. I guess he'll be fired. I certainly hope so. Maybe Tom too, I don't know.

LAURA. They put two and two together?

BILL. Yes, Laura.

LAURA. I suppose this is all over school by now.

BILL. I'm afraid so.

LAURA. And most of the boys know.

BILL. Yes.

LAURA. So what's going to happen to Tom?

BILL (*takes pipe from mantel piece and cleans it*). I know you won't like this, Laura, but I think he should be kicked out. I think you've got to let people know the school doesn't stand for even a hint of this sort of thing. He should be booted.

LAURA. For what?

BILL. Look, a boy's caught coming out of Ellie Martin's rooms across the river. That's enough evidence. Nobody asks particulars. They don't go to Ellie's room to play Canasta. It's the same here.

LAURA (*hardly daring to suggest it*). But, Bill . . . you don't think . . . I mean, you don't think Tom is . . . (*She stops.* BILL *looks at her a moment, his answer is in his silence.*) Oh, Bill!

BILL. And I'm ashamed and sorry as hell for his father. Herb Lee was always damned good to me . . . came down from college when I was playing football here . . . helped me get into college . . . looked after me when I was in college and he was in law school . . . And I know he put the boy in my house hoping I could do something with him. (*He dials number.*)

LAURA. And you feel you've failed.

BILL. Yes. (*He pauses.*) With your help, I might say. (*Busy signal. He hangs up.*)

LAURA. How?

BILL. Because, Laura, the boy would rather sit around here and talk with you and listen to music and strum his guitar.

LAURA. Bill, I'm not to blame for everything. Everything's not my fault.

BILL (*disregarding this*). What a lousy thing for Herb. (*He looks at a small picture of a team on his desk.*) That's Herb. He was Graduate Manager of the team when I was a sophomore in college. He was always the manager of the teams, and he really wanted his son to be there in the center of the picture.

LAURA. Why are you calling the Dean?

BILL. I'm going to find out what's being done.

LAURA. I've never seen you like this before.

BILL. This is something that touches me very closely. The name of the school, it's reputation, the reputation of all of us here. I went here and my father before me, and one day I hope our children will come here, when we have them. And, of course, one day I hope to be headmaster.

LAURA. Let's assume that you're right about Harris. It's a terrible thing to say on the evidence you've got, but let's assume you're right. Does it necessarily follow that Tom—

BILL. Tom was his friend. Everyone knew that.

LAURA. Harris encouraged him in his music.

BILL. Come on, Laura.

LAURA. What if Tom's roommate, Al, or some other great big athlete had been out with Harris?

BILL. He wouldn't have been.

LAURA. I'm saying what if he had been? Would you have jumped to the same conclusion?

BILL. It would have been different. Tom's always been an off-horse. And now it's quite obvious why. If he's kicked out, maybe it'll bring him to his senses. But he won't change if nothing's done about it. (LAURA *turns away.* BILL *starts to look over his mail again.*) Anyway, why are you so concerned over what happens to Tom Lee?

LAURA. I've come to know him. You even imply that I am somewhat responsible for his present reputation.

BILL. All right. I shouldn't have said that. But you watch, now that it's out in the open. Look at the way he walks, the way he sometimes stands.

LAURA. Oh, Bill!

BILL. All right, so a woman doesn't notice these things. But a man knows a queer when he sees one. (*He has opened a letter. Reads.*) The bookstore now has the book you wanted . . . *The Rose and The Thorn.* What's that?

LAURA. A book of poems. Do you know, Bill, I'll bet he doesn't even know the meaning of the word . . . queer.

BILL. What do you think he is?

LAURA. I think he's a nice sensitive kid who doesn't know the meaning of the word.

BILL. He's eighteen, or almost. I don't know.

LAURA. How much did you know at eighteen?

BILL. A lot. (*At the desk he now notices the Canada literature.*) What are these?

LAURA. What?

BILL. These.

LAURA. Oh, nothing.

BILL (*he throws them in wastebasket, then notices her look*). Well, they're obviously something. (*He takes them out of wastebasket.*)

LAURA (*the joy of it gone for her*). I was thinking we might take a motor trip up there this summer.

BILL (*dialing phone again*). I wish you'd said something about it earlier. I've already invited some of the scholarship boys up to the lodge. I can't disappoint them.

LAURA. Of course not.

BILL. If you'd said something earlier.

LAURA. It's my fault.

BILL. It's nobody's fault, it's just—Hello, Fitz, Bill Reynolds—I was wondering if you're going to be in tonight after supper . . . Oh . . . oh, I see . . . Supper? Well, sure I could talk about it at supper. . . . Well, no, I think I'd better drop over alone. . . . All right. I'll see you at the house then . . . Good-by.

(LAURA *looks at him, trying to understand him.* BILL *comes to her to speak softly to her. Seeing him come, she holds out her arms to be embraced, but he just takes her chin in his hand.*)

BILL. Look, Laura, when I brought you here a year ago, I told you it was a tough place for a woman with a heart like yours. I told you you'd run across boys, big and little boys, full of problems, problems which for the moment seem gigantic and heartbreaking. And you promised me then you wouldn't get all taken up with them. Remember?

LAURA. Yes.

BILL. When I was a kid in school here, I had my problems too. There's a place up by the golf course where I used to go off alone Sunday afternoons and cry my eyes out. I used to lie on my bed just the way Tom does, listening to phonograph records hour after hour. (LAURA, *touched by this, kneels at his side.*) But I got over it, Laura. I learned how to take it. (LAURA *looks at him. This touches her.*) When the headmaster's wife gave you this teapot, she told you what she tells all new masters' wives. You have to be an interested bystander.

LAURA. I know.

BILL. Just as she said, all you're supposed to do is every once in a while give the boys a little tea and sympathy. Do you remember?

LAURA. Yes, I remember. It's just that . . .

BILL. What?

LAURA. This age—seventeen, eighteen—it's so . . .

BILL. I know.

LAURA. John was this age when I married him.

BILL. Look, Laura . . .

LAURA. I know. You don't like me to talk about John, but . . .

BILL. It's not that. It's . . .

LAURA. He was just this age, eighteen or so, when I married him. We both were. And I know now how this age can suffer. It's a heartbreaking time . . . no longer a boy . . . not yet a man . . . Bill? Bill?

BILL (*looks at her awkwardly a moment, then starts to move off*). I'd better clean up if I'm going to get to the Dean's for supper. You don't mind, do you?

LAURA (*very quietly*). I got things in for dinner here. But they'll keep.

BILL (*awkwardly*). I'm sorry, Laura. But you understand, don't you? About this business? (LAURA *shakes her head, "No."* BILL *stands over her, a little put out that she has not understood his reasoning. He starts to say something several times, then stops. Finally he notices the Five-and-Dime engagement ring around her neck. He touches it.*) You're not going to wear this thing to the dining hall, are you?

LAURA. Why not?

BILL. It was just a gag. It means something to you, but to them . . .

LAURA (*bearing in, but gently*). Does it mean anything to you, Bill?

BILL. Well, it did, but . . . (*He stops with a gesture, unwilling to go into it all.*)

LAURA. I think you're ashamed of the night you gave it to me. That you ever let me see you needed help. That night in Italy, in some vague way you cried out . . .

BILL. What is the matter with you today? *Me* crying out for help. (*He heads for the other room. A knock on the study door is heard.*)

BILL. It's probably Tom.

(LAURA *goes to door.*)

HERB (*This is* HERBERT LEE, TOM's *father. He is a middle-sized man, fancying himself a man of the world and an extrovert. He is dressed as a conservative Boston businessman, but with still a touch of the collegiate in his attire—button-down shirt, etc.*). Mrs. Reynolds?

LAURA. Yes?

BILL (*stopped by the voice, turns*). Herb! Come in.

HERB (*coming in*). Hiya, Bill. How are you, fella?

BILL (*taking his hand*). I'm fine, Herb.

HERB (*poking his finger into* BILL's *chest*). Great to see you. (*Looks around to* LAURA.) Oh, uh . . .

BILL. I don't think you've met Laura, Herb. This is Laura. Laura this is Herb Lee, Tom's father.

HERB (*hearty and friendly, meant to put people at their ease*). Hello, Laura.

LAURA. I've heard so much about you.

HERB (*after looking at her for a moment*). I like her, Bill. I like her very much. (LAURA *blushes and is a little taken aback by this. To* LAURA) What I'd like to know is how did you manage to do it? (*Cuffing* BILL) I'll bet you make her life miserable . . . You look good, Bill.

BILL. You don't look so bad yourself. (*He takes in a notch in his belt.*)

HERB. No, *you're* in shape. I never had anything to keep in shape, but you . . . You should have seen this boy, Laura.

LAURA. I've seen pictures.

HERB. Only exercise I get these days is bending the elbow.

LAURA. May I get you something? A drink?

HERB. No, thanks. I haven't got much time.

BILL. You drive out from Boston, Herb?

HERB. No, train. You know, Bill, I think that's the same old train you and I used to ride in when we came here.

BILL. Probably is.

HERB. If I don't catch the six-fifty-four, I'll have to stay all night, and I'd rather not.

BILL. We'd be glad to put you up.

HERB. No. You're putting me up in a couple of weeks at the reunion. That's imposing enough. (*There is an awkward pause. Both men sit down.*) I . . . uh . . . was over at the Dean's this afternoon.

BILL. Oh, he called you?

HERB. Why, no. I was up discussing Alumni Fund matters with him . . . and . . . Do you know about it?

BILL. You mean about Tom?

HERB. Yes. (*Looks at* LAURA.)

BILL. Laura knows too. (*He reaches for her to come to him, and he puts his arm around her waist.*)

HERB. Well, after we discussed the Fund, he told me about that. Thought I ought to hear about it from him. Pretty casual about it, I thought.

BILL. Well, that's Fitz.

HERB. What I want to know is, what was a guy like Harris doing at the school?

BILL. I tried to tell them.

HERB. Was there anyone around like that in our day, Bill?

BILL. No. You're right.

HERB. I tried to find the guy. I wanted to punch his face for him. But he's cleared out. Is Tom around?

LAURA. He's in his room.

HERB. How'd he get mixed up with a guy like that?

BILL. I don't know, Herb . . .

HERB. I know. I shouldn't ask you. I know. Of course I don't believe Tom was really involved with this fellow. If I believed that, I'd . . . well, I don't know what I'd do. You don't believe it, do you, Bill?

BILL. Why . . . (*Looks at* LAURA.)

HERB (*cutting in*). Of course you don't. But what's the matter? What's happened, Bill? Why isn't my boy a regular fellow? He's had every chance to be since he was knee-high to a grasshopper—boys' camps every summer, boarding schools. What do you think, Laura?

LAURA. I'm afraid I'm not the one to ask, Mr. Lee. (*She breaks away from* BILL.)

HERB. He's always been with men and boys. Why doesn't some of it rub off?

LAURA. You see, I feel he's a "regular fellow" . . . whatever that is.

HERB. You do?

LAURA. If it's sports that matter, he's an excellent tennis player.

HERB. But Laura, he doesn't even play tennis like a regular fellow. No hard drives and cannon-ball serves. He's a cut artist. He can put more damn twists on that ball.

LAURA. He wins. He's the school champion. And isn't he the champion of your club back home?

(TOM *comes down the stairs and enters his bedroom with the costume skirt and towel.*)

HERB. I'm glad you mentioned that . . . because that's just what I mean. Do you know, Laura, his winning that championship brought me one of my greatest humiliations? I hadn't been able to watch the match. I was supposed to be in from a round of golf in time, but we got held up on every hole . . . And when I got back to the locker room, I heard a couple of men talking about Tom's match in the next locker section. And what they said, cut me to the quick, Laura. One of them said, "It's a damn shame Tom Lee won the match. He's a good player, all right, but John Batty is such a regular guy." John Batty was his opponent. Now what pleasure was there for me in that?

BILL. I know what you mean.

HERB. I *want* to be proud of him. My God, that's why I had him in the first place. That's why I took him from his mother when we split up, but . . . Look, this is a terrible thing to say, but you know the scholarships the University Club sponsors for needy kids . . .

BILL. Sure.

HERB. Well, I contribute pretty heavily to it, and I happened to latch on to one of the kids we help—an orphan. I sort of talk to him like a father, go up to see him at his school once in a while, and that kid listens to me . . . and you know what, he's shaping up better than my own son.

(*There is an awkward pause. Upstairs* TOM *has put a record on the phonograph. It starts playing now.*)

BILL. You saw the Dean, Herb?

HERB. Yes.

BILL. And?

HERB. He told me the circumstances. Told me he was confident that Tom was innocently involved. He actually apologized for the whole thing. He did say that some of the faculty had suggested —though he didn't go along with this— that Tom would be more comfortable if I took him out of school. But I'm not going to. He's had nothing but comfort all his life, and look what's happened. My associates ask me what he wants to be, and I tell them he hasn't made up his mind. Because I'll be damned if I'll tell them he wants to be a singer of folk songs.

(TOM *lies on the bed listening to the music.*)

BILL. So you're going to leave him in?

HERB. Of course. Let him stick it out. It'll be a good lesson.

LAURA. Mightn't it be more than just a lesson, Mr. Lee?

HERB. Oh, he'll take some kidding. He'll have to work extra hard to prove to them he's . . . well, manly. It may be the thing that brings him to his senses.

LAURA. Mr. Lee, Tom's a very sensitive boy. He's a very lonely boy.

HERB. Why should he be lonely? I've always seen to it that he's been with people . . . at camps, at boarding schools.

BILL. He's certainly an off-horse, Herb.

HERB. That's a good way of putting it, Bill. An off-horse. Well, he's going to have to learn to run with the other horses. Well, I'd better be going up.

LAURA. Mr. Lee, this may sound terribly naïve of me, and perhaps a trifle indelicate, but I don't believe your son knows what this is all about. Why Mr. Harris was fired, why the boys will kid him.

HERB. You mean . . . (*Stops.*)

LAURA. I'm only guessing. But I think when it comes to these boys, we often take too much knowledge for granted. And I think it's going to come as a terrible shock when he finds out what they're talking about. Not just a lesson, a shock.

HERB. I don't believe he's as naïve as all that. I just don't. Well . . . (*He starts for the door.*)

BILL (*takes* HERB's *arm and they go into the hall*). I'm going over to the Dean's for supper, Herb. If you're through with Tom come by here and I'll walk you part way to the station.

HERB. All right. (*Stops on the stairs.*) How do you talk to the boys, Bill?

BILL. I don't know. I just talk to them.

HERB. They're not your sons. I only talked with Tom, I mean, really talked with him, once before. It was after a Sunday dinner and I made up my mind it was time we sat in a room together and talked about important things. He got sick to his stomach. That's a terrible effect to have on your boy . . . Well, I'll drop down. (*He takes a roll of money from his pocket and looks at it, then starts up the stairs.*)

BILL (*coming into his study*). Laura, you shouldn't try to tell him about his own son. After all, if he doesn't know the boy, who does?

LAURA. I'm sorry.

(BILL *exits into the other part of the house, pulling off his tie.* HERB *has gone up the stairs. Knocks on the study door.* LAURA *settles down in her chair and eventually goes on with her sewing.*)

AL (*inside, calls*). Come in.

(HERB *goes in and shuts the door.*)

HERB (*opens* TOM's *bedroom door and sticks his head in*). Hello, there.

TOM (*looks up from the bed, surprised*). Oh . . . Hi . . .

HERB. I got held up at the Dean's.

TOM. Oh. (*He has risen, and attempts to kiss his father on the cheek. But his father holds him off with a firm handshake.*)

HERB. How's everything? You look bushed.

TOM. I'm okay.

HERB (*looking at him closely*). You sure?

TOM. Sure.

HERB (*looking around room*). This room looks smaller than I remember. (*He throws on light switch.*) I used to have the bed over here. Used to rain in some nights. (*Comes across phonograph.*) This the one I gave you for Christmas?

TOM. Yeah. It works fine.

HERB (*turns phonograph off*). You're neater than I was. My vest was always behind the radiator, or somewhere. (*Sees part of dress costume.*) What's this?

TOM (*hesitates for a moment. Then*). A costume Mrs. Reynolds made for me. I'm in the play.

HERB. You didn't write about it.

TOM. I know.

HERB. What are you playing? (*Looks at dress.*)

TOM. You know *The School For Scandal.* I'm playing Lady Teazle.

HERB. Tom, I want to talk to you. Last time we tried to talk, it didn't work out so well.

TOM. What's up?

HERB. Tom, I'd like to be your friend. I guess there's something between fathers and sons that keeps them from being friends, but I'd like to try.

TOM (*embarrassed*). Sure, Dad. (*He sits on the bed.*)

HERB. Now when you came here, I told you to make friends slowly. I told you to make sure they were the right kind of friends. You're known by the company you keep. Remember I said that?

TOM. Yes.

HERB. And I told you if you didn't want to go out for sports like football, hockey . . . that was all right with me. But you'd get in with the right kind of fellow if you managed these teams. They're usually pretty good guys. You remember.

TOM. Yes.

HERB. Didn't you believe me?

TOM. Yes, I believed you.

HERB. Okay, then let's say you believed me, but you decided to go your own way. That's all right too, only you see what it's led to.

TOM. What?

HERB. You made friends with people like this Harris guy who got himself fired.

TOM. Why is he getting fired?

HERB. He's being fired because he was seen in the dunes with you.

TOM. Look, I don't—

HERB. Naked.

TOM. You too?

HERB. So you know what I'm talking about?

TOM. No, I don't.

HERB. You do too know. I heard my sister tell you once. She warned you about a janitor in the building down the street.

TOM (*incredulous*). Mr. Harris . . . ?

HERB. Yes. He's being fired because he's been doing a lot of suspicious things around apparently, and this finished it. All right, I'll say it plain, Tom. He's a fairy. A homosexual.

TOM. Who says so?

HERB. Now, Tom—

TOM. And seeing us on the beach . . .

HERB. Yes.

TOM. And what does that make me?

HERB. Listen, I know you're all right.

TOM. Thanks.

HERB. Now wait a minute.

TOM. Look, we were just swimming.

HERB. All right, all right. So perhaps you didn't know.

TOM. What do you mean perhaps?

HERB. It's the school's fault for having a guy like that around. But it's your fault for being a damned fool in picking your friends.

TOM. So that's what the guys meant.

HERB. You're going to get a ribbing for a while, but you're going to be a man about it and you're going to take it and you're going to come through much more careful how you make your friends.

TOM. He's kicked out because he was seen with me on the beach, and I'm telling you that nothing, absolutely nothing . . . Look, I'm going to the Dean and tell him that Harris did nothing, that—

HERB (*stopping him*). Look, don't be a fool. It's going to be hard enough for you without sticking your neck out, asking for it.

TOM. But, Dad!

HERB. He's not going to be reappointed next year. Nothing you can say is going to change anyone's mind. You got to think about yourself. Now, first of all, get your hair cut. (TOM *looks at father, disgusted.*) Look, this isn't easy for me. Stop thinking about yourself, and give me a break. (TOM *looks up at this appeal.*) I suppose you think it's going to be fun for *me* to have to live this down back home. It'll get around, and it'll affect me, too. So we've got to see this thing through together. You've got to do your part. Get your hair cut. And then . . . No, the first thing I want you to do is call whoever is putting on this play, and tell them you're not playing this lady whatever her name is.

TOM. Why shouldn't I play it? It's the best part in the play, and I was chosen to play it.

HERB. I should think you'd have the sense to see why you shouldn't.

TOM. Wait a minute. You mean . . . do you mean, you think I'm . . . whatever you call it? Do you, Dad?

HERB. I told you "no."

TOM. But the fellows are going to think that I'm . . . and Mrs. Reynolds?

HERB. Yes. You're going to have to fight their thinking it. Yes.

(TOM *sits on the bed, the full realization of it dawning.*)

RALPH (*sticks his head around the stairs from upstairs, and yells*). Hey, Grace, who's taking you to the dance Saturday night? Hey, Grace! (*He disappears again up the stairs.*)

HERB. What's that all about?

TOM. I don't know.

(LAURA, *as the noise comes in, rises and goes to door to stop it, but* AL *comes into the hall and goes upstairs yelling at the boys and* LAURA *goes back to her chair.*)

HERB (*looks at his watch*). Now . . . Do you want me to stay over? If I'm not going to stay over tonight, I've got to catch the six-fifty-four.

TOM. Stay over?

HERB. Yes, I didn't bring a change of clothes along, but if you want me to stay over . . .

TOM. Why should you stay over?

HERB (*stung a little by this*). All right. Now come on down to Bill's room and telephone this drama fellow. So I'll know you're making a start of it. And bring the dress.

TOM. I'll do it tomorrow.

HERB. I'd feel better if you did it to-night. Come on. I'm walking out with Bill. And incidentally, the Dean said if the ribbing goes beyond bounds . . . you know . . . you're to come to him and he'll take some steps. He's not going to do anything now, because these things take care of themselves. They're better ignored . . .

(*They have both started out of the bed-room, but during the above* HERB *goes back for the dress.* TOM *continues out and stands on the stairs looking at the telephone in the hall.*)

HERB (*comes out of the study. Calls back*). See you Al. Take good care of my boy here. (*Starts down stairs. Stops.*) You need any money?

TOM. No.

HERB. I'm lining you up with a counselor's job at camp this year. If this thing doesn't spoil it. (*Stops.*) You sure you've got enough money to come home?

TOM. Yes, sure. Look Dad, let me call about the play from here. (*He takes receiver off hook.*)

HERB. Why not use Bill's phone? He won't mind. Come on. (TOM *reluctantly puts phone back on hook.*) Look, if you've got any problems, talk them over with Bill —Mr. Reynolds. He's an old friend, and I think he'd tell you about what I'd tell you in a spot. (*Goes into master's study.*) Is Bill ready?

LAURA. He'll be right down. How does the costume work?

TOM. I guess it's all right, only . . .

HERB. I'd like Tom to use your phone if he may—to call whoever's putting on the play. He's giving up the part.

LAURA. Giving up the part?

HERB. Yes. I've . . . I want him to. He's doing it for me.

LAURA. Mr. Lee, it was a great honor for him to be chosen to play the part.

HERB. Bill will understand. Bill! (*He thrusts costume into* LAURA's *hand and goes off through alcove.*) Bill, what's the number of the man putting on the play. Tom wants to call him.

(LAURA *looks at* TOM *who keeps his eyes from her. She makes a move towards him, but he takes a step away.*)

BILL (*off stage*). Fred Mayberry . . . Three-two-six . . . You ready, Herb?

HERB (*off stage*). Yes. You don't mind if Tom uses your phone, do you?

BILL. Of course not.

HERB (*comes in*). When do you go on your mountain-climbing week-end, Bill?

BILL (*comes in*). This week-end's the outing.

HERB. Maybe Tom could go with you.

BILL. He's on the dance committee, I think. Of course he's welcome if he wants to. Always has been.

HERB (*holding out phone to* TOM). Tom. (TOM *hesitates to cross to phone. As* LAURA *watches him with concern, he makes a move to escape out the door.*) Three-two-six.

(TOM *slowly and painfully crosses the stage, takes the phone and sits.*)

BILL. Will you walk along with us as far as the dining hall, Laura?

LAURA. I don't think I feel like supper, thanks.

BILL (*looks from her to* TOM). What?

HERB. I've got to get along if I want to catch my train.

(TOM *dials phone.*)

BILL. Laura?

(LAURA *shakes her head, tightlipped.*)

HERB. Well, then, good-by, Laura . . . I still like you.

LAURA. Still going to the Dean's, Bill?

BILL. Yes. I'll be right back after supper. Sure you don't want to walk along with us to the dining hall?

(LAURA *shakes her head.*)

TOM. Busy.

HERB (*pats his son's arm*). Keep trying him. We're in this together. Anything you want? (TOM *shakes his head "no."*) Just remember, anything you want, let me know. (*To* LAURA) See you at reunion time . . . This'll all be blown over by then. (*He goes.*)

BILL. Laura, I wish you'd . . . Laura! (*He is disturbed by her mood. He sees it's hopeless, and goes after* HERB, *leaving door open.*)

TOM (*at phone*). Hello, Mr. Mayberry . . . This is Tom Lee . . . Yes, I know it's time to go to supper, Mr. Mayberry . . . (*Looks around at open door.* LAURA *shuts it.*) but I wanted you to know . . . (*This comes hard.*) I wanted you to know I'm not going to be able to play in the play . . . No . . . I . . . well, I just can't. (*He is about to break. He doesn't trust himself to speak.*)

LAURA (*quickly crosses and takes phone from* TOM). Give it to me. Hello, Fred . . . Laura. Yes, Tom's father, well, he wants Tom—he thinks Tom is tired, needs to concentrate on his final exams. You had someone covering the part, didn't you? . . . Yes, of course it's a terrible disappointment to Tom. I'll see you tomorrow.

(*She hangs up.* TOM *is ashamed and humiliated. Here is the woman he loves, hearing all about him . . . perhaps believing the things . . .* LAURA *stands above him for a moment, looking at the back of his head with pity. Then he rises and starts for the door without looking at her.* RALPH *and* STEVE *come stampeding down the stairway.*)

RALPH (*as he goes*). Okay, you can sit next to him if you want. Not me.

STEVE. Well, if you won't . . . why should I?

RALPH. Two bits nobody will.

(*They slam out the front door.* TOM *has shut the door quickly again when he has heard* RALPH *and* STEVE *start down. Now stands against the door listening.*)

AL (*comes out from his door, pulling on his jacket. Calls*). Tom . . . Tom! (*Getting no answer, he goes down the stairs and out.*)

LAURA. Tom . . .

TOM (*opens the study door*). I'll bet my father thinks I'm . . . (*Stops.*)

LAURA. Now, Tom! I thought I'd call Joan Harrison and ask her to come over for tea tomorrow. I want you to come too. I want you to ask her to go to the dance with you.

TOM (*turns in anguish and looks at her for several moments. Then*). You were to go with me.

LAURA. I know, but . . .

TOM. Do you think so too, like the others? Like my father?

LAURA. Tom!

TOM. Is that why you're shoving me off on Joan?

LAURA (*moving towards him*). Tom, I asked her over so that we could lick this thing.

TOM (*turns on her*). What thing? What thing? (*He looks at her a moment, filled with indignation, then he bolts up the stairs. But on the way up,* PHIL *is coming down.* TOM *feels like a trapped rat. He starts to turn down the stairs again, but he doesn't want to face* LAURA, *as he is about to break. He tries to hide his face and cowers along one side going up.*)

PHIL. What's the matter with you?

(TOM *doesn't answer. Goes on up and into the study door.* PHIL *shrugs his shoulders and goes on down the stairs and out.* TOM *comes into his own bedroom and shuts the door and leans against the door- jamb.* LAURA *goes to the partly opened door. Her impulse is to go up to* TOM *to comfort him, but she checks herself, and turns in the doorway and closes the door, then walks back to her chair and sits down and reaches out and touches the teapot, as though she were half-unconsciously rub- bing out a spot. She is puzzled and wor- ried. Upstairs we hear the first few sobs from* TOM *as the lights dim out, and*

THE CURTAIN FALLS

ACT TWO

SCENE ONE

The scene is the same.
The time is two days later.
As the curtain rises, AL *is standing at the public telephone fastened to the wall on the first landing. He seems to be doing more listening than talking.*

AL. Yeah . . . (*He patiently waits through a long tirade.*) Yeah, Dad. I know, Dad . . . No, I haven't done anything about it, yet . . . Yes, Mr. Hudson says he has a room in his house for me next year . . . But I haven't done anything about it here yet . . . Yeah, okay, Dad . . . I know what you mean . . . (*Gets angry.*) I swear to God I don't . . . I lived with him a year, and I don't . . . All right, okay, Dad . . . No, don't *you* call. I'll do it. Right now. (*He hangs up. He stands and puts his hands in his pocket and tries to think this out. It's something he doesn't like.*)

RALPH (*comes in the house door and starts up the steps*). Hey, Al?

AL. Yeah?

RALPH. The guys over at the Beta house want to know has it happened yet?

AL. Has what happened?

RALPH. Has Tom made a pass at you yet?

AL (*reaches out to swat* RALPH). For crying out loud!

RALPH. Okay, okay! You can borrow my chastity belt if you need it.

AL. That's not funny.

RALPH (*shifting his meaning to hurt* AL). No, I know it's not. The guys on the ball team don't think it's funny at all.

AL. What do you mean?

RALPH. The guy they're supposed to elect captain rooming with a queer.

AL (*looks at him for a moment, then rejects the idea*). Aw . . . knock it off, huh!

RALPH. So you don't believe me . . . Wait and see. (*Putting on a dirty grin.*) Anyway, my mother said I should save myself for the girl I marry. Hell, how would you like to have to tell your wife, "Honey, I've been saving myself for you, except for one night when a guy—" (AL *roughs* RALPH *up with no intention of hurting him.*) Okay, okay. So you don't want to be captain of the baseball team. So who the hell cares. I don't, I'm sure.

AL. Look. Why don't you mind your own business?

RALPH. What the hell fun would there be in that?

AL. Ralph, Tom's a nice kid.

RALPH. Yeah. That's why all the guys leave the shower room at the gym when he walks in.

AL. When?

RALPH. Yesterday . . . Today. You didn't hear about it?

AL. No. What are they trying to do?

RALPH. Hell, they don't want some queer looking at them and—

AL. Oh, can it! Go on up and bury your horny nose in your *Art Models* magazine.

RALPH. At least I'm normal. I like to look at pictures of naked girls, not men, the way Tom does.

AL. Jeeze, I'm gonna push your face in in a—

RALPH. Didn't you notice all those strong man poses he's got in his bottom drawer?

AL. Yes, I've noticed them. His old man wants him to be a muscle man, and he wrote away for this course in muscle building, and they send those pictures. Any objections?

RALPH. Go on, stick up for him. Stick your neck out. You'll get it chopped off with a baseball bat, you crazy bastard. (*Exits upstairs.* AL *looks at the phone, then up the way* RALPH *went. He is upset. He throws himself into a few push-ups, using the bannisters. Then still not happy with what he's doing, he walks down the stairs and knocks on the study door.*)

LAURA (*comes from inside the house and opens the door*). Oh, hello, Al.

AL. Is Mr. Reynolds in?

LAURA. Why, no, he isn't. Can I do something?

AL. I guess I better drop down when he's in.

LAURA. All right. I don't really expect him home till after supper tonight.

AL (*thinks for a moment*). Well . . . well, you might tell him just so he'll know and can make other plans . . . I won't be rooming in this house next year. This is the last day for changing, and I want him to know that.

LAURA (*moves into the room to get a cigarette*). I see. Well, I know he'll be sorry to hear that, Al.

AL. I'm going across the street to Harmon House.

LAURA. Both you and Tom going over?

AL. No.

LAURA. Oh.

AL. Just me.

LAURA. I see. Does Tom know this?

AL. No. I haven't told him.

LAURA. You'll have to tell him, won't you, so he'll be able to make other plans.

AL. Yes, I suppose so.

LAURA. Al, won't you sit down for a moment, please? (AL *hesitates, but comes in and sits down. Offers* AL *a cigarette.*) Cigarette?

AL (*reaches for one automatically, then stops*). No, thanks. I'm in training. (*He slips a pack of cigarettes from his shirt pocket to his trousers pocket.*)

LAURA. That's right. I'm going to watch you play Saturday afternoon. (AL *smiles at her.*) You're not looking forward to telling Tom, are you, Al? (AL *shakes his head, "No."*) I suppose I can guess why you're not rooming with him next year.

(AL *shrugs his shoulders.*) I wonder if you know how much it has meant for him to room with you this year. It's done a lot for him too. It's given him a confidence to know he was rooming with one of the big men of the school.

AL (*embarrassed*). Oh . . .

LAURA. You wouldn't understand what it means to be befriended. You're one of the strong people. I'm surprised, Al.

AL (*blurting it out*). My father's called me three times. How he ever found out about Harris and Tom, I don't know. But he did. And some guy called him and asked him, "Isn't that the boy your son is rooming with?" . . . and he wants me to change for next year.

LAURA. What did you tell your father?

AL. I told him Tom wasn't so bad, and . . . I'd better wait and see Mr. Reynolds.

LAURA. Al, you've lived with Tom. You know him better than anyone else knows him. If you do this, it's as good as finishing him so far as this school is concerned, and maybe farther.

AL (*almost whispering it*). Well, he *does* act sort of queer, Mrs. Reynolds. He . . .

LAURA. You never said this before. You never paid any attention before. What do you mean, "queer?"

AL. Well, like the fellows say, he sort of walks lightly, if you know what I mean. Sometimes the way he moves . . . the things he talks about . . . long hair music all the time.

LAURA. All right. He wants to be a singer. So he talks about it.

AL. He's never had a girl up for any of the dances.

LAURA. Al, there are good explanations for all these things you're saying. They're silly . . . and prejudiced . . . and arguments all dug up to suit a point of view. They're all after the fact.

AL. I'd better speak to Mr. Reynolds. (*He starts for the door.*)

LAURA. Al, look at me. (*She holds his eyes for a long time, wondering whether to say what she wants to say.*)

AL. Yes?

LAURA (*she decides to do it*). Al, what if I were to start the rumor tomorrow that you were . . . well, queer, as you put it.

AL. No one would believe it.

LAURA. Why not?

AL. Well, because . . .

LAURA. Because you're big and brawny and an athlete. What they call a top guy and a hard hitter?

AL. Well, yes.

LAURA. You've got some things to learn, Al. I've been around a little, and I've met men, just like you—same setup—who weren't men, some of them married and with children.

AL. Mrs. Reynolds, you wouldn't do a thing like that.

LAURA. No, Al, I probably wouldn't. But I could, and I almost would to show you how easy it is to smear a person, and once I got them believing it, you'd be surprised how quickly your . . . manly virtues would be changed into suspicious characteristics.

AL (*has been standing with his hands on his hips.* LAURA *looks pointedly at this stance.* AL *thrusts his hands down to his side, and then behind his back*). Mrs. Reynolds, I got a chance to be captain of the baseball team next year.

LAURA. I know. And I have no right to ask you to give up that chance. But I wish somehow or other you could figure out a way . . . so it wouldn't hurt Tom.

(TOM *comes in the hall and goes up the stairs. He's pretty broken up, and mad. After a few moments he appears in his room, shuts the door, and sits on the bed, trying to figure something out.*

AL (*as* TOM *enters house*). Well . . .

LAURA. That's Tom now. (AL *looks at her, wondering how she knows.*) I know all your footsteps. He's coming in for tea. (AL *starts to move to door.*) Well, Al? (AL *makes a helpless motion.*) You still want me to tell Mr. Reynolds about your moving next year?

AL (*after a moment*). No.

LAURA. Good.

AL. I mean, I'll tell him when I see him.

LAURA. Oh.

AL (*turns on her*). What can I do?

LAURA. I don't know.

AL. Excuse me for saying so, but it's easy for you to talk the way you have. You're not involved. You're just a bystander. You're not going to be hurt. Nothing's going to happen to you one way or the other. I'm sorry.

LAURA. That's a fair criticism, Al. I'm sorry I asked you . . . As you say, I'm not involved.

AL. I'm sorry. I think you're swell, Mrs.

Reynolds. You're the nicest housemaster's wife I've ever ran into . . . I mean . . . Well, you know what I mean. It's only that . . . (*He is flustered. He opens the door.*) I'm sorry.

LAURA. I'm sorry too, Al. (*She smiles at him.* AL *stands in the doorway for a moment, not knowing whether to go out the hall door or go upstairs. Finally, he goes upstairs, and into the study door.* LAURA *stands thinking over what* AL *has said, even repeating to herself, "I'm not involved." She then goes into the alcove and off.*)

AL (*outside* TOM'S *bedroom door*). Tom? (TOM *moves quietly away from the door.*) Tom? (*He opens the door.*) Hey.

TOM. I was sleeping.

AL. Standing up, huh? (TOM *turns away.*) You want to be alone?

TOM. No. You want to look. Go ahead. (*He indicates the window.*)

AL. No, I don't want to look, I . . . (*He looks at* TOM, *not knowing how to begin . . . He stalls . . . smiling*) Nice tie you got there.

TOM (*starts to undo tie*). Yeah, it's yours. You want it?

AL. No. Why? I can only wear one tie at a time. (TOM *leaves it hanging around his neck. After an awkward pause*) I . . . uh . . .

TOM. I guess I don't need to ask you what's the matter?

AL. It's been rough today, huh?

TOM. Yeah. (*He turns away, very upset. He's been holding it in . . . but here's his closest friend asking him to open up.*) Jesus Christ! (AL *doesn't know what to say. He goes to* TOM'S *bureau and picks up his hairbrush, gives his hair a few brushes.*) Anybody talk to you?

AL. Sure. You know they would.

TOM. What do they say?

AL (*yanks his tie off*). Hell, I don't know.

TOM. I went to a meeting of the dance committee. I'm no longer on the dance committee. Said that since I'd backed out of playing the part in the play, I didn't show the proper spirit. That's what they *said* was the reason.

AL (*loud*). Why the hell don't you do something about it?

TOM (*yelling back*). About what?

AL. About what they're saying.

TOM. What the hell can I do?

AL. Jeeze, you could . . . (*He suddenl*￼ *wonders what* TOM *could do.*) I don'￼ know.

TOM. I tried to pass it off. Christ, yo￼ can't pass it off. You know, when I wen￼ into the showers today after my tenni￼ match, everyone who was in there, grabbe￼ a towel and . . . and . . . walked out.

AL. They're stupid. Just a bunch o￼ stupid bastards. (*He leaves the room.*￼

TOM (*following him into sitting room*)￼ Goddamn it, the awful thing I found my￼ self . . . Jesus, I don't know . . . I foun￼ myself self-conscious about things I've bee￼ doing for years. Dressing, undressing. . .￼ I keep my eyes on the floor . . . (*Re￼ enters his own room.*) Jeeze, if I even look￼ at a guy that doesn't have any clothes on￼ I'm afraid someone's gonna say something￼ or . . . Jesus, I don't know.

AL (*during this,* AL *has come back int*￼ *the room, unbuttoning his shirt, taking i*￼ *off, etc. Suddenly he stops*). What the hel￼ am I doing? I've had a shower today. (*H*￼ *tries to laugh.*)

TOM (*looks at him a moment*). Undres￼ in your own room, will ya? You don'￼ want them talking about you too, do you￼

AL. No I don't. (*He has said this ver*￼ *definitely and with meaning.*)

TOM (*looks up at his tone of voice*). O￼ course you don't. (*He looks at* AL *a lon*￼ *time. He hardly dares say this.*) You . .￼ uh . . . you moving out?

AL (*doesn't want to answer*). Look￼ Tom, do you mind if I try to help you￼

TOM. Hell, no. How?

AL. I know this is gonna burn your tai￼ and I know it sounds stupid as hell. Bu￼ it isn't stupid. It's the way people loo￼ at things. You could do a lot for your￼ self, just the way you talk and look.

TOM. You mean get my hair cut?

AL. For one thing.

TOM. Why the hell should a man wit￼ a crew cut look more manly than a gu￼ who—

AL. Look, I don't know the reasons fo￼ these things. It's just the way they are.

TOM (*looking at himself in bureau mir*￼ *ror*). I tried a crew cut a coupla times.￼ haven't got that kind of hair, or that kin￼ of head. (*After a moment*) Sorry, I didn'￼ mean to yell at you. Thanks for trying t￼ help.

AL (*finds a baseball on the radiator an*￼ *throws it at* TOM. TOM *smiles, and throw*￼

back). Look, Tom, the way you walk ...

TOM. Oh, Jesus.

AL (*flaring*). Look, I'm only trying to help you.

TOM. No one gave a goddamn about how I walked till last Saturday!

AL (*starts to go*). Okay, okay. Forget it. (*He goes out.*)

TOM (*stands there a few moments, then slams the baseball into the bed and walks out after* AL *into sitting room*). Al?

AL (*off*). Yeah?

TOM. Tell me about how I walk.

AL (*in the sitting room*). Go ahead, walk!

TOM (*walks back into the bedroom.* AL *follows him, wiping his face on a towel and watching* TOM *walk. After he has walked a bit*). Now I'm not going to be able to walk any more. Everything I been doing all my life makes me look like a fairy.

AL. Go on.

TOM. All right, now I'm walking. Tell me.

AL. Tom, I don't know. You walk sort of light.

TOM. Light? (*He looks at himself take a step.*)

AL. Yeah.

TOM. Show me.

AL. No, I can't do it.

TOM. Okay. You walk. Let me watch you. I never noticed how you walked. (AL *stands there for a moment, never having realized before how difficult it could be to walk if you think about it. Finally he walks.*) Do it again.

AL. If you go telling any of the guys about this . . .

TOM. Do you think I would? . . . (AL *walks again.*) That's a good walk. I'll try to copy it. (*He tries to copy the walk, but never succeeds in taking even a step.*) Do you really think that'll make any difference?

AL. I dunno.

TOM. Not now it won't. Thanks anyway.

AL (*comes and sits on bed beside* TOM. *Puts his arm around* TOM's *shoulder and thinks this thing out*). Look, Tom . . . You've been in on a lot of bull sessions. You heard the guys talking about stopping over in Boston on the way home . . . getting girls . . . you know.

TOM. Sure. What about it?

AL. You're not going to the dance Saturday night?

TOM. No. Not now.

AL. You know Ellie Martin. The gal who waits on table down at the soda joint?

TOM. Yeah. What about her?

AL. You've heard the guys talking about her.

TOM. What do you mean?

AL. Hell, do you want me to draw a picture?

TOM (*with disgust*). Ellie Martin?

AL. Okay. I know she's a dog, but . . .

TOM. So what good's that going to do? I get caught there, I get thrown out of school.

AL. No one ever gets caught. Sunday morning people'd hear about it . . . not the Dean . . . I mean the fellows. Hell, Ellie tells and tells and tells . . . Boy, you'd be made!

TOM. Are you kidding?

AL. No.

TOM (*with disgust*). Ellie Martin!

AL (*after a long pause*). Look, I've said so much already, I might as well be a complete bastard . . . You ever been with a woman?

TOM. What do you think?

AL. I don't think you have.

TOM. So?

AL. You want to know something?

TOM. What?

AL. Neither have I. But if you tell the guys, I'll murder you.

TOM. All those stories you told . . .

AL. Okay, I'll be sorry I told you.

TOM. Then why don't you go see Ellie Martin Saturday night?

AL. Why the hell should I?

TOM. You mean you don't have to prove anything?

AL. Aw, forget it. It's probably a lousy idea anyway. (*He starts out.*)

TOM. Yeah.

AL (*stops*). Look, about next—(*Stops.*)

TOM. Next year? Yes?

AL. Hap Hudson's asked me to come to his house. He's got a single there. A lot of the fellows from the team are over there, and . . . well . . . (*He doesn't look at* TOM.)

TOM. I understand!

AL (*looks up at last. He hates himself but he's done it, and it's a load off his chest*). See ya. (*He starts to go.*)

TOM (*as* AL *gets to door*). Al . . . (AL

stops and looks back. Taking tie from around his neck) Here.

AL *(looks at tie, embarrassed)*. I said wear it. Keep it.

TOM. It's yours.

AL *(looks at the tie for a long time, then without taking it, goes through the door)*. See ya.

(TOM *folds the tie neatly, dazed, then seeing what he's doing, he throws it viciously in the direction of the bureau, and turns and stares out the window. He puts a record on the phonograph.)*

BILL *(comes in to study from the hall, carrying a pair of shoes and a slim book. As he opens his study door, he hears the music upstairs. He stands in the door and listens, remembering his miserable boyhood. Then he comes in and closes the door)*. Laura. *(Throws shoes on floor near footstool.)*

LAURA *(off stage, calling)*. Bill?

BILL. Yes.

LAURA *(coming in with tea things)*. I didn't think you'd be back before your class. Have some tea.

BILL. I beat young Harvey at handball.

LAURA. Good.

BILL. At last. It took some doing, though. He was after my scalp because of that D minus I gave him in his last exam. *(Gives her book.)* You wanted this . . . book of poems.

LAURA *(looks at book. Her eyes shift quickly to the same book in the chair)*. Why yes. How did you know?

BILL *(trying to be offhand about it)*. The notice from the bookstore.

LAURA. That's very nice of you. *(She moves towards him to kiss him, but at this moment, in picking some wrapping paper from the armchair, he notices the duplicate copy.)*

BILL *(a little angry)*. You've already got it.

LAURA. Why, yes . . . I . . . well, I . . . (BILL *picking it up . . . opens it.)* That is, someone gave it to me. (BILL *reads the inscription.)* Tom knew I wanted it, and . . .

BILL *(looks at her, a terrible look coming into his face. Then he slowly rips the book in two and hurls it into the fireplace)*. Damn!

LAURA. Bill! (BILL *goes to footstool and sits down and begins to change his shoes.)* Bill, what difference does it make that he

gave me the book? He knew I wanted it too.

BILL. I don't know. It's just that every time I try to do something . . .

LAURA. Bill, how can you say that? It isn't so.

BILL. It is.

LAURA. Bill, this thing of the book is funny.

BILL. I don't think it's very funny.

LAURA *(going behind him, and kneeling by his side)*. Bill, I'm very touched that you should have remembered. Thank you. *(He turns away from her and goes on with his shoes.)* Bill, don't turn away. I want to thank you. *(As she gets no response from him, she rises.)* Is it such a chore to let yourself be thanked? *(She puts her hands on his shoulders, trying to embrace him.)* Oh, Bill, we so rarely touch any more. I keep feeling I'm losing contact with you. Don't you feel that?

BILL *(looking at his watch)*. Laura, I . . .

LAURA *(she backs away from him)*. I know, you've got to go. But it's just that, I don't know, we don't touch any more. It's a silly way of putting it, but you seem to hold yourself aloof from me. A tension seems to grow between us . . . and then when we do . . . touch . . . it's a violent thing . . . almost a compulsive thing. (BILL *is uncomfortable at this accurate description of their relationship. He sits troubled. She puts her arms around his neck and embraces him, bending over him.)* You don't feel it? You don't feel yourself holding away from me until it becomes overpowering? There's no growing together any more . . . no quiet times, just holding hands, the feeling of closeness, like it was in Italy. Now it's long separations and then this almost brutal coming together, and . . . Oh, Bill, you do see, you do see. (BILL *suddenly straightens up, toughens, and looks at her.* LAURA *repulsed, slowly draws her arms from around his shoulders.)*

BILL. For God's sake, Laura, what are you talking about? *(He rises and goes to his desk.)* It can't always be a honeymoon.

(Upstairs in his room, TOM *turns off the phonograph, and leaves the room, going out into the hall and up the stairs.)*

LAURA. Do you think that's what I'm talking about?

BILL. I don't know why you chose a

time like this to talk about things like . . .

LAURA. . . . I don't know why, either. I just wanted to thank you for the book . . . (*Moves away and looks in book.*) What did you write in it?

BILL (*starts to mark exam papers*). Nothing. Why? Should I write in it? I just thought you wanted the book.

LAURA. Of course . . . Are you sure you won't have some tea? (*She bends over the tea things.*)

BILL. Yes.

LAURA (*straightening up, trying another tack of returning to normality*). Little Joan Harrison is coming over for tea.

BILL. No, she isn't. (LAURA *looks inquiringly.*) I just saw her father at the gym. I don't think that was a very smart thing for you to do, Laura.

LAURA. I thought Tom might take her to the dance Saturday. He's on the committee, and he has no girl to take.

BILL. I understand he's no longer on the committee. You're a hostess, aren't you?

LAURA. Yes.

BILL. I've got the mountain-climbing business this week end. Weather man predicts rain.

LAURA (*almost breaks. Hides her face in her hands. Then recovers*). That's too bad. (*After a moment*) Bill?

BILL. Yes?

LAURA. I think someone should go to the Dean about Tom and the hazing he's getting.

BILL. What could the Dean do? Announce from chapel, "You've got to stop riding Tom. You've got to stop calling him Grace?" Is that what you'd like him to do?

LAURA. No. I suppose not.

BILL. You know we're losing Al next year because of Tom.

LAURA. Oh, you've heard?

BILL. Yes, Hudson tells me he's moving over to his house. He'll probably be captain of the baseball team. Last time we had a major sport captain was eight years ago.

LAURA. Yes, I'm sorry.

BILL. However, we'll also be losing Tom.

LAURA. Oh?

BILL (*noting her increased interest*). Yes. We have no singles in this house, and he'll be rooming alone.

LAURA. I'm sorry to hear that.

BILL (*he turns to look at her*). I knew you would be.

LAURA. Why should my interest in this boy make you angry?

BILL. I'm not angry.

LAURA. You're not only angry. It's almost as though you were, well, jealous.

BILL. Oh, come on now.

LAURA. Well, how else can you explain your . . . your vindictive attitude towards him?

BILL. Why go into it again? Jealous! (*He has his books together now. Goes to the door.*) I'll go directly from class to the dining hall. All right?

LAURA. Yes, of course.

BILL. And please, please, Laura . . . (*He stops.*)

LAURA. I'll try.

BILL. I know you like to be different, just for the sake of being different . . . and I like you for that . . . But this time, lay off. Show your fine free spirit on something else.

LAURA. On something that can't hurt us.

BILL. All right. Sure. I don't mind putting it that way. And Laura?

LAURA. Yes?

BILL. Seeing Tom so much . . . having him down for tea alone all the time . . .

LAURA. Yes?

BILL. I think you should have him down only when you have the other boys . . . for his own good. I mean that. Well, I'll see you in the dining hall. Try to be on time. (*He goes out.* LAURA *brings her hands to her face, and cries, leaning against the back of the chair.* AL *has come tumbling out of the door to his room with books in hand, and is coming down stairs. Going down the hall*) You going to class, Al?

AL. Hello, Mr. Reynolds. Yes I am.

BILL (*as they go*). Let's walk together. I'm sorry to hear that you're moving across the street next year. (*And they are gone out the door.*)

TOM (*has come down the stairs, and now stands looking at the hall telephone. He is carrying his coat. After a long moment's deliberation he puts in a coin and dials*). Hello, I'd like to speak to Ellie Martin, please. (LAURA *has moved to pick up the torn book which her husband has thrown in the fireplace. She is smoothing it out, as she suddenly hears* TOM's *voice in the hall. She can't help but hear what he is saying. She stands stock still and listens, her alarm and concern showing on her face.*) Hello, Ellie? This is Tom Lee

. . . Tom Lee. I'm down at the soda fountain all the time with my roommate, Al Thompson . . . Yeah, the guys do sometimes call me that . . . Well, I'll tell you what I wanted. I wondered if . . . you see, I'm not going to the dance Saturday night, and I wondered if you're doing anything? Yeah, I guess that is a hell of a way to ask for a date . . . but I just wondered if I could maybe drop by and pick you up after work on Saturday . . . I don't know what's *in* it for you, Ellie . . . but something I guess. I just thought I'd like to see you . . . What time do you get through work? . . . Okay, nine o'clock. (LAURA, *having heard this, goes out through the alcove. About to hang up*) Oh, thanks. (*He stands for a moment, contemplating what he's done, then he slips on his jacket, and goes to the study door and knocks. After a moment, he opens the door and enters.*)

LAURA (*coming from the other room with a plate of cookies*). Oh, there you are. I've got your favorites today.

TOM. Mrs. Reynolds, do you mind if I don't come to tea this afternoon?

LAURA. Why . . . if you don't want to . . . How are you? (*She really means this question.*)

TOM. I'm okay.

LAURA. Good.

TOM. It's just I don't feel like tea.

LAURA. Perhaps, it's just as well . . . Joan can't make it today, either.

TOM. I didn't expect she would. She's nothing special; just a kid.

LAURA. Something about a dentist appointment or something.

TOM. It wouldn't have done any good anyway. I'm not going to the dance.

LAURA. Oh?

TOM. Another member of the committee will stop around for you.

LAURA. What will you be doing?

TOM. I don't know. I can take care of myself.

LAURA. If you're not going, that gives me an easy out. I won't have to go.

TOM. Just because I'm not going?

LAURA (*in an effort to keep him from going to Ellie*). Look, Tom . . . now that neither of us is going, why don't you drop down here after supper, Saturday night. We could listen to some records, or play gin, or we can just talk.

TOM. I . . . I don't think you'd better

count on me.

LAURA. I'd like to.

TOM. No, really. I don't want to sound rude . . . but I . . . I may have another engagement.

LAURA. Oh?

TOM. I'd like to come. Please understand that. It's what I'd like to do . . . but . . .

LAURA. Well, I'll be here just in case just in case you decide to come in. (LAURA *extends her hand.*) I hope you'll be feeling better.

TOM (*hesitates, then takes her hand*) Thanks.

LAURA. Maybe your plans will change.

(TOM *looks at her, wishing they would knowing they won't. He runs out and down the hall as the lights fade out on* LAURA *standing at the door.*)

SCENE TWO

The time is eight-forty-five on Saturday night.

In the study a low fire is burning. As the curtain rises, the town clock is striking the three-quarter hour. LAURA *is sitting in her chair sipping a cup of coffee. The door to the study is open slightly. She is waiting for* TOM. *She is wearing a lovely but informal dress, and a single flower. In his room,* TOM *listens to the clock strike. He has just been shaving. He is putting shaving lotion on his face. His face is tense and nervous. There is no joy in the preparations. In a moment, he turns and leaves the room, taking off his belt as he goes.*

After a moment, LILLY *comes to the study door, knocks and comes in.*

LILLY. Laura?

LAURA. Oh, Lilly.

LILLY (*standing in the doorway, a rain coat held over her head. She is dressed in a low-cut evening gown, which she wears very well*). You're not dressed yet. Why aren't you dressed for the dance?

LAURA (*still in her chair*). I'm not going I thought I told you.

LILLY (*deposits raincoat and goes immediately to look at herself in mirror next to the door*). Oh, for Heaven's sake, why not? Just because Bill's away with his oathsome little mountain climbers?

LAURA. Well . . .

LILLY. Come along with us. It's raining on and off, so Harry's going to drive us in the car.

LAURA. No, thanks.

LILLY. If you come, Harry will dance with you all evening. You won't be lonely, I promise you. (LAURA *shakes her head, "no."*) You're the only one who can dance those funny steps with him.

LAURA. It's very sweet of you, but no.

LILLY (*at the mirror*). Do you think this neck is too low?

LAURA. I think you look lovely.

LILLY. Harry says this neck will drive all the little boys crazy.

LAURA. I don't think so.

LILLY. Well, that's not very flattering.

LAURA. I mean, I think they'll appreciate it, but as for driving them crazy . . .

LILLY. After all I want to give them some reward for dancing their duty dances with me.

LAURA. I'm sure when they dance with you, it's no duty, Lilly. I've seen you at these dances.

LILLY. It's not this . . . (*indicating her bosom*) it's my line of chatter. I'm oh so interested in what courses they're taking, where they come from and where they learned to dance so divinely.

LAURA (*laughing.*) Lilly, you're lost in a boys' school. You were meant to shine some place much more glamorous.

LILLY. I wouldn't trade it for the world. Where else could a girl indulge in three hundred innocent flirtations a year?

LAURA. Lilly, I've often wondered what you'd do if one of the three hundred attempted to go, well, a little further than innocent flirtation.

LILLY. I'd slap him down . . . the little beast. (*She laughs and admires herself in mirror.*) Harry says if I'm not careful I'll get to looking like Ellie Martin. You've seen Ellie.

LAURA. I saw her this afternoon for the first time.

LILLY. Really? The first time?

LAURA. Yes. I went into the place where she works . . . the soda shop . . .

LILLY. You!

LAURA. Yes . . . uh . . . for a package of cigarettes. (*After a moment she says with some sadness*) She's not even pretty, is she?

LILLY (*turns from admiring herself at the tone in* LAURA's *voice*). Well, honey, don't sound so sad. What difference should it make to you if she's pretty or not?

LAURA. I don't know. It just seems so . . . they're so young.

LILLY. If they're stupid enough to go to Ellie Martin, they deserve whatever happens to them. Anyway, Laura, the boys *talk* more about Ellie than anything else. So don't fret about it.

LAURA (*arranges chair for* TOM *facing fireplace. Notices* LILLY *primping*). You look lovely, Lilly.

LILLY. Maybe I'd better wear that corsage the dance committee sent, after all . . . right here. (*She indicates low point in dress*) I was going to carry it—or rather Harry was going to help me carry it. You know, it's like one of those things people put on Civil War monuments on Decoration Day.

LAURA. Yes, I've seen them.

LILLY (*indicating the flower* LAURA *is wearing*). Now that's tasteful. Where'd you get that?

LAURA. Uh . . . I bought it for myself.

LILLY. Oh, now.

LAURA. It's always been a favorite of mine and I saw it in the florist's window.

LILLY. Well, Harry will be waiting for me to tie his bow tie. (*Starts towards door.*) Will you be up when we get back?

LAURA (*giving* LILLY *her raincoat*). Probably not.

LILLY. If there's a light on, I'll drop in and tell you how many I had to slap down . . . Night-night. (*She leaves.* LAURA *stands at the closed door until she hears the outside door close. Then she opens her door a bit. She takes her cup of coffee and stands in front of the fireplace and listens.*)

TOM (*as* LILLY *goes, he returns to his room, dressed in a blue suit. He stands there deliberating a moment, then reaches under his pillow and brings out a pint bottle of whisky. He takes a short swig. It gags him. He corks it and puts it back under the pillow*). Christ, I'll never make it. (*He reaches in his closet and pulls out a raincoat, then turns and snaps out the room light, and goes out. A moment later, he appears on the stairs. He sees* LAURA's *door partly open, and while he's putting on his raincoat, he walks warily past it.*)

LAURA (*when she hears* TOM's *door close,*

she stands still and listens more intently. She hears him pass her door and go to the front door. She puts down the cup of coffee, and goes to the study door. She calls). Tom? *(After some moments,* TOM *appears in the door, and she opens it wide.)* I've been expecting you.

TOM. I . . . I . . .

LAURA *(opening the door wide).* Are you going to the dance, after all?

TOM *(comes in the door).* No . . . You can report me if you want. Out after hours. Or . . . *(He looks up at her finally.)* Or you can give me permission. Can I have permission to go out?

LAURA *(moving into the room, says pleasantly).* I think I'd better get you some coffee.

TOM *(at her back, truculent).* You can tell them that, too . . . that I've been drinking. There'll be lots to tell before— *(He stops.)* I didn't drink much. But I didn't eat much either.

LAURA. Let me get you something to eat.

TOM *(as though convincing himself).* No. I can't stay!

LAURA. All right. But I'm glad you dropped in. I was counting on it.

TOM *(chip on shoulder).* I said I might not. When you invited me.

LAURA. I know. *(She looks at him a moment. He is to her a heartbreaking sight . . . all dressed up as though he were going to a prom, but instead he's going to Ellie . . . the innocence and the desperation touch her deeply . . . and this shows in her face as she circles behind him to the door.)* It's a nasty night out, isn't it?

TOM. Yes.

LAURA. I'm just as glad I'm not going to the dance. *(She shuts the door gently.* TOM, *at the sound of the door, turns and sees what she has done.)* It'll be nice just to stay here by the fire.

TOM. I wasn't planning to come in.

LAURA. Then why the flower . . . and the card? "For a pleasant evening?"

TOM. It was for the dance. I forgot to cancel it.

LAURA. I'm glad you didn't.

TOM. Why? *(He stops studying the curtains and looks at her.)*

LAURA *(moving into the room again).* Well, for one thing I like to get flowers. For another thing . . . *(*TOM *shakes his head a little to clear it.)* Let me make you some coffee.

TOM. No. I am just about right.

LAURA. Or you can drink this . . . I just had a sip. *(She holds up the cup.* TOM *looks at the proffered coffee.)* You can drink from this side. *(She indicates the other side of the cup.)*

TOM *(takes the cup, and looks at the side where her lips have touched and then slowly turns it around to the other and takes a sip).* And for another thing?

LAURA. What do you mean?

TOM. For one thing you like to get flowers . . .

LAURA. For another it's nice to have flowers on my anniversary.

TOM. Anniversary?

LAURA. Yes.

TOM *(waving the cup and saucer around).* And Mr. Reynolds on a mountain top with twenty stalwart youths, soaking wet . . . Didn't he remember?

LAURA *(rescues the cup and saucer).* It's not that anniversary. *(*TOM *looks at her wondering. Seeing that she has interested him, she moves towards him.)* Let me take your coat.

TOM *(definitely).* I can't—

LAURA. I know. You can't stay. But . . . *(She comes up behind him and puts her hand on his shoulders to take off his coat. He can hardly stand her touch. She gently peels his coat from him and stands back to look at him.)* How nice you look!

TOM *(disarranging his hair or tie).* Put me in a blue suit and I look like a kid.

LAURA. How did you know I liked this flower?

TOM. You mentioned it.

LAURA. You're very quick to notice these things. So was he.

TOM *(after a moment, his curiosity aroused).* Who?

LAURA. My first husband. That's the anniversary.

TOM. I didn't know.

LAURA *(she sits in her chair).* Mr. Reynolds doesn't like me to talk about my first husband. He was, I'd say, about your age. How old are you, Tom?

TOM. Eighteen . . . tomorrow.

LAURA. Tomorrow . . . We must celebrate.

TOM. You'd better not make any plans.

LAURA. He was just your age then. *(She looks at him again with slight wonder.)* It doesn't seem possible now, looking at you . . .

TOM. Why, do I look like such a child?

LAURA. Why no.

TOM. Men are married at my age.

LAURA. Of course, they are. *He* was. Maybe a few months older. Such a lonely boy, away from home for the first time . . . and . . . and going off to war. (TOM *looks up inquiringly.*) Yes, he was killed.

TOM. I'm sorry . . . but I'm glad to hear about him.

LAURA. Glad?

TOM. Yes. I don't know . . . He sounds like someone you *should* have been married to, not . . . (*Stops.*) I'm sorry if I . . . (*Stops.*)

LAURA (*after a moment*). He was killed being conspicuously brave. He had to be conspicuously brave, you see, because something had happened in training camp . . . I don't know what . . . and he was afraid the others thought him a coward . . . He showed them he wasn't.

TOM. He had that satisfaction.

LAURA. What was it worth if it killed him?

TOM. I don't know. But I can understand.

LAURA. Of course you can. You're very like him.

TOM. Me?

LAURA (*holding out the coffee cup*). Before I finish it all? (TOM *comes over and takes a sip from his side of the cup.*) He was kind and gentle, and lonely. (TOM *turns away in embarrassment at hearing himself so described.*) We knew it wouldn't last . . . We sensed it . . . But he always said, "Why must the test of everything be its durability?"

TOM. I'm sorry he was killed.

LAURA. Yes, so am I. I'm sorry he was killed the way he was killed . . . trying to prove how brave he was. In trying to prove he was a man, he died a boy.

TOM. Still he must have died happy.

LAURA. Because he proved his courage?

TOM. That . . . and because he was married to you. (*Embarrassed, he walks to his coat which she has been holding in her lap.*) I've got to go.

LAURA. Tom, please.

TOM. I've got to.

LAURA. It must be a very important engagement.

TOM. It is.

LAURA. If you go now, I'll think I bored you, talking all about myself.

TOM. You haven't.

LAURA. I probably shouldn't have gone on like that. It's just that I felt like it . . . a rainy night . . . a fire. I guess I'm in a reminiscent mood. Do you ever get in reminiscing moods on nights like this?

TOM. About what?

LAURA. Oh, come now . . . there must be something pleasant to remember, or someone. (TOM *stands by the door beginning to think back, his raincoat in his hand, but still dragging on the floor.*) Isn't there? . . . Of course there is. Who was it, or don't you want to tell?

TOM (*after a long silence*). May I have a cigarette?

LAURA (*relieved that she has won another moment's delay*). Yes, Of course. (*Hands him a box, then lights his cigarette.*)

TOM. My seventh-grade teacher.

LAURA. What?

TOM. That's who I remember.

LAURA. Oh.

TOM. Miss Middleton . . .

LAURA. How sweet.

TOM (*drops the raincoat again, and moves into the room*). It wasn't sweet. It was terrible.

LAURA. At that time, of course . . . Tell me about her.

TOM. She was just out of college . . . tall, blonde, honey-colored hair . . . and she wore a polo coat, and drove a convertible.

LAURA. Sounds very fetching.

TOM. Ever since then I've been a sucker for girls in polo coats.

LAURA (*smiling*). I have one somewhere.

TOM. Yes, I know. (*He looks at her.*)

LAURA. What happened?

TOM. What could happen? As usual I made a fool of myself. I guess everyone knew I was in love with her. People I like, I can't help showing it.

LAURA. That's a good trait.

TOM. When she used to go on errands and she needed one of the boys to go along and help carry something, there I was.

LAURA. She liked you too, then.

TOM. This is a stupid thing to talk about.

LAURA. I can see why she liked you.

TOM. I thought she . . . I thought she loved me. I was twelve years old.

LAURA. Maybe she did.

TOM. Anyway, when I was in eighth grade, she got married. And you know what they made me do? They gave a

luncheon at school in her honor, and I had to be the toastmaster and wish her happiness and everything . . . I had to write a poem . . . (*He quotes*)
"Now that you are going to be married,
And away from us be carried,
Before you promise to love, honor and obey,
There are a few things I want to say."
(*He shakes his head as they both laugh.*)
From there on it turned out to be more of a love poem than anything else.

LAURA (*as she stops laughing*). Puppy love can be heartbreaking.

TOM (*the smile dying quickly as he looks at her. Then after what seems like forever*). I'm always falling in love with the wrong people.

LAURA. Who isn't?

TOM. You too?

LAURA. It wouldn't be any fun if we didn't. Of course, nothing ever comes of it, but there are bittersweet memories, and they can be pleasant. (*Kidding him as friend to friend, trying to get him to smile again.*) Who else have you been desperately in love with?

TOM (*he doesn't answer. Then he looks at his watch*). It's almost nine . . . I'm late. (*Starts to go.*)

LAURA (*rising*). I can't persuade you to stay? (TOM *shakes his head, "no."*) We were getting on so well.

TOM. Thanks.

LAURA. In another moment I would have told you all the deep, dark secrets of my life.

TOM. I'm sorry. (*He picks up his coat from the floor.*)

LAURA (*desperately trying to think of something to keep him from going*). Won't you stay even for a dance?

TOM. I don't dance.

LAURA. I was going to teach you. (*She goes over to the phonograph and snaps on the button.*)

TOM (*opens the door*). Some other time . . .

LAURA. Please, for me. (*She comes back.*)

TOM (*after a moment he closes the door*). Tell me something.

LAURA. Yes? (*The record starts to play, something soft and melodic. It plays through to the end of the act.*)

TOM. Why are you so nice to me?

LAURA. Why . . . I . . .

TOM. You're not this way to the rest of the fellows.

LAURA. No, I know I'm not. Do you mind my being nice to you?

TOM (*shakes his head, "no"*). I just wondered why.

LAURA (*in a perfectly open way*). I guess Tom . . . I guess it's because I like you.

TOM. No one else seems to. Why do you?

LAURA. I don't know . . . I . . .

TOM. Is it *because* no one else likes me? Is it just pity?

LAURA. No, Tom, of course not . . . It's well . . . it's because you've been very nice to me . . . very considerate. It wasn't easy for me, you know, coming into a school, my first year. You seemed to sense that. I don't know, we just seem to have hit it off. (*She smiles at him.*)

TOM. Mr. Reynolds knows you like me.

LAURA. I suppose so. I haven't kept it a secret.

TOM. Is that why he hates me so?

LAURA. I don't think he hates you.

TOM. Yes, he hates me. Why lie? I think everyone here hates me but you. But they won't.

LAURA. Of course they won't.

TOM. He hates me because he made a flop with me. I know all about it. My father put me in this house when I first came here, and when he left me he said to your husband, "Make a man out of him." He's failed, and he's mad, and then you come along, and were nice to me . . . out of pity.

LAURA. No, Tom, not pity. I'm too selfish a woman to like you just out of pity.

TOM (*he has worked himself up into a state of confusion, and anger, and desperation*). There's so much I . . . there's so much I don't understand.

LAURA (*reaches out and touches his arm*). Tom, don't go out tonight.

TOM. I've got to. That's one thing that's clear. I've got to!

LAURA (*holds up her arms for dancing*). Won't you let me teach you how to dance.

TOM (*suddenly and impulsively he throws his arms around her, and kisses her passionately, awkwardly, and then in embarrassment he buries his head in her shoulder*). Oh, God . . . God.

LAURA. Tom . . . Tom . . . (TOM *raises his face and looks at her, and would kiss her again.*) No, Tom . . . No, I . . . (*At the first "No," TOM breaks from her and* runs out the door halfway up the stairs. *Calling*) Tom! . . . Tom! (TOM *stops at the sound of her voice and turns around and looks down the stairs.* LAURA *moves to the open door.*) Tom, I . . . (*The front door opens and two of the mountain-climbing boys,* PHIL *and* PAUL *come in, with their packs.*)

PHIL (*seeing* TOM *poised on the stairs*). What the hell are you doing? (TOM *just looks at him.*) What's the matter with you? (*He goes on up the stairs.*)

TOM. What are you doing back?

PAUL. The whole bunch is back. Who wants to go mountain climbing in the rain?

BILL (*outside his study door*). Say, any of you fellows want to go across the street for something to eat when you get changed, go ahead. (PHIL *and* PAUL *go up the stairs past* TOM. BILL *goes into his own room, leaving door open.*) Hi. (*He takes off his equipment and puts it on the floor.*)

LAURA (*has been standing motionless where* TOM *has left her*). Hello.

BILL (*comes to her and kisses her on the cheek*). One lousy week end a year we get to go climbing and it rains. (*Throws the rest of his stuff down.*) The fellows are damned disappointed.

LAURA (*hardly paying any attention to him*). That's too bad.

BILL (*going up to alcove*). I think they wanted me to invite them down for a feed. But I didn't want to. I thought we'd be alone. Okay? (*He looks across at her.*)

LAURA (*she is listening for footsteps outside*). Sure. (BILL *goes out through alcove.* LAURA *stoops and picks up the raincoat which* TOM *has dropped and hides it in the cabinet by the fireplace.*)

BILL (*appears in door momentarily wiping his hands with towel*). Boy it really rained. (*He disappears again.* LAURA *sadly goes to the door and slowly and gently closes it. When she is finished, she leans against the door, listening, hoping against hope that* TOM *will go upstairs. When* TOM *sees the door close, he stands there for a moment, then turns his coat collar up and goes down the hall and out. Off stage as* TOM *starts to go down the hall*) We never made it to the timberline. The rain started to come down. Another hour or so and we would have got to the hut and spent the night, but the fellows wouldn't hear of it . . . (*The door slams.*

LAURA *turns away from the study door in despair. Still off stage*) What was that?

LAURA. Nothing . . . Nothing at all.

BILL (*enters and gets pipe from mantelpiece*). Good to get out, though. Makes you feel alive. Think I'll go out again next Saturday, alone. Won't be bothered by the fellows wanting to turn back. (*He has settled down in the chair intended for* TOM. *The school bells start to ring nine.* BILL *reaches out his hand for* LAURA. *Standing by the door, she looks at his outstretched hand, as the lights fade, and*

THE CURTAIN FALLS

ACT THREE

The time is late the next afternoon.

As the curtain rises, TOM *is in his room. His door is shut and bolted. He is lying on his back on the bed, staring up at the ceiling.*

———

RALPH (*he is at the phone*). Hello, Mary . . . Ralph . . . Yeah, I just wanted you to know I'd be a little delayed picking you up . . . Yeah . . . everyone was taking a shower over here, and there's only one shower for eight guys . . . No it's not the same place as last night . . . The tea dance is at the Inn . . . (*He suddenly looks very uncomfortable.*) Look, I'll tell you when I see you . . . Okay . . . (*Almost whispers it.*) I love you . . . (STEVE, RALPH's *sidekick, comes running in from the outside. He's all dressed up and he's got something to tell.*) Yeah, Mary. Well, I can't say it over again . . . Didn't you hear me the first time? (*Loud so she'll hear it*) Hi, Steve.

STEVE. Come on, get off. I got something to tell you.

RALPH. Mary—Mary, I'll get there faster if I stop talking now. Okay? Okay. See you a little after four. (*He hangs up.*) What the hell's the matter with you?

STEVE. Have you seen Tom?

RALPH. No.

STEVE. You know what the hell he did last night?

RALPH. What?

STEVE. He went and saw Ellie.

RALPH. Who are you bulling?

STEVE. No, honest. Ellie told Jackson over at the kitchen. Everybody knows now.

RALPH. What did he want to go and do a thing like that for?

STEVE. But wait a minute. You haven't heard the half of it.

RALPH. Listen, I gotta get dressed. (*Starts upstairs.*)

STEVE (*on the way up the stairs*). The way Ellie tells it, he went there, all the hell dressed up like he was going to the dance, and . . . (*They disappear up the stairs.* BILL *after a moment comes in the hall, and goes quickly up the stairs. He goes right into* AL *and* TOM's *main room without knocking. We then hear him try the handle of* TOM's *bedroom door.* TOM *looks at the door defiantly and sullenly.*)

BILL (*knocks sharply*). Tom! (*Rattles door some more.*) Tom, this is Mr. Reynolds. Let me in.

TOM. I don't want to see anyone.

BILL. You've got to see me. Come on. Open up! I've got to talk to the Dean at four, and I want to speak to you first.

TOM. There's nothing to say.

BILL. I can break the door down. Then your father would have to pay for a new door. Do you want that? Are you afraid to see me? (TOM *after a moment, goes to the door and pulls back the bolt.* BILL *comes in quickly.*) Well. (TOM *goes back and sits on the bed. Doesn't look at* BILL.) Now I've got to have the full story. All the details so that when I see the Dean . . .

TOM. You've got the full story. What the the hell do you want?

BILL. We don't seem to have the full story.

TOM. When the school cops brought me in last night they told you I was with Ellie Martin.

BILL. That's just it. It seems you weren't *with* her.

TOM (*after a moment*). What do you mean?

BILL. You weren't *with* her. You couldn't be *with* her. Do you understand what I mean?

TOM (*trying to brave it out*). Who says so?

BILL. She says so. And she ought to know. (TOM *turns away.*) She says that you couldn't . . . and that you jumped up and grabbed a knife in her kitchen and tried to kill yourself . . . and she had to fight with you and that's what attracted the school cops.

TOM. What difference does it make?

BILL. I just wanted the record to be straight. You'll undoubtedly be expelled, no matter what . . . but I wanted the record straight.

TOM (*turning on him*). You couldn't have stood it, could you, if I'd proved you wrong?

BILL. Where do you get off talking like that to a master?

TOM. You'd made up your mind long ago, and it would have killed you if I'd proved you wrong.

BILL. Talking like that isn't going to help you any.

TOM. Nothing's going to help. I'm gonna be kicked out, and then you're gonna be happy.

BILL. I'm not going to be happy. I'm going to be very sorry . . . sorry for your father.

TOM. All right, now you know. Go on, spread the news. How can you wait?

BILL. I won't tell anyone . . . but the Dean, of course.

TOM. And my father . . .

BILL. Perhaps . . .

TOM (*after a long pause*). And Mrs. Reynolds.

BILL (*looks at* TOM). Yes. I think she ought to know. (*He turns and leaves the room. Goes through the sitting room and up the stairs, calling "Ralph."* TOM *closes the door and locks it, goes and sits down in the chair.*)

LAURA (*as* BILL *goes upstairs to* RALPH, *she comes into the master's study. She is wearing a wool suit. She goes to the cupboard and brings out* TOM's *raincoat. She moves with it to the door. There is a knock. She opens the door*). Oh, hello, Mr. Lee.

HERB (*coming in, he seems for some reason rather pleased*). Hello, Laura.

LAURA. Bill isn't in just now, though I'm expecting him any moment.

HERB. My train was twenty minutes late. I was afraid I'd missed him. We have an appointment with the Dean in a few minutes . . .

LAURA (*is coolly polite*). Oh, I see.

HERB. Have I done something to displease you, Laura? You seem a little . . . (HERB *shrugs and makes a gesture with his hands meaning cool.*)

LAURA. I'm sorry. Forgive me. Won't you sit down?

HERB. I remember that you were displeased at my leaving Tom in school a week ago. Well, you see I was right in a sense. Though, perhaps being a lady you wouldn't understand.

LAURA. I'm not sure that I do.

HERB. Well, now, look here. If I had taken Tom out of school after that scandal with Mr. . . . uh . . . what was his name?

LAURA. Mr. Harris.

HERB. Yes. If I'd taken Tom out then, he would have been marked for the rest of his life.

LAURA. You know that Tom will be expelled, of course.

HERB. Yes, but the circumstances are so much more normal.

LAURA (*after looking at him a moment*). I think, Mr. Lee, I'm not quite sure, but I think, in a sense, you're proud of Tom.

HERB. Well.

LAURA. Probably for the first time you're proud of him because the school police found him out of bounds with a . . .

HERB. I shouldn't have expected you to understand. Bill will see what I mean.

(BILL *starts down the stairs.*)

LAURA. Yes. He probably will.

(BILL *comes in the room.*)

HERB. Bill.

BILL. Hello, Herb.

(HERB *looks from* LAURA *to* BILL. *Notices the coldness between them.*)

BILL. I was just seeing Tom.

HERB. Yes. I intend to go up after we've seen the Dean. How is he?

BILL. All right.

HERB (*expansive*). Sitting around telling the boys all about it.

BILL. No, he's in his room alone. The others are going to the tea dance at the Inn. Laura . . . (*Sees* LAURA *is leaving the room.*) Oh, Laura, I wish you'd stay.

(LAURA *takes one step back into the room.*)

HERB. I was telling your wife here, trying to make her understand the male point of view on this matter. I mean, how being kicked out for a thing like this, while not exactly desirable, is still not so serious. It's sort of one of the calculated risks of being a man. (*He smiles at his way of putting it.*)

BILL (*preparing to tell* HERB). Herb?

HERB. Yes, Bill. I mean, you agree with me on that, don't you?

BILL. Yes, Herb, only the situation is not exactly as it was reported to you over the phone. It's true that Tom went to this girl Ellie's place, and it's true that he went for the usual purpose. However . . . however, it didn't work out that way.

HERB. What do you mean?

BILL. Nothing happened.

HERB. You mean she . . . she wouldn't have him?

BILL. I mean, Tom . . . I don't know . . . he didn't go through with it. He couldn't. (*He looks at* LAURA.) It's true. The girl says so. And when it didn't work, he tried to kill himself with a knife in the kitchen, and she struggled with him, and that brought the school cops, and that's that. (LAURA *turns away, shocked and moved.* MR. LEE *sits down in a chair bewildered.*) I'm sorry, Herb. Of course the fact that he was with Ellie at her place is enough to get him expelled.

HERB. Does everyone know this?

BILL. Well, Ellie talks. She's got no shame . . . and this is apparently something to talk about.

LAURA (*to* MR. LEE). Do you still think it will make a good smoking-car story?

BILL. What do you mean?

HERB. Why did he do it? Before, maybe he could talk it down, but to go do a thing like this and leave no doubts.

LAURA. In whose mind?

BILL. Laura, please.

LAURA (*angry*). You asked me to stay.

BILL (*flaring back at her*). Well, now you've heard. We won't keep you.

LAURA (*knowing without asking*). Why did you want me to hear?

BILL (*going to her*). I wanted you to know the facts. That's all. The whole story.

(LAURA *stands in the alcove.*)

HERB. Bill, Bill! Maybe there's some way of getting this girl so she wouldn't spread the story.

BILL. I'm afraid it's too late for that.

HERB. I don't know. Some things don't make any sense. What am I going to do now?

LAURA (*re-entering*). Mr. Lee, please don't go on drawing the wrong conclusions!

HERB. I'm drawing no conclusions. This sort of thing can happen to a normal boy. But it's what the others will think . . . Added to the Harris business. And that's all that's important. What they'll think.

LAURA. Isn't it important what Tom thinks?

BILL. Herb, we'd better be getting on over to the Dean's . . .

HERB (*indicating upstairs*). Is he in his room?

BILL. Yes.

HERB. Packing?

BILL. No.

HERB. I told him to come to you to talk things over. Did he?

BILL. No.

HERB. What am I going to say to him now?

BILL. We're expected at four.

HERB. I know. But I've got to go up . . . Maybe I should have left him with his mother. She might have known what to do, what to say . . . (*He starts out.*) You want to come along with me?

BILL (*moving to hall*). All right.

LAURA (*serious*). Bill, I'd like to talk with you.

BILL. I'll be back.

(*Goes with* HERB *to the landing.* LAURA *exits, taking off her jacket.*)

HERB. Maybe I ought to do this alone.

BILL. He's probably locked in his bedroom.

(HERB *goes up the stairs and inside the study.* BILL *stays in the hall.* TOM, *as he hears his father knocking on the bedroom door, stiffens.* HERB *tries the door handle.*)

HERB (*off, in the study*). Tom . . . Tom . . . it's Dad. (TOM *gets up, but just stands there.*) Tom, are you asleep? (*After a few moments, he reappears on the landing. He is deeply hurt that his son wouldn't speak to him.*) I think he's asleep.

BILL (*making a move to go in and get* TOM). He can't be . . .

HERB (*stops*). Yes, I think he is. He was always a sound sleeper. We used to have to drag him out of bed when he was a kid.

BILL. But he should see you.

HERB. It'll be better later, anyhow. (*He starts down the stairs, troubled, puzzled.*)

BILL. I'll go right with you, Herb. (*They re-enter the study, and* BILL *goes out through the alcove.* HERB *stays in the master's study.*)

TOM (*when his father is downstairs, he opens his bedroom door and faintly calls*). Dad?

(HERB *looks up, thinking he's heard something but then figures it must have been something else.* RALPH, STEVE *and* PHIL *come crashing down the stairs, dressed for the tea dance, ad libbing comments about the girls at the dance.* TOM *closes his door. When they have gone, he opens it again and calls "Dad" faintly. When there is no response, he closes the door, and goes and lies on the bed.*)

BILL (*re-entering*). Laura, I'm going to the Dean's now with Herb. I'm playing squash with the headmaster at five. So I'll see you at the dining room at six-thirty.

LAURA (*entering after him*). I wish you'd come back here after.

BILL. Laura, I can't.

LAURA. Bill, I wish you would.

BILL (*sees that there is some strange determination in* LAURA's *face*). Herb, I'll be with you in a minute. Why don't you walk along?

HERB. All right . . . Good-by, Laura. See you again.

BILL. You'll see her in a couple of days at the reunion.

HERB. I may not be coming up for it now . . . Maybe I will. I don't know. I'll be walking along. Good-by, Laura. Tell Tom I tried to see him. (*He goes out.*)

BILL. Now, Laura, what's the matter? I've got to get to the Dean's rooms to discuss this matter.

LAURA. Yes, of course. But first I'd like to discuss the boys who made him do this . . . the men and boys who made him do this.

BILL. No one made him do anything.

LAURA. Is there to be no blame, no punishment for the boys and men who taunted him into doing this? What if he had succeeded in killing himself? What then?

BILL. You're being entirely too emotional about this.

LAURA. If he had succeeded in killing himself in Ellie's rooms wouldn't you have felt some guilt?

BILL. I?

LAURA. Yes, you.

BILL. I wish you'd look at the facts and not be so emotional about this.

LAURA. The facts! What facts! an innocent boy goes swimming with an instructor . . . an instructor whom he likes because this instructor is one of the few who encourage him, who don't ride him . . . And because he's an off-horse, you and the rest of them are only too glad to put two and two together and get a false answer . . . anything which will let you go on and persecute a boy whom you basically don't like. If it had happened with Al or anybody else, you would have done nothing.

BILL. It would have been an entirely different matter. You can't escape from what you are . . . your character. Why do they spend so much time in the law courts on character witnesses? To prove this was the kind of man who could or couldn't commit such and such a crime.

LAURA. I resent this judgment by prejudice. He's not like me, therefore, he is capable of all possible crimes. He's not one of us . . . a member of the tribe!

BILL. Now look, Laura, I know this is a shock to you, because you were fond of this boy. But you did all you could for him, more than anyone would expect. After all, your responsibility doesn't go beyond—

LAURA. I know. Doesn't go beyond giving him tea and sympathy on Sunday afternoons. Well, I want to tell you something. It's going to shock you . . . but I'm going to tell you.

BILL. Laura, it's late.

LAURA. Last night I knew what Tom had in mind to do. I heard him making the date with Ellie on the phone.

BILL. And you didn't stop him? Then you're the one responsible.

LAURA. Yes, I am responsible, but not as you think. I did try to stop him, but not by locking him in his room, or calling the school police. I tried to stop him by being nice to him, by being affectionate. By showing him that he was liked . . . yes, even loved. I knew what he was going to do . . . and why he was going to do it. He had to prove to you bullies that he was a man, and he was going to prove it with Ellie Martin. Well . . . last night . . . last night, I wished he had proved it with me.

BILL. What in Christ's name are you saying?

LAURA. Yes, I shock you. I shock myself. But you are right. I am responsible here. I know what I should have done. I knew it then. My heart cried out for this boy in his misery . . . a misery imposed by my husband. And I wanted to help him as one human being to another . . . and I failed. At the last moment, I sent him

away . . . sent him to . . .

BILL. You mean you managed to overcome your exaggerated sense of pity.

LAURA. No, it was not just pity. My heart in its loneliness . . . Yes, I've been lonely here, miserably lonely . . . and my heart in its loneliness cried out for this boy . . . cried out for the comfort he could give me too.

BILL. You don't know what you're saying.

LAURA. But I was a good woman. Good in what sense of the word? Good to whom . . . and for whom?

BILL. Laura, we'll discuss this, if we must, later on . . .

LAURA. Bill! There'll be no later on. I'm leaving you.

BILL. Over this thing?

LAURA (*after a moment*). Yes, this *thing* and all the other *things* in our marriage.

BILL. For God's sake, Laura, what are you talking about?

LAURA. I'm talking about love and honor and manliness, and tenderness, and persecution. I'm talking about a lot. You haven't understood any of it.

BILL. Laura, you can't leave over a thing like this. You know what it means.

LAURA. I wouldn't worry too much about it. When I'm gone, it will probably be agreed by all that I was an off-horse too, and didn't really belong to the clan, and it's good riddance.

BILL. And you're doing this . . . all because of this . . . this fairy?

LAURA (*after a moment*). This boy, Bill . . . this boy is more of a man than you are.

BILL. Sure. Ask Ellie.

LAURA. Because it was distasteful for him. Because for him there has to be love. He's more of a man than you are.

BILL. Yes, sure.

LAURA. Manliness is not all swagger and swearing and mountain climbing. Manliness is also tenderness, gentleness, consideration. You men think you can decide on who is a man, when only a woman can really know.

BILL. Ellie's a woman. Ask Ellie.

LAURA. I don't need to ask anyone.

BILL. What do you know about a man? Married first to that boy . . . again, a pitiable boy . . . You want to mother a boy, not love a man. That's why you never really loved me. Because I was not a boy you could mother.

LAURA. You're quite wrong about my not loving you. I did love you. But not just for your outward show of manliness, but because you needed me . . . For one unguarded moment you let me know you needed me, and I have tried to find that moment again the year we've been married . . . Why did you marry me, Bill? In God's name, why?

BILL. Because I loved you. Why else?

LAURA. You've resented me . . . almost from the day you married me, you've resented me. You never wanted to marry really . . . Did they kid you into it? Does a would-be headmaster have to be married? Or what was it, Bill? You would have been far happier going off on your jaunts with the boys, having them to your rooms for feeds and bull sessions . . .

BILL. That's part of being a master.

LAURA. Other masters and their wives do not take two boys always with them whenever they go away on vacations or week ends.

BILL. They are boys without privileges.

LAURA. And I became a wife without privileges.

BILL. You became a wife . . . (*He stops.*)

LAURA. Yes?

BILL. You did *not* become a wife.

LAURA. I know. I know I failed you. In some terrible way I've failed you.

BILL. You were more interested in mothering that fairy up there than in being my wife.

LAURA. But you wouldn't let me, Bill. You wouldn't let me.

BILL (*grabbing her by the shoulders*). What do you mean I wouldn't let you?

LAURA (*quietly, almost afraid to say it*). Did it ever occur to you that you persecute in Tom, that boy up there, you persecute in him the thing you fear in yourself? (BILL *looks at her for a long moment of hatred. She has hit close to the truth he has never let himself be conscious of. There is a moment when he might hurt her, but then he draws away, still staring at her. He backs away, slowly, and then turns to the door.*) Bill!

BILL (*not looking at her*). I hope you will be gone when I come back from dinner.

LAURA (*quietly*). I will be . . . (*Going towards him*) Oh, Bill, I'm sorry. I shouldn't have said that . . . it was cruel.

(*She reaches for him as he goes out the door.*) This was the weakness you cried out for me to save you from, wasn't it . . . And I have tried. (*He is gone.*) I have tried. (*Slowly she turns back into the room and looks at it.*) I did try. (*For a few moments she stands stunned and tired from her outburst. Then she moves slowly to* TOM's *raincoat, picks it up and turns and goes out of the room and to the stair-landing. She goes to the boys' study door and knocks.*) Tom. (*She opens it and goes in out of sight. At* TOM's *door, she calls again.*) Tom. (TOM *turns his head slightly and listens.* LAURA *opens* TOM's *door and come in.*) Oh, I'm sorry. May I come in? (*She sees she's not going to get an answer from him, so she goes in.*) I brought back your raincoat. You left it last night. (*She puts it on chair. She looks at him.*) This is a nice room . . . I've never seen it before . . . As a matter of fact I've never been up here in this part of the house. (*Still getting no response, she goes on.* TOM *slowly turns and looks at her back, while she is examining something on the walls. She turns, speaking.*) It's very cozy. It's really quite . . . (*She stops when she sees he has turned around looking at her.*) Hello.

TOM (*barely audible*). Hello.

LAURA. Do you mind my being here?

TOM. You're not supposed to be.

LAURA. I know. But everyone's out, and will be for some time . . . I wanted to return your raincoat.

TOM. Thank you. (*After a pause he sits up on the bed, his back to her.*) I didn't think you'd ever want to see me again.

LAURA. Why not?

TOM. After last night. I'm sorry about what happened downstairs.

LAURA (*she looks at him awhile, then*). I'm not.

TOM (*looks at her. Can't quite make it out*). You've heard everything I suppose.

LAURA. Yes.

TOM. Everything?

LAURA. Everything.

TOM. I knew your husband would be anxious to give you the details.

LAURA. He did. (*She stands there quietly looking down at the boy.*)

TOM. So now you know too.

LAURA. What?

TOM. That everything they said about me is true.

LAURA. Tom!

TOM. Well, it is, isn't it?

LAURA. Tom?

TOM. I'm no man. Ellie knows it. Everybody knows it. It seems everybody knew it, except me. And now I know it.

LAURA (*moves towards him*). Tom . . . Tom . . . dear. (TOM *turns away from her.*) You don't think that just because . . .

TOM. What else am I to think?

LAURA (*very gently*). Tom, that didn't work because you didn't believe in it . . . in such a test.

TOM (*with great difficulty*). I touched her, and there was nothing.

LAURA. You aren't in love with Ellie.

TOM. That's not supposed to matter.

LAURA. But it does.

TOM. I wish they'd let me kill myself.

LAURA. Tom, look at me. (TOM *shakes his head.*) Tom, last night you kissed me.

TOM. Jesus!

LAURA. Why did you kiss me?

TOM (*turns suddenly*). And it made you sick, didn't it? Didn't it? (*Turns away from her again.*)

LAURA. How can you think such a thing?

TOM. You sent me away . . . you . . . Anyway, when you heard this morning it must have made you sick.

LAURA (*sits on the edge of bed*). Tom, I'm going to tell you something. (TOM *won't turn.*) Tom? (*He still won't turn.*) It was the nicest kiss I've ever had . . . from anybody. (TOM *slowly turns and looks at her.*) Tom, I came to say goodby. (TOM *shakes his head, looking at her.*) I'm going away . . . I'll probably never see you again. I'm leaving Bill. (TOM *knits his brows, questioning.*) For a lot of reasons . . . one of them, what he's done to you. But before I left, I wanted you to know, for your own comfort, you're more of a man now than he ever was or will be. And one day you'll meet a girl, and it will be right. (TOM *turns away in disbelief.*) Tom, believe me.

TOM. I wish I could. But a person knows . . . knows inside. Jesus, do you think after last night I'd ever . . . (*He stops. After a moment, he smiles at her.*) But

thanks . . . thanks a lot. (*He closes his eyes.* LAURA *looks at him a long time. Her face shows the great compassion and tenderness she feels for this miserable boy. After some time, she gets up and goes out the door. A moment later she appears in the hall door. She pauses for a moment, then reaches out and closes it, and stays inside.*

(TOM, *when he hears the door close, his eyes open. He sees she has left his bedroom. Then in complete misery, he lies down on the bed, like a wounded animal, his head at the foot of the bed.*

(LAURA *in a few moments appears in the bedroom doorway. She stands there, and then comes in, always looking at the slender figure of the boy on the bed. She closes the bedroom door.*

(TOM *hears the sound and looks around. When he sees she has come back, he turns around slowly, wonderingly, and lies on his back, watching her.*

(LAURA *seeing a bolt on the door, slides it to. Then she stands looking at* TOM, *her hand at her neck. With a slight and delicate movement, she unbuttons the top button of her blouse, and moves towards* TOM. *When she gets alongside the bed, she reaches out her hand, still keeping one hand at her blouse.* TOM *makes no move. Just watches her.*

(LAURA *makes a little move with the outstretched hand, asking for his hand.* TOM *slowly moves his hand to hers.*)

LAURA (*stands there holding his hand and smiling gently at him. Then she sits and looks down at the boy, and after a moment, barely audible*). And now . . . nothing?

(TOM'S *other hand comes up and with both his hands he brings her hand to his lips.*)

LAURA (*smiles tenderly at this gesture, and after a moment*). Years from now . . . when you talk about this . . . and you will . . . be kind. (*Gently she brings the boy's hands toward her opened blouse, as the lights slowly dim out . . . and . . .*

THE CURTAIN FALLS

A VIEW FROM THE BRIDGE

Arthur Miller

First presented by Kermit Bloomgarden and Whitehead-Stevens
at the Coronet Theatre in New York on September 29,
1955, with the following cast:

LOUIS David Clarke

MIKE Tom Pedi

ALFIERI J. Carrol Naish

EDDIE Van Heflin

CATHERINE Gloria Marlowe

BEATRICE Eileen Heckart

MARCO Jack Warden

TONY Antony Vorno

RODOLPHO Richard Davalos

FIRST IMMIGRATION OFFICER Curt Conway

SECOND IMMIGRATION OFFICER Ralph Bell

MR. LIPARI Russell Collins

MRS. LIPARI Anne Driscoll

TWO "SUBMARINES" Leo Penn,
Milton Carney

NOTE: The above data refers to the Broadway production, when the play, a long one-acter,
appeared on the same bill with another one-acter, *A Memory of Two Mondays.* The
version published in this volume is the expanded one prepared by the author for
presentation in two acts in London. It is presented here because it is in this version that the play
has been produced in the United States after its Broadway première. Although the
expansion has resulted in some sacrifice of power, it has the advantage of being performable
without having to be joined with another play. For the original version the
reader should consult The Viking Press, New York, 1955 volume titled
A View From the Bridge: Two one-act plays by Arthur Miller.

INTRODUCTION

A View from the Bridge was originally produced on Broadway as a long one-act play in a two-play program. The "curtain-raiser," *A Memory of two Mondays*, was a sensitive and admirably uncontrived genre-piece about life in a factory during the Depression of the 1930's. It made no great impression, and it was unmistakably overshadowed by its companion piece. For the London production the author prepared an expanded version of *A View from the Bridge* so that it could provide a full evening of theatre. Some concentration of power was lost in the process, but the practicality of the solution was in its favor. The new version proved to be extraordinarily successful in London, and it has since been used satisfactorily in all American productions.

One other feature of the new version is that it lacks the numerous references to classic tragedy employed in the prologue and epilogue of the original one-acter. For Miller had once more set his sights on Tragedy, and this time he found a geographical connection between his play and the themes of classic drama. His characters were of Italian origin, and the immigrant characters had but recently left the island of Sicily where the classic Greeks had built flourishing centers such as Syracuse. Elemental drama and passion transferred to the Brooklyn waterfront were expected by Miller to yield the concentrated force and the timelessness of high tragedy. Nor did Miller veer particularly from his moral preoccupations when he took for his theme the conflict between desire and honor, which involved the specific issue that continued to absorb the author— namely, the indignity and immorality of acting as an informer.

The original prologue, spoken by the waterfront lawyer Alfieri, contained the following passages in verse:

When the tide is right
And the wind blows the sea against these houses,
I sit here in my office
Thinking it is all so timeless here.
I think of Sicily, from where these people came,
The Roman rocks of Calabria,
Siracusa on the cliff, where Carthaginian and Greek
Fought such fights . . .

It's different now, of course.
I no longer keep a pistol in my filing cabinet;
We are quite American, quite civilized—
Now we settle for half. And I like it better.

And yet, when the tide is right
And the green smell of the sea
Floats through my window
I must look up at the circling pigeons of the poor,
And I see falcons there,
The hunting eagles of the olden time,
Fierce above Italian forests . . .

Once in every few years there is a case,
And as the parties tell me what the trouble is,

I see cobwebs tearing, Adriatic ruins rebuilding themselves; Calabria;

The eyes of the plaintiff seem suddenly carved,
His voice booming toward me over many fallen stones.

And Alfieri's epilogue concludes:

Most of the time we settle for half,
And I like it better.
And yet when the tide is right,
And the green smell of the sea
Floats in through my window,
The waves of this bay
Are the waves against Siracusa,
And I see a face that suddenly seems carved;
The eyes look like tunnels
Leading back toward some ancestral beach
Where all of us once lived

And I wonder at those times
How much of all of us
Really lives there yet,
And when we will truly have moved on,
On and away from that dark place,
The world that has fallen to stone?

The reader may decide for himself whether or not these passages from the original one-act drama should have been retained in the expanded two-act version that follows. An opinion in the negative was forcefully rendered by Woolcott Gibbs in *The New Yorker* of October 8, 1955, when he complained against "a sort of extra and, in my opinion, distractingly literary touch that has been provided in the shape of the lawyer." But this statement followed that reviewer's conviction that "No writer in the theatre understands better how to combine the poverty-stricken imagery, the broken rhythms and mindless repetitions, and the interminable clichés of illiterate speech into something that has a certain harsh and grotesque eloquence."

ACT ONE

The street and house front of a tenement building. The front is skeletal entirely. The main acting area is the living room-dining room of Eddie's apartment. It is a worker's flat, clean, sparse, homely. There is a rocker down front; a round dining table at center, with chairs; and a portable phonograph.

At back are a bedroom door and an opening to the kitchen; none of these interiors are seen.

At the right, forestage, a desk. This is Mr. Alfieri's law office.

There is also a telephone booth. This is not used until the last scenes, so it may be covered or left in view.

A stairway leads up to the apartment, and then farther up to the next story, which is not seen.

Ramps, representing the street, run upstage and off to right and left.

As the curtain rises, LOUIS *and* MIKE, *longshoremen, are pitching coins against the building at left.*

A distant foghorn blows.

Enter ALFIERI, *a lawyer in his fifties turning gray; he is portly, good-humored, and thoughtful. The two pitchers nod to him as he passes. He crosses the stage to his desk, removes his hat, runs his fingers through his hair, and grinning, speaks to the audience.*

———

ALFIERI. You wouldn't have known it, but something amusing has just happened. You see how uneasily they nod to me? That's because I am a lawyer. In this neighborhood to meet a lawyer or a priest on the street is unlucky. We're only thought of in connection with disasters, and they'd rather not get too close.

I often think that behind that suspicious little nod of theirs lie three thousand years of distrust. A lawyer means the law, and in Sicily, from where their fathers came, the law has not been a friendly idea since the Greeks were beaten.

I am inclined to notice the ruins in things, perhaps because I was born in Italy. . . . I only came here when I was twenty-five. In those days, Al Capone, the greatest Carthaginian of all, was learning his trade on these pavements, and Frankie Yale himself was cut precisely in half by a machine gun on the corner of Union Street, two blocks away. Oh, there were many here who were justly shot by unjust men. Justice is very important here.

But this is Red Hook, not Sicily. This is the slum that faces the bay on the seaward side of Brooklyn Bridge. This is the gullet of New York swallowing the tonnage of the world. And now we are quite civilized, quite American. Now we settle for half, and I like it better. I no longer keep a pistol in my filing cabinet.

And my practice is entirely unromantic.

My wife has warned me, so have my friends; they tell me the people in this neighborhood lack elegance, glamour. After all, who have I dealt with in my life? Longshoremen and their wives, and fathers and grandfathers, compensation cases, evictions, family squabbles—the petty troubles of the poor—and yet . . . every few years there is still a case, and as the parties tell me what the trouble is, the flat air in my office suddenly washes in with the green scent of the sea, the dust in this air is blown away and the thought comes that in some Caesar's year, in Calabria perhaps or on the cliff at Syracuse, another lawyer, quite differently dressed, heard the same complaint and sat there as powerless as I, and watched it run its bloody course.

(EDDIE *has appeared and has been pitching coins with the men and is highlighted among them. He is forty—a husky, slightly overweight longshoreman.*)

This one's name was Eddie Carbone, a longshoreman working the docks from Brooklyn Bridge to the breakwater where the open sea begins.

(ALFIERI *walks into darkness.*)

EDDIE (*moving up steps into doorway*). Well, I'll see ya, fellas.

(CATHERINE *enters from kitchen, crosses down to window, looks out.*)

LOUIS. You workin' tomorrow?

EDDIE. Yeah, there's another day yet on that ship. See ya, Louis.

(EDDIE *goes into the house, as light rises in the apartment.* CATHERINE *is waving to* LOUIS *from the window and turns to him.*)

CATHERINE. Hi, Eddie!

(EDDIE *is pleased and therefore shy about it; he hangs up his cap and jacket.*)

EDDIE. Where you goin' all dressed up?

CATHERINE (*running her hands over her skirt*). I just got it. You like it?

EDDIE. Yeah, it's nice. And what happened to your hair?

CATHERINE. You like it? I fixed it different. (*Calling to kitchen.*) He's here, B.!

EDDIE. Beautiful. Turn around, lemme see in the back. (*She turns for him.*) Oh, if your mother was alive to see you now! She wouldn't believe it.

CATHERINE. You like it, huh?

EDDIE. You look like one of them girls that went to college. Where you goin'?

CATHERINE (*taking his arm*). Wait'll B. comes in, I'll tell you something. Here, sit down. (*She is walking him to the armchair. Calling offstage.*) Hurry up, will you, B.?

EDDIE (*sitting*). What's goin' on?

CATHERINE. I'll get you a beer, all right?

EDDIE. Well, tell me what happened. Come over here, talk to me.

CATHERINE. I want to wait till B. comes in. (*She sits on her heels beside him.*) Guess how much we paid for the skirt.

EDDIE. I think it's too short, ain't it?

CATHERINE (*standing*). No! not when I stand up.

EDDIE. Yeah, but you gotta sit down sometimes.

CATHERINE. Eddie, it's the style now. (*She walks to show him.*) I mean, if you see me walkin' down the street—

EDDIE. Listen, you been givin' me the willies the way you walk down the street, I mean it.

CATHERINE. Why?

EDDIE. Catherine, I don't want to be a pest, but I'm tellin' you you're walkin' wavy.

CATHERINE. I'm walkin' wavy?

EDDIE. Now don't aggravate me, Katie, you are walkin' wavy! I don't like the looks they're givin' you in the candy store. And with them new high heels on the sidewalk—clack, clack, clack. The heads are turnin' like windmills.

CATHERINE. But those guys look at all the girls, you know that.

EDDIE. You ain't "all the girls."

CATHERINE (*almost in tears because he disapproves*). What do you want me to do? You want me to—

EDDIE. Now don't get mad, kid.

CATHERINE. Well, I don't know what you want from me.

EDDIE. Katie, I promised your mother on her deathbed. I'm responsible for you. You're a baby, you don't understand these things. I mean like when you stand here

by the window, wavin' outside.

CATHERINE. I was wavin' to Louis!

EDDIE. Listen, I could tell you things about Louis which you wouldn't wave to him no more.

CATHERINE (*trying to joke him out of his warning*). Eddie, I wish there was one guy you couldn't tell me things about!

EDDIE. Catherine, do me a favor, will you? You're gettin' to be a big girl now, you gotta keep yourself more, you can't be so friendly, kid. (*Calls.*) Hey, B., what're you doin' in there? (*To* CATHERINE.) Get her in here, will you? I got news for her.

CATHERINE (*starting out*). What?

EDDIE. Her cousins landed.

CATHERINE (*clapping her hands together*). No! (*She turns instantly and starts for the kitchen.*) B.! Your cousins!

(BEATRICE *enters, wiping her hands with a towel.*)

BEATRICE (*in the face of* CATHERINE's *shout*). What?

CATHERINE. Your cousins got in!

BEATRICE (*astounded, turns to* EDDIE). What are you talkin' about? Where?

EDDIE. I was just knockin' off work before and Tony Bereli come over to me; he says the ship is in the North River.

BEATRICE (*her hands are clasped at her breast; she seems half in fear, half in unutterable joy*). They're all right?

EDDIE. He didn't see them yet, they're still on board. But as soon as they get off he'll meet them. He figures about ten o'clock they'll be here.

BEATRICE (*sits, almost weak from tension*). And they'll let them off the ship all right? That's fixed, heh?

EDDIE. Sure, they give them regular seamen papers and they walk off with the crew. Don't worry about it, B., there's nothin' to it. Couple of hours they'll be here.

BEATRICE. What happened? They wasn't supposed to be till next Thursday.

EDDIE. I don't know; they put them on any ship they can get them out on. Maybe the other ship they was supposed to take there was some danger— What you cryin' about?

BEATRICE (*astounded and afraid*). I'm— I just—I can't believe it! I didn't even buy a new table cloth; I was gonna wash the walls—

EDDIE. Listen, they'll think it's a millionaire's house compared to the way they live. Don't worry about the walls. They'll be thankful. (*To* CATHERINE.) Whyn't you run down buy a table cloth. Go ahead, here. (*He is reaching into his pocket.*)

CATHERINE. There's no stores open now.

EDDIE (*to* BEATRICE). You was gonna put a new cover on the chair.

BEATRICE. I know—well, I thought it was gonna be next week! I was gonna clean the walls, I was gonna wax the floors. (*She stands disturbed.*)

CATHERINE (*pointing upward*). Maybe Mrs. Dondero upstairs—

BEATRICE (*of the table cloth*). No, hers is worse than this one. (*Suddenly.*) My God, I don't even have nothin' to eat for them! (*She starts for the kitchen.*)

EDDIE (*reaching out and grabbing her arm*). Hey, hey! Take it easy.

BEATRICE. No, I'm just nervous, that's all. (*To* CATHERINE.) I'll make the fish.

EDDIE. You're savin' their lives, what're you worryin' about the table cloth? They probably didn't see a table cloth in their whole life where they come from.

BEATRICE (*looking into his eyes*). I'm just worried about you, that's all I'm worried.

EDDIE. Listen, as long as they know where they're gonna sleep.

BEATRICE. I told them in the letters. They're sleepin' on the floor.

EDDIE. Beatrice, all I'm worried about is you got such a heart that I'll end up on the floor with you, and they'll be in our bed.

BEATRICE. All right, stop it.

EDDIE. Because as soon as you see a tired relative, I end up on the floor.

BEATRICE. When did you end up on the floor?

EDDIE. When your father's house burned down I didn't end up on the floor?

BEATRICE. Well, their house burned down!

EDDIE. Yeah, but it didn't keep burnin' for two weeks!

BEATRICE. All right, look, I'll tell them to go someplace else. (*She starts into the kitchen.*)

EDDIE. Now wait a minute. Beatrice! (*She halts. He goes to her.*) I just don't want you bein' pushed around, that's all. You got too big a heart. (*He touches her hand.*) What're you so touchy?

BEATRICE. I'm just afraid if it don't turn out good you'll be mad at me.

EDDIE. Listen, if everybody keeps his mouth shut, nothin' can happen. They'll pay for their board.

BEATRICE. Oh, I told them.

EDDIE. Then what the hell. (*Pause. He moves.*) It's an honor, B. I mean it. I was just thinkin' before, comin' home, suppose my father didn't come to this country, and I was starvin' like them over there . . . and I had people in America could keep me a couple of months? The man would be honored to lend me a place to sleep.

BEATRICE (*there are tears in her eyes. She turns to* CATHERINE). You see what he is? (*She turns and grabs* EDDIE's *face in her hands.*) Mmm! You're an angel! God'll bless you. (*He is gratefully smiling.*) You'll see, you'll get a blessing for this!

EDDIE (*laughing*). I'll settle for my own bed.

BEATRICE. Go, Baby, set the table.

CATHERINE. We didn't tell him about me yet.

BEATRICE. Let him eat first, then we'll tell him. Bring everything in. (*She hurries* CATHERINE *out.*)

EDDIE (*sitting at the table*). What's all that about? Where's she goin'?

BEATRICE. Noplace. It's very good news, Eddie. I want you to be happy.

EDDIE. What's goin' on?

(CATHERINE *enters with plates, forks.*)

BEATRICE. She's got a job.

(*Pause.* EDDIE *looks at* CATHERINE, *then back to* BEATRICE.)

EDDIE. What job? She's gonna finish school.

CATHERINE. Eddie, you won't believe it—

EDDIE. No—no, you gonna finish school. What kinda job, what do you mean? All of a sudden you—

CATHERINE. Listen a minute, it's wonderful.

EDDIE. It's not wonderful. You'll never get nowheres unless you finish school. You can't take no job. Why didn't you ask me before you take a job?

BEATRICE. She's askin' you now, she didn't take nothin' yet.

CATHERINE. Listen a minute! I came to school this morning and the principal called me out of the class, see? To go to his office.

EDDIE. Yeah?

CATHERINE. So I went in and he says to me he's got my records, y'know? And there's a company wants a girl right away.

It ain't exactly a secretary, it's a stenographer first, but pretty soon you get to be secretary. And he says to me that I'm the best student in the whole class—

BEATRICE. You hear that?

EDDIE. Well why not? Sure she's the best.

CATHERINE. I'm the best student, he says, and if I want, I should take the job and the end of the year he'll let me take the examination and he'll give me the certificate. So I'll save practically a year!

EDDIE (*strangely nervous*). Where's the job? What company?

CATHERINE. It's a big plumbing company over Nostrand Avenue.

EDDIE. Nostrand Avenue and where?

CATHERINE. It's someplace by the Navy Yard.

BEATRICE. Fifty dollars a week, Eddie.

EDDIE (*to* CATHERINE, *surprised*). Fifty?

CATHERINE. I swear.

(*Pause.*)

EDDIE. What about all the stuff you wouldn't learn this year, though?

CATHERINE. There's nothin' more to learn, Eddie, I just gotta practice from now on. I know all the symbols and I know the keyboard. I'll just get faster, that's all. And when I'm workin' I'll keep gettin' better and better, you see?

BEATRICE. Work is the best practice anyway.

EDDIE. That ain't what I wanted, though.

CATHERINE. Why! It's a great big company—

EDDIE. I don't like that neighborhood over there.

CATHERINE. It's a block and half from the subway, he says.

EDDIE. Near the Navy Yard plenty can happen in a block and a half. And a plumbin' company! That's one step over the water front. They're practically longshoremen.

BEATRICE. Yeah, but she'll be in the office, Eddie.

EDDIE. I know she'll be in the office, but that ain't what I had in mind.

BEATRICE. Listen, she's gotta go to work sometime.

EDDIE. Listen, B., she'll be with a lotta plumbers? And sailors up and down the street? So what did she go to school for?

CATHERINE. But it's fifty a week, Eddie.

EDDIE. Look, did I ask you for money? I supported you this long I support you a little more. Please, do me a favor, will ya?

I want you to be with different kind of people. I want you to be in a nice office. Maybe a lawyer's office someplace in New York in one of them nice buildings. I mean if you're gonna get outa here then get out; don't go practically in the same kind of neighborhood.

(*Pause.* CATHERINE *lowers her eyes.*)

BEATRICE. Go, Baby, bring in the supper. (CATHERINE *goes out.*) Think about it a little bit, Eddie. Please. She's crazy to start work. It's not a little shop, it's a big company. Some day she could be a secretary. They picked her out of the whole class. (*He is silent, staring down at the table cloth, fingering the pattern.*) What are you worried about? She could take care of herself. She'll get out of the subway and be in the office in two minutes.

EDDIE (*somehow sickened*). I know that neighborhood, B., I don't like it.

BEATRICE. Listen, if nothin' happened to her in this neighborhood it ain't gonna happen noplace else. (*She turns his face to her.*) Look, you gotta get used to it, she's no baby no more. Tell her to take it. (*He turns his head away.*) You hear me? (*She is angering.*) I don't understand you; she's seventeen years old, you gonna keep her in the house all her life?

EDDIE (*insulted*). What kinda remark is that?

BEATRICE (*with sympathy but insistent force*). Well, I don't understand when it ends. First it was gonna be when she graduated high school, so she graduated high school. Then it was gonna be when she learned stenographer, so she learned stenographer. So what're we gonna wait for now? I mean it, Eddie, sometimes I don't understand you; they picked her out of the whole class, it's an honor for her.

(CATHERINE *enters with food, which she silently sets on the table. After a moment of watching her face,* EDDIE *breaks into a smile, but it almost seems that tears will form in his eyes.*)

EDDIE. With your hair that way you look like a madonna, you know that? You're the madonna type. (*She doesn't look at him, but continues ladling out food onto the plates.*) You wanna go to work, heh, Madonna?

CATHERINE (*softly*). Yeah.

EDDIE (*with a sense of her childhood, her babyhood, and the years*). All right, go to work. (*She looks at him, then rushes* and hugs him.) Hey, hey! Take it easy! (*He holds her face away from him to look at her.*) What're you cryin' about? (*He is affected by her, but smiles his emotion away.*)

CATHERINE (*sitting at her place*). I just— (*Bursting out.*) I'm gonna buy all new dishes with my first pay! (*They laugh warmly.*) I mean it. I'll fix up the whole house! I'll buy a rug!

EDDIE. And then you'll move away.

CATHERINE. No, Eddie!

EDDIE (*grinning*). Why not? That's life. And you'll come visit on Sundays, then once a month, then Christmas and New Year's, finally.

CATHERINE (*grasping his arm to reassure him and to erase the accusation*). No, please!

EDDIE (*smiling but hurt*). I only ask you one thing—don't trust nobody. You got a good aunt but she's got too big a heart, you learned bad from her. Believe me.

BEATRICE. Be the way you are, Katie, don't listen to him.

EDDIE (*to* BEATRICE—*strangely and quickly resentful*). You lived in a house all your life, what do you know about it? You never worked in your life.

BEATRICE. She likes people. What's wrong with that?

EDDIE. Because most people ain't people. She's goin' to work; plumbers; they'll chew her to pieces if she don't watch out. (*To* CATHERINE.) Believe me, Katie, the less you trust, the less you be sorry. (EDDIE *crosses himself and the women do the same, and they eat.*)

CATHERINE. First thing I'll buy is a rug, heh, B.?

BEATRICE. I don't mind. (*To* EDDIE.) I smelled coffee all day today. You unloadin' coffee today?

EDDIE. Yeah, a Brazil ship.

CATHERINE. I smelled it too. It smelled all over the neighborhood.

EDDIE. That's one time, boy, to be a longshoreman is a pleasure. I could work coffee ships twenty hours a day. You go down in the hold, y'know? It's like flowers, that smell. We'll bust a bag tomorrow, I'll bring you some.

BEATRICE. Just be sure there's no spiders in it, will ya? I mean it. (*She directs this to* CATHERINE, *rolling her eyes upward.*) I still remember that spider coming out of that bag he brung home. I nearly died.

EDDIE. You call that a spider? You oughta see what comes outa the bananas sometimes.

BEATRICE. Don't talk about it!

EDDIE. I seen spiders could stop a Buick.

BEATRICE (*clapping her hands over her ears*). All right, shut up!

EDDIE (*laughing and taking a watch out of his pocket*). Well, who started with spiders?

BEATRICE. All right, I'm sorry, I didn't mean it. Just don't bring none home again. What time is it?

EDDIE. Quarter nine. (*Puts watch back in his pocket. They continue eating in silence.*)

CATHERINE. He's bringin' them ten o'clock, Tony?

EDDIE. Around, yeah. (*He eats.*)

CATHERINE. Eddie, suppose somebody asks if they're livin' here. (*He looks at her as though already she had divulged something publicly. Defensively:*) I mean if they ask.

EDDIE. Now look, Baby, I can see we're gettin' mixed up again here.

CATHERINE. No, I just mean . . . people'll see them goin' in and out.

EDDIE. I don't care who sees them goin' in and out as long as you don't see them goin' in and out. And this goes for you too, B. You don't see nothin' and you don't know nothin'.

BEATRICE. What do you mean? I understand.

EDDIE. You don't understand; you still think you can talk about this to somebody just a little bit. Now lemme say it once and for all, because you're makin' me nervous again, both of you. I don't care if somebody comes in the house and sees them sleepin' on the floor, it never comes out of your mouth who they are or what they're doin' here.

BEATRICE. Yeah, but my mother'll know—

EDDIE. Sure she'll know, but just don't you be the one who told her, that's all. This is the United States government you're playin' with now, this is the Immigration Bureau. If you said it you knew it, if you didn't say it you didn't know it.

CATHERINE. Yeah, but Eddie, suppose somebody—

EDDIE. I don't care what question it is. You—don't—know—nothin'. They got stool pigeons all over this neighborhood they're payin' them every week for information, and you don't know who they are. It could be your best friend. You hear? (*To* BEATRICE.) Like Vinny Bolzano, remember Vinny?

BEATRICE. Oh, yeah. God forbid.

EDDIE. Tell her about Vinny. (*To* CATHERINE.) You think I'm blowin' steam here? (*To* BEATRICE.) Go ahead, tell her. (*To* CATHERINE.) You was a baby then. There was a family lived next door to her mother, he was about sixteen—

BEATRICE. No, he was no more than fourteen, cause I was to his confirmation in Saint Agnes. But the family had an uncle that they were hidin' in the house, and he snitched to the Immigration.

CATHERINE. The kid snitched?

EDDIE. On his own uncle!

CATHERINE. What, was he crazy?

EDDIE. He was crazy after, I tell you that, boy.

BEATRICE. Oh, it was terrible. He had five brothers and the old father. And they grabbed him in the kitchen and pulled him down the stairs—three flights his head was bouncin' like a coconut. And they spit on him in the street, his own father and his brothers. The whole neighborhood was cryin'.

CATHERINE. Ts! So what happened to him?

BEATRICE. I think he went away. (*To* EDDIE.) I never seen him again, did you?

EDDIE (*rises during this, taking out his watch*). Him? You'll never see him no more, a guy do a thing like that? How's he gonna show his face? (*To* CATHERINE, *as he gets up uneasily:*) Just remember, kid, you can quicker get back a million dollars that was stole than a word that you gave away. (*He is standing now, stretching his back.*)

CATHERINE. Okay, I won't say a word to nobody, I swear.

EDDIE. Gonna rain tomorrow. We'll be slidin' all over the decks. Maybe you oughta put something on for them, they be here soon.

BEATRICE. I only got fish, I hate to spoil it if they ate already. I'll wait, it only takes a few minutes; I could broil it.

CATHERINE. What happens, Eddie, when that ship pulls out and they ain't on it, though? Don't the captain say nothin'?

EDDIE (*slicing an apple with his pocket knife*). Captain's pieced off, what do you mean?

CATHERINE. Even the captain?

EDDIE. What's the matter, the captain don't have to live? Captain gets a piece, maybe one of the mates, piece for the guy in Italy who fixed the papers for them, Tony here'll get a little bite. . . .

BEATRICE. I just hope they get work here, that's all I hope.

EDDIE. Oh, the syndicate'll fix jobs for them; till they pay 'em off they'll get them work every day. It's after the pay-off, then they'll have to scramble like the rest of us.

BEATRICE. Well, it be better than they got there.

EDDIE. Oh sure, well, listen. So you gonna start Monday, heh, Madonna?

CATHERINE (*embarrassed*). I'm supposed to, yeah.

(EDDIE *is standing facing the two seated women. First* BEATRICE *smiles, then* CATHERINE, *for a powerful emotion is on him, a childish one and a knowing fear, and the tears show in his eyes—and they are shy before the avowal.*)

EDDIE (*sadly smiling, yet somehow proud of her*). Well . . . I hope you have good luck. I wish you the best. You know that, kid.

CATHERINE (*rising, trying to laugh*). You sound like I'm goin' a million miles!

EDDIE. I know. I guess I just never figured on one thing.

CATHERINE (*smiling*). What?

EDDIE. That you would ever grow up. (*He utters a soundless laugh at himself, feeling his breast pocket of his shirt.*) I left a cigar in my other coat, I think. (*He starts for the bedroom.*)

CATHERINE. Stay there! I'll get it for you.

(*She hurries out. There is a slight pause, and* EDDIE *turns to* BEATRICE, *who has been avoiding his gaze.*)

EDDIE. What are you mad at me lately?

BEATRICE. Who's mad? (*She gets up, clearing the dishes.*) I'm not mad. (*She picks up the dishes and turns to him.*) You're the one is mad. (*She turns and goes into the kitchen as* CATHERINE *enters from the bedroom with a cigar and a pack of matches.*)

CATHERINE. Here! I'll light it for you! (*She strikes a match and holds it to his cigar. He puffs. Quietly:*) Don't worry about me, Eddie, heh?

EDDIE. Don't burn yourself. (*Just in time she blows out the match.*) You better go in help her with the dishes.

CATHERINE (*turns quickly to the table, and, seeing the table cleared, she says, almost guiltily*). Oh! (*She hurries into the kitchen, and as she exits there.*) I'll do the dishes, B.!

(*Alone,* EDDIE *stands looking toward the kitchen for a moment. Then he takes out his watch, glances at it, replaces it in his pocket, sits in the armchair, and stares at the smoke flowing out of his mouth.*

(*The lights go down, then come up on* ALFIERI, *who has moved onto the forestage.*)

ALFIERI. He was as good a man as he had to be in a life that was hard and even. He worked on the piers when there was work, he brought home his pay, and he lived. And toward ten o'clock of that night, after they had eaten, the cousins came.

(*The lights fade on* ALFIERI *and rise on the street.*

(*Enter* TONY, *escorting* MARCO *and* RODOLPHO, *each with a valise.* TONY *halts, indicates the house. They stand for a moment looking at it.*)

MARCO (*he is a square-built peasant of thirty-two, suspicious, tender, and quiet-voiced*). Thank you.

TONY. You're on your own now. Just be careful, that's all. Ground floor.

MARCO. Thank you.

TONY (*indicating the house*). I'll see you on the pier tomorrow. You'll go to work.

(MARCO *nods.* TONY *continues on walking down the street.*)

RODOLPHO. This will be the first house I ever walked into in America! Imagine! She said they were poor!

MARCO. Ssh! Come. (*They go to door.*)

(MARCO *knocks. The lights rise in the room.* EDDIE *goes and opens the door. Enter* MARCO *and* RODOLPHO, *removing their caps.* BEATRICE *and* CATHERINE *enter from the kitchen. The lights fade in the street.*)

EDDIE. You Marco?

MARCO. Marco.

EDDIE. Come on in! (*He shakes* MARCO'S *hand.*)

BEATRICE. Here, take the bags!

MARCO (*nods, looks to the women and fixes on* BEATRICE. *Crosses to* BEATRICE.) Are you my cousin?

(*She nods. He kisses her hand.*)

BEATRICE (*above the table, touching her chest with her hand*). Beatrice. This is my husband, Eddie. (*All nod.*) Catherine, my

sister Nancy's daughter. (*The brothers nod.*)

MARCO (*indicating* RODOLPHO). My brother. Rodolpho. (RODOLPHO *nods.* MARCO *comes with a certain formal stiffness to* EDDIE.) I want to tell you now Eddie—when you say go, we will go.

EDDIE. Oh, no . . . (*Takes* MARCO'S *bag.*)

MARCO. I see it's a small house, but soon, maybe, we can have our own house.

EDDIE. You're welcome, Marco, we got plenty of room here. Katie, give them supper, heh? (*Exits into bedroom with their bags.*)

CATHERINE. Come here, sit down. I'll get you some soup.

MARCO (*as they go to the table*). We ate on the ship. Thank you. (*To* EDDIE, *calling off to bedroom:*) Thank you.

BEATRICE. Get some coffee. We'll all have coffee. Come sit down. (RODOLPHO *and* MARCO *sit, at the table.*)

CATHERINE (*wondrously*). How come he's so dark and you're so light, Rodolpho?

RODOLPHO (*ready to laugh*). I don't know. A thousand years ago, they say, the Danes invaded Sicily.

(BEATRICE *kisses* RODOLPHO. *They laugh as* EDDIE *enters.*)

CATHERINE (*to* BEATRICE). He's practically blond!

EDDIE. How's the coffee doin'?

CATHERINE (*brought up*). I'm gettin' it. (*She hurries out to kitchen.*)

EDDIE (*sits on his rocker*). Yiz have a nice trip?

MARCO. The ocean is always rough. But we are good sailors.

EDDIE. No trouble gettin' here?

MARCO. No. The man brought us. Very nice man.

RODOLPHO (*to* EDDIE). He says we start to work tomorrow. Is he honest?

EDDIE (*laughing*). No. But as long as you owe them money, they'll get you plenty of work. (*To* MARCO.) Yiz ever work on the piers in Italy?

MARCO. Piers? Ts!—no.

RODOLPHO (*smiling at the smallness of his town*). In our town there are no piers, only the beach, and little fishing boats.

BEATRICE. So what kinda work did yiz do?

MARCO (*shrugging shyly, even embarrassed*). Whatever there is, anything.

RODOLPHO. Sometimes they build a house, or if they fix the bridge—Marco is a mason and I bring him the cement. (*He laughs.*) In harvest time we work in the fields . . . if there is work. Anything.

EDDIE. Still bad there, heh?

MARCO. Bad, yes.

RODOLPHO (*laughing*). It's terrible! We stand around all day in the piazza listening to the fountain like birds. Everybody waits only for the train.

BEATRICE. What's on the train?

RODOLPHO. Nothing. But if there are many passengers and you're lucky you make a few lire to push the taxi up the hill.

(*Enter* CATHERINE; *she listens.*)

BEATRICE. You gotta push a taxi?

RODOLPHO (*laughing*). Oh, sure! It's a feature in our town. The horses in our town are skinnier than goats. So if there are too many passengers we help to push the carriages up to the hotel. (*He laughs.*) In our town the horses are only for show.

CATHERINE. Why don't they have automobile taxis?

RODOLPHO. There is one. We push that too. (*They laugh.*) Everything in our town, you gotta push!

BEATRICE (*to* EDDIE). How do you like that!

EDDIE (*to* MARCO). So what're you wanna do, you gonna stay here in this country or you wanna go back?

MARCO (*surprised*). Go back?

EDDIE. Well, you're married, ain't you?

MARCO. Yes. I have three children.

BEATRICE. Three! I thought only one.

MARCO. Oh, no. I have three now. Four years, five years, six years.

BEATRICE. Ah . . . I bet they're cryin' for you already, heh?

MARCO. What can I do? The older one is sick in his chest. My wife—she feeds them from her own mouth. I tell you the truth, if I stay there they will never grow up. They eat the sunshine.

BEATRICE. My God. So how long you want to stay?

MARCO. With your permission, we will stay maybe a—

EDDIE. She don't mean in this house, she means in the country.

MARCO. Oh. Maybe four, five, six years, I think.

RODOLPHO (*smiling*). He trusts his wife.

BEATRICE. Yeah, but maybe you'll get enough, you'll be able to go back quicker.

MARCO. I hope. I don't know. (*To* EDDIE:) I understand it's not so good here either.

EDDIE. Oh, you guys'll be all right—till you pay them off, anyway. After that, you'll have to scramble, that's all. But you'll make better here than you could there.

RODOLPHO. How much? We hear all kinds of figures. How much can a man make? We work hard, we'll work all day, all night—

(MARCO *raises a hand to hush him.*)

EDDIE (*he is coming more and more to address* MARCO *only*). On the average a whole year? Maybe—well, it's hard to say, see. Sometimes we lay off, there's no ships three four weeks.

MARCO. Three, four weeks!—Ts!

EDDIE. But I think you could probably—thiry, forty a week, over the whole twelve months of the year.

MARCO (*rises, crosses to* EDDIE). Dollars.

EDDIE. Sure dollars.

(MARCO *puts an arm round* RODOLPHO *and they laugh.*)

MARCO. If we can stay here a few months, Beatrice—

BEATRICE. Listen, you're welcome, Marco—

MARCO. Because I could send them a little more if I stay here.

BEATRICE. As long as you want, we got plenty a room.

MARCO (*his eyes are showing tears*). My wife—(*To* EDDIE:) My wife—I want to send right away maybe twenty dollars—

EDDIE. You could send them something next week already.

MARCO (*he is near tears*). Eduardo . . . (*He goes to* EDDIE, *offering his hand.*)

EDDIE. Don't thank me. Listen, what the hell, it's no skin off me. (*To* CATHERINE:) What happened to the coffee?

CATHERINE. I got it on. (*To* RODOLPHO:) You married too? No.

RODOLPHO (*rises*). Oh, no . . .

BEATRICE (*to* CATHERINE). I told you he—

CATHERINE. I know, I just thought maybe he got married recently.

RODOLPHO. I have no money to get married. I have a nice face, but no money. (*He laughs.*)

CATHERINE (*to* BEATRICE). He's a real blond!

BEATRICE (*to* RODOLPHO). You want to stay here too, heh? For good?

RODOLPHO. Me? Yes, forever! Me, I want

to be an American. And then I want to go back to Italy when I am rich, and I will buy a motorcycle. (*He smiles.* MARCO *shakes him affectionately.*)

CATHERINE. A motorcycle!

RODOLPHO. With a motorcycle in Italy you will never starve any more.

BEATRICE. I'll get you coffee. (*She exits to the kitchen.*)

EDDIE. What you do with a motorcycle?

MARCO. He dreams, he dreams.

RODOLPHO (*to* MARCO). Why? (*To* EDDIE:) *Messages!* The rich people in the hotel always need someone who will carry a message. But quickly, and with a great noise. With a blue motorcycle I would station myself in the courtyard of the hotel, and in a little while I would have messages.

MARCO. When you have no wife you have dreams.

EDDIE. Why can't you just walk, or take a trolley or sump'm?

(*Enter* BEATRICE *with coffee.*)

RODOLPHO. Oh, no, the machine, the machine is necessary. A man comes into a great hotel and says, I am a messenger. Who is this man? He disappears walking, there is no noise, nothing. Maybe he will never come back, maybe he will never deliver the message. But a man who rides up on a great machine, this man is responsible, this man exists. He will be given messages. (*He helps* BEATRICE *set out the coffee things.*) I am also a singer, though.

EDDIE. You mean a regular—?

RODOLPHO. Oh, yes. One night last year Andreola got sick. Baritone. And I took his place in the garden of the hotel. Three arias I sang without a mistake! Thousand-lire notes they threw from the tables, money was falling like a storm in the treasury. It was magnificent. We lived six months on that night, eh, Marco?

(MARCO *nods doubtfully.*)

MARCO. Two months.

(EDDIE *laughs.*)

BEATRICE. Can't you get a job in that place?

RODOLPHO. Andreola got better. He's a baritone, very strong.

(BEATRICE *laughs.*)

MARCO (*regretfully, to* BEATRICE). He sang too loud.

RODOLPHO. Why too loud?

MARCO. Too loud. The guests in that hotel are all Englishmen. They don't like too loud.

RODOLPHO (*to* CATHERINE). Nobody ever said it was too loud!

MARCO. I say. It was too loud. (*To* BEATRICE:) I knew it as soon as he started to sing. Too loud.

RODOLPHO. Then why did they throw so much money?

MARCO. They paid for your courage. The English like courage. But once is enough.

RODOLPHO (*to all but* MARCO). I never heard anybody say it was too loud.

CATHERINE. Did you ever hear of jazz?

RODOLPHO. Oh, sure! I *sing* jazz.

CATHERINE (*rises*). You could sing jazz?

RODOLPHO. Oh, I sing Napolidan, jazz, bel canto— I sing "Paper Doll," you like "Paper Doll"?

CATHERINE. Oh, sure, I'm crazy for "Paper Doll." Go ahead, sing it.

RODOLPHO (*takes his stance after getting a nod of permission from* MARCO, *and with a high tenor voice begins singing.*)

"I'll tell you boys it's tough to be alone, And it's tough to love a doll that's not your own.

I'm through with all of them, I'll never fall again, Hey, boy, what you gonna do? I'm gonna buy a paper doll that I can call my own, A doll that other fellows cannot steal. (EDDIE *rises and moves upstage.*) And then those flirty, flirty guys With their flirty, flirty eyes Will have to flirt with dollies that are real—

EDDIE. Hey, kid—hey, wait a minute—

CATHERINE (*enthralled*). Leave him finish, it's beautiful! (*To* BEATRICE:) He's terrific! It's terrific, Rodolpho.

EDDIE. Look, kid; you don't want to be picked up, do ya?

MARCO. No—no! (*He rises.*)

EDDIE (*indicating the rest of the building*). Because we never had no singers here . . . and all of a sudden there's a singer in the house, y'know what I mean?

MARCO. Yes, yes. You'll be quiet, Rodolpho.

EDDIE (*he is flushed*). They got guys all over the place, Marco. I mean.

MARCO. Yes. He'll be quiet. (*To* RODOLPHO:) You'll be quiet.

(RODOLPHO *nods.* EDDIE *has risen, with iron control, even a smile. He moves to* CATHERINE.)

EDDIE. What's the high heels for, Garbo?

CATHERINE. I figured for tonight—

EDDIE. Do me a favor, will you? Go ahead.

(*Embarrassed now, angered,* CATHERINE *goes out into the bedroom.* BEATRICE *watches her go and gets up; in passing, she gives* EDDIE *a cold look, restrained only by the strangers, and goes to the table to pour coffee.*)

EDDIE (*striving to laugh, and to* MARCO, *but directed as much to* BEATRICE). All actresses they want to be around here.

RODOLPHO (*happy about it*). In Italy too! All the girls.

(CATHERINE *emerges from the bedroom in low-heel shoes, comes to the table.* RODOLPHO *is lifting a cup.*)

EDDIE (*he is sizing up* RODOLPHO, *and there is a concealed suspicion*). Yeah, heh?

RODOLPHO. Yes! (*Laughs, indicating* CATHERINE). Especially when they are so beautiful!

CATHERINE. You like sugar?

RODOLPHO. Sugar? Yes! I like sugar very much!

(EDDIE *is downstage, watching as she pours a spoonful of sugar into his cup, his face puffed with trouble, and the room dies.*)

(*Lights rise on* ALFIERI.)

ALFIERI. Who can ever know what will be discovered? Eddie Carbone had never expected to have a destiny. A man works, raises his family, goes bowling, eats, gets old, and then he dies. Now, as the weeks passed, there was a future, there was a trouble that would not go away.

(*The lights fade on* ALFIERI, *then rise on* EDDIE *standing at the doorway of the house.* BEATRICE *enters on the street. She sees* EDDIE, *smiles at him. He looks away. She starts to enter the house when* EDDIE *speaks.*)

EDDIE. It's after eight.

BEATRICE. Well, it's a long show at the Paramount.

EDDIE. They must've seen every picture in Brooklyn by now. He's supposed to stay in the house when he ain't working. He ain't supposed to go advertising himself.

BEATRICE. Well that's his trouble, what do you care? If they pick him up they pick him up, that's all. Come in the house.

EDDIE. What happened to the stenography? I don't see her practice no more.

BEATRICE. She'll get back to it. She's excited, Eddie.

EDDIE. She tell you anything?

BEATRICE (*comes to him, now the subject is opened*). What's the matter with you? He's a nice kid, what do you want from him?

EDDIE. That's a nice kid? He gives me the heeby-jeebies.

BEATRICE (*smiling*). Ah, go on, you're just jealous.

EDDIE. Of *him*? Boy, you don't think much of me.

BEATRICE. I don't understand you. What's so terrible about him?

EDDIE. You mean it's all right with you? That's gonna be her husband?

BEATRICE. Why? He's a nice fella, hard workin', he's a good-lookin' fella.

EDDIE. He sings on the ships, didja know that?

BEATRICE. What do you mean, he sings?

EDDIE. Just what I said, he sings. Right on the deck, all of a sudden, a whole song comes out of his mouth—with motions. You know what they're callin' him now? Paper Doll they're callin' him, Canary. He's like a weird. He comes out on the pier, one-two-three, it's a regular free show.

BEATRICE. Well, he's a kid; he don't know how to behave himself yet.

EDDIE. And with that wacky hair; he's like a chorus girl or sump'm.

BEATRICE. So he's blond, so—

EDDIE. I just hope that's his regular hair, that's all I hope.

BEATRICE. You crazy or sump'm? (*She tries to turn him to her.*)

EDDIE (*he keeps his head turned away*). What's so crazy? I don't like his whole way.

BEATRICE. Listen, you never seen a blond guy in your life? What about Whitey Balso?

EDDIE (*turning to her victoriously*). Sure, but Whitey don't sing; he don't do like that on the ships.

BEATRICE. Well, maybe that's the way they do in Italy.

EDDIE. Then why don't his brother sing? Marco goes around like a man; nobody kids Marco. (*He moves from her, halts. She realizes there is a campaign solidified in him.*) I tell you the truth I'm surprised I have to tell you all this. I mean I'm surprised, B.

BEATRICE (*she goes to him with purpose*

now). Listen, you ain't gonna start nothin' here.

EDDIE. I ain't startin' nothin', but I ain't gonna stand around lookin' at that. For that character I didn't bring her up. I swear, B., I'm surprised at you; I sit there waitin' for you to wake up but everything is great with you.

BEATRICE. No, everything ain't great with me.

EDDIE. No?

BEATRICE. No. But I got other worries.

EDDIE. Yeah. (*He is already weakening.*)

BEATRICE. Yeah, you want me to tell you?

EDDIE (*in retreat*). Why? What worries you got?

BEATRICE. When am I gonna be a wife again, Eddie?

EDDIE. I ain't been feelin' good. They bother me since they came.

BEATRICE. It's almost three months you don't feel good; they're only here a couple of weeks. It's three months, Eddie.

EDDIE. I don't know, B. I don't want to talk about it.

BEATRICE. What's the matter, Eddie, you don't like me, heh?

EDDIE. What do you mean, I don't like you? I said I don't feel good, that's all.

BEATRICE. Well, tell me, am I doing something wrong? Talk to me.

EDDIE (*Pause. He can't speak, then*). I can't. I can't talk about it.

BEATRICE. Well tell me what—

EDDIE. I got nothin' to say about it!

(*She stands for a moment; he is looking off; she turns to go into the house.*)

EDDIE. I'll be all right, B.; just lay off me, will ya? I'm worried about her.

BEATRICE. The girl is gonna be eighteen years old, it's time already.

EDDIE. B., he's taking her for a ride!

BEATRICE. All right, that's her ride. What're you gonna stand over her till she's forty? Eddie, I want you to cut it out now, you hear me? I don't like it! Now come in the house.

EDDIE. I want to take a walk, I'll be in right away.

BEATRICE. They ain't goin' to come any quicker if you stand in the street. It ain't nice, Eddie.

EDDIE. I'll be in right away. Go ahead. (*He walks off.*)

(*She goes into the house.* EDDIE *glances up the street, sees* LOUIS *and* MIKE *coming, and sits on an iron railing.* LOUIS *and* MIKE *enter.*)

LOUIS. Wanna go bowlin' tonight?

EDDIE. I'm too tired. Goin' to sleep.

LOUIS. How's your two submarines?

EDDIE. They're okay.

LOUIS. I see they're gettin' work allatime.

EDDIE. Oh yeah, they're doin' all right.

MIKE. That's what we oughta do. We oughta leave the country and come in under the water. Then we get work.

EDDIE. You ain't kiddin'.

LOUIS. Well, what the hell. Y'know?

EDDIE. Sure.

LOUIS (*sits on railing beside* EDDIE). Believe me, Eddie, you got a lotta credit comin' to you.

EDDIE. Aah, they don't bother me, don't cost me nutt'n.

MIKE. That older one, boy, he's a regular bull. I seen him the other day liftin' coffee bags over the Matson Line. They leave him alone he woulda load the whole ship by himself.

EDDIE. Yeah, he's a strong guy, that guy. Their father was a regular giant, supposed to be.

LOUIS. Yeah, you could see. He's a regular slave.

MIKE (*grinning*). That blond one, though—(EDDIE *looks at him.*) He's got a sense of humor. (LOUIS *snickers.*)

EDDIE (*searchingly*). Yeah. He's funny—

MIKE (*starting to laugh*). Well he ain't exackly funny, but he's always like makin' remarks like, y'know? He comes around, everybody's laughin'. (LOUIS *laughs.*)

EDDIE (*uncomfortably, grinning*). Yeah, well . . . he's got a sense of humor.

MIKE (*laughing*). Yeah, I mean, he's always makin' like remarks, like, y'know?

EDDIE. Yeah, I know. But he's a kid yet, y'know? He—he's just a kid, that's all.

MIKE (*getting hysterical with* LOUIS). I know. You take one look at him—everybody's happy. (LOUIS *laughs.*) I worked one day with him last week over the Moore-MacCormack Line, I'm tellin' you they was all hysterical. (LOUIS *and he explode in laughter.*)

EDDIE. Why? What'd he do?

MIKE. I don't know . . . he was just humorous. You never can remember what he says, y'know? But it's the way he says it. I mean he gives you a look sometimes and you start laughin'!

EDDIE. Yeah. (*Troubled:*) He's got a

sense of humor.

MIKE (*gasping*). Yeah.

LOUIS (*rising*). Well, we see ya, Eddie.

EDDIE. Take it easy.

LOUIS. Yeah. See ya.

MIKE. If you wanna come bowlin' later we're goin' Flatbush Avenue.

(*Laughing, they move to exit, meeting* RODOLPHO *and* CATHERINE *entering on the street. Their laughter rises as they see* RODOLPHO, *who does not understand but joins in.* EDDIE *moves to enter the house as* LOUIS *and* MIKE *exit.* CATHERINE *stops him at the door.*)

CATHERINE. Hey, Eddie—what a picture we saw! Did we laugh!

EDDIE (*he can't help smiling at sight of her*). Where'd you go?

CATHERINE. Paramount. It was with those two guys, y'know? That—

EDDIE. Brooklyn Paramount?

CATHERINE (*with an edge of anger, embarrassed before* RODOLPHO). Sure, the Brooklyn Paramount. I told you we wasn't goin' to New York.

EDDIE (*retreating before the threat of her anger*). All right, I only asked you. (*To* RODOLPHO.) I just don't want her hangin' around Times Square, see? It's full of tramps over there.

RODOLPHO. I would like to go to Broadway once, Eddie. I would like to walk with her once where the theaters are and the opera. Since I was a boy I see pictures of those lights.

EDDIE (*his little patience waning*). I want to talk to her a minute, Rodolpho. Go inside, will you?

RODOLPHO. Eddie, we only walk together in the streets. She teaches me.

CATHERINE. You know what he can't get over? That there's no fountains in Brooklyn!

EDDIE (*smiling unwillingly*). Fountains? (RODOLPHO *smiles at his own naïveté.*)

CATHERINE. In Italy he says, every town's got fountains, and they meet there. And you know what? They got oranges on the trees where he comes from, and lemons. Imagine—on the trees? I mean it's interesting. But he's crazy for New York.

RODOLPHO (*attempting familiarity*). Eddie, why can't we go once to Broadway—?

EDDIE. Look, I gotta tell her something—

RODOLPHO. Maybe you can come too. I want to see all those lights. (*He sees no response in* EDDIE's *face. He glances at*

CATHERINE.) I'll walk by the river before I go to sleep. (*He walks off down the street.*)

CATHERINE. Why don't you talk to him, Eddie? He blesses you, and you don't talk to him hardly.

EDDIE (*enveloping her with his eyes*). I bless you and you don't talk to me. (*He tries to smile.*)

CATHERINE. *I* don't talk to you? (*She hits his arm.*) What do you mean?

EDDIE. I don't see you no more. I come home you're runnin' around someplace—

CATHERINE. Well, he wants to see everything, that's all, so we go. . . . You mad at me?

EDDIE. No. (*He moves from her, smiling sadly.*) It's just I used to come home, you was always there. Now, I turn around, you're a big girl. I don't know how to talk to you.

CATHERINE. Why?

EDDIE. I don't know, you're runnin', you're runnin', Katie. I don't think you listening any more to me.

CATHERINE (*going to him*). Ah, Eddie, sure I am. What's the matter? You don't like him?

(*Slight pause.*)

EDDIE (*turns to her*). You like him, Katie?

CATHERINE (*with a blush but holding her ground*). Yeah. I like him.

EDDIE (*his smile goes*). You like him.

CATHERINE (*looking down*). Yeah. (*Now she looks at him for the consequences, smiling but tense. He looks at her like a lost boy.*) What're you got against him? I don't understand. He only blesses you.

EDDIE (*turns away*). He don't bless me, Katie.

CATHERINE. He does! You're like a father to him!

EDDIE (*turns to her*). Katie.

CATHERINE. What, Eddie?

EDDIE. You gonna marry him?

CATHERINE. I don't know. We just been . . . goin' around, that's all. (*Turns to him.*) What're you got against him, Eddie? Please, tell me. What?

EDDIE. He don't respect you.

CATHERINE. Why?

EDDIE. Katie . . . if you wasn't an orphan, wouldn't he ask your father's permission before he run around with you like this?

CATHERINE. Oh, well, he didn't think

you'd mind.

EDDIE. He knows I mind, but it don't bother him if I mind, don't you see that?

CATHERINE. No, Eddie, he's got all kinds of respect for me. And you too! We walk across the street he takes my arm—he almost bows to me! You got him all wrong, Eddie; I mean it, you—

EDDIE. Katie, he's only bowin' to his passport.

CATHERINE. His passport!

EDDIE. That's right. He marries you he's got the right to be an American citizen. That's what's goin' on here. (*She is puzzled and surprised.*) You understand what I'm tellin' you? The guy is lookin' for his break, that's all he's lookin' for.

CATHERINE (*pained*). Oh, no, Eddie, I don't think so.

EDDIE. You don't think so! Katie, you're gonna make me cry here. Is that a workin' man? What does he do with his first money? A snappy new jacket he buys, records, a pointy pair new shoes and his brother's kids are starvin' over there with tuberculosis? That's a hit-and-run guy, baby; he's got bright lights in his head, Broadway. Them guys don't think of nobody but theirself! You marry him and the next time you see him it'll be for divorce!

CATHERINE (*steps toward him*). Eddie, he never said a word about his papers or—

EDDIE. You mean he's supposed to tell you that?

CATHERINE. I don't think he's even thinking about it.

EDDIE. What's better for him to think about! He could be picked up any day here and he's back pushin' taxis up the hill!

CATHERINE. No, I don't believe it.

EDDIE. Katie, don't break my heart, listen to me.

CATHERINE. I don't want to hear it.

EDDIE. Katie, listen . . .

CATHERINE. He loves me!

EDDIE (*with deep alarm*). Don't say that, for God's sake! This is the oldest racket in the country—

CATHERINE (*desperately, as though he had made his imprint*). I don't believe it! (*She rushes to the house.*)

EDDIE (*following her*). They been pullin' this since the Immigration Law was put in! They grab a green kid that don't know nothin' and they—

CATHERINE (*sobbing*). I don't believe it and I wish to hell you'd stop it!

EDDIE. Katie!

(*They enter the apartment. The lights in the living room have risen and* BEATRICE *is there. She looks past the sobbing* CATHERINE *at* EDDIE, *who in the presence of his wife, makes an awkward gesture of eroded command, indicating* CATHERINE.)

EDDIE. Why don't you straighten her out?

BEATRICE (*inwardly angered at his flowing emotion, which in itself alarms her*). When are you going to leave her alone?

EDDIE. B., the guy is no good!

BEATRICE (*suddenly, with open fright and fury*). You going to leave her alone? Or you gonna drive me crazy? (*He turns, striving to retain his dignity, but nevertheless in guilt walks out of the house, into the street and away.* CATHERINE *starts into a bedroom.*) Listen, Catherine. (CATHERINE *halts, turns to her sheepishly.*) What are you going to do with yourself?

CATHERINE. I don't know.

BEATRICE. Don't tell me you don't know; you're not a baby any more, what are you going to do with yourself?

CATHERINE. He won't listen to me.

BEATRICE. I don't understand this. He's not your father, Catherine. I don't understand what's going on here.

CATHERINE (*as one who herself is trying to rationalize a buried impulse*). What am I going to do, just kick him in the face with it?

BEATRICE. Look, honey, you wanna get married, or don't you wanna get married? What are you worried about, Katie?

CATHERINE (*quietly, trembling*). I don't know B. It just seems wrong if he's against it so much.

BEATRICE (*never losing her aroused alarm*). Sit down, honey, I want to tell you something. Here, sit down. Was there ever any fella he liked for you? There wasn't, was there?

CATHERINE. But he says Rodolpho's just after his papers.

BEATRICE. Look, he'll say anything. What does he care what he says? If it was a prince came here for you it would be no different. You know that, don't you?

CATHERINE. Yeah, I guess.

BEATRICE. So what does that mean?

CATHERINE (*slowly turns her head to* BEATRICE). What?

BEATRICE. It means you gotta be your own self more. You still think you're a little girl, honey. But nobody else can make up your mind for you any more, you understand? You gotta give him to understand that he can't give you orders no more.

CATHERINE. Yeah, but how am I going to do that? He thinks I'm a baby.

BEATRICE. Because *you* think you're a baby. I told you fifty times already, you can't act the way you act. You still walk around in front of him in your slip—

CATHERINE. Well I forgot.

BEATRICE. Well you can't do it. Or like you sit on the edge of the bathtub talkin' to him when he's shavin' in his underwear.

CATHERINE. When'd I do that?

BEATRICE. I seen you in there this morning.

CATHERINE. Oh . . . well, I wanted to tell him something and I—

BEATRICE. I know, honey. But if you act like a baby and he be treatin' you like a baby. Like when he comes home sometimes you throw yourself at him like when you was twelve years old.

CATHERINE. Well I like to see him and I'm happy so I—

BEATRICE. Look, I'm not tellin' you what to do honey, but—

CATHERINE. No, you could tell me, B.! Gee, I'm all mixed up. See, I— He looks so sad now and it hurts me.

BEATRICE. Well look Katie, if it's goin' to hurt you so much you're gonna end up an old maid here.

CATHERINE. No!

BEATRICE. I'm tellin' you, I'm not makin' a joke. I tried to tell you a couple of times in the last year or so. That's why I was so happy you were going to go out and get work, you wouldn't be here so much, you'd be a little more independent. I mean it. It's wonderful for a whole family to love each other, but you're a grown woman and you're in the same house with a grown man. So you'll act different now, heh?

CATHERINE. Yeah, I will. I'll remember.

BEATRICE. Because it ain't only up to him, Katie, you understand? I told him the same thing already.

CATHERINE (*quickly*). What?

BEATRICE. That he should let you go. But, you see, if only I tell him, he thinks I'm just bawlin' him out, or maybe I'm jealous or somethin', you know?

CATHERINE (*astonished*). He said you was jealous?

BEATRICE. No, I'm just sayin' maybe that's what he thinks. (*She reaches over to* CATHERINE's *hand; with a strained smile.*) You think I'm jealous of you, honey?

CATHERINE. No! It's the first I thought of it.

BEATRICE (*with a quiet sad laugh*). Well you should have thought of it before . . . but I'm not. We'll be all right. Just give him to understand; you don't have to fight, you're just— You're a woman, that's all, and you got a nice boy, and now the time came when you said good-by. All right?

CATHERINE (*strangely moved at the prospect*). All right. . . . If I can.

BEATRICE. Honey . . . you gotta.

(CATHERINE, *sensing now an imperious demand, turns with some fear, with a discovery, to* BEATRICE. *She is at the edge of tears, as though a familiar world had shattered.*)

CATHERINE. Okay.

(*Lights out on them and up on* ALFIERI, *seated behind his desk.*)

ALFIERI. It was at this time that he first came to me. I had represented his father in an accident case some years before, and I was acquainted with the family in a casual way. I remember him now as he walked through my doorway— (*Enter* EDDIE *down right ramp.*) His eyes were like tunnels; my first thought was that he had committed a crime, (EDDIE *sits beside the desk, cap in hand, looking out.*) but soon I saw it was only a passion that had moved into his body, like a stranger. (ALFIERI *pauses, looks down at his desk, then to* EDDIE *as though he were continuing a conversation with him.*) I don't quite understand what I can do for you. Is there a question of law somewhere?

EDDIE. That's what I want to ask you.

ALFIERI. Because there's nothing illegal about a girl falling in love with an immigrant.

EDDIE. Yeah, but what about it if the only reason for it is to get his papers?

ALFIERI. First of all you don't know that.

EDDIE. I see it in his eyes; he's laughin' at her and he's laughin' at me.

ALFIERI. Eddie, I'm a lawyer. I can only deal in what's provable. You understand that, don't you? Can you prove that?

EDDIE. *I know what's in his mind, Mr.*

Alfieri!

ALFIERI. Eddie, even if you could prove that—

EDDIE. Listen . . . will you listen to me a minute? My father always said you was a smart man. I want you to listen to me.

ALFIERI. I'm only a lawyer, Eddie.

EDDIE. Will you listen a minute? I'm talkin' about the law. Lemme just bring out what I mean. A man, which he comes into the country illegal, don't it stand to reason he's gonna take every penny and put it in the sock? Because they don't know from one day to another, right?

ALFIERI. All right.

EDDIE. He's spendin'. Records he buys now. Shoes. Jackets. Y'understand me? This guy ain't worried. This guy is *here*. So it must be that he's got it all laid out in his mind already—he's stayin'. Right?

ALFIERI. Well? What about it?

EDDIE. All right. (*He glances at* ALFIERI, *then down to the floor.*) I'm talking to you confidential, ain't I?

ALFIERI. Certainly.

EDDIE. I mean it don't go no place but here. Because I don't like to say this about anybody. Even my wife I didn't exactly say this.

ALFIERI. What is it?

EDDIE (*takes a breath and glances briefly over each shoulder*). The guy ain't right, Mr. Alfieri.

ALFIERI. What do you mean?

EDDIE. I mean he ain't right.

ALFIERI. I don't get you.

EDDIE (*shifts to another position in the chair*). Dja ever get a look at him?

ALFIERI. Not that I know of, no.

EDDIE. He's a blond guy. Like . . . platinum. You know what I mean?

ALFIERI. No.

EDDIE. I mean if you close the paper fast —you could blow him over.

ALFIERI. Well that doesn't mean—

EDDIE. Wait a minute, I'm tellin' you sump'm. He sings, see. Which is—I mean it's all right, but sometimes he hits a note, see. I turn around. I mean—high. You know what I mean?

ALFIERI. Well, that's a tenor.

EDDIE. I know a tenor, Mr. Alfieri. This ain't no tenor. I mean if you came in the house and you didn't know who was singin', you wouldn't be lookin' for him you be lookin' for her.

ALFIERI. Yes, but that's not—

EDDIE. I'm tellin' you sump'm, wait a minute. Please, Mr. Alfieri. I'm tryin' to bring out my thoughts here. Couple of nights ago my niece brings out a dress which it's too small for her, because she shot up like a light this last year. He takes the dress, lays it on the table, he cuts it up; one-two-three, he makes a new dress. I mean he looked so sweet there, like an angel—you could kiss him he was so sweet.

ALFIERI. Now look, Eddie—

EDDIE. Mr. Alfieri, they're laughin' at him on the piers. I'm ashamed. Paper Doll they call him. Blondie now. His brother thinks it's because he's got a sense of humor, see—which he's got—but that ain't what they're laughin'. Which they're not goin' to come out with it because they know he's my relative, which they have to see me if they make a crack, y'know? But I know what they're laughin' at, and when I think of that guy layin' his hands on her I could—I mean it's eatin' me out, Mr. Alfieri, because I struggled for that girl. And now he comes in my house and—

ALFIERI. Eddie, look—I have my own children. I understand you. But the law is very specific. The law does not . . .

EDDIE (*with a fuller flow of indignation*). You mean to tell me that there's no law that a guy which he ain't right can go to work and marry a girl and—?

ALFIERI. You have no recourse in the law, Eddie.

EDDIE. Yeah, but if he ain't right, Mr. Alfieri, you mean to tell me—

ALFIERI. There is nothing you can do, Eddie, believe me.

EDDIE. Nothin'.

ALFIERI. Nothing at all. There's only one legal question here.

EDDIE. What?

ALFIERI. The manner in which they entered the country. But I don't think you want to do anything about that, do you?

EDDIE. You mean—?

ALFIERI. Well, they entered illegally.

EDDIE. Oh, Jesus, no, I wouldn't do nothin' about that, I mean—

ALFIERI. All right, then, let me talk now, eh?

EDDIE. Mr. Alfieri, I can't believe what you tell me. I mean there must be some kinda law which—

ALFIERI. Eddie, I want you to listen to me. (*Pause.*) You know, sometimes God mixes up the people. We all love some-body, the wife, the kids—every man's got somebody that he loves, heh? But some-times . . . there's too much. You know? There's too much, and it goes where it mustn't. A man works hard, he brings up a child, sometimes it's a niece, some-times even a daughter, and he never realizes it, but through the years—there is too much love for the daughter, there is too much love for the niece. Do you under-stand what I'm saying to you?

EDDIE (*sardonically*). What do you mean, I shouldn't look out for her good?

ALFIERI. Yes, but these things have to end, Eddie, that's all. The child has to grow up and go away, and the man has to learn to forget. Because after all, Eddie— what other way can it end? (*Pause.*) Let her go. That's my advice. You did your job, now it's her life; wish her luck, and let her go. (*Pause.*) Will you do that? Because there's no law, Eddie; make up your mind to it; the law is not interested in this.

EDDIE. You mean to tell me, even if he's a punk?—if he's—

ALFIERI. There's nothing you can do.

(EDDIE *stands.*)

EDDIE. Well, all right, thanks. Thanks very much.

ALFIERI. What are you going to do?

EDDIE (*with a helpless but ironic ges-ture*). What can I do? I'm a patsy, what can a patsy do? I worked like a dog twenty years so a punk could have her, so that's what I done. I mean, in the worst times, in the worst, when there wasn't a ship comin' in the harbor, I didn't stand around lookin' for relief—I hustled. When there was empty piers in Brooklyn I went to Hoboken, Staten Island, the West Side, Jersey, all over—because I made a promise. I took out of my own mouth to give to her. I took out of my wife's mouth. I walked hungry plenty days in this city! (*It begins to break through.*) And now I gotta sit in my own house and look at a son-of-a-bitch punk like that—which he came out of nowhere! I give him my house to sleep! I take the blankets off my bed for him, and he takes and puts his dirty filthy hands on her like a goddam thief!

ALFIERI (*rising*). But, Eddie, she's a woman now.

EDDIE. He's stealing from me!

ALFIERI. She wants to get married, Ed-die. She can't marry you, can she?

EDDIE (*furiously*). What're you talkin' about, marry me! I don't know what the hell you're talkin' about!

(*Pause.*)

ALFIERI. I gave you my advice, Eddie. That's it.

(EDDIE *gathers himself. A pause.*)

EDDIE. Well, thanks. Thanks very much. It just—it's breakin' my heart, y'know. I—

ALFIERI. I understand. Put it out of your mind. Can you do that?

EDDIE. I'm— (*He feels the threat of sobs, and with a helpless wave.*) I'll see you around. (*He goes out up the right ramp.*)

ALFIERI (*sits on desk*). There are times when you want to spread an alarm, but nothing has happened. I knew, I knew then and there—I could have finished the whole story that afternoon. It wasn't as though there was a mystery to unravel. I could see every step coming, step after step, like a dark figure walking down a hall toward a certain door. I knew where he was heading for, I knew where he was going to end. And I sat here many after-noons asking myself why, being an intel-ligent man, I was so powerless to stop it. I even went to a certain old lady in the neighborhood, a very wise old woman, and I told her, and she only nodded, and said, "Pray for him . . ." And so I— waited here.

(*As lights go out on* ALFIERI, *they rise in the apartment where all are finishing dinner.* BEATRICE *and* CATHERINE *are clear-ing the table.*)

CATHERINE. You know where they went?

BEATRICE. Where?

CATHERINE. They went to Africa once. On a fishing boat. (EDDIE *glances at her.*) It's true, Eddie.

(BEATRICE *exits into the kitchen with dishes.*)

EDDIE. I didn't say nothin'. (*He goes to his rocker, picks up a newspaper.*)

CATHERINE. And I was never even in Staten Island.

EDDIE (*sitting with the paper*). You didn't miss nothin'. (*Pause.* CATHERINE *takes dishes out.*) How long that take you, Marco—to get to Africa?

MARCO (*rising*). Oh . . . two days. We go all over.

RODOLPHO (*rising*). Once we went to Yugoslavia.

EDDIE (*to* MARCO). They pay all right on them boats?

(BEATRICE *enters. She and* RODOLPHO *stack the remaining dishes.*)

MARCO. If they catch fish they pay all right. (*Sits on a stool.*)

RODOLPHO. They're family boats, though. And nobody in our family owned one. So we only worked when one of the families was sick.

BEATRICE. Y'know, Marco, what I don't understand—there's an ocean full of fish and yiz are all starvin'.

EDDIE. They gotta have boats, nets, you need money.

(CATHERINE *enters.*)

BEATRICE. Yeah, but couldn't they like fish from the beach? You see them down Coney Island—

MARCO. Sardines.

EDDIE. Sure. (*Laughing:*) How you gonna catch sardines on a hook?

BEATRICE. Oh, I didn't know they're sardines. (*To* CATHERINE.) They're sardines!

CATHERINE. Yeah, they follow them all over the ocean, Africa, Yugoslavia . . . (*She sits and begins to look through a movie magazine.* RODOLPHO *joins her.*)

BEATRICE (*to* EDDIE). It's funny, y'know. You never think of it, that sardines are swimming in the ocean! (*She exits to kitchen with dishes.*)

CATHERINE. I know. It's like oranges and lemons on a tree. (*To* EDDIE:) I mean you ever think of oranges and lemons on a tree?

EDDIE. Yeah, I know. It's funny. (*To* MARCO:) I heard that they paint the oranges to make them look orange.

(BEATRICE *enters.*)

MARCO (*he has been reading a letter*). Paint?

EDDIE. Yeah, I heard that they grow like green.

MARCO. No, in Italy the oranges are orange.

RODOLPHO. Lemons are green.

EDDIE (*resenting his instruction*). I know lemons are green, for Christ's sake, you see them in the store they're green sometimes. I said oranges they paint, I didn't say nothin' about lemons.

BEATRICE (*sitting; diverting their attention*). Your wife is gettin' the money all right, Marco?

MARCO. Oh, yes. She bought medicine for my boy.

BEATRICE. That's wonderful. You feel better, heh?

MARCO. Oh, yes! But I'm lonesome.

BEATRICE. I just hope you ain't gonna do like some of them around here. They're here twenty-five years, some men, and they didn't get enough together to go back twice.

MARCO. Oh, I know. We have many families in our town, the children never saw the father. But I will go home. Three, four years, I think.

BEATRICE. Maybe you should keep more here. Because maybe she thinks it comes so easy you'll never get ahead of yourself.

MARCO. Oh, no, she saves. I send everything. My wife is very lonesome. (*He smiles shyly.*)

BEATRICE. She must be nice. She pretty? I bet, heh?

MARCO (*blushing*). No, but she understand everything.

RODOLPHO. Oh, he's got a clever wife!

EDDIE. I betcha there's plenty surprises sometimes when those guys get back there, heh?

MARCO. Surprises?

EDDIE (*laughing*). I mean, you know—they count the kids and there's a couple extra than when they left?

MARCO. No—no . . . The women wait, Eddie. Most. Most. Very few surprises.

RODOLPHO. It's more strict in our town. (EDDIE *looks at him now.*) It's not so free.

EDDIE (*rises, paces up and down*). It ain't so free here either, Rodolpho, like you think. I seen greenhorns sometimes get in trouble that way—they think just because a girl don't go around with a shawl over her head that she ain't strict, y'know? Girl don't have to wear black dress to be strict. Know what I mean?

RODOLPHO. Well, I always have respect—

EDDIE. I know, but in your town you wouldn't just drag off some girl without permission, I mean. (*He turns.*) You know what I mean, Marco? It ain't that much different here.

MARCO (*cautiously*). Yes.

BEATRICE. Well, he didn't exactly drag her off though, Eddie.

EDDIE. I know, but I seen some of them get the wrong idea sometimes. (*To* RODOLPHO:) I mean it might be a little more free here but it's just as strict.

RODOLPHO. I have respect for her, Eddie.

I do anything wrong?

EDDIE. Look, kid, I ain't her father, I'm only her uncle—

BEATRICE. Well then, be an uncle then. (EDDIE *looks at her, aware of her criticizing force.*) I mean.

MARCO. No, Beatrice, if he does wrong you must tell him. (*To* EDDIE:) What does he do wrong?

EDDIE. Well, Marco, till he came here she was never out on the street twelve o'clock at night.

MARCO (*to* RODOLPHO). You come home early now.

BEATRICE (*to* CATHERINE). Well, you said the movie ended late, didn't you?

CATHERINE. Yeah.

BEATRICE. Well, tell him, honey. (*To* EDDIE:) The movie ended late.

EDDIE. Look, B., I'm just sayin'—he thinks she always stayed out like that.

MARCO. You come home early now, Rodolpho.

RODOLPHO (*embarrassed*). All right, sure. But I can't stay in the house all the time, Eddie.

EDDIE. Look, kid, I'm not only talkin' about her. The more you run around like that the more chance you're takin'. (*To* BEATRICE:) I mean suppose he gets hit by a car or something. (*To* MARCO:) Where's his papers, who is he? Know what I mean?

BEATRICE. Yeah, but who is he in the daytime, though? It's the same chance in the daytime.

EDDIE (*holding back a voice full of anger*). Yeah, but he don't have to go lookin' for it, Beatrice. If he's here to work, then he should work; if he's here for a good time then he could fool around! (*To* MARCO:) But I understood, Marco, that you was both comin' to make a livin' for your family. You understand me, don't you, Marco? (*He goes to his rocker.*)

MARCO. I beg your pardon, Eddie.

EDDIE. I mean, that's what I understood in the first place, see.

MARCO. Yes. That's why we came.

EDDIE (*sits on his rocker*). Well, that's all I'm askin'. (EDDIE *reads his paper. There is a pause, an awkwardness. Now* CATHERINE *gets up and puts a record on the phonograph—* "Paper Doll.")

CATHERINE (*flushed with revolt*). You wanna dance, Rodolpho?

(EDDIE *freezes.*)

RODOLPHO (*in deference to* EDDIE). No, I —I'm tired.

BEATRICE. Go ahead, dance, Rodolpho.

CATHERINE. Ah, come on. They got a beautiful quartet, these guys. Come. (*She has taken his hand and he stiffly rises, feeling* EDDIE's *eyes on his back, and they dance.*)

EDDIE (*to* CATHERINE). What's that, a new record?

CATHERINE. It's the same one. We bought it the other day.

BEATRICE (*to* EDDIE). They only bought three records. (*She watches them dance;* EDDIE *turns his head away.* MARCO *just sits there, waiting. Now* BEATRICE *turns to* EDDIE.) Must be nice to go all over in one of them fishin' boats. I would like that myself. See all them other countries?

EDDIE. Yeah.

BEATRICE (*to* MARCO). But the women don't go along, I bet.

MARCO. No, not on the boats. Hard work.

BEATRICE. What're you got, a regular kitchen and everything?

MARCO. Yes, we eat very good on the boats—especially when Rodolpho comes along; everybody gets fat.

BEATRICE. Oh, he cooks?

MARCO. Sure, very good cook. Rice, pasta, fish, everything.

(EDDIE *lowers his paper.*)

EDDIE. He's a cook, too! (*Looking at* RODOLPHO:) He sings, he cooks . . .

(RODOLPHO *smiles thankfully.*)

BEATRICE. Well it's good, he could always make a living.

EDDIE. It's wonderful. He sings, he cooks, he could make dresses . . .

CATHERINE. They get some high pay, them guys. The head chefs in all the big hotels are men. You read about them.

EDDIE. That's what I'm sayin'.

(CATHERINE *and* RODOLPHO *continue dancing.*)

CATHERINE. Yeah, well, I mean.

EDDIE (*to* BEATRICE). He's lucky, believe me. (*Slight pause. He looks away, then back to* BEATRICE.) That's why the water front is no place for him. (*They stop dancing.* RODOLPHO *turns off phonograph.*) I mean like me—I can't cook, I can't sing, I can't make dresses, so I'm on the water front. But if I could cook, if I could sing, if I could make dresses, I wouldn't be on the water front. (*He has been unconsciously twisting the newspaper into a tight roll. They are all regarding him now; he senses he is exposing the issue and he is driven on.*) I would be someplace else. I would be like in a dress store. (*He has bent the rolled paper and it suddenly tears in two. He suddenly gets up and pulls his pants up over his belly and goes to* MARCO.) What do you say, Marco, we go to the bouts next Saturday night. You never seen a fight, did you?

MARCO (*uneasily*). Only in the moving pictures.

EDDIE (*going to* RODOLPHO). I'll treat yiz. What do you say, Danish? You wanna come along? I'll buy the tickets.

RODOLPHO. Sure. I like to go.

CATHERINE (*goes to* EDDIE; *nervously happy now*). I'll make some coffee, all right?

EDDIE. Go ahead, make some! Make it nice and strong. (*Mystified, she smiles and exits to kitchen. He is weirdly elated, rubbing his fists into his palms. He strides to* MARCO.) You wait, Marco, you see some real fights here. You ever do any boxing?

MARCO. No, I never.

EDDIE (*to* RODOLPHO). Betcha you have done some, heh?

RODOLPHO. No.

EDDIE. Well, come on, I'll teach you.

BEATRICE. What's he got to learn that for?

EDDIE. Ya can't tell, one a these days somebody's liable to step on his foot or sump'm. Come on, Rodolpho, I show you a couple of passes. (*He stands below table.*)

BEATRICE. Go ahead, Rodolpho. He's a good boxer, he could teach you.

RODOLPHO (*embarrassed*). Well, I don't know how to— (*He moves down to* EDDIE.)

EDDIE. Just put your hands up. Like this, see? That's right. That's very good, keep your left up, because you lead with the left, see, like this. (*He gently moves his left into* RODOLPHO's *face.*) See? Now what you gotta do is you gotta block me, so when I come in like that you—(RODOLPHO *parries his left.*) Hey, that's very good! (RODOLPHO *laughs.*) All right, now come into me. Come on.

RODOLPHO. I don't want to hit you, Eddie.

EDDIE. Don't pity me, come on. Throw it, I'll show you how to block it. (RO-DOLPHO *jabs at him, laughing. The others*

join.) 'At's it. Come on again. For the jaw right here. (RODOLPHO *jabs with more assurance.*) Very good!

BEATRICE (*to* MARCO). He's very good!

(EDDIE *crosses directly upstage of* RO-DOLPHO.)

EDDIE. Sure, he's great! Come on, kid, put sump'm behind it, you can't hurt me. (RODOLPHO, *more seriously, jabs at* EDDIE's *jaw and grazes it.*) Attaboy. (CATHERINE *comes from the kitchen, watches.*) Now I'm gonna hit you, so block me, see?

CATHERINE (*with beginning alarm*). What are they doin'?

(*They are lightly boxing now.*)

BEATRICE (*she senses only the comradeship in it now*). He's teachin' him; he's very good!

EDDIE. Sure, he's terrific! Look at him go! (RODOLPHO *lands a blow.*) 'At's it! Now, watch out, here I come, Danish! (*He feints with his left hand and lands with his right. It mildly staggers* RODOLPHO. MARCO *rises.*)

CATHERINE (*rushing to* RODOLPHO). Eddie!

EDDIE. Why? I didn't hurt him. Did I hurt you, kid? (*He rubs the back of his hand across his mouth.*)

RODOLPHO. No, no, he didn't hurt me. (*To* EDDIE *with a certain gleam and a smile.*) I was only surprised.

BEATRICE (*pulling* EDDIE *down into the rocker*). That's enough, Eddie; he did pretty good, though.

EDDIE. Yeah. (*Rubbing his fists together:*) He could be very good, Marco. I'll teach him again.

(MARCO *nods at him dubiously.*)

RODOLPHO. Dance, Catherine. Come. (*He takes her hand; they go to phonograph and start it. It plays "Paper Doll."*)

(RODOLPHO *takes her in his arms. They dance.* EDDIE *in thought sits in his chair, and* MARCO *takes a chair, places it in front of* EDDIE, *and looks down at it.* BEATRICE *and* EDDIE *watch him.*)

MARCO. Can you lift this chair?

EDDIE. What do you mean?

MARCO. From here. (*He gets on one knee with one hand behind his back, and grasps the bottom of one of the chair legs but does not raise it.*

EDDIE. Sure, why not? (*He comes to the chair, kneels, grasps the leg, raises the chair one inch, but it leans over to the floor.*) Gee, that's hard, I never knew that.

(*He tries again, and again fails.*) It's on an angle, that's why, heh?

MARCO. Here. (*He kneels, grasps, and with strain slowly raises the chair higher and higher, getting to his feet now.* RODOLPHO *and* CATHERINE *have stopped dancing as* MARCO *raises the chair over his head.*

(MARCO *is face to face with* EDDIE, *a strained tension gripping his eyes and jaw, his neck stiff, the chair raised like a weapon over* EDDIE's *head—and he transforms what might appear like a glare of warning into a smile of triumph, and* EDDIE's *grin vanishes as he absorbs his look.*)

CURTAIN

ACT TWO

Light rises on ALFIERI *at his desk.*

ALFIERI. On the twenty-third of that December a case of Scotch whisky slipped from a net while being unloaded—as a case of Scotch whisky is inclined to do on the twenty-third of December on Pier Forty-one. There was no snow, but it was cold, his wife was out shopping. Marco was still at work. The boy had not been hired that day; Catherine told me later that this was the first time they had been alone together in the house.

(*Light is rising on* CATHERINE *in the apartment.* RODOLPHO *is watching as she arranges a paper pattern on cloth spread on the table.*)

CATHERINE. You hungry?

RODOLPHO. Not for anything to eat. (*Pause.*) I have nearly three hundred dollars. Catherine?

CATHERINE. I heard you.

RODOLPHO. You don't like to talk about it any more?

CATHERINE. Sure, I don't mind talkin' about it.

RODOLPHO. What worries you, Catherine?

CATHERINE. I been wantin' to ask you about something. Could I?

RODOLPHO. All the answers are in my eyes, Catherine. But you don't look in my eyes lately. You're full of secrets. (*She looks at him. She seems withdrawn.*) What is the question?

CATHERINE. Suppose I wanted to live in Italy.

RODOLPHO (*smiling at the incongruity*). You going to marry somebody rich?

CATHERINE. No, I mean live there—you and me.

RODOLPHO (*his smile vanishing*). When?

CATHERINE. Well . . . when we get married.

RODOLPHO (*astonished*). You want to be an Italian?

CATHERINE. No, but I could live there without being Italian. Americans live there.

RODOLPHO. Forever?

CATHERINE. Yeah.

RODOLPHO (*crosses to rocker*). You're fooling.

CATHERINE. No, I mean it.

RODOLPHO. Where do you get such an idea?

CATHERINE. Well, you're always saying it's so beautiful there, with the mountains and the ocean and all the—

RODOLPHO. You're fooling me.

CATHERINE. I mean it.

RODOLPHO (*goes to her slowly*). Catherine, if I ever brought you home with no money, no business, nothing, they would call the priest and the doctor and they would say Rodolpho is crazy.

CATHERINE. I know, but I think we would be happier there.

RODOLPHO. Happier! What would you eat? You can't cook the view!

CATHERINE. Maybe you could be a singer, like in Rome or—

RODOLPHO. Rome! Rome is full of singers.

CATHERINE. Well, I could work then.

RODOLPHO. Where?

CATHERINE. God, there must be jobs somewhere!

RODOLPHO. There's nothing! Nothing, nothing, nothing. Now tell me what you're talking about. How can I bring you from a rich country to suffer in a poor country? What are you talking about? (*She searches for words.*) I would be a criminal stealing your face. In two years you would have an old, hungry face. When my brother's babies cry they give them water, water that boiled a bone. Don't you believe that?

CATHERINE (*quietly*). I'm afraid of Eddie here.

(*Slight pause.*)

RODOLPHO (*steps closer to her*). We wouldn't live here. Once I am a citizen I could work anywhere and I would find better jobs and we would have a house,

Catherine. If I were not afraid to be arrested I would start to be something wonderful here!

CATHERINE (*steeling herself*). Tell me something. I mean just tell me, Rodolpho —would you still want to do it if it turned out we had to go live in Italy? I mean just if it turned out that way.

RODOLPHO. This is your question or his question?

CATHERINE. I would like to know, Rodolpho. I mean it.

RODOLPHO. To go there with nothing.

CATHERINE. Yeah.

RODOLPHO. No. (*She looks at him wide-eyed.*) No.

CATHERINE. You wouldn't?

RODOLPHO. No; I will not marry you to live in Italy. I want you to be my wife, and I want to be a citizen. Tell him that, or I will. Yes. (*He moves about angrily.*) And tell him also, and tell yourself, please, that I am not a beggar, and you are not a horse, a gift, a favor for a poor immigrant.

CATHERINE. Well, don't get mad!

RODOLPHO. I am furious! (*Goes to her.*) Do you think I am so desperate? My brother is desperate, not me. You think I would carry on my back the rest of my life a woman I didn't love just to be an American? It's so wonderful? You think we have no tall buildings in Italy? Electric lights? No wide streets? No flags? No automobiles? Only work we don't have. I want to be an American so I can work, that is the only wonder here—work! How can you insult me, Catherine?

CATHERINE. I didn't mean that—

RODOLPHO. My heart dies to look at you. Why are you so afraid of him?

CATHERINE (*near tears*). I don't know!

RODOLPHO. Do you trust me, Catherine? You?

CATHERINE. It's only that I—He was good to me, Rodolpho. You don't know him; he was always the sweetest guy to me. Good. He razzes me all the time but he don't mean it. I know. I would—just feel ashamed if I made him sad. 'Cause I always dreamt that when I got married he would be happy at the wedding, and laughin'—and now he's—mad all the time and nasty—(*She is weeping.*) Tell him you'd live in Italy—just tell him, and maybe he would start to trust you a little, see? Because I want him to be happy; I mean—I like him, Rodolpho—and I can't

stand it!

RODOLPHO. Oh, Catherine—oh, little girl.

CATHERINE. I love you, Rodolpho, I love you.

RODOLPHO. Then why are you afraid? That he'll spank you?

CATHERINE. Don't, don't laugh at me! I've been here all my life. . . . Every day I saw him when he left in the morning and when he came home at night. You think it's so easy to turn around and say to a man he's nothin' to you no more?

RODOLPHO. I know, but—

CATHERINE. You don't know; nobody knows! I'm not a baby, I know a lot more than people think I know. Beatrice says to be a woman, but—

RODOLPHO. Yes.

CATHERINE. Then why don't she be a woman? If I was a wife I would make a man happy instead of goin' at him all the time. I can tell a block away when he's blue in his mind and just wants to talk to somebody quiet and nice. . . . I can tell when he's hungry or wants a beer before he even says anything. I know when his feet hurt him, I mean I *know* him and now I'm supposed to turn around and make a stranger out of him? I don't know why I have to do that, I mean.

RODOLPHO. Catherine. If I take in my hands a little bird. And she grows and wishes to fly. But I will not let her out of my hands because I love her so much, is that right for me to do? I don't say you must hate him; but anyway you must go, mustn't you? Catherine?

CATHERINE (*softly*). Hold me.

RODOLPHO (*clasping her to him*). Oh, my little girl.

CATHERINE. Teach me. (*She is weeping.*) I don't know anything, teach me, Rodolpho, hold me.

RODOLPHO. There's nobody here now. Come inside. Come. (*He is leading her toward the bedrooms.*) And don't cry any more.

(*Light rises on the street. In a moment* EDDIE *appears. He is unsteady, drunk. He mounts the stairs. He enters the apartment, looks around, takes out a bottle from one pocket, puts it on the table. Then another bottle from another pocket, and a third from an inside pocket. He sees the pattern and cloth, goes over to it and touches it, and turns toward upstage.*)

EDDIE. Beatrice? (*He goes to the open

kitchen door and looks in.) Beatrice? Beatrice?

(CATHERINE *enters from bedroom; under his gaze she adjusts her dress.*)

CATHERINE. You got home early.

EDDIE. Knocked off for Christmas early. (*Indicating the pattern.*) Rodolpho makin' you a dress?

CATHERINE. No. I'm makin' a blouse.

(RODOLPHO *appears in the bedroom doorway.* EDDIE *sees him and his arm jerks slightly in shock.* RODOLPHO *nods to him testingly.*)

RODOLPHO. Beatrice went to buy presents for her mother.

(*Pause.*)

EDDIE. Pack it up. Go ahead. Get your stuff and get outa here. (CATHERINE *instantly turns and walks toward the bedroom, and* EDDIE *grabs her arm.*) Where you goin'?

CATHERINE (*trembling with fright*). I think I have to get out of here, Eddie.

EDDIE. No, you ain't goin' nowheres, he's the one.

CATHERINE. I think I can't stay here no more. (*She frees her arm, steps back toward the bedroom.*) I'm sorry, Eddie. (*She sees the tears in his eyes.*) Well, don't cry. I'll be around the neighborhood; I'll see you. I just can't stay here no more. You know I can't. (*Her sobs of pity and love for him break her composure.*) Don't you know I can't? You know that, don't you? (*She goes to him.*) Wish me luck. (*She clasps her hands prayerfully.*) Oh, Eddie, don't be like that!

EDDIE. You ain't goin' nowheres.

CATHERINE. Eddie, I'm not gonna be a baby any more! You—

(*He reaches out suddenly, draws her to him, and as she strives to free herself he kisses her on the mouth.*)

RODOLPHO. Don't! (*He pulls on* EDDIE's *arm.*) Stop that! Have respect for her!

EDDIE (*spun round by* RODOLPHO). You want something?

RODOLPHO. Yes! She'll be my wife. That is what I want. My wife!

EDDIE. But what're you gonna be?

RODOLPHO. I show you what I be!

CATHERINE. Wait outside; don't argue with him!

EDDIE. Come on, show me! What're you gonna be? Show me!

RODOLPHO (*with tears of rage*). Don't say that to me! (RODOLPHO *flies at him in*

attack. EDDIE *pins his arms, laughing, and suddenly kisses him.*)

CATHERINE. Eddie! Let go, ya hear me! I'll kill you! Leggo of him! (*She tears at* EDDIE's *face and* EDDIE *releases* RODOLPHO. EDDIE *stands there with tears rolling down his face as he laughs mockingly at* RODOLPHO. *She is staring at him in horror.* RODOLPHO *is rigid. They are like animals that have torn at one another and broken up without a decision, each waiting for the other's mood.*)

EDDIE (*to* CATHERINE). You see? (*To* RODOLPHO:) I give you till tomorrow, kid. Get outa here. Alone. You hear me? Alone.

CATHERINE. I'm going with him, Eddie. (*She starts toward* RODOLPHO.)

EDDIE (*indicating* RODOLPHO *with his head*). Not with that. (*She halts, frightened. He sits, still panting for breath, and they watch him helplessly as he leans toward them over the table.*) Don't make me do nuttin', Catherine. Watch your step, submarine. By rights they oughta throw you back in the water. But I got pity for you. (*He moves unsteadily toward the door, always facing* RODOLPHO.) Just get outa here and don't lay another hand on her unless you wanna go out feet first. (*He goes out of the apartment.*)

(*The lights go down, as they rise on* ALFIERI.)

ALFIERI. On December twenty-seventh I saw him next. I normally go home well before six, but that day I sat around looking out my window at the bay, and when I saw him walking through my doorway, I knew why I had waited. And if I seem to tell this like a dream, it was that way. Several moments arrived in the course of the two talks we had when it occurred to me how—almost transfixed I had come to feel. I had lost my strength somewhere. (EDDIE *enters, removing his cap, sits in the chair, looks thoughtfully out.*) I looked in his eyes more than I listened—in fact, I can hardly remember the conversation. But I will never forget how dark the room became when he looked at me; his eyes were like tunnels. I kept wanting to call the police, but nothing had happened. Nothing at all had really happened. (*He breaks off and looks down at the desk. Then he turns to* EDDIE.) So in other words, he won't leave?

EDDIE. My wife is talkin' about renting

a room upstairs for them. An old lady on the top floor is got an empty room.

ALFIERI. What does Marco say?

EDDIE. He just sits there. Marco don't say much.

ALFIERI. I guess they didn't tell him, heh? What happened?

EDDIE. I don't know; Marco don't say much.

ALFIERI. What does your wife say?

EDDIE (*unwilling to pursue this*). Nobody's talkin' much in the house. So what about that?

ALFIERI. But you didn't prove anything about him. It sounds like he just wasn't strong enough to break your grip.

EDDIE. I'm tellin' you I know—he ain't right. Somebody that don't want it can break it. Even a mouse, if you catch a teeny mouse and you hold it in your hand, that mouse can give you the right kind of fight. He didn't give me the right kind of fight, I know it, Mr. Alfieri, the guy ain't right.

ALFIERI. What did you do that for, Eddie?

EDDIE. To show her what he is! So she would see, once and for all! Her mother'll turn over in the grave! (*He gathers himself almost peremptorily.*) So what do I gotta do now? Tell me what to do.

ALFIERI. She actually said she's marrying him?

EDDIE. She told me, yeah. So what do I do?

(*Slight pause.*)

ALFIERI. This is my last word, Eddie, take it or not, that's your business. Morally and legally you have no rights, you cannot stop it; she is a free agent.

EDDIE (*angering*). Didn't you hear what I told you?

ALFIERI (*with a tougher tone*). I heard what you told me, and I'm telling you what the answer is. I'm not only telling you now, I'm warning you—the law is nature. The law is only a word for what has a right to happen. When the law is wrong it's because it's unnatural, but in this case it is natural and a river will drown you if you buck it now. Let her go. And bless her. (*A phone booth begins to glow on the opposite side of the stage; a faint, lonely blue.* EDDIE *stands up, jaws clenched.*) Somebody had to come for her, Eddie, sooner or later. (EDDIE *starts turning to go and* ALFIERI *rises with new*

anxiety.*) You won't have a friend in the world, Eddie! Even those who understand will turn against you, even the ones who feel the same will despise you! (EDDIE *moves off.*) Put it out of your mind! Eddie! (*He follows into the darkness, calling desperately.*)

(EDDIE *is gone. The phone is glowing in light now. Light is out on* ALFIERI. EDDIE *has at the same time appeared beside the phone.*)

EDDIE. Give me the number of the Immigration Bureau. Thanks. (*He dials.*) I want to report something. Illegal immigrants. Two of them. That's right. Four-forty-one Saxon Street, Brooklyn, yeah. Ground floor. Heh? (*With greater difficulty.*) I'm just around the neighborhood, that's all. Heh? (*Evidently he is being questioned further, and he slowly hangs up. He leaves the phone just as* LOUIS *and* MIKE *come down the street.*)

LOUIS. Go bowlin', Eddie?

EDDIE. No, I'm due home.

LOUIS. Well, take it easy.

EDDIE. I'll see yiz.

(*They leave him, exiting right, and he watches them go. He glances about, then goes up into the house. The lights go on in the apartment.* BEATRICE *is taking down Christmas decorations and packing them in a box.*)

EDDIE. Where is everybody? (BEATRICE *does not answer.*) I says where is everybody?

BEATRICE (*looking up at him, wearied with it, and concealing a fear of him*). I decided to move them upstairs with Mrs. Dondero.

EDDIE. Oh, they're all moved up there already?

BEATRICE. Yeah.

EDDIE. Where's Catherine? She up there?

BEATRICE. Only to bring pillow cases.

EDDIE. She ain't movin' in with them.

BEATRICE. Look, I'm sick and tired of it. I'm sick and tired of it!

EDDIE. All right, all right, take it easy.

BEATRICE. I don't wanna hear no more about it, you understand? Nothin'!

EDDIE. What're you blowin' off about? Who brought them in here?

BEATRICE. All right, I'm sorry; I wish I'd a drop dead before I told them to come. In the ground I wish I was.

EDDIE. Don't drop dead, just keep in

mind who brought them in here, that's all. (*He moves about restlessly.*) I mean I got a couple of rights here. (*He moves, wanting to beat down her evident disapproval of him.*) This is my house here not their house.

BEATRICE. What do you want from me? They're moved out; what do you want now?

EDDIE. I want my respect!

BEATRICE. So I moved them out, what more do you want? You got your house now, you got your respect.

EDDIE (*he moves about biting his lip*). I don't like the way you talk to me, Beatrice.

BEATRICE. I'm just tellin' you I done what you want!

EDDIE. I don't like it! The way you talk to me and the way you look at me. This is my house. And she is my niece and I'm responsible for her.

BEATRICE. So that's why you done that to him?

EDDIE. I done what to him?

BEATRICE. What you done to him in front of her; you know what I'm talkin' about. She goes around shakin' all the time, she can't go to sleep! That's what you call responsible for her?

EDDIE (*quietly*). The guy ain't right, Beatrice. (*She is silent.*) Did you hear what I said?

BEATRICE. Look, I'm finished with it. That's all. (*She resumes her work.*)

EDDIE (*helping her to pack the tinsel*). I'm gonna have it out with you one of these days, Beatrice.

BEATRICE. Nothin' to have out with me, it's all settled. Now we gonna be like it never happened, that's all.

EDDIE. I want my respect, Beatrice, and you know what I'm talkin' about.

BEATRICE. What?

(*Pause.*)

EDDIE (*finally his resolution hardens*). What I feel like doin' in the bed and what I don't feel like doin'. I don't want no—

BEATRICE. When'd I say anything about that?

EDDIE. You said, you said, I ain't deaf. I don't want no more conversations about that, Beatrice. I do what I feel like doin' or what I don't feel like doin'.

BEATRICE. Okay.

(*Pause.*)

EDDIE. You used to be different, Bea-trice. You had a whole different way.

BEATRICE. *I'm* no different.

EDDIE. You didn't used to jump me all the time about everything. The last year or two I come in the house I don't know what's gonna hit me. It's a shootin' gallery in here and I'm the pigeon.

BEATRICE. Okay, okay.

EDDIE. Don't tell me okay, okay, I'm tellin' you the truth. A wife is supposed to believe the husband. If I tell you that guy ain't right don't tell me he is right.

BEATRICE. But how do you know?

EDDIE. Because I know. I don't go around makin' accusations. He give me the heeby-jeebies the first minute I seen him. And I don't like you sayin' I don't want her marryin' anybody. I broke my back payin' her stenography lessons so she could go out and meet a better class of people. Would I do that if I didn't want her to get married? Sometimes you talk like I was a crazy man or sump'm.

BEATRICE. But she likes him.

EDDIE. Beatrice, she's a baby, how is she gonna know what she likes?

BEATRICE. Well, you kept her a baby, you wouldn't let her go out. I told you a hundred times.

(*Pause.*)

EDDIE. All right. Let her go out, then.

BEATRICE. She don't wanna go out now. It's too late, Eddie.

(*Pause.*)

EDDIE. Suppose I told her to go out. Suppose I—

BEATRICE. They're going to get married next week, Eddie.

EDDIE (*his head jerks around to her*). She said that?

BEATRICE. Eddie, if you want my advice, go to her and tell her good luck. I think maybe now that you had it out you learned better.

EDDIE. What's the hurry next week?

BEATRICE. Well, she's been worried about him bein' picked up; this way he could start to be a citizen. She loves him, Eddie. (*He gets up, moves about uneasily, restlessly.*) Why don't you give her a good word? Because I still think she would like you to be a friend, y'know? (*He is standing, looking at the floor.*) I mean like if you told her you'd go to the wedding.

EDDIE. She asked you that?

BEATRICE. I know she would like it. I'd like to make a party here for her. I mean

there oughta be some kinda send-off. Heh?
I mean she'll have trouble enough in her
life, let's start it off happy. What do you
say? Cause in her heart she still loves you,
Eddie. I know it. (*He presses his fingers
against his eyes.*) What're you, cryin'?
(*She goes to him, holds his face.*) Go
. . . whyn't you go tell her you're sorry?
(CATHERINE *is seen on the upper landing
of the stairway, and they hear her descending.*) There . . . she's comin' down.
Come on, shake hands with her.

EDDIE (*moving with suppressed sudden-
ness*). No, I can't, I can't talk to her.

BEATRICE. Eddie, give her a break; a
wedding should be happy!

EDDIE. I'm goin', I'm goin' for a walk.
(*He goes upstage for his jacket.* CATHERINE
enters and starts for the bedroom door.)

BEATRICE. Katie? . . . Eddie, don't go,
wait a minute. (*She embraces* EDDIE'S *arm
with warmth.*) Ask him, Katie. Come on,
honey.

EDDIE. It's all right, I'm—(*He starts to
go and she holds him.*)

BEATRICE. No, she wants to ask you.
Come on, Katie, ask him. We'll have a
party! What're we gonna do, hate each
other? Come on!

CATHERINE. I'm gonna get married,
Eddie. So if you wanna come, the wedding
be on Saturday.

(*Pause.*)

EDDIE. Okay. I only wanted the best for
you, Katie. I hope you know that.

CATHERINE. Okay. (*She starts out again.*)

EDDIE. Catherine? (*She turns to him.*) I
was just tellin' Beatrice . . . if you wanna
go out, like . . . I mean I realize maybe I
kept you home too much. Because he's the
first guy you ever knew, y'know? I mean
now that you got a job, you might meet
some fellas, and you get a different idea,
y'know? I mean you could always come
back to him, you're still only kids, the both
of yiz. What's the hurry? Maybe you'll get
around a little bit, you grow up a little
more, maybe you'll see different in a couple
of months. I mean you be surprised, it
don't have to be him.

CATHERINE. No, we made it up already.

EDDIE (*with increasing anxiety*). Katie,
wait a minute.

CATHERINE. No, I made up my mind.

EDDIE. But you never knew no other
fella, Katie! How could you make up your
mind?

CATHERINE. Cause I did. I don't want nobody else.

EDDIE. But, Katie, suppose he gets picked
up.

CATHERINE. That's why we gonna do it
right away. Soon as we finish the wedding
he's goin' right over and start to be a citizen. I made up my mind, Eddie. I'm sorry.
(*To* BEATRICE:) Could I take two more
pillow cases for the other guys?

BEATRICE. Sure, go ahead. Only don't let
her forget where they came from.

(CATHERINE *goes into a bedroom.*)

EDDIE. She's got other boarders up there?

BEATRICE. Yeah, there's two guys that
just came over.

EDDIE. What do you mean, came over?

BEATRICE. From Italy. Lipari the butcher
—his nephew. They come from Bari, they
just got here yesterday. I didn't even know
till Marco and Rodolpho moved up there
before. (CATHERINE *enters, going toward
exit with two pillow cases.*) It'll be nice,
they could all talk together.

EDDIE. Catherine! (*She halts near the
exit door. He takes in* BEATRICE *too.*)
What're you, got no brains? You put them
up there with two other submarines?

CATHERINE. Why?

EDDIE (*in a driving fright and anger*).
Why! How do you know they're not
trackin' these guys? They'll come up for
them and find Marco and Rodolpho! Get
them out of the house!

BEATRICE. But they been here so long
already—

EDDIE. How do you know what enemies
Lipari's got? Which they'd love to stab
him in the back?

CATHERINE. Well what'll I do with
them?

EDDIE. The neighborhood is full of
rooms. Can't you stand to live a couple of
blocks away from him? Get them out of
the house!

CATHERINE. Well maybe tomorrow night
I'll—

EDDIE. Not tomorrow, do it now. Catherine, you never mix yourself with somebody else's family! These guys get picked
up, Lipari's liable to blame you or me and
we got his whole family on our head. They
got a temper, that family.

(*Two men in overcoats appear outside,
start into the house.*)

CATHERINE. How'm I gonna find a place
tonight?

EDDIE. Will you stop arguin' with me and get them out! You think I'm always tryin' to fool you or sump'm? What's the matter with you, don't you believe I could think of your good? Did I ever ask sump'm for myself? You think I got no feelin's? I never told you nothin' in my life that wasn't for your good. Nothin'! And look at the way you talk to me! Like I was an enemy! Like I—(*A knock on the door. His head swerves. They all stand motionless. Another knock.* EDDIE, *in a whisper, pointing upstage.*) Go up the fire escape, get them out over the back fence.

(CATHERINE *stands motionless, uncomprehending.*)

FIRST OFFICER (*in the hall*). Immigration! Open up in there!

EDDIE. Go, go. Hurry up! (*She stands a moment staring at him in a realized horror.*) Well, what're you lookin' at!

FIRST OFFICER. Open up!

EDDIE (*calling toward door*). Who's that there?

FIRST OFFICER. Immigration, open up.

(EDDIE *turns, looks at* BEATRICE. *She sits. Then he looks at* CATHERINE. *With a sob of fury* CATHERINE *streaks into a bedroom. Knock is repeated.*)

EDDIE. All right, take it easy, take it easy. (*He goes and opens the door. The* OFFICER *steps inside.*) What's all this?

FIRST OFFICER. Where are they?

(SECOND OFFICER *sweeps past and, glancing about, goes into the kitchen.*)

EDDIE. Where's who?

FIRST OFFICER. Come on, come on, where are they? (*He hurries into the bedrooms.*)

EDDIE. Who? We got nobody here. (*He looks at* BEATRICE, *who turns her head away. Pugnaciously, furious, he steps toward* BEATRICE.) What's the matter with you?

(FIRST OFFICER *enters from the bedroom, calls to the kitchen.*)

FIRST OFFICER. Dominick?

(*Enter* SECOND OFFICER *from kitchen.*)

SECOND OFFICER. Maybe it's a different apartment.

FIRST OFFICER. There's only two more floors up there. I'll take the front, you go up the fire escape. I'll let you in. Watch your step up there.

SECOND OFFICER. Okay, right, Charley. (FIRST OFFICER *goes out apartment door and runs up the stairs.*) This is Four-forty-one, isn't it?

EDDIE. That's right.

(SECOND OFFICER *goes out into the kitchen.*

(EDDIE *turns to* BEATRICE. *She looks at him now and sees his terror.*)

BEATRICE (*weakened with fear*). Oh, Jesus, Eddie.

EDDIE. What's the matter with *you*?

BEATRICE (*pressing her palms against her face*). Oh, my God, my God.

EDDIE. What're you, accusin' me?

BEATRICE (*her final thrust is to turn toward him instead of running from him*). My God, what did you do?

(*Many steps on the outer stair draw his attention. We see the* FIRST OFFICER *descending, with* MARCO, *behind him* RODOLPHO, *and* CATHERINE *and the two strange immigrants, followed by* SECOND OFFICER. BEATRICE *hurries to door.*)

CATHERINE (*backing down stairs, fighting with* FIRST OFFICER; *as they appear on the stairs*). What do yiz want from them? They work, that's all. They're boarders upstairs, they work on the piers.

BEATRICE (*to* FIRST OFFICER). Ah, Mister, what do you want from them, who do they hurt?

CATHERINE (*pointing to* RODOLPHO). They ain't no submarines, he was born in Philadelphia.

FIRST OFFICER. Step aside, lady.

CATHERINE. What do you mean? You can't just come in a house and—

FIRST OFFICER. All right, take it easy. (*To* RODOLPHO:) What street were you born in Philadelphia?

CATHERINE. What do you mean, what street? Could you tell me what street you were born?

FIRST OFFICER. Sure. Four blocks away, One-eleven Union Street. Let's go fellas.

CATHERINE (*fending him off* RODOLPHO). No, you can't! Now, get outa here!

FIRST OFFICER. Look, girlie, if they're all right they'll be out tomorrow. If they're illegal they go back where they came from. If you want, get yourself a lawyer, although I'm tellin' you now you're wasting your money. Let's get them in the car, Dom. (*To the men:*) Andiamo, Andiamo, let's go.

(*The men start, but* MARCO *hangs back.*)

BEATRICE (*from doorway*). Who're they hurtin', for God's sake, what do you want from them? They're starvin' over there, what do you want! Marco!

(MARCO *suddenly breaks from the group and dashes into the room and faces* EDDIE; BEATRICE *and* FIRST OFFICER *rush in as* MARCO *spits into* EDDIE's *face.*

(CATHERINE *runs into hallway and throws herself into* RODOLPHO's *arms.* EDDIE, *with an enraged cry, lunges for* MARCO.)

EDDIE. Oh, you mother's—!

(FIRST OFFICER *quickly intercedes and pushes* EDDIE *from* MARCO, *who stands there accusingly.*)

FIRST OFFICER (*between them, pushing* EDDIE *from* MARCO). Cut it out!

EDDIE (*over the* FIRST OFFICER's *shoulder, to* MARCO). I'll kill you for that, you son of a bitch!

FIRST OFFICER. Hey! (*Shakes him.*) Stay in here now, don't come out, don't bother him. You hear me? Don't come out, fella.

(*For an instant there is silence. Then* FIRST OFFICER *turns and takes* MARCO's *arm and then gives a last, informative look at* EDDIE. *As he and* MARCO *are going out into the hall,* EDDIE *erupts.*)

EDDIE. I don't forget that, Marco! You hear what I'm sayin'?

(*Out in the hall,* FIRST OFFICER *and* MARCO *go down the stairs. Now, in the street,* LOUIS, MIKE, *and several neighbors including the butcher,* LIPARI—*a stout, intense, middle-aged man—are gathering around the stoop.*)

(LIPARI, *the butcher, walks over to the two strange men and kisses them. His wife, keening, goes and kisses their hands.* EDDIE *is emerging from the house shouting after* MARCO. BEATRICE *is trying to restrain him.*)

EDDIE. That's the thanks I get? Which I took the blankets off my bed for yiz? You gonna apologize to me, Marco! *Marco!*

FIRST OFFICER (*in the doorway with* MARCO). All right, lady, let them go. Get in the car, fellas, it's right over there.

(RODOLPHO *is almost carrying the sobbing* CATHERINE *off up the street, left.*)

CATHERINE. He was born in Philadelphia! What do you want from him?

FIRST OFFICER. Step aside, lady, come on now . . .

(*The* SECOND OFFICER *has moved off with the two strange men.* MARCO, *taking advantage of the* FIRST OFFICER's *being occupied with* CATHERINE, *suddenly frees himself and points back at* EDDIE.)

MARCO. That one! I accuse that one!

(EDDIE *brushes* BEATRICE *aside and rushes out to the stoop.*)

FIRST OFFICER (*grabbing him and moving him quickly off up the left street*). Come on!

MARCO (*as he is taken off, pointing back at* EDDIE). That one! He killed my children! That one stole the food from my children!

(MARCO *is gone. The crowd has turned to* EDDIE.)

EDDIE (*to* LIPARI *and wife*). He's crazy! I give them the blankets off my bed. Six months I kept them like my own brothers!

(LIPARI, *the butcher, turns and starts up left with his arm around his wife.*)

EDDIE. Lipari! (*He follows* LIPARI *up left.*) For Christ's sake, I kept them, I give them the blankets off my bed!

(LIPARI *and wife exit.* EDDIE *turns and starts crossing down right to* LOUIS *and* MIKE.)

EDDIE. Louis! *Louis!*

(LOUIS *barely turns, then walks off and exits down right with* MIKE. *Only* BEATRICE *is left on the stoop.* CATHERINE *now returns, blank-eyed, from offstage and the car.* EDDIE *calls after* LOUIS *and* MIKE.)

EDDIE. He's gonna take that back. He's gonna take that back or I'll kill him! You hear me? I'll kill him! I'll kill him! (*He exits up street calling.*)

(*There is a pause of darkness before the lights rise, on the reception room of a prison.* MARCO *is seated;* ALFIERI, CATHERINE, *and* RODOLPHO *standing.*)

ALFIERI. I'm waiting, Marco, what do you say?

RODOLPHO. Marco never hurt anybody.

ALFIERI. I can bail you out until your hearing comes up. But I'm not going to do it, you understand me? Unless I have your promise. You're an honorable man, I will believe your promise. Now what do you say?

MARCO. In my country he would be dead now. He would not live this long.

ALFIERI. All right, Rodolpho—you come with me now.

RODOLPHO. No! Please, Mister. Marco—promise the man. Please, I want you to watch the wedding. How can I be married and you're in here? Please, you're not going to do anything; you know you're not.

(MARCO *is silent.*)

CATHERINE (*kneeling left of* MARCO). Marco, don't you understand? He can't bail you out if you're gonna do something bad. To hell with Eddie. Nobody is gonna talk to him again if he lives to a hundred. Everybody knows you spit in his face, that's enough, isn't it? Give me the satisfaction—I want you at the wedding. You got a wife and kids, Marco. You could be workin' till the hearing comes up, instead of layin' around here.

MARCO (*to* ALFIERI). I have no chance?

ALFIERI (*crosses to behind* MARCO). No, Marco. You're going back. The hearing is a formality, that's all.

MARCO. But him? There is a chance, eh?

ALFIERI. When she marries him he can start to become an American. They permit that, if the wife is born here.

MARCO (*looking at* RODOLPHO). Well— we did something. (*He lays a palm on* RODOLPHO's *arm and* RODOLPHO *covers it.*)

RODOLPHO. Marco, tell the man.

MARCO (*pulling his hand away*). What will I tell him? He knows such a promise is dishonorable.

ALFIERI. To promise not to kill is not dishonorable.

MARCO (*looking at* ALFIERI). No?

ALFIERI. No.

MARCO (*gesturing with his head—this is a new idea*). Then what is done with such a man?

ALFIERI. Nothing. If he obeys the law, he lives. That's all.

MARCO (*rises, turns to* ALFIERI). The law? All the law is not in a book.

ALFIERI. Yes. In a book. There is no other law.

MARCO (*his anger rising*). He degraded my brother. My blood. He robbed my children, he mocks my work. I work to come here, mister!

ALFIERI. I know, Marco—

MARCO. There is no law for that? Where is the law for that?

ALFIERI. There is none.

MARCO (*shaking his head, sitting*). I don't understand this country.

ALFIERI. Well? What is your answer? You have five or six weeks you could work. Or else you sit here. What do you say to me?

MARCO (*lowers his eyes. It almost seems he is ashamed*). All right.

ALFIERI. You won't touch him. This is your promise.

(*Slight pause.*)

MARCO. Maybe he wants to apologize to me.

(MARCO *is staring away.* ALFIERI *takes one of his hands.*)

ALFIERI. This is not God, Marco. You hear? Only God makes justice.

MARCO. All right.

ALFIERI (*nodding, not with assurance*). Good! Catherine, Rodolpho, Marco, let us go.

(CATHERINE *kisses* RODOLPHO *and* MARCO, *then kisses* ALFIERI's *hand.*)

CATHERINE. I'll get Beatrice and meet you at the church. (*She leaves quickly.*)

(MARCO *rises.* RODOLPHO *suddenly embraces him.* MARCO *pats him on the back and* RODOLPHO *exits after* CATHERINE. MARCO *faces* ALFIERI.)

ALFIERI. Only God, Marco.

(MARCO *turns and walks out.* ALFIERI *with a certain processional tread leaves the stage. The lights dim out.*)

(*The lights rise in the apartment.* EDDIE *is alone in the rocker, rocking back and forth in little surges. Pause. Now* BEATRICE *emerges from a bedroom. She is in her best clothes, wearing a hat.*)

BEATRICE (*with fear, going to* EDDIE). I'll be back in about an hour, Eddie. All right?

EDDIE (*quietly, almost inaudibly, as though drained*). What, have I been talkin' to myself?

BEATRICE. Eddie, for God's sake, it's her wedding.

EDDIE. Didn't you hear what I told you? You walk out that door to that wedding you ain't comin' back here, Beatrice.

BEATRICE. Why! What do you want?

EDDIE. I want my respect. Didn't you ever hear of that? From my wife?

(CATHERINE *enters from bedroom.*)

CATHERINE. It's after three; we're supposed to be there already, Beatrice. The priest won't wait.

BEATRICE. Eddie. It's her wedding. There'll be nobody there from her family. For my sister let me go. I'm goin' for my sister.

EDDIE (*as though hurt*). Look, I been arguin' with you all day already, Beatrice, and I said what I'm gonna say. He's gonna come here and apologize to me or nobody from this house is goin' into that church today. Now if that's more to you than I am, then go. But don't come back. You be on my side or on their side, that's all.

CATHERINE (*suddenly*). Who the hell do you think you are?

BEATRICE. Sssh!

CATHERINE. You got no more right to tell nobody nothin'! Nobody! The rest of your life, nobody!

BEATRICE. Shut up, Katie! (*She turns* CATHERINE *around.*)

CATHERINE You're gonna come with me!

BEATRICE. I can't Katie, I can't . . .

CATHERINE. How can you listen to him? This rat!

BEATRICE (*shaking* CATHERINE). Don't you call him that!

CATHERINE (*clearing from* BEATRICE). What're you scared of? He's a rat! He belongs in the sewer!

BEATRICE. Stop it!

CATHERINE (*weeping*). He bites people when they sleep! He comes when nobody's lookin' and poisons decent people. In the garbage he belongs!

(EDDIE *seems about to pick up the table and fling it at her.*)

BEATRICE. No, Eddie! Eddie! (*To* CATHERINE:) Then we all belong in the garbage. You, and me too. Don't say that. Whatever happened we all done it, and don't you ever forget it, Catherine. (*She goes to* CATHERINE.) Now go, go to your wedding, Katie, I'll stay home. Go. God bless you, God bless your children.

(*Enter* RODOLPHO.)

RODOLPHO. Eddie?

EDDIE. Who said you could come in here? Get outa here!

RODOLPHO. Marco is coming, Eddie. (*Pause.* BEATRICE *raises her hands in terror.*) He's praying in the church. You understand? (*Pause.* RODOLPHO *advances into the room.*) Catherine, I think it is better we go. Come with me.

CATHERINE. Eddie go away please.

BEATRICE (*quietly*). Eddie. Let's go someplace. Come. You and me. (*He has not moved.*) I don't want you to be here when he comes. I'll get your coat.

EDDIE. Where? Where am I goin'? This is my house.

BEATRICE (*crying out*). What's the use of of it! He's crazy now, you know the way they get, what good is it! You got nothin' against Marco, you always liked Marco!

EDDIE. I got nothin' against Marco? Which he called me a rat in front of the whole neighborhood? Which he said I killed his children! Where you been?

RODOLPHO (*quite suddenly, stepping up to* EDDIE). It is my fault, Eddie. Every-

thing. I wish to apologize. It was wrong that I do not ask your permission. I kiss your hand. (*He reaches for* EDDIE's *hand, but* EDDIE *snaps it away from him.*)

BEATRICE. Eddie, he's apologizing!

RODOLPHO. I have made all our troubles. But you have insult me too. Maybe God understand why you did that to me. Maybe you did not mean to insult me at all—

BEATRICE. Listen to him! Eddie, listen what 'he's tellin' you!

RODOLPHO. I think, maybe when Marco comes, if we can tell him we are comrades now, and we have no more argument between us. Then maybe Marco will not—

EDDIE. Now, listen—

CATHERINE. Eddie, give him a chance!

BEATRICE. What do you want! Eddie, what do you want!

EDDIE. I want my name! He didn't take my name; he's only a punk. Marco's got my name—(*to* RODOLPHO:) and you can run tell him, kid, that he's gonna give it back to me in front of this neighborhood, or we have it out. (*Hoisting up his pants:*) Come on, where is he? Take me to him.

BEATRICE. Eddie, listen—

EDDIE. I heard enough! Come on, let's go!

BEATRICE. Only blood is good? He kissed your hand!

EDDIE. What he does don't mean nothin' to nobody! (*To* RODOLPHO:) Come on!

BEATRICE (*barring his way to the stairs*). What's gonna mean somethin'? Eddie, listen to me. Who could give you your name? Listen to me, I love you, I'm talkin' to you, I love you; if Marco'll kiss your hand outside, if he goes on his knees, what is he got to give you? That's not what you want.

EDDIE. Don't bother me!

BEATRICE. You want somethin' else, Eddie, and you can never have her!

CATHERINE (*in horror*). B.!

EDDIE (*shocked, horrified, his fists clenching*). Beatrice!

(MARCO *appears outside, walking toward the door from a distant point.*)

BEATRICE (*crying out, weeping*). The truth is not as bad as blood, Eddie! I'm tellin' you the truth—tell her good-by forever!

EDDIE (*crying out in agony*). That's what you think of me—that I would have such a thoughts? (*His fists clench his head as though it will burst.*)

MARCO (*calling near the door outside*). Eddie Carbone!

(EDDIE *swerves about; all stand transfixed for an instant. People appear outside.*)

EDDIE (*as though flinging his challenge*). Yeah, Marco! Eddie Carbone. Eddie Carbone. Eddie Carbone. (*He goes up the stairs and emerges from the apartment.* RODOLPHO *streaks up and out past him and runs to* MARCO.)

RODOLPHO. No, Marco, please! Eddie, please, he has children! You will kill a family!

BEATRICE. Go in the house! Eddie, go in the house!

EDDIE (*he gradually comes to address the people*). Maybe he come to apologize to me. Heh, Marco? For what you said about me in front of the neighborhood? (*He is incensing himself and little bits of laughter even escape him as his eyes are murderous and he cracks his knuckles in his hands with a strange sort of relaxation.*) He knows that ain't right. To do like that? To a man? Which I put my roof over their head and my food in their mouth? Like in the Bible? Strangers I never seen in my whole life? To come out of the water and grab a girl for a passport? To go and take from your own family like from the stable—and never a word to me? And now accusations in the bargain! (*Directly to* MARCO:) Wipin' the neighborhood with my name like a dirty rag! I want my name, Marco. (*He is moving now, carefully, toward* MARCO.) Now gimme my name and we go together to the wedding.

BEATRICE *and* CATHERINE (*keening*). Eddie! Eddie, don't! Eddie!

EDDIE. No, Marco knows what's right from wrong. Tell the people, Marco, tell them what a liar you are! (*He has his arms spread and* MARCO *is spreading his.*) Come on, liar, you know what you done! (*He lunges for* MARCO *as a great hushed shout goes up from the people.*)

(MARCO *strikes* EDDIE *beside the neck.*)

MARCO. Animal! You go on your knees to me!

(EDDIE *goes down with the blow and* MARCO *starts to raise a foot to stomp him when* EDDIE *springs a knife into his hand and* MARCO *steps back.* LOUIS *rushes in toward* EDDIE.)

LOUIS. Eddie, for Christ's sake!

(EDDIE *raises the knife and* LOUIS *halts and steps back.*)

EDDIE. You lied about me, Marco. Now say it. Come on now, say it!

MARCO. Anima-a-a-l!

(EDDIE *lunges with the knife.* MARCO *grabs his arm, turning the blade inward and pressing it home as the women and* LOUIS *and* MIKE *rush in and separate them, and* EDDIE, *the knife still in his hand, falls to his knees before* MARCO. *The two women support him for a moment, calling his name again and again.*)

CATHERINE. Eddie I never meant to do nothing bad to you.

EDDIE. Then why—Oh, B.!

BEATRICE. Yes, yes!

EDDIE. My B.!

(*He dies in her arms, and* BEATRICE *covers him with her body.* ALFIERI, *who is in the crowd, turns out to the audience. The lights have gone down, leaving him in a glow, while behind him the dull prayers of the people and the keening of the women continue.*)

ALFIERI. Most of the time now we settle for half and I like it better. But the truth is holy, and even as I know how wrong he was, and his death useless, I tremble, for I confess that something perversely pure calls to me from his memory—not purely good, but himself purely, for he allowed himself to be wholly known and for that I think I will love him more than all my sensible clients. And yet, it is better to settle for half, it must be! And so I mourn him—I admit it—with a certain . . . alarm.

CURTAIN

THE CRUCIBLE

(With a new scene written for the revised production of the play)

Arthur Miller

First presented by Kermit Bloomgarden at the Martin
Beck Theatre, New York, on January 22, 1953,
with the following cast:

REVEREND PARRIS Fred Stewart

BETTY PARRIS Janet Alexander

TITUBA Jacqueline Andre

ABIGAIL WILLIAMS Madeleine Sherwood

SUSANNA WALCOTT Barbara Stanton

MRS. ANN PUTNAM Jane Hoffman

THOMAS PUTNAM Raymond Bramley

MERCY LEWIS Dorothy Joliffe

MARY WARREN Jenny Egan

JOHN PROCTOR Arthur Kennedy

REBECCA NURSE Jean Adair

GILES COREY Joseph Sweeney

REVEREND JOHN HALE E. G. Marshall

ELIZABETH PROCTOR Beatrice Straight

FRANCIS NURSE Graham Velsey

EZEKIEL CHEEVER Don McHenry

MARSHAL HERRICK George Mitchell

JUDGE HATHORNE Philip Coolidge

DEPUTY GOVERNOR DANFORTH
  Walter Hampden

SARAH GOOD Adele Fortin

HOPKINS Donald Marye

NOTE: In the restaged Broadway production, which opened at the Martin Beck Theatre
on January 22, 1953, Philip Coolidge replaced Walter Hampden, and the roles of John
Proctor and his wife were played by E. G. Marshall and Maureen Stapleton.

INTRODUCTION

The Crucible was actually staged twice for Broadway—once by Jed Harris, and a second time, six months later, by the author himself. For that occasion he added a new scene, a meeting between Proctor and Abigail that would strengthen the latter's motivation in precipitating the scandalous witchhunt in Salem. At the same time, in restaging the production prior to its national tour, Miller abolished the scenery and placed the action in front of drapes and an expressively lit cyclorama. In securing greater fluency for the work, he also drew attention to a timelessness of tragic implication expressed in his declaration that he wished to write a play that "would lift out of the morass of subjectivism the squirming, single defined process which would show that the sin of public terror is that it divests man of conscience, of himself."

Miller, our theatre's chief moralist, is correct in stating that "It was a theme not unrelated to those that had invested the previous plays," and that "I had grown increasingly conscious of this theme in my past work . . ." Nor is there any doubt that the pressure upon him to turn to it directly was both personal and, given his strong sense of the responsibilities of a writer, social. He had strong feelings about the state of the public mind, and it is apparent from both the play and the explanation of it offered in his introduction to his *Collected Plays* (The Viking Press, 1957) that the political situation of the period had acquired moral and spiritual connotations for him. "It was not only the rise of 'McCarthyism' that moved me," he declares, "but something which was much more weird and mysterious. It was the fact that a political, objective, knowledgeable campaign from the far Right was capable of creating not only a terror, but a new subjective reality, a veritable mystique which was gradually assuming even a holy resonance. That so interior and subjective an emotion could have been so manifestly created from without was a marvel to me. It underlies every word in *The Crucible*." To the author's contentions, in so far as they are intended to explain *The Crucible*, it is possible to object that while it is true that Salem had no witches, it is not true that contemporary America had no Communists. But it is true that Miller's concern was with a rather different matter—namely, the matter of conscience.

The subject of "confessing" to guilt concerned him especially, in both public life and in the play, where the tragic climax revolves around whether John Proctor will validate the Salem witchhunt by signing a statement to the effect that the Devil came to him and his neighbors. Miller writes, "I saw forming [in the 1950's] a kind of interior mechanism of confession and forgiveness of sins which until now had not been rightly categorized as sins. New sins were being created monthly. It was very odd how quickly these were accepted into the new orthodoxy, quite as though they had been there since the beginning of time. . . .

"Above all, above all horrors," Miller concludes, "I saw accepted the notion that conscience was no longer a private matter but one of state administration. I saw men handing conscience to other men and thanking other men for the opportunity of doing so." Therein lies the real tragic gambit of the play, whether or not Miller played it as well as we think he should have. Miller does not say so, but this theme could have reminded him of Sophocles' *Antigone* and given him the assurance that he was speaking with the voice of high-tragic tradition.

That he did not quite do so was the result of the intrigue in the plot, as well as of a limitation of literary talent, and perhaps also of point of view. That *The Crucible* was not a warmer and less abstract play, despite the author's concentration on personal motivation, has also been noted, eliciting Miller's reply that in plays of broad social awareness emotion and private feeling should be held in check. The resistance of some of the reviewers was strong enough for them to resort to charges of "contrivance" and "melodrama," including much dependency "on a slut's malicious lie," as *Time* magazine put it. Nevertheless, the first Broadway audiences were, in the main, greatly stirred. And a London production directed by George Devine and Tony Richardson at the Royal Court Theatre on April 10, 1956, eighteen months after a rather lukewarm premiere by the Bristol Old Vic Company, roused general enthusiasm despite reservations concerning weakness of characterization and some melodrama. The London *Times* complimented the author on "generating, nevertheless, a genuine dramatic force" and the author could accept the praise in this instance without granting the reservation. He believed he was sustained by the historical record in not providing "any mitigation of the unrelieved, straightforward, and absolute dedication to evil displayed by the judges of these trials and the prosecutors . . . There was a sadism here that was breathtaking." He blamed himself, on the contrary, for mitigating the evil of Danforth in the play, whereas the record of the trials does not support any mitigation. "I believe now," he declared in his preface to *Collected Plays,* "as I did not conceive then, that there are people dedicated to evil in the world," which view carries Miller out of the camp of old-fashioned liberalism and almost into the camp of his chief antagonists, the literati of the New Conservatism. . . . He concluded with a criticism that would have surprised the Broadway critics of the play in 1953: *"The Crucible* is a tough play. My criticism of it now would be that it is not tough enough."

AUTHOR'S NOTE ON THE HISTORICAL ACCURACY
OF THIS PLAY

This play is not history in the sense in which the word is used by the academic historian. Dramatic purposes have sometimes required many characters to be fused into one; the number of girls involved in the "crying-out" has been reduced; Abigail's age has been raised; while there were several judges of almost equal authority, I have symbolized them all in Hathorne and Danforth. However, I believe that the reader will discover here the essential nature of one of the strangest and most awful chapters in human history. The fate of each character is exactly that of his historical model, and there is no one in the drama who did not play a similar—and in some cases exactly the same—role in history.

As for the characters of the persons, little is known about most of them excepting what may be surmised from a few letters, the trial record, certain broadsides written at the time, and references to their conduct in sources of varying reliability. They may therefore be taken as creations of my own, drawn to the best of my ability in conformity with their known behavior, except as indicated in the commentary I have written for this text.

ACT ONE

A small upper bedroom in the home of Reverend Samuel Parris, Salem, Massachusetts, in the spring of the year 1692.

There is a narrow window at the left. Through its leaded panes the morning sunlight streams. A candle still burns near the bed, which is at the right. A chest, a chair, and a small table are the other furnishings. At the back a door opens on the landing of the stairway to the ground floor. The room gives off an air of clean spareness. The roof rafters are exposed, and the wood colors are raw and unmellowed.

As the curtain rises, REVEREND PARRIS *is discovered kneeling beside the bed, evidently in prayer. His daughter,* BETTY PARRIS, *aged ten, is lying on the bed, inert.*

At the time of these events Parris was in his middle forties. In history he cut a villainous path, and there is very little good to be said for him. He believed he was being persecuted wherever he went, despite his best efforts to win people and God to his side. In meeting, he felt insulted if someone rose to shut the door without first asking his permission. He was a widower with no interest in children, or talent with them. He regarded them as young adults, and until this strange crisis he, like the rest of Salem, never conceived that the children were anything but thankful for being permitted to walk straight, eyes slightly lowered, arms at the sides, and mouths shut until bidden to speak.

His house stood in the "town"—but we today would hardly call it a village. The meeting house was nearby, and from this point outward—toward the bay or inland —there were a few small-windowed, dark houses snuggling against the raw Massachusetts winter. Salem had been established hardly forty years before. To the European world the whole province was a barbaric frontier inhabited by a sect of fanatics who, nevertheless, were shipping out products of slowly increasing quantity and value.

No one can really know what their lives were like. They had no novelists—and would not have permitted anyone to read a novel if one were handy. Their creed forbade anything resembling a theater or "vain enjoyment." They did not celebrate Christmas, and a holiday from work meant only that they must concentrate even more upon prayer.

Which is not to say that nothing broke into this strict and somber way of life. When a new farmhouse was built, friends assembled to "raise the roof," and there would be special foods cooked and probably some potent cider passed around. There was a good supply of ne'er-do-wells in Salem, who dallied at the shovelboard in Bridget Bishop's tavern. Probably more than the creed, hard work kept the morals of the place from spoiling, for the people were forced to fight the land like heroes for every grain of corn, and no man had very much time for fooling around.

That there were some jokers, however, is indicated by the practice of appointing a two-man patrol whose duty was to "walk forth in the time of God's worship to take notice of such as either lye about the meeting house, without attending to the word and ordinances, or that lye at home or in the fields without giving good account thereof, and to take the names of such persons, and to present them to the magistrates, whereby they may be accordingly proceeded against." This predilection for minding other people's business was time-honored among the people of Salem, and it undoubtedly created many of the suspicions which were to feed the coming madness. It was also, in my opinion, one of the things that a John Proctor would rebel against, for the time of the armed camp had almost passed, and since the country was reasonably—although not wholly— safe, the old disciplines were beginning to rankle. But, as in all such matters, the issue was not clear-cut, for danger was still a possibility, and in unity still lay the best promise of safety.

The edge of the wilderness was close by. The American continent stretched endlessly west, and it was full of mystery for them. It stood, dark and threatening, over their shoulders night and day, for out of it Indian tribes marauded from time to time, and Reverend Parris had parishioners who had lost relatives to these heathen.

The parochial snobbery of these people was partly responsible for their failure to convert the Indians. Probably they also preferred to take land from heathens rather than from fellow Christians. At any rate, very few Indians were converted, and the Salem folk believed that the virgin forest was the Devil's last preserve, his home base and the citadel of his final stand. To the best of their knowledge the American forest was the last place on earth that was not paying homage to God.

For these reasons, among others, they carried about an air of innate resistance, even of persecution. Their fathers had, of course, been persecuted in England. So now they and their church found it necessary to deny any other sect its freedom, lest their New Jersualem be defiled and corrupted by wrong ways and deceitful ideas.

They believed, in short, that they held in their steady hands the candle that would light the world. We have inherited this belief, and it has helped and hurt us. It helped them with the discipline it gave them. They were a dedicated folk, by and large, and they had to be to survive the life they had chosen or been born into in this country.

The proof of their belief's value to them may be taken from the opposite character of the first Jamestown settlement, farther south, in Virginia. The Englishmen who landed there were motivated mainly by a hunt for profit. They had thought to pick off the wealth of the new country and then return rich to England. They were a band of individualists, and a much more ingratiating group than the Massachusetts men. But Virginia destroyed them. Massachusetts tried to kill off the Puritans, but they combined; they set up a communal society which, in the beginning, was little more than an armed camp with an autocratic and very devoted leadership. It was, however, an autocracy by consent, for they were united from top to bottom by a commonly held ideology whose perpetuation was the reason and justification for all their sufferings. So their self-denial, their purposefulness, their suspicion of all vain pursuits, their hard-handed justice, were altogether perfect instruments for the conquest of this space so antagonistic to man.

But the people of Salem in 1692 were not quite the dedicated folk that arrived on the *Mayflower*. A vast differentiation had taken place, and in their own time a revolution had unseated the royal government and substituted a junta which was at this moment in power. The times, to their eyes, must have been out of joint, and to the common folk must have seemed as insoluble and complicated as do ours today. It is not hard to see how easily many could have been led to believe that the time of confusion had been brought upon them by deep and darkling forces. No hint of such speculation appears on the court record, but social disorder in any age breeds such mystical suspicions, and when, as in Salem, wonders are brought forth from below the social surface, it is too much to expect people to hold back very long from laying on the victims with all the force of their frustrations.

The Salem tragedy, which is about to begin in these pages, developed from a paradox. It is a paradox in whose grip we still live, and there is no prospect yet that we will discover its resolution. Simply, it was this: for good purposes, even high purposes, the people of Salem developed a theocracy, a combine of state and religious power whose function was to keep the community together, and to prevent any kind of disunity that might open it to destruction by material or ideological enemies. It was forged for a necessary purpose and accomplished that purpose. But all organization is and must be grounded on the idea of exclusion and prohibition, just as two objects cannot occupy the same space. Evidently the time came in New England when the repressions of order were heavier than seemed warranted by the dangers against which the order was organized. The witchhunt was a perverse manifestation of the panic which set in among all classes when the balance began to turn toward greater individual freedom.

When one rises above the individual villainy displayed, one can only pity them all, just as we shall be pitied someday. It is still impossible for man to organize his social life without repressions, and the balance has yet to be struck between order and freedom.

The witchhunt was not, however, a mere repression. It was also, and as importantly, a long overdue opportunity for everyone so inclined to express publicly his guilt and sins, under the cover of accusations against the victims. It suddenly became possible—and patriotic and holy—for a man to say that Martha Corey had come into his bedroom at night, and that, while his wife was sleeping at his side,

Martha laid herself down on his chest and "nearly suffocated him." Of course it was her spirit only, but his satisfaction at confessing himself was no lighter than if it had been Martha herself. One could not ordinarily speak such things in public.

Long-held hatreds of neighbors could now be openly expressed, and vengeance taken, despite the Bible's charitable injunctions. Land-lust which had been expressed before by constant bickering over boundaries and deeds, could now be elevated to the arena of morality; one could cry witch against one's neighbor and feel perfectly justified in the bargain. Old scores could be settled on a plane of heavenly combat between Lucifer and the Lord; suspicions and the envy of the miserable toward the happy could and did burst out in the general revenge.

REVEREND PARRIS *is praying now, and, though we cannot hear his words, a sense of his confusion hangs about him. He mumbles, then seems about to weep; then he weeps, then prays again; but his daughter does not stir on the bed.*

The door opens, and his Negro slave enters. TITUBA *is in her forties.* PARRIS *brought her with him from Barbados, where he spent some years as a merchant before entering the ministry. She enters as one does who can no longer bear to be barred from the sight of her beloved, but she is also very frightened because her slave sense has warned her that, as always, trouble in this house eventually lands on her back.*

TITUBA (*already taking a step backward*). My Betty be hearty soon?

PARRIS. Out of here!

TITUBA (*backing to the door*). My Betty not goin' die . . .

PARRIS (*scrambling to his feet in a fury*). Out of my sight! (*She is gone.*) Out of my—(*He is overcome with sobs. He clamps his teeth against them and closes the door and leans against it, exhausted.*) Oh, my God! God help me! (*Quaking with fear, mumbling to himself through his sobs, he goes to the bed and gently takes* BETTY's *hand.*) Betty. Child. Dear child. Will you wake, will you open up your eyes! Betty, little one . . .

(*He is bending to kneel again when his niece,* ABIGAIL WILLIAMS, *seventeen, enters —a strikingly beautiful girl, an orphan, with an endless capacity for dissembling. Now she is all worry and apprehension and propriety.*)

ABIGAIL. Uncle? (*He looks to her.*) Susanna Walcott's here from Doctor Griggs.

PARRIS. Oh? Let her come, let her come.

ABIGAIL (*leaning out the door to call to* SUSANNA, *who is down the hall a few steps*). Come in, Susanna.

(SUSANNA WALCOTT, *a little younger than* ABIGAIL, *a nervous, hurried girl, enters.*)

PARRIS (*eagerly*). What does the doctor say, child?

SUSANNA (*craning around* PARRIS *to get a look at* BETTY). He bid me come and tell you, reverend sir, that he cannot discover no medicine for it in his books.

PARRIS. Then he must search on.

SUSANNA. Aye, sir, he have been searchin' his books since he left you, sir. But he bid me tell you, that you might look to unnatural things for the cause of it.

PARRIS (*his eyes going wide*). No—no. There be no unnatural cause here. Tell him I have sent for Reverend Hale of Beverly, and Mr. Hale will surely confirm that. Let him look to medicine and put out all thought of unnatural causes here. There be none.

SUSANNA. Aye, sir. He bid me tell you. (*She turns to go.*)

ABIGAIL. Speak nothin' of it in the village, Susanna.

PARRIS. Go directly home and speak nothing of unnatural causes.

SUSANNA. Aye, sir. I pray for her. (*She goes out.*)

ABIGAIL. Uncle, the rumor of witchcraft is all about; I think you'd best go down and deny it yourself. The parlor's packed with people, sir. I'll sit with her.

PARRIS (*pressed, turns on her*). And what shall I say to them? That my daughter and my niece I discovered dancing like heathen in the forest?

ABIGAIL. Uncle, we did dance; let you tell them I confessed it—and I'll be whipped if I must be. But they're speakin' of witchcraft. Betty's not witched.

PARRIS. Abigail, I cannot go before the congregation when I know you have not opened with me. What did you do with her in the forest?

ABIGAIL. We did dance, uncle, and when you leaped out of the bush so suddenly, Betty was frightened and then she fainted. And there's the whole of it.

PARRIS. Child. Sit you down.

ABIGAIL (*quavering, as she sits*). I would never hurt Betty. I love her dearly.

PARRIS. Now look you, child, your punishment will come in its time. But if you trafficked with spirits in the forest I must know it now, for surely my enemies will, and they will ruin me with it.

ABIGAIL. But we never conjured spirits.

PARRIS. Then why can she not move herself since midnight? This child is desperate! (ABIGAIL *lowers her eyes.*) It must come out—my enemies will bring it out. Let me know what you done there. Abigail, do you understand that I have many enemies?

ABIGAIL. I have heard of it, uncle.

PARRIS. There is a faction that is sworn to drive me from my pulpit. Do you understand that?

ABIGAIL. I think so, sir.

PARRIS. Now then, in the midst of such disruption, my own household is discovered to be the very center of some obscene practice. Abominations are done in the forest—

ABIGAIL. It were sport, uncle!

PARRIS (*pointing at* BETTY). You call this sport? (*She lowers her eyes. He pleads.*) Abigail, if you know something that may help the doctor, for God's sake tell it to me. (*She is silent.*) I saw Tituba waving her arms over the fire when I came on you. Why was she doing that? And I heard a screeching and gibberish coming from her mouth. She were swaying like a dumb beast over that fire!

ABIGAIL. She always sings her Barbados songs, and we dance.

PARRIS. I cannot blink what I saw, Abigail, for my enemies will not blink it. I saw a dress lying on the grass.

ABIGAIL (*innocently*). A dress?

PARRIS (*—it is very hard to say*). Aye, a dress. And I thought I saw—someone naked running through the trees!

ABIGAIL (*in terror*). No one was naked! You mistake yourself, uncle!

PARRIS (*with anger*). I saw it! (*He moves from her. Then, resolved.*) Now tell me true, Abigail. And I pray you feel the weight of truth upon you, for now my ministry's at stake, my ministry and perhaps your cousin's life. Whatever abomination you have done, give me all of it now, for I dare not be taken unaware when I go before them down there.

ABIGAIL. There is nothin' more. I swear it, uncle.

PARRIS (*studies her, then nods, half convinced*). Abigail, I have fought here three long years to bend these stiff-necked people to me, and now, just now when some good respect is rising for me in the parish, you compromise my very character. I have given you a home, child, I have put clothes upon your back—now give me upright answer. Your name in the town—it is entirely white, is it not?

ABIGAIL (*with an edge of resentment*). Why, I am sure it is, sir. There be no blush about my name.

PARRIS (*to the point*). Abigail, is there any other cause than you have told me, for your being discharged from Goody Proctor's service? I have heard it said, and I tell you as I heard it, that she comes so rarely to the church this year for she will not sit so close to something soiled. What signified that remark?

ABIGAIL. She hates me, uncle, she must, for I would not be her slave. It's a bitter woman, a lying, cold, sniveling woman, and I will not work for such a woman!

PARRIS. She may be. And yet it has troubled me that you are now seven month out of their house, and in all this time no other family has ever called for your service.

ABIGAIL. They want slaves, not such as I. Let them send to Barbados for that. I will not black my face for any of them! (*With ill-concealed resentment at him.*) Do you begrudge my bed, uncle?

PARRIS. No—no.

ABIGAIL (*in a temper*). My name is good in the village! I will not have it said my name is soiled! Goody Proctor is a gossiping liar!

(*Enter* MRS. ANN PUTNAM. *She is a twisted soul of forty-five, a death-ridden woman, haunted by dreams.*)

PARRIS (*as soon as the door begins to open*). No—no, I cannot have anyone. (*He sees her, and a certain deference springs into him, although his worry remains.*) Why, Goody Putnam, come in.

MRS. PUTNAM (*full of breath, shiny-eyed*). It is a marvel. It is surely a stroke of hell upon you.

PARRIS. No, Goody Putnam, it is—

MRS. PUTNAM (*glancing at* BETTY). How high did she fly, how high?

PARRIS. No, no, she never flew—

MRS. PUTNAM (*very pleased with it*). Why, it's sure she did. Mr. Collins saw her goin' over Ingersoll's barn, and come down light as bird, he says!

PARRIS. Now, look you, Goody Putnam, she never—(*Enter* THOMAS PUTNAM, *a well-to-do, hard-handed landowner, near fifty.*) Oh, good morning, Mr. Putnam.

PUTNAM. It is a providence the thing is out now! It is a providence. (*He goes directly to the bed.*)

PARRIS. What's out, sir, what's—?

(MRS. PUTNAM *goes to the bed.*)

PUTNAM (*looking down at* BETTY). Why, her eyes is closed! Look you, Ann.

MRS. PUTNAM. Why, that's strange. (*To* PARRIS.) Ours is open.

PARRIS (*shocked*). Your Ruth is sick?

MRS. PUTNAM (*with vicious certainty*). I'd not call it sick; the Devil's touch is heavier than sick. It's death, y'know, it's death drivin' into them, forked and hoofed.

PARRIS. Oh, pray not! Why, how does Ruth ail?

MRS. PUTNAM. She ails as she must—she never waked this morning, but her eyes open and she walks, and hears naught, sees naught, and cannot eat. Her soul is taken, surely.

(PARRIS *is struck.*)

PUTNAM (*as though for further details*). They say you've sent for Reverend Hale of Beverly?

PARRIS (*with dwindling conviction now*). A precaution only. He has much experience in all demonic arts, and I—

MRS. PUTNAM. He has indeed; and found a witch in Beverly last year, and let you remember that.

PARRIS. Now, Goody Ann, they only thought that were a witch, and I am certain there be no element of witchcraft here.

PUTNAM. No witchcraft! Now look you, Mr. Parris—

PARRIS. Thomas, Thomas, I pray you, leap not to witchcraft. I know that you —you least of all, Thomas, would ever wish so disastrous a charge laid upon me. We cannot leap to witchcraft. They will howl me out of Salem for such corruption in my house.

———

A word about Thomas Putnam. He was a man with many grievances, at least one of which appears justified. Some time before, his wife's brother-in-law, James Bayley, had been turned down as minister of Salem. Bayley had all the qualifications, and a two-thirds vote into the bargain, but a faction stopped his acceptance, for reasons that are not clear.

Thomas Putnam was the eldest son of the richest man in the village. He had fought the Indians at Narragansett, and was deeply interested in parish affairs. He undoubtedly felt it poor payment that the village should so blatantly disregard his candidate for one of its more important offices, especially since he regarded himself as the intellectual superior of most of the people around him.

His vindictive nature was demonstrated long before the witchcraft began. Another former Salem minister, George Burroughs, had had to borrow money to pay for his wife's funeral, and, since the parish was remiss in his salary, he was soon bankrupt. Thomas and his brother John had Burroughs jailed for debts the man did not owe. The incident is important only in that Burroughs succeeded in becoming minister where Bayley, Thomas Putnam's brother-in-law, had been rejected; the motif of resentment is clear here. Thomas Putnam felt that his own name and the honor of his family had been smirched by the village, and he meant to right matters however he could.

Another reason to believe him a deeply embittered man was his attempt to break his father's will, which left a disproportionate amount to a step-brother. As with every other public cause in which he tried to force his way, he failed in this.

So it is not surprising to find that so many accusations against people are in the handwriting of Thomas Putnam, or that his name is so often found as a witness corroborating the supernatural testimony, or that his daughter led the crying-out at the most opportune junctures of the trials, especially when—But we'll speak of that when we come to it.

———

PUTNAM (—*at the moment he is intent upon getting* PARRIS, *for whom he has only contempt, to move toward the abyss*). Mr. Parris, I have taken your part in all contention here, and I would continue; but I cannot if you hold back in this. There are hurtful, vengeful spirits layin' hands on these children.

PARRIS. But, Thomas, you cannot—

PUTNAM. Ann! Tell Mr. Parris what you have done.

MRS. PUTNAM. Reverend Parris, I have laid seven babies unbaptized in the earth. Believe me, sir, you never saw more hearty babies born. And yet, each would wither in my arms the very night of their birth. I have spoke nothin', but my heart has clamored intimations. And now, this year, my Ruth, my only— I see her turning strange. A secret child she has become this year, and shrivels like a sucking mouth were pullin' on her life too. And so I thought to send her to your Tituba—

PARRIS. To Tituba! What may Tituba—?

MRS. PUTNAM. Tituba knows how to speak to the dead, Mr. Parris.

PARRIS. Goody Ann, it is a formidable sin to conjure up the dead!

MRS. PUTNAM. I take it on my soul, but who else may surely tell us what person murdered my babies?

PARRIS (*horrified*). Woman!

MRS. PUTNAM. They were murdered, Mr. Parris! And mark this proof! Mark it! Last night my Ruth were ever so close to their little spirits; I know it, sir. For how else is she struck dumb now except some power of darkness would stop her mouth? It is a marvelous sign, Mr. Parris!

PUTNAM. Don't you understand it, sir? There is a murdering witch among us, bound to keep herself in the dark. (PARRIS *turns to* BETTY, *a frantic terror rising in him.*) Let your enemies make of it what they will, you cannot blink it more.

PARRIS (*to* ABIGAIL). Then you were conjuring spirits last night.

ABIGAIL (*whispering*). Not I, sir—Tituba and Ruth.

PARRIS (*turns now, with new fear, and goes to* BETTY, *looks down at her, and then, gazing off*). Oh, Abigail, what proper payment for my charity! Now I am undone.

PUTNAM. You are not undone! Let you take hold here. Wait for no one to charge you—declare it yourself. You have discovered witchcraft—

PARRIS. In my house? In my house, Thomas? They will topple me with this! They will make of it a—

(*Enter* MERCY LEWIS, *the Putnams' servant, a fat, sly, merciless girl of eighteen.*)

MERCY. Your pardons. I only thought to see how Betty is.

PUTNAM. Why aren't you home? Who's with Ruth?

MERCY. Her grandma come. She's improved a little, I think—she give a powerful sneeze before.

MRS. PUTNAM. Ah, there's a sign of life!

MERCY. I'd fear no more, Goody Putnam. It were a grand sneeze; another like it will shake her wits together, I'm sure. (*She goes to the bed to look.*)

PARRIS. Will you leave me now, Thomas? I would pray a while alone.

ABIGAIL. Uncle, you've prayed since midnight. Why do you not go down and—

PARRIS. No—no. (*To* PUTNAM.) I have no answer for that crowd. I'll wait till Mr. Hale arrives. (*To get* MRS. PUTNAM *to leave.*) If you will, Goody Ann . . .

PUTNAM. Now look you, sir. Let you strike out against the Devil, and the village will bless you for it! Come down, speak to them—pray with them. They're thirsting for your word, Mister! Surely you'll pray with them.

PARRIS (*swayed*). I'll lead them in a psalm, but let you say nothing of witchcraft yet. I will not discuss it. The cause is yet unknown. I have had enough contention since I came; I want no more.

MRS. PUTNAM. Mercy, you go home to Ruth, d'y'hear?

MERCY. Aye, mum.

(MRS. PUTNAM *goes out.*)

PARRIS (*to* ABIGAIL). If she starts for the window, cry for me at once.

ABIGAIL. I will, uncle.

PARRIS (*to* PUTNAM). There is a terrible power in her arms today. (*He goes out with* PUTNAM.)

ABIGAIL (*with hushed trepidation*). How is Ruth sick?

MERCY. It's weirdish, I know not—she seems to walk like a dead one since last night.

ABIGAIL (*turns at once and goes to* BETTY, *and now, with fear in her voice*). Betty? (BETTY *doesn't move. She shakes her.*) Now stop this! Betty! Sit up now!

(BETTY *doesn't stir.* MERCY *comes over.*)

MERCY. Have you tried beatin' her? I gave Ruth a good one and it waked her for a minute. Here, let me have her.

ABIGAIL (*holding* MERCY *back*). No, he'll be comin' up. Listen, now; if they be questioning us, tell them we danced—I told him as much already.

MERCY. Aye. And what more?

ABIGAIL. He knows Tituba conjured

356 ARTHUR MILLER

Ruth's sisters to come out of the grave.

MERCY. And what more?

ABIGAIL. He saw you naked.

MERCY (*clapping her hands together with a frightened laugh*). Oh, Jesus!

(*Enter* MARY WARREN, *breathless. She is seventeen, a subservient, naïve, lonely girl.*)

MARY WARREN. What'll we do? The village is out! I just come from the farm; the whole country's talkin' witchcraft! They'll be callin' us witches, Abby!

MERCY (*pointing and looking at* MARY WARREN). She means to tell, I know it.

MARY WARREN. Abby, we've got to tell. Witchery's a hangin' error, a hangin' like they done in Boston two year ago! We must tell the truth, Abby! You'll only be whipped for dancin', and the other things!

ABIGAIL. Oh, *we'll* be whipped!

MARY WARREN. I never done none of it, Abby. I only looked!

MERCY (*moving menacingly toward* MARY). Oh, you're a great one for lookin', aren't you, Mary Warren? What a grand peeping courage you have!

(BETTY, *on the bed, whimpers.* ABIGAIL *turns to her at once.*)

ABIGAIL. Betty? (*She goes to* BETTY.) Now, Betty, dear, wake up now. It's Abigail. (*She sits* BETTY *up and furiously shakes her.*) I'll beat you, Betty! (BETTY *whimpers.*) My, you seem improving. I talked to your papa and I told him everything. So there's nothing to—

BETTY (*darts off the bed, frightened of* ABIGAIL, *and flattens herself against the wall*). I want my mama!

ABIGAIL (*with alarm, as she cautiously approaches* BETTY). What ails you, Betty? Your mama's dead and buried.

BETTY. I'll fly to Mama. Let me fly! (*She raises her arms as though to fly, and streaks for the window, gets one leg out.*)

ABIGAIL (*pulling her away from the window*). I told him everything; he knows now, he knows everything we—

BETTY. You drank blood, Abby! You didn't tell him that!

ABIGAIL. Betty, you never say that again! You will never—

BETTY. You did, you did! You drank a charm to kill John Proctor's wife! You drank a charm to kill Goody Proctor!

ABIGAIL (*smashes her across the face*). Shut it! Now shut it!

BETTY (*collapsing on the bed*). Mama, Mama! (*She dissolves into sobs.*)

ABIGAIL. Now look you. All of you. We danced. And Tituba conjured Ruth Putnam's dead sisters. And that is all. And mark this. Let either of you breathe a word, or the edge of a word, about the other things, and I will come to you in the black of some terrible night and I will bring a pointy reckoning that will shudder you. And you know I can do it; I saw Indians smash my dear parents' heads on the pillow next to mine, and I have seen some reddish work done at night, and I can make you wish you had never seen the sun go down! (*She goes to* BETTY *and roughly sits her up.*) Now, you—sit up and stop this!

(*But* BETTY *collapses in her hands and lies inert on the bed.*)

MARY WARREN (*with hysterical fright*). What's got her? (ABIGAIL *stares in fright at* BETTY.) Abby, she's going to die! It's a sin to conjure, and we—

ABIGAIL (*starting for* MARY). I say shut it, Mary Warren!

(*Enter* JOHN PROCTOR. *On seeing him,* MARY WARREN *leaps in fright.*)

———

Proctor was a farmer in his middle thirties. He need not have been a partisan of any faction in the town, but there is evidence to suggest that he had a sharp and biting way with hypocrites. He was the kind of man—powerful of body, even-tempered, and not easily led—who cannot refuse support to partisans without drawing their deepest resentment. In Proctor's presence a fool felt his foolishness instantly —and a Proctor is always marked for calumny therefore.

But as we shall see, the steady manner he displays does not spring from an untroubled soul. He is a sinner, a sinner not only against the moral fashion of the time, but against his own vision of decent conduct. These people had no ritual for the washing away of sins. It is another trait we inherited from them, and it has helped to discipline us as well as to breed hypocrisy among us. Proctor, respected and even feared in Salem, has come to regard himself as a kind of fraud. But no hint of this has yet appeared on the surface, and as he enters from the crowded parlor below it is a man in his prime we see, with a quiet confidence and an unexpressed, hidden force. Mary Warren, his servant, can barely speak for embarrassment and fear. _____

MARY WARREN. Oh! I'm just going home, Mr. Proctor.

PROCTOR. Be you foolish, Mary Warren? Be you deaf? I forbid you leave the house, did I not? Why shall I pay you? I am looking for you more often than my cows!

MARY WARREN. I only come to see the great doings in the world.

PROCTOR. I'll show you a great doin' on your arse one of these days. Now get you home; my wife is waitin' with your work! (*Trying to retain a shred of dignity, she goes slowly out.*)

MERCY LEWIS (*both afraid of him and strangely titillated*). I'd best be off. I have my Ruth to watch. Good morning, Mr. Proctor.

(MERCY *sidles out. Since* PROCTOR'S *entrance,* ABIGAIL *has stood as though on tiptoe, absorbing his presence, wide-eyed. He glances at her, then goes to* BETTY *on the bed.*)

ABIGAIL. Gah! I'd almost forgot how strong you are, John Proctor!

PROCTOR (*looking at* ABIGAIL *now, the faintest suggestion of a knowing smile on his face*). What's this mischief here?

ABIGAIL (*with a nervous laugh*). Oh, she's only gone silly somehow.

PROCTOR. The road past my house is a pilgrimage to Salem all morning. The town's mumbling witchcraft.

ABIGAIL. Oh, posh! (*Winningly she comes a little closer, with a confidential, wicked air.*) We were dancin' in the woods last night, and my uncle leaped in on us. She took fright, is all.

PROCTOR (*his smile widening*). Ah, you're wicked yet, aren't y'! (*A trill of expectant laughter escapes her, and she dares come closer, feverishly looking into his eyes.*) You'll be clapped in the stocks before you're twenty.

(*He takes a step to go, and she springs into his path.*)

ABIGAIL. Give me a word, John. A soft word. (*Her concentrated desire destroys his smile.*)

PROCTOR. No, no, Abby. That's done with.

ABIGAIL (*tauntingly*). You come five mile to see a silly girl fly? I know you better.

PROCTOR (*setting her firmly out of his path*). I come to see what mischief your uncle's brewin' now. (*With final emphasis.*) Put it out of mind, Abby.

ABIGAIL (*grasping his hand before he can release her*). John—I am waitin' for you every night.

PROCTOR. Abby, I never give you hope to wait for me.

ABIGAIL (*now beginning to anger—she can't believe it*). I have something better than hope, I think!

PROCTOR. Abby, you'll put it out of mind. I'll not be comin' for you more.

ABIGAIL. You're surely sportin' with me.

PROCTOR. You know me better.

ABIGAIL. I know how you clutched my back behind your house and sweated like a stallion whenever I come near! Or did I dream that? It's she put me out, you cannot pretend it were you. I saw your face when she put me out, and you loved me then and you do now!

PROCTOR. Abby, that's a wild thing to say—

ABIGAIL. A wild thing may say wild things. But not so wild, I think. I have seen you since she put me out; I have seen you nights.

PROCTOR. I have hardly stepped off my farm this sevenmonth.

ABIGAIL. I have a sense for heat, John, and yours has drawn me to my window, and I have seen you looking up, burning in your loneliness. Do you tell me you've never looked up at my window?

PROCTOR. I may have looked up.

ABIGAIL (*now softening*). And you must. You are no wintry man. I know you, John. I *know* you. (*She is weeping.*) I cannot sleep for dreamin'; I cannot dream but I wake and walk about the house as though I'd find you comin' through some door. (*She clutches him desperately.*)

PROCTOR (*gently pressing her from him, with great sympathy but firmly*). Child—

ABIGAIL (*with a flash of anger*). How do you call me child!

PROCTOR. Abby, I may think of you softly from time to time. But I will cut off my hand before I'll ever reach for you again. Wipe it out of mind. We never touched, Abby.

ABIGAIL. Aye, but we did.

PROCTOR. Aye, but we did not.

ABIGAIL (*with a bitter anger*). Oh, I marvel how such a strong man may let such a sickly wife be—

PROCTOR (*angered—at himself as well*).

You'll sp~ak nothin' of Elizabeth!

ABIGAIL. She is blackening my name in the village! She is telling lies about me! She is a cold, sniveling woman, and you bend to her! Let her turn you like a—

PROCTOR (*shaking her*). Do you look for whippin'?

(*A psalm is heard being sung below.*)

ABIGAIL (*in tears*). I look for John Proctor that took me from my sleep and put knowledge in my heart! I never knew what pretense Salem was, I never knew the lying lessons I was taught by all these Christian women and their covenanted men! And now you bid me tear the light out of my eyes? I will not, I cannot! You loved me, John Proctor, and whatever sin it is, you love me yet! (*He turns abruptly to go out. She rushes to him.*) John, pity me, pity me!

(*The words "going up to Jesus" are heard in the psalm, and* BETTY *claps her ears suddenly and whines loudly.*)

ABIGAIL. Betty? (*She hurries to* BETTY, *who is now sitting up and screaming.* PROCTOR *goes to* BETTY *as* ABIGAIL *is trying to pull her hands down, calling "Betty!"*)

PROCTOR (*growing unnerved*). What's she doing? Girl, what ails you? Stop that wailing!

(*The singing has stopped in the midst of this, and now* PARRIS *rushes in.*)

PARRIS. What happened? What are you doing to her? Betty! (*He rushes to the bed, crying, "Betty, Betty!"* MRS. PUTNAM *enters, feverish with curiosity, and with her* THOMAS PUTNAM *and* MERCY LEWIS. PARRIS, *at the bed, keeps lightly slapping* BETTY's *face, while she moans and tries to get up.*)

ABIGAIL. She heard you singin' and suddenly she's up and screamin'.

MRS. PUTNAM. The psalm! The psalm! She cannot bear to hear the Lord's name!

PARRIS. No, God forbid. Mercy, run to the doctor! Tell him what's happened here! (MERCY LEWIS *rushes out.*)

MRS. PUTNAM. Mark it for a sign, mark it!

(REBECCA NURSE, *seventy-two, enters. She is white-haired, leaning upon her walking-stick.*)

PUTNAM (*pointing at the whimpering* BETTY). That is a notorious sign of witchcraft afoot, Goody Nurse, a prodigious sign!

MRS. PUTNAM. My mother told me that!

When they cannot bear to hear the name of—

PARRIS (*trembling*). Rebecca, Rebecca, go to her, we're lost. She suddenly cannot bear to hear the Lord's—

(GILES COREY, *eighty-three, enters. He is knotted with muscle, canny, inquisitive, and still powerful.*)

REBECCA. There is hard sickness here, Giles Corey, so please to keep the quiet.

GILES. I've not said a word. No one here can testify I've said a word. Is she going to fly again? I hear she flies.

PUTNAM. Man, be quiet now!

(*Everything is quiet.* REBECCA *walks across the room to the bed. Gentleness exudes from her.* BETTY *is quietly whimpering, eyes shut.* REBECCA *simply stands over the child, who gradually quiets.*)

———

And while they are so absorbed, we may put a word in for Rebecca. Rebecca was the wife of Francis Nurse, who, from all accounts, was one of those men for whom both sides of the argument had to have respect. He was called upon to arbitrate disputes as though he were an unofficial judge, and Rebecca also enjoyed the high opinion most people had for him. By the time of the delusion, they had three hundred acres, and their children were settled in separate homesteads within the same estate. However, Francis had originally rented the land, and one theory has it that, as he gradually paid for it and raised his social status, there were those who resented his rise.

Another suggestion to explain the systematic campaign against Rebecca, and inferentially against Francis, is the land war he fought with his neighbors, one of whom was a Putnam. This squabble grew to the proportions of a battle in the woods between partisans of both sides, and it is said to have lasted for two days. As for Rebecca herself, the general opinion of her character was so high that to explain how anyone dared cry her out for a witch—and more, how adults could bring themselves to lay hands on her—we must look to the fields and boundaries of that time.

As we have seen, Thomas Putnam's man for the Salem ministry was Bayley. The Nurse clan had been in the faction that prevented Bayley's taking office. In addition, certain families allied to the Nurses by blood or friendship, and whose farms were contiguous with the Nurse farm or close to it, combined to break away from the Salem town authority and set up Topsfield, a new and independent entity whose existence was resented by old Salemites.

That the guiding hand behind the outcry was Putnam's is indicated by the fact that, as soon as it began, this Topsfield-Nurse faction absented themselves from church in protest and disbelief. It was Edward and Jonathan Putnam who signed the first complaint against Rebecca; and Thomas Putnam's little daughter was the one who fell into a fit at the hearing and pointed to Rebecca as her attacker. To top it all, Mrs. Putnam—who is now staring at the bewitched child on the bed—soon accused Rebecca's spirit of "tempting her to iniquity," a charge that had more truth in it than Mrs. Putnam could know.

MRS. PUTNAM (*astonished*). What have you done?

(REBECCA, *in thought, now leaves the bedside and sits.*)

PARRIS (*wondrous and relieved*). What do you make of it, Rebecca?

PUTNAM (*eagerly*). Goody Nurse, will you go to my Ruth and see if you can wake her?

REBECCA (*sitting*). I think she'll wake in time. Pray calm yourselves. I have eleven children, and I am twenty-six times a grandma, and I have seen them all through their silly seasons, and when it come on them they will run the Devil bowlegged keeping up with their mischief. I think she'll wake when she tires of it. A child's spirit is like a child, you can never catch it by running after it; you must stand still, and, for love, it will soon itself come back.

PROCTOR. Aye, that's the truth of it, Rebecca.

MRS. PUTNAM. This is no silly season, Rebecca. My Ruth is bewildered, Rebecca; she cannot eat.

REBECCA. Perhaps she is not hungered yet. (*To* PARRIS.) I hope you are not decided to go in search of loose spirits, Mr. Parris. I've heard promise of that outside.

PARRIS. A wide opinion's running in the parish that the Devil may be among us, and I would satisfy them that they are wrong.

PROCTOR. Then let you come out and call them wrong. Did you consult the wardens before you called this minister to look for devils?

PARRIS. He is not coming to look for devils!

PROCTOR. Then what's he coming for?

PUTNAM. There be children dyin' in the village, Mister!

PROCTOR. I seen none dyin'. This society will not be a bag to swing around your head, Mr. Putnam. (*To* PARRIS.) Did you call a meeting before you—?

PUTNAM. I am sick of meetings; cannot the man turn his head without he have a meeting?

PROCTOR. He may turn his head, but not to Hell!

REBECCA. Pray, John, be calm. (*Pause. He defers to her.*) Mr. Parris, I think you'd best send Reverend Hale back as soon as he come. This will set us all to arguin' again in the society, and we thought to have peace this year. I think we ought rely on the doctor now, and good prayer.

MRS. PUTNAM. Rebecca, the doctor's baffled!

REBECCA. If so he is, then let us go to God for the cause of it. There is prodigious danger in the seeking of loose spirits. I fear it, I fear it. Let us rather blame ourselves and—

PUTNAM. How may we blame ourselves? I am one of nine sons; the Putnam seed have peopled this province. And yet I have but one child left of eight—and now she shrivels!

REBECCA. I cannot fathom that.

MRS. PUTNAM (*with a growing edge of sarcasm*). But I must! You think it God's work you should never lose a child, nor grandchild either, and I bury all but one? There are wheels within wheels in this village, and fires within fires!

PUTNAM (*to* PARRIS). When Reverend Hale comes, you will proceed to look for signs of witchcraft here.

PROCTOR (*to* PUTNAM). You cannot command Mr. Parris. We vote by name in this society, not by acreage.

PUTNAM. I never heard you worried so on this society, Mr. Proctor. I do not think I saw you at Sabbath meeting since snow flew.

PROCTOR. I have trouble enough without I come five mile to hear him preach only hellfire and bloody damnation. Take it to heart, Mr. Parris. There are many others who stay away from church these days because you hardly ever mention God any more.

PARRIS (*now aroused*). Why, that's a drastic charge!

REBECCA. It's somewhat true; there are many that quail to bring their children—

PARRIS. I do not preach for children, Rebecca. It is not the children who are unmindful of their obligations toward this ministry.

REBECCA. Are there really those unmindful?

PARRIS. I should say the better half of Salem village—

PUTNAM. And more than that!

PARRIS. Where is my wood? My contract provides I be supplied with all my firewood. I am waiting since November for a stick, and even in November I had to show my frostbitten hands like some London beggar!

GILES. You are allowed six pound a year to buy your wood, Mr. Parris.

PARRIS. I regard that six pound as part of my salary. I am paid little enough without I spend six pound on firewood.

PROCTOR. Sixty, plus six for firewood—

PARRIS. The salary is sixty-six pound, Mr. Proctor! I am not some preaching farmer with a book under my arm; I am a graduate of Harvard College.

GILES. Aye, and well instructed in arithmetic!

PARRIS. Mr. Corey, you will look far for a man of my kind at sixty pound a year! I am not used to this poverty; I left a thrifty business in the Barbados to serve the Lord. I do not fathom it, why am I persecuted here? I cannot offer one proposition but there be a howling riot of argument. I have often wondered if the Devil be in it somewhere; I cannot understand you people otherwise.

PROCTOR. Mr. Parris, you are the first minister ever did demand the deed to this house—

PARRIS. Man! Don't a minister deserve a house to live in?

PROCTOR. To live in, yes. But to ask ownership is like you shall own the meeting house itself; the last meeting I were at you spoke so long on deeds and mortgages I thought it were an auction.

PARRIS. I want a mark of confidence, is all! I am your third preacher in seven years. I do not wish to be put out like the cat whenever some majority feels the whim. You people seem not to comprehend that a minister is the Lord's man in the parish; a minister is not to be so lightly crossed and contradicted—

PUTNAM. Aye!

PARRIS. There is either obedience or the church will burn like Hell is burning!

PROCTOR. Can you speak one minute without we land in Hell again? I am sick of Hell!

PARRIS. It is not for you to say what is good for you to hear!

PROCTOR. I may speak my heart, I think!

PARRIS (*in a fury*). What, are we Quakers? We are not Quakers here yet, Mr. Proctor. And you may tell that to your followers!

PROCTOR. My followers!

PARRIS (*—now he's out with it*). There is a party in this church. I am not blind; there is a faction and a party.

PROCTOR. Against you?

PUTNAM. Against him and all authority!

PROCTOR. Why, then I must find it and join it.

(*There is shock among the others.*)

REBECCA. He does not mean that.

PUTNAM. He confessed it now!

PROCTOR. I mean it solemnly, Rebecca; I like not the smell of this "authority."

REBECCA. No, you cannot break charity with your minister. You are another kind, John. Clasp his hand, make your peace.

PROCTOR. I have a crop to sow and lumber to drag home. (*He goes angrily to the door and turns to* COREY *with a smile.*) What say you, Giles, let's find the party. He says there's a party.

GILES. I've changed my opinion of this man, John. Mr. Parris, I beg your pardon. I never thought you had so much iron in you.

PARRIS (*surprised*). Why, thank you, Giles!

GILES. It suggests to the mind what the trouble be among us all these years. (*To all.*) Think on it. Wherefore is everybody suing everybody else? Think on it now, it's a deep thing, and dark as a pit. I have been six time in court this year—

PROCTOR (*familiarly, with warmth, although he knows he is approaching the edge of* GILES' *tolerance with this*). Is it the Devil's fault that a man cannot say you good morning without you clap him for defamation? You're old, Giles, and you're not hearin' so well as you did.

GILES (*—he cannot be crossed*). John Proctor, I have only last month collected four pound damages for you publicly sayin' I burned the roof off your house, and I—

PROCTOR (*laughing*). I never said no such thing, but I've paid you for it, so I hope I can call you deaf without charge. Now come along, Giles, and help me drag my lumber home.

PUTNAM. A moment, Mr. Proctor. What lumber is that you're draggin', if I may ask you?

PROCTOR. My lumber. From out my forest by the riverside.

PUTNAM. Why, we are surely gone wild this year. What anarchy is this? That tract is in my bounds, it's in my bounds, Mr. Proctor.

PROCTOR. In your bounds! (*Indicating* REBECCA.) I bought that tract from Goody Nurse's husband five months ago.

PUTNAM. He had no right to sell it. It stands clear in my grandfather's will that all the land between the river and—

PROCTOR. Your grandfather had a habit of willing land that never belonged to him, if I may say it plain.

GILES. That's God's truth; he nearly willed away my north pasture but he knew I'd break his fingers before he'd set his name to it. Let's get your lumber home, John. I feel a sudden will to work coming on.

PUTNAM. You load one oak of mine and you'll fight to drag it home!

GILES. Aye, and we'll win too, Putnam—this fool and I. Come on! (*He turns to* PROCTOR *and starts out.*)

PUTNAM. I'll have my men on you, Corey! I'll clap a writ on you!

(*Enter* REVEREND JOHN HALE *of Beverly.*)

———

Mr. Hale is nearing forty, a tight-skinned, eager-eyed intellectual. This is a beloved errand for him; on being called here to ascertain witchcraft he felt the pride of the specialist whose unique knowledge has at last been publicly called for. Like almost all men of learning, he spent a good deal of his time pondering the invisible world, especially since he had himself encountered a witch in his parish not long before. That woman, however, turned into a mere pest under his searching scrutiny, and the child she had allegedly been afflicting recovered her normal behavior after Hale had given her his kindness and a few days of rest in his own house. However, that experience never raised a doubt in his mind as to the reality of the underworld or the existence of Lucifer's many-faced lieutenants. And his belief is not to his discredit. Better minds than Hale's were —and still are—convinced that there is a society of spirits beyond our ken. One cannot help noting that one of his lines has never yet raised a laugh in any audience that has seen this play; it is his assurance that "We cannot look to superstition in this. The Devil is precise." Evidently we are not quite certain even now whether diabolism is holy and not to be scoffed at. And it is no accident that we should be so bemused.

Like Reverend Hale and the others on this stage, we conceive the Devil as a necessary part of a respectable view of cosmology. Ours is a divided empire in which certain ideas and emotions and actions are of God, and their opposites are of Lucifer. It is as impossible for most men to conceive of a morality without sin as of an earth without "sky." Since 1692 a great but superficial change has wiped out God's beard and the Devil's horns, but the world is still gripped between two diametrically opposed absolutes. The concept of unity, in which positive and negative are attributes of the same force, in which good and evil are relative, ever-changing, and always joined to the same phenomenon— such a concept is still reserved to the physical sciences and to the few who have grasped the history of ideas. When it is recalled that until the Christian era the underworld was never regarded as a hostile area, that all gods were useful and essentially friendly to man despite occasional lapses; when we see the steady and methodical inculcation into humanity of the idea of man's worthlessness—until redeemed—the necessity of the Devil may become evident as a weapon, a weapon designed and used time and time again in every age to whip men into a surrender to a particular church or church-state.

Our difficulty in believing the—for want of a better word—political inspiration of the Devil is due in great part to the fact that he is called up and damned not only by our social antagonists but by our own side, whatever it may be. The Catholic Church, through its Inquisition, is famous for cultivating Lucifer as the arch-fiend, but the Church's enemies relied no less upon the Old Boy to keep the human mind enthralled. Luther was himself accused of alliance with Hell, and he in turn accused his enemies. To complicate matters further, he believed that he had had contact with the Devil and had argued theology with him. I am not surprised at this, for at my own university a professor of history—a Lutheran, by the way—used to assemble his graduate students, draw the shades, and commune in the classroom with Erasmus. He was never, to my knowledge, officially scoffed at for this, the reason being that the university officials, like most of us, are the children of a history which still sucks at the Devil's teats. At this writing, only England has held back before the temptations of contemporary diabolism. In the countries of the Communist ideology, all resistance of any import is linked to the totally malign capitalist succubi, and in America any man who is not reactionary in his views is open to the charge of alliance with the Red hell. Political opposition, thereby, is given an inhumane overlay which then justifies the abrogation of all normally applied customs of civilized intercourse. A political policy is equated with moral right, and opposition to it with diabolical malevolence. Once such an equation is effectively made, society becomes a congerie of plots and counterplots, and the main role of government changes from that of the arbiter to that of the scourge of God.

The results of this process are no different now from what they were, except sometimes in the degree of cruelty inflicted, and not always even in that department. Normally the actions and deeds of a man were all that society felt comfortable in judging. The secret intent of an action was left to the ministers, priests, and rabbis to deal with. When diabolism rises, however, actions are the least important manifests of the true nature of a man. The Devil, as Reverend Hale said, is a wily one, and, until an hour before he fell, even God thought him beautiful in Heaven.

The analogy, however, seems to falter when one considers that, while there were no witches then, there are Communists and capitalists now, and in each camp there is certain proof that spies of each side are at work undermining the other. But this is a snobbish objection and not at all warranted by the facts. I have no doubt that people *were* communing with, and even worshiping, the Devil in Salem, and if the whole truth could be known in this case, as it is in others, we should discover a regular and conventionalized propitiation of the dark spirit. One certain evidence of this is the confession of Tituba, the slave of Reverend Parris, and another is the behavior of the children who were known to have indulged in sorceries with her.

There are accounts of similar *klatches* in Europe, where the daughters of the towns would assemble at night and, sometimes with fetishes, sometimes with a selected young man, give themselves to love, with some bastardly results. The Church, sharp-eyed as it must be when gods long dead are brought to life, condemned these orgies as witchcraft and interpreted them, rightly, as a resurgence of the Dionysiac forces it had crushed long before. Sex, sin, and the Devil were early linked, and so they continued to be in Salem, and are today. From all accounts there are no more puritanical mores in the world than those enforced by the Communists in Russia, where women's fashions, for instance, are as prudent and all-covering as any American Baptist would desire. The divorce laws lay a tremendous responsibility on the father for the care of his children. Even the laxity of divorce regulations in the early years of the revolution was undoubtedly a revulsion from the nineteenth-century Victorian immobility of marriage and the consequent hypocrisy that developed from it. If for no other reasons, a state so powerful, so jealous of the uniformity of its citizens, cannot long tolerate the atomization of the family. And yet, in American eyes at least, there remains the conviction that the Russian attitude toward women is lascivious. It is the Devil working again, just as he is working within the Slav who is shocked at the very idea of a woman's disrobing herself in a burlesque show. Our opposites are always robed in sexual sin, and it is from this unconscious conviction that demonology gains both its attractive sensuality and its capacity to infuriate and frighten.

Coming into Salem now, Reverend Hale conceives of himself much as a young doctor on his first call. His painfully acquired armory of symptoms, catchwords, and diagnostic procedures are now to be put to use at last. The road from Beverly is unusually busy this morning, and he has passed a hundred rumors that make him smile at the ignorance of the yeomanry in this most precise science. He feels himself allied with the best minds of Europe—kings, philosophers, scientists, and ecclesiasts of all churches. His goal is light, goodness and its preservation, and he knows the exaltation of the blessed whose intelligence, sharpened by minute examinations of enormous tracts, is finally called upon to face what may be a bloody fight with the Fiend himself.

———

(*He appears loaded down with half a dozen heavy books.*)

HALE. Pray you, someone take these!

PARRIS (*delighted*). Mr. Hale! Oh! it's good to see you again! (*Taking some books.*) My, they're heavy!

HALE (*setting down his books*). They must be; they are weighted with authority.

PARRIS (*a little scared*). Well, you do come prepared!

HALE. We shall need hard study if it comes to tracking down the Old Boy. (*Noticing* REBECCA:) You cannot be Rebecca Nurse?

REBECCA. I am, sir. Do you know me?

HALE. It's strange how I knew you, but I suppose you look as such a good soul should. We have all heard of your great charities in Beverly.

PARRIS. Do you know this gentleman? Mr. Thomas Putnam. And his good wife Ann.

HALE. Putnam! I had not expected such distinguished company, sir.

PUTNAM (*pleased*). It does not seem to help us today, Mr. Hale. We look to you to come to our house and save our child.

HALE. Your child ails too?

MRS. PUTNAM. Her soul, her soul seems flown away. She sleeps and yet she walks . . .

PUTNAM. She cannot eat.

HALE. Cannot eat! (*Thinks on it. Then, to* PROCTOR *and* GILES COREY:) Do you men have afflicted children?

PARRIS. No, no, these are farmers. John Proctor—

GILES COREY. He don't believe in witches.

PROCTOR (*to* HALE). I never spoke on witches one way or the other. Will you come, Giles?

GILES. No—no, John, I think not. I have some few queer questions of my own to ask this fellow.

PROCTOR. I've heard you to be a sensible man, Mr. Hale. I hope you'll leave some of it in Salem.

(PROCTOR *goes.* HALE *stands embarrassed for an instant.*)

PARRIS (*quickly*). Will you look at my daughter, sir? (*Leads* HALE *to the bed.*) She has tried to leap out the window; we discovered her this morning on the highroad, waving her arms as though she'd fly.

HALE (*narrowing his eyes*). Tries to fly.

PUTNAM. She cannot bear to hear the Lord's name, Mr. Hale; that's a sure sign of witchcraft afloat.

HALE (*holding up his hands*). No, no. Now let me instruct you. We cannot look to superstition in this. The Devil is precise; the marks of his presence are definite as stone, and I must tell you all that I shall not proceed unless you are prepared to believe me if I should find no bruise of hell upon her.

PARRIS. It is agreed, sir—it is agreed—we will abide by your judgment.

HALE. Good then. (*He goes to the bed, looks down at* BETTY. *To* PARRIS:) Now, sir, what were your first warning of this strangeness?

PARRIS. Why, sir—I discovered her—(*indicating* ABIGAIL)—and my niece and ten or twelve of the other girls, dancing in the forest last night.

HALE (*surprised*). You permit dancing?

PARRIS. No, no, it were secret—

MRS. PUTNAM (*unable to wait*). Mr. Parris's slave has knowledge of conjurin', sir.

PARRIS (*to* MRS. PUTNAM). We cannot be sure of that, Goody Ann—

MRS. PUTNAM (*frightened, very softly*). I know it, sir. I sent my child—she should learn from Tituba who murdered her sisters.

REBECCA (*horrified*). Goody Ann! You sent a child to conjure up the dead?

MRS. PUTNAM. Let God blame me, not you, not you, Rebecca! I'll not have you judging me any more! (*To* HALE:) Is it a natural work to lose seven children before they live a day?

PARRIS. Sssh!

(REBECCA, *with great pain, turns her face away. There is a pause.*)

HALE. Seven dead in childbirth.

MRS. PUTNAM (*softly*). Aye. (*Her voice breaks; she looks up at him. Silence.* HALE *is impressed.* PARRIS *looks to him. He goes to his books, opens one, turns pages, then reads. All wait, avidly.*)

PARRIS (*hushed*). What book is that?

MRS. PUTNAM. What's there, sir?

HALE (*with a tasty love of intellectual pursuit*). Here is all the invisible world, caught, defined, and calculated. In these books the Devil stands stripped of all his brute disguises. Here are all your familiar spirits—your incubi and succubi; your witches that go by land, by air, and by sea; your wizards of the night and of the day. Have no fear now—we shall find him out if he has come among us, and I mean to crush him utterly if he has shown his face! (*He starts for the bed.*)

REBECCA. Will it hurt the child, sir?

HALE. I cannot tell. If she is truly in the Devil's grip we may have to rip and tear to get her free.

REBECCA. I think I'll go, then. I am too old for this. (*She rises.*)

PARRIS (*striving for conviction*). Why, Rebecca, we may open up the boil of all our troubles today!

REBECCA. Let us hope for that. I go to God for you, sir.

PARRIS (*with trepidation—and resentment*). I hope you do not mean we go to Satan here! (*Slight pause.*)

REBECCA. I wish I knew. (*She goes out; they feel resentful of her note of moral superiority.*)

PUTNAM (*abruptly*). Come, Mr. Hale, let's get on. Sit you here.

GILES. Mr. Hale, I have always wanted to ask a learned man—what signifies the readin' of strange books?

HALE. What books?

GILES. I cannot tell; she hides them.

HALE. Who does this?

GILES. Martha, my wife. I have waked at night many a time and found her in a corner, readin' of a book. Now what do you make of that?

HALE. Why, that's not necessarily—

GILES. It discomfits me! Last night—mark this—I tried and tried and could not say my prayers. And then she close her book and walks out of the house, and suddenly—mark this—I could pray again!

Old Giles must be spoken for, if only because his fate was to be so remarkable and so different from that of all the others. He was in his early eighties at this time, and was the most comical hero in the history. No man has ever been blamed for so much. If a cow was missed, the first thought was to look for her around Corey's house; a fire blazing up at night brought suspicion of arson to his door. He didn't give a hoot for public opinion, and only in his last years—after he had married Martha—did he bother much with the church. That she stopped his prayer is very probable, but he forgot to say that he'd only recently learned any prayers and it didn't take much to make him stumble over them. He was a crank and a nuisance, but withal a deeply innocent and brave man. In court, once, he was asked if it were true that he had been frightened by the strange behavior of a hog and had then said he knew it to be the Devil in an animal's shape. "What frighted you?" he was asked. He forgot everything but the word "frighted," and instantly replied, "I do not know that I ever spoke that word in my life."

———

HALE. Ah! The stoppage of prayer—that is strange. I'll speak further on that with you.

GILES. I'm not sayin' she's touched the Devil, now, but I'd admire to know what books she reads and why she hides them. She'll not answer me, y'see.

HALE. Aye, we'll discuss it. (*To all:*) Now mark me, if the Devil is in her you will witness some frightful wonders in this room, so please to keep your wits about you. Mr. Putnam, stand close in case she flies. Now Betty, dear, will you sit up? (PUTNAM *comes in closer, ready-handed.* HALE *sits* BETTY *up, but she hangs limp in his hands.*) Hmmm. (*He observes her carefully. The others watch breathlessly.*) Can you hear me? I am John Hale, minister of Beverly. I have come to help you, dear. Do you remember my two little girls in Beverly? (*She does not stir in his hands.*)

PARRIS (*in fright*). How can it be the Devil? Why would he choose my house to strike? We have all manner of licentious people in the village!

HALE. What victory would the Devil have to win a soul already bad? It is the best the Devil wants, and who is better than the minister?

GILES. That's deep, Mr. Parris, deep, deep!

PARRIS (*with resolution now*). Betty! Answer Mr. Hale! Betty!

HALE. Does someone afflict you, child? It need not be a woman, mind you, or a man. Perhaps some bird invisible to others comes to you—perhaps a pig, a mouse, or any beast at all. Is there some figure bids you fly? (*The child remains limp in his hands. In silence he lays her back on the pillow. Now, holding out his hands toward her, he intones:*) In nomine Domini Sabaoth sui filiique ite ad infernos. (*She does not stir. He turns to* ABIGAIL, *his eyes narrowing.*) Abigail, what sort of dancing were you doing with her in the forest?

ABIGAIL. Why—common dancing is all.

PARRIS. I think I ought to say that I—I saw a kettle in the grass where they were dancing.

ABIGAIL. That were only soup.

HALE. What sort of soup were in this kettle, Abigail?

ABIGAIL. Why, it were beans—and lentils, I think, and—

HALE. Mr. Parris, you did not notice, did you, any living thing in the kettle? A mouse, perhaps, a spider, a frog—?

PARRIS (*fearfully*). I—do believe there were some movement—in the soup.

ABIGAIL. That jumped in, we never put it in!

HALE (*quickly*). What jumped in?

ABIGAIL. Why, a very little frog jumped—

PARRIS. A frog, Abby!

HALE (*grasping* ABIGAIL). Abigail, it may be your cousin is dying. Did you call the Devil last night?

ABIGAIL. I never called him! Tituba, Tituba . . .

PARRIS (*blanched*). She called the Devil?

HALE. I should like to speak with Tituba.

PARRIS. Goody Ann, will you bring her up? (MRS. PUTNAM *exits.*)

HALE. How did she call him?

ABIGAIL. I know not—she spoke Barbados.

HALE. Did you feel any strangeness when she called him? A sudden cold wind, perhaps? A trembling below the ground?

ABIGAIL. I didn't see no Devil! (*Shaking* BETTY:) Betty, wake up. Betty! Betty!

HALE. You cannot evade me, Abigail. Did your cousin drink any of the brew in that kettle?

ABIGAIL. She never drank it!

HALE. Did you drink it?

ABIGAIL. No, sir!

HALE. Did Tituba ask you to drink it?

ABIGAIL. She tried, but I refused.

HALE. Why are you concealing? Have you sold yourself to Lucifer?

ABIGAIL. I never sold myself! I'm a good girl! I'm a proper girl!

(MRS. PUTNAM *enters with* TITUBA, *and instantly* ABIGAIL *points at* TITUBA.)

ABIGAIL. She made me do it! She made Betty do it!

TITUBA (*shocked and angry*). Abby!

ABIGAIL. She makes me drink blood!

PARRIS. Blood!!

MRS. PUTNAM. My baby's blood?

TITUBA. No, no, chicken blood. I give she chicken blood!

HALE. Woman, have you enlisted these children for the Devil?

TITUBA. No, no, sir, I don't truck with no Devil!

HALE. Why can she not wake? Are you silencing this child?

TITUBA. I love me Betty!

HALE. You have sent your spirit out upon this child, have you not? Are you gathering souls for the Devil?

ABIGAIL. She sends her spirit on me in church; she makes me laugh at prayer!

PARRIS. She have often laughed at prayer!

ABIGAIL. She comes to me every night to go and drink blood!

TITUBA. You beg *me* to conjure! She beg *me* make charm—

ABIGAIL. Don't lie! (*To* HALE:) She comes to me while I sleep; she's always making me dream corruptions!

TITUBA. Why you say that, Abby?

ABIGAIL. Sometimes I wake and find myself standing in the open doorway and not a stitch on my body! I always hear her laughing in my sleep. I hear her singing her Barbados songs and tempting me with—

TITUBA. Mister Reverend, I never—

HALE (*resolved now*). Tituba, I want you to wake this child.

TITUBA. I have no power on this child, sir.

HALE. You most certainly do, and you will free her from it now! When did you compact with the Devil?

TITUBA. I don't compact with no Devil!

PARRIS. You will confess yourself or I

will take you out and whip you to your death, Tituba!

PUTNAM. This woman must be hanged! She must be taken and hanged!

TITUBA (*terrified, falls to her knees*). No, no, don't hang Tituba! I tell him I don't desire to work for him, sir.

PARRIS. The Devil?

HALE. Then you saw him! (TITUBA *weeps.*) Now Tituba, I know that when we bind ourselves to Hell it is very hard to break with it. We are going to help you tear yourself free—

TITUBA (*frightened by the coming process*). Mister Reverend, I do believe somebody else be witchin' these children.

HALE. Who?

TITUBA. I don't know, sir, but the Devil got him numerous witches.

HALE. Does he! (*It is a clue.*) Tituba, look into my eyes. Come, look into me. (*She raises her eyes to his fearfully.*) You would be a good Christian woman, would you not, Tituba?

TITUBA. Aye, sir, a good Christian woman.

HALE. And you love these little children?

TITUBA. Oh, yes, sir, I don't desire to hurt little children.

HALE. And you love God, Tituba?

TITUBA. I love God with all my bein'.

HALE. Now, in God's holy name—

TITUBA. Bless Him. Bless Him. (*She is rocking on her knees, sobbing in terror.*)

HALE. And to His glory—

TITUBA. Eternal glory. Bless Him—bless God . . .

HALE. Open yourself, Tituba—open yourself and let God's holy light shine on you.

TITUBA. Oh, bless the Lord.

HALE. When the Devil comes to you does he ever come—with another person? (*She stares up into his face.*) Perhaps another person in the village? Someone you know.

PARRIS. Who came with him?

PUTNAM. Sarah Good? Did you ever see Sarah Good with him? Or Osburn?

PARRIS. Was it man or woman came with him?

TITUBA. Man or woman. Was—was woman.

PARRIS. What woman? A woman, you said. What woman?

TITUBA. It was black dark, and I—

PARRIS. You could see him, why could you not see her?

TITUBA. Well, they was always talking; they was always runnin' round and carryin' on—

PARRIS. You mean out of Salem? Salem witches?

TITUBA. I believe so, yes, sir.

(*Now* HALE *takes her hand. She is surprised.*)

HALE. Tituba. You must have no fear to tell us who they are, do you understand? We will protect you. The Devil can never overcome a minister. You know that, do you not?

TITUBA (*kisses* HALE's *hand*). Aye, sir, oh, I do.

HALE. You have confessed yourself to witchcraft, and that speaks a wish to come to Heaven's side. And we will bless you, Tituba.

TITUBA (*deeply relieved*). Oh, God bless you, Mr. Hale!

HALE (*with rising exaltation*). You are God's instrument put in our hands to discover the Devil's agents among us. You are selected, Tituba, you are chosen to help us cleanse our village. So speak utterly, Tituba, turn your back on him and face God—face God, Tituba, and God will protect you.

TITUBA (*joining with him*). Oh, God, protect Tituba!

HALE (*kindly*). Who came to you with the Devil? Two? Three? Four? How many?

(TITUBA *pants, and begins rocking back and forth again, staring ahead.*)

TITUBA. There was four. There was four.

PARRIS (*pressing in on her*). Who? Who? Their names, their names!

TITUBA (*suddenly bursting out*). Oh, how many times he bid me kill you, Mr. Parris!

PARRIS. Kill me!

TITUBA (*in a fury*). He say Mr. Parris must be kill! Mr. Parris no goodly man, Mr. Parris mean man and no gentle man, and he bid me rise out of my bed and cut your throat! (*They gasp.*) But I tell him "No! I don't hate that man. I don't want kill that man." But he say, "You work for me, Tituba, and I make you free! I give you pretty dress to wear, and put you way high up in the air, and you gone fly back to Barbados!" And I say, "You lie, Devil, you lie!" And then he come one stormy night to me, and he say, "Look! I have *white* people belong to me." And I look—and there was Goody Good.

PARRIS. Sarah Good!

TITUBA (*rocking and weeping*). Aye, sir, and Goody Osburn.

MRS. PUTNAM. I knew it! Goody Osburn were midwife to me three times. I begged you, Thomas, did I not? I begged him not to call Osburn because I feared her. My babies always shriveled in her hands!

HALE. Take courage, you must give us all their names. How can you bear to see this child suffering? Look at her, Tituba. (*He is indicating* BETTY *on the bed.*) Look at her God-given innocence; her soul is so tender; we must protect her, Tituba; the Devil is out and preying on her like a beast upon the flesh of the pure lamb. God will bless you for your help.

(ABIGAIL *rises, staring as though inspired, and cries out.*)

ABIGAIL. I want to open myself! (*They turn to her, startled. She is enraptured, as though in a pearly light.*) I want the light of God, I want the sweet love of Jesus! I danced for the Devil; I saw him; I wrote in his book; I go back to Jesus; I kiss His hand. I saw Sarah Good with the Devil! I saw Goody Osburn with the Devil! I saw Bridget Bishop with the Devil!

(*As she is speaking,* BETTY *is rising from the bed, a fever in her eyes, and picks up the chant.*)

BETTY (*staring too*). I saw George Jacobs with the Devil! I saw Goody Howe with the Devil!

PARRIS. She speaks! (*He rushes to embrace* BETTY.) She speaks!

HALE. Glory to God! It is broken, they are free!

BETTY (*calling out hysterically and with great relief*). I saw Martha Bellows with the Devil!

ABIGAIL. I saw Goody Sibber with the Devil! (*It is rising to a great glee.*)

PUTNAM. The marshal, I'll call the marshal!

(PARRIS *is shouting a prayer of thanksgiving.*)

BETTY. I saw Alice Barrow with the Devil!

(*The curtain begins to fall.*)

HALE (*as* PUTNAM *goes out*). Let the marshal bring irons!

ABIGAIL. I saw Goody Hawkins with the Devil!

BETTY. I saw Goody Bibber with the Devil!

ABIGAIL. I saw Goody Booth with the Devil!

On their ecstatic cries

THE CURTAIN FALLS

ACT TWO

The common room of PROCTOR's *house, eight days later.*

At the right is a door opening on the fields outside. A fireplace is at the left, and behind it a stairway leading upstairs. It is the low, dark, and rather long living room of the time. As the curtain rises, the room is empty. From above, ELIZABETH *is heard softly singing to the children. Presently the door opens and* JOHN PROCTOR *enters, carrying his gun. He glances about the room as he comes toward the fireplace, then halts for an instant as he hears her singing. He continues on to the fireplace, leans the gun against the wall as he swings a pot out of the fire and smells it. Then he lifts out the ladle and tastes. He is not quite pleased. He reaches to a cupboard, takes a pinch of salt, and drops it into the pot. As he is tasting again, her footsteps are heard on the stair. He swings the pot into the fireplace and goes to a basin and washes his hands and face.* ELIZABETH *enters.*

ELIZABETH. What keeps you so late? It's almost dark.

PROCTOR. I were planting far out to the forest edge.

ELIZABETH. Oh, you're done then.

PROCTOR. Aye, the farm is seeded. The boys asleep?

ELIZABETH. They will be soon. (*And she goes to the fireplace, proceeds to ladle up stew in a dish.*)

PROCTOR. Pray now for a fair summer.

ELIZABETH. Aye.

PROCTOR. Are you well today?

ELIZABETH. I am. (*She brings the plate to the table, and, indicating the food.*) It is a rabbit.

PROCTOR (*going to the table*). Oh, is it! In Jonathan's trap?

ELIZABETH. No, she walked into the house this afternoon; I found her sittin' in the corner like she come to visit.

PROCTOR. Oh, that's a good sign walkin' in.

ELIZABETH. Pray God. It hurt my heart to strip her, poor rabbit. (*She sits and watches him taste it.*)

PROCTOR. It's well seasoned.

ELIZABETH (*blushing with pleasure*). I took great care. She's tender?

PROCTOR. Aye. (*He eats. She watches him.*) I think we'll see green fields soon. It's warm as blood beneath the clods.

ELIZABETH. That's well.

(PROCTOR *eats, then looks up.*)

PROCTOR. If the crop is good I'll buy George Jacobs' ·heifer. How would that please you?

ELIZABETH. Aye, it would.

PROCTOR (*with a grin*). I mean to please you, Elizabeth.

ELIZABETH (*—it is hard to say*). I know it, John.

(*He gets up, goes to her, kisses her. She receives it. With a certain disappointment, he returns to the table.*)

PROCTOR (*as gently as he can*). Cider?

ELIZABETH (*with a sense of reprimanding herself for having forgot*). Aye! (*She gets up and goes and pours a glass for him. He now arches his back.*)

PROCTOR. This farm's a continent when you go foot by foot droppin' seeds in it.

ELIZABETH (*coming with the cider*). It must be.

PROCTOR (*drinks a long draught, then, putting the glass down*). You ought to bring some flowers in the house.

ELIZABETH. Oh! I forgot! I will tomorrow.

PROCTOR. It's winter in here yet. On Sunday let you come with me, and we'll walk the farm together; I never see such a load of flowers on the earth. (*With a good feeling he goes and looks up at the sky through the open doorway.*) Lilacs have a purple smell. Lilac is the smell of nightfall, I think. Massachusetts is a beauty in the spring!

ELIZABETH. Aye, it is.

(*There is a pause. She is watching him from the table as he stands there absorbing the night. It is as though she would speak but cannot. Instead, now, she takes up his plate and glass and fork and goes with them to the basin. Her back is turned to him. He turns to her and watches her. A sense of their separation rises.*)

PROCTOR. I think you're sad again. Are you?

ELIZABETH (*—she doesn't want friction, and yet she must*). You come so late I thought you'd gone to Salem this afternoon.

PROCTOR. Why? I have no business in Salem.

ELIZABETH. You did speak of going, earlier this week.

PROCTOR (*—he knows what she means*). I thought better of it since.

ELIZABETH. Mary Warren's there today.

PROCTOR. Why'd you let her? You heard me forbid her go to Salem any more!

ELIZABETH. I couldn't stop her.

PROCTOR (*holding back a full condemnation of her*). It is a fault, it is a fault, Elizabeth—you're the mistress here, not Mary Warren.

ELIZABETH. She frightened all my strength away.

PROCTOR. How may that mouse frighten you, Elizabeth? You—

ELIZABETH. It is a mouse no more. I forbid her go, and she raises up her chin like the daughter of a prince and says to me, "I must go to Salem, Goody Proctor; I am an official of the court!"

PROCTOR. Court! What court?

ELIZABETH. Aye, it is a proper court they have now. They've sent four judges out of Boston, she says, weighty magistrates of the General Court, and at the head sits the Deputy Governor of the Province.

PROCTOR (*astonished*). Why, she's mad.

ELIZABETH. I would to God she were. There be fourteen people in the jail now, she says. (PROCTOR *simply looks at her, unable to grasp it.*) And they'll be tried, and the court have power to hang them too, she says.

PROCTOR (*scoffing, but without conviction*). Ah, they'd never hang—

ELIZABETH. The Deputy Governor promises hangin' if they'll not confess, John. The town's gone wild, I think. She speak of Abigail, and I thought she were a saint, to hear her. Abigail brings the other girls into the court, and where she walks the crowd will part like the sea for Israel. And folks are brought before them, and if they scream and howl and fall to the floor—the person's clapped in the jail for bewitchin' them.

PROCTOR (*wide-eyed*). Oh, it is a black mischief.

ELIZABETH. I think you must go to Salem, John. (*He turns to her.*) I think so. You must tell them it is a fraud.

PROCTOR (*thinking beyond this*). Aye, it is, it is surely.

ELIZABETH. Let you go to Ezekiel Cheever—he knows you well. And tell him what she said to you last week in her uncle's house. She said it had naught to do with witchcraft, did she not?

PROCTOR (*in thought*). Aye, she did, she did. (*Now, a pause.*)

ELIZABETH (*quietly fearing to anger him by prodding*). God forbid you keep that from the court, John. I think they must be told.

PROCTOR (*quietly, struggling with his thought*). Aye, they must, they must. It is a wonder they do believe her.

ELIZABETH. I would go to Salem now, John—let you go tonight.

PROCTOR. I'll think on it.

ELIZABETH (*with her courage now*). You cannot keep it, John.

PROCTOR (*angering*). I know I cannot keep it. I say I will think on it!

ELIZABETH (*hurt and very coldly*). Good, then, let you think on it. (*She stands and starts to walk out of the room.*)

PROCTOR. I am only wondering how I may prove what she told me, Elizabeth. If the girl's a saint now, I think it is not easy to prove she's fraud, and the town gone so silly. She told it to me in a room alone—I have no proof for it.

ELIZABETH. You were alone with her?

PROCTOR (*stubbornly*). For a moment alone, aye.

ELIZABETH. Why, then, it is not as you told me.

PROCTOR (*his anger rising*). For a moment, I say. The others come in soon after.

ELIZABETH (*quietly—she has suddenly lost all faith in him*). Do as you wish, then. (*She starts to turn.*)

PROCTOR. Woman. (*She turns to him.*) I'll not have your suspicion any more.

ELIZABETH (*a little loftily*). I have no—

PROCTOR. I'll not have it!

ELIZABETH. Then let you not earn it.

PROCTOR (*with a violent undertone*). You doubt me yet?

ELIZABETH (*with a smile, to keep her dignity*). John, if it were not Abigail that you must go to hurt, would you falter now? I think not.

PROCTOR. Now look you—

ELIZABETH. I see what I see, John.

PROCTOR (*with solemn warning*). You will not judge me more, Elizabeth. I have good reason to think before I charge fraud on Abigail, and I will think on it. Let you look to your own improvement before you go to judge your husband any more. I have forgot Abigail, and—

ELIZABETH. And I.

PROCTOR. Spare me! You forget nothin' and forgive nothin'. Learn charity, woman. I have gone tiptoe in this house all seven month since she is gone. I have not moved from there to there without I think to please you, and still an everlasting funeral marches round your heart. I cannot speak but I am doubted, every moment judged for lies, as though I come into a court when I come into this house!

ELIZABETH. John, you are not open with me. You saw her with a crowd, you said. Now you—

PROCTOR. I'll plead my honesty no more, Elizabeth.

ELIZABETH (*—now she would justify herself*). John, I am only—

PROCTOR. No more! I should have roared you down when first you told me your suspicion. But I wilted, and, like a Christian, I confessed. Confessed! Some dream I had must have mistaken you for God that day. But you're not, you're not, and let you remember it! Let you look sometimes for the goodness in me, and judge me not.

ELIZABETH. I do not judge you. The magistrate sits in your heart that judges you. I never thought you but a good man, John—(*with a smile—*) only somewhat bewildered.

PROCTOR (*laughing bitterly*). Oh, Elizabeth, your justice would freeze beer! (*He turns suddenly toward a sound outside. He starts for the door as MARY WARREN enters. As soon as he sees her, he goes directly to her and grabs her by her cloak, furious.*) How do you go to Salem when I forbid it? Do you mock me? (*Shaking her.*) I'll whip you if you dare leave this house again!

(*Strangely, she doesn't resist him, but hangs limply by his grip.*)

MARY WARREN. I am sick, I am sick, Mr. Proctor. Pray, pray, hurt me not. (*Her strangeness throws him off, and her evident pallor and weakness. He frees her.*) My insides are all shuddery; I am in the proceedings all day, sir.

PROCTOR (*with draining anger—his curiosity is draining it*). And what of these proceedings here? When will you proceed to keep this house, as you are paid nine pound a year to do—and my wife not wholly well?

(*As though to compensate,* MARY WARREN *goes to* ELIZABETH *with a small rag doll.*)

MARY WARREN. I made a gift for you today, Goody Proctor. I had to sit long hours in a chair, and passed the time with sewing.

ELIZABETH (*perplexed, looking at the doll*). Why, thank you, it's a fair poppet.

MARY WARREN (*with a trembling, decayed voice*). We must all love each other now, Goody Proctor.

ELIZABETH (*amazed at her strangeness*). Aye, indeed we must.

MARY WARREN (*glancing at the room*). I'll get up early in the morning and clean the house. I must sleep now. (*She turns and starts off.*)

PROCTOR. Mary. (*She halts.*) Is it true? There be fourteen women arrested?

MARY WARREN. No, sir. There be thirty-nine now—(*She suddenly breaks off and sobs and sits down, exhausted.*)

ELIZABETH. Why, she's weepin'! What ails you, child?

MARY WARREN. Goody Osburn—will hang!

(*There is a shocked pause, while she sobs.*)

PROCTOR. Hang! (*He calls into her face.*) Hang, y'say?

MARY WARREN (*through her weeping*). Aye.

PROCTOR. The Deputy Governor will permit it?

MARY WARREN. He sentenced her. He must. (*To ameliorate it:*) But not Sarah Good. For Sarah Good confessed, y'see.

PROCTOR. Confessed! To what?

MARY WARREN. That she—(*In horror at the memory—*) she sometimes made a compact with Lucifer, and wrote her name in his black book—with her blood—and bound herself to torment Christians till God's thrown down—and we all must worship Hell forevermore.

(*Pause.*)

PROCTOR. But—surely you know what a jabberer she is. Did you tell them that?

MARY WARREN. Mr. Proctor, in open court she near to choked us all to death.

PROCTOR. How, choked you?

MARY WARREN. She sent her spirit out.

ELIZABETH. Oh, Mary, Mary, surely you—

MARY WARREN (*with an indignant edge*). She tried to kill me many times, Goody Proctor!

ELIZABETH. Why, I never heard you mention that before.

MARY WARREN. I never knew it before. I never knew anything before. When she come into the court I say to myself, I must not accuse this woman, for she sleep in ditches, and so very old and poor. But then —then she sit there, denying and denying, and I feel a misty coldness climbin' up my back, and the skin on my skull begin to creep, and I feel a clamp around my neck and I cannot breathe air; and then—(*Entranced—*) I hear a voice, a screamin' voice, and it were my voice—and all at once I remembered everything she done to me!

PROCTOR. Why? What did she do to you?

MARY WARREN (*like one awakened to a marvelous secret insight*). So many time, Mr. Proctor, she come to this very door, beggin' bread and a cup of cider—and mark this: whenever I turned her away empty, she *mumbled*.

ELIZABETH. Mumbled. She may mumble if she's hungry.

MARY WARREN. But *what* does she mumble? You must remember, Goody Proctor. Last month—a Monday, I think— she walked away, and I thought my guts would burst for two days after. Do you remember it?

ELIZABETH. Why—I do, I think, but—

MARY WARREN. And so I told that to Judge Hathorne, and he asks her so. "Goody Osburn," says he, "what curse do you mumble that this girl must fall sick after turning you away?" And then she replies—(*Mimicking an old crone—*) "Why, your excellence, no curse at all. I only say my commandments; I hope I may say my commandments," says she!

ELIZABETH. And that's an upright answer.

MARY WARREN. Aye, but then Judge Hathorne say, "Recite for us your commandments!"—(*Leaning avidly toward them—*) and of all the ten she could not say a single one. She never knew no commandments, and they had her in a flat lie!

PROCTOR. And so condemned her?

MARY WARREN (*now a little strained, seeing his stubborn doubt*). Why, they must when she condemned herself.

PROCTOR. But the proof, the proof!

MARY WARREN (*with greater impatience with him*). I told you the proof. It's hard proof, hard as rock, the judges said.

PROCTOR (*pauses an instant then*). You will not go to court again, Mary Warren.

MARY WARREN. I must tell you, sir, I will be gone every day now. I am amazed you do not see what weighty work we do.

PROCTOR. What work you do! It's strange work for a Christian girl to hang old women!

MARY WARREN. But, Mr. Proctor, they will not hang them if they confess. Sarah Good will only sit in jail some time— (*Recalling*—) and here's a wonder for you; think on this. Goody Good is pregnant!

ELIZABETH. Pregnant! Are they mad? The woman's near to sixty!

MARY WARREN. They had Doctor Griggs examine her, and she's full to the brim. And smokin' a pipe all these years, and no husband either! But she's safe, thank God, for they'll not hurt the innocent child. But be that not a marvel? You must see it, sir, it's God's work we do. So I'll be gone every day for some time. I'm—I am an official of the court, they say, and I— (*She has been edging toward offstage.*)

PROCTOR. I'll official you! (*He strides to the mantel, takes down the whip hanging there.*)

MARY WARREN (*terrified, but coming erect, striving for her authority*). I'll not stand whipping any more!

ELIZABETH (*hurriedly, as* PROCTOR *approaches*). Mary, promise now you'll stay at home—

MARY WARREN (*backing from him, but keeping her erect posture, striving, striving for her way*). The Devil's loose in Salem, Mr. Proctor; we must discover where he's hiding!

PROCTOR. I'll whip the Devil out of you! (*With whip raised he reaches out for her, and she streaks away and yells.*)

MARY WARREN (*pointing at* ELIZABETH). I saved her life today!

(*Silence. His whip comes down.*)

ELIZABETH (*softly*). I am accused?

MARY WARREN (*quaking*). Somewhat mentioned. But I said I never see no sign you ever sent your spirit out to hurt no one, and seeing I do live so closely with you, they dismissed it.

ELIZABETH. Who accused me?

MARY WARREN. I am bound by law, I cannot tell it. (*To* PROCTOR:) I only hope you'll not be so sarcastical no more. Four judges and the King's deputy sat to dinner with us but an hour ago. I—I would have you speak civilly to me, from this out.

PROCTOR (*in horror, muttering in disgust at her*). Go to bed.

MARY WARREN (*with a stamp of her foot*). I'll not be ordered to bed no more, Mr. Proctor! I am eighteen and a woman, however single!

PROCTOR. Do you wish to sit up? Then sit up.

MARY WARREN. I wish to go to bed!

PROCTOR (*in anger*). Good night, then!

MARY WARREN. Good night. (*Dissatisfied, uncertain of herself, she goes out. Wide-eyed, both,* PROCTOR *and* ELIZABETH *stand staring.*)

ELIZABETH (*quietly*). Oh, the noose, the noose is up!

PROCTOR. There'll be no noose.

ELIZABETH. She wants me dead. I knew all week it would come to this!

PROCTOR (*without conviction*). They dismissed it. You heard her say—

ELIZABETH. And what of tomorrow? She will cry me out until they take me!

PROCTOR. Sit you down.

ELIZABETH. She wants me dead, John, you know it!

PROCTOR. I say sit down! (*She sits, trembling. He speaks quietly, trying to keep his wits.*) Now we must be wise, Elizabeth.

ELIZABETH (*with sarcasm, and a sense of being lost*). Oh, indeed, indeed!

PROCTOR. Fear nothing. I'll find Ezekiel Cheever. I'll tell him she said it were all sport.

ELIZABETH. John, with so many in the jail, more than Cheever's help is needed now, I think. Would you favor me with this? Go to Abigail.

PROCTOR (*his soul hardening as he senses*). What have I to say to Abigail?

ELIZABETH (*delicately*). John—grant me this. You have a faulty understanding of young girls. There is a promise made in any bed—

PROCTOR (*striving against his anger*). What promise!

ELIZABETH. Spoke or silent, a promise is surely made. And she may dote on it now—I am sure she does—and thinks to kill me, then to take my place.

(PROCTOR's *anger is rising; he cannot speak.*)

ELIZABETH. It is her dearest hope, John, I know it. There be a thousand names; why does she call mine? There be a certain danger in calling such a name—I am no Goody Good that sleeps in ditches, nor Osburn, drunk and half-witted. She'd dare not call out such a farmer's wife but there be monstrous profit in it. She thinks to take my place, John.

PROCTOR. She cannot think it! (*He knows it is true.*)

ELIZABETH (*"reasonably"*). John, have you ever shown her somewhat of contempt? She cannot pass you in the church but you will blush—

PROCTOR. I may blush for my sin.

ELIZABETH. I think she sees another meaning in that blush.

PROCTOR. And what see you? What see you, Elizabeth?

ELIZABETH (*"conceding"*). I think you be somewhat ashamed, for I am there, and she so close.

PROCTOR. When will you know me, woman? Were I stone I would have cracked for shame this seven month!

ELIZABETH. Then go and tell her she's a whore. Whatever promise she may sense—break it, John, break it.

PROCTOR (*between his teeth*). Good, then. I'll go. (*He starts for his rifle.*)

ELIZABETH (*trembling, fearfully*). Oh, how unwillingly!

PROCTOR (*turning on her, rifle in hand*). I will curse her hotter than the oldest cinder in hell. But pray, begrudge me not my anger!

ELIZABETH. Your anger! I only ask you—

PROCTOR. Woman, am I so base? Do you truly think me base?

ELIZABETH. I never called you base.

PROCTOR. Then how do you charge me with such a promise? The promise that a stallion gives a mare I gave that girl!

ELIZABETH. Then why do you anger with me when I bid you break it?

PROCTOR. Because it speaks deceit, and I am honest! But I'll plead no more! I see now your spirit twists around the single error of my life, and I will never tear it free!

ELIZABETH (*crying out*). You'll tear it free—when you come to know that I will be your only wife, or no wife at all! She has an arrow in you yet, John Proctor, and you know it well!

(*Quite suddenly, as though from the air, a figure appears in the doorway. They start slightly. It is* MR. HALE. *He is different now—drawn a little, and there is a quality of deference, even of guilt, about his manner now.*)

HALE. Good evening.

PROCTOR (*still in his shock*). Why, Mr. Hale! Good evening to you, sir. Come in, come in.

HALE (*to* ELIZABETH). I hope I do not startle you.

ELIZABETH. No, no, it's only that I heard no horse—

HALE. You are Goodwife Proctor.

PROCTOR. Aye; Elizabeth.

HALE (*nods then*). I hope you're not off to bed yet.

PROCTOR (*setting down his gun*). No, no. (HALE *comes further into the room. And* PROCTOR, *to explain his nervousness:*) We are not used to visitors after dark, but you're welcome here. Will you sit you down, sir?

HALE. I will. (*He sits.*) Let you sit, Goodwife Proctor.

(*She does, never letting him out of her sight. There is a pause as* HALE *looks about the room.*)

PROCTOR (*to break the silence*). Will you drink cider, Mr. Hale?

HALE. No, it rebels my stomach; I have some further traveling yet tonight. Sit you down, sir. (PROCTOR *sits.*) I will not keep you long, but I have some business with you.

PROCTOR. Business of the court?

HALE. No—no, I come of my own, without the court's authority. Hear me. (*He wets his lips.*) I know not if you are aware, but your wife's name is—mentioned in the court.

PROCTOR. We know it, sir. Our Mary Warren told us. We are entirely amazed.

HALE. I am a stranger here, as you know. And in my ignorance I find it hard to draw a clear opinion of them that come accused before the court. And so this afternoon, and now tonight, I go from house to house—I come now from Rebecca Nurse's house and—

ELIZABETH (*shocked*). Rebecca's charged!

HALE. God forbid such a one be charged. She is, however—mentioned somewhat.

ELIZABETH (*with an attempt at a laugh*). You will never believe, I hope, that Rebecca trafficked with the Devil.

HALE. Woman, it is possible.

PROCTOR (*taken aback*). Surely you cannot think so.

HALE. This is a strange time, Mister. No man may longer doubt the powers of the dark are gathered in monstrous attack upon this village. There is too much evidence now to deny it. You will agree, sir?

PROCTOR (*evading*). I—have no knowledge in that line. But it's hard to think so pious a woman be secretly a Devil's bitch after seventy year of such good prayer.

HALE. Aye. But the Devil is a wily one, you cannot deny it. However, she is far from accused, and I know she will not be. (*Pause.*) I thought, sir, to put some questions as to the Christian character of this house, if you'll permit me.

PROCTOR (*coldly, resentful*). Why, we—have no fear of questions, sir.

HALE. Good, then. (*He makes himself more comfortable.*) In the book of record that Mr. Parris keeps, I note that you are rarely in the church on Sabbath Day.

PROCTOR. No, sir, you are mistaken.

HALE. Twenty-six time in seventeen month, sir. I must call that rare. Will you tell me why you are so absent?

PROCTOR. Mr. Hale, I never knew I must account to that man for I come to church or stay at home. My wife were sick this winter.

HALE. So I am told. But you, Mister, why could you not come alone?

PROCTOR. I surely did come when I could, and when I could not I prayed in this house.

HALE. Mr. Proctor, your house is not a church; your theology must tell you that.

PROCTOR. It does, sir, it does; and it tells me that a minister may pray to God without he have golden candlesticks upon the altar.

HALE. What golden candlesticks?

PROCTOR. Since we built the church there were pewter candlesticks upon the altar; Francis Nurse made them, y'know, and a sweeter hand never touched the metal. But Parris came, and for twenty week he preach nothin' but golden candlesticks until he had them. I labor the earth from dawn of day to blink of night, and I tell you true, when I look to heaven and see my money glaring at his elbows—it hurt my prayer, sir, it hurt my prayer. I think, sometimes, the man dreams cathedrals, not clapboard meetin' houses.

HALE (*thinks, then*). And yet, Mister, a Christian on Sabbath Day must be in church. (*Pause.*) Tell me—you have three children?

PROCTOR. Aye. Boys.

HALE. How comes it that only two are baptized?

PROCTOR (*starts to speak, then stops, then, as though unable to restrain this*). I like it not that Mr. Parris should lay his hand upon my baby. I see no light of God in that man. I'll not conceal it.

HALE. I must say it, Mr. Proctor; that is not for you to decide. The man's ordained, therefore the light of God is in him.

PROCTOR (*flushed with resentment but trying to smile*). What's your suspicion, Mr. Hale?

HALE. No, no, I have no—

PROCTOR. I nailed the roof upon the church, I hung the door—

HALE. Oh, did you! That's a good sign, then.

PROCTOR. It may be I have been too quick to bring the man to book, but you cannot think we ever desired the destruction of religion. I think that's in your mind, is it not?

HALE (*not altogether giving way*). I—have—there is a softness in your record, sir, a softness.

ELIZABETH. I think, maybe, we have been too hard with Mr. Parris. I think so. But sure we never loved the Devil here.

HALE (*nods, deliberating this. Then, with the voice of one administering a secret test*). Do you know your Commandments, Elizabeth?

ELIZABETH (*without hesitation, even eagerly*). I surely do. There be no mark of blame upon my life, Mr. Hale. I am a covenanted Christian woman.

HALE. And you, Mister?

PROCTOR (*a trifle unsteadily*). I—am sure I do, sir.

HALE (*glances at her open face, then at John, then*). Let you repeat them, if you will.

PROCTOR. The Commandments.

HALE. Aye.

PROCTOR (*looking off, beginning to sweat*). Thou shalt not kill.

HALE. Aye.

PROCTOR (*counting on his fingers*). Thou shalt not steal. Thou shalt not covet thy neighbor's goods, nor make unto thee any graven image. Thou shalt not take the name of the Lord in vain; thou shalt have no other gods before me. (*With some hesitation.*) Thou shalt remember the Sabbath Day and keep it holy. (*Pause. Then:*) Thou shalt honor thy father and mother. Thou shalt not bear false witness. (*He is stuck. He counts back on his fingers, knowing one is missing.*) Thou shalt not make unto thee any graven image.

HALE. You have said that twice, sir.

PROCTO (*lost*). Aye. (*He is flailing for it.*)

ELIZABETH (*delicately*). Adultery, John.

PROCTOR (*as though a secret arrow had pained his heart*). Aye. (*Trying to grin it away—to* HALE:) You see, sir, between the two of us we do know them all. (HALE *only looks at* PROCTOR, *deep in his attempt to define this man.* PROCTOR *grows more uneasy.*) I think it be a small fault.

HALE. Theology, sir, is a fortress; no crack in a fortress may be accounted small. (*He rises; he seems worried now. He paces a little, in deep thought.*)

PROCTOR. There be no love for Satan in this house, Mister.

HALE. I pray it, I pray it dearly. (*He looks to both of them, an attempt at a smile on his face, but his misgivings are clear.*) Well, then—I'll bid you good night.

ELIZABETH (*unable to restrain herself*). Mr. Hale. (*He turns.*) I do think you are suspecting me somewhat? Are you not?

HALE (*obviously disturbed—and evasive*). Goody Proctor, I do not judge you. My duty is to add what I may to the godly wisdom of the court. I pray you both good health and good fortune. (*To* JOHN:) Good night, sir. (*He starts out.*)

ELIZABETH (*with a note of desperation*). I think you must tell him, John.

HALE. What's that?

ELIZABETH (*restraining a call*). Will you tell him?

(*Slight pause. Hale looks questioningly at* JOHN.)

PROCTOR (*with difficulty*). I—I have no witness and cannot prove it, except my word be taken. But I know the children's sickness had naught to do with witchcraft.

HALE (*stopped, struck*). Naught to do—?

PROCTOR. Mr. Parris discovered them sportin' in the woods. They were startled and took sick.

(*Pause.*)

HALE. Who told you this?

PROCTOR (*hesitates, then*). Abigail Williams.

HALE. Abigail!

PROCTOR. Aye.

HALE (*his eyes wide*). Abigail Williams told you it had naught to do with witchcraft!

PROCTOR. She told me the day you came, sir.

HALE (*suspiciously*). Why—why did you keep this?

PROCTOR. I never knew until tonight that the world is gone daft with this nonsense.

HALE. Nonsense! Mister, I have myself examined Tituba, Sarah Good, and numerous others that have confessed to dealing with the Devil. They have *confessed* it.

PROCTOR. And why not, if they must hang for denyin' it? There are them that will swear to anything before they'll hang; have you never thought of that?

HALE. I have. I—I have indeed. (*It is his own suspicion, but he resists it. He glances at* ELIZABETH, *then at* JOHN.) And you—would you testify to this in court?

PROCTOR. I—had not reckoned with goin' into court. But if I must I will.

HALE. Do you falter here?

PROCTOR. I falter nothing, but I may wonder if my story will be credited in such a court. I do wonder on it, when such a steady-minded minister as you will suspicion such a woman that never lied, and cannot, and the world knows she cannot! I may falter somewhat, Mister; I am no fool.

HALE (*quietly—it has impressed him*). Proctor, let you open with me now, for I have a rumor that troubles me. It's said you hold no belief that there may even be witches in the world. Is that true, sir?

PROCTOR (*—he knows this is critical, and is striving against his disgust with* HALE *and with himself for even answering*). I know not what I have said, I may have said it. I have wondered if there be witches in the world—although I cannot believe they come among us now.

HALE. Then you do not believe—

PROCTOR. I have no knowledge of it; the

Bible speaks of witches, and I will not deny them.

HALE. And you, woman?

ELIZABETH. I—I cannot believe it.

HALE (*shocked*). You cannot!

PROCTOR. Elizabeth, you bewilder him!

ELIZABETH (*to* HALE). I cannot think the Devil may own a woman's soul, Mr. Hale, when she keeps an upright way, as I have. I am a good woman, I know it; and if you believe I may do only good work in the world, and yet be secretly bound to Satan, then I must tell you, sir, I do not believe it.

HALE. But, woman, you do believe there are witches in—

ELIZABETH. If you think that I am one, then I say there are none.

HALE. You surely do not fly against the Gospel, the Gospel—

PROCTOR. She believe in the Gospel, every word!

ELIZABETH. Question Abigail Williams about the Gospel, not myself!

(HALE *stares at her.*)

PROCTOR. She do not mean to doubt the Gospel, sir, you cannot think it. This be a Christian house, sir, a Christian house.

HALE. God keep you both; let the third child be quickly baptized, and go you without fail each Sunday in to Sabbath prayer; and keep a solemn, quiet way among you. I think—

(GILES COREY *appears in doorway.*)

GILES. John!

PROCTOR. Giles! What's the matter?

GILES. They take my wife.

(FRANCIS NURSE *enters.*)

GILES. And his Rebecca!

PROCTOR (*to* FRANCIS). Rebecca's in the *jail!*

FRANCIS. Aye, Cheever come and take her in his wagon. We've only now come from the jail, and they'll not even let us in to see them.

ELIZABETH. They've surely gone wild now, Mr. Hale!

FRANCIS (*going to* HALE). Reverend Hale! Can you not speak to the Deputy Governor? I'm sure he mistakes these people—

HALE. Pray calm yourself, Mr. Nurse.

FRANCIS. My wife is the very brick and mortar of the church, Mr. Hale—(*Indicating* GILES—) and Martha Corey, there cannot be a woman closer yet to God than Martha.

HALE. How is Rebecca charged, Mr. Nurse?

FRANCIS (*with a mocking, half-hearted laugh*). For murder, she's charged! (*Mockingly quoting the warrant.*) "For the marvelous and supernatural murder of Goody Putnam's babies." What am I to do, Mr. Hale?

HALE (*turns from* FRANCIS, *deeply troubled, then*). Believe me, Mr. Nurse, if Rebecca Nurse be tainted, then nothing's left to stop the whole green world from burning. Let you rest upon the justice of the court; the court will send her home, I know it.

FRANCIS. You cannot mean she will be tried in court!

HALE (*pleading*). Nurse, though our hearts break, we cannot flinch; these are new times, sir. There is a misty plot afoot so subtle we should be criminal to cling to old respects and ancient friendships. I have seen too many frightful proofs in court—the Devil is alive in Salem, and we dare not quail to follow wherever the accusing finger points!

PROCTOR (*angered*). How may such a woman murder children?

HALE (*in great pain*). Man, remember, until an hour before the Devil fell, God thought him beautiful in Heaven.

GILES. I never said my wife were a witch, Mr. Hale; I only said she were reading books!

HALE. Mr. Corey, exactly what complaint were made on your wife?

GILES. That bloody mongrel Walcott charge her. Y'see, he buy a pig of my wife four or five year ago, and the pig died soon after. So he come dancin' in for his money back. So my Martha, she says to him, "Walcott, if you haven't the wit to feed a pig properly, you'll not live to own many," she says. Now he goes to court and claims that from that day to this he cannot keep a pig alive for more than four weeks because my Martha bewitch them with her books!

(*Enter* EZEKIEL CHEEVER. *A shocked silence.*)

CHEEVER. Good evening to you, Proctor.

PROCTOR. Why, Mr. Cheever. Good evening.

CHEEVER. Good evening, all. Good evening, Mr. Hale.

PROCTOR. I hope you come not on business of the court.

CHEEVER. I do, Proctor, aye. I am clerk

of the court now, y'know.

(*Enter* MARSHAL HERRICK, *a man in his early thirties, who is somewhat shamefaced at the moment.*)

GILES. It's a pity, Ezekiel, that an honest tailor might have gone to Heaven must burn in Hell. You'll burn for this, do you know it?

CHEEVER. You know yourself I must do as I'm told. You surely know that, Giles. And I'd as lief you'd not be sending me to Hell. I like not the sound of it, I tell you; I like not the sound of it. (*He fears* PROCTOR, *but starts to reach inside his coat.*) Now believe me, Proctor, how heavy be the law, all its tonnage I do carry on my back tonight. (*He takes out a warrant.*) I have a warrant for your wife.

PROCTOR (*to* HALE). You said she were not charged!

HALE. I know nothin' of it. (*To* CHEEVER:) When were she charged?

CHEEVER. I am given sixteen warrant tonight, sir, and she is one.

PROCTOR. Who charged her?

CHEEVER. Why, Abigail Williams charge her.

PROCTOR. On what proof, what proof?

CHEEVER (*looking about the room*). Mr. Proctor, I have little time. The court bid me search your house, but I like not to search a house. So will you hand me any poppets that your wife may keep here?

PROCTOR. Poppets?

ELIZABETH. I never kept no poppets, not since I were a girl.

CHEEVER (*embarrassed, glancing toward the mantel where sits* MARY WARREN's *poppet*). I spy a poppet, Goody Proctor.

ELIZABETH. Oh! (*Going for it:*) Why, this is Mary's.

CHEEVER (*shyly*). Would you please to give it to me?

ELIZABETH (*handing it to him, asks* HALE). Has the court discovered a text in poppets now?

CHEEVER (*carefully holding the poppet*). Do you keep any others in this house?

PROCTOR. No, nor this one either till tonight. What signifies a poppet?

CHEEVER. Why, a poppet—(*he gingerly turns the poppet over—*) a poppet may signify—Now, woman, will you please to come with me?

PROCTOR. She will not! (*To* ELIZABETH:) Fetch Mary here.

CHEEVER (*ineptly reaching toward* ELIZA-BETH). No, no, I am forbid to leave her from my sight.

PROCTOR (*pushing his arm away*). You'll leave her out of sight and out of mind, Mister. Fetch Mary, Elizabeth. (ELIZABETH *goes upstairs.*)

HALE. What signifies a poppet, Mr. Cheever?

CHEEVER (*turning the poppet over in his hands*). Why, they say it may signify that she—(*He has lifted the poppet's skirt, and his eyes widen in astonished fear.*) Why, this, this—

PROCTOR (*reaching for the poppet*). What's there?

CHEEVER. Why—(*He draws out a long needle from the poppet—*) it is a needle! Herrick, Herrick, it is a needle!

(HERRICK *comes toward him.*)

PROCTOR (*angrily, bewildered*). And what signifies a needle!

CHEEVER (*his hands shaking*). Why, this go hard with her, Proctor, this—I had my doubts, Proctor, I had my doubts, but here's calamity. (*To* HALE, *showing the needle:*) You see it, sir, it is a needle!

HALE. Why? What meanin' has it?

CHEEVER (*wide-eyed, trembling*). The girl, the Williams girl, Abigail Williams, sir. She sat to dinner in Reverend Parris's house tonight, and without word nor warnin' she falls to the floor. Like a struck beast, he says, and screamed a scream that a bull would weep to hear. And he goes to save her, and, stuck two inches in the flesh of her belly, he draw a needle out. And demandin' of her how she come to be so stabbed, she—(*to* PROCTOR *now—*) testify it were your wife's familiar spirit pushed it in.

PROCTOR. Why, she done it herself! (*To* HALE:) I hope you're not takin' this for proof, Mister!

(HALE, *struck by the proof, is silent.*)

CHEEVER. 'Tis hard proof! (*To* HALE:) I find here a poppet Goody Proctor keeps. I have found it, sir. And in the belly of the poppet a needle's stuck. I tell you true, Proctor, I never warranted to see such proof of Hell, and I bid you obstruct me not, for I—

(*Enter* ELIZABETH *with* MARY WARREN. PROCTOR, *seeing* MARY WARREN, *draws her by the arm to* HALE.)

PROCTOR. Here now! Mary, how did this poppet come into my house?

MARY WARREN (*frightened for herself,*

her voice very small). What poppet's that, sir?

PROCTOR (*impatiently, pointing at the doll in* CHEEVER's *hand*). This poppet, this poppet.

MARY WARREN (*evasively, looking at it*). Why, I—I think it is mine.

PROCTOR. It is your poppet, is it not?

MARY WARREN (*not understanding the direction of this*). It—is, sir.

PROCTOR. And how did it come into this house?

MARY WARREN (*glancing about at the avid faces*). Why—I made it in the court, sir, and—give it to Goody Proctor tonight.

PROCTOR (*to* HALE). Now, sir—do you have it?

HALE. Mary Warren, a needle have been found inside this poppet.

MARY WARREN (*bewildered*). Why, I meant no harm by it, sir.

PROCTOR (*quickly*). You stuck that needle in yourself?

MARY WARREN. I—I believe I did, sir, I—

PROCTOR (*to* HALE). What say you now?

HALE (*watching* MARY WARREN *closely*). Child, you are certain this be your natural memory? May it be, perhaps, that someone conjures you even now to say this?

MARY WARREN. Conjures me? Why, no, sir, I am entirely myself, I think. Let you ask Susanna Walcott—she saw me sewin' it in court. (*Or better still:*) Ask Abby, Abby sat beside me when I made it.

PROCTOR (*to* HALE, *of* CHEEVER). Bid him begone. Your mind is surely settled now. Bid him out, Mr. Hale.

ELIZABETH. What signifies a needle?

HALE. Mary—you charge a cold and cruel murder on Abigail.

MARY WARREN. Murder! I charge no—

HALE. Abigail were stabbed tonight; a needle were found stuck into her belly—

ELIZABETH. And she charges me?

HALE. Aye.

ELIZABETH (*her breath knocked out*). Why—! The girl is murder! She must be ripped out of the world!

CHEEVER (*pointing at* ELIZABETH). You've heard that, sir! Ripped out of the world! Herrick, you heard it!

PROCTOR (*suddenly snatching the warrant out of* CHEEVER's *hands*). Out with you.

CHEEVER. Proctor, you dare not touch the warrant.

PROCTOR (*ripping the warrant*). Out with you!

CHEEVER. You've ripped the Deputy Governor's warrant, man!

PROCTOR. Damn the Deputy Governor! Out of my house!

HALE. Now, Proctor, Proctor!

PROCTOR. Get y'gone with them! You are a broken minister.

HALE. Proctor, if she is innocent, the court—

PROCTOR. If *she* is innocent! Why do you never wonder if Parris be innocent, or Abigail? Is the accuser always holy now? Were they born this morning as clean as God's fingers? I'll tell you what's walking Salem—vengeance is walking Salem. We are what we always were in Salem, but now the little crazy children are jangling the keys of the kingdom, and common vengeance writes the law! This warrant's vengeance! I'll not give my wife to vengeance!

ELIZABETH. I'll go, John—

PROCTOR. You will not go!

HERRICK. I have nine men outside. You cannot keep her. The law binds me, John, I cannot budge.

PROCTOR (*to* HALE, *ready to break him*). Will you see her taken?

HALE. Proctor, the court is just—

PROCTOR. Pontius Pilate! God will not let you wash your hands of this!

ELIZABETH. John—I think I must go with them. (*He cannot bear to look at her.*) Mary, there is bread enough for the morning; you will bake, in the afternoon. Help Mr. Proctor as you were his daughter—you owe me that, and much more. (*She is fighting her weeping. To* PROCTOR:) When the children wake, speak nothing of witchcraft—it will frighten them. (*She cannot go on.*)

PROCTOR. I will bring you home. I will bring you soon.

ELIZABETH. Oh, John, bring me soon!

PROCTOR. I will fall like an ocean on that court! Fear nothing, Elizabeth.

ELIZABETH (*with great fear*). I will fear nothing. (*She looks about the room, as though to fix it in her mind.*) Tell the children I have gone to visit someone sick.

(*She walks out the door,* HERRICK *and* CHEEVER *behind her. For a moment,* PROCTOR *watches from the doorway. The clank of chain is heard.*)

PROCTOR. Herrick! Herrick, don't chain her! (*He rushes out the door. From outside:*) Damn you, man, you will not chain her! Off with them! I'll not have it! I will not have her chained!

(*There are other men's voices against his.* HALE, *in a fever of guilt and uncertainty, turns from the door to avoid the sight;* MARY WARREN *bursts into tears and sits weeping.* GILES COREY *calls to* HALE.)

GILES. And yet silent, minister? It is fraud, you know it is fraud! What keeps you, man?

(PROCTOR *is half braced, half pushed into the room by two deputies and* HERRICK.)

PROCTOR. I'll pay you, Herrick, I will surely pay you!

HERRICK (*panting*). In God's name, John, I cannot help myself. I must chain them all. Now let you keep inside this house till I am gone! (*He goes out with his deputies.*)

(PROCTOR *stands there, gulping air. Horses and a wagon creaking are heard.*)

HALE (*in great uncertainty*). Mr. Proctor—

PROCTOR. Out of my sight!

HALE. Charity, Proctor, charity. What I have heard in her favor, I will not fear to testify in court. God help me, I cannot judge her guilty or innocent—I know not. Only this consider: the world goes mad, and it profit nothing you should lay the cause to the vengeance of a little girl.

PROCTOR. You are a coward! Though you be ordained in God's own tears, you are a coward now!

HALE. Proctor, I cannot think God be provoked so grandly by such a petty cause. The jails are packed—our greatest judges sit in Salem now—and hangin's promised. Man, we must look to cause proportionate. Were there murder done, perhaps, and never brought to light? Abominations? Some secret blasphemy that stinks to Heaven? Think on cause, man, and let you help me to discover it. For there's your way, believe it, there is your only way, when such confusion strikes upon the world. (*He goes to* GILES *and* FRANCIS.) Let you counsel among yourselves; think on your village and what may have drawn from heaven such thundering wrath upon you all. I shall pray God open up our eyes.

(HALE *goes out.*)

FRANCIS (*struck by* HALE's *mood*). I never heard no murder done in Salem.

PROCTOR (*—he has been reached by* HALE's *words*). Leave me, Francis, leave me.

GILES (*shaken*). John—tell me, are we lost?

PROCTOR. Go home now, Giles. We'll speak on it tomorrow.

GILES. Let you think on it. We'll come early, eh?

PROCTOR. Aye. Go now, Giles.

GILES. Good night, then.

(GILES COREY *goes out. After a moment:*)

MARY WARREN (*in a fearful squeak of a voice*). Mr. Proctor, very likely they'll let her come home once they're given proper evidence.

PROCTOR. You're coming to the court with me, Mary. You will tell it in the court.

MARY WARREN. I cannot charge murder on Abigail.

PROCTOR (*moving menacingly toward her*). You will tell the court how that poppet come here and who stuck the needle in.

MARY WARREN. She'll kill me for sayin' that! (PROCTOR *continues toward her.*) Abby'll charge lechery on you, Mr. Proctor!

PROCTOR (*halting*). She's told you!

MARY WARREN. I have known it, sir. She'll ruin you with it, I know she will.

PROCTOR (*hesitating, and with deep hatred of himself*). Good. Then her saintliness is done with. (MARY *backs from him.*) We will slide together into our pit; you will tell the court what you know.

MARY WARREN (*in terror*). I cannot, they'll turn on me—

(PROCTOR *strides and catches her, and she is repeating,* "I cannot, I cannot!")

PROCTOR. My wife will never die for me! I will bring your guts into your mouth but that goodness will not die for me!

MARY WARREN (*struggling to escape him*). I cannot do it, I cannot!

PROCTOR (*grasping her by the throat as though he would strangle her*). Make your peace with it! Now Hell and Heaven grapple on our backs, and all our old pretense is ripped away—make your peace! (*He throws her to the floor, where she sobs,* "I cannot, I cannot . . ." *And now, half to himself, staring, and turning to the open door.*) Peace. It is a providence, and no great change; we are only what we always were, but naked now. (*He walks as though toward a great horror, facing the open sky.*) Aye, naked! And the wind,

God's icy wind, will blow!

And she is over and over again sobbing, "I cannot, I cannot, I cannot," as

THE CURTAIN FALLS

[The following sequence was added to Act Two by Arthur Miller for his revised version of the play, which had its first production in New York in July, 1953.]

SCENE: *A wood. Night.*

PROCTOR *appears with lantern. He enters glancing behind him, then halts, holding the lantern raised.* ABIGAIL *appears with a wrap over her nightgown, her hair down. A moment of questioning silence.*

———

PROCTOR (*searching*). I must speak with you, Abigail. (*She does not move, staring at him.*) Will you sit?

ABIGAIL. How do you come?

PROCTOR. Friendly.

ABIGAIL (*glancing about*). I don't like the woods at night. Pray you, stand closer. (*He comes closer to her, but keeps separated in spirit.*) I knew it must be you. When I heard the pebbles on the window, before I opened up my eyes I knew. I thought you would come a good time sooner.

PROCTOR. I had thought to come many times.

ABIGAIL. Why didn't you? I am so alone in the world now.

PROCTOR (*as a fact. Not bitterly*). Are you? I've heard that people come a hundred mile to see your face these days.

ABIGAIL. Aye, my face. Can you see my face?

PROCTOR (*holds the lantern to her face*). Then you're troubled?

ABIGAIL. Have you come to mock me?

PROCTOR (*sets lantern and sits down*). No, no, but I hear only that you go to the tavern every night, and play shovelboard with the Deputy Governor, and they give you cider.

ABIGAIL (*as though that did not count*). I have once or twice played the shovelboard. But I have no joy in it.

PROCTOR (*he is probing her*). This is a surprise, Abby. I'd thought to find you gayer than this. I'm told a troop of boys go step for step with you wherever you walk these days.

ABIGAIL. Aye, they do. But I have only lewd looks from the boys.

PROCTOR. And you like that not?

ABIGAIL. I cannot bear lewd looks no more, John. My spirit's changed entirely. I ought to be given Godly looks when I suffer for them as I do.

PROCTOR. Oh? How do you suffer, Abby?

ABIGAIL (*pulls up dress*). Why, look at my leg. I'm holes all over from their damned needles and pins. (*Touching her stomach.*) The jab your wife gave me's not healed yet, y'know.

PROCTOR (*seeing her madness now*). Oh, it isn't.

ABIGAIL. I think sometimes she pricks it open again while I sleep.

PROCTOR. Ah?

ABIGAIL. And George Jacobs . . . (*Sliding up her sleeve.*) He comes again and again and raps me with his stick—the same spot every night all this week. Look at the lump I have.

PROCTOR. Abby—George Jacobs is in the jail all this month.

ABIGAIL. Thank God he is, and bless the day he hangs and lets me sleep in peace again! Oh, John, the world's so full of hypocrites. (*Astonished, outraged:*) They pray in jail! I'm told they all pray in jail!

PROCTOR. They may not pray?

ABIGAIL. And torture me in my bed while sacred words are comin' from their mouths? Oh, it will need God himself to cleanse this town properly!

PROCTOR. Abby—you mean to cry out still others?

ABIGAIL. If I live, if I am not murdered, I surely will, until the last hypocrite is dead.

PROCTOR. Then there is no one good?

ABIGAIL (*softly*). Aye, there is one. *You* are good.

PROCTOR. Am I? How am I good?

ABIGAIL. Why, you taught me goodness, therefore you are good. It were a fire you walked me through, and all my ignorance was burned away. It were a fire, John, we lay in fire. And from that night no woman dare call me wicked anymore but I knew my answer. I used to weep for my sins when the wind lifted up my skirts; and blushed for shame because some old Rebecca called me loose. And then you burned my ignorance away. As bare as some December tree I saw them all—walking like saints to church, running to feed the sick, and hypocrites in their hearts! And God gave me strength to call them liars, and God made men to listen to me, and by God I will scrub the world clean for the love of Him! Oh, John, I will make you such a wife when the world is white again! (*She kisses his hand in high emotion.*) You will be amazed to see me every day, a light of heaven in your house, a . . . (*He rises and backs away, frightened, amazed.*) Why are you cold?

PROCTOR (*in a business-like way, but with uneasiness, as though before an unearthly thing*). My wife goes to trial in the morning, Abigail.

ABIGAIL (*distantly*). Your wife?

PROCTOR. Surely you knew of it?

ABIGAIL (*coming awake to that*). I do remember it now. (*As a duty:*) How—how—is she well?

PROCTOR. As well as she may be, thirty-six days in that place.

ABIGAIL. You said you came friendly.

PROCTOR. She will not be condemned, Abby.

ABIGAIL (*her holy feelings outraged. But she is questioning*). You brought me from my bed to speak of her?

PROCTOR. I come to tell you, Abby, what I will do tomorrow in the court. I would not take you by surprise, but give you all good time to think on what to do to save yourself.

ABIGAIL (*incredibly, and with beginning fear*). Save myself!

PROCTOR. If you do not free my wife tomorrow, I am set and bound to ruin you, Abby.

ABIGAIL (*her voice small—astonished*). How—ruin me?

PROCTOR. I have rocky proof in documents that you knew that poppet were none of my wife's; and that you yourself bade Mary Warren stab that needle into it.

ABIGAIL (*a wildness stirs in her; a child is standing here who is unutterably frustrated, denied her wish; but she is still grasping for her wits*). I bade Mary Warren . . . ?

PROCTOR. You know what you do, you are not so mad!

ABIGAIL (*she calls upwards*). Oh, hypocrites! Have you won him, too? (*Directly to him:*) John, why do you let them send you?

PROCTOR. I warn you, Abby.

ABIGAIL. They send you! They steal your honesty and . . .

PROCTOR. I have found my honesty.

ABIGAIL. No, this is your wife pleading, your sniveling, envious wife! This is Rebecca's voice, Martha Corey's voice. You were no hypocrite!

PROCTOR (*he grasps her arm and holds her*). I will prove you for the fraud you are!

ABIGAIL. And if they ask you why Abigail would ever do so murderous a deed, what will you tell them?

PROCTOR (*it is hard even to say it*). I will tell them why.

ABIGAIL. What will you tell? You will confess to fornication? In the court?

PROCTOR. If you will have it so, so I will tell it! (*She utters a disbelieving laugh.*) I say I will! (*She laughs louder, now with more assurance he will never do it. He shakes her roughly.*) If you can still hear, hear this! Can you hear! (*She is trembling, staring up at him as though he were out of his mind.*) You will tell the court you are blind to spirits; you cannot see them anymore, and you will never cry witchery again, or I will make you famous for the whore you are!

ABIGAIL (*she grabs him*). Never in this world! I know you, John—you are this moment singing secret Hallelujahs that your wife will hang!

PROCTOR (*throws her down*). You mad, you murderous bitch!

ABIGAIL (*rises*). Oh, how hard it is when pretense falls! But it falls, it falls! (*She wraps herself up as though to go.*) You have done your duty by her. I hope it is your last hypocrisy. I pray you will come again with sweeter news for me. I know you will—now that your duty's done. Good night, John. (*She is backing away, raising her hand in farewell.*) Fear naught. I will save you tomorrow. From yourself I will save you. (*She is gone.*)

PROCTOR *is left alone, amazed in terror. He takes up his lantern and slowly exits as*

THE CURTAIN FALLS

ACT THREE

The vestry room of the Salem meeting house, now serving as the anteroom of the General Court.

*As the curtain rises, the room is empty,
but for sunlight pouring through two high
windows in the back wall. The room is
solemn, even forbidding. Heavy beams jut
out, boards of random widths make up the
walls. At the right are two doors leading
into the meeting house proper, where the
court is being held. At the left another
door leads outside.*

*There is a plain bench at the left, and
another at the right. In the center a rather
long meeting table, with stools and a considerable armchair snugged up to it.*

*Through the partitioning wall at the
right we hear a prosecutor's voice,* JUDGE
HATHORNE's, *asking a question; then a
woman's voice,* MARTHA COREY's, *replying.*

HATHORNE'S VOICE. Now, Martha Corey,
there is abundant evidence in our hands to
show that you have given yourself to the
reading of fortunes. Do you deny it?

MARTHA COREY'S VOICE. I am innocent to
a witch. I know not what a witch is.

HATHORNE'S VOICE. How do you know,
then, that you are not a witch?

MARTHA COREY'S VOICE. If I were, I would
know it.

HATHORNE'S VOICE. Why do you hurt
these children?

MARTHA COREY'S VOICE. I do not hurt
them. I scorn it!

GILES' VOICE (*roaring*). I have evidence
for the court!

(*Voices of townspeople rise in excitement.*)

DANFORTH'S VOICE. You will keep your
seat!

GILES' VOICE. Thomas Putnam is reaching out for land!

DANFORTH'S VOICE. Remove that man,
Marshal!

GILES' VOICE. You're hearing lies, lies!

(*A roaring goes up from the people.*)

HATHORNE'S VOICE. Arrest him, excellency!

GILES' VOICE. I have evidence. Why will
you not hear my evidence?

(*The door opens and* GILES *is half carried into the vestry room by* HERRICK.)

GILES. Hands off, damn you, let me go!

HERRICK. Giles, Giles!

GILES. Out of my way, Herrick! I bring
evidence—

HERRICK. You cannot go in there, Giles;
it's a court!

(*Enter* HALE *from the court.*)

HALE. Pray be calm a moment.

GILES. You, Mr. Hale, go in there and
demand I speak.

HALE. A moment, sir, a moment.

GILES. They'll be hangin' my wife!

(JUDGE HATHORNE *enters. He is in his
sixties, a bitter, remorseless Salem judge.*)

HATHORNE. How do you dare come
roarin' into this court! Are you gone daft,
Corey?

GILES. You're not a Boston judge yet,
Hathorne. You'll not call me daft!

(*Enter* DEPUTY GOVERNOR DANFORTH *and,
behind him,* EZEKIEL CHEEVER *and* PARRIS.
On his appearance, silence falls. DANFORTH
*is a grave man in his sixties, of some hu-
mor and sophistication that does not, however, interfere with an exact loyalty to his
position and his cause. He comes down to*
GILES, *who awaits his wrath.*)

DANFORTH (*looking directly at* GILES).
Who is this man?

PARRIS. Giles Corey, sir, and a more con-
tentious—

GILES (*to* PARRIS). I am asked the question, and I am old enough to answer it!
(*To* DANFORTH, *who impresses him and to
whom he smiles through his strain*). My
name is Corey, sir, Giles Corey. I have
six hundred acres, and timber in addition.
It is my wife you be condemning now.
(*He indicates the courtroom.*)

DANFORTH. And how do you imagine to
help her cause with such contemptuous
riot? Now be gone. Your old age alone
keeps you out of jail for this.

GILES (*beginning to plead*). They be
tellin' lies about my wife, sir, I—

DANFORTH. Do you take it upon yourself to determine what this court shall believe and what it shall set aside?

GILES. Your excellency, we mean no disrespect for—

DANFORTH. Disrespect indeed! It is disruption, Mister. This is the highest court
of the supreme government of this province, do you know it?

GILES (*beginning to weep*). Your excellency, I only said she were readin' books,
sir, and they come and take her out of my
house for—

DANFORTH (*mystified*). Books! What
books?

GILES (*through helpless sobs*). It is my
third wife, sir; I never had no wife that
be so taken with books, and I thought to
find the cause of it, d'y'see, but it were no

witch I blamed her for. (*He is openly weeping.*) I have broke charity with the woman, I have broke charity with her. (*He covers his face ashamed.* DANFORTH *is respectfully silent.*)

HALE. Excellency, he claims hard evidence for his wife's defense. I think that in all justice you must—

DANFORTH. Then let him submit his evidence in proper affidavit. You are certainly aware of our procedure here, Mr. Hale. (*To* HERRICK:) Clear this room.

HERRICK. Come now, Giles. (*He gently pushes* COREY *out.*)

FRANCIS. We are desperate, sir; we come here three days now and cannot be heard.

DANFORTH. Who is this man?

FRANCIS. Francis Nurse, Your Excellency.

HALE. His wife's Rebecca that were condemned this morning.

DANFORTH. Indeed! I am amazed to find you in such uproar. I have only good report of your character, Mr. Nurse.

HATHORNE. I think they must both be arrested in contempt, sir.

DANFORTH (*to* FRANCIS). Let you write your plea, and in due time I will—

FRANCIS. Excellency, we have proof for your eyes; God forbid you shut them to it. The girls, sir, the girls are frauds.

DANFORTH. What's that?

FRANCIS. We have proof of it, sir. They are all deceiving you.

(DANFORTH *is shocked, but studying* FRANCIS.)

HATHORNE. This is contempt, sir, contempt!

DANFORTH. Peace, Judge Hathorne. Do you know who I am, Mr. Nurse?

FRANCIS. I surely do, sir, and I think you must be a wise judge to be what you are.

DANFORTH. And do you know that near to four hundred are in the jails from Marblehead to Lynn, and upon my signature?

FRANCIS. I—

DANFORTH. And seventy-two condemned to hang by that signature?

FRANCIS. Excellency, I never thought to say it to such a weighty judge, but you are deceived.

(*Enter* GILES COREY *from left. All turn to see as he beckons in* MARY WARREN *with* PROCTOR. MARY *is keeping her eyes to the ground;* PROCTOR *has her elbow as though she were near collapse.*)

PARRIS (*on seeing her, in shock*). Mary Warren! (*He goes directly to bend close to her face.*) What are you about here?

PROCTOR (*pressing* PARRIS *away from her with a gentle but firm motion of protectiveness*). She would speak with the Deputy Governor.

DANFORTH (*shocked by this, turns to* HERRICK). Did you not tell me Mary Warren were sick in bed?

HERRICK. She were, Your Honor. When I go to fetch her to the court last week, she said she were sick.

GILES. She has been strivin' with her soul all week, Your Honor; she comes now to tell the truth of this to you.

DANFORTH. Who is this?

PROCTOR. John Proctor, sir. Elizabeth Proctor is my wife.

PARRIS. Beware this man, Your Excellency, this man is mischief.

HALE (*excitedly*). I think you must hear the girl, sir, she—

DANFORTH (*who has become very interested in* MARY WARREN *and only raises a hand toward* HALE). Peace. What would you tell us, Mary Warren?

(PROCTOR *looks at her, but she cannot speak.*)

PROCTOR. She never saw no spirits, sir.

DANFORTH (*with great alarm and surprise, to* MARY). Never saw no spirits!

GILES (*eagerly*). Never.

PROCTOR (*reaching into his jacket*). She has signed a deposition, sir—

DANFORTH (*instantly*). No, no, I accept no depositions. (*He is rapidly calculating this; he turns from her to* PROCTOR.) Tell me, Mr. Proctor, have you given out this story in the village?

PROCTOR. We have not.

PARRIS. They've come to overthrow the court, sir! This man is—

DANFORTH. I pray you, Mr. Parris. Do you know, Mr. Proctor, that the entire contention of the state in these trials is that the voice of Heaven is speaking through the children?

PROCTOR. I know that, sir.

DANFORTH (*thinks, staring at* PROCTOR, *then turns to* MARY WARREN). And you, Mary Warren, how came you to cry out people for sending their spirits against you?

MARY WARREN. It were pretense, sir.

DANFORTH. I cannot hear you.

PROCTOR. It were pretense, she says.

DANFORTH. Ah? And the other girls? Susanna Walcott, and—the others? They are also pretending?

MARY WARREN. Aye, sir.

DANFORTH (*wide-eyed*). Indeed. (*Pause. He is baffled by this. He turns to study* PROCTOR's *face.*)

PARRIS (*in a sweat*). Excellency, you surely cannot think to let so vile a lie be spread in open court!

DANFORTH. Indeed not, but it strike hard upon me that she will dare come here with such a tale. Now, Mr. Proctor, before I decide whether I shall hear you or not, it is my duty to tell you this. We burn a hot fire here; it melts down all concealment.

PROCTOR. I know that, sir.

DANFORTH. Let me continue. I understand well, a husband's tenderness may drive him to extravagance in defense of a wife. Are you certain in your conscience, Mister, that your evidence is the truth?

PROCTOR. It is. And you will surely know it.

DANFORTH. And you thought to declare this revelation in the open court before the public?

PROCTOR. I thought I would, aye—with your permission.

DANFORTH (*his eyes narrowing*). Now, sir, what is your purpose in so doing?

PROCTOR. Why, I—I would free my wife, sir.

DANFORTH. There lurks nowhere in your heart, nor hidden in your spirit, any desire to undermine this court?

PROCTOR (*with the faintest faltering*). Why, no, sir.

CHEEVER (*clears his throat, awakening*). I— Your Excellency.

DANFORTH. Mr. Cheever.

CHEEVER. I think it be my duty, sir— (*Kindly, to* PROCTOR:) You'll not deny it, John. (*To* DANFORTH:) When we come to take his wife, he damned the court and ripped your warrant.

PARRIS. Now you have it!

DANFORTH. He did that, Mr. Hale?

HALE (*takes a breath*). Aye, he did.

PROCTOR. It were a temper, sir. I knew not what I did.

DANFORTH (*studying him*). Mr. Proctor.

PROCTOR. Aye, sir.

DANFORTH (*straight into his eyes*). Have you ever seen the Devil?

PROCTOR. No, sir.

DANFORTH. You are in all respects a Gospel Christian?

PROCTOR. I am, sir.

PARRIS. Such a Christian that will not come to church but once in a month!

DANFORTH (*restrained—he is curious*). Not come to church?

PROCTOR. I—I have no love for Mr. Parris. It is no secret. But God I surely love.

CHEEVER. He plow on Sunday, sir.

DANFORTH. Plow on Sunday!

CHEEVER (*apologetically*). I think it be evidence, John. I am an official of the court, I cannot keep it.

PROCTOR. I—I have once or twice plowed on Sunday. I have three children, sir, and until last year my land give little.

GILES. You'll find other Christians that do plow on Sunday if the truth be known.

HALE. Your Honor, I cannot think you may judge the man on such evidence.

DANFORTH. I judge nothing. (*Pause. He keeps watching* PROCTOR, *who tries to meet his gaze.*) I tell you straight, Mister—I have seen marvels in this court. I have seen people choked before my eyes by spirits; I have seen them stuck by pins and slashed by daggers. I have until this moment not the slightest reason to suspect that the children may be deceiving me. Do you understand my meaning?

PROCTOR. Excellency, does it not strike upon you that so many of these women have lived so long with such upright reputation, and—

PARRIS. Do you read the Gospel, Mr. Proctor?

PROCTOR. I read the Gospel.

PARRIS. I think not, or you should surely know that Cain were an upright man, and yet he did kill Abel.

PROCTOR. Aye, God tells us that. (*To* DANFORTH:) But who tells us Rebecca Nurse murdered seven babies by sending out her spirit on them? It is the children only, and this one will swear she lied to you.

(DANFORTH *considers, then beckons* HATHORNE *to him.* HATHORNE *leans in, and he speaks in his ear.* HATHORNE *nods.*)

HATHORNE. Aye, she's the one.

DANFORTH. Mr. Proctor, this morning, your wife send me a claim in which she states that she is pregnant now!

PROCTOR. My wife pregnant!

DANFORTH. There be no sign of it—we have examined her body.

PROCTOR. But if she say she is pregnant, then she must be! That woman will never lie, Mr. Danforth.

DANFORTH. She will not?

PROCTOR. Never, sir, never.

DANFORTH. We have thought it too convenient to be credited. However, if I should tell you now that I will let her be kept another month; and if she begin to show her natural signs, you shall have her living yet another year until she is delivered—what say you to that? (JOHN PROCTOR *is struck silent.*) Come now. You say your only purpose is to save your wife. Good, then, she is saved at least this year, and a year is long. What say you, sir? It is done now. (*In conflict,* PROCTOR *glances at* FRANCIS *and* GILES.) Will you drop this charge?

PROCTOR. I—I think I cannot.

DANFORTH (*now an almost imperceptible hardness in his voice*). Then your purpose is somewhat larger.

PARRIS. He's come to overthrow this court, Your Honor!

PROCTOR. These are my friends. Their wives are also accused—

DANFORTH (*with a sudden briskness of manner*). I judge you not, sir. I am ready to hear your evidence.

PROCTOR. I come not to hurt the court; I only—

DANFORTH (*cutting him off*). Marshal, go into the court and bid Judge Stoughton and Judge Sewall declare recess for one hour. And let them go to the tavern, if they will. All witnesses and prisoners are to be kept in the building.

HERRICK. Aye, sir. (*Very deferentially:*) If I may say it, sir, I know this man all my life. It is a good man, sir.

DANFORTH (—*it is the reflection on himself he resents*). I am sure of it, Marshal. (HERRICK *nods, then goes out.*) Now, what deposition do you have for us, Mr. Proctor? And I beg you be clear, open as the sky, and honest.

PROCTOR (*as he takes out several papers*). I am no lawyer, so I'll—

DANFORTH. The pure in heart need no lawyers. Proceed as you will.

PROCTOR (*handing* DANFORTH *a paper*). Will you read this first, sir? It's a sort of testament. The people signing it declare their good opinion of Rebecca, and my wife, and Martha Corey. (DANFORTH *looks down at the paper.*)

PARRIS (*to enlist* DANFORTH's *sarcasm*). Their good opinion! (*But* DANFORTH *goes on reading, and* PROCTOR *is heartened.*)

PROCTOR. These are all landholding farmers, members of the church. (*Delicately, trying to point out a paragraph:*) If you'll notice, sir—they've known the women many years and never saw no sign they had dealings with the Devil.

(PARRIS *nervously moves over and reads over* DANFORTH's *shoulder.*)

DANFORTH (*glancing down a long list*). How many names are here?

FRANCIS. Ninety-one, Your Excellency.

PARRIS (*sweating*). These people should be summoned. (DANFORTH *looks up at him questioningly.*) For questioning.

FRANCIS (*trembling with anger*). Mr. Danforth, I gave them all my word no harm would come to them for signing this.

PARRIS. This is a clear attack upon the court!

HALE (*to* PARRIS, *trying to contain himself*). Is every defense an attack upon the court? Can no one—?

PARRIS. All innocent and Christian people are happy for the courts in Salem! These people are gloomy for it. (*To* DANFORTH *directly:*) And I think you will want to know, from each and every one of them, what discontents them with you!

HATHORNE. I think they ought to be examined, sir.

DANFORTH. It is not necessarily an attack, I think. Yet—

FRANCIS. These are all covenanted Christians, sir.

DANFORTH. Then I am sure they may have nothing to fear. (*Hands* CHEEVER *the paper.*) Mr. Cheever, have warrants drawn for all of these—arrest for examination. (*To* PROCTOR:) Now, Mister, what other information do you have for us? (FRANCIS *is still standing, horrified.*) You may sit, Mr. Nurse.

FRANCIS. I have brought trouble on these people; I have—

DANFORTH. No, old man, you have not hurt these people if they are of good conscience. But you must understand, sir, that a person is either with this court or he must be counted against it, there be no road between. This is a sharp time, now, a precise time—we live no longer in the dusky afternoon when evil mixed itself with good and befuddled the world. Now, by God's grace, the shining sun is up, and them that fear not light will surely praise it. I hope you will be one of those. (MARY WARREN *suddenly sobs.*) She's not hearty, I see.

PROCTOR. No, she's not, sir. (*To* MARY, *bending to her, holding her hand, quietly:*) Now remember what the angel Raphael said to the boy Tobias. Remember it.

MARY WARREN (*hardly audible*). Aye.

PROCTOR. "Do that which is good, and no harm shall come to thee."

MARY WARREN. Aye.

DANFORTH. Come, man, we wait you.

(MARSHAL HERRICK *returns, and takes his post at the door.*)

GILES. John, my deposition, give him mine.

PROCTOR. Aye. (*He hands* DANFORTH *another paper.*) This is Mr. Corey's deposition.

DANFORTH. Oh? (*He looks down at it. Now* HATHORNE *comes behind him and reads with him.*)

HATHORNE (*suspiciously*). What lawyer drew this, Corey?

GILES. You know I never hired a lawyer in my life, Hathorne.

DANFORTH (*finishes the reading*). It is very well phrased. My compliments. Mr. Parris, if Mr. Putnam is in the court, will you bring him in? (HATHORNE *takes the deposition, and walks to the window with it.* PARRIS *goes into the court.*) You have no legal training, Mr. Corey?

GILES (*very pleased*). I have the best, sir —I am thirty-three time in court in my life. And always plaintiff, too.

DANFORTH. Oh, then you're much put-upon.

GILES. I am never put-upon; I know my rights, sir, and I will have them. You know, your father tried a case of mine— might be thirty-five year ago, I think.

DANFORTH. Indeed.

GILES. He never spoke to you of it?

DANFORTH. No, I cannot recall it.

GILES. That's strange, he give me nine pound damages. He were a fair judge, your father. Y'see, I had a white mare that time, and this fellow come to borrow the mare— (*Enter* PARRIS *with* THOMAS PUTNAM. *When he sees* PUTNAM, GILES' *ease goes; he is hard.*) Aye, there he is.

DANFORTH. Mr. Putnam, I have here an accusation by Mr. Corey against you. He states that you coldly prompted your daughter to cry witchery upon George Jacobs that is now in jail.

PUTNAM. It is a lie.

DANFORTH (*turning to* GILES). Mr. Putnam states your charge is a lie. What say you to that?

GILES (*furious, his fists clenched*). A fart on Thomas Putnam, that is what I say to that!

DANFORTH. What proof do you submit for your charge, sir?

GILES. My proof is there! (*Pointing to the paper.*) If Jacobs hangs for a witch he forfeit up his property—that's law! And there is none but Putnam with the coin to buy so great a piece. This man is killing his neighbors for their land!

DANFORTH. But proof, sir, proof.

GILES (*pointing at his deposition*). The proof is there! I have it from an honest man who heard Putnam say it! The day his daughter cried out on Jacobs, he said she'd given him a fair gift of land.

HATHORNE. And the name of this man?

GILES (*taken aback*). What name?

HATHORNE. The man that give you this information.

GILES (*hesitates, then*). Why, I—I cannot give you his name.

HATHORNE. And why not?

GILES (*hesitates, then bursts out*). You know well why not! He'll lay in jail if I give his name!

HATHORNE. This is contempt of the court, Mr. Danforth!

DANFORTH (*to avoid that*). You will surely tell us the name.

GILES. I will not give you no name. I mentioned my wife's name once and I'll burn in hell long enough for that. I stand mute.

DANFORTH. In that case, I have no choice but to arrest you for contempt of this court, do you know that?

GILES. This is a hearing; you cannot clap me for contempt of a hearing.

DANFORTH. Oh, it is a proper lawyer! Do you wish me to declare the court in full session here? Or will you give me good reply?

GILES (*faltering*). I cannot give you no name, sir, I cannot.

DANFORTH. You are a foolish old man. Mr. Cheever, begin the record. The court is now in session. I ask you, Mr. Corey—

PROCTOR (*breaking in*). Your Honor— he has the story in confidence, sir, and he—

PARRIS. The Devil lives on such confidences! (*To* DANFORTH:) Without confidences there could be no conspiracy, Your Honor!

HATHORNE. I think it must be broken, sir.

DANFORTH (*to* GILES). Old man, if your informant tells the truth let him come here openly like a decent man. But if he hide in anonymity I must know why. Now sir, the government and central church demand of you the name of him who reported Mr. Thomas Putnam a common murderer.

HALE. Excellency—

DANFORTH. Mr. Hale.

HALE. We cannot blink it more. There is a prodigious fear of this court in the country—

DANFORTH. Then there is a prodigious guilt in the country. Are *you* afraid to be questioned here?

HALE. I may only fear the Lord, sir, but there is fear in the country nevertheless.

DANFORTH (*angered now*). Reproach me not with the fear in the country; there is fear in the country because there is a moving plot to topple Christ in the country!

HALE. But it does not follow that everyone accused is part of it.

DANFORTH. No uncorrupted man may fear this court, Mr. Hale! None! (*To* GILES:) You are under arrest in contempt of this court. Now sit you down and take counsel with yourself, or you will be set in the jail until you decide to answer all questions.

(GILES COREY *makes a rush for* PUTNAM. PROCTOR *lunges and holds him.*)

PROCTOR. No, Giles!

GILES (*over* PROCTOR'S *shoulder at* PUTNAM). I'll cut your throat, Putnam, I'll kill you yet!

PROCTOR (*forcing him into a chair*). Peace, Giles, peace. (*Releasing him:*) We'll prove ourselves. Now we will. (*He starts to turn to* DANFORTH.)

GILES. Say nothin' more, John. (*Pointing at* DANFORTH:) He's only playin' you! He means to hang us all!

(MARY WARREN *bursts into sobs.*)

DANFORTH. This is a court of law, Mister. I'll have no effrontery here!

PROCTOR. Forgive him, sir, for his old age. Peace, Giles, we'll prove it all now. (*He lifts up* MARY'S *chin.*) You cannot weep, Mary. Remember the angel, what

he say to the boy. Hold to it, now; there is your rock. (MARY *quiets. He takes out a paper, and turns to* DANFORTH.) This is Mary Warren's deposition. I—I would ask you remember, sir, while you read it, that until two week ago she were no different than the other children are today. (*He is speaking reasonably, restraining all his fears, his anger, his anxiety.*) You saw her scream, she howled, she swore familiar spirits choked her; she even testified that Satan, in the form of women now in jail, tried to win her soul away, and then when she refused—

DANFORTH. We know all this.

PROCTOR. Aye, sir. She swears now that she never saw Satan; nor any spirit, vague or clear, that Satan may have sent to hurt her. And she declares her friends are lying now.

(PROCTOR *starts to hand* DANFORTH *the deposition, and* HALE *comes up to* DANFORTH *in a trembling state.*)

HALE. Excellency, a moment. I think this goes to the heart of the matter.

DANFORTH (*with deep misgivings*). It surely does.

HALE. I cannot say he is an honest man; I know him little. But in all justice, sir, a claim so weighty cannot be argued by a farmer. In God's name sir, stop here; send him home and let him come again with a lawyer—

DANFORTH (*patiently*). Now look you Mr. Hale—

HALE. Excellency, I have signed seventy-two death warrants; I am a minister of the Lord, and I dare not take a life without there be a proof so immaculate no slightest qualm of conscience may doubt it.

DANFORTH. Mr. Hale, you surely do not doubt my justice.

HALE. I have this morning signed away the soul of Rebecca Nurse, Your Honor. I'll not conceal it, my hand shakes yet as with a wound! I pray you, sir, this argument let lawyers present to you.

DANFORTH. Mr. Hale, believe me; for a man of such terrible learning you are most bewildered—I hope you will forgive me. I have been thirty-two year at the bar, sir, and I should be confounded were I called upon to defend these people. Let you consider, now—(*To* PROCTOR *and the others:*) And I bid you all do likewise. In an ordinary crime, how does one defend the accused? One calls up witnesses to prove his innocence. But witchcraft is *ipso facto,* on its face and by its nature, an invisible crime, is it not? Therefore, who may possibly be witness to it? The witch and the victim. None other. Now we cannot hope the witch will accuse herself; granted? Therefore, we must rely upon her victims —and they do testify, the children certainly do testify. As for the witches, none will deny that we are most eager for all their confessions. Therefore, what is left for a lawyer to bring out? I think I have made my point. Have I not?

HALE. But this child claims the girls are not truthful, and if they are not—

DANFORTH. That is precisely what I am about to consider, sir. What more may you ask of me? Unless you doubt my probity?

HALE (*defeated*). I surely do not, sir. Let you consider it, then.

DANFORTH. And let you put your heart to rest. Her deposition, Mr. Proctor.

(PROCTOR *hands it to him.* HATHORNE *rises, goes beside* DANFORTH, *and starts reading.* PARRIS *comes to his other side.* DANFORTH *looks at* JOHN PROCTOR, *then proceeds to read.* HALE *gets up, finds position near the judge, reads too.* PROCTOR *glances at* GILES. FRANCIS *prays silently, hands pressed together.* CHEEVER *waits placidly, the sublime official, dutiful.* MARY WARREN *sobs once.* JOHN PROCTOR *touches her head reassuringly. Presently* DANFORTH *lifts his eyes, stands up, takes out a kerchief and blows his nose. The others stand aside as he moves in thought toward the window.*)

PARRIS (*hardly able to contain his anger and fear*). I should like to question—

DANFORTH (*—his first real outburst, in which his contempt for* PARRIS *is clear*). Mr. Parris, I bid you be silent! (*He stands in silence, looking out the window. Now, having established that he will set the gait:*) Mr. Cheever, will you go into the court and bring the children here? (CHEEVER *gets up and goes out upstage.* DANFORTH *now turns to* MARY.) Mary Warren, how came you to this turnabout? Has Mr. Proctor threatened you for this deposition?

MARY WARREN. No, sir.

DANFORTH. Has he ever threatened you?

MARY WARREN (*weaker*). No, sir.

DANFORTH (*sensing a weakening*). Has he threatened you?

MARY WARREN. No, sir.

DANFORTH. Then you tell me that you sat in my court, callously lying, when you knew that people would hang by your evidence? (*She does not answer.*) Answer me!

MARY WARREN (*almost inaudibly*). I did, sir.

DANFORTH. How were you instructed in your life? Do you not know that God damns all liars? (*She cannot speak.*) Or is it now that you lie?

MARY WARREN. No, sir—I am with God now.

DANFORTH. You are with God now.

MARY WARREN. Aye, sir.

DANFORTH (*containing himself*). I will tell you this—you are either lying now, or you were lying in the court, and in either case you have committed perjury and you will go to jail for it. You cannot lightly say you lied, Mary. Do you know that?

MARY WARREN. I cannot lie no more. I am with God, I am with God.

(*But she breaks into sobs at the thought of it, and the right door opens, and enter* SUSANNA WALCOTT, MERCY LEWIS, BETTY PARRIS, *and finally* ABIGAIL. CHEEVER *comes to* DANFORTH.)

CHEEVER. Ruth Putnam's not in the court, sir, nor the other children.

DANFORTH. These will be sufficient. Sit you down, children. (*Silently they sit.*) Your friend, Mary Warren, has given us a deposition. In which she swears that she never saw familiar spirits, apparitions, nor any manifest of the Devil. She claims as well that none of you have seen these things either. (*Slight pause.*) Now, children, this is a court of law. The law, based upon the Bible, and the Bible, writ by Almighty God, forbid the practice of witchcraft, and describe death as the penalty thereof. But likewise, children, the law and Bible damn all bearers of false witness. (*Slight pause.*) Now then. It does not escape me that this deposition may be devised to blind us; it may well be that Mary Warren has been conquered by Satan, who sends her here to distract our sacred purpose. If so, her neck will break for it. But if she speak true, I bid you now drop your guile and confess your pretense, for a quick confession will go easier with you. (*Pause.*) Abigail Williams, rise. (ABIGAIL *slowly rises.*) Is there any truth in this?

ABIGAIL. No, sir.

DANFORTH (*thinks, glances at* MARY, *then back to* ABIGAIL). Children, a very augur bit will now be turned into your souls until your honesty is proved. Will either of you change your positions now, or do you force me to hard questioning?

ABIGAIL. I have naught to change, sir. She lies.

DANFORTH (*to* MARY). You would still go on with this?

MARY WARREN (*faintly*). Aye, sir.

DANFORTH (*turning to* ABIGAIL). A poppet were discovered in Mr. Proctor's house, stabbed by a needle. Mary Warren claims that you sat beside her in the court when she made it, and that you saw her make it and witnessed how she herself stuck her needle into it for safe-keeping. What say you to that?

ABIGAIL (*with a slight note of indignation*). It is a lie, sir.

DANFORTH (*after a slight pause*). While you worked for Mr. Proctor, did you see poppets in that house?

ABIGAIL. Goody Proctor always kept poppets.

PROCTOR. Your Honor, my wife never kept no poppets. Mary Warren confesses it was her poppet.

CHEEVER. Your Excellency.

DANFORTH. Mr. Cheever.

CHEEVER. When I spoke with Goody Proctor in that house, she said she never kept no poppets. But she said she did keep poppets when she were a girl.

PROCTOR. She has not been a girl these fifteen years, Your Honor.

HATHORNE. But a poppet will keep fifteen years, will it not?

PROCTOR. It will keep if it is kept, but Mary Warren swears she never saw no poppets in my house, nor anyone else.

PARRIS. Why could there not have been poppets hid where no one ever saw them?

PROCTOR (*furious*). There might also be a dragon with five legs in my house, but no one has ever seen it.

PARRIS. We are here, Your Honor, precisely to discover what no one has ever seen.

PROCTOR. Mr. Danforth, what profit this girl to turn herself about? What may Mary Warren gain but hard questioning and worse?

DANFORTH. You are charging Abigail Williams with a marvelous cool plot to murder, do you understand that?

PROCTOR. I do, sir. I believe she means to murder.

DANFORTH (*pointing at* ABIGAIL, *incredulously*). This child would murder your wife?

PROCTOR. It is not a child. Now hear me, sir. In the sight of the congregation she were twice this year put out of this meetin' house for laughter during prayer.

DANFORTH (*shocked, turning to* ABIGAIL). What's this? Laughter during—!

PARRIS. Excellency, she were under Tituba's power at that time, but she is solemn now.

GILES. Aye, now she is solemn and goes to hang people!

DANFORTH. Quiet, man.

HATHORNE. Surely it have no bearing on the question, sir. He charges contemplation of murder.

DANFORTH. Aye. (*He studies* ABIGAIL *for a moment, then:*) Continue, Mr. Proctor.

PROCTOR. Mary. Now tell the Governor how you danced in the woods.

PARRIS (*instantly*). Excellency, since I come to Salem this man is blackening my name. He—

DANFORTH. In a moment, sir. (*To* MARY WARREN, *sternly, and surprised:*) What is this dancing?

MARY WARREN. I—(*She glances at* ABIGAIL, *who is staring down at her remorselessly. Then, appealing to* PROCTOR:) Mr. Proctor—

PROCTOR (*taking it right up*). Abigail leads the girls to the woods, Your Honor, and they have danced there naked—

PARRIS. Your Honor, this—

PROCTOR (*at once*). Mr. Parris discovered them himself in the dead of night! There's the "child" she is!

DANFORTH (—*it is growing into a nightmare, and he turns, astonished, to* PARRIS). Mr. Parris—

PARRIS. I can only say, sir, that I never found any of them naked, and this man is—

DANFORTH. But you discovered them dancing in the woods? (*Eyes on* PARRIS, *he points at* ABIGAIL.) Abigail?

HALE. Excellency, when I first arrived from Beverly, Mr. Parris told me that.

DANFORTH. Do you deny it, Mr. Parris?

PARRIS. I do not, sir, but I never saw any of them naked.

DANFORTH. But she have *danced*?

PARRIS (*unwillingly*). Aye, sir.

(DANFORTH, *as though with new eyes, looks at* ABIGAIL.)

HATHORNE. Excellency, will you permit me? (*He points at* MARY WARREN.)

DANFORTH (*with great worry*). Pray, proceed.

HATHORNE. You say you never saw no spirits, Mary, were never threatened or afflicted by any manifest of the Devil or the Devil's agents.

MARY WARREN (*very faintly*). No, sir.

HATHORNE (*with a gleam of victory*). And yet, when people accused of witchery confronted you in court, you would faint, saying their spirits came out of their bodies and choked you—

MARY WARREN. That were pretense, sir.

DANFORTH. I cannot hear you.

MARY WARREN. Pretense, sir.

PARRIS. But you did turn cold, did you not? I myself picked you up many times, and your skin were icy. Mr. Danforth, you—

DANFORTH. I saw that many times.

PROCTOR. She only pretended to faint, Your Excellency. They're all marvelous pretenders.

HATHORNE. Then can she pretend to faint now?

PROCTOR. Now?

PARRIS. Why not? Now there are no spirits attacking her, for none in this room is accused of witchcraft. So let her turn herself cold now, let her pretend she is attacked now, let her faint. (*He turns to* MARY WARREN.) Faint!

PARRIS. Aye, faint. Prove to us how you pretended in the court so many times.

MARY WARREN (*looking to* PROCTOR). I—cannot faint now, sir.

PROCTOR (*alarmed, quietly*). Can you not pretend it?

MARY WARREN. I—(*She looks about as though searching for the passion to faint.*) I—have no *sense* of it now, I—

DANFORTH. Why? What is lacking now?

MARY WARREN. I—cannot tell, sir, I—

DANFORTH. Might it be that here we have no afflicting spirit loose, but in the court there were some?

MARY WARREN. I never saw no spirits.

PARRIS. Then see no spirits now, and prove to us that you can faint by your own will, as you claim.

MARY WARREN (*stares, searching for the emotion of it, and then shakes her head*). I—cannot do it.

PARRIS. Then you will confess, will you not? It were attacking spirits made you faint!

MARY WARREN. No, sir, I—

PARRIS. Your Excellency, this is a trick to blind the court!

MARY WARREN. It's not a trick! (*She stands.*) I—I used to faint because I—I thought I saw spirits.

DANFORTH. *Thought* you saw them!

MARY WARREN. But I did not, Your Honor.

HATHORNE. How could you think you saw them unless you saw them?

MARY WARREN. I—I cannot tell how, but I did. I—I heard the other girls screaming, and you, Your Honor, you seemed to believe them, and I— It were only sport in the beginning, sir, but then the whole world cried spirits, spirits, and I—I promise you Mr. Danforth, I only thought I saw them but I did not.

(DANFORTH *peers at her.*)

PARRIS (*smiling, but nervous because* DANFORTH *seems to be struck by* MARY WARREN's *story.*) Surely Your Excellency is not taken by this simple lie.

DANFORTH (*turning worriedly to* ABIGAIL). Abigail. I bid you now search your heart and tell me this—and beware of it, child, to God every soul is precious and His vengeance is terrible on them that take life without cause. Is it possible, child, that the spirits you have seen are illusion only, some deception that may cross your mind when—

ABIGAIL. Why, this—this—is a base question, sir.

DANFORTH. Child, I would have you consider it—

ABIGAIL. I have been hurt, Mr. Danforth; I have seen my blood runnin' out! I have been near to murdered every day because I done my duty pointing out the Devil's people—and this is my reward? To be mistrusted, denied, questioned like a—

DANFORTH (*weakening*). Child, I do not mistrust you—

ABIGAIL (*in an open threat*). Let *you* beware, Mr. Danforth. Think you to be so mighty that the power of Hell may not turn *your* wits? Beware of it! There is— (*Suddenly, from an accusatory attitude, her face turns, looking into the air above —it is truly frightened.*)

DANFORTH (*apprehensively*). What is it, child?

ABIGAIL (*looking about in the air, clasping her arms about her as though cold*). I—I know not. A wind, a cold wind, has come. (*Her eyes fall on* MARY WARREN.)

MARY WARREN (*terrified, pleading*). Abby!

MERCY LEWIS (*shivering*). Your Honor, I freeze!

PROCTOR. They're pretending!

HATHORNE (*touching* ABIGAIL's *hand*). She is cold, Your Honor, touch her!

MERCY LEWIS (*through chattering teeth*). Mary, do you send this shadow on me?

MARY WARREN. Lord, save me!

SUSANNA WALCOTT. I freeze, I freeze!

ABIGAIL (*shivering visibly*). It is a wind, a wind!

MARY WARREN. Abby, don't do that!

DANFORTH (*himself engaged and entered by* ABIGAIL). Mary Warren, do you witch her? I say to you, do you send your spirit out?

(*With a hysterical cry* MARY WARREN *starts to run.* PROCTOR *catches her.*)

MARY WARREN (*almost collapsing*). Let me go, Mr. Proctor, I cannot, I cannot—

ABIGAIL (*crying to Heaven*). Oh, Heavenly Father, take away this shadow!

(*Without warning or hesitation,* PROCTOR *leaps at* ABIGAIL *and, grabbing her by the hair, pulls her to her feet. She screams in pain.* DANFORTH, *astonished, cries,* "*What are you about?*" *and* HATHORNE *and* PARRIS *call,* "*Take your hands off her!*" *and out of it all comes* PROCTOR's *roaring voice.*)

PROCTOR. How do you call Heaven! Whore! Whore!

(HERRICK *breaks* PROCTOR *from her.*)

HERRICK. John!

DANFORTH. Man! Man, what do you—

PROCTOR (*breathless and in agony*). It is a whore!

DANFORTH (*dumfounded*). You charge—?

ABIGAIL. Mr. Danforth, he is lying!

PROCTOR. Mark her! Now she'll suck a scream to stab me with, but—

DANFORTH. You will prove this! This will not pass!

PROCTOR (*trembling, his life collapsing about him*). I have known her, sir. I have known her.

DANFORTH. You—you are a lecher?

FRANCIS (*horrified*). John, you cannot say such a—

PROCTOR. Oh, Francis, I wish you had some evil in you that you might know

me! (*To* DANFORTH:) A man will not cast away his good name. You surely know that.

DANFORTH (*dumfounded*). In—in what time? In what place?

PROCTOR (*his voice about to break, and his shame great*). In the proper place—where my beasts are bedded. On the last night of my joy, some eight months past. She used to serve me in my house, sir. (*He has to clamp his jaw to keep from weeping.*) A man may think God sleeps, but God sees everything. I know it now. I beg you, sir, I beg you—see her what she is. My wife, my dear good wife, took this girl soon after, sir, and put her out on the highroad. And being what she is, a lump of vanity, sir—(*He is being overcome.*) Excellency, forgive me, forgive me. (*Angrily against himself, he turns away from the Governor for a moment. Then, as though to cry out is his only means of speech left.*) She thinks to dance with me on my wife's grave! And well she might, for I thought of her softly. God help me, I lusted, and there *is* a promise in such sweat. But it is a whore's vengeance, and you must see it; I set myself entirely in your hands. I know you must see it now.

DANFORTH (*blanched, in horror, turning to* ABIGAIL). You deny every scrap and tittle of this?

ABIGAIL. If I must answer that, I will leave and I will not come back again!

(DANFORTH *seems unsteady.*)

PROCTOR. I have made a bell of my honor! I have rung the doom of my good name—you will believe me, Mr. Danforth! My wife is innocent, except she knew a whore when she saw one!

ABIGAIL (*stepping up to* DANFORTH). What look do you give me? (DANFORTH *cannot speak.*) I'll not have such looks! (*She turns and starts for the door.*)

DANFORTH. You will remain where you are! (HERRICK *steps into her path. She comes up short, fire in her eyes.*) Mr. Parris, go into the court and bring Goodwife Proctor out.

PARRIS (*objecting*). Your Honor, this is all a—

DANFORTH (*sharply to* PARRIS). Bring her out! And tell her not one word of what's been spoken here. And let you knock before you enter. (PARRIS *goes out.*) Now we shall touch the bottom of this swamp. (*To* PROCTOR:) Your wife, you say, is an honest woman.

PROCTOR. In her life, sir, she have never lied. There are them that cannot sing, and them that cannot weep—my wife cannot lie. I have paid much to learn it, sir.

DANFORTH. And when she put this girl out of your house, she put her out for a harlot?

PROCTOR. Aye, sir.

DANFORTH. And knew her for a harlot?

PROCTOR. Aye, sir, she knew her for a harlot.

DANFORTH. Good then. (*To* ABIGAIL:) And if she tell me, child, it were for harlotry, may God spread His mercy on you! (*There is a knock. He calls to the door.*) Hold! (*To* ABIGAIL:) Turn your back. Turn your back. (*To* PROCTOR:) Do likewise. (*Both turn their backs—*ABIGAIL *indignantly slow.*) Now let neither of you turn to face Goody Proctor. No one in this room is to speak one word, or raise a gesture aye or nay. (*He turns toward the door, calls:*) Enter! (*The door opens.* ELIZABETH *enters with* PARRIS. PARRIS *leaves her. She stands alone, her eyes looking for* PROCTOR.) Mr. Cheever, report this testimony in all exactness. Are you ready?

CHEEVER. Ready sir.

DANFORTH. Come here, woman. (ELIZABETH *comes to him, glancing at* PROCTOR's *back.*) Look at me only, not at your husband. In my eyes only.

ELIZABETH (*faintly*). Good, sir.

DANFORTH. We are given to understand that at one time you dismissed your servant, Abigail Williams.

ELIZABETH. That is true, sir.

DANFORTH. For what cause did you dismiss her? (*Slight pause. Then* ELIZABETH *tries to glance at* PROCTOR.) You will look in my eyes only and not at your husband. The answer is in your memory and you need no help to give it to me. Why did you dismiss Abigail Williams?

ELIZABETH (*not knowing what to say, sensing a situation, wetting her lips to stall for time*). She—dissatisfied me. (*Pause.*) And my husband.

DANFORTH. In what way dissatisfied you?

ELIZABETH. She were—(*She glances at* PROCTOR *for a cue.*)

DANFORTH. Woman, look at me! (ELIZABETH *does.*) Were she slovenly? Lazy? What disturbance did she cause?

ELIZABETH. Your Honor, I—in that time I were sick. And I— My husband is a good

and righteous man. He is never drunk as some are, nor wastin' his time at the shovelboard, but always at his work. But in my sickness—you see, sir, I were a long time sick after my last baby, and I thought I saw my husband somewhat turning from me. And this girl—(*She turns to* ABIGAIL.)

DANFORTH. Look at me.

ELIZABETH. Aye, sir. Abigail Williams—(*She breaks off.*)

DANFORTH. What of Abigail Williams?

ELIZABETH. I came to think he fancied her. And so one night I lost my wits, I think, and put her out on the highroad.

DANFORTH. Your husband—did he indeed turn from you?

ELIZABETH (*in agony*). My husband—is a goodly man, sir.

DANFORTH. Then he did not turn from you.

ELIZABETH (*starting to glance at* PROCTOR). He—

DANFORTH (*reaches out and holds her face, then*). Look at me! To your own knowledge, has John Proctor ever committed the crime of lechery? (*In a crisis of indecision she cannot speak.*) Answer my question! Is your husband a lecher!

ELIZABETH (*faintly*). No, sir.

DANFORTH. Remove her, Marshal.

PROCTOR. Elizabeth, tell the truth!

DANFORTH. She has spoken. Remove her!

PROCTOR (*crying out*). Elizabeth, I have confessed it!

ELIZABETH. Oh, God! (*The door closes behind her.*)

PROCTOR. She only thought to save my name!

HALE. Excellency, it is a natural lie to tell; I beg you, stop now before another is condemned! I may shut my conscience to it no more—private vengeance is working through this testimony! From the beginning this man has struck me true. By my oath to Heaven, I believe him now, and I pray you call back his wife before we—

DANFORTH. She spoke nothing of lechery, and this man has lied!

HALE. I believe him! (*Pointing at* ABIGAIL:) This girl has always struck me false! She has—

(ABIGAIL, *with a weird, wild, chilling cry, screams up to the ceiling.*)

ABIGAIL. You will not! Begone! Begone, I say!

DANFORTH. What is it, child? (*But* ABI-

GAIL, *pointing with fear is now raising up her frightened eyes, her awed face, toward the ceiling—the girls are doing the same—and now* HATHORNE, HALE, PUT-NAM, CHEEVER, HERRICK, *and* DANFORTH *do the same.*) What's there? (*He lowers his eyes from the ceiling, and now he is frightened; there is real tension in his voice.*) Child! (*She is transfixed—with all the girls, she is whimpering open-mouthed, agape at the ceiling.*) Girls! Why do you—?

MERCY LEWIS (*pointing*). It's on the beam! Behind the rafter!

DANFORTH (*looking up*). Where!

ABIGAIL. Why?—(*She gulps.*) Why do you come, yellow bird?

PROCTOR. Where's a bird! I see no bird!

ABIGAIL (*to ceiling*). My face? My face?

PROCTOR. Mr. Hale—

DANFORTH. Be quiet!

PROCTOR. (*to* HALE). Do you see a bird?

DANFORTH. Be quiet!!

ABIGAIL (*to the ceiling, in a genuine conversation with the "bird," as though trying to talk it out of attacking her*). But God made my face; you cannot want to tear my face. Envy is a deadly sin, Mary.

MARY WARREN (*on her feet with a spring, and horrified, pleading*). Abby!

ABIGAIL (*unperturbed, continuing to the "bird"*). Oh, Mary, this is a black art to change your shape. No, I cannot, I cannot stop my mouth; it's God's work I do.

MARY WARREN. Abby, I'm *here!*

PROCTOR (*frantically*). They're pretending, Mr. Danforth!

ABIGAIL (*—now she takes a backward step, as though in fear the bird will swoop down momentarily*). Oh, please, Mary! Don't come down.

SUSANNA WALCOTT. Her claws, she's stretching her claws!

PROCTOR. Lies, lies.

ABIGAIL (*backing further, eyes still fixed above*). Mary, please don't hurt me!

MARY WARREN (*to* DANFORTH). I'm not hurting her!

DANFORTH (*to* MARY WARREN). Why does she see this vision?

MARY WARREN. She sees nothin'!

ABIGAIL (*now staring full front as though hypnotized, and mimicking the exact tone of* MARY WARREN'S *cry*). She sees nothin'!

MARY WARREN (*pleading*). Abby, you mustn't!

ABIGAIL AND ALL THE GIRLS (*all transfixed*). Abby, you mustn't!

MARY WARREN (*to all the girls*). I'm here, I'm here!

GIRLS. I'm here, I'm here!

DANFORTH (*horrified*). Mary Warren! Draw back your spirit out of them!

MARY WARREN. Mr. Danforth!

GIRLS (*cutting her off*). Mr. Danforth!

DANFORTH. Have you compacted with the Devil? Have you?

MARY WARREN. Never, never!

GIRLS. Never, never!

DANFORTH (*growing hysterical*). Why can they only repeat you?

PROCTOR. Give me a whip—I'll stop it!

MARY WARREN. They're sporting. They—!

GIRLS. They're sporting!

MARY WARREN (*turning on them all hysterically and stamping her feet*). Abby, stop it!

GIRLS (*stamping their feet*). Abby, stop it!

MARY WARREN. Stop it!

GIRLS. Stop it!

MARY WARREN (*screaming it out at the top of her lungs, and raising her fists*). Stop it!!

GIRLS (*raising their fists*). Stop it!!

(MARY WARREN, *utterly confounded, and becoming overwhelmed by* ABIGAIL'S—*and the girls'—utter conviction, starts to whimper, hands half raised, powerless, and all the girls begin whimpering exactly as she does.*)

DANFORTH. A little while ago you were afflicted. Now it seems you afflict others; where did you find this power?

MARY WARREN (*staring at* ABIGAIL). I—have no power.

GIRLS. I have no power.

PROCTOR. They're gulling you, Mister!

DANFORTH. Why did you turn about this past two weeks? You have seen the Devil, have you not?

HALE (*indicating* ABIGAIL *and the girls*). You cannot believe them!

MARY WARREN. I—

PROCTOR (*sensing her weakening*). Mary, God damns all liars!

DANFORTH (*pounding it into her*). You have seen the Devil, you have made compact with Lucifer, have you not?

PROCTOR. God damns liars, Mary!

(MARY *utters something unintelligible, staring at* ABIGAIL, *who keeps watching the "bird" above.*)

DANFORTH. I cannot hear you. What do you say? (MARY *utters again unintelligi-*

bly.) You will confess yourself or you will hang! (*He turns her roughly to face him.*) Do you know who I am? I say you will hang if you do not open with me!

PROCTOR. Mary, remember the angel Raphael—do that which is good and—

ABIGAIL (*pointing upward*). The wings! Her wings are spreading! Mary, please, don't, don't—!

HALE. I see nothing, Your Honor!

DANFORTH. Do you confess this power! (*He is an inch from her face.*) Speak!

ABIGAIL. She's going to come down! She's walking the beam!

DANFORTH. Will you speak!

MARY WARREN (*staring in horror*). I cannot!

GIRLS. I cannot!

PARRIS. Cast the Devil out! Look him in the face! Trample him! We'll save you, Mary, only stand fast against him and—

ABIGAIL (*looking up*). Look out! She's coming down!

(*She and all the girls run to one wall, shielding their eyes. And now, as though cornered, they let out a gigantic scream, and* MARY, *as though infected, opens her mouth and screams with them. Gradually* ABIGAIL *and the girls leave off, until only* MARY *is left there, staring up at the "bird," screaming madly. All watch her, horrified by this evident fit.* PROCTOR *strides to her.*)

PROCTOR. Mary, tell the governor what they—(*He has hardly got a word out, when, seeing him coming for her, she rushes out of his reach, screaming in horror.*)

MARY WARREN. Don't touch me—don't touch me! (*At which the girls halt at the door.*)

PROCTOR (*astonished*). Mary!

MARY WARREN (*pointing at* PROCTOR). You're the Devil's man!

(*He is stopped in his tracks.*)

PARRIS. Praise God!

GIRLS. Praise God!

PROCTOR (*numbed*). Mary, how—?

MARY WARREN. I'll not hang with you! I love God, I love God.

DANFORTH (*to* MARY). He bid you do the Devil's work?

MARY WARREN (*hysterically, indicating* PROCTOR). He come at me by night and every day to sign, to sign, to—

DANFORTH. Sign what?

PARRIS. The Devil's book? He come with a book?

MARY WARREN (*hysterically, pointing at* PROCTOR, *fearful of him*). My name, he want my name. "I'll murder you," he says, "if my wife hangs! We must go and overthrow the court," he says!

(DANFORTH's *head jerks toward* PROCTOR, *shock and horror in his face.*)

PROCTOR (*turning, appealing to* HALE). Mr. Hale!

MARY WARREN (*her sobs beginning*). He wake me every night, his eyes were like coals and his fingers claw my neck, and I sign, I sign . . .

HALE. Excellency, this child's gone wild!

PROCTOR (*as* DANFORTH's *wide eyes pour on him*). Mary, Mary!

MARY WARREN (*screaming at him*). No, I love God; I go your way no more. I love God, I bless God. (*Sobbing, she rushes to* ABIGAIL.) Abby, Abby, I'll never hurt you more! (*They all watch, as* ABIGAIL, *out of her infinite charity, reaches out and draws the sobbing* MARY *to her, and then looks up to* DANFORTH.)

DANFORTH (*to* PROCTOR). What are you? (PROCTOR *is beyond speech in his anger.*) You are combined with anti-Christ, are you not? I have seen your power; you will not deny it! What say you, Mister?

HALE. Excellency—

DANFORTH. I will have nothing from you, Mr. Hale! (*To* PROCTOR:) Will you confess yourself befouled with Hell, or do you keep that black allegiance yet? What say you?

PROCTOR (*his mind wild, breathless*). I say—I say—God is dead!

PARRIS. Hear it, hear it!

PROCTOR (*laughs insanely, then*). A fire, a fire is burning! I hear the boot of Lucifer, I see his filthy face! And it is my face, and yours, Danforth! For them that quail to bring men out of ignorance, as I have quailed, and as you quail now when you know in all your black hearts that this be fraud—God damns our kind especially, and we will burn, we will burn together!

DANFORTH. Marshal! Take him and Corey with him to the jail!

HALE (*starting across to the door*). I denounce these proceedings!

PROCTOR. You are pulling Heaven down and raising up a whore!

HALE. I denounce these proceedings, I quit this court! (*He slams the door to the outside behind him.*)

DANFORTH (*calling to him in a fury*). Mr. Hale! Mr. Hale!

THE CURTAIN FALLS

ACT FOUR

A cell in Salem jail, that fall.

At the back is a high barred window; near it, a great, heavy door. Along the walls are two benches.

The place is in darkness but for the moonlight seeping through the bars. It appears empty. Presently footsteps are heard coming down a corridor beyond the wall, keys rattle, and the door swings open. MARSHAL HERRICK *enters with a lantern.*

He is nearly drunk, and heavy-footed. He goes to a bench and nudges a bundle of rags lying on it.

———

HERRICK. Sarah, wake up! Sarah Good! (*He then crosses to the other bench.*)

SARAH GOOD (*rising in her rags*). Oh, Majesty! Comin', comin'! Tituba, he's here, His Majesty's come!

HERRICK. Go to the north cell; this place is wanted now. (*He hangs his lantern on the wall.* TITUBA *sits up.*)

TITUBA. That don't look to me like His Majesty; look to me like the marshal.

HERRICK (*taking out a flask*). Get along with you now, clear this place. (*He drinks, and* SARAH GOOD *comes and peers into his face.*)

SARAH GOOD. Oh, is it you, Marshal! I thought sure you be the devil comin' for us. Could I have a sip of cider for me goin-away?

HERRICK (*handing her the flask*). And where are you off to, Sarah?

TITUBA (*as* SARAH *drinks*). We goin' to Barbados, soon the Devil gits here with the feathers and the wings.

HERRICK. Oh? A happy voyage to you.

SARAH GOOD. A pair of bluebirds wingin' southerly, the two of us! Oh, it be a grand transformation, Marshal! (*She raises the flask to drink again.*)

HERRICK (*taking the flask from her lips*). You'd best give me that or you'll never rise off the ground. Come along now.

TITUBA. I'll speak to him for you, if you desires to come along, Marshal.

HERRICK. I'd not refuse it, Tituba; it's the proper morning to fly into Hell.

TITUBA. Oh, it be no Hell in Barbados. Devil, him be pleasure-man in Barbados, him be singin' and dancin' in Barbados. It's you folks—you riles him up 'round here; it be too cold 'round here for that Old Boy. He freeze his soul in Massachusetts, but in Barbados he just as sweet and —(*A bellowing cow is heard, and* TITUBA *leaps up and calls to the window:*) Aye, sir! That's him, Sarah!

SARAH GOOD. I'm here, Majesty! (*They hurriedly pick up their rags as* HOPKINS, *a guard, enters.*)

HOPKINS. The Deputy Governor's arrived.

HERRICK (*grabbing* TITUBA). Come along, come along.

TITUBA (*resisting him*). No, he comin' for me. I goin' home!

HERRICK (*pulling her to the door*). That's not Satan, just a poor old cow with a hatful of milk. Come along now, out with you!

TITUBA (*calling to the window*). Take me home, Devil! Take me home!

SARAH GOOD (*following the shouting* TITUBA *out*). Tell him I'm goin', Tituba! Now you tell him Sarah Good is goin' too!

(*In the corridor outside* TITUBA *calls on* —"*Take me home, Devil; Devil take me home!*" *and* HOPKINS' *voice orders her to move on.* HERRICK *returns and begins to push old rags and straw into a corner. Hearing footsteps, he turns, and enter* DANFORTH *and* JUDGE HATHORNE. *They are in greatcoats and wear hats against the bitter cold. They are followed in by* CHEEVER, *who carries a dispatch case and a flat wooden box containing his writing materials.*)

HERRICK. Good morning, Excellency.

DANFORTH. Where is Mr. Parris?

HERRICK. I'll fetch him. (*He starts for the door.*)

DANFORTH. Marshal (HERRICK *stops.*) When did Reverend Hale arrive?

HERRICK. It were toward midnight, I think.

DANFORTH (*suspiciously*). What is he about here?

HERRICK. He goes among them that will hang, sir. And he prays with them. He sits with Goody Nurse now. And Mr. Parris with him.

DANFORTH. Indeed. That man have no authority to enter here, Marshal. Why have you let him in?

HERRICK. Why, Mr. Parris command me, sir. I cannot deny him.

DANFORTH. Are you drunk, Marshal?

HERRICK. No, sir; it is a bitter night, and I have no fire here.

DANFORTH (*containing his anger*). Fetch Mr. Parris.

HERRICK. Aye, sir.

DANFORTH. There is a prodigious stench in this place.

HERRICK. I have only now cleared the people out for you.

DANFORTH. Beware hard drink, Marshal.

HERRICK. Aye, sir. (*He waits an instant for further orders. But* DANFORTH, *in dissatisfaction, turns his back on him, and* HERRICK *goes out. There is a pause.* DANFORTH *stands in thought.*)

HATHORNE. Let you question Hale, Excellency; I should not be surprised he have been preaching in Andover lately.

DANFORTH. We'll come to that; speak nothing of Andover. Parris prays with him. That's strange. (*He blows on his hands, moves toward the window, and looks out.*)

HATHORNE. Excellency, I wonder if it be wise to let Mr. Parris so continuously with the prisoners. (DANFORTH *turns to him, interested.*) I think, sometimes, the man has a mad look these days.

DANFORTH. Mad?

HATHORNE. I met him yesterday coming out of his house, and I bid him good morning—and he wept and went his way. I think it is not well the village sees him so unsteady.

DANFORTH. Perhaps he have some sorrow.

CHEEVER (*stamping his feet against the cold*). I think it be the cows, sir.

DANFORTH. Cows?

CHEEVER. There be so many cows wanderin' the highroads, now their masters are in the jails, and much disagreement who they will belong to now. I know Mr. Parris be arguin' with farmers all yesterday—there is great contention, sir, about the cows. Contention make him weep, sir; it were always a man that weep for contention. (*He turns, as do* HATHORNE *and* DANFORTH, *hearing someone coming up the corridor.* DANFORTH *raises his head as* PARRIS *enters. He is gaunt, frightened, and sweating in his greatcoat.*)

PARRIS (*to* DANFORTH, *instantly*). Oh, good morning, sir, thank you for coming, I beg your pardon wakin' you so early.

Good morning, Judge Hathorne.

DANFORTH. Reverend Hale have no right to enter this—

PARRIS. Excellency, a moment. (*He hurries back and shuts the door.*)

HATHORNE. Do you leave him alone with the prisoners?

DANFORTH. What's his business here?

PARRIS (*prayerfully holding up his hands*). Excellency, hear me. It is a providence. Reverend Hale has returned to bring Rebecca Nurse to God.

DANFORTH (*surprised*). He bids her confess?

PARRIS (*sitting*). Hear me. Rebecca have not given me a word this three month since she came. Now she sits with him, and her sister and Martha Corey and two or three others, and he pleads with them, confess their crimes and save their lives.

DANFORTH. Why—this is indeed a providence. And they soften, they soften?

PARRIS. Not yet, not yet. But I thought to summon you, sir, that we might think on whether it be not wise, to—(*He dares not say it.*) I had thought to put a question, sir, and I hope you will not—

DANFORTH. Mr. Parris, be plain, what troubles you?

PARRIS. There is news, sir, that the court—the court must reckon with. My niece, sir, my niece—I believe she has vanished.

DANFORTH. Vanished!

PARRIS. I had thought to advise you of it earlier in the week, but—

DANFORTH. Why? How long is she gone?

PARRIS. This be the third night. You see, sir, she told me she would stay a night with Mercy Lewis. And next day, when she does not return, I send to Mr. Lewis to inquire. Mercy told him she would sleep in *my* house for a night.

DANFORTH. They are both gone?!

PARRIS (*in fear of him*). They are, sir.

DANFORTH (*alarmed*). I will send a party for them. Where may they be?

PARRIS. Excellency, I think they be aboard a ship. (DANFORTH *stands agape.*) My daughter tells me how she heard them speaking of ships last week, and tonight I discover my—my strongbox is broke into. (*He presses his fingers against his eyes to keep back tears.*)

HATHORNE (*astonished*). She have robbed you?

PARRIS. Thirty-one pound is gone. I am penniless. (*He covers his face and sobs.*)

DANFORTH. Mr. Parris, you are a brainless man! (*He walks in thought, deeply worried.*)

PARRIS. Excellency, it profit nothing you should blame me. I cannot think they would run off except they fear to keep in Salem any more. (*He is pleading.*) Mark it, sir, Abigail had close knowledge of the town, and since the news of Andover has broken here—

DANFORTH. Andover is remedied. The court returns there on Friday, and will resume examinations.

PARRIS. I am sure of it, sir. But the rumor here speaks rebellion in Andover, and it—

DANFORTH. There is no rebellion in Andover!

PARRIS. I tell you what is said here, sir. Andover have thrown out the court, they say, and will have no part of witchcraft. There be a faction here, feeding on the news, and I tell you true, sir, I fear there will be riot here.

HATHORNE. Riot! Why at every execution I have seen naught but high satisfaction in the town.

PARRIS. Judge Hathorne—it were another sort that hanged till now. Rebecca Nurse is no Bridget that lived three year with Bishop before she married him. John Proctor is not Isaac Ward that drink his family to ruin. (*To* DANFORTH:) I would to God it were not so, Excellency, but these people have great weight yet in the town. Let Rebecca stand upon the gibbet and send up some righteous prayer, and I fear she'll wake a vengeance on you.

HATHORNE. Excellency, she is condemned a witch. The court have—

DANFORTH (*in deep concern, raising a hand to* HATHORNE.) Pray you. (*To* PARRIS:) How do you propose, then?

PARRIS. Excellency, I would postpone these hangin's for a time.

DANFORTH. There will be no postponement.

PARRIS. Now Mr. Hale's returned, there s hope, I think—for if he bring even one)f these to God, that confession surely lamns the others in the public eye, and lone may doubt more that they are all inked to Hell. This way, unconfessed and laiming innocence, doubts are multiplied, nany honest people will weep for them, nd our good purpose is lost in their tears.

DANFORTH (*after thinking a moment, then going to* CHEEVER). Give me the list.

(CHEEVER *opens the dispatch case, searches.*)

PARRIS. It cannot be forgot, sir, that when I summoned the congregation for John Proctor's excommunication there were hardly thirty people come to hear it. That speak a discontent, I think, and—

DANFORTH (*studying the list*). There will be no postponement.

PARRIS. Excellency—

DANFORTH. Now, sir—which of these in your opinion may be brought to God? I will myself strive with him till dawn. (*He hands the list to* PARRIS, *who merely glances at it.*)

PARRIS. There is not sufficient time till dawn.

DANFORTH. I shall do my utmost. Which of them do you have hope for?

PARRIS (*not even glancing at the list now, and in a quavering voice, quietly*). Excellency—a dagger—(*He chokes up.*)

DANFORTH. What do you say?

PARRIS. Tonight, when I open my door to leave my house—a dagger clattered to the ground. (*Silence.* DANFORTH *absorbs this. Now* PARRIS *cries out.*) You cannot hang this sort. There is danger for me. I dare not step outside at night! (*REVEREND HALE enters. They look at him for an instant in silence. He is steeped in sorrow, exhausted, and more direct than he ever was.*)

DANFORTH. Accept my congratulations, Reverend Hale; we are gladdened to see you returned to your good work.

HALE (*coming to* DANFORTH *now*). You must pardon them. They will not budge.

(HERRICK *enters, waits.*)

DANFORTH (*conciliatory*). You misunderstand, sir; I cannot pardon these when twelve are already hanged for the same crime. It is not just.

PARRIS (*with failing heart*). Rebecca will not confess?

HALE. The sun will rise in a few minutes. Excellency, I must have more time.

DANFORTH. Now hear me, and beguile yourselves no more. I will not receive a single plea for pardon or postponement. Them that will not confess will hang. Twelve are already executed; the names of these seven are given out, and the village expects to see them die this morning. Postponement now speaks a floundering on my part; reprieve or pardon must cast doubt upon the guilt of them that died till now. While I speak God's law, I will not crack its voice with whimpering. If retaliation is your fear, know this—I should hang ten thousand that dared to rise against 'the law, and an ocean of salt tears could not melt the resolution of the statutes. Now draw yourselves up like men and help me, as you are bound by Heaven to do. Have you spoken with them all, Mr. Hale?

HALE. All but Proctor. He is in the dungeon.

DANFORTH (*to* HERRICK). What's Proctor's way now?

HERRICK. He sits like some great bird; you'd not know he lived except he will take food from time to time.

DANFORTH (*after thinking a moment*). His wife—his wife must be well on with child now.

HERRICK. She is, sir.

DANFORTH. What think you, Mr. Parris? You have closer knowledge of this man; might her presence soften him?

PARRIS. It is possible, sir. He have not laid eyes on her these three months. I should summon her.

DANFORTH (*to* HERRICK). Is he yet adamant? Has he struck at you again?

HERRICK. He cannot, sir, he is chained to the wall now.

DANFORTH (*after thinking on it*). Fetch Goody Proctor to me. Then let you bring him up.

HERRICK. Aye, sir. (HERRICK *goes. There is silence.*)

HALE. Excellency, if you postpone a week and publish to the town that you are striving for their confessions, that speak mercy on your part, not faltering.

DANFORTH. Mr. Hale, as God have not empowered me like Joshua to stop this sun from rising, so I cannot withhold from them the perfection of their punishment.

HALE (*harder now*). If you think God wills you to raise rebellion, Mr. Danforth, you are mistaken!

DANFORTH (*instantly*). You have heard rebellion spoken in the town?

HALE. Excellency, there are orphans wandering from house to house; abandoned cattle bellow on the highroads, the stink of rotting crops hangs everywhere, and no man knows when the harlots' cry will end his life—and you wonder yet if rebellion's spoke? Better you should mar-

vel how they do not burn your province!

DANFORTH. Mr. Hale, have you preached in Andover this month?

HALE. Thank God they have no need of me in Andover.

DANFORTH. You baffle me, sir. Why have you returned here?

HALE. Why, it is all simple. I come to do the Devil's work. I come to counsel Christians they should belie themselves. (*His sarcasm collapses.*) There is blood on my head! Can you not see the blood on my head!!

PARRIS. Hush! (*For he has heard footsteps. They all face the door.* HERRICK *enters with* ELIZABETH. *Her wrists are linked by heavy chain, which* HERRICK *now removes. Her clothes are dirty; her face is pale and gaunt.* HERRICK *goes out.*)

DANFORTH (*very politely*). Goody Proctor. (*She is silent.*) I hope you are hearty?

ELIZABETH (*as a warning reminder*). I am yet six months before my time.

DANFORTH. Pray be at your ease, we come not for your life. We—(*Uncertain how to plead, for he is not accustomed to it.*) Mr. Hale, will you speak with the woman?

HALE. Goody Proctor, your husband is marked to hang this morning.

(*Pause.*)

ELIZABETH (*quietly*). I have heard it.

HALE. You know, do you not, that I have no connection with the court? (*She seems to doubt it.*) I come of my own, Goody Proctor. I would save your husband's life, for if he is taken I count myself his murderer. Do you understand me?

ELIZABETH. What do you want of me?

HALE. Goody Proctor, I have gone this three month like our Lord into the wilderness. I have sought a Christian way, for damnation's doubled on a minister who counsels men to lie.

HATHORNE. It is no lie, you cannot speak of lies.

HALE. It is a lie! They are innocent!

DANFORTH. I'll hear no more of that!

HALE (*continuing to* ELIZABETH). Let you not mistake your duty as I mistook my own. I came into this village like a bridegroom to his beloved, bearing gifts of high religion; the very crowns of holy law I brought, and what I touched with my bright confidence, it died; and where I turned the eye of my great faith, blood flowed up. Beware, Goody Proctor—cleave to no faith when faith brings blood. It is mistaken law that leads you to sacrifice. Life, woman, life is God's most precious gift; no principle, however glorious, may justify the taking of it. I beg you, woman, prevail upon your husband to confess. Let him give his lie. Quail not before God's judgment in this, for it may well be God damns a liar less than he that throws his life away for pride. Will you plead with him? I cannot think he will listen to another.

ELIZABETH (*quietly*). I think that be the Devil's argument.

HALE (*with climactic desperation*). Woman, before the laws of God we are as swine! We cannot read His will!

ELIZABETH. I cannot dispute with you, sir; I lack learning for it.

DANFORTH (*going to her*). Goody Proctor, you are not summoned here for disputation. Be there no wifely tenderness within you? He will die with the sunrise. Your husband. Do you understand it? (*She only looks at him.*) What say you? Will you contend with him? (*She is silent.*) Are you stone? I tell you true, woman, had I no other proof of your unnatural life, your dry eyes now would be sufficient evidence that you delivered up your soul to Hell! A very ape would weep at such calamity! Have the devil dried up any tear of pity in you? (*She is silent.*) Take her out. It profit nothing she should speak to him!

ELIZABETH (*quietly*). Let me speak with him, Excellency.

PARRIS (*with hope*). You'll strive with him? (*She hesitates.*)

DANFORTH. Will you plead for his confession or will you not?

ELIZABETH. I promise nothing. Let me speak with him.

(*A sound—the sibilance of dragging feet on stone. They turn. A pause.* HERRICK *enters with* JOHN PROCTOR. *His wrists are chained. He is another man, bearded, filthy, his eyes misty as though webs had overgrown them. He halts inside the doorway, his eye caught by the sight of* ELIZABETH. *The emotion flowing between them prevents anyone from speaking for an instant. Now* HALE, *visibly affected, goes to* DANFORTH *and speaks quietly.*)

HALE. Pray, leave them, Excellency.

DANFORTH (*pressing* HALE *impatiently aside*). Mr. Proctor, you have been notified, have you not? (*PROCTOR is silent, staring at* ELIZABETH.) I see light in the sky, Mister; let you counsel with your wife, and may God help you turn your back on Hell. (*PROCTOR is silent, staring at* ELIZABETH.)

HALE (*quietly*). Excellency, let—

(*DANFORTH brushes past* HALE *and walks out.* HALE *follows.* CHEEVER *stands and follows,* HATHORNE *behind.* HERRICK *goes.* PARRIS, *from a safe distance, offers:*)

PARRIS. If you desire a cup of cider, Mr. Proctor, I am sure I—(*PROCTOR turns an icy stare at him, and he breaks off.* PARRIS *raises his palms toward* PROCTOR.) God lead you now. (*PARRIS goes out.*)

(*Alone,* PROCTOR *walks to her, halts. It is as though they stood in a spinning world. It is beyond sorrow, above it. He reaches out his hand as though toward an embodiment not quite real, and as he touches her, a strange soft sound, half laughter, half amazement, comes from his throat. He pats her hand. She covers his hand with hers. And then, weak, he sits. Then she sits, facing him.*)

PROCTOR. The child?

ELIZABETH. It grows.

PROCTOR. There is no word of the boys?

ELIZABETH. They're well. Rebecca's Samuel keeps them.

PROCTOR. You have not seen them?

ELIZABETH. I have not. (*She catches a weakening in herself and downs it.*)

PROCTOR. You are a—marvel, Elizabeth.

ELIZABETH. You—have been tortured?

PROCTOR. Aye. (*Pause. She will not let herself be drowned in the sea that threatens her.*) They come for my life now.

ELIZABETH. I know it.

(*Pause.*)

PROCTOR. None—have yet confessed?

ELIZABETH. There be many confessed.

PROCTOR. Who are they?

ELIZABETH. There be a hundred or more, they say. Goody Ballard is one; Isaiah Goodkind is one. There be many.

PROCTOR. Rebecca?

ELIZABETH. Not Rebecca. She is one foot in Heaven now; naught may hurt her more.

PROCTOR. And Giles?

ELIZABETH. You have not heard of it?

PROCTOR. I hear nothin', where I am kept.

ELIZABETH. Giles is dead.

(*He looks at her incredulously.*)

PROCTOR. When were he hanged?

ELIZABETH (*quietly, factually*). He were

not hanged. He would not answer aye or nay to his indictment; for if he denied the charge they'd hang him surely, and auction out his property. So he stand mute, and died Christian under the law. And so his sons will have his farm. It is the law, for he could not be condemned a wizard without he answer the indictment, aye or nay.

PROCTOR. Then how does he die?

ELIZABETH (*gently*). They press him, John.

PROCTOR. Press?

ELIZABETH. Great stones they lay upon his chest until he plead aye or nay. (*With a tender smile for the old man:*) They say he give them but two words. "More weight," he says. And died.

PROCTOR (*numbed—a thread to weave into his agony*). "More weight."

ELIZABETH. Aye. It were a fearsome man, Giles Corey.

(*Pause.*)

PROCTOR (*with great force of will, but not quite looking at her*). I have been thinking I would confess to them, Elizabeth. (*She shows nothing.*) What say you? If I give them that?

ELIZABETH. I cannot judge you, John.

(*Pause.*)

PROCTOR (*simply—a pure question*). What would you have me do?

ELIZABETH. As you will, I would have it. (*Slight pause.*) I want you living, John. That's sure.

PROCTOR (*pauses, then with a flailing of hope*). Giles' wife? Have she confessed?

ELIZABETH. She will not.

(*Pause.*)

PROCTOR. It is a pretense, Elizabeth.

ELIZABETH. What is?

PROCTOR. I cannot mount the gibbet like a saint. It is a fraud. I am not that man. (*She is silent.*) My honesty is broke, Elizabeth; I am no good man. Nothing's spoiled by giving them this lie that were not rotten long before.

ELIZABETH. And yet you've not confessed till now. That speak goodness in you.

PROCTOR. Spite only keeps me silent. It is hard to give a lie to dogs. (*Pause, for the first time he turns directly to her.*) I would have your forgiveness, Elizabeth.

ELIZABETH. It is not for me to give, John, I am—

PROCTOR. I'd have you see some honesty in it. Let them that never lied die now to keep their souls. It is pretense for me, a vanity that will not blind God nor keep my children out of the wind. (*Pause.*) What say you?

ELIZABETH (*upon a heaving sob that always threatens*). John, it come to naught that I should forgive you, if you'll not forgive yourself. (*Now he turns away a little, in great agony.*) It is not my soul, John, it is yours. (*He stands, as though in physical pain, slowly rising to his feet with a great immortal longing to find his answer. It is difficult to say, and she is on the verge of tears.*) Only be sure of this, for I know it now: Whatever you will do, it is a good man does it. (*He turns his doubting, searching gaze upon her.*) I have read my heart this three month, John. (*Pause.*) I have sins of my own to count. It needs a cold wife to prompt lechery.

PROCTOR (*in great pain*). Enough, enough—

ELIZABETH (*now pouring out her heart*). Better you should know me!

PROCTOR. I will not hear it! I know you!

ELIZABETH. You take my sins upon you, John—

PROCTOR (*in agony*). No, I take my own, my own!

ELIZABETH. John, I counted myself so plain, so poorly made, no honest love could come to me! Suspicion kissed you when I did; I never knew how I should say my love. It were a cold house I kept! (*In fright, she swerves, as* HATHORNE *enters.*)

HATHORNE. What say you, Proctor? The sun is soon up.

(PROCTOR, *his chest heaving, stares, turns to* ELIZABETH. *She comes to him as though to plead, her voice quaking.*)

ELIZABETH. Do what you will. But let none be your judge. There be no higher judge under Heaven than Proctor is! Forgive me, forgive me, John—I never knew such goodness in the world! (*She covers her face, weeping.*)

(PROCTOR *turns from her to* HATHORNE; *he is off the earth, his voice hollow.*)

PROCTOR. I want my life.

HATHORNE (*electrified, surprised*). You'll confess yourself?

PROCTOR. I will have my life.

HATHORNE (*with a mystical tone*). God be praised! It is a providence! (*He rushes out the door, and his voice is heard calling down the corridor.*) He will confess! Proctor will confess!

PROCTOR (*with a cry, as he strides to the door*). Why do you cry it? (*In great pain he turns back to her.*) It is evil, is it not? It is evil.

ELIZABETH (*in terror, weeping*). I cannot judge you, John, I cannot!

PROCTOR. Then who will judge ,me? (*Suddenly clasping his hands:*) God in Heaven, what is John Proctor, what is John Proctor? (*He moves as an animal, and a fury is riding in him, a tantalized search.*) I think it is honest, I think so; I am no saint. (*As though she had denied this he calls angrily at her:*) Let Rebecca go like a saint; for me it is fraud!

(*Voices are heard in the hall, speaking together in suppressed excitement.*)

ELIZABETH. I am not your judge, I cannot be. (*As though giving him release:*) Do as you will, do as you will!

PROCTOR. Would you give them such a lie? Say it. Would you ever give them this? (*She cannot answer.*) You would not; if tongs of fire were singeing you, you would not! It is evil. Good, then—it is evil, and I do it!

(HATHORNE *enters with* DANFORTH, *and, with them,* CHEEVER, PARRIS, *and* HALE. *It is a businesslike, rapid entrance, as though the ice had been broken.*)

DANFORTH (*with great relief and gratitude*). Praise to God, man, praise to God; you shall be blessed in Heaven for this. (CHEEVER *has hurried to the bench with pen, ink, and paper.* PROCTOR *watches him.*) Now then, let us have it. Are you ready, Mr. Cheever?

PROCTOR (*with a cold, cold horror at their efficiency*). Why must it be written?

DANFORTH. Why, for the good instruction of the village, Mister; this we shall post upon the church door! (*To* PARRIS, *urgently:*) Where is the marshal?

PARRIS (*runs to the door and calls down the corridor*). Marshal! Hurry!

DANFORTH. Now, then, Mister, will you speak slowly, and directly to the point, for Mr. Cheever's sake. (*He is on record now, and is really dictating to* CHEEVER, *who writes.*) Mr. Proctor, have you seen the Devil in your life? (PROCTOR's *jaws lock.*) Come, man, there is light in the sky; the town waits at the scaffold; I would give out this news. Did you see the Devil?

PROCTOR. I did.

PARRIS. Praise God!

DANFORTH. And when he come to you, what were his demand? (PROCTOR *is silent.* DANFORTH *helps.*) Did he bid you to do his work upon the earth?

PROCTOR. He did.

DANFORTH. And you bound yourself to his service? (DANFORTH *turns, as* REBECCA NURSE *enters, with* HERRICK *helping to support her. She is barely able to walk.*) Come in, come in, woman!

REBECCA (*brightening as she sees* PROCTOR). Ah, John! You are well, then, eh? (PROCTOR *turns his face to the wall.*)

DANFORTH. Courage, man, courage—let her witness your good example that she may come to God herself. Now hear it, Goody Nurse! Say on, Mr. Proctor. Did you bind yourself to the Devil's service?

REBECCA (*astonished*).Why, John!

PROCTOR (*through his teeth, his face turned from* REBECCA). I did.

DANFORTH. Now, woman, you surely see it profit nothin' to keep this conspiracy any further. Will you confess yourself with him?

REBECCA. Oh, John—God send his mercy on you!

DANFORTH. I say, will you confess yourself, Goody Nurse?

REBECCA. Why, it is a lie, it is a lie, how may I damn myself? I cannot, I cannot.

DANFORTH. Mr. Proctor. When the Devil came to you did you see Rebecca Nurse in his company? (PROCTOR *is silent.*) Come, man, take courage—did you ever see her with the Devil?

PROCTOR (*almost inaudibly*). No.

(DANFORTH, *now sensing trouble, glances at* JOHN *and goes to the table, and picks up a sheet—the list of condemned.*)

DANFORTH. Did you ever see her sister, Mary Easty, with the Devil?

PROCTOR. No, I did not.

DANFORTH (*his eyes narrow on* PROCTOR). Did you ever see Martha Corey with the Devil?

PROCTOR. I did not.

DANFORTH (*realizing, slowly putting the sheet down*). Did you ever see anyone with the Devil?

PROCTOR. I did not.

DANFORTH. Proctor, you mistake me. I am not empowered to trade your life for a lie. You have most certainly seen some person with the Devil. (PROCTOR *is silent.*) Mr. Proctor, a score of people have already testified they saw this woman with the Devil.

PROCTOR. Then it is proved. Why must I say it?

DANFORTH. Why "must" you say it! Why, you should rejoice to say it if your soul is truly purged of any love for Hell!

PROCTOR. They think to go like saints. I like not to spoil their names.

DANFORTH (*inquiring, incredulous*). Mr. Proctor, do you think they go like saints?

PROCTOR (*evading*). This woman never thought she done the Devil's work.

DANFORTH. Look you, sir. I think you mistake your duty here. It matters nothing what she thought—she is convicted of the unnatural murder of children, and you for sending your spirit out upon Mary Warren. Your soul alone is the issue here, Mister, and you will prove its whiteness or you cannot live in a Christian country. Will you tell me now what persons conspired with you in the Devil's company? (PROCTOR *is silent.*) To your knowledge was Rebecca Nurse ever—

PROCTOR. I speak my own sins; I cannot judge another. (*Crying out, with hatred:*) I have no tongue for it.

HALE (*quickly to* DANFORTH.) Excellency, it is enough he confess himself. Let him sign it, let him sign it.

PARRIS (*feverishly*). It is a great service, sir. It is a weighty name; it will strike the village that Proctor confess. I beg you, let him sign it. The sun is up, Excellency!

DANFORTH (*considers; then with dissatisfaction*). Come, then, sign your testimony. (*To* CHEEVER:) Give it to him. (CHEEVER *goes to* PROCTOR, *the confession and a pen in hand.* PROCTOR *does not look at it.*) Come, man, sign it.

PROCTOR (*after glancing at the confession*). You have all witnessed it—it is enough.

DANFORTH. You will not sign it?

PROCTOR. You have all witnessed it; what more is needed?

DANFORTH. Do you sport with me? You will sign your name or it is no confession, Mister! (*His breast heaving with agonized breathing,* PROCTOR *now lays the paper down and signs his name.*)

PARRIS. Praise be to the Lord!

(PROCTOR *has just finished signing when* DANFORTH *reaches for the paper. But* PROCTOR *snatches it up, and now a wild terror is rising in him, and a boundless anger.*)

DANFORTH (*perplexed, but politely extending his hand*). If you please, sir.

PROCTOR. No.

DANFORTH (*as though* PROCTOR *did not understand*). Mr. Proctor, I must have—

PROCTOR. No, no. I have signed it. You have seen me. It is done! You have no need for this.

PARRIS. Proctor, the village must have proof that—

PROCTOR. Damn the village! I confess to God, and God has seen my name on this! It is enough!

DANFORTH. No, sir, it is—

PROCTOR. You came to save my soul, did you not? Here! I have confessed myself; it is enough!

DANFORTH. You have not con—

PROCTOR. I have confessed myself! Is there no good penitence but it be public? God does not need my name nailed upon the church! God sees my name; God knows how black my sins are! It is enough!

DANFORTH. Mr. Proctor—

PROCTOR. You will not use me! I am no Sarah Good or Tituba, I am John Proctor! You will not use me! It is no part of salvation that you should use me!

DANFORTH. I do not wish to—

PROCTOR. I have three children—how may I teach them to walk like men in the world, and I sold my friends?

DANFORTH. You have not sold your friends—

PROCTOR. Beguile me not! I blacken all of them when this is nailed to the church the very day they hang for silence!

DANFORTH. Mr. Proctor, I must have good and legal proof that you—

PROCTOR. You are the high court, your word is good enough! Tell them I confessed myself; say Proctor broke his knees and wept like a woman; say what you will, but my name cannot—

DANFORTH (*with suspicion*). It is the same, is it not? If I report it or you sign to it?

PROCTOR (*—he knows it is insane*). No, it is not the same! What others say and what I sign to is not the same!

DANFORTH. Why? Do you mean to deny this confession when you are free?

PROCTOR. I mean to deny nothing!

DANFORTH. Then explain to me, Mr. Proctor, why you will not let—

PROCTOR (*with a cry of his whole soul*). Because it is my name! Because I cannot have another in my life! Because I lie and sign myself to lies! Because I am not worth the dust on the feet of them that hang! How may I live without my name? I have given you my soul; leave me my name!

DANFORTH (*pointing at the confession in* PROCTOR's *hand*). Is that document a lie? If it is a lie I will not accept it! What say you? I will not deal in lies, Mister! (PROCTOR *is motionless.*) You will give me your honest confession in my hand, or I cannot keep you from the rope. (PROCTOR *does not reply.*) Which way do you go, Mister?

(*His breast heaving, his eyes staring,* PROCTOR *tears the paper and crumples it, and he is weeping in fury, but erect.*)

DANFORTH. Marshal!

PARRIS (*hysterically, as though the tearing paper were his life*). Proctor, Proctor!

HALE. Man, you will hang! You cannot!

PROCTOR (*his eyes full of tears*). I can. And there's your first marvel, that I can. You have made your magic now, for now I do think I see some shred of goodness in John Proctor. Not enough to weave a banner with, but white enough to keep it from such dogs. (ELIZABETH, *in a burst of terror, rushes to him and weeps against his hand.*) Give them no tear! Tears pleasure them! Show honor now, show a stony heart and sink them with it! (*He has lifted her, and kisses her now with great passion.*)

REBECCA. Let you fear nothing! Another judgment waits us all!

DANFORTH. Hang them high over the town! Who weeps for these, weeps for corruption! (*He sweeps out past them.* HERRICK *starts to lead* REBECCA, *who almost collapses, but* PROCTOR *catches her, and she glances up at him apologetically.*)

REBECCA. I've had no breakfast.

HERRICK. Come, man.

(HERRICK *escorts them out,* HATHORNE *and* CHEEVER *behind them.* ELIZABETH *stands staring at the empty doorway.*)

PARRIS (*in deadly fear, to* ELIZABETH). Go to him, Goody Proctor! There is yet time!

(*From outside a drumroll strikes the air.* PARRIS *is startled.* ELIZABETH *jerks about toward the window.*)

PARRIS. Go to him! (*He rushes out the door, as though to hold back his fate.*) Proctor! Proctor!

(*Again, a short burst of drums.*)

HALE. Woman, plead with him! (*He starts to rush out the door, and then goes back to her.*) Woman! It is pride, it is vanity. (*She avoids his eyes, and moves to the window. He drops to his knees.*) Be his helper!— What profit him to bleed? Shall the dust praise him? Shall the worms declare his truth? Go to him, take his shame away!

ELIZABETH (*supporting herself against collapse, grips the bars of the window, and with a cry.*) He have his goodness now. God forbid I take it from him!

(*The final drumroll crashes, then heightens violently.* HALE *weeps in frantic prayer, and the new sun is pouring in upon her face, and the drums rattle like bones in the morning air.*)

THE CURTAIN FALLS

ECHOES DOWN THE CORRIDOR

Not long after the fever died, Parris was voted from office, walked out on the highroad, and was never heard of again.

The legend has it that Abigail turned up later as a prostitute in Boston.

Twenty years after the last execution, the government awarded compensation to the victims still living, and to the families of the dead. However, it is evident that some people still were unwilling to admit their total guilt, and also that the factionalism was still alive, for some beneficiaries were actually not victims at all, but informers.

Elizabeth Proctor married again, four years after Proctor's death.

In solemn meeting, the congregation rescinded the excommunications—this in March 1712. But they did so upon order of the government. The jury, however, wrote a statement praying forgiveness of all who had suffered.

Certain farms which had belonged to the victims were left to ruin, and for more than a century no one would buy them or live on them.

To all intents and purposes, the power of theocracy in Massachusetts was broken.

INHERIT THE WIND

Jerome Lawrence AND *Robert E. Lee*

First presented at Theatre '55, Dallas, on January 10, 1955.
First presented on Broadway by Herman Shumlin,
in association with Margo Jones, at the National Theatre,
New York, April 21, 1955, with the following cast:

RACHEL BROWN • Bethel Leslie

MEEKER • Robert P. Lieb

BERTRAM CATES • Karl Light

MR. GOODFELLOW • Salem Ludwig

MRS. KREBS • Sara Floyd

REV. JEREMIAH BROWN • Staats Cotsworth

CORKIN • Fred Herrick

BOLLINGER • Donald Elson

PLATT • Fred Miller

MR. BANNISTER • Charles Thompson

MELINDA • Mary Kevin Kelly

HOWARD • Eric Berne

MRS. LOOMIS • Rita Newton

HOT DOG MAN • Howard Caine

MRS. MCCLAIN • Margherita Sargent

MRS. BLAIR • Ruth Newton

ELIJAH • Charles Brin

E. K. HORNBECK • Tony Randall

HURDY GURDY MAN • Harry Shaw

TIMMY • Jack Banning

MAYOR • James Maloney

MATTHEW HARRISON BRADY • Ed Begley

MRS. BRADY • Muriel Kirkland

TOM DAVENPORT • William Darrid

HENRY DRUMMOND • Paul Muni

JUDGE • Louis Hector

DUNLAP • Fred Miller

SILLERS • Fred Herrick

REUTER'S MAN • Edmund Williams

HARRY Y. ESTERBROOK • Perry Fiske

TOWNSPEOPLE, HAWKERS, REPORTERS, JURORS, SPECTATORS played by:
Lou Adelman, Joseph Brownstone, Clifford Carpenter, Michael
Constantine, Michael Del Medico, James Greene, Ruth Hope, Sally Jessup,
Julie Knox, Patricia Larson, Michael Lewin, Evelyn Mando, Sarah Meade,
Gian Pace, Richard Poston, Jack Riano, Gordon Russell, Carroll Saint,
Robert Shannon, Maurice Shrog.

TIME: Summer. Not too long ago.   PLACE: A small town.

Inherit the Wind was first presented at the Dallas Theatre '55 on January
10, 1955. The cast included Edward Cullen, J. Frank Lucas, James Field,
Louise Latham, Harry Bergman, Michael Dolan, Kathleen Phelan,
Gilbert Milton, Edwin Whitner, Joe Walker, Dolores Walker, John
Maddox, Sadie French, Sam Brunstein, Tommy Wright, Joe Parker, Joan
Breymer, Harriet Slaughter, Eddie Gale, Oscar Wilson, Jr., Charlie
West and Fred Hoskins. Margo Jones directed.

PREFACE

Inherit the Wind is not history. The events which took place in Dayton, Tennessee, during the scorching July of 1925 are clearly the genesis of this play. It has, however, an exodus entirely its own.

Only a handful of phrases have been taken from the actual transcript of the famous Scopes trial. Some of the characters of the play are related to the colorful figures in that battle of giants; but they have life and language of their own—and, therefore, names of their own.

The greatest reporters and historians of the century have written millions of words about the "monkey trial." We are indebted to them for their brilliant reportage. And we are grateful to the late Arthur Garfield Hays, who recounted to us much of the unwritten vividness of the Dayton adventure from his own memory and experience.

The collision of Bryan and Darrow at Dayton was dramatic, but it was not a drama. Moreover, the issues of their conflict have acquired new dimensions and meaning in the thirty years since they clashed at the Rhea County Courthouse. So *Inherit the Wind* does not pretend to be journalism. It is theatre. It is not 1925. The stage directions set the time as "Not too long ago." It might have been yesterday. It could be tomorrow.

INTRODUCTION

JEROME LAWRENCE and Robert E. Lee were young Broadway playwrights when *Inherit the Wind* reached New York; that is, they were still in their thirties. Mr. Lawrence came from Cleveland, an Ohio State University graduate and a *bona fide* holder of a Phi Beta Kappa key; he also has a Master of Arts degree and was the author of a dissertation on Maxwell Anderson. Mr. Lee, reputed to be a descendant of the Confederacy's commander-in-chief, came from Elyria, Ohio, and had majored in astronomy at Ohio Wesleyan. They conceived *Inherit the Wind* while working together in radio, Mr. Lee as a director and Mr. Lawrence as a director-writer. The outbreak of World War II directed their energies into other channels; they became enlisted men and were assigned to the Armed Forces Radio network. After the war, they returned to civilian radio and television, and won two Peabody awards for meritorious service in the mass-communication media.

They began to collaborate as writers in 1942, and they invaded Broadway in 1948 with the musical comedy *Look Ma, I'm Dancing*. Turning toward more serious matters, they completed a first draft of *Inherit the Wind* in 1950. But they decided that the times were unfavorable for a play with liberal leanings, that "the intellectual climate was not right." For it was their intention, according to a *New York Times* report (April 17, 1955), to use the Scopes trial as an illustration of "the great danger to freedom, particularly academic freedom," and they wanted to show that "what happened in Dayton in 1925 was not in the remote past and could have happened yesterday." In 1950, the scion of Southern aristocracy recalls, one trusts facetiously, "I wouldn't have dared write a letter to my Congressman." Five years later, however, the authors thought that the "climate" had improved. They gave the play to the late Margo Jones for production at her Dallas Theatre in Texas, where it ran for three weeks. It was in Dallas that Herman Shumlin, always partial to socially significant drama and the original producer-director of such plays as *The Corn Is Green* and *The Male Animal*, acquired the work for Broadway. He saw the play "as one in which a representative stratum of America is in opposition to new ideas" and as "a battle of giants" in a representative town.

ACT ONE

SCENE ONE

In and around the Hillsboro Courthouse. The foreground is the actual courtroom, with jury box, judge's bench, a raised witness chair and a scattering of trial-scarred · chairs and counsel tables. The back wall of the courtroom, from waist-level up, is non-existent. In full stage, at a raked elevation, is the courthouse square and the Main Street of Hillsboro, including a practical drug store and dry-goods store.

It is important to the concept of the play that the town is visible always, looming there, as much on trial as the individual defendant. The crowd is equally important throughout, so that the courtroom becomes a cock-pit, an arena, with the active spectators on all sides of it.

During some portions of the play, the action on the street and the courthouse lawn fills the entire stage; at such times, the furnishings of the courtroom are barely visible. When the action is in the courtroom, the street is dimmed in shadow. In some instances, where action is simultaneous, the lighting is balanced equally between the two areas. This change of emphasis is never abrupt, but fluid—a gentle blend of attention focus from exterior to interior action. This is not so much a literal view of Hillsboro as it is an impression of a sleepy, obscure country town about to be vigorously awakened.

It is an hour after dawn on a July day that promises to be a scorcher.

RACHEL enters. She is twenty-two, pretty, but not beautiful. She wears a cotton summer dress. She carries a small composition-paper suitcase. There is a tense, distraught air about her. She may have been crying. She looks about nervously, as if she doesn't want to be seen. She bumps into a chair, and jumps, as if somebody had touched her. The courtroom is· strange ground to her. Unsure, she looks about. Then, with resolution, she crosses and touches the empty jury-box.

RACHEL (*tentatively, calling*). Mr. Meeker . . . ?

(*After a pause,* MR. MEEKER, *the bailiff, enters. There is no collar on his shirt; his hair is tousled, and there is shaving soap on his face, which he is wiping off with a towel as he enters.*)

MEEKER (*a little irritably*). Who is it? (*Surprised*) Why, hello, Rachel. 'Scuse the way I look. (*He wipes the soap out of his ear. Then he notices her suitcase.*) Not goin' away, are you? Excitement's just startin'.

RACHEL (*earnestly*). Mr. Meeker, don't let my father know I came here.

MEEKER (*shrugs*). The Reverend don't tell me his business. Don't know why I should tell him mine.

RACHEL. I want to see Bert Cates. Is he all right?

MEEKER. Don't know why he shouldn't be. I always figured the safest place in the world is a jail.

RACHEL. Can I go down and see him?

MEEKER. Ain't a very proper place for a minister's daughter.

RACHEL. I only want to see him for a minute.

MEEKER. Sit down, Rachel. I'll bring him up. You can talk to him right here in the courtroom. (RACHEL *sits in one of the stiff wooden chairs.* MEEKER *starts out, then pauses.*) Long as I've been bailiff here, we've never had nothin' but drunks, vagrants, couple of chicken thieves. (*A little dreamily*) Our best catch was that fella from Minnesota that chopped up his wife; we had to extradite him. (*Shakes his head.*) Seems kinda queer havin' a school-teacher in our jail. (*Shrugs.*) Might improve the writin' on the walls.

(MEEKER *goes out. Nervously,* RACHEL *looks around at the cold, official furnishings of the courtroom.* MEEKER *returns to the courtroom, followed by* BERT CATES. CATES *is a pale, thin young man of twenty-four. He is quiet, shy, well-mannered, not particularly good-looking.* RACHEL *and* CATES *face each other expressionlessly, without speaking.* MEEKER *pauses in the doorway.*)

MEEKER. I'll leave you two alone to talk. Don't run off, Bert.

(MEEKER *goes out.* RACHEL *and* CATES *look at each other.*)

RACHEL. Hello, Bert.

CATES. Rache, I told you not to come here.

RACHEL. I couldn't help it. Nobody saw me. Mr. Meeker won't tell. (*Troubled.*) I keep thinking of you, locked up here—

CATES (*trying to cheer her up*). You

know something funny? The food's better than the boarding house. And you'd better not tell anybody how cool it is down here, or we'll have a crime wave every summer.

RACHEL. I stopped by your place and picked up some of your things. A clean shirt, your best tie, some handkerchiefs.

CATES. Thanks.

RACHEL (*rushing to him*). Bert, why don't you tell 'em it was all a joke? Tell 'em you didn't mean to break a law, and you won't do it again!

CATES. I suppose everybody's all steamed up about Brady coming.

RACHEL. He's coming in on a special train out of Chattanooga. Pa's going to the station to meet him. Everybody is!

CATES. Strike up the band.

RACHEL. Bert, it's still not too late. Why can't you admit you're wrong? If the biggest man in the country—next to the President, maybe—if Matthew Harrison Brady comes here to tell the whole world how wrong you are—

CATES. You still think I did wrong?

RACHEL. Why did you do it?

CATES. You know why I did it. I had the book in my hand, Hunter's *Civic Biology*. I opened it up, and read my sophomore science class Chapter 17, Darwin's *Origin of Species*. (RACHEL *starts to protest*.) All it says is that man wasn't just stuck here like a geranium in a flower pot; that living comes from a *long* miracle, it didn't just happen in seven days.

RACHEL. There's a law against it.

CATES. I know that.

RACHEL. Everybody says what you did is bad.

CATES. It isn't as simple as that. Good or bad, black or white, night or day. Do you know, at the top of the world the twilight is six months long?

RACHEL. But we don't live at the top of the world. We live in Hillsboro, and when the sun goes down, it's dark. And why do you try to make it different? (RACHEL *gets the shirt, tie, and handkerchiefs from the suitcase*.) Here.

CATES. Thanks, Rache.

RACHEL. Why can't you be on the right side of things?

CATES. Your father's side. (RACHEL *starts to leave*. CATES *runs after her*.) Rache—love me!

(*They embrace*. MEEKER *enters with a long-handled broom*.)

MEEKER (*clears his throat*). I gotta sweep.

(RACHEL *breaks away and hurries off*.)

CATES (*calling*). Thanks for the shirt!

(MEEKER, *who has been sweeping impassively, now stops and leans on the broom*.)

MEEKER. Imagine Matthew Harrison Brady, comin' here. I voted for him for President. Twice. In nineteen hundred, and again in oh-eight. Wasn't old enough to vote for him the first time he ran. But my pa did. (*Turns proudly to* CATES.) I *seen* him once. At a Chautauqua meeting in Chattanooga. (*Impressed, remembering*.) The tent poles shook! (CATES *moves nervously*.) Who's gonna be your lawyer, son?

CATES. I don't know yet. I wrote to that newspaper in Baltimore. They're sending somebody.

MEEKER (*resumes sweeping*). He better be loud.

CATES (*picking up the shirt*). You want me to go back down?

MEEKER. No need. You can stay up here if you want.

CATES (*going toward the jail*). I'm supposed to be in jail; I'd better be in jail!

(MEEKER *shrugs and follows* CATES *off. The lights fade in the courtroom area, and come up on the town: morning of a hot July day. The* STOREKEEPER *enters, unlocking his store*. MRS. KREBS *saunters across the square*.)

STOREKEEPER. Warm enough for you, Mrs. Krebs?

MRS. KREBS. The Good Lord guv us the heat, and the Good Lord guv us the glands to sweat with.

STOREKEEPER. I bet the Devil ain't so obliging.

MRS. KREBS. Don't intend to find out.

(*The* REVEREND JEREMIAH BROWN, *a gaunt, thin-lipped man, strides on. He looks around, scowling*.)

STOREKEEPER. Good morning, Reverend.

BROWN. 'Morning.

MRS. KREBS. 'Morning, Reverend.

BROWN. Mrs. Krebs. (*Shouting off*.) Where's the banner? Why haven't you raised the banner?

CORKIN (*entering, followed by another workman*). Paint didn't dry 'til jist now. (*They are carrying a rolled-up canvas banner*.)

BROWN. See that you have it up before

Mr. Brady arrives.

(COOPER *enters, gestures "hello" to the others.*)

CORKIN. Fast as we can do it, Reverend.

BROWN. We must show him at once what kind of a community this is.

CORKIN. Yes, Reverend. Come on, Phil. Hep. (*They rig the banner to halyards between the buildings.*)

MRS. KREBS. Big day, Reverend.

CORKIN. Indeed it is. Picnic lunch ready, Mrs. Krebs?

MRS. KREBS. Fitt'n fer a king.

(BANNISTER, PLATT *and other townspeople gather excitedly. They are colorful small-town citizens, but not caricatured rubes.*)

BOLLINGER (*running on, carrying his cornet*). Station master says old 94's on time out of Chattanooga. And Brady's on board all right!

COOPER. The minute Brady gets here, people gonna pour in. Town's gonna fill up like a rain barrel in a flood.

STOREKEEPER. That means business!

(MELINDA *and her mother come on and set up a lemonade stand.*)

BANNISTER. Where they gonna stay? Where we gonna sleep all them people?

MRS. KREBS. They got money, we'll sleep 'em.

PLATT. Looks like the biggest day for this town since we put up Coxey's army!

HOWARD (*bolting on*). Hey! Ted Finney's got out his big bass drum. And y'oughta see what they done to the depot! Ribbons all over the rainspouts!

MELINDA. Lemonade! Lemonade!

(*The workmen hoist the banner above the heads of the crowd, where it hangs for the remainder of the action. The banner blares: "READ YOUR BIBLE."*)

CORKIN. It's all ready, Reverend.

(*The townspeople applaud.* BOLLINGER *toots a ragged fanfare. A* HAWKER *in a white apron wheels on a hot-dog stand. The crowd mills about, in holiday spirit.*)

HAWKER. Hot dogs! Get your red-hots! Hot dogs!

(MRS. MCCLAIN *enters with a shopping bag full of frond fans.*)

MRS. MCCLAIN. Get your fans. Compliments of Maley's Funeral Home. Thirty-five cents.

(*The stage is now full of eager and expectant people.* MRS. BLAIR *shoves her way through the crowd, looking for her son.*)

MRS. BLAIR (*calling*). Howard. Howard!

HOWARD (*racing to her*). Hey, Ma. This is just like the county fair.

MRS. BLAIR. Now you settle down and stop runnin' around and pay some attention when Mr. Brady gets here. Spit down your hair. (HOWARD *spits in her hand, and she pastes down a cowlick.*) Hold still!

(HOWARD *flashes off through the crowd.* ELIJAH, *a "holy man" from the hills, comes on with a wooden vegetable crate full of books. He is bearded, wild-haired, dressed in a tattered burlap smock. His feet are bare. He sets up shop between the hot dogs and the lemonade, with a placard reading:* "WHERE WILL YOU SPEND ETERNITY?")

ELIJAH (*in a shrill, screeching voice*). Buy a Bible! Your guidebook to eternal life!

(E. K. HORNBECK *wanders on, carrying a suitcase. He is a newspaperman in his middle thirties, who sneers politely at everything, including himself. His clothes—those of a sophisticated city-dweller—contrast sharply with the attire of the townspeople.* HORNBECK *looks around, with wonderful contempt.*)

MRS. MCCLAIN (*to* HORNBECK). Want a fan? Compliments of Maley's Funeral Home—thirty-five cents!

HORNBECK. I'd die first.

MRS. KREBS (*unctuously, to* HORNBECK). You're a stranger, aren't you, mister? Want a nice clean place to stay?

HORNBECK. I had a nice clean place to stay, madame, and I left it to come here.

MRS. KREBS (*undaunted*). You're gonna need a room.

HORNBECK. I have a reservation at the Mansion House.

MRS. KREBS. Oh? (*She sniffs.*) That's all right, I suppose, for them as *likes* havin' a privy practically in the bedroom!

HORNBECK (*tipping his straw hat*). The unplumbed and plumbing-less depths! Ahhh, Hillsboro—Heavenly Hillsboro. The buckle on the Bible Belt.

(*The* HAWKER *and* ELIJAH *converge on* HORNBECK *from opposite sides.*)

HAWKER. Hot dog?

ELIJAH. Bible?

(HORNBECK *upends his suitcase and sits on it.*)

HORNBECK. Now that poses a pretty problem! Which is hungrier—my stomach or my soul? (HORNBECK *buys a hot dog.*) My stomach.

ELIJAH (*miffed*). Are you an Evolutionist? An infidel? A sinner?

HORNBECK (*munching the hot dog*). Isn't everybody? (*An* ORGAN-GRINDER *enters, with a live monkey on a string.* HORNBECK *spies the monkey gleefully; he greets the monkey with arms outstretched.*) Grandpa! (*Crosses to the monkey, bends down and shakes the monkey's hand.*) Welcome to Hillsboro, sir! Have you come to testify for the defense or for the prosecution? (*The monkey, oddly enough, doesn't answer.*) No comment? That's fairly safe. But I warn you, sir, you can't compete with all these monkeyshines.

(MELINDA *hands the monkey a penny.*)

MELINDA. Look. He took my penny.

HORNBECK. How could you ask for better proof than that? *There's* the father of the human race!

TIMMY (*running on, breathlessly*). Train's coming! I seen the smoke 'way up the track! (*The train whistle sounds, off.*)

BROWN (*taking command*). All the members of the Bible League, get ready! Let us show Mr. Brady the spirit in which we welcome him to Hillsboro.

(MRS. BLAIR *blows her pitch pipe and the townspeople parade off singing "Marching to Zion." Even the* ORGAN-GRINDER *leaves his monkey tied to the hurdy-gurdy and joins the departing crowd. But* HORNBECK *stays behind.*)

HORNBECK. Amen. (*To the monkey.*) Shield your eyes, monk! You're about to meet the mightiest of your descendants: a man who wears a cathedral for a cloak, a church spire for a hat, whose tread has the thunder of the legions of the Lion-Hearted! (*The* STOREKEEPER *emerges from his establishment and looks in his own store window.* HORNBECK *turns to him.*) You're missing the show.

STOREKEEPER. Somebody's got to mind the store.

HORNBECK. May I ask your opinion, sir, on Evolution?

STOREKEEPER. Don't have any opinions. They're bad for business.

(*Off stage, a cheer. Then the thumping drum into "Gimme That Old-Time Religion" sung by the unseen townspeople.*)

HORNBECK (*to the monkey*). Sound the trumpet, beat the drum. Everybody's come to town to see your competition, monk. Alive and breathing in the county cooler: a high-school teacher—wild, untamed!

(*The crowd surges back, augmented, in a jubilant parade. Many are carrying banners, reading:*

ARE YOU A MAN OR A MONKEY?
AMEND THE CONSTITUTION—PROHIBIT DARWIN
SAVE OUR SCHOOLS FROM SIN
MY ANCESTORS AIN'T APES!
WELCOME MATTHEW HARRISON BRADY
DOWN WITH DARWIN
BE A SWEET ANGEL
DON'T MONKEY WITH OUR SCHOOLS!
DARWIN IS WRONG!
DOWN WITH EVOLUTION
SWEETHEART, COME UNTO THE LORD)

(HORNBECK *goes to the background to watch the show.* MATTHEW HARRISON BRADY *comes on, a benign giant of a man, wearing a pith helmet. He basks in the cheers and the excitement, like a patriarch surrounded by his children. He is gray, balding, paunchy, an indeterminate sixty-five. He is followed by* MRS. BRADY; *the* MAYOR; REVEREND BROWN; TOM DAVENPORT, *the circuit district attorney; some newspapermen, and an army of the curious.*)

ALL (*singing*). Gimme that old-time religion,
Gimme that old-time religion,
Gimme that old-time religion,
It's good enough for me!

It was good enough for father,
It was good enough for father,
It was good enough for father,
And it's good enough for me!

It was good for the Hebrew children,
It was good for the Hebrew children,
It was good for the Hebrew children,
And it's good enough for me!

Gimme that old-time religion,
Gimme that old-time religion,
Gimme that old-time religion,
It's good enough for me!

MAYOR (*speaks*). Mr. Brady, if you please.

REVEREND (*singing*). It is good enough for Brady.

CROWD. It is good enough for Brady,
It is good enough for Brady,
And it's good enough for me!

(*Cheers and applause.* BRADY *seems to carry with him a built-in spotlight. So* MRS. BRADY—*pretty, fashionably dressed, a proper "Second Lady" to the nation's "Sec-*

ond Man"—seems always to be in his shadow. This does not annoy her. SARAH BRADY *is content that all her thoughts and emotions should gain the name of action through her husband.* BRADY *removes his hat and raises his hand. Obediently, the crowd falls to a hushed anticipatory silence.*)

BRADY. Friends—and I can see most of you are my friends, from the way you have decked out your beautiful city of Hillsboro —(*There is a pleased reaction, and a spattering of applause. When* BRADY *speaks, there can be no doubt of his personal magnetism. Even* HORNBECK, *who slouches contemptuously at far left, is impressed with the speaker's power; for here is a man to be reckoned with.*) Mrs. Brady and I are delighted to be among you! (BRADY *takes his wife's hand and draws her to his side.*) I could only wish one thing: that you had not given us quite so warm a welcome! (BRADY *removes his alpaca coat. The crowd laughs.* BRADY *beams.* MRS. MCCLAIN *hands him a frond fan.* BRADY *takes it.*) Bless you. (*He fans himself vigorously.*) My friends of Hillsboro, you know why I have come here. I have not come merely to prosecute a law-breaker, an arrogant youth who has spoken out against the Revealed Word. I have come because what has happened in a schoolroom of your town has unloosed a wicked attack from the big cities of the North!—an attack upon the law which you have so wisely placed among the statutes of this state. I am here to defend that which is most precious in the hearts of all of us: the Living Truth of the Scriptures!

(*Applause and emotional cheering.*)

PHOTOGRAPHER. Mr. Brady. Mr. Brady, a picture?

BRADY. I shall be happy to oblige! (*The townspeople, chanting "Go Tell It on the Mountain," move upstage.* BRADY *begins to organize a group photograph. To his wife*) Sarah . . .

MRS. BRADY (*moving out of the camera range*). No, Matt. Just you and the dignitaries.

BRADY. You are the Mayor, are you not?

MAYOR (*stepping forward, awkwardly*). I am, sir.

BRADY (*extending his hand*). My name is Matthew Harrison Brady.

MAYOR. Oh, I know. Everybody knows that. I had a speech of welcome ready, but somehow it didn't seem necessary.

BRADY. I shall be honored to hear your greeting, sir.

(*The* MAYOR *clears his throat and takes some notes from his pocket.*)

MAYOR (*sincerely*). Mr. Matthew Harrison Brady, this municipality is proud to have within its city limits the warrior who has always fought for us ordinary people. The lady folks of this town wouldn't have the vote if it wasn't for you, fightin' to give 'em all that suffrage. Mr. President Wilson wouldn't never have got to the White House and won the war if it wasn't for you supportin' him. And, in conclusion, the Governor of our state . . .

PHOTOGRAPHER. Hold it! (*The camera clicks.*) Thank you.

(MRS. BRADY *is disturbed by the informality of the pose.*)

MRS. BRADY. Matt—you didn't have your coat on.

BRADY (*to the* PHOTOGRAPHER). Perhaps we should have a more formal pose. (*As* MRS. BRADY *helps him on with his coat*) Who is the spiritual leader of the community?

MAYOR. That would be the Reverend Jeremiah Brown.

(REVEREND BROWN *steps forward.*)

BROWN. Your servant, and the Lord's. (BRADY *and* BROWN *shake hands.*)

BRADY. The Reverend at my left, the Mayor at my right. (*Stiffly, they face the camera.*) We must look grave, gentlemen, but not too serious. Hopeful, I think is the word. We must look hopeful.

(BRADY *assumes the familiar oratorical pose. The camera clicks. Unnoticed, the barefoot* HOWARD *has stuck his head, mouth agape, into the picture. The* MAYOR *refers to the last page of his undelivered speech.*)

MAYOR. In conclusion, the Governor of our state has vested in me the authority to confer upon you a commission as Honorary Colonel in the State Militia. (*Applause*)

BRADY (*savoring it*). "Colonel Brady." I like the sound of that!

BROWN. We thought you might be hungry, Colonel Brady, after your train ride.

MAYOR. So the members of our Ladies' Aid have prepared a buffet lunch.

BRADY. Splendid, splendid—I could do with a little snack.

(*Some of the townspeople, at* BROWN'S

direction, carry on a long picnic table, loaded with foodstuffs, potato salad, fried turkey, pickled fruits, cold meats and all the picnic paraphernalia. RACHEL *comes on following the table, carrying a pitcher of lemonade which she places on the table.*)

BANNISTER (*an eager beaver*). You know, Mr. Brady—*Colonel* Brady—all of us here voted for you three times.

BRADY. I trust it was in three separate elections!

(*There is laughter.* TOM DAVENPORT, *a crisp, businesslike young man, offers his hand to* BRADY.)

DAVENPORT. Sir, I'm Tom Davenport.

BRADY (*beaming*). Of course. Circuit district attorney. (*Putting his arm around* DAVENPORT's *shoulder*) We'll be a team, won't we, young man! Quite a team! (*The picnic table is in place. The sight of the food being uncovered is a magnetic attraction to* BRADY. *He beams and moistens his lips.*) Ahhhh, what a handsome repast! (*Some of the women grin sheepishly at the flattery.* BRADY *is a great eater, and he piles mountains of food on his plate.*) What a challenge it is, to fit on the old armor again! To test the steel of our Truth against the blasphemies of Science! To stand—

MRS. BRADY. Matthew, it's a warm day. Remember, the doctor told you not to overeat.

BRADY. Don't worry, Mother. Just a bite or two. (*He hoists a huge drumstick on his plate, then assails a mountain of potato salad.*) Who among you knows the defendant?—Cates, is that his name?

DAVENPORT. Well, we *all* know him, sir.

MAYOR. Just about everybody in Hillsboro knows everybody else.

BRADY. Can someone tell me—is this fellow Cates a criminal by nature?

RACHEL (*almost involuntarily*). Bert isn't a criminal. He's good, really. He's just—(RACHEL *seems to shrink from the attention that centers on her. She takes an empty bowl and starts off with it.*)

BRADY. Wait, my child. Is Mr. Cates your friend?

RACHEL (*looking down, trying to get away*). I can't tell you anything about him—

BROWN (*fiercely*). Rachel! (*To* BRADY) My daughter will be pleased to answer any questions about Bertram Cates.

BRADY. Your daughter, Reverend? You must be proud, indeed. (BROWN *nods.* BRADY *takes a mouthful of potato salad, turns to* RACHEL.) Now. How did you come to be acquainted with Mr. Cates?

RACHEL (*suffering*). At school. I'm a schoolteacher, too.

BRADY. I'm sure you teach according to the precepts of the Lord.

RACHEL. I try. My pupils are only second-graders.

BRADY. Has Mr. Cates ever tried to pollute your mind with his heathen dogma?

RACHEL. Bert isn't a heathen!

BRADY (*sympathetically*). I understand your loyalty, my child. This man, the man in your jailhouse, is a fellow schoolteacher. Likeable, no doubt. And you are loath to speak out against him before all these people. (BRADY *takes her arm, still carrying his plate. He moves her easily away from the others. As they move*) Think of me as a friend, Rachel. And tell me what troubles you. (BRADY *moves her upstage and their conversation continues, inaudible to us.* BRADY *continues to eat,* RACHEL *speaks to him earnestly. The townspeople stand around the picnic table, munching the buffet lunch.*)

BANNISTER. Who's gonna be the defense attorney?

DAVENPORT. We don't know yet. It hasn't been announced.

MAYOR (*he hands a modest picnic plate to* MRS. BRADY). Whoever it is, he won't have much of a chance against your husband, will he, Mrs. Brady!

(*There are chortles of self-confident amusement. But* HORNBECK *saunters toward the picnic table.*)

HORNBECK. I disagree.

MAYOR. Who are you?

HORNBECK. Hornbeck. E. K. Hornbeck, of the Baltimore *Herald*.

BROWN (*can't quite place the name, but it has unpleasant connotations*). Hornbeck. . . . Hornbeck . . .

HORNBECK. I am a newspaperman, bearing news. When this sovereign state determined to indict the sovereign mind of a less-than-sovereign schoolteacher, my editors decided there was more than a headline here. The Baltimore *Herald*, therefore, is happy to announce that it is sending two representatives to "Heavenly Hillsboro": the most brilliant reporter in America today. (*He tips his straw hat.*) Myself. (*With emphasis*) And the most agile legal mind of the Twentieth Century, Henry Drummond.

(*This name is like a whip-crack.*)

MRS. BRADY (*stunned*). Drummond!

BROWN. Henry Drummond, the agnostic?

BANNISTER. I heard about him. He got those two Chicago child-murderers off just the other day.

BROWN. A vicious, godless man!

(*Blithely,* HORNBECK *reaches across the picnic table and chooses a drumstick. He waves it jauntily toward the astonished party.*)

HORNBECK. A Merry Christmas and a Jolly Fourth of July!

(*Munching the drumstick,* HORNBECK *goes off. Unnoticed,* BRADY *and* RACHEL *have left the scene, missing this significant disclosure. There is a stunned pause.*)

DAVENPORT (*genuinely impressed*). Henry Drummond for the defense. Well!

BROWN. Henry Drummond is an agent of darkness. (*With resolution*) We won't let him in the town!

DAVENPORT. I don't know by what law you could keep him out.

MAYOR (*rubbing his chin*). I'll look it up in the town ordinances.

BROWN. I saw Drummond once. In a courtroom in Ohio. A man was on trial for a most brutal crime. Although he knew—and admitted—the man was guilty, Drummond was perverting the evidence to cast the guilt away from the accused and onto you and me and all of society.

MRS. BRADY. Henry Drummond. Oh, dear me.

BROWN. I can still see him. A slouching hulk of a man, whose head juts out like an animal's. (*He imitates* DRUMMOND'S *slouch.* MELINDA *watches, frightened.*) You look into his face, and you wonder why God made such a man. And then you know that God didn't make him, that he is a creature of the Devil, perhaps even the Devil himself!

(*Little* MELINDA *utters a frightened cry, and buries her head in the folds of her mother's skirt.* BRADY *re-enters with* RACHEL, *who has a confused and guilty look.* BRADY'S *plate has been scraped clean; only the fossil of the turkey leg remains. He looks at the ring of faces, which have been disturbed by* BROWN'S *description of the heretic* DRUMMOND. MRS. BRADY *comes toward him.*)

MRS. BRADY. Matt—they're bringing Henry Drummond for the defense.

BRADY (*pale*). Drummond? (*The townspeople are impressed by the impact of this name on* BRADY.) Henry Drummond!

BROWN. We won't allow him in the town!

MAYOR (*lamely*). I think—maybe the Board of Health—(*He trails off.*)

BRADY (*crossing thoughtfully*). No. (*He turns.*) I believe we should *welcome* Henry Drummond.

MAYOR (*astonished*). Welcome him!

BRADY. If the enemy sends its Goliath into battle, it magnifies our cause. Henry Drummond has stalked the courtrooms of this land for forty years. Where he fights, headlines follow. (*With growing fervor*) The whole world will be watching our victory over Drummond. (*Dramatically*) If St. George had slain a dragonfly, who would remember him.

(*Cheers and pleased reactions from the crowd.*)

MRS. BLAIR. Would you care to finish off the pickled apricots, Mr. Brady?

(BRADY *takes them.*)

BRADY. It would be a pity to see them go to waste.

MRS. BRADY. Matt, do you think—

BRADY. Have to build up my strength, Mother, for the battle ahead. (*Munching thoughtfully*) Now what will Drummond do? He'll try to make us forget the lawbreaker and put the law on trial. (*He turns to* RACHEL.) But we'll have the *answer* for Mr. Drummond. Right here, in some of the things this sweet young lady has told me.

RACHEL. But Mr. Brady—

BRADY. A fine girl, Reverend. Fine girl!

(RACHEL *seems tormented, but helpless.*)

BROWN. Rachel has always been taught to do the righteous thing.

(RACHEL *moves off.*)

BRADY. I'm sure she has.

(MELINDA *hands him a glass of lemonade.*)

BRADY. Thank you. A toast, then! A toast to tomorrow! To the beginning of the trial and the success of our cause. A toast, in good American lemonade! (*He stands lifting his glass. Others rise and join the toast.* BRADY *downs his drink.*)

MRS. BRADY. Mr. Mayor, it's time now for Mr. Brady's nap. He always likes to nap after a meal.

MAYOR. We have a suite ready for you at the Mansion House. I think you'll find your bags already there.

BRADY. Very thoughtful, considerate of you.

MAYOR. If you'll come with me—it's only across the square.

BRADY. I want to thank all the members of the Ladies' Aid for preparing this nice little picnic repast.

MRS. KREBS (*beaming*). Our pleasure, sir.

BRADY. And if I seemed to pick at my food, I don't want you to think I didn't enjoy it. (*Apologetically*) But you see, we had a box lunch on the train.

(*There is a good-humored reaction to this, and the* BRADYS *move off accompanied by the throng of admirers, singing "It is good enough for Brady." Simultaneously the lights fade down on the courthouse lawn and fade up on the courtroom area.* HORNBECK *saunters on, chewing at an apple. He glances about the courtroom as if he were searching for something. When* RACHEL *hurries on,* HORNBECK *drops back into a shadow and she does not see him.*)

RACHEL (*distressed*). Mr. Meeker. Mr. Meeker? (*She calls down toward the jail.*) Bert, can you hear me? Bert, you've got to tell me what to do. I don't know what to do—

(HORNBECK *takes a bite out of his apple.* RACHEL *turns sharply at the sound, surprised to find someone else in the courtroom.*)

HORNBECK (*quietly*). I give advice, at remarkably low hourly rates. Ten per cent off to unmarried young ladies, and special discounts to the clergy and their daughters.

RACHEL. What are you doing here?

HORNBECK. I'm inspecting the battlefield —the night before the battle. Before it's cluttered with the debris of journalistic camp followers. (*Hiking himself up on a window ledge*) I'm scouting myself an observation post to watch the fray. (RA-CHEL *starts to go off.*) Wait. Why do you want to see Bert Cates? What's he to you, or you to him? Can it be that both beauty and biology are on our side? (*Again she starts to leave. But* HORNBECK *jumps down from his ledge and crosses toward her.*) There's a newspaper here I'd like to have you see. It just arrived from the wicked modern Sodom and Gomorrah, Baltimore! (RACHEL *looks at him quizzically as he fishes a tear sheet out of his pocket.*) Not the entire edition, of course. No Happy Hooligan, Barney Google, Abe Kabibble. Merely the part worth reading: E. K. Hornbeck's brilliant little symphony of words. (*He offers her the sheet, but she doesn't take it.*) You should read it. (*Almost reluctantly, she takes it and starts to read.*) My typewriter's been singing a sweet, sad song about the Hillsboro heretic. B. Cates: boy-Socrates, latter-day Dreyfus, Romeo with a biology book. (*He looks over her shoulder, admiring his own writing. He takes another bite out of the apple.*) I may be rancid butter, but I'm on your side of the bread.

RACHEL (*looking up, surprised*). This sounds as if you're a friend of Bert's.

HORNBECK. As much as a critic can be a friend to anyone. (*He sits backward on a chair, watching her read. He takes another bite out of his apple, then offers it to her.*) Have a bite? (RACHEL, *busily reading, shakes her head.*) Don't worry, I'm not the serpent, Little Eva. This isn't from the Tree of Knowledge. You won't find one in the orchards of Heavenly Hillsboro. Birches, beeches, butternuts. A few ignorance bushes. No Tree of Knowledge.

(RACHEL *has finished reading the copy; she looks up at* HORNBECK *with a new respect.*)

RACHEL. Will this be published here, in the local paper?

HORNBECK. In the *Weekly Bugle?* Or whatever it is they call the leaden stuff they blow through the local linotypes? I doubt it.

RACHEL. It would help Bert if people here could read this. It would help them understand. (*She appraises* HORNBECK, *puzzled.*) I never would have expected you to write an article like this. You seem so—

HORNBECK. Cynical? That's my fascination. I do hateful things, for which people love me, and lovable things for which they hate me. I am the friend of enemies, the enemy of friends; I am admired for my detestability. I am both poles and the equator with no temperate zones between.

RACHEL. You make it sound as if Bert is a hero. I'd like to think that, but I can't. A schoolteacher is a public servant: I think he should do what the law and the school board want him to. If the superintendent says, "Miss Brown, you're to teach from

Whitley's *Second Reader*," I don't feel I have to give him an argument.

HORNBECK. Ever give your pupils a snap-quiz on existence?

RACHEL. What?

HORNBECK. Where we came from, where we are, where we're going?

RACHEL. All the answers to those questions are in the Bible.

HORNBECK (*with genuine incredulity*). *All?!* You feed the youth of Hillsboro from the little truck-garden of your mind?

RACHEL (*offended, angry*). I think there must be something wrong in what Bert believes, if a great man like Mr. Brady comes here to speak out against him.

HORNBECK. Matthew Harrison Brady came here to find himself a stump to shout from. That's all.

RACHEL. You couldn't understand. Mr. Brady is the champion of ordinary people, like us.

HORNBECK. Wake up, Sleeping Beauty. The ordinary people played a dirty trick on Colonel Brady. They ceased to exist. (RACHEL *looks puzzled.*) Time was when Brady was the hero of the hinterland, water-boy for the great unwashed. But they've got inside plumbing in their heads these days! There's a highway through the backwoods now, and the trees of the forest have reluctantly made room for their leaf-less cousins, the telephone poles. Henry's Lizzie rattles into town and leaves behind the Yesterday-Messiah, standing in the road alone in a cloud of flivver dust. (*Emphatically, he brandishes the apple.*) The boob has been de-boobed. Colonel Brady's virginal small-towner has been *had*—by Marconi and Montgomery Ward. (*Again, he offers the apple.*) Sure you don't want a bite? Awful good.

(HORNBECK *strolls out of the courtroom and onto the town square; the lights dissolve as before from one area to the other.* RACHEL *goes off in the darkness. The store fronts glow with sunset light. The* STORE-KEEPER *pulls the shade in his store window and locks the door.* MRS. MCCLAIN *crosses, fanning herself wearily.*)

SHOPKEEPER. Gonna be a hot night, Mrs. McClain.

MRS. MCCLAIN. I thought we'd get some relief when the sun went down.

(HORNBECK *tosses away his apple core, then leans back and watches as the* SHOP-KEEPER *and* MRS. MCCLAIN *go off. The* ORGAN-GRINDER *comes on idly with his monkey.* MELINDA *enters attracted by the melody which tinkles in the twilight. She gives the monkey a penny. The* ORGAN-GRINDER *thanks her, and moves off.* MELINDA *is alone, back to the audience, in center stage.* HORNBECK, *silent and motionless, watches from the side. The faces of the buildings are now red with the dying moment of sunset.*

A long, ominous shadow appears across the buildings, cast from a figure approaching off stage. MELINDA, *awed, watches the shadow grow.* HENRY DRUMMOND *enters, carrying a valise. He is hunched over, head jutting forward, exactly as* BROWN *described him. The red of the sun behind him hits his slouching back, and his face is in shadow.* MELINDA *turns and looks at* DRUMMOND, *full in the face.*)

MELINDA (*terrified*). It's the Devil!

(*Screaming with fear* MELINDA *runs off.* HORNBECK *crosses slowly toward* DRUMMOND, *and offers his hand.*)

HORNBECK. Hello, Devil. Welcome to Hell.

The lights fade.

SCENE TWO

The courtroom. A few days later.

The townspeople are packed into the sweltering courtroom. The shapes of the buildings are dimly visible in the background, as if Hillsboro itself were on trial. Court is in session, fans are pumping. The humorless JUDGE *sits at his bench; he has a nervous habit of flashing an automatic smile after every ruling.* CATES *sits beside* DRUMMOND *at a counsel table.* BRADY *sits grandly at another table, fanning himself with benign self-assurance.* HORNBECK *is seated on his window ledge.* RACHEL, *tense, is among the spectators. In the jury box, ten of the twelve jurors are already seated.* BANNISTER *is on the witness stand.* DAVEN-PORT *is examining him.*

DAVENPORT. Do you attend church regularly, Mr. Bannister?

BANNISTER. Only on Sundays.

DAVENPORT. That's good enough for the prosecution. Your Honor, we will accept this man as a member of the jury.

(BANNISTER *starts toward the jury box.*)

JUDGE. One moment, Mr. Bannister. You're not excused.

BANNISTER (*a little petulant*). I wanted that there front seat in the jury box.

DRUMMOND (*rising*). Well, hold your horses, Bannister. You may get it yet!

(BANNISTER *returns to the witness chair.*)

JUDGE. Mr. Drummond, you may examine the venireman.

DRUMMOND. Thank you, Your Honor. Mr. Bannister, how come you're so anxious to get that front seat over there?

BANNISTER. Everybody says this is going to be quite a show.

DRUMMOND. I hear the same thing. Ever read anything in a book about Evolution?

BANNISTER. Nope.

DRUMMOND. Or about a fella named Darwin?

BANNISTER. Can't say I have.

DRUMMOND. I'll bet you read your Bible.

BANNISTER. Nope.

DRUMMOND. How come?

BANNISTER. Can't read.

DRUMMOND. Well, you are fortunate. (*There are a few titters through the courtroom.*) He'll do.

(BANNISTER *turns toward the* JUDGE, *poised.*)

JUDGE. Take your seat, Mr. Bannister. (BANNISTER *races to the jury box as if shot from a gun, and sits in the remaining front seat, beaming.*) Mr. Meeker, will you call a venireman to fill the twelfth and last seat on the jury?

BRADY (*rising*). Your Honor, before we continue, will the court entertain a motion on a matter of procedure?

MEEKER (*calling toward the spectators*). Jesse H. Dunlap. You're next, Jesse.

JUDGE. Will the learned prosecutor state the motion?

BRADY. It has been called to my attention that the temperature in this courtroom is now 97 degrees Fahrenheit. (*He mops his forehead with a large handkerchief.*) And it may get hotter! (*There is laughter.* BRADY *basks in the warmth of his popularity.*) I do not feel that the dignity of the court will suffer if we remove a few superfluous outer garments. (BRADY *indicates his alpaca coat.*)

JUDGE. Does the defense have any objection to Colonel Brady's motion?

DRUMMOND (*askance*). I don't know if the dignity of the court can be upheld with these galluses I've got on.

JUDGE. We'll take the chance, Mr. Drummond. Those who wish to remove their coats may do so.

(*With relief, many of the spectators take off their coats and loosen their collar buttons.* DRUMMOND *wears wide, bright purple suspenders. The spectators react.*)

BRADY (*with affable sarcasm*). Is the counsel for the defense showing us the latest fashion in the great metropolitan city of Chicago?

DRUMMOND (*pleased*). Glad you asked me that. I brought these along special. (*He cocks his thumbs in the suspenders.*) Just so happens I bought these galluses at Peabody's General Store in *your* home town, Mr. Brady. Weeping Water, Nebraska.

(DRUMMOND *snaps the suspenders jauntily. There is amused reaction at this.* BRADY *is nettled: this is his show, and he wants all the laughs. The* JUDGE *pounds for order.*)

JUDGE. Let us proceed with the selection of the final juror.

(MEEKER *brings* JESSE DUNLAP *to the stand. He is a rugged, righteous-looking man.*)

MEEKER. State your name and occupation.

DUNLAP. Jesse H. Dunlap. Farmer and cabinetmaker.

DAVENPORT. Do you believe in the Bible, Mr. Dunlap?

DUNLAP (*vigorously*). I believe in the Holy Word of God. And I believe in Matthew Harrison Brady!

(*There is some applause, and a few scattered "Amens."* BRADY *waves acceptance.*)

DAVENPORT. This man is acceptable to the prosecution.

JUDGE. Very well. Mr. Drummond?

DRUMMOND (*quietly, without rising*). No questions. Not acceptable.

BRADY (*annoyed*). Does Mr. Drummond refuse this man a place on the jury simply because he believes in the Bible?

DRUMMOND. If you find an Evolutionist in this town, you can refuse him.

BRADY (*angrily*). I object to the defense attorney rejecting a worthy citizen without so much as asking him a question!

DRUMMOND (*agreeably*). All right. I'll ask him a question. (*Saunters over to* DUNLAP.) How are you?

DUNLAP (*a little surprised*). Kinda hot.

DRUMMOND. So am I. Excused.

(DUNLAP *looks at the* JUDGE, *confused.*)

JUDGE. You are excused from jury duty, Mr. Dunlap. You may step down.

(DUNLAP *goes back and joins the spectators, a little miffed.*)

BRADY (*piously*). I object to the note of levity which the counsel for the defense is introducing into these proceedings.

JUDGE. The bench agrees with you in spirit, Colonel Brady.

DRUMMOND (*rising angrily*). And *I* object to all this damned "Colonel" talk. I am not familiar with Mr. Brady's military record.

JUDGE. Well—he was made an Honorary Colonel in our State Militia. The day he arrived in Hillsboro.

DRUMMOND. The use of this title prejudices the case of my client: it calls up a picture of the prosecution, astride a' white horse, ablaze in the uniform of a militia colonel, with all the forces of right and righteousness marshaled behind him.

JUDGE. What can we do?

DRUMMOND. Break him. Make him a private. I have no serious objection to the honorary title of "Private Brady."

(*There is a buzz of reaction. The* JUDGE *gestures for the* MAYOR *to come over for a hurried, whispered conference.*)

MAYOR (*after some whispering*). Well, we can't take it back—! (*There is another whispered exchange. Then the* MAYOR *steps gingerly toward* DRUMMOND.) By—by authority of—well, I'm sure the Governor won't have any objection—I hereby appoint you, Mr. Drummond, a temporary Honorary Colonel in the State Militia.

DRUMMOND (*shaking his head, amused*). Gentlemen, what can I say? It is not often in a man's life that he attains the exalted rank of "temporary Honorary Colonel."

MAYOR. It will be made permanent, of course, pending the arrival of the proper papers over the Governor's signature.

DRUMMOND (*looking at the floor*). I thank you.

JUDGE. Colonel Brady. Colonel Drummond. You will examine the next venireman.

(MEEKER *brings* GEORGE SILLERS *to the stand.*)

MEEKER. State your name and occupation.

SILLERS. George Sillers. I work at the feed store.

DAVENPORT. Tell me, sir. Would you call yourself a religious man?

SILLERS. I guess I'm as religious as the next man.

(BRADY *rises.* DAVENPORT *immediately steps back, deferring to his superior.*)

BRADY. In Hillsboro, sir, that means a great deal. Do you have any children, Mr. Sillers?

SILLERS. Not as I know of.

BRADY. If you had a son, Mr. Sillers, or a daughter, what would you think if that sweet child came home from school and told you that a Godless teacher—

DRUMMOND. Objection! We're supposed to be choosing jury members! The prosecution's denouncing the defendant before the trial has even begun!

JUDGE. Objection sustained. (*The* JUDGE *and* BRADY *exchange meaningless smiles.*)

BRADY. Mr. Sillers. Do you have any personal opinions with regard to the defendant that might prejudice you on his behalf?

SILLERS. Cates? I don't hardly know him. He bought some peat moss from me once, and paid his bill.

BRADY. Mr. Sillers impresses me as an honest, God-fearing man. I accept him.

JUDGE. Thank you, Colonel Brady. *Colonel* Drummond?

DRUMMOND (*strolling toward the witness chair*). Mr. Sillers, you just said you were a religious man. Tell me something. Do you work at it very hard?

SILLERS. Well, I'm pretty busy down at the feed store. My wife tends to the religion for both of us.

DRUMMOND. In other words, you take care of this life, and your wife takes care of the next one?

DAVENPORT. Objection.

JUDGE. Objection sustained.

DRUMMOND. While your wife was tending to the religion, Mr. Sillers, did you ever happen to bump into a fella named Charles Darwin?

SILLERS. Not till recent.

DRUMMOND. From what you've heard about this Darwin, do you think your wife would want to have him over for Sunday dinner?

(BRADY *rises magnificently.*)

BRADY. Your Honor, my worthy opponent from Chicago is cluttering the issue with hypothetical questions—

DRUMMOND (*wheeling*). I'm doing *your* job, Colonel.

DAVENPORT (*leaping up*). The prosecution is perfectly able to handle its own arguments.

DRUMMOND. Look, I've established that Mr. Sillers isn't working very hard at religion. Now, for your sake, I want to make sure he isn't working at Evolution.

SILLERS (*simply*). I'm just working at the feed store.

DRUMMOND (*to the* JUDGE). This man's all right. (*Turning*) Take a box seat, Mr. Sillers.

BRADY. I am not altogether satisfied that Mr. Sillers will render impartial—

DRUMMOND. Out of order. The prosecution has already accepted this man.

(*The following becomes a simultaneous wrangle among the attorneys.*)

BRADY. I want a fair trial.

DRUMMOND. So do I!

BRADY. Unless the state of mind of the members of the jury conforms to the laws and patterns of society—

DRUMMOND. Conform! Conform! What do you want to do—run the jury through a meat-grinder, so they all come out the same?

DAVENPORT. Your Honor!

BRADY. I've seen what you can do to a jury. Twist and tangle them. Nobody's forgotten the Endicott Publishing case—where you made the jury believe the obscenity was in their own minds, not on the printed page. It was immoral what you did to that jury. Tricking them. Judgment by confusion. Think you can get away with it here?

DRUMMOND. All I want is to prevent the clock-stoppers from dumping a load of medieval nonsense into the United States Constitution.

JUDGE. This is not a Federal court.

DRUMMOND (*slapping his hand on the table*). Well, dammit, you've got to stop 'em somewhere.

(*The* JUDGE *beats with his gavel.*)

JUDGE. Gentlemen, you are *both* out of order. The bench holds that the jury has been selected. (BRADY *lets his arms fall, with a gesture of sweet charity.*) Because of the lateness of the hour and the unusual heat, the court is recessed until ten o'clock tomorrow morning. (JUDGE *raps the gavel, and the court begins to break up. Then the* JUDGE *notices a slip of paper, and raps for order again.*) Oh. The Reverend Brown has asked me to make this announcement. There will be a prayer meet-

ing tonight on the courthouse lawn, to pray for justice and guidance. All are invited.

DRUMMOND. Your Honor. I object to this commercial announcement.

JUDGE. Commercial announcement?

DRUMMOND. For Reverend Brown's product. Why don't you announce that there will be an Evolutionist meeting?

JUDGE. I have no knowledge of such a meeting.

DRUMMOND. That's understandable. It's bad enough that everybody coming into this courtroom has to walk underneath a banner that says: "Read Your Bible!" Your Honor, I want that sign taken down! Or else I want another one put up—just as big, just as big letters—saying "Read Your Darwin!"

JUDGE. That's preposterous!

DRUMMOND. It certainly is!

JUDGE. You are out of order, Colonel Drummond. The court stands recessed.

(*As the formality of the courtroom is relaxed, there is a general feeling of relief. Spectators and jury members adjust their sticky clothes, and start moving off. Many of the townspeople gather around* BRADY, *to shake his hand, get his autograph, and so stand for a moment in the great man's presence. They cluster about him, and follow* BRADY *as he goes off, the shepherd leading his flock. In marked contrast,* DRUMMOND *packs away his brief in a tattered leather case; but no one comes near him.* RACHEL *moves toward* BERT. *They stand face to face, wordlessly. Both seem to wish the whole painful turmoil were over. Suddenly,* RACHEL *darts to* DRUMMOND's *side.* CATES *opens his mouth to stop her, but she speaks rapidly, with pent-up tension.*)

RACHEL. Mr. Drummond. You've got to call the whole thing off. It's not too late. Bert knows he did wrong. He didn't mean to. And he's sorry. Now why can't he just stand up and say to everybody: "I did wrong. I broke a law. I admit it. I won't do it again." Then they'd stop all this fuss, and—everything would be like it was.

(DRUMMOND *looks at* RACHEL, *not unkindly.*)

DRUMMOND. Who are you?

RACHEL. I'm—a friend of Bert's.

(DRUMMOND *turns to* CATES.)

DRUMMOND. How about it boy? Getting cold feet?

CATES. I never thought it would be like this. Like Barnum and Bailey coming to town.

DRUMMOND (*easily*). We can call it off. You want to quit?

RACHEL (*coming to* BERT's *side*). Yes!

CATES. People look at me as if I was a murderer. Worse than a murderer! That fella from Minnesota who killed his wife —remember, Rachel—half the town turned out to see 'em put him on the train. They just looked at him as if he was a curiosity —not like they *hated* him! Not like he'd done anything really wrong! Just different!

DRUMMOND (*laughs a little to himself*). There's nothing very original about murdering your wife.

CATES. People I thought were my friends look at me now as if I had horns growing out of my head.

DRUMMOND. You murder a wife, it isn't nearly as bad as murdering an old wives' tale. Kill one of their fairy-tale notions, and they call down the wrath of God, Brady, and the state legislature.

RACHEL. You make a joke out of everything. You seem to think it's so funny!

DRUMMOND. Lady, when you lose your power to laugh, you lose your power to think straight.

CATES. Mr. Drummond, I can't laugh. I'm scared.

DRUMMOND. Good. You'd be a damned fool if you weren't.

RACHEL (*bitterly*). You're supposed to help Bert; but every time you swear you make it worse for him.

DRUMMOND (*honestly*). I'm sorry if I offend you. (*He smiles.*) But I don't swear just for the hell of it. (*He fingers his galluses.*) You see, I figure language is a poor enough means of communication as it is. So we ought to use all the words we've got. Besides, there are damned few words that everybody understands.

RACHEL. You don't care anything about Bert! You just want a chance to make speeches against the Bible!

DRUMMOND. I care a great deal about Bert. I care a great deal about what Bert thinks.

RACHEL. Well, I care about what the people in this town think of *him*.

DRUMMOND (*quietly*). Can you buy back his respectability by making him a coward? (*He spades his hands in his hip pockets.*) I understand what Bert's going

through. It's the loneliest feeling in the world—to find yourself standing up when everybody else is sitting down. To have everybody look at you and say, "What's the matter with him?" I know. I know what it feels like. Walking down an empty street, listening to the sound of your own footsteps. Shutters closed, blinds drawn, doors locked against you. And you aren't sure whether you're walking toward something, or if you're just walking away. (*He takes a deep breath, then turns abruptly.*) Cates, I'll change your plea and we'll call off the whole business—on one condition. If you honestly believe you committed a criminal act against the citizens of this state and the minds of their children. If you honestly believe that you're wrong and the law's right. Then the hell with it. I'll pack my grip and go back to Chicago, where it's a cool hundred in the shade.

RACHEL (*eagerly*). Bert knows he's wrong. Don't you, Bert?

DRUMMOND. Don't prompt the witness.

CATES (*indecisive*). What do you think, Mr. Drummond?

DRUMMOND. I'm here. That tells you what I think. (*He looks squarely at* CATES.) Well, what's the verdict, Bert? You want to find yourself guilty before the jury does?

CATES (*quietly, with determination*). No, sir. I'm not gonna quit.

RACHEL (*protesting*). Bert!

CATES. It wouldn't do any good now, anyhow. (*He turns to* RACHEL.) If you'll stick by me, Rache—well, we can fight it out.

(*He smiles at her wanly. All the others have gone now, except* MEEKER *and* DRUMMOND. RACHEL *shakes her head, bewildered, tears forming in her eyes.*)

RACHEL. I don't know what to do; I don't know what to do.

CATES (*frowning*). What's the matter, Rache?

RACHEL. I don't want to do it, Bert; but Mr. Brady says—

DRUMMOND. What does Brady say?

RACHEL (*looking down*). They want me to testify against Bert.

CATES (*stunned*). You can't!

MEEKER. I don't mean to rush you, Bert; but we gotta close up the shop.

(CATES *is genuinely panicked.*)

CATES. Rache, some of the things I've

talked to you about are things you just say to your own heart. (*He starts to go with* MEEKER, *then turns back*.) If you get up on the stand and say those things out loud— (*He shakes his head*.) Don't you understand? The words I've said to you—softly, in the dark—just trying to figure out what the stars are for, or what might be on the back side of the moon—

MEEKER. Bert—

CATES. They were questions, Rache. I was just asking questions. If you repeat those things on the witness stand, Brady'll make 'em sound like answers. And they'll crucify me!

(CATES *and* MEEKER *go off. The lights are slowly dimming*. DRUMMOND *puts on his coat, sizing up* RACHEL *as he does so*. RACHEL, *torn, is almost unconscious of his presence or of her surroundings*.)

DRUMMOND (*kindly, quietly*). What's your name? Rachel what?

RACHEL. Rachel Brown. Can they make me testify?

DRUMMOND. I'm afraid so. It would be nice if nobody ever had to *make* anybody do anything. But—(*He takes his brief case*.) Don't let Brady scare you. He only *seems* to be bigger than the law.

RACHEL. It's not Mr. Brady. It's my father.

DRUMMOND. Who's your father?

RACHEL. The Reverend Jeremiah Brown. (DRUMMOND *whistles softly through his teeth*.) I remember feeling this way when I was a little girl. I would wake up at night, terrified of the dark. I'd think sometimes that my bed was on the ceiling, and the whole house was upside down; and if I didn't hang onto the mattress, I might fall outward into the stars. (*She shivers a little, remembering*.) I wanted to run to my father, and have him tell me I was safe, that everything was all right. But I was always more frightened of him than I was of falling. It's the same way now.

DRUMMOND (*softly*). Is your mother dead?

RACHEL. I never knew my mother. (*Distraught*) Is it true? *Is* Bert wicked?

DRUMMOND (*with simple conviction*). Bert Cates is a good man. Maybe even a great one. And it takes strength for a woman to love such a man. Especially when he's a pariah in the community.

RACHEL. I'm only confusing Bert. And he's confused enough as it is.

DRUMMOND. The man who has everything figured out is probably a fool. College examinations notwithstanding, it takes a very smart fella to say "I don't know the answer!" (DRUMMOND *puts on his hat, touches the brim of it as a gesture of good-by and goes slowly off*.)

CURTAIN

ACT TWO

SCENE ONE

The courthouse lawn. The same night. The oppressive heat of the day has softened into a pleasant summer evening. Two lampposts spread a glow over the town square, and TWO WORKMEN *are assembling the platform for the prayer meeting. One of the* WORKMEN *glances up at the* READ YOUR BIBLE *banner*.

———

FIRST WORKMAN. What're we gonna do about this sign?

SECOND WORKMAN. The Devil don't run this town. Leave it up.

(BRADY *enters, followed by a knot of reporters.* HORNBECK *brings up the rear; he alone is not bothering to take notes. Apparently this informal press conference has been in progress for some time, and* BRADY *is now bringing it to a climax*.)

BRADY. —and I hope that you will tell the readers of your newspapers that here in Hillsboro we are fighting the fight of the Faithful throughout the world! (*All write.* BRADY *eyes* HORNBECK, *leaning lazily, not writing*.)

REPORTER (*British accent*). A question, Mr. Brady.

BRADY. Certainly. Where are you from, young man?

REPORTER. London, sir. Reuters News Agency.

BRADY. Excellent. I have many friends in the United Kingdom.

REPORTER. What is your personal opinion of Henry Drummond?

BRADY. I'm glad you asked me that. I want people everywhere to know I bear no personal animosity toward Henry Drummond. There was a time when we were on the same side of the fence. He gave me active support in my campaign of 1908 —and I welcomed it. (*Almost impas-*

sioned, *speaking at writing tempo, so all the reporters can get it down*) But I say that if my own *brother* challenged the faith of millions, as Mr. Drummond is doing, I would oppose him still! (*The* WORKMEN *pound; the townspeople begin to gather.*) I think that's all for this evening, gentlemen. (*The reporters scatter.* BRADY *turns to* HORNBECK.) Mr. Hornbeck, my clipping service has sent me some of your dispatches.

HORNBECK. How flattering to know I'm being clipped.

BRADY. It grieves me to read reporting that is so—biased.

HORNBECK. I'm no reporter, Colonel. I'm a critic.

BRADY. I hope you will stay for Reverend Brown's prayer meeting. It may bring you some enlightenment..

HORNBECK. It may. I'm here on a press pass, and I don't intend to miss any part of the show.

(REVEREND BROWN *enters with* MRS. BRADY *on his arm.* HORNBECK *passes them jauntily, and crosses downstage.*)

BRADY. Good evening, Reverend. How are you, Mother?

MRS. BRADY. The Reverend Brown was good enough to escort me.

BRADY. Reverend, I'm looking forward to your prayer meeting.

BROWN. You will find our people are fervent in their belief.

(MRS. BRADY *crosses to her husband.*)

MRS. BRADY. I know it's warm, Matt; but these night breezes can be treacherous. And you know how you perspire. (*She takes a small kerchief out of her handbag and tucks it around his neck. He laughs a little.*)

BRADY. Mother is always so worried about my throat.

BROWN (*consulting his watch*). I always like to begin my meetings at the time announced.

BRADY. Most commendable. Proceed, Reverend. After you.

(BROWN *mounts the few steps to the platform.* BRADY *follows him, loving the feel of the board beneath his feet. This is the squared circle where he has fought so many bouts with the English language, and won. The prayer meeting is motion picture, radio, and tent show to these people. To them, the* REVEREND BROWN *is a combination Milton Sills and Douglas*

Fairbanks. He grasps the podium and stares down at them sternly. BRADY *is benign. He sits with his legs crossed, an arm crooked over one corner of his chair.* BROWN *is milking the expectant pause. Just as he is ready to speak,* DRUMMOND *comes in and stands at the fringe of the crowd.* BROWN *glowers at* DRUMMOND. *The crowd chants.*)

BROWN. Brothers and sisters, I come to you on the Wings of the Word. The Wings of the Word are beating loud in the treetops! The Lord's Word is howling in the Wind, and flashing in the belly of the Cloud!

WOMAN. I hear it!

MAN. I see it, Reverend!

BROWN. And we *believe* the Word!

ALL. We believe!

BROWN. We believe the Glory of the Word!

ALL. Glory, glory! Amen, amen!

(RACHEL *comes on, but remains at the fringes of the crowd.*)

BROWN. Hearken to the Word! (*He lowers his voice.*) The Word tells us that the World was created in Seven Days. In the beginning, the earth was without form, and void. And the Lord said, "Let there be light!"

VOICES. Ahhhh . . . !

BROWN. And there *was* light! And the Lord saw the Light and the Light saw the Lord, and the Light said, "Am I good, Lord?" and the Lord said, "Thou art good!"

MAN (*deep-voiced, singing*). And the evening and the morning were the first day!

VOICES. Amen, amen!

BROWN (*calling out*). The Lord said, "Let there be Firmament!" And even as He spoke, it was so! And the Firmament bowed down before Him and said, "Am I good, Lord?" And the Lord said, "Thou art good!"

MAN (*singing*). And the evening and the morning were the second day!

VOICES. Amen, amen!

BROWN. On the Third Day brought He forth the Dry Land, and the Grass, and the Fruit Tree! And on the Fourth Day made He the Sun, the Moon, and the Stars —and He pronounced them Good!

VOICES. Amen.

BROWN. On the Fifth Day He peopled the sea with fish. And the air with fowl.

And made He great whales. And He blessed them all. But on the morning of the Sixth Day, the Lord rose, and His eye was dark, and a scowl lay across His face. (*Shouts.*) Why? Why was the Lord troubled?

ALL. Why? Tell us why! Tell us the troubles of the Lord!

BROWN (*dropping his voice almost to a whisper*). He looked about Him, did the Lord; at all His handiwork, bowed down before Him. And He said, "It is not good, it is not enough, it is not finished. I . . . shall . . . make . . . Me . . . a . . . Man!"

(*The crowd bursts out into an orgy of hosannahs and waving arms.*)

ALL. Glory! Hosannah! Bless the Lord who created us!

WOMAN (*shouting out*). Bow down! Bow down before the Lord!

MAN. Are we good, Lord? Tell us! Are we good?

BROWN (*answering*). The Lord said, "Yea, thou art good! For I have created ye in My Image, after My Likeness! Be fruitful, and multiply, and replenish the Earth, and subdue it!"

MAN (*deep-voiced, singing*). The Lord made Man master of the Earth . . . !

ALL. Glory, glory! Bless the Lord!

BROWN (*whipping 'em up*). Do we believe?

ALL (*in chorus*). Yes!

BROWN. Do we believe the Word?

ALL (*coming back like a whip-crack*). Yes!

BROWN. Do we believe the Truth of the Word?

ALL. Yes!

BROWN (*pointing a finger toward the jail*). Do we curse the man who denies the Word?

ALL (*crescendo, each answer mightier than the one before*). Yes!

BROWN. Do we cast out this sinner in our midst?

ALL. Yes!

(*Each crash of sound from the crowd seems to strike RACHEL physically, and shake her.*)

BROWN. Do we call down hellfire on the man who has sinned against the Word?

ALL (*roaring*). Yes!

BROWN (*deliberately shattering the rhythm, to go into a frenzied prayer, hands clasped together and lifted heavenward*). O Lord of the Tempest and the Thunder!

O Lord of Righteousness and Wrath! We pray that Thou wilt make a sign unto us! Strike down this sinner, as Thou didst Thine enemies of old, in the days of the Pharaohs! (*All lean forward, almost expecting the heavens to open with a thunderbolt. RACHEL is white. BRADY shifts uncomfortably in his chair; this is pretty strong stuff, even for him.*) Let him feel the terror of Thy sword! For all eternity, let his soul writhe in anguish and damnation—

RACHEL. *No!* (*She rushes to the platform.*) No, Father. Don't pray to destroy Bert!

BROWN. Lord, we call down the same curse on those who ask grace for this sinner—though they be blood of my blood, and flesh of my flesh!

BRADY (*rising, grasping BROWN's arm*). Reverend Brown, I know it is the great zeal of your faith which makes you utter this prayer! But it is possible to be overzealous, to destroy that which you hope to save—so that nothing is left but emptiness. (*BROWN turns.*) Remember the wisdom of Solomon in the Book of Proverbs— (*Softly.*) "He that troubleth his own house . . . shall inherit the wind." (*BRADY leads BROWN to a chair, then turns to the townspeople.*) The Bible also tells us that God forgives His children. And we, the Children of God, should forgive each other. (*RACHEL slips off.*) My good friends, return to your homes. The blessings of the Lord be with you all. (*Slowly the townspeople move off, singing and humming "Go, Tell It On the Mountain." BRADY is left alone on stage with DRUMMOND, who still watches him impassively. BRADY crosses to DRUMMOND.*) We were good friends once. I was always glad of your support. What happened between us? There used to be a mutuality of understanding and admiration. Why is it, my old friend, that you have moved so far away from me? (*A pause. They study each other.*)

DRUMMOND (*slowly*). All motion is relative. Perhaps it is *you* who have moved away—by standing still.

(*The words have a sharp impact on BRADY. For a moment, he stands still, his mouth open, staring at DRUMMOND. Then he takes two faltering steps backward, looks at DRUMMOND again, then moves off the stage. DRUMMOND stands alone. Slowly the* lights fade on the silent man. The curtain falls momentarily.)

SCENE TWO

The courtroom, two days later. It is bright midday, and the trial is in full swing. The JUDGE is on the bench; the jury, lawyers, officials and spectators crowd the courtroom. HOWARD, the thirteen-year-old boy, is on the witness stand. He is wretched in a starched collar and Sunday suit. The weather is as relentlessly hot as before. BRADY is examining the boy, who is a witness for the prosecution.

BRADY. Go on, Howard. Tell them what else Mr. Cates told you in the classroom.

HOWARD. Well, he said at first the earth was too hot for any life. Then it cooled off a mite, and cells and things begun to live.

BRADY. Cells?

HOWARD. Little bugs like, in the water. After that, the little bugs got to be bigger bugs, and sprouted legs and crawled up on the land.

BRADY. How long did this take, according to Mr. Cates?

HOWARD. Couple million years. Maybe longer. Then comes the fishes and the reptiles and the mammals. Man's a mammal.

BRADY. Along with the dogs and the cattle in the field: did he say that?

HOWARD. Yes, sir.

(DRUMMOND is about to protest against prompting the witness; then he decides it isn't worth the trouble.)

BRADY. Now, Howard, how did man come out of this slimy mess of bugs and serpents, according to your—"Professor"?

HOWARD. Man was sort of evoluted. From the "Old World Monkeys."

(BRADY slaps his thigh.)

BRADY. Did you hear that, my friends? "Old World Monkeys"! According to Mr. Cates, you and I aren't even descended from good American monkeys! (There is laughter.) Howard, listen carefully. In all this talk of bugs and "Evil-ution," of slime and ooze, did Mr. Cates ever make any reference to God?

HOWARD. Not as I remember.

BRADY. Or the miracle He achieved in seven days as described in the beautiful Book of Genesis?

HOWARD. No, sir.

(BRADY stretches out his arms in an all-embracing gesture.)

BRADY. Ladies and gentlemen—

DRUMMOND. Objection! I ask that the court remind the learned counsel that this is not a Chautauqua tent. He is supposed to be submitting evidence to a jury. There are no ladies on the jury.

BRADY. Your Honor, I have no intention of making a speech. There is no need. I am sure that everyone on the jury, everyone within the sound of this boy's voice, is moved by his tragic confusion. He has been taught that he wriggled up like an animal from the filth and the muck below! (Continuing fervently, the spirit is upon him.) I say that these Bible-haters, these "Evil-utionists," are brewers of poison. And the legislature of this sovereign state has had the wisdom to demand that the peddlers of poison—in bottles or in books —clearly label the products they attempt to sell! (There is applause. HOWARD gulps. BRADY points at the boy.) I tell you, if this law is not upheld, this boy will become one of a generation shorn of its faith by the teachings of Godless science! But if the full penalty of the law is meted out to Bertram Cates, the faithful the whole world over, who are watching us here, and listening to our every word, will call this courtroom blessed! (Applause. Dramatically, BRADY moves to his chair. Condescendingly, he waves to DRUMMOND.)

BRADY. Your witness, sir.

(BRADY sits. DRUMMOND rises, slouches toward the witness stand.)

DRUMMOND. Well, I sure am glad Colonel Brady didn't make a speech! (Nobody laughs. The courtroom seems to resent DRUMMOND's gentle ridicule of the orator. To many, there is an effrontery in DRUMMOND's very voice—folksy and relaxed. It's rather like a harmonica following a symphony concert.) Howard, I heard you say that the world used to be pretty hot.

HOWARD. That's what Mr. Cates said.

DRUMMOND. You figure it was any hotter then than it is right now?

HOWARD. Guess it musta been. Mr. Cates read it to us from a book.

DRUMMOND. Do you know what book?

HOWARD. I guess that Mr. Darwin thought it up.

DRUMMOND (leaning on the arm of the boy's chair). You figure anything's wrong about that, Howard?

HOWARD. Well, I dunno—

DAVENPORT (*leaping up, crisply*). Objection, Your Honor. The defense is asking that a thirteen-year-old boy hand down an opinion on a question of morality!

DRUMMOND (*to the* JUDGE). I am trying to establish, Your Honor, that Howard—or Colonel Brady—or Charles Darwin—or anyone in this courtroom—or *you,* sir—has the right to *think!*

JUDGE. Colonel Drummond, the right to think is not on trial here.

DRUMMOND (*energetically*). With all respect to the bench, I hold that the right to think is very much on trial! It is fearfully in danger in the proceedings of this court!

BRADY (*rises*). A *man* is on trial!

DRUMMOND. A thinking man! And he is threatened with fine and imprisonment because he chooses to speak what he thinks.

JUDGE. Colonel Drummond, would you please rephrase your question.

DRUMMOND (*to* HOWARD). Let's put it this way, Howard. All this fuss and feathers about Evolution, do you think it hurt you any?

HOWARD. Sir?

DRUMMOND. Did it do you any harm? You still feel reasonably fit? What Mr. Cates told you, did it hurt your baseball game any? Affect your pitching arm? (*He punches* HOWARD's *right arm playfully.*)

HOWARD. No, sir. I'm a leftie.

DRUMMOND. A southpaw, eh? Still honor your father and mother?

HOWARD. Sure.

DRUMMOND. Haven't murdered anybody since breakfast?

DAVENPORT. Objection.

JUDGE. Objection sustained.

(DRUMMOND *shrugs.*)

BRADY. Ask him if his Holy Faith in the scriptures has been shattered—

DRUMMOND. When I need your *valuable* help, Colonel, you may rest assured I shall humbly ask for it. (*Turning*) Howard, do you believe everything Mr. Cates told you?

HOWARD (*frowning*). I'm not sure. I gotta think it over.

DRUMMOND. Good for you. Your pa's a farmer, isn't he?

HOWARD. Yes, sir.

DRUMMOND. Got a tractor?

HOWARD. Brand new one.

DRUMMOND. You figure a tractor's sinful, because it isn't mentioned in the Bible?

HOWARD (*thinking*). Don't know.

DRUMMOND. Moses never made a phone call. Suppose that makes the telephone an instrument of the Devil?

HOWARD. I never thought of it that way.

BRADY (*rising, booming*). Neither did anybody else! Your Honor, the defense makes the same old error of all Godless men! They confuse material things with the great spiritual realities of the Revealed Word! (*Turning to* DRUMMOND) Why do you bewilder this child? Does Right have no meaning to you, sir? (BRADY's *hands are outstretched, palms upward, pleading.* DRUMMOND *stares at* BRADY *long and thoughtfully.*)

DRUMMOND (*in a low voice*). Realizing that I may prejudice the case of my client, I must say that "Right" has no meaning to me whatsoever! (*There is a buzz of reaction in the courtroom.*) *Truth* has meaning—as a direction. But one of the peculiar imbecilities of our time is the grid of morality we have placed on human behavior: so that every act of man must be measured against an arbitrary latitude of right and longitude of wrong—in exact minutes, seconds, and degrees! (*He turns to* HOWARD.) Do you have any idea what I'm talking about, Howard?

HOWARD. No, sir.

DRUMMOND. Well, maybe you will. Someday. Thank you, son. That's all.

JUDGE. The witness is excused. (*He raps his gavel, but* HOWARD *remains in the chair, staring goop-eyed at his newly found idol.*) We won't need you any more, Howard: you can go back to your pa now. (HOWARD *gets up, and joins the spectators.*) Next witness.

DAVENPORT. Will Miss Rachel Brown come forward, please?

(RACHEL *emerges from among the spectators. She comes forward quickly, as if wanting to get the whole thing over with. She looks at no one.* CATES *watches her with a hopeless expression:* Et tu, Brute. MEEKER *swears her in perfunctorily.*)

BRADY. Miss Brown. You are a teacher at the Hillsboro Consolidated School?

RACHEL (*flat*). Yes.

BRADY. So you have had ample opportunity to know the defendant, Mr. Cates, professionally?

RACHEL. Yes.

BRADY (*with exaggerated gentleness*). Is Mr. Cates a member of the spiritual community to which you belong?

DRUMMOND (*rises*). Objection! I don't understand this chatter about "spiritual communities." If the prosecution wants to know if they go to the same church, why doesn't he ask that?

JUDGE. Uh—objection overruled. (DRUMMOND *slouches, disgruntled.* CATES *stares at* RACHEL *disbelievingly, while her eyes remain on the floor. The exchange between* DRUMMOND *and the* JUDGE *seems to have unnerved her, however.*) You will answer the question, please.

RACHEL. I did answer it, didn't I? What was the question?

BRADY. Do you and Mr. Cates attend the same church?

RACHEL. Not any more. Bert dropped out two summers ago.

BRADY. Why?

RACHEL. It was what happened with the little Stebbins boy.

BRADY. Would you tell us about that, please?

RACHEL. The boy was eleven years old, and he went swimming in the river, and got a cramp, and drowned. Bert felt awful about it. He lived right next door, and Tommy Stebbins used to come over to the boarding house and look through Bert's microscope. Bert said the boy had a quick mind, and he might even be a scientist when he grew up. At the funeral, Pa preached that Tommy didn't die in a state of grace, because his folks had never had him baptized—

(CATES, *who has been smoldering through this recitation, suddenly leaps angrily to his feet.*)

CATES. Tell 'em what your father really said! That Tommy's soul was damned, writhing in hellfire!

DUNLAP (*shaking a fist at* CATES). Cates, you sinner!

(*The* JUDGE *raps for order. There is confusion in the courtroom.*)

CATES. Religion's supposed to comfort people, isn't it? Not frighten them to death!

JUDGE. We will have order, please!

(DRUMMOND *tugs* CATES *back to his seat.*)

DRUMMOND. Your Honor, I request that the defendant's remarks be stricken from the record.

(*The* JUDGE *nods.*)

BRADY. But how can we strike this young man's bigoted opinions from the memory

of this community? (BRADY *turns, about to play his trump card.*) Now, my dear. Will you tell the jury some more of Mr. Cates' opinions on the subject of religion?

DRUMMOND. Objection! Objection! Objection! Hearsay testimony is not admissible.

JUDGE. The court sees no objection to this line of questioning. Proceed, Colonel Brady.

BRADY. Will you merely repeat in your own words some of the conversations you had with the defendant?

(RACHEL's *eyes meet* BERT's. *She hesitates.*)

RACHEL. I don't remember exactly—

BRADY (*helpfully*). What you told me the other day. That presumably "humorous" remark Mr. Cates made about the Heavenly Father.

RACHEL. Bert said— (*She stops.*)

BRADY. Go ahead, my dear.

RACHEL (*pathetically*). I can't—

JUDGE. May I remind you, Miss Brown, that you are testifying under oath, and it is unlawful to withhold pertinent information.

RACHEL. Bert was just talking about some of the things he'd read. He—He—

BRADY. Were you shocked when he told you these things? (RACHEL *looks down.*) Describe to the court your innermost feelings when Bertram Cates said to you: "God did not create Man! Man created God!" (*There is a flurry of reaction.*)

DRUMMOND (*leaping to his feet*). Objection!

RACHEL (*blurting*). Bert didn't say that! He was just joking. What he said was: "God created Man in His own image—and Man, being a gentleman, returned the compliment."

(HORNBECK *guffaws and pointedly scribbles this down.* BRADY *is pleased.* RACHEL *seems hopelessly torn.*)

BRADY. Go on, my dear. Tell us some more. What did he say about the holy state of matrimony? Did he compare it with the breeding of animals?

RACHEL. No, he didn't say that— He didn't *mean* that. That's not what I told you. All he said was—(*She opens her mouth to speak, but nothing comes out. An emotional block makes her unable to utter a sound. Her lips move wordlessly.*)

JUDGE. Are you ill, Miss Brown? Would you care for a glass of water?

(*The fatuity of this suggestion makes*

RACHEL *crumble into a near breakdown.*)

BRADY. Under the circumstances, I believe the witness should be dismissed.

DRUMMOND. And will the defense have no chance to challenge some of these statements the prosecutor has put in the mouth of the witness?

(CATES *is moved by* RACHEL's *obvious distress.*)

CATES (*to* DRUMMOND). Don't plague her. Let her go.

DRUMMOND (*pauses, then sighs*). No questions.

JUDGE. For the time being, the witness is excused. (REVEREND BROWN *comes forward to help his daughter from the stand. His demeanor is unsympathetic as he escorts her from the courtroom. There is a hushed babble of excitement.*) Does the prosecution wish to call any further witnesses?

DAVENPORT. Not at the present time, Your Honor.

JUDGE. We shall proceed with the case for the defense. Colonel Drummond.

DRUMMOND (*rising*). Your Honor, I wish to call Dr. Amos D. Keller, head of the Department of Zoology at the University of Chicago.

BRADY. Objection.

(DRUMMOND *turns, startled.*)

DRUMMOND. On what grounds?

BRADY. I wish to inquire what possible relevance the testimony of a Zoo-ology professor can have in this trial.

DRUMMOND (*reasonably*). It has every relevance! My client is on trial for teaching Evolution. Any testimony relating to his alleged infringement of the law must be admitted!

BRADY. Irrelevant, immaterial, inadmissible.

DRUMMOND (*sharply*). Why? If Bertram Cates were accused of murder, would it be irrelevant to call expert witnesses to examine the weapon? Would you rule out testimony that the so-called murder weapon was incapable of firing a bullet?

JUDGE. I fail to grasp the learned counsel's meaning.

DRUMMOND. Oh. (*With exaggerated gestures, as if explaining things to a small child*) Your Honor, the defense wishes to place Dr. Keller on the stand to explain to the gentlemen of the jury exactly what the evolutionary theory is. How can they pass judgment on it if they don't know what it's all about?

BRADY. I hold that the very law we are here to enforce excludes such testimony! The people of this state have made it very clear that they do not want this *zoo*-ological hogwash slobbered around the schoolrooms! And I refuse to allow these agnostic scientists to employ this courtroom as a sounding board, as a platform from which they can shout their heresies into the headlines!

JUDGE (*after some thoughtful hesitation*). Colonel Drummond, the court rules that zoology is irrelevant to the case. (*The* JUDGE *flashes his customary mechanical and humorless grin.*)

DRUMMOND. Agnostic scientists! Then I call Dr. Allen Page—(*Staring straight at* BRADY) Deacon of the Congregational Church—and professor of geology and archeology at Oberlin College.

BRADY (*dryly*). Objection!

JUDGE. Objection sustained. (*Again, the meaningless grin*)

DRUMMOND (*astonished*). In one breath, does the court deny the existence of zoology, geology and archeology?

JUDGE. We do not deny the existence of these sciences: but they do not relate to this point of law.

DRUMMOND (*fiery*). I call Walter Aaronson, philosopher, anthropologist, author! One of the most brilliant minds in the world today! Objection, Colonel Brady?

BRADY (*nodding, smugly*). Objection.

DRUMMOND. Your Honor! The defense has brought to Hillsboro—at great expense and inconvenience—fifteen noted scientists! The great thinkers of our time! Their testimony is basic to the defense of my client. For it is my intent to show this court that what Bertram Cates spoke quietly one spring afternoon in the Hillsboro High School is no crime! It is incontrovertible as geometry in every enlightened community of minds!

JUDGE. In *this* community, Colonel Drummond—and in this sovereign state— exactly the opposite is the case. The language of the law is clear; we do not need experts to question the validity of a law that is already on the books.

(DRUMMOND, *for once in his life, has hit a legal roadblock.*)

DRUMMOND (*scowling*). In other words, the court rules out any expert testimony on Charles Darwin's *Origin of Species or Descent of Man?*

JUDGE. The court so rules.

(DRUMMOND *is flabbergasted. His case is cooked and he knows it. He looks around helplessly.*)

DRUMMOND (*there's the glint of an idea in his eye*). Would the court admit expert testimony regarding a book known as the Holy Bible?

JUDGE (*hesitates, turns to* BRADY). Any objection, Colonel Brady?

BRADY. If the counsel can advance the case of the defendant through the use of the Holy Scriptures, the prosecution will take no exception!

DRUMMOND. Good! (*With relish*) I call to the stand one of the world's foremost experts on the Bible and its teachings—Matthew Harrison Brady!

(*There is an uproar in the courtroom. The* JUDGE *raps for order.*)

DAVENPORT. Your Honor, this is preposterous!

JUDGE (*confused*). I—well, it's highly unorthodox. I've never known an instance where the defense called the prosecuting attorney as a witness.

(BRADY *rises. Waits for the crowd's reaction to subside.*)

BRADY. Your Honor, this entire trial is unorthodox. If the interests of Right and Justice will be served, I will take the stand.

DAVENPORT (*helplessly*). But Colonel Brady—

(*Buzz of awed reaction. The giants are about to meet head-on. The* JUDGE *raps the gavel again, nervously.*)

JUDGE (*to* BRADY). The court will support you if you wish to decline to testify—as a witness against your own case. . . .

BRADY (*with conviction*). Your Honor, I shall not testify *against* anything. I shall speak out, as I have all my life—on behalf of the Living Truth of the Holy Scriptures!

(DAVENPORT *sits, resigned but nervous.*)

JUDGE (*to* MEEKER, *in a nervous whisper*). Uh—Mr. Meeker, you'd better swear in the witness, please . . .

(DRUMMOND *moistens his lips in anticipation.* BRADY *moves to the witness stand in grandiose style.* MEEKER *holds out a Bible.* BRADY *puts his left hand on the book, and raises his right hand.*)

MEEKER. Do you solemnly swear to tell the truth, the whole truth, and nothing but the truth, so help you God?

BRADY (*booming*). I do.

MRS. KREBS. And he will!

(BRADY *sits, confident and assured. His air is that of a benign and learned mathematician about to be quizzed by a schoolboy on matters of short division.*)

DRUMMOND. Am I correct, sir, in calling on you as an authority on the Bible?

BRADY. I believe it is not boastful to say that I have studied the Bible as much as any layman. And I have tried to live according to its precepts.

DRUMMOND. Bully for you. Now, I suppose you can quote me chapter and verse right straight through the King James Version, can't you?

BRADY. There are many portions of the Holy Bible that I have committed to memory.

(DRUMMOND *crosses to counsel table and picks up a copy of Darwin.*)

DRUMMOND. I don't suppose you've memorized many passages from the *Origin of Species*?

BRADY. I am not in the least interested in the pagan hypotheses of that book.

DRUMMOND. Never read it?

BRADY. And I never will.

DRUMMOND. Then how in perdition do you have the gall to whoop up this holy war against something you don't know anything about? How can you be so cocksure that the body of scientific knowledge systematized in the writings of Charles Darwin is, in any way, irreconcilable with the spirit of the Book of Genesis?

BRADY. Would you state that question again, please?

DRUMMOND. Let me put it this way. (*He flips several pages in the book*) On page nineteen of *Origin of Species*, Darwin states—

(DAVENPORT *leaps up.*)

DAVENPORT. I object to this, Your Honor. Colonel Brady has been called as an authority on the Bible. Now the "gentleman from Chicago" is using this opportunity to read into the record scientific testimony which you, Your Honor, have previously ruled is irrelevant. If he's going to examine Colonel Brady on the Bible, let him stick to the Bible, the Holy Bible, and only the Bible!

(DRUMMOND *cocks an eye at the bench.*)

JUDGE (*clears his throat*). You will confine your questions to the Bible.

(DRUMMOND *slaps shut the volume of Darwin.*)

DRUMMOND (*not angrily*). All right. I get the scent in the wind. (*He tosses the volume of Darwin on the counsel table.*) We'll play in *your* ball park, Colonel. (*He searches for a copy of the Bible, finally gets* MEEKER'S. *Without opening it* DRUMMOND *scrutinizes the binding from several angles.*) Now let's get this straight. Let's get it clear. This *is* the book that you're an expert on?

(BRADY *is annoyed at* DRUMMOND'S *elementary attitude and condescension.*)

BRADY. That is correct.

DRUMMOND. Now tell me. Do you feel that every word that's written in this book should be taken literally?

BRADY. Everything in the Bible should be accepted, exactly as it is given there.

DRUMMOND (*leafing through the Bible*). Now take this place where the whale swallows Jonah. Do you figure that actually happened?

BRADY. The Bible does not say "a whale," it says "a big fish."

DRUMMOND. Matter of fact, it says "a great fish"—but it's pretty much the same thing. What's your feeling about that?

BRADY. I believe in a God who can make a whale and who can make a man and make both do what He pleases!

VOICES. Amen, amen!

DRUMMOND (*turning sharply to the clerk*). I want those "Amens" in the record! (*He wheels back to* BRADY.) I recollect a story about Joshua, making the sun stand still. Now as an expert, you tell me that's as true as the Jonah business. Right? (BRADY *nods, blandly.*) That's a pretty neat trick. You suppose Houdini could do it?

BRADY. I do not question or scoff at the miracles of the Lord—as do ye of little faith.

DRUMMOND. Have you ever pondered just what would naturally happen to the earth if the sun stood still?

BRADY. You can testify to that if I get you on the stand. (*There is laughter.*)

DRUMMOND. If they say that the sun stood still, they must've had a notion that the sun moves around the earth. Think that's the way of things? Or don't you believe the earth moves around the sun?

BRADY. I have faith in the Bible!

DRUMMOND. You don't have much faith in the solar system.

BRADY (*doggedly*). The sun stopped.

DRUMMOND. Good. (*Level and direct*) Now if what you say factually happened—if Joshua halted the sun in the sky—that means the earth stopped spinning on its axis; continents toppled over each other, mountains flew out into space. And the earth, arrested in its orbit, shriveled to a cinder and crashed into the sun. (*Turning*) How come they missed *this* tidbit of news.

BRADY. They missed it because it didn't happen.

DRUMMOND. It must've happened! According to natural law. Or don't you believe in natural law, Colonel? Would you like to ban Copernicus from the classroom, along with Charles Darwin? Pass a law to wipe out all the scientific development since Joshua. Revelations—period!

BRADY (*calmly, as if instructing a child*). Natural law was born in the mind of the Heavenly Father. He can change it, cancel it, use it as He pleases. It constantly amazes me that you apostles of science, for all your supposed wisdom, fail to grasp this simple fact.

(DRUMMOND *flips a few pages in the Bible.*)

DRUMMOND. Listen to this: Genesis 4—16. "And Cain went out from the presence of the Lord, and dwelt in the land of Nod, on the East of Eden. And Cain *knew his wife!*" Where the hell did *she* come from?

BRADY. Who?

DRUMMOND. Mrs. Cain. Cain's wife. If, "In the beginning" there were only Adam and Eve, and Cain and Abel, where'd this extra woman spring from? Ever figure that out?

BRADY (*cool*). No, sir. I will leave the agnostics to hunt for her. (*Laughter*)

DRUMMOND. Never bothered you?

BRADY. Never bothered me.

DRUMMOND. Never tried to find out?

BRADY. No.

DRUMMOND. Figure somebody pulled off another creation, over in the next county?

BRADY. The Bible satisfies me, it is enough.

DRUMMOND. It frightens me to imagine the state of learning in this world if everyone had your driving curiosity. (DRUMMOND *is still probing for a weakness in Goliath's armor. He thumbs a few pages further in the Bible.*) This book now goes into a lot of "begats." (*He reads.*) "And Aphraxad begat Salah; and Salah begat Eber" and so on and so on. These pretty important folks?

BRADY. They are the generations of the holy men and women of the Bible.

DRUMMOND. How did they go about all this "begatting"?

BRADY. What do you mean?

DRUMMOND. I mean, did people "begat" in those days about the same way they get themselves "begat" today?

BRADY. The process is about the same. I don't think your scientists have improved it any. (*Laughter*)

DRUMMOND. In other words, these folks were conceived and brought forth through the normal biological function known as *sex*. (*There is hush-hush reaction through the court.* HOWARD's *mother clamps her hands over the boy's ears, but he wriggles free.*) What do you think of sex, Colonel Brady?

BRADY. In what spirit is this question asked?

DRUMMOND. I'm not asking what you think of sex as a father, or as a husband. Or a Presidential candidate. You're up here as an expert on the Bible. What's the Biblical evaluation of sex?

BRADY. It is considered "Original Sin."

DRUMMOND (*with mock amazement*). And all these holy people got themselves "begat" through "Original Sin"? (BRADY *does not answer. He scowls, and shifts his weight in his chair.*) All this sinning make 'em any less holy?

DAVENPORT. Your Honor, where is this leading us? What does it have to do with the State versus Bertram Cates.

JUDGE. Colonel Drummond, the court must be satisfied that this line of questioning has some bearing on the case.

DRUMMOND (*fiery*). You've ruled out all my witnesses. I must be allowed to examine the one witness you've left me in my own way!

BRADY (*with dignity*). Your Honor, I am willing to sit here and endure Mr. Drummond's sneering and his disrespect. For he is pleading the case of the prosecution by his contempt for all that is holy.

DRUMMOND. I object, I object, I object.

BRADY. On what grounds? It is possible that something *is* holy to the celebrated agnostic?

DRUMMOND. Yes! (*His voices drops, intensely*). The individual human mind. In a child's power to master the multiplication table there is more sanctity than in all

your shouted "Amens!" "Holy, Holies!" and "Hosannahs!" An idea is a greater monument than a cathedral. And the advance of man's knowledge is more of a miracle than any sticks turned to snakes, or the parting of waters! But are we now to halt the march of progress because Mr. Brady frightens us with a fable? (*Turning to the jury, reasonably*) Gentlemen, progress has never been a bargain. You've got to pay for it. Sometimes I think there's a man behind a counter who says, "All right, you can have a telephone; but you'll have to give up privacy, the charm of distance. Madam, you may vote; but at a price; you lose the right to retreat behind a powder-puff or a petticoat. Mister, you may conquer the air; but the birds will lose their wonder, and the clouds will smell of gasoline!" (*Thoughtfully, seeming to look beyond the courtroom*) Darwin moved us forward to a hilltop, where we could look back and see the way from which we came. But for this view, this insight, this knowledge, we must abandon our faith in the pleasant poetry of Genesis.

BRADY. We must *not* abandon faith! Faith is the important thing!

DRUMMOND. Then why did God plague us with the power to think? Mr. Brady, why do you deny the *one* faculty which lifts man above all other creatures on the earth: the power of his brain to reason. What other merit have we? The elephant is larger, the horse is stronger and swifter, the butterfly more beautiful, the mosquito more prolific, even the simple sponge is more durable! (*Wheeling on* BRADY) Or does a *sponge* think?

BRADY. I don't know. I'm a man, not a sponge.

(*There are a few snickers at this; the crowd seems to be slipping away from* BRADY *and aligning itself more and more with* DRUMMOND.)

DRUMMOND. Do you think a sponge thinks?

BRADY. If the Lord wishes a sponge to think, it thinks.

DRUMMOND. Does a man have the same privileges that a sponge does?

BRADY. Of course.

DRUMMOND (*roaring, for the first time: stretching his arm toward* CATES). This man wishes to be accorded the same privilege as a sponge! *He wishes to think!*

(*There is some applause. The sound of*

it strikes BRADY *exactly as if he had been slapped in the face.*)

BRADY. But your client is wrong! He is deluded! He has lost his way!

DRUMMOND. It's sad that we aren't all gifted with your positive knowledge of Right and Wrong, Mr. Brady. (DRUMMOND *strides to one of the uncalled witnesses seated behind him, and takes from him a rock, about the size of a tennis ball.* DRUMMOND *weighs the rock in his hand as he saunters back toward* BRADY.) How old do you think this rock is?

BRADY (*intoning*). I am more interested in the Rock of Ages, than I am in the Age of Rocks.

(*A couple of die-hard "Amens."* DRUMMOND *ignores this glib gag.*)

DRUMMOND. Dr. Page of Oberlin College tells me that this rock is at least ten million years old.

BRADY (*sarcastically*). Well, well, Colonel Drummond! You managed to sneak in some of that scientific testimony after all.

(DRUMMOND *opens up the rock, which splits into two halves. He shows it to* BRADY.)

DRUMMOND. Look, Mr. Brady. These are the fossil remains of a pre-historic marine creature, which was found in this very county—and which lived here millions of years ago, when these very mountain ranges were submerged in water.

BRADY. I know. The Bible gives a fine account of the flood. But your professor is a little mixed up on his dates. That rock is not more than six thousand years old.

DRUMMOND. How do you know?

BRADY. A fine Biblical scholar, Bishop Usher, has determined for us the exact date and hour of the Creation. It occurred in the Year 4,004 B.C.

DRUMMOND. That's Bishop Usher's opinion.

BRADY. It is not an opinion. It is literal fact, which the good Bishop arrived at through careful computation of the ages of the prophets as set down in the Old Testament. In fact, he determined that the Lord began the Creation on the 23rd of October in the Year 4,004 B.C. at—uh, 9 A.M.!

DRUMMOND. That Eastern Standard Time? (*Laughter.*) Or Rocky Mountain Time? (*More laughter.*) It wasn't daylight-saving time, was it? Because the Lord didn't make the sun until the fourth day!

BRADY (*fidgeting*). That is correct.

DRUMMOND (*sharply*). That first day. Was it a twenty-four-hour day?

BRADY. The Bible says it was a day.

DRUMMOND. There wasn't any sun. How do you know how long it was?

BRADY (*determined*). The Bible says it was a day.

DRUMMOND. A normal day, a literal day, a twenty-four-hour day?

(*Pause.* BRADY *is unsure.*)

BRADY. I do not know.

DRUMMOND. What do you think?

BRADY (*floundering*). I do not think about things that . . . I do not think about!

DRUMMOND. Do you ever think about things that you *do* think about? (*There is some laughter. But it is dampened by the knowledge and awareness throughout the courtroom that the trap is about to be sprung.*) Isn't it possible that first day was twenty-five hours long? There was no way to measure it, no way to tell! *Could* it have been twenty-five hours?

(*Pause. The entire courtroom seems to lean forward.*)

BRADY (*hesitates—then*). It is . . . possible . . .

(DRUMMOND'S *got him. And he knows it! This is the turning point. From here on, the tempo mounts.* DRUMMOND *is now fully in the driver's seat. He pounds his questions faster and faster.*)

DRUMMOND. Oh. You interpret that the first day recorded in the Book of Genesis could be of indeterminate length.

BRADY (*wriggling*). I mean to state that the day referred to is not necessarily a twenty-four-hour day.

DRUMMOND. It could have been thirty hours! Or a month! Or a year! Or a hundred years! (*He brandishes the rock underneath* BRADY'S *nose.*) Or *ten million years!*

(DAVENPORT *is able to restrain himself no longer. He realizes that* DRUMMOND *has* BRADY *in his pocket. Red-faced, he leaps up to protest.*)

DAVENPORT. I protest! This is not only irrelevant, immaterial—it is *illegal!* (*There is excited reaction in the courtroom. The* JUDGE *pounds for order, but the emotional tension will not subside.*) I demand to know the purpose of Mr. Drummond's examination! What is he trying to do?

(*Both* BRADY *and* DRUMMOND *crane forward, hurling their answers not at the court, but at each other.*)

BRADY. I'll tell you what he's trying to do! He wants to destroy everybody's belief in the Bible, and in God!

DRUMMOND. You know that's not true. I'm trying to stop you bigots and ignoramuses from controlling the education of the United States! And you know it!

(*Arms out,* DAVENPORT *pleads to the court, but is unheard. The* JUDGE *hammers for order.*)

JUDGE (*shouting*). I shall ask the bailiff to clear the court, unless there is order here.

BRADY. How dare you attack the Bible?

DRUMMOND. The Bible is a book. A good book. But it's not the *only* book.

BRADY. It is the revealed word of the Almighty. God spake to the men who wrote the Bible.

DRUMMOND. And how do you know that God didn't "spake" to Charles Darwin?

BRADY. I know, because God tells me to oppose the evil teachings of that man.

DRUMMOND. Oh. God speaks to you.

BRADY. Yes.

DRUMMOND. He tells you exactly what's right and what's wrong?

BRADY (*doggedly*). Yes.

DRUMMOND. And you act accordingly?

BRADY. Yes.

DRUMMOND. So you, Matthew Harrison Brady, through oratory, legislation, or whatever, pass along God's orders to the rest of the world! (*Laughter begins.*) Gentlemen, meet the "Prophet From Nebraska!"

(BRADY'S *oratory is unassailable; but his vanity—exposed by* DRUMMOND'S *prodding —is only funny. The laughter is painful to* BRADY. *He starts to answer* DRUMMOND, *then turns toward the spectators and tries, almost physically, to suppress the amused reaction. This only makes it worse.*)

BRADY (*almost inarticulate*). I—Please—!

DRUMMOND (*with increasing tempo, closing in*). Is that the way of things?

BRADY. No.

DRUMMOND. God tells Brady what is good!

BRADY. No.

DRUMMOND. To be against Brady is to be against God! (*More laughter.*)

BRADY (*confused*). No, no! Each man is a free agent—

DRUMMOND. Then what is Bertram Cates doing in the Hillsboro jail? (*Some applause.*) Suppose Mr. Cates had enough influence and lung power to railroad through the State Legislature a law that only *Darwin* should be taught in the schools!

BRADY. Ridiculous, ridiculous! There is only one great Truth in the world—

DRUMMOND. The Gospel according to Brady! God speaks to Brady, and Brady tells the world! Brady, Brady, Brady, Almighty! (DRUMMOND *bows grandly. The crowd laughs.*)

BRADY. The Lord is my strength—

DRUMMOND. What if a lesser human being—a Cates, or a Darwin—has the audacity to think that God might whisper to *him*? That an un-Brady thought might still be holy? Must men go to prison because they are at odds with the self-appointed prophet? (BRADY *is now trembling so that it is impossible for him to speak. He rises, towering above his tormentor— rather like a clumsy, lumbering bear that is baited by an agile dog.*) Extend the Testaments! Let us have a Book of Brady! We shall hex the Pentateuch, and slip you in neatly between Numbers and Deuteronomy!

(*At this, there is another burst of laughter.* BRADY *is almost in a frenzy.*)

BRADY (*reaching for a sympathetic ear, trying to find the loyal audience which has slipped away from him*). My friends— Your Honor—My Followers—Ladies and Gentlemen—

DRUMMOND. The witness is excused.

BRADY (*unheeding*). All of you know what I stand for! What I believe! I believe, I believe in the truth of the Book of Genesis! (*Beginning to chant.*) Exodus, Leviticus, Numbers, Deuteronomy, Joshua, Judges, Ruth, First Samuel, Second Samuel, First Kings, Second Kings—

DRUMMOND. Your Honor, this completes the testimony. The witness is excused!

BRADY (*pounding the air with his fists*). Isaiah, Jeremiah, Lamentations, Ezekiel, Daniel, Hosea, Joel, Amos, Obadiah—

(*There is confusion in the court. The* JUDGE *raps.*)

JUDGE. You are excused, Colonel Brady—

BRADY. Jonah, Micah, Nahum, Habakkuk, Zephaniah— (BRADY *beats his clenched fists in the air with every name.*

There is a rising counterpoint of reaction from the spectators. Gavel.)

JUDGE (*over the confusion*). Court is adjourned until ten o'clock tomorrow morning!

(*Gavel. The spectators begin to mill about. A number of them, reporters and curiosity seekers, cluster around* DRUMMOND. DAVENPORT *follows the* JUDGE *out.*)

DAVENPORT. Your Honor, I want to speak to you about striking all of this from the record. (*They go out.*)

BRADY (*still erect on the witness stand*). Haggai, Zechariah, Malachi . . .

(*His voice trails off. He sinks, limp and exhausted into the witness chair.* MRS. BRADY *looks at her husband, worried and distraught. She looks at* DRUMMOND *with helpless anger.* DRUMMOND *moves out of the courtroom, and most of the crowd goes with him; reporters cluster tight about* DRUMMOND, *pads and pencils hard at work.* BRADY *sits, ignored, on the witness chair.* MEEKER *takes* CATES *back to the jail.* MRS. BRADY *goes to her husband, who still sits on the raised witness chair.*)

MRS. BRADY (*taking his hand*). Matt—

(BRADY *looks about to see if everyone has left the courtroom, before he speaks.*)

BRADY. Mother. They're laughing at me, Mother!

MRS. BRADY (*unconvincingly*). No, Matt. No, they're not!

BRADY. I can't stand it when they laugh at me!

(MRS. BRADY *steps up onto the raised level of the witness chair. She stands beside and behind her husband, putting her arms around the massive shoulders and cradling his head against her breast.*)

MRS. BRADY (*soothing*). It's all right, baby. It's all right. (MRS. BRADY *sways gently back and forth, as if rocking her husband to sleep.*) Baby . . . Baby . . . !

THE CURTAIN FALLS

ACT THREE

The courtroom, the following day. The lighting is low, somber. A spot burns down on the defense table, where DRUMMOND *and* CATES *sit, waiting for the jury to return.* DRUMMOND *leans back in a meditative mood, feet propped on a chair.* CATES, *the focus of the furor, is resting his head on his arms. The courtroom is almost empty. Two spectators doze in their chairs. In comparative shadow,* BRADY *sits, eating a box lunch. He is drowning his troubles with food, as an alcoholic escapes from reality with a straight shot.* HORNBECK *enters, bows low to* BRADY.

—

HORNBECK. Afternoon, Colonel. Having high tea, I see. (BRADY *ignores him.*) Is the jury still out? Swatting flies and wrestling with justice—in that order? (HORNBECK *crosses to* DRUMMOND. CATES *lifts his head.*) I'll hate to see the jury filing in; won't you, Colonel? I'll miss Hillsboro—especially this courthouse: a mélange of Moorish and Methodist; it must have been designed by a congressman. (HORNBECK *smirks at his own joke, then lies down in the shadows and pores over a newspaper. Neither* CATES *nor* DRUMMOND *have paid the slightest attention to him.*)

CATES (*staring straight ahead*). Mr. Drummond. What's going to happen?

DRUMMOND. What do you think is going to happen, Bert?

CATES. Do you think they'll send me to prison?

DRUMMOND. They could.

CATES. They don't ever let you see anybody from the outside, do they? I mean —you can just talk to a visitor—through a window—the way they show it in the movies?

DRUMMOND. Oh, it's not as bad as all that. (*Turning toward the town*) When they started this fire here, they never figured it would light up the whole sky. A lot of people's shoes are getting hot. But you can't be too sure.

(*At the other side of the stage,* BRADY *rises majestically from his debris of paper napkins and banana peels, and goes off.*)

CATES (*watching* BRADY *go off*). He seems so sure. He seems to know what the verdict's going to be.

DRUMMOND. Nobody knows. (*He tugs on one ear.*) I've got a pretty good idea. When you've been a lawyer as long as I have—a thousand years, more or less— you get so you can smell the way a jury's thinking.

CATES. What are they thinking right now?

DRUMMOND (*sighing*). Someday I'm going to get me an *easy* case. An open-and-shut case. I've got a friend up in Chicago. Big lawyer. Lord how the money rolls in! You know why? He never takes a case unless it's a sure thing. Like a jockey who won't go in a race unless he can ride the favorite.

CATES. You sure picked the long shot this time, Mr. Drummond.

DRUMMOND. Sometimes I think the law *is* like a horse race. Sometimes it seems to me I ride like fury, just to end up back where I started. Might as well be on a merry-go-round, or a rocking horse . . . or . . . (*He half-closes his eyes. His voice is far away, his lips barely move.*) Golden Dancer. . . .

CATES. What did you say?

DRUMMOND. That was the name of my first long shot. Golden Dancer. She was in the big side window of the general store in Wakeman, Ohio. I used to stand out in the street and say to myself, "If I had Golden Dancer I'd have everything in the world that I wanted." (*He cocks an eyebrow.*) I was seven years old, and a very fine judge of rocking horses. (*He looks off again into the distance.*) Golden Dancer had a bright red mane, blue eyes, and she was gold all over, with purple spots. When the sun hit her stirrups, she was a dazzling sight to see. But she was a week's wages for my father. So Golden Dancer and I always had a plate glass window between us. (*Reaching back for the memory*) But—let's see, it wasn't Christmas; must've been my birthday—I woke up in the morning and there was Golden Dancer at the foot of my bed! Ma had skimped on the groceries, and my father'd worked nights for a month. (*Reliving the moment*) I jumped into the saddle and started to rock—(*Almost a whisper*) And it *broke!* It split in two! The wood was rotten, the whole thing was put together with spit and sealing wax! All shine, and no substance! (*Turning to* CATES) Bert, whenever you see something bright, shining, perfect-seeming—all gold, with purple spots—look behind the paint! And if it's a lie—show it up for what it really is!

(*A* RADIO MAN *comes on, lugging an old-fashioned carbon microphone. The* JUDGE, *carrying his robe over his arm, comes on and scowls at the microphone.*)

RADIO MAN (*to* JUDGE). I think this is the best place to put it—if it's all right with you, Your Honor.

JUDGE. There's no precedent for this sort of thing.

RADIO MAN. You understand, sir, we're making history here today. This is the first time a public event has ever been broadcast.

JUDGE. Well, I'll allow it—provided you don't interfere with the business of the court.

(*The* RADIO MAN *starts to string his wires. The* MAYOR *hurries on, worried, brandishing a telegram.*)

MAYOR (*to* JUDGE). Merle, gotta talk to you. Over here. (*He draws the* JUDGE *aside, not wanting to be heard.*) This wire just came. The boys over at the state capitol are getting worried about how things are going. Newspapers all over are raising such a hullaballoo. After all, November ain't too far off, and it don't do any of us any good to have any of the voters gettin' all steamed up. Wouldn't do no harm to just let things simmer down. (*The* RADIO MAN *reappears.*) Well, go easy, Merle. (*Tipping his hat to* DRUMMOND, *the* MAYOR *hurries off.*)

RADIO MAN (*crisply, into the mike*). Testing. Testing.

(DRUMMOND *crosses to the microphone.*)

DRUMMOND (*to the* RADIO MAN). What's that?

RADIO MAN. An enunciator.

DRUMMOND. You going to broadcast?

RADIO MAN. We have a direct wire to WGN, Chicago. As soon as the jury comes in, we'll announce the verdict.

(DRUMMOND *takes a good look at the microphone, fingers the base.*)

DRUMMOND. Radio! God, this is going to break down a lot of walls.

RADIO MAN (*hastily*). You're—you're not supposed to say "God" on the radio!

DRUMMOND. Why the hell not?

(*The* RADIO MAN *looks at the microphone, as if it were a toddler that had just been told the facts of life.*)

RADIO MAN. You're not supposed to say "Hell," either.

DRUMMOND (*sauntering away*). *This* is going to be a barren source of amusement!

(BRADY *re-enters and crosses ponderously to the* RADIO MAN.)

BRADY. Can one speak into either side of this machine?

(*The* RADIO MAN *starts at this rumbling thunder, so close to the ear of his delicate child*.)

RADIO MAN (*in an exaggerated whisper*). Yes, sir. Either side.

(BRADY *attempts to lower his voice, but it is like putting a leash on an elephant.*)

BRADY. Kindly signal me while I am speaking, if my voice does not have sufficient projection for your radio apparatus.

(RADIO MAN *nods, a little annoyed.* HORNBECK *smirks, amused. Suddenly the air in the courtroom is charged with excitement.* MEEKER *hurries on—and the spectators begin to scurry expectantly back into the courtroom. Voices mutter: "They're comin' in now. Verdict's been reached. Jury's comin' back in."* MEEKER *crosses to the* JUDGE's *bench, reaches up for the gavel and raps it several times.*)

MEEKER. Everybody rise. (*The spectators come to attention.*) Hear ye, hear ye. Court will reconvene in the case of the State versus Bertram Cates. (MEEKER *crosses to lead in the jury. They enter, faces fixed and stern.*)

CATES (*whispers to* DRUMMOND). What do you think? Can you tell from their faces?

(DRUMMOND *is nervous, too. He squints at the returning jurors, drumming his fingers on the table top.* CATES *looks around, as if hoping to see* RACHEL—*but she is not there. His disappointment is evident. The* RADIO MAN *has received his signal from off stage, and he begins to speak into the microphone.*)

RADIO MAN (*low, with dramatic intensity*). Ladies and gentlemen, this is Harry Esterbrook, speaking to you from the courthouse in Hillsboro, where the jury is just returning to the courtroom to render its verdict in the famous Hillsboro Monkey Trial case. The Judge has just taken the bench. And in the next few minutes we shall know whether Bertram Cates will be found innocent or guilty.

(*The* JUDGE *looks at him with annoyance. Gingerly the* RADIO MAN *aims his microphone at the* JUDGE *and steps back. There is hushed tension all through the courtroom.*)

JUDGE (*clears his throat*). Gentlemen of the Jury, have you reached a decision?

SILLERS (*rising*). Yeah. Yes, sir, we have, Your Honor.

(MEEKER *crosses to* SILLERS *and takes a slip of paper from him. Silently, he crosses to the* JUDGE's *bench again, all eyes*

following the slip of paper. The JUDGE *takes it, opens it, raps his gavel.*)

JUDGE. The jury's decision is unanimous. Bertram Cates is found guilty as charged!

(*There is tremendous reaction in the courtroom. Some cheers, applause, "Amens." Some boos.* BRADY *is pleased. But it is not the beaming, powerful, assured* BRADY *of the Chautauqua tent. It is a spiteful, bitter victory for him, not a conquest with a cavalcade of angels.* CATES *stares at his lap.* DRUMMOND *taps a pencil. The* RADIO MAN *talks rapidly, softly into his microphone. The* JUDGE *does not attempt to control the reaction.*)

HORNBECK (*in the manner of a hawker or pitchman*). Step right up, and get your tickets for the Middle Ages! You only *thought* you missed the Coronation of Charlemagne!

JUDGE (*rapping his gavel, shouting over the noise*). Quiet, please! Order! This court is still in session. (*The noise quiets down.*) The prisoner will rise, to hear the sentence of this court. (DRUMMOND *looks up quizzically, alert.*) Bertram Cates, I hereby sentence you to—

DRUMMOND (*sharply*). Your Honor! A question of procedure!

JUDGE (*nettled*). Well, sir?

DRUMMOND. It is not customary in this state to allow the defendant to make a statement before sentence is passed?

(*The* JUDGE *is red-faced.*)

JUDGE. Colonel Drummond, I regret this omission. In the confusion, and the—I neglected— (*Up, to* CATES) Uh, Mr. Cates, if you wish to make any statement before sentence is passed on you, why, you may proceed. (*Clears throat again.* CATES *rises. The courtroom quickly grows silent again.*)

CATES (*simply*). Your Honor, I am not a public speaker. I do not have the eloquence of some of the people you have heard in the last few days. I'm just a schoolteacher.

MRS. BLAIR. Not any more you ain't!

CATES (*Pause. Quietly*). I *was* a schoolteacher. (*With difficulty*) I feel I am . . . I have been convicted of violating an unjust law. I will continue in the future, as I have in the past, to oppose this law in any way I can. I—

(CATES *isn't sure exactly what to say next. He hesitates, then sits down. There is a crack of applause. Not from every-*

*body, but from many of the spectators.
BRADY is fretful and disturbed. He's won
the case. The prize is his, but he can't
reach for the candy. In his hour of triumph, BRADY expected to be swept from
the courtroom on the shoulders of his ex-
ultant followers. But the drama isn't proceeding according to plan. The gavel
again. The court quiets down.)*

JUDGE. Bertram Cates, this court has
found you guilty of violating Public Act
Volume 37, Statute Number 31428, as
charged. This violation is punishable by
fine and/or imprisonment. (*He coughs.*)
But since there has been no previous violation of this statute, there is no precedent
to guide the bench in passing sentence.
(*He flashes the automatic smile.*) The
court deems it proper—(*He glances at the
MAYOR.*)—to sentence Bertram Cates to
pay a fine of—(*He coughs.*) one hundred
dollars.

(*The mighty Evolution Law explodes
with the pale puff of a wet firecracker.
There is a murmur of surprise through the
courtroom. BRADY is indignant. He rises,
incredulous.*)

BRADY. Did Your Honor say one hundred dollars?

JUDGE. That is correct. (*Trying to get it
over with*) This seems to conclude the
business of the trial—

BRADY (*thundering*). Your Honor, the
prosecution takes exception! Where the
issues are so titanic, the court must mete
out more drastic punishment—

DRUMMOND (*biting in*). I object!

BRADY. To make an example of this
transgressor! To show the world—

DRUMMOND. Just a minute. Just a minute. The amount of the fine is of no concern to me. Bertram Cates has no intention whatsoever of paying this or any
other fine. He would not pay it if it were
one single dollar. We will appeal this
decision to the Supreme Court of this
state. Will the court grant thirty days to
prepare our appeal?

JUDGE. Granted. The court fixes bond at
. . . five hundred dollars. I believe this
concludes the business of this trial. Therefore, I declare this court is adjour—

BRADY (*hastily*). Your Honor! (*He
reaches for a thick manuscript.*) Your
Honor, with the court's permission, I
should like to read into the record a few
short remarks which I have prepared—

DRUMMOND. I object to that. Mr. Brady
may make any remarks he likes—long,
short or otherwise. In a Chautauqua tent
or in a political campaign. Our business
in Hillsboro is completed. The defense
holds that the court shall be adjourned.

BRADY (*frustrated*). But I have a few
remarks—

JUDGE. And we are all anxious to hear
them, sir. But Colonel Drummond's point
of procedure is well taken. I am sure that
everyone here will wish to remain after
the court is adjourned to hear your address. (*BRADY lowers his head slightly, in
gracious deference to procedure. The
JUDGE raps the gavel.*) I hereby declare
this court is adjourned, sine die.

(*There is a babble of confusion and reaction. HORNBECK promptly crosses to
MEEKER and confers with him in whispers.
Spectators, relieved of the court's formality, take a seventh-inning stretch. Fans
pump, sticky clothes are plucked away
from the skin.*)

MELINDA (*calling to HOWARD, across the
courtroom*). Which side won?

HOWARD (*calling back*). I ain't sure. But
the whole thing's over!

(*A couple of HAWKERS slip in the courtroom with Eskimo Pies and buckets of
lemonade.*)

HAWKER. Eskimo Pies. Get your Eskimo
Pies!

(*JUDGE raps with his gavel.*)

JUDGE (*projecting*). Quiet! Order in the
—I mean, your attention, please. (*The
spectators quiet down some, but not completely.*) We are honored to hear a few
words from Colonel Brady, who wishes
to address you—

(*The JUDGE is interrupted in his introduction by MEEKER and HORNBECK. They
confer sotto voce. The babble of voices
crescendos.*)

HAWKER. Get your Eskimo Pies! Cool
off with an Eskimo Pie!

(*Spectators flock to get ice cream and
lemonade. BRADY preens himself for the
speech, but is annoyed by the confusion.
HORNBECK hands the JUDGE several bills
from his wallet, and MEEKER pencils a re-
ceipt. The JUDGE bangs the gavel again.*)

JUDGE. We beg your attention, please,
ladies and gentlemen! Colonel Brady has
some remarks to make which I am sure
will interest us all!

(*A few of the faithful fall dutifully si-*

lent. But the milling about and the slopping of lemonade continues. *Two kids chase each other in and out among the spectators, annoying the perspiring* RADIO MAN. BRADY *stretches out his arms, in the great attention-getting gesture.*)

BRADY. My dear friends . . . ! Your attention, please! (*The bugle voice reduces the noise somewhat further. But it is not the eager, anticipatory hush of olden days. Attention is given him, not as the inevitable due of a mighty monarch, but grudgingly and resentfully.*) Fellow citizens, and friends of the unseen audience. From the hallowed hills of sacred Sinai, in the days of remote antiquity, came the law which has been our bulwark and our shield. Age upon age, men have looked to the law as they would look to the mountains, whence cometh our strength. And here, here in this—

(*The* RADIO MAN *approaches* BRADY *nervously.*)

RADIO MAN. Excuse me, Mr.—uh, Colonel Brady; would you . . . uh . . . point more in the direction of the enunciator . . . ?

(*The* RADIO MAN *pushes* BRADY *bodily toward the microphone. As the orator is maneuvered into position, he seems almost to be an inanimate object, like a huge ornate vase which must be precisely centered on a mantel. In this momentary lull, the audience has slipped away from him again. There's a backwash of restless shifting and murmuring.* BRADY'S *vanity and cussedness won't let him give up, even though he realizes this is a sputtering anticlimax. By God, he'll make them listen!*)

BRADY (*red-faced, his larynx taut, roaring stridently*). As they would look to the mountains whence cometh our strength. And here, here in this courtroom, we have seen vindicated— (*A few people leave. He watches them desperately, out of the corner of his eye.*) We have seen vindicated—

RADIO MAN (*after an off-stage signal*). Ladies and gentlemen, our program director in Chicago advises us that our time here is completed. Harry Y. Esterbrook speaking. We return you now to our studios and "Matinee Musicale."

(*He takes the microphone and goes off. This is the final indignity to* BRADY; *he realizes that a great portion of his audience has left him as he watches it go.* BRADY *brandishes his speech, as if it were Excali-*bur. His eyes start from his head, the voice is a tight, frantic rasp.*)

BRADY. From the hallowed hills of sacred Sinai . . . (*He freezes. His lips move, but nothing comes out. Paradoxically, his silence brings silence. The orator can hold his audience only by not speaking.*)

STOREKEEPER. Look at him!

MRS. BRADY (*with terror*). Matt—

(*There seems to be some violent, volcanic upheaval within him. His lower lip quivers, his eyes stare. Very slowly, he seems to be leaning toward the audience. Then, like a figure in a waxworks, toppling from its pedestal, he falls stiffly, face forward.* MEEKER *and* DAVENPORT *spring forward, catch* BRADY *by the shoulders and break his fall. The sheaf of manuscript, clutched in his raised hand, scatters in mid air. The great words flutter innocuously to the courtroom floor. There is a burst of reaction.* MRS. BRADY *screams.*)

DAVENPORT. Get a doctor!

(*Several men lift the prostrate* BRADY, *and stretch him across three chairs.* MRS. BRADY *rushes to his side.*)

JUDGE. Room! Room! Give him room!

MRS. BRADY. Matt! Dear God in Heaven! Matt!

(DRUMMOND, HORNBECK *and* CATES *watch, silent and concerned—somewhat apart from the crowd. The silence is tense. It is suddenly broken by a frantic old* WOMAN, *who shoves her face close to* BRADY'S *and shrieks.*)

WOMAN (*wailing*). O Lord, work us a miracle and save our Holy Prophet!

(*Rudely,* MEEKER *pushes her back.*)

MEEKER (*contemptuously*). Get away! (*Crisply*) Move him out of here. Fast as we can. Hank. Bill. Give us a hand here. Get him across the street to Doc's office.

(*Several men lift* BRADY, *with difficulty, and begin to carry him out. A strange thing happens.* BRADY *begins to speak in a hollow, distant voice—as if something sealed up inside of him were finally broken, and the precious contents spilled out into the open at last.*)

BRADY (*as he is carried out; in a strange, unreal voice*). Mr. Chief Justice, Citizens of these United States. During my term in the White House, I pledge to carry out my program for the betterment of the common people of this country. As your new President, I say what I have said all of my life. . . .

(*The crowd tags along, curious and awed. Only* DRUMMOND, CATES *and* HORNBECK *remain, their eyes fixed on* BRADY'S *exit.* DRUMMOND *stares after him.*)

DRUMMOND. How quickly they can turn. And how painful it can be when you don't expect it. (*He turns.*) I wonder how it feels to be Almost-President three times—with a skull full of undelivered inauguration speeches.

HORNBECK. Something happens to an Also-Ran. Something happens to the feet of a man who always comes in second in a foot-race. He becomes a national unloved child, a balding orphan, an aging adolescent who never got the biggest piece of candy. Unloved children, of all ages, insinuate themselves into spotlights and rotogravures. They stand on their hands and wiggle their feet. Split pulpits with their pounding! And their tonsils turn to organ pipes. Show me a shouter and I'll show you an Also-Ran. A might-have-been. An almost-was.

CATES (*softly*). Did you see his face? He looked terrible. . . .

(MEEKER *enters.* CATES *turns to him.* MEEKER *shakes his head: "I don't know."*)

MEEKER. I'm surprised more folks ain't keeled over in this heat.

HORNBECK. He's all right. Give him an hour or so to sweat away the pickles and the pumpernickel; to let his tongue forget the acid taste of vinegar victory. Mount Brady will erupt again by nightfall, spouting lukewarm fire and irrelevant ashes.

(CATES *shakes his head, bewildered.* DRUMMOND *watches him, concerned.*)

DRUMMOND. What's the matter, boy?

CATES. I'm not sure. Did I win or did I lose?

DRUMMOND. You won.

CATES. But the jury found me—

DRUMMOND. What jury? Twelve men? Millions of people will say you won. They'll read in their papers tonight that you smashed a bad law. You made it a joke!

CATES. Yeah. But what's going to happen now? I haven't got a job. I'll bet they won't even let me back in the boarding house.

DRUMMOND. Sure, it's gonna be tough, it's not gonna be any church social for a while. But you'll live. And while they're making you sweat, remember—you've helped the next fella.

CATES. What do you mean?

DRUMMOND. You don't suppose this kind of thing is ever finished, do you? Tomorrow it'll be something else—and another fella will have to stand up. And you've helped give him the guts to do it!

CATES (*turning to* MEEKER, *with new pride in what he's done*). Mr. Meeker, don't you have to lock me up?

MEEKER. They fixed bail.

CATES. You don't expect a schoolteacher to have five hundred dollars.

MEEKER (*jerking his head toward* HORNBECK). This fella here put up the money.

HORNBECK. With a year's subscription to the Baltimore *Herald*, we give away—at no cost or obligation—a year of freedom.

(RACHEL *enters, carrying a suitcase. She is smiling, and there is a new lift to her head.* CATES *turns and sees her.*)

CATES. Rachel!

RACHEL. Hello, Bert.

CATES (*indicating her suitcase*). I won't need any more shirts. I'm free—for a while anyway.

RACHEL. These are *my* things, Bert. I'm going away.

CATES. Where are you going?

RACHEL. I'm not sure. But I'm leaving my father.

CATES. Rache . . .

RACHEL. Bert, it's my fault the jury found you guilty. (*He starts to protest.*) Partly my fault. I helped. (RACHEL *hands* BERT *a book.*) This is your book, Bert. (*Silently, he takes it.*) I've read it. All the way through. I don't understand it. What I do understand, I don't like. I don't want to think that men come from apes and monkeys. But I think that's beside the point.

(DRUMMOND *looks at the girl admiringly.*)

DRUMMOND. That's right. That's beside the point.

(RACHEL *crosses to* DRUMMOND.)

RACHEL. Mr. Drummond, I hope I haven't said anything to offend you. You see, I haven't really thought very much. I was always afraid of what I might think—so it seemed safer not to think at all. But now I know. A thought is like a child inside our body. It has to be born. If it dies inside you, part of you dies, too! (*Pointing to the book*) Maybe what Mr. Darwin wrote is bad. I don't know. Bad or good, it doesn't make any difference.

The ideas have to come out—like children. Some of 'em healthy as a bean plant, some sickly. I think the sickly ideas die mostly, don't you, Bert?

(BERT *nods yes, but he's too lost in new admiration for her to do anything but stare. He does not move to her side.* DRUMMOND *smiles, as if to say: "That's quite a girl!" The* JUDGE *walks in slowly.*)

JUDGE (*quietly*). Brady's dead. (*They all react. The* JUDGE *starts toward his chambers.*)

DRUMMOND. I can't imagine the world without Matthew Harrison Brady.

CATES (*to the* JUDGE). What caused it? Did they say?

(*Dazed, the* JUDGE *goes off without answering.*)

HORNBECK. Matthew Harrison Brady died of a busted belly.

(DRUMMOND *slams down his brief case.*)

HORNBECK. Be frank! Why should we weep for him? He cried enough for himself! The national tear duct from Weeping Water, Nebraska, who flooded the whole nation like a one-man Mississippi! You know what he was: a Barnum-bunkum Bible-beating bastard!

(DRUMMOND *rises, fiercely angry.*)

DRUMMOND. You smart-aleck! You have no more right to spit on his religion than you have a right to spit on *my* religion! Or my lack of it!

HORNBECK (*askance*). Well, what do you know! Henry Drummond for the defense —even of his enemies!

DRUMMOND (*low, moved*). There was much greatness in this man.

HORNBECK. Shall I put that in the obituary?

(DRUMMOND *starts to pack up his brief case.*)

DRUMMOND. Write anything you damn please.

HORNBECK. How do you write an obituary for a man who's been dead thirty years? "In Memoriam—M. H. B." Then what? Hail the apostle whose letters to the Corinthians were lost in the mail? Two years, ten years—and tourists will ask the guide, "Who died here? Matthew Harrison Who?" (*A sudden thought.*) What did he say to the minister? It fits! He delivered his own obituary! (HORNBECK *searches, finds the Bible on the* JUDGE's *bench.*) Here it is: his book! (*Thumbing hastily*) Proverbs, wasn't it?

DRUMMOND (*quietly*). "He that troubleth his own house shall inherit the wind: and the fool shall be servant to the wise in heart."

(HORNBECK *looks at* DRUMMOND, *surprised. He snaps the Bible shut, and lays it on the* JUDGE's *bench.* HORNBECK *folds his arms and crosses slowly toward* DRUMMOND, *his eyes narrowing.*)

HORNBECK. We're growing an odd crop of agnostics this year!

(DRUMMOND's *patience is wearing thin.*)

DRUMMOND (*evenly*). I'm getting damned tired of you, Hornbeck.

HORNBECK. Why?

DRUMMOND. You never pushed a noun against a verb except to blow up something.

HORNBECK. That's a typical lawyer's trick: accusing the accuser!

DRUMMOND. What am I accused of?

HORNBECK. I charge you with contempt of conscience! Self-perjury. Kindness aforethought! Sentimentality in the first degree.

DRUMMOND. Why? Because I refuse to erase a man's lifetime? I tell you Brady had the same right as Cates: the right to be wrong!

HORNBECK. "Be-Kind-To-Bigots" Week. Since Brady's dead, we must be kind. God, how the world is rotten with kindness!

DRUMMOND. A giant once lived in that body. (*Quietly*) But Matt Brady got lost. Because he was looking for God too high up and too far away.

HORNBECK. You hypocrite! You fraud! (*With a growing sense of discovery*) You're more religious than *he* was! (DRUMMOND *doesn't answer.* HORNBECK *crosses toward the exit hurriedly.*) Excuse me, gentlemen. I must get me to a typewriter and hammer out the story of an atheist—who believes in God! (*He goes off.*)

CATES. Colonel Drummond.

DRUMMOND. Bert, I am resigning my commission in the State Militia. I hand in my sword!

CATES. Doesn't it cost a lot of money for an appeal? I couldn't pay you . . .

(DRUMMOND *waves him off.*)

DRUMMOND. I didn't come here to be paid. (*He turns.*) Well, I'd better get myself on a train.

RACHEL. There's one out at five-thirteen. Bert, you and I can be on that train, too!

CATES (*smiling, happy*). I'll get my stuff!

RACHEL. I'll help you! (*They start off. RACHEL comes back for her suitcase. CATES grabs his suit jacket, clasps DRUMMOND's arm.*)

CATES (*calling over his shoulder*). See you at the depot! (*RACHEL and CATES go off. DRUMMOND is left alone on stage. Suddenly he notices RACHEL's copy of Darwin on the table.*)

DRUMMOND (*calling*). Say—you forgot—

(*But RACHEL and CATES are out of earshot. He weighs the volume in his hand;* this one book has been the center of the whirlwind. Then DRUMMOND notices the Bible, on the JUDGE's bench. He picks up the Bible in his other hand; he looks from one volume to the other, balancing them thoughtfully, as if his hands were scales. He half-smiles, half-shrugs. Then DRUMMOND slaps the two books together and jams them in his brief case, side by side. Slowly, he climbs to the street level and crosses the empty square.*)

THE CURTAIN FALLS

THE CAINE MUTINY

COURT-MARTIAL

Herman Wouk

First presented by Paul Gregory in the Granada Theatre,
Santa Barbara, California, on October 12, 1953. After
a tour across the United States it opened in New York at the
Plymouth Theatre on January 20, 1954, with
the same cast, as follows:

LT. STEPHEN MARYK   John Hodiak
LT. BARNEY GREENWALD   Henry Fonda
LT. COM. JOHN CHALLEE   Ainslie Pryor
CAPTAIN BLAKELY   Russell Hicks
LT. COM. PHILIP FRANCIS QUEEG
          Lloyd Nolan
LT. THOMAS KEEFER   Robert Gist
SIGNALMAN THIRD CLASS JUNIUS URBAN
          Eddie Firestone

LT. (JR. GRADE) WILLIS SEWARD KEITH
          Charles Nolte
CAPT. RANDOLPH SOUTHARD   Paul Birch
DR. FORREST LUNDEEN   Stephen Chase
DR. BIRD   Herbert Anderson
STENOGRAPHER   John Huffman
ORDERLY   Greg Roman
MEMBERS OF THE COURT*   Larry Barton,
Jim Bumgarner, T. H. Jourdan, Richard
Farmer, Richard Norris, Pat Waltz

The time of the play is February 1945. The scene is the General
Court-Martial Room of the Twelfth Naval District, San
Francisco. At the end of Act 2 the scene shifts to a banquet room
in the Hotel Fairmont, San Francisco.

ACT ONE: The Prosecution.

ACT TWO: The Defense.

NOTE: THE CAINE MUTINY COURT-MARTIAL is purely imaginary. No ship named
U.S.S. *Caine* ever existed. The records show no instance of a U.S. Navy captain relieved
at sea under Articles 184-186. The fictitious figure of the deposed captain was derived from a
study of psychoneurotic case histories, and is not a portrait of a real military person or
a type; this statement is made because of the existing tendency to seek lampoons of living
people in imaginary stories. The author served under two captains of the regular Navy aboard
destroyer-minesweepers, both of whom were decorated for valor. One technical note:
court-martial regulations have been extensively revised since the Second World War. This trial
takes place according to instructions then in force. Certain minor omissions have been
made for purposes of brevity; otherwise the play strictly follows procedures
stipulated in *Naval Courts and Boards*.

* Taken from second-night program.

INTRODUCTION

The Caine Mutiny Court-Martial was extracted by Herman Wouk from his very successful novel *The Caine Mutiny,* his third published book, which won the Pulitzer Prize in 1951. Herman Wouk, born in New York City in 1915, and educated at Columbia College where he was a favorite pupil of the late philosopher and wit Irwin Edman, served four years in the Navy during World War II. He ended up as the executive officer of a destroyer-minesweeper. Prior to composing his *Caine Mutiny* drama in 1954, Mr. Wouk wrote a provocative melodrama about a scientist-traitor, *The Traitor,* which had a short run on Broadway in 1949.

Even a critic disposed to question the validity of *The Caine Mutiny Court-Martial* as a drama of real depth must acknowledge the exceptional efficiency of the action and the theatrical force and ingenuity of the writing. One thinks of such canny twists of drama as Greenwald's winning a case he did not want to take on, Commander Queeg's starting out as Lieutenant Maryk's accuser and ending up as the accused, and Greenwald's turning on the cheap-jack writer Keefer after scoring his courtroom victory. Although essentially a novelist, Mr. Wouk proved himself a first-rate theatrician. It is true that in his eagerness to discharge the United States Navy of any blame he did switch his signals at the end of the play. But even that maneuver was theatrically effective; in giving an extra fillip of interest to the play, it was a good maneuver. And Mr. Wouk had made some preparation for it in Greenwald's reluctance to serve as attorney for the defense and his early declaration, "Maryk, I'd rather be prosecuting you than defending you." For some reviewers the second scene of the final act was an additional *tour de force* rather than anticlimax: Said Walter Kerr in the *New York Herald Tribune* of January 22, 1954: *"The Caine Mutiny Court-Martial* is a theatrical adventure which builds a second-act climax of such hair-raising intensity that you are sure nothing, and no one, can ever top it. Someone then proceeds to top it."

FROM THE NAVY REGULATIONS:

ARTICLE 184. *Unusual circumstances.* It is conceivable that most unusual and extraordinary circumstances may arise in which the relief from duty of a commanding officer by a subordinate becomes necessary, either by placing him under arrest or on the sick list; but such action shall never be taken without the approval of the Navy Department or other appropriate higher authority, except when reference to such higher authority is undoubtedly impracticable because of the delay involved or for other clearly obvious reason. Such reference must set forth all facts in the case, and the reasons for the recommendation, with particular regard to the degree of urgency involved.

ARTICLE 185. *Conditions to fulfill.* In order that a subordinate officer, acting upon his own initiative, may be vindicated for relieving a commanding officer from duty, the situation must be obvious and clear, and must admit of the single conclusion that the retention of command by such commanding officer will seriously and irretrievably prejudice the public interests. The subordinate officer so acting must be next in lawful succession to command; must be unable to refer the matter to a common superior for one of the reasons set down in Article 184; must be certain that the prejudicial actions of his commanding officer are not caused by secret instructions unknown to the subordinate; must have given the matter such careful consideration, and must have made such exhaustive investigation of all the circumstances, as may be practicable; and finally must be thoroughly convinced that the conclusion to relieve his commanding officer is one which a reasonable, prudent, and experienced officer would regard as a necessary consequence from the facts thus determined to exist.

ARTICLE 186. *Responsibility.* Intelligently fearless initiative is an important trait of military character, and it is not the purpose to discourage its employment in cases of this nature. However, as the action of relieving a superior from command involves most serious possibilities, a decision so to do or so to recommend should be based upon facts established by substantial evidence, and upon the official views of others in a position to form valuable opinions, particularly of a technical character. An officer relieving his commanding officer or recommending such action together with all others who so counsel, must bear the legitimate responsibility for, and must be prepared to justify, such action.

ACT ONE

THE PROSECUTION

THE SCENE: *The curtain is up when the audience enters the theater. Dimly visible is a gray-draped stage barren except for the chairs, tables, and witness box of a court-martial. The big raised curved judge's bench, Stage Right, is covered with green baize, and behind it on the draperies is a large American flag. Upstage Left is* LIEUTENANT COMMANDER CHALLEE's *desk. Next to his desk, placed out of the way, is* GREENWALD's *desk, with two chairs placed on top. Behind, Upstage, is the witness stand: a chair on a raised round platform which rolls on casters. There is a chair for the* ORDERLY, *Stage Center, by the end of the judge's bench, and a chair and small desk for the* STENOGRAPHER, *Downstage Right, below* CAPTAIN BLAKELY's *place on the bench. The single entrance to the stage is through the curtains, deep Center Stage.*

The start of the play is marked by the dimming of the house lights and the brightening of the stage. The ORDERLY *and* STENOGRAPHER, *two sailors in dress blues, enter. They pick up* GREENWALD's *desk and chairs, carry them Downstage Left, and put the chairs in place.* GREENWALD *enters, and as the* ORDERLY *and* STENOGRAPHER *roll the witness stand into place, Center Stage, he puts his brief case down on his desk. Exit the two sailors.* GREENWALD, *a lanky lieutenant in a green flier's uniform with wings and campaign ribbons, strolls to the witness stand. His face is stern and abstracted. He stares at the stand for a few moments, then leans his elbows on the arms of the chair and puts his hand to his face. Enter* MARYK, *a big, powerfully built lieutenant in blues, with close-cropped hair. He comes down to the other side of the witness stand and peers at* GREENWALD *for a moment.*

———

MARYK (*bursting out*). What are they

doing out there? This is a hell of a long recess. This is the longest recess yet.

GREENWALD. I've seen longer.

MARYK. I thought the trial would be over by now. All they do is swear in somebody, recess, look at a paper, recess, look at another paper, recess, mumble some legal words, recess some more—when does the court-martial start?

GREENWALD. Maryk, take it easy. It's going to be a long trial.

MARYK. But you won't tell me what you're doing, how you're going to conduct my case, what I'm supposed to say—nothing.

GREENWALD. It would only confuse you.

MARYK. I couldn't be more confused than I am.

GREENWALD. Well, you've got something there.

MARYK. I don't like the way you're handling me.

GREENWALD. Good. That makes us even.

MARYK. How's that?

GREENWALD. I don't like handling you.

MARYK. What? Well, then, maybe I'd better—

GREENWALD (*crossing to desk and taking papers from brief case*). Maryk, I'd rather be prosecuting you than defending you. I told you that the first time we met. Nevertheless, I'm defending you. If it's humanly possible to win an acquittal in this case I'm going to win you an acquittal. If you want a prediction, I believe I'm going to get you off. But you can't help me. So just leave me be.

MARYK. You're a damn peculiar fish.

GREENWALD. My mother thinks I'm beautiful.

MARYK. That's a hell of a thing to say, you know.

GREENWALD. What?

MARYK. You'd rather be prosecuting me than defending me. How d'you suppose that makes me feel?

GREENWALD (*looks at him, crosses to him*). You're nervous.

MARYK. Sure I am.

GREENWALD. I am too, a bit. Sorry.

MARYK. I can ask the court for a different counsel.

GREENWALD. Forget it. I don't take on a case to lose it.

MARYK. You do think I was right to relieve Captain Queeg?

GREENWALD. I can't say that.

MARYK. After everything I told you, you still don't think he was nuts?

GREENWALD. No, I don't.

MARYK. Then I get hung.

GREENWALD. Not necessarily.

MARYK. Maybe I should plead guilty. Eight legal officers advised me to plead guilty. The court would go easy on me—

GREENWALD. I don't care if every legal officer in the Navy says otherwise. I think I can get you off.

MARYK. I'll get all fouled up.

GREENWALD. You'll do nobly. You may come out of this a great naval hero.

MARYK (*stares at him*). Greenwald, is there something eating you?

GREENWALD. I don't know. (*Paces in silence for a moment. Halts.*) I'm a damn good lawyer, Maryk, and I'm a pretty poor flier. Took quite a shellacking at flight school from snotty ensign instructors four or five years younger than me. I didn't like it. Baby-faced kids couldn't do such things to Greenwald the hot-shot lawyer. I used to daydream about a court-martial coming up on that base. And some poor joe would need defending. And I'd step in, and take over, and twist the Navy's arm, and make it holler Uncle. Now—here's my dream come true. You know something? I don't look forward to twisting the Navy's arm. Not one bit.

MARYK. Scared of the brass, eh?

GREENWALD. Worse.

MARYK. What?

GREENWALD. Respectful.

MARYK. Listen, I put in for transfer to the regulars. I respect the Navy too.

GREENWALD. Maryk, they took us in naked. Just a lot of pink forked animals with belly buttons. And they worked us over, and kicked us around, and put us through a bunch of silly rituals, and stuffed us full of the dullest bloody books in the world, and slapped funny uniforms on us. And there we were all of a sudden with big flaming machines in our hands, sinking U-boats and shooting down Zeros. A lot of guys take it in stride. Me, it's sort of turned all my old ideas wrong side out. And this is a war that sure needs winning, for my dough.

MARYK. Well, I don't go along with you all the way.

GREENWALD. You don't.

MARYK. There's still a big pile of foolishness connected with the Navy. In fact—I sometimes think the Navy is a master plan designed by geniuses for execution by idiots.

GREENWALD (*startled*). You think what?

MARYK (*self-conscious*). The Navy is a master plan designed by genuises for execution by idiots.

GREENWALD. Where'd you hear that?

MARYK (*injured*). Couldn't I just have made it up?

GREENWALD. You could just have made up the Gettysburg Address, too. Where'd you hear it?

MARYK (*grins reluctantly*). Well, matter of fact, it's one of Tom Keefer's favorite cracks.

GREENWALD (*nods*). Ah yes. You echo your novelist friend quite a bit, don't you?

MARYK. Tom's got the keenest mind on the ship. About the keenest I've ever run into.

GREENWALD. He's keen, all right.

MARYK. I'm sure glad Tom is going to testify.

GREENWALD. You are?

MARYK. Hell! He knows everything Captain Queeg did. He knows psychiatry. I'm a stoop about those things. I'll foul myself up. Tom Keefer can tell the thing straight.

GREENWALD. If I had my way, Lieutenant Thomas Keefer would never appear in this court.

MARYK. What?

GREENWALD. He's not going to do you any good on the witness stand, Maryk, you mark my word. One man I'd really enjoy prosecuting is Mister Thomas Keefer, the eminent novelist.

MARYK. Greenwald, you're not to go pinning anything on Tom Keefer . . . It was my responsibility—

GREENWALD. That's right. You did what you did. (*Enter the six* COURT MEMBERS, *the* STENOGRAPHER, *and the* ORDERLY, *who take their places.*) Well, here we go . . . It's better you did it out of your own noble judgment than that you took the advice of a sensitive novelist. (CHALLEE *enters, and crosses to his desk. Puts his brief case down, looks to the entrance.*)

CHALLEE. Attention!

(*All stand to attention as* CAPTAIN BLAKELY *enters and goes to his place in silence. All officers are in dress blues; so are all witnesses in the trial.*)

BLAKELY. We're spending excessive time in all these recesses. (*He rings his desk bell. All sit.*) I appreciate the judge advocate's desire to have the record letter-perfect. But let's get on with the case and hereafter keep technicalities to a minimum.

CHALLEE. Aye aye, sir.

BLAKELY (*holds out paper to* CHALLEE). Court finds the charge and specification in due form and technically correct. Is the accused ready for trial?

(GREENWALD *motions to* MARYK *to rise.* MARYK *rises.*)

MARYK. Yes, sir.

(BLAKELY *nods to* CHALLEE, *who reads from the paper.*)

CHALLEE. "Charge. Conduct to the prejudice of good order and discipline. Specification. In that Lieutenant Stephen Maryk, U.S.N.R., on or about 18 December, 1944, aboard the U.S.S. *Caine,* willfully, without proper authority, and without justifiable cause, did relieve from his duty as commanding officer Lieutenant Commander Philip Francis Queeg, U.S.N., the duly assigned commanding officer of said ship, who was then and there in lawful exercise of his command, the United States then being in a state of war." . . . Stephen Maryk, Lieutenant, United States Naval Reserve, you have heard the charge and specification preferred against you; how say you, guilty or not guilty?

MARYK. Not guilty.

GREENWALD (*rises*). Accused admits he is Lieutenant Stephen Maryk, U.S.N.R., and that he was the executive officer of the U.S.S. *Caine* on December 18, 1944.

MARYK (*haltingly*). The admission is made with my authority.

BLAKELY. Judge advocate, present your case.

CHALLEE (*to* ORDERLY). Call Lieutenant Commander Queeg.

(*Exit* ORDERLY. *He returns in a moment with* QUEEG, *who is tanned, natty, erect, the picture of a correct naval officer. He is a short man in his thirties with scanty hair.* CHALLEE *holds a Bible for him. He places left hand on it and raises right hand.*)

BLAKELY (*stands, raises his right hand*). You do solemnly swear that the evidence you shall give in this court shall be the truth, the whole truth, and nothing but the truth, so help you God.

QUEEG. I do.

CHALLEE. State your name, rank, and present position.

QUEEG. Philip Francis Queeg, Lieutenant

Commander, United States Navy, temporarily assigned to Commandant, Twelfth Naval District, awaiting reassignment by BuPers.

CHALLEE. If you recognize the accused, state as whom.

QUEEG (*glancing briefly at* MARYK). Lieutenant Stephen Maryk, U.S.N.R.

CHALLEE. Commander Queeg, on December 18, 1944, were you in command of the U.S.S. *Caine?*

QUEEG. I was.

CHALLEE. What type of vessel is the *Caine?*

QUEEG. Her official designation is high-speed minesweeper. What she is, is a four-piper, one of those flush-deck twelve-hundred-ton destroyers from World War I, fixed up with minesweeping gear.

CHALLEE. An old ship, then?

QUEEG. I guess about the oldest type still doing combatant duty.

CHALLEE. What is her primary mission?

QUEEG (*smiling*). That's a hard one. These old buckets are regarded as pretty expendable. By and large we were doing the usual destroyer duty—anti-submarine screening—also ran the mail, transported marines, carried aviation gas and torpedoes, gave fire support in minor landings, or what have you? Also swept mines now and then.

CHALLEE. Commander, on December 18, 1944, were you relieved of command of the *Caine?*

QUEEG (*slight pause*). Yes.

CHALLEE. By whom?

QUEEG. By the accused.

CHALLEE. Was this a regular relief?

QUEEG. It was totally irregular, sir.

CHALLEE. How would you describe it?

QUEEG. Well, the most charitable description would be that it was an incident, a regrettable incident of temporary and total collapse of military discipline.

CHALLEE. Commander, please relate all the facts that bear on this unauthorized relief.

QUEEG. Kay, I'll try to do this consecutively, here. The *Caine* sortied from Ulithi Atoll on the sixteenth of December, I believe, the fifteenth or the sixteenth. We were a screening vessel with a group of fleet oilers. Our mission was to rendezvous with and refuel Admiral Halsey's fast carrier force in the Philippine Sea. Kay. Well, we made the rendezvous. And then this typhoon came along. The fueling was broken off and the fleet began to maneuver to evade the storm. Now, the storm was traveling due west—(*Gestures with hands.*) —so Admiral Halsey set fleet course due south and we began to make a run for the safe semi-circle.

CHALLEE. What was the date and time of that course change?

QUEEG. That would be early morning of the eighteenth, sir. Well, as I say, the storm was pretty bad at this point. Visibility was almost zero. Couldn't see the guide or even the next ship in the screen, we were just steaming blindly through rain and spray. And of course with the wind and sea and all, we had to maneuver pretty smartly with engines and rudder to hold fleet course and speed. But we were doing fine. My executive officer, however, pretty early in the game began to show unusual symptoms of nervousness. And I had to—

CHALLEE. What were these symptoms of nervousness?

QUEEG. Well, for instance, he began talking very early—oh, it couldn't have been half an hour after the fleet started to run south—that we should operate independently and come around north.

CHALLEE. Why did he want to do that?

QUEEG (*with illustrative gestures*). Well, to give you the picture on that—you see the typhoon was coming at us from the east. We were on the western edge of it. Now as you know these blows spin counterclockwise above the equator. That means where we were the wind was from due north. Admiral Halsey, of course, was running south with the wind, to get out of the storm's path. Now that's in accordance with all existing storm doctrine from Bowditch on up. But my exec insisted that the ship was on the verge of foundering, and we'd better come around and head into the wind—that is, north—if we were to survive. Of course we weren't in any such bad shape at all. And that's what I mean by nervousness.

CHALLEE. What was your objection to coming north, as the executive officer suggested?

QUEEG. Why, everything was wrong with that idea that could be wrong with it, sir. In the first place my orders were to proceed south. My mission was screening. My ship was in no danger and was functioning normally. Why to drop out of station and act independently under those conditions was unthinkable. Coming around to north would have headed the ship directly into the heart of the typhoon. It was not only a senseless suggestion in the circumstances, it was almost suicidal. I might add that I've since checked my decisions of December eighteenth with the finest ship handlers I know up to the rank of rear admiral, and they've unanimously agreed that the only course in that situation was south.

(CHALLEE *glances at* GREENWALD. *He is doodling obliviously.* CHALLEE *hesitates.*)

CHALLEE. Commander, your last remark was hearsay evidence. That is not acceptable.

QUEEG. Oh. I'm sorry, sir. I'm not up on those legal distinctions as much as I should be, I guess.

CHALLEE. Perfectly all right.

(CHALLEE *and* BLAKELY *stare at* GREENWALD.)

BLAKELY. Will defense counsel move to strike out that part of the testimony which was hearsay evidence?

GREENWALD (*half rises*). All right, sir. I so move. (*Sits.*)

CHALLEE. No objection.

(BLAKELY, *with a disgusted look at* GREENWALD, *turns to* STENOGRAPHER.)

BLAKELY. Strike out the last sentence.

CHALLEE. A ship-handling expert will be called, Commander, to testify on that point.

QUEEG. I see. I'm very glad to know that, sir. Thank you.

CHALLEE. Proceed with your description of the relief.

QUEEG. Kay . . . Well, it was just that Maryk kept insisting on coming north, more and more stridently as the weather deteriorated. Finally I began to be a little concerned about him. Then suddenly he walked up to me out of a clear sky, and told me I was on the sick list and he was relieving me. To be honest, I couldn't believe my ears, and was a little slow in catching on. It was only when he started shouting orders at the officer of the deck and countermanding my instructions to the helm that I began to realize what was going on.

CHALLEE. Commander, can you recall anything in your own bearing or manner that could have provoked your executive officer's act?

QUEEG. Well—truthfully, sir, I cannot. Frankly, I don't think my bearing or manner had anything to do with it. It was a pretty scary situation in the wheelhouse. The wind was force 10 to 12, screeching and all that, the waves were mountainous. The barometer was about as low as it's ever been in the U. S. Navy history. We took one very bad roll—and I mean a bad one, and I've done a lot of North Atlantic rolling, too—and I think Maryk simply went into panic.

CHALLEE. Was the *Caine* in grave danger at that moment?

QUEEG. I wouldn't say that—no sir. We righted very nicely from that bad roll. He repeatedly tried to order me off the bridge, but I stayed right where I was. I gave him orders only when it seemed necessary for the safety of the ship. In the situation I thought the chief hazard was any further acts of frenzy on his part. And to the extent that the *Caine* did come safely through the storm despite this unprecedented running amuck of my executive officer, I believe my handling of the emergency was the correct one.

CHALLEE. Did Maryk cite any authority at all when he relieved you?

QUEEG. He mumbled something about Article 184. I didn't even catch it at the time. Later he said his authority was Articles 184, 185, and 186 of the Naval Regulations.

CHALLEE. Are you familiar with those articles?

QUEEG. Certainly.

CHALLEE. In substance, what do they provide?

QUEEG. Well, as I understand it, they make it possible for an executive officer to take over in an emergency, a highly unusual emergency where the captain is— well, frankly, where the captain's gone absolutely and hopelessly loony.

CHALLEE. Were those articles properly invoked in your situation?

QUEEG (*smiling wryly*). Well, I'm sort of an interested party here. But you won't have to take my word for it. I was successfully conning my ship through a typhoon. Fortunately there are a hundred thirty witnesses to that fact, every man who was aboard that ship.

CHALLEE (*glancing toward* GREENWALD). There again, sir, you're testifying to the conclusions of others.

QUEEG (*smiling*). Sorry. I'm obviously no legal expert. I'll withdraw that last sentence. (*With a glance at* BLAKELY.)

(BLAKELY *glances annoyed at* GREENWALD, *who seems to be paying no attention, doodling on a scratch pad.*)

BLAKELY (*to* STENOGRAPHER). Strike the last sentence of the answer from the record.

CHALLEE. Have you ever been mentally ill, sir?

QUEEG. No, sir.

CHALLEE. Were you ill in any way when Mister Maryk relieved you?

QUEEG. I was not.

CHALLEE. Did you warn your executive officer of the consequences of his act?

QUEEG. I told him he was performing a mutinous act.

CHALLEE. What was his reply?

QUEEG. That he expected to be court-martialed, but was going to retain command anyway.

CHALLEE. What was the attitude of Lieutenant Junior Grade Keith, the officer of the deck?

QUEEG. He was in a state of panic as bad as Maryk's.

CHALLEE. What was the attitude of the helmsman?

QUEEG. Stilwell was emotionally unbalanced, and for some reason was very devoted to Mister Keith. They both backed up Maryk.

CHALLEE (*glances at the court*). Is there anything else, Commander Queeg, that you care to state in connection with the events of 18 December aboard the *Caine*?

QUEEG. Well, I have thought a lot about it all, of course. It's the gravest occurrence in my career, and the only questionable one that I'm aware of. It was an unfortunate freak accident. If the OOD had been anyone but this immature Keith, and the helmsman anyone but Stilwell, I don't think it would have happened. A competent officer of the deck would have repudiated Maryk's orders and a normal sailor at the helm would have disregarded both officers and obeyed me. It was just bad luck that those three men—Maryk, Keith, and Stilwell—were combined against me at a crucial time. Bad luck for me, and I'm afraid worse luck for them.

(MARYK *writes a note to* GREENWALD, *who glances at it negligently, shakes his head, and tears it up.*)

BLAKELY. The court would like to question the witness. Commander Queeg, you have taken all the prescribed physical and mental examinations incident to entrance to the Academy, graduation, commissioning, promotion, and so forth?

QUEEG. Yes, sir, for fourteen years.

BLAKELY. Does your medical record contain any history of illness, mental or physical?

QUEEG. It does not, sir. My tonsils were removed in the fall of 1938.

BLAKELY. Have you ever had an unsatisfactory fitness report, Commander Queeg?

QUEEG. Negative, sir. I have one letter of commendation in my jacket.

BLAKELY. Now, Commander, can you account for Lieutenant Maryk's opinion that you were mentally ill?

QUEEG (*smiling*). Well—that's rather a tough one, sir.

BLAKELY. I appreciate that, but it might be helpful.

QUEEG. Well, sir, I'll have to say that I assumed command of an extremely disorganized and dirty ship. Now that's no reflection on the officer I relieved. The *Caine* had had a year and a half of the most arduous combat duty, and it was understandable. Still, the safety of that ship and its crew demanded its being brought up to snuff. I took many stern measures. Lieutenant Maryk, I may say, from the first, didn't see eye to eye with me at all on this idea of making the *Caine* a taut ship again. Maybe he thought I was crazy to keep trying. I guess that's the picture, sir.

CHALLEE. No more questions. (*He goes back to his desk.* GREENWALD *rises and approaches* QUEEG.)

GREENWALD. Commander Queeg, I should like to ask you whether you have ever heard the expression, "Old Yellowstain."

QUEEG (*looking genuinely puzzled*). In what connection?

GREENWALD. In any connection.

QUEEG. Old Yellowstone?

GREENWALD. Old Yellowstain, sir.

QUEEG. I have not.

GREENWALD. You aren't aware, then, that all the officers of the *Caine* habitually referred to you as Old Yellowstain?

CHALLEE (*jumping to his feet*). I object to the question! It is impertinent badgering of the witness.

BLAKELY (*frostily*). How does defense

counsel Greenwald justify this line of questioning?

GREENWALD. If the court please, the nickname, "Old Yellowstain," used by the officers of the *Caine,* will be relevant to the issue of mental competence.

BLAKELY (*staring very hard at* GREENWALD). Before ruling, the court wishes to caution defense counsel. This is a most unusual and delicate case. The honor and career of an officer with an unblemished military record of fourteen years' standing is involved. The defense counsel will have to bear full responsibility for the conduct of his case. (*Pause.*) Subject to the foregoing comment, the judge advocate's objection is overruled. Court stenographer will repeat the question.

STENOGRAPHER (*tonelessly*). "You aren't aware, then, that all the officers of the *Caine* habitually referred to you as Old Yellowstain?"

QUEEG. I am not aware of it.

GREENWALD. No further questions at this time.

BLAKELY. Is that the extent of your cross-examination, Lieutenant Greenwald?

GREENWALD. Commander Queeg will be called as a witness for the defense, sir.

BLAKELY. For the *defense?*

GREENWALD. Yes, sir.

(BLAKELY *stares, shrugs, turns to* CHALLEE, *who shakes his head.*)

BLAKELY (*to* QUEEG). Commander, you'll refrain from conversing with any person whatsoever concerning the details of your testimony today.

QUEEG. Aye aye, sir.

BLAKELY. You're excused, and thank you.

QUEEG. Thank you, Captain. (QUEEG *goes out.* ORDERLY *stands to attention.* JUDGES *all write notes.*)

CHALLEE. Call Lieutenant Thomas Keefer.

(*Exit* ORDERLY. KEEFER *enters, a tall, clever-looking officer, crosses down to* CHALLEE. *Puts hand on Bible.*)

BLAKELY. You do solemnly swear that the evidence you shall give in this court shall be the truth, the whole truth, and nothing but the truth. So help you God.

KEEFER. I do so swear. (KEEFER *takes witness stand.* ORDERLY *re-enters, sits in his chair Upstage.*)

CHALLEE. State your name, rank, and present station.

KEEFER. Thomas Keefer, Lieutenant, U.S.N.R., communication officer of the U.S.S. *Caine.*

CHALLEE. If you recognize the accused, state as whom.

KEEFER. Steve Maryk, Lieutenant Stephen Maryk, executive officer of the *Caine.*

CHALLEE. What is your occupation in civilian life?

KEEFER. I'm a writer.

(GREENWALD *turns, looks at* KEEFER.)

CHALLEE. And has your work been published?

KEEFER. A number of my short stories have been published, yes, sir. (*To the court:*) In national magazines.

CHALLEE. Have you done any writing in your spare time while in service?

KEEFER. Yes, I've completed half a war novel.

CHALLEE. What is the title?

KEEFER. *Multitudes, Multitudes.*

BLAKELY. What was that?

KEEFER. *Multitudes, Multitudes,* sir.

BLAKELY. Oh. Thank you. (*Makes a note.*)

CHALLEE. And has this novel, *Multitudes, Multitudes,* though incomplete, recently been accepted by a New York publisher?

KEEFER (*a little puzzled*). Yes.

CHALLEE. I'm asking these questions to establish your reliability as an observer of personalities.

KEEFER. I understand, sir.

CHALLEE. Now, Lieutenant Keefer, were you serving aboard the *Caine* in your present capacity on December 18, 1944?

KEEFER. Yes, sir.

CHALLEE. Was Captain Queeg relieved of command on that date?

KEEFER. He was, sir.

CHALLEE. By whom?

KEEFER. The accused.

CHALLEE. Describe how you learned that the captain had been relieved.

KEEFER. Well, Mister Maryk passed the word over the loudspeakers for all officers to lay up to the wheelhouse. When we got there he told us that the captain was sick and he had assumed command.

CHALLEE. Did Captain Queeg show any external signs of being sick?

(KEEFER *shifts in his seat and encounters* MARYK's *painfully intense glance.*)

KEEFER. Well, at the height of a typhoon nobody aboard a four-piper looks very well . . .

(MARYK *reacts;* GREENWALD *writes a note.*)

CHALLEE. Was he raving, or foaming?

KEEFER. No.

CHALLEE. Did he look any worse than, say, Lieutenant Keith?

KEEFER. No, sir.

CHALLEE. Or Maryk?

KEEFER. We were all tired, dripping, and knocked out.

(MARYK *starts to move,* GREENWALD *passes him the note.* MARYK *turns away from* KEEFER.)

CHALLEE. Mister Keefer, did you make any effort to persuade Maryk to restore Queeg to command?

KEEFER. I did not.

CHALLEE. Didn't you feel the seriousness of the situation?

KEEFER. I certainly did, sir.

CHALLEE. Why did you take no remedial action?

KEEFER. I wasn't present when the captain was relieved. Maryk was in full command. The entire ship was obeying his orders. I decided that for the safety of the ship my best course was to obey his orders. That was what I did.

CHALLEE. Mister Keefer, were you aboard the *Caine* throughout the period when Captain Queeg was in command?

KEEFER. Yes.

CHALLEE. Did you ever observe any evidences of insanity in him?

(KEEFER *hesitates.* GREENWALD *turns in chair, looks at* KEEFER. MARYK *stretches his arms out in tension.*)

KEEFER. I don't—I can't answer that question, not being a psychiatrist.

(GREENWALD *puts his hand on* MARYK's *arm.* MARYK *pulls away.*)

CHALLEE. Well, surely now, Mister Keefer, as a writer you're certainly not wholly ignorant of such matters.

KEEFER (*leans back in witness chair*). Well, I hope not wholly ignorant—no, sir.

CHALLEE. What, for instance, is the Rorschach Test?

KEEFER. I believe that's the inkblot test. The analyst detects psychopathic tendencies in a person by showing him inkblots and getting the person to say what the shapes resemble.

CHALLEE (*nods*). And who is Alfred Adler?

KEEFER. These things are very elementary. Adler split off from Freud. Any college man knows that much, sir.

CHALLEE. A novelist, however, is apt to understand and appreciate these things more than the average man.

KEEFER. Well, our work is the narration of human conduct.

(GREENWALD *turns, looks at* KEEFER, *then turns away, disgusted.*)

CHALLEE. Naturally. Now then, Mister Keefer, with your grasp of such matters— if you saw a man rushing up and down passageways screaming that a tiger was after him when there was no tiger, would you venture to say that that man was temporarily deranged?

KEEFER (*smiling wryly*). I would, sir.

CHALLEE. Did Commander Queeg ever exhibit such behavior?

KEEFER. No. Nothing like that.

CHALLEE. Did you ever think he might be insane?

(MARYK *frantically scribbles a note.*)

GREENWALD (*rising*). Objection. Witness isn't an expert. Matters of opinion are not admissible evidence.

(MARYK *pulls at* GREENWALD's *sleeve, hands him the note.* GREENWALD *sits, reads note, then tears it up.*)

CHALLEE (*with a slight smile*). I withdraw the question. Mister Keefer, at any time prior to 18 December were you informed that Maryk suspected Queeg of being mentally ill?

KEEFER. Yes, sir.

CHALLEE. Describe how you learned this fact.

KEEFER. Well—now let me see—two weeks before the typhoon, Maryk showed me a "medical log" he'd kept on Queeg's behavior. He asked me to come with him to the *New Jersey* to report the situation to Admiral Halsey.

CHALLEE. Did you consent to go with him?

KEEFER. Yes, I did.

CHALLEE. Why?

KEEFER. He was my superior officer and also my close friend.

(MARYK *turns away.*)

CHALLEE. Did you believe that the log justified the relief of Queeg?

KEEFER. No—no, when we arrived aboard the *New Jersey,* I told him as forcibly as I could that in my opinion the log would not justify the action.

CHALLEE. What was his response?

KEEFER. Well, after a lot of arguing, he

followed my advice. We returned to the *Caine*.

CHALLEE. Were you surprised, two weeks later, when he relieved the captain?

KEEFER. I was flabbergasted.

CHALLEE. Were you pleased, Mister Keefer?

KEEFER. I was badly disturbed. I anticipated that at best he would be involved in grave difficulties. I thought it was a terrible situation.

(MARYK *turns, rests head on hand.*)

CHALLEE. No further questions.

(*Nods at* GREENWALD.)

GREENWALD (*half rises and then sits*). No questions.

BLAKELY. Does the defense intend to recall the witness at a later time?

GREENWALD. No, sir.

BLAKELY. No cross-examination of this highly material witness?

GREENWALD. No, sir.

BLAKELY. The court will question the witness . . . Mister Keefer, now as to this so-called medical log. The facts it contained, which convinced Lieutenant Maryk that he should report the captain to Admiral Halsey, didn't convince you. Is that right?

KEEFER. They did not, sir.

BLAKELY. Why not?

KEEFER. Sir, it's not something a layman can intelligently discuss.

BLAKELY. You've stated you're a close friend of Mister Maryk.

KEEFER. Yes, sir.

BLAKELY. This court is trying to find out among other things any possible extenuating circumstances for his acts. Did this medical log merely indicate to you that Captain Queeg was a highly normal and competent officer?

KEEFER. Sir, speaking from ignorance, it's always seemed to me that mental disability was a relative thing. Captain Queeg was a very strict disciplinarian and extremely meticulous in hunting down the smallest matters. He was not the easiest person in the world to reason with. There were several occasions when I thought he bore down too hard and spent excessive time on small matters. Those were the things that were recorded in the medical log. They were very unpleasant. But to jump from them to a conclusion that the captain was a maniac—no—I was compelled in all honesty to warn Maryk

against doing that.

BLAKELY. No further questions. You will not discuss your testimony outside this courtroom. Witness excused.

(KEEFER *steps down, turns, and walks out rapidly.* MARYK *looks after him.*)

CHALLEE. Call Signalman Third Class Urban.

MARYK (*pulls* GREENWALD's *arm*). Why didn't you cross-examine Tom Keefer? Why did you let him off like that?

GREENWALD. It was the only thing to do.

MARYK. Why?

GREENWALD. It would have made things worse for you. You'll get your chance on the stand.

MARYK. I'll never say a word about Tom Keefer. Not me. God damn it, he should have talked himself.

GREENWALD. Sure he should. You don't understand, do you? (*Enter* URBAN, *a little sailor in blues, crosses down to* CHALLEE, *puts hand on Bible.*) Not about Keefer. Not even about yourself.

(BLAKELY *rises, raises right hand.*)

BLAKELY. You do solemnly swear that the evidence you shall give in this court shall be the truth, the whole truth, and nothing but the truth. So help you God.

URBAN. Aye aye, sir. (URBAN *sits in witness chair.* ORDERLY *re-enters, sits in his chair.*)

CHALLEE. State your name, rating, and present station.

URBAN. Junius Hannaford Urban, Signalman Third Class, U.S.N., of the U.S.S. *Caine,* sir.

CHALLEE. If you recognize the accused, state as whom.

URBAN. Sir?

CHALLEE. Do you recognize the accused?

URBAN. Sir?

CHALLEE (*pointing*). Do you recognize the officer at that table?

URBAN. Which one, sir? There are two.

CHALLEE. Name the one you recognize.

URBAN. That's the exec, sir.

CHALLEE. What's his name?

URBAN. He's Mister Maryk.

CHALLEE. What is he exec of?

URBAN. The ship.

CHALLEE. Name the ship.

URBAN. The *Caine*.

CHALLEE. Thank you.

URBAN. Sorry, sir.

CHALLEE. Urban, on December 18, 1944, were you serving aboard the U.S.S. *Caine* in your present capacity?

URBAN. Is that the day it happened?

CHALLEE. The day what happened?

URBAN. I don't know.

CHALLEE. That was the day of the typhoon.

URBAN. Sure, I was aboard.

CHALLEE. Were you in the pilothouse when Mister Maryk relieved Captain Queeg?

URBAN. Yes, sir.

CHALLEE. Who else was in the wheelhouse at that time?

URBAN. Well, there was the captain and Mister Maryk.

CHALLEE. Yes.

URBAN. And the helmsman.

CHALLEE. His name?

URBAN. Stilwell.

CHALLEE. Who else?

URBAN. The OOD.

CHALLEE. His name.

URBAN. Mister Keith.

CHALLEE. What were you doing in the wheelhouse?

URBAN. I had the watch, sir.

CHALLEE. Urban, describe in your own words how Lieutenant Maryk relieved the captain.

URBAN. He said, "I relieve you, sir."

CHALLEE. What was happening at the time?

URBAN. Well . . . The ship was rolling very bad.

CHALLEE. Urban, describe everything that happened in the ten minutes before Captain Queeg was relieved.

URBAN. Well, like I say, the ship was rolling very bad.

(*A long silence.* CHALLEE *waits, with his eyes on* URBAN.)

CHALLEE. That's all? Did the exec say anything? Did the captain say anything? Did the OOD say anything? Did the ship just roll in silence for ten minutes?

URBAN. Well, sir, it was a typhoon.

BLAKELY. Urban, you're under oath.

URBAN. Well, I think the captain wanted to come north and the exec wanted to come south, or the other way around, or something like that.

CHALLEE. Why did the captain want to come south?

URBAN. I don't know, sir.

CHALLEE. Why did the exec want to come north?

URBAN. Sir, I'm a signalman.

CHALLEE. Did the captain act crazy?

URBAN. No, sir.

CHALLEE. Did the exec seem scared?

URBAN. No, sir.

CHALLEE. Did the captain?

URBAN. No, sir.

CHALLEE. Did anyone?

URBAN. *I* was goddam scared, sir. (*To* BLAKELY, *standing:*) I beg your pardon, sir. (*Sits.*)

CHALLEE. But the captain definitely did not act queer or crazy in any way at any time that morning—correct?

URBAN. The captain was the same as always, sir.

CHALLEE (*at the end of his patience*). Crazy, or sane, Urban?

URBAN. He was sane, sir, so far as I knew.

BLAKELY. Urban, how old are you?

URBAN. Twenty, sir.

BLAKELY. What schooling have you had?

URBAN. One year in high school.

BLAKELY. Have you been telling the whole truth here, or haven't you?

URBAN. Sir, a signalman isn't supposed to listen to arguments between the captain and the exec.

BLAKELY. Did you like the captain?

URBAN (*miserably*). *Sure* I liked him, sir.

BLAKELY (*to* CHALLEE). Continue your examination.

CHALLEE. No further questions.

(CHALLEE *crosses up to his desk, sits.* GREENWALD *approaches the witness platform, rolling the pencil against his palm.*)

GREENWALD. Urban, were you aboard when the *Caine* cut her own tow cable the time she was towing targets outside Pearl Harbor?

URBAN. Yes, sir.

GREENWALD. What were you doing at the time that it happened?

URBAN. I was—that is, the captain was eating my—(*Catches himself just short of an obscenity, glances in horror at* BLAKELY.) bawling me out—on the bridge, sir.

GREENWALD. What for?

URBAN. My shirttail was out.

GREENWALD. Was the captain very strict on the subject of shirttails?

URBAN. Sir, he was a nut on—yes, sir. He was very strict on shirttails, sir.

GREENWALD (*with an illustrative gesture*). And while the captain was discussing your shirttail the ship went right around in a circle and steamed over its own towline? Is that the way it hap—

(CHALLEE *jumps up*.)

CHALLEE. Object to this line of questioning. Counsel has tricked the witness with leading questions into asserting as a fact that the *Caine* cut a towline, a material point that was not touched upon in direct examination.

GREENWALD. Please the court, the witness stated he had never seen the captain do anything crazy. I am attempting to refute this.

BLAKELY. Defense counsel will have the opportunity to originate evidence later. Objection sustained. Cross-examination thus far will be stricken from the record.

GREENWALD. Urban, what is a paranoid personality?

URBAN. Huh?

GREENWALD. What is a paranoid personality?

URBAN. Sir?

GREENWALD. Could you recognize a psychotic person?

URBAN. Me?

GREENWALD. No further questions. (*Crosses to chair and sits*.)

BLAKELY. Urban. (URBAN *rises*.) You will not discuss your testimony in this courtroom with anybody, understand?

URBAN. Who, sir? Me, sir? No, sir.

BLAKELY. Excused.

URBAN. Thank you, sir. (*Exits*.)

CHALLEE. Call Chief Water Tender Budge. (*An* ORDERLY *starts out*.)

GREENWALD. One moment. (ORDERLY *halts*.) If it please the court. I understand that the judge advocate intends to call a dozen members of the crew of the *Caine*.

CHALLEE. That's correct.

GREENWALD. Is the purpose to confirm the testimony of Urban that the captain was never seen to do anything crazy?

CHALLEE. That is the purpose.

GREENWALD. The defense will concede that the testimony of all these witnesses will corroborate Urban's . . . if the judge advocate will concede that these twelve men don't know any more about a paranoid personality than Urban.

CHALLEE (*to* BLAKELY). I'll gladly accept that concession on those terms, sir.

BLAKELY. Lieutenant Greenwald, you're making a weighty concession.

GREENWALD. By your leave, sir, however, the defense makes that concession. (*Sits*.)

BLAKELY (*to* STENOGRAPHER). One moment. Don't record that . . . Mister Greenwald.

GREENWALD (*stands*). Yes, sir?

BLAKELY. The court understands that you were appointed as defense counsel by the judge advocate.

GREENWALD. Yes, sir.

BLAKELY. When were you appointed?

GREENWALD. Four days ago, sir.

BLAKELY. Do you feel you've had enough time to prepare your case?

GREENWALD. Yes, sir.

BLAKELY. Did you undertake this assignment willingly? (GREENWALD *hesitates*.)

CHALLEE (*rises*). If it please the court. Lieutenant Greenwald accepted the assignment at my earnest request.

BLAKELY. I see by your uniform that you're a flying officer.

GREENWALD. Yes, sir.

BLAKELY. What do you fly?

GREENWALD. F6F, sir.

BLAKELY. What are you doing on the beach? Were you grounded?

GREENWALD. Hospitalized for third degree burns, sir.

BLAKELY (*a little more sympathetically*). I see. How did you get burned?

GREENWALD. Crashed a barrier on the U.S.S. *Wasp*, sir.

BLAKELY. Did you have a chance to practice much law before the war came along?

GREENWALD (*hesitantly*). A little, sir.

BLAKELY. Court will speak to the accused off the record. (GREENWALD *sits, motions to* MARYK *to rise. He does*.)

MARYK. Yes, sir?

BLAKELY. It seems the court's duty at this point to inquire whether your counsel's conduct of the defense meets with your approval.

(MARYK *hesitates, looking from* GREENWALD *to* BLAKELY. GREENWALD *rises*.)

GREENWALD. May it please the court. If the accused answers that question now he must do so on blind faith. I beg the court for an opportunity to speak to my client first.

BLAKELY. We've had too many recesses here.

GREENWALD. Not a recess, sir—a brief delay—two minutes, sir—

BLAKELY. Court will remain in session. We'll have a two-minute pause in the proceedings. (*Rings the bell*.)

GREENWALD. Well, do you want to get rid of me?

MARYK. I don't know.

GREENWALD. Take my word for it. Everything's all right up to now.

MARYK. I think I'm sunk at this point.

GREENWALD. You're not.

MARYK. Fifteen years in the brig—

GREENWALD. You won't go to the brig.

MARYK. Why didn't you cross-examine these twelve guys?

GREENWALD. Two minutes isn't much time to explain elementary trial tactics.

MARYK. Explain one thing and maybe I'll go along with you. Why didn't you cross-examine Tom Keefer?

GREENWALD. Maryk, there isn't time to tell—

MARYK. Tom Keefer knows everything that the captain did. Everything!

GREENWALD. Sure he does.

MARYK. If he wouldn't talk it was up to you to drag it out of him. Wasn't it?

GREENWALD. You don't begin to understand.

MARYK. I don't understand what you're doing, mister, that's for sure.

GREENWALD. I just happen to want to fight this case.

MARYK. Why? What does it mean to you? You're a total stranger.

GREENWALD. I want to win it!

MARYK. I want to believe you.

GREENWALD. It's God's truth.

MARYK. You said you'd rather be prosecuting me than defending me. Maybe this is your screwy way of prosecuting me.

GREENWALD. All right. (*A harried glance at the court and at his wrist watch.*) Listen carefully. Implicating Keefer harms you.

MARYK. What?

GREENWALD. Two disgruntled bastards' instead of one heroic exec. (MARYK *stares uncomprehending.*) I've got a chance with a lone heroic exec. Making that picture stick is my only chance to win for you. Please try to let that sink in, Maryk. (MARYK *keeps looking at him. Understanding slowly dawns on him as* CHALLEE *and* BLAKELY *talk.*)

BLAKELY (*motions to* CHALLEE *to come closer*). Challee. (*In a confidential undertone:*) What's going on here, Jack? Where'd you get this bird?

CHALLEE. Sir, Barney Greenwald and I went to Georgetown Law together. Before the war he was one of the most successful young lawyers in Washington.

BLAKELY (*staring at* GREENWALD). He was? Don't you think he's putting up a damned queer show?

CHALLEE. Well, yes, sir . . . But he has a reputation for defending the underdog, sir. He used to handle Indian cases back in Washington—(GREENWALD *rises, crosses over to* MARYK, *and puts his hand on* MARYK's *shoulder.*)—where Indians were getting pushed around by the officials—and didn't charge for it.

BLAKELY. Jewish fellow, isn't he?

CHALLEE. Yes, sir. Barney's Jewish.

BLAKELY. Well, maybe he's a hell of a lot smarter than he seems. (BLAKELY *rings bell.* MARYK *rises.* GREENWALD *crosses back to his chair.*) The court again asks the accused—are you satisfied?

MARYK (*after a long stare at* GREENWALD, *shakily*). I'm satisfied, sir.

BLAKELY. Court will not reopen this question.

MARYK. I understand, sir. I'm satisfied with Lieutenant Greenwald.

BLAKELY (*nods to* CHALLEE). Proceed with your case, Commander Challee.

CHALLEE. Call Lieutenant Keith. (OR-DERLY *goes.* LIEUTENANT (*j.g.*) WILLIS KEITH *enters, a handsome youngster with reddish-blond hair.* CHALLEE *holds Bible for him.*)

BLAKELY. You do solemnly swear that the evidence you shall give in this court shall be the truth, the whole truth, and nothing but the truth. So help you God.

KEITH. I do. (KEITH *takes the stand.* ORDERLY *re-enters, sits.*)

CHALLEE. State your name, rank, and present station.

KEITH. Willis Seward Keith, Lieutenant Junior Grade, U.S.N.R., assistant communication officer of the U.S.S. *Caine*.

CHALLEE. If you recognize the accused, state as whom.

KEITH. Steve Maryk, my executive officer on the *Caine*.

CHALLEE. Mister Keith, were you officer of the deck of the *Caine* during the forenoon watch on 18 December, 1944?

KEITH. I was.

CHALLEE. Was the captain relieved of his command during your watch?

KEITH. Yes.

CHALLEE. Do you know why the executive officer relieved the captain?

KEITH. Yes. Captain Queeg had lost control of himself, and the ship was in grave danger of foundering.

CHALLEE. How many years have you served at sea, Lieutenant?

KEITH. One year and three months.

CHALLEE. Do you know how many years Commander Queeg has served at sea?

KEITH. I guess about ten years.

CHALLEE. Which of you is better qualified to judge whether a ship is foundering or not?

KEITH. Myself, sir, if I'm in possession of my faculties and Commander Queeg isn't.

CHALLEE. What makes you think he isn't in possession of his faculties?

KEITH. He wasn't on the morning of December eighteenth.

CHALLEE. Have you studied medicine or psychiatry?

KEITH. No.

CHALLEE. Did the captain foam, or rave, or make insane gestures?

KEITH. No, but what he did do was just as bad.

CHALLEE. Clarify that a bit, if you will.

KEITH. His orders were vague and sluggish and—not appropriate. He insisted on going south, when we had a north wind of ninety miles an hour behind us. With a stern wind that strong the ship couldn't be controlled.

CHALLEE. In your expert opinion as a ship handler, that is.

KEITH. Steve Maryk thought so, and he's an expert ship handler.

CHALLEE. Were you wholeheartedly loyal to your captain or antagonistic to him, prior to 18 December?

KEITH. I was antagonistic to Captain Queeg at certain isolated times.

CHALLEE. At what isolated times were you antagonistic?

KEITH. When Captain Queeg maltreated the men, I opposed him.

CHALLEE. When did the captain ever maltreat the men?

KEITH. Well, for one thing, he systematically persecuted Gunner's Mate Second Class Stilwell.

CHALLEE. In what way?

KEITH. First he restricted him to the ship for six months for reading on watch. He refused to grant him leave in the States when we were back here in December '43. The man was getting anonymous letters about his wife's infidelity. Maryk gave Stil- well a seventy-two-hour emergency leave and he returned a few hours overleave and—

CHALLEE. You say Maryk gave Stilwell a pass. Did Maryk know that the captain had denied leave to Stilwell?

KEITH. Yes, sir.

CHALLEE. Did Maryk check with the captain before issuing this pass?

KEITH. No, sir.

CHALLEE (*pleased and surprised*). Are you testifying, Mister Keith, that Maryk deliberately violated his captain's orders?

KEITH (*rattled*). Well, I mean it was my fault, actually. I begged him to. I was morale officer, and I thought the man's morale—I mean—

CHALLEE. Mister Keith, we now have your testimony that you and Maryk and Stilwell connived to circumvent an express order of your commanding officer, a whole year before the typhoon of 18 December . . . Now, please tell the court any other instances of maltreatment that occur to you.

KEITH (*pause*). He cut off the movies for six months just because he wasn't invited to a showing by mistake—he cut off the water at the equator because he said the men were using too much and had to be taught a lesson—and he—

CHALLEE. Mister Keith, did the captain ever issue rules or punishments not permitted by regulations?

KEITH. He never did anything not allowed by regulations.

CHALLEE. You didn't like the captain, did you, Lieutenant?

KEITH. I did at first, very much. But I gradually realized that he was a petty tyrant and utterly incompetent.

CHALLEE. Did you think he was insane, too?

KEITH. Not until the day of the typhoon.

CHALLEE. Very well, come to the day of the typhoon. Was your decision to obey Maryk based on your judgment that the captain had gone mad, or was it based on your hatred of Captain Queeg?

KEITH (*miserably, after a betraying pause and glance at* MARYK). I just don't remember my state of mind that long ago.

CHALLEE (*contemptuously*). No further questions. (*Turns on his heel and sits down.* GREENWALD *rises.*)

GREENWALD. Mister Keith, you have stated you disliked Captain Queeg.

KEITH. I did dislike him.

GREENWALD. Did you state under direct examination all your reasons for disliking him?

KEITH. Not at all.

GREENWALD. State the rest of your reasons now, please.

KEITH. Well, for one thing, he extorted a hundred dollars from me—

CHALLEE. Objection. The issue in this case is not whether Captain Queeg was a model officer, but whether he was insane on 18 December. Defense counsel hasn't even touched this issue.

GREENWALD. Please the court, this will bear directly on the mental fitness of Captain Queeg to command a naval vessel, and as evidence it is nothing but clarification of Keith's dislike of his commanding officer, a fact established by the judge advocate at great pains in direct examination.

BLAKELY. The objection is overruled.

GREENWALD. Describe this so-called extortion, Mister Keith.

KEITH. Well, this was back last December in San Francisco Bay. The captain had this big crate full of cheap tax-free whiskey from Pearl Harbor that he wanted to sneak into Oakland, avoiding the customs. He appointed me boat officer, and a working party started to load the crate into the gig. It was terrifically heavy. Captain Queeg got excited and screeched a whole bunch of contradictory orders. The sailors got rattled and dropped the crate into the water. It sank like a stone. And I was out a hundred and ten dollars.

GREENWALD. You mean the captain was?

KEITH. No, sir, I was . . . The captain informed me that I was responsible because I was boat officer in charge of the loading. And he asked me to think over what I ought to do about it. Well, I was supposed to go on leave the next day. My girl friend had flown out from New York to be with me. So I went to the captain and I apologized for my stupidity and said I'd like to pay for the lost crate. He took my money gladly. Then he signed my leave papers.

GREENWALD. What further reason did you have for disliking Queeg?

KEITH (a pause to gather his nerve). My chief reason for disliking Captain Queeg was his cowardice in battle.

GREENWALD. What cowardice?

KEITH. He repeatedly ran from shore batteries—

CHALLEE (infuriated). Objection! Counsel is originating evidence beyond the scope of direct examination. He is leading the witness into irresponsible libels of an officer of the Navy! (BLAKELY starts looking through Naval Regulations.)

GREENWALD. Please the court, the witness's dislike of Queeg was not only in the scope of direct examination, it was the key fact brought out. The witness has confessed ignorance of psychiatry. Things Queeg did, which caused the witness in his ignorance to dislike him, may in fact have been the helpless acts of a sick man.

CHALLEE. I respectfully urge my objection, sir!

BLAKELY. One moment. (JUDGES write ballots.) For the benefit of all parties, court will read from the Articles for the Government of the Navy on cowardice. (Reads.) "The punishment of death, or such other punishment as a court-martial may adjudge, may be inflicted on any person in the naval service, who in time of battle, displays cowardice, negligence, or disaffection, or withdraws from or keeps out of danger to which he should expose himself . . ." (JUDGES pass ballots to BLAKELY.) The defense counsel and the witness are warned that they are on the most dangerous possible ground. In charging an officer of the United States Navy with an offense punishable by death, and that the most odious offense in military life, they take on themselves the heaviest responsibility. The court now asks defense counsel in view of the foregoing whether he desires to withdraw his question.

GREENWALD. I do not so desire, sir.

BLAKELY. The court asks the witness to state whether he desires to withdraw his answers.

KEITH. I do not so desire, sir.

BLAKELY (with icy gravity). Court finds that the question is within the scope of direct examination, and that the answer is material. The objection of the judge advocate is overruled. (Tears ballots. Nods to GREENWALD.) Proceed.

GREENWALD. Where and when did Captain Queeg run from shore batteries?

KEITH. Practically every time we heard gunfire from the beach. I guess the worst time was at Kwajalein. That's where he got the nickname, "Old Yellowstain."

GREENWALD. What did this nickname,

"Old Yellowstain," imply?

KEITH. Well, cowardice, of course. It referred to a yellow dye marker he dropped over the side.

GREENWALD. Describe this Yellow Stain incident.

KEITH. Well, I wasn't on the bridge, so I only heard about it afterwards. What happened was that Captain Queeg—

CHALLEE. Objection. Does defense counsel seriously expect to enter these hearsay libels on the record?

GREENWALD. I withdraw the question. Defense will introduce direct evidence on the Yellow Stain incident.

BLAKELY. Strike the question and answer from the record.

GREENWALD. Can you describe incidents of cowardice to which you were an eye-witness?

KEITH. Well, in any combat situation Captain Queeg was always found on the side of the bridge away from the firing. I saw that a dozen times when I was OOD.

GREENWALD. No further questions. (*Goes to his seat.*)

CHALLEE. Mister Keith, has Commander Queeg been court-martialed by higher authority for any of the alleged acts of cowardice you describe?

KEITH. No.

CHALLEE. Can you cite any official records that will substantiate any of these fantastic and libelous stories you've been telling under the guidance of defense counsel?

KEITH. Official records? No.

CHALLEE. Mister Keith, do you know for a fact that the crate that was lost contained smuggled liquor?

KEITH. It was common knowledge.

CHALLEE. Common knowledge. Did you see the liquor in the crate?

KEITH. No—

CHALLEE. Can you name one person who will testify that they saw liquor in the crate?

KEITH. Well, naturally, he was pretty careful about that.

CHALLEE. Not one person.

KEITH. I just don't know who would have actually seen it.

CHALLEE. Mister Keith, you've testified that you hate Captain Queeg. You're reporting as fact every evil rumor about him and you're making wild, irresponsible charges under oath. Isn't that the plain

truth about your testimony, Mister Keith?

KEITH. I haven't lied once.

CHALLEE. Mister Keith, on the morning when the captain was relieved, did you really think he had gone crazy?

KEITH (*losing assurance*). I said before I can't say for sure what my state of mind was.

CHALLEE. No more questions.

(BLAKELY *looks at* GREENWALD, *who shakes his head.*)

BLAKELY (*to* KEITH). You'll not discuss any details of your testimony outside this courtroom, Lieutenant.

KEITH. Aye aye, sir.

BLAKELY. You're excused.

(*Exit* KEITH, *with a glance at* MARYK *and a slight despairing shrug.*)

CHALLEE. Call Captain Southard. (*Exit* ORDERLY, *returning with a dapper, lean officer. Close-cropped head, hard-bitten face, three rows of ribbons and stars. Business with Bible.*)

BLAKELY. You do solemnly swear that the evidence you shall give in this court shall be the truth, the whole truth, and nothing but the truth. So help you God.

SOUTHARD. I do. (*Takes the witness chair.*)

CHALLEE. State your name, rank, and present station.

SOUTHARD. Randolph Patterson Southard, Captain, U. S. Navy, commander, Destroyer Squadron Eight.

CHALLEE. You understand that you've been called as an expert witness on destroyer ship handling?

SOUTHARD. I do.

CHALLEE. State your qualifications.

SOUTHARD. Some twenty years in destroyers. Ten years of commanding all types, from the World War I 4-piper on up to the newest 2200 tonner.

CHALLEE. Now, sir, I'm going to describe a hypothetical ship handling problem for your expert opinion.

SOUTHARD. Very well.

CHALLEE. You're in command of a destroyer in the Philippine Sea. A typhoon blows up without warning, traveling west. You're directly in the path of it. The wind keeps increasing, its direction holding steady from the north. Soon your wind is force 10 to 12, and your seas are mountainous. Under the circumstances, what would you do?

SOUTHARD. I believe I'd execute the classic naval maneuver known as getting the hell out of there.

CHALLEE (*smiling*). How would you go about that, Captain?

SOUTHARD. Well, it's almost rule, of thumb. You say the wind's from the north at ninety knots, the center of the typhoon coming at you from the west. Best course is south. You might have to head a couple of points one way or the other, depending on your seas, but there's only one way out of that mess—south.

CHALLEE. But then you have a terribly strong stern wind, don't you?

SOUTHARD. What about it?

CHALLEE. Can a destroyer ride safely downwind in such conditions?

SOUTHARD. She'll ride just as well going downwind as upwind. In fact, with your high freeboard forward, a destroyer tends to back into the wind. Other things being equal, she'll do slightly better going downwind.

CHALLEE. How about turning north in those circumstances and heading into the wind?

SOUTHARD. That would be dubious and dangerous, not to say idiotic.

CHALLEE. Why, Captain?

SOUTHARD. You're heading yourself right back into the path of the typhoon. Unless you're interested in sinking, that's not smart.

CHALLEE. That's all, sir. (CHALLEE *crosses to his desk and sits.* GREENWALD *arises.*)

GREENWALD. Captain, have you ever conned a ship through the center of a typhoon?

SOUTHARD. Negative. Been on the fringes often but always managed to avoid the center.

GREENWALD. Have you ever commanded a destroyer-minesweeper, sir?

SOUTHARD. Negative.

GREENWALD. This case, sir, concerns a destroyer-minesweeper at the center of a typhoon—

SOUTHARD (*frostily*). I'm aware of that. I've had DMS's under my command in screens, and I've read the book on 'em. They don't differ from destroyers except in details of topside weight characteristics.

GREENWALD. I ask these questions, Captain, because you are the only expert witness on ship handling, and the extent of your expert knowledge should be clear to the court.

SOUTHARD. That's all right. I've handled destroyer types in almost every conceivable situation for ten years. Haven't handled a DMS at the center of a typhoon, no, but I don't know who has besides the skipper of the *Caine*. It's a thousand-to-one shot.

GREENWALD. Will you state without reservation that the rules of destroyer handling would hold for a DMS in the center of a typhoon?

SOUTHARD. Well, at the center of a typhoon there are no hard-and-fast rules. That's one situation where it's all up to the commanding officer. Too many strange things happen too fast.

GREENWALD. Sir, you remember the hypothetical question of the judge advocate about the typhoon.

SOUTHARD. I do.

GREENWALD. Now in that situation, I ask you to assume that the winds and seas become worse than any you've ever experienced. Your ship is wallowing broadside. You actually believe your ship is foundering. You're in the last extremity. Would you bring your ship north, into the wind, or continue on south, stern to wind?

SOUTHARD. You're getting mighty hypothetical.

GREENWALD. Yes, sir. You prefer not to answer that question, Captain?

SOUTHARD. I'll answer it. In the last extremity I'd come around to north and head into the wind, if I could. But *only* in the last extremity.

GREENWALD. Why, sir?

SOUTHARD. Why, because your engines and rudder have the best purchase that way, that's all. It's your last chance to keep control of your ship.

GREENWALD. But wouldn't coming north head you back into the path of the storm?

SOUTHARD. First things first. If you're on the verge of foundering you're as bad off as you can get. Mind you, you said the last extremity.

GREENWALD. Yes, sir, no further questions. (*Sits.*)

CHALLEE (*rises*). Captain, who in your opinion is the best judge as to whether a ship is in its last extremity?

SOUTHARD. There's only one judge. The commanding officer.

CHALLEE. Why sir?

SOUTHARD. The Navy's made him captain because his knowledge of the sea and of ships is better than anyone else's on the ship. It's very common for some subordinate officers to think the ship is sinking when all they're having is a little weather.

CHALLEE. Don't you think, sir, that when his subordinates all agree that the ship is going down the captain ought to listen to them?

SOUTHARD. Negative! Panic is a common hazard at sea. The highest function of command is to override it and to listen to nothing but the voice of his own professional judgment.

CHALLEE. Thank you, Captain. (CHALLEE *sits.*)

BLAKELY (*with the smile of an old friend at* SOUTHARD). You will not discuss your testimony outside the courtroom, Captain.

SOUTHARD. Understood.

BLAKELY. You're excused, and thank you. (*Exit* SOUTHARD.)

CHALLEE. Call Dr. Forrest Lundeen. (*Exit* ORDERLY. *Returns with a captain, intelligent plump man in his fifties, rimless glasses. Bible business.*)

BLAKELY. You do solemnly swear that the evidence you shall give in this court shall be the truth, the whole truth, and nothing but the truth. So help you God.

LUNDEEN. I do. (*Takes stand.*)

CHALLEE. State name, rank, and present station.

LUNDEEN. Forrest Lundeen, M.D., Captain, U. S. Navy. Head of psychiatry, U. S. Naval Hospital, San Francisco.

CHALLEE. Were you the head of the medical board which examined Lieutenant Commander Queeg?

LUNDEEN. I was.

CHALLEE. How long did your examination last, Doctor?

LUNDEEN. We had the commander under constant observation and testing for three weeks.

CHALLEE. What was the finding of the board?

LUNDEEN. Commander Queeg was discharged with a clean bill of health.

CHALLEE. Doctor, is it possible that two months ago, on December 18, he was in such a state of psychotic collapse that relieving him from a naval command would be justified?

LUNDEEN. It's utterly impossible.

CHALLEE. Is it possible for a sane man to perform offensive, disagreeable, foolish acts?

LUNDEEN. It happens every day. We

didn't find that the commander was a perfect officer.

CHALLEE. Yet you still say that to relieve him from naval command because of mental illness would be unjustified?

LUNDEEN. Completely unjustified.

CHALLEE. We will place your report in evidence and hear Dr. Bird. Thank you, Doctor. (CHALLEE *glances directly into* GREENWALD's *eyes, with a thin cold grin.* GREENWALD *shuffles toward witness platform, rubbing his nose with the back of his hand, looking down at his feet, and presenting a general picture of flustered embarrassment.*)

GREENWALD. Dr. Lundeen, my background is legal, not medical. I hope you'll bear with me if I try to clarify technical terms.

LUNDEEN. Of course, of course.

GREENWALD. I'll probably ask some elementary questions.

LUNDEEN (*with an expansive smile*). That's perfectly all right.

GREENWALD. Would you say that Commander Queeg is absolutely normal?

LUNDEEN. Well, normality, you know, is a fiction in psychiatry. No adult is without problems except a happy imbecile.

GREENWALD. Describe Commander Queeg's problems.

LUNDEEN. Well, you might say the overall problem is one of inferiority feelings generated by an unfavorable childhood and aggravated by certain adult experiences.

GREENWALD. Unfavorable childhood in what way?

LUNDEEN. Disturbed background. Divorced parents, financial trouble, schooling problems.

GREENWALD. And the aggravating factors in adult life?

LUNDEEN (*hesitant*). In general, the commander is rather troubled by his short stature, his low standing in his class, and such factors. But the commander is well adjusted to all these things.

GREENWALD. Can you describe the nature of the adjustment?

LUNDEEN. Yes, I can. His identity as a naval officer is the essential balancing factor. It's the key to his personal security. Therefore he has a fixed anxiety about protecting his standing. That would account for the harshness and ill temper.

GREENWALD. Would he be disinclined to

admit to mistakes?

LUNDEEN. Yes. Of course there's nothing unbalanced in that.

GREENWALD. Would he be a perfectionist?

LUNDEEN. Such a personality would be.

GREENWALD. Suspicious of his subordinates? Inclined to hound them about small details?

LUNDEEN. Any mistake of a subordinate is intolerable because it might endanger him.

GREENWALD. Yet he will not admit mistakes when he makes them himself.

LUNDEEN. You might say he revises reality in his own mind so that he comes out blameless.

GREENWALD. Doctor, isn't distorting reality a symptom of mental illness?

LUNDEEN. It's a question of degree. None of us wholly faces reality.

GREENWALD. But doesn't the commander distort reality more than, say, you do?

LUNDEEN. That's his weakness. Other people have other weaknesses. It's definitely not disabling.

GREENWALD. If criticized from above, would he be inclined to think he was being unjustly persecuted?

LUNDEEN. It's all one pattern, all stemming from one basic premise, that he must try to be perfect.

GREENWALD. Would he be inclined to stubbornness?

LUNDEEN. Well, you'll have a certain rigidity of personality in such an individual. The inner insecurity checks him from admitting that those who differ with him may be right.

GREENWALD (*suddenly switching from the fumbling manner to clicking preciseness*). Doctor, you've testified that the following symptoms exist in the commander's behavior: rigidity of personality, feelings of persecution, unreasonable suspicion, withdrawal from reality, perfectionist anxiety, an unreal basic premise, and an obsessive sense of self-righteousness.

LUNDEEN (*looking startled, then appreciatively amused*). All mild, sir, all well compensated.

GREENWALD. Yes, Doctor. Is there an inclusive psychiatric term—one label—for this syndrome?

LUNDEEN. Syndrome? Who said anything about a syndrome? You're misusing a term. There's no syndrome, because there's no disease.

GREENWALD. Thank you for the correction, Doctor. I'll rephrase it. Do the symptoms fall into a single pattern of neurotic disturbance—a common psychiatric class?

LUNDEEN. I know what you're driving at, of course. It's a paranoid personality, but that is not a disabling affliction.

GREENWALD. What kind of personality, Doctor?

LUNDEEN. Paranoid.

GREENWALD. Paranoid, Doctor?

LUNDEEN. Yes, paranoid.

(GREENWALD *glances at* CHALLEE, *then looks around slowly one by one at the faces of the* COURT MEMBERS. *He starts back to his desk.* CHALLEE *rises.* GREENWALD *shakes his head at* CHALLEE, *who sits, annoyed. A moment of silence.* GREENWALD *shuffles papers at his desk.*)

GREENWALD. Doctor, in a paranoid personality like Commander Queeg's—well, let me put this hypothetically. Could a man have a paranoid personality which would not disable him for any subordinate duties, but would disable him for command?

LUNDEEN (*rather irritated*). It's conceivable.

GREENWALD. Is the disabling factor likely to show up in personal interviews?

LUNDEEN. With a skilled psychiatrist, yes.

GREENWALD. Why is a psychiatrist needed, Doctor? Can't an educated intelligent person, like myself, or the judge advocate, or the court, detect a paranoid?

LUNDEEN (*sarcastically*). You evidently are not too well acquainted with the pattern. The distinguishing mark of this neurosis is extreme plausibility and a most convincing normal manner on the surface. Particularly in self-justification.

GREENWALD. Thank you, Doctor. No more questions. (*Returns to seat. The other* COURT MEMBERS *look tensely at* BLAKELY.)

BLAKELY. The court wishes to clear up one point. Doctor, is such a thing possible? (*Hesitates.*) Well, let me put it this way. Let's say a man with a mild condition is not disabled for all the usual stresses of command. Now let's say the stresses are multiplied manifold by an extreme emergency. Would there be a tendency to make erroneous judgments?

LUNDEEN. Well, there might be. Extreme

stress does that to almost anybody, sir.

BLAKELY (*sternly*). It's not supposed to do it to commanding officers.

LUNDEEN. No, but practically speaking, sir, they're human, too.

BLAKELY. You are not to discuss your testimony outside the courtroom. You're excused.

LUNDEEN. Yes, sir.

BLAKELY. Thank you, Doctor. (*Exit LUNDEEN.*)

CHALLEE. Dr. Bird will be my last witness, sir. (CHALLEE *nods to* ORDERLY. *Exit* ORDERLY, *returning with a lieutenant, good-looking, young, of an intellectual and ascetic appearance. Bible business.*)

BLAKELY. You do solemnly swear that the evidence you shall give in this court shall be the truth, the whole truth, and nothing but the truth. So help you God.

BIRD. I do. (*Takes the stand.*)

CHALLEE. State your name, rank, and present station.

BIRD. Allen Winston Bird, M.D., Lieutenant, U.S.N.R. On the psychiatric staff of U. S. Naval Hospital, San Francisco.

CHALLEE. Were you a member of the board headed by Dr. Lundeen which recently inquired into the mental health of Lieutenant Commander Queeg?

BIRD. Yes, sir.

CHALLEE. What was the finding of the board?

BIRD. We found that the commander is mentally fit for command now and has never been unfit.

CHALLEE (*after a pause*). Did you find any indication that Commander Queeg had what is known as a paranoid personality?

BIRD. Well, I prefer to call it an obsessive personality with paranoid features.

CHALLEE. This did not indicate mental unfitness, however?

BIRD. Oh, no.

CHALLEE. You unanimously agreed, then, Doctor, that Commander Queeg is mentally fit now and must have been mentally fit on 18 December, when he was relieved on the grounds of mental illness?

BIRD. That was our unanimous conclusion.

CHALLEE. Thank you, Doctor. No further questions.

(GREENWALD *appraises* DR. BIRD *with a cold eye, slowly gets out of his chair, and approaches him.*)

GREENWALD. Doctor, you have special training in Freudian technique?

BIRD. Yes.

GREENWALD. In the Freudian analysis is there such a thing as mental illness?

BIRD. Well, there are disturbed people and adjusted people.

GREENWALD. But *disturbed* and *adjusted* correspond roughly, don't they, to the terms *sick* and *well* as laymen use them?

BIRD. Very roughly, yes.

GREENWALD. Doctor, would you say Commander Queeg suffers from inferiority feelings?

BIRD. Yes, but they are well compensated.

GREENWALD. Is there a difference between *compensated* and *adjusted*?

BIRD. Most definitely.

GREENWALD. Can you explain it?

BIRD (*smiles and settles back in his chair*). Well—let's say a man has some deep-seated psychological disturbance. He can *compensate* by finding outlets for his peculiar drives. He can never *adjust* without undergoing psychoanalysis.

GREENWALD. Has Commander Queeg ever been psychoanalyzed?

BIRD. No.

GREENWALD. He is, then, a disturbed person.

BIRD. Yes, he is. Not disabled, however, by the disturbance. (*Smiles.*)

GREENWALD. How has he compensated?

BIRD. In two ways, mainly. The paranoid pattern, which is useless and not desirable, and his naval career, which is extremely useful and desirable.

GREENWALD. You say his military career is a result of his disturbance?

BIRD. Most military careers are.

GREENWALD. Doctor, did you note any peculiar habit Commander Queeg had? Something he did with his hands?

BIRD. Do you mean rolling the steel balls?

GREENWALD. Yes, describe the habit, please.

BIRD. Well, it's an incessant rolling or rattling of two marbles in his hand—either hand.

GREENWALD. Why does he do it?

BIRD. His hands tremble. He does it to still his hands and conceal the trembling. It makes him feel more comfortable.

GREENWALD. Why do his hands tremble?

BIRD. The inner tension. It's one of the surface symptoms.

GREENWALD. Does this rolling motion have significance in Freudian analysis?

BIRD. It's an obvious sexual symbol, of course. Now, as to the precise meaning, I—

CHALLEE (*stands*). How far is this totally irrelevant technical discussion going to be pushed?

BLAKELY (*scowling*). Are you objecting to the question?

CHALLEE. I'm requesting the court to set limits to time-wasting by the defense.

BLAKELY. Your request is noted. (*To* GREENWALD:) Proceed with cross-examination.

GREENWALD. Doctor, you have testified that the commander is a disturbed, not an adjusted, person.

BIRD. Yes.

GREENWALD. He is then, in laymen's terms, sick.

BIRD (*smiles*). I remember agreeing to the rough resemblance of the terms *disturbed* and *sick*. But by those terms an awful lot of people are sick . . .

GREENWALD. But this trial only has Commander Queeg's sickness at issue. If he's sick, how could your board have given him a clean bill of health?

BIRD. You're playing on words, I'm afraid. We found no disability.

GREENWALD. Doctor, supposing the requirements of command were many times as severe as you believe them to be—wouldn't even this mild sickness disable Queeg?

BIRD. That's absurdly hypothetical, because—

GREENWALD. Is it? Have you ever had sea duty, Doctor?

BIRD. No.

GREENWALD. Have you ever *been* to sea? (BIRD *is losing his self-possessed look.*)

BIRD. No.

GREENWALD. How long have you been in the Navy?

BIRD. Five months—no, six, I guess, now—

GREENWALD. Have you had any dealings with ships' captains before this case?

BIRD. No.

GREENWALD. On what do you base your estimate of the stresses of command?

BIRD. Well, my general knowledge—

GREENWALD. Do you think command requires a highly gifted, exceptional person?

BIRD. Well, no—

GREENWALD. It doesn't?

BIRD. Not highly gifted, no. Adequate responses, fairly good intelligence, and sufficient training and experience, but—

GREENWALD. Is that enough equipment for, say, a skilled psychiatrist?

BIRD. Well, not exactly—

GREENWALD. In other words, it takes more ability to be a psychiatrist than the captain of a naval vessel?

BIRD. It takes—(*Looks toward* BLAKELY.) That is, different abilities are required. You're making the invidious comparison, not I.

GREENWALD. Doctor, you've admitted Commander Queeg is sick. The only remaining question is *how* sick. You don't think he's sick enough to be disabled for command. I suggest that since evidently you don't know much about the requirements of command you may be wrong in your conclusion.

BIRD (*looking like an insulted boy, his voice quivers*). I repudiate your suggestion. You've deliberately substituted the word *sick,* which is a loose, a polarized word, for the correct—

GREENWALD. Pardon me, what kind of word?

BIRD. Polarized—loaded, invidious . . . I never said sick. My grasp of the requirements of command is adequate or I would have disqualified myself from serving on the board—

GREENWALD. Maybe you should have.

CHALLEE (*rises, shouts*). The witness is being badgered!

GREENWALD. I withdraw my last statement. No further questions. (GREENWALD *strides to his seat.* CHALLEE *crosses to* BIRD *in witness chair.*)

CHALLEE. Dr. Bird, defense counsel managed to put words into your mouth that I'm certain you don't mean, and I'd like to—

BIRD. I'm not aware that he succeeded in putting any words into my mouth.

CHALLEE (*with an exasperated glance at* GREENWALD). Doctor, he drew the implication from you that Captain Queeg is sick. Surely you don't—

BIRD. Sir, I'm careful in my use of terminology. I did not introduce the term *sick.* I don't regard it as a precise term. Nevertheless, if you're going to use such a loose term, Captain Queeg, like a vast number of seemingly healthy people, is sick. However, he is definitely not disabled for command, which is the only issue here.

CHALLEE. But that sounds like a contradiction, sir, which surely you don't intend—

BIRD. We live in a sick civilization. The well people are the exceptions, and Captain Queeg certainly isn't exceptional in that regard, and furthermore—

CHALLEE (*hastily, with a worried glance at* BLAKELY). Thank you, thank you, Doctor. That certainly clarifies the matter. No more questions. (CHALLEE *goes quickly to his seat.*)

BLAKELY. Doctor—(*Stares at* BIRD *as though considering questioning him, then shrugs.*) Doctor, you will not discuss your testimony outside this courtroom.

BIRD. No, sir.

BLAKELY. Excused. (*Exit* BIRD.)

CHALLEE. Prosecution rests.

(BLAKELY *glances at wrist watch, then at* GREENWALD, *who comes forward as* CHALLEE *sits.*)

BLAKELY. Is defense ready to present its case?

GREENWALD. Yes, sir.

BLAKELY. How many witnesses are you calling?

GREENWALD. Only two, sir. The first is the accused.

BLAKELY. Then we can button it all up tomorrow morning.

GREENWALD. I believe so, sir.

BLAKELY (*rings his bell*). Recess until 0900.

(COURT *rises.* BLAKELY *goes out.* COURT *follows.* ORDERLY *and* STENOGRAPHER *leave.* CHALLEE *gathers his papers.* GREENWALD *sits slumped in his chair, leaning on one hand, doodling.*)

CHALLEE (*to* GREENWALD, *when all are gone*). Quite a job you did on Dr. Bird.

GREENWALD (*looks up; in a weary, flat tone*). Thanks, Jack.

CHALLEE. It won't cut any ice.

GREENWALD. No?

CHALLEE. Captain Blakely's headed up a lot of these courts. He doesn't go for vaudeville.

GREENWALD (*shrugs*). See you tomorrow.

CHALLEE. See you tomorrow. (*He goes out.*)

MARYK. Boy, that was marvelous, cutting up that doctor. Wise little bastard.

GREENWALD (*strolls to witness chair and slumps in it*). Have you ever read it?

MARYK. What?

GREENWALD. Your friend Tom Keefer's novel.

MARYK. Huh?

GREENWALD. *Multitudes, Multitudes.* Have you ever read it?

MARYK. Tom's novel? No, he's always kept it in a black satchel, locked.

GREENWALD. I'd like to read it.

MARYK. You would?

GREENWALD. I'm sure it exposes this war in all its grim futility, and shows up the regular army and navy officers—just a lot of stupid sadists, bitching up the campaigns, and throwing away the lives of fatalistic, humorous, lovable citizen soldiers. Lots of sexy scenes where the prose becomes rhythmic and beautiful, while the girl gets her pants pulled down.

MARYK. What's eating you?

GREENWALD. I hate this case, do you know? The more so because I want to win it so bad. Because of what I've got to do to win it.

MARYK. I'm beginning to think I've got a chance. You're pretty keen, all right.

GREENWALD (*gets up and paces*). Almost as keen as Mr. Keefer?

MARYK (*abashed*). You were sure right about him. Why did he do it? He didn't have to implicate himself. He could have said what he really thought of Queeg.

GREENWALD. What, to Blakely? Blakely's sniffing around the edges of Keefer as it is. No sir. Your novelist friend's one course was to clam up. He's smart.

MARYK. You don't like Tom much.

GREENWALD. Well, I look at Keefer and I see my own self of a couple of years ago. Only like in a crazy-house mirror, all distorted and upside down. I'm not amused. Maybe Keefer didn't enjoy sailing under Queeg for half a year. Maybe he'd enjoy it less if the Nazis and the Japs were shaking hands right now at the Mississippi River. I guess what I've found out, Maryk, is that there's a time for everything, including rebellious youth. Possibly you and Mr. Keefer were dead wrong in your timing. In which case the next question is, Who's the real victim in this courtroom? You? Or Captain Queeg?

MARYK. Captain Queeg was nuts!

GREENWALD. You heard Dr. Lundeen. It's a question of degree. If you're in a war and your command personnel is stretched thin, maybe you've got to use him because he's got the training. I'll grant you that Captain Queeg was a mean, stupid son of a bitch, but that doesn't mean—

MARYK. Okay!

GREENWALD. Maryk, if that was grounds for deposing your superior officer we wouldn't have an army or a navy. That's a widespread opinion of superior officers.

MARYK. They're not all Queegs.

GREENWALD. Superiors all tend to look like Queeg from underneath. It's an unflattering angle.

MARYK. What do you do when you really get a Queeg?

GREENWALD. You fight the war. Where can we get drunk? I mean drunk.

MARYK. Mister, you've got a day's work to do in court tomorrow.

GREENWALD. I know exactly what I've got to do in court tomorrow. That's why I want to get drunk. Come on, let's go. (*They go out. Stage lights fade. House lights come on.*)

ACT TWO

THE DEFENSE

SCENE ONE

THE SCENE: *House lights dim. The lights brighten on an empty stage, the setting unchanged from the end of* ACT I. *Enter* ORDERLY, STENOGRAPHER, GREENWALD, MARYK, CHALLEE, *and the six* COURT MEMBERS. *All take their places, standing.*

CHALLEE. Attention!

(BLAKELY *enters and goes to his seat.*)

BLAKELY (*rings bell*). Defense, present your case. (*All sit except* GREENWALD.)

GREENWALD. I call the accused. (MARYK *stands.*)

BLAKELY. Does the accused request that he be permitted to testify?

MARYK. I do so request, sir.

BLAKELY. You have the right to do so. You also have the right not to take the stand. If you don't take the stand that fact won't be to your prejudice. If you take the stand you may be subjected to a rigorous cross-examination.

MARYK. I understand that, sir.

BLAKELY. Court stenographer will affirmatively record that the statutory request was made. (MARYK *does Bible busi-*

ness.) You do solemnly swear that the evidence you shall give in this court shall be the truth, the whole truth, and nothing but the truth. So help you God.

MARYK. I do. (MARYK *takes witness stand.*)

GREENWALD. State your name, rank, and present station.

MARYK. Stephen Maryk, Lieutenant, U.S.N.R., executive officer of the U.S.S. *Caine.*

GREENWALD. Are you the accused in this court-martial?

MARYK. I am.

GREENWALD. What was your occupation in civilian life?

MARYK. Helping out in my father's fishing business. We own a couple of boats.

GREENWALD. Where?

MARYK. Here in San Francisco.

GREENWALD. Then you were familiar with the problems of ocean-going ship handling before entering the Navy?

MARYK. Well, I've been on the boats since I was fourteen.

GREENWALD. Did you relieve the commanding officer of the *Caine* of his command on December 18, 1944?

MARYK. I did.

GREENWALD. Was the *Caine* in the last extremity when you relieved the captain?

MARYK. It was.

GREENWALD. On what facts do you base that judgment?

MARYK (*nervous*). Well, several things, like—well, we were unable to hold course. We broached to three times in an hour.

GREENWALD. Broached to.

MARYK. Yes. Wind and sea took charge and tossed us sideways for ten minutes at a time. We were rolling too steeply for the inclinometer to record. We were shipping solid green water in the wheelhouse. The generators were cutting out. The ship wasn't answering to emergency rudder and engine settings. We were lost and out of control.

GREENWALD. Did you point these things out to the captain?

MARYK. Repeatedly for an hour. I begged him to come north and head into the wind.

GREENWALD. What was his response?

MARYK. Well, mostly a glazed look and no answer or a repetition of his own desires.

GREENWALD. Which were what?

MARYK. I guess to hold fleet course until

we went down.

GREENWALD. Mister Maryk, when did you start keeping your medical log on Captain Queeg?

MARYK. Shortly after the Kwajalein invasion.

GREENWALD. Why did you start it?

MARYK. Well, I began to think the captain might be mentally ill.

GREENWALD. Why?

MARYK. That yellow dye marker business.

GREENWALD. Was that the incident in which Captain Queeg acquired the nickname, Old Yellowstain?

MARYK. Yes, it was.

GREENWALD. You witnessed the occurrence yourself?

MARYK. I was navigator. I was right there on the bridge.

GREENWALD. Describe the Yellow Stain incident, please.

MARYK. Well, it was the first morning of the invasion. We were ordered to lead a group of attack boats in to the beach. That is, we had to take them to their line of departure, one thousand yards from the beach. These little boats lay so low in the water they couldn't see to navigate for themselves. They needed a guide to make sure they hit the right island and the right beach. Captain Queeg rang up ten knots and we started to head in toward this island. It had some funny Jap name. Our code name for it was Jacob Island. Well, it was a choppy sea. These assault boats could only make five or six knots. And at that they were shipping solid water, and the marines were getting just about drowned in spray. They began to fall way behind. Naturally they signaled for us to slow down. But the captain just ignored them. We pulled further and further ahead until we could hardly see them. Then, when we were about twenty-five hundred yards from the beach, we heard some gunfire. The captain suddenly yelled, "We're running up on the beach! Reverse course! Make thirty knots!" And while we were turning he threw over one of these yellow dye markers you use to mark water where there's a floating mine or something. So we went barreling out of there. The attack boats were just a lot of specks way off in the distance. All you could see behind us was this big spread of yellow, all over the water.

(*A long pause.*)

GREENWALD. Now, Mister Maryk—

(BLAKELY *rings his bell.*)

BLAKELY. Court wants to question the witness. Lieutenant, how do you know you were twenty-five hundred yards from the beach when you turned?

MARYK. Sir, I was navigating. There wasn't a doubt in the world where we were, by visual plot. And our radar range to the beach was also twenty-five hundred when we turned.

BLAKELY. Did you inform your captain that he was turning fifteen hundred yards short?

MARYK. Sir, I shouted it at him, over and over. He just stood there smiling.

BLAKELY (*making notes*). You say these boats signaled to you to slow down.

MARYK. Yes, sir. By semaphore.

BLAKELY. Was the signal reported to your captain?

MARYK. I reported it myself.

BLAKELY. Was he aware of the fact that you were running away from the boats?

MARYK. He was looking right at them, sir. I pointed out that if we got too far ahead, the boats wouldn't know where the line of departure was. That's when he said, "Well, we'll throw over a dye marker, then." (BLAKELY *nods to* GREENWALD.)

GREENWALD. Mister Maryk, why didn't you go to higher authority at once with your doubts about the captain's mental health?

MARYK. I figured if I only had a record I'd be on stronger ground. So I decided to start the log. I figured if ever I saw that I was all wrong I'd just burn it. I kept it under lock and key.

GREENWALD. What, in your view, made an incident worthy of record in your medical log?

MARYK. Just any act that seemed strange or abnormal. Like the Silex business.

GREENWALD. Describe the Silex business.

MARYK. A mess boy slopped coffee on a Silex and burned it out. None of the mess boys would admit which one did it. So the captain ordered all the officers of the ship to sit as a court of inquiry till we found out who burned out the Silex. I mean in itself it's a silly little thing. But it went on and on for thirty-six hours. All ship's work stopped. There we were, all of us in the wardroom, dying for sleep, needing shaves, and still trying to find out which of those poor colored boys burned out the Silex. By then those kids thought whoever did it was going to get hung. They would have died before telling us. So finally I had to go to the captain and tell him that all the officers admitted they were incompetent investigators and would take cuts in their fitness reports, but they couldn't find out who slopped coffee on the Silex. So, he made a note in his black book and called off the inquiry. Things like that. Or like the water business.

GREENWALD. Describe the water business.

MARYK. It's all in the log. How he cut off the water at the equator for two days for the whole ship. Just because he caught one simple deck hand stealing a drink during water conservation hours. Or plain crazy things, like the strawberry business.

GREENWALD. Describe the strawberry business.

MARYK. Well, there—

CHALLEE. Objection. The so-called medical log was introduced in evidence at the start of these proceedings. All this is just repeating a lot of trivial disloyal gripes.

GREENWALD. If the court concurs, I'll pass over the medical log.

BLAKELY (with a glance around at the MEMBERS OF THE COURT, uneasily). Well, let's not take up time here.

GREENWALD. Aye aye, sir.

BLAKELY. Only—there seems to be some confusion about the so-called strawberry business. It started out as a search for a quart of strawberries, didn't it?

MARYK. Yes, sir.

BLAKELY. Then it somehow became a search for a key.

MARYK. That's right.

BLAKELY. How was that?

MARYK. That was on account of the cheese business.

BLAKELY. Cheese business? I don't recall any cheese business.

MARYK. That was on the first ship Captain Queeg served on, sir, when he was an ensign. Cheese had been disappearing from ship's stores. He investigated and caught a sailor who had made himself a duplicate key to a padlock on the refrigerator. Well, for catching this cheese thief the captain had gotten a letter of commendation. This was peacetime. Naturally, he was real proud of it. When this strawberry thing came up he insisted it was the same thing, and all we had to do was find out who had

made a duplicate key to the wardroom icebox. But of course it was ridiculous. It was the mess boys again. We all knew they'd eaten up this quart of strawberries. It was just the leavings from the wardroom mess, and they were entitled to eat it, that was the custom. But naturally when the captain started to roar around about "those strawberries," why, the boys just froze up and swore they hadn't eaten them. And the captain, he was so steamed up on this key theory, he believed them.

BLAKELY. So he ordered the search for the key?

MARYK. Yes, sir. We never saw Captain Queeg so happy before or since. He was living the cheese business all over again. He organized the search himself. All ship's work was suspended. We collected every single key on the ship—boxes of keys, barrels of keys, about twenty-eight hundred of them all tagged with the owner's name. Then to make sure we had them all we searched the ship from stem to stern, from the crow's nest to the bilge. We stripped the crew stark-naked, every one of them, and shook out their clothes. We searched their lockers. We crawled into every hole and every space in the ship. We crawled under the boilers and pulled out the lead ballast blocks, two hundred pounds apiece. This went on for three days, and all of it over a key that never existed. Well, when I saw Captain Queeg sitting by the icebox, taking those keys one by one out of the barrels and trying them on the padlock, hours on end, with a gleam in his eye, I gave up. That was when I showed the medical log to Lieutenant Keefer.

BLAKELY. Mister Maryk, when Lieutenant Keefer finished reading your medical log, what was his first comment?

(All six COURT MEMBERS stare intently at MARYK.)

MARYK (pause). Sir, I'm afraid I don't remember.

BLAKELY. Did he encourage you to go to Admiral Halsey?

MARYK. I did that on my own responsibility, sir.

BLAKELY. But he went with you to the New Jersey?

MARYK. He did, sir.

BLAKELY. So at first—he didn't discourage you?

MARYK. Well, sir, when we got aboard the New Jersey he discouraged me. He said we shouldn't go through with it. And we didn't.

BLAKELY. Would you say his testimony on the subject was substantially correct?

MARYK. Yes, sir. It was all my doing, sir. (BLAKELY *nods to* GREENWALD.)

GREENWALD. Mister Maryk, when the typhoon was over, did Captain Queeg make any effort to regain command?

MARYK. Yes, on the morning of the nineteenth. The storm had blown out. We'd just sighted the fleet.

GREENWALD. Describe what happened.

MARYK. Well, I was in the charthouse writing up a despatch to report the relief to Admiral Halsey. The captain came in and said, "Do you mind coming to my cabin and having a talk before you send that?" I went below and we talked. It was the same thing at first—about how I'd be court-martialed for mutiny. He said, "You've applied for transfer to the regular navy. You know this means the end of all that, don't you?" Then he went into a long thing about how he loved the Navy and had no other interest in life, and even if he was cleared this would ruin his record. I said I felt sorry for him, and I really did. Finally he came out with his proposal. He said he'd forget the whole thing and never report me. He would resume command, and the whole matter would be forgotten and written off—

GREENWALD. What did you say to the proposal?

MARYK. Well, I was amazed. I said, "Captain, the whole ship knows about it. It's written up in the quartermaster's log and the OOD's log." Well, he hemmed and hawed, and finally said it wouldn't be the first time a penciled rough log had been corrected and fixed up after the fact.

GREENWALD. Did you remind him of the rule against erasures?

MARYK. Yes, and he kind of laughed and said it was either that or a court-martial for mutiny for me, and a black mark on his record which he didn't deserve. And he didn't see that a few penciled lines were worth all that.

GREENWALD. What followed?

MARYK. Well he began to plead and beg —he cried at one point—in the end he became terrifically angry, and ordered me out of his cabin. So I sent the despatch.

GREENWALD. Then you had the chance, twenty-four hours later, of expunging the whole event from the official record with the captain's knowledge and approval?

MARYK. Yes.

GREENWALD. Mister Maryk, were you panicky at all during the typhoon?

MARYK. I was not.

GREENWALD. Now, Lieutenant, you're charged with relieving your captain willfully, without authority, and without justifiable cause. Did you relieve Captain Queeg willfully?

MARYK. Yes, I knew what I was doing.

GREENWALD. Did you relieve without authority?

MARYK. No. My authority was Articles 184, 185, and 186.

GREENWALD. Did you relieve without justifiable cause?

MARYK. No. My justifiable cause was the captain's mental breakdown at a time when the ship was in danger.

GREENWALD. No further questions. (*Sits.* CHALLEE *approaches* MARYK.)

CHALLEE. Mister Maryk, this amazing interview in which the captain offered to falsify official records. Were there any witnesses to it?

MARYK. We were alone in the captain's cabin. No.

CHALLEE. This incident at Kwajalein. Did anyone else see this chart which, according to you, indicated your ship turned away from the beach too soon?

MARYK. About an hour after it happened the captain asked to see the chart and took it to his cabin. When I got it back all my bearings and course lines had been erased.

CHALLEE. Then you have no documentary corroboration of this story.

MARYK. No.

CHALLEE. How about the radar men who called off the ranges? Won't they confirm your story?

MARYK. Sir, you can't expect them to remember one single radar range, when they called them by the thousands in every invasion.

CHALLEE. These poor abandoned marines in the assault boats never complained to higher authority of the dastardly conduct of the *Caine?*

MARYK. No.

CHALLEE. Strange.

MARYK. Sir, they landed against machine gun fire. The ones that survived, I don't think they remembered much else besides that landing.

CHALLEE. Mister Maryk, who coined this scurrilous nickname, "Old Yellowstain"?

MARYK (*a worried glance at* GREENWALD). Well, it just sprang into existence.

CHALLEE. Throughout the ship? Or just among the officers?

MARYK. Among the officers.

CHALLEE. You're sure you didn't coin it yourself?

MARYK. I didn't.

CHALLEE. Mister Maryk, what kind of rating would you give yourself for loyalty to your captain?

MARYK. I think I was a loyal officer.

CHALLEE. Did you issue a seventy-two-hour pass to Stilwell in December '43 against the captain's express instructions?

MARYK. I did.

CHALLEE. Do you call that a loyal act?

MARYK. No.

CHALLEE. You admit to a disloyal act in your first days as executive officer?

MARYK. Yes.

CHALLEE. Mister Maryk—where did you get your schooling?

MARYK. Public schools, San Francisco. And San Francisco University.

CHALLEE. How were your grades in elementary school?

MARYK. Okay.

CHALLEE. Average? Above average? Below average?

MARYK. Average.

CHALLEE. How about your high school grades?

MARYK. Well, I didn't do so good there. Below average.

CHALLEE. What kind of course did you take at college?

MARYK. Business course.

CHALLEE. Any pre-medical courses?

MARYK. No.

CHALLEE. Any psychology or psychiatry courses?

MARYK. No.

CHALLEE. How were your grades at college?

MARYK. I scraped by.

CHALLEE. Below average?

MARYK. Yes.

CHALLEE. Then where did you get all of these highfalutin ideas about paranoia?

MARYK (*with a worried glance toward* GREENWALD). I—out of books.

CHALLEE. What books? Name the titles.

MARYK. Medical-type books about mental illness.

CHALLEE. Was that your intellectual hobby—reading about psychiatry?

MARYK. No.

CHALLEE. Then where did you get these books?

MARYK. I—borrowed them off ships' doctors here and there.

CHALLEE. And with your background, your scholastic record—did you imagine you understood these highly technical scientific works?

MARYK. Well, I got something out of them.

CHALLEE. What is a conditioned reflex?

MARYK. I don't know.

CHALLEE. What is schizophrenia?

MARYK. I think it's a mental illness.

CHALLEE. You think so. What are its symptoms?

MARYK. I don't know.

CHALLEE. In fact, you don't know what you're talking about when you discuss mental illness, is that right? .

MARYK. I didn't say I knew much about it.

CHALLEE. Have you ever heard the expression, "A little learning is a dangerous thing"?

MARYK. Yes.

CHALLEE. You got a headful of terms you didn't understand, and on that basis you had the temerity to depose a commanding officer on the grounds of mental illness. Is that correct?

MARYK. I didn't relieve him because of what the books said. The ship was in danger—

CHALLEE. Never mind the ship. We're discussing your grasp of psychiatry. Have you heard the diagnosis of the qualified psychiatrists who examined your captain?

MARYK. Yes.

CHALLEE. What was their diagnosis—was he crazy or wasn't he, on 18 December?

MARYK. They say he wasn't.

CHALLEE. But, you, with your whining gripes about strawberries and Silexes, know better. Mister Maryk, who was the third ranking officer on your ship?

MARYK. Lieutenant Keefer.

CHALLEE. Was he a good officer?

MARYK. Yes.

CHALLEE. Do you consider his mind as good as yours? Or perhaps better?

MARYK. Better.

CHALLEE. You showed this medical log

of yours to him.

MARYK. Yes.

CHALLEE. He wasn't convinced by it that the captain was mentally ill.

MARYK. No.

CHALLEE. He talked you out of trying to have the captain relieved.

MARYK. Yes.

CHALLEE. And yet two weeks later—despite the whole weight of naval discipline —despite the arguments of the next officer in rank to you, a superior intellect—despite all this, you went ahead and seized command of your ship?

MARYK. I relieved him because he definitely seemed sick during the typhoon.

CHALLEE. You *still* imagine your diagnosis of Captain Queeg is superior to the doctor's?

MARYK. Only about Queeg on the morning of the typhoon.

CHALLEE. No more questions.

GREENWALD. No re-examination.

BLAKELY. You may step down, Lieutenant. (MARYK *leaves the stand with a stunned expression and goes to his seat.* BLAKELY *glances at* GREENWALD.)

GREENWALD. Call Lieutenant Commander Queeg. (*Exit* ORDERLY. *Returns with* QUEEG, *who looks as debonair and assured as on the first day. He hesitates before taking witness chair, expecting to be sworn.*)

BLAKELY. Commander, the oath previously taken by you is still binding.

QUEEG. Yes, sir. (QUEEG *takes witness chair.* GREENWALD *approaches* QUEEG.)

GREENWALD. Commander, on the morning of 19 December, did you have an interview in your room with Lieutenant Maryk?

QUEEG. Let's see. That's the day after the typhoon. Yes, I did.

GREENWALD. Was it at your request?

QUEEG. Yes.

GREENWALD. What was the substance of that interview?

QUEEG. Well, as I say, I felt sorry for him. I hated to see him ruining his life with one panicky mistake. Particularly as I knew his ambition was to make the Navy his career. I tried as hard as I could to show him what a mistake he had made. I recommended that he relinquish command to me, and I offered to be as lenient as I could in reporting what had happened.

GREENWALD. You never offered not to re-port the incident?

QUEEG. How could I? It was already recorded in the logs.

GREENWALD. Were the logs in pencil, or typed, or what?

QUEEG. That would make no difference.

GREENWALD. Were they in pencil, Commander?

QUEEG. Well, let's see. Probably they were—quartermaster log and OOD rough log always are. I doubt the yeoman would have gotten around to typing smooth logs in all the excitement.

GREENWALD. Did you offer to erase the incident from the penciled logs and make no report at all?

QUEEG. I did not. Erasures aren't permitted in penciled logs.

GREENWALD. Lieutenant Maryk has testified under oath, Commander, that you made such an offer. Not only that, but you begged and pleaded and even wept to get him to agree to erase those few pencil lines, in return for which you promised to hush up the incident completely and make no report.

QUEEG (*calmly and pleasantly*). That isn't true.

GREENWALD. There isn't any truth in it at all?

QUEEG. Well, it's a distortion of what I told you. My version is the exact truth.

GREENWALD. You deny the proposal to erase the logs and hush up the story?

QUEEG. I deny it completely. That's the part he made up . . . And the weeping and the pleading. That's fantastic.

GREENWALD. You are accusing Mister Maryk of perjury?

QUEEG. I'm not accusing him. He's accused of enough as it stands. You're likely to hear a lot of strange things from Mister Maryk about me, that's all.

GREENWALD. Isn't one of you obviously not telling the truth about that interview?

QUEEG. It appears so.

GREENWALD. Can you prove it isn't you?

QUEEG. Only by citing a clean record of over fourteen years as a naval officer, against the word of a man on trial for a mutinous act.

GREENWALD. Commander, did you ever receive a hundred ten dollars from Lieutenant Junior Grade Keith?

QUEEG. I don't recall offhand that I did.

GREENWALD. He testified that you did.

QUEEG. I did? On what occasion?

GREENWALD. On the occasion of a loss of a crate of yours in San Francisco Bay.

QUEEG. Yes. I remember now. It was over a year ago. December or thereabouts. He was responsible for the loss and insisted on paying, and so he did.

GREENWALD. What was in the crate, Commander, that cost a hundred and ten dollars?

QUEEG. Oh, uniforms, books, navigating instruments—the usual.

GREENWALD. How was Keith responsible for the loss?

QUEEG. Well, he was boat officer and in charge of the loading. He issued foolish and contradictory orders. The men got rattled and the crate fell into the water and sank.

GREENWALD. A wooden crate full of clothes sank?

QUEEG. There were other things in it, I guess. I had some souvenir coral rocks.

GREENWALD. Commander, wasn't the crate entirely full of bottles of intoxicating liquor?

QUEEG (after a barely perceptible pause). Certainly not.

GREENWALD. Keith has testified you charged him for a crate of liquor.

QUEEG. You'll hear plenty of strange distortions about me from Keith and Maryk. They're the two culprits here and they're apt to make all kinds of strange statements.

GREENWALD. Did you make this crate yourself?

QUEEG. No. My carpenter's mate did.

GREENWALD. What was his name?

QUEEG. I don't recall. It'll be on the personnel records. He's been gone from the ship a long time.

GREENWALD. Where is this carpenter's mate now, Commander?

QUEEG. I don't know. I transferred him to the beach at Funafuti at the request of the commodore for a carpenter. This was back in May.

GREENWALD. You don't recall his name?

QUEEG. No.

GREENWALD. Was it Carpenter's Mate Second Class Otis F. Langhorne?

QUEEG. Lang, Langhorne. Sounds right.

GREENWALD. Commander, there is a Carpenter's Mate First Class Otis F. Langhorne at present in damage-control school at Treasure Island, right here in the bay. Defense has arranged to subpoena him if

necessary.

QUEEG (shoots a look at CHALLEE). You're sure it's the same one?

GREENWALD. His service record shows twenty-one months aboard the Caine. Your signature is in it. Would it be useful to have him subpoenaed, sir?

CHALLEE. Objection to this entire irrelevancy about the crate, and request it be stricken from the record.

GREENWALD. The credibility of the witness is being established. I submit to the court that nothing could be more relevant to this trial.

BLAKELY. Overruled. (Nods to STENOGRAPHER.)

STENOGRAPHER (reads). "Would it be useful to have him subpoenaed, sir?"

QUEEG. Well, it's a question which crate Langhorne nailed up. I had two crates, as I recall now.

GREENWALD. Oh? (Pause.) Well. This a new angle, not mentioned by Keith. Did Langhorne make both crates, sir?

QUEEG. Well, I don't recall whether I had both crates on that occasion or two crates on two different occasions. It's all very trivial and happened a long time ago and I've had a year of combat steaming in between and a typhoon and all this hospital business and I'm not too clear.

GREENWALD. Commander, there are many points in this trial which turn on the issue of credibility between yourself and other officers. If you wish I will request a five-minute recess while you clear your mind as well as you can on the matter of these crates.

QUEEG. That won't be necessary. Just let me think for a moment, please. (In the silence BLAKELY's pencil makes a thin rattling noise as he rolls it under his palm on the bench. QUEEG sits staring from under his eyebrows.) Kay. I have it straight now. I made a misstatement. I lost a crate in San Diego Harbor back in '38 or '39 I think it was, under similar circumstances. That was the one containing clothes. The crate Keith lost did contain liquor.

GREENWALD. Was it entirely full of liquor?

QUEEG. I believe it was.

GREENWALD. How did you obtain a crate full of whiskey, Commander, in wartime?

QUEEG. Bought up the rations of my officers at the wine mess in Pearl Harbor.

GREENWALD. You transported this liquor

from Pearl to the States in your ship? Do you know the regulations—

QUEEG (*breaks in*). I'm aware of regulations. The crate was sealed prior to getting under way. I gave it the same locked stowage I gave the medicinal brandy. Liquor was damned scarce and expensive in the States. I'd had three years of steady combat duty. I gave myself this leeway as captain of the *Caine* and it was a common practice and I believe rank has its privileges, as they say. I had no intentions of concealing it from the court and I'm not ashamed of it. I simply mixed up the two crates in my mind.

GREENWALD. Keith testified, Commander, that you gave all the orders to the boat crew which caused the loss of the crate.

QUEEG. That's a lie.

GREENWALD. Also that you refused to sign his leave papers until he paid for the loss.

QUEEG. That's another lie.

GREENWALD. It seems to be the issue of credibility again, sir—this time your word against Keith's. Correct?

QUEEG. You'll hear nothing but lies about me from Keith. He has an insane hatred of me.

GREENWALD. Do you know why, sir?

QUEEG. I can't say, unless it's his resentment against fancied injuries to his crony, this sailor Stilwell. Those two were mighty affectionate.

GREENWALD. Affectionate, sir?

QUEEG. Well, it seems to me every time Keith thought I looked crosseyed at Stilwell there was all kinds of screeching and hollering from Keith as though I were picking on his wife or something. And those two sure ganged up mighty fast to back Maryk when he relieved me.

GREENWALD. Commander, are you suggesting there were abnormal relations between Lieutenant Keith and the sailor Stilwell?

QUEEG. I'm not suggesting a thing. I'm stating plain facts that everybody knew who had eyes to see.

GREENWALD (*looking around at* BLAKELY). Does the court desire to caution the witness about the gravity of the insinuated charge?

QUEEG (*nasally*). I'm not insinuating a thing, sir! I don't know of anything improper between those two men and I deny insinuating anything. All I said was that

Keith was always taking Stilwell's part and and it's the easiest thing in the world to prove and that's all I said or meant. I resent the twisting of my words.

BLAKELY. Are you going to pursue this—topic?

GREENWALD. No, sir.

BLAKELY. Very well. Go ahead.

GREENWALD. Commander, during the period when the *Caine* was towing targets at Pearl Harbor did you ever steam over your own towline and cut it?

CHALLEE (*stands*). Objection! This towline business is the last straw. The tactics of the defense counsel are an outrage on the dignity of these proceedings. He's systematically turning this trial into a court-martial of Commander Queeg.

GREENWALD. Sir, the judge advocate has made it perfectly clear that he thinks he has a prima facie case in the report of the two psychiatrists. But I say it's still up to the court, not to shore-bound doctors, however brilliant, to decide whether the captain of the *Caine* was mentally well enough to retain his self-control and his post during a typhoon.

BLAKELY. The objection is overruled. The witness will answer the question. (*Nods to* STENOGRAPHER. CHALLEE *appears stunned, sitting down slowly.*)

STENOGRAPHER (*reads*). "Commander Queeg, during the period when the *Caine* was towing targets at Pearl Harbor did you ever steam over your own towline and cut it?"

QUEEG (*promptly*). Kay, now—here's the story on that particular slander. I started to make a turn, when I noticed some anti-aircraft bursts close aboard to starboard. I was gravely concerned that my ship might be within range of somebody's firing. We were in a gunnery area. I was watching the bursts. This same sailor Stilwell, a very dreamy and unreliable man, was at the helm. He failed to warn me that we were coming around the full 360 degrees. I saw what was happening, finally, and instantly reversed course, and I avoided passing over the towline, to my best knowledge. However, the line parted during the turn.

GREENWALD. You say you were distracted by AA bursts. Did anything else distract you?

QUEEG. Not that I recall.

GREENWALD. Were you engaged in reprimanding a signalman named Urban at length for having his shirttail out, while your ship was turning 360 degrees?

QUEEG. Who says that—Keith again?

GREENWALD. Will you answer the question, Commander?

QUEEG. It's a malicious lie, of course.

GREENWALD. Was Urban on the bridge at the time?

QUEEG. Yes.

GREENWALD. Was his shirttail out?

QUEEG. Yes, and I reprimanded him. That took me about two seconds. I'm not in the habit of dwelling on those things. Then there were those AA bursts, and that was what distracted me.

GREENWALD. Did you point out these AA bursts to the officer of the deck or the exec?

QUEEG. I may have. I don't recall. I didn't run weeping to my OOD on every occasion. I may very well have kept my own counsel. And since this shirttail thing has been brought up—I'd like to say that Ensign Keith as morale officer was in charge of enforcing uniform regulations and completely soldiered on the job. When I took over the ship it was like the Chinese Navy. And I bore down on Keith to watch those shirttails and for all I know that's another reason he hated me and circulated all this about my cutting the towline.

GREENWALD. Did you drop a yellow dye marker off Jacob Island on the first morning of the invasion of Kwajalein?

QUEEG. I may have. I don't recall.

GREENWALD. Do you recall what your first mission was during the invasion?

QUEEG. Yes. To lead a group of attack boats to the line of departure for Jacob Island.

GREENWALD. Did you fulfill that mission?

QUEEG. Yes.

GREENWALD. Why did you drop the dye marker?

QUEEG. I don't know for sure that I did drop one. Maybe I dropped one to mark the line of departure plainly.

GREENWALD. How far was the line of departure from the beach?

QUEEG. As I recall, a thousand yards.

GREENWALD. Commander, didn't you run a mile ahead of the attack boats, drop your dye marker more than half a mile short, and retire at high speed, leaving the boats to grope their way to the line of departure as best they could?

CHALLEE (rises). The question is abusive and flagrantly leading.

GREENWALD (wearily). I am willing to withdraw the question, in view of the commander's dim memory, and proceed to more recent events.

BLAKELY. Court desires to question the witness. (GREENWALD crosses to his desk.) Commander Queeg, in view of the implications in this line of testimony, I urge you to search your memory for correct answers.

QUEEG. I am certainly trying to do that, sir. But these are very small points. I've been through several campaigns since Kwajalein and the typhoon and now all this business—

BLAKELY. I appreciate that. It will facilitate justice if you can remember enough to give a few definite answers on points of fact. First of all, were those boats on the line of departure when you turned away from the beach?

QUEEG. As near as I could calculate, yes.

BLAKELY. In that case, Commander, if they were already on the line, what purpose did the dye marker serve?

QUEEG (hesitates). Well, you might say a safety factor. Just another added mark. Now—maybe I erred in being overcautious and making sure they knew where they were but then again, sir, I've always believed you can't err on the side of safety.

BLAKELY (slight acrid impatience). Did you have the conn?

QUEEG (pauses). As I recall now Lieutenant Maryk had the conn, and I now recall I had to caution him for opening the gap too wide between us and the boats.

BLAKELY. How wide?

QUEEG. I can't say, but at one point there was definitely too much open water and I called him aside and I admonished him not to run away from the boats.

BLAKELY. Didn't you direct him to slow down when you saw the gap widening?

QUEEG. Well, but it was all happening very fast and I may have been watching the beach for a few seconds and then I saw we were running away. And so that's why I dropped the marker, to compensate for Maryk's running away from the boats.

BLAKELY (pauses, face grave). These are your factual recollections, Commander?

QUEEG. Those are the facts, sir.

BLAKELY (to GREENWALD). Resume your examination.

GREENWALD (speaks at once). Commander Queeg, did you make it a practice, during invasions, to station yourself on the side of the bridge that was sheltered from the beach?

QUEEG (*angrily*). That's an insulting question, and the answer is no, I had to be on all sides of the bridge at once, constantly moving from one side to the other because Maryk was navigator and Keith was my OOD at general quarters and both of them were invariably scurrying to the safe side of the bridge so I was captain and navigator and OOD all rolled in one and that's why I had to move constantly from one side of the bridge to the other. And that's the truth, whatever lies may have been said about me in this court. (QUEEG *takes two steel balls out of his pocket.*)

BLAKELY (*rings bell*). The court will question the witness.

CHALLEE (*stands*). Sir, the witness is obviously and understandably agitated by this ordeal, and I request a recess to give him a breathing space—

QUEEG. I am not in the least agitated, and I'm glad to answer any and all questions here and in fact I demand a chance to set the record straight on anything derogatory to me in the testimony that's gone before. I did not make a single mistake in fifteen months aboard the *Caine* and I can prove it and my record has been spotless until now and I don't want it smirched by a whole lot of lies and distortions by disloyal officers.

BLAKELY. Commander, would you like a recess?

QUEEG. Definitely not, sir. I request there be no recess if it's up to me.

BLAKELY. Very well. I simply want to ask—if the performance of these two officers was so unspeakably bad, why did you tolerate it? Why didn't you beach them? Or at least rotate them to less responsible battle stations?

QUEEG. Well, sir, strange as it may seem, the fact is I'm a very soft-hearted guy. Not many people know that. I never despaired of training those two men up and making naval officers of them. I kept them under my eye just because I wanted to train them up. The last thing I wanted to do was wreck their careers. Not that they had any similar concern for me, either of them.

BLAKELY. Defense counsel . . .

GREENWALD. Commander, on the morning of 18 December, at the moment you were relieved, was the *Caine* in the last extremity?

QUEEG. It certainly was not!

GREENWALD. Was it in grave danger at that moment?

QUEEG. Absolutely not. I had that ship under complete control. (*Puts steel balls away.*)

GREENWALD. Did you ever indicate to your other officers that it had been your intention to change course and come north at ten o'clock—or fifteen minutes after Maryk did?

QUEEG (*pause*). Yes, I did make that statement, and such had been my intention.

GREENWALD. Why did you intend to abandon fleet course, Commander, if the ship wasn't in danger?

QUEEG (*after a long silence*). Well, I don't see any inconsistency there. I've repeatedly stated in my testimony that my rule is safety first. As I say the ship wasn't in danger but a typhoon is still a typhoon and I'd just about decided that we'd do as well coming around to north. I might have executed my intention at ten o'clock and then again I might not have.

GREENWALD. Then Maryk's decision to come north was not a panicky, irrational blunder?

QUEEG. His panicky blunder was relieving me. I kept him from making any disastrous mistakes thereafter. I didn't intend to vindicate myself at the cost of all the lives on the *Caine*.

GREENWALD. Commander Queeg, have you read Lieutenant Maryk's medical log?

QUEEG. Oh, yes, I have read that interesting document, yes, sir, I have. It's the biggest conglomeration of lies and distortions and half-truths I've ever seen and I'm extremely glad you asked me because I want to get my side of it all on the record.

GREENWALD. Please state your version, or any factual comments on the episodes in the log, sir.

QUEEG. Kay. Now, starting right with that strawberry business the real truth is that I was betrayed and thrown and double-crossed by my executive officer and this precious gentleman Mister Keith who between them corrupted my wardroom so that I was one man against a whole ship without any support from my officers . . . Kay. Now, you take that strawberry business—why, if that wasn't a case of outright conspiracy to protect a malefactor from justice—Maryk carefully leaves out the little fact that I had conclusively proved by a process of elimination that someone had a key to the icebox. He says it was the steward's mates who ate the strawberries but if I wanted to take the trouble I could prove to this court geometrically that they couldn't have. It's the water business all over again, like when the crew was taking baths seven times a day and our evaps were definitely on the fritz half the time and I was trying to inculcate the simplest principles of water conservation, but no, Mister Maryk the hero of the crew wanted to go right on mollycoddling them and— Or you take the coffee business . . . No! Well, the strawberry thing first—it all hinged on a thorough search for the key and that was where Mister Maryk as usual with the help of Mister Keith fudged it. Just went through a lot of phony motions that proved nothing and— Like thinking the incessant burning out of Silexes which were government property was a joke, which was the attitude of everybody from Maryk down, no sense of responsibility though I emphasized over and over that the war wouldn't last forever, that all these things would have to be accounted for. It was a constant battle, always the same thing, Maryk and Keith undermining my authority, always arguments, though I personally liked Keith and kept trying to train him up only to get stabbed in the back when— Kay, I think I've covered the strawberry business and— Oh, yes, this mess account business. I had to watch them like a hawk. And believe me I did. They didn't sneak any fast ones by but it wasn't for not trying. Instead of paying some attention to their accounts and their inventories which I had to check over and over, always a few pennies short or a few dollars over— what did it matter to them, keeping accurate records? Let the captain worry. And I did, by God. I defy anyone to check over a single wardroom mess statement or ship's service inventory filed aboard the U.S.S. *Caine* while I was captain and find a mistake of one single solitary cent, and I mean I defy a certified public accountant to do it. Kay, what else? There was so much tripe in that precious log of Mister Maryk's — Oh, yes, the movie business. Kay. No respect for command was the whole trouble with that ship, and the movie operator, who had a disrespectful surly manner anyway, blithely started the movie without waiting for the arrival of the commanding officer. And out of that whole ship's crew, officers and men, did one person call a halt or even notice that the captain wasn't present? I missed those movies more than they did, but I banned them and by God I'd do it again. What was I supposed to do, issue letters of commendation to all of them for this gratuitous insult to the commanding officer? Not that I took it personally, it was the principle, the principle of respect for command. That principle was dead when I came aboard that ship but I brought it to life and I nagged and I crabbed and I bitched and I hollered but by God I made it stick while I was the captain. And as I say—like the Silexes. It wasn't only the Silexes, it was a matter of respect, when I ask a sailor a question I want a straight answer and nobody's going to get away with shifty evasions if I have to hold a court of inquiry for a week. What do I care for strawberries? It was a question of principle, pilfering is pilfering, and on my ship—not that we had so many treats, either. With those slow-motion treasurers of ours—not like when I was an ensign, believe me, they made me jump sure enough—when we did get something pleasant like strawberries once in a blue moon it was an outrage not to have another helping if I felt like it, and I wasn't going to let them get away with that, and I didn't, by God, there was no more of that again on that ship. And so, as I say— Kay, how many of these things have I covered? I can only do this roughly from memory, but you ask me specific questions and I'll tackle them one by one.

(*During this speech* GREENWALD *strolls to his desk and leans against it, listening respectfully. The* COURT MEMBERS *stare at* QUEEG *and at each other and at their wrist watches after a while.* CHALLEE *slouches, biting his nails.*)

GREENWALD. It was a very thorough and complete answer, Commander, thank you. (*Goes to* STENOGRAPHER.) May I have exhibit twelve? (STENOGRAPHER *hands him a glossy black photostat.*) Commander, I show you an authenticated copy of a fitness report you wrote on Lieutenant Maryk, dated 1 July 1944. Do you recognize it as such?

(QUEEG *takes paper, glances at it.*)

QUEEG (*grumpily*). Yes.

GREENWALD. By that date, had the following incidents already occurred: the water shortage, the Silex investigation, the suspension of movies—among others?

QUEEG (*hesitates*). Well, by then, yes, I think.

GREENWALD. Please read to the court your comment of 1 July on Lieutenant Maryk.

QUEEG (*stares at the paper. In a choked voice*). Naturally, not being vindictive, I don't write down every single thing—a fitness report goes into a man's record, and I—I try to go easy, I always have, I always will—

GREENWALD. I appreciate that, sir. Please read your comment.

QUEEG (*mumbling, hunched over, after a long pause*). "This officer has if anything improved in his performance of duty since the last fitness report. He is consistently loyal, unflagging, thorough, courageous, and efficient. He is considered at present fully qualified for command of a 1200-ton DMS. His professional zeal and integrity set him apart as an outstanding example for other officers, reserve and regular alike. He cannot be too highly commended. He is recommended for transfer to the regular navy."

GREENWALD. Thank you, Commander. No further questions. (GREENWALD *walks to his desk and sits.* CHALLEE *stands slowly, like an old man with rheumatism. He approaches the witness stand, seems about to speak, then turns to* BLAKELY.)

CHALLEE. No cross-examination.

BLAKELY. You are excused, Commander. (*Exit* QUEEG.)

GREENWALD. Defense rests.

BLAKELY. Is the judge advocate ready to present his argument?

CHALLEE. Sir, I believe I'll waive the argument.

BLAKELY. No argument at all?

CHALLEE. If it please the court, I'm at a loss to discuss the case the defense has presented. I have nothing to refute. It's no case at all. It has nothing to do with the charge or the specification. The defense counsel's very first question in this trial was, "Commander, have you ever heard the expression, 'Old Yellowstain'?" That was the key to his entire strategy—which was simply to twist the proceedings around so that the accused would become not Maryk but Commander Queeg. He's dragged out every possible vicious and malicious criticism of the commander from the other witnesses, and forced Queeg to defend himself against them in open court, on the spur of the moment, without advice of counsel, without any of the normal privileges and safeguards of an accused man under naval law.

Can this court possibly endorse the precedent that a captain who doesn't please his underlings can be deposed by them? And that the captain's only recourse afterward is to be placed on the witness stand at a general court-martial to answer every petty gripe and justify all his command decisions to a hostile lawyer taking the part of his insubordinate inferiors? Such a precedent is nothing but a blank check for mutiny. It is the absolute destruction of the chain of command.

However all this doesn't worry me, sir. I'm confident that this court hasn't been impressed by such shyster tactics. I know the court is going to reject this cynical play on its emotions, this insult to its intelligence, and find the specification proven by the facts. I've only this to say, sir. Whatever the verdict on the accused, I formally recommend that defense counsel Greenwald be reprimanded by this court for conduct unbecoming an officer of the Navy —and that this reprimand be made part of his service record. (CHALLEE *sits*.)

BLAKELY. Defense counsel—closing argument?

GREENWALD (*rises, stands by his desk*). Please the court, I undertook the defense of the accused very reluctantly, and only at the urging of the judge advocate that no other defense counsel was available. I was reluctant because I knew that the only possible defense was to show in court the mental incompetence of an officer of the Navy. It has been the most unpleasant duty I've ever had to perform. Once having undertaken it, I did what I could to win an acquittal. I thought this was my duty, both as defense counsel appointed by the Navy, and as a member of the bar. (*Comes forward slowly.*) Let me make one thing clear. It is not, and never has been, the contention of the defense that Commander Queeg is a coward. The entire case of the defense rests on the assumption that no man who rises to command of a United States naval ship can possibly be a coward. And that therefore if he commits questionable acts under fire, the explanation must lie elsewhere. The court saw the bearing of Captain Queeg on the stand. The court can picture what his bearing must have been at the height of a typhoon. On that basis the court will decide the fate of the accused. (*Sits.*)

BLAKELY. Before recessing, the court will rule on the recommendation to reprimand. (COURT MEMBERS *write their votes and pass papers to him.*) Lieutenant Greenwald.

GREENWALD (*rises, comes to Center Stage at attention*). Yes, sir.

BLAKELY. Lieutenant, this has been a strange and tragic trial. You have conducted your case with striking ingenuity. The judge advocate's remark about "shyster tactics" was an unfortunate personal slur. But your conduct has been puzzling, and it does raise questions. With talent goes responsibility. Has your conduct here been responsible, Lieutenant Greenwald? (*Glances through votes and tears them up. In a dry cold tone:*) The reprimand, if there's to be one, must come from your own conscience. Counsel's words and acts are privileged within the broad limits of contempt of court. Court finds defense counsel has not been in contempt. Recommendation to reprimand denied. (*Rings bell.*) Recess.

(*Exit all but* MARYK *and* GREENWALD. *During next lines* ORDERLY *and* STENOGRAPHER *put back the witness stand and* GREENWALD's *desk as they were when the play began; then they go out.*)

MARYK. What happens now?

GREENWALD. That's the ball game.

MARYK. When do we find out?

GREENWALD. If it's an acquittal, you'll find out in an hour or so. If it isn't they may not publish the findings for weeks.

MARYK. Meantime would I be confined?

GREENWALD. No, hardly.

MARYK. What do you think?

GREENWALD. I'd stick around for an hour or so.

MARYK. You were terrific.

GREENWALD. Thanks.

MARYK. You murdered Queeg.

GREENWALD. Yes, I murdered him.

MARYK. I'm grateful to you. Win or lose.

GREENWALD. Okay.

MARYK. What's the matter?

GREENWALD. Not a thing.

MARYK. You bothered by what Challee said? Or Blakely?

GREENWALD. Why should I be? I had a job to do. I did it. That's all.

MARYK. That's the spirit. Look. I want to ask your advice.

GREENWALD. What now?

MARYK. Tom Keefer's throwing a party tonight at the Fairmont Hotel. This morning he got a thousand-buck check—advance on his novel.

GREENWALD. Bully for him. I hope he sells a million copies, and wins the Pulitzer Prize, the Nobel Prize, and the Congressional Medal of Honor, and gets his bust in the Hall of Fame. That'll wrap this thing up in a pink ribbon.

MARYK. We're both invited to the party.

GREENWALD. What!

MARYK. Well, I know what you probably think. But hell, one way or another it's all over. I don't know what I'd have done in Tom's place.

GREENWALD. You'd go to Keefer's party?

MARYK. Tom's always called me a good-natured slob. I'll go if you will. If you think we should.

GREENWALD (*staring at him*). All right. Maybe we'll both go and help Mr. Keefer celebrate.

(BLACKOUT. *Drunken singing of many male voices in the darkness, "I've Got Sixpence."*)

Scene Two

THE SCENE: *The scene is the private dining room in the Fairmont Hotel. A long table has been moved on. It is covered with a green cloth and a garland of flowers is stretched along the front. A green curtain masks the center of the courtroom, and the rest is in darkness. The lights concentrate narrowly on the table. The table is stacked with bottles of champagne and glasses, and a huge cake baked in the form of a book.*

Seven officers in blues are grouped around the table, including MARYK, KEITH, *and* KEEFER. *They are all pretty drunk. They are sitting at various angles, waving glasses and bottles, and trying to drown each other out in the singing of "I've Got Sixpence."* WILLIE KEITH *is trying desperately to sing, all alone, "Bell Bottom Trousers."* KEEFER *and* MARYK *tell him he is singing the wrong song and finally get him to*

join in their singing of "Sixpence." GREEN-
WALD *enters Stage Left, unnoticed by the
group, and stands silently watching their
party.* KEEFER *glances off and sees* GREEN-
WALD *standing there.*

———

KEEFER. Quiet!

Quiet! All right, QUIET, you drunken
bums of the *Caine!* Here he is! The guest
of honor! Fill your glasses! A toast to the
conquering hero! Greenwald the Magnificent! The man who won the acquittal!

(*One of the members of the party walks
over to* GREENWALD *and takes him by the
arm and moves* GREENWALD *closer to the
table.*)

GREENWALD. Party's pretty far along,
hey?

KEEFER. A toast I say! to Lieutenant—

KEITH. Make it rhyme, Tom! Like you
did at the ship's party!

ALL. Yes, yes. That's right. Rhymes!
Rhymes! A toast in rhyme.

MARYK (*to* GREENWALD). He makes 'em
up as he goes along, Barney.

KEITH. You've never heard anything like
it.

MARYK. Come on, Tom.

KEITH. Rhymes!

KEEFER. Well, I'm a bit drunk to be
doing Thomas the Rhymer tonight—
(*Drunken protests from the others.*) But,
to honor this great man, I'll try my best.
Fill your glasses, I say!

To Lieutenant Barney Greenwald,
Who fought with might and main.
The terror of judge advocates,
The massive legal brain.
(*They all cheer.*)
Who hit the Navy where it lived
And made it writhe with pain.
Who sees through brass and gold stripes
Like so much cellophane.
(*They all cheer.*)
The man who licked the regulars
Right on their own terrain,
Who wrought the great deliverance
For the galley slaves of the *Caine.*
(*They all cheer.*)
And gave us all the Fifth Freedom—
Freedom from Old Yellowstain!

(*They all cheer loudly, and burst into
"For He's a Jolly Good Fellow." Then,
"Speech, Barney, speech," etc.*)

GREENWALD. No, no, no. I'm drunker'n
any of you. I've been out drinking with
the judge advocate—trying to get him to
take back some of the dirty names he
called me—finally got him to shake hands
on the ninth whiskey sour—maybe the
tenth—

MARYK. That's good.

GREENWALD. Had to talk loud 'n' fast,
Steve—I played pretty dirty pool, you
know, in court—poor Jack Challee. (*Peers
blearily at cake.*) What's this?

KEEFER. It's a double celebration.

GREENWALD. Cake baked like a book—

KEEFER. A thousand bucks came in the
mail today. Advance on my novel.

GREENWALD. Very nice. (*Reads icing.*)
Multitudes, Multitudes, by Thomas Keefer
—I got something in the mail, too.

MARYK. What, Barney?

GREENWALD. Medical okay. Orders back
to my squadron. Sailing tomorrow. (*They
all cheer.*)

MARYK. That's great.

GREENWALD. A thousand bucks. Guess I
ought to return the celebrated author's
toast, at that—li'l speech—thanks for that
elegant poem, Mr. Keefer. War novel, isn't
it?

KEEFER. What else?

GREENWALD. I assume you give the Navy
a good pasting?

KEEFER. I don't think Public Relations
would clear it, at any rate.

GREENWALD. Fine. Someone should show
up these stodgy, stupid Prussians. Who's
the hero, you?

KEEFER. Well, any resemblance, you
know, is purely accidental—

(*A few laughs.*)

GREENWALD. 'Course I'm warped, and
I'm drunk, but it suddenly seems to me
that if I wrote a war novel I'd try to make
a hero out of Old Yellowstain. (*All
whoop.*) No, I'm serious, I would. Tell
you why. Tell you how I'm warped. I'm a
Jew, guess most of you know that. Jack
Challee said I used smart Jew-lawyer tactics—'course he took it back, apologized,
after I told him a few things about the
case he never knew. Well, anyway—the
reason I'd make Old Yellowstain a hero
is on account of my mother, little gray-
headed Jewish lady, fat. Well, sure you
guys all have mothers, but they wouldn't
be in the same bad shape mine would if
we'd of lost this war. See, the Germans
aren't kidding about the Jews. They're
cooking us down to soap over there. They
think we're vermin and should be 'stermi-

nated and our corpses turned into something useful. Granting the premise—being warped, I don't, but granting the premise—soap is as good an idea as any. But I just can't cotton to the idea of my mom melted down to a bar of soap. (*One of the officers, drunker than the rest, mutters thickly something ad lib: "What's all this got to do with Old Yellowstain?" or words to that effect. The others swiftly quiet him.* GREENWALD *rides over the interruption.*) Now I'm coming to Old Yellowstain. Coming to him. See, Mr. Keefer, while I was studying law, and you were writing your short stories for national magazines, and little Willie here was on the playing fields of Princeton, why, all that time these birds we call regulars, these stuffy stupid Prussians, they were standing guard on this fat, dumb, and happy country of ours. 'Course they were doing it for dough, same as everybody does what they do. Question is in the last anal—last analysis, what do you do for dough? You and me, for dough, were advancing our free little non-Prussian careers. So, when all hell broke loose and the Germans started running out of soap and figured, well, time to come over and melt down old Mrs. Greenwald, who's gonna stop 'em? Not her boy Barney. Can't stop a Nazi with a lawbook. So, I dropped the lawbooks, and ran to learn how to fly. Stout fellow. Meantime, and it took a year and a half before I was any good, who was keeping Mama out of the soapdish? Tom Keefer? Communication school. Willie Keith? Midshipman school. Old Yellowstain, maybe? Why, yes, even poor sad Queeg. And most of them not sad at all, fellows, a lot of them sharper boys than any of us, don't kid yourself, you can't be good in the Army or Navy unless you're goddamn good. Though maybe not up on Proust, 'n' *Finnegan's Wake* 'n' all.

MARYK. Barney, forget it, it's all over, let's enjoy the dinner—

GREENWALD. Steve, this dinner's a phony. You're guilty. Course you're only half guilty. There's another guy who's stayed very neatly out of the picture. The guy who started the whole idea that Queeg was a dangerous paranoiac—who argued you into it for half a year—who invented the name Old Yellowstain—who kept feeding you those psychiatry books—who pointed out Article 184 and kept hammer-

ing it at you—

KEEFER. Now wait a minute—

GREENWALD. Oh, had to drag it out of Steve, Mister Keefer. Big dumb fisherman, tried to tell me it was all his own idea. Doesn't know the difference between a paranoid and an anthropoid. But you knew. Told him his medical log was a clinical picture of a paranoid. Advised him to go to Halsey. Offered to go with him. Didn't get cold feet till you stood outside Halsey's cabin on the *New Jersey.* Then ducked, and been ducking ever since.

KEEFER (*angrily*). I don't know where in hell you got all this, but—

GREENWALD. Biggest favor you could have done Steve, so far as winning an acquittal went, though I doubt you realized it. But if there's a guilty party at this table, it's you. If you hadn't filled Steve Maryk's thick head full of paranoia and Article 184, why he'd have got Queeg to come north, or he'd have helped the poor bastard pull through to the south, and the *Caine* wouldn't have been yanked out of action in the hottest part of the war. That's your contribution to the good old U.S.A., my friend. Pulling a minesweeper out of the South Pacific when it was most needed. That, and *Multitudes, Multitudes.*

KEEFER. Just a minute—you're really drunk—

GREENWALD. 'Scuse me, I'm all finished, Mister Keefer. I'm up to the toast. Here's to you. You bowled a perfect score. You went after Queeg and got him. You kept your own skirts all white and starchy. You'll publish your novel proving that the Navy stinks, and you'll make a million dollars and marry Hedy Lamarr. So you won't mind a li'l verbal reprimand from me. What does it mean? I defended Steve because I found out the wrong guy was on trial. Only way I could defend him was to murder Queeg for you. I'm sore that I was pushed into that spot, and ashamed of what I did, and thass why I'm drunk. Queeg deserved better at my hands. I owed him a favor, don't you see? He stopped Hermann Goering from washing his fat behind with my mother. So I'm not going to eat your dinner, Mister Keefer, or drink your wine, but simply make my toast and go. Here's to you, Mister *Caine's* favorite author, and here's to your book. (GREENWALD *throws the wine in* KEEFER'S

face. Shocked murmurs. KEEFER *crumples.*)
You can wipe for the rest of your life,
Mister. You'll never wipe off that yellow
stain.

MARYK. Barney—

GREENWALD (*a wry smile, a hand brushed on* MARYK's *head*). See you in Tokyo, you mutineer. (GREENWALD *staggers out.*)

CURTAIN

THE FOURPOSTER

Jan de Hartog

First presented by The Playwrights' Company at the Ethel
Barrymore Theatre, New York, on October 24,
1951, with the following cast:

AGNES Jessica Tandy   MICHAEL Hume Cronyn

ACT ONE. SCENE I: 1890. SCENE II: A year later.

ACT TWO. SCENE I: 1901. SCENE II: Seven years later.

ACT THREE. SCENE I: 1913. SCENE II: Twelve years later.

INTRODUCTION

JAN DE HARTOG, author of *The Fourposter,* a Dutch writer born in Haarlem in 1914, fled to England in 1943 during the German occupation of Holland and was condemned to death by the Nazis. He first attracted attention in the American theatre in 1948 with *Skipper Next to God* (previously produced in London), the drama of a sea captain who transported Jewish refugees to Palestine and refused to allow international politics to rule his conscience. It was not a play contrived for Broadway, but it attracted attention with its strenuous idealism when staged in New York with the late John Garfield in the role of the skipper. *The Fourposter* is, of course, work of a completely different character, and in the fall of 1951 it revealed a facet of the author's dramatic talent hitherto unsuspected on Broadway. Actually, Jan de Hartog who also had a fantastic drama, *This Time Tomorrow,* produced in 1947, has demonstrated considerable versatility. He is also the author of a comprehensive picaresque novel about a physician's struggles in the South Pacific, *The Spiral Road,* published in 1957, and of earlier books, praised as warm and humorous, *The Distant Shore* and *A Sailor's Life.*

Jan de Hartog has many interests. Fortunately humor is one of them, and it was a warm sense of comedy that made *The Fourposter* one of the pleasantest of Broadway plays. And the author also has a disposition to like people and to view human relationships in terms of average humanity. The background of *The Fourposter* is vividly American, but in treating married life, the author dealt with timeless traits and foibles, even while availing himself of elements of period comedy. "In cameo size," according to Brooks Atkinson, *"The Fourposter* is the story of all marriages." When the play was revived at New York's City Center on January 6, 1955, with Jessica Tandy and Hume Cronyn reenacting their original roles, it was appreciated no less than on its first appearance on Broadway proper. Dissent was possible on the grounds that the humor and sentiment were rather standardized. But a critic could be mollified on reflecting that familiarity has been a requirement of domestic comedy ever since the ancients, and the standardization of humor in De Hartog's play was certainly mitigated by the rich acting roles provided by the author.

ACT ONE

SCENE ONE

1890. Night.

Bedroom. Fourposter. Door in back wall, window to the right, washstand and low chair to the left. The room is dark. Low-burning gas lamps shimmer bluishly to the right of arch and at bed, left.

The door is opened clumsily, and HE *enters, carrying* HER *in his arms into the room out of the lighted passage.* HE *wears a top hat on the back of his head;* SHE *is in her bridal gown.* HE *stops in the moonlight, kisses her, whirls and carries her to bed.*

———

SHE. Oh, Micky, whoo! Hold me! Hold me tight! Whoo! Whoo! I'm falling. I can't . . . (HE *throws her onto the bed and tries to kiss her again.*) Michael, the door! The door! (HE *runs to the door and closes it.* SHE *gets off the bed, straightens her hat and dress.*) Oh, goodness, my hair . . . and look at my dress! (SHE *turns on the gas bracket on wall beside the bed.* HE *goes to her, takes off gloves, puts one in each pocket and kneels before her.*) What are you doing?

HE. I'm worshipping you.

SHE. Get up immediately! (*Tries to lift him up.*) Michael, get up, I say!

HE. Can't I worship you?

SHE. Are you out of your senses? If our Lord should see you . . .

HE. He could only rejoice in such happiness.

SHE. Michael, you mustn't blaspheme, you know you mustn't. Just because you've had a little too much to drink . . .

HE. I haven't drunk a thing. (*Teeters on his knees.*) If I'm drunk, I'm drunk only with happiness . . .

SHE. You wouldn't be praying with everything on if you weren't. (*Turns.*) Oh! Goodness! I think I am too.

HE. Happy?

SHE. Tipsy. Let me see if I can stand on one leg. (*Holding her hands out to him, tries and fails.*) Whoo!

HE (*rises*). Angel! (*Tries to kiss her, but* SHE *dodges.*)

SHE. Michael, that hat . . .

HE. What? Oh. (*Takes hat off.*) What have you got in your hand?

SHE. A little rose . . . a little rose from our wedding cake.

HE. Let's eat it.

SHE. No—I want to keep it—always . . . (SHE *puts it in her dress.* HE *puts hat on.*)

HE. Agnes . . . tell me that you are happy.

SHE. Please, Michael, do say something else for a change.

HE. I can't. I've only one word left to express what I feel: happy. Happy, happy, happy, happy! Happy! (*Twirls and, stumbling against dais, sprawls back against bed.*)

SHE. Are you all right?

HE. Happy!

SHE. I suddenly feel like saying all sorts of shocking things.

HE. Go on.

SHE. Listen—no, in your ear . . . (SHE *wants to whisper something but is checked by what she sees.*) Oh! Michael . . .

HE (*faces her*). What?

SHE. No, don't move. (*Looks at ear again.*) Let me see the other one. (HE *turns his head and* SHE *looks at his other ear.*) You pig!

HE. What is it?

SHE. Don't you ever wash?

HE. Every day.

SHE. All over?

HE. Oh, well—the main things.

SHE. What *are* the main things?

HE (*trying to kiss her*). My precious . . .

SHE. Your what?

HE. You are my precious. Wouldn't you like to kiss me?

SHE. I would like to go over you from top to bottom, with hot water and soap; that's what I would like to do.

HE. Please do.

SHE. Oh, well—don't let's dwell on it. (SHE *sits on trunk.*) Ouch!

HE. Sweetheart! What's the matter?

SHE. Ouch! My shoes are hurting me. I must take them off or I'll faint.

HE. Let me do it! Please . . . (SHE *puts out her foot.* HE *kneels and tenderly pulls her skirt back and kisses her shoe.*)

SHE. Michael, please, they hurt me so.

HE (*kisses her foot again; when* SHE *wants to take shoe off herself.*) No, no, dearest! Let me do it, please let me do it. (HE *takes her shoe again.*)

SHE. But you take such a long time.

HE (*untying bow on shoe*). Isn't that heaven? I could spend the whole night undressing you.

SHE. I didn't ask you to undress me. I only asked you to help me out of my shoes.

HE. I would help you out of anything you ask, dear heart. (*Takes off shoe.*)

SHE (*withdraws her foot*). Now that's one, and now . . . (*As* SHE *leans forward to take off other shoe herself, sees him, still on his knees, leaning back and staring at her.*) Please, Michael, don't look at me so creepily. Please get undre . . . Take your hat off! (HE *takes hat off, puts it on trunk.*)

HE. Agnes, do you remember what I told you when we first met?

SHE. No . . .

HE. That we had met in a former existence.

SHE. Oh, that.

HE. I am absolutely certain of it now.

SHE. Of what?

HE. That moment, just now, I suddenly had the feeling of having experienced all this before.

SHE. Did you really?

HE. You sitting here just as you are, I on my knees in front of you in a hired suit, just before we . . .

SHE. What?

HE (*putting shoe down,* HE *leans against her knee*). Oh, darling, I am happy.

SHE. *Must* you make me cry?

HE. You should, you know. This is a very sad occasion, really. Your youth is over.

SHE (*pushing him back and getting up*). I want to go home.

HE. What . . .

SHE. I can't! I want to go home!

HE (*still on knees*). Darling, what's the matter? What have I done?

SHE (*picks up shoe*). I want to go home. I should never have married you.

HE (*rises*). Agnes . . .

SHE. How can you! How dare you say such a thing!

HE. But what . . . I haven't said a thing all night but that I was . . .

SHE. My youth over! That's what you would like! Undressing me, the whole night long, with your hat on and unwashed ears and . . . oh! (SHE *puts her arms around his neck and weeps.*)

HE (*comforting her inexperiencedly*). That's right, darling; that's it; you cry, my dearest; that's the spirit.

SHE. That's . . . that's why you made

me drink such a lot, taking nothing yourself all the time.

HE. Why, I've had at least three bottles.

SHE. Then what did you say? What did you say, when you threw me on the bed?

HE. Threw?

SHE. "If I'm drunk, I'm drunk with happiness." That's what you said.

HE. But, darling, only a minute ago you ·said yourself . . .

SHE. I did not!

HE. Well, of all the . . . (*Takes her by the shoulders.*) Here—smell! (*Breathes at her with his mouth wide open.*) Ho, ho, ho!

SHE (*escaping the kiss she wants by hiding her face against his shoulder*). Oh, I'm so dizzy.

HE. I love you.

SHE. I'm so embarrassed.

HE. Why?

SHE. Because I'm so dizzy.

HE. So am I.

SHE. Dizzy?

HE. Embarrassed.

SHE. Why?

HE. Oh, well, you know. It would have been such a relief if I could have spent the whole night taking off your shoes.

SHE. And then have breakfast, straightaway, yes?

HE. Yes. Agnes, I . . . I don't revolt you, do I?

SHE. You? Why on earth should you?

HE. Well, I mean—those ears and . . . things, you know.

SHE. But, darling, I said that only because of other people. What do I care?

HE. And Agnes . . . there's something I should tell you.

SHE. Why tell it just now?

HE. You're right. (*Puts hat on.*) I'm such a fool that I . . . (SHE *frowns.* HE *takes hat off again and puts it on trunk.*) Would you like something to drink?

SHE. Heavens, no. Don't talk about drinking.

HE. A glass of water, I mean. (*Picks up glass and carafe.*) After all that champagne.

SHE. Michael, please talk about something else. I—I really couldn't just now, honestly.

HE. Well, I think I will. (*Pours glass of water.*)

SHE. Did you write a poem for tonight?

HE. No.

SHE. What a pity! I thought you would have written something beautiful for our wedding.

HE. No.

SHE. Nothing at all?

HE. No.

SHE. You're blushing. Please read it to me.

HE. I haven't got one, darling, really, I haven't.

SHE. You're lying. I can tell by your eyes that you are lying.

HE. As a matter of fact, you wouldn't like it, darling; it's rather modern. There is another one I'm writing just now . . .

SHE. I want to hear the one about our wedding.

HE. Never before in my whole life have I told anybody anything about a poem I hadn't finished . . .

SHE. Is it in your pocket? (*Starts to pick his pockets.*)

HE (*trying to keep her hands back, sits in chair*). I think it's going to be wonderful. "The Fountain of the Royal Gardens."

SHE. Why may I not hear the one about our wedding?

HE. Darling, don't you think it much more special, just now, something nobody else has ever heard before?

SHE. Has anybody heard the one about our wedding, then?

HE (*takes poems from pocket*). Listen, tell me what you think of the permutation of the consonants, the onomatopoeia, I mean: "Hissing shoots the slender shower; out of shining, slimy stone. . . ."

SHE. No.

HE. "Swaying shivers sparkling flower; rainbow shimmers in the foam." (SHE *starts toward door.*) "Flashing, dashing, splashing, crashing . . ." (SHE *hurries to the door, picking up suitcase from chest as she goes.*) Where are you going?

SHE (*opens door, taking the key from the lock*). Back in a minute. (*Exits, shuts door, locks it.*)

HE. Why are you taking your suitcase? (*Rises and runs to door; drops poems on chest as he goes.*) Agnes, darling! Agnes! Agnes! (*Tries to open the locked door. HE turns, sees her shoes, picks them up and smiles. Suddenly, a thought strikes him. He drops the shoes, runs onto dais, picks up suitcase there, starts to put it on bed, stops, turns, then puts suitcase on arms of chair. He opens the case, takes out night-cap and puts it on his head. He rips off his coat and vest, shirt and tie. As he starts to take his trousers off, he stops, listens, runs to door, listens again. He then takes the trousers off. He takes nightshirt from case, goes to foot of bed, throws nightshirt on bed and sits on chest and hurriedly takes off his shoes. Then he pauses, looks toward the door in embarrassment. He quickly puts the shoes back on again, gets into the nightshirt, pulls his trousers on over it; then his coat. He moves a few steps, turns, sees his vest, shirt and tie on trunk where he had thrown them. He tosses them into the suitcase, fastens it, puts suitcase in wardrobe; starts to washstand, stops, looks toward door. Then he quickly goes down to washstand, picks up towel, dampens one corner of it in pitcher of water and starts to wash his right ear. SHE enters. As HE hears door open, he sits in chair and folds his arms. SHE closes the door and puts the key back in the lock. Her dress is changed somehow; it looks untidier and she has taken off her wedding hat. SHE turns from door, spots him sitting in the chair, the collar of his jacket upturned and the night-cap on his head.*)

HE. Hullo.

SHE. What—what are you doing?

HE. Sitting.

SHE. What on earth is that?

HE. What?

SHE. On your head?

HE. Oh . . .

SHE. Do you wear a nightcap?

HE. Oh, no. Just now when there's a draft. (*Rises, takes cap off and puts it in his pocket.*)

SHE. Is that a nightshirt?

HE. What have you got on?

SHE. My father has been wearing pajamas for ages.

HE. Oh, has he really? Well, I don't.

SHE. Why have you . . . changed?

HE. Why have you?

SHE. I? Oh . . . I'm sleepy.

HE. So am I.

SHE. Well, then, shall we . . .

HE. Why, yes . . . let's.

SHE. All right. Which side do you want?

HE. I? Oh, well. . . . I don't care, really. Any side that suits you is all right with me.

SHE. I think I would like the far side. Because of the door.

HE. The door?

SHE (*turns back quilt*). Because of breakfast, and in case somebody should knock. You could answer it.

HE. I see.

SHE (*picks up "God Is Love" pillow from bed*). What's this?

HE. What?

SHE. This little pillow? Did you put that there?

HE. Of course not! What's it got written on it?

SHE. "God Is Love." Oh, how sweet! Mother must have done that. Wasn't that lovely of her? (*Puts pillow back on bed.*)

HE (*looks at door*). Yes, lovely.

(SHE *turns away and starts undressing.* HE *takes off his coat.* SHE *turns. After an embarrassing moment in which neither of them can think of anything to say.*)

SHE. Michael, please turn 'round.

HE. Oh, I'm so sorry . . . I didn't realize . . .

(HE *sits down on the edge of the chest, putting his coat beside him, and takes off his shoes and socks.* SHE *steps out of dress and hangs it in wardrobe. Goes back up onto dais.*)

SHE. It's rather a pretty bed, isn't it?

HE. Yes, it is, isn't it? It was my father's, you know.

SHE. Not your mother's?

HE. Yes, of course, my parents'. I was born in it, you know.

SHE. Michael . . .

HE (*turning toward her*). Yes, darling?

SHE (*backing up*). No, don't look! Michael?

HE (*turning away*). Yes?

SHE. Tell me how much you love me, once more.

HE. I can't any more.

SHE. What?

HE. I can't love you any more than I'm doing. I wor . . . I'm the hap . . . I'm mad about you.

SHE. That's what I am about you. Honestly.

HE. That is nice, dear.

SHE. I am so happy, I couldn't be happier.

HE. That is lovely, darling.

SHE. And I wouldn't want to be, either.

HE. What?

SHE. Happier.

HE. I see.

SHE. I wish that everything could stay as it was—before today. I couldn't stand any more—happiness. Could you?

HE. God, no.

SHE. How coldly you say that!

HE. But what the blazing hell do you expect me to say?

SHE. Michael! Is that language for the wedding ni . . . before going to sleep? You ought to be ashamed of yourself!

HE. But damn it, Agnes . . . (*Sneezes.*) I—I've got a splitting headache and I'm dying of cold feet. (*Takes nightcap from pocket and puts it on.*)

SHE (*takes off her slippers*). Then why don't you get into bed, silly? (HE *rises.*) No! A moment! A moment! (HE *turns away.* SHE *gets into bed, the "God Is Love" pillow beneath her head.* HE *stands for a moment in embarrassment, starts to take off his trousers, then realizing that the room is still brightly lit, he goes to bracket, right of arch, and turns it off.*)

HE. May I turn 'round now?

SHE. Yes.

(HE *reaches to turn down the bracket but is stopped by her interruption.*)

SHE. Wait! It can't leak, can it? The lamp, I mean?

HE. Of course not.

SHE. But I think I smell gas.

HE (*reaches behind him and takes her hand*). Darling, listen. You are an angel, and I'm madly in love with you, and I'm embarrassed to death and so are you, and that's the reason why we . . . Good night. (HE *reaches up and turns down the bracket.*)

SHE. Good night. (HE *takes off his trousers and puts them on chair.*) Can you find your way?

HE. Yes, yes . . . (*Going back up to bed, stubs his toe.*) Ouch!

SHE. Michael! What are you doing?

HE (*on dais*). Nothing. I hurt my toe. (HE *gets into bed.*)

SHE. Oh, I'm so sorry. (*Long silence.*) Do get into bed carefully, won't you?

HE. I'm in it already.

SHE (*after another silence*). Michael?

HE. Yes?

SHE. Michael, what was it you didn't want to tell me tonight?

HE. Ah . . .

SHE. You may tell me now, if you like. I'm not embarrassed any more, somehow.

HE. Well . . .

SHE. If you tell me what it was, I'll tell you something as well.

HE. What?

SHE. But you must tell me as well. Promise me.

HE. Yes.

SHE. No, promise me first.

HE. All right. I promise.

SHE. I . . . I've never seen a man . . . before . . . completely. Never.

HE. Oh, well—you haven't missed much.

SHE. And you?

HE. Oh.

SHE. Have you ever seen a woman before . . . completely?

HE. Well . . .

SHE. What does that mean?

HE. You know, I once had my fortune told by a gypsy.

SHE. Oh . . .

HE. She said I'd have a very happy married life, that I'd live to a ripe old age, and she said that everything would turn out all right.

SHE. And was she . . . naked?

HE. Of course not! She went from house to house with a goat.

SHE. Oh . . . Good night.

HE. Good night. (*Pause.*) Are you comfy?

SHE. Oh, yes.

HE. Not too cold?

SHE. Heavens, no. I'm simply boiling. And you?

HE. Rather cold, really.

SHE (*after a silence*). Michael!

HE. Yes?

SHE. Michael! Now I'm sure that I smell gas. (SHE *sits up.*)

HE. That must be the drink.

SHE. Do you still smell of drink that much? I can't believe it.

HE. Yes.

SHE. Let me smell your breath again.

HE. Oh, please, Agnes, let's try to go to sleep.

SHE. No, Michael, I want to smell it. If it is the gas, we may be dead tomorrow, both of us.

HE. Oh, well . . .

SHE. Oh, well! Do you want to die?

HE. Sometimes.

SHE. Now?

HE. No, no.

SHE. Please, Michael, let me have a little sniff before I go to sleep; otherwise, I won't close an eye. (*Lies down.*) Please, Michael.

HE (*sits up and leans over her*). Ho!

Ho! Ho! (*Lies back on his pillow.*) There.

SHE (*sits up and leans over him*). I don't smell a thing. Do it again.

HE. Ho! Ho!

SHE. Again?

HE. Ho, ho.

SHE. Again . . .

CURTAIN

SCENE TWO

1891. Late Afternoon.

The same bedroom. To the right, a cradle.

HE *is lying in the fourposter, with a towel wrapped around his head. The bed is strewn with books, papers, an oversized dinner bell and his dressing gown. Heaps of books and papers are on the dais at foot of bed.*

When the curtain rises, HE *awakens.*

———

HE (*from beneath the blankets*). Agnes! Agnes! (*Sits up.*) Agnes! (*Picks up bell and rings loudly and insistently.*)

SHE (*enters hurriedly carrying a pile of clean laundry.* SHE *is very pregnant*). Yes, yes, yes, yes, yes. What is it?

HE. I've got such a pain! (SHE *returns to door and closes it.*) I can't stand it any longer!

SHE (*putting laundry on chest*). Now, come, come, darling. Don't dramatize. I'll soak your towel again.

HE. No! It isn't my head. It's shifted to here. (*Puts his hand on his back.*)

SHE. Where?

HE. Here! (*Leans forward. Places her hand on the painful spot.*) Here! What is there? Do you feel anything?

SHE. You've got a pain there?

HE. As if I'd been stabbed. No, don't take your hand away . . . Oh, that's nice.

SHE (*suspiciously*). But what sort of pain? Does it come in—in waves? First almost nothing and then growing until you could scream?

HE. That's right. How do you know . . .

SHE. Micky, that's impossible.

HE. What's impossible? Do you think I'm shamming?

SHE. You're having labor pains!

HE. You're crazy!

SHE. And all the time . . . all the time

I've put up a brave front because I thought you were really ill!

HE. But I *am* ill! What do you think? That I lay here groaning and sweating just for the fun of it?

SHE. All the time I've been thinking of *you!*

HE. I've done nothing else, day and night, but think of *you!* How else do you think I got the pains *you're* supposed to have? (SHE *sobs.*) Oh, hell! This is driving me mad! (HE *jumps out of bed.*)

SHE. Micky! (HE *tears open the wardrobe.*) Micky, what are you doing?

HE. Where are my shoes?

SHE. Michael! You aren't running away, are you?

HE (*gets clothes from wardrobe*). I'm going to get that doctor.

SHE (*rises*). No. Michael, you mustn't.

HE (*puts clothes on chair*). If I drop dead on the pavement, I'm going to get that doctor! I'm not going to leave you in this condition a minute longer. He said so himself, the moment you got those pains . . . (*Kneels, looks under bed.*)

SHE. When *I* got them! Not when *you* got them!

HE. Don't you feel anything?

SHE. Nothing! Nothing at all.

HE. Then I don't understand why you were crying just now.

SHE. Please, darling, please go back to bed. You'll catch a cold with those bare feet and you're perspiring so freely. Please, darling.

HE. But I don't want to.

SHE (*pops him into bed*). I want you to. Uppy-pie, in you go!

HE. Anyone would think you wanted me to be ill.

SHE. No grumbling, no growling. (*Puts "God Is Love" pillow behind his head.*) There! Comfy? (*Goes to chest.*)

HE. No! (HE *throws pillow to floor.*) I'm scared.

SHE. What on earth of?

HE. Of—of the baby. Aren't you?

SHE. Good Heavens, no. Why should I? It's the most natural thing in the world, isn't it? And I'm feeling all right. (*Picks up sewing.*)

HE. You have changed a lot, do you know that?

SHE (*starts sewing*). Since when?

HE. Since you became a mother.

SHE. But I'm not a mother yet.

HE. Then you don't realize it yourself. Suddenly you have become a woman.

SHE. Have I ever been anything else?

HE. A silly child.

SHE. So that's what you thought of me when we married?

HE. When we married, my feet were off the ground.

SHE. Well, you've changed a lot, too.

HE. Of course I have. I have become a man.

SHE. Hah!

HE. Well, haven't I? Aren't I much more calm, composed . . .

SHE (*picks up rattle from bassinette and throws it to him*). You're a baby!

HE (*throws covers back and sits on edge of bed*). That's right! Humiliate me! Lose no opportunity of reminding me that I'm the male animal that's done its duty and now can be dismissed! (*Jumps out.*)

SHE. Michael!

HE. Yes! A drone, that's what I am! The one thing lacking is that you should devour me. The bees . . .

SHE. Michael, Michael, what's the matter? (*Reaches out to him.*)

HE. I'm afraid!

SHE. But I'm not, Michael, honestly, not a bit.

HE. I'm afraid of something else.

SHE. What?

HE. That I've lost you.

SHE (*rises, goes to him*). Michael, look at me . . . What did the doctor tell you?

HE. It's got nothing to do with the doctor. It's got nothing to do with you either. It's got to do with me.

SHE (*puts arms about him*). But you're going to be all right, aren't you?

HE (*breaks away*). I'd never be all right again, if I've lost you.

SHE. What are you talking about? You've got me right here, haven't you?

HE. But your heart, that's gone. I wish I was lying in that cradle.

SHE (*puts her arms around him again*). You fool . . . (*Kisses him.*) You can't be as stupid as all that. No, Michael.

HE. Listen! Before that cuckoo pushes me out of the nest, I want to tell you once more that I love you. Love you, just as you are . . . I thought I loved you when I married you, but that wasn't you at all. That was a romantic illusion. I loved a sort of fairy princess with a doll's smile and a . . . well, anyway not a princess with hiccoughs and cold feet, scratching her stomach in her sleep . . .

SHE. Michael!

HE (*takes her hand*). I thought I was marrying a princess and I woke up to find a friend, a wife . . . You know, sometimes when I lay awake longer than you, with my arm around your shoulder and your head on my chest, I thought with pity of all those lonely men staring at the ceiling or writing poems . . . pity, and such happiness that I knew at that very moment it wouldn't last. I was right, that's all.

SHE. Well, if you thought about a princess, I thought about a poet.

HE. Oh?

SHE. You didn't know that I had cold feet, and every now and again I get an attack of hiccoughs . . .

HE. You don't do anything else the whole night long.

SHE. What?

HE. Scratch your stomach and sniff and snort and smack your lips, but go on.

SHE. And you lie listening to all this without waking me up?

HE. Yes. Because I don't know anything in the world I'd rather listen to. (*Kisses her.*) Got anything to say to that?

SHE. Yes, but I won't say it.

HE. Why not?

SHE. Never mind, darling, you stay just as you are.

HE. Miserable, deserted, alone? You do nothing else all day and night but fuss over that child—eight months now! First it was knitting panties, then sewing dresses, fitting out the layette, rigging the cradle . . .

SHE. And all this time you sat quietly in your corner, didn't you?

HE. I retired into the background as becomes a man who recognizes that he is one too many.

SHE (*rises, goes to him*). Oh, angel! (*Puts her arms around his neck and kisses him.*) Do you still not understand why I love you so much?

HE. You . . . you noticed how I blotted myself out?

SHE. Did I!

HE. I didn't think you did.

SHE. You helped me more than all model husbands put together. Without you I would have been frightened to death for eight whole months. But now I simply had

no time.

HE. I believe you're teasing me.

SHE. I love you. Do you believe that?

HE. Of course.

SHE. Must I prove it to you?

HE. Oh, no. I'm perfectly prepared to take your word for it.

SHE. All right, if you like, we'll send the child to a home.

HE. What?

SHE. And then we'll go and look at it every Sunday.

HE. Agnes, why do you tease me?

SHE. Darling, I'm not teasing you. I'm telling you the truth. Even if I were going to have twenty children, you are my husband and I'd rather leave them as foundlings . . . (SHE *grasps at her back and turns.* HE *stares at her in horror.*)

HE. Darling, what—what is it? Agnes!

SHE (*clutching the bed post*). Oh!

HE (*picks up clothes, goes to her*). The doctor! For God's sake, the doctor!

SHE. No . . . oh, oh! Don't . . . not the doctor. Stay here.

HE. Darling, darling! Angel! Agnes, my love! What must I do? For God's sake, I must do something!

SHE (*sings, convulsed by pain, loudly*). "Yankee Doodle went to town, Riding on a pony . . ."

HE. Agnes!

SHE (*sings on*). "He stuck a feather in his hat, And called it macaroni."

HE (*takes her by shoulders*). Agnes!

SHE. Oh, Micky . . . What are you doing?

HE. I—I thought you were going mad.

SHE. I? Why?

HE (*seats her on chest*). You started to sing.

SHE (*sitting*). Oh, yes. The doctor said if those pains started, I had to sing. That would help. I must have done it automatically.

HE. Are you all right now?

SHE. Oh, yes, yes.

HE. Now you just sit here quietly. I'll get the doctor.

SHE. No, Michael, you mustn't. He said we weren't to bother him until the pains came regularly.

HE. Regularly? But I won't be a minute. (*Picks up clothes.*)

SHE. Oh, please, please don't go away. Oh, I wish Mother were here.

HE (*puts clothes on bed*). Now, don't worry! This is the most natural thing in the world. You just sit here quietly. I'll put some clothes on and . . .

SHE. Oh, no, no Micky, please, please don't fuss. I wish it didn't have to happen so soon.

HE (*turns upstage with back to audience, takes off pajama pants. Puts on trousers*). Yes.

SHE (*picks up pajama pants*). I'm not nearly ready for it yet . . .

HE (*taking off robe and putting it on bed*). Well, I am. Honestly, I am. I can't wait to—to go fishing with him, if it's a boy, and—and, if it's a girl, go for walks, nature rambles. . . . (*Goes to wardrobe and gets tie.*)

SHE. But that won't happen for years. First, there will be years of crying and diapers and bottles . . .

HE (*ties tie*). I don't mind, darling. Honestly, I don't. I'll—find something to do. I'll work and—and go fishing alone. You're never going to have to worry about . . .

SHE (*in pain again*). Oh!

HE (*goes to her, kneels*). Another one?

SHE. No. No, I don't think so.

HE. Now, why don't you go to bed? (*Throws robe and coat on chest. Fixes bed linen.*) You go to bed. I'll finish dressing and make you a nice cup of tea, yes?

SHE. No, no, thank you, darling. I think I'll stay right where I am. Oh, I haven't done nearly all the things I should have done. There's still half the laundry out on the roof and . . .

HE (*stops her*). Agnes, do stop worrying. As soon as I've finished dressing, I'll go to the roof and take the washing in for you. (*Seats her on chest.*)

SHE (*puts arms about his waist*). No, please don't leave me alone.

HE (*puts his arms about her shoulders*). All right, all right. There's nothing to be afraid of. This has been going on for millions and millions of years. Now what would you like? Shall I read you something? (*Goes to the bed. Picks up books.*) Schopenhauer, *Alice in Wonderland*?

SHE. No.

HE. I know. I've started a new book. It's only half a page. Shall I read you that? Yes? (*He picks up writing pad.*)

SHE (*biting her lip*). Yes . . .

HE (*sits on foot of bed*). It's going to be a trilogy. It's called "Burnt Corn, the Story of a Rural Love." Do you like that as a title?

SHE (*biting her lips*). I think that's wonderful.

HE. Now this is how it opens . . . (*Takes hold of her hand.*) Are you all right?

SHE. Fine.

HE (*reads*). "When she entered the attic with the double bed, she bent her head, partly out of reverence for the temple where she had worshipped and sacrificed, partly because the ceiling was so low. It was not the first time she had returned to that shrine . . ." (SHE *has a pain.*) Are you all right?

SHE. Oh, Micky, I love you so. Don't, don't let's ever . . . (SHE *has another pain.* HE *drops pad and kneels before her.*)

SHE (*buries her head in his shoulder, then looks up*). Now . . . now, I think you'd better go and call him.

HE. I will, my darling. (*Puts on his coat. Goes to door, stops, returns to her.*) Now, you just sit tight. (*Goes to door, returns and kisses her. Goes back to door, turns, sees bassinette, runs to it and pulls it over close to her and exits.*)

CURTAIN

ACT TWO

SCENE ONE

1901. Night.

The same room, ten years later. The only piece of furniture left from the preceding scene is the fourposter, but it has been fitted out with new brocade curtains. Paintings hang on the walls; expensive furniture crowds the room. No washstand any more, but a bathroom to the left. Where the wardrobe stood in the preceding act, the wall has been removed and this has become an entrance to a dressing room. The whole thing is very costly, very grand and very new. Only one side of the bed has been made; there is only one pillow on the bed with the "God Is Love" pillow on top of it.

AT RISE, *there is no one in the room.* SHE *enters and slams the door behind her.* SHE *stands at the foot of the bed, removing her evening gloves. Goes to dressing table, throws gloves on the table, and is stopped by a knock at the door.* SHE *stands for a moment. The knock is repeated, more insistently.*

SHE (*after a pause*). Come in.

HE (*enters, closes door*). Excuse me. (*Goes to the dressing room, gets his night clothes, re-enters and crosses to door.*) Good night.

SHE (*as* HE *opens door*). You certainly were the life and soul of the party this evening, with your interminable little stories.

HE (*starts out, stops, turns*). My dear, if you don't enjoy playing second fiddle, I suggest you either quit the orchestra or form one of your own. (*Goes out and shuts door.*)

SHE (*mutters after a moment's stupefaction*). Now, I've had enough! (*Runs to door, rips it open, stands in hallway and calls off:*) Michael! (*Then bellows:*) Michael! Come here!

HE (*pops in. Has top hat and cane in hand and evening cape over arm*). Have you taken leave of your senses? The servants . . .

SHE. I don't care if the whole town hears it. (HE *exits.*) Come back, I say!

HE (*re-enters*). All right. This situation is no longer bearable! (*Closes door.*)

SHE. What on earth is the matter with you?

HE. Now, let me tell you one thing, calmly. (SHE *goes to dressing table, takes off plume, throws it on table.*) My greatest mistake has been to play up to you, plying you with presents . . .

SHE. I like that! (*Picks up gloves.*)

HE. Calmly! Do you know what I should have done? I should have packed you off to boarding school, big as you are, to learn deportment.

SHE. Deportment for what?

HE. To be worthy of *me*.

SHE. The pompous ass whose book sold three hundred thousand copies!

HE. That is entirely beside the point.

SHE. It is right to the point! Before you had written that cursed novel, the rest of the world helped me to keep you sane. Every time you had finished a book or a play or God knows what, and considered yourself to be the greatest genius since Shakespeare . . . (HE *says,* "Now really!") I was frightened to death that it might turn out to be a success. But, thank Heaven, it turned out to be such a thorough failure every time, that I won the battle with your megalomania. But now, now this book, the only book you ever confessed to be trash until you read the papers . . . Oh, what's the use!

HE. My dear woman, I may be vain, but you are making a tragic mistake.

SHE (*laughs*). Now listen! Just listen to him! To be married to a man for eleven years, and then to be addressed like a public meeting. Tragic mistake! Can't you hear yourself, you poor darling idiot, that you've sold your soul to a sentimental novel?

HE. Agnes, are you going on like this, or must I . . .

SHE. Yes, yes, you must! You *shall* hear it. (HE *pounds floor with evening cane.*) And don't interrupt me! There is only one person in this world who loves you in spite of what you are, and let me tell you . . .

HE. You are mistaken. There is a person in this world who loves me—because of what I am.

SHE. And what are you, my darling?

HE. Ask her.

SHE. Her . . .

HE. Yes.

SHE. Oh . . . (*Holds onto bed post.*) Who is she?

HE. You don't know her.

SHE. Is she . . . young? How young?

HE. No. I'll be damned if I go on with this. You look like a corpse.

SHE. A corpse?

HE. So pale, I mean. (*At door.*) Agnes, I'm not such a monster, that . . . Sit down. Please, Agnes, do sit . . . Agnes!

SHE (*turns away*). No, no . . . it's nothing. I'm all right. What do you think? That I should faint in my thirty-first year because of something so . . . so ordinary?

HE. Ordinary?

SHE. With two children? I didn't faint when Robert had the mumps, did I?

HE. Don't you think this is a little different?

SHE. No, Michael. This belongs to the family medicine chest.

HE. I love her!

SHE. So, not me any more? (HE *doesn't reply.*) I don't mean as a friend, or as . . . as the mother of your children, but as a wife? You may tell me honestly, really. Is that why you've been sleeping in the study?

HE. I haven't slept a wink.

SHE. I see. It must be Cook who snores.

HE. Since when do I snore?

SHE. Not you, dear, Cook. Every night when I went down the passage.

HE (*goes to the door, opens it*). Good night!

SHE. Sleep well.

HE. What was that?

SHE. Sleep well.

HE. Oh . . . (*Stops at door, then slams it shut.*) No! I'll be damned, I won't stand it!

SHE. What is the matter?

HE. Cook snores! Agnes, I love somebody else! It's driving me crazy! You, the children, she, the children, you . . . for three weeks I have lived through hell, and all you've got to say is "Cook snores!"

SHE. But, darling . . .

HE. No, no, no, no! You are so damned sure of yourself that it makes me sick! I know you don't take this seriously, but believe me, I love that woman! I must have that woman or I'll go mad!

SHE. Haven't you . . . had her yet?

HE. At last! Thank God, a sign of life. Why haven't you looked at me like that before? I have begged, implored, crawled to you for a little understanding and warmth, and love, and got nothing. Even my book, that was inspired by you, longing for you—right from the beginning you have seen it as a rival. Whatever I did, whatever I tried: a carriage, servants, money, dresses, paintings, everything . . . you hated that book. And now? Now you have driven me into somebody else's arms. Somebody else, who understands at least one thing clearly: that she will have to share me with my work.

SHE. Does she understand that she will have to share you with other women as well?

HE. She doesn't need to. At last I have found a woman who'll live with my work, and a better guarantee of my faithfulness nobody could have.

SHE. But how does she live with it? What does she do?

HE. She listens. She encourages me—with a look, a touch, a—well, an encouragement. When I cheer, she cheers with me, when I meditate, she meditates with me . . .

SHE. And when you throw crockery, she throws crockery with you?

HE. Haven't you understood one single word of what I have been saying? Won't you, can't you see that I have changed?

SHE. No.

HE. Then you are blind! That's all I can say. At any rate, *you've* changed.

SHE. I!

HE. No, don't let's start that.

SHE. Go on.

HE. No, it's senseless. No reason to torture you any longer, once I have . . .

SHE. Once you have tasted blood.

HE. I . . . I'm sorry it was necessary for me to hurt you. It couldn't very well have been done otherwise. I'm at the mercy of a feeling stronger than I.

SHE. Rotten, isn't it?

HE. Horrible.

SHE. And yet . . . at the same time not altogether.

HE. No. On the other hand, it's delicious.

SHE. The greatest thing a human being can experience.

HE. I'm glad you understand it so well.

SHE. Understand? Why, of course. It's human isn't it?

HE. How do you come to know that?

SHE. What?

HE. That it's—human?

SHE. Well, I'm a human being, aren't I?

HE. I never heard you talk like this before. What's the matter with you?

SHE. Well, I might have my experiences too, mightn't I? Good night.

HE. Just a minute! I want to hear a little more about this!

SHE. But I know it now, dear.

HE. Yes, you do! But I don't! What sort of experiences are you referring to?

SHE. Now, listen, my little friend! You have dismissed me without notice, and I haven't complained once as any other housekeeper would have done. I have accepted the facts because I know a human being is at the mercy of this feeling, however horrible and at the same time delicious it may be.

HE. Agnes!

SHE. I really don't understand you. I am not thwarting you in the least, and instead of your going away happily and relieved that you are not leaving a helpless wreck behind . . .

HE. You might answer just one plain question before . . . we finish this business. Have you . . . aren't you going to be alone, if I leave you?

SHE. Alone? I've got the children, haven't I?

HE. That's not at all certain.

SHE (*after a shaky silence*). You had better leave this room very quickly now, before you get to know a side of me that might surprise you a lot.

HE. I have, I'm afraid. I demand an answer. Have you a lover?

SHE (*goes to door, opens it*). Good night.

HE. For eleven long years I have believed in you! You were the purest, the . . .

SHE (*interrupting*). The noblest thing in my life! Good night!

HE. If you don't answer my question, you'll never see me again.

SHE. Get out of here!

HE. No.

SHE. All right. Then there's only one thing left to be done. (SHE *picks up wrap from bed and exits into dressing room.*)

HE. What? What did you want to say? (SHE *does not answer.* SHE *returns with second wrap and overnight case; puts them both on chair and opens case.*) What's the meaning of that? (SHE *picks up nightgown and negligee, packs them in case.*) Darling, believe me, I won't blame you for anything, only tell me—where are you going?

SHE (*goes to dressing table and gets brushes and comb*). Would you mind calling a cab for me?

HE. Agnes!

SHE (*packs brushes and comb in case*). Please, Michael, I can't arrive there too late. It is such an embarrassing time already. Pass me my alarm clock, will you?

HE. No, I can't have been mistaken about you that much! Only yesterday you said that I had qualities . . .

SHE. Excuse me. (*Passes him, gets her alarm clock, puts clock in case.*)

HE (*wants to stop her when she passes, but checks himself*). All right. It *is* a solution, anyhow.

SHE (*closes overnight case, picks it up, puts wrap over arm, goes around chair to him and puts out her hand*). Good-by, Michael. (HE *blocks her way.*)

HE. Do you really think I'm going to let you do this? Do you?

SHE. A gentleman does not use force when a lady wishes to leave the room.

HE. Oh, I'm so sorry. (*Steps aside.*)

SHE. Thank you. (HE *grabs her arm and pulls her back.* SHE *drops her suitcase and wrap in the struggle;* HE *flings her up onto the bed.*) Michael! Let me go! Let me go! I . . .

HE. Now look, I've put up with all the nonsense from you . . . (SHE *succeeds in tearing herself free, gets off the bed and kicks his shin.*) Ouch! (HE *grasps at his shinbone and limps, leans against arm of sofa.*)

SHE. Get out!

HE. Right on my scar!

SHE. Get out! (HE *takes off his coat, throws it on chair. As* HE *starts toward her:*) I'll scream the house down if you dare come near me! (SHE *scrambles back up onto bed.*)

HE. Where's my pillow?

SHE (*reaching for bell pull*). Get out or I'll ring the bell!

HE (*as he exits to dressing room*). Make up that bed properly.

SHE. You're the vilest swine God ever created!

HE (*re-enters carrying pillow*). If I have to make you hoarse and broken for the rest of your life, you'll know that I am a man. Make up that bed! (*Throws pillow at her.*)

SHE. I would rather . . .

HE. And shut up! Get off there!

SHE (*strikes at him with "God Is Love" pillow*). You are the silliest hack-writer I ever . . .

HE (*grabs "God Is Love" pillow and throws it*). Get off, or I'll drag you off!

SHE (*gets off bed*). And that book of yours is rubbish.

HE. What did I tell you after I finished it? Listening to me once in awhile wouldn't do you any harm. Here! (*Throws comforter at her.*) Fold that!

SHE (*throws it back*). Fold it yourself!

HE (*throws it back*). Fold it!

(SHE *goes at him and* HE *grasps her hands.* SHE *still tries to flail him.* HE *slips in the struggle and sits on dais.* SHE *tries to pound his head.* HE *regains his feet and pinions her arms behind her.*)

SHE (*as* HE *grasps her face with left hand*). I'll bite you!

HE. If you could see your eyes now, you'd close them. They're blinding.

SHE. With hatred!

HE. With love. (*gives her a quick kiss;* SHE *breaks free.* HE *gets on guard.*)

SHE (*looks at him speechless for a moment, then sits on the bed, away from him, sobbing*). I wish I were dead. I want to be dead, dead . . .

HE (*sits on edge of bed, holding shin*). Before you die, look in my eyes, just once. Look! (*Turns her to him.* SHE *looks.*) What do you see there?

SHE. Wrinkles!

HE (*picks up evening pumps which have come off in the scuffle and goes back onto dais*). That's how long it is since you last looked. (*Sits on bed and puts one pump on.*) What else?

SHE. But . . . what about her?

HE. I was lonely.

SHE (*stands*). You'd better go now.

HE. Weren't you?

SHE. Please go.

HE (*picks up evening coat.* SHE *picks up his pillow and puts it on chair. At archway, as* HE *puts on other pump.*) I've started writing a new book.

SHE. When?

HE. A couple of weeks ago.

SHE. And you haven't read me anything yet? Impossible.

HE. I read it to her.

SHE. Oh . . . and?

HE. She liked it all right. But she thought it a little . . . well, coarse.

SHE. You, coarse? What kind of sheep is she?

HE. Shall I go and get the manuscript?

SHE (*picks up his pillow*). Tomorrow.

HE (*moves quickly to door and puts hand on door knob*). No, now!

SHE (*goes onto dais, puts his pillow on bed*). Please . . . tomorrow.

(HE *throws coat onto bench at foot of bed and goes around onto dais and embraces her.*)

CURTAIN

SCENE TWO

1908. 4:00 A.M. to dawn.

When the curtain rises, the stage is dark. The door is opened brusquely and HE *enters, wearing an overcoat over his pajamas.* HE *is carrying a bourbon bottle and riding crop.* SHE *is asleep in the fourposter.*

HE (*as* HE *enters*). Agnes! (*Goes to dressing table right of arch and turns on dressing-table lamps.*) Agnes, Agnes, look at this! (*Turns on bed-table lamp.* HE *shows her brown bourbon bottle.*)

SHE (*waking up and shielding her eyes with arm*). Huh? What's the matter?

HE. In his drawer, behind a pile of junk —this!

SHE. What?

HE. He's seventeen—eighteen! And it's four o'clock in the morning! And—and now, this!

SHE (*sitting up*). What, for Heaven's sake?

HE (*hands her the bottle*). Look!

SHE (*takes bottle and looks at it*). Bourbon!

HE. Your son. The result of your modern upbringing.

SHE. But what—where . . . (*Puts bottle down on bed.*) What does all this mean? What's the time? (*Leans over and picks up clock.*)

HE (*as* HE *exits into bathroom*). It's time I took over his education.

SHE. But he told you he would be late tonight. He specially asked permission to go to that dance. I gave him the key myself!

HE (*re-enters and exits again into dressing room*). Where did you put that thing?

SHE. What thing?

HE. My old shaving strop.

SHE. What do you want that for? (*Lying back in bed.*) Come back to bed.

HE (*re-enters*). So you approve of all this? You think it's perfectly natural that a child boozes in his bedroom and paints the town until four o'clock in the morning?

SHE. But, darling, he told you! And surely the child has a right to a bit of gaiety.

HE. One day let me explain the difference between gaiety and delirium tremens!

SHE. What are you going to do, Michael?

HE (*turns round in the doorway*). I am going downstairs where I have been since one o'clock this morning. And when he comes home, I . . .

SHE (*climbs out of bed. Picks up robe*). I won't let you! If you are going to beat that child, you will have to do so over my dead body!

HE. Don't interfere, Agnes.

SHE. I mean it, Michael! Whatever happens, even if he has taken to opium, I will not let you beat that child!

HE. All right. In that case, we had better call the police.

SHE. But you knew he was coming in late! These children's parties go on till dawn!

HE (*with a politician's gesture of despair*). Now, in my young days, if I was told to be in at a certain hour—(*Turns to her for the beginning of a big speech.*) I—(*Sees her for the first time.*) What in the name of sanity have you got on your head?

SHE. Now, now, that's the very latest thing—everyone's wearing them—

HE. But what *is* it?

SHE. A slumber helmet.

HE. Slumber helmet! Bourbon in the bedroom, children's parties that go on till dawn and slumber helmets. All right. (*Throws riding crop on bench at foot of bed and rips off overcoat.*) I am going to bed.

SHE. Listen to me, will you?

HE (*steps out of slippers*). I have the choice between bed and the madhouse. I prefer bed. I have a life to live. Good night! (HE *gets into bed and pulls the blanket up.* SHE *goes above sofa.* HE *sits up.*) I hope you enjoy being a drunkard's mother! (*Lies back.*)

SHE. I don't want to spoil your performance as an irate father, but I can't help thinking what your attitude would be if it were not Robert, but Lizzie who stayed out late.

HE (*sits up*). Exactly the same! With this difference, that Lizzie would never do such a thing.

SHE. Ha!

HE. Because she happens to be the only sane member of this family, except me. (*Lies back.*)

SHE (*at arch*). I could tell you something about her that would . . . No, I'd better not.

HE (*sits up*). If you think that I am going to fall for that stone-age woman's trick of hinting at something and then stopping . . . That child is as straight and as sensible as—as a glass of milk. (*Lies back.*)

SHE. Milk!

HE (*finds bottle in bed, sits up, puts bottle on bed table, lies back*). At least she doesn't go to bed with a bottle of bourbon.

SHE. Mmm.

HE (*sitting up*). What—Mmm?

SHE. Nothing, nothing.

HE. Agnes, you aren't by any chance suggesting that she goes to bed with anything else, are you?

SHE. I am not suggesting anything. I am just sick and tired of your coming down like a ton of bricks on that poor boy every time, while she is allowed to do whatever she pleases.

HE. So! I have an unhealthy preference for my daughter. Is that it?

SHE. I am not saying that. I . . .

HE. All right, say it! Say it!

SHE. What?

HE. Oedipus!

SHE. Who?

HE. Oh! Leave me alone. (*Under the blankets again.*)

SHE. In his drawer, did you say?

HE. Shut up.

SHE. Darling, I know you never concern yourself with the children's education except for an occasional bout of fatherly hysteria, but I think that this time you are going a little too far, if you don't mind my saying so.

HE. What else do you want me to do? I have to spend every waking hour earning money. You are my second in command. I have to leave certain things to you; but if I see that they are obviously going wrong, it is my duty to intervene.

SHE. If that is your conception of our relationship, then you ought to think of something better than a shaving crop and a riding strop.

HE. Riding crop! And it's not a matter of thinking of something better, it's . . . (HE *stops because she has suddenly got up and gone to the window, as if she heard something.*)

SHE. Michael!

HE. Is that him? (*As* SHE *does not answer,* HE *gets out of bed and grabs his overcoat.*)

SHE (*peeking out the window*). I thought I heard the gate.

HE (*from the doorway*). Robert! (*Exits and calls offstage.*) Is that you, Robert? (*No answer, so he comes back.*) No.

SHE (*sits at dressing table, opens powder box*). Why don't you go back to bed?

HE. Because I'm worried.

SHE (*picking up hand mirror and puff and powdering her face*). Why, that's nonsense!

HE. And so are you.

SHE. What on earth gives you that idea?

HE. That you are powdering your face at four o'clock in the morning.

SHE (*puts down mirror, puff. Realizes that there is no use pretending any longer, goes to the bottle and picks it up from bed table*). What drawer was it?

HE. The one where he keeps all his junk.

SHE. I can't believe it. It can't be true.

HE. Well, there you are.

SHE. How did you find it?

HE. I was sitting downstairs waiting. I got more and more worried so I decided to go up to his room and see whether perhaps he had climbed in through the window, and then I happened to glance into an open drawer, and there it was.

SHE. But it isn't possible. A child can't be drinking on the sly without his mother knowing it.

HE. We'll have to face it, my dear. He is no longer a child. When I looked into that drawer and found his old teddy bears, his steam engine, and then that bottle, I—I can't tell you what I felt.

SHE. Suppose—of course it isn't—but suppose—it is true, whatever shall we do?

HE. I don't know—see a doctor.

SHE. Nonsense. It's perfectly natural childish curiosity. A boy has to try everything once.

HE. If that's going to be your attitude, he'll end by trying murder once. By the way, what were you going to say about Lizzie?

SHE (*smiles*). She is in love.

HE. What?

SHE. She's secretly engaged.

HE. To whom?

SHE. To the boy next door.

HE. To that—ape? To that pie face?

SHE. I think it's quite serious.

HE. The child is only . . . nonsense!

SHE. She is not a child any more. She's . . . well, the same thing Robert is, I suppose. I wouldn't be surprised if one of these days the boy came to see you to ask for her hand.

HE. If he does, I'll shoot him.

SHE. But, darling . . .

HE. But she's only sixteen! Agnes, this is a nightmare!

SHE. But, sweetheart . . .

HE. She can't be in love, and certainly

not with *that!*

SHE. Why not?

HE. After spending her whole life with me, she can't fall in love with something hatched out of an egg.

SHE. Are you suggesting that the only person the child will be allowed to fall in love with is a younger edition of yourself?

HE. Of course not. Don't be indecent. What I mean is that at least we should have given them taste! They should have inherited our taste!

SHE. Well, he seems to have inherited a taste for bourbon.

HE. I don't understand how you can joke about it. This happens to be the worst night of my life.

SHE. I'm not joking, darling. I just don't think that there's much point in us sitting up all night worrying ourselves sick about something we obviously can't do anything about until the morning. Come, go back to bed.

HE. You go to bed . . . I'll wait up for him.

SHE. Shall I make you a cup of tea?

HE. Tea! Do you know that we haven't had a single crisis in our life yet for which your ultimate solution wasn't a cup of tea?

SHE. I'm sorry. I was only trying to be sensible about it.

HE. I know you are. I apologize if I've said things that I didn't mean. (*Picks up the bourbon bottle and uncorks it with his left hand.*) I think what we both need is a swig of this. Have we got any glasses up here?

SHE. Only tooth-glasses. (HE *takes a swig, then with a horrified expression thrusts the bottle and cork into her hands and runs to the bathroom.*) Michael! (SHE *smells the bottle, grimaces.*)

HE (*rushing out of bathroom with a nauseated look on his face*). What is that?

SHE. Cod liver oil!

HE. Oh! (*Runs back into bathroom.*)

SHE (*takes handkerchief from pocket, wipes bottle*). How on earth did it get into this bottle?

HE. God knows! (*Re-enters to just outside bathroom door.* HE *carries a glass of water.*) I think that little monster must have been trying to set a trap for me! (*Runs back into bathroom.*)

SHE (*holding bottle up, puzzling over*

contents). Michael, wait a minute! (SHE *is interrupted by the sound of his gargling.*) I know! Well, this is the limit!

HE (*re-enters, wiping mouth with towel*). What?

SHE. Do you remember, three years ago, that he had to take a spoonful of cod liver oil every night and that he didn't want to take it in my presence? Of course I measured the bottle every morning, but he poured it into this!

HE. Agnes, do you mean to say that that stuff I swallowed is three years old?

SHE. The little monkey! Oh, now I am going to wait till he gets home!

HE. I think perhaps we'd better call the doctor. This stuff must be putrid by now.

SHE. You'll have to speak to him, Michael. This is one time that you'll have to speak to him. I . . . (*Hears something.*) Michael, there he is! (*Rises, goes to door.* HE *rushes to door, stops, returns to bench and picks up riding crop. Starts out.* SHE *stops him.*) No, Michael, not that! Don't go that far!

HE. Three-year-old cod liver oil! (HE *whips the air with the riding crop. Exits.* SHE *listens for a moment, very worried. Then she runs into the bathroom and leaves the bottle there. Re-enters, to door, listens, goes down to bench at foot of bed and sits on end of it, all the while muttering to herself.* HE *appears in the doorway, dejectedly holding his riding crop in his hand.* HE *looks offstage, incredulously.* SHE *turns to him.*)

SHE. Well, what did you say?

HE (*closes door; distracted, turns to her*). I beg your pardon?

SHE. What did you *say* to him?

HE. Oh—er—"Good morning."

SHE. Is that all?

HE. Yes.

SHE. Well, I must say! To go through all this rigmarole and then to end up with . . . I honestly think you could have said something more.

HE (*sits on sofa*). I couldn't.

SHE. Why not?

HE. He was wearing a top hat.

(HE *makes a helpless gesture and rests his head in his hands.* SHE *laughs, crosses to him and puts her arms about him, then kisses him on the top of his head.*)

CURTAIN

ACT THREE

SCENE ONE

1913. Late afternoon.

The same bedroom. The bed canopy has been changed, as have the drapes and articles of furniture. It is all in more conservative taste now.

As the curtain rises, SHE *is seated at the dressing table, holding a wedding bouquet that matches her gown and hat. After a moment,* HE *is heard humming the Wedding March.*

———

HE (*from dressing room*). Agnes! (*Hums a bit more, then whistles for her.* HE *enters, arranging his smoking jacket. Goes to foot of bed, humming again. Sees her.*) Oh, there you are. Your hat still on? Agnes!

SHE (*starts*). Yes?

HE. Hey! Are you asleep?

SHE (*sighs and smiles absently*). Yes . . .

HE. Come on, darling. The only thing to think is: little children grow up. Let's be glad she ended up so well.

SHE. Yes . . .

HE. Thank God, Robert is a boy. I couldn't stand to go through that a second time, to see my child abducted by such a . . . Oh, well, love is blind.

SHE (*putting down bouquet*). Michael.

HE. Yes? (*Opens humidor and picks up pipe.*) What is the matter with you? The whole day long you've been so . . . so strange.

SHE. How?

HE. You aren't ill, are you?

SHE. No.

HE. That's all right then. (*Starts filling his pipe.*) What did you want to say?

SHE. Today is the first day of Lizzie's marriage.

HE. It is. And?

SHE. And the last day of ours.

HE. Beg pardon?

SHE. I waited to tell you, perhaps too long. I didn't want to spoil your fun.

HE. My *fun*?

SHE. Yes. I haven't seen you so cheerful for ages.

HE. Well . . . I'm . . . For your sake I have made a fool of myself. For your sake I have walked around all these days with the face of a professional comedian, with a flower in my buttonhole and death in my heart! Do you know what I would have liked to do? To hurl my glass in the pie face of that bore, take my child under my arm—and as for that couple of parents-in-law . . . (*Looks heavenward.*) And now you start telling me you didn't want to spoil my fun! (*Searches pockets for match.*)

SHE. With the information that I am going away.

HE. You are what . . .

SHE. I'm going away.

HE. Huh?

SHE. Away.

HE. How do you mean?

SHE. Can't you help me just a little by understanding quickly what I mean?

HE. But, darling . . .

SHE. Michael, I'll say it to you plainly once, and please try to listen quietly. If you don't understand me after having heard it once, I'll . . . I'll have to write it to you.

HE. But, darling, we needn't make such a fuss about it. You want to have a holiday now the children have left the house. What could be more sensible? No need to announce it to me like an undertaker.

SHE. Not for a holiday, Michael—forever.

HE. You want to move into another house?

SHE. I want to go away from *you.*

HE. From me?

SHE. Yes.

HE. You want to . . . visit friends, or something?

SHE. Please, darling, stop it. You knew ages ago what I meant; please don't try and play for time. It makes it all so . . . so difficult.

HE. I don't know a damned thing. What have I done?

SHE. Nothing, nothing. You are an angel. But I am . . . not.

HE. Agnes, what is the matter with you?

SHE. I would appreciate it if you would stop asking me what is the matter with me. There never has been anything the matter with me, and there couldn't be less the matter with me now. The only thing is, I can't . . .

HE. Can't what?

SHE. Die behind the stove, like a domestic animal.

HE. Good Heavens . . .

SHE. You wouldn't understand. You are a man. You'll be able to do what you like until you are seventy.

HE. But my dear good woman . . .

SHE. I won't! Today I stopped being a mother; in a few years' time, perhaps next year even, I'll stop being a woman.

HE. And that's what you don't want?

SHE. I can't help it. That happens to be the way a benevolent Providence arranged things.

HE. But, darling, then it's madness.

SHE. I want to be a woman just once, before . . . before I become a grandmother. Is that so unreasonable?

HE. But my angel . . .

SHE. For Heaven's sake, stop angeling me! You treat me as if I were sitting in a wheelchair already. I want to live, can't you understand that? My life long I have been a mother; my life long I've had to be at somebody's beck and call; I've never been able to be really myself, completely, wholeheartedly. No, never! From the very first day you have handcuffed me and gagged me and shut me in the dark. When I was still a child who didn't even know what it meant to be a woman, you turned me into a mother.

HE. But, darling, Robert is only . . .

SHE. No, not through Robert, not through Lizzie, through yourself, your selfishness, your . . . Oh, Michael. (*Puts her hand on his shoulder.*) I didn't intend to say all this, honestly, I didn't. I only wanted to be honest and quiet and nice about it, but . . . but I can't help it. I can't! The mere way you look at me, now, this very moment! That amazement, that heartbreaking stupidity . . . Don't you feel yourself that there is nothing between us any more in the way of tenderness, of real feeling, of love; that we are dead, as dead as doornails, that we move and think and talk like . . . like puppets? Making the same gestures every day, the same words, the same kisses . . . Today, in the carriage, it was sinister. The same, the same, everything was the same; the coachman's boots behind the little window, the sound of the hooves on the pavement, the scent of flowers, the . . . I wanted to throw open the door, jump out, fall, hurt myself, I don't know what . . . only to feel that I was alive! I, I, not that innocent, gay child in front, who was experiencing all this for the first time, who played the part I had rehearsed for her . . . but I couldn't. I said "yes" and "no" and "darling" and "Isn't it cold," but I heard my own voice, and saw my own face mirrored in the little window, in the coachman's boots, like a ghost, and as I put my hat straight, to prove to myself that I wasn't a ghost, driving to my own burial, I remembered how, twenty-three years ago, I had looked at myself in exactly the same way, in the same window perhaps, to see if my bridal veil . . . (HER *voice breaks;* SHE *covers her face with her hands; goes up onto dais and falls onto bed, weeping.* HE *rises, puts his pipe into his pocket, goes up onto dais and puts his hands on her waist.*) No! Don't touch me! (*Sits up, gets handkerchief from bed-table drawer and wipes her eyes.*) I don't want to, I don't want to blame you for anything. You've always been an angel to me; you've always done whatever you could, as much as you could . . . (HE *sits on bed.*) although you never opened a door for me, always got on the streetcar first, never bought me anything nice . . . Oh, yes, I know, darling, you have given me many beautiful presents. But something real —if it had only been one book you didn't want to read yourself; or one box of chocolates you didn't like yourself, but nothing. Absolutely nothing. (*Shows him her hands.*) Look, just look! Only wrinkles and a wedding ring, and a new cash book for the household every year. (HE *takes her hand, raises it to his lips, kisses the palm of her hand.*) No, Michael. That's so easy, so mean, really. You've always known how to make that one little gesture, say that one little word . . . but now it doesn't work any more. This is what I've been trying to tell you all along. It's the most difficult part of all, and I don't know if I . . . No, I can't.

HE. Say it.

SHE. I'm afraid—I think—I'm sure I don't love you any more. I don't say this to hurt you, darling, honestly I don't. I only want you to understand. Do you? Do you a little?

HE. Yes. I think so.

SHE. I even remember the moment I realized I didn't love you. One clear, terrible moment.

HE. When was that?

SHE. About a month ago, one Sunday morning, in the bathroom. I came in to bring your coffee and you were rubbing your head with your scalp lotion. I said something about that boy's poems that you had given me to read; I don't remember what I said—and then you said, "I could tell him where to put them" . . . with both hands on your head. (*Puts hands on her head.*) And then . . . then it was suddenly as if I were seeing you for the first time. It was horrible.

HE (*after a silence*). Where had you thought of going?

SHE. Oh, I don't know. I thought a room in a boarding house somewhere.

HE. Not a trip, abroad for instance?

SHE. Good Heavens, no.

HE. Why not?

SHE. Because I don't feel like it . . . (*Turns to him.*) You don't think that I . . . that there is something the matter with me?

HE. No.

SHE. Do you understand now why I *must* go away?

HE. Well, if I were to come into the bathroom with my head full of love lyrics, like you, only to see you rubbing your face with skin food or shaving your arm pits, I don't think I'd have been overcome by any wave of tenderness for you . . . but I wouldn't go and live in a boarding house.

SHE. That was not the point. The point was what you said.

HE. "I could tell him where to put them." H'm. You're sure that was the point?

SHE. Why?

HE. Who wrote those poems you were talking about?

SHE. Well, that boy . . . that boy, who keeps asking you what you think about his work.

HE. You liked what he wrote, didn't you?

SHE. Oh, yes. I thought it young, promising . . . honestly. It had something so . . . so . . .

HE. So . . . well?

SHE. Well, what?

HE. I seem to remember this same description, twenty-three years ago.

SHE. You aren't trying to tell me that I'm . . . ? I won't say another word to you! The very idea that I, with a boy like that, such a . . . such . . . It's just that the boy has talent! At least as much as you had, when you were still rhyming about gazelles with golden horns.

HE. I was rhyming about you.

SHE. He must be rhyming about somebody as well, but . . .

HE. Of course he is. About you, too.

SHE. Me?

HE. What did he write on the title page? "Dedicated in reverent admiration to the woman who inspired my master." Well, I have been his master only insofar that I wrote him a letter: "Dear Sir, I have read your poems twice. I would advise you to do the same." Still, I don't know. Perhaps I'm growing old-fashioned. After all, he's new school and all that. I should like to read those poems again. Have you got them here?

SHE. Yes.

HE. Where are they?

SHE (*gets poems from lower drawer of bedside table; walks to foot of bed and starts to hand him the poems, then stops*). You aren't going to make fun of them, are you?

HE (*takes out glasses, puts them on, takes poems from her*). Fun? Why should I? I think this occasion is serious enough for both of us to find out what exactly we're talking about. Perhaps you're right. Perhaps I need this lesson. Well, let's have it. (*Reads the title*.) "Flashing Foam— Jetsam on the Beach of Youth." H'm. That seems to cover quite a lot. First Sonnet: "Nocturnal Embrace."

SHE. Michael, if you're going to make a fool of this poor boy who is just starting, only because you. . . .

HE. Who is doing the starting here? Me! After thirty years I'm just starting to discover how difficult it is to write something that is worth reading, and I *shall* write something worth reading one day unless . . . well, "Nocturnal Embrace." (*Reads*.)

"We are lying in the double bed,
On the windows have thrown a net
The dead leaves of an acorn tree."

Do you understand why it has to be an acorn tree? Why not an oak?

SHE. Because it's beautiful. Because it gives atmosphere.

HE. I see. I'm sorry. (HE *reads*.)

"From a church tower far unseen,
A solemn bell strikes twelve."

Well, now that rhyme could definitely be improved.

"From a church tower far unseen,
A solemn bell strikes just thirteen."

(SHE *doesn't answer.* HE *reads on.*)

"Strikes twelve,
O'er the darkened fields,
The silent sea.

But then we start and clasp
A frightened, sickening gasp,
For a foot has stopped behind the door."

Now this I understand. No wonder they are startled. Suppose you're just busy clasping each other, and then a foot walks along the corridor and stops right outside your door . . . (HE *shudders*.)

SHE. I'm not laughing, if that's what you're after.

HE. That's not what he was after in any case, but let's see how it ends. (HE *reads*.)

"For a foot has stopped behind the door.

Silence. Thumping. It's our hearts
Waiting with our breath . . ."

Wondering where the other foot's got to, I suppose . . .

SHE. Michael, please stop it!

HE. Why? Am I his master or am I not? And has he had the cheek to dedicate this bad pornography to my Agnes or has he not?

SHE. He meant it for the best.

HE. Oh, now, did he really? Do you call that for the best, to turn the head of a woman, the best wife any man could wish himself, at the moment when she's standing empty-handed because she imagines her job is over? To catch her at a time when she can't think of anything better to do than to become young again and wants to start for a second time fashioning the first damn fool at hand into a writer like me?

SHE. But you don't need me any more.

HE. Oh, no? Well, let me tell you something. People may buy my books by the thousands, they may write me letters and tell me how I broke their hearts and made them bawl their damn heads off, but I know the truth all right. It's *you* who make me sing . . . and if I sing like a frog in a pond, it's not my fault.

(SHE *is so amused and relieved that she cries and laughs at the same time. The laughter gets the upper hand.*)

SHE. Oh, Michael!

HE. What are you laughing at?

SHE (*sitting on sofa beside him*). Oh, Michael . . . I'm not laughing. . . . I'm not laughing. (SHE *embraces him and sobs on his shoulder.*)

HE (*comforts her like a man who suddenly feels very tired*). I'll be damned if I understand that. (HE *rests his head on her shoulder.*)

CURTAIN

SCENE TWO

1925. Dawn.

Same bedroom, twelve years later. It is apparent that they are moving out—pictures have been taken off the walls, leaving discolored squares on the wallpaper; a stepladder leans against the wall of archway; all drapes have been removed with the exception of the bed canopy and spread on the fourposter which is the only piece of furniture remaining in the room. Several large suitcases, packed and closed.

AT RISE, HE is heard messing about in the bathroom. Then HE comes out, humming and carrying toilet articles. HE goes to the suitcases, finds them shut, carries the stuff to the bed. HE goes again to the suitcases, opens one. It is full. HE slams the lid shut and fastens the locks, at the same time noticing that a small piece of clothing is left hanging out. HE disregards it and drags a second case on top of the first one, opens it, finds that it is fully packed as well. However, HE re-arranges the contents to make room for his toilet articles. As HE starts back to bed, he again notices the piece of clothing hanging out of the bottom case. HE looks toward the door, then leans down and rips off the piece of material, puts it in his pocket and walks up onto dais. HE picks up his toilet articles from the bed, turns, then drops them on the floor. HE mutters, "Damn!" and gets down on his hands and knees to pick them up. At that moment, when HE is out of sight of the door, SHE comes in carrying the little "God Is Love" pillow. The moment SHE realizes he is there, SHE quickly hides the pillow behind her back.

SHE. What are you doing?

HE (*rises*). Packing.

SHE (*picks up knitting bag from floor at foot of bed and puts it with the suitcases*). Well, hurry up, darling. The car comes at eight and it's almost twenty of. What have you been doing all this time?

HE. Taking down the soap dish in the bathroom.

SHE. The soap dish? What on earth for?

HE. I thought it might come in useful.

SHE. But, darling, you mustn't. It's a fixture.

HE. Nonsense. Anything that is screwed on isn't a fixture. Only things that are nailed.

SHE. That's not true at all. The agent explained it most carefully. Anything that's been fixed for more than twenty-five years is a fixture.

HE (*hands her the soap dish*). Then I'm a fixture, too.

SHE. Don't be witty, darling. There isn't time.

HE (*seeing little pillow under her arm*). Hey! (SHE *stops.*) We don't have to take that little horror with us, do we?

SHE. No. (*Exits into bathroom.*)

HE (*picks up part of his toilet things*). What about the bed?

SHE (*offstage*). What?

HE. Are you going to unmake the bed or have we sold the blankets and the sheets with it? (*Starts packing toilet things.*)

SHE (*offstage*). What is it, dear?

HE. Have we only sold the horse or the saddle as well?

SHE (*re-enters, holding the little pillow*). Horse, what horse?

HE. What's to become of those things? (SHE *still does not understand.*) Have we sold the bed clothes or haven't we?

SHE. Oh, no, dear. Only the spread. I'll pack the rest. (*Puts little pillow under arm and strips pillow cases.*)

HE. In what? These suitcases are landmines. Why are you nursing that thing? (SHE *mumbles something and tucks little pillow more firmly under her arm.* HE *goes up to her.*) Just what are you planning to do with it?

SHE. I thought I'd leave it as a surprise.

HE. A surprise?

SHE. Yes, for the new tenants. Such a nice young couple. (*Places pillow at the head of the bed.*)

HE. Have you visualized that surprise, may I ask?

SHE. Why?

HE. Two young people entering the bedroom on their first night of their marriage, uncovering the bed and finding a pillow a foot across with "God Is Love" written on it.

SHE (*picks up rest of toilet articles and newspaper from bed. Puts them down on dais, the newspaper on top.*) You've got nothing to do with it.

HE. Oh, I haven't, have I? Well, I have.

I've only met those people once, but I'm not going to make a fool of myself.

SHE. But, darling . . .

HE. There's going to be no arguing about it, and that's final. (*Snatches pillow and throws it on trunk. Mutters.*) God Is Love!

SHE (*stripping blanket and sheets from bed*). All right. Now, why don't you run downstairs and have a look at the cellar?

HE. Why?

SHE (*stuffs bed linen in pillow case*). To see if there's anything left there.

HE. Suppose there is something left there, what do you suggest we do with it? Take it with us? You don't seem to realize that the apartment won't hold the stuff from one floor of this house.

SHE. Please, darling, don't bicker. We agreed that it was silly to stay on here with all these empty rooms.

HE. But where are we going to put all this stuff?

SHE. Now, I've arranged all that. Why don't you go down and see if there's anything left in the wine cellar?

HE. Ah, now you're talking.

(HE *goes out.* SHE *twirls the pillow case tight and leaves it by the suitcases. Picks up the "God Is Love" pillow, returns to the bed, and places it on top of the regular bed pillows, then stands back and admires it. With one hand on bedpost,* SHE *glances over the entire bed and smiles fondly. Then straightens the spread, moves around to side, smooths out the cover, goes to foot of bed, stops, hears him coming; walks around again and quickly covers the "God Is Love" pillow with spread.*)

HE (*entering with champagne bottle*). Look what I've found!

SHE (*going to foot of bed and arranging the cover there*). What?

HE. Champagne! (*Blows dust from bottle.*) Must be one that was left over from Robert's wedding.

SHE. Oh.

HE. Have we got any glasses up here?

SHE. Only the tooth glasses.

HE (*sits on edge of bed*). All right, get them.

SHE. You aren't going to drink it now?

HE. Of course. Now, don't tell me this is a fixture! (*Tears off foil from bottle.*)

SHE. But, darling, we can't drink champagne at eight o'clock in the morning.

HE. Why not?

SHE. We'll be reeling about when we get there. That would be a nice first impression to make on the landlady!

HE. I'd be delighted. I'd go up to that female sergeant major and say, "Hiya! Hah! Hah!" (*Blows his breath in her face as in the First Act. The memory strikes them both. They stay for a moment motionless.* SHE *pats his cheek.*)

SHE. I'll go get those glasses. (SHE *exits into bathroom.*)

(HE *rises, throws the foil into the wastebasket at foot of bed, goes to suitcases and puts bottle on floor. Goes back to bed and looks for the rest of his toilet articles.* HE *pulls back the spread, picks up the "God Is Love" pillow, looks under it, tosses it back, looks under the other pillows, then suddenly realizes that the "God Is Love" pillow has been put back in the bed. Picks it up and calls.*)

HE. Agnes.

SHE (*offstage*). What?

HE. Agnes.

SHE (*re-enters carrying towel and two glasses*). What? Oh . . . (SHE *is upset when she sees what it is, and very self-conscious.*)

HE. Agnes, did you put this back in the bed?

SHE (*standing at bathroom door*). Yes.

HE. Why, for Heaven's sake?

SHE. I told you . . . I wanted to leave something . . . friendly for that young couple . . . a sort of message.

HE. What message?

SHE. I'd like to tell them how happy we'd been—and that it was a very good bed . . . I mean, it's had a very nice history, and that . . . marriage was a good thing.

HE. Well, believe me, that's not the message they'll read from this pillow. Agnes, we'll do anything you like, we'll write them a letter, or carve our initials in the bed, but I won't let you do this to that boy . . .

SHE. Why not? (SHE *puts glasses and towel on floor beside knitting bag, takes little pillow from him and goes up to bed.*) When I found this very same little pillow in this very same bed on the first night of our marriage, I nearly burst into tears!

HE. Oh, you did, did you? Well, so did I! And it's time you heard about it! When, on that night, at that moment, I first saw that pillow, I suddenly felt as if I'd been caught in a world of women. Yes, women! I suddenly saw loom up behind you the biggest trade union in the world, and if I hadn't been a coward in long woolen underwear with my shoes off, I would have made a dive for freedom.

SHE. That's a fine thing to say! After all these years . . .

HE. Now, we'll have none of that. You can burst into tears, you can stand on your head, you can divorce me, but I'm not going to let you paralyze that boy at a crucial moment.

SHE. But it isn't a crucial moment!

HE. It is *the* crucial moment!

SHE. It is not! She would find it before, when she made the bed. That's why I put it there. It is meant for her, not for him, not for you, for her, from me! (*Puts little pillow on bed as before.*)

HE. Whomever it's for, the answer is NO! (HE *takes the little pillow and puts it on the trunk again.* SHE *pulls the spread up over the bed pillows.*) Whatever did I do with the rest of my toilet things?

(SHE *picks them up from floor by bed, goes to him, hands them to him, puts newspaper in wastebasket, sets basket down near arch.* HE *is very carefully packing his things. When he is finished, he closes the lid to the suitcase, tries to lock it, but doesn't succeed.*)

HE. You'll have to sit on this with me. I'll never get it shut alone. (SHE *sits down beside him.*) Now, get hold of the lock and when I say "Yes," we'll both do—that. (HE *bounces on the suitcase.*) Ready? Yes! (*They bounce.* HE *fastens his lock.*) Is it shut?

SHE (*trying to fix catch*). Not quite.

HE. What do you mean, not quite? Either it's shut or it isn't.

SHE. It isn't.

HE. All right. Here we go again. Ready? Yes! (*They bounce again.*) All right?

SHE. Yes.

HE (*picks up champagne bottle*). Now, do we drink this champagne or don't we?

SHE (*picks up glasses, towel, packs them in knitting bag*). No.

HE. All right. I just thought it would be a nice idea. Sort of round things off. (*Puts champagne bottle back on floor.*) Well, what do we do? Sit here on the suitcase till the car comes, or go downstairs and wait in the hall?

SHE. I don't know. (HE *looks at her, then at the little pillow on trunk, then smiles at her anger.*)

HE. It's odd, you know, how after you have lived in a place for so long, a room gets full of echoes. Almost everything we've said this morning we have said before . . . It's the bed, really, that I regret most. Pity it wouldn't fit. I wonder how the next couple will get along. Do you know what he does?

SHE. He's a salesman.

HE. A salesman, eh? Well, why not? So was I. Only I realized it too late. The nights that I lay awake in that bed thinking how I'd beat Shakespeare at the game . . .

SHE. Never mind, darling, you've given a lot of invalids a very nice time. (*In his reaction, as* HE *turns to reply, the doorbell rings.*)

(HE *rises and looks out window. He goes to door, opens it.* SHE *rises and turns top suitcase up.* HE *puts bed linen under left arm, picks up top suitcase in left hand.* SHE *turns up the other suitcase and* HE *picks that one up in his right hand; turns to go.* SHE *quickly gets the knitting bag, stops him and tucks it under his right arm.* HE *exits.*

SHE *picks up purse, gloves, from off of trunk, then quickly takes the little pillow and goes to bed but stops suddenly, hearing him return, and hides the pillow under her coat.* HE *goes to trunk, leans over to grasp its handle, sees that the little pillow is not there, but proceeds to drag the trunk out. At the door, as* HE *swings trunk around,* HE *looks back at her.* SHE *is standing, leaning against the bedpost, pulling on her gloves. As soon as* HE *is out of sight,* SHE *hurriedly puts the pillow back into the bed and covers it.*

HE *re-enters, wearing his hat, picks up bottle of champagne, goes up to bed, drops hat on foot of bed, flings back the covers, picks up the little pillow and throws it to her side of the bed; then throws the bottle of champagne down on the pillow on his side and flips the spread back into place.* HE *picks up his hat and goes to her. They stand there for a moment, looking about the room.* HE *puts his hat on, smiles, leans down and hesitantly, but surely, picks her up.* SHE *cries, "Michael!"* HE *stands there for a moment, kisses her, then turns and carries her out of the room.*)

CURTAIN

THE SEVEN YEAR ITCH

George Axelrod

First presented by Courtney Burr and Elliott Nugent at the
Fulton Theatre, New York, on November 20, 1952,
with the following cast:

RICHARD SHERMAN Tom Ewell

RICKY Johnny Klein

HELEN SHERMAN Neva Patterson

MISS MORRIS Marilyn Clark

ELAINE Joan Donovan

MARIE WHATEVER-HER-NAME-WAS
                         Irene Moore

THE GIRL Vanessa Brown

DR. BRUBAKER Robert Emhardt

TOM MACKENZIE George Keane

RICHARD'S VOICE George Ives

THE GIRL'S VOICE Pat Fowler

ACT ONE. SCENE I: About eight o'clock on a summer evening.

SCENE II: Immediately following.

ACT TWO. SCENE I: Evening, the following day. SCENE II: Two
hours later.

ACT THREE. The following morning.

The action of the play takes place in the apartment of the Richard
Shermans, in the Gramercy Park section of New York City. The
time is the present.

INTRODUCTION

GEORGE AXELROD, the thirty-year-old New York author of *The Seven-Year Itch,* is wholly a devotee of show business. He had served the noble cause of entertainment his entire adult life by the time he saw his fabulously successful comedy on the stage. Previously, his energies had gone mainly into the channels of radio and television, to which he has contributed nearly five hundred plays or approximations of plays, although he also wrote some novels and some revue sketches for the stage. The revue, on which he had collaborated with Max Wilk, was called *Curtain Going Up.* Unfortunately it was subtitled—much too accurately, he recalls—"People Running Out." He was also occupied with a radio show called *Grand Old Opry* and a "fancy saloon show" called *All About Love,* which the young author considered "a good deal" since the management for whom the show was put on "was nice about letting us drink on the arm." After all this experience, *"Itch,"* he recalls, "was an easy one." (These *memorabilia* are taken from the author's article in the January, 1954, issue of *Theatre Arts.*)

Encouraged by the success of his first bout with Broadway showmanship, which also resulted in the successful filming of *The Seven Year Itch,* Mr. Axelrod tried his luck again. It held out rather well. Although *Will Success Spoil Rock Hunter?* collected few cheers from the New York press, the more coveted approbation of Broadway's cash customers was not slow in coming and the author had a second hit with which to replenish the United States Treasury. Mr. Axelrod's father had collaborated on variety shows at Columbia University with Oscar Hammerstein II, but had retreated to the relative security of a business career. It seemed as if his son were wholeheartedly bent upon erasing the blot upon the Axelrod scutcheon caused by this defection from the theatre.

ACT ONE

Scene One

The apartment of the RICHARD SHERMANS, *about half a block from Gramercy Park in New York City.*

We see the foyer, the living room and the back terrace of a four-room apartment —the parlor floor through—in a remodeled private house.

A flight of stairs on the back wall lead to the ceiling where they stop. In one of the earlier phases of remodeling, this apartment and the one above it were a duplex. But now they are rented separately and the ceiling is boarded up.

A door, also on the back wall, leads to the kitchen. French doors, right, open onto the terrace. The terrace, while it increases the rent about thirty dollars a month, is small and rather uninviting. It looks out into the back court and because of the buildings around it you get the feeling of being at the bottom of a well. From the terrace we see some of the skyline of the city and a good deal of the backs of the buildings across the court. On the terrace there is a chaise, a table and a few shrubs.

On the left wall of the living room are high, sliding doors which lead to the bedrooms and bath. There is a fireplace in the living room. The whole apartment has a summer look. The rugs are up and the summer slip covers are on the furniture. The living room contains a piano, bookshelves, a large radio phonograph and a liquor cabinet.

When the curtain rises it is about eight o'clock on an evening in July. It is a hot, airless night. It is not yet completely dark. It grows darker gradually through the scene.

RICHARD SHERMAN, *a young-looking man of thirty-eight, is lying on the chaise on the terrace. He wears a shirt, gabardine pants, loafers and no socks.*

It is hard to know what to say about RICHARD. *He has a crew haircut. He has a good job. He's vice-president in charge of sales at a twenty-five-cent publishing house. He made eighteen thousand dollars last year. He buys his clothes at Brooks.*

At the moment, he has moved a small, portable radio out to the table on the terrace and is listening to the first game of a twi-night double header between Brooklyn and Boston. He is listening to the game and drinking unenthusiastically from a bottle of Seven-Up.

At rise we hear the ball game softly on the radio. We have come in at a rather tense moment. The bases are loaded and Hodges is up. He bunts and is thrown out. RICHARD *is disgusted. He snaps off the radio.*

———

RICHARD (*rising*). Bunt? Two runs behind, the bases loaded and they send Hodges up to bunt! (*Shaking his head, he goes into the kitchen. He reappears carrying a bottle of raspberry soda. Still appalled*) Bunt, for God's sake! Well, what are you going to do? (*He looks around aimlessly for a moment.*) I'm hungry. Well, that's what comes of having dinner at Schrafft's! Schrafft's! I wanted to have dinner in the saloon across the street—but you can't have dinner in a saloon and then not . . . They don't like it. Oh, I suppose I could have ordered a drink and then not drunk it . . . But I figure it's easier just to eat at Schrafft's. (*He drops wearily onto the chaise.*) It's hard on a man when the family goes away. It's peaceful, though, with everybody gone. It's sure as hell peaceful. (*He settles back in the chaise and grins. Music sneaks in very softly, and the light on him dims to a spot.*) Ricky was really upset this morning when they left for the station. It was very flattering. I thought the kid was going to cry . . . (*He sits, smiling, remembering the scene. Dream lighting by the front door picks up* HELEN *and* RICKY *leaving.*)

RICKY. But what about Daddy? Isn't Daddy coming with us?

HELEN. Daddy'll come up Friday night.

RICKY. But, Mommy, why can't Daddy come up with us now?

HELEN. Poor Daddy has to stay in the hot city and make money. We're going to spend the whole summer at the beach but poor Daddy can only come up week ends.

RICKY. Poor Daddy . . .

HELEN. Daddy is going to work very hard. He's going to eat properly and not smoke like Dr. Murphy told him and he's going to stay on the wagon for a while like Dr. Summers told him, to take care of his nervous indigestion . . .

(*In the spot,* RICHARD *drinks from the bottle of raspberry soda. He is somewhat awed by the taste. He looks curiously at the label and then reads it.*)

RICHARD. "Contains carbonated water, citric acid, corn syrup, artificial raspberry flavoring, pure vegetable colors and preservative." Since I've been on the wagon, I've had one continuous upset stomach. (*He looks sadly at the bottle and drinks some more.*)

HELEN. And just to make sure Daddy's all right, Mommy is going to call Daddy at ten o'clock tonight . . .

RICKY. Poor Daddy . . .

(*The music fades and so does the dream light by the door.* HELEN *and* RICKY *disappear. The lighting returns to normal.*)

RICHARD (*coming out of his reverie*). Ten o'clock! I don't even know how I'm going to stay awake till ten o'clock! (*He stares moodily off into the growing dusk. Suddenly he notices something in an apartment across the court. He is momentarily fascinated and rises for a better look.*) Hey, lady! I know it's a hot night but . . . You sit out on this terrace, it's like having a television set with about thirty channels all going at once . . . Don't give me any dirty look, lady. I pay rent for this terrace. If you don't like it, pull your blind down! (*As she apparently does so*) Oh. Well, that's life. (*He yawns. Restlessly, he rises and wanders into the living room. He yawns again and then, suddenly, in mid-yawn, something occurs to him.*) Helen has a lot of nerve calling me at ten o'clock. It shows a very definite lack of trust. What's she think I'm going to do? Start smoking the minute she turns her back? Start drinking? Maybe she thinks I'm going to have girls up here! . . . You know, that's a hell of a thing! . . . Seven years, we've been married. And not once have I done anything like that. Not *once!* And don't think I couldn't have, either. Because I could have. But plenty . . . (*Music sneaks in and in dream lighting we see* HELEN *seated on the couch knitting. She laughs.*) Don't laugh. There's plenty of women who think I'm *pretty* attractive, for your information!

HELEN. For instance, who?

RICHARD (*indignant*). What do you mean, for instance, who? There've been plenty of them, that's all.

HELEN. Name one. (*There is a considerable pause while he thinks about this.*) Go ahead. Just one.

RICHARD. It's hard, I mean just offhand. There're plenty of them, though. (HELEN *laughs.* RICHARD *is stung.*) Well, there's Miss Morris, for instance. She's practically thrown herself at me. You should see the way she gives me the business every time she comes into my office. . . . (MISS MORRIS, *a sexy-looking blonde in a backless summer blouse and a skirt with an exaggerated slit, drifts into the scene carrying a dictation pad and pencil.*) She wears those backless things and she's always telling me it's so hot she's not wearing any underwear . . .

HELEN. It sounds perfectly sordid. Does she sit on your lap when she takes dictation?

RICHARD. Of course not!

(MISS MORRIS *sits on his lap.*)

MISS MORRIS. Good morning, Mr. Sherman.

RICHARD. Good morning, Miss Morris. (MISS MORRIS *runs her fingers through his hair and covers his cheek and neck with little kisses.*) That will be all. (MISS MORRIS *gets up and drifts away, giving him a private wave and a wink.*) I just happened to bring her up as an example, that's all. Just an example . . .

HELEN. I'm quite sure you're a great success with the stenographers in your office.

RICHARD. I could be a great success with a couple of your high-class friends if you're going to get snooty about it. Elaine, for instance. You may not know this, but for *two years* that dame has been trying to get me into the sack . . . (ELAINE, *a luscious-looking dame in a gold-lamé evening gown, appears on the terrace. She is carrying a glass of champagne.*) The night of your birthday party, she got loaded and went after me right here on the terrace . . . (*Dream lighting on* HELEN *dims out.*)

ELAINE (*coming up behind him and draping her arms around his neck*). Do you know something, darling? I look at you and I just melt. You must know that. Men always know . . . (*Quite casually she tosses her champagne glass off the terrace and grabs him and kisses him violently.*)

RICHARD. What's the matter? Are you crazy or something?

ELAINE. Let's get out of here, darling. Come on. Nobody'll even know we're gone . . .

RICHARD. You don't know what you're

saying!

ELAINE. Oh, yes, I do! Come on, darling! Let's be a little mad! (*She drifts away, giving him the eye as she goes.*)

RICHARD. Now, Elaine may be a little mad, but she's plenty attractive! And *she's* not the only one either! You probably don't even remember that Marie whatever-her-name-was, from the UN who was staying with the Petersons in Wesport last summer . . . We went swimming together one night. Without any bathing suits. You didn't know that, did you? It was that Saturday night the MacKenzies came up and I drove over to the beach by myself . . .

(MARIE WHAT-EVER-HER-NAME-WAS *has materialized beside him. A gorgeous girl in shorts and man's shirt.*)

MARIE (*speaking in rapid but somehow sexy-sounding French. She kicks off her shorts and as she talks begins to unbutton her shirt*). Hello, Dick. You too, without doubt, like to swim at night. I like it because the wearing of a bathing costume is unnecessary . . . You see that rock over there. The men leave their bathing costumes on one side and the girls leave theirs on the other. Sometimes the bathing costumes get mixed up.

RICHARD. I don't speak very good French, but I knew what she was talking about.

MARIE. The water at night is magnificent. There is a warmness and a feeling of black velvet. Especially when one is without bathing costume . . .

RICHARD (*weakly, unable to take his eyes off the buttons*). Mais oui. Mais oui.

MARIE. Don't peek now. I am not wearing a bathing costume.

(*Her shirt is almost off. The lights dim out just in time.*)

RICHARD (*with great self-righteousness*). We didn't do anything but swim. As a matter of fact, she was plenty disappointed we didn't do anything but swim. (*The lights have dimmed back to normal.*) So, all I can say is, in the light of the circumstances, I resent your calling me at ten o'clock to check up on me. If Helen is going to start worrying about me after seven years, it's pretty ridiculous, that's all. (*He rises and begins to pace nervously.*) And she is worried too. Even if she doesn't show it. I don't know. She probably figures she isn't as young as she used to be. She's thirty-one years old. One of these days she's going to wake up and find her looks

are gone. Then where will she be? No wonder she's worried. . . . Especially since I don't look a bit different than I did when I was twenty-eight. It's not my fault I don't. It's just a simple biological fact. Women age quicker than men. I probably won't look any different when I'm sixty. I have that kind of a face. Everybody'll think she's my mother. (*He sighs a mournful sigh and sinks into chair. The downstairs door buzzer rings.*) Now who's that? (*He goes to the foyer and presses the wall button. Then he opens the front door and peers out calling.*) Hello? Hello? Who is it?

GIRL'S VOICE (*off stage*). I'm terribly sorry to bother you . . .

RICHARD. What? (*Then as he sees her, he reacts.*) Oh. Oh. Well, hello . . .

GIRL'S VOICE (*off stage*). I feel so silly. I forgot my key. I locked myself out. So I pressed your bell. I hope you don't mind.

RICHARD. No. No. I don't mind. No trouble at all.

GIRL'S VOICE (*off stage*). I'm awfully sorry.

RICHARD. Don't worry about it. Any time. It's a pleasure.

GIRL'S VOICE (*off stage*). Thank you. Well, good-by . . .

RICHARD. Good-by . . . (*He closes the door. Then, after a moment opens it again and peers out, craning his neck to see up the stairs. He comes back inside, closes the door. He is shaking his head.*)

RICHARD. Where did *that* come from? I didn't know they made them like that any more. Oh, she must be the one who sublet the Kaufmans' apartment. I should have asked her in for a drink. Oh, no, I shouldn't have. Not me, kid. (*The telephone rings.* RICHARD *glances at his watch. Then hurries to answer it.*) Hello? Oh. Hello, Helen. I wasn't expecting you to call till ten. Is everything okay? . . . Good. . . . I was just sitting here listening to the ball game. They're two runs behind and they send Hodges up to bunt. . . . Yeah, I'm sleepy too. . . . The old place is pretty empty without you. I can't wait till Friday. Ricky okay? . . . He did? Well, he hasn't done that for a long time. It was probably just the excitement . . . That's nice. No, I don't . . . Who did you meet at the A&P? . . . What's Tom MacKenzie doing up there? . . . Look, my advice to you is avoid Tom MacKenzie like the plague. If you keep meeting him at the A&P, switch to Bohack's! . . . Look, are you sure everything else is all right? Good. . . . Me too. Yeah, I'm pretty tired myself. Good night . . . Night. (*He hangs up phone.*) Well, I might as well go to sleep myself. But I'm not sleepy. I suddenly realize I am not even a little bit sleepy. Maybe I could call up Charlie Peterson. No. That's a real bad idea. Under no circumstances should I call up Charlie Peterson. . . . I'll get in bed and read. God knows I've got enough stuff here I'm supposed to read. (*Picks up brief case and begins to take out manuscripts.*) I've got a conference with Dr. Brubaker tomorrow night. It might be amusing if I'd finished his miserable book before I talk to him about it. I don't know why every psychiatrist in America feels he has to write a book. And let's see what else. *The Scarlet Letter.* I read that in school. I don't have to read that again. But I'd better. Dr. Brubaker and *The Scarlet Letter.* It looks like a big night. (*Picks up soda bottle, notices that it is empty.*) Well, one more of these for a night cap and we're all set . . . (*Sighing heavily, he goes to kitchen for a fresh bottle of soda. He walks back out to the terrace and sits for a moment on the chaise. Automatically, he switches on the radio.*)

RADIO VOICE. . . . and so as we go into the last half of the eighth inning, Boston is leading, seven to four. In the last of the eighth, for Brooklyn, it'll be Robinson, Hodges and Furillo . . .

(RICHARD *reaches over and snaps off the radio.*)

RICHARD. Frankly, I don't give a damn. (*He rises and walks to the edge of the terrace, looking hopefully toward the apartment across the court.*)

(*At that moment there is a violent crash. Apparently from the sky, an enormous iron pot with a plant in it comes plummeting down. It lands with a sickening thud on the chaise where he was sitting a moment before.*)

(RICHARD *looks at it in horror-struck silence for a moment or two.*)

RICHARD. Look at that damn thing! Right where I was sitting! I could have been killed, for God's sake! (*Cautiously, with a nervous glance upward, he leans over to examine it.*) Jes-sus! (*He darts back inside, looks wildly around for a* cigarette, *finally finds a crumbled pack in the pocket of a raincoat hanging in the hall closet. He starts to light it. Then, stops himself.*) I forgot—I'm not smoking. Oh, the hell with *that!* (*He lights the cigarette.*) I could have been killed. Just then. Like that. Right now I could be lying out there on the lousy terrace dead. I should stop smoking because twenty years from now it might affect my goddamn lungs! (*He inhales deeply with great enjoyment.*) Oh, that tastes beautiful. The first one in six weeks. (*He lets the smoke out slowly.*) All those lovely injurious tars and resins! (*Suddenly he is dizzy.*) I'm dizzy . . . (*He sinks to the piano bench, coughing.*) Another week of not smoking and I'd really've been dead! (*He picks up the bottle of soda and starts to take a slug of that. He chokes on it.*) The hell with this stuff too! (*He goes quickly to liquor cabinet and pours an inch or two of whiskey into a glass and belts it down. Then he mixes another one and carries it onto the terrace. He sets the drink on the table and in a very gingerly fashion tries to pick up the pot. It is real heavy.*) My God! This thing weighs a ton! I could have been killed! (*Suddenly, his anger finds a direction.*) Hey, up there! What's the big idea! You want to kill somebody or something? What do you think you're doing anyway?

GIRL'S VOICE (*from terrace above*). What's the matter?

RICHARD (*yelling*). What's the matter? This goddamn cast-iron chamber pot damn near killed me, that's what's the matter. What the hell! . . . Oh. Oh. It's you. Hello.

GIRL'S VOICE. What hap———Oh, golly! The tomato plant fell over!

RICHARD. It sure did.

GIRL'S VOICE. I'm terribly sorry.

RICHARD. That's okay.

GIRL'S VOICE. I seem to be giving you a terrible time tonight. First the door and now this. I don't know what to do . . .

RICHARD. Don't worry about it. (*He drains drink.*) Hey, up there!

GIRL'S VOICE. Yes?

RICHARD. I'll tell you what you can do about it. You can come down and have a drink.

GIRL'S VOICE. But that doesn't seem . . .

RICHARD. Sure it seems . . . Come on now . . . I insist . . .

GIRL'S VOICE. Well, all right . . .

RICHARD. I'll see you in a minute.

GIRL'S VOICE. All right. I'm really terribly sorry . . .

RICHARD. That's okay. Don't worry about it. As a matter of fact, it's wonderful. See you in a minute . . .

GIRL'S VOICE. All right . . .

(RICHARD *gallops frantically into the living room. The sound of the telephone brings him up short. He goes quickly to phone and answers it.*)

RICHARD. Hi there! Oh. Oh, Helen! (*With great, if somewhat forced enthusiasm.*) Well, Helen! This *is* a surprise! And a very pleasant one if I may say so! How *are you?* . . . Sure, sure I'm all right. Why shouldn't I be all right? In what way do I sound funny? I was just out on the terrace listening to the ball game. They're two runs behind and they send Hodges up to bunt . . . What? Sure . . . Sure I will. Your yellow skirt . . . (*As she talks on the other end of the phone he is reaching around straightening up the room.*) Yes, of course I'm listening to you. You want me to send up your yellow skirt, because you're having Tom MacKenzie and some people over for cocktails. Good old Tom! How is he? . . . No. I haven't been drinking. I just had . . . What? Your yellow skirt. In the hall closet. On a wire hanger. Sure. By parcel post. The first thing in the morning. Without fail. . . . No. I don't feel a bit funny. I was just out on the terrace listening to the ball game. They're two runs behind and they send Hodges up . . . Yes . . . well, good night. Good night. Night. (*He hangs up phone. Then, galvanized into action, he starts to straighten up the place. In the middle of this he realizes he looks a little sloppy himself and he dashes off through the bedroom doors. Music swells and the lights dim out.*)

CURTAIN

SCENE TWO

The music continues through the blackout.

After a moment the curtain rises and the lights dim back up to normal.

RICHARD *reappears from the bedroom. He has put on the jacket to his pants and is frantically tying his tie.*

He is visibly agitated. He starts to arrange the room for his guest. He pauses and turns off a lamp. Catches himself and quickly turns it back on again.

RICHARD. What am I *doing* anyway! . . . This is absolutely ridiculous. The first night Helen leaves and I'm bringing dames into the apartment. . . . Now take it easy. The girl upstairs damn near kills me with a cast-iron bucket. So I ask her down for a drink. What's wrong with that? . . . If Helen was here, she'd do the same thing. It's only polite. . . . And what the hell is she doing asking Tom MacKenzie over for cocktails, for God's sake! . . . Besides, I want to get another look at that girl. She must be some kind of a model or actress or something. (*He is busily arranging things. Laying out ice and soda. Puffing cushions. Picking up his socks.*) There is absolutely nothing wrong with asking a neighbor down for a drink. Nothing. . . . I just hope *she* doesn't get the wrong idea, that's all. If this dame thinks she's coming down here for some kind of a big time or something—well, she's got a big surprise. One drink and out! That's all! I'm a happily married man, for God's sake! (*He surveys his work.*) Maybe we ought to have a little soft music, just for atmosphere. (*He goes to phonograph and starts looking through records.*) Let's see. How about the Second Piano Concerto? Maybe Rachmaninoff would be overdoing it a little. This kid is probably more for old show tunes . . . (*He finds a record: "Just One of Those Things"—it is obviously an old one with a real thirties orchestration. He puts it on and listens to it for a moment or two with great satisfaction.*) That's more like it. The old nostalgia. Never misses. . . . Never misses? What am I trying to do? I'll call her and tell her not to come. That's all. Why ask for trouble? (*He starts for phone—stops.*) I don't even know her phone number. I don't even know her name. What am I doing? And what the hell is she doing? She could have been down here, had her lousy drink, and gone home already! . . . She's probably getting all fixed up. She'll probably be wearing some kind of a damn evening dress! . . . Oh, my God! What have I done? (*Very quickly he has another drink.*) If anything happens, it happens. That's all. It's up to her. She looked kind of sophisticated. She must know what she's doing. . . . I'm pretty sophisticated myself. At least I used to be. I've been married so damn long I don't remember. (*Suddenly, he becomes very polished.*) Drink? . . . Thanks. (*He pours himself a drink.*) Soda? . . . A dash. (*He toasts.*) Cheers. (*He leans nonchalantly against the piano. The "real" lighting begins to dim and music: "Just One of Those Things" fades in. The front door lights up and swings majestically open flooding the room with "dream light." He moves toward the door, almost dancing. In this particular flight of fancy he is very suave, very Noel Coward.*)

(THE GIRL *is standing in the doorway. She is an extraordinarily beautiful girl in her early twenties. She wears an extravagantly glamorous evening gown. There is a wise, half-mocking, half-enticing smile on her face. She looks like nothing so much as a Tabu perfume ad.*)

THE GIRL. I came.

RICHARD. I'm so glad.

THE GIRL. Didn't you know I'd come?

RICHARD. Of course. Of course I knew. Won't you come in?

THE GIRL. Thank you. (*She comes in. The door swings closed behind her.*)

(RICHARD *turns and we suddenly notice that he is wearing a black patch over one eye.*)

RICHARD. How lovely you are! Tell me, who are you? What is your name?

THE GIRL. Does it matter?

RICHARD. No. Of course not. I was a boor to ask.

THE GIRL. Why have you invited me here?

RICHARD (*spoken—like dialogue*). Oh, it was just one of those things. Just one of those foolish things. A trip to the moon—on gossamer wings . . .

THE GIRL. How sweet! Oh—a Steinway. Do you play?

RICHARD (*somewhat wistfully. Thinking, perhaps, of other, happier days*). Just a little now—for myself . . .

THE GIRL. Play something for me . . .

RICHARD. All right. You'll be sorry you asked . . .

THE GIRL. I'm sure I'll not . . .

RICHARD (*sitting at piano*). You'll see . . . (*Very dramatically he prepares to play. His preparations, while vastly complicated, do not, however, include raising the lid from the keys. Finally he begins to play—or rather pantomime playing on the closed lid. We hear, however, the opening bars of the C-Sharp Minor Prelude played brilliantly.*)

RICHARD (*playing*). I'm afraid I'm a little rusty. (*She is overcome. She sinks to the piano bench beside him. He turns to her.*) Tell me, what would you think, if, quite suddenly, I were to seize you in my arms and cover your neck with kisses?

THE GIRL. I would think: What a mad impetuous fool he is!

RICHARD. And if I merely continued to sit here, mooning at you, as I have done for the last half-hour—what would you think then?

THE GIRL. I would simply think: What a fool he is!

(RICHARD *takes her dramatically in his arms. They embrace. He kisses her violently. Music sweeps in and the lights black out.*)

(*In the darkness, we hear the sound of the door buzzer. It rings twice.*)

(*The lights dim back to normal.* RICHARD *is standing where we left him, leaning against the piano, lost in reverie. The buzzer rings again and he is jarred back to reality. He puts down his drink, and falling all over himself in nervous and undignified haste dashes to the door.*)

RICHARD. Come in . . . Come in . . .

(*Revealed in the doorway is* DR. BRUBAKER. *He is a round, somewhat messy, imperious man in his middle fifties. He carries a large brief case.*)

RICHARD (*completely taken aback*). Dr. Brubaker!

DR. BRUBAKER. Good evening. I hope I'm not late. Monday is my day at the clinic plus my regular patients and of course I'm on The Author Meets the Critic Friday night. I have been preparing my denunciation. I hope I haven't kept you waiting . . .

RICHARD. Look, Dr. Brubaker. Wasn't our . . .?

DR. BRUBAKER. Your office sent me the galleys of the last five chapters. I have them here with me. They are a mass of errors. I want to go over the whole thing with you very carefully.

RICHARD. Dr. Brubaker. I'm terribly sorry. Our appointment—I believe it was for tomorrow night . . .

(DR. BRUBAKER *has opened his brief case*

and has begun to spread papers all over the table.)

DR. BRUBAKER. I understand, of course, that your firm wishes to reach as wide an audience as possible. But I must protest— and very strongly—the changing of the title of my book from *Of Man and the Unconscious* to *Of Sex and Violence* . . .

RICHARD. Dr. Brubaker, I'm terribly sorry. I know how important this is. But I'm afraid our appointment was for tomorrow night.

DR. BRUBAKER. Tomorrow night?

RICHARD. Tuesday night. I understood it was definite for Tuesday night.

DR. BRUBAKER. Good Lord!

RICHARD. And I'm afraid I have someone coming in tonight. Another appointment. With an author. And she'll be here any minute. In fact she's late.

DR. BRUBAKER. Astounding. Really incredible.

RICHARD. It's probably my fault. I probably wasn't clear on the phone.

DR. BRUBAKER. No. No. You were perfectly clear . . .

RICHARD. I can't understand how it happened.

DR. BRUBAKER. Perfectly simple. Repressed uxoricide.

RICHARD. I beg your pardon?

DR. BRUBAKER. Repressed uxoricide. I came tonight because I want to murder my wife.

RICHARD. I see . . . Yes . . . Of course . . .

DR. BRUBAKER. A perfectly natural phenomenon. It happens every day.

RICHARD. It does?

DR. BRUBAKER. Certainly. Upon leaving the clinic and being faced with the necessity of returning to my home, I felt a strong unconscious impulse to murder my wife. Naturally, not wanting to do the good woman any bodily harm, my mind conveniently changed our appointment to tonight. What could be more simple?

RICHARD. I see . . .

DR. BRUBAKER. I am most sorry to have inconvenienced you, sir . . .

RICHARD. No, no. That's quite all right . . .

DR. BRUBAKER. And I shall see you here tomorrow evening.

RICHARD. Fine, Doctor. We could just as easily have our conference tonight—except that I do have this other author coming . . .

DR. BRUBAKER. Of course. I understand perfectly. Oh . . . Have you finished reading the book?

RICHARD. Well, I got as far as Chapter Three. The Meyerholt Case.

DR. BRUBAKER. Meyer*heim*. You read very slowly. Well, sir. Good night. (*He turns and starts to go. He is almost to the door when he stops and turns back.*) Sir. I trust you will not be offended if I call to your attention the fact that you are not wearing socks . . .

RICHARD (*looking down*). Good Lord!

DR. BRUBAKER. I was interested in knowing if you were aware of it? And I gather from your expression that you were not. In Chapter Three on Gustav Meyerheim I point out that he invariably removed his socks. Before he struck.

RICHARD. Before he *struck*?

DR. BRUBAKER. Yes. Surely you recall Meyerheim. A fascinating character! A rapist! I was certain you would be amused by the coincidence. Until tomorrow then, good evening. (*The* DOCTOR *bows and exits.*)

(RICHARD *looks helplessly down at his sockless ankles, then looks wildly around, finds his socks and struggles into them, muttering angrily as he does so something that sounds vaguely like: "Damn psychiatrists—write books—make a Federal case out of everything . . . I bet his wife is a nervous wreck—every time he takes off his socks she probably hides in the closet . . .")*

(*As he is fighting his way into his loafers the door buzzer sounds.*)

RICHARD. Coming . . . (*He dashes to door and opens it.* THE GIRL *is standing in the doorway. Her real-life entrance is very different from the way he imagined it. She is quite lovely but far from the exotic creature he envisioned. She wears a checked shirt and rolled dungarees. She looks at him for a moment and then smiles tentatively.*)

THE GIRL. Hi.

RICHARD (*he looks at her blankly for an instant*). Hi.

THE GIRL. Can I come in?

RICHARD. Sure . . . I mean, of course. Please do.

THE GIRL. I'm sorry I took so long but I've been watering the garden. I promised the Kaufmans I'd take good care of it, and I'm afraid I kind of neglected it. I didn't even find the hose until tonight.

RICHARD. I didn't know the Kaufmans had a garden . . .

THE GIRL. Oh, yes. They do.

RICHARD. It must be very nice.

THE GIRL. It is. But it's a lot of work. Before I found the hose I'd been using the cocktail shaker—that was the only thing I could find . . .

RICHARD. The cocktail shaker . . .

THE GIRL. Yes. They have a big glass one. It must hold about a gallon. I'm just sick about the tomato plant. Did it survive, do you think?

RICHARD. I really don't know. We could look at it, I suppose. It's out on the terrace. Right where it landed.

THE GIRL. That's awful . . . I can't figure out how it happened . . .

(RICHARD *leads way to terrace.*)

RICHARD. It's right there. I haven't touched it . . .

THE GIRL. Golly, look at that! I'll pay for it, of course. Do you think you could lift it up . . . ?

RICHARD. Sure. (*He lifts the pot off the chaise with a great deal of effort.*) This damn thing weighs a ton . . . There . . .

THE GIRL. I just thought. If you'd been sitting in that chair . . . When it fell, I mean. It might have, well—practically killed you . . .

RICHARD. That occurred to me, too.

THE GIRL. I'm really awfully sorry. It's probably criminal negligence or manslaughter or something. You could have sued somebody. Me, probably. Or your family could have. Of course I don't know what they would have collected. If they'd sued me, I mean. But anyway, they'd have had a very good case.

RICHARD. There's no use getting all upset. I wasn't sitting there, thank God, so it's all right. Look, I asked you down for a drink. Would you like one? I mean you really don't look old enough to drink . . .

THE GIRL. I do, though. I drink like a fish. Do you have Scotch?

RICHARD. Sure. At least I'm pretty sure I do. I've been drinking something for the last half hour. I'm not sure now what it was. I was a little upset . . .

THE GIRL (*following him back into the living room*). I don't blame you. You could have been killed, practically. I feel just terrible about it. I mean . . .

RICHARD. Let's don't start that again.

Let's just have a drink.

THE GIRL. All right. I'm glad you're taking it this way. You have every right to be just furious. I know I would be. If somebody practically dropped a tomato plant on my head.

RICHARD. Let's see, what I *was* drinking? (*Picks up glass and tastes it.*) Bourbon. But we do have Scotch around here somewhere. Yeah—here we are. How do you like it?

THE GIRL. Scotch and soda, I guess. That's what you're supposed to say, isn't it? Back home the boys drink Scotch and Pepsi-Cola a lot. Before I knew anything at all, I knew *that* was wrong.

RICHARD. That's about as wrong as you can get, yes.

THE GIRL. I knew it was. When I was very young I liked it, though. It sort of killed the taste of the Scotch.

RICHARD (*mixing drink*). I can see how it would tend to do that.

THE GIRL. Do you have a cigarette around? I left mine upstairs.

RICHARD. Oh, yes. Sure. I'm sorry. Right here. (*He takes the crumpled pack from his pocket. There is one left in it.*) It may be a little stale. I haven't been smoking. In fact, before tonight, I hadn't had a cigarette in six weeks.

THE GIRL. That's wonderful! I wish I had the will power to stop. I don't, though. I smoke like a chimney. Sometimes three packs a day.

RICHARD. My God! That's terrifying.

THE GIRL. I know. It doesn't seem to affect me, though. I guess I'm pretty healthy. What made you start aga—Oh. I'll bet you started smoking after the plant fell down. To steady your nerves.

RICHARD. Well, something like that.

THE GIRL. Now I really *do* feel awful. If I'd just had the sense to move it off the wall. Or call the janitor and have him move it. It's pretty heavy. . . . Oh, I just feel . . .

RICHARD. Please, now, that's enough. Let me get some more cigarettes. I think there's an unopened carton out in the kitchen. Excuse me a minute . . . (*He exits into the kitchen.*)

(THE GIRL *looks around the apartment then drifts over to the piano. She hits a random note or two.* RICHARD *reappears.*)

THE GIRL. Do you play the piano?

(*For one mad instant,* RICHARD *consid-*

ers the question. The faraway "Just-a-little-now-for-myself" look comes into his eye. But he quickly suppresses it.)

RICHARD (*truthfully*). I'm afraid not. I'm tone deaf. My wife plays, though . . .

THE GIRL. Oh, you're married?

RICHARD. Yes. I am.

THE GIRL. I knew it! I could tell. You *look* married.

RICHARD. I do?

THE GIRL. Mmm! It's funny. Back home practically nobody was married. And in New York everybody is. Men, I mean.

RICHARD. That's a remarkable observation.

THE GIRL. It's really true.

RICHARD. I guess so. I never really thought about it.

THE GIRL (*as he hands her drink*). Thanks. I think about it quite a lot. This is good. Do you mind if I put my feet up? I'll take my shoes off.

RICHARD. No. Of course not. Go right ahead. Make yourself comfortable.

THE GIRL. Your wife is away for the summer, isn't she?

RICHARD. Yes, as a matter of fact she is. How did you know?

THE GIRL. They all are. It's really amazing.

RICHARD. They *all* are?

THE GIRL. Mmm. Everybody's wife. Back home practically nobody goes away for the summer. Especially anybody's wife.

RICHARD. Have you been away long? In New York, that is?

THE GIRL. Oh, years. Almost a year and a half. It seems like years. I love it. Especially now that I've got my own apartment. When I lived at the club I didn't like it so much. You had to be in by one o'clock. Now I can stay out all night if I want to. I was really glad when they practically asked me to leave.

RICHARD. Why did they practically ask you to leave?

THE GIRL. It was so silly. I used to do modeling when I first came to New York and when this picture of me was published in *US Camera* they got all upset. You should have seen Miss Stephenson's face. She was the house mother.

RICHARD. What was the matter with the picture?

THE GIRL. I was nude.

RICHARD. Oh.

THE GIRL. On the beach with some drift-wood. It got honorable mention. It was called "Textures." Because you could see the three different textures. The drift-wood, the sand and me. I got twenty-five dollars an hour. And it took hours and hours, you'd be surprised. And the first day the sun wasn't right and I got paid for that too.

RICHARD. That seems only fair.

THE GIRL. Sure. You get paid from the time you're called. No matter how long it takes to make the picture. But I don't do modeling any more. Since I got this steady job . . .

RICHARD. Now you have a steady job?

THE GIRL. I take in washing . . .

RICHARD. What?

THE GIRL. That's just a joke. I'm on this television program. The commercial part. First I wash my husband's shirt in *ordinary* soap flakes. Then I wash it with Trill. So when people ask me what I do I always say I take in washing. I'm on for a minute and forty-five seconds. It's really a very good part . . .

RICHARD. Oh, so you're an actress. Is that it?

THE GIRL. Mmm. It's really very interesting. People don't realize, but every time I wash a shirt on television, I'm appearing before more people than Sarah Bernhardt appeared before in her whole career. It's something to think about.

RICHARD. It certainly is.

THE GIRL. I wish *I* were old enough to have seen Sarah Bernhardt. Was she magnificent?

(RICHARD *is somewhat shaken by this question. For a moment he sits there, grinning weakly.*)

RICHARD. I really wouldn't know. I'm not quite that old myself . . .

THE GIRL. I guess you're really not, are you?

RICHARD. I am thirty-nine. Or I will be the day after tomorrow. At the moment I'm still only thirty-eight.

THE GIRL. The day after tomorrow?

RICHARD. That's right.

THE GIRL. Isn't that amazing? We were born under the same sign. I was twenty-two yesterday. I didn't do anything about it, though. I didn't even tell anyone. Oh, I did one thing. I bought a bottle of champagne. I thought I'd sit there and drink it all by myself . . .

RICHARD. That sounds absolutely sad . . .

THE GIRL. Oh, no. It would have been fun. Sitting in my own apartment drinking champagne. But I couldn't get the bottle open. You're not supposed to use a corkscrew. You're supposed to work the cork loose with your thumbs. I just couldn't seem to do it. I suppose I could have called the janitor or something. But, somehow, I didn't feel like calling the janitor to open a bottle of champagne on my birthday. Look, I got blisters on both thumbs. Well, not really blisters, but I sort of pulled the thumb part away from the nail . . .

RICHARD. It's not really a matter of brute force. It's more of a trick. (*Demonstrating with thumbs*) You kind of get one side and then the other and it finally works loose. . . . You have to have strong thumbs, though . . .

THE GIRL. I've got a wonderful idea. Let me go up and get it. It's just sitting there in the ice box. We could both drink it. Since we both have birthdays. If you can really get it open . . .

RICHARD. I'm pretty sure I could get it open—but I don't want to drink your . . .

THE GIRL. It would be fun. After I couldn't get it open I sort of lost interest in sitting up there and drinking it alone. Let me go up and get it and we'll have a double birthday party. It's very good champagne. The man said.

RICHARD. I don't really think . . .

THE GIRL. I told him to be sure and give me very good champagne. Because I couldn't tell the difference myself. Wouldn't you like to?

RICHARD. Sure. As a matter of fact, I'd love to. I think we've got some champagne glasses in the kitchen . . .

THE GIRL. Okay. I'll go up and get it. I'll be right back. Should I bring the potato chips too?

RICHARD. Sure. Let's shoot the works!

THE GIRL. That's just the way I felt. I'll be right back.

RICHARD. Okay.

THE GIRL. See you in a minute . . . (*She exits, closing the door behind her.*)

(RICHARD *stares after her, somewhat bewildered. He picks up his glass, drains it, shakes his head, picks up her glass and starts toward the kitchen. Suddenly, he stops and turns back, a reflective expression on his face.*)

RICHARD. *US Camera* . . . (*He puts down the glasses and goes to the bookshelf. He looks for a moment and then finds what he is looking for. He takes down a book. It is a very large book, very clearly marked:* US Camera. *He begins, in a casual way, to riffle through the pages. Muttering*) News events . . . Children and Animals . . . The Human Body . . . (*He turns the pages slowly and then suddenly stops. He stares. He closes the book, puts it back on the shelf, picks up the glasses and goes swiftly into the kitchen. After a moment he comes back again, carrying two champagne glasses. He polishes them, sets them down, starts for the book and stops himself. Instead he pours a little whiskey into one of the champagne glasses, gulps it down, then wipes it out with his handkerchief. Finally he pulls himself together.*) Let's see . . . Birthday party! (*He starts to fix things up a little bit. Goes to phonograph and looks through records.*) Show tunes . . . (*He puts on a record:* "Falling in Love with Love.") In seven years I never did anything like this! In another seven years I won't be able to.

(*On this sobering thought, he sits down and stares moodily into space—the music from the record fades softly down.*)

HIS VOICE. Hey, Dick. Dickie boy . . .

RICHARD. Yeah, Richard?

HIS VOICE. What do you think you're doing?

RICHARD. I don't know. I don't know what I'm doing.

HIS VOICE. This kid is just a little young, don't you think?

RICHARD. Look, let me alone, will you?

HIS VOICE. Okay. You know what you're doing.

RICHARD. No, I don't. I really don't.

HIS VOICE. Relax. You're not doing anything. Even if you wanted to—you haven't got a chance . . .

RICHARD. Oh yeah? That's what you think. She seems to like me. She seems kind of fascinated by me.

HIS VOICE. She thinks you're that nice Sarah Bernhardt fan who lives downstairs. You're getting older, boy. You got bags under your eyes. You're getting fat.

RICHARD. Fat? Where?

HIS VOICE. Under your chin there. You're getting a martini pouch. And that crewcut stuff! You're not kidding anybody. One of these mornings you're going to look in the mirror and that's all, brother.

The Portrait of Dorian Gray.

(RICHARD *examines himself nervously in the mirror. He is only slightly reassured*.)

RICHARD. Look, pal. I'm going to level with you. This is a real pretty girl—and, as we pointed out, I'm not getting any younger—so . . .

HIS VOICE. Okay, pal. You're on your own . . .

(*He stands there for a moment of nervous indecision. The buzzer sounds. He decides—and with a new briskness in his step heads gaily for the door. He opens the door, admitting the girl. She comes in. She has changed to a sophisticated cocktail dress. She carries champagne and a bag of potato chips*.)

THE GIRL. Hi. I'm sorry I took so long. I thought I ought to change. I got this dress at Ohrbach's. But I don't think you could tell, could you?

RICHARD. You look lovely. (*She reacts slightly, sensing a difference in his tone*.)

THE GIRL. Thank you. Here's the champagne. You can see where I was working on it . . .

RICHARD. Let me take a crack at it. (*He takes bottle and begins to thumb cork*.) This is a tough one . . .

THE GIRL. Should I do anything?

RICHARD. I don't think so. Just stand well back . . . (*He struggles with cork*.)

THE GIRL. We could call the janitor. He's probably got some kind of an instrument . . .

RICHARD (*through clenched teeth as he struggles*). No—let's—keep—the janitor out of this . . . Damn it . . . This thing is in here like . . .

THE GIRL. I told you. You can imagine what I went through. On my birthday and everything.

RICHARD (*he stops to rest*). You know, this is just a lot of damn chi-chi nonsense. They could put a regular cork in this stuff and you could just pull it with a corkscrew . . . (*He attacks it again*.) Come on, you stinker! . . . Hey—I think—watch out— maybe you better get a glass just in case she . . . (*The cork finally pops*.) Catch it! Catch it! (*She catches it*.)

THE GIRL. Got it! Boy, you sure have powerful thumbs . . .

RICHARD (*he is rather pleased by this*). I used to play a lot of tennis . . .

THE GIRL. Do you think it's cold enough?

I just had it sitting in the ice box . . .

RICHARD. It's fine . . . Well, happy birthday.

THE GIRL. Happy birthday. (*They touch glasses and drink*.) Is it all right? I mean is that how it's supposed to taste . . . ?

RICHARD. That's how.

(*She takes another tentative taste*.)

THE GIRL. You know, it's pretty good. I was sort of afraid it would taste like Seven-Up or something . . .

RICHARD. Hey, I forgot . . . (*He leans forward and plants a quick, nervous kiss on her forehead*.) Birthday kiss. Happy Birthday.

THE GIRL. Thank you. Same to you.

RICHARD. Maybe we ought to have some music or something. Since this a party . . .

THE GIRL. That's a good idea . . .

RICHARD. I've got about a million records here. We can probably find something appropriate. Ready for some more?

THE GIRL. Not quite yet.

(*He refills his own glass*.)

THE GIRL. I've kind of stopped buying records. I mean I didn't have a machine for so long. Now that I've got one again— or anyway the Kaufmans have one—I'm all out of the habit . . .

RICHARD. Do you like show tunes?

THE GIRL. Sure. Do you have *The King and I*?

RICHARD. I'm afraid I don't. That's a little recent for me. I've got mostly old Rodgers and Hart and Cole Porter and Gershwin. . . . How about this one? From *Knickerbocker Holiday*. (*He is offering a prized possession: the Walter Huston recording of "September Song." He puts it on and they listen for a moment in silence*.)

THE GIRL. Oh, I love that. I didn't even know it was from a show or anything. I thought it was just a song . . .

RICHARD. Walter Huston sang it. He had a wooden leg—in the show. You better have some more champagne. It's really very good. (*He puts a little more in her glass which is still half-full. He refills his own. She takes off her shoes*.)

THE GIRL. This is pretty nice . . .

RICHARD. Isn't it? It's a lot better than sitting out there listening to the ball game. Two runs behind and they send Hodges up to bunt!

THE GIRL. Is that bad?

RICHARD. It's awful.

THE GIRL. I didn't know. I was never

very good at baseball. I was going to wash my hair tonight. But after I got through with the garden I just didn't feel like it.

RICHARD. I was going to bed and read *Of Sex and Violence* and *The Scarlet Letter*. We're publishing them in the fall and I'm supposed to read them.

THE GIRL. You're a book publisher?

RICHARD. In a way. I'm the advertising manager for a firm called Pocket Classics. Two bits in any drugstore. I'm supposed to figure out a new title for *The Scarlet Letter*. They want something a little catchier . . .

THE GIRL. I think I read *The Scarlet Letter* in school . . . I don't remember much about it . . .

RICHARD. Neither do I. I sent a memo to Mr. Brady—he's the head of the company —advising him not to change the title. But we had the title tested and eighty per cent of the people didn't know what it meant. So we're changing it . . . (*He gets up and fills glass again.*) Do you know what Mr. Brady wanted to call it? (*She shakes her head.*) *I Was an Adulteress.* But he's not going to, thank God. And do you know why? Because we had *it* tested and sixty-three per cent of the people didn't know what *that* meant. I wish you'd drink some more of your champagne . . .

THE GIRL. No, thanks . . . (*She rises and drifts over to the bookcase.*) You've certainly got a lot of books . . .

RICHARD. There's cases more in the closets . . .

THE GIRL (*suddenly*). Oh! Look! You've got *US Camera!*

RICHARD (*a little flustered*). Do we? I didn't even know it. How about that! *US Camera!*

THE GIRL (*she takes it down*). I bet I bought a dozen copies of this. But I don't have a single one left. Boys and people used to keep stealing 'em . . .

RICHARD. I can't think why . . .

THE GIRL. Did you ever notice me in it? It's a picture called "Textures."

RICHARD. I'm afraid I didn't . . .

THE GIRL. I told you about it, don't you remember? See, that's me, right there on the beach. My hair was a little longer then, did you notice?

RICHARD. No, actually—I didn't . . .

THE GIRL. And of course I've taken off some weight. I weighed 124 then. Gene Belding—Gene took the picture—used to

call it baby fat.

RICHARD. Baby fat?

THE GIRL. Mmm! I'm much thinner now . . .

(*They both study the picture for a moment.*)

RICHARD. This was taken at the beach?

THE GIRL. Mmm . . .

RICHARD. *What beach?*

THE GIRL. Right on Fire Island . . . Oh . . . I see what you mean. It was taken very early in the morning. Nobody was even up yet.

RICHARD. Just you and Miss Belding?

THE GIRL. *Mr.* Belding. Gene Belding. With a G . . .

RICHARD. Oh. Well, it certainly is a fine picture.

THE GIRL. I'll autograph it for you if you want. People keep asking me to . . .

RICHARD (*weakly*). That would be wonderful. . . . Maybe we'd better have some more champagne . . .

THE GIRL. Good. You know, this is suddenly beginning to feel like a party . . . (*He refills her glass which is only half-empty and fills his own all the way, emptying the bottle.*) It was awfully sweet of you to ask me down here in the first place . . . (*He drains his glass of champagne—looks at her for a moment.*)

RICHARD. Oh, it was just one of those things. Just one of those foolish things. A trip to the moon—on gossamer wings . . . Do you play the piano?

THE GIRL. The piano?

RICHARD. Yeah. Somebody should play the piano. Do you play?

THE GIRL. I really don't. Do you?

RICHARD. Just a little. For myself . . .

THE GIRL. *You* play then . . .

RICHARD. You'll be sorry you asked . . . (*He sits at piano and after a very impressive moment begins to play "Chopsticks." She listens and is delighted.*)

THE GIRL. Oh! I was afraid you could *really* play. I can play *that* too!

(*She sits on the bench beside him and they play "Chopsticks" as a duet. When they finish:*)

RICHARD. That was lovely . . . (*His manner changes.*) Tell me, what would you say if, quite suddenly, I were to seize you in my . . . Hey, come here . . . (*He reaches over and takes her in his arms.*)

THE GIRL. Hey, now wait a minute . . .

(*For a moment they bounce precariously*

THE SEVEN YEAR ITCH 517

around on the piano bench, then RICHARD loses his balance and they both fall off knocking over the bench with a crash and landing in a tangle of arms and legs.)

RICHARD (panic-stricken). Are you all right? I'm sorry— I don't know what happened—I must be out of my mind . . .

THE GIRL. I'm fine . . .

RICHARD. I don't know what happened . . .

THE GIRL. Well, I think I'd better go now . . . (Putting on her shoes.)

RICHARD. Please don't . . . I'm sorry . . .

THE GIRL. I'd better. Good night . . .

RICHARD. Please . . . I'm so sorry . . .

THE GIRL. That's all right. Good night. (She goes, closing the door behind her.)

(RICHARD looks miserably at the door. Then turns and kicks viciously at the piano bench. He succeeds in injuring his toe. Sadly, still shaking his wounded foot, he limps to the kitchen and reappears a moment later with a bottle of raspberry soda. He goes to the phonograph and puts on "September Song." He listens to it with morbid fascination. In a melancholy voice he joins Mr. Huston in a line or two about what a long, long while it is from May to December. He shakes his head and crosses sadly to the terrace. He stands there—a mournful figure clutching a bottle of raspberry soda.)

(As he stands there, a potted geranium comes crashing down from the terrace above and shatters at his feet.)

(He does not even bother to look around. He merely glances over his shoulder and says:)

RICHARD (quietly). Oh, now, for God's sake, let's not start that again . . .

THE GIRL'S VOICE (from above). Oh, golly! I was just taking them in so there wouldn't be another accident. I'm really sorry . . . I mean this is awful . . . I could have practically killed you again . . .

RICHARD. It doesn't matter . . .

THE GIRL'S VOICE (from above). I'm really sorry. It was an accident . . . Are you all right . . . ?

RICHARD. I'm fine.

THE GIRL'S VOICE (from above). Well, good night . . .

RICHARD. Good night . . .

THE GIRL'S VOICE (from above). Good night. See you tomorrow, maybe . . .

RICHARD. Huh? (He straightens up.) Yeah! I'll see you tomorrow!

THE GIRL'S VOICE (from above). Good night!

(He starts to drink from the soda bottle. Stops himself. Puts it down in disgust. Then strides back to living room with renewed vigor. He goes to the liquor cabinet and begins to pour himself another drink. From the phonograph comes the happy chorus of "September Song.")

(RICHARD, a peculiar expression on his face, sings cheerfully with the record as:)

THE CURTAIN FALLS

ACT TWO

SCENE ONE

The same.

It is early evening the following day. RICHARD, back in full control and very businesslike, is deep in conference with DR. BRUBAKER.

Both are somewhat tense and it is evident that the conference has been proceeding with difficulty. The DOCTOR is seated amid a litter of papers and galley sheets. RICHARD holds a duplicate set of galleys. As the curtain rises RICHARD clears his throat and prepares to renew his attack.

———

RICHARD. On page one hundred and ten, Doctor, if we could somehow simplify the whole passage . . .

DR. BRUBAKER. Simplify? In what way simplify?

RICHARD. In the sense of making it—well —simpler. Both Mr. Brady and I have gone over it a number of times, and, to be perfectly frank with you, neither of us has any clear idea of what it's actually about . . .

DR. BRUBAKER. Your Mr. Brady, sir, is, if I may also speak with frankness, a moron.

RICHARD. It is Mr. Brady's business, as an editor, to keep the point of view of the average reader very clearly in mind. If something is beyond Mr. Brady's comprehension, he can only assume that it will also be over the head of our readership.

DR. BRUBAKER. It was, I take it, at Mr. Brady's suggestion that the title of my book was changed from *Of Man and the Unconscious* to, and I shudder to say these words aloud, *Of Sex and Violence* . . .

RICHARD. That is correct. Mr. Brady felt that the new title would have a broader popular appeal.

DR. BRUBAKER. I regret to inform you, sir, that Mr. Brady is a psychopathic inferior . . .

RICHARD. Cheer up, Doctor. If you think you've got troubles, Mr. Brady wants to change *The Scarlet Letter* to *I Was an Adulteress*. I know it all seems a little odd to you—but Mr. Brady understands the twenty-five-cent book field. Both Mr. Brady and I *want* to publish worthwhile books. Books like yours. Like *The Scarlet Letter*. But you must remember that you and Nathaniel Hawthorne are competing in every drugstore with the basic writings of Mickey Spillane.

(*As* DR. BRUBAKER *is unacquainted with this author,* RICHARD's *bon mot gets no reaction.*)

DR. BRUBAKER. This is therefore why my book is to be published with a cover depicting Gustav Meyerheim in the very act of attacking one of his victims . . . (DR. BRUBAKER *has picked up a large full-color painting of the cover of his book which shows in lurid detail a wild-eyed man with a beard attempting to disrobe an already pretty-well disrobed young lady. It also bears the following line of copy: "Hotter Than the Kinsey Report." Both regard the cover for a moment.*)

RICHARD (*with a certain nervous heartiness*). I must take the responsibility for the cover myself, Doctor . . .

DR. BRUBAKER. And also for making Meyerheim's victim—all of whom incidentally, were middle-aged women—resemble in a number of basic characteristics, Miss Marilyn Monroe?

RICHARD. I'm afraid so, Doctor. Don't you think there would be something just a little bit distasteful about a book jacket showing a man attempting to attack a middle-aged lady?

DR. BRUBAKER. And it is less distasteful if the lady is young and beautiful?

RICHARD. At least, if a man attacks a young and beautiful girl, it seems more . . . Oh, my God! (*He remembers last night and shudders.*)

DR. BRUBAKER. I beg your pardon?

RICHARD. Nothing. Doctor, if you don't like the cover, I'll see if I can have it changed . . .

DR. BRUBAKER. I would be most grateful.

RICHARD. Doctor.

DR. BRUBAKER. Yes?

RICHARD. You say in the book that ninety per cent of the population is in need of some sort of psychiatric help?

DR. BRUBAKER. This is theoretically true. It is not however practical. There is the matter of cost . . .

RICHARD. With your own patients—are you very expensive?

DR. BRUBAKER (*his Third Ear has caught the direction this conversation is leading and his defenses go up immediately*). Very.

RICHARD. I'm sure you occasionally make exceptions . . .

DR. BRUBAKER. Never.

RICHARD. I mean, once in a while a case must come along that really interests you . . .

DR. BRUBAKER (*primly*). At fifty dollars an hour—all my cases interest me.

RICHARD (*undaunted*). I mean if you should run into something really spectacular. Another Gustav Meyerheim, for example . . . Doctor, tell me frankly. Do you think, just for example, that *I* need to be psychoanalyzed?

DR. BRUBAKER. Very possibly. I could recommend several very excellent men who might, perhaps, be a little cheaper.

RICHARD. How much cheaper?

DR. BRUBAKER (*considering*). Ohhhhh . . .

RICHARD. I couldn't even afford *that* . . .

DR. BRUBAKER. I thought not. (*He turns back to his papers.*) Now to get back to . . .

RICHARD (*seating himself casually on the couch*). I wondered if possibly you might give me some advice . . .

DR. BRUBAKER. I know. Everyone wonders that.

(*Still moving casually,* RICHARD *swings his feet onto the couch until he is lying flat on his back in the classic position.*)

RICHARD. I'm desperate, Doctor. Last night after you left, I was just sitting there listening to the ball game . . .

DR. BRUBAKER (*outmaneuvered, but still game*). This fact in itself is not really sufficient cause to undertake analysis . . .

RICHARD. No, I don't mean that. I *started out* listening to the ball game and do you know what I ended up doing?

DR. BRUBAKER. I have no idea . . .

RICHARD. I ended up attempting to commit what I guess they call criminal assault . . .

DR. BRUBAKER (*defeated, he takes a pad and pencil from his pocket*). From the way you phrase it, I assume the attempt was unsuccessful . . .

RICHARD. Thank God! All I did was knock us both off the piano bench . . .

DR. BRUBAKER (*a flicker of interest—he begins to write*). You attempted to commit criminal assault on a *piano bench?*

RICHARD. Yes.

DR. BRUBAKER. And on whose person was this obviously maladroit attempt committed?

(RICHARD *rises and goes to bookshelf. Gets* US Camera *and shows it to* DOCTOR.)

RICHARD. That's her. Her hair was a little longer then.

DR. BRUBAKER (*after a moment*). Splendid. I congratulate you on your taste. However, you ask for my advice. I give it to you. Do not attempt it again. (*A brief pause while the* DOCTOR *re-examines the photograph.*) If you *should,* however, give yourself plenty of room to work in. In any case do not attempt it precariously balanced on a piano bench. Such an attempt is doomed from the start. Now, my boy, I must go. I have many things to . . .

RICHARD. But look, Doctor—I'm married. I've always been married. Suppose this girl tells people about this. She's likely to mention it to someone. Like my wife.

DR. BRUBAKER. This is, of course, not beyond the realm of possibility. In that event I would recommend a course of vigorous denial. It would be simply your word against hers. Very possibly, if you were convincing enough, you could make it stick. And now I must really go. I thank you for your help. It is agreed that I shall make the necessary clarifications in Chapter Eight and you will devote your best efforts to making the cover of my book look less like a French postal card. I shall be in touch with your office the first of next week . . .

RICHARD. If she tells anyone about this —I'll, I'll—kill her! I'll kill her with my bare hands!

DR. BRUBAKER (*who has started to leave, turns back*). This is also a possible solution. However, I submit that murder is the most difficult of all crimes to commit successfully. Therefore, until you are able to commit a simple criminal assault, I strongly advise that you avoid anything so complex as murder. One must learn to walk before one can run. I thank you again and good night. (*He exits briskly.*)

(RICHARD *stands blankly staring after the good Doctor. He shakes his head.*)

(*Music sneaks in—he turns and there grouped about the couch and coffee table, in "dream lighting" are* HELEN, THE GIRL, MISS MORRIS, ELAINE, MARIE WHATEVER-HER-NAME-WAS *and an unidentified* YOUNG LADY *in brassiere and panties. They all brandish tea cups and in very hen-party fashion are engaged in dishing the dirt about someone. It is, after all, a figment of* RICHARD's *imagination, so the cups are raised and lowered in unison and the little clucking noises of disapproval are done in chorus.*)

THE GIRL (*very chatty*). Actually, Mrs. Sherman, it was terribly embarrassing. He seemed to go berserk. He'd been sitting playing "Chopsticks" when suddenly he grabbed me and practically tried to tear my clothes off . . .

ELAINE. My dear, the night of your birthday party he made himself perfectly obnoxious right out there on the terrace. I don't like to say this, but he attempted to take advantage of me.

(*All the girls shake their heads and make small clucking noises of shocked disapproval.*)

MISS MORRIS. It's just terrible, Mrs. Sherman. I'm positively scared to go into his office to take dictation. Why, the way that man looks at me, it makes me feel kinda naked.

(*All drink tea.*)

ELAINE. I said, Richard darling, at least have the decency not to try something like this practically in front of poor Helen's eyes!

THE GIRL. He'd been drinking heavily, of course . . . He practically guzzled a whole bottle of my champagne . . .

MARIE (*in French*). Madame! Madame! He was like a human beast! He tore off my belt, he tore off my shirt, he tore off my pants and he chased me into the sea without a bathing costume.

(*All shake heads and "Tsk-tsk." Then the unidentified* YOUNG LADY *in the bra and pants speaks up.*)

YOUNG LADY. And *me!* I'm not even safe in my own apartment! Every time I start getting ready for bed that man sits out there on the terrace—staring at me! I just hate a Peeping Tom!

HELEN. I've always suspected that Richard was not quite sane.

THE GIRL. Oh, he's sane, all right. He's just a nasty, evil-minded, middle-aged man . . .

(RICHARD *can stand it no longer.*)

RICHARD. Helen! Listen to me . . .

(*The girls raise their tea cups and vanish. Music in and out and lighting back to normal.*)

RICHARD (*in a panic, lights a cigarette*). I've got to do something. That girl's probably told fifty people about this already. If I just sent her some flowers . . . That's no good. . . . I've got to talk to her. Reason with her. Plead with her. Tell her I was drunk, which God knows I was, and beg her not to mention this to anyone or my life could be ruined . . . (*He has found telephone book and is riffling through pages.*) Twelve solid pages of Kaufman . . . Here it is . . . ORegon 3-7221. (*He lifts receiver, starts to dial, then stops.*) I can't do it. What can I possibly say to her? (*He practices—holding receiver switch down.*)

RICHARD (*with great charm*). My dear Miss— *I don't even know what the hell her name is*—My dear Young Woman— I have simply called to apologize for my absurd behavior last night. It was inexcusable, but I had been drinking. I can barely remember what happened, but I'm under the impression that I made a terrible fool of myself. I beg you to forgive me and put the whole distasteful incident out of your mind. (*Stops and puts down phone.*) No good. I can't do it. . . . And what about Helen? She hasn't called. She's probably heard about it by now. Oh, that's out of the question. How could she possibly have heard anything? But she could have. The word gets around. It's like jungle drums. . . . If she hasn't heard anything—why hasn't she called? . . . I could call her. The minute I heard her voice I could tell if she knew anything. . . . Come on. Call her. . . . Stop stalling. Pick up the telephone and call her. It's the only way you'll know. . . . Okay. Okay. (*He picks up the phone and dials the Long-Distance Operator.*) Long Distance? I want to call Cohasset. Cohasset, Massachusetts, 4-2831-J. Yeah . . . My number? ORegon 9-4437. Thank you. . . . Okay—fasten your seat belts . . . Hello? Hello, Helen? Who? Who is this? Look, I want to talk to Mrs. Richard Sherman. Is she there? Who is this anyway? Oh. The baby sitter. Look, this is Mr. Sherman calling from New York. What do you mean she's out for the evening. With whom is she out for the evening? Mr. MacKenzie and some people? *What people?* Well, what *was* the message she left for me? . . . Oh. Oh, my God. Her yellow skirt. No, no, I didn't. Something unexpected came up. But tell her I will. The first thing in the morning. Without fail. . . . Look, I want to ask you. How did Mrs. Sherman seem? I mean did she seem upset in any way? Like she'd heard some bad news or anything like that? . . . Just about the yellow skirt. Well, good. Tell her I'll send it up the first thing in the morning. Is Ricky all right? Good. When Mrs. Sherman comes in, tell her everything is fine here and I'll talk to her tomorrow . . . Fine . . . Good-by . . . Good-by. (*He hangs up phone.*) Well, thank God! (*He sits down and lights a cigarette.*) The only thing I cannot understand is, what the hell is she doing having dinner with Tom MacKenzie. I wish she wouldn't hang around with people like that. He gets away with murder because he's a writer. Well, he's a damn lousy writer. That last book! . . . Helen should know better than to go around with people like that. She isn't even safe. . . . I know for a positive fact that he's been after her for years. Tom MacKenzie happens to be a real bum, if you want to know! And there probably aren't any other people. . . . She doesn't know what she's getting herself into. She's been married so long she forgets what it's like. . . . Helen happens to be a damned attractive woman. A man like Tom MacKenzie is perfectly capable of making a pass at her. (*By now he has begun to pace the floor.*) And don't think she doesn't know what she's doing. She's getting older. She's used to me. In many ways I'm probably very dull. And Tom MacKenzie's a writer. She probably thinks he's fascinating as hell! . . . She thought that last book of his was great! All that inwardly-downwardly-pulsating-and-afterward-her-hair-spilled-across-the-pillow crap! Strictly for little old ladies at Womrath's. . . . But Helen is just the kind of middle-aged dame who would fall for it. . . . Well, good luck! That's all! (*Brooding, he sits in easy chair, a grim expression on his face.)*

(Music sneaks in and the "dream lighting" comes up on the far side of the stage by the fireplace. We hear the sound of wind mingled with the music. A door opens and slams shut and TOM MACKENZIE *and* HELEN *enter, laughing.* TOM MACKENZIE *is a handsome, glamorous-type author with a mustache. He looks quite a lot like his photograph on the book jackets. He wears a tweed coat with the collar up and a hunting shirt.* HELEN *wears a sweater and skirt with a man's raincoat thrown about her shoulders. Both are very gay.)*

HELEN *(as he helps her off with raincoat).* It's been years since I took a walk on the beach in the rain . . .

TOM. I love the rain on the sea. It's so wild and untamed . . .

HELEN *(looking around).* Where are the other people?

TOM. I have a confession to make.

HELEN. Yes?

TOM. There are no other people. Don't be angry.

HELEN *(after a moment).* I'm not angry.

TOM. I hoped you wouldn't be. Come over here by the fire.

HELEN. I love an open fire.

TOM. I always say, What good is the rain without an open fire?

RICHARD *(from his chair across the room).* Oh, brother!

TOM. Let me get you a little whiskey to take out the chill . . .

HELEN. Thank you . . .

(He pours whiskey from flask. She drinks, then hands the cup to him. He drinks—but first kisses the spot on the cup where her lips have been.)

RICHARD *(muttering scornfully).* H. B. Warner . . .

TOM. But wait. You're shivering . . .

HELEN. It's nothing. I'll be warm in a moment . . .

TOM. No, no . . . You're soaked to the skin. You'll catch your death of cold . . .

RICHARD. Here it comes . . .

TOM. Why don't you take off your things and hang them by the fire? I'll get you something dry . . .

RICHARD *(appalled).* He used *that* in his book, for God's sake! As who didn't!

HELEN. All right. Turn your back . . .

(He turns his back and she removes her shoes. She takes off her skirt and hangs it

on the fire screen.)*

TOM. May I turn around now?

HELEN. If you like . . .

(Suddenly, the mood has changed. His voice is now husky with passion.)

TOM. Helen, darling!

HELEN. Yes, Tom?

TOM. Did anyone ever tell you that you are a very beautiful woman?

HELEN. No. Not recently anyway . . .

TOM. But surely Richard . . .

HELEN. I'm afraid Richard rather takes me for granted now . . .

TOM. That blind, utter fool!

HELEN. Oh, darling!

TOM. Darling! *(The music swells.* TOM *takes her in his arms. Murmuring as he covers her with kisses)* Inwardly, downwardly, pulsating, striving, now together, ending and unending, now, now, now! *(They are in a full mad clinch as the lights black out.)*

(On his side of the room, RICHARD *jumps to his feet and angrily pounds the table.)*

RICHARD. Okay! If that's the way you want it! Okay!

(With great purpose he strides to the telephone. Gets phone book, thumbs through it, finds number and dials. He whistles softly through his teeth. . . . The tune he is whistling might, if he were not tone deaf, almost be "Just One of Those Things." After a moment someone obviously answers the phone.)

RICHARD *(with great charm).* Hi. Did you know you left your tomato plant down here last night? I could have the janitor bring it back—or—if you want—I was thinking maybe I could . . . *(He is talking into the phone with great animation by the time the lights have dimmed and:)*

THE CURTAIN IS DOWN

SCENE TWO

The same. It is later that evening.

The apartment is empty. A single light in the foyer.

After a moment, the sound of a key in the lock and RICHARD *and* THE GIRL *enter. He switches on the lights.*

RICHARD. Well, we made it.

THE GIRL. I'm so full of steak I can

barely wobble . . .

RICHARD. Me too.

THE GIRL. I feel wonderful . . .

RICHARD. Did anyone ever tell you that you have a very, very beautiful digestive tract?

THE GIRL. Yes. But they don't usually say it like that. Mostly they just say: Boy, did you ever stuff yourself!

RICHARD. Would you like a drink or something?

THE GIRL. No, thanks. But you go ahead and have one. Don't mind me . . .

RICHARD. Not me. I'm back on the wagon again . . .

THE GIRL. This was awfully nice of you. It was enough to have you carry that heavy plant all the way upstairs. You didn't have to ask me out for dinner. I hope you didn't hurt yourself. Or strain something . . .

RICHARD. It wasn't that heavy. I was going to call the janitor to help me, but then I decided not to . . .

THE GIRL. You're in pretty good shape . . .

RICHARD. For an old man . . .

THE GIRL. You're not *that* old. You don't look a day over twenty-eight.

RICHARD. I know . . .

THE GIRL. Anyway it was very nice of you.

RICHARD. I just took a chance and called. I didn't really think you'd be home. You know, I thought you'd be out or something.

THE GIRL. No, I don't go out very much . . .

RICHARD. That's funny. I should think you'd have a line of suitors halfway round the block. Like Easter show at Radio City . . .

THE GIRL. Last night, I went to the movies by myself . . .

RICHARD. Last night?

THE GIRL (*diplomatically*). After I left here.

RICHARD (*moving the conversation past a trouble spot*). All by yourself! You must have a boy friend or something . . .

THE GIRL. I don't go out with most people who ask me. I know it sounds silly but people are always falling desperately in love with me and everything and it makes things so complicated. I mean, it's just easier to pay the fifty-five cents and go to the movies by myself.

RICHARD. It doesn't sound very excit-ing . . .

THE GIRL. It is, though. This is the first time I've had my own apartment and everything.

RICHARD. You went out with me when I asked you . . .

THE GIRL. Well, that's different. I mean, it's all right going out with you. After all, you're married.

RICHARD. I see. I *think*.

THE GIRL. No. What I mean is, it's all right to have dinner with you because you're not likely to fall desperately in love with me or anything. You're more mature . . .

RICHARD. I don't feel so—mature . . .

THE GIRL. Well, you know what I mean. (*Pause.*)

RICHARD. You're absolutely sure you wouldn't like a drink?

THE GIRL. Absolutely.

RICHARD. I think maybe I'll have one. Just a little one. (*He goes to bar and fixes himself a drink.*) Not even a Coke or something?

THE GIRL. Not right now.

RICHARD. Well, happy birthday. (*Pause.*)

THE GIRL. This certainly is a beautiful apartment.

RICHARD. It's all right. It's a little ridiculous in some ways . . . The stairs, for instance . . .

THE GIRL. I think they're beautiful. I like an apartment with stairs.

RICHARD. But these don't go any place. They just go up to the ceiling and stop. They give the joint a kind of Jean Paul Sartre quality.

THE GIRL. I see what you mean. No exit. A stairway to nowhere.

RICHARD. I tried to get the landlord to take them out. See, this used to be the bottom half of a duplex. This place and the Kaufmans' were all one apartment. So when he divided them separately he just boarded up the ceiling—or in your case the floor . . .

THE GIRL. Yes, I noticed the place in the floor. I lost an orange stick down the crack. Anyway, I think the apartment's just charming . . .

RICHARD. Yeah. But we're moving into a larger place in September . . .

THE GIRL. Oh, that's too bad. But still, people in New York are always moving. You certainly have a lot of books. The last book I read was *The Catcher in the Rye* . . .

RICHARD. The last book I read was *The Scarlet Letter*. Mr. Brady thinks we can sell it. If we make it sound sexy enough.

THE GIRL. Is it sexy? I don't seem to remember.

RICHARD. No. Actually, it's kind of dull. In fact, people are going to want their quarters back. But Mr. Brady feels we can sell it if I can just figure out a way to tell people what the Scarlet Letter is.

THE GIRL. What *is* it?

RICHARD. Well, the Scarlet Letter was a big red "A." For Adultery. Anyone who was convicted of adultery had to wear it.

THE GIRL. How awful!

RICHARD. The cover will be a picture of Hester Prynne with a cigarette hanging out of her mouth. She'll be in a real tight, low-cut dress. Our big problem is—if the dress is cut low enough to sell any copies, there won't be any space on the front for a big red letter . . .

THE GIRL. The publishing business sounds fascinating.

RICHARD. Oh, it is. It is.

(*Pause.*)

THE GIRL. It's getting late. I really ought to go . . .

RICHARD. You've got plenty of time.

THE GIRL. I guess so. That's the wonderful thing about having my own apartment. I mean at the club you had to be in at one o'clock or they locked the doors.

RICHARD. It sounds barbaric . . .

THE GIRL. Oh, it practically was. It was really very funny. I mean, all the girls at the club were actresses. So naturally they were always asking each other what they called the big question . . .

RICHARD. The big question?

THE GIRL. Mmm! They were always asking each other: Would you sleep with a producer to get a part?

RICHARD. That is a big question . . .

THE GIRL. But it's so silly. If you live at the club anyway. I used to tell them, producers don't even *go* to bed before one o'clock. So the whole thing is academic, if you see what I mean. You'd be surprised how much time they spent discussing it, though.

RICHARD. I can see where they might give the matter some thought.

THE GIRL. Oh, sure. But they never dis-

cussed it in a *practical* way. When they asked me, I always used to say: It depends. How big is the part? Is the producer handsome? Things like that . . .

RICHARD. Practical things . . .

THE GIRL. Mmm! I was at the club for eight months and as far as I know no producer ever mentioned the subject to any of the girls.

RICHARD. That must have been very disappointing for them.

THE GIRL. It was.

RICHARD. But what if he was very handsome? And it was a very good part? And you didn't have to be in by one o'clock? What *would* you do?

THE GIRL. In that case . . . If I was sure he wouldn't fall desperately in love with me and ask me to marry him and everything.

RICHARD. What's so bad about that?

THE GIRL. Oh, that would spoil everything. Marrying him, I mean. It would be worse than living at the club. Then I'd have to start getting in at one o'clock again. I mean it's taken me twenty-two years to get my own apartment. It would be pretty silly if the first thing I did was get married and spoil everything. I mean, I want to have a chance to be independent first. For a few years anyway. You can't imagine how exciting it is to live by yourself—after you've had somebody practically running your life for as long as you can remember. . . . You just can't imagine . . .

(*As* RICHARD *stops listening to* THE GIRL *and gradually becomes absorbed in his own thoughts, the lights dim down till there is only a dream spot on* RICHARD.)

RICHARD. Yes, I can. As a matter of fact we have a great deal in common.

HIS VOICE (*Mockingly—imitating* HELEN's *tone*). Daddy's going to work very hard. And he's going to stay on the wagon, like Dr. Summers told him. And he's going to eat properly and not smoke, like Dr. Murphy told him. And Mommy is going to call Daddy tonight just to make sure he's all right . . . *Poor Daddy!*

RICHARD. Poor Daddy!

HIS VOICE. The girl is absolutely right. Not want to get married. You—you dope. The minute you were old enough to have any fun—the only thing you could think of to do was to get married.

RICHARD. I know. I know. It was a kind

of nervousness. But I made the best of it. I've been a pretty good husband. When I think of the chances I've had . . .

HIS VOICE. We've been through all this before . . .

RICHARD. I know. I know. I just thought I'd mention it.

HIS VOICE. Has it ever dawned on you that you're kidding yourself?

RICHARD. What do you mean by that?

HIS VOICE. All those dames you could have had if you weren't such a noble husband. The only reason you didn't do anything about 'em is that you didn't want to . . .

RICHARD. Why didn't I want to?

HIS VOICE. Laziness, pal. Laziness. It was too much trouble. You just didn't want to get involved. Elaine, for instance. It would have taken six months. And all those phone calls and taxis and excuses.

RICHARD. Yeah. (*Pause*) Why does it always have to be so complicated?

HIS VOICE. If you could answer that one, pal-pal, they'd make you President of the United States.

(RICHARD *sighs and the lights dim back to normal.* THE GIRL *is still speaking, unaware of the fact that his mind has been far away.*)

THE GIRL. . . . so when you asked me to go out for dinner with you it was all right. You're married and naturally, you don't want to fall desperately in love with anyone any more than I want anyone to fall desperately in love with me. Do you know what I mean?

RICHARD. Sure. It's too much trouble.

THE GIRL. Exactly.

RICHARD. I know just what you mean.

THE GIRL. That's right.

RICHARD. We both happen to be in positions where we can't possibly let ourselves get involved in anything . . .

THE GIRL. Mmm.

RICHARD. All the damn phone calls and taxis and everything.

THE GIRL. That's right. I mean I certainly wouldn't be sitting alone with some man in his apartment at eleven-thirty at night if he wasn't married.

RICHARD. Certainly not. (*Pause*) When you said about the producer—it would depend on if he were handsome—what did you mean by that? I mean, just out of curiosity . . . what would be your idea of handsome?

THE GIRL. Well, let's see. I really don't know. I suppose he should be tall—and kind of mature-looking . . .

RICHARD. Like me?

THE GIRL (*thoughtfully*). Mmmmm . . . (*Pause*) You're not going to start falling desperately in love with me or anything, are you?

RICHARD. No. No. Definitely not. I mean I think you're very pretty and sweet and I certainly enjoyed having dinner with you. But . . .

THE GIRL. That's just the way *I* feel about you. You're very nice-looking and charming and mature. You're someone I can be with and count on him not falling desperately in love with me . . .

RICHARD. That's right. I'm almost—well—I'm a lot older than you are. And one thing I've learned. Nothing is ever as simple as you think it's going to be. You take the simplest damn thing and, before you know it, it gets all loused up. I don't know how it happens or why it happens but it always happens . . .

THE GIRL. That's very true. You're absolutely right.

(*As* THE GIRL *stops listening to* RICHARD *and gradually becomes absorbed in her own thoughts the lights dim to a single dream spot on her.*)

HER VOICE. Well, what do you think?

THE GIRL. Mmm . . .

HER VOICE. What do you mean—mmm?

THE GIRL. I mean—I don't know . . .

HER VOICE. That's ridiculous. What is there not to know? He certainly is nice—and he's mature without being—you know—decrepit or anything . . .

THE GIRL. He certainly seems well-preserved . . .

HER VOICE. He's sweet and intelligent and married. What more do you want?

THE GIRL. I don't know.

HER VOICE. You're the one who wants to be the big-deal woman of the world. It's all your idea. It's not as if you were some kind of a virginal creature or something.

THE GIRL. Oh—shut up— I mean you make it sound so—so clinical. Besides, you certainly can't count Jerry . . .

HER VOICE. What do you mean we can't count Jerry?

THE GIRL. Well, I mean it was a big mistake—and it was so—so—and then he got all hysterical and wanted to marry me . . .

HER VOICE. It counts.

THE GIRL. I mean you can understand a person wanting to find out something about life and everything before she gets married and all settled down and has to start getting in by one o'clock again . . . Besides, what makes you think he's interested in me that way? I must seem like some kind of a juvenile delinquent to him . . .

HER VOICE. You're twenty-two years old. And he's interested.

THE GIRL. How can you tell?

HER VOICE. I can tell . . .

THE GIRL. How?

HER VOICE. I can tell. . . . What have you got to lose?

THE GIRL. Well, nothing, I guess—if you're really going to make Jerry count.

HER VOICE. He counts . . .

THE GIRL. Well, then . . .

(*The lights come back to normal.* RICHARD *is still talking, unaware that* THE GIRL'S *mind has been far away.*)

RICHARD. . . . what I'm trying to say is, that people who are really mature weigh things more carefully. They impose a discipline on themselves. They understand the cost. . . . I mean, they finally learn that sometimes something that seems very wonderful and desirable isn't really worth . . . I mean—all the hysteria it's going to cause . . . (*Pause*) Then, of course, you can over-do that line of thinking too. I mean a man—a person—anyone doesn't like to feel that he's some kind of a vegetable or something. You know. What it amounts to is this: You've got to decide which is the most painful—doing something and regretting it—or not doing something and—regretting it. Do you see what I mean?

THE GIRL. I think so . . .

RICHARD. I didn't mean to start making a speech. Look, are you sure you don't want a drink?

THE GIRL. No, thanks. Really. (*Starts to go.*)

RICHARD. Now look, really. It's not late. You don't have to go yet . . .

THE GIRL. I really should . . .

RICHARD. Well, whatever you think. Let me take you up to your door . . .

THE GIRL. No. That's all right. It's just upstairs . . .

RICHARD. Well, all right. If you have to go.

THE GIRL. I want to thank you for the dinner. It was lovely . . .

RICHARD. It was fun . . .

THE GIRL. And for carrying that heavy plant all the way upstairs . . .

RICHARD. It wasn't so heavy . . . (*They have edged almost to the door by now.*)

THE GIRL. Well, good night. And thanks —again . . .

RICHARD. Well, good night . . . (*She leans forward and kisses him lightly on the cheek.*) Well, good night . . .

(*Suddenly they move together in a tight embrace which they hold for a moment. She breaks away, then kisses him again and in the same motion goes quickly out the door closing it behind her.*)

(RICHARD *is visibly shaken. He starts after her. Stops himself. Closes the door again. And locks it. He shakes his head and then puts on the chain lock.*)

(*Comes inside, starts for the phone, stops again. Tries to pull himself together. Picks up the galley sheets and sits down on the couch and tries to work on them.*)

(*As he sits, a square in the ceiling at the top of the stairs lifts out and a moment later the girl appears. She backs down the first few steps, lowering the floor-ceiling back into place. He is oblivious to this. She turns and starts down the stairs. We see that she is carrying a small claw hammer.*)

(*Quietly she comes down into the room. She looks at him and smiles. She pauses for a moment.*)

THE GIRL. (*with a small, ineffectual wave of the hand*). Hi . . .

(RICHARD *almost jumps out of his skin. He sees her. After a moment he sees the hammer and realizes where she has come from. Then, after a long time, he smiles and makes a similar, ineffectual wave of the hand.*)

RICHARD. Hi . . .

CURTAIN

ACT THREE

The same.

It is about eight o'clock the following morning. The blinds on the French doors are drawn, but outside the sun is shining brightly. It is going to be another hot day.

As the curtain rises, RICHARD *stands by the French doors. He is in his shirt sleeves.*

He opens the blinds and then the doors. He steps out onto the terrace and breathes deeply. He comes back into the living room and notices the girl's shoes. Somewhat tentatively, he picks them up and carries them to the bedroom doors. He stops and listens for a moment. He puts the shoes back where he found them and goes to the front door. He listens again, then unlocks the door without unfastening the chain.

He kneels down and reaching around through the slightly open door fishes in milk and the newspaper. He carries the paper down to the armchair and tries to read. He can't, however.

After a moment he looks up and speaks to himself in a very reassuring voice.

RICHARD. There's not a thing in the world to worry about. Two very attractive, intelligent people happened to meet under circumstances that seemed to be —propitious—and, well, it happened. It was very charming and gay. As a matter of fact it was wonderful. But now it's over. (*He rises and starts for the bedroom.*) We'll say good-by, like two intelligent people. We'll have coffee . . . (*He knocks gently on the door. He listens. He knocks again. His calm is rapidly evaporating.*) How can she possibly sleep like that? . . . What's the matter with her anyway? Maybe she's sick or something. Maybe she's dead. . . . Maybe the excitement was too much for her and she passed away in her sleep. . . . Oh, my God! That means the police. And the reporters. "Actress found dead in publisher's apartment"! . . . (*He looks desperately around. His eye lights on the staircase.*) No. No. I'll just haul the body upstairs. That's all. Right back upstairs, nail up the floor again and that's all. They'd have no reason to suspect me. I'd wear gloves, of course. They'd never prove a thing. . . . Now stop it. You're getting hysterical again. (*Pause*) Well, if she isn't dead, why the hell doesn't she just get up and go home? It's late! It's—late—it's *really* late —it's . . . (*He picks up his wrist watch from table.*) . . . ten after eight? It seemed later than *that* . . . (*He is somewhat relieved by the time.*) Well. I'll give her another half-hour to catch up on her beauty sleep. Then, I'll very politely wake her. We'll have coffee like two intelligent

people. And then, I'll kiss her good-by. (*Confidently acting out the scene*) It's been fun, darling, but now, of course, it's over . . . No tears—no regrets . . . (*He stands waving as if she were walking up the stairs.*) Just good-by. It's been—swell . . . (*He blows a kiss upward, waves and then stands transfixed, a foolish expression on his face.*)

HIS VOICE. Pal.

RICHARD. Huh?

HIS VOICE. I don't want you to get upset or anything, but it might not be as easy as all that. You know. Be realistic.

RICHARD. What? What are you talking about?

HIS VOICE. I was just pointing out. Women don't take these things as lightly as men, you know. There *could* be complications. For example, suppose she's fallen desperately in love with you . . .

RICHARD. She can't do that. It isn't fair. She knows she can't.

HIS VOICE. After all, pal, you had a little something to do with this yourself . . .

RICHARD. Don't worry. I can handle it. Just don't worry. I can be tough if I have to. I can be pretty damn tough. If I set my mind to it, I can be a terrible heel . . .

HIS VOICE (*mocking*). Ha-*ha!*

RICHARD. Shut up . . . (*He stands for a moment, setting his mind to being a terrible heel. The lights dim and music sneaks in. "Dream lighting" lights up the bedroom doors. They open and the girl emerges. She is dressed like an Al Parker illustration for a story called "Glorious Honeymoon" in* The Woman's Home Companion. *She is radiant.*)

THE GIRL (*radiantly*). Good morning, my darling . . . Good morning . . . Good morning . . .

RICHARD (*very tough. He lights a cigarette and stares at her for a moment through ice-blue eyes*). Oh. It's about time you dragged your dead pratt out of the sack . . .

THE GIRL. Oh, darling, darling, darling . . . (*He exhales smoke.*) What is it, my darling, you seem troubled . . .

RICHARD. Shut up, baby, and listen to me. I got something to tell you.

THE GIRL. And I've something to tell you. I've grown older, somehow, overnight. I know now that all our brave talk of independence—our not wanting to get involved—our being—actually—*afraid* of love—it was all childish nonsense. I'm not afraid to say it, darling. I love you. I want you. You belong to me.

RICHARD. Look, baby. Let's get one thing straight. I belong to nobody, see. If some dumb little dame wants to throw herself at me—that's her lookout, see. I'm strictly a one-night guy. I've left a string of broken hearts from here to—to Westport, Connecticut, and back. Now, the smartest little move you could make is to pack your stuff and scram . . .

THE GIRL. Go? Not I! Not now! Not ever! Don't you see, my darling, after what we've been to each other . . .

RICHARD. I spell trouble, baby, with a capital "T". We're poison to each other —you and me. Don't you see that?

THE GIRL. When two people care for each other as we do . . .

RICHARD (*a little "Pal Joey" creeping in*). What do I care for a dame? Every damn dame is the same. I'm going to own a night club . . .

THE GIRL. That doesn't matter. Nothing matters. This thing is bigger than both of us. We'll *flaunt* our love. Shout it from the highest housetops. We're on a great toboggan. We can't stop it. We can't steer it. It's too late to run, the Beguine has begun . . .

RICHARD (*weakly*). Oh, Jesus Christ . . .

THE GIRL (*coolly taking charge*). Now then. Do you want to be the one to tell Helen, or shall I?

RICHARD (*with an anguished moan*). Tell Helen?

THE GIRL. Of course. We must. It's the only way . . .

RICHARD. No, no, no! You can't do that! You can't! (*He is now kneeling at her feet, pleading. She puts her arm about his shoulder. From somewhere comes the brave sound of a solo violin which plays behind her next speech.*)

THE GIRL. We can and we must. We'll face her together. Hand in hand. Proudly. Our heads held high. Oh, we'll be social outcasts, but we won't care. It'll be you and I together against the world. I'll go and dress now, darling. But I wanted you to know how I felt. I couldn't wait to tell you. Good-by, for now, my darling. I won't be long . . .

(*As the music swells, she floats off into the bedroom, waving and blowing kisses with both hands. The "dream light" fades out and the lighting returns to normal.*

RICHARD *stands panic-stricken in the middle of the living-room floor. He shakes his head.*)

RICHARD. I'm crazy. I'm going crazy. That's all. I've run amok. Helen goes away and I run amok. Raping and looting and . . . (*He notices the cigarette in his hand.*) smoking cigarettes . . . (*He quickly puts out the cigarette.*) What have I done? What did I think I was doing? What did I possibly think I was doing? . . . Damn it! I begged Helen not to go away for the summer. I begged her! . . . What am I going to do! That girl in there undoubtedly expects me to get a divorce and marry her.

HIS VOICE. Well, why don't you?

RICHARD. Are you kidding? What about Helen?

HIS VOICE. What about her? Maybe this is all for the best. Maybe this is the best thing that could have happened to you. After all, Helen's not as young as she used to be. In a couple of years you'll look like her son.

RICHARD. Now wait a minute. Wait a minute. Helen is still pretty attractive. She happens to be a damn beautiful woman, if you want to know. And we've been through a lot together. The time I was fired from Random House. And when little Ricky was sick—and I caught the damn mumps from him. She's taken a lot of punishment from me, if you want to know. And she's been pretty nice about it . . .

HIS VOICE. The point, however is: Do you love her?

RICHARD. Love her? Well, sure. Sure, I love her. Of course I love her. I'm *used to her!*

HIS VOICE. Used to her? That doesn't sound very exciting. Of course I imagine when a man enters middle life, he doesn't want someone exciting. He wants someone comfortable. Someone he's *used* to . . .

RICHARD. Now, just a second. You've got the wrong idea. Helen's not so—*comfortable*. She's pretty exciting. You should see the way people look at her at parties and on the street and everywhere . . .

HIS VOICE. What people?

RICHARD. Men. That's what people. For instance, Tom MacKenzie, if you want to know. When Helen wears that green dress —the backless one with hardly any front— there's nothing comfortable about that at all . . . (RICHARD *sinks into chair and leans back*.) She wore it one night last spring when Tom MacKenzie was over— and you just couldn't get him out of here . . . (*Music sneaks in and the lights dim. "Dream lighting" fills the stage*.) It looked like he was going to go home about four different times but he just couldn't tear himself away . . .

(TOM *and* HELEN *appear.* HELEN *is wearing the green dress. It is everything* RICHARD *has said it is*.)

TOM. Helen, you look particularly lovely tonight . . .

HELEN. Why, thank you, Tom . . .

TOM. You're a lucky boy, Dickie, even if you don't know it.

RICHARD. I know all about it and don't call me Dickie . . .

TOM. Helen—Helen, that name is so like you. "Helen, thy beauty is to me as those Nicaean barks of yore" . . .

HELEN. Gracious . . .

TOM. No, no, I mean it. Stand there a moment. Let me drink you in. Turn around. Slowly, that's it . . . (HELEN *models dress*.) You look particularly lovely in a backless gown . . .

RICHARD (*muttering*). Backless, frontless, topless, bottomless, I'm on to you, you son of a bitch . . .

TOM (*from across the room*). What was that, old man?

HELEN (*quickly*). Don't pay any attention to Dick. You know what happens to him and martinis . . .

RICHARD. Two martinis. Two lousy martinis.

HELEN. Dr. Summers has told him time and time again that he should go on the wagon for a while till his stomach gets better . . .

TOM. That's good advice, Dick. When a man can't handle the stuff he should leave it alone completely. That's what I say. Once a year—just to test my will power— I stop everything.

RICHARD (*he starts to say something, but finally stops himself*). No comment.

HELEN (*leaping once again into the breach*). You really like this dress—do you, Tom?

TOM. I certainly do. It's a Potter original, isn't it?

HELEN. Yes—but that's wonderful! How did you know?

TOM. I'm a bit of an authority on wom-en's clothes. You should really take me with you the next time you go shopping. We could have a bite of lunch first and really make a day of it . . . (*He has finally got to the door*.) Good night, Dick . . . (RICHARD *waves unenthusiastically*.) Good night, Helen . . . (*He kisses her*.)

HELEN. Good night, Tom . . .

TOM. I'll call you one day next week . . .

HELEN. I'll be looking forward to it. (*She closes the door behind him*.) I thought he was never going home . . .

RICHARD (*in rather feeble imitation of* TOM). "Helen, thy beauty is to me as those Nicaean barks of yore"—is he kidding?

HELEN. You know Tom. He beats his chest and makes noises but it doesn't really mean anything . . .

RICHARD. I know. His Nicaean bark is worse than his Nicaean bite . . . (*He is pleasantly surprised by how well this came out*.) Hey, that's pretty good. That came out better than I thought it was going to. Nicaean bark—Nicaean bite . . .

HELEN (*unfractured*). Actually, in some ways, Tom is very sweet. I mean it's nice to have people notice your clothes . . .

RICHARD. Notice your clothes! He did a lot more than notice. . . . He practically . . . You know, you really ought to do something about that dress. Just the front part there . . .

HELEN. Do something about it?

RICHARD. I mean sort of . . . (*He gestures ineffectually about raising or tightening or something the front*.) I don't know. Maybe we ought to empty the ash trays or something. You should see the way he was looking at you . . .

HELEN. You should have been flattered. Don't you want people to think your wife is attractive?

RICHARD. Sure, but . . . Why don't we clean this place up a little? It looks like a cocktail lounge on West Tenth Street . . . (*He picks up an ash tray full of cigarette butts*.)

(HELEN *comes over to him*.)

HELEN. Darling . . .

RICHARD. We ought to at least empty the ash trays . . .

HELEN. Not now . . .

RICHARD (*looks at her questioningly*). Huh?

HELEN. I mean not now . . .

(*He looks at her for another moment*

and then very casually tosses away the tray full of butts and takes her in his arms.)

(*The lights black out and the music swells in the darkness.*)

(*When the lights come on again the lighting is back to normal and* RICHARD *is leaning back in the chair where we left him, a self-satisfied grin on his face.*)

HIS VOICE. Then you really do love Helen?

RICHARD. What do you want—an affidavit?

HIS VOICE. Well, good. So that leaves you with only one problem. I'm warning you, pal, it may not be as easy to get rid of this girl as you think.

RICHARD. Huh?

HIS VOICE. My dear boy, did you ever hear of a thing called blackmail?

RICHARD. *Blackmail?*

HIS VOICE. One often hears of unscrupulous young girls who prey on foolish, wealthy, middle-aged men . . .

RICHARD. Now, really . . .

HIS VOICE. You got her into bed without any great effort. Why do you suppose she was so willing?

RICHARD (*weakly*). But she said—she told me—she went on record—she didn't want to get involved . . . (HIS VOICE *laughs coarsely.*) A minute ago you were saying she was madly in love with me . . .

HIS VOICE. *You poor, foolish, wealthy, middle-aged man.*

RICHARD. Wait a minute—in the first place I'm not wealthy . . .

HIS VOICE. Blackmail, pal, it happens every day. She'll bleed you white.

RICHARD. Oh, my God. I'll have to sell the kid's bonds. . . . Poor Ricky. Poor Helen. There's only one thing to do. Confess everything and throw myself on her mercy. We're both intelligent people. She'll forgive me.

HIS VOICE. I wouldn't be a bit surprised if she shot you dead.

RICHARD. You're out of your mind. Not Helen. If she shot anyone it would much more likely be herself. Oh, my God. She'd probably shoot us both . . . I can't go on torturing myself like this. I'll have to tell her. Oh, she'll be hurt. For a while. But she'll get over it. There's no other way. I've got to tell her and take my chances . . .

(*Music and "dream lighting" in.*)

RICHARD (*calling*). Helen! Helen!

HELEN (*from kitchen*). Yes, darling . . .

RICHARD. Can you come in here a moment, please? There's something I must tell you.

(*Helen enters from the kitchen. This is the domestic, very un-green-dress* HELEN. *She wears an apron and carries a bowl which she stirs with a wooden spoon.*)

HELEN (*sweetly*). Yes, Dick? I was just making a cherry pie. I know how you hate the pies from Gristede's and I wanted to surprise you. . . .

RICHARD. I don't know how to say this to you . . .

HELEN. Yes, Dick?

RICHARD. We've been married a long time . . .

HELEN. Seven years, darling. Seven glorious years. These are sweetheart cherries . . .

RICHARD. And in all that time, I've never looked at another woman . . .

HELEN. I know that, Dick. And I want to tell you what it's meant to me. You may not know this, darling, but you're terribly attractive to women . . .

RICHARD. I am?

HELEN. Yes, you funny Richard you—you are. But in all those seven years I've never once worried. Oh, don't I know there are plenty of women who would give their eye teeth to get you. Elaine. Miss Morris. That Marie What-ever-her-name-was up in Westport. But I trust you, Dick. I always have. I always will. Do you know something?

RICHARD. What?

HELEN. I . . . Oh, I can't even say it. It's too foolish . . .

RICHARD. Go ahead. Go ahead, say it. Be foolish.

HELEN. Well—I honestly believe that if you were ever unfaithful to me—I'd know it. I'd know it instantly.

RICHARD. You would?

HELEN. Oh, yes . . .

RICHARD. How?

HELEN. Wives have ways. Little ways.

RICHARD. And what would you do?

HELEN. Oh, darling, don't be . . .

RICHARD. No. Really. I'm interested. What would you do?

HELEN. Oh, I think I'd probably shoot you dead. Afterwards, of course, I'd shoot myself. Life wouldn't be worth living after that . . .

RICHARD. Oh, no! (*A pause*) Helen . . .

HELEN. Yes?

RICHARD. Nothing. Nothing.

HELEN. Yes, there is something. I can tell.

RICHARD. No, now take it easy . . .

HELEN. I can tell. I can suddenly feel it. The vibrations—something happened while I was away this summer . . .

RICHARD. It was an accident. A crazy accident. There was this tomato . . . That is—this tomato plant fell down. It landed right out there on the terrace. But nobody was hurt, thank God. I didn't want to tell you about it. I was afraid you'd worry . . .

HELEN (sadly). Who was she?

RICHARD. Now, Helen—you're making this up . . .

HELEN (turning on him). Who was she!

RICHARD. Now please, really . . .

HELEN. Then it's true. It is true.

RICHARD. Look, we're both intelligent people. I knew you'd be hurt. But I know that somehow, someday, you'll forgive me. . . . (He suddenly notices that HELEN is holding a revolver in her hand.) Now put that thing down. What are you going to do?

HELEN. You've left me nothing else to do. I'm going to shoot you dead. Then I'm going to kill myself.

RICHARD. But what about—the child?

HELEN. You should have thought of that before. Good-by, Richard . . . (She fires five times.)

(For a moment, RICHARD stands erect, weathering the hail of bullets. . . . Then slowly, tragically, in the best gangster movie tradition—clutching his middle—and making small Bogart-like sounds he sinks to the floor.)

RICHARD (gasping—the beads of sweat standing out on his forehead.) Helen—I'm—going—fast . . . Give me a cigarette . . .

HELEN (always the wife, even in times of crisis). A cigarette! You know what Dr. Murphy told you about smoking!

RICHARD. Good-by . . . Helen . . .

(She turns and walks sadly to the kitchen. At the door she stops, waves sadly with the wooden spoon, blows one final kiss and as the music swells she exits into kitchen. An instant later we hear the final shot.)

(RICHARD collapses in a final spasm of agony and the lights black out.)

(As the lights dim back to reality RICHARD is seated where we left him, a horror-struck expression on his face.)

RICHARD. Oh, the hell with that! I'll be goddamned if I'll tell her! (For a moment, RICHARD stands shaking his head.) But I've got to . . . I've just got to . . . (He is heading for the telephone when the sound of the door buzzer stops him.)

(He freezes, panic-stricken. Glances quickly at the bedroom. The buzzer sounds again. Then a third time.)

(When it is quite clear that whoever it is is not going to go away, RICHARD presses the buzzer, then opens the door a crack, still leaving the chain fastened.)

RICHARD (hoarsely). Who is it?

DR. BRUBAKER (off stage). Once again, sir, I must trouble you . . .

RICHARD. Dr. Brubaker!

DR. BRUBAKER (off stage). Yes . . .

RICHARD. What it is? What can I do for you?

DR. BRUBAKER (through door). Last evening, after our conference, I appear to have left your apartment without my brief case.

RICHARD. No, no, Doctor. That's impossible. I'm afraid you're mistaken. I'm quite sure you had it with you. In fact, I remember quite clearly seeing . . . (He looks wildly around the room and then sees the brief case.) Oh. Oh, there it is. . . . You're right. Isn't that amazing? It's right there. I'm sorry I can't ask you in but the place is kind of a mess and . . . (He is trying to get the brief case through the door without unfastening the chain. It doesn't fit. He attempts brute force, but it just isn't going to fit. He pounds at it wildly and then finally realizes that he is going to have to open the chain. He does so.) Here you are, Doctor . . . Good-by . . .

DR. BRUBAKER (an unstoppable force, he moves into the living room). I thank you. If you will permit me, I'll just make sure that everything is in order . . . (Opening the brief case and riffling through the contents) You can see what a strong unconscious resistance this whole project has stimulated in me. . . . I cannot understand this mass compulsion on the part of the psychiatric profession to write and publish books . . .

RICHARD. Don't worry about it, Doctor. Books by psychiatrists almost always sell well. I'll talk to you again the first of the week . . .

DR. BRUBAKER. Thank you, sir. And once again I must apologize for troubling you. Particularly in the midst of such a delicate situation . . .

RICHARD. Yes. Well . . . *What?* What do you mean? What delicate situation?

DR. BRUBAKER. I meant only that, as, quite clearly, your second assault on the person of the young lady was more successful than the first, my visit could not have been more inopportune. Good-by, sir, and good luck! (DR. BRUBAKER *starts to go.* RICHARD *stops him.*)

RICHARD. Now wait a minute, Doctor. Now wait a minute. You can't just say something like that and then go . . .

DR. BRUBAKER. My boy, I have a full day ahead of me . . .

RICHARD. Look, I can't stand it. You've got to tell me. How did you know—about —what happened?

DR. BRUBAKER. In the light of our conversation of last evening, it is quite obvious. I return this morning to find you behind barred doors in an extreme state of sexomasochistic excitement bordering on hysteria . . .

RICHARD. What the hell is sexomasochistic excitement?

DR. BRUBAKER. Guilt feelings, sir. Guilt feelings. A state of deep and utter enjoyment induced by reveling in one's guilt feelings. One punishes oneself and one is pardoned of one's crime. And now, my boy, I must really go. Enjoy yourself!

RICHARD. Look, this may not seem like very much to you—you spend eight hours a day with rapists and all kinds of—but I've never done anything like this before . . .

DR. BRUBAKER. This is quite obvious.

RICHARD. This is the first time. And, by God, it's the last time . . .

DR. BRUBAKER. An excellent decision.

RICHARD. I mean, I love my wife!

DR. BRUBAKER. Don't we all? And now, sir . . .

RICHARD. If she ever finds out about this she'll—kill us both. She'll kill *herself* anyway—and I don't want her to do that. Maybe it would be better if I didn't tell her . . .

DR. BRUBAKER. Possibly . . .

RICHARD. But she'd find out some way. I know she would. What was that you said the other night? There was some phrase you used. What was it?

DR. BRUBAKER (*he has wandered over to the bookshelf and taken down the copy of* US Camera). Vigorous denial. This popular theory of omniscience of wives is completely untrue. They almost never know. Because they don't want to.

RICHARD. Yeah. Yeah. Vigorous denial. Suppose I denied it. That's all. She'd have to take my word for it. As a matter of fact, you know, it's probably a damn good thing this happened. I mean, a couple of days ago—I wasn't even sure if I did love her. Now I know I do. Helen ought to be damn glad this happened, if you want to know . . . (*He notices* DR. BRUBAKER *holding* US Camera) You can take that with you if you want to . . .

DR. BRUBAKER. No. No, thank you.

RICHARD. You know, suddenly I feel much better. Everything's going to be all right. You're absolutely right, Doctor. I just won't tell her and everything'll be fine. And if she should find out, I'll deny it . . .

DR. BRUBAKER. Vigorously.

RICHARD. Gee, Doctor—I'd like to give you fifty dollars or something . . .

DR. BRUBAKER (*considers this briefly, but rejects it*). Well . . . No, no. It will not be necessary . . . (*He is casually thumbing through* US Camera *and stops at* THE GIRL's *picture.*) However, if the young lady should by any chance suffer any severe traumatic or emotional disturbances due to your decision to go back to your wife . . . If, in other words, she appears to be in need of psychiatric aid—I trust you will mention my name . . . Thank you once again, sir, and good day . . . (*He hands* US Camera *back to* RICHARD *and exits.* RICHARD *looks after him thoughtfully for a moment or two. Then, the doors to the bedrooms slide open and* THE GIRL *emerges. She is dressed and is bright and cheerful and very much herself.*)

THE GIRL. Hi.

RICHARD. Oh. Hi.

THE GIRL. *Golly,* I didn't know it was so late. I don't know what happened to me. I've got to be at the studio in half an hour. . . .

RICHARD. The studio . . .

THE GIRL. Sure. The television show. Forty million people are waiting to see me wash my husband's shirt in Trill—that exciting new, no-rinse detergent . . .

RICHARD. Oh.

THE GIRL. Well, I'd better go now. . . .

RICHARD. I was going to make some coffee. . . .

THE GIRL. That's all right. I'll get some on the way.

RICHARD. I don't know how to say this —but you're . . . I mean, I . . .

THE GIRL. I know. Me too . . .

RICHARD. Will I see you—again, I mean?

THE GIRL. I think better not . . .

RICHARD. This whole thing—it's been swell. Only . . .

THE GIRL. Only one thing. We mustn't forget that . . .

RICHARD. What's that?

THE GIRL. This is your birthday.

RICHARD. Gee, that's right. It is.

THE GIRL. Well, I want this to be a happy birthday . . .

RICHARD. Look. You're not upset about anything, are you?

THE GIRL. No. No, I feel fine. Are you?

RICHARD. Are you sure? I mean, well . . .

THE GIRL. No, really, I feel wonderful. . . . Only . . . Well, suddenly I feel like maybe it wouldn't be so bad to have to start getting in at one o'clock again . . .

RICHARD. Didn't you say—I mean— wouldn't that spoil everything?

THE GIRL. You don't understand—I mean it would be pretty nice to have to start getting in at one o'clock again. As soon as I find someone who's fallen desperately in love with me—someone who's sweet and intelligent and married—to me . . . I don't mean you—I mean—you know— someone who . . .

RICHARD. Someone who never saw Sarah Bernhardt?

THE GIRL. Well, yes . . . Good-by, and thanks for everything . . . (She kisses him lightly on the cheek.) Birthday kiss. Happy birthday, Richard.

RICHARD. Thank you . . .

(She starts up the stairs then turns and stops.)

THE GIRL. Hey—I forgot my hammer.

RICHARD. Yeah—you better take that . . .

(Both laugh and are released. She goes up the stairs. The trap closes and she is gone.)

(RICHARD is a little awed. In a dazed way he wanders over to the bar and pours himself a glass of milk. Then, he looks at his watch, pulls himself together, picks up US Camera and heads for bedroom. He puts US Camera on shelf, starts out. Comes back and drops it behind the row of books, hiding it. He starts out again and the door buzzer sounds. He goes to the door and opens it. TOM MACKENZIE is standing in the doorway.)

TOM. Hi, there . . .

RICHARD. Hello.

TOM. How are you? Hope I didn't wake you . . .

RICHARD. What do you want?

TOM. I'm sorry to bust in on you at this ungodly hour, boy, but I'm here on business. Family business. Got any coffee?

RICHARD. No. What are you doing here? I thought you were up in the country.

TOM. I was. I just drove in this morning. Got an appointment with my agent so Helen asked me to stop by and ask you . . .

RICHARD. Oh! Oh, she did. Well, I'm damn glad she did. I want to talk to you.

TOM. What's the matter with you, boy? You're acting mighty peculiar.

RICHARD. Never mind how I'm acting. You think you're pretty fancy with your rain and your damn fireplaces . . .

TOM. What are you talking about? What fireplaces?

RICHARD. You know what fireplaces.

TOM. I don't even have a fireplace.

RICHARD. That's your story.

TOM. I put in radiant heat. It's the latest thing. Cost me three thousand dollars.

RICHARD. Oh, yeah?

TOM. Yeah! They take the coils and they bury them right in the floor . . . What the hell is all this about fireplaces? Are you drunk or something?

RICHARD. No, I am not drunk! (From above comes the sound of hammering, a nail being driven into the floor.) She had dinner with you last night, didn't she?

TOM. Sure. Sure. (More hammering.) What's wrong with that?

RICHARD. And she was wearing that green dress from Clare Potter wasn't she?

TOM. How the hell do I know where she bought that green dress?

RICHARD. Oh, then she was wearing it! Worse than I thought!

TOM. You are drunk. (More hammering. This time TOM looks up.) What's that?

RICHARD. That's nothing. This used to be a duplex. I just had a glass of milk!

TOM (patiently). Now see here, old man. Why shouldn't Helen have dinner with me? She's stuck up there in the country while you're down here doing God knows what . . .

RICHARD. What do you mean by that?

TOM. I know what happens with guys like you when their wives are away. Don't forget, I used to be married myself.

RICHARD. I got a good mind to punch you right in the nose.

TOM. Why?

RICHARD. Why—because you're too old —that's why!

TOM. Too old—what are you talking about?

RICHARD. You're getting fat—you look like the portrait of Dorian Gray!

TOM. Drunk. Blind, stinking drunk at nine o'clock in the morning. Where am I getting fat?

RICHARD. Everywhere! You know, there's something really repulsive about old men who run after young wives! Now you get out of here and get back to Helen and tell her I refuse to give her a divorce . . .

TOM. *A divorce?*

RICHARD. You heard me! You can tell her for me that I'll fight it in every court in the country!

TOM. You're crazy! Helen doesn't want a divorce . . . (*Yelling, he can no longer control himself.*) She wants her yellow skirt!

RICHARD. Her yellow skirt? Oh, my God . . .

TOM (*bellowing*). She's having people over for dinner and she needs it! (*He exits slamming the door furiously.*)

RICHARD. Her yellow skirt . . . (*He reaches into hall closet and finds it on the wire hanger. Tenderly, he folds it over his arm.*) I'll take her yellow skirt up to her myself. She needs it. She's having people over for dinner. . . . People over for dinner? *What* people? . . . *Me!* That's what people! (*Takes his hat from closet, puts it on his head at a rakish angle and with a great flourish exits out the door as:*)

THE CURTAIN FALLS

THE MATCHMAKER

Thornton Wilder

The Merchant of Yonkers was produced by Herman Shumlin and the cast included Jane Cowl, June Walker, Nydia Westman, Minna Phillips, Percy Waram, Tom Ewell, John Call, Joseph Sweeney, Philip Coolidge and Edward Nannery. It was first performed on December 12, 1938, at the Colonial Theatre, Boston. The New York engagement opened at the Guild Theatre on December 28, 1938. *The Matchmaker* was produced for the Edinburgh Festival by Tennent Productions. The first performance was at the Royal Lyceum Theatre, Edinburgh, on August 23, 1954. It was directed by Tyrone Guthrie with settings and costumes by Tanya Moiseiwitsch. The same production opened at the Theatre Royal, Haymarket, London, on November 4, 1954. Without changes in the principal roles—with the exception of that of Mr. Vandergelder, which was played successively by Sam Levene, Eddie Mayehoff and Loring Smith—the play was performed at the Locust Street Theatre, Philadelphia, on October 27, 1955. The cast of the play from Edinburgh to New York, with the exceptions noted, included:

HORACE VANDERGELDER Loring Smith

CORNELIUS HACKL Arthur Hill

BARNABY TUCKER Robert Morse (following Alec McCowen)

MALACHI STACK Patrick McAlinney

AMBROSE KEMPER Alexander Davion (following Lee Montague)

WAITERS Timothy Findley, John Milligan

CABMAN Peter Bayliss

DOLLY LEVI Ruth Gordon

IRENE MOLLOY Eileen Herlie

MINNIE FAY Rosamund Greenwood

ERMENGARDE Prunella Scales

GERTRUDE Charity Grace (following Henzie Raeburn)

FLORA VAN HUYSEN Esme Church

COOK Christine Thomas (following Daphne Newton)

This play is a rewritten version of *The Merchant of Yonkers*, which was directed in 1938 by Max Reinhardt and is again dedicated to Max Reinhardt with deep admiration and indebtedness.

TIME: The early 80's.

ACT I. Vandergelder's house in Yonkers, New York. ACT II. Mrs. Molloy's hat shop, New York. ACT III. The Harmonia Gardens Restaurant on the Battery, New York. ACT IV. Miss Van Huysen's house, New York.

This play is based upon a comedy by Johann Nestroy, *Einen Jux will er sich Machen* (Vienna, 1842), which was in turn based upon an English original, *A Day Well Spent* (London, 1835) by John Oxenford.

INTRODUCTION

Novelist, playwright, and gentleman of the world, Thornton Niven Wilder has been the foremost American in the theatre of the imagination, whether intensely "serious" in *The Skin of Our Teeth* or intensely "frivolous" in *The Matchmaker*. Moreover, his seriousness and frivolity have often appeared together and sometimes indistinguishably; Mr. Wilder has been weighty and mercurial, a formal writer and a casual one, a neo-classicist and a romantic, a poet and a wit. He defies definition, and a critic who would keep up with Mr. Wilder's wonder-filled course would need seven-league boots in order to catch up with him. Alertness is also needed in keeping a record of all the distinctions that have come to this author and gay philosopher. The latest of these came in 1957 from the West German book industry; it was a Peace Prize for the balm he brought to war-shattered Germany with *The Skin of Our Teeth*, which the German public came to know after 1945 under the title of *Wir sind noch einmal davongekommen*.

Born in Wisconsin in 1897, Mr. Wilder started his wide-ranging career early by spending a part of his childhood in China and then returning to the United States in order to complete his high-school education. Subsequently, he took a B.A. at Yale and an M.A. at Princeton, completing his graduate studies after service with the Coast Artillery Corps during World War I. He then spent a year in studying archaeology at the American Academy in Rome, and these studies may have remotely influenced his decision to write one of his best works, *The Ides of March*, a novel about Julius Caesar published in 1948. During and after his graduate work at Princeton he taught for seven years at the Lawrenceville School, and from 1930 to 1936 at the University of Chicago. This was a fruitful period for the writer, who had a success of esteem with his novel *The Cabala* in 1925 and both a popular and critical success with the Pulitzer Prize novel *The Bridge of San Luis Rey* two years later. Two other novels followed in the next decade, *The Woman of Andros*, in 1930, and *Heaven's My Destination*, in 1935. During this period, too, Mr. Wilder became a playwright of note with volumes of one-act plays (*The Angel That Troubled the Waters* and *The Long Christmas Dinner*, published in 1928 and 1931 respectively), with adaptations of Obey's *Lucrèce* for Katharine Cornell and Ibsen's *A Doll's House* for Ruth Gordon, and, in 1938, with his masterpiece *Our Town*. In 1942, Mr. Wilder wrote the outstanding play of the World War II period, *The Skin of Our Teeth*, a philosophical extravaganza noteworthy alike for its reflectiveness and exuberance, its depth and playfulness, its literary quality and its theatricality.

After service in the United States Air Corps Intelligence as a lieutenant colonel during World War II, Mr. Wilder increased his stature as a novelist with *The Ides of March*, adapted Sartre's French Resistance drama, *Morts sans Sépulture*, under the title of *The Victors*, and revised *The Merchant of Yonkers*, his play of the year 1938, under the title of *The Matchmaker*. It was staged very successfully in London in 1954 by Tyrone Guthrie, with Ruth Gordon in the main role, and another Tyrone Guthrie production of the play opened on Broadway successfully in December, 1955. A learned discourse on *The Matchmaker* is no doubt in order, for it is the adaptation of Wilder's earlier adaptation of an Austrian farce by Johann Nestroy, who died in 1862, but the present editor respectfully begs off. *The Matchmaker* gave him such wonderful release from rationality and learning that he isn't fool enough to put on his shackles again, not even for the reader, who is probably not fool enough to want the obvious explained and his pleasure ruined by pedantry. Just a hint should suffice—imagine the action and look to the soliloquies for anything else you need!

ACT ONE

Living room of MR. VANDERGELDER's *house, over his hay, feed and provision store in Yonkers, fifteen miles north of New York City. Articles from the store have overflowed into this room; it has not been cleaned for a long time and is in some disorder, but it is not sordid or gloomy.*

There are three entrances. One at the center back leads into the principal rooms of the house. One on the back right (all the directions are from the point of view of the actors) opens on steps which descend to the street door. One on the left leads to ERMENGARDE's *room.*

In the center of the room is a trap door; below it is a ladder descending to the store below.

Behind the trap door and to the left of it is a tall accountant's desk; to the left of it is an old-fashioned stove with a stove-pipe going up into the ceiling. Before the desk is a tall stool. On the right of the stage is a table with some chairs about it.

MR. VANDERGELDER's *Gladstone bag, packed for a journey, is beside the desk.*

It is early morning.

VANDERGELDER, *sixty, choleric, vain and sly, wears a soiled dressing gown. He is seated with a towel about his neck, in a chair beside the desk, being shaved by* JOE SCANLON. VANDERGELDER *is smoking a cigar and holding a hand mirror.* AMBROSE KEMPER *is angrily striding about the room.*

VANDERGELDER (*loudly*). I tell you for the hundredth time you will never marry my niece.

AMBROSE (*thirty; dressed as an "artist"*). And I tell you for the thousandth time that I will marry your niece; and right soon, too.

VANDERGELDER. Never!

AMBROSE. Your niece is of age, Mr. Vandergelder. Your niece has consented to marry me. This is a free country, Mr. Vandergelder—not a private kingdom of your own.

VANDERGELDER. There are no free countries for fools, Mr. Kemper. Thank you for the honor of your visit—good morning.

JOE (*fifty; lanky, mass of gray hair falling into his eyes*). Mr. Vandergelder, will you please sit still one minute? If I cut your throat it'll be practically unintentional.

VANDERGELDER. Ermengarde is not for you, nor for anybody else who can't support her.

AMBROSE. I tell you I can support her. I make a very good living.

VANDERGELDER. No, sir! A living is made, Mr. Kemper, by selling something that everybody needs at least once a year. Yes, sir! And a million is made by producing something that everybody needs every day. You artists produce something that nobody needs at any time. You may sell a picture once in a while, but you'll make no living. Joe, go over there and stamp three times. I want to talk to Cornelius. (JOE *crosses to trap door and stamps three times.*)

AMBROSE. Not only can I support her now, but I have considerable expectations.

VANDERGELDER. *Expectations!* We merchants don't do business with them. I don't keep accounts with people who promise somehow to pay something someday, and I don't allow my niece to marry such people.

AMBROSE. Very well, from now on you might as well know that I regard any way we can find to get married is right and fair. Ermengarde is of age, and there's no law . . . (VANDERGELDER *rises and crosses toward* AMBROSE. JOE SCANLON *follows him complainingly and tries to find a chance to cut his hair even while he is standing.*)

VANDERGELDER. Law? Let me tell you something, Mr. Kemper: most of the people in the world are fools. The law is there to prevent crime; we men of sense are there to prevent foolishness. It's I, and not the law, that will prevent Ermengarde from marrying you, and I've taken some steps already. I've sent her away to get this nonsense out of her head.

AMBROSE. Ermengarde's . . . not here?

VANDERGELDER. She's gone—east, west, north, south. I thank you for the honor of your visit.

(*Enter* GERTRUDE—*eighty; deaf; half blind; and very pleased with herself.*)

GERTRUDE. Everything's ready, Mr. Vandergelder. Ermengarde and I have just finished packing the trunk.

VANDERGELDER. Hold your tongue! (JOE *is shaving* VANDERGELDER's *throat, so he can only wave his hands vainly.*)

GERTRUDE. Yes, Mr. Vandergelder, Ermengarde's ready to leave. Her trunk's all marked. Care Miss Van Huysen, 8 Jackson Street, New York.

VANDERGELDER (*breaking away from* JOE). Hell and damnation! Didn't I tell you it was a secret?

AMBROSE (*picks up hat and coat—kisses* GERTRUDE). Care Miss Van Huysen, 8 Jackson Street, New York. Thank you very much. Good morning, Mr. Vandergelder. (*Exit* AMBROSE, *to the street.*)

VANDERGELDER. It won't help you, Mr. Kemper—(*To* GERTRUDE.) Deaf! And blind! At least you can do me the favor of being dumb!

GERTRUDE. Chk—chk! Such a temper! Lord save us!

(CORNELIUS *puts his head up through the trap door. He is thirty-three; mock-deferential—he wears a green apron and is in his shirt-sleeves.*)

CORNELIUS. Yes, Mr. Vandergelder?

VANDERGELDER. Go in and get my niece's trunk and carry it over to the station. Wait! Gertrude, has Mrs. Levi arrived yet?

(CORNELIUS *comes up the trap door, steps into the room and closes the trap door behind him.*)

GERTRUDE. Don't shout. I can hear perfectly well. Everything's clearly marked. (*Exit left.*)

VANDERGELDER. Have the buggy brought round to the front of the store in half an hour.

CORNELIUS. Yes, Mr. Vandergelder.

VANDERGELDER. This morning I'm joining my lodge parade and this afternoon I'm going to New York. Before I go, I have something important to say to you and Barnaby. Good news. Fact is—I'm going to promote you. How old are you?

CORNELIUS. Thirty-three, Mr. Vandergelder.

VANDERGELDER. What?

CORNELIUS. Thirty-three.

VANDERGELDER. That all? That's a foolish age to be at. I thought you were forty.

CORNELIUS. Thirty-three.

VANDERGELDER. A man's not worth a cent until he's forty. We just pay 'em wages to make mistakes—don't we, Joe?

JOE. You almost lost an ear on it, Mr. Vandergelder.

VANDERGELDER. I was thinking of promoting you to chief clerk.

CORNELIUS. What am I now, Mr. Vandergelder?

VANDERGELDER. You're an impertinent fool, that's what you are. Now, if you be-

have yourself, I'll promote you from impertinent fool to chief clerk, with a raise in your wages. And Barnaby may be promoted from idiot apprentice to incompetent clerk.

CORNELIUS. Thank you, Mr. Vandergelder.

VANDERGELDER. However, I want to see you again before I go. Go in and get my niece's trunk.

CORNELIUS. Yes, Mr. Vandergelder. (*Exit* CORNELIUS, *left.*)

VANDERGELDER. Joe—the world's getting crazier every minute. Like my father used to say: the horses'll be taking over the world soon.

JOE (*presenting mirror*). I did what I could, Mr. Vandergelder, what with you flying in and out of the chair. (*He wipes last of the soap from* VANDERGELDER'S *face.*)

VANDERGELDER. Fine, fine. Joe, you do a fine job, the same fine job you've done me for twenty years. Joe . . . I've got special reasons for looking my best today . . . isn't there something a little extry you could do, something a little special? I'll pay you right up to fifty cents—see what I mean? Do some of those things you do to the young fellas. Touch me up; smarten me up a bit.

JOE. All I know is fifteen cents' worth, like usual, Mr. Vandergelder; and that includes everything that's decent to do to a man.

VANDERGELDER. Now hold your horses, Joe—all I meant was . . .

JOE. I've shaved you for twenty years and you never asked me no such question before.

VANDERGELDER. Hold your horses, I say, Joe! I'm going to tell you a secret. But I don't want you telling it to that riffraff down to the barbershop what I'm going to tell you now. All I ask of you is a little extry because I'm thinking of getting married again; and this very afternoon I'm going to New York to call on my intended, a very refined lady.

JOE. Your gettin' married is none of my business, Mr. Vandergelder. I done everything to you I know, and the charge is fifteen cents like it always was, and . . . (CORNELIUS *crosses, left to right, and exits, carrying a trunk on his shoulder.* ERMENGARDE *and* GERTRUDE *enter from left.*) I don't dye no hair, not even for fifty cents I don't!

VANDERGELDER. Joe Scanlon, get out!

JOE. And lastly, it looks to me like you're pretty rash to judge which is fools and which isn't fools, Mr. Vandergelder. People that's et onions is bad judges of who's et onions and who ain't. Good morning, ladies; good morning, Mr. Vandergelder. (*Exit* JOE.)

VANDERGELDER. Well, what do you want?

ERMENGARDE (*twenty-four; pretty, sentimental*). Uncle! You said you wanted to talk to us.

VANDERGELDER. Oh yes. Gertrude, go and get my parade regalia—the uniform for my lodge parade.

GERTRUDE. What? Oh yes. Lord have mercy! (*Exit* GERTRUDE, *back center*.)

VANDERGELDER. I had a talk with that artist of yours. He's a fool. (ERMENGARDE *starts to cry*.) Weeping! Weeping! You can go down and weep for a while in New York where it won't be noticed. (*He sits on desk chair, puts tie round neck and calls her over to tie it for him.*) Ermengarde! I told him that when you were old enough to marry you'd marry someone who could support you. I've done you a good turn. You'll come and thank me when you're fifty.

ERMENGARDE. But Uncle, I love him!

VANDERGELDER. I tell you you don't.

ERMENGARDE. But I *do!*

VANDERGELDER. And I tell you you don't. Leave those things to me.

ERMENGARDE. If I don't marry Ambrose I know I'll die.

VANDERGELDER. What of?

ERMENGARDE. A broken heart.

VANDERGELDER. Never heard of it. Mrs. Levi is coming in a moment to take you to New York. You are going to stay two or three weeks with Miss Van Huysen, an old friend of your mother's. (GERTRUDE *re-enters with coat, sash and sword. Enter from the street, right,* MALACHI STACK.) You're not to receive any letters except from me. I'm coming to New York myself today and I'll call on you tomorrow. (*To* MALACHI.) Who are you?

MALACHI (*fifty. Sardonic. Apparently innocent smile; pretense of humility.*) Malachi Stack, your honor. I heard you wanted an apprentice in the hay, feed, provision and hardware business.

VANDERGELDER. An apprentice at your age?

MALACHI. Yes, your honor; I bring a lot of experience to it.

VANDERGELDER. Have you any letters of recommendation?

MALACHI (*extending a sheaf of soiled papers*). Yes, indeed, your honor! First-class recommendation.

VANDERGELDER. Ermengarde! Are you ready to start?

ERMENGARDE. Yes.

VANDERGELDER. Well, go and get ready some more. Ermengarde! Let me know the minute Mrs. Levi gets here.

ERMENGARDE. Yes, Uncle Horace. (ERMENGARDE *and* GERTRUDE *exit*.)

(VANDERGELDER *examines the letters, putting them down one by one.*)

VANDERGELDER. I don't want an able seaman. Nor a typesetter. And I don't want a hospital cook.

MALACHI. No, your honor, but it's all experience. Excuse me! (*Selects a letter.*) This one is from your former partner, Joshua Van Tuyl, in Albany. (*He puts letters from table back into pocket.*)

VANDERGELDER. ". . . for the most part honest and reliable . . . occasionally willing and diligent." There seems to be a certain amount of hesitation about these recommendations.

MALACHI. Businessmen aren't writers, your honor. There's only one businessman in a thousand that can write a good letter of recommendation, your honor. Mr. Van Tuyl sends his best wishes and wants to know if you can use me in the provision and hardware business.

VANDERGELDER. Not so fast, not so fast! What's this "your honor" you use so much?

MALACHI. Mr. Van Tuyl says you're President of the Hudson River Provision Dealers' Recreational, Musical and Burial Society.

VANDERGELDER. I am; but there's no "your honor" that goes with it. Why did you come to Yonkers?

MALACHI. I heard that you'd had an apprentice that was a good-for-nothing, and that you were at your wit's end for another.

VANDERGELDER. Wit's end, wit's end! There's no dearth of good-for-nothing apprentices.

MALACHI. That's right, Mr. Vandergelder. It's employers there's a dearth of. Seems like you hear of a new one dying every day.

VANDERGELDER. What's that? Hold your tongue. I see you've been a barber, and a valet too. Why have you changed your place so often?

MALACHI. Changed my place, Mr. Vandergelder? When a man's interested in experience . . .

VANDERGELDER. Do you drink?

MALACHI. No, thanks. I've just had breakfast.

VANDERGELDER. I didn't ask you whether —Idiot! I asked you if you were a drunkard.

MALACHI. No, sir! No! Why, looking at it from all sides I don't even like liquor.

VANDERGELDER. Well, if you keep on looking at it from all sides, out you go. Remember that. Here. (*Gives him remaining letters.*) With all your faults, I'm going to give you a try.

MALACHI. You'll never regret it, Mr. Vandergelder. You'll never regret it.

VANDERGELDER. Now today I want to use you in New York. I judge you know your way around New York?

MALACHI. Do I know New York? Mr. Vandergelder, I know every hole and corner in New York.

VANDERGELDER. Here's a dollar. A train leaves in a minute. Take that bag to the Central Hotel on Water Street, have them save me a room. Wait for me. I'll be there about four o'clock.

MALACHI. Yes, Mr. Vandergelder. (*Picks up the bag, starts out, then comes back.*) Oh, but first, I'd like to meet the other clerks I'm to work with.

VANDERGELDER. You haven't time. Hurry now. The station's across the street.

MALACHI. Yes, sir. (*Away—then back once more.*) You'll see, sir, you'll never regret it. . . .

VANDERGELDER. I regret it already. Go on. Off with you.

(*Exit* MALACHI, *right.*)

(*The following speech is addressed to the audience. During it* MR. VANDERGELDER *takes off his dressing gown, puts on his scarlet sash, his sword and his bright-colored coat. He is already wearing light blue trousers with a red stripe down the sides.*)

VANDERGELDER. Ninety-nine per cent of the people in the world are fools and the rest of us are in great danger of contagion. But I wasn't always free of foolishness as I am now. I was once young, which was foolish; I fell in love, which was foolish; and I got married, which was foolish; and for a while I was poor, which was more foolish than all the other things put together. Then my wife died, which was foolish of her; I grew older, which was sensible of me; then I became a rich man, which is as sensible as it is rare. Since you see I'm a man of sense, I guess you were surprised to hear that I'm planning to get married again. Well, I've two reasons for it. In the first place, I like my house run with order, comfort and economy. That's a woman's work; but even a woman can't do it well if she's merely being paid for it. In order to run a house well, a woman must have the feeling that she owns it. Marriage is a bribe to make a housekeeper think she's a householder. Did you ever watch an ant carry a burden twice its size? What excitement! What patience! What will! Well, that's what I think of when I see a woman running a house. What giant passions in those little bodies—what quarrels with the butcher for the best cut— what fury at discovering a moth in a cupboard! Believe me!—if women could harness their natures to something bigger than a house and a baby carriage—tck! tck!— they'd change the world. And the second reason, ladies and gentlemen? Well, I see by your faces you've guessed it already. There's nothing like mixing with women to bring out all the foolishness in a man of sense. And that's a risk I'm willing to take. I've just turned sixty, and I've just laid side by side the last dollar of my first half million. So if I should lose my head a little, I still have enough money to buy it back. After many years' caution and hard work, I have a right to a little risk and adventure, and I'm thinking of getting married. Yes, like all you other fools, I'm willing to risk a little security for a certain amount of adventure. Think it over. (*Exit back center.*)

(AMBROSE *enters from the street, crosses left, and whistles softly.* ERMENGARDE *enters from left.*)

ERMENGARDE. Ambrose! If my uncle saw you!

AMBROSE. Sh! Get your hat.

ERMENGARDE. My hat!

AMBROSE. Quick! Your trunk's at the station. Now quick! We're running away.

ERMENGARDE. Running away!

AMBROSE. Sh!

ERMENGARDE. Where?

AMBROSE. To New York. To get married.

ERMENGARDE. Oh, Ambrose, I can't do that. Ambrose dear—it wouldn't be proper!

AMBROSE. Listen. I'm taking you to my friend's house. His wife will take care of you.

ERMENGARDE. But, Ambrose, a girl can't go on a train with a man. I can see you don't know anything about girls.

AMBROSE. But I'm telling you we're going to get married!

ERMENGARDE. Married! But what would *Uncle* say?

AMBROSE. We don't care what Uncle'd say—we're eloping.

ERMENGARDE. Ambrose Kemper! How can you use such an awful word!

AMBROSE. Ermengarde, you have the soul of a field mouse.

ERMENGARDE (*crying*). Ambrose, why do you say such cruel things to me?

(*Enter* MRS. LEVI, *from the street, right. She stands listening.*)

AMBROSE. For the last time I beg you—get your hat and coat. The train leaves in a few minutes. Ermengarde, we'll get married tomorrow. . . .

ERMENGARDE. Oh, Ambrose! I see you don't understand anything about weddings. Ambrose, don't you *respect* me? . . .

MRS. LEVI (*uncertain age; mass of sandy hair; impoverished elegance; large, shrewd but generous nature, an assumption of worldly cynicism conceals a tireless amused enjoyment of life. She carries a handbag and a small brown paper bag*). Good morning, darling girl—how are you? (*They kiss.*)

ERMENGARDE. Oh, good morning, Mrs. Levi.

MRS. LEVI. And who is this gentleman who is so devoted to you?

ERMENGARDE. This is Mr. Kemper, Mrs. Levi. Ambrose, this is . . . Mrs. Levi . . . she's an old friend. . . .

MRS. LEVI. Mrs. Levi, born Gallagher. Very happy to meet you, Mr. Kemper.

AMBROSE. Good morning, Mrs. Levi.

MRS. LEVI. Mr. Kemper, *the artist!* Delighted! Mr. Kemper, may I say something very frankly?

AMBROSE. Yes, Mrs. Levi.

MRS. LEVI. This thing you were planning to do is a very great mistake.

ERMENGARDE. Oh, Mrs. Levi, please explain to Ambrose—of *course!* I want to marry him, but to *elope!* . . . How . . .

MRS. LEVI. Now, my dear girl, you go in and keep one eye on your uncle. I wish to talk to Mr. Kemper for a moment. You give us a warning when you hear your Uncle Horace coming. . . .

ERMENGARDE. Ye-es, Mrs. Levi (*Exit* ERMENGARDE, *back center.*)

MRS. LEVI. Mr. Kemper, I was this dear girl's mother's oldest friend. Believe me, I am on your side. I hope you two will be married very soon, and I think I can be of real service to you. Mr. Kemper, I always go right to the point.

AMBROSE. What is the point, Mrs. Levi?

MRS. LEVI. Mr. Vandergelder is a very rich man, Mr. Kemper, and Ermengarde is his only relative.

AMBROSE. But I am not interested in Mr. Vandergelder's money. I have enough to support a wife and family.

MRS. LEVI. Enough? How much is enough when one is thinking about children and the future? The future is the most expensive luxury in the world, Mr. Kemper.

AMBROSE. Mrs. Levi, what is the point?

MRS. LEVI. Believe me, Mr. Vandergelder wishes to get rid of Ermengarde, and if you follow my suggestions he will even permit her to marry you. You see, Mr. Vandergelder is planning to get married himself.

AMBROSE. What? That monster!

MRS. LEVI. Mr. Kemper!

AMBROSE. Married! To you, Mrs. Levi?

MRS. LEVI (*taken aback*). Oh, no, no . . . NO! I am merely arranging it. I am helping him find a suitable bride.

AMBROSE. For Mr. Vandergelder there are no suitable brides.

. MRS. LEVI. I think we can safely say that Mr. Vandergelder will be married to someone by the end of next week.

AMBROSE. What are you suggesting, Mrs. Levi?

MRS. LEVI. I am taking Ermengarde to New York on the next train. I shall not take her to Miss Van Huysen's, as is planned; I shall take her to my house. I wish you to call for her at my house at five-thirty. Here is my card.

AMBROSE. "Mrs. Dolly Gallagher Levi. Varicose veins reduced."

MRS. LEVI (*trying to take back card*). I beg your pardon . . .

AMBROSE (*holding card*). I beg *your* pardon. "Consultations free."

MRS. LEVI. I meant to give you my other card. Here.

AMBROSE. "Mrs. Dolly Gallagher Levi. Aurora Hosiery. Instruction in the guitar and mandolin." You do all these things, Mrs. Levi?

MRS. LEVI. Two and two make four, Mr. Kemper—always did. So you will come to my house at five-thirty. At about six I shall take you both with me to the Harmonia Gardens Restaurant on the Battery; Mr. Vandergelder will be there and everything will be arranged.

AMBROSE. How?

MRS. LEVI. Oh, I don't know. One thing will lead to another.

AMBROSE. How do I know that I can trust you, Mrs. Levi? You could easily make our situation worse.

MRS. LEVI. Mr. Kemper, your situation could not possibly be worse.

AMBROSE. I wish I knew what you get out of this, Mrs. Levi.

MRS. LEVI. That is a very proper question. I get two things: profit and pleasure.

AMBROSE. How?

MRS. LEVI. Mr. Kemper, I am a woman who arranges things. At present I am arranging Mr. Vandergelder's domestic affairs. Out of it I get—shall we call it: little pickings? I need little pickings, Mr. Kemper, and especially just now, when I haven't got my train fare back to New York. You see: I am frank with you.

AMBROSE. That's your profit, Mrs. Levi; but where do you get your pleasure?

MRS. LEVI. My pleasure? Mr. Kemper, when you artists paint a hillside or a river you change everything a little, you make thousands of little changes, don't you? Nature is never completely satisfactory and must be corrected. Well, I'm like you artists. Life as it is is never quite interesting enough for me—I'm bored, Mr. Kemper, with life as it is—and so I do things. I put my hand in here, and I put my hand in there, and I watch and I listen—and often I'm very much amused.

AMBROSE (*rises*). Not in my affairs, Mrs. Levi.

MRS. LEVI. Wait, I haven't finished. There's another thing. I'm very interested in this household here—in Mr. Vander-

gelder and all that idle, frozen money of his. I don't like the thought of it lying in great piles, useless, motionless, in the bank, Mr. Kemper. Money should circulate like rain water. It should be flowing down among the people, through dressmakers and restaurants and cabmen, setting up a little business here, and furnishing a good time there. Do you see what I mean?

AMBROSE. Yes, I do.

MRS. LEVI. New York should be a very happy city, Mr. Kemper, but it isn't. My late husband came from Vienna; now there's a city that understands this. I want New York to be more like Vienna and less like a collection of nervous and tired ants. And if you and Ermengarde get a good deal of Mr. Vandergelder's money, I want you to see that it starts flowing in and around a lot of people's lives. And for that reason I want you to come with me to the Harmonia Gardens Restaurant tonight. (*Enter* ERMENGARDE.)

ERMENGARDE. Mrs. Levi, Uncle Horace is coming.

MRS. LEVI. Mr. Kemper, I think you'd better be going. . . . (AMBROSE *crosses to trap door and disappears down the ladder, closing trap as he goes.*) Darling girl, Mr. Kemper and I have had a very good talk. You'll see: Mr. Vandergelder and I will be dancing at your wedding very soon—(*Enter* VANDERGELDER *at back. He has now added a splendid plumed hat to his costume and is carrying a standard or small flag bearing the initials of his lodge.*) Oh, Mr. Vandergelder, how handsome you look! You take my breath away. Yes, my dear girl, I'll see you soon. (*Exit* ERMENGARDE *back center.*) Oh, Mr. Vandergelder, I wish Irene Molloy could see you now. But then! I don't know what's come over you lately. You seem to be growing younger every day.

VANDERGELDER. Allowing for exaggeration, Mrs. Levi. If a man eats careful there's no reason why he should look old.

MRS. LEVI. You never said a truer word.

VANDERGELDER. I'll never see fifty-five again.

MRS. LEVI. Fifty-five! Why, I can see at a glance that you're the sort that will be stamping about at a hundred—and eating five meals a day, like my Uncle Harry. At fifty-five my Uncle Harry was a mere boy. I'm a judge of hands, Mr. Vandergelder—show me your hand. (*Looks at it.*) Lord in heaven! What a life line!

VANDERGELDER. Where?

MRS. LEVI. From *here* to *here*. It runs right off your hand. I don't know where it goes. They'll have to hit you on the head with a mallet. They'll have to stifle you with a sofa pillow. You'll bury us all! However, to return to our business—Mr. Vandergelder, I suppose you've changed your mind again. I suppose you've given up all idea of getting married.

VANDERGELDER (*complacently*). Not at all, Mrs. Levi. I have news for you.

MRS. LEVI. News?

VANDERGELDER. Mrs. Levi, I've practically decided to ask Mrs. Molloy to be my wife.

MRS. LEVI (*taken aback*). You have?

VANDERGELDER. Yes, I have.

MRS. LEVI. Oh, you have! Well, I guess that's just about the best news I ever heard. So there's nothing more for me to do but wish you every happiness under the sun and say good-by. (*Crosses as if to leave.*)

VANDERGELDER (*stopping her*). Well—Mrs. Levi—Surely I thought—

MRS. LEVI. Well, I did have a little suggestion to make—but I won't. You're going to marry Irene Molloy, and that closes the matter.

VANDERGELDER. What suggestion was that, Mrs. Levi?

MRS. LEVI. Well—I *had* found *another* girl for you.

VANDERGELDER. Another?

MRS. LEVI. The most wonderful girl, the ideal wife.

VANDERGELDER. Another, eh? What's her name?

MRS. LEVI. Her name?

VANDERGELDER. Yes!

MRS. LEVI (*groping for it*). Err . . . er . . . her *name?*—Ernestina—Simple. *Miss Ernestina Simple.* But now of course all that's too late. After all, you're engaged—you're practically engaged to marry Irene Molloy.

VANDERGELDER. Oh, I ain't engaged to Mrs. Molloy!

MRS. LEVI. Nonsense! you can't break poor Irene's heart now and change to another girl. . . . When a man at your time of life calls four times on an attractive widow like that—and sends her a pot of geraniums—that's practically an engagement!

VANDERGELDER. That ain't an engagement!

MRS. LEVI. And yet—! If only you were free! I've found this treasure of a girl. Every moment I felt like a traitor to Irene Molloy—but let me tell you: I couldn't help it. I told this girl all about you, just as though you were a free man. Isn't that dreadful? The fact is: she has fallen in love with you already.

VANDERGELDER. Ernestina?

MRS. LEVI. Ernestina Simple.

VANDERGELDER. Ernestina Simple.

MRS. LEVI. Of course she's a very different idea from Mrs. Molloy, Ernestina is. Like her name—simple, domestic, practical.

VANDERGELDER. Can she cook?

MRS. LEVI. Cook, Mr. Vandergelder? I've had two meals from her hands, and—as I live—I don't know what I've done that God should reward me with such meals.

[*The following passage—adapted from a scene in Molière's L'Avare—has been cut in recent performances:*

MRS. LEVI (*continues*). Her duck! Her steak!

VANDERGELDER. Eh! Eh! In this house we don't eat duck and steak every day, Mrs. Levi.

MRS. LEVI. But didn't I tell you?—that's the wonderful part about it. Her duck—what was it? Pigeon! I'm alive to tell you. I don't know how she does it. It's a secret that's come down in her family. The greatest chefs would give their right hands to know it. And the steaks? Shoulder of beef—four cents a pound. Dogs wouldn't eat. But when Ernestina passes her hands over it—!!

VANDERGELDER. Allowing for exaggeration, Mrs. Levi.

MRS. LEVI. No exaggeration.]

I'm the best cook in the world myself, and I *know* what's good.

VANDERGELDER. Hm. How old is she, Mrs. Levi?

MRS. LEVI. Nineteen, well—say twenty.

VANDERGELDER. Twenty, Mrs. Levi? Girls of twenty are apt to favor young fellows of their own age.

MRS. LEVI. But you don't listen to me. And you don't know the girl. Mr. Vandergelder, she has a positive horror of flighty, brainless young men. A fine head of gray hair, she says, is worth twenty shined up with goose grease. No, sir. "I like a man that's *settled*"—in so many words she said it.

VANDERGELDER. That's . . . that's not usual, Mrs. Levi.

MRS. LEVI. Usual? I'm not wearing myself to the bone hunting up *usual* girls to interest you, Mr. Vandergelder. Usual, indeed. Listen to me. Do you know the sort of pictures she has on her wall? Is it any of these young Romeos and Lochinvars? No! —it's Moses on the Mountain—that's what she's got. If you want to make her happy, you give her a picture of Methuselah surrounded by his grandchildren. That's my advice to you.

[*Following passage—also based on Molière—has generally been cut in performance:*

VANDERGELDER. I hope . . . hm . . . that she has some means, Mrs. Levi. I have a large household to run.

MRS. LEVI. Ernestina? She'll bring you five thousand dollars a year.

VANDERGELDER. Eh! Eh!

MRS. LEVI. Listen to me, Mr. Vandergelder. You're a man of sense, I hope. A man that can reckon. In the first place, she's an orphan. She's been brought up with a great saving of food. What does she eat herself? Apples and lettuce. It's what she's been used to eat and what she likes best. She saves you two thousand a year right there. Secondly, she makes her own clothes—out of old tablecloths and window curtains. And she's the best-dressed woman in Brooklyn this minute. She saves you a thousand dollars right there. Thirdly, her health is of iron—

VANDERGELDER. But, Mrs. Levi, that's not money in the pocket.

MRS. LEVI. We're talking about marriage, aren't we, Mr. Vandergelder? The money she saves while she's in Brooklyn is none of your affair—but if she were your wife that would be *money*. Yes, sir, that's money.]

VANDERGELDER. What's her family?

MRS. LEVI. Her father?—God be good to him! He was the best—what am I trying to say?—the best undertaker in Brooklyn, respected, esteemed. He knew all the best people—knew them well, even before they died. So—well, that's the way it is.

(*Lowering her voice, intimately*) Now let me tell you a little more of her appearance. Can you hear me: as I say, a beautiful girl, beautiful, I've seen her go down the street —you know what I mean?—the young men get dizzy. They have to lean against lampposts. And she? Modest, eyes on the ground—I'm not going to tell you any more. . . . Couldn't you come to New York today?

VANDERGELDER. I was thinking of coming to New York this afternoon. . . .

MRS. LEVI. You were? Well now, I wonder if something could be arranged—oh, she's so eager to see you! Let me see . . .

VANDERGELDER. Could I . . . Mrs. Levi, could I give you a little dinner, maybe?

MRS. LEVI. Really, come to think of it, I don't see where I could get the time. I'm so busy over that wretched lawsuit of mine. Yes. If I win it, I don't mind telling you, I'll be what's called a very rich woman. I'll own half of Long Island, that's a fact. But just now I'm at my wit's end for a little help, just enough money to finish it off. My wit's end! (*She looks in her handbag. In order not hear this,* VANDERGELDER *has a series of coughs, sneezes and minor convulsions.*) But perhaps I could arrange a little dinner; I'll see. Yes, for that lawsuit all I need is fifty dollars, and Staten Island's as good as mine. I've been trotting all over New York for you, trying to find you a suitable wife.

VANDERGELDER. Fifty dollars!!

MRS. LEVI. Two whole months I've been . . .

VANDERGELDER. Fifty dollars, Mrs. Levi . . . is no joke. (*Producing purse*) I don't know where money's gone to these days. It's in hiding. . . . There's twenty . . . well, there's twenty-five. I can't spare no more, not now I can't.

MRS. LEVI. Well, this will help—will help somewhat. Now let me tell you what we'll do. I'll bring Ernestina to that restaurant on the Battery. You know it: the Harmonia Gardens. It's good, but it's not flashy. Now, Mr. Vandergelder, I think it'd be nice if just this once you'd order a real nice dinner. I guess you can afford it.

VANDERGELDER. Well, just this once.

MRS. LEVI. A chicken wouldn't hurt.

VANDERGELDER. Chicken!!— Well, just this once.

MRS. LEVI. And a little wine.

VANDERGELDER. Wine? Well, just this

once.

MRS. LEVI. Now about Mrs. Molloy—what do you think? Shall we call that subject closed?

VANDERGELDER. No, not at all, Mrs. Levi, I want to have dinner with Miss . . . with Miss . . .

MRS. LEVI. Simple.

VANDERGELDER. With Miss Simple; but first I want to make another call on Mrs. Molloy.

MRS. LEVI. Dear, dear, dear! And Miss Simple? What races you make me run! Very well; I'll meet you on one of those benches in front of Mrs. Molloy's hat store at four-thirty, as usual. (*Trap door rises, and* CORNELIUS' *head appears.*)

CORNELIUS. The buggy's here, ready for the parade, Mr. Vandergelder.

VANDERGELDER. Call Barnaby. I want to talk to both of you.

CORNELIUS. Yes, Mr. Vandergelder. (*Exit* CORNELIUS *down trap door. Leaves trap open.*)

MRS. LEVI. Now do put your thoughts in order, Mr. Vandergelder. I can't keep up setting and disturbing the finest women in New York City unless you mean business.

VANDERGELDER. Oh, I mean business all right!

MRS. LEVI. I hope so. Because, you know, you're playing a very dangerous game.

VANDERGELDER. Dangerous?—Dangerous, Mrs. Levi?

MRS. LEVI. Of course, it's dangerous—and there's a name for it! You're tampering with these women's affections, aren't you? And the only way you can save yourself now is to be married to *someone* by the end of next week. So think that over! (*Exit center back.*)

(*Enter* CORNELIUS *and* BARNABY, *by the trap door.*)

VANDERGELDER. This morning I'm joining my lodge parade, and this afternoon I'm going to New York. When I come back, there are going to be some changes in the house here. I'll tell you what the change is, but I don't want you discussing it amongst yourselves: you're going to have a mistress.

BARNABY (*seventeen; round-faced, wide-eyed innocence; wearing a green apron*). I'm too young, Mr. Vandergelder!!

VANDERGELDER. Not yours! Death and damnation! Not yours, idiot—*mine!* (*Then, realizing:*) Hey! Hold your tongue until you're spoken to! I'm thinking of getting married.

CORNELIUS (*crosses, hand outstretched*). Many congratulations, Mr. Vandergelder, and my compliments to the lady.

VANDERGELDER. That's none of your business. Now go back to the store. (*The* BOYS *start down the ladder,* BARNABY *first.*) Have you got any questions you want to ask before I go?

CORNELIUS. Mr. Vandergelder—er—Mr. Vandergelder, does the chief clerk get one evening off every week?

VANDERGELDER. So that's the way you begin being chief clerk, is it? When I was your age I got up at five; I didn't close the shop until ten at night, and then I put in a good hour at the account books. The world's going to pieces. You elegant ladies lie in bed until six and at nine o'clock at night you rush to close the door so fast the line of customers bark their noses. No, sir—you'll attend to the store as usual, and on Friday and Saturday nights you'll remain open until ten—now hear what I say! This is the first time I've been away from the store overnight. When I come back I want to hear that you've run the place perfectly in my absence. If I hear of any foolishness, I'll discharge you. An evening free! Do you suppose that *I* had evenings free? (*At the top of his complacency*) If I'd had evenings free I wouldn't be what I am now! (*He marches out, right.*)

BARNABY (*watching him go*). The horses nearly ran away when they saw him. What's the matter, Cornelius?

CORNELIUS (*sits in dejected thought*). Chief clerk! Promoted from chief clerk to chief clerk.

BARNABY. Don't you like it?

CORNELIUS. Chief clerk!—and if I'm good, in ten years I'll be promoted to chief clerk again. Thirty-three years old and I still don't get an evening free? When am I going to begin to live?

BARNABY. Well—ah . . . you can begin to live on Sundays, Cornelius.

CORNELIUS. That's not living. Twice to church, and old Wolf-trap's eyes on the back of my head the whole time. And as for holidays! What did we do last Christmas? All those canned tomatoes went bad and exploded. We had to clean up the mess all afternoon. Was that living?

BARNABY (*holding his nose at the mem-*

ory of the bad smell). No!!!

CORNELIUS (*rising with sudden resolution*). Barnaby, how much money have you got—where you can get at it?

BARNABY. Oh—three dollars. Why, Cornelius?

CORNELIUS. You and I are going to New York.

BARNABY. Cornelius!!! We can't! Close the store?

CORNELIUS. Some more rotten-tomato cans are going to explode.

BARNABY. Holy cabooses! How do you know?

CORNELIUS. I know they're rotten. All you have to do is to light a match under them. They'll make such a smell that customers can't come into the place for twenty-four hours. That'll get us an evening free. We're going to New York too, Barnaby, we're going to live! I'm going to have enough adventures to last me until I'm *partner*. So go and get your Sunday clothes on.

BARNABY. Wha-a-a-t?

CORNELIUS. Yes, I mean it. We're going to have a good meal; and we're going to be in danger; and we're going to get almost arrested; and we're going to spend all our money.

BARNABY. Holy cabooses!!

CORNELIUS. And one more thing: we're not coming back to Yonkers until we've kissed a girl.

BARNABY. Kissed a girl! Cornelius, you can't do that. You don't know any girls.

CORNELIUS. I'm thirty-three. I've got to begin sometime.

BARNABY. I'm only seventeen, Cornelius. It isn't so urgent for me.

CORNELIUS. Don't start backing down now—if the worst comes to the worst and we get discharged from here we can always join the Army.

BARNABY. Uh—did I hear you say that you'd be old Wolf-trap's partner?

CORNELIUS. How can I help it? He's growing old. If you go to bed at nine and open the store at six, you get promoted upward whether you like it or not.

BARNABY. My! Partner.

CORNELIUS. Oh, there's no way of getting away from it. You and I will be Vandergelders.

BARNABY. I? Oh, no—I may rise a little, but I'll never be a Vandergelder.

CORNELIUS. Listen—everybody thinks when he gets rich he'll be a different kind of rich person from the rich people he sees around him; later on he finds out there's only one kind of rich person, and he's it.

BARNABY. Oh, but I'll—

CORNELIUS. No. The best of all would be a person who has all the good things a poor person has, and all the good meals a rich person has, but that's never been known. No, you and I are going to be Vandergelders; all the more reason, then, for us to try and get some living and some adventure into us now—will you come, Barnaby?

BARNABY (*in a struggle with his fears, a whirlwind of words*). But Wolf-trap—KRR-pt, Gertrude—KRR-pt—(*With a sudden cry of agreement*) Yes, Cornelius!

(*Enter* MRS. LEVI, ERMENGARDE *and* GERTRUDE *from back center. The* BOYS *start down the ladder,* CORNELIUS *last.*)

MRS. LEVI. Mr. Hackl, is the trunk waiting at the station?

CORNELIUS. Yes, Mrs. Levi. (*Closes the trap door.*)

MRS. LEVI. Take a last look, Ermengarde.

ERMENGARDE. What?

MRS. LEVI. Take a last look at your girlhood home, dear. I remember when I left my home. I gave a whinny like a young colt, and off I went.

(ERMENGARDE *and* GERTRUDE *exit.*)

ERMENGARDE (*as they go*). Oh, Gertrude, do you think I ought to get married this way? A young girl has to be so careful!

(MRS. LEVI *is alone. She addresses the audience.*)

MRS. LEVI. You know, I think I'm going to have this room with *blue* wallpaper,—yes, in blue! (*Hurries out after the others.*)

(BARNABY *comes up trap door, looks off right, then lies on floor, gazing down through the trap door.*)

BARNABY. All clear up here, Cornelius! Cornelius—hold the candle steady a minute—the bottom row's all right—but try the top now . . . they're swelled up like they are ready to bust! (*BANG.*) Holy CABOOSES! (*BANG, BANG.*) Cornelius! I can smell it up here! (*Rises and dances about, holding his nose.*)

CORNELIUS (*rushing up the trap door*). Get into your Sunday clothes, Barnaby. We're going to New York!

As they run out . . . there is a big ex-

plosion. A shower of tomato cans comes up from below, as—

THE CURTAIN FALLS

ACT TWO

MRS. MOLLOY's *hat shop, New York City. There are two entrances. One door at the extreme right of the back wall, to* MRS. MOLLOY's *workroom; one at the back left corner, to the street. The whole left wall is taken up with the show windows, filled with hats. It is separated from the shop by a low brass rail, hung with net; during the act both* MRS. MOLLOY *and* BARNABY *stoop under the rail and go into the shop window. By the street door stands a large cheval glass. In the middle of the back wall is a large wardrobe or clothes cupboard, filled with ladies' coats, large enough for* CORNELIUS *to hide in. At the left, beginning at the back wall, between the wardrobe and the workroom door, a long counter extends toward the audience, almost to the footlights. In the center of the room is a large round table with a low-hanging red cloth. There are a small gilt chair by the wardrobe and two chairs in front of the counter. Over the street door and the workroom door are bells which ring when the doors are opened.*

As the curtain rises, MRS. MOLLOY *is in the window, standing on a box, reaching up to put hats on the stand.* MINNIE FAY *is sewing by the counter.* MRS. MOLLOY *has a pair of felt overshoes, to be removed later.*

MRS. MOLLOY. Minnie, you're a fool. Of course I shall marry Horace Vandergelder.

MINNIE. Oh, Mrs. Molloy! I didn't ask you. I wouldn't dream of asking you such a personal question.

MRS. MOLLOY. Well, it's what you meant, isn't it? And there's your answer. I shall certainly marry Horace Vandergelder if he asks me. (*Crawls under window rail, into the room, singing loudly.*)

MINNIE. I know it's none of my business . . .

MRS. MOLLOY. Speak up, Minnie, I can't hear you.

MINNIE. . . . but do you . . . do you . . . ?

MRS. MOLLOY (*having crossed the room, is busy at the counter*). Minnie, you're a

fool. Say it: Do I love him? Of course, I don't love him. But I have two good reasons for marrying him just the same. Minnie, put something on that hat. It's not ugly enough. (*Throws hat over counter.*)

MINNIE (*catching and taking hat to table*). Not ugly enough!

MRS. MOLLOY. I couldn't sell it. Put a . . . put a sponge on it.

MINNIE. Why, Mrs. Molloy, you're in such a *mood* today.

MRS. MOLLOY. In the first place I shall marry Mr. Vandergelder to get away from the millinery business. I've hated it from the first day I had anything to do with it. Minnie, I hate hats. (*Sings loudly again.*)

MINNIE. Why, what's the matter with the millinery business?

MRS. MOLLOY (*crossing to window with two hats*). I can no longer stand being suspected of being a wicked woman, while I have nothing to show for it. I can't stand it. (*She crawls under rail into window.*)

MINNIE. Why, no one would dream of suspecting you—

MRS. MOLLOY (*on her knees, she looks over the rail*). Minnie, you're a fool. All millineresses are suspected of being wicked women. Why, half the time all those women come into the shop merely to look at me.

MINNIE. Oh!

MRS. MOLLOY. They enjoy the suspicion. But they aren't certain. If they were *certain* I was a wicked woman, they wouldn't put foot in this place again. Do I go to restaurants? No, it would be bad for business. Do I go to balls, or theatres, or operas? No, it would be bad for business. The only men I ever meet are feather merchants. (*Crawls out of window, but gazes intently into the street.*) What are those two young men doing out there on that park bench? Take my word for it, Minnie, either I marry Horace Vandergelder, or I break out of this place like a fire engine. I'll go to every theatre and ball and opera in New York City. (*Returns to counter, singing again.*)

MINNIE. But Mr. Vandergelder's not . . .

MRS. MOLLOY. Speak up, Minnie, I can't hear you.

MINNIE. . . . I don't think he's attractive.

MRS. MOLLOY. But what I think he is—and it's very important—I think he'd make a good fighter.

MINNIE. Mrs. Molloy!

MRS. MOLLOY. Take my word for it, Minnie: the best part of married life is the fights. The rest is merely so-so.

MINNIE (*fingers in ears*). I won't listen.

MRS. MOLLOY. *Peter Molloy*—God rest him!—was a fine arguing man. I pity the woman whose husband slams the door and walks out of the house at the beginning of an argument. Peter Molloy would stand up and fight for hours on end. He'd even throw things, Minnie, and there's no pleasure to equal that. When I felt tired I'd start a good bloodwarming fight and it'd take ten years off my age; now Horace Vandergelder would put up a good fight; I know it. I've a mind to marry him.

MINNIE. I think they're just awful, the things you're saying today.

MRS. MOLLOY. Well, I'm enjoying them myself, too.

MINNIE (*at the window*). Mrs. Molloy, those two men out in the street—

MRS. MOLLOY. What?

MINNIE. Those men. It looks as if they meant to come in here.

MRS. MOLLOY. Well now, it's time some men came into this place. I give you the younger one, Minnie.

MINNIE. Aren't you terrible!

(MRS. MOLLOY *sits on center table, while* MINNIE *takes off her felt overshoes.*)

MRS. MOLLOY. Wait till I get my hands on that older one! Mark my words, Minnie, we'll get an adventure out of this yet. Adventure, adventure! Why does everybody have adventures except me, Minnie? Because I have no spirit, I have no gumption. Minnie, they're coming in here. Let's go into the workroom and make them wait for us for a minute.

MINNIE. Oh, but Mrs. Molloy . . . my work! . . .

MRS. MOLLOY (*running to workroom*). Hurry up, be quick now, Minnie!

(*They go out to workroom.* BARNABY *and* CORNELIUS *run in from street, leaving front door open. They are dressed in the stiff discomfort of their Sunday clothes.* CORNELIUS *wears a bowler hat,* BARNABY *a straw hat too large for him.*)

BARNABY. No one's here.

CORNELIUS. Some women were here a minute ago. I saw them. (*They jump back to the street door and peer down the street.*) That's Wolf-trap all right! (*Com-ing back.*) Well, we've got to hide here until he passes by.

BARNABY. He's sitting down on that bench. It may be quite a while.

CORNELIUS. When these women come in, we'll have to make conversation until he's gone away. We'll pretend we're buying a hat. How much money have you got now?

BARNABY (*counting his money*). Forty cents for the train—seventy cents for dinner—twenty cents to see the whale—and a dollar I lost—I have seventy cents.

CORNELIUS. And I have a dollar seventy-five. I wish I knew how much hats cost!

BARNABY. Is this an adventure, Cornelius?

CORNELIUS. No, but it may be.

BARNABY. I think it is. There we wander around New York all day and nothing happens; and then we come to the quietest street in the whole city and suddenly Mr. Vandergelder turns the corner. (*Going to door.*) I think that's an adventure. I think . . . Cornelius! That Mrs. Levi is there now. She's sitting down on the bench with him.

CORNELIUS. What do you know about that! We know only one person in all New York City, and there she is!

BARNABY. Even if our adventure came along now I'd be too tired to enjoy it. Cornelius, why isn't this an adventure?

CORNELIUS. Don't be asking that. When you're in an adventure, you'll know it all right.

BARNABY. Maybe I wouldn't Cornelius, let's arrange a signal for you to give me when an adventure's really going on. For instance, Cornelius, you say . . . uh . . . uh . . . *pudding;* you say *pudding* to me if it's an adventure we're in.

CORNELIUS. I wonder where the lady who runs this store is? What's her name again?

BARNABY. "Mrs. Molloy, hats for ladies."

CORNELIUS. Oh yes. I must think over what I'm going to say when she comes in. (*To counter.*) "Good afternoon, Mrs. Molloy, wonderful weather we're having. We've been looking everywhere for some beautiful hats."

BARNABY. That's fine, Cornelius!

CORNELIUS. "Good afternoon, Mrs. Molloy; wonderful weather . . ." We'll make her think we're very rich. (*One hand in trouser pocket, the other on back of chair.*) "Good afternoon, Mrs. Molloy . . ." You keep one eye on the door the whole time.

"We've been looking everywhere for . . ."
(*Enter* MRS. MOLLOY *from the workroom.*)

MRS. MOLLOY (*behind the counter*). Oh, I'm sorry. Have I kept you waiting? Good afternoon, gentlemen.

CORNELIUS (*hat off*). Here, Cornelius Hackl.

BARNABY (*hat off*). Here, Barnaby Tucker.

MRS. MOLLOY. I'm very happy to meet you. Perhaps I can help you. Won't you sit down?

CORNELIUS. Thank you, we will. (*The* BOYS *place their hats on the table, then sit down at the counter facing* MRS. MOLLOY.) You see, Mrs. Molloy, we're looking for hats. We've looked everywhere. Do you know what we heard? Go to Mrs. Molloy's, they said. So we came here. Only place we *could* go . . .

MRS. MOLLOY. Well now, that's *very* complimentary.

CORNELIUS. . . . and we were right. Everybody was right.

MRS. MOLLOY. You wish to choose some hats for a friend?

CORNELIUS. Yes, exactly. (*Kicks* BARNABY.)

BARNABY. Yes, exactly.

CORNELIUS. We were thinking of five or six, weren't we, Barnaby?

BARNABY. Er—five.

CORNELIUS. You see, Mrs. Molloy, money's no object with us. None at all.

MRS. MOLLOY. Why, Mr. Hackl . . .

CORNELIUS (*rises and goes toward street door*). . . . I beg your pardon, what an interesting street! Something happening every minute. Passers-by, and . . . (BARNABY *runs to join him.*)

MRS. MOLLOY. You're from out of town, Mr. Hackl?

CORNELIUS (*coming back*). Yes, ma'am —Barnaby, just keep your eye on the street, will you? You won't see that in Yonkers every day. (BARNABY *remains kneeling at street door.*)

BARNABY. Oh yes, I will.

CORNELIUS. Not all of it.

MRS. MOLLOY. Now this friend of yours —couldn't she come in with you someday and choose her hats herself?

CORNELIUS (*sits at counter*). No. Oh, no. It's a surprise for her.

MRS. MOLLOY. Indeed? That may be a little difficult, Mr. Hackl. It's not entirely customary.—Your friend's very interested in the street, Mr. Hackl.

CORNELIUS. Oh yes. Yes. He has reason to be.

MRS. MOLLOY. You said you were from out of town?

CORNELIUS. Yes, we're from Yonkers.

MRS. MOLLOY. Yonkers?

CORNELIUS. Yonkers . . . yes, Yonkers. (*He gazes rapt into her eyes.*) You should know Yonkers, Mrs. Molloy. Hudson River; Palisades; drives; some say it's the most beautiful town in the world; that's what they say.

MRS. MOLLOY. Is that so!

CORNELIUS (*rises*). Mrs. Molloy, if you ever had a Sunday free, I'd . . . we'd like to show you Yonkers. Y' know, it's very historic, too.

MRS. MOLLOY. That's very kind of you. Well, perhaps . . . now about those hats. (*Takes two hats from under counter, and crosses to back center of the room.*)

CORNELIUS (*following*). Is there . . . Have you a . . . Maybe Mr. Molloy would like to see Yonkers too?

MRS. MOLLOY. Oh, I'm a widow, Mr. Hackl.

CORNELIUS (*joyfully*). You are! (*With sudden gravity*) Oh, that's too bad. Mr. Molloy would have enjoyed Yonkers.

MRS. MOLLOY. Very likely. Now about these hats. Is your friend dark or light?

CORNELIUS. Don't think about that for a minute. Any hat you'd like would be perfectly all right with her.

MRS. MOLLOY. Really! (*She puts one on.*) Do you like this one?

CORNELIUS (*in awe-struck admiration*). Barnaby! (*In sudden anger*) Barnaby! Look! (BARNABY *turns; unimpressed, he laughs vaguely, and turns to door again.*) Mrs. Molloy, that's the most beautiful hat I ever saw. (BARNABY *now crawls under the rail into the window.*)

MRS. MOLLOY. Your friend is acting very strangely, Mr. Hackl.

CORNELIUS. Barnaby, stop acting strangely. When the street's quiet and empty, come back and talk to us. What was I saying? Oh yes: Mrs. Molloy, you should know Yonkers.

MRS. MOLLOY (*hat off*). The fact is, I have a friend in Yonkers. Perhaps you know him. It's always so foolish to ask in cases like that, isn't it? (*They both laugh over this with increasing congeniality.* MRS.

MOLLOY *goes to counter with hats from table.* CORNELIUS *follows.*) It's a Mr. Vandergelder.

CORNELIUS (*stops abruptly*). What was that you said?

MRS. MOLLOY. Then you do know him?

CORNELIUS. Horace Vandergelder?

MRS. MOLLOY. Yes, that's right.

CORNÉLIUS. Know him! (*Look to* BARNABY.) Why, no. No!

BARNABY. No! No!

CORNELIUS (*starting to glide about the room, in search of a hiding place*). I beg your pardon, Mrs. Molloy—what an attractive shop you have! (*Smiling fixedly at her he moves to the workshop door.*) And where does this door lead to? (*Opens it, and is alarmed by the bell which rings above it.*)

MRS. MOLLOY. Why, Mr. Hackl, that's my workroom.

CORNELIUS. Everything here is so interesting. (*Looks under counter.*) Every corner. Every door, Mrs. Molloy. Barnaby, notice the interesting doors and cupboards. (*He opens the cupboard door.*) Deeply interesting. Coats for ladies. (*Laughs.*) Barnaby, make a note of the table. Precious piece of furniture, with a low-hanging cloth, I see. (*Stretches his leg under table.*)

MRS. MOLLOY (*taking a hat from box left of wardrobe*). Perhaps your friend might like some of this new Italian straw. Mr. Vandergelder's a substantial man and very well liked, they tell me.

CORNELIUS. A lovely man, Mrs. Molloy.

MRS. MOLLOY. Oh yes—charming, charming!

CORNELIUS (*smiling sweetly*). Has only one fault, as far as I know; he's hard as nails; but apart from that, as you say, a charming nature, ma'am.

MRS. MOLLOY. And a large circle of friends—?

CORNELIUS. Yes, indeed, yes indeed—five or six.

BARNABY. Five!

CORNELIUS. He comes and calls on you here from time to time, I suppose.

MRS. MOLLOY (*turns from mirror where she has been putting a hat on*). This summer we'll be wearing ribbons down our back. Yes, as a matter of fact I am expecting a call from him this afternoon. (*Hat off.*)

BARNABY. I think . . . Cornelius! I think . . . !!

MRS. MOLLOY. Now to show you some more hats—

BARNABY. Look out! (*He takes a flying leap over the rail and flings himself under the table.*)

CORNELIUS. Begging your pardon, Mrs. Molloy. (*He jumps into the cupboard.*)

MRS. MOLLOY. Gentlemen! Mr. Hackl! Come right out of there this minute!

CORNELIUS (*sticking his head out of the wardrobe door*). Help us just this once, Mrs. Molloy! We'll explain later!

MRS. MOLLOY. Mr. Hackl!

BARNABY. We're as innocent as can be, Mrs. Molloy.

MRS. MOLLOY. But really! Gentlemen! I can't have this! *What are you doing?*

BARNABY. Cornelius! Cornelius! Pudding?

CORNELIUS (*a shout*). Pudding!

(*They disappear. Enter from the street* MRS. LEVI, *followed by* MR. VANDERGELDER. VANDERGELDER *is dressed in a too-bright checked suit, and wears a green derby—or bowler—hat. He is carrying a large ornate box of chocolates in one hand, and a cane in the other.*)

MRS. LEVI. Irene, my darling child, how *are* you? Heaven be good to us, how well you look! (*They kiss.*)

MRS. MOLLOY. But what a surprise! And Mr. Vandergelder in New York—what a pleasure!

VANDERGELDER (*swaying back and forth on his heels complacently*). Good afternoon, Mrs. Molloy. (*They shake hands.* MRS. MOLLOY *brings chair from counter for him. He sits at left of table.*)

MRS. LEVI. Yes, Mr. Vandergelder's in New York. Yonkers lies up there—*decimated* today. Irene, we thought we'd pay you a very short call. Now you'll tell us if it's inconvenient, won't you?

MRS. MOLLOY (*placing a chair for* MRS. LEVI *at right of table*). Inconvenient, Dolly! The idea! Why, it's sweet of you to come. (*She notices the boys' hats on the table—sticks a spray of flowers into crown of* CORNELIUS' *bowler and winds a piece of chiffon round* BARNABY's *panama.*)

VANDERGELDER. We waited outside a moment.

MRS. LEVI. Mr. Vandergelder thought he saw two customers coming in—two men.

MRS. MOLLOY. Men! Men, Mr. Vandergelder? Why, what will you be saying next?

MRS. LEVI. Then we'll sit down for a minute or two. . . .

MRS. MOLLOY (*wishing to get them out of the shop into the workroom*). Before you sit down—(*She pushes them both.*) Before you sit down, there's something I want to show you. I want to show Mr. Vandergelder my workroom, too.

MRS. LEVI. I've seen the workroom a hundred times. I'll stay right here and try on some of these hats.

MRS. MOLLOY. No, Dolly, you come too. I have something for you. Come along, everybody. (*Exit* MRS. LEVI *to workroom.*) Mr. Vandergelder, I want your advice. You don't know how helpless a woman in business is. Oh, I feel I need advice every minute from a fine business head like yours. (*Exit* VANDERGELDER *to workroom.* MRS. MOLLOY *shouts this line and then slams the workroom door.*) Now I shut the door!! (*Exit* MRS. MOLLOY.)

(CORNELIUS *puts his head out of the wardrobe door and gradually comes out into the room, leaving door open.*)

CORNELIUS. Hsst!

BARNABY (*pokes his head out from under the table*). Maybe she wants us to go, Cornelius?

CORNELIUS. Certainly I won't go. Mrs. Molloy would think we were just thoughtless fellows. No, all I want is to stretch a minute.

BARNABY. What are you going to do when he's gone, Cornelius? Are we just going to run away?

CORNELIUS. Well . . . I don't know yet. I like Mrs. Molloy a lot. I wouldn't like her to think badly of me. I think I'll buy a hat. We can walk home to Yonkers, even if it takes us all night. I wonder how much hats cost. Barnaby, give me all the money you've got. (*As he leans over to take the money, he sneezes. Both return to their hiding places in alarm; then emerge again.*) My, all those perfumes in that cupboard tickle my nose! But I like it in there . . . it's a woman's world, and very different.

BARNABY. I like it where I am, too; only I'd like it better if I had a pillow.

CORNELIUS (*taking coat from wardrobe*). Here, take one of these coats. I'll roll it up for you so it won't get mussed. Ladies don't like to have their coats mussed.

BARNABY. That's fine. Now I can just lie here and hear Mr. Vandergelder talk.

(CORNELIUS *goes slowly above table toward cheval mirror, repeating* MRS. MOLLOY's *line dreamily.*)

CORNELIUS. This summer we'll be wearing ribbons down our back. . . .

BARNABY. Can I take off my shoes, Cornelius?

(CORNELIUS *does not reply. He comes to the footlights and addresses the audience, in completely simple naïve sincerity.*)

CORNELIUS. Isn't the world full of wonderful things. There we sit cooped up in Yonkers for years and years and all the time wonderful people like Mrs. Molloy are walking around in New York and we don't know them at all. I don't know whether—from where you're sitting—you can see—well, for instance, the way (*He points to the edge of his right eye.*) her eye and forehead and cheek come together, up here. Can you? And the kind of fireworks that shoot out of her eyes all the time. I tell you right now: a fine woman is the greatest work of God. You can talk all you like about Niagara Falls and the Pyramids; they aren't in it at all. Of course, up there at Yonkers they came into the store all the time, and bought this and that, and I said, "Yes, ma'am," and "That'll be seventy-five cents, ma'am"; and I *watched* them. But today I've talked to one, equal to equal, equal to equal, and to the finest one that ever existed, in my opinion. They're so different from men! Everything that they say and do is so different that you feel like laughing all the time. (*He laughs.*) Golly, they're different from men. And they're awfully mysterious, too. You never can be really sure what's going on in their heads. They have a kind of wall around them all the time—of pride and a sort of play-acting: I bet you could know a woman a hundred years without ever being really sure whether she liked you or not. This minute I'm in danger. I'm in danger of losing my job and my future and everything that people think is important; but I don't care. Even if I have to dig ditches for the rest of my life, I'll be a ditch digger who once had a wonderful day.

Barnaby!

BARNABY. Oh, you woke me up!

CORNELIUS (*kneels*). Barnaby, we can't go back to Yonkers yet and you know why.

BARNABY. Why not?

CORNELIUS. We've had a good meal. We've had an adventure. We've been in danger of getting arrested. There's only one more thing we've got to do before we go back to be successes in Yonkers.

BARNABY. Cornelius! You're never going to kiss Mrs. Molloy!

CORNELIUS. Maybe.

BARNABY. But she'll scream.

CORNELIUS. Barnaby, you don't know anything at all. You might as well know right now that everybody except us goes through life kissing right and left all the time.

BARNABY (*pauses for reflection: humbly*). Well, thanks for telling me, Cornelius. I often wondered. (*Enter* MRS. LEVI *from workroom.*)

MRS. LEVI. Just a minute, Irene. I must find my handkerchief. (CORNELIUS, *caught by the arrival of* MRS. LEVI, *drops to his hands and knees, and starts very slowly to crawl back to the wardrobe, as though the slowness rendered him invisible.* MRS. LEVI, *leaning over the counter, watches him. From the cupboard he puts his head out of it and looks pleadingly at her.*) Why, Mr. Hackl, I thought you were up in Yonkers.

CORNELIUS. I almost always am, Mrs. Levi. Oh, Mrs. Levi, don't tell Mr. Vandergelder! I'll explain everything later.

BARNABY (*puts head out*). We're terribly innocent, Mrs. Levi.

MRS. LEVI. Why, who's that?

BARNABY. Barnaby Tucker—just paying a call.

MRS. LEVI (*looking under counter and even shaking out her skirts*). Well, who else is here?

CORNELIUS. Just the two of us, Mrs. Levi, that's all.

MRS. LEVI. Old friends of Mrs. Molloy's, is that it?

CORNELIUS. We never knew her before a few minutes ago, but we like her a lot—don't we, Barnaby? In fact, I think she's . . . I think she's the finest person in the world. I'm ready to tell that to anybody.

MRS. LEVI. And does she think *you're* the finest person in the world?

CORNELIUS. Oh, no. I don't suppose she even notices that I'm alive.

MRS. LEVI. Well, I think she must notice that you're alive in that cupboard, Mr. Hackl. Well, if I were you, I'd get back into it right away. Somebody could be coming in any minute.

(CORNELIUS *disappears. She sits unconcernedly in chair right. Enter* MRS. MOL-LOY.)

MRS. MOLLOY (*leaving door open and looking about in concealed alarm*). Can I help you, Dolly?

MRS. LEVI. No, no, no. I was just blowing my nose.

(*Enter* VANDERGELDER *from workroom.*)

VANDERGELDER. Mrs. Molloy, I've got some advice to give you about your business.

(MRS. MOLLOY *comes to the center of the room and puts* BARNABY's *hat on floor in window, then Cornelius' hat on the counter.*)

MRS. LEVI. Oh, advice from Mr. Vandergelder! The whole city should hear this.

VANDERGELDER (*standing in the workroom door, pompously*). In the first place, the aim of business is to make profit.

MRS. MOLLOY. Is that so?

MRS. LEVI. I never heard it put so clearly before. Did you hear it?

VANDERGELDER (*crossing the room to the left*). You pay those girls of yours too much. You pay them as much as men. Girls like that enjoy their work. Wages, Mrs. Molloy, are paid to make people do work they don't want to do.

MRS. LEVI. Mr. Vandergelder thinks so ably. And that's exactly the way his business is run up in Yonkers.

VANDERGELDER (*patting her hand*). Mrs. Molloy, I'd like for you to come up to Yonkers.

MRS. MOLLOY. That would be very nice. (*He hands her the box of chocolates.*) Oh, thank you. As a matter of fact, I know someone from Yonkers, someone else.

VANDERGELDER (*hangs hat on the cheval mirror*). Oh? Who's that?

(MRS. MOLLOY *puts chocolates on table and brings gilt chair forward and sits center at table facing the audience.*)

MRS. MOLLOY. Someone quite well-to-do, I believe, though a little free and easy in his behavior. Mr. Vandergelder, do you know Mr. Cornelius Hackl in Yonkers?

VANDERGELDER. I know him like I know my own boot. He's my head clerk.

MRS. MOLLOY. Is that so?

VANDERGELDER. He's been in my store for ten years.

MRS. MOLLOY. Well, I never!

VANDERGELDER. Where would you have known him?

(MRS. MOLLOY *is in silent confusion. She looks for help to* MRS. LEVI, *seated at right end of table.*)

MRS. LEVI (*groping for means to help* MRS. MOLLOY). Err . . . blah . . . err . . . bl . . . er . . . Oh, just one of those chance meetings, I suppose.

MRS. MOLLOY. Yes, oh yes! One of those chance meetings.

VANDERGELDER. What? Chance meetings? Cornelius Hackl has no right to chance meetings. Where was it?

MRS. MOLLOY. Really, Mr. Vandergelder, it's very unlike you to question me in such a way. I think Mr. Hackl is better known than you think he is.

VANDERGELDER. Nonsense.

MRS. MOLLOY. He's in New York often, and he's very well liked.

MRS. LEVI (*having found her idea, with decision*). Well, the truth might as well come out now as later. Mr. Vandergelder, Irene is quite right. Your head clerk is often in New York. Goes everywhere; has an army of friends. Everybody knows Cornelius Hackl.

VANDERGELDER (*laughs blandly and sits in chair at left of table*). He never comes to New York. He works all day in my store and at nine o'clock at night he goes to sleep in the bran room.

MRS. LEVI. So you think. But it's not true.

VANDERGELDER. Dolly Gallagher, you're crazy.

MRS. LEVI. Listen to me. You keep your nose so deep in your account books you don't know what goes on. Yes, by day, Cornelius Hackl is your faithful trusted clerk—that's true; but by night! Well, he leads a double life, that's all! He's here at the opera; at the great restaurants; in all the fashionable homes . . . why, he's at the Harmonia Gardens Restaurant three nights a week. The fact is, he's the wittiest, gayest, naughtiest, most delightful man in New York. Well, he's just *the* famous Cornelius Hackl!

VANDERGELDER (*sure of himself*). It ain't the same man. If I ever thought Cornelius Hackl came to New York, I'd discharge him.

MRS. LEVI. Who took the horses out of Jenny Lind's carriage and pulled her through the streets?

MRS. MOLLOY. Who?

MRS. LEVI. Cornelius Hackl! Who dressed up as waiter at the Fifth Avenue Hotel the other night and took an oyster and dropped it right down Mrs. . . . (*Rises.*)

No, it's too wicked to tell you!

MRS. MOLLOY. Oh yes, Dolly, tell it! Go on!

MRS. LEVI. No. But it *was* Cornelius Hackl.

VANDERGELDER (*loud*). It ain't the same man. Where'd he get the money?

MRS. LEVI. But he's very rich.

VANDERGELDER (*rises*). Rich! I keep his money in my own safe. He has a hundred and forty-six dollars and thirty-five cents.

MRS. LEVI. Oh, Mr. Vandergelder, you're killing me! Do come to your senses. He's one of *the* Hackls.

(MRS. MOLLOY *sits at chair right of table where* MRS. LEVI *has been sitting.*)

VANDERGELDER. *The* Hackls?

MRS. LEVI. They built the Raritan Canal.

VANDERGELDER. Then why should he work in my store?

MRS. LEVI. Well, I'll tell you. (*Sits at the center of the table, facing the audience.*)

VANDERGELDER (*striding about*). I don't want to hear! I've got a headache! I'm going home. *It ain't the same man!!* He sleeps in my bran room. You can't get away from facts. I just made him my chief clerk.

MRS. LEVI. If you had any sense you'd make him partner. (*Rises, crosses to* MRS. MOLLOY.) Now Irene, I can see you were as taken with him as everybody else is.

MRS. MOLLOY. Why, I only met him once, very hastily.

MRS. LEVI. Yes, but I can see that you were taken with him. Now don't you be thinking of marrying him!

MRS. MOLLOY (*her hands on her cheeks*). Dolly! What are you saying! Oh!

MRS. LEVI. Maybe it'd be fine. But think it over carefully. He breaks hearts like hickory nuts.

VANDERGELDER. Who?

MRS. LEVI. Cornelius Hackl!

VANDERGELDER. Mrs. Molloy, how often has he called on you?

MRS. MOLLOY. Oh, I'm telling the truth. I've only seen him once in my life. Dolly Levi's been exaggerating so. I don't know where to look!

(*Enter* MINNIE *from workroom and crosses to window.*)

MINNIE. Excuse me, Mrs. Molloy. I must get together that order for Mrs. Parkinson.

MRS. MOLLOY. Yes, we must get that off before closing.

MINNIE. I want to send it off by the errand girl. (*Having taken a hat from the window.*) Oh, I almost forgot the coat. (*She starts for the wardrobe.*)

MRS. MOLLOY (*running to the wardrobe to prevent her*). Oh, oh! I'll do that, Minnie! (*But she is too late.* MINNIE *opens the right-hand cupboard door and falls back in terror, and screams.*)

MINNIE. Oh, Mrs. Molloy! Help! There's a man!

(MRS. MOLLOY *with the following speech pushes her back to the workroom door.* MINNIE *walks with one arm pointing at the cupboard. At the end of each of* MRS. MOLLOY'S *sentences she repeats—at the same pitch and degree—the words: "There's a man!"*)

MRS. MOLLOY (*slamming cupboard door*). Minnie, you imagined it. You're tired, dear. You go back in the workroom and lie down. Minnie, you're a fool; hold your tongue!

MINNIE. There's a man! (*Exit* MINNIE *to workroom.*)

(MRS. MOLLOY *returns to the front of the stage.* VANDERGELDER *raises his stick threateningly.*)

VANDERGELDER. If there's a man there, we'll get him out. Whoever you are, come out of there! (*Strikes table with his stick.*)

MRS. LEVI (*goes masterfully to the cupboard—sweeps her umbrella around among the coats and closes each door as she does so*). Nonsense! There is no man there. See! Miss Fay's nerves have been playing tricks on her. Come now, let's sit down again. What were you saying, Mr. Vandergelder? (*They sit,* MRS. MOLLOY *right,* MRS. LEVI *center,* VANDERGELDER *left. A sneeze is heard from the cupboard. They all rise, look toward cupboard, then sit again.*) Well now . . . (*Another tremendous sneeze. With a gesture that says, "I can do no more."*) God bless you!

(*They all rise.* MRS. MOLLOY *stands with her back to the cupboard.*)

MRS. MOLLOY (*to* VANDERGELDER). Yes, there is a man in there. I'll explain it all to you another time. Thank you very much for coming to see me. Good afternoon, Dolly. Good afternoon, Mr. Vandergelder.

VANDERGELDER. You're protecting a man in there!

MRS. MOLLOY (*with back to cupboard*). There's a very simple explanation, but for the present, good afternoon.

(BARNABY *now sneezes twice, lifting the table each time.* VANDERGELDER, *right of table, jerks off the tablecloth.* BARNABY *pulls cloth under table and rolls himself up in it.* MRS. MOLLOY *picks up the box of chocolates, which has rolled on to the floor.*)

MRS. LEVI. Lord, the whole room's *crawling* with men! I'll never get over it.

VANDERGELDER. The world is going to pieces! I can't believe my own eyes!

MRS. LEVI. Come, Mr. Vandergelder. Ernestina Simple is waiting for us.

VANDERGELDER (*finds his hat and puts it on*). Mrs. Molloy, I shan't trouble you again, and *vice versa.*

(MRS. MOLLOY *is standing transfixed in front of cupboard, clasping the box of chocolates.* VANDERGELDER *snatches the box from her and goes out.*)

MRS. LEVI (*crosses to her*). Irene, when I think of all the interesting things you have in this room! (*Kisses her.*) Make the most of it, dear. (*Raps cupboard.*) Good-by! (*Raps on table with umbrella.*) Good-by! (*Exit* MRS. LEVI.)

(MRS. MOLLOY *opens door of cupboard.* CORNELIUS *steps out.*)

MRS. MOLLOY. So that was one of your practical jokes, Mr. Hackl?

CORNELIUS. No, no, Mrs. Molloy!

MRS. MOLLOY. Come out from under that, Barnaby Tucker, you troublemaker! (*She snatches the cloth and spreads it back on table.* MINNIE *enters.*) There's nothing to be afraid of, Minnie, I know all about these gentlemen.

CORNELIUS. Mrs. Molloy, we realize that what happened here—

MRS. MOLLOY. You think because you're rich you can make up for all the harm you do, is that it?

CORNELIUS. No, no!

BARNABY (*on the floor putting shoes on*). No, no!

MRS. MOLLOY. Minnie, this is the famous Cornelius Hackl who goes round New York tying people into knots; and that's Barnaby Tucker, another troublemaker.

BARNABY. How d'you do?

MRS. MOLLOY. Minnie, choose yourself any hat and coat in the store. We're going out to dinner. If this Mr. Hackl is so rich and gay and charming, he's going to be rich and gay and charming to us. He dines three nights a week at the Harmonia Gardens Restaurant, does he? Well, he's taking us there now.

MINNIE. Mrs. Molloy, are you sure it's safe?

MRS. MOLLOY. Minnie, hold your tongue. We're in a position to put these men into jail if they so much as squeak.

CORNELIUS. Jail, Mrs. Molloy?

MRS. MOLLOY. Jail, Mr. Hackl. Officer Cogarty does everything I tell him to do. Minnie, you and I have been respectable for years; now we're in disgrace, we might as well make the most of it. Come into the workroom with me; I know some ways we can perk up our appearances. Gentlemen, we'll be back in a minute.

CORNELIUS. Uh—Mrs. Molloy, I hear there's an awfully good restaurant at the railway station.

MRS. MOLLOY (*high indignation*). Railway station? Railway station? Certainly not! No, sir! You're going to give us a good dinner in the heart of the fashionable world. Go on in, Minnie! Don't you boys forget that you've made us lose our reputations, and now the fashionable world's the only place we *can* eat. (MRS. MOLLOY *exits to workroom.*)

BARNABY. She's angry at us, Cornelius. Maybe we'd better run away now.

CORNELIUS. No, I'm going to go through with this if it kills me. Barnaby, for a woman like that a man could consent to go back to Yonkers and be a success.

BARNABY. All I know is no woman's going to make a success out of me.

CORNELIUS. Jail or no jail, we're going to take those ladies out to dinner. So grit your teeth.

(*Enter* MRS. MOLLOY *and* MINNIE *from workroom dressed for the street.*)

MRS. MOLLOY. Gentlemen, the cabs are at the corner, so forward march! (*She takes a hat—which will be* BARNABY's *at the end of Act III—and gives it to* MINNIE.)

CORNELIUS. Yes, ma'am. (BARNABY *stands shaking his empty pockets warningly.*) Oh, Mrs. Molloy . . . is it far to the restaurant? Couldn't we walk?

MRS. MOLLOY (*pauses a moment, then*). Minnie, take off your things. We're not going.

OTHERS. Mrs. Molloy!

MRS. MOLLOY. Mr. Hackl, I don't go anywhere I'm not wanted. Good night. I'm not very happy to have met you. (*She crosses the stage as though going to the workroom door.*)

OTHERS. Mrs. Molloy!

MRS. MOLLOY. I suppose you think we're not fashionable enough for you? Well, I won't be a burden to you. Good night, Mr. Tucker. (*The others follow her behind counter:* CORNELIUS, BARNABY, *then* MINNIE.)

CORNELIUS. We want you to come with us more than anything in the world, Mrs. Molloy.

(MRS. MOLLOY *turns and pushes the three back. They are now near the center of the stage, to the right of the table,* MRS. MOLLOY *facing the audience.*)

MRS. MOLLOY. No, you don't! Look at you! Look at the pair of them, Minnie! Scowling, both of them!

CORNELIUS. Please, Mrs. Molloy!

MRS. MOLLOY. Then smile. (*To* BARNABY) Go on, smile! No, that's not enough. Minnie, you come with me and we'll get our own supper.

CORNELIUS. Smile, Barnaby, you lout!

BARNABY. My face can't smile any stronger than that.

MRS MOLLOY. Then do something! Show some interest. Do something lively: sing!

CORNELIUS. I can't sing, really I can't.

MRS. MOLLOY. We're wasting our time, Minnie. They don't want us.

CORNELIUS. Barnaby, what can you sing? Mrs. Molloy, all we know are sad songs.

MRS. MOLLOY. That doesn't matter. If you want us to go out with you, you've got to sing something.

(*All this has been very rapid; the* BOYS *turn up to counter, put their heads together, confer and abruptly turn, stand stiffly and sing "Tenting tonight; tenting tonight; tenting on the old camp ground." The four of them now repeat the refrain, softly harmonizing.*)

(*At the end of the song, after a pause,* MRS. MOLLOY, *moved, says.*)

MRS. MOLLOY. We'll come! (*The* BOYS *shout joyfully.*) You boys go ahead. (CORNELIUS *gets his hat from counter; as he puts it on he discovers the flowers on it.* BARNABY *gets his hat from window. They go out whistling.* MINNIE *turns and puts her hat on at the mirror.*) Minnie, get the front door key—I'll lock the workroom.

(MRS MOLLOY *goes to workroom.* MINNIE *takes key from hook left of wardrobe and goes to* MRS. MOLLOY, *at the workroom door. She turns her around.*)

MINNIE. Why, Mrs. Molloy, you're crying! (MRS. MOLLOY *flings her arms round*

MINNIE.)

MRS. MOLLOY. Oh, Minnie, the world is full of wonderful things. Watch me, dear, and tell me if my petticoat's showing. (*She crosses to door, followed by* MINNIE, *as—*

THE CURTAIN FALLS

ACT THREE

Veranda at the Harmonia Gardens Restaurant on the Battery, New York.

This room is informal and rustic. The main restaurant is indicated to be off stage back right.

There are three entrances: swinging double doors at the center of the back wall leading to the kitchen; one on the right wall (perhaps up a few steps and flanked by potted palms) to the street; one on the left wall to the staircase leading to the rooms above.

On the stage are two tables, left and right, each with four chairs. It is now afternoon and they are not yet set for dinner.

Against the back wall is a large folding screen. Also against the back wall are hat and coat racks.

As the curtain rises, VANDERGELDER *is standing, giving orders to* RUDOLPH, *a waiter.* MALACHI STACK *sits at table left.*

VANDERGELDER. Now, hear what I say. I don't want you to make any mistakes. I want a table for three.

RUDOLPH (*tall "snob" waiter, alternating between cold superiority and rage. German accent*). For three.

VANDERGELDER. There'll be two ladies and myself.

MALACHI. It's a bad combination, Mr. Vandergelder. You'll regret it.

VANDERGELDER. And I want a chicken.

MALACHI. A chicken! You'll regret it.

VANDERGELDER. Hold your tongue. Write it down: chicken.

RUDOLPH. Yes, sir. Chicken Esterhazy? Chicken cacciatore? Chicken à la crème —?

VANDERGELDER (*exploding*). A chicken! A chicken like everybody else has. And with the chicken I want a bottle of wine.

RUDOLPH. Moselle? Chablis? Vouvray?

MALACHI. He doesn't understand you, Mr. Vandergelder. You'd better speak louder.

VANDERGELDER (*spelling*). W-I-N-E.

RUDOLPH. Wine.

VANDERGELDER. Wine! And I want this table removed. We'll eat at that table alone. (*Exit* RUDOLPH *through service door at back.*)

MALACHI. There are some people coming in here now, Mr. Vandergelder.

(VANDERGELDER *goes to back right to look at the newcomers.*)

VANDERGELDER. What! Thunder and damnation! It's my niece Ermengarde! What's she doing here?!—Wait till I get my hands on her.

MALACHI (*running up to him*). Mr. Vandergelder! You must keep your temper!

VANDERGELDER. And there's that rascal artist with her. Why, it's a plot. I'll throw them in jail.

MALACHI. Mr. Vandergelder! They're old enough to come to New York. You can't throw people into jail for coming to New York.

VANDERGELDER. And there's Mrs. Levi! What's she doing with them? It's a plot. It's a conspiracy! What's she saying to the cabman? Go up and hear what she's saying.

MALACHI (*listening at entrance, right*). She's telling the cabman to wait, Mr. Vandergelder. She's telling the young people to come in and have a good dinner, Mr. Vandergelder.

VANDERGELDER. I'll put an end to this.

MALACHI. Now, Mr. Vandergelder, if you lose your temper, you'll make matters worse. Mr. Vandergelder, come here and take my advice.

VANDERGELDER. Stop pulling my coat. What's your advice?

MALACHI. Hide, Mr. Vandergelder. Hide behind this screen, and listen to what they're saying.

VANDERGELDER (*being pulled behind the screen*). Stop pulling at me. (*They hide behind the screen as* MRS. LEVI, ERMENGARDE *and* AMBROSE *enter from the right.* AMBROSE *is carrying* ERMENGARDE'S *luggage.*)

ERMENGARDE. But I don't want to eat in a restaurant. It's not proper.

MRS. LEVI. Now, Ermengarde, dear, there's nothing wicked about eating in a restaurant. There's nothing wicked, even, about being in New York. Clergymen just make those things up to fill out their sermons.

ERMENGARDE. Oh, I wish I were in Yonkers, where *nothing* ever happens!

MRS. LEVI. Ermengarde, you're hungry. That's what's troubling you.

ERMENGARDE. Anyway, after dinner you must promise to take me to Aunt Flora's. She's been waiting for me all day and she must be half dead of fright.

MRS. LEVI. All right but of course, you know at Miss Van Huysen's you'll be back in your uncle's hands.

AMBROSE (*hands raised to heaven*). I can't stand it.

MRS. LEVI (*to* AMBROSE). Just keep telling yourself how pretty she is. Pretty girls have very little opportunity to improve their other advantages.

AMBROSE. Listen, Ermengarde! You don't want to go back to your uncle. Stop and think! That old man with one foot in the grave!

MRS. LEVI. And the other three in the cashbox.

AMBROSE. Smelling of oats—

MRS. LEVI. And axle grease.

MALACHI. That's not true. It's only partly true.

VANDERGELDER (*loudly*). Hold your tongue! I'm going to teach them a lesson.

MALACHI (*whisper*). Keep your temper, Mr. Vandergelder. Listen to what they say.

MRS. LEVI (*hears this; throws a quick glance toward the screen; her whole manner changes*). Oh dear, what was I saying? The Lord be praised, how glad I am that I found you two dreadful children just as you were about to break poor dear Mr. Vandergelder's heart.

AMBROSE. He's got no heart to break!

MRS. LEVI (*vainly signaling*). Mr. Vandergelder's a much kinder man than you think.

AMBROSE. Kinder? He's a wolf.

MRS. LEVI. Remember that he leads a very lonely life. Now you're going to have dinner upstairs. There are some private rooms up there,—just meant for shy timid girls like Ermengarde. Come with me. (*She pushes the young people out left,* AMBROSE *carrying the luggage.*)

VANDERGELDER (*coming forward*). I'll show them! (*He sits at table right.*)

MALACHI. Everybody should eavesdrop once in a while, I always say. There's nothing like eavesdropping to show you

that the world outside your head is different from the world inside your head.

VANDERGELDER (*producing a pencil and paper*). I want to write a note. Go and call that cabman in here. I want to talk to him.

MALACHI. No one asks advice of a cabman, Mr. Vandergelder. They see so much of life that they have no ideas left.

VANDERGELDER. Do as I tell you.

MALACHI. Yes, sir. Advice of a cabman! (*Exit right.*)

(VANDERGELDER *writes his letter.*)

VANDERGELDER. "My dear Miss Van Huysen"—(*To audience.*) Everybody's dear in a letter. It's enough to make you give up writing 'em. "My dear Miss Van Huysen. This is Ermengarde and that rascal Ambrose Kemper. They are trying to run away. Keep them in your house until I come."

(MALACHI *returns with an enormous* CABMAN *in a high hat and a long coat. He carries a whip.*)

CABMAN (*entering*). What's he want?

VANDERGELDER. I want to talk to you.

CABMAN. I'm engaged. I'm waiting for my parties.

VANDERGELDER (*folding letter and writing address*). I know you are. Do you want to earn five dollars?

CABMAN. Eh?

VANDERGELDER. I asked you, do you want to earn five dollars?

CABMAN. I don't know. I never tried.

VANDERGELDER. When those parties of yours come downstairs, I want you to drive them to this address. Never mind what they say, drive them to this address. Ring the bell: give this letter to the lady of the house: see that they get in the door and keep them there.

CABMAN. I can't make people go into a house if they don't want to.

VANDERGELDER (*producing purse*). Can you for ten dollars?

CABMAN. Even for ten dollars, I can't do it alone.

VANDERGELDER. This fellow here will help you.

MALACHI (*sitting at table left*). Now I'm pushing people into houses.

VANDERGELDER. There's the address: Miss Flora Van Huysen, 8 Jackson Street.

CABMAN. Even if I get them in the door I can't be sure they'll stay there.

VANDERGELDER. For fifteen dollars you

can.

MALACHI. Murder begins at twenty-five.

VANDERGELDER. Hold your tongue! (*To* CABMAN.) The lady of the house will help you. All you have to do is to sit in the front hall and see that the man doesn't run off with the girl. I'll be at Miss Van Huysen's in an hour or two and I'll pay you then.

CABMAN. If they call the police, I can't do anything.

VANDERGELDER. It's perfectly honest business. Perfectly honest.

MALACHI. Every man's the best judge of his own honesty.

VANDERGELDER. The young lady is my niece. (*The* CABMAN *laughs, skeptically.*) The young lady is my niece!! (*The* CABMAN *looks at* MALACHI *and shrugs.*) She's trying to run away with a good-for-nothing and we're preventing it.

CABMAN. Oh, I know them, sir. They'll win in the end. Rivers don't run uphill.

MALACHI. What did I tell you, Mr. Vandergelder? Advice of a cabman.

VANDERGELDER (*hits table with his stick*). Stack! I'll be back in half an hour. See that the table's set for three. See that nobody else eats here. Then go and join the cabman on the box.

MALACHI. Yes, sir.

(*Exit* VANDERGELDER *right.*)

CABMAN. Who's your friend?

MALACHI. Friend!! That's not a friend; that's an employer I'm trying out for a few days.

CABMAN. You won't like him.

MALACHI. I can see you're in business for yourself because you talk about liking employers. No one's ever liked an employer since business began.

CABMAN. AW—!

MALACHI. No, sir. I suppose you think *your horse* likes you?

CABMAN. My old Clementine? She'd give her right feet for me.

MALACHI. That's what all employers think. You imagine it. The streets of New York are full of cab horses winking at one another. Let's go in the kitchen and get some whiskey. I can't push people into houses when I'm sober. No, I've had about fifty employers in my life, but this is the most employer of them all. He talks to everybody as though he were paying them.

CABMAN. I had an employer once. He watched me from eight in the morning until six at night—just sat there and watched me. Oh, dear! Even my mother didn't think I was as interesting as that. (CABMAN *exits through service door.*)

MALACHI (*following him off*). Yes, being employed is like being loved: you know that somebody's thinking about you the whole time. (*Exits.*)

(*Enter right,* MRS. MOLLOY, MINNIE, BARNABY *and* CORNELIUS.)

MRS. MOLLOY. See! Here's the place I meant! Isn't it fine? Minnie, take off your things; we'll be here for hours.

CORNELIUS (*stopping at door*). Mrs. Molloy, are you sure you'll like it here? I think I feel a draught.

MRS. MOLLOY. Indeed, I do like it. We're going to have a fine dinner right in this room; it's private, and it's elegant. Now we're all going to forget our troubles and call each other by our first names. Cornelius! Call the waiter.

CORNELIUS. Wait—wait—I can't make a sound. I must have caught a cold on that ride. Wai—No! It won't come.

MRS. MOLLOY. I don't believe you. Barnaby, you call him.

BARNABY (*boldly*). Waiter! Waiter! (CORNELIUS *threatens him.* BARNABY *runs left.*)

MINNIE. I never thought I'd be in such a place in my whole life. Mrs. Molloy, is this what they call a "café"?

MRS. MOLLOY (*sits at table left, facing audience*). Yes, this is a café. Sit down, Minnie. Cornelius, Mrs. Levi gave us to understand that every waiter in New York knew you.

CORNELIUS. They will. (BARNABY *sits at chair left;* MINNIE *in chair back to audience. Enter* RUDOLPH *from service door.*)

RUDOLPH. Good evening, ladies and gentlemen.

CORNELIUS (*shaking his hand*). How are you, Fritz? How are you, my friend?

RUDOLPH. I am Rudolph.

CORNELIUS. Of course. Rudolph, of course. Well, Rudolph, these ladies want a little something to eat—you know what I mean? Just if you can find the time—we know how busy you are.

MRS. MOLLOY. Cornelius, there's no need to be so familiar with the waiter. (*Takes menu from* RUDOLPH.)

CORNELIUS. Oh, yes, there is.

MRS. MOLLOY (*passing menu across*). Minnie, what do you want to eat?

MINNIE. Just anything, Irene.

MRS. MOLLOY. No, speak up, Minnie. What do you want?

MINNIE. No, really, I have no appetite at all. (*Swings round in her chair and studies the menu, horrified at the prices.*) Oh . . . Oh . . . I'd like some sardines on toast and a glass of milk.

CORNELIUS (*takes menu from her*). Great grindstones! What a sensible girl. Barnaby, shake Minnie's hand. She's the most sensible girl in the world. Rudolph, bring us gentlemen two glasses of beer, a loaf of bread and some cheese.

MRS. MOLLOY (*takes menu*). I never heard such nonsense. Cornelius, we've come here for a good dinner and a good time. Minnie, have you ever eaten pheasant?

MINNIE. Pheasant? No-o-o-o!

MRS. MOLLOY. Rudolph, have you any pheasant?

RUDOLPH. Yes, ma'am. Just in from New Jersey today.

MRS. MOLLOY. Even the pheasants are leaving New Jersey. (*She laughs loudly, pushing* CORNELIUS, *then* RUDOLPH; *not from menu.*) Now, Rudolph, write this down: mock turtle soup; pheasant; mashed chestnuts; green salad; and some nice red wine.

(RUDOLPH *repeats each item after her.*)

CORNELIUS (*losing all his fears, boldly*). All right, Barnaby, you watch me. (*He reads from the bill of fare.*) Rudolph, write this down: Neapolitan ice cream; hothouse peaches; champagne . . .

ALL. Champagne!

(BARNABY *spins round in his chair.*)

CORNELIUS (*holds up a finger*). . . . and a German band. Have you got a German band?

MRS. MOLLOY. No, Cornelius, I won't let you be extravagant. Champagne, but no band. Now, Rudolph, be quick about this. We're hungry. (*Exit* RUDOLPH *to kitchen.* MRS. MOLLOY *crosses to right.*) Minnie, come upstairs. I have an idea about your hair. I think it'd be nice in two wee horns—

MINNIE (*hurrying after her, turns and looks at the boys*). Oh! Horns! (*They go out right.*)

(*There is a long pause.* CORNELIUS *sits staring after them.*)

BARNABY. Cornelius, in the Army, you have to peel potatoes all the time.

CORNELIUS (*not turning*). Oh, that doesn't matter. By the time we get out of jail we can move right over to the Old Men's Home.

(*Another waiter,* AUGUST, *enters from service door bearing a bottle of champagne in cooler, and five glasses.* MRS. MOLLOY *re-enters right, followed by* MINNIE, *and stops* AUGUST.)

MRS. MOLLOY. Waiter! What's that? What's that you have?

AUGUST (*young waiter; baby face; is continually bursting into tears*). It's some champagne, ma'am.

MRS. MOLLOY. Cornelius; it's our champagne. (ALL *gather round* AUGUST.)

AUGUST. No, no. It's for His Honor the Mayor of New York and he's very impatient.

MRS. MOLLOY. Shame on him! The Mayor of New York has more important things to be impatient about. Cornelius, open it.

(CORNELIUS *takes the bottle, opens it and fills the glasses.*)

AUGUST. Ma'am, he'll kill me.

MRS. MOLLOY. Well, have a glass first and die happy.

AUGUST (*sits at table right, weeping*). He'll kill me.

(RUDOLPH *lays the cloth on the table, left.*)

MRS. MOLLOY. I go to a public restaurant for the first time in ten years and all the waiters burst into tears. There, take that and stop crying, love. (*She takes a glass to* AUGUST *and pats his head, then comes back.*) Barnaby, make a toast!

BARNABY (*center of the group, with naïve sincerity*). I? . . . uh . . . To all the the ladies in the world . . . may I get to know more of them . . . and . . . may I get to know them better.

(*There is a hushed pause.*)

CORNELIUS (*softly*). To the ladies!

MRS. MOLLOY. That's *very* sweet and *very* refined. Minnie, for that I'm going to give Barnaby a kiss.

MINNIE. Oh!

MRS. MOLLOY. Hold your tongue, Minnie. I'm old enough to be his mother, and— (*Indicating a height three feet from the floor*) a dear wee mother I would have been too. Barnaby, this is for you from all the ladies in the world. (*She kisses him.* BARNABY *is at first silent and dazed, then:*)

BARNABY. Now I can go back to Yonkers, Cornelius. Pudding. Pudding. Pudding!

(*He spins round and falls on his knees.*)

MRS. MOLLOY. Look at Barnaby. He's not strong enough for a kiss. His head can't stand it. (*Exit* AUGUST, *right service door, with tray and cooler. The sound of "Les Patineurs" waltz comes from off left.* CORNELIUS *sits in chair facing audience, top of table.* MINNIE *at left.* BARNABY *at right and* MRS. MOLLOY *back to audience.*) Minnie, I'm enjoying myself. To think that this goes on in hundreds of places every night, while I sit at home darning my stockings. (MRS. MOLLOY *rises and dances, alone, slowly about the stage.*) Cornelius, dance with me.

CORNELIUS (*rises*). Irene, the Hackls don't dance. We're Presbyterian.

MRS. MOLLOY. Minnie, you dance with me.

(MINNIE *joins her.* CORNELIUS *sits again.*)

MINNIE. Lovely music.

MRS. MOLLOY. Why, Minnie, you dance beautifully.

MINNIE. We girls dance in the workroom when you're not looking, Irene.

MRS. MOLLOY. You thought I'd be angry! Oh dear, no one in the world understands anyone else in the world. (*The girls separate.* MINNIE *dances off to her place at the table.* MRS. MOLLOY *sits thoughtfully at table right. The music fades away.*) Cornelius! Jenny Lind and all those other ladies —do you see them all the time?

CORNELIUS (*rises and joins her at table right*). Irene, I've put them right out of my head. I'm interested in . . .

(RUDOLPH *has entered by the service door. He now flings a tablecloth between them on table.*)

MRS. MOLLOY. Rudolph, what are you doing?

RUDOLPH. A table's been reserved here. Special orders.

MRS. MOLLOY. Stop right where you are. That party can eat inside. This veranda's ours.

RUDOLPH. I'm very sorry. This veranda is open to anybody who wants it. Ah, there comes the man who brought the order.

(*Enter* MALACHI *from the kitchen, drunk.*)

MRS. MOLLOY (*to* MALACHI). Take your table away from here. We got here first, Cornelius, throw him out.

MALACHI. Ma'am, my employer reserved this room at four o'clock this afternoon.

You can go and eat in the restaurant. My employer said it was very important that he have a table alone.

MRS. MOLLOY. No, sir. We got here first and we're going to stay here—alone, too.

(MINNIE *and* BARNABY *come forward.*)

RUDOLPH. Ladies and gentlemen!

MRS. MOLLOY. Shut up, you! (*To* MALACHI.) You're an impertinent, idiotic killjoy.

MALACHI (*very pleased*). That's an insult!

MRS. MOLLOY. All the facts about you are insults. (*To* CORNELIUS.) Cornelius, do something. Knock it over! The table.

CORNELIUS. Knock it over. (*After a shocked struggle with himself* CORNELIUS *calmly overturns the table.* AUGUST *rights the table and picks up cutlery, weeping copiously.*)

RUDOLPH (*in cold fury*). I'm sorry, but this room can't be reserved for anyone. If you want to eat alone, you must go upstairs. I'm sorry, but that's the rule.

MRS. MOLLOY. We're having a nice dinner alone and we're going to stay here. Cornelius, knock it over.

(CORNELIUS *overturns the table again. The girls squeal with pleasure. The waiter* AUGUST *again scrambles for the silver.*)

MALACHI. Wait till you see my employer!

RUDOLPH (*bringing screen down*). Ladies and gentlemen! I tell you what we'll do. There's a big screen here. We'll put the screen up between the tables. August, come and help me.

MRS. MOLLOY. I won't eat behind a screen. I won't. Minnie, make a noise. We're not animals in a menagerie. Cornelius, no screen. Minnie, there's a fight. I feel ten years younger. No screen! No screen!

(*During the struggle with the screen all talk at once.*)

MALACHI (*loud and clear and pointing to entrance right*). Now you'll learn something. There comes my employer now, getting out of that cab.

CORNELIUS (*coming to him, taking off his coat*). Where? I'll knock him down too.

(BARNABY *has gone up to right entrance. He turns and shouts clearly.*)

BARNABY. Cornelius, it's Wolf-trap. Yes, it is!

CORNELIUS. Wolf-trap! Listen, everybody. I think the screen's a good idea. Have you got any more screens, Rudolph? We could use three or four. (*He pulls the screen forward again.*)

MRS. MOLLOY. Quiet down, Cornelius, and stop changing your mind. Hurry up, Rudolph, we're ready for the soup.

(*During the following scene* RUDOLPH *serves the meal at the table left, as unobtrusively as possible.*

(*The stage is now divided in half. The quartet's table is at the left. Enter* VANDERGELDER *from the right. Now wears overcoat and carries the box of chocolates.*)

VANDERGELDER. Stack! What's the meaning of this? I told you I wanted a table alone. What's that? (VANDERGELDER *hits the screen twice with his stick.* MRS. MOLLOY *hits back twice with a spoon. The four young people sit:* BARNABY *facing audience;* MRS. MOLLOY *right,* MINNIE *left, and* CORNELIUS *back to audience.*)

MALACHI. Mr. Vandergelder, I did what I could. Mr. Vandergelder, you wouldn't believe what wild savages the people of New York are. There's a woman over there, Mr. Vandergelder—civilization hasn't touched her.

VANDERGELDER. Everything's wrong. You can't even manage a thing like that. Help me off with my coat. Don't kill me. Don't kill me. (*During the struggle with the overcoat* MR. VANDERGELDER's *purse flies out of his pocket and falls by the screen.* VANDERGELDER *goes to the coat tree and hangs his coat up.*)

MRS. MOLLOY. Speak up! I can't hear you.

CORNELIUS. My voice again. Barnaby, how's your throat? Can you speak?

BARNABY. Can't make a sound.

MRS. MOLLOY. Oh, all right. Bring your heads together and we'll whisper.

VANDERGELDER. Who are those people over there?

MALACHI. Some city sparks and their girls, Mr. Vandergelder. What goes on in big cities, Mr. Vandergelder—best not think of it.

VANDERGELDER. Has that couple come down from upstairs yet? I hope they haven't gone off without your seeing them.

MALACHI. No, sir. Myself and the cabman have kept our eyes on everything.

VANDERGELDER (*sits at right of table right, profile to the audience*). I'll sit here and wait for my guests. You go out to the cab.

MALACHI. Yes, sir. (VANDERGELDER *unfurls newspaper and starts to read.* MALACHI *sees the purse on the floor and picks it up.*) Eh? What's that? A purse. Did you drop something, Mr. Vandergelder?

VANDERGELDER. No. Don't bother me any more. Do as I tell you.

MALACHI (*stooping over. Coming center*). A purse. That fellow over there must have let it fall during the misunderstanding about the screen. No, I won't look inside. Twenty-dollar bills, dozens of them. I'll go over and give it to him. (*Starts toward* CORNELIUS, *then turns and says to audience.*) You're surprised? You're surprised to see me getting rid of this money so quickly, eh? I'll explain it to you. There was a time in my life when my chief interest was picking up money that didn't belong to me. The law is there to protect property, but—sure, the law doesn't care whether a property owner deserves his property or not, and the law has to be corrected. There are several thousands of people in this country engaged in correcting the law. For a while, I too was engaged in the redistribution of superfluities. A man works all his life and leaves a million to his widow. She sits in hotels and eats great meals and plays cards all afternoon and evening, with ten diamonds on her fingers. Call in the robbers! Call in the robbers! Or a man leaves it to his son who stands leaning against bars all night boring a bartender. Call in the robbers! Stealing's a weakness. There are some people who say you shouldn't have any weaknesses at all—no vices. But if a man has no vices, he's in great danger of making vices out of his virtues, and there's a spectacle. We've all seen them: men who were monsters of philanthropy and women who were dragons of purity. We've seen people who told the truth, though the Heavens fall,—and the Heavens fell. No, no—nurse one vice in your bosom. Give it the attention it deserves and let your virtues spring up modestly around it. Then you'll have the miser who's no liar; and the drunkard who's the benefactor of a whole city. Well, after I'd had that weakness of stealing for a while, I found another: I took to whisky —whisky took to me. And then I discovered an important rule that I'm going to pass on to you: Never support two weaknesses at the same time. It's your combination sinners—your lecherous liars and your miserly drunkards—who dishonor the vices and bring them into bad repute. So now you see why I want to get rid of this money: I want to keep my mind free to do the credit to whisky that it deserves. And my last word to you, ladies and gentlemen, is this: one vice at a time. (*Goes over to* CORNELIUS.) Can I speak to you for a minute?

CORNELIUS (*rises*). You certainly can. We all want to apologize to you about that screen—that little misunderstanding. (*They all rise, with exclamations of apology.*) What's your name, sir?

MALACHI. Stack, sir. Malachi Stack. If the ladies will excuse you, I'd like to speak to you for a minute. (*Draws* CORNELIUS *down to front of stage.*)Listen, boy, have you lost . . . ? Come here . . . (*Leads him further down, out of* VANDERGELDER'S *hearing.*) Have you lost something?

CORNELIUS. Mr. Stack, in this one day I've lost everything I own.

MALACHI. There it is. (*Gives him purse.*) Don't mention it.

CORNELIUS. Why, Mr. Stack . . . you know what it is? It's a miracle. (*Looks toward the ceiling.*)

MALACHI. Don't mention it.

CORNELIUS. Barnaby, come here a minute. I want you to shake hands with Mr. Stack. (BARNABY, *napkin tucked into his collar, joins them.*) Mr. Stack's just found the purse I lost, Barnaby. You know—the purse full of money.

BARNABY (*shaking his hand vigorously*). You're a wonderful man, Mr. Stack.

MALACHI. Oh, it's nothing—nothing.

CORNELIUS. I'm certainly glad I went to church all these years. You're a good person to know, Mr. Stack. In a way. Mr. Stack, where do you work?

MALACHI. Well, I've just begun. I work for a Mr. Vandergelder in Yonkers. (CORNELIUS *is thunderstruck. He glances at* BARNABY *and turns to* MALACHI *with awe. All three are swaying slightly, back and forth.*)

CORNELIUS. You do? It's a miracle. (*He points to the ceiling.*) Mr. Stack, I know you don't need it—but can I give you something for . . . for the good work?

MALACHI (*putting out his hand*). Don't mention it. It's nothing. (*Starts to go left.*)

CORNELIUS. Take that. (*Hands him a note.*)

MALACHI (*taking note*). Don't mention it.

CORNELIUS. And that. (*Another note.*)

MALACHI (*takes it and moves away*). I'd better be going.

CORNELIUS. Oh, here. And that.

MALACHI (*hands third note back*). No . . . I might get to like them. (*Exit left.*) (CORNELIUS *bounds exultantly back to table.*)

CORNELIUS. Irene, I feel a lot better about everything. Irene, I feel so well that I'm going to tell the truth.

MRS. MOLLOY. I'd forgotten that, Minnie. Men get drunk so differently from women. All right, what is the truth?

CORNELIUS. If I tell the truth, will you let me . . . will you let me put my arm around your waist?

(MINNIE *screams and flings her napkin over her face.*)

MRS. MOLLOY. Hold your tongue, Minnie. All right, you can put your arm around my waist just to show it can be done in a gentlemanly way; but I might as well warn you: a corset is a corset.

CORNELIUS (*his arm around her; softly*). You're a wonderful person, Mrs. Molloy.

MRS. MOLLOY. Thank you. (*She removes his hand from around her waist.*) All right, now that's enough. What is the truth?

CORNELIUS. Irene, I'm not rich as Mrs. Levi said I was.

MRS. MOLLOY. Not rich!

CORNELIUS. I almost never came to New York. And I'm not like she said I was,—bad. And I think you ought to know that at this very minute Mr. Vandergelder's sitting on the other side of that screen.

MRS. MOLLOY. What! Well, he's not going to spoil any party of mine. So *that's* why we've been whispering? Let's forget all about Mr. Vandergelder and have some more wine.

(*They start to sing softly: "The Sidewalks of New York." Enter* MRS. LEVI, *from the street, in an elaborate dress.* VANDERGELDER *rises.*)

MRS. LEVI. Good evening, Mr. Vandergelder.

VANDERGELDER. Where's—where's Miss Simple?

MRS. LEVI. Mr. Vandergelder, I'll never trust a woman again as long as I live.

VANDERGELDER. Well? What is it?

MRS. LEVI. She ran away this afternoon and got married!

VANDERGELDER. She did?

MRS. LEVI. Married, Mr. Vandergelder, to a young boy of fifty.

VANDERGELDER. She did?

MRS. LEVI. Oh, I'm as disappointed as you are. I-can't-eat-a-thing-what-have-you-ordered?

VANDERGELDER. I ordered what you told me to, a chicken.

(*Enter* AUGUST. *He goes to* VANDERGELDER's *table.*)

MRS. LEVI. I don't think I could face a chicken. Oh, waiter. How do you do? What's your name?

AUGUST. August, ma'am.

MRS. LEVI. August, this is Mr. Vandergelder of Yonkers—Yonkers' most influential citizen, in fact. I want you to see that he's served with the best you have and served promptly. And there'll only be the two of us. (MRS. LEVI *gives one set of cutlery to* AUGUST. VANDERGELDER *puts chocolate box under table.*) Mr. Vandergelder's been through some trying experiences today—what with men hidden all over Mrs. Molloy's store—like Indians in ambush.

VANDERGELDER (*between his teeth*). Mrs. Levi, you don't have to tell him everything about me.

(*The quartet commences singing again very softly.*)

MRS. LEVI. Mr. Vandergelder, if you're thinking about getting married, you might as well learn right now you have to let women be women. Now, August, we want excellent service.

AUGUST. Yes, ma'am. (*Exits to kitchen.*)

VANDERGELDER. You've managed things very badly. When I plan a thing it takes place. (MRS. LEVI *rises.*) Where are you going?

MRS. LEVI. Oh, I'd just like to see who's on the other side of that screen. (MRS. LEVI *crosses to the other side of the stage and sees the quartet. They are frightened and fall silent.*)

CORNELIUS (*rising*). Good evening, Mrs. Levi.

(MRS. LEVI *takes no notice, but, taking up the refrain where they left off, returns to her place at the table right.*)

VANDERGELDER. Well, who was it?

MRS. LEVI. Oh, just some city sparks entertaining their girls, I guess.

VANDERGELDER. Always wanting to know everything; always curious about everything; always putting your nose into other people's affairs. Anybody who lived with

you would get as nervous as a cat.

MRS. LEVI. What? What's that you're saying?

VANDERGELDER. I said anybody who lived with you would—

MRS. LEVI. Horace Vandergelder, get that idea right out of your head this minute. I'm surprised that you even mentioned such a thing. Understand once and for all that I have no intention of marrying you.

VANDERGELDER. I didn't mean that.

MRS. LEVI. You've been hinting around at such a thing for some time, but from now on put such ideas right out of your head.

VANDERGELDER. Stop talking that way. That's not what I meant at all.

MRS. LEVI. I hope not. I should hope not. Horace Vandergelder, you go your way (*Points a finger.*) and I'll go mine. (*Points again in same direction.*) I'm not some Irene Molloy, whose head can be turned by a pot of geraniums. Why, the idea of your even suggesting such a thing.

VANDERGELDER. Mrs. Levi, you misunderstood me.

MRS. LEVI. I certainly hope I did. If I had any intention of marrying again it would be to a far more pleasure-loving man than you. Why I'd marry Cornelius Hackl before I'd marry you. (CORNELIUS *raises his head in alarm. The others stop eating and listen.*) However, we won't discuss it any more. (*Enter* AUGUST *with a tray.*) Here's August with our food. I'll serve it, August.

AUGUST. Yes, ma'am. (*Exit* AUGUST.)

MRS. LEVI. Here's some white meat for you, and some giblets, very tender and very good for you. No, as I said before, you go your way and I'll go mine.—Start right in on the wine. I think you'll feel better at once. However, since you brought the matter up, there's one more thing I think I ought to say.

VANDERGELDER (*rising in rage*). I didn't bring the matter up at all.

MRS. LEVI. We'll have forgotten all about it in a moment, but—sit down, sit down, we'll close the matter forever in just a moment, but there's one more thing I ought to say: (VANDERGELDER *sits down.*) It's true, I'm a woman who likes to know everything that's going on; who likes to manage things, you're perfectly right about that. But I wouldn't like to manage anything as disorderly as your household, as out of control, as untidy. You'll have to do that yourself, God helping you.

VANDERGELDER. It's not out of control.

MRS. LEVI. Very well, let's not say another word about it. Take some more of that squash, it's good. No, Horace, a complaining, quarrelsome, friendless soul like you is no sort of companion for me. You go your way (*Peppers her own plate.*) and I'll go mine. (*Peppers his plate.*)

VANDERGELDER. Stop saying that.

MRS. LEVI. I won't say another word.

VANDERGELDER. Besides . . . I'm not those things you said I am.

MRS. LEVI. What?—Well, I guess you're friendless, aren't you? Ermengarde told me this morning you'd even quarreled with your barber—a man who's held a razor to your throat for twenty years! Seems to me that that's sinking pretty low.

VANDERGELDER. Well, . . . but . . . my clerks, they . . .

MRS. LEVI. They like you? Cornelius Hackl and that Barnaby? Behind your back they call you Wolf-trap.

(*Quietly the quartet at the other table have moved up to the screens—bringing chairs for* MRS. MOLLOY *and* MINNIE. *Wine glasses in hand, they overhear this conversation.*)

VANDERGELDER (*blanching*). They don't.

MRS. LEVI. No, Horace. It looks to me as though I were the last person in the world that liked you, and even I'm just so-so. No, for the rest of my life I intend to have a good time. You'll be able to find some housekeeper who can prepare you three meals for a dollar a day—it can be done, you know, if you like cold baked beans. You'll spend your last days listening at keyholes, for fear someone's cheating you. Take some more of that.

VANDERGELDER. Dolly, you're a damned exasperating woman.

MRS. LEVI. There! You see? That's the difference between us. I'd be nagging you all day to get some spirit into you. You could be a perfectly charming, witty, amiable man, if you wanted to.

VANDERGELDER (*rising, bellowing*). I don't want to be charming.

MRS. LEVI. But you are. Look at you now. You can't hide it.

VANDERGELDER (*sits*). Listening at keyholes! Dolly, you have no right to say such things to me.

MRS. LEVI. At your age you ought to enjoy hearing the honest truth.

VANDERGELDER. My age! My age! You're always talking about my age.

MRS. LEVI. I don't know what your age is, but I do know that up at Yonkers with bad food and bad temper you'll double it in six months. Let's talk of something else; but before we leave the subject there's one more thing I *am* going to say.

VANDERGELDER. Don't!

MRS. LEVI. Sometimes, just sometimes, I think I'd be tempted to marry you out of sheer pity; and if the confusion in your house gets any worse I may *have* to.

VANDERGELDER. I haven't asked you to marry me.

MRS. LEVI. Well, *please don't.*

VANDERGELDER. And my house is not in confusion.

MRS. LEVI. What? With your niece upstairs in the restaurant right now?

VANDERGELDER. I've fixed that better than you know.

MRS. LEVI. And your clerks skipping around New York behind your back?

VANDERGELDER. They're in Yonkers where they always are.

MRS. LEVI. Nonsense!

VANDERGELDER. What do you mean, nonsense?

MRS. LEVI. Cornelius Hackl's the other side of that screen this very minute.

VANDERGELDER. It ain't the same man!

MRS. LEVI. All right. Go on. Push it, knock it down. Go and see.

VANDERGELDER (*goes to screen, pauses in doubt, then returns to his chair again*). I don't believe it.

MRS. LEVI. All right. All right. Eat your chicken. Of course, Horace, if your affairs went from bad to worse and you became actually miserable, I might feel that it was my duty to come up to Yonkers and be of some assistance to you. After all, I was your wife's oldest friend.

VANDERGELDER. I don't know how you ever got any such notion. Now understand, once and for all, I have *no intention of marrying anybody.* Now, I'm tired and I don't want to talk.

(CORNELIUS *crosses to extreme left,* MRS. MOLLOY *following him.*)

MRS. LEVI. I won't say another word, either.

CORNELIUS. Irene, I think we'd better go. You take this money and pay the bill. Oh, don't worry, it's not mine.

MRS. MOLLOY. No, no, I'll tell you what we'll do. You boys put on our coats and veils, and if he comes stamping over here, he'll think you're girls.

CORNELIUS. What! Those things!

MRS. MOLLOY. Yes. Come on. (*She and* MINNIE *take the clothes from the stand.*)

VANDERGELDER (*rises*). I've got a headache. I've had a bad day. I'm going to Flora Van Huysen's, and then I'm going back to my hotel. (*Reaches for his purse.*) So, here's the money to pay for the dinner. (*Searching another pocket.*) Here's the money to pay for the . . . (*Going through all his pockets.*) Here's the money . . . I've lost my purse!!

MRS. LEVI. Impossible! I can't imagine you without your purse.

VANDERGELDER. It's been stolen. (*Searching overcoat.*) Or I left it in the cab. What am I going to do? I'm new at the hotel; they don't know me. I've never been here before. . . . Stop eating the chicken, I can't pay for it!

MRS. LEVI (*laughing gaily*). Horace, I'll be able to find some money. Sit down and calm yourself.

VANDERGELDER. Dolly Gallagher, I gave you twenty-five dollars this morning.

MRS. LEVI. I haven't a cent, I gave it to my lawyer. We can borrow it from Ambrose Kemper, upstairs.

VANDERGELDER. I wouldn't take it.

MRS. LEVI. Cornelius Hackl will lend it to us.

VANDERGELDER. He's in Yonkers.— Waiter!

(CORNELIUS *comes forward dressed in* MRS. MOLLOY'S *coat, thrown over his shoulder like a cape.* MRS. LEVI *is enjoying herself immensely.* VANDERGELDER *again goes to back wall to examine the pockets of his overcoat.*)

MRS. MOLLOY. Cornelius, is that Mr. Vandergelder's purse?

CORNELIUS. I didn't know it myself. I thought it was money just wandering around loose that didn't belong to anybody.

MRS. MOLLOY. Goodness! That's what politicians think!

VANDERGELDER. Waiter!

(*A band off left starts playing a polka.* BARNABY *comes forward dresed in* MINNIE'S *hat, coat and veil.*)

MINNIE. Irene, doesn't Barnaby make a lovely girl? He just ought to stay that way.

(MRS. LEVI *and* VANDERGELDER *move their table upstage while searching for the purse.*)

MRS. MOLLOY. Why should we have our evening spoiled? Cornelius, I can teach you to dance in a few minutes. Oh, he won't recognize you.

MINNIE. Barnaby, it's the easiest thing in the world. (*They move their table up against the back wall.*)

MRS. LEVI. Horace, you danced with me at your wedding and you danced with me at mine. Do you remember?

VANDERGELDER. No. Yes.

MRS. LEVI. Horace, you were a good dancer then. Don't confess to me that you're too old to dance.

VANDERGELDER. I'm not too old. I just don't want to dance.

MRS. LEVI. Listen to that music. Horace, do you remember the dances in the firehouse at Yonkers on Saturday nights? You gave me a fan. Come, come on!

(VANDERGELDER *and* MRS. LEVI *start to dance.* CORNELIUS, *dancing with* MRS. MOLLOY, *bumps into* VANDERGELDER, *back to back.* VANDERGELDER, *turning, fails at first to recognize him, then does and roars.*)

VANDERGELDER. You're discharged! Not a word! You're fired! Where's that idiot, Barnaby Tucker? He's fired, too. (*The four young people, laughing, start rushing out the door to the street.* VANDERGELDER, *pointing at* MRS. MOLLOY, *shouts.*) You're discharged!

MRS. MOLLOY (*pointing at him*). You're discharged! (*Exit.*)

VANDERGELDER. You're discharged! (*Enter from left,* AMBROSE *and* ERMENGARDE. *To* ERMENGARDE) I'll lock you up for the rest of your life, young lady.

ERMENGARDE. Uncle! (*She faints in* AMBROSE'S *arms.*)

VANDERGELDER (*to* AMBROSE). I'll have you arrested. Get out of my sight. I never want to see you again.

AMBROSE (*carrying* ERMENGARDE *across to exit right*). You can't do anything to me, Mr. Vandergelder. (*Exit* AMBROSE *and* ERMENGARDE.)

MRS. LEVI (*who has been laughing heartily, follows the distraught* VANDERGELDER *about the stage as he continues to hunt for his purse*). Well, there's your life, Mr. Vandergelder! Without niece—without clerks—without bride—and without your purse. *Will you marry me now?*

VANDERGELDER. No! (*To get away from her, he dashes into the kitchen.* MRS. LEVI, *still laughing, exclaims to the audience.*)

MRS. LEVI. Damn!! (*And rushes off right.*)

THE CURTAIN FALLS

ACT FOUR

MISS FLORA VAN HUYSEN'S *house.*

This is a prosperous spinster's living room and is filled with knickknacks, all in bright colors, and hung with family portraits, bird cages, shawls, etc.

There is only one entrance—a large double door in the center of the back wall. Beyond it one sees the hall which leads left to the street door and right to the kitchen and the rest of the house. On the left are big windows hung with lace curtains on heavy draperies. Front left is MISS VAN HUYSEN'S *sofa, covered with bright-colored cushions, and behind it a table. On the right is another smaller sofa.* MISS VAN HUYSEN *is lying on the sofa. The* COOK *is at the window, left.* MISS VAN HUYSEN, *fifty, florid, stout and sentimental, is sniffing at smelling salts.* COOK (*enormous*) *holds a china mixing bowl.*

COOK. No, ma'am. I could swear I heard a cab drawing up to the door.

MISS VAN H. You imagined it. Imagination. Everything in life . . . like that . . . disappointment . . . illusion. Our plans . . . our hopes . . . what becomes of them? Nothing. The story of my life. (*She sings for a moment.*)

COOK. Pray God nothing's happened to the dear girl. Is it a long journey from Yonkers?

MISS VAN H. No; but long enough for a thousand things to happen.

COOK. Well, we've been waiting all day. Don't you think we ought to call the police about it?

MISS VAN H. The police! If it's God's will, the police can't prevent it. Oh, in three days, in a week, in a year, we'll know what's happened. . . . And if anything *has* happened to Ermengarde, it'll be a lesson to *him*—that's what it'll be.

COOK. To who?

MISS VAN H. To that cruel uncle of hers, of course,—to Horace Vandergelder, and to everyone else who tries to separate young lovers. Young lovers have enough to contend with as it is. Who should know that better than I? No one. The story of my life. (*Sings for a moment, then:*) There! Now I hear a cab. Quick!

COOK. No. No, ma'am. I don't see anything.

MISS VAN H. There! What did I tell you? Everything's imagination—illusion.

COOK. But surely, if they'd changed their plans Mr. Vandergelder would have sent you a message.

MISS VAN H. Oh, I know what's the matter. That poor child probably thought she was coming to another prison—to another tyrant. If she'd known that I was her friend, and a friend of all young lovers, she'd be here by now. Oh, yes, she would. Her life shall not be crossed with obstacles and disappointments as . . . Cook, a minute ago my smelling salts were on this table. Now they've completely disappeared.

COOK. Why, there they are, ma'am, right there in your hand.

MISS VAN H. Goodness! How did they get there? I won't inquire. Stranger things have happened!

COOK. I suppose Mr. Vandergelder was sending her down with someone?

MISS VAN H. Two can go astray as easily as . . . (*She sneezes.*)

COOK. God bless you! (*Runs to window.*) Now, here's a carriage stopping. (*The doorbell rings.*)

MISS VAN H. Well, open the door, Cook. (COOK *exits.*) It's probably some mistake . . . (*Sneezes again.*) God bless you! (*Sounds of altercation off in hall.*) It almost sounds as though I heard voices.

CORNELIUS (*off*). I don't want to come in. This is a free country, I tell you.

CABMAN (*off*). Forward march!

MALACHI (*off*). In you go. We have orders.

CORNELIUS (*off*). You can't make a person go where he doesn't want to go.

(*Enter* MALACHI, *followed by* COOK. *The* CABMAN *bundles* BARNABY *and* CORNELIUS *into the room, but they fight their way back into the hall.* CORNELIUS *has lost* MRS. MOLLOY'S *coat, but* BARNABY *is wearing* MINNIE'S *clothes.*)

MALACHI. Begging your pardon, ma'am, are you Miss Van Huysen?

MISS VAN H. Yes, I am, unfortunately. What's all this noise about?

MALACHI. There are two people here that Mr. Vandergelder said must be brought to this house and kept here until he comes. And here's his letter to you.

MISS VAN H. No one has any right to tell me whom I'm to keep in my house if they don't want to stay.

MALACHI. You're right, ma'am. Everybody's always talking about people breaking into houses, ma'am; but there are more people in the world who want to break out of houses, that's what I always say.—Bring them in, Joe.

(*Enter* CORNELIUS *and* BARNABY *being pushed by the* CABMAN.)

CORNELIUS. This young lady and I have no business here. We jumped into a cab and asked to be driven to the station and these men brought us to the house and forced us to come inside. There's been a mistake.

CABMAN. Is your name Miss Van Huysen?

MISS VAN H. Everybody's asking me if my name's Miss Van Huysen. I think that's a matter I can decide for myself. Now will you all be quiet while I read this letter? . . . "This is Ermengarde and that rascal Ambrose Kemper . . ." Now I know who you two are, anyway. "They are trying to run away . . ." Story of my life. "Keep them in your house until I come." Mr. Kemper, you have nothing to fear. (*To* CABMAN) Who are you?

CABMAN. I'm Joe. I stay here until the old man comes. He owes me fifteen dollars.

MALACHI. That's right, Miss Van Huysen, we must stay here to see they don't escape.

MISS VAN H. (*to* BARNABY). My dear child, take off your things. We'll all have some coffee. (*To* MALACHI *and* CABMAN) You two go out and wait in the hall. I'll send coffee out to you. Cook, take them.

(COOK *pushes* MALACHI *and* CABMAN *into the hall.*)

CORNELIUS. Ma'am, we're not the people you're expecting, and there's no reason . . .

MISS VAN H. Mr. Kemper, I'm not the tyrant you think I am. . . . You don't have to be afraid of me. . . . I know you're trying to run away with this innocent girl. . . . All my life I have suffered from the interference of others. You shall not suffer as I did. So put yourself entirely in my hands. (*She lifts* BARNABY's *veil.*) Ermengarde! (*Kisses him on both cheeks.*) Where's your luggage?

BARNABY. It's—uh—uh—it's . . .

CORNELIUS. Oh, I'll find it in the morning. It's been mislaid.

MISS VAN H. Mislaid! How like life! Well, Ermengarde; you shall put on some of my clothes.

BARNABY. Oh, I know I wouldn't be happy, really.

MISS VAN H. She's a shy little thing, isn't she? Timid little darling! . . . Cook! Put some gingerbread in the oven and get the coffee ready . . .

COOK. Yes, ma'am. (*Exits to kitchen.*)

MISS VAN H. . . . while I go and draw a good hot bath for Ermengarde.

CORNELIUS. Oh, oh—Miss Van Huysen . . .

MISS VAN H. Believe me, Ermengarde, your troubles are at an end. You two will be married tomorrow. (*To* BARNABY) My dear, you look just like I did at your age, and your sufferings have been as mine. While you're bathing, I'll come and tell you the story of my life.

BARNABY. Oh, I don't want to take a bath. I always catch cold.

MISS VAN H. No, dear, you won't catch cold. I'll slap you all over. I'll be back in a minute. (*Exit.*)

CORNELIUS (*looking out of window*). Barnaby, do you think we could jump down from this window?

BARNABY. Yes—we'd kill ourselves.

CORNELIUS. We'll just have to stay here and watch for something to happen. Barnaby, the situation's desperate.

BARNABY. It began getting desperate about half-past four and it's been getting worse ever since. Now I have to take a bath and get slapped all over.

(*Enter* MISS VAN HUYSEN *from kitchen.*)

MISS VAN H. Ermengarde, you've still got those wet things on. Your bath's nearly ready. Mr. Kemper, you come into the kitchen and put your feet in the oven. (*The doorbell rings. Enter* COOK.) What's that? It's the doorbell. I expect it's your uncle.

COOK. There's the doorbell. (*At window.*) It's *another* man and a girl in a cab!

MISS VAN H. Well, go and let them in, Cook. Now, come with me, you two.

Come, Ermengarde. (*Exit* COOK. MISS VAN HUYSEN *drags* CORNELIUS *and the protesting* BARNABY *off into the kitchen.*)

COOK (*off*). No, that's impossible. Come in, anyway. (*Enter* ERMENGARDE, *followed by* AMBROSE, *carrying the two pieces of luggage.*) There's some mistake. I'll tell Miss Van Huysen, but there's some mistake.

ERMENGARDE. But, I tell you, I *am* Mr. Vandergelder's niece; I'm Ermengarde.

COOK. Beg your pardon, Miss, but you *can't* be Miss Ermengarde.

ERMENGARDE. But—but—here I *am*. And that's my baggage.

COOK. Well, I'll tell Miss Van Huysen who you *think* you are, but she won't like it. (*Exits.*)

AMBROSE. You'll be all right now, Ermengarde. I'd better go before she sees me.

ERMENGARDE. Oh, no. You must stay, I feel so strange here.

AMBROSE. I know, but Mr. Vandergelder will be here in a minute. . . .

ERMENGARDE. Ambrose, you can't go. You can't leave me in this crazy house with those drunken men in the hall. Ambrose . . . Ambrose, let's say you're someone else that my uncle sent down to take care of me. Let's say you're—you're Cornelius Hackl!

AMBROSE. Who's Cornelius Hackl?

ERMENGARDE. You know. He's chief clerk in Uncle's store.

AMBROSE. I don't want to be Cornelius Hackl. No, no, Ermengarde, come away with me now. I'll take you to my friend's house. Or I'll take you to Mrs. Levi's house.

ERMENGARDE. Why, it was Mrs. Levi who threw us right at Uncle Horace's face. Oh, I wish I were back in Yonkers where nothing ever happens.

(*Enter* MISS VAN HUYSEN.)

MISS VAN H. What's all this I hear? Who do you say you are?

ERMENGARDE. Aunt Flora . . . don't you remember me? I'm Ermengarde.

MISS VAN H. And you're Mr. Vandergelder's niece?

ERMENGARDE. Yes, I am.

MISS VAN H. Well, that's very strange indeed, because he has just sent me another niece named Ermengarde. She came with a letter from him, explaining everything. Have you got a letter from him?

ERMENGARDE. No . . .

MISS VAN H. Really!—And who is this?

ERMENGARDE. This is Cornelius Hackl, Aunt Flora.

MISS VAN H. Never heard of him.

ERMENGARDE. He's chief clerk in Uncle's store.

MISS VAN H. Never heard of him. The other Ermengarde came with the man she's in·love with, and that *proves* it. She came with Mr. Ambrose Kemper.

AMBROSE (*shouts*). Ambrose Kemper!

MISS VAN H. Yes, Mr. Hackl, and Mr. Ambrose Kemper is in the kitchen there now *with his feet in the oven.* (ERMENGARDE *starts to cry.* MISS VAN HUYSEN *takes her to the sofa. They both sit.*) Dear child, what is your trouble?

ERMENGARDE. Oh, dear. I don't know what to do.

MISS VAN H. (*in a low voice*). Are you in love with this man?

ERMENGARDE. Yes, I am.

MISS VAN H. I could see it—and are people trying to separate you?

ERMENGARDE. Yes, they are.

MISS VAN H. I could see it—who? Horace Vandergelder?

ERMENGARDE. Yes.

MISS VAN H. That's enough for me. I'll put a stop to Horace Vandergelder's goings on. (MISS VAN HUYSEN *draws* AMBROSE *down to sit on her other side.*) Mr. Hackl, think of me as your friend. Come in the kitchen and get warm. . . . (*She rises and starts to go out.*) We can decide later who everybody is. My dear, would you like a good hot bath?

ERMENGARDE. Yes, I would.

MISS VAN H. Well, when Ermengarde comes out you can go in. (*Enter* CORNELIUS *from the kitchen.*)

CORNELIUS. Oh, Miss Van Huysen . . .

ERMENGARDE. Why, Mr. Hack—!!

CORNELIUS (*sliding up to her, urgently*). Not yet! I'll explain. I'll explain everything.

MISS VAN H. Mr. Kemper!—Mr. Kemper! This is Mr. Cornelius Hackl. (*To* AMBROSE) Mr. Hackl, this is Mr. Ambrose Kemper. (*Pause, while the men glare at one another.*) Perhaps you two know one another?

AMBROSE. No!

CORNELIUS. No, we don't.

AMBROSE (*hotly*). Miss Van Huysen, I know that man is not Ambrose Kemper.

CORNELIUS (*ditto*). And he's not Cornelius Hackl.

MISS VAN H. My dear young men, what does it matter what your names are? The important thing is that you are you. (*To* AMBROSE) You are alive and breathing, aren't you, Mr. Hackl? (*Pinches* AMBROSE's *left arm.*)

AMBROSE. Ouch, Miss Van Huysen.

MISS VAN H. This dear child imagines she is Horace Vandergelder's niece Ermengarde.

ERMENGARDE. But I am.

MISS VAN H. The important thing is that you're all in love. Everything else is illusion. (*She pinches* CORNELIUS' *arm.*)

CORNELIUS. Ouch! Miss Van Huysen!

MISS VAN H. (*comes down and addresses the audience*). Everybody keeps asking me if I'm Miss Van Huys . . . (*She seems suddenly to be stricken with doubt as to who she is; her face shows bewildered alarm. She pinches herself on the upper arm and is abruptly and happily relieved.*) Now, you two gentlemen sit down and have a nice chat while this dear child has a good hot bath. (*The doorbell rings.* ERMENGARDE *exit,* MISS VAN HUYSEN *about to follow her, but stops. Enter* COOK.)

COOK. There's the doorbell again.

MISS VAN H. Well, answer it.

(ERMENGARDE *exits to kitchen.*)

COOK (*at window, very happy about all these guests*). It's a cab and three ladies. I never saw such a night. (*Exit to front door.*)

MISS VAN H. Gentlemen, you can rest easy. I'll see that Mr. Vandergelder lets his nieces marry you both.

(*Enter* MRS. LEVI.)

MRS. LEVI. Flora, how are you?

MISS VAN H. Dolly Gallagher! What brings you here?

MRS. LEVI. Great Heavens, Flora, what are those two drunken men doing in your hall?

MISS VAN H. I don't know. Horace Vandergelder sent them to me.

MRS. LEVI. Well, I've brought you two girls in much the same condition. Otherwise they're the finest girls in the world. (*She goes up to the door and leads in* MRS. MOLLOY. MINNIE *follows.*) I want you to meet Irene Molloy and Minnie Fay.

MISS VAN H. Delighted to know you.

MRS. LEVI. Oh, I see you two gentlemen are here, too. Mr. Hackl, I was about to look for you (*pointing about the room*)

somewhere here.

CORNELIUS. No, Mrs. Levi. I'm ready to face anything now.

MRS. LEVI. Mr. Vandergelder will be here in a minute. He's downstairs trying to pay for a cab without any money.

MRS. MOLLOY (*holding* VANDERGELDER's *purse*). Oh, I'll help him.

MRS. LEVI. Yes, will you, dear? You had to pay the restaurant bills. You must have hundreds of dollars there it seems.

MRS. MOLLOY. This is his own purse he lost. I can't give it back to him without seeming . . .

MRS. LEVI. I'll give it back to him.— There, you help him with this now. (*She gives* MRS. MOLLOY *a bill and puts the purse airily under her arm.*)

VANDERGELDER (*off*). Will somebody please pay for this cab?

(MRS. MOLLOY *exits to front door.*)

MRS. MOLLOY (*off stage*). I'll take care of that, Mr. Vandergelder.

(*As* MR. VANDERGELDER *enters,* MALACHI *and the* CABMAN *follow him in.* VANDERGELDER *carries overcoat, stick and box of chocolates.*)

CABMAN. Fifteen dollars, Mr. Vandergelder.

MALACHI. Hello, Mr. Vandergelder .

VANDERGELDER (*to* MALACHI). You're discharged! (*To* CABMAN) You too! (MALACHI *and* CABMAN *go out and wait in the hall.*) So I've caught up with you at last! (*To* AMBROSE) I never want to see you again! (*To* CORNELIUS) You're discharged! Get out of the house, both of you. (*He strikes sofa with his stick; a second after,* MISS VAN HUYSEN *strikes him on the shoulder with a folded newspaper or magazine.*)

MISS VAN H. (*forcefully*). Now then you. Stop ordering people out of my house. You can shout and carry on in Yonkers, but when you're in my house you'll behave yourself.

VANDERGELDER. They're both dishonest scoundrels.

MISS VAN H. Take your hat off. Gentlemen, you stay right where you are.

CORNELIUS. Mr. Vandergelder, I can explain—

MISS VAN H. There aren't going to be any explanations. Horace, stop scowling at Mr. Kemper and forgive him.

VANDERGELDER. That's not Kemper, that's a dishonest rogue named Cornelius Hackl.

MISS VAN H. You're crazy. (*Points to*

AMBROSE.) That's Cornelius Hackl.

VANDERGELDER. I guess I know my own chief clerk.

MISS VAN H. I don't care what their names are. You shake hands with them both, or out you go.

VANDERGELDER. Shake hands with those dogs and scoundrels!

MRS. LEVI. Mr. Vandergelder, you've had a hard day. You don't want to go out in the rain now. Just for form's sake, you shake hands with them. You can start quarreling with them tomorrow.

VANDERGELDER (*gives* CORNELIUS *one finger to shake*). There! Don't regard that as a handshake. (*He turns to* AMBROSE, *who mockingly offers him one finger.*) Hey! I never want to see you again.

(MRS. MOLLOY *enters from front door.*)

MRS. MOLLOY. Miss Van Huysen.

MISS VAN H. Yes, dear?

MRS. MOLLOY. Do I smell coffee?

MISS VAN H. Yes, dear.

MRS. MOLLOY. Can I have some, good and black?

MISS VAN H. Come along, everybody. We'll all go into the kitchen and have some coffee. (*As they all go:*) Horace, you'll be interested to know there are two Ermengardes in there. . . .

VANDERGELDER. Two!!

(*Last to go is* MINNIE, *who revolves about the room dreamily waltzing, a finger on her forehead.* MRS. LEVI *has been standing at one side. She now comes forward, in thoughtful mood.* MINNIE *continues her waltz round the left sofa and out to the kitchen.*)

(MRS. LEVI, *left alone, comes to front, addressing an imaginary Ephraim.*)

MRS. LEVI. Ephraim Levi, I'm going to get married again. Ephraim, I'm marrying Horace Vandergelder for his money. I'm going to send his money out doing all the things you taught me. Oh, it won't be a marriage in the sense that we had one—but I shall certainly make him happy, and Ephraim—I'm tired. I'm tired of living from hand to mouth, and I'm asking your permission, Ephraim—will you give me away? (*Now addressing the audience, she holds up the purse.*) Money! Money!—it's like the sun we walk under; it can kill or cure.—Mr. Vandergelder's money! Vandergelder's never tired of saying most of the people in the world are fools, and in a way he's right, isn't he? Himself, Irene,

Cornelius, myself! But there comes a moment in everybody's life when he must decide whether he'll live among human beings or not—a fool among fools or a fool alone.

As for me, I've decided to live among them.

I wasn't always so. After my husband's death I retired into myself. Yes, in the evenings, I'd put out the cat, and I'd lock the door, and I'd make myself a little rum toddy; and before I went to bed I'd say a little prayer, thanking God that I was independent—that no one else's life was mixed up with mine. And when ten o'clock sounded from Trinity Church tower, I fell off to sleep and I was a perfectly contented woman. And one night, after two years of this, an oak leaf fell out of my Bible. I had placed it there on the day my husband asked me to marry him; perfectly good oak leaf—but without color and without life. And suddenly I realized that for a long time I had not shed one tear; nor had I been filled with the wonderful hope that something or other would turn out well. I saw that I was like that oak leaf, and on that night I decided to rejoin the human race.

Yes, we're all fools and we're all in danger of destroying the world with our folly. But the surest way to keep us out of harm is to give us the four or five human pleasures that are our right in the world,—and that takes a little *money!*

The difference between a little money and no money at all is enormous—and can shatter the world. And the difference between a little money and an enormous amount of money is very slight—and that, also, can shatter the world.

Money, I've always felt, money—pardon my expression—is like manure; it's not worth a thing unless it's spread about encouraging young things to grow.

Anyway,—that's the opinion of the second Mrs. Vandergelder. (VANDERGELDER *enters with two cups of coffee. With his back, he closes both doors.*)

VANDERGELDER. Miss Van Huysen asked me to bring you this.

MRS. LEVI. Thank you both. Sit down and rest yourself. What's been going on in the kitchen?

VANDERGELDER. A lot of foolishness. Everybody falling in love with everybody. I forgave 'em; Ermengarde and that artist.

MRS. LEVI. I knew you would.

VANDERGELDER. I made Cornelius Hackl my partner.

MRS. LEVI. You won't regret it.

VANDERGELDER. Dolly, you said some mighty unpleasant things to me in the restaurant tonight . . . all that about my house . . . and everything.

MRS. LEVI. Let's not say another word about it.

VANDERGELDER. Dolly, you have a lot of faults—

MRS. LEVI. Oh, I know what you mean.

VANDERGELDER. You're bossy, scheming, inquisitive . . .

MRS. LEVI. Go on.

VANDERGELDER. But you're a wonderful woman. Dolly, marry me.

MRS. LEVI. Horace! (*Rises.*) Stop right there.

VANDERGELDER. I know I've been a fool about Mrs. Molloy, and that other woman. But, Dolly, forgive me and marry me. (*He goes on his knees.*)

MRS. LEVI. Horace, I don't dare. No. I don't dare.

VANDERGELDER. What do you mean?

MRS. LEVI. You know as well as I do that you're the first citizen of Yonkers. Naturally, you'd expect your wife to keep open house, to have scores of friends in and out all the time. Any wife of yours should be used to that kind of thing.

VANDERGELDER (*after a brief struggle with himself*). Dolly, you can live any way you like.

MRS. LEVI. Horace, you can't deny it, your wife would have to be a *somebody.* Answer me: am I a somebody?

VANDERGELDER. You are . . . you are. Wonderful woman.

MRS. LEVI. Oh, you're partial. (*She crosses, giving a big wink at the audience, and sits on sofa right. VANDERGELDER follows her on his knees.*) Horace, it won't be enough for you to load your wife with money and jewels; to insist that she be a benefactress to half the town. (*He rises and, still struggling with himself, coughs so as not to hear this.*) No, she must be a somebody. Do you really think I have it in me to be a credit to you?

VANDERGELDER. Dolly, everybody knows that you could do anything you wanted to do.

MRS. LEVI. I'll try. With your help, I'll try—and by the way, I found your purse. (*Holds it up.*)

VANDERGELDER. Where did you—! Wonderful woman!

MRS. LEVI. It just walked into my hand. I don't know how I do it. Sometimes I frighten myself. Horace, take it. Money walks out of my hands, too.

VANDERGELDER. Keep it. Keep it.

MRS. LEVI. Horace! (*Half laughing, half weeping, and with an air of real affection for him.*) I never thought . . . I'd ever . . . hear you say a thing like that!

(BARNABY *dashes in from the kitchen in great excitement. He has discarded* MINNIE's *clothes.*)

BARNABY. Oh! Excuse me. I didn't know anybody was here.

VANDERGELDER (*bellowing*). Didn't know anybody was here. Idiot!

MRS. LEVI (*putting her hand on* VANDERGELDER's *arm; amiably*). Come in, Barnaby. Come in.

(VANDERGELDER *looks at her a minute; then says, imitating her tone.*)

VANDERGELDER. Come in, Barnaby. Come in.

BARNABY. Cornelius is going to marry Mrs. Molloy!!

MRS. LEVI. Isn't that fine! Horace! . . . (MRS. LEVI *rises, and indicates that he has an announcement to make.*)

VANDERGELDER. Barnaby, go in and tell the rest of them that Mrs. Levi has consented—

MRS. LEVI. *Finally* consented!

VANDERGELDER. Finally consented to become my wife.

BARNABY. Holy cabooses. (*Dashes back to the doorway.*) Hey! *Listen, everybody!* Wolf-trap—I mean—Mr. Vandergelder is going to marry Mrs. Levi.

(MISS VAN HUYSEN *enters followed by all the people in this act. She is now carrying the box of chocolates.*)

MISS VAN H. Dolly, that's the best news I ever heard. (*She addresses the audience.*) There isn't any more coffee; there isn't any more gingerbread; but there are three couples in my house and they're all going to get married. And do you know, one of those Ermengardes wasn't a dear little girl at all—she was a boy! Well, that's what life is: disappointment, illusion.

MRS. LEVI (*to audience*). There isn't any more coffee; there isn't any more gingerbread, and there isn't any more play—but there is one more thing we have to do. . . .

Barnaby, come here. (*She whispers to him, pointing to the audience. Then she says to the audience:*) I think the youngest person here ought to tell us what the moral of the play is.

(BARNABY *is reluctantly pushed forward to the footlights.*)

BARNABY. Oh, I think it's about . . . I think it's about adventure. The test of an adventure is that when you're in the middle of it, you say to yourself, "Oh, now I've got myself into an awful mess; I wish I were sitting quietly at home." And the sign that something's wrong with you is when you sit quietly at home wishing you were out having lots of adventure. So that now we all want to thank you for coming tonight, and we all hope that in your lives you have just the right amount of—adventure!

THE CURTAIN FALLS

NO TIME FOR SERGEANTS

Ira Levin

(*Adapted from the novel by* MAC HYMAN)

First presented by Maurice Evans, in association with
Emmett Rogers, at the Alvin Theatre, New York,
October 20, 1955, with the following cast:

PREACHER Don Knotts
WILL STOCKDALE Andy Griffith
PA STOCKDALE Floyd Buckley
DRAFT MAN O. Tolbert-Hewitt
BUS DRIVER Michael Thoma
IRVIN BLANCHARD Robert Webber
ROSABELLE Maree Dow

INDUCTEES
- Cecil Rutherford
- Robert McQuade
- Carl Albertson
- Arthur P. Keegan
- Van Williams
- Jules Racine
- Wynn Pearce

BEN WHITLEDGE Roddy McDowall
SERGEANT KING Myron McCormick
A CAPTAIN Ed Peck
A NURSE Maree Dow
FIRST CLASSIFICATION CORPORAL
　　　　　Robert McQuade
SECOND CLASSIFICATION CORPORAL
　　　　　Don Knotts

THIRD CLASSIFICATION CORPORAL
　　　　　Ray Johnson
A LIEUTENANT Earle Hyman
A PSYCHIATRIST James Millhollin
CIGARETTE GIRL Maree Dow
AN INFANTRYMAN Arthur P. Keegan
AIR FORCE POLICEMAN Jules Racine
A COLONEL Rex Everhart
LT. BRIDGES (PILOT) Hazen Gifford
LT. GARDELLA (CO-PILOT) Carl Albertson
LT. KENDALL (ENGINEER)
　　　　　Cecil Rutherford
LT. COVER (NAVIGATOR) Bill Hinnant
GENERAL BUSH Howard Freeman
GENERAL POLLARD Royal Beal
A SENATOR O. Tolbert-Hewitt
AIDE TO GENERAL POLLARD Ray Johnson
LT. ABEL Rex Everhart
LT. BAKER Edmund Johnston
CAPT. CHARLES Wynn Pearce

The action of the play takes place in and above the United States
of America. Some of it is happening now and some of it happened
a while back. There are two acts.

INTRODUCTION

No Time for Sergeants is the joint work of a novelist and a playwright, both graduates from the military services. Mac Hyman, a native of Cordele, Georgia, born in 1923, is the novelist. He was much traveled in the academic world, having attended four institutions of higher learning: North Georgia College, Auburn, Duke University, and Columbia. With the help of all this learning, he became a lieutenant in the Air Force during World War II and, incidentally, an author. *No Time for Sergeants* was his first novel. The New Yorker Ira Levin, who dramatized it, was born six years later than the future novelist and became a private in the Army Signal Corps during the Korean War. He spent two years at Drake University and took a bachelor's degree at New York University. He, too, wrote a novel, somewhat luridly titled *A Kiss Before Dying;* it won an annual award—an "Edgar," presumably in memory of Edgar Allan Poe—from the Mystery Writers of America.

Mac Hyman's novel was acclaimed as a sort of American *Good Soldier Schweik,* and comparisons with the works of Mark Twain and Ring Lardner were also fittingly made. William Faulkner called it "one of the funniest stories of war or peace I ever read." The Broadway play was received just as gratefully and was variously applauded by the metropolitan play reviewers as "a wonderful bit of folklore out of modern times" (Brooks Atkinson of the *Times*), as "patently outrageous buffoonery" (Walter Kerr of the *Herald Tribune*), as an almost continuously hilarious joke (Richard Watts, Jr. of the *Post*), and as "a Southern-fried tale about a modern Huckleberry Finn" (John Chapman of the *Daily News*).

ACT ONE

The house curtain rises on a second curtain, that of the "Callville Township Meeting Hall," on which is depicted a horde of Confederate soldiers surging on toward victory. The house lights dim, amateur musicians are heard, and the PREACHER *enters from the wings, applauding solicitously.*

PREACHER. Thank you, members of the Civic Orchestra, for fillin' in so beautifully, but now our speaker has finally arrived. And here he is, Callville's favorite son in uniform—Will Stockdale. (*He motions toward the wings, coaxes applause from audience—but no one appears.*) Will Stockdale!

(WILL STOCKDALE *enters, wearing a private's uniform. He watches the* PREACHER *exit, then finds the mark at the center of the stage and faces the audience. He would rather be anywhere else in the world.*)

WILL. Howdy. How I Won My Medal. (*Pause.*) There's this medal that I got in the draft and I'm supposed to tell you how I won it. Well I didn't *win* it exactly; more like this fellow just *slipped* it to me. I tell you the truth, I'd just as soon somebody come up here and sung a song or somethin'. (*He heads for the wings, stops, nods obediently several times and returns to center stage.*) Well, How I Won My Medal. The whole thing begun, of course, when I went into the draft. Well, I didn't exactly go *in* to the draft, neither. What it was, was the draft *come out* to me. Last spring that was, one evenin' around the time the chickens was quietin' down. You know. (*Through the "Meeting Hall" curtain, a ramshackle cabin is seen, surrounded by scrubby trees.* PA STOCKDALE *is sitting on the porch steps, his chin in his hands, angry-looking. An ancient radio on a shelf is straining out hillbilly music. A rifle is propped against the front of the cabin; near it, a sleeping hound-dog whose head droops over the edge of the porch.*) Pa and I had gone fishin' that day and he was settin' on the front steps of our place with his neck all red and his foot tappin'—angry, kind of. I'd caught a bigger fish than him. Anyhow, things was right peaceful, with my dog Blue asleep there, and the radio playin' some good music and all. (PA *has heard something. He stands and looks off right.*) And then, all of a sudden,

Pa stood up. Now that surprised me a good bit right there, because usually when we go fishin' it takes Pa two-three hours to get over it.

PA (*calling, still looking off*). Will!

(*"Meeting Hall" curtain rises as* WILL *turns upstage.*)

WILL. What is it, Pa? (*Starts to undo his tie.*)

PA. Come over here!

(WILL *heads for porch, taking off tie.*)

WILL (*to audience*). I warn't in uniform then. (*Goes up to* PA, *unbuttoning shirt.*)

PA. Listen. Your ears are better than mine. Somebody's comin'.

WILL. I don't hear nothin'.

PA. Turn off that whatchamacallit.

WILL. Radio.

PA. I know what you call it. Turn it off. (WILL *turns it off, drops shirt and tie on porch. He is now in T-shirt and khaki trousers.*) First I heared one of them cars, and then it stopped, and now somebody's comin'. (*Sound of twigs breaking and mumbled cursing off right.*) Hear?

DRAFT MAN (*off*). You stay right here and if I call come a'running.

(PA *snatches up rifle, holds it ready.*)

WILL (*trying to restrain him*). Pa . . . That ain't no way to welcome folks. Maybe it's kin.

PA. Kin don't come in cars. See if you can wake that hound-dog.

WILL (*crouching beside dog*). Hey, Blue. C'mon Blue. Got a big old hambone for you. C'mon Blue . . .

(*Approaching sounds have been growing louder. Now* DRAFT MAN *comes bursting in; a short, fat man in a white linen suit. He is sweating, fuming, and picking branches from his ankles.*)

DRAFT MAN. Never seen such a prickly path in all my whole life! . . . Damn! (*Coming up for air before* WILL, *who is still crouching.*) You Will Stockdale?

WILL (*rising*). Howdy . . .

DRAFT MAN (*pointing vigorously*). Three damn times I been out here this month!

PA (*raising rifle*). Don't you pint your finger in my boy's face!

DRAFT MAN (*retreating a step*). Are you threatening me with a firearm? I'm a government representative on government business!

PA. Bustin' up here without sayin' Howdy or nothin' . . . What government?

DRAFT MAN. U.S. Government! The draft board! This boy's been called for the April draft and never reported. He's a draft-dodger! (*He points again.*)

PA. Fold in that finger, sir! I'm warnin' you, fold in that finger!

DRAFT MAN (*lowering his hand*). He can be put in jail for that. He's in tomorrow's group. (*Turning to* WILL) This is your last chance, and by God, if you don't leave with that group at seven A.M. you're gonna be in more trouble than you ever seen! You already got one offense against you for not answering my letters!

WILL. I never got no letters.

DRAFT MAN. And don't tell me you can't read because you could've got somebody to read 'em to you, so that ain't no excuse! (WILL, *shocked, turns to* PA.)

PA. Do you mean to stand here and say to my face that my son can't read?

DRAFT MAN. Now look . . .

PA. Do you think my son, who has *gone to school* and who has read *more times* than you could shake a stick at, couldn't read a puny little ole letter if he wanted to? By God, sir!

WILL. I never *got* no letters.

PA. I don't think I can stand to *listen* to any more of this, by God! Get that book! (WILL *exits into cabin. To* DRAFT MAN) No sir! What you think don't mean nothin' to me . . . (*Levels rifle again.*) But we're gonna settle this here question here and now, and not have no more foolishness about it! (WILL *enters from cabin with book.*) Read at 'im!

WILL (*clears throat. Reads slowly*). Once there was a boy named Tony who wanted a pony. He went to his Mama and said, "May I have a pony?" and his Mama said, (*Turns page.*) "No, Tony, you may not have a pony." (*Looks at* PA, *who signals him to continue.*) So he went to his Papa and said, "May I have a pony?" and his Papa said, "No, Tony, you may not have— (*Turns page.*)—a pony." (PA *lifts hand grandly.* WILL *closes book. To* DRAFT MAN:) End of the book, he gets the pony anyhow.

PA (*advancing on* DRAFT MAN). Now that we've settled whether or not my boy can read . . .

WILL. Pa . . .

PA. . . . you best be gettin' off'n my property and into that car of yourn and out of range of—

WILL. Pa . . . Be Christian to him.

PA. Christian? You know what Christ woulda done if a man come stompin' onto *His* property . . . not sayin' Howdy or nothin' . . . sayin' folks couldn't read? *I* know what He woulda done. He woulda sent that man straight to *hell,* by God!

WILL. Pa! (*Taking* PA's *shoulder, gently.*) Now, I want to talk to you for a minute. Come here. (PA *turns to* WILL, *who backs toward cabin.* PA *looks back at* DRAFT MAN, *lowers rifle reluctantly and joins* WILL. *They sit on porch steps.*) Now, Pa, listen. I don't think this here draft is such a bad idea. I mean, I'd kind of like to go. There's a whole bunch of fellows there and they all march along right snappy-like—

PA. You listen to me, boy. Goin' into the draft don't mean just goin' into town. It means Macon and Atlanta, and farther still. I been to Atlanta—you know that—when I was no older than you. I told you how them folks . . . laughed at me and called me smart names. You don't want that, boy.

WILL. Pa, now ain't the same as it was then.

PA. The hell it ain't.

WILL. But they *want* me. They even sent a man to come and fetch me, didn't they? And that ain't all. Last spring I seen this sign out on the sidewalk down there in town. This big picture of Uncle Sam. And "*Uncle Sam* wants you," he's sayin'—just like this fellow here, Pa, pintin' straight in my face. And don't you think this soldier fellow come up to me right then and there, invitin' me to' come along with all the other fellows? I told him how you was ailin' then and would he kindly wait a while. (*Pause.*) You been tearin' up them letters, haven't you, Pa? And you ain't ailin' no more. (*He rises.*) Say good-by to Blue for me when he wakes up, will you? (*Holds out his hand.*)

PA. You'll see, things ain't no different. They'll make fun of you . . . and talk sassy 'cause you ain't a town boy . . . (*Rises, grabs* WILL's *hand.*) Write to me regular, you hear?

WILL. Sure, Pa. (WILL *backs toward* DRAFT MAN.)

PA. Print big!

DRAFT MAN. All right now . . .

PA. Draft man! You tell them folks out there to be nice to that boy, hear? (DRAFT MAN *mutters an impatient affirmative.*) He's a *good* boy. And it's my fault he didn't come when he should'a.

(WILL *and* DRAFT MAN *start off.*)

DRAFT MAN. Yeah, yeah . . .

WILL. 'By, Pa.

PA. 'By, Will . . . (*He picks up "Tony and The Pony," holds it out.*) You want your book?

WILL. No, Pa . . . 'By.

(PA *watches them off, looks at book, wipes it slowly with his sleeve. The lights dim out.*)

(*Lights come up on the town square. A bus stands upstage. There is a statue at stage right and a gas station with two pumps at stage left.* INDUCTEES *are lounging around; one strumming a guitar and singing softly, one embracing a girl. As more* INDUCTEES *drift in, a civilian* BUS DRIVER *takes forms which they carry and gives them blue cards in exchange.*)

DRIVER. Fill it out. Last name first, first name, middle name last. (*Gives a card to another* INDUCTEE.) Fill it out. Last name first, first name, middle name last.

(IRVIN BLANCHARD *enters, wearing a leather jacket and dark glasses. He looks about disdainfully.*)

IRVIN. This the group going to the Air Force?

DRIVER. That's where I'm driving the bus to. You want me to reserve you a seat?

IRVIN. All right, save the jokes for the plowboys.

DRIVER (*glaring at* IRVIN, *giving him card*). Fill it out. Last name first, first name, middle name last.

IRVIN. I know. (IRVIN *moves aside and begins writing as* DRAFT MAN *enters, his right wrist handcuffed to* WILL'S *left.*)

DRAFT MAN. Stand back, everybody. Stand back. Don't come too close. Keep away from him. (INDUCTEES *who have been lying down, sit up. Guitar stops.* WILL *looks shamefaced as* DRAFT MAN *transfers cuff from his own wrist to gas pump.*) Reckon this'll hold you.

WILL. Yes, sir.

DRIVER. Have any trouble bringing him over, Mr. McKinney?

DRAFT MAN (*finished with handcuffs, stepping back and surveying* WILL). Uh-uh. Night in jail simmered all the wildness out of him. (*Takes forms and cards from* DRIVER. DRAFT MAN *gives card and pencil to* WILL.) Fill it out. Last name first, first name, middle name last. Lean on the pump there.

WILL. Last name first . . .

DRAFT MAN. First name, middle name last. (WILL, *looking confused, holds card against pump and begins to write.*) Any of you boys had any R.O.T.C.?

IRVIN. I did. Close to a year.

DRAFT MAN. What's your name?

IRVIN. Blanchard, Irvin S.

DRAFT MAN. Okay, Irvin, I'm setting you in charge of the group. When the bus gets to the Classification Center, report to the Sergeant there. Give him these here forms.

IRVIN (*nodding toward* WILL). What about *him*?

DRAFT MAN. Better keep the cuffs on him. Here's the key. It took me two months to flush him out of the hills, so see that he don't get away.

DRIVER. Mr. McKinney . . .

(DRAFT MAN *goes over to* DRIVER. IRVIN *goes to* WILL.)

IRVIN. You hear what he said, plowboy? I don't want any trouble, you understand?

WILL. Oh, me neither, Irvin.

IRVIN. My name to you is Blanchard.

WILL (*extending his hand*). It's a real pleasure.

IRVIN. Are you getting smart with me, plowboy? (WILL *shakes his head.*) I don't want to hear one peep out of you. Not a peep! (IRVIN *moves aside.* WILL *resumes writing.*)

DRAFT MAN. All right, boys. Irvin here is in charge. Do like he tells you and don't give him any trouble. Callville is proud of her sons in uniform. Show them what kind of men we raise down here. Be good, and if you can't be good, be careful. (*He laughs uproariously at his joke, then catches sight of the* INDUCTEE *and* GIRL *embracing by bus.*) Rosabelle!

ROSABELLE (*breaking away from the* INDUCTEE). Pa!

DRAFT MAN. Get on home!

ROSABELLE. Yes, Pa! (*She runs off.*)

DRAFT MAN. I told you to stay home this time. Now git! Ma'll kill you! (*To* INDUCTEES) Well, 'by, boys. Don't take any wooden nickels! (*This line really kills him. He exits in a roar of laughter, which is echoed mockingly by the* INDUCTEES. IRVIN *moves to center and silences them.*)

IRVIN. Okay. Okay! Into the bus when I call your name. DeRoy, Richard S.

FIRST INDUCTEE. Here! (*Gives card to* IRVIN *and exits around bus. Other* INDUCTEES *do the same when their names are called.*)

IRVIN. Farnum, Robert E.

SECOND INDUCTEE. Here!

IRVIN. Hooper, Junior C.

THIRD INDUCTEE. Here!

IRVIN. Lemon, Henry P.

FOURTH INDUCTEE. Here!

IRVIN. Stockdale, Will.

WILL (*pause*). Here . . .

IRVIN. Swinburne, Armand A.

FIFTH INDUCTEE. Here!

IRVIN. Whitledge, Benjamin B. (*Pause.*) Whitledge, Benjamin B.!

(WHITLEDGE, BENJAMIN B., *comes running in, an overnight bag in one hand, a pink envelope in the other. He is small, spindly and frenetic.*)

BEN. Here! Here! Whitledge! Here! Benjamin B.! Is Mr. McKinney here? Mr. McKinney—the man on the draft board! Where is he?

IRVIN. Who?

BEN. Mr. McKinney, the man on the draft board! Where'd he go? I got a letter for him!

IRVIN. Take it easy, sonny. You just missed him.

BEN. I got to find him! I got a letter for him!

IRVIN. He left *me* in charge. (*Plucks the letter out of* BEN's *hand.*)

BEN. Hey, give me that! That's a private letter! You can't take that! It's official business, for Mr. McKinney! Give it back!

(IRVIN *pushes* BEN *away from him roughly.* WILL *extends his free arm and keeps* BEN *from falling over backwards.*)

IRVIN. Don't you understand English? *I'm* in charge. (*Shoves card at* BEN.) Fill out this card.

BEN. That's a private letter . . . (IRVIN *glares at him, moving upstage.*) You big . . .

WILL. Don't get sore at Irvin, fellow. He's had R.O.T.C.

BEN. That don't give him no right to push me around. (*Starts to fill out card.*)

WILL. You put your last name, and then your first name, and then . . . (*Shows his card to* BEN.) Like this.

BEN (*reading*). Stockdale, Will, Will, Stockdale, Stockdale, Stockdale . . . (*Shaking head.*) All you need is one of each.

WILL. That's all? (*Scratches head, begins crossing out extra names.*)

BEN (*glaring toward* IRVIN). Wise guy . . .

(WILL *drops pencil, has difficulty re-*trieving it because of handcuffs, BEN *picks it up for him, notices handcuffs.*)

BEN. What's the matter with you?

WILL. They think I'm a draft-dodger, but I ain't.

BEN (*taking* WILL's *card*). Here, give me . . . You can't write good with handcuffs.

WILL. Thanks. Can't write much good *without* 'em, neither.

BEN (*glares at* IRVIN). Big shot! (*To* WILL) Ever have measles?

WILL. No.

BEN (*making checks on card*). The mumps?

WILL. No.

BEN. Chicken pox . . .

WILL. No.

BEN. Any other communicable diseases?

WILL. Reckon not. (*Watches* BEN *write.*) You figger they're gonna make me go back home?

IRVIN (*reading letter*). Hey Wiggins, come here! (INDUCTEE *comes to* IRVIN, *reads over his shoulder.*)

BEN. Ever break any bones?

WILL. Leg bone once.

BEN. Which leg?

WILL. The right. No, it was the left. Yeah, the left.

BEN (*writing*). Any member of your family belong to groups planning to overthrow the government by unconstitutional means?

WILL (*thinks*). No, we're pretty satisfied. (BEN *writes.* WILL *thinks.*) He still limps a mite.

BEN. Who does?

WILL. That fellow whose leg bone I broke. (BEN *looks annoyedly at* WILL, *begins erasing.*) He hit me first . . .

WIGGINS. Hey, Young! (*Another* INDUCTEE *joins* IRVIN *and* WIGGINS. *They chuckle over the letter.*)

BEN. Did you ever have R.O.T.C.?

WILL. No. (*Pause.*) Irvin had it—close to a year. I figure he still got a touch of it in him.

BEN. Look, Stockdale—

WILL. Will's my name.

BEN. Listen . . .

WILL. What's yours again?

BEN. Ben Whitledge.

WILL. Howdy. (*He extends his hand.* BEN *shakes it.*)

BEN. Hi. Look, Will, R.O.T.C. ain't a disease. It's training. Reserve, Officer,

Training—uh—Corporation.

WILL. Is that the truth . . .

BEN. Sure. There's different kinds. There's Cavalry R.O.T.C., Artillery R.O.T.C., Infantry R.O.T.C. . . . Infantry's the best.

WILL. Yeah . . . that's what I always thought . . . (BEN *writes on his own card.*) Ben, Irvin ain't sick?

BEN. No. And he don't rank no higher than we do, neither, 'cause R.O.T.C. don't mean nothing unless you finish the course.

IRVIN (*removing glasses and holding up sheet of pink paper*). "So I beg of you, Mr. McKinney, please get my enclosed letter to the Commanding Officer in the Air Force."

BEN. Hey, you . . . (BEN *flies at* IRVIN *but* WIGGINS *and* YOUNG *grab him.*)

IRVIN. ". . . so that my son Ben will be put into the Infantry the same as his six brothers . . ."

BEN. Give me that! You big—let go! Let go of me!

IRVIN. "All his life little Ben has been dreaming of being a real Infantry soldier like all the men in our family." (INDUCTEES *roar.*) Little Ben wanna be a big soldier!

WILL (*loud, silencing them*). Irvin! That there letter belongs to Ben. You give it to him.

IRVIN. I told you to keep your mouth shut, plowboy! (*Resumes reading.*) "It will break his poor heart if he's put in the Air Force instead of—"

(WILL *wrenches his arm free, along with a piece of the gas pump.*)

WILL. Give Ben his letter, Irvin.

IRVIN (*a bit pale*). I'm in charge here . . . I'm warning you . . .

WILL. Ben, are you absolutely sure about that R.O.T.C.? (BEN, *still held captive, nods,* WILL *hits* IRVIN; *a blockbuster. As* IRVIN *collapses,* WILL *plucks the letter out of his hand and gives it to* BEN. *Light irises down to a pin-spot on* WILL. *He turns, comes downstage and addresses audience, attempting to conceal the handcuffs, which embarrass him.*) After laying there in that jail till seven o'clock in the morning it was right good to finally git some exercise. Well anyhow, we had a real nice ride up to the Classification Center. Ben and I got us a seat in the back of the bus and what we done was every fifteen minutes we switched around—you know, so there

wouldn't be neither one of us settin' next to the window no longer than the other. We rode up through Pinehurst, and then another town just as big, and then another town as big as Pinehurst and Callville put together! You never seen nothin' like it. And then we come to Macon. Whew! Half an hour to get through it! And it was real fun, with all the fellows hangin' out the bus windows, whistlin' at the gals and hollerin' "Oh, you kid" and "I want you in my stockin' for Christmas" and a whole lot of funny sayings like that. I did enjoy it that day. But somewhere between Macon and Atlanta, Ben and I both dozed off and didn't wake up until we was at the Classification Center.

(*Lights fade on him. Whistle blows in darkness. Light comes up on* SERGEANT KING, *standing before a section of wall on which is a bulletin board marked "Barracks #10—Sgt. King."* KING *looks very tired and somewhat pained by it all. He gives another blast on the whistle.*)

KING. Please . . . let's keep it quiet . . . (*He waits for silence, glances at his wrist watch, and starts unreeling his orientation speech in a somnambulistic monotone, avoiding any inflection that might give meaning to the words. He takes a breath whenever he feels the need—usually in mid-sentence.*) On behalf of the President of the United States, the Secretary of the Air Force and the Commanders of the base and this squadron, I want to welcome you gentlemen to the United States Air Force. This is a classification center where you will undergo a series of tests both physical and mental designed to determine your abilities and potentialities so that you may be trained for the position from which you and the Air Force will derive the greatest benefit, tests are for your own good so do your best in every test. My name is King, K-I-N-G, Sergeant King, and I'm in charge of this barracks in which you will be billeted for approximately two weeks. During this period the barracks *will* be kept spotlessly clean, maybe it's just a stopping place to you, but to me—*it's home.* Before turning in tonight every one of you will write a letter to your nearest of kin informing them that you have arrived safely and *are in the best of health.* If at any time a problem should arise, feel free to consult me about its solution. (*Opens door of his room.*) I am here to help you during these first difficult days of military service. *Knock before entering.* (*He exits, closing door. Blackout. Lights come up in* KING's *room, a cosy place with many homelike touches.* KING *stands just within door, garrison cap in hand, wiping his forehead. He hangs cap on hook, goes to radio on shelf and turns it on. Pausing to straighten framed sampler on which "Mother" is embroidered in prominent letters, he goes down to small table with hotplate and percolator.* KING *jiggles percolator, nods, sets it on hotplate, flicks switch, and looks at his watch. Knock on door.*)

KING. Come in.

(IRVIN *enters, still in civilian clothes, holding the forms that* DRAFT MAN *gave him. He comes to attention.*)

IRVIN. Private Blanchard delivering forms on eight inductees as ordered.

KING (*a contemplative pause*). You keep standing like that, you're gonna pull a muscle. (*Starts taking off tie.*) Just put them down. (IRVIN *starts to put forms on bunk.*) Not on the bed please. (IRVIN *looks around for someplace else.* KING *nods toward the table.* IRVIN *puts forms there, hesitates.*) Anything else?

IRVIN. Sergeant, I feel it's my duty to tell you about one of the men. Fellow named Stockdale. A draft-dodger. He gave me a lot of trouble. (*Takes handcuffs out of pocket.*) They brought him to the bus in these.

KING (*a bit taken aback by handcuffs*). I'll make a note of it.

IRVIN. I think he ought to be given disciplinary action. He took a swing at—one of the men. Even knocked him out. He jumped this man from behind and knocked him out.

KING. In the barracks here?

IRVIN. Back at the bus.

KING (*pause*). I'll make a note of it.

IRVIN. I thought he ought to be reported to the Squadron Commander, that's what. (KING *freezes for a moment.*) I mean, I think it's my duty to see that he—

KING. Any reporting is done around here, *I* do it.

IRVIN. Sure you do, and this fellow Stockdale is a real troublemaker and he—

KING (*sitting on bed*). Sonny, look; how long have you been in the service?

IRVIN. About six hours, I guess. I had R.O.T.C., though.

KING. Uh-huh . . . And they told you it was all efficiency and getting things done and standing at attention and running around? (*Taking off shoes.*) I been in for eighteen years, and it ain't like you think at all. It's a quiet, peaceful life . . . if everybody minds their own business. It's like there's a big lake, nice and calm; I'm in one canoe, you're in another, the Captain's in a canoe, the Colonel . . . You know what you do when you complain to somebody, or report somebody, or request something? (IRVIN *shakes his head.*) You make waves. (*Puts his feet into big woolly slippers, rises, goes to table, takes cup and saucer from shelf, pours coffee.* IRVIN, *meanwhile, puts handcuffs on forms and goes to door.*)

IRVIN. Well, I thought the Captain would want to know, if he's got a troublemaker in the outfit.

KING. Look, Sonny, I hate to pull rank, but for your information, you got the smallest canoe in the whole damn lake! Good afternoon, Private. (IRVIN *exits, closing door.* KING *stretches out on his bunk.*)

RADIO ANNOUNCER. Our next request comes from Master Sergeant Orville C. King at the Air Force Classification Center. Here you are, Sergeant. (KING *beams. The radio plays "Flow Gently, Sweet Afton,"* KING *sips his coffee thoughtfully, and the lights slowly fade.*)

(*Lights come up on a double-decker bunk.* BEN, *in underwear, manages to climb on to upper bunk, with* WILL's *assistance.*)

BEN. Don't boost—I can make it.

WILL. Ben, I wish you would take the bottom one.

BEN. No, sir. Just hand me my bag.

WILL (*doing so*). Honest, I like sleeping high.

BEN. No, sir. You sat on the bottom bunk first.

WILL. I didn't mean nothin' by it. Honest I didn't.

BEN. First come, first served. That's the military way.

VOICE (*off*). Lights out in five minutes.

WILL (*pulling on* BEN's *bag*). C'mon, Ben.

BEN. I won't, I tell you!

(IRVIN *and two* INDUCTEES *enter from right.*)

IRVIN. Let that man alone, Stockdale! Get your hands off that man's things! (WILL, *wide-eyed, withdraws his hand.*

BEN *falls back on bunk.*) They brought you to the bus in handcuffs and I'm beginning to think I never should've taken 'em off you!

WILL. Irvin, I wasn't doin' anythin'. I was just—

IRVIN. I've stood about as much as I'm *gonna* stand out of you! One lucky punch don't make no champion. If you want to start some more fighting go after somebody your own size, not some skinny little —

BEN (*swinging his feet off top bunk*). You watch your mouth! Why don't you mind your own business anyhow?

IRVIN. Look, this fellow was going to—

BEN. That's between him and me! Nobody asked you to butt in!

WILL. Now, Ben, don't . . .

IRVIN. I was only trying to do you a favor, Junior!

BEN. Who you calling Junior? Who asked you anything anyhow?

IRVIN. All right. If that's the way you feel about it, all right. You want to be buddies with the draft-dodger, *be* buddies with the draft-dodger. Go ahead . . .

BEN. That's the way I feel about it.

IRVIN (*backing away*). You better just get into bed and *don't start no trouble in this barracks!* Get into bed!

WILL. I was just goin' to, Irvin.

FIRST INDUCTEE. Give him time, Irvin. Beds is strange to Plowboy; he's used to sleepin' with the hogs!

(INDUCTEES *laugh*, WILL *joins in*, BEN *glares.* IRVIN *and* INDUCTEES, *laughing, move off.*)

BEN (*livid*). What's the matter with you anyhow?

WILL. Me?

BEN. Taking their insults all day and hee-hawing like a danged donkey!

WILL. Ah, they don't mean nothin', Ben. And besides, that one about sleepin' with the hogs was kind of funny. (*Starts taking off pants.*)

BEN (*getting under blankets*). Aw . . .

WILL. I figger if we just laugh with 'em, Ben, pretty soon they'll get tired of carryin' on, and that way there won't be no ruckus or nothin'.

BEN. You think laughing is gonna stop these guys? A good licking is all they understand!

WILL (*hangs pants on end of bunk*). You think so?

BEN. I know so! . . . And you hee-hawing like a danged donkey! (*He turns over, putting his back to* WILL. WILL *scratches his head, sits on bottom bunk. Lights dim down and a bugle starts playing "Taps."* WILL *listens for a moment.*)

WILL (*to audience*). Somebody brung their trumpet.

(THIRD INDUCTEE *crosses.*)

FIRST INDUCTEE. Lonesome for the hogs, Plowboy?

(WILL *laughs half-heartedly.*)

WILL (*to audience*). I reckon Ben knew what he was talkin' about when he said laughin' warn't gonna do no good. But I figgered I couldn't start bangin' away at 'em with no reason so I set around waitin' for someone to give me a reason.

FOURTH INDUCTEE (*passing* WILL). Ain't used to sleeping indoors, are you, Plowboy?

WILL (*to audience*). I didn't feel as how that was quite enough.

(IRVIN *and his two sidekicks return.*)

IRVIN. Get in bed, Plowboy.

WILL (*to audience*). That warn't enough.

IRVIN (*to* WILL). That is, if you can lift those big clumsy feet of yours.

WILL (*to audience*). That warn't enough either.

IRVIN (*to* BEN). Don't wet the bed, Junior, or Mama will spank.

WILL (*to audience*). That were. (*He slugs* IRVIN *and* IRVIN *goes down.*) No stayin' power at all. (*Other* INDUCTEES *attack.* BEN *hops onto one's shoulders and pummels his head.* WILL *dispatches the others with great ease, punctuating the action with the following lines.*) No more muscle than a rabbit . . . Livin' in town, that's what does it . . . They stay up till close on to ten o'clock every night! Eat all them fancy foods . . . Orange juice. . . . Won't touch green peas unless the shells is off 'em! Surprises me they got what little strength they have . . . (*All the assailants are floored by now. They stagger away.* WILL *comes downstage, brushing off his hands.*) But there was a whole lot of 'em, so it was a pretty good fight anyhow! (*Turning up to* BEN.) Warn't it, Ben?

BEN. Aww . . .

WILL. Could've been better, but it wasn't bad.

BEN. Dog it, Will. This will mess up everything!

WILL. What will, Ben?

BEN. Fighting—in the barracks.

WILL. But you said a lickin' was all they'd understand.

BEN. Not in the barracks! One of them's bound to talk about it. Dog it, I'll never get into the Infantry now . . . starting a big ruckus . . . I figgered if we kept our mouths shut and didn't do nothin' to nobody we might get transferred—but now—

WILL. Both of us?

BEN. But now they're sure to talk about the fight—they're bound to!

WILL. No they won't, Ben. If one of them says anythin', I'll take him out back and whomp him good.

BEN. Now there you go again, Will! You think they want folks in the Infantry that acts like that? No sir, they want folks who can take it and keep their mouths shut, the way a man ought to do. Transfer? We'll be lucky if they don't transfer us into the Navy—walking around in them li'l ole white uniforms!

WILL. You want both of us to transfer, Ben?

BEN. Don't you understand, Will? It's the Infantry does the real fighting . . . the rest is just helpers. Look at The War Between The States. How about that?

WILL. Yeh! How about that!

BEN. See what I mean? Listen, every man in my whole family's been in the Infantry, clear back to Great-Grandpa! You know what he done? Fought with Stonewall Jackson at Chancellorsville, that's what!

WILL. Licked him good too, I bet!

BEN. By dog, first thing tomorrow morning I'm going to get the Sergeant's permission to see the Captain. I'll give him Ma's letter . . . (Takes letter from under pillow, looks at it.) Aww . . . (Throws letter disgustedly on floor.) What's the use! (Climbs into bunk and under blankets.)

WILL. But, Ben, maybe you'll get to like the Air Force. Zoomin' all over the sky, shoutin' Roger and Wilco and everythin'. Maybe it won't be so bad.

BEN. Bad! You know what they call men in the Air Force? Airmen! Like something out of a danged funny book! How you gonna like it when somebody calls you Airman?

WILL. By God, I just don't think I'd stand for it.

BEN. AIRMAN! (He buries his head in the pillow.)

WILL. Ben! (No response.) Hey, Ben! (Still no reply. WILL picks up the letter which BEN has discarded. He looks at the envelope.) By dog! (Lights fade, leaving only a pin-spot on WILL as he takes trousers from bunk, pulls them on, tiptoes down to door of KING's room and knocks lightly. He buttons trousers and knocks again, harder. He fastens belt and knocks once more, a real rafter-shaker. There is an excited bumping and fumbling from KING's room.)

KING. All right! I'm up! I'm up! All right! (More bumping and fumbling. Lights come up; KING's table lamp. He almost knocks it over. One leg is in his trousers, one arm in his shirt. WILL enters room.) All right! I'm up!

WILL. Howdy! I'm Will Stockdale.

KING (struggling into uniform). I didn't hear no whistle. Tell the men to line up in back. If the Captain comes around tell him I'm checking on who overslept. I'll be out as soon as I . . . (Looks at WILL, looks around, looks at wrist watch.) It's ten o'clock . . . at night.

WILL. It is? (KING shoves his wrist watch under WILL's nose.) Ooh! That's the prettiest watch . . .

KING (dazed by the enormity of the sin). You woke me.

WILL. You said to knock before enterin'.

KING (sinking on bunk, removing uniform). Why did you wake me?

WILL. Well, this ain't nothin' personal against you, Sergeant, or that we don't like your barracks or nothin' like that. What it is is Ben's got these six brothers that are all Infantry—that's my new buddy Ben that's sleepin' out there—so naturally he don't want to be in the Air Force, I mean with the Infantry doin' the real fightin' and the Air Force just bein' the helpers. You know, like in The War Between The States. So he wants to transfer to the Infantry and he asked me to go along with him. I figgered you could do it for us. I heared what you said out there, about how you was here to help us durin' these first difficult days of military service.

KING (stares, turns away). Why do they send all the bums and idiots to my barracks?

WILL. They do?

KING (turning to him again). Yes. Yes, they do.

WILL. Sho' must be a mess.

KING (*rising*). Now look, whatever-your-name-is, I want you to get—

WILL. Stockdale.

KING. Stockdale. I want you to get out of this room and—Stockdale . . . (*Turns to table, lifts handcuffs.*) Stockdale . . . (*Turning to* WILL *again*) Now don't start anything with me, you hear. Just get out of here and go to sleep, that's all.

WILL. Yes, sir. (*As he exits*) Ben *did* say the Captain was the one to see.

KING. STOCKDALE! (*Rushes after him.*) Where are you going?

WILL. To the Captain.

KING. No . . . no . . . You can't . . . (*Pushes* WILL *back into room.*)

WILL. Ben knows all about doin' things military-like, and he said the Captain was—

KING. Stockdale, you're . . . you're . . . (*Makes wave-making gesture.*) You can't *do* this. This Captain'll rip off your stripes as soon as look at you.

WILL. I ain't got no stripes.

KING. You'll never get transfers waking him up. He won't understand; believe me, he won't!

WILL. I'll go over it real slow.

KING. Oh Lord . . . Look, this Captain . . . he . . . he won't do a favor for anybody unless they do a favor for him first! That's it. Now how would you like to do a big favor for the Captain?

WILL. Me?

KING. Come on. (*Virtually drags* WILL *across stage.*) You do one for him, he'll do one for me, and I do one for you. That's the way it works in the service.

(*Lights come up in latrine and fade out in* KING's *room.*)

KING. Do you know what this is, Stockdale?

WILL. Well, it's kind of a big outhouse, ain't it?

KING. We call it the latrine.

WILL (*looking around*). La-trine . . . How about that . . .

KING. You might say it's the Captain's hobby. He inspects it every chance he gets, and when everything is sparkling, the Captain sparkles too. (*Takes long-handled brush from wall and gives it to* WILL.) You stay in here and get things all cleaned up. You are the Officer in Charge.

WILL (*overwhelmed*). In charge?

KING. Every last one! All yours!

WILL. Golly!

KING (*going to door*). Now stay in here, you understand? Don't go no place.

WILL. You bet! Good night!

KING (*incredulously*). Good night . . . (*Exits, shaking head wonderingly.*)

WILL (*calling after him*). Say, thanks! (*He tucks handle of brush under his belt and begins collecting trash from floor. Door of* KING's *room is heard slamming. To audience*) Well! It just goes to show you how good things happen to you when you least expect 'em. (*Hums at his work.*) I stayed Officer in Charge of this here latrine all night, a'rubbin' and a'scrubbin' and doin' my best to make things sparkle like Sergeant King said. (*Puts trash in can.*) And by the time mornin' come—if you'll excuse my braggin'—I think I done a right good job of it. Sergeant King was real pleased with how things come out.

(KING *enters latrine.*)

KING. Beautiful! Beautiful . . . beautiful . . . (*At commodes.*) . . . beau—ti—ful!

WILL. Shucks, it ain't hard . . .

KING (*looks around incredulously*). Wait till the *Captain* sees this! He inspects this place like it was an operating room where they was getting ready to *cut out his heart!* Never in your life have you seen such a man for sticking his head *right down into* things!

WILL. You figger he'll like what I done?

KING. He'll be a new man. . . . (KING *stares some more, then goes to* WILL *and puts his hand solemnly on his shoulder.*) Will . . . How would you like to be . . . Permanent Latrine Orderly?

WILL. Permanent Latrine Orderly . . .

KING. P.L.O.!

WILL. Golly . . .

KING. You'll keep this place all the time like it is now, the Captain'll get off my back . . .

WILL. Gee, I sure would like to do it, Sergeant. Only I was set on helpin' Ben get those transfers. He's my buddy.

KING. Ain't I your buddy?

WILL. You are?

KING. You help me, I'll help Ben. But don't say a word about this outside of this room, you understand? I'm going straight over to the Record Section and fix it with some friends of mine.

WILL. Don't I have to go get them tests you talked about yesterday, to get myself classified?

KING. (*at door*). No, Will . . . (*A final enraptured look at latrine*) . . . you've *been* classified. (*He exits.* WILL *turns happily to audience.*)

WILL. Well, didn't *that* make me feel pretty good? (*Hangs brush on wall, takes tie and khaki shirt from hook, puts them on during following.*) I worked just as hard as I could all week long. Of course, every time I seen Ben, he took on right fierce about how it was against the rules for me to be permanent in the latrine. He didn't mean nothin' by it, though. Anyhow I worked real hard; I scrubbed what was for scrubbin' and polished what was for polishin', and what was left over, I painted. And by Saturday, when the Captain come to inspect, I had everythin' so white and shiny you couldn't hardly look at it without squenchin' up your eyes. Them faucets for instance; I polished them so hard they don't say hot and cold no more! (*Smooths down his hair and comes to attention facing the door. Door flies open.*)

KING. Ten-hut! (KING *holds door for* CAPTAIN, *then follows him in.*)

WILL (*saluting*). Latrine ready for inspection, sir!

(CAPTAIN *returns salute, sees glittering latrine, lowers arm slowly.* WILL *drops salute.* CAPTAIN, *wide-eyed, turns to* KING. KING *smiles complacently.* CAPTAIN *moves incredulously about latrine.*)

CAPTAIN. This is incredible . . . This is absolutely . . . incredible! I'm pleased! No, no . . . no, I'm *happy!*

KING. Thank you, sir, thank you.

CAPTAIN (*inspects commodes, thoroughly, then beams at* WILL). You the one on latrine duty today, Private?

WILL. Yes, sir. All week, sir.

(KING *clears his throat forebodingly.*)

CAPTAIN. Well, you are to be congratulated. (*Examines sink.*) Just look at the— (*Turns to* WILL.) What did you say?

WILL. Me? Nothin', sir.

CAPTAIN. Something about all week.

WILL. Well, I done my best in one day, but to be fair with you it took a week of rubbin' and scrubbin' to get it like this.

CAPTAIN (*to* KING). Is this man being punished for—

WILL. Heck no, sir! I'm P.L.O.!

CAPTAIN. What?

WILL. Permanent Latrine Orderly.

KING. Stockdale . . .

WILL. Don't credit me none, sir. It's *all* Sergeant King's doin'. He's even got it fixed up so's I don't have to get classified!

KING. Sir—

CAPTAIN. That's . . . that's impossible!

WILL. Oh no, sir. He fixed it with some friends of his.

KING. Stockdale . . .

WILL. It was him got me to work so hard, tellin' me how latrines is your hobby and stickin' your head into things and all.

KING. Sir, I can . . .

WILL. Now don't be bashful, Sergeant! Sir, I been wantin' to tell you what a good sergeant he is. He solves our problems for us, and he helps us out on our difficult days of military service, and I reckon he's just about the best danged sergeant there is in the whole danged Air Force! (*Pause.*) Sir, you really ought to get up off'n his back.

(CAPTAIN *turns slowly to* KING; KING *turns slowly to liquid.*)

CAPTAIN. How long have you been a sergeant? (KING *gives an incomprehensible mumble.*) Speak up!

KING. Sixteen years, sir.

CAPTAIN. How long do you expect to remain a sergeant?

KING (*hopefully*). Twelve years?

CAPTAIN. You will remain a sergeant for exactly one week. One week! Unless this man completes the entire classification process and is shipped out with the group he came in with. Do you understand? Unless this man is out of here by the end of next week, you will not be in charge of this barracks, you will not be a sergeant; you will in all probability be a permanent latrine orderly. P.L.O.!

KING (*saluting weakly*). Yes, sir! (CAPTAIN *returns salute and goes to door. Stops outside latrine doorway, turns and speaks to* WILL.)

CAPTAIN. This is not your fault, Private. You've done a fine job. This is the cleanest latrine I've seen in my entire career.

WILL. Thank you, sir. My aim was to get it just as clean as that operatin' room where they're gettin' ready to cut out your heart. (*Before* WILL *has finished the above,* KING *has leaped across room and slammed door in* CATPAIN's *face. He remains against door, staring at* WILL, *trembling.*) You forgot to ask him about the transfers.

KING. What happened? What did you do it for?

WILL. Well, I couldn't see no sense in *me* gettin' all the credit.

KING (*coming close to* WILL, *not daring to touch him*). Look, Will, we got to get you classified. We got to get you out of here . . .

WILL (*pause*). You don't want me around no more? I thought we was buddies.

KING (*quickly*). It ain't what I want, Will; it's what the Captain wants. (*Leading* WILL *out of latrine.*) Come on, we gotta get you classified in a hurry. There's all kinds of tests you'll have to take, and people you'll have to talk with. You'll have to work real hard. (KING *and* WILL *are now spotlighted downstage, as rest of stage fades into darkness.*)

WILL. I'll work hard, all right, but I don't know . . . The last time I took a test was close on to five years ago, and then it was just one of them tests where you try this fellow's toothpaste for ten days and see if'n your teeth don't get brighter. (*Pause.*) I failed.

KING (*looks desperate. He shows* WILL *his wrist watch*). Look, you been admiring this watch of mine, haven't you?

WILL. I sure have! It's the prettiest . . .

KING. If you're ready to ship out by next Saturday like the Captain said—it's yours!

WILL. Mine?

KING. Yours!

WILL. Gol-ly!

KING. So you're going to try your hardest, right?

WILL. Right!

KING. And not waste no time?

WILL. No sir!

KING. Good! Good boy! Now first thing Monday morning we start Classification. You just stay right here and relax, rest your head. I'm going over to the testing area and see if I can . . . uh, borrow some of the tests. (*He vanishes into the darkness.* WILL *turns to audience.*)

WILL. That Classification was really somethin'. They got this great big buildin' all full of doctors and nurses and officers— all of 'em walkin' around real quickety-quick and not smilin' at nobody. And first thing you knowed, one of 'em was mashin' down your tongue with an ice cream stick! You think I'm makin' this up. It's the truth! One of them fellows was even goin' around poppin' everybody in the knee with a little rubber hammer!

(*Lights fade up on a hallway with three doors marked "Manual Dexterity," "Psy-chiatrist" and "Oculist."* OFFICERS, INDUCTEES, NURSES *and* DOCTORS *cross back and forth. Typewriters and tabulators can be heard.* WILL *sets about rolling a cigarette.*)

FIRST CORPORAL (*crossing*). Hey, you there! (WILL *turns.*) No smoking! (*Points to wall sign.*) Don't you know how to read?

WILL (*to audience*). Good thing Pa ain't around to hear that. Well, anyhow, I did pretty good on it all. The written tests was exactly the same as the ones Sergeant King borrowed, but the only trouble was the Sergeant spent so much time drummin' the answers into me, there was hardly no time left to study the questions they joined up with. So in the tests, the answers was easy, but the questions was real hard. By Friday afternoon, I was down to the last three tests, and Sergeant King said it looked like maybe I might get myself classified for Gunnery School.

(*"Manual Dexterity" door opens.* KING *sticks his head out.*)

KING. Will! Come on! (WILL *goes up to* KING.) Corporal's waiting for you.

(*Lights come up in "Manual Dexterity" room and fade out in hallway. An officious little* CORPORAL *stands waiting; a large irregularly shaped link in each hand.*)

SECOND CORPORAL (*motions* WILL *into chair*). What we do here, Private, is evaluate your manual dexterity. On a time scale in relation to digital-visual co-ordination. (*He holds up links.*) Two irregular steel links . . . (*He fits them together, a complex job.*) . . . which can be interconnected . . . thusly. (*Holds them up, joined, then separates them.*) I separate them . . . (*Joins them again.*) . . . I join them. It will be your task, Private, when I give the signal, to place the two links in the interconnected relationship I have just demonstrated. (*He puts a link in each of* WILL's *hands.* WILL *looks at them confusedly.*)

WILL. I put 'em together?

SECOND CORPORAL. That's right, you "put them together." I'll time you. Three minutes is passing. (*Winds stop watch.*)

KING. Whatever you do, don't get nervous.

SECOND CORPORAL. Ready? (*Raises watch.*) Go!

(WILL *slowly touches one link against the other, baffled.* KING *is on top of him.*)

KING. There we go! At-a-boy! Put 'em

together!

SECOND CORPORAL. Sergeant! Please. No one ever does it in less than two minutes! Please! You're not even supposed to be in here! (*He pulls* KING *away. They move aside, conversing in low tones.*)

KING. No, no. It's okay. You see, I'm rushing him through so he can catch up with the group he came in with. He's a special case.

SECOND CORPORAL. Well, I'll have to ask you not to speak to him during the actual testing. It's a difficult problem and requires his full attention. (*As* KING *and* SECOND CORPORAL *continue their exchange,* WILL *is busily wrenching open one link, shoving it through its mate and compressing the pair into something resembling a bowknot.*)

WILL. I'm done.

KING. Stop the watch!

SECOND CORPORAL. Done? (*Looking at watch*) In fourteen seconds? (*Takes links from* WILL.) He . . . look what he . . . look! (*Tries to separate links.*)

KING. He put them together, didn't he?

SECOND CORPORAL (*running into hallway.* KING *and* WILL *follow. Lights dim out in room and come up in hallway.*) Corporal!

KING. Now what are you making a fuss about? You said put 'em together and he—

SECOND CORPORAL (*to* FIRST CORPORAL *as he enters*). Look! Look what he's done, for Pete's sake. How you supposed to mark him on that?

FIRST CORPORAL. You're supposed to be grading this. Can't you do a simple thing like that? (*Exits.*)

SECOND CORPORAL (*calling after him*). I'm supposed to mark it down if they put it back together or not and there ain't supposed to be but one way of doing it, and he sure didn't do it that way. . . . How you gonna mark a thing like that? And who's gonna pay for these things? (*To* WILL) Sixteen dollars they cost. If you think I'm gonna pay sixteen lousy dollars . . .

KING (*advancing on him, soothingly*). Corporal, Corporal . . .

SECOND CORPORAL. Sixteen lousy dollars!

KING. Corporal . . . I'll be *glad* to pay the sixteen lousy dollars.

SECOND CORPORAL. You will?

KING. Sure. If he passed the test . . .

SECOND CORPORAL. But he did it completely wrong. He was supposed to—

KING (*taking* CORPORAL's *arm and leading him off*). Now let's take this logically; you need some money and I need for him to pass the test. . . .

(WILL *watches them go. Door of* PSYCHIATRIST's *office opens and* BEN *emerges.*)

BEN (*seeing* WILL). Will!

WILL (*turning*). Ben! (*They rush to each other and pump hands.*)

BEN. I ain't hardly seen you all day! What you been doing, classifying?

WILL. Yeah!

BEN. Find out where you're going?

WILL. Sergeant King says if I pass the eye test I'll be goin' to Gunnery School!

BEN. That's where I'm going if I pass the eye test!

WILL. How about that—(*Flips* BEN's *tie out of his shirt.*)

BEN (*suddenly deflated*). Yeah. How about that.

WILL. Ben, you ain't *still* sad about not bein' in the Infantry?

BEN. The Captain never even read my letter. I even asked that there psychiatrist.

WILL. What did he say?

BEN. He didn't say nothing. I don't think he understands so good. Looks like I'm stuck with the Air Force.

WILL. But Ben, maybe it's really the Air Force that's the real soldiers and the Infantry that's just the helpers.

BEN. Never.

WILL. What about that movie they showed us, about that airplane that goes up *fifty* thousand feet, and makes the blood boil up inside you and kills you in ten seconds! It's the Air Age, Ben! And the gunner is right up there with the pilot and the bombardier and all the others!

BEN. Yeah! Bombardier! Throws bombs! But who does he throw 'em at? The infantry, that's who!

WILL. And medals! Ooh, the way that fellow took on! You get one for practically everythin' in the Air Force. They even give you one for just bein' there and not doin' nothin' wrong. How about that!

BEN. Wait till my brothers find out. Airman! (BEN *pulls his cap from his belt and hurls it to the floor. As he does so, a Negro* LIEUTENANT *is passing by. He stops.*)

LIEUTENANT. Private!

BEN (*snapping to attention*). Sir!

LIEUTENANT. That's no way to treat government property.

BEN. Yes, sir!

LIEUTENANT. Pick up your cap, Private.

BEN. Yes, sir. (*Stoops to retrieve cap.*)

LIEUTENANT. You shouldn't be loitering here anyhow.

BEN. (*rising quickly and coming to attention again*). We're being classified, sir.

LIEUTENANT (*to* WILL). I'm looking for Sergeant King. Do you know him?

WILL (*gaping*). Sure do . . . He's ourn . . .

LIEUTENANT. Where is he?

WILL. He went down there with a corporal in tow. He's havin' trouble gettin' me classified.

LIEUTENANT (*knowingly*). Uh-huh. (*Starting to go.*) Pick up that cap, Private.

BEN (*retrieves cap*). Yes, sir.

LIEUTENANT. And let's get that tie tucked in. (*Exits.*)

BEN. Yes, sir. (*To* WILL) What's the matter with you? Don't you know enough to stand at attention and salute an officer?

WILL (*still gaping after the* LIEUTENANT). You know, he talked whiter than I do.

BEN. Whiter than you do? Listen, he was an officer, that's all!

WILL. And I'll bet he's a good one, too, so snappy and all . . . (*Pause*) I'm homesick . . .

BEN. Will, when a man's in uniform, he ain't black or white or yellow or nothing! You ain't supposed to notice the color of a man in uniform!

WILL. You ain't?

BEN. No sir!

WILL. Ben, you mean . . . when that Lieutenant come over . . . you didn't notice he was . . . is it all right if I say colored?

BEN. All I saw was a lieutenant, period!

WILL. A colored lieutenant.

BEN. A lieutenant! Can't you understand nothing, Will? The only thing that's important in the service is rank! If a man's an officer, he's higher than you, even if he's green with purple spots!

WILL. Oh, now, Ben . . .

BEN. Rank! That's all! A man in uniform don't see nothing else!

WILL. Well, dang it, Ben . . . I'm a man in uniform all right and the minute he come in here I seen his face was darker than ourn!

BEN. Honest, Will. Sometimes I wonder how come they ever took you in the draft at all!

(KING *and* SECOND CORPORAL *re-enter, both smiling,* KING *pocketing his wallet.* SECOND CORPORAL *exits into "Manual Dexterity" room.*)

KING. Well, it looks like we're just liable to get you classified after all. It goes to show what the Air Force has come down to.

THIRD CORPORAL (*entering from* PSYCHIATRIST's *office with form in hand. To* KING). Is this fellow Whitledge in your group?

BEN. That's me, Corporal.

KING. Yeah—that's him.

THIRD CORPORAL. Psychiatrist says he has a secondary anxiety with inferiority and systematized delusions of persecution.

KING. I ain't surprised.

THIRD CORPORAL. Recommends he be considered for transfer to the Infantry.

BEN. The *Infantry!*

THIRD CORPORAL. Don't get excited. He didn't say you have to.

WILL. That's what Ben's always wantin', Corporal.

BEN. Just what do I have to do?

THIRD CORPORAL (*gives* BEN *a form*). Here—fill this out. (*To* KING) Soon as he's finished, buck it through to the Colonel for approval.

KING. Okay. If that's what the crazy kid wants.

WILL. How about that, Ben—you made it!

BEN. Just wait till I tell my brothers!

THIRD CORPORAL (*holding out another form*). Okay, Stockdale—Psychiatrist.

KING (*takes form from* CORPORAL, *who exits*). Oh Lord. Now Will, listen carefully. The psychiatrist test is one I couldn't get the questions for because there ain't any. The doctor just asks you whatever pops into his head. So keep your wits about you.

WILL. I'll try. Maybe I can get a transfer too, huh, Ben?

KING. He'll just ask you stuff like "What do you dream?"

WILL. Okay. (*Touches* BEN.) Maybe he'll give me a transfer too, huh, Ben?

BEN. Yeah, sure . . .

KING. Safest thing, I guess, is to say you never dream at all.

WILL. See you later, Ben. (*Exits into* PSYCHIATRIST's *office.*)

KING. No dreams! Oh, jeez . . . (*Begins pacing.*)

BEN. Do you think he can?

KING. Can what?

BEN. Get transferred too? Maybe you could talk to the doctor.

KING. Listen! Don't you complicate things.

BEN. I just wish Will was going too. I mean it'd be more fun . . .

KING. Listen, Whitledge, you take care of yourself. *I'll* take care of *him.*

BEN. Okay, okay . . . (BEN *begins filling out his form as the lights fade out in hallway and fade up in* PSYCHIATRIST'S *office.* PSYCHIATRIST, *a major, signs and stamps a paper before him, then takes form from* WILL, *seated next to desk.* PSYCHIATRIST *looks at form, looks at* WILL. *A moment of silence.*)

WILL. I never have no dreams at all.

PSYCHIATRIST (*a pause. He looks carefully at* WILL, *looks at form*). Where you from, Stockdale?

WILL. Georgia.

PSYCHIATRIST. That's . . . not much of a state, is it?

WILL. Well . . . I don't live all over the state. I just live in this one little place in it.

PSYCHIATRIST. That's where "Tobacco Road" is, Georgia.

WILL. Not around my section. (*Pause*) Maybe you're from a different part than me?

PSYCHIATRIST. I've never been there. What's more I don't think I would ever *want* to go there. What's your reaction to that?

WILL. Well, I don't know.

PSYCHIATRIST. I think I would sooner live in the rottenest pigsty in Alabama or Tennessee than in the fanciest mansion in all of Georgia. What about that?

WILL. Well, sir, I think where you want to live is your business.

PSYCHIATRIST (*pause, staring*). You don't mind if someone says something bad about Georgia?

WILL. I ain't heared nobody say nothin' bad about Georgia.

PSYCHIATRIST. What do you think I've been saying?

WILL. Well, to tell you the truth, I ain't been able to get too much sense out of it. Don't you know?

PSYCHIATRIST. Watch your step, young man. (*Pause*) We psychiatrists call this attitude of yours "resistance."

WILL. You do?

PSYCHIATRIST. You sense that this interview is a threat to your security. You feel yourself in danger.

WILL. Well, kind of I do. If'n I don't get classified Sergeant King won't give me the wrist watch. (PSYCHIATRIST *stares at* WILL *uncomprehendingly.*) He *won't!* He said I only gets it if I'm classified inside a week.

PSYCHIATRIST (*turns forlornly to papers on desk. A bit subdued*). You get along all right with your mother?

WILL. No, sir, I can't hardly say that I do—

PSYCHIATRIST (*cutting in*). She's very strict? Always hovering over you?

WILL. No, sir, just the opposite—

PSYCHIATRIST. She's never there.

WILL. That's right.

PSYCHIATRIST. You resent this neglect, don't you?

WILL. No, I don't resent nothin'.

PSYCHIATRIST (*leaning forward paternally*). There's nothing to be ashamed of, son. It's a common situation. Does she ever beat you?

WILL. No!

PSYCHIATRIST (*silkily*). So defensive. It's not easy to talk about your mother, is it.

WILL. No, sir. She died when I was borned.

PSYCHIATRIST (*a long, sick pause*). You . . . could have told me that sooner . . .

WILL (*looks hang-dog.* PSYCHIATRIST *returns to papers.* WILL *glances up at him*). Do you hate *your* Mama? (PSYCHIATRIST'S *head snaps up, glaring.*) I figgered as how you said it was so common . . .

PSYCHIATRIST. I do not hate my mother.

WILL. I should hope not! (*Pause*) What does she beat you or somethin'?

PSYCHIATRIST (*glares again, drums his fingers briefly on table. Steeling himself, more to self than* WILL). This is a transference. You're taking all your stored up antagonisms and loosing them in my direction. Transference. It happens every day. . . .

WILL (*excited*). It does? To the Infantry?

PSYCHIATRIST (*aghast*). The Infantry?

WILL. You give Ben a transfer. I wish you'd give me one too. I'd sure love to go along with him.

PSYCHIATRIST. Stop! (*The pause is a long one this time. Finally* PSYCHIATRIST *points at papers.*) There are a few more topics we have to cover. We will not talk about transfers, we will not talk about my mother. We will only talk about what *I* want to talk about, do you understand?

WILL. Yes, sir.

PSYCHIATRIST. Now then—your father. (*Quickly*) Living?

WILL. Yes, sir.

PSYCHIATRIST. Do you get along with him okay?

WILL. Yes, sir.

PSYCHIATRIST. Does he ever beat you?

WILL. You bet!

PSYCHIATRIST. Hard?

WILL. And how! Boy, there ain't nobody can beat like my Pa can!

PSYCHIATRIST (*beaming*). So *this* is where the antagonism comes from! (*Pause*) You hate your father, don't you.

WILL. No . . . I got an uncle I hate! Every time he comes out to the house he's always wantin' to rassle with the mule, and the mule gets all wore out, and *he* gets all wore out . . . Well, I don't really *hate* him; I just ain't exactly partial to him.

PSYCHIATRIST (*pause*). Did I ask you about your uncle?

WILL. I thought you wanted to talk about hatin' people.

PSYCHIATRIST (*glares, drums his fingers; retreats to form. Barely audible*). Now—girls. How do you like girls?

WILL. What girls is that, sir?

PSYCHIATRIST. Just girls. Just any girls.

WILL. Well, I don't like just any girls. There's one old girl back home that ain't got hair no longer than a hound dog's and she's always—

PSYCHIATRIST. No! Look, when I say girls I don't mean any one specific girl. I mean girls in general; women, sex! Didn't that father of yours ever sit down and have a talk with you?

WILL. Sure he did.

PSYCHIATRIST. Well?

WILL. Well what?

PSYCHIATRIST. What did he say?

WILL (*with a snicker*). Well, there was this one about these two travelin' salesmen that their car breaks down in the middle of this terrible storm—

PSYCHIATRIST. Stop!

WILL. —so they stop at this farmhouse where the farmer has fourteen daughters who was—

PSYCHIATRIST. *Stop!*

WILL. You heared it already?

PSYCHIATRIST (*writing furiously on form*). No, I did not hear it already . . .

WILL. Well, what did you stop me for? It's a real knee-slapper. You see, the fourteen daughters is all studyin' to be trombone players and—

PSYCHIATRIST (*shoving form at* WILL). Here. Go. Good-by. You're through. You're normal. Good-by. Go. Go.

WILL (*takes form and stands, a bit confused by it all*). Sir, if girls is what you want to talk about, you ought to come down to the barracks some night. The younger fellows there is always tellin' spicy stories and all like that.

(*Lights fade out in* PSYCHIATRIST'S *office and come up in hallway.* KING *and* BEN *are as before.* IRVIN *emerges from oculist's office, putting on his dark glasses.* BEN *exits into oculist's office.*)

KING. Irvin! How's the eye test?

IRVIN. A snap.

KING. Listen, I want you to coach Stockdale. He's going in there next.

IRVIN. Now, listen, Sarge . . .

KING. You'll coach him!

(*Door of* PSYCHIATRIST'S *office opens and* WILL *emerges.*)

WILL (*over his shoulder*). Excuse me for sayin' it, sir, but I don't think a fellow your age would be so confused about it all if you went out and *seen* some girls once in a while. (*Closes door.*)

KING (*seizing him*). What are you doing? Are you crazy?

WILL. That fellow's in pretty bad shape, Sergeant. (*Handing* KING *his form.*)

KING (*looking at form*). What did he say? (BEN *comes out of oculist's office.*) Thank the Lord! Good boy! Normal!

WILL. Hey, Ben. You fill out that transfer yet?

BEN. It's only an application, Will. Don't mean a thing unless the Colonel okays it. (*Hands application form to* KING.)

WILL. I asked that fellow in there to give me a transfer too, but all he done was squench up his eyes.

(*The Negro* LIEUTENANT *enters.*)

LIEUTENANT. Sergeant, is your group all through?

KING. Just these two to go and that's the lot.

LIEUTENANT (*consulting his clipboard*). Names?

BEN (*saluting*). Whitledge, Benjamin B.

WILL (*saluting, outdoing* BEN). Will

Stockdale, sir!

LIEUTENANT. Make sure they finish today. The ones chosen for Gunnery School will be leaving tomorrow, right after the Colonel's lecture.

KING. Yes, sir.

LIEUTENANT. The Colonel is taking the inspection himself. Thought you might like to know.

KING. Thanks for the tip, sir.

LIEUTENANT (to BEN, WILL and IRVIN). Good luck, fellows.

WILL (saluting vigorously). Thank you, Lieutenant! It's been real nice bein' here! We'll sure miss yall!

LIEUTENANT (smiles). Thanks, Private. (Salutes and exits. WILL looks at BEN for approval.)

KING (to IRVIN). Why in hell does the Colonel want to come nosing around? Irvin, you better get back to the section and start slicking up the place.

IRVIN. Me?

BEN. Sergeant, can I take the clean-up detail? I'll do a real good job of it for the Colonel.

WILL. I'll lend you a hand, Ben, soon as I'm through the eye test.

KING. Lord, the eye test. (To IRVIN) Tell him all about it. Okay, Whitledge, you're in charge of clean-up. (To WILL) Have you been eating them carrots like I told you?

WILL (taking carrot from pocket). Just one more to go.

KING. Eat fast, but chew it well—good for your eyes. And none of them wise cracks to the eye doctor. Just be nice and polite.

IRVIN (crossing to WILL). He'll be polite, all right. (Saluting) "Yes, sir. No, sir. Been real nice bein' here, sir!" You're even polite to niggers, ain't you?

WILL. I don't know what you're talkin' about, Irvin.

IRVIN. That Lieutenant, that's what.

WILL. Was the Lieutenant . . . colored? (Glances at BEN.)

IRVIN. What are you, blind?

WILL. I didn't notice whether he was black or white or what. (Glances at BEN.)

KING (looking at WILL with dawning horror). You . . . didn't . . . notice . . .

WILL. I don't notice no color. He might've been black or white or yellow or even green with purple dots; it's all the same to me. All I seen was the uniform.

I never notice color nohow. (WILL looks at BEN; BEN grins. Door of oculist's office opens and FIRST CORPORAL sticks his head out.)

FIRST CORPORAL. Stockdale! Eye test!

KING (paralyzed). No, no . . . it couldn't be . . .

WILL. See you at the bunk, Ben. We'll clean up good for the Colonel, huh, Ben?

BEN. Yeah. Okay, Will. (WILL exits into oculist's office.)

KING. He's color-blind . . .

IRVIN. I don't know what you're going to do now. Half that test is matching red and green squares.

BEN. Sergeant, could I look at that application a minute?

KING (hands him application). I'm doomed . . . (BEN tears application in half and hands pieces back to KING.) What the hell are you . . .

BEN (starting to exit). Guess I changed my mind.

KING. For Pete's sake, this all started from you wanting to go in the Infantry!

BEN (gruffly). I changed my mind! (Exits.)

KING. I get all the nuts! Now what am I going to do with that one? If he's color-blind, Gunnery won't take him, and if they won't take him, nobody'll take him. I'm going to be a permanent latrine orderly . . .

IRVIN. Yeah . . . looks that way . . . unless . . .

KING. Unless what?

IRVIN. Unless Stockdale gets into some real trouble.

KING. What kind of trouble can he get into? He makes trouble.

IRVIN. He could get into plenty of trouble at the Purple Grotto.

KING (horrified). The Purple Grotto?

IRVIN. Sure. We could invite him there . . . you know, to celebrate . . . you know—a couple of drinks . . .

KING. That's a pretty stinking idea, Irvin. After all, he ain't a bad kid. I even got to like him in a way . . .

IRVIN. His being a nice kid ain't gonna get the Captain off your back.

KING (pause). Yeah, let him be a nice kid on his own time.

IRVIN. We could take him there tonight. . . .

KING (starting to go). I guess we could . . . Yeah, I guess we better. . . . Tell you one thing though, Irvin . . . I'm glad I didn't think of it.

(*They exit. Blackout. Low-down music is heard, and lights come up on "The Purple Grotto," a sordid den reeking of vice and corruption.* WILL *sits at a bottle-laden table downstage, looking about with innocent enjoyment. A* CIGARETTE GIRL *undulates toward him.*)

CIGARETTE GIRL. Cigars, cigarettes, anything else you want to smoke . . . (*Snakes her way around* WILL *to his other side and repeats.*) Cigars, cigarettes, anything else you want to smoke . . .

WILL (*flashing tobacco pouch*). Thank you, ma'am, but I roll my own.

(*With a contemptuous sniff,* CIGARETTE GIRL *heads upstage.* KING *and* IRVIN *enter, their arms loaded with bottles, their feet a wee bit rubbery.*)

KING. Here we are, Will. Round two. (*Sets bottles on table.*)

WILL. I sure appreciate it. But I don't feel right my glass bein' so much bigger'n yourn. (*Holds up enormous brandy balloon.*)

IRVIN. Guest of honor always gets the biggest glass. That's the honor. (*Raising glass*) To Will.

WILL. Again? (KING *quells him with a glance.* WILL *drinks.* KING *and* IRVIN *toss down their shots and watch, fascinated, as* WILL *drains his glass. He sets down empty glass and makes a slight grimace.*) This here Scotch stuff tastes kind of sharp. I like the other stuff you give me better.

IRVIN (*pouring it for* WILL). The rye.

WILL. No, the gin.

(KING *grabs gin bottle and adds it to the rye that* IRVIN *is pouring.*)

KING. How you feeling, Will?

WILL. Fine, fine.

KING. That eye doctor wouldn't tell you nothing, huh?

WILL. Nope. Seemed kind of angry most of the time.

KING. What made you think he was angry?

WILL. Well, he got sort of fussed when I was readin' this here sign they had on the wall. That was kind of hard at first 'cause they was right peculiar words like IP and GNXL and BUGLUMP.

IRVIN. You were supposed to read them letters one at a time.

WILL. Didn't make no sense that way neither.

KING. You're not drinking your rye and gin.

WILL. After this one I reckon we ought to be headin' back to Ben at the barracks. With the Colonel coming the place has got to be fixed up special. (*Drinks, then rises.*)

KING. Now, wait a minute . . . (*Gets to his feet—sort of.*) I promised you my watch, and I'm gonna give you my watch, and we gotta have several, several drinks on that! (*Unfastens watch strap.*)

WILL. Oh, golly! (WILL *sits.*)

KING. My mother give it to me . . . (*He's got it off now. He clears his throat.*) To Will Stockdale because, because—because I'm proud of him for doing such a good job getting classified and cleaning the latrine and all . . . (*He hands watch to* WILL *and resumes seat.*)

WILL. Thank you, thank you . . . (*Starts fastening watch, realizes he should be standing, rises.*) I—I sure am glad I come into the draft! (*Snatches up his glass.*) To Sergeant King! The best danged sergeant in the whole danged Air Force! (*He drinks.* KING *and* IRVIN, *less eagerly, down their drinks.* WILL *sits, examines watch happily.*)

KING. Will . . . are you absolutely sure you never drank no whisky before?

WILL. Never no *store* whisky. Only some ole stuff that my Pa makes.

KING. Stuff that . . .

WILL. Corn likker, kind of. Corn, and grain . . . (*Sips his drink*) . . . and kerosene . . .

KING AND IRVIN. *Kerosene!*

WILL. Just a mite. For flavorin'.

(CIGARETTE GIRL *crosses.*)

KING (*despondently*). Where we gonna get kerosene?

CIGARETTE GIRL. Cigars, cigarettes, anything else you want to smoke . . .

IRVIN (*thrusting dollar bill into her tray*). Here's some lighter fluid. . . .

KING. He *wants* kerosene, he *gets* kerosene!

(IRVIN *fires a few squirts of fluid into* WILL's *glass.* KING *and* IRVIN *sit raptly as* WILL *lifts glass, inspects it, sips, and savors the aftertaste.*)

WILL. It's familiar. (KING *and* IRVIN *groan.*) Hey, there's an Infantry man! Hey, Infantry! (*A burly* INFANTRY PRIVATE *staggers to their table.*)

INFANTRY. Hi, Jack!

WILL. Have a drink! We're celebratin'!

INFANTRY (*pulling up a chair*). Thanks a lot. I do not mind if I do.

WILL (*to* KING *and* IRVIN). Let's drink one to the Infantry.

INFANTRY (*grabbing* WILL'S *upraised glass*). To the Infantry! (*He drinks, stiffens, sets glass on table, shakes his head.*) Smooth . . . Say, I never seen fly-boys so nice to the Infantry.

WILL. Well, heck, this is the Air Age, and you're our helpers, ain't you?

KING AND IRVIN. Will, Will . . .

INFANTRY. Your what?

WILL. Our helpers. And don't think we don't appreciate it.

INFANTRY. Listen, you guys got it easier than anybody, even the Navy!

IRVIN. For your information they drill us fifteen miles every day!

INFANTRY. Twenty miles, we drill! When it rains, twenty-five!

KING. Do you have to put up with all the stupid kid officers we do?

IRVIN. And sergeants . . . we got the roughest, toughest, meanest sergeants in the whole service!

INFANTRY. Go on, you don't know what a tough sergeant is till you've been in the Infantry!

IRVIN. Ain't nobody tougher than my sergeant! He's *tough!*

KING. I sure am!

WILL. Now, Sergeant, I wouldn't say that.

KING. I'm a louse, ain't I, Irvin?

IRVIN. Yes, sir, you are.

KING. Thanks, Irvin.

INFANTRY. I don't know, you look like a pretty decent Joe to me.

KING (*rising*). You take that back!

INFANTRY. All right, I'll bet you five bucks *I'm* a bigger louse than you. And I'm just a private!

IRVIN. Put up or shut up. (*Throws money on table.*)

INFANTRY (*to* KING). What's a bigger louse that'll drink your booze and then punch you in the guts?

IRVIN. Put up or shut up!

INFANTRY. Sure. (INFANTRY *punches* KING *in the stomach.* KING *doubles up.* INFANTRY *turns to* IRVIN, *who violates the Marquess of Queensberry Rules with his right knee. A brawl ensues, in the midst of which* WILL *attempts to disengage* KING.)

WILL. Sergeant, I think we better go home now. Ben's waitin' for me to—

KING (*strangling someone*). Go on away! You're drunk!

WILL. No I ain't. My fingers is a mite tingly, but—

KING. Go 'way!

(*With bottles flying and a siren wailing, the lights fade out on "The Purple Grotto" as* WILL, *in a pin-spot, reluctantly comes downstage. He addresses the audience.*)

WILL. Well, I finally figgered I better quit bein' a wet blanket and stop spoilin' the Sergeant's fun. So . . . much as I hated to miss the fun myself—you know, quit a party early and the best things happen after you're gone—I went on back to the barracks 'cause I had a lot to do before the Colonel come.

(*An* AIR FORCE POLICEMAN *rushes across.*)

AIR FORCE POLICEMAN. Hey! Which way's that Purple Grotto?

WILL. Right down yonder there. (*To audience*) There's a thirsty fellow for you! Well, anyhow, I went on back to the barracks and give Ben a hand with the cleanin'. And afterwards, when everyone was asleep, I got me some nails and a board and some wires and I fixed up somethin' special for the Colonel. Then in the mornin', right before inspection, I give it the finishin' touches.

(*Lights come up on barracks set.* WILL *takes a wire-entangled board from within latrine door and stands straightening the wires as* BEN *approaches.*)

BEN. What you been doing in there?

WILL. Fixin' up somethin' special. It ain't every day a Colonel inspects.

BEN. I sure wish the Sergeant was here.

WILL. He'll show up. Sergeant King ain't gonna miss no inspection if he can help it.

BEN. The heck he ain't. Here comes the Captain now—and the Colonel!

WILL. Oh, golly.

BEN. Who's going to report?

WILL. You're in charge.

BEN. Me? Oh! (*Rehearsing salute*) Barracks ready for inspection, sir. Barracks ready for inspection, sir . . .

WILL. Now mind, when you throw open this door, holler "attention" just as loud as you can!

BEN (*preoccupied*). Yeah, yeah . . . (*Closes latrine door.*) Barracks ready for inspection, sir. Barracks ready . . . (CAPTAIN *and* COLONEL *enter in conversation.* BEN, *between latrine and* KING'S *room, keeps rehearsing until officers are upon him. He calls to* INDUCTEES *in back*.) Tenshun! (*Saluting officers*) Barracks ready for inspection, sir!

(OFFICERS, *flinching at his vehemence, return salute*. WILL, *in latrine, is placing the wired board on the floor before commodes, fussing with wires, etc.*)

CAPTAIN. Where's Sergeant King?

BEN. I don't know, sir, but (*Saluting*) the barracks are ready for inspection, sir!

CAPTAIN (*saluting mechanically*). All right, all right . . . (*To Colonel*) Sir, before we go any further, I'd like you to take a look at this latrine. There's a man in this barracks whose latrine work is quite surprising.

(BEN *flings open latrine door*.)

BEN. *Ten-shun!*

(*Up comes* WILL's *arm in a snappy salute, down stomps his foot, up fly the toilet seats; clattering, banging, quivering at attention*.)

WILL. Latrine ready for inspection, sir!

(OFFICERS *recoil through the door, then peer in again timorously. They enter latrine, hesitantly approach the commodes. The seats waver*. WILL *gives the board a further push and the seats regain their precision*. OFFICERS *turn their dumbfounded gaze at* WILL.)

WILL. Latrine ready for inspection, sir!

CAPTAIN (*dazedly returns salute*. WILL *drops his hand*). What is . . . the *idea* behind this?

WILL. Welcomin' the Colonel, sir.

CAPTAIN (*to Colonel*). I'm sorry, sir.

COLONEL. It's all right, Captain . . . I've been welcomed in many ways; with tickertape, with waving flags, the women of a French village once threw rosebuds at me . . . But this . . . this . . . (*Shaking his head, he and* CAPTAIN *leave latrine and exit into barracks proper. The clatter of the falling seats speeds them.*)

WILL (*joining* BEN *outside latrine*). They didn't hardly inspect the latrine at all.

(KING *comes staggering in, looking back cautiously over his shoulder. He is a bruised and battered wreck, his uniform in shreds. His stripes are hanging by a thread, literally and figuratively*.)

BEN (*as* KING *totters up*). Sergeant!

KING. Lieutenant there . . . almost spotted me . . .

WILL. You all right?

KING. I'm not sure . . .

WILL. Where's Irvin?

KING. The M.P.s got him.

WILL. Golly . . .

COLONEL (*off*). Excellent! Excellent!

KING (*wide-eyed*). The Colonel? (WILL *nods excitedly*.)

BEN. They inspected the latrine already!

WILL. Watch out for the treadle!

(KING *ducks into latrine*. COLONEL *and* CAPTAIN *reappear*. CAPTAIN *opens door of* KING's *room*. COLONEL *pokes his head in*.)

COLONEL. Excellent! Excellent! (*To* BEN) Were you in charge during your sergeant's absence?

BEN. Yes, sir. Complete charge.

COLONEL. Captain, I think you should make a note of this man's name.

(KING *is examining himself in the mirror*.)

CAPTAIN. Yes indeed, sir. What is it, Private?

BEN. Private Ben Whitledge, sir!

(KING *backs away from mirror to get better look at himself. He steps on the treadle. The seats fly up with a horrendous clatter. As he turns to see what the clatter is he steps off the treadle and the seats crash down again.*)

CAPTAIN (*when the noise subsides*). What was that again? (*Produces pencil and note pad.*)

BEN. Whitledge, sir. W—H—I—T—

(KING *has been cautiously tiptoeing toward seats to examine them. He steps on the treadle. The seats fly up. As he bucks up, they crash down.*)

COLONEL. What in blazes?

CAPTAIN. What's going on in there? (COLONEL *and* CAPTAIN *move to latrine door*. WILL *blocks it.*)

WILL. Latrine's out of order, sir. You'll have to use the one next door.

(CAPTAIN *gestures* WILL *aside, flings open the door*. KING *retreats to the far corner of the latrine and attempts a salute, but with the hangover and the shock he can't quite make it.*)

CAPTAIN. *This* is the barracks sergeant!

KING. How are ya, sir. . . .

CAPTAIN. All slicked up for inspection! (KING *withers. Pause*.) Explain!

KING. Explain . . . uh . . . mm . . . Well, sir . . . I went to a movie last night. And there were these . . . *eight infantrymen* sitting behind me. And they took to cussing the Air Force, and saying how our officers wasn't as . . . understanding . . .

as Infantry officers.

COLONEL. So you fought them. All night long.

KING. Yes sir. It was awful.

CAPTAIN. What was the name of the movie?

KING. The movie . . . ?

CAPTAIN. The movie!

KING. Uh . . . Forward March . . . American Battalion . . . of the Air . . . in the Wild Blue . . . It was a sneak preview.

COLONEL. I don't know how this man ever got *on* my base, Captain, but he certainly isn't going to remain here, corrupting new airmen with his—hideous example. Ship him out!

CAPTAIN. There's a group leaving today for Gunnery School.

COLONEL. Splendid! General Bush can always use another private.

KING. Private?

COLONEL (*plucks dangling stripes from* KING's *arms and drops them to the floor*). Private!

(KING *clasps his arms as though wounded.* COLONEL *and* CAPTAIN *leave latrine.* BEN *confronts them outside.*)

BEN. That was Whitledge, sir. W—H—I—T—L—

CAPTAIN. Whitledge, eh? This is going on your record, Whitledge! This is going on everybody's record! (COLONEL *and* CAPTAIN *exit furiously.* WILL *enters latrine.*)

KING (*pointing at commodes, flapping his hand*). Something special for the Colonel . . .

WILL (*nods*). You ain't a sergeant no more?

KING. No I ain't a sergeant no more! I'm a private, a forty-five-year-old private!

WILL. Oh, gosh, I—

BEN (*coming to door*). He's putting it on my record . . .

WILL. Gosh, Ben, I didn't . . .

KING. There's a silver lining to this cloud, by God! You're staying here, but I'm going to Gunnery School, a thousand miles away! (*Comes out of latrine.* WILL *and* BEN *follow.*)

WILL. Sergeant . . .

KING. Private!

WILL. I ain't stayin' here. I'm goin' to Gunnery School, just like you.

KING. They . . . took you?

WILL. It's right on the bulletin board. It was your helpin' that done it for me.

KING. No . . .

WILL (*hesitantly*). We're gonna be together.

KING. Now listen, I've had all I can take, you understand? You and him be together; leave me out of it!

WILL. But we're buddies.

KING. *Buddies?*

WILL. Last night you said you was proud of me . . .

KING. I was drunk! I didn't know what I was saying!

WILL. You give me your watch . . .

KING. I was drunk!

WILL. Not when you set me in charge of this latrine!

KING. Oh, my God! (*To* BEN) You tell him! Maybe you can get through!

BEN. Cleaning the latrine isn't a good job, Will. It's the worst job there is. It's a punishment job.

WILL (*turns slowly from* BEN *to* KING). It is? (*Begins unfastening watch strap.*)

KING (*uncomfortable now*). Now do you understand? There's your buddy. Make some trouble for *him* for a change. (WILL *holds out the watch.* KING *hesitates, then crosses and snatches it from him. To* BEN) You glad now you tore up your transfer? (*He exits into his room. There is a moment of silence.*)

WILL. You tore up your transfer, Ben?

BEN (*inching away*). It was just an application, that's all.

WILL. To the Infantry!

BEN (*heading for wings. More for himself than for* WILL). Nothing would've come of it!

WILL. I didn't know you done that. I'll make it up to you, honest I will. Ben . . . (BEN *stops, turns, holds himself in check.*)

BEN. I got to go pack for Gunnery School . . . (*He exits. After a moment,* WILL *turns downstage, looking at floor. He becomes aware of the audience watching.*)

WILL. I didn't realize . . . honest . . . I was just . . . (*He turns, putting his back toward them. The lights fade slowly.*)

CURTAIN

ACT TWO

WILL *comes on in front of the "Meeting Hall" curtain. He holds a slip of paper in his hand.*

WILL. Feels right good to move around after settin' still so long, don't it? (*Glances at slip of paper.*) Uh . . . Preacher says that Mrs. Henry Calhoun couldn't find one of her shoes when yall went out for that orange drink. Would all them around her look under you and if it's there just pass it on back to her? Thank you. (*Pockets paper.*) Let's see . . . where was I—oh yeh. Well, the three of us—Ben and Sergeant King and me—we went to Gunnery School together, like the Three Musketeers. Only to be real honest, we warn't really much like the Three Musketeers; it was more like three fellows that two of 'em warn't talkin' with one of 'em any more'n they could help. Anyway, after Gunnery School they put me and Ben on the same flight crew, because they put you accordin' to how you come out in the class, and we was the bottom two. Sergeant King, though, he come out on top. He did. The instructors said they never seen nothin' like it. It was just as if he had copies of the tests before they give them. He done so good that General Bush he's kind of like the principal of the school— General Bush give him his stripes back and made him his orderly, and an orderly is kind of important; it's like a right-hand man . . . or an assistant . . . or a helper . . . Well, it's really more like a servant is what it is. Everybody said this crew Ben and me was on was the worst one on the base, on account of the officers was all from the bottom of their class too. The other crews had a nickname for our'n, only I can't say it with the ladies here. In fact I don't think I could say it with the *men* here. Ben and me, though, we went on most of the missions; it warn't much trouble and there warn't nothin' else to do anyhow. (*"Meeting Hall" curtain rises on an airstrip. A medium-sized plane stands ready for take-off, a mounting ladder reaching up into its underbelly.*) Ben was pretty upset about it. You know how he is. (BEN, *in flying gear, comes striding in from left.*)

BEN. If this ain't the sorriest crew on the whole danged base! We're supposed to take off five minutes ago, and do you know what? Every one of our officers would still be fast asleep if I hadn't gone and shook them awake! What a crew!

WILL. It's just that they ain't used to gettin' up at three in the mornin', Ben.

BEN. All the other planes got off on time except ours. These officers are a disgrace to the Air Force!

WILL. Now, Ben, they ain't so bad. Easy goin', that's all.

BEN. All I know is that if you're going to fly a plane you ought to be awake first. I'm going aboard. (*He climbs the ladder into the plane.*)

WILL (*calling after him*). Here's Lieutenant Bridges now, Ben. (LIEUTENANT BRIDGES *enters sleepily, his parachute at half-mast.* WILL *salutes smartly.*) Good mornin', Lieutenant Bridges!

BRIDGES. Good morning, Lieutenant Bridges . . . (*He continues across stage somnambulistically.* WILL *calls after him.*)

WILL. The plane's right here, sir. (BRIDGES, *without stopping, turns back and drags himself up the ladder and into the plane.*) That's the pilot. Easy goin' fellow. (LIEUTENANT GARDELLA *and* LIEUTENANT KENDALL *enter. They pause a few feet onstage and* GARDELLA *helps* KENDALL *adjust his parachute straps.*) This here is Lieutenant Kendall, the engineer, and Lieutenant Gardella, the co-pilot. Lieutenant Kendall ain't quite got the hang of puttin' on a parachute yet. (*The pair approach.* WILL *salutes.*) Good morning, sirs!

KENDALL AND GARDELLA (*saluting*). Good morning . . .

WILL. Lieutenant Gardella. (GARDELLA *stops.* KENDALL *exits into plane.*)

GARDELLA. Yes?

WILL. Sir, would it be all right if I come up to the front of the plane for a while and watch what yall do up there?

GARDELLA. Sorry. Only crew members allowed on board.

WILL. I'm a crew member, sir.

GARDELLA. You are?

WILL. Yes, sir. I been on the crew for close on to a month now. Is it okay if I come up front and—

GARDELLA. Sure. Sure. Come on up. There ain't much to see though. All I do is let the wheels up after we take off and let them down again when we're ready to land.

WILL. That might be nice. Thank you, sir.

GARDELLA. I *knew* I'd seen you *some* place. (*Exits into plane.* WILL *takes parachute from behind ladder, puts it on during following.*)

WILL (*to audience*). I think he really

knowed who I was. It's just the sleep ain't wore off yet. You see, we never had to go up this early before. This here mission is we're supposed to fly to Denver, Colorado, and when we get to Denver, Colorado, we're supposed to turn around and fly back again. That's the biggest mission we got so far. Usually, all they ask is for us to get the plane up off'n the ground and keep it up for half an hour or so without smackin' into nothin'.

(LIEUTENANT COVER *comes scurrying on, his arms loaded with maps, sextants, slide rules, books, etc. He climbs the ladder, muttering a hasty inventory, oblivious of* WILL's *salute.*)

COVER. Maps . . . sextant . . . slide rule . . . scale . . . dramamine . . . I forgot the—No, here it is. (*He is gone.*)

WILL. That's Lieutenant Cover, the navigator. He's the serious one of the bunch. (*Glances at his wrist watch but he doesn't have one. Rubs wrist.*) Well, I guess I'll just get on the—

(SERGEANT KING *and two* MECHANICS *enter.* KING *wears a staff armband and carries a clipboard. Engines rev up as* MECHANICS *busy themselves underneath the plane.*)

KING (*to* MECHANICS). Get this one off and we can all go back to sleep.

WILL. Hey, look at you! An armband and a writin' board and everythin'!

KING. All right, get this plane off on the double.

WILL. We can't. Everyone ain't here yet. The radio operator and the front gunner—

KING. You heard me, get moving!

WILL. How come we're goin' up so early?

KING. To break the sound barrier. You gotta sneak up on it when nobody's looking.

(GENERAL BUSH *enters.*)

BUSH. Oh, there you are, Sergeant. Is this the last of them?

KING. Yes, General.

BUSH. Fine. That does it for tonight. Don't disturb me unless there's a big emergency. Breakfast a little later than usual, I think . . .

KING. Yes, sir. What about your eggs, sir?

BUSH. My eggs? What eggs?

KING. For breakfast. Poached or scrambled?

BUSH. Scrambled, I think . . . nice and loose. No, no . . . poached.

KING. Yes, sir, poached.

BUSH. Poached. I feel like poached.

WILL. Scrambled is tastier, sir. Especially with chitlins.

KING. Get on that plane!

BUSH. Chitlins?

WILL. Yes, sir, at home we always have scrambled eggs with chitlins.

BUSH. Poached! (*Exits.*)

KING. Yes, sir! (*To* WILL) Can't you keep your mouth shut? Scrambled with chitlins!

WILL. A bit of red pepper helps.

KING. Get on that plane!

WILL (*climbing ladder*). Sure, Sergeant.

VOICE ON P.A. Sergeant King! Sergeant King! Report to General Bush immediately. (*Incredulous*) With chitlins?

(*Blackout.*)

(*The roar of the engines grows louder. Clouds are seen, and running lights blinking in a rhythmic pattern. Lights come up on a cross-section of the plane in flight. In front,* BRIDGES *and* GARDELLA *are seated at the controls, asleep. Behind them,* KENDALL *sits by his needles and gauges, asleep. Farther back,* COVER *is at his work table, frantically operating six instruments at once. Toward the rear of the plane,* BEN *sits reading a comic book.* WILL *is peering at the audience from the tail blister. After a moment the sound of the engines fades low and* WILL *moves forward. He crouches beside* BEN.)

WILL. I got my penknife. Want to play mumbly-peg?

BEN. That's a kid's game. (*Turns a page of his comic book.*)

WILL. We could play for money. (*No comment from* BEN.) Well, I guess I'll go see what they do up front.

BEN. We're supposed to stay at our stations.

WILL. I asked Lieutenant Gardella. He said it was all right. Want to come along?

(BEN *shakes his head.* WILL *hesitates, then moves forward.* COVER *is working like a man possessed; marking charts, measuring, drawing circles, searching for instruments and papers.* WILL *watches him, fascinated.*)

COVER (*talking to himself*). Compass, compass . . . ah . . . mmm . . . now . . . scale. Where's the . . . (*Snaps his fingers.*) Ruler, ruler . . . (WILL *hands it to him.*) Ah . . . there . . . (*Copying data from various sheets of paper onto central sheet.*) Ground speed . . . mmm air speed . . . mmm . . . wind direction — Wind direction, wind direction . . . (*Searches furiously through papers.* WILL, *behind him, licks his forefinger and holds it up. He taps* COVER.)

WILL. Wind's comin' from that way, sir. (*Points forward.*)

COVER (*turning*). Dead ahead?

WILL. Yes, sir.

COVER (*returning to charts*). Then something's wrong with the compass. We're supposed to be . . . that couldn't . . . (*He is beginning to get a bit desperate.* WILL *watches him for a moment, then heads forward.*) Now wait a minute, let's start all over again. If we took off at 0315 . . .

WILL (*stepping over* KENDALL's *outstretched legs*). Excuse me, sir . . . (*He comes up behind* BRIDGES *and* GARDELLA, *who are slumped over the steering wheels.*) Howdy, sirs! (*They sit bolt upright and whirl around in their chairs.*)

GARDELLA. It's all right, George; he's one of the crew.

BRIDGES. Lord! Don't come sneaking up on people, fella.

WILL. Sorry, sir. Just wanted to watch what yall do up here.

(*Pause.* BRIDGES *and* GARDELLA *resume their sleeping positions.*)

BRIDGES. Automatic pilot.

WILL. You already let up the wheels?

GARDELLA. Hell, yes.

WILL. Shucks.

BRIDGES. What do yall do in back?

WILL. Oh, nothin' much. I mostly look out the blister and sweep up a little. (*Pause. Apprehensively*) You don't have to guide this here thing?

BRIDGES. Automatic. Everything's automatic. Every little ole thing.

GARDELLA. You come back when we're ready to land and you can watch me let down the wheels.

BRIDGES. It's a real spectacle.

GARDELLA. I do it all with one hand.

WILL. Well, thank you, sir. Guess I'll go look out the blister some. (*Pause*) Good night. (*He heads for the rear of the plane, stepping over* KENDALL's *legs* . . .) Excuse me, sir. (. . . *and stopping behind* COVER, *who is staring straight ahead with a stoned expression, his hands flat on the work table.*)

COVER. We're off our course.

WILL. We are?

COVER. If we're heading straight into a south wind then we can't be going west, can we? (WILL *licks his finger and holds it up.*) Are they in contact with the base up there?

WILL. Well, no . . .

COVER (*putting on earphones*). What the hell *are* they doing?

WILL. Well, sir, you might say they're kind of sleepin'.

COVER. Sleeping! Navigator to pilot, navigator to pilot. Over. (BRIDGES *lifts one hand and pulls down earphones without opening his eyes. He holds one phone to ear.*) Navigator to pilot, navigator to pilot. Over.

BRIDGES. Pilot to navigator. Fred, I wish you wouldn't call me once we're off the ground. Over.

COVER. I just thought you might like to know that we're heading for Mexico, that's all. Over.

BRIDGES. Now Fred, everything is automatic and you know it. Every time we go off on a mission you start fussing with those maps and things, and all you do is confuse everybody. Over.

COVER. Well, for your information we got a south wind and we're heading straight into it and we're supposed to be going west. Over.

BRIDGES (*extends his toe and does something with the instrument panel*). All right. I just moved us up ninety degrees. Are you happy? Over and out.

(*Hangs up earphones.*)

COVER. I don't see why you guys should get to sleep when I have to work like a dog back here. None of *my* instruments are automatic and they're pretty damn complicated, let me tell you. Over. Navigator to pilot, navigator to . . . Damn! (*Hangs up earphones.*) Sometimes I think he doesn't take a serious attitude.

WILL. I noticed that.

COVER. Now let's see . . . moved us up ninety degrees . . . wind from the south . . . flying since 0315 hours . . .

(WILL *retreats toward rear of plane.*)

BEN (*not looking up from comic book*). Taking an awful long time to get to Denver, Colorado. What are they doing up there?

WILL. Oh, you'd be right proud of them, Ben! They're workin' real hard; navigatin' and steerin' and engineerin' and all.

BEN. Yeah, I'll bet.

WILL. They're about as good a crew as you can find, when they're sober like this.

(*Lights fade, engine sound rises, clouds and running lights are seen. After a moment, interior lights come up again.* BEN *is sleeping,* WILL *is sweeping,* COVER *is shouting frantically into his microphone.*)

COVER. Navigator to pilot, navigator to pilot, over! Navigator to pilot, navigator to pilot!

BRIDGES (*snatching earphones*). Fred, what the hell's the matter with you?

COVER. We're over the Gulf of Mexico, you idiot!

BRIDGES. Now, Fred, how can we be over the Gulf of Mexico when there's a city below us half the size of New York?

COVER. You want to come back here and check the maps? I figured our position by dead reckoning and we're smack-dab in the middle of the Gulf of Mexico!

BRIDGES. Well, by God, I can see, can't I? I can look right out the window and *see,* can't I?

KENDALL (*taking earphones, partially awake*). Engineer to pilot. Are we lost again?

COVER. No, Kendall, we know exactly where we are. Smack dab in the middle of the Gulf of Mexico.

BRIDGES. There ain't any towns in the middle of the Gulf of Mexico!

GARDELLA. Maybe we're across the Gulf already.

COVER. You stay out of this, Gardella!

KENDALL (*a bit surprised*). Hey, fellows. Number two engine is dead.

GARDELLA AND COVER. Oh Lord!

BRIDGES. Prepare for landing!

COVER. This is *not* a seaplane!

BRIDGES. Cover, will you please look out the ever-loving window. What do you think that is down there?

GARDELLA. Wait a minute, wait a minute! That gunner fellow said he was going to watch from the blister . . . Co-pilot to rear gunner, co-pilot to rear gunner, over. Co-pilot to rear gunner . . .

(*A red light blinks in rear of plane.* WILL *goes to it, takes earphones.*)

WILL. Howdy. Over.

GARDELLA. Hey, you seen anything below that might've been a body of water?

WILL. No sir, I ain't seen nothin'. I been sweepin' up.

BRIDGES. What the hell's the radio operator doing? Pilot to radio operator, pilot to radio operator, over.

GARDELLA. Co-pilot to radio operator. Over.

COVER. Navigator to radio operator, over.

WILL. Rear gunner to everybody. Radio operator missed the plane. Over.

OFFICERS. Oh, no!

BRIDGES. Listen, rear gunner, get on the radio and see if you can find out where we are. This is an emergency. Over.

WILL. It is?

COVER (*tossing aside earphones, gathering up maps*). We know *exactly* where we are! (*Storms toward the front of plane.*)

WILL. Hey, sir, you ought to give the job to the other gunner! I reckon he'd be just about the best danged radio operator in the whole danged Air Force!

BRIDGES (*over him*). All right, get him on it.

WILL (*going right on*). He's a real smart fellow and right military-like. His whole family been—

BRIDGES. ALL RIGHT! Just get *somebody* on the damn radio! Over and out!

WILL. Roger! (*Hangs up earphones, drops broom and goes to* BEN.)

COVER (*thrusting maps over* BRIDGES' *shoulder*). You want to see the map? Here's the Gulf of Mexico right here! (BRIDGES *pushes him away.*)

WILL (*shaking* BEN *gently*). Ben? Hey, Ben. Wake up, Ben.

BEN. What . . .

WILL. It's an emergency! We're lost and Lieutenant Bridges wants you to be the radio operator and find out where we are! It's up to you to save the plane and us and everythin'!

BEN. Me?

WILL. They heared what a good soldier you was. (*Drags* BEN *to his feet and leads him to radio equipment.*)

BEN. Me? . . . Oh golly . . . oh Lord . . .

WILL (*picks up pamphlet, looks at it*). Here's some instructions . . .

BEN (*sitting at equipment*). Good. Read them off. I'll operate and you'll be my assistant. (*Puts on earphones.*)

WILL. Assistant? Yes, sir! (*He opens pamphlet, while* BEN *straightens his jacket, sitting proudly erect.*)

KENDALL. Watch out! Those are mountains there!

GARDELLA. Pull up! Pull up! *Pull up!*

BRIDGES. How do you pull up with only one engine, Mr. Rickenbacker?

GARDELLA. *You're* the pilot, Mr. Lindbergh.

COVER. There aren't any mountains on the map . . .

WILL· (*reading with difficulty*). Congrat-u-lations. As an Air Force radio operator yours is one of the most important jobs in—

BEN. Skip that part. Get to the instructions.

WILL. Yes, sir. (*Turns several pages, skimming them as he does so. Reads again.*) Important notice. The taxpayers of the United States paid their hard-earned—

BEN. The instructions! How to operate it.

WILL (*turns several more pages, which brings him to the end of the pamphlet. Shows* BEN). Just half a page. (*Squints, reads*) One. Turn the power switch to the on position.

BEN. Here, this one. This is it. (*Pause*) Here goes . . . (*Turns switch. Lights appear on equipment.*) Hey . . .

WILL. How about that!

BRIDGES. Pilot to radio operator. You getting anything back there? Over.

BEN (*as baritone as he can get*). Radio operator to pilot, sir! Roger! Wilco! We're working on it. Over! How about that?

WILL. Pretty good! Two. Turn . . . turn . . . O-S-C-I-L-L-A-T-O-R . . .

BEN. Oscillator.

WILL. Turn—what-you-just-said—control knob to tran . . . tran . . . T-R-A-N-S—

BEN (*taking off earphones, rising*). Here. You operate, I'll read. (*Gives* WILL *earphones, takes pamphlet.*)

WILL. But they give you the job, Ben!

BEN. Go on! I got to think of the good of the outfit!

(WILL *sits, puts on earphones. During following* BEN *strips off parachute, up-ends it beside* WILL *and sits on it. He reads with less difficulty than* WILL.)

BEN. Two. Turn oscillator control knob —I think that's the big one there—to transmission frequency desired.

WILL (*turns knob*). What frequency we desire?

BEN. Oh . . . I'll leave it up to you.

WILL (*makes careful adjustment*). All righty . . .

BEN. Three. Adjust knob B so as to obtain minimum impedance.

WILL (*pause*). Ben, listen, we got a little radio on the porch back home, and when it won't start, Pa spits in the back of it and whomps it a good one. Works every time. (BEN *shrugs noncommittally.* WILL *leans over radio, spits in the back of it and whomps it a good one. A red bulb on top lights up.*) There y'are! She's workin'! (*Picking up microphone*) Hello? Hello? I don't hear nothin'.

BEN. You got to keep saying it over and over again until somebody picks up your signal.

WILL. Hello? Hello? Hello?

BRIDGES. I told you I'd find an airport!

GARDELLA, KENDALL AND COVER. *That's a drive-in movie! Pull up!*

(*Lights begin to fade, light on* WILL *and* BEN *going last.*)

WILL. Hello? Hello?

BEN. If you get somebody, be careful what you say. They might be the enemy.

WILL. What enemy?

BEN. I don't know, but be careful.

WILL. Hello? Hello? (*Spits at microphone.*) Anybody out there? Hello?

(*Fade-out complete. Lights come up on a sandbagged bunker at extreme right of stage.* GENERAL POLLARD, *the ramrod type of officer, stands scanning the horizon with powerful binoculars. His aide, a* LIEUTENANT, *is seated at a bank of radio, telephone and radar equipment. A* SENATOR *approaches from right, where there apparently is an extension of the bunker.*)

SENATOR. Did you just hear an airplane?

POLLARD. An airplane? You're joking, Senator.

SENATOR. No, no, I'm perfectly serious.

POLLARD. My dear Senator, a plane couldn't conceivably slip in here unless they had Lindbergh for pilot and Rickenbacker for co-pilot. Ha, ha, ha. When General Pollard is in charge of an operation, safety is the prime consideration. You can mention that in your report to your Committee if you'd like.

SENATOR. I could have sworn I heard engines . . .

POLLARD (*ushering the* SENATOR *off right*). The desert plays strange tricks on the ear. Auditory mirages, so to speak.

LIEUTENANT. Excuse me, sir, but I'm getting a very odd signal here. Listen . . .

RADIO. Tphhh . . . tphhh . . . tphhh . . . tphhh . . .

POLLARD. Hmmm, that *is* odd . . . Sounds like somebody spitting.

BEN'S VOICE (*filter. Off mike*). Okay, Will. Try again.

WILL'S VOICE (*filter. Off mike*). Yes, sir. (*On*) Hello? Hello? Anybody there? Hello?

POLLARD (*seizing a microphone*). Hello.

WILL'S VOICE. Hello?

POLLARD. Hello!

WILL'S VOICE. HOWDY! (*Off mike*) Ben, I got somebody!

POLLARD. Who are you? Where are you?

WILL'S VOICE (*off mike*). Ben, he wants to know who we are.

POLLARD. Answer me, dammit. Who the hell are you?

WILL'S VOICE (*off mike*). He talks like an American, Ben.

POLLARD. Who are you?

WILL'S VOICE. Ben says, first who are you?

POLLARD. This is Command Post, "Operation Prometheus." Are you in . . . an airplane?

WILL'S VOICE. Sure are!

POLLARD. Oh Lord . . .

LIEUTENANT. I've got them on the PPI scope, sir! They're heading straight for the tower!

POLLARD. Oh my God!

WILL'S VOICE. Is this the Gulf of Mexico?

POLLARD. No, you idiot! (*To* LIEUTENANT) Send word to stop the detonator!

LIEUTENANT. It's too late, sir! Zero minus three!

WILL'S VOICE. Where'd you say we was?

POLLARD. You're right over Yucca Flats! Now listen to me, you turn that plane around and go right back where you came from! This minute!

LIEUTENANT (*pointing to radarscope*). There they are! See? Straight toward the tower!

WILL'S VOICE. Ben says sorry, our orders come from General Bush. Gotta do like he says.

POLLARD. Eugene Bush?

WILL'S VOICE. Our Commandin' General. Short fellow with a mustache.

POLLARD. I might have known. Get a line through to that idiot! I'll kill him for this! (*LIEUTENANT picks up the telephone, ad libs putting through of call.* POLLARD *speaks into microphone again.*) All right now, I don't care what Ben says or what Eugene Bush said. I'm a General too, in the U.S. Infantry—

WILL'S VOICE. The Infantry?

POLLARD. Yes! I'm ordering you to turn that plane around this instant! You're heading straight into . . . Hello? Hello? Oh God, I lost them! (*He twirls radio dials furiously.* SENATOR *enters from right.*) Hello? Hello?

SENATOR. Has something gone wrong?

POLLARD. No, no, no! Everything's fine. Lieutenant, help the Senator into his ear plugs and blinders. (*LIEUTENANT does so and through the rest of the scene the* SENATOR, *now deaf, smiles benignly in anticipation.*) Where's Bush? Where is he?

LIEUTENANT. I've put the call through, sir. (*Looks at watch.*) Zero minus two.

POLLARD (*taking telephone*). Hello? Hello? Hello? Hello?

(*At the other side of the stage, lights come up on a corner of* BUSH'S *office.* KING *stands behind desk, telephone in hand.* BUSH *enters.*)

KING (*overlapping* POLLARD). Hello? Hello? Hello?—Here he is now, sir! (*BUSH grabs phone from* KING.)

BUSH. Bush here.

POLLARD. Eugene? This is Vernon Pollard!

BUSH. Vernon! How are you, old boy?

POLLARD. You've sabotaged my operation, you miserable idiot! You were ordered to send your planes as far away as you could, and one of them is right here!

BUSH. I sent them away, Vernon! I sent them to Denver!

POLLARD. I don't care where you sent them! What's wrong with your communication?

BUSH. What's wrong with your security measures?

POLLARD. Shut up and listen! I'm trying to re-establish radio contact. What kind of idiot radio operators did you *put* in those planes?

BUSH (*to* KING). What kind of idiot radio operators did you *put* in those planes?

POLLARD. I'll skin you for this, Eugene.

LIEUTENANT. Sir, I've got that signal again!

POLLARD. Hold it! Don't move, Eugene!

RADIO. Tphhh . . . tphhhh . . . tphhhh . . . tphhhh . . .

WILL'S VOICE. Hello? Hello?

POLLARD (*seizing microphone*). Hello! Listen! Here's your General Bush!

WILL'S VOICE (*off mike*). He's got General Bush there, Ben!

POLLARD (*into phone*). Eugene, I'm putting the telephone next to the microphone. Tell this idiot to turn back! (*He holds telephone and microphone together.*)

BUSH. Hello? Who is this?

WILL'S VOICE. Private Stockdale, sir.

BUSH. This is General Bush, Stockdale.

KING. Stockdale! (*Starts for door.*)

BUSH. Don't move, King! Tell your pilot to reverse course immediately, Stockdale. You're in extreme danger.

WILL'S VOICE. Roger, sir! Wilco. (*Pause*) Ben says how do we know you're General Bush?

BUSH. What? I can't go up there and identify myself!

KING (*frantically*). Tell him Sergeant King will give him his watch!

BUSH. What?

KING. It's the only way, sir!

BUSH. Sergeant King will give you his watch!

WILL'S VOICE. He will!

BUSH. I *think* so . . .

WILL'S VOICE. That's good enough for me! Ben, tell Lieutenant Bridges to reverse course!

LIEUTENANT (*over this*). Twenty seconds, sir!

POLLARD (*looking at radarscope*). They're turning. There they go. They're still turning! They're heading for the tower again! (*Drops mike, raises telephone.*)

LIEUTENANT. Ten seconds! Nine . . . eight . . . seven . . . six . . . five . . . four . . . three . . . two . . . one . . . zero!

(*During count-down, simultaneously.*)

POLLARD. It's all your fault, Eugene! You've never forgiven me for those hazings back at the Point. For thirty years you've been out to get me and now you've wrecked my career!

BUSH (*to* KING). It's all your fault, you blundering idiot! How in the name of Creation did you let that plane get off the ground without a radio operator?

(*As* LIEUTENANT *reaches zero, both* GENERALS' *tirades are cut short by a blinding flash of light and a thunderous explosion. The stage blacks out.*)

(*Pre-dawn sky.* WILL *descends into view swaying from a parachute. He holds* BEN *by the scruff of the neck.*)

BEN. Pull to the left! Pull to the right!

WILL. Hold still, Ben.

BEN. What did you do it for? You snatched me right out of the plane! What did you do it for?

WILL. Well, I knowed you done took off your parachute. Heck, you'da done the same for me.

BEN. I wouldn't! Our post was the tail of the plane and nobody told us to quit it!

WILL. But the tail was on fire, Ben. Our post was quittin' us.

BEN. Do you know what we are now?

WILL. We're alive . . .

BEN. *We are deserters!* Deserters!

WILL. Stop wrigglin', Ben. *Please.*

BEN. Here's the first lick of danger and you snatch me away from it! (*Folds arms belligerently.*) I'd rather be a dead hero than a live deserter.

WILL (*pause. Stubbornly*). I ain't gonna drop you, no matter *what* you say.

BEN (*sullenly*). Out in the middle of no place . . . take us *weeks* to get back to the base. Can't even see where we are . . .

WILL. Sun'll be up in a few minutes, Ben. Don't worry. (*Pause. Conversationally*) It's always darkest before the dawn.

(BEN *squirms disgustedly, putting an end to the talk.* WILL *looks at audience, gives an uncomprehending shrug. Lights fade out.*)

(*A spotlight appears on* GENERAL BUSH, *standing before a microphone, downstage near portal. He reads from a sheet of paper.*)

BUSH. "Ten days ago, in 'Operation Prometheus,' the power of the atom bomb was challenged by a band of battle-hardened air aces. When General Pollard and I planned this shining symbol of man's unconquerability we had no idea that the newspapers would give it so very much publicity. To these brave volunteers I award the air medal for valor beyond the call of duty: Lieutenants Bridges, Gardella, Kendall and Cover." How does it sound, King?

(KING, *wearing earphones, sticks his head out from behind portal.*)

KING. Very sincere, sir.

BUSH. I just hope I don't choke on their names. When this whole thing quiets down I'm sending those men to Iceland.

KING. Ready to hear the playback?

BUSH. Wait, there's more. (KING *disappears.*) "Two did not return. In the shattered tail of the plane, all that remained were two charred helmets and a handful of dust. I ask you now to rise as I award these medals posthumously to the gallant heroes who gave the last measure of devotion, Privates Stackpole and Whitehead."

KING (*appearing again*). Stockdale and Whitledge, sir.

BUSH (*squinting at script*). "Stockdale and Whitledge . . ." This is where the bugler plays Taps, right?

KING. Yes, sir. And the flags go to half-mast.

BUSH. Be sure that second bugler is stationed up in the hills to play the echo.

KING. I'll check on it, sir. (*Martial music is heard.*) I'll just rewind the tape and give you the playback.

BUSH. There isn't time. The band has started.

(*Lights come up on* BUSH's *office and anteroom.*)

LIEUTENANT ABEL (*in office, holding* BUSH's *jacket*). General Bush! Only five minutes, sir!

(BUSH *goes upstage into office.* KING *takes microphone and exits into wings. In office* CAPTAIN CHARLES *is crouching by the radio, busily brushing the visor of* BUSH's *garrison cap.* LIEUTENANT BAKER *is looking out the window with a pair of binoculars.* BUSH *slips into the jacket which* ABEL *is holding for him.*)

BUSH (*to* CHARLES). Brush, man, brush! That's genuine leather! (*To* ABEL) Watch the sleeve there . . .

BAKER. The grandstands are full, sir!

BUSH. You're darn right they are! Those men are on duty. All leaves were canceled today. (*Mumbling from radio.*) What? What did he say?

CHARLES. Senator Hawk and Senator Winkle are in the reviewing stand!

BUSH. Good, Good! Baker, bring the car around!

BAKER. Yes, sir. (*Exits.*)

BUSH. Abel, check on those reporters!

ABEL. Yes, sir. (*Exits. More mumbling from radio.*)

BUSH. What was that? What did he say?

CHARLES. General Pollard just came in!

BUSH (*snatching cap from* CHARLES). Shut that off! (CHARLES *turns off radio and hurries out.* BUSH *dons cap, unfurls speech, rehearses.*) Two did not return . . . (BEN *and* WILL *come into the anteroom.*) Two did *not* return . . .

(BEN *moves closer to dividing door, which is open.* WILL *follows.*)

BEN. Excuse me, sir, I—

BUSH. Your uniform is *filthy*, boy!

BEN. I know, sir. We hitchhiked some but we had to walk a lot and—

BUSH. You know? And do you know what day this is?

BEN. Saturday, sir. I wanted to—

BUSH. The proudest day in the history of this base, that's all! People have come from miles around—generals, senators—to do homage to two enlisted men, your brothers-in-arms, and you don't even have enough courtesy and respect to put on a decent uniform!

BEN. Sir, please, I want to turn myself in.

WILL (*over him*). He didn't jump, sir! I pulled him out!

BAKER (*at the door*). The car is ready, sir.

BUSH. What squadron are you in?

BEN. The Ninth Squadron, sir.

BUSH. The Ninth! Stackpole and Whitehead's own outfit . . . !

WILL AND BEN (*coming to attention and saluting*). Stockdale and Whitledge, sir!

BUSH. Well, whoever they were. By God, you're going to stay right here until I finish the ceremony and then we'll see if we can put a little decency and esprit de corps into you! I don't want our visitors to get even a *glimpse* of you! Dirty uniforms, today of all days! (*He exits.* WILL *and* BEN *look at each other, drop salutes.*)

WILL. Well, we turned ourselves in. I think . . .

BEN. Yeah, wait till he finds out that besides wearing dirty uniforms, we're deserters. (BEN *stalks into anteroom.* WILL *follows, closing connecting door.* BEN *sits on bench, grimly snaps up a copy of* Time *from adjacent table.*)

WILL. I told him I pulled you out, Ben. I'll tell him again . . .

BEN. Aww . . . (BEN *riffles pages of magazine gloomily.* WILL, *watching uneasily, sits beside him.* KING *enters office, whistling "Flow Gently, Sweet Afton." He flicks radio on, and martial music is heard.* KING *sits at* GENERAL's *desk. In anteroom,* WILL *is watching* BEN's *black mood with concern.*)

WILL. Say, Ben, did I ever tell you the story about the turkey that got in with a coopful of chickens?

BEN. I don't want to hear it . . .

WILL. You'll enjoy it, Ben . . . You see, this turkey got in with these chickens—

BEN. I don't want to hear it.

WILL. It's a right good story, Ben.

BEN. Don't you understand, we'll probably be shot!

WILL. Well, then, you don't hear it now, you're likely never to hear it.

BEN (*rising, magazine in hand*). Oh!

WILL. What's the matter, Ben?

BEN. Lieutenant Bridges on the cover.

WILL. I wish you'd look!

VOICE ON RADIO (*as music fades*). General Bush has just taken his place on the reviewing stand . . . and now the four Lieutenants who are to receive the Air Medal are bravely mounting the platform. (KING *is removing his shoes, putting them beside desk.*)

BEN (*looking from magazine to radio*). The Lieutenants are getting medals! They're heroes!

WILL. Gol-ly!

BEN. If we'd stayed on the plane, we would be heroes!

VOICE ON RADIO. It's a solemn moment, ladies and gentlemen; the many visiting dignitaries standing at attention, the flags at half-mast in honor of the two men who gave their lives in "Operation Prometheus," Privates Stockdale and Whitledge . . .

WILL AND BEN. Stockdale and Whitledge?

VOICE ON RADIO. Yes, Stockdale and Whitledge! Names that will live as long as men are free! (*Martial music comes up again.*)

WILL. We *are* heroes, Ben!

BEN. But we ain't dead!

WILL. Well, that makes it even better, don't it?

BEN. They think we're heroes and we're a couple of rotten no-good deserters . . .

WILL. Golly, will they be surprised!

(KING *rises, crosses office.*)

BEN. They'll kill us, that's what they'll do! They'll kill us!

(KING *opens anteroom door, takes magazine from table, closes door, heads back for desk. He stops, looks back at closed door, shakes his head vigorously and continues to desk.*)

WILL. Come on, Ben. They'll be real glad we're alive, you'll see. (WILL *goes to connecting door, opens it.* BEN *follows.* KING *has his feet up on the desk and the*

magazine held open before his face. WILL *and* BEN *enter office.*) Howdy, Sergeant!

BEN (*saluting*). Private Ben Whitledge reporting for duty after an unforeseen delay, sir!

WILL. I'll bet you never expected to see us again, but here we are!

KING (*slowly lowering magazine*). No . . . No . . . No . . .

WILL. Didn't I tell you he'd be surprised, Ben?

KING. Why—ain't—you—dead?

(BEN *remains at petrified attention.*)

WILL. No excuse, sir!

KING. You ain't dead. . . . You ain't dead . . .

WILL. Well, I had my parachute on.

KING. . . . and I'm the one who identified your remains. . . . Two charred helmets and a pile of dust . . . they're having a ceremony down there. . . .

BUSH (*on radio*). Ten days ago, in "Operation Prometheus," the power of the atom bomb was challenged by a band of battle-hardened air aces. When General Pollard and I planned this shining symbol of man's unconquerability, we had no idea—

WILL (*over the above, pointing to radio*). Is that the General? Is he gonna give us medals?

KING. The General . . . ! (*Flings himself at radio, shuts it off, beats on it.*) Oh, God! Oh, my God!

WILL. Now that ain't no way to act, Sergeant. Here Ben and me is alive and you—

KING (*pushing them into anteroom*). Medals! He's giving you medals! (*Slamming door on* WILL *and* BEN, *he rushes from the office.*) Lieutenant! Lieutenant!

BEN. We'll be shot. We'll be shot!

WILL (*leading* BEN *to the bench*). No, it's just that he's kind of surprised right now. Later on, they'll be right happy we're here, you'll see.

(KING *and* ABEL *come running into office.*)

ABEL. *What?* (KING, *nodding points to door.* ABEL *throws it open.* BEN *snaps to attention.*) No . . . No, no . . . Don't move, do you understand, don't move! (*He slams door, then flings it open again.*) Don't move or I'll have you shot! (*He slams door again.* BEN *wilts.* ABEL *grabs* KING.) You get over to the reviewing stand on the double and tell the General to stop the proceedings. There's radio and television and newsreel cameras there, and if he gives posthumous medals to two men who are standing right here in his own office he'll be the laughing stock of the whole country! Step on it! (KING *runs.* ABEL *flings connecting door open.* BEN *snaps to attention.*) Stay away from the windows, you understand? Stay away from the doors! Just don't move! And if anybody comes in here you tell them you're John Jones and Jack Smith, you got that?

WILL. Yes, sir! (ABEL *slams door and mops his brow.* BEN *collapses.*)

BEN. They're gonna kill us . . . they're gonna kill us . . .

WILL (*taking up* Time *and fanning* BEN *with it*). No they ain't. Breathe deep.

(CHARLES *bursts into office.*)

CHARLES (*to* ABEL). What the hell's going on here? King just jumped an Air Policeman and stole his motorcycle.

ABEL. The two men who are getting the posthumous medals . . . they're inside.

CHARLES. The medals?

ABEL. The men.

CHARLES. You're drunk.

ABEL. Go ahead, look!

CHARLES (*opens connecting door slowly. Peers in.* WILL *turns from his fanning*). Who are you?

WILL. I'm John Jones and this here is Jack Smith.

CHARLES (*slams door*). Listen, Jim, if you're trying to pull my leg, it'll be the last time, because joking about the dead is carrying it just a little too far.

ABEL. Dead? That's them, right there! That idiot gave those names because I told them to! They're the ones; Sergeant King identified them.

CHARLES. I'm beginning to think that doesn't mean too much! *He identified them once before, didn't he?*

ABEL (*snatching newspaper from desk*). Here's their pictures! You want more proof?

CHARLES. Lord. Lordy Lord . . .

(WILL *stops fanning, looks at back of magazine.*)

WILL. Lieutenant Gardella don't really smoke Camels, does he? (WILL *resumes fanning.* KING *runs into office.*)

ABEL. Well? Did you stop him in time?

KING. Sir, I reported to the General and informed him as to the situation and advised him that under the very unusual circumstances, as it has been found out that contrary to all Intelligence reports to the contrary, he desist . . .

ABEL. In English, damn it! Had he already presented the medals or not?

KING. Yes sir, he had.

ABEL. Lord! (*Runs from office.*)

CHARLES. Lordy Lord. What did he say?

KING. He said that—

BUSH (*a fearful bellow from offstage*). *I'll court-martial everybody in the whole damn Air Force!*

KING. That's what he said, sir.

(BUSH, *livid, bursts into office.* BAKER *follows him.*)

BUSH. Where are they? Where are they? Where are the two privates who hold my career in the palm of their hands?

CHARLES. In there, sir. (*Points to door.* BUSH *flings it open and steps into anteroom.* BEN *and* WILL *come to attention and salute.*)

BUSH. You two!

WILL. Yes, sir. We got back here as quick as we could. (*Pause.* BUSH *stares.*) And we sure do appreciate you givin' us medals and all and settin' the flags at half-mast. (WILL *shakes* BUSH's *hand.* BUSH *winces sickly.*) And I got the whole thing figured out, sir. I have. You see, before all the excitement started in the plane up there, I was cleanin' and sweepin' in the back. Well, you know that handful of dust Sergeant King was talkin' about? (BUSH *nods dumbly.*) That's what it was, a handful of dust. If I'da knowed yall was gonna think it was *us,* I'da swept it under a seat or somethin'! Well, anyhow, what it all comes down to is, we ain't dead!

(BUSH *totters back into office, closing the door.* WILL *lowers* BEN's *saluting arm and resumes fanning him.* BUSH *stares at* KING.)

BUSH. Ten minutes ago, in front of half the brass in the continental United States, I awarded the Air Medal to a pile of dust. Do you know what this is going to do to me, Sergeant King, when this story gets out?

KING. Sir, I didn't know that they were—

BUSH. For thirty-two years I've been building a reputation! For dignity, for responsibility, for coolness in the crisis and clear-thinking in the clutch! Tomorrow I will probably be known throughout the entire Pentagon as "Old Dustpan!"

KING. Sir, there were these two charred

helmets and this—

BUSH. I am not interested in how you *knew* these men in there were dead, Sergeant King! You are responsible for this whole mess!

KING (*saluting rapidly*). Yes, sir! Yes, sir!

ABEL (*entering office*). The reporters, sir! They're on their way over. They want to know why you ran out in the middle of Taps.

BUSH. Stall them! Keep them away! Show them the new gymnasium! (ABEL *exits.*) I've got to get those men off my base. If anybody sees them—if anybody hears them—

KING. You could transfer them to another base, sir—

BUSH. Shut up! . . . What? Of course! (*To* CHARLES) Go down to the basement and get as many DD-613 forms as you can lay your hands on.

CHARLES. You mean DAF-39-J, don't you, sir?

BUSH. I mean DD-613! (CHARLES *exits.* BUSH *calls after him.*) Well, if you find any DAF-39-J's . . . (*To* BAKER) You. Go get a car and bring it around back. Quietly. See if you can find one of those old jobs, with window shades.

BAKER. Yes, sir! (*Exits.*)

BUSH. You!

KING (*saluting, heading for door*). Yes, sir!

BUSH. The phone. Get through to General Hooper, down in Texas. See if he's got room for a couple of new privates on his base. Bright, hardworking boys.

KING. Yes, sir. (*Goes to phone.*)

BUSH. But first get those miserable men in here!

KING. Yes, sir. (*Heads for anteroom.*)

BUSH. And put your shoes on!

KING. Yes, sir. (*Snatches shoes from floor, opens anteroom door and beckons* WILL *and* BEN *into office.* KING *returns to telephone.* WILL *and* BEN *enter office hesitantly.* BUSH *draws himself up, glares at them, then melts into a department-store-Santa-Claus chuckle.*)

BUSH. Ha-ha-ha-ho-ho-ho. Well, it looks like we've had a little mix-up, boys, doesn't it?

WILL. Yes sir, it sure do.

BUSH. *It sure do,* all right, ha-ha-ha-ho-ho. But I guess we can straighten it out, can't we? You can straighten most things

out if everybody co-operates. That's all it takes, just a little co-operation isn't that so? Ha-ha-ha.

BEN (*through chattering teeth*). Yes, sir, yes, sir, yes, sir, yes, sir . . .

BUSH. Well, I'm mighty glad to hear you feel that way about it, because if you didn't there could be all kinds of trouble! You boys could even get court-martialed and you wouldn't like that, would you? Ha-ha-ha. No sir, that's the reason we're—

BEN. Give it to us, sir! We deserve it!

BUSH. No, no, no, we're just going to co-operate and everything will—

BEN. We deserted when we should've stuck to our posts!

BUSH. Well, accidents will happen, and sometimes—

BEN. Throw the book at us, sir!

BUSH (*to* WILL). What's the matter with *him?*

WILL. He's worryin' he ain't dead.

BUSH. Oh, for pity's sake!

BEN. I plead guilty, sir. There was no excuse, sir.

ABEL (*entering*). The reporters, sir. They've seen the gymnasium and they still want to see *you.*

BUSH. Oh, no . . .

BEN. I'll make a full confession, sir!

BUSH. No! Don't let them in. Tell them I'm sick. Tell them I've gone home. (ABEL *exits.*)

BAKER (*entering through anteroom*). I've got the car, sir.

BUSH. Good! Good! Get rid of this idiot!

BEN (*as* BAKER *hustles him out*). The Universal Code of Military Justice says that a soldier who deserts his post should be tried by court-martial!

BUSH (*calling after them*). Lock him in!

WILL. Sir, listen—

BUSH. Get into that car out there.

WILL. Sir, listen, I don't want you to give Ben no punishment. It's my fault he warn't killed, not his'n.

BUSH. Now *look,* nobody's going to punish anybody! I'm just going to transfer the two of you to another air base, that's all! Now will you please get into that car?

WILL (*snapping his fingers*). Sir, as long as you're fixin' to transfer us, couldn't it please be into the Infantry?

BUSH. No, no! I said I wasn't going to punish you and I meant it!

WILL. But it's where we *want* to go, sir!

BUSH. Out of the question! Airmen can

not transfer into the Infantry. Now if you don't get into that car before someone sees you, so help me Hannah, I'm going to have you court-martialed!

WILL (*starts to go, then stops*). Excuse me for sayin' it, sir, but if you done that a whole lot of people would see me, wouldn't they?

BUSH. What! . . . (*Dazed, turns slowly to* KING. *Softly*) Every bit of this is your fault, Sergeant. If you hadn't sent that plane up with this nincompoop at the radio—

KING (*rising, covering mouthpiece of phone*). Me, sir? *My* fault! Now look, sir—

BUSH. Stockdale, be reasonable! I'll find an air base right near your home! That would make you happy, wouldn't it?

WILL. I'm sorry, sir, but if Ben and me can't go into the Infantry I reckon we're better off staying right here.

KING. Will, what do you want to upset the General for? The Infantry's murder. Believe me.

WILL. Ben had a chance to go and he tore it up. You know that.

KING. I'll give you back the watch, Will.

BUSH. I'll give you mine too.

WILL. I'm sorry, sir. The Infantry's what we want.

(BUSH *and* KING *look at each other.* KING *becomes conscious of phone in his hand, hangs up.* ABEL *enters.*)

ABEL. The reporters are *here,* sir.

BUSH. You're asking the impossible, Stockdale! It would take an Act of Congress! Absolutely impossible!

(*Blackout—except for a spot on* WILL. *He grins, comes downstage and addresses audience.*)

WILL. Now *you* know, when you put your mind to it there ain't *nothin'* impossible. General Bush, he got them reporters in there and told 'em all about how it was such a proud day in the history of the base and all like that, and then the reporters left and him and Sergeant King let me out of the closet . . . And then General Pollard come over and him and General Bush talked some . . . argued, you might say . . . well, what it was was cussin'. All I said to General Pollard was "Howdy" and he knowed who I was right off. He did. Then he left and the next thing you know, me and Sergeant King and General Bush was all pilin' into this great big car. With

window shades. And did we drive! Till after dark and then some. And all the time General Bush kept mumblin' to hisself. After a while I made out what he was mumblin'. He was sayin' over and over again, "Where there's a will, there's a way." I asked him to stop, 'cause it's right embarrassin' to hear someone praisin' you like that. Well, finally we was done drivin', and I could tell by the smell of the pines and the sound of the frogs we was out in the woods. Just then the moon come up and things commenced to happen.

(*Spot on* WILL *blacks out, and lights dim up on a clearing in the woods. The rear end of an* AIR FORCE *sedan projects onstage right. There is a tent upstage, with its side rolled up. Within the tent, a* CORPORAL *sits typing by lantern light.* WILL *steps back into the scene and watches as* KING *gives orders to a line of armed sentries.*)

KING. All right, have you got it straight now? Challenge everybody. The password is "Nightmare." If they don't give it, *shoot!* Okay—sentries, take your posts. On the double!

(SENTRIES *trot off in various directions.* BUSH *enters, followed by* ABEL, BAKER *and* CHARLES, *who go into tent.*)

BUSH. Are you sure we've got the whole area surrounded?

KING. I think so, sir. Tell you the truth, I've never done anything like this before.

BUSH. Do you think I have? Guns. Passwords . . .

WILL. It sure is excitin', ain't it?

BUSH. Look, you just stand over there and let me handle this. Please! (*To* KING) Where's General Pollard?

KING. On his way, sir.

BUSH. Are the forms ready for him to sign?

KING. The corporal's working on them, sir.

(*An approaching car is heard from the left.*)

BUSH. Well, speed him up! That must be Pollard's car now.

KING. Yes, sir. (*Goes to tent.*)

SENTRY (*off*). Halt! Give the password! (*Silence, then a volley of shots ring out.*)

BUSH. Great Scott, they've shot Pollard!

POLLARD (*off*). Eugene! Tell these idiots to stop shooting! It's me! Vernon! (*Another shot.*)

BUSH. Give the password!

POLLARD (*off*). I've forgotten the damn

thing.

BUSH. Nightmare!

WILL. Nightmare! (*Another shot.*)

POLLARD (*off*). Nightmare, goddammit! (*He storms into the clearing, brandishing a shooting stick.*) Look here, Eugene, you're carrying this thing just a little too far!

BUSH. I'm sorry, Vernon, the sentries are as nervous as I am.

(*There is loud hammering from the trunk of the sedan.* BUSH *and* POLLARD *throw up their arms.*)

BUSH AND POLLARD. Nightmare!

BUSH. It's the other dead hero, Vernon. The talkative one. I hid him in the trunk for total security.

WILL. Ben's in the trunk? (*More hammering.*)

BUSH. All right, Stockdale. Get the keys and let him out. (WILL *goes around car for keys.*)

POLLARD. Listen, Eugene, we could both get into a hell of a lot of trouble, pulling a deal like this.

BUSH. We are in trouble, Vernon. Clear up to our pensions. Now come on, sign those papers. (*They go up to tent.* WILL *unlocks trunk of car, raises lid.* BEN *sticks his head out, peers around.*)

WILL. Howdy, Ben!

BEN. I knew it . . . they got us out in no-man's land . . .

WILL (*helping him out*). Come on . . . here you go . . .

BEN. Good-by, Will.

WILL. We just now got here, Ben.

BEN. And we ain't never going back. Will, I know you didn't do it on purpose and I know there wasn't no meanness behind it. (*Extends hand.*) I forgive you.

WILL (*shaking hands*). You mean we're buddies again?

BEN. For a little while . . .

KING (*coming down from tent*). All right, Whitledge, you're first. Sentry! Take him inside. See that he signs everything in triplicate. (*A* SENTRY *drags* BEN *up to the tent.*)

BEN. 'By, Will.

WILL. 'By, Ben. (*To* KING) Golly, is he gonna be surprised!

KING. We can say good-by too, Will.

WILL. I'm sure gonna miss you, Sergeant!

KING. Me too. I could hardly type your transfers for the tears in my eyes.

WILL. You know—everyone's all the time sayin' how sergeants is mean and tough, so I'm right glad you was my first one. You showed me different.

KING. Thanks, Will. (*They shake hands.* WILL *looks at* KING's *watch.*) Okay, I'm going to give you the watch anyway. Here. Go on, take it.

WILL. Gee, I never held that against you . . .

KING (*backing away*). We're square now. I don't owe you nothing; you don't owe me nothing. We're square.

(BUSH *and* POLLARD *come down from tent.*)

BUSH. King, what's the matter with that Whitledge? He keeps saying he's sorry he has only one life to give for his country.

(KING *makes crazy sign, goes up to tent.*)

WILL. He figgers you brought us here to get shot, sir.

BUSH AND POLLARD. Shot? (*They look at each other speculatively.*)

BUSH. Ridiculous . . . All these witnesses, Vernon . . . (POLLARD *returns to tent.* BUSH *flourishes a clipboard.*) All right, Stockdale, I've just got a couple of letters for you to sign and then we'll be through with this mess. This one is to your folks, saying that you're on a very important secret mission, and this one certifies that you've never heard of "Operation Prometheus" and have never been on my base in your entire life. Sign here. (*Shoves pen at* WILL.)

WILL. But if we never heard of "Operation Whatchamacallit," then we don't get no medals, do we?

BUSH. Medals! Of course not! Sign here . . .

WILL. Ben sets a lot of stock in medals and all like that.

BUSH. Now look—you just sign these letters! You're going into the Infantry; what more do you want?

WILL. But if we don't sign, then we're still dead—and Ben's medal will be sent to his folks and he could just go home and pick it up, couldn't he?

BUSH. Well, yes . . . well, no! . . . well . . .

WILL. Looks to me like we're *best* off just stayin' dead!

BUSH. You can't *do* that! All right, all right. (*Detaches a ribbon from his jacket.*) Here's a ribbon. Now sign.

WILL. This way is okay for me, sir, but couldn't you do it up right for Ben?

BUSH. Do it up—

WILL. You know, give him a real medal, not just a little ribbon. And everybody standin' up stifflike and you sayin' a whole lot of words.

BUSH. You want me to *present* a medal . . . out here in the woods . . . in the middle of the night?

WILL. That's right! We'll get everybody standin' up over there, and we could turn some of the cars around so their lights is shinin'! Maybe we can get some music on the radio! Hey, driver, could you turn that car around! (*Runs off right.*)

BUSH. No! No! I don't have any medals!

POLLARD (*coming down from tent*). How long is this going to take, Eugene?

BUSH (*calling after* WILL). I didn't bring any medals!

POLLARD. I want to get to bed.

BUSH (*turning to the be-medaled* POLLARD). I don't have any med— Ohhh . . . !

POLLARD. What are you staring at?

BUSH. Vernon . . . old man . . . I wonder if you could give me . . . one of your . . . medals?

POLLARD. What?

BUSH. Just one, Vernon! You've got so many of them!

POLLARD. What are you talking about, Eugene?

BUSH. Stockdale wants a medal!

POLLARD. To hell with him!

BUSH. No! Vernon, if you give me one of yours . . . I'll give you *two* of mine. I swear I will.

POLLARD. But these medals are sewn on!

BUSH. Sewn?

(WILL *re-enters, approaches them.*)

POLLARD. Yes, dammit!

BUSH (*to* WILL, *pleadingly*). His medals are *sewn* on . . .

WILL. I got my mumbly-peg knife. (*Producing it.*)

BUSH (*handing* POLLARD *the knife*). A small one, Vernon . . . Please . . .

POLLARD (*snatching knife*). I'll do this in private, if you don't mind! (POLLARD *storms off into the trees. From the right, a pair of headlight beams swing around, and an orchestra playing "Goody, Goody" is heard.*)

BUSH. There's nothing else you can think of at the moment, is there, Stockdale? You do understand why we don't have a brass band, don't you?

WILL. I wouldn't worry about it none. This'll do fine. I'll just get the fellows lined up. Hey, Corporal! (CORPORAL *comes out of tent.* WILL *salutes.*) Howdy. Would you please go over there and stand up at attention, real smart-like.

CORPORAL. Do what?

BUSH. Just do as you're told! On the double!

WILL. Captain, could you and the Lieutenants come out here a minute, please? (CHARLES, BAKER *and* ABEL *emerge from tent.* WILL *salutes.*) Howdy. Would you fellows go over there with the Corporal and stand up at attention, please?

THREE OFFICERS. DO WHAT?

BUSH. Get over there! You ought to know enough to obey orders by now!

(POLLARD *storms back on, the front of his jacket slashed and torn. He thrusts a medal at* BUSH.)

POLLARD. I've been blackmailed, I've been shanghaied, I've been shot at, and now I've been robbed.

WILL. Boy, Ben's gonna pop his shirt when both you Generals snap to attention!

POLLARD. DO WHAT?

BUSH. Vernon, please . . .

POLLARD. Never! Not on your life! (*Flips open his shooting stick and sits on it.*)

BUSH. *I'll* stand at attention! I'll stand on my head! Please sign!

WILL (*taking pen*). Clean forgot! Last name first, first name, middle name last?

BUSH. Just your regular signature. (SENTRIES *enter.*) You men get over there with the others! (SENTRIES *join group standing at attention.*)

WILL. I'll go fetch Ben. (WILL *exits into tent as* KING *emerges, a sheaf of papers in his hand.*)

BUSH. King, have you got those orders?

KING. Yes, sir.

BUSH (*calling to tent*). All right, dammit, come out and get it!

WILL (*leading* BEN *out*). Go ahead, Ben. Strut right up to the General and he's gonna give you somethin'.

BEN. I know. Good-by, Will.

BUSH. King . . .

KING (*reading*). "The following enlisted men are hereby relieved of duty and removed from the records of Major General Eugene Bush, and transferred to the command of Major General Vernon I. Pollard, U.S. Army, Infantry."

BEN. What?

WILL. We're in the Infantry, Ben.

BEN. The Infantry?

WILL. You finally made it, Ben.

BEN. Oh, no . . . oh, golly . . . oh. . . .

KING (*crossing and handing papers to them*). Private Benjamin B. Whitledge . . . Private Will Stockdale . . . So long, boys. It's been swell knowing you!

WILL AND BEN. So long, Sergeant.

KING. Wish I could go along with you, but that's life!

WILL (*to* BUSH). Gee, couldn't he, sir? Go along with us?

BUSH. Brilliant idea, Stockdale! Vernon?

POLLARD. Wonderful!

KING. No, no, no—

WILL (*throwing his arm around* KING'*s shoulder*). We're still gonna be together!

BEN. In the Infantry!

KING. What happened?

BUSH. Detail, atten-shun!

POLLARD (*sitting with his arms folded*). Damned if I'll stand at attention!

VOICE ON RADIO. . . . broadcasting on 1200 kilocycles. Good night. (*Drum roll.*)

BUSH. It gives me great pleasure to award this medal which through a regrettable error was previously awarded posthumously, to Private Benjamin B. Whitledge, U.S. Army, Infantry.

(*Band on radio plays "The Star-Spangled Banner."* POLLARD *leaps to attention and salutes.* BEN *marches up to* BUSH *to receive his medal.* WILL *comes downstage and addresses audience as "Meeting Hall" curtain falls and the scene behind it slowly fades out.*)

WILL. Everythin' come out as good as Tony and the Pony, didn't it? Well, that's how I got my ribbon and Ben got his medal, and how us Three Musketeers wound up in the Infantry after all. I want to thank yall for bein' such good listeners and not leavin' the hall no more'n you had to. Mrs. Calhoun got her shoe back? Good. Well, I guess I better quit now, because— (*Looks carefully at watch.*)—Mickey Mouse got his hands way up to goin' home time! Good night! Good night! (*He runs off into the wings.*)

CURTAIN

THE SOLID GOLD CADILLAC

George S. Kaufman AND Howard Teichmann

First presented by Max Gordon at the New Parsons Theatre in Hartford,
Connecticut, on October 1, 1953. After the customary
vicissitudes—plus a few extra ones—in Washington and Philadelphia,
it opened at the Belasco Theatre in New York on November 5,
1954. The cast was as follows:

T. JOHN BLESSINGTON	Geoffrey Lumb	MISS LOGAN	Vera Fuller Mellish
ALFRED METCALFE	Wendell K. Phillips	THE A.P.	Carl Judd
WARREN GILLIE	Reynolds Evans	THE U.P.	Al McGranary
CLIFFORD SNELL	Henry Jones	I.N.S.	Howard Adelman
MRS. LAURA PARTRIDGE	Josephine Hull	A LITTLE OLD LADY	Gloria Maitland
MISS AMELIA SHOTGRAVEN	Mary Welch	NEWS BROADCASTERS	
MARK JENKINS	Jack Ruth	BILL PARKER	Henry Norell
MISS L'ARRIERE	Charlotte Van Lein	DWIGHT BROOKFIELD	Mark Allen
EDWARD L. MCKEEVER	Loring Smith	ESTELLE EVANS	Lorraine MacMartin

The action of the play takes place in New York and Washington.

The recitation by Edward L. McKeever, "Spartacus to the
Gladiators," complete with gestures, is the invention of
Marc Connelly.

And Fred Allen recorded the narration. . . . Damned
comically, too.

The Solid Gold Cadillac's original author, Howard Teichmann, born in Chicago, studied journalism at the University of Wisconsin, graduating in 1938, but turned to the theatre in the late 1930's. He was first Orson Welles' playreader at the notably experimental Mercury Theatre and then a stage manager for the same organization. Subsequently he began to work for radio as a writer for Orson Welles, Helen Hayes, and the Ford Theatre, and he supplemented his labors with some teaching at Columbia University. He has also dramatized Nathaniel West's satiric novel *Miss Lonelyhearts* for Broadway and Hollywood and sold a comedy called *Girls in 509* to Alfred de Liagre, Jr., for production in the fall of 1958.

Mr. Teichmann's collaborator, George S. Kaufman, certainly needs no introduction to readers of the *Best American Plays* volumes. Born in Pittsburgh in 1889, a journalist on the *Washington Times* by 1912, and a drama editor for *The New York Times* in the early 1920's, Mr. Kaufman became author or co-author of many successful comedies (*Dulcy, The Butter and Egg Man, Beggar on Horseback, Merton of the Movies, The Royal Family, June Moon, You Can't Take It With You,* and *The Man Who Came to Dinner*), as well as musical comedies such as *Of Thee I Sing* and *I'd Rather Be Right.* Mr. Kaufman has also often distinguished himself as a stage director. There are indeed few precincts of the Broadway theatre to which he has not brought expert dramaturgy, humor, wit, and genial mockery. He has been altogether a good workman and great gentleman of the theatre.

The well-tested talents of an expert were rewarded by a farce-comedy which combined genial cartooning and a "darlin'" characterization—namely, Mrs. Laura Partridge who was superbly played by the lovable Josephine Hull—with spoofs on big business, politics, television, and other subjects suitable for humorous comment. The play has no literary pretensions whatsoever, nor was credibility an ambition of the authors of this entertainment. It was a fairy tale, and Fred Allen was almost literally correct in declaring that it was the story of Cinderella and the Four Ugly Directors. It was also the story of Cinderella on Wall Street, which amounts to a compounding of fairy-tale elements. *The Solid Gold Cadillac* is undoubtedly a random piece of playwriting, but its kind of improvisation is of the essence in the game of farce, which probably has to kick up its heels faster and higher on Broadway than at any other Vanity Fair in the world.

ACT ONE

SCENE ONE

The curtain rises to reveal four over-stuffed shirts, each one with a man inside it.

They are seated behind a great directors' table—and, indeed, directors are what they are. For this is a stockholders' meeting, somewhere in downtown New York, and our four directors are on hand strictly in their own interests, and not at all concerned with the welfare of the stockholders. But that can wait, since it is the story of the play.

Then, as they stiffly sit there, a voice comes over the loud-speaker. It comes over in the raspy tone of Mr. Fred Allen, and we trust that the reader, if any, will imagine Mr. Allen's wonderful voice as he reads this narration:

THIS IS A FAIRY STORY—THE STORY OF CINDERELLA AND THE FOUR UGLY CORPORATION DIRECTORS. ONCE UPON A TIME, NOT SO LONG AGO, CINDERELLA WENT DOWN TO WALL STREET, NOT IN A GOLD COACH DRAWN BY SIX WHITE HORSES, BUT IN THE I.R.T. SUBWAY.

(One of the stuffed shirts rises and pounds a gavel. His name is T. JOHN BLESSINGTON, *and he looks it. The other three, from whom we presently will hear, are named* ALFRED METCALFE, WARREN GILLIE, *and* CLIFFORD SNELL. *Not that it matters.)*

(But soft! MR. BLESSINGTON *is speaking.)*

———

BLESSINGTON. Order, please, order! The meeting will come to order. The fifty-ninth annual meeting of the stockholders is hereby declared in session. Stockholders, that is, of the General Products Corporation of America. (MR. BLESSINGTON *looks the stockholders over.*) No doubt many of you are surprised to find me acting as chairman of this meeting. No more so than I. My seat has always been Mr. Metcalfe's—that is, where Mr. Metcalfe is *sitting*. However, due to our great and irreplaceable loss—I have naturally, and legally too, I am informed, moved up one notch. Not that I shall ever be able to fill the place left vacant by our beloved Ed McKeever—Big Ed, as he was known to those who loved him. (*The others look appropriately solemn.*) Edward L. Mc-

Keever made this great company what it is today—one of the largest corporations in the United States. In his nineteen years as President and Chairman of the Board he saw your company grow until it now manufactures everything from pins to automobiles, from a nail file to tractors and locomotives. Yes, I can safely say: if General Products doesn't make it, there's no money in it. Now I will call upon your new President—Acting President, I should say, until you make your new President, who will tell you what your Board of Directors proposes to do to honor our great former leader. . . . Mr. Alfred Metcalfe.

METCALFE (*the rough-diamond type*). Thank you, Mr. Blessington. Yes, General Products lost a good man when the President called Ed McKeever to Washington. You all remember what happened down there—I'm sure you read about it in the papers. Before they would give him the job he was forced by the Government to take a profit of three million dollars in General Products stock. But did he hesitate? Only for a week or so. That is why we are sending him this scroll: "To Edward Leon McKeever, slag hauler, furnace feeder, assembly-line worker, foreman, shop supervisor, plant manager, Vice-President, and, for nineteen years, President and Chairman of the Board of the General Products Corporation of America —with the gratitude and affection of labor, management and capital." I just want to add that in the good old days I worked on the slag pile with Ed McKeever, and that nobody ever slung as much slag as Big Ed.

(A smattering of applause, for no good reason.)

BLESSINGTON. Thank you, Mr. Metcalfe. The chair will entertain a motion to have the scroll duly delivered to Mr. McKeever in Washington.

METCALFE. So moved.

BLESSINGTON. Thank you. Do I hear a second?

GILLIE. Second.

SNELL (*indicates a great pile of proxies*). Voting 750,000 shares by duly authorized proxy, I say aye.

BLESSINGTON. Thank you. Opposed? . . . Motion carried by acclamation. . . . And now the next business of the meeting —the report of your Secretary, Mr. Warren Gillie.

GILLIE (*really a dull fellow*). The stockholders will have found on their chairs a little white booklet—(*He holds one up as example; reads the title.*)—"Compendium of Minutes of Quarterly Meetings of Directors of General Products Corporation." . . . As the stockholders know, the posts of Chairman of the Board and President of the Corporation were both held by Mr. McKeever. In the new alignment, delegation of responsibility is proposed as follows: T. John Blessington, from First Vice-President to Chairman of the Board; (BLESSINGTON *smiles, fatuously.*) Alfred Metcalfe, from Second Vice-President to President of the company. (METCALFE *pretends to be embarrassed.*) Clifford Snell, from Treasurer to Administrative Vice-President *and* Treasurer. (SNELL *grins—a phony if ever there was one.*) Warren Gillie, Secretary, to remain as Secretary. Respectfully submitted, Warren Gillie, Secretary. (*And he sits, before anyone can throw an egg.*)

BLESSINGTON (*rises*). Thank you, Mr. Gillie. Do I hear a motion to accept Mr. Gillie's report?

SNELL. Moved.

METCALFE. Second.

SNELL (*right on the job*). 750,000 proxies vote aye.

BLESSINGTON. Opposed? Carried. And now, the report of the man you're really waiting to hear from, your Treasurer, Mr. Clifford Snell.

SNELL (*we don't have to mince words here—*SNELL *is a plain crook*). Thank you, Jack. (*The big smile*) Well folks, I'm the fellow you either like or dislike. Depending on the size of the dividend check, eh? (*The other three laugh it up, even if the audience doesn't.*) And here's the report on how we did this year. I'm sure all of you have found it on your chairs, alongside of Mr. Gillie's little booklet. It isn't as compact as Warren's report, but then you can't do things with figures the way you can with words. (*Another laugh from his associates. Jolly good fellows they.*) Anyhow, suppose you and I kind of thumb through it together. . . . Let's see. Page 11—just as one example. Page 11. Assets—26 billion, one million, seven hundred and ninety-two thousand, eight hundred and ninety-one dollars and seventy-two cents. Now, I think that's pretty good, don't you? (*The big grin again. Here is a fellow to avoid even in a light alley*)

BLESSINGTON. Fine, Clifford. Just fine.

GILLIE. Fine!

SNELL. Page 32. Inventory. Starts on Page 32, runs to Page 57, and you'll find a pretty complete list there, from the raw stock in our Allegheny steel plant to the little cellophane price tags in our Denver merchandising rooms. (*Idly flipping pages*) Pages 161, 162, all the way up to 170—gross profits, net gains, interest charges, dividend payments, and the like . . . Well, folks, that's the story. I might add that now, at long last, since we finally have an administration in Washington that understands business—our dividend this quarter will be slightly smaller. Of course, that's only temporary. . . . (*He sits, but bounces up again.*) The smaller dividend will be temporary, I mean, not the administration in Washington. (*And he is finished.*)

BLESSINGTON. Thank you, Mr. Snell. Now will anyone move for the adoption of Mr. Snell's report?

METCALFE (*fast as hell*). Moved.

GILLIE (*even faster than hell*). Second.

SNELL (*much faster than hell*). Proxies vote aye.

BLESSINGTON. It's been moved and seconded that the report of the Treasurer, Mr. Clifford Snell, be unanimously adopted. All those in favor—Yes, Madame?

(*A dumpy little woman has got to her feet. A real charmer, but tough. Having got up, she is really never going to sit down again till the show is over.*)

THE WOMAN. Oh! Well, I'm sorry—it's nothing, really.

BLESSINGTON. Then you don't wish the chair to recognize you?

THE WOMAN (*looking around a little uncertainly*). The—chair?

BLESSINGTON. I am the chair, Madame.

THE WOMAN. Oh. I didn't quite—

BLESSINGTON. Do you wish the chair to recognize you?

THE WOMAN. I *did* have something I wanted to ask, but—

BLESSINGTON. Certainly, Madame. What was it you wanted to know?

THE WOMAN. Well, it's not really something I want to know, exactly—it's—kind of something I don't like.

SNELL. Can't we get ahead with this, Jack?

BLESSINGTON. Something you don't like? What is it?

THE WOMAN. Well, it's—this. (*She holds up the blue book.*)

BLESSINGTON. You don't like Mr. Snell's report? All of it?

THE WOMAN. No, I don't mean all of it. I—I like the color.

SNELL. Isn't this a little ridiculous?

THE WOMAN. I'm sorry, I—I've never attended a stockholders' meeting before. Maybe I'd better sit down.

BLESSINGTON. Just as you wish, Madame.

THE WOMAN. Thank you.

BLESSINGTON. Now, there is a motion—

THE WOMAN. On the other hand—it says here that the salary for the Chairman of the Board next year will be $175,000. (*Gossipy*) Tell me—is that true?

BLESSINGTON. Well—uh—wherever did you get a notion like that, Miss—uh—

THE WOMAN. *Mrs.* Mrs. Partridge. It's on Page 96. Right here.

BLESSINGTON. I see. Uh—Mr. Snell, as Treasurer, would you care to answer that question?

SNELL (*brightly*). Yes, indeed! Happy to oblige . . . The—uh—could I hear the question again, please?

MRS. PARTRIDGE. I don't want anyone to think I'm nosy, but is it true that the Chairman will get $175,000 next year? It seems such a lot of money.

SNELL. Why—Madame. In a company of this size that is not considered a large salary. Not a large salary at all. I believe that answers the question. (*And pretty smug he is.*)

BLESSINGTON. Yes. There is a motion—

MRS. PARTRIDGE (*not one to give up*). Well, would I be just awful if I asked another question? What does the Chairman of the Board do?

SNELL. My dear lady, as an attorney I can assure you that the office of Chairman of the Board is one prescribed by law. New York State Corporation Code, Section 23. We have very little to say about it —we're just obeying the law.

MRS. PARTRIDGE. Oh, I'm sure of that. Only—what does he do?

BLESSINGTON (*The four look at each other. This is really a tough one*). He presides over the board. The Chairman of the Board presides over the board of directors.

MRS. PARTRIDGE. Now I understand. Thank you so much.

(*The stuffed shirts breathe easier.*)

BLESSINGTON. Not at all. We are always happy to—

MRS. PARTRIDGE. How often does he do that?

BLESSINGTON. I beg your pardon?

MRS. PARTRIDGE. How often does he preside over the board?

BLESSINGTON (*damned if he knows*). Why—uh—how often *is* that, Mr. Gillie?

GILLIE (*with his dreams*). How's that?

BLESSINGTON. How often does the Board meet?

GILLIE. Why—four times a year, isn't it? (*Firmly, to* MRS. PARTRIDGE) Four times every year.

SNELL. That is also prescribed by law.

MRS. PARTRIDGE. Now I know I'm asking a lot of questions, but—how long do the meetings last?

BLESSINGTON (*walking right into it*). Oh, several hours. At least several hours.

MRS. PARTRIDGE. *Two* hours, would you say?

BLESSINGTON. Yes. Yes, indeed. And then there's the annual stockholders' meeting.

MRS. PARTRIDGE. So that makes five times?

SNELL. Excuse me, Jack . . . Uh—Mrs. Partridge—that's right, Partridge?

MRS. PARTRIDGE. Yes, sir.

SNELL (*as to a child*). You understand this is a stockholders' meeting?

MRS. PARTRIDGE. Oh, yes.

SNELL. You *are* a—stockholder?

MRS. PARTRIDGE Oh yes. I have ten shares. I've had them for a long time, only I've never come to a meeting before.

SNELL. Your full name and address, Mrs. uh—(*He motions to* GILLIE *to confirm.*)

MRS. PARTRIDGE. Mrs. Laura Partridge, 226-a 18th St., Jackson Heights, Long Island.

GILLIE (*looks in the book*). Paddington, Partridge . . . (*Reluctantly*) Mrs. Laura Partridge. Ten shares, stock certificate No. 18973635. (*The boys are anything but pleased at this.*)

MRS. PARTRIDGE. Yes. I haven't got it with me. It's in my top bureau drawer.

SNELL (*escorting her toward her chair*). Now we have many points on the agenda, so—

MRS. PARTRIDGE (*not to be silenced*). Well, five meetings a year—that's ten hours in all—you mean he gets $175,000 for just working ten hours?

SNELL (*he can answer that—he thinks*).

Not at all. The Chairman of the Board must be intimately conversant with every detail of the company at all times—that requires constant study, brain work.

BLESSINGTON. It's a big job, Mrs. Partridge—a very big job. Responsibilities to the company, to the nation, and, in these times, to the world.

MRS. PARTRIDGE. Ye-es . . . Still—$175,-000. And you're going to get $100,000, Mr. Snell.

SNELL (*blandly*). And don't you think I'm worth $100,000, Mrs. Partridge?

MRS. PARTRIDGE. Not if we can get somebody for less. (*Well,* SNELL *asked for it.*) You see, the reason I came here today, it says it's a good day to attend to financial matters.

BLESSINGTON. I beg your pardon?

MRS. PARTRIDGE. My horoscope. I'm Leo the Lion. It says: (*She reads.*) "Cultivate friends and attend to financial matters."

BLESSINGTON (*he hadn't figured on this*). I see.

SNELL. Isn't there a motion before the house?

MRS. PARTRIDGE. Mind you, I don't really pay much attention to it. Now that I'm here I'm much more interested in the salaries.

BLESSINGTON (*so sweet*). And we want you to be. Now what is it you would like to know?

MRS. PARTRIDGE. Well, it says you used to get $75,000 and now it's going to be $175,-000—that's $100,0000 more—now, how much did *you* used to get, Mr. Snell?

SNELL (*Let's not go into that*). Madame, that is not the point.

MRS. PARTRIDGE. Goodness, I know it isn't but let's add up, just for fun. Shall we? May I borrow your pencil?—Thank you. (*She takes* SNELL's *pencil out of his pocket.*) Now, how much did you say you used to get, Mr. Snell?

SNELL (what *a nuisance!*) You'll find everything in the report. I don't recall that—

MRS. PARTRIDGE. Oh, here it is. Fifty thousand dollars. Of course, to the ordinary person, fifty thousand dollars—gracious!

SNELL (*a desperate look to* BLESSINGTON). This seems to me hardly a matter for—

MRS. PARTRIDGE. Well, I don't mean to be a nuisance, but—can just anybody make a motion?

BLESSINGTON. Certainly, Madame.

MRS. PARTRIDGE. Oh, good! Well, I move the salaries are too big. (*Having tossed this bombshell, she sits down.*)

BLESSINGTON (*trapped*). It is not quite the proper form for a motion, Mrs. Partridge—however, if someone seconds it—do I hear a second to Mrs. Partridge's motion?

(*There is no response for a moment, but then it comes.*)

MRS. PARTRIDGE (*brightly*). I second it.

SNELL. Madame, you cannot second your own motion.

MRS. PARTRIDGE. Why not? I'm for it.

SNELL. It's a matter of parliamentary law.

MRS. PARTRIDGE. I don't care what they do in Parliament—I think the salaries are too big, and that some of us here ought to form a stockholders' committee.

BLESSINGTON (*stunned*). A committee?

GILLIE. Committee? (*There is an impromptu conference at the table.*)

MRS. PARTRIDGE. To look into the salaries of our company's directors. And until we come back with our report—

SNELL. I object, Mr. Chairman!

METCALFE. Mrs. Partridge, I don't think this is the time—

MRS. PARTRIDGE. Because I've known a lot of directors and they didn't get anything like that. So if the committee finds—

BLESSINGTON (*a panicky look at his fellows*). Mrs. Partridge, the chair has decided not to act on the matter of salaries today. The meeting is adjourned, if someone will so move.

SNELL (*lightning-fast*). Moved.

METCALFE. Second.

BLESSINGTON. It's moved and seconded that we adjourn—opposed? Carried. (*Bangs gavel, thank God that's over.*) The meeting is adjourned. The meeting is adjourned for six weeks.

MRS. PARTRIDGE. Six weeks! I can come.

BLESSINGTON. That's splendid! (*But we doubt if he means it. In fact, a council of war is taking place among our four boy friends. Something has to be done.* MR. BLESSINGTON, *accordingly, takes the bull by the horns.*) Madame, would you remain a moment, please?

MRS. PARTRIDGE. Me?

BLESSINGTON. If you please. I'd like to talk to you a moment.

MRS. PARTRIDGE. You're going to scold

me. I know. I've behaved badly.

BLESSINGTON. Not at all. You showed very fine business sense.

METCALFE (*coming through for a pal*). Very fine.

MRS. PARTRIDGE. I did?

BLESSINGTON. You did indeed. So much so that—(*He is feeling his way, with an eye on his associates*)—I wonder if we shouldn't take advantage of your business abilities—I mean, here at General Products. How would you like to come to work with us here?

MRS. PARTRIDGE. What kind of work?

BLESSINGTON. Well, I don't know exactly. But you seem to have a keen insight into business affairs. I'm sure you can be of aid to us.

MRS. PARTRIDGE. Oh, but I've never worked in my life, Mr. Blessington. I'm an actress.

BLESSINGTON (*with feigned interest*). An actress!

SNELL. Well, well!

METCALFE. An actress! Would I—would I have seen you on the stage?

MRS. PARTRIDGE. Well, I don't know—did you see *Ah, Wilderness*?

BLESSINGTON. *Ah, Wilderness* . . . I believe so. You were the—uh—

MRS. PARTRIDGE. I was one of the women.

BLESSINGTON. Oh, yes.

METCALFE. I think I remember. Very good. Yes.

BLESSINGTON. You're not acting in a play now?

MRS. PARTRIDGE. No, I'm not.

BLESSINGTON. Then would you be free to associate yourself with us?

SNELL. Are you sure Mrs. Partridge wants to come with us, Jack? Maybe she wouldn't like it.

MRS. PARTRIDGE. Oh, I'd love it. (*Down to business*) What about salary?

BLESSINGTON. A *hundred dollars*, Mrs. Partridge. *A hundred dollars a week*. How's *that*?

MRS. PARTRIDGE. Well, I got a hundred and a quarter from the Theatre Guild.

BLESSINGTON. Well, Mrs. Partridge, we *want* you *here* with *us*. So what would you say to a hundred and fifty?

MRS. PARTRIDGE. A hundred and fifty. Yes, that would be better.

BLESSINGTON. Then it's all settled. Let's say you report to me—that's on the thirty-fifth floor—Monday morning at nine o'clock?

MRS. PARTRIDGE (What *an idea*). Nine o'clock!

BLESSINGTON. Would you rather come at some other hour?

MRS. PARTRIDGE. Well, in the theatre we don't generally start until eleven.

BLESSINGTON. Eleven would be quite agreeable. That's Monday morning at eleven.

MRS. PARTRIDGE. Yes, that's fine. (*Going through her astrology book*) Wait a minute. I can't start Monday. It's a bad day for me to go out—see?

BLESSINGTON. Tuesday then?

MRS. PARTRIDGE. Tuesday . . . (*Consulting her book*) "Start new enterprises"—it's perfect. And it's the 17th—that's my lucky number—17. . . . You know, you ought to get one of these.

BLESSINGTON. Well, maybe we can use yours.

MRS. PARTRIDGE. Certainly. Because whoever picked the day for this meeting—(*She beams at them.*)—well, it wasn't a very good time for you, was it?

AND THAT IS SCENE ONE

The Narrator: SO CINDERELLA WENT TO WORK FOR THE FOUR UGLY CORPORATION DIRECTORS AT $150 A WEEK. BUT IN ONE RESPECT, CINDERELLA WAS JUST LIKE THE REST OF US. THEY SOAKED HER FOR WITHHOLDING TAX, WORKMEN'S COMPENSATION TAX, PERSONAL PROPERTY TAX, STATE INCOME TAX, CITY TAX, COUNTY TAX, UNEMPLOYMENT TAX, HOSPITALIZATION TAX, SOCIAL SECURITY TAX, AND SOCIAL INSECURITY TAX.

SCENE TWO

An almost pathetically small office. A desk and two chairs, bookcase and hat rack.

CLIFFORD SNELL *and a severely tailored secretary are talking together.*

SNELL. I want to emphasize one thing, Miss Shotgraven. Mrs. Partridge's activities on behalf of the company must be very slight. It is your job to see that she does little or nothing. Is that clear?

MISS SHOTGRAVEN. You'll find me most co-operative, Mr. Snell.

SNELL. Then we understand each other.

You will report to me if anything unusual happens.

MISS SHOTGRAVEN. Yes, sir. May I ask how long Mrs. Partridge will be with us?

(BLESSINGTON *enters with* MRS. PARTRIDGE.)

BLESSINGTON. Yes, here we are. You remember Mr. Snell of course!

MRS. PARTRIDGE. Yes, indeed.

SNELL. Good morning, Mrs. Partridge! This is your secretary, Miss Shotgraven.

MISS SHOTGRAVEN. How do you do, Mrs. Partridge?

MRS. PARTRIDGE. Good morning, dear . . . My, the business world is fascinating. I know I'm going to love it. Only you gentlemen haven't told me yet just what I'm supposed to do.

BLESSINGTON. Mrs. Partridge, we are going to make you Director of Stockholder Relations.

MRS. PARTRIDGE. How nice!

BLESSINGTON. I hoped you'd like it.

MRS. PARTRIDGE. What is it?

BLESSINGTON. Why—uh—we have a great many stockholders, Mrs. Partridge—many of them women, like yourself, who own just a few shares—and it will be your job to keep them happy, make friends for the company.

MRS. PARTRIDGE. I see. Will they be coming in?

BLESSINGTON. No, no.

SNELL. We hope not.

BLESSINGTON. But occasionally we receive letters from them, and—uh—when we do receive such letters, they will be turned over to you to answer.

MRS. PARTRIDGE. And that's all I'm to do?

BLESSINGTON. That's quite a lot, Mrs. Partridge. We have more than four million stockholders.

MRS. PARTRIDGE. My!

SNELL. Jack, the meeting on short-term debentures is set for 11:20.

BLESSINGTON. Right! Good luck, Mrs. Partridge, and we're so pleased to have you with us.

MRS. PARTRIDGE. Thank you. Good-by.

BLESSINGTON. Good-by.

SNELL. Good-by.

(*The two men go.*)

MRS. PARTRIDGE (*right on the job*). How soon is lunch?

MISS SHOTGRAVEN. How's that?

MRS. PARTRIDGE (*discovers a dictaphone on her desk*). What's that?

MISS SHOTGRAVEN. Your dictaphone. On evenings that you work late, and choose not to keep me on overtime, you use that for your dictation. Then I transcribe the following morning.

MRS. PARTRIDGE. Oh, I've heard of these. Those rich radio actors have them.

MISS SHOTGRAVEN. Simply pick up the microphone and press that button. That's right. Do you have something to say?

MRS. PARTRIDGE. I don't know. (*A thoughtful pause; then into the machine*) "The quality of mercy is not strained. It droppeth as—"

(*A stocky but handsome young man enters—shirt-sleeved, and carrying a clipboard to which are affixed a stack of papers. Also a thick, heavy pencil.*)

THE YOUNG MAN (*businesslike as hell*). Partridge?

MISS SHOTGRAVEN (*with dignity*). This is Mrs. Partridge's office.

THE YOUNG MAN. Jenkins, Incoming Mail . . . How do you spell that name?

MRS. PARTRIDGE. P-a-r-t—

MISS SHOTGRAVEN (*taking it away from her*). R-i-d-g-e.

JENKINS. First name?

MRS. PARTRIDGE. Laura.

MISS SHOTGRAVEN (*a look at her*). Laura.

JENKINS. Yours or hers?

MISS SHOTGRAVEN. Mrs. Laura Partridge.

JENKINS. Okay! Room 2762. (*He makes a quick note.*) Any mail comes, you'll get it.

(*He goes.*)

MISS SHOTGRAVEN (*pulling herself together. The young man has obviously made an impression*). Shall we begin?

MRS. PARTRIDGE. Yes . . . Begin what?

MISS SHOTGRAVEN. Begin work.

MRS. PARTRIDGE. Oh yes. Where are the letters from the stockholders?

MISS SHOTGRAVEN. I haven't seen any, Mrs. Partridge.

MRS. PARTRIDGE. But Mr. Blessington just said—

MISS SHOTGRAVEN. He said if any should come in.

MRS. PARTRIDGE. Oh! Then what do we do? Just wait?

MISS SHOTGRAVEN. Your schedule is clear until 11:55. All executives are required in the main lobby at 11:55 for the unveiling of a bust of Mr. McKeever.

MRS. PARTRIDGE. Well, that'll be interesting. (*Studies* MISS SHOTGRAVEN *a second.*)

Do you always wear your hair that way, dear?

MISS SHOTGRAVEN. I do.

MRS. PARTRIDGE. There's a little hairdresser on 53rd Street . . .

MISS SHOTGRAVEN (*briskly*). Please, Mrs. Partridge. Not during business hours.

MRS. PARTRIDGE. I'm sorry.

(MR. GILLIE *comes in—all business.*)

GILLIE. Good morning, Mrs. Partridge.

MRS. PARTRIDGE. Good morning, Mr. Gillie.

GILLIE (*pompously*). Mrs. Partridge, we're giving a dinner next week to honor Mr. Blessington on his promotion to Chairman of the Board, and we'd be so pleased if you would attend. Tickets are twenty-five dollars.

MRS. PARTRIDGE. Twenty-five dollars! What are you going to have for dinner?

GILLIE. Mrs. Partridge, that is not the point.

MRS. PARTRIDGE. The hell it isn't!

(MR. GILLIE *gets out of there fast—happy to escape.*)

MRS. PARTRIDGE (*to* MISS SHOTGRAVEN). Now, where were we?

MISS SHOTGRAVEN. You were about to dictate.

MRS. PARTRIDGE. Yes. (*But unable to leave the subject*) Do you have any beaus? I suppose you have a lot of beaus. Tell me about them.

MISS SHOTGRAVEN. Please, Mrs. Partridge, I must insist upon a business relationship. Either you must dictate or I shall have to leave the office.

MRS. PARTRIDGE. I'm so sorry. Now let me see . . . Whom can I—Oh, I know. "Dear Eddie:"

MISS SHOTGRAVEN. But whom is it going to?

MRS. PARTRIDGE. To Eddie.

MISS SHOTGRAVEN. But first you have to give me his full name and address, and then you can begin "Dear Eddie."

MRS. PARTRIDGE. But that's all the name he has—Eddie—and I don't know his address.

MISS SHOTGRAVEN. Then how will it reach him?

MRS. PARTRIDGE. I'll just put it in the milk bottle. "Dear Eddie. Please do not leave the half pint of cream every morning, as I will not be home for lunch any more. So just leave it every other day. Thank you. Mrs. Partridge." (*The tele-phone rings. She quickly picks up the receiver.*) Hello.

MISS SHOTGRAVEN (*horrified*). Mrs. Partridge! (*She takes the receiver from her.*) Mrs. Partridge's secretary speaking . . . Who wants to speak to Mrs. Partridge? . . . One moment please—I'll see if she is in.

MRS. PARTRIDGE. I'm in.

MISS SHOTGRAVEN (*refusing to give her the phone*). What does he want to talk to Mrs. Partridge about?

MRS. PARTRIDGE. I haven't anything to do—isn't it all right if I talk to him?

MISS SHOTGRAVEN (*covering phone*). Not to a theatrical agent, Mrs. Partridge.

MRS. PARTRIDGE. A theatrical agent! (*Takes phone from her.*) Who's this—Tom Lynch? . . . How on earth did you find me? . . . Oh, yes, my answering service . . . Yes, I *am* working again . . . No, I've quit the theatre . . . $150 a week . . . Well, I don't see why you should get 10 per cent of *that,* Tom. . . . All right, *take* me off your list! You haven't got me a job in six years, not even modeling! (*Hangs up.*)

MISS SHOTGRAVEN (*a new respect*). Why, Mrs. Partridge! I didn't know you'd been in the theatre.

MRS. PARTRIDGE (*quite calmly*). Really, dear?

MISS SHOTGRAVEN. It must have been terribly exciting! Especially in the old days!

MRS. PARTRIDGE. The old days, Miss Shotgraven, were strictly n.g. That means no good. Rehearse for ten weeks without pay, go on the road and the company manager would make off with the receipts. That happened to me once. And the worst of it was that I was married to him. That was the last time I saw him, except at the funeral. Poor Harry. Now, Miss—uh—what's that name of yours again?

MISS SHOTGRAVEN. Shotgraven. Amelia Shotgraven.

MRS. PARTRIDGE (*with new authority*). Oh, I'd change that if I were you.

MISS SHOTGRAVEN. Tell me some more of your experiences when you were acting.

MRS. PARTRIDGE. Not during business hours, Miss Shotgraven.

MISS SHOTGRAVEN (*back into her shell*). Quite right. Sorry.

MRS. PARTRIDGE. Now, Miss Shotgraven, is there any way of finding out some of the stockholders' names?

MISS SHOTGRAVEN. Well, there's the—uh—stockholders' directory.

MRS. PARTRIDGE. Would you bring it to me, please? (MISS SHOTGRAVEN *does so*.) Thank you.

MISS SHOTGRAVEN. This is somewhat irregular, Mrs. Partridge.

MRS. PARTRIDGE. Alabama, Arizona, Arkansas. I don't want anybody from Arkansas. We starved to death there. . . . Louisiana, Maine, Maryland. We did good business in Maryland. . . . Take a letter, Miss Shotgraven.

MISS SHOTGRAVEN. A letter, Mrs. Partridge?

MRS. PARTRIDGE. Yes.

MISS SHOTGRAVEN. To a stockholder?

MRS. PARTRIDGE. Mr. Blessington told me to make friends. . . . Ready?

MISS SHOTGRAVEN (*stiffly*). Yes, Mrs. Partridge.

MRS. PARTRIDGE. Mrs. Emily Woodbury—that's a friendly name, don't you think? Two-sixteen Fremont Street, Hagerstown, Maryland. Twenty-five shares. That's not too many—twenty-five—so she can't be rich. "Dear Mrs. Woodbury: My name is Laura Partridge, and I am a woman just like yourself, except that you probably have a husband and children, and I haven't. However, I am helping out here at General Products these days—just making suggestions. But I'm sure you also have some suggestions you would like to make—just little homey ones, about their stoves or sewing machines and things—or maybe you would like them to invent something. Because we have a lot of inventors here, and they haven't anything to do except invent. Hoping to hear from you soon" . . . Do you have all that written down, dear?

MISS SHOTGRAVEN. Yes, Mrs. Partridge.

MRS. PARTRIDGE. Well, you typewrite it out, and I'll go through the book for more places and names that sound good.

MISS SHOTGRAVEN. More?

MRS. PARTRIDGE. Now—Massachusetts, Minnesota, Mississippi . . .

(*She is turning pages of the directory*.)

THE CURTAINS CLOSE

The Narrator: MEANWHILE THE FOUR UGLY CORPORATION DIRECTORS WERE HAVING A WONDERFUL TIME. THEY WERE RUNNING THE COMPANY ALL OVER THE PLACE. TWICE A DAY THEY WATERED THE STOCK, TO KEEP IT FRESH. AND EVERY SATURDAY THEY TOOK A LONG PAIR OF GARDEN SHEARS AND TRIMMED THE DIVIDEND. ALL IN ALL, YOU WOULD NOT FIND A NICER BUNCH OF FELLOWS OUTSIDE OF A POLICE LINE-UP.

SCENE THREE

The big office.

*Three of the governing board of four are present—*METCALFE, BLESSINGTON *and* SNELL.

They are studiously regarding a beautiful blonde in a skimpy bathing suit—a luscious dame who is obviously there on business, but still luscious. She is holding a pose—about to dive. BLESSINGTON *circles around her, appraisingly.*

———

BLESSINGTON. Excellent, Miss L'Arriere. Excellent. . . . All right with you boys?

METCALFE (*a grunt*). All right.

(SNELL *grunts an assent and then* GILLIE *enters. Stops short on seeing the girl.*)

GILLIE. What's this?

BLESSINGTON. Advertising department. She's a model. She's from the advertising department.

GILLIE. We're not making bathing suits, are we?

BLESSINGTON. It's not for bathing suits, Warren. It's for—what is it again, Miss L'Arriere? What's the slogan?

MISS L'ARRIERE (*one of those awful voices*). "I had my swimming pool dug by a General Products steam shovel."

BLESSINGTON. There you are—it's for steam shovels.

GILLIE. Oh! Then why don't they use a steam shovel?

BLESSINGTON. Because nobody would want to look at a steam shovel. . . . All right, Miss L'Arriere.

MISS L'ARRIERE. Thank you, Mr. Blessington. (*She goes.*)

(METCALFE *goes to work at a little work table, sanding a piece of wood at an electrically run sand-papering machine. It makes a terrific whirr as he works it.*)

GILLIE. I've just been on the phone with Mr. McKeever down in Washington.

SNELL. What?

GILLIE. I say I've just been talking to Mr. McKeever on the phone.

SNELL (*unable to hear above the whirr*). Stop that thing a minute, will you, Al?

(METCALFE *shuts off the machine*.) What are you doing anyhow?

METCALFE. I'm making a chair leg.

SNELL. I wish you wouldn't do it when we're talking.

METCALFE. Look! You've got your hobbies, I've got mine.

SNELL (*ever the logician*). Yes, but my hobbies don't irritate me.

METCALFE. Okay—don't get sore.

SNELL (*turns to* GILLIE). What'd he say?

GILLIE. Who?

SNELL. McKeever, of course. What'd he *say?*

GILLIE. Nothing in particular.

SNELL. You mean you didn't take it up with him?

GILLIE. No.

SNELL. Why not? . . . Do you men realize we haven't had a single Government order since McKeever took that job?

BLESSINGTON. He's just leaning over backwards, that's all.

SNELL. Do you know what corporate earnings are going to look like this year?

METCALFE. Ed'll come through for us. I've known Ed for thirty years.

SNELL. Last December our gross dealings with the Government came to a hundred million dollars. That's before McKeever went down there. Since then, nothing.

GILLIE (*pulling a trick pen from his pocket*). Say, fellows, did I show you this gadget? Picked it up in a novelty store. It's a pen that lights up, so that you can write in the dark. . . . See?

BLESSINGTON. Is that what you do in the dark?

GILLIE. Well, I thought if you all liked it we might buy the patent and manufacture it ourselves.

(MISS L'ARRIERE *returns, dressed now in a feminine version of a railroad engineer's cap, gauntlets, and little else. She carries an idealized oil can*.)

BLESSINGTON (*hurrying to her*). Yes?— What's the slogan this time, Miss L'Arriere?

MISS L'ARRIERE. "My train is pulled by a General Products Diesel."

BLESSINGTON. Oh, yes . . . Excellent!

METCALFE (*studying the ensemble*). The neck ain't right.

BLESSINGTON. What?

METCALFE. The neck ain't right.

BLESSINGTON. What's the matter with her neck?

METCALFE. Not *hers*. The oil can's.

BLESSINGTON. Oh.

METCALFE. Ought to be straight. A Diesel oil can has a straight neck.

BLESSINGTON (*angrily*). I'll send a memo to Wilcox on it.

METCALFE. Okay.

BLESSINGTON (*now very sweet*). All right, Miss L'Arriere.

MISS L'ARRIERE. Thank you, Mr. Blessington. (*She goes*.)

GILLIE. Say! I have something to tell you fellows.

SNELL. About McKeever?

GILLIE. No! You know that little Apex Company? Massachusetts. We put them into bankruptcy yesterday.

BLESSINGTON. Splendid, Warren!

METCALFE. What's the Apex Company?

GILLIE. Apex Electric Clock Company. Pittsfield, Massachusetts. I found out we were taking a trimming from some little clock manufacturer up in New England—remember?

SNELL. Yes, yes.

GILLIE. Well, we aren't taking it from now on.

METCALFE. We buy 'em out?

GILLIE. Not me! I stole a leaf out of Mr. McKeever's book—*forced* 'em out. Undersold them by 50 per cent and kept on doing it until they cried "Uncle!" So yesterday, under they went.

BLESSINGTON. Marvelous, Warren!

GILLIE (*modestly*). Well, it'll look good in the annual report.

METCALFE. I don't know. Think we should have done that?

BLESSINGTON. Free enterprise, Al.

METCALFE (*returns to his machine*). Just the same, I can't forget that we were a little company once. (*Turns on his machine*.)

SNELL. Now if you fellows are finished there's something *I* want to take up.

METCALFE (*turns off his machine*). I just don't like the idea of putting little companies out of business.

SNELL. You know something, Al? You always turn that thing off when *you* talk, so that you can hear what *you're* going to say.

METCALFE. Okay, it's off. Now what is it?

SNELL. Well, it's that pheasant woman.

BLESSINGTON. Who?

SNELL. Pheasant, Partridge, whatever her

name is.

BLESSINGTON. What about her? It's only three weeks—can't let her go yet.

SNELL. I'll tell you what about her. She's costing us ninety-five dollars a week for postage, that's what about her.

(GILLIE *meanwhile has gone to the light switch and now plunges the room into darkness. He holds up the lighted pen triumphantly.*)

GILLIE. See what I mean!?

SNELL. Oh, for God's sake, Warren!

GILLIE (*puts on the lights*). How do you know she's costing us all that postage?

SNELL. I know because I got the figures from the mail room. She's writing letters to the stockholders, hundreds of them.

METCALFE. To the stockholders?

GILLIE. What's she doing that for?

SNELL. Some idea of Jack's—I don't know.

BLESSINGTON. Hold on! Just a moment! I didn't tell her to write to the stockholders. I said if any letters came in from the stockholders—

SNELL. Well, she's not waiting for 'em to come in.

GILLIE. What's *in* the letters—did you read 'em?

SNELL. Certainly I read 'em—some of them. Couldn't read 'em all.

GILLIE. What'd she say?

SNELL. Oh, how are you, and have they got any suggestions, and stuff like that.

METCALFE. Sounds harmless.

SNELL. What do *we* want with their suggestions? Damned fool idea in the first place, putting her in here. I must say, Jack, I didn't like the way you handled her, that day at the meeting.

BLESSINGTON. We've been over that a dozen times. She's here now, and we've got to keep her another three weeks. Do you want her to show up at the meeting again and raise hell!

SNELL. All I know is I don't like her writing those letters to the stockholders. It's not safe.

BLESSINGTON. What can we do about it? We can't fire her.

SNELL. I'll tell you what we can do about it. We can take her secretary away from her. Let her write six hundred letters a day by hand and see how she likes it.

(MISS L'ARRIERE *enters again. She is fully clothed, this time.*)

BLESSINGTON. Well? Something wrong,

Miss L'Arriere?

MISS L'ARRIERE (*indicating her hair*). "I'm wearing General Products bobby pins."

BLESSINGTON (*looks her up and down. He doesn't like it*). That's no good—no good at all. Very disappointing, Miss L'Arriere. Tell Mr. Wilcox I don't like it at all.

MISS L'ARRIERE. Yes, Mr. Blessington. (*She goes.*)

BLESSINGTON (*outraged*). Sending a girl in here dressed like that! What the hell's he thinking of!

(*And then the noon whistle blows.*)

THE FOUR OF THEM. Lunch! (*They hurry out. Lunch is lunch.*)

THE CURTAINS CLOSE

The Narrator: SO EVERY DAY CINDERELLA PUNCHED THE TIME CLOCK AND ATE WATERCRESS SANDWICHES IN THE COMPANY CAFETERIA. NOW ONE DAY SHE WAS WORKING AWAY IN HER OFFICE, HER LITTLE HEAD FILLED WITH HAPPY THOUGHTS, AND WONDERING WHETHER PRINCE CHARMING AND THE GOLDEN COACH WERE EVER GOING TO COME ALONG. AND AS SHE BUBBLED AND TOILED, TRYING TO TURN AN HONEST BUCK, SHE DREAMED ABOUT THE TIME WHEN THE PRINCE WOULD FIT THE GLASS SLIPPER ONTO HER DAINTY FOOT. LITTLE DID SHE THINK, AS SHE SAT THERE, THAT WHAT SHE WAS GOING TO GET WAS NOT A GLASS SLIPPER, BUT A GOOD SWIFT BOOT.

SCENE FOUR

LAURA PARTRIDGE's *office again.* MRS. PARTRIDGE *is alone, and dictating into the machine in a brisk and businesslike manner.*

MRS. PARTRIDGE (*consulting a letter in her hand*). . . . Salt Lake City, Utah. Dear Mrs. Avery, semicolon, paragraph. I was so delighted that you answered my letter of last week, period. Yes, comma, I have been in Salt Lake City twice, dash dash, once in 1906 and once in 1925, period. It is a beautiful city. I am so pleased that you are satisfied with the way General Products is being managed, period. I can assure you that earnings will be much higher for the next period, period. But remember, comma, dear Mrs. Avery, comma, if you ever have a suggestion to offer to your company, dash dash, I am always at the above address. I hope that I will hear from you again, comma, real soon, comma. I remain your new friend, and so forth, and so forth, et cetera. (*She puts the letter on the desk; picks up another*) Colonel William B. Butler, one-seven Ashton—A-s-h-t-o-n Street, Natchez, Miss. My dear Colonel, semi-colon, paragraph. Stop. Miss Shotgraven, use Form Letter for Men No. 5 here. And in the second paragraph insert, quote: "I have not had the pleasure of visiting your beautiful and romantic city since 1911, period. However, its memory is still with me, and I agree with you completely that Natchez is indeed the Jewel of the Swamps. (*She stops as* MISS SHOTGRAVEN *enters, carrying a large stack of letters.* MISS SHOTGRAVEN *has been to that little hairdresser, and the severe hairdo has been exchanged for a curly sweep-up.*)

MISS SHOTGRAVEN. Form Letter for Women, No. 8. A thousand of them.

MRS. PARTRIDGE. Thank you, dear. It's nice to have them on hand.

MISS SHOTGRAVEN. Lucky I got there when I did. The mimeograph department was getting ready to close.

MRS. PARTRIDGE. *This* early?

MISS SHOTGRAVEN. It's a quarter to five, Mrs. Partridge.

MRS. PARTRIDGE. Oh, dear. Already? Time just seems to fly. . . . So much work. We *are* doing a good job, aren't we, Miss Shotgraven?

MISS SHOTGRAVEN. *I* think so.

MRS. PARTRIDGE. I think so, too.

(JENKINS, *from the mail room, comes in, a few letters in his hand.*)

JENKINS. Afternoon, Mrs. Partridge.

MRS. PARTRIDGE. Hello, Mark.

JENKINS (*to* MISS SHOTGRAVEN). Hi.

MISS SHOTGRAVEN (*primly*). Good afternoon, Mr. Jenkins.

JENKINS. Few misdirected strays came in. Thought I'd deliver them myself. (*Handing her the letters*)

MRS. PARTRIDGE. That's very kind of you, Mark.

JENKINS. Service—that's all. (*To* MISS SHOTGRAVEN) How about dinner tomorrow night?

MISS SHOTGRAVEN. All right.

JENKINS. And next week we gotta go to the Music Hall. They're putting in a new screen that's twice as wide as the theatre (*He goes.*)

MRS. PARTRIDGE. Well! Next time I'm up around 53rd Street, I'm certainly going to drop in and compliment that little hairdresser.

MISS SHOTGRAVEN (*changing the subject*). I—I passed Mr. Snell's secretary in the hall. She gave me a memo for you.

MRS. PARTRIDGE. Thank you, dear. (*She glances at the memo and is rocked by what she reads.*) Oh!

MISS SHOTGRAVEN. Mrs. Partridge!

MRS. PARTRIDGE. They're—taking you away from me, Miss Shotgraven.

MISS SHOTGRAVEN. What?

MRS. PARTRIDGE. Mr. Snell. He says there's a retrenchment policy. And you have to leave. As of the close of this business day. That means—now.

MISS SHOTGRAVEN. But I don't want to leave you, Mrs. Partridge.

MRS. PARTRIDGE. What'll I do? I don't know how to typewrite. I don't know where the mimeograph department is. Or where they keep the postage stamps.

MISS SHOTGRAVEN. Perhaps I could drop in during my lunch hour, Mrs. Partridge.

MRS. PARTRIDGE. You are a very lovable young lady, Miss Shotgraven. And staunch, too. But, no. All of this will have to stop now.

MISS SHOTGRAVEN. I—I don't know what to say.

MRS. PARTRIDGE. They don't want me here. They don't want me here at all.

MISS SHOTGRAVEN. Mrs. Partridge, I'd like you to know that every minute I've worked for you . . . (*She chokes up; goes for her hat and purse.*)

MRS. PARTRIDGE. Miss Shotgraven, before you go, would you type one little note for me? Just make it a memo. *From:* Laura Partridge, *to:* Mr. Clifford Snell. Until now, I have enjoyed working for the General Products Corporation. As my usefulness is at an end, please accept my resignation. . . . Will you typewrite that now, dear?

MISS SHOTGRAVEN. No. Mrs. Partridge, this is a large organization. Sit here. Collect your check every week.

MRS. PARTRIDGE. It's getting late, dear. . . . Would you mind?

MISS SHOTGRAVEN. Do you want me to drop it at Mr. Snell's office on the way out?

MRS. PARTRIDGE. Would you?

MISS SHOTGRAVEN. Mrs. Partridge . . .

MRS. PARTRIDGE. What is it, dear? (*Her eyes, unseeing, are on another letter.*)

MISS SHOTGRAVEN. Good-by.

MRS. PARTRIDGE. Thank you for everything, Amelia. (MISS SHOTGRAVEN *goes.* MRS. PARTRIDGE *concentrates a little more on the letter before her, as though to check her own emotion. Presently she is actually reading it. She concentrates a little more —now she is both reading it and digesting it. She jumps to her feet.*) Miss Shotgraven! . . . Miss Shotgraven! (MISS SHOTGRAVEN *returns, hurriedly.*)

MISS SHOTGRAVEN. Yes, Mrs. Partridge?

MRS. PARTRIDGE. Miss Shotgraven, did you read the Company newspaper this morning? Didn't it say that General Products had eliminated one of its competitors —some company that makes clocks or something up in Pittsfield?

MISS SHOTGRAVEN. I—believe so. But—

MRS. PARTRIDGE. Then listen to this. It's from Pittsfield. "I received your letter and am writing to you right away because the strangest thing has happened. My husband has just lost his job after working for the same company for twenty-two years. It is one of our best companies here—the Apex Electric Clock Company. And the funny thing is that General Products bought the company just two years ago, and now everybody is saying that it was General Products that drove it out of business. Why would they do that to their own company, is what I want to know. Please answer as soon as possible."

MISS SHOTGRAVEN. I don't understand.

MRS. PARTRIDGE. Neither do I. . . . I wonder if it's true. (*Takes up the phone.*) Long distance! (*Back to* MISS SHOTGRAVEN) It does seem a funny thing to do, doesn't it—put one of their own companies out of business! (*Back to the phone*) I want Pittsfield, Massachusetts. I want the telephone number of Mrs. Henry Brooks, 141 Oak Street. . . . I'll pay for the call myself—this is Mrs. Partridge speaking.

MISS SHOTGRAVEN. Don't bother checking, Mrs. Partridge! It's our own company, all right. Here it is in our directory. (*Reads*) "Clocks, pendulum—General Products Divisions: Moline, Illinois, Baton Rouge, Louisiana; San Bernardino, California. . . . Clocks, electric: Apex Electric Clock Company, Pittsfield, Massachusetts!

MRS. PARTRIDGE. Cancel the call, operator! (*She hangs up.*)

MISS SHOTGRAVEN. What do you make of it?

MRS. PARTRIDGE. Their own company! Putting it into bankruptcy and it's their own company! . . . Boy! What I can do with this at the next stockholders' meeting! (*The phone again*) Mr. Snell's office, please! . . . What did you do with my resignation?

MISS SHOTGRAVEN. I put it in Mr. Snell's box.

MRS. PARTRIDGE. Get it back!

MISS SHOTGRAVEN. I can't! It's locked!

MRS. PARTRIDGE. Break it open! (*Into telephone*) I want to talk to Mr. Snell! . . . Take an axe if you want to—I guarantee he won't say a word! Those big geniuses! . . . Gone for the day! Well, it's pretty early for *him* to be waltzing out. . . . Yes, you *can* give him a message. What does he mean by taking away my secretary! . . . This is Laura Partridge! . . . .Yes, that's what I said, and tell him I'll be in to see him first thing in the morning. And I want those three other dummies there too. Good-by! (*She hangs up with a bang.*)

THE CURTAINS CLOSE

The Narrator: SO THE FOUR UGLY CORPORATION DIRECTORS TORE THEIR HAIR AND GNASHED THEIR TEETH, WHICH DID NOT MAKE THEM ANY LESS UGLY, AS YOU CAN IMAGINE. BUT NO MATTER HOW MUCH THEY SQUIRMED, ONE SIMPLE LITTLE FACT REMAINED: CINDERELLA HAD THEM BY THE SWANNEE RIVER.

SCENE FIVE

The big office again.
The Board of Directors are seated in discomfort on the edges of their chairs, like schoolboys. Behind the desk sits MRS. PARTRIDGE, *enjoying herself in the big chair.*

MRS. PARTRIDGE. Now let's see. Miss Shotgraven comes back to work as my secretary. (*She makes a big check mark on a list before her.*) Agreed?

BLESSINGTON (*swallowing hard*). Agreed.

MRS. PARTRIDGE. And she gets a ten dollar a week raise? (*Another check mark*) Is that agreed, Mr. Snell?

SNELL (*nearly choking on the words*). That's—right.

MRS. PARTRIDGE. And I can mail all the letters I want to? . . . That's agreed, too? (*They nod glumly.*) Now, what else was there?

BLESSINGTON (*after a pause*). Do you—do you mind if I smoke, Mrs. Partridge?

MRS. PARTRIDGE. Oh, good heavens no, go right ahead. It's your office, all of you. I do hope you're comfortable—those little chairs.

BLESSINGTON. Yes, indeed. Are you comfortable in that chair, Mrs. Partridge?

MRS. PARTRIDGE (*leaning back luxuriously*). Oh, very comfortable, thank you. (*The phone rings.*)

GILLIE. McKeever!

METCALFE. This must be our call. Do you mind, Mrs. Partridge?

MRS. PARTRIDGE (*rises*). Not at all.

METCALFE (*taking the phone*). Yeah? . . . I'm ready. (*Covering mouthpiece*) Washington . . . It's McKeever, all right.

BLESSINGTON. Be nice to him.

SNELL. Nice nothing! Give him the facts.

METCALFE. Hello, Ed. . . . Gosh, it's good to hear your voice again. How are you? . . . That's great. . . . Oh, just sitting around your old office. Cliff, and Jack, and Warren, and—uh—(*He decides not to mention* MRS. PARTRIDGE, *natch.*) . . . No, I finished the lamp table. Working on a chair now. Early American.

BLESSINGTON. Let *me* talk to him. . . . How've you been, Ed? . . . That's splendid . . . How'd you like yourself on the cover of *Time* last week? Looked very impressive, I thought. . . .

SNELL. Oh, for God's—give it to me! . . . McKeever, this is Cliff Snell. . . . Look, we can't understand why we haven't been awarded any Government contracts this year. . . . I'm aware there's no law that we have to get 'em. . . . Well, don't you think that if you looked into it personally . . . I'm aware it's up to the Government, but if you were to . . . Hello . . . Hello. (*Realizes he has hung up*) Won't even talk about it.

BLESSINGTON. There's gratitude for you. After that half-million dollar bonus we gave him.

SNELL. He didn't take it.

BLESSINGTON. He didn't. Where is it?

SNELL. It's in the treasury.

BLESSINGTON. What treasury?

SNELL. Ours, of course. Whose did you think?

BLESSINGTON. I was afraid you meant the United States Treasury.

SNELL. I can understand his being careful, but not to award us a single contract! Just because he used to head the company!

MRS. PARTRIDGE. But I don't think that's fair.

BLESSINGTON. Of *course* it isn't fair!

MRS. PARTRIDGE. What do I write my stockholders about the dividend?

SNELL (*annoyed*). Write 'em that because there's a stubborn old goat in Washington, the dividend will be less, that's all.

MRS. PARTRIDGE. But I've already written them that the dividend will be higher this year. They'll be so disappointed.

SNELL. Tell 'em to blame Ed McKeever, not us.

MRS. PARTRIDGE. I just can't do it. Those poor stockholders—the little ones, I mean.

GILLIE. The little ones don't lose as much as the big ones.

SNELL. We're sorry about the little stockholders, Mrs. Partridge, but they've got to take it as it comes. And it's not coming.

MRS. PARTRIDGE. But suppose I talked to Mr. McKeever, and told him about the little stockholders? You see, I've *promised* them.

GILLIE. I'm afraid it wouldn't do any good, Mrs. Partridge.

BLESSINGTON. No.

METCALFE (*slowly*). Mrs. Partridge is mighty good at talking.

BLESSINGTON (*thinks it out*). And she does represent the little stockholders. She's one herself.

GILLIE. He just might listen to her.

SNELL (*a quick decision*). Get him back on the phone!

METCALFE. That's no good. She's got to talk to him—face to face.

BLESSINGTON. Exactly the way she's just done with us.

SNELL (*wheeling on* MRS. PARTRIDGE). Do you think you could do it? . . . Would you, Mrs. Partridge, go down to Washington, and tell Mr. McKeever about the little stockholders?

GILLIE. Just the little ones, mind you!

BLESSINGTON. Don't mention the big ones!

MRS. PARTRIDGE. Well, if you think I could do any good . . .

BLESSINGTON. Certainly you could do good. Take some of their letters along.

MRS. PARTRIDGE. Yes . . . Yes . . . When would you want me to go?

METCALFE. The sooner the better!

BLESSINGTON. Tomorrow! Can you go tomorrow?

MRS. PARTRIDGE. I—I guess so. What time?

BLESSINGTON. Eight-thirty train! Would you mind, *one morning,* eight-thirty?

SNELL. Just one morning.

MRS. PARTRIDGE. But—what do I do?

SNELL. Just tell him about the little stockholders!

GILLIE. The littler the better!

MRS. PARTRIDGE. Yes, I know, but—

BLESSINGTON. We'll get you a ticket—drawing room, everything!

MRS. PARTRIDGE. But—when I get to Washington—

BLESSINGTON. We'll have somebody at the station—take you right to him. All you've got to do is to talk!

METCALFE. Just the way you did here.

GILLIE. Remember the little stockholders!

MRS. PARTRIDGE (*the big decision*). I'll do it!

SNELL. Good for you!

METCALFE. That's great!

BLESSINGTON. Good luck!

GILLIE. And thank you, Mrs. Partridge.

MRS. PARTRIDGE. You're welcome.

BLESSINGTON. I can't tell you how grateful we all are.

MRS. PARTRIDGE. Oh, that's all right—well—I won't see you gentlemen again, then, before I . . . Good-by. . . . Good-by. . . . Good-by. . . . Good-by. (*She makes the rounds*) I'll just tell him it isn't fair.

GILLIE. To the little stockholders!

SNELL. And make him listen to you!

MRS. PARTRIDGE. Now don't you worry about a thing. Any of you. (*She addresses them all.*) I've played Washington before. (*She goes.*)

THE CURTAINS CLOSE

The Narrator: SO CINDERELLA WENT TO MEET HER PRINCE CHARMING. PRINCE CHARMING WAS BALD AS A HONEYDEW AND FIFTEEN POUNDS OVERWEIGHT, BUT HE ALSO HAD FIFTEEN MILLION DOLLARS, WHICH DID NOT MAKE HIM ANY LESS CHARMING, AS YOU CAN IMAGINE. RIGHT NOW THE PRINCE HAD THE ENTIRE UNITED STATES GOVERNMENT ON HIS NECK, AND IT IS WELL KNOWN THAT THE PENTAGON ALONE WEIGHS FOUR HUNDRED MILLION TONS.

SCENE SIX

MC KEEVER's *office in Washington.*

An enormous room with an enormous desk—on it a phone and nothing else. In the background an American flag.

MC KEEVER *is alone in the room. In his shirt sleeves, he is pacing and reading a report.*

The phone rings. It will ring a lot.

MC KEEVER. McKeever! . . . Clarence! . . . What the hell happened to South America? . . . I know it's down there, but what's happening? . . . And where are those cruisers? . . . What cruisers do you think? The same ones that I've been yelling about for six months! . . . Well, I want a meeting of all bureau chiefs tomorrow morning at eight o'clock. Fly 'em in—I want 'em here. (*Puts down the report. Takes off coat; runs around the desk.* MISS LOGAN, *his secretary, enters with a letter for him to sign. The phone rings.*) McKeever! . . . The note to Malenkov? How do *I* know? . . . Just Moscow, Russia, ought to reach him. (*Hangs up. Growls to himself.*) Call me for everything! (*He starts a squatting exercise.* MISS LOGAN *enters with a newspaper. He continues squatting up and down. She starts to squat up and down in unison with him as he reads the paper. The phone rings.*) McKeever! . . . No, I can't give you the data on Nato—the Nato on data—(*Desperate, but gets it out*) The data on Nato! (*He stretches out on the desk and starts doing a bicycle exercise. The phone rings again.*) Miss Logan! (MISS LOGAN *runs on, picks up the phone and puts it to his ear.*) McKeever! . . . No! We can't christen any more ships with champagne. Use seltzer. We're trying to balance the budget. (*He flops back on the desk again.* MISS LOGAN *replaces the phone, then kneels down deside him and whispers in his ear.*) Who? (*She whispers again.*) Send her in. (*He gets off his desk and dons his coat. Meanwhile* MISS LOGAN *ushers in* MRS. PARTRIDGE. *She has donned her best bib and tucker for the occasion.*)

MRS. PARTRIDGE. How do you do?

MC KEEVER. How do you do? Now I'll do all the talking! I've got to make this fast, because any minute the phone'll ring and it'll be the goddam Senate wanting me to come over for some more questions.

The Senate, Mrs.—you're Mrs.—uh—

MRS. PARTRIDGE. Partridge. Mr. Blessington said—

MC KEEVER. Yes. Jack Blessington told me you were coming. The Senate, Mrs. Partridge, is driving me crazy. Absolutely crazy! I'm there every day, seems to me. Just settling down to work here, getting out the stuff, and bang! The goddam Senate says come over and answer questions— what I'm doing, what I'm not doing, *why!* A Senator, Mrs. Partridge, is the only man on God's green earth who is allowed to talk forever without knowing what he's talking about and nobody can stop him! Nobody! Greatest timewaster in the world, the United States Senate, and there's nothing anybody can do about it! Absolutely nothing! I'm there for hours—days! Weeks!

MRS. PARTRIDGE. Well—

MC KEEVER (*as the phone rings*). McKeever! . . . NO! The French can't have it! (*Hangs up.*) Now, I know why you're here, Mrs. Partridge—I know just what you're after! The answer is NO.

MRS. PARTRIDGE. But—

MC KEEVER. Remember—this isn't business, down here. Not like business at all. I've made a discovery, here in Washington, and I'll tell you what it is. Honesty! Just plain honesty. I'm not used to it yet, but I'm starting to get the hang of it. Been in business all my life and a man can't change overnight. Anyhow, I'm working on it, and in another month or so I'll turn the trick. Because if you're not honest down here they catch you at it and then you *do* get hell. (*The phone rings.*) McKeever! . . . Okay for the Eskimos. (*Hangs up.*) So the answer is no. No contracts for General Products, Mrs. Partridge! (*He is now reading and signing still another report.*) Because if I give 'em to 'em the goddam Senate will be on my neck and I've had about all I can stand.

MRS. PARTRIDGE. You know, I sort of thought you'd be a big silent man. You're big, but you're not silent.

MC KEEVER. I've got nothing to be silent about.

MRS. PARTRIDGE. Now, why don't you sit down behind that desk and just be silent! It'll be good for you. Go on. Try it.—

(MC KEEVER *looks at her a second, then, as though hypnotized, sits in his chair. He looks at her for the next move.*)

MRS. PARTRIDGE. Fine! . . . I'd have

known you anywhere. You look just like your bust downstairs.

MC KEEVER. That isn't me. That's Stonewall Jackson.

MRS. PARTRIDGE. Oh, not here. Downstairs in the General Products Building.

MC KEEVER. Oh! (*He gets interested.*) There's a bust of me in the General Products Building?

MRS. PARTRIDGE. Yes, didn't you know? . . . It's very good, too.

MC KEEVER. A statue, eh? . . . Now, they didn't have to go and do a thing like that. How big is it?

MRS. PARTRIDGE. Oh, it's big. (*She indicates the size.*)

MC KEEVER. Whereabouts is it?

MRS. PARTRIDGE. Right across from the elevators. So it's the first thing you see coming in and going out.

MC KEEVER. Yeah?

MRS. PARTRIDGE. And on dark days there's a light in the ceiling that shines right down on your head.

MC KEEVER. Sort of a halo.

MRS. PARTRIDGE. Now don't tell me they forgot to write you about it.

MC KEEVER. I don't see a third of the mail that comes in. No time. And if I do get a minute the goddam Senate—

MRS. PARTRIDGE. Now, now!

MC KEEVER. What's the matter?

MRS. PARTRIDGE. You mustn't even think about the goddam Senate. That's what gets you all worked up.

MC KEEVER. How can I keep from thinking about it when—

MRS. PARTRIDGE. It just occurred to me. Are you Taurus the Bull?

MC KEEVER. How's that?

MRS. PARTRIDGE. I'm Leo the Lion. I was born July 25th. When's your birthday?

MC KEEVER. April 7th.

MRS. PARTRIDGE. Oh! You're Aries the Ram. No wonder you're successful in business. J. P. Morgan was a Ram too.

MC KEEVER. I don't think I'm following you, Mrs. Partridge.

MRS. PARTRIDGE. I have a hobby. Horoscopes.

MC KEEVER. Horoscopes? . . . Really? Can you tell fortunes?

MRS. PARTRIDGE. Heavens, no. That sort of thing is silly. But the Zodiac—it may not always be accurate, but you'd be surprised how often—well, let's take *you,* for example. You're a regular Ram. I can understand how you did all those things with General Products. Building it up to such a big company.

MC KEEVER. Tell me, Mrs. Partridge, how long have you been with the company?

MRS. PARTRIDGE. Not long.

MC KEEVER. What company you with before that?

MRS. PARTRIDGE. I wasn't with a company before. I was on the stage.

MC KEEVER (*high interest*). The stage? You mean an actress?

MRS. PARTRIDGE. Forty-six productions.

MC KEEVER. You don't say? You know something? I always had an idea *I*'d have liked to've been an actor.

MRS. PARTRIDGE. Oh, I'm glad you didn't, Mr. McKeever. It's a terrible business.

MC KEEVER. Always kind of fascinated me. Clyde Fitch, Shakespeare—did you ever do Shakespeare, Mrs. Partridge?

MRS. PARTRIDGE. Little bit. Not much.

MC KEEVER. Must have been wonderful.

MRS. PARTRIDGE. I never cared much for Shakespeare. He's so tiring. You never get to sit down unless you're a king.

MC KEEVER. I used to recite a lot when I was a boy. All kinds of things. Then—I didn't know—something happened—all of a sudden I was a businessman.

MRS. PARTRIDGE. You're lucky. Almost nobody makes a living in the theatre any more.

MC KEEVER. People used to think I was pretty good—well, for an amateur. Used to do recitations Friday afternoons—you know, in school.

MRS. PARTRIDGE. Oh, I'm glad you didn't go on the stage, Mr. McKeever. You're better off even *here*.

MC KEEVER. Still, would have been fun. Had one recitation—they used to applaud like anything after I finished.

MRS. PARTRIDGE. The applause is very nice, but the rest of it!

MC KEEVER. Then Professor Sleeth—that was our elocution teacher—he had me do it for the parents and everybody at the end of the term. They put it in the paper—nice write-up. "Spoke with real fire," it said. "Real fire."

MRS. PARTRIDGE. That's a good notice.

MC KEEVER. "Spartacus to the Gladiators."

MRS. PARTRIDGE. What?

MC KEEVER. That was the name of the piece—"Spartacus to the Gladiators."

MRS. PARTRIDGE. Oh.

MC KEEVER. You know, I still remember it.

MRS. PARTRIDGE. Really? Well, that happens—something that you learned when you were young, why, all your life—

MC KEEVER. "Ye call me Chief"—you wouldn't do me a big favor and listen to it, would you?—tell me what you really think?

MRS. PARTRIDGE. I'd love to.

MC KEEVER. Mind you, if you don't like it, say so.

MRS. PARTRIDGE. Oh, I will. Whenever I go backstage to somebody's dressing room . . .

MC KEEVER. Because *hell!* I'm never going to be an actor *now!* Be foolish, at my age. (*Hopefully*) Wouldn't it?

MRS. PARTRIDGE. Yes, it would.

MC KEEVER (*not the answer he wanted*). Uh—yes . . . Anyhow, here it is. I haven't done this for years, mind you.

MRS. PARTRIDGE. I know.

MC KEEVER. Not since I was a boy. (*All over again*) "Spartacus to the Gladiators": (NOTE: *This recitation is accompanied by overdramatic gestures. You'll just have to imagine them.*)

"Ye call me chief, and ye do well to call me chief who, for twelve long years, has met in the arena every shape of man and beast that the broad empire of Rome could furnish and has never yet lowered his arm. And yet I was not always thus, the savage chief of still more savage men. My ancestors came from old Sparta and settled among the vine-clad hills and citron groves of Cyracella. My early life ran quiet as the brook by which I sported. And when, at noon, I gathered the sheep beneath the shade and played upon my shepherd's flute, there was a friend, the son of a neighbor, who joined me in my pastime. One evening after the sheep were folded and we were seated beneath the myrtle which girded our cottage, my grandsire—an old man—was telling of Marathon and how a little band of Spartans, in a defile of the mountain, had withstood a whole army. I knew not then what war was, but my cheeks burned—I knew not why—and I grasped the knees of that venerable man until my mother, parting the hair from off my forehead, kissed my throbbing temples and bade me go to rest and think no more of savage wars. . . . That night the Romans landed on our coast. I saw the bleeding body of my father cast among the blazing rafters of our dwelling. . . . Today I killed a man in the arena. And when I broke his helmet clasp, behold! he was my boyhood friend. He knew me, smiled faintly, gasped, and died. The same sweet smile that I had marked when, in adventurous boyhood, we had scaled the lofty cliff to pluck the first ripe grape and bear it home in childish triumph. I told the Praetor that the dead man had been my friend and begged that I might bear away the body to burn it on the funeral pyre and mourn over it in silence. Aye, amid the dust of the arena did I beg that poor boon. But the Praetor drew back as though I were pollution and sternly said, "Let the carrion rot. There are no noblemen but Romans." (*He bows to* MRS. PARTRIDGE *by way of signifying its finish. And about time.*)

MRS. PARTRIDGE. Oh, I'm awfully glad you didn't try to be an actor, Mr. McKeever.

MC KEEVER. You are?

MRS. PARTRIDGE. Yes, because—

MC KEEVER (*the phone rings*). McKeever! . . . Oh, good morning, Senator! . . . Yes, I'm fine. And you? . . . Did you read my report? . . . Well, just between us, what did you think of it? . . . What? . . . Before your committee? . . . But I was there yesterday. And twice last week. (*Sighs heavily.*) Very well, Senator. . . . Nine-thirty tomorrow morning. . . . Copies of all contracts. I'll be there. (*Hangs up.*) Well, there you are! . . . How they expect a man to get anything done—Miss Logan!—When he has to keep running to those committee rooms all the time—Miss Logan! (*She enters.*) Get everything ready—every contract, every letter! Every memorandum! I'm up before the goddam Senate again tomorrow morning. (*Pacing*) Enough to drive a man crazy! Senate, Senate, Senate!

MRS. PARTRIDGE. Poor Mr. McKeever! Why do you do it?

MC KEEVER. What?

MRS. PARTRIDGE. Why don't you refuse?

MC KEEVER. Refuse! It's the goddam Senate!

MRS. PARTRIDGE. Then why don't you quit?

MC KEEVER. What do you mean—quit?

MRS. PARTRIDGE. Just quit! Walk out and don't come back. You don't *have* to do this, Mr. McKeever—not if it's going to do this to you.

MC KEEVER. That's so, I don't.

MRS. PARTRIDGE. Besides, they need you back at General Products. I didn't want to come right out and say so, but those other men are terrible. They're going to ruin the company. There won't be any dividends at all.

MC KEEVER. Ruin the company? Miss Logan! . . . Mrs. Partridge, would you have lunch with me and talk some more about this?

MRS. PARTRIDGE. I'd be glad to.

MC KEEVER. I'm going out to lunch, Miss Logan. I'll be back in an hour—*two* hours, I don't know. . . . Where would you like to eat, Mrs. Partridge? Anywhere you say.

MRS. PARTRIDGE. You know what I've heard a lot about—where I'd love to go? The Senate Restaurant.

MC KEEVER. Oh, my God!

THE CURTAINS CLOSE

SCENE SEVEN

A giant television set.
A few wavy lines on the screen and an image comes into focus.
Sound: A bell

A VOICE. The Six O'clock News Roundup, Bill Parker Reporting!
(*We see a newsroom, teletype machines clanging, clocks in background. A chair, microphone, a reporter*)

PARKER. Good evening, ladies and gentlemen—here are the headlines. A resignation in Washington, a tornado in Texas, and a lady with fourteen children in Alaska sells her cow! Now let's have a look at the top story of the day. This afternoon, in the nation's capital, one of the Government's key figures, Edward L. McKeever, handed in his resignation. Members of both parties were stunned. Senate leaders in particular are at a loss as to why McKeever decided to leave Washington. And here are first films rushed directly to our news-room of McKeever as he left the nation's capital this afternoon.

(*The film shows* MC KEEVER *standing beside a plane. In front of him is a reporter with cable and microphone.*)

REPORTER. What significance, Mr. McKeever, does your resignation have?

MC KEEVER. I just decided to quit. No significance. No significance at all.

(*Back to the Announcer*)

PARKER. Mr. McKeever was accompanied by an unidentified friend.

(*Shot of* LAURA PARTRIDGE *as* MC KEEVER *helps her up the first step. She turns, apparently in response to a question. There is an enigmatic smile on her face.*)

(*More wavy lines on the screen, indicating a passage of time. Another newsroom. A map on the wall, a new reporter sitting behind another desk.*)

REPORTER. A very good evening, ladies and gentlemen. This is Dwight Brookfield bringing the eleven o'clock news right into your own living room. And the big news tonight still centers about the sudden move made earlier today—a move *out* of Washington, *out* of the Government. One high administration source was quoted as saying that McKeever's abrupt departure is causing grave inconvenience to certain parties in certain parties. McKeever, meanwhile, was undergoing an inconvenience of his own. Heavy thunderstorms over the Middle Atlantic States forced his plane down in Philadelphia a few hours ago. Told of the furore his action had caused in Washington, Mr. McKeever refused to comment.

(MC KEEVER *and* LAURA PARTRIDGE *are seen descending the plane stairway, greeted by reporters.*)

MC KEEVER. Sorry, boys, no comment. I'm not a talker, you know.

(*Back to the studio*)

REPORTER. Mr. McKeever was accompanied by a woman reported to be a business associate.

(MC KEEVER *steps aside—and guess who has been behind him all the time. You're right.*)

(*More wavy lines and again a passage of time. This time it is a woman reporter—behind her a bookcase flanked by two windows with chintzy curtains.*)

A VOICE. And now, Estelle Evans and the high noon news bulletin, a compendium of events of local, national and international importance to you and your family. . . . Miss Evans.

MISS EVANS. Good afternoon, ladies. I'll have the weather, the fashions and the shopping for you in just a second. But first, I'd like to tell you in word *and* picture about the latest developments in a front-page story that I know will interest you as much as it fascinates me. Edward L. McKeever—you all know who *he* is—he resigned from that big job in Washington yesterday—well, this morning Mr. McKeever arrived at his New York office from Philadelphia. And—this is what will interest you ladies—still accompanying him was the mystery woman who traveled with him from Washington late last night.

(*Shot of* MC KEEVER *and* LAURA *getting out of a limousine in front of the General Products building*)

A REPORTER. Pardon me, lady, would you mind telling us who you are?

MRS. PARTRIDGE. Oh, I'm not anybody. Not anybody at all.

(*Back to the studio*)

MISS EVANS. Well! Despite the mystery woman's denial, informed circles in Washington were busy speculating this morning on the strange circumstances of Mr. McKeever's resignation. Did he break with the administration or did the millionaire widower leave his high post because of a woman? In other words, ladies, is Edward McKeever a modern Marc Antony, captivated by a wily and seductive Cleopatra?

(*The television set goes off.*)

SCENE EIGHT

Back at General Products.

MC KEEVER *is at the desk—the other directors grouped at his side.*

Several reporters are present, and they have apparently been giving MC KEEVER *a time.*

The flashlights snap.

MC KEEVER. All right, boys, that's enough pictures! Let's run this just the way the President runs his conferences. First a statement, then questions.

A. P. MAN. Excuse me, Mr. McKeever—Sullivan, A. P.

MC KEEVER. Questions afterwards—here's your statement. Ready?

U. P. MAN. I'm Turner, Mr. McKeever—U.P.

I. N. S. Mathewson, I. N. S. We'd like—

MC KEEVER. I know what you'd like—get out your pencils. I'm only going to say it once, so get it down. "Political differences had absolutely no bearing on my resignation. My confidence in the Administration and its policies—"

I. N. S. Sorry, Mr. McKeever—that's not the story we're after.

U. P. What about the woman?

A. P. Yeah—who's the woman?

MC KEEVER. Nobody at all.

BLESSINGTON. Nobody at all.

(*The three other men murmur assent.*)

MC KEEVER. Just an old friend.

I. N. S. Where is she?

A. P. What's her name?

MC KEEVER. Her name is Mrs. Laura Partridge and she works for this company.

BLESSINGTON. Yes.

MC KEEVER. She came to see me on business and *that's all*.

BLESSINGTON. Absolutely all.

(*The other men agree. They will agree to anything, in their present spot.*)

U. P. Where is she?

I. N. S. Can we see her?

MC KEEVER. Certainly. We have nothing to conceal. Always willing to co-operate with the press.

BLESSINGTON. Yes indeed.

MC KEEVER. Come in, Mrs. Partridge.

(MRS. PARTRIDGE *enters—somewhat cautiously. It is clear that this entrance has been rehearsed.*)

U. P. How do you do, Mrs. Partridge?

MRS. PARTRIDGE. (*carefully*). How do you do?

U. P. You work for the company, Mrs. Partridge?

MC KEEVER. Yes, she does.

(*The other men concur.*)

MRS. PARTRIDGE. Yes, I do.

I. N. S. Doing what?

MC KEEVER. She's in charge of—er—

BLESSINGTON. Of stockholder relations.

MRS. PARTRIDGE. I'm in charge of stockholder relations.

MC KEEVER (*somewhat gratuitous*). She's in charge of stockholder relations.

A. P. Why did you go to see Mr. Mc-Keever?

MC KEEVER. She came to see me on business.

BLESSINGTON. Yes. On business.

(*The others agree.*)

MRS. PARTRIDGE. I went to see him on business.

U. P. Had you known him long?

MC KEEVER. No, no.

(*The other men deny it also.*)

MRS. PARTRIDGE. Goodness, no. I hadn't met him until yesterday.

I. N. S. You left Washington yesterday afternoon.

MC KEEVER. Yes, she did.

(*More concurring*)

MRS. PARTRIDGE. Yes, I did.

U. P. And you got here this morning?

MC KEEVER. Yes, sir.

(*The yes-men are right on the job.*)

MRS. PARTRIDGE. Yes, sir.

I. N. S. Where did you spend the night?

MC KEEVER (*he had not expected this*). Why—uh—

THE OTHER MEN. Uh—(*But they are stumped.*)

MRS. PARTRIDGE (*this one had not been rehearsed, but she is an honest woman*). We were at the Hotel Barclay in Philadelphia.

MC KEEVER (*quickly*). On separate floors!

THE FOUR OTHER MEN. Separate floors!

MRS. PARTRIDGE (*a little late, would you say?*) On separate floors.

(*But the newspaper boys have swung into action. A couple of them whip* MRS. PARTRIDGE *up onto the desk. One and all are ready with their cameras.* MC KEEVER *and the four stooges don't even want to look. They turn away, hiding their faces frantically beneath their coattails.*)

MRS. PARTRIDGE (*smoothing down her ruffled skirt*). Now, now! No cheesecake!

(*The flashlights pop. And it is rather surprising, in the circumstances, that a couple of arteries don't pop too.*)

THE CURTAIN FALLS ON ACT ONE

ACT TWO

SCENE ONE

The General Products office again.

The office is empty. But just when you are beginning to think that the boys have all shot themselves, BLESSINGTON *enters—a pile of newspapers under his arm.*

He settles down at the desk; reads busily if not happily.

METCALFE *is next. Also with papers.*

METCALFE. Have you seen the papers? (*Getting no answer, he too settles down to read.*)

(*Then* WARREN GILLIE. *More papers.*)

GILLIE (*he has the hard luck to pick the same line*). Have you seen the papers?

BLESSINGTON (*with full sarcasm*). No, Warren, we have *not seen* the *papers*. For the past twenty-four hours we have been living in a tree.

GILLIE. Well, what are we going to do about it? It's dreadful.

BLESSINGTON. It's not as bad for you as it is for me. You're not married.

GILLIE. I don't see what that's got to do with it.

BLESSINGTON. Well, if you were married to Mrs. Blessington you'd damn well see! According to her, *I* took that woman to Philadelphia.

GILLIE. Well, at choir practice last night, the whole choir was buzzing about it. Right in the middle of a Handel oratorio.

METCALFE. What's there to buzz about? This has got nothing to do with General Products!

BLESSINGTON. She works for us, doesn't she? The Partridge woman!

METCALFE. A lot of women work for us. Maybe they've *all* been to Philadelphia.

BLESSINGTON. Just the same, it's not good for the company. We sell things for the *home,* don't forget. Have you seen the wires we got this morning? Have you heard about the phone calls?

GILLIE. I've got an idea. Why don't we take a big ad? Full page in every paper in the country.

METCALFE. What'll we say in it?

GILLIE. Well, I . . . haven't gotten that far yet.

METCALFE. "Take a General Products diesel locomotive next time you go to Philadelphia."

GILLIE. Well, it wouldn't cost anything. It would come off taxes. And, maybe we could get that Hotel Barclay in Philadelphia to pay part of it.

BLESSINGTON. We've got to get rid of her, that's all.

METCALFE. We can't do that. That would only make it look worse.

BLESSINGTON. Well, if we don't get rid of her, it looks as though we're afraid of her.

GILLIE. Well, aren't we?

(CLIFFORD SNELL *arrives.*)

SNELL. Well, I hope you're satisfied! You boys have got us in a hell of a spot.

BLESSINGTON. This wasn't any idea of mine, Clifford. When I go to Philadelphia, I always stay at the Bellevue-Stratford.

SNELL. I don't give a damn about Philadelphia. It's her bringing McKeever back that's going to make trouble.

BLESSINGTON. You don't think he's going to want his old job again, do you?

SNELL. I know this. He's going through the building right now shaking hands with all the employees.

GILLIE. What's he doing that for?

SNELL. How do I know? Some habit he picked up in Washington.

BLESSINGTON. But if he comes back he'll want to be Chairman of the Board again.

METCALFE. And President of the company.

BLESSINGTON. A lousy Vice-President again. Back to the masses.

SNELL. Now, listen. . . . If the four of us stick together, we can freeze him out. We've got the votes, haven't we?

BLESSINGTON. True enough.

GILLIE. Do you think we should?

METCALFE. I don't like doing this to Ed.

SNELL. We've got to do it. You want to keep your jobs, don't you? Your bonuses? Your stock options?

GILLIE (*a thoughtful pause*). Well—if you put it *that* way.

SNELL. Then don't any of you weaken. McKeever's a hell of a talker.

BLESSINGTON. But what about the woman? God knows what she's going to do next!

SNELL. Leave the woman to me.

METCALFE. Think you know how to handle her, Cliff?

SNELL. I know how to keep her away from the stockholders' meeting. And that's the main thing!

BLESSINGTON. How?

GILLIE. Yes, how?

SNELL. While you boys have been reading those newspapers, *I've* been doing some thinking. There's one sure way to reach her. Astrology. (*He unrolls a horoscope chart which he brought in with him.*) Now, here's the way this thing works. (*He looks them over.*) Once you're born, you're done for.

(*The heads of the four uglies come*

closer together as they study the chart.)
(*The lights fade.*)

The Narrator: WELL, I WOULDN'T SAY THAT THE BOYS WERE GETTING GREEDY, EXACTLY, BUT THEY WERE NOT FAR FROM IT. AT THE VERY LEAST, THEY WERE BEGINNING TO FEEL THEIR OATS—AND SERVED WITH PLENTY OF RICH CREAM THEY MADE A TASTY DISH. YES, SIR, THE BOYS WERE IN THE SADDLE, AND THEY THOUGHT THAT NOTHING COULD STOP THEM. BUT A FEW HUNDRED YEARS AGO A WISE OLD PHILOSOPHER MADE A VERY WONDERFUL REMARK—ONE THAT WE SHOULD ALWAYS REMEMBER. HE SAID: "JOE, YOU NEVER CAN TELL."

SCENE TWO

Back to MRS. PARTRIDGE's *office.*

MISS SHOTGRAVEN *and* JENKINS *are locked in a long, long embrace. You could definitely say they like each other.*

As MRS. PARTRIDGE *enters they spring apart.*

JENKINS. Oh! (*He darts out.*)

MISS SHOTGRAVEN (*pulling herself together as well as she can*). I'm sorry, Mrs. Partridge. I promise you it won't happen again.

MRS. PARTRIDGE. Why not, darling?

MISS SHOTGRAVEN (*trying to be business-like*). The telephone has been ringing steadily. You have a great many messages.

MRS. PARTRIDGE. More? . . . Those terrible headlines! Weren't they wonderful?

MISS SHOTGRAVEN. *Life* magazine called up, and *Look,* and *Sensible Sex Weekly.* I don't know what *they* wanted.

MRS. PARTRIDGE. Pictures, probably. Send everyone who wants a picture to Vandamm. They took some lovely ones of me in 1926.

MISS SHOTGRAVEN. And several television producers, and—a lot of agents. I couldn't find out what they were agents *for.*

MRS. PARTRIDGE. Flesh, dear. Just flesh.

MISS SHOTGRAVEN. I beg your pardon?

MRS. PARTRIDGE. It's been a long time, Miss Shotgraven, since *they* called *me.* . . . Of course, it all comes a little late. . . . Don't let life go past you, Miss Shotgraven. Jump aboard it while you're young.

MISS SHOTGRAVEN (*on the edge of tears*).

Oh, Mrs. Partridge, if I only could!

MRS. PARTRIDGE. Why, Amelia, darling, what's the matter? (*But* MISS SHOTGRAVEN *just bursts into tears.*) Sit down here. (*An arm around her*) Now tell me what it is. (*More tears*) Are you in trouble? (*Fresh tears*) Bad trouble? . . . Who's the man? (MISS SHOTGRAVEN *gestures vaguely.*) Mark? It's all my fault. You were so unattractive with your hair the other way. And now see what's happened! . . . I suppose it wouldn't help now to put your hair back again. (*Tears again*) Have you told him?

MISS SHOTGRAVEN. Told him what?

MRS. PARTRIDGE. About your condition?

MISS SHOTGRAVEN. What condition?

MRS. PARTRIDGE. Then you're not going to—I mean, you aren't—

MISS SHOTGRAVEN. Of course not! How could you think such a thing?

MRS. PARTRIDGE. Well, in my day, when a girl said she was in trouble—she was in trouble.

MISS SHOTGRAVEN. We can't afford to get married. He has to support his mother and sister, and I don't want to live with them.

MRS. PARTRIDGE. It *would* be crowded, wouldn't it?

(*More tears, broken by the entrance of* MR. SNELL.)

SNELL. Well, well! Good afternoon, Mrs. Partridge.

MISS SHOTGRAVEN. Excuse me, please. (*She hurries out.*)

SNELL (*looking after her*). Something wrong?

MRS. PARTRIDGE. Cinders. Both eyes.

SNELL (*squaring off*). Mrs. Partridge, when is your birthday?

MRS. PARTRIDGE. Oh, Mr. Snell, you don't have to give me anything.

SNELL. It so happens, Mrs. Partridge, that the stockholders' meeting has been changed to the 14th of the month. And on the 14th, Mrs. Partridge, Saggitarius will be in the ascendency for those born under the Lion. You realize what that means.

MRS. PARTRIDGE. Oh! You're talking about my horoscope.

SNELL. Yes, Mrs. Partridge. It will be a very bad day for you to go out.

MRS. PARTRIDGE. Oh, you don't expect me to go by *that* damned nonsense.

SNELL (*somewhat stunned*). You—don't believe in astrology?

MRS. PARTRIDGE. Not for stockholders'

meetings.

SNELL. I see. (*It needs a new attack.*) Mrs. Partridge, I wonder if you realize the position in which you have placed us.

MRS. PARTRIDGE. I'm terribly sorry.

SNELL. You were sent to Washington, Mrs. Partridge, to persuade Mr. McKeever to revise his attitude toward this company. Instead, you brought Mr. McKeever back to New York.

MRS. PARTRIDGE. But he was so unhappy there. He was a nervous wreck—you should have seen him.

SNELL. We want to protect you, Mrs. Partridge. We are very fond of you here at General Products.

MRS. PARTRIDGE. Oh, Mr. Snell.

SNELL. So we don't want you to feel that you *must* attend the forthcoming stockholders' meeting. You would be stared at, whispered about. We don't want you to be embarrassed.

MRS. PARTRIDGE. Oh, I'd like it.

SNELL. So to spare your feelings, Mrs. Partridge, we are prepared to buy your stock in the company. You're a good business woman. What would you say to five thousand dollars? That would be seventeen points over the market value.

MRS. PARTRIDGE. Seventeen? That's my lucky number. I signed for the best part I ever had on the 17th. It was in 1917, and the play ran for 17 months.

SNELL. Fine! Now if you'll just sign this form, transferring the stock to us, you can bring the certificate in tomorrow. And here is our check for $5,000.

MRS. PARTRIDGE. Oh, I want more than that if I'm going to be bribed, Mr. Snell.

SNELL. Bribed! Who said anything about being bribed?

MRS. PARTRIDGE. You did. Why, when I show this to the other stockholders—

SNELL. Show what to the other stockholders? (*He is stuffing the paper and check into his pocket.*) May I remind you, Mrs. Partridge, that you have no witnesses?

(*And* MC KEEVER *enters.*)

MC KEEVER. Hope I'm not interrupting business.

MRS. PARTRIDGE. Oh, good afternoon, Mr. McKeever.

SNELL. Excuse me, Old-timer. (*And he goes.*)

MCKEEVER. Old-timer! In the Klondike I would have killed a man for that.

MRS. PARTRIDGE. Klondike! Did you ever see *Belle of the Klondike?*

MC KEEVER. I didn't see any women in the Klondike. I went there for gold. Dug for it with my bare hands.

MRS. PARTRIDGE. Mercy! Did you get any?

MC KEEVER (*shakes his head*). Fellows with shovels were ahead of me. That's where I learned my first lesson: the little man doesn't stand a chance. But the trip was worth it. I met Robert W. Service. (*This reminds him, and at once he goes into* "The Shooting of Dan McGrew," *with gestures.*) "A bunch of the boys were whooping it up in the Malamute Saloon"—

MRS. PARTRIDGE (*hastily*). Yes, yes. . . . And after the Klondike?

MC KEEVER. Johannesburg. Diamonds. But the more I knocked around the more I realized: can't get ahead being a little fellow. Got to be big. So I came home. Worked my way back as a common seaman—(*Stiffens up*)—lashed to the mast for seventy-two hours—typhoon.

MRS. PARTRIDGE. Gracious!

MC KEEVER Landed in Frisco—started my own business.

MRS. PARTRIDGE. At last!

MC KEEVER. Lumber. Six months later they broke me. The Trust!

MRS. PARTRIDGE. Wasn't that mean of them?

MC KEEVER. No. It was business. Big business. So I made up my mind then and there. Looked around for the biggest outfit I could find and went to work at the bottom of the pile.

MRS. PARTRIDGE. The slag pile. I remember.

MC KEEVER. Old-timer! I should have fired him fifteen years ago, when I caught him taking paper clips home. So what happened? I'm out and they're in! And why? Because I sold my stock. There's the goddam Senate for you again!

MRS. PARTRIDGE. You've got to do something, Mr. McKeever.

MC KEEVER. Thirty-nine years with this company. When I went to Washington they gave me a gold key to this building. It's about all I have left.

MRS. PARTRIDGE. There'll be no dividends at all, with those men running things! Think of the stockholders!

MC KEEVER. Are you a stockholder?

MRS. PARTRIDGE. Ten shares.

MC KEEVER. Do you want my help?

MRS. PARTRIDGE. Oh, yes, Mr. McKeever!

MC KEEVER. You've got it! (*He weighs the situation.*) Now to get *them* out and take this company over again.

MRS. PARTRIDGE (*encouragingly*). That's it!

MC KEEVER. First time was easy. But these boys are smart—that's the reason I put 'em *in* there. . . . (*Thinking hard*) Must be a way. All's fair in war and business, and by God! This is both!

MRS. PARTRIDGE. I only wish I could help.

MC KEEVER (*the glimmer of an idea*). Maybe you can.

MRS. PARTRIDGE. I'll do anything!

MC KEEVER. Tell me. When they sent you down to Washington—(*He stops, thoughtfully.*)

MRS. PARTRIDGE. Yes? (*He is still thinking.*) What is it?

MC KEEVER. They *did* send you down to Washington, *didn't* they?

MRS. PARTRIDGE. Yes!

MC KEEVER (*an edge of excitement in his voice*). They bought your railroad ticket, and they had you met at the station, and they delivered you to my office!

MRS. PARTRIDGE. Yes, they did.

MC KEEVER. To get Government contracts! Contracts for General Products!

MRS. PARTRIDGE (*catching a little of his excitement*). Yes!

MC KEEVER. Will you testify to that? Will you testify to that in court?

MRS. PARTRIDGE. Of course!

MC KEEVER. Then we've got them! There just happens to be a law against that, Mrs. Partridge! A Federal law!

MRS. PARTRIDGE (*a flash of divination*). I know! The Mann Act! (*And that's that.*)

SCENE THREE

Again the television screen.
A bell rings.

A VOICE. The six o'clock news round up, Bill Parker reporting.

PARKER. Good evening, ladies and gentlemen. First a look at the top story of the day—the United States Government versus General Products, Incorporated.

(*Shot of* LAURA *and* ED MC KEEVER *ascending the courthouse steps. They are both smiling and happy, and nod gayly to passers-by.*)

PARKER (*his voice heard over the film clip*). Up the steps of the Federal Courthouse in New York's Foley Square this morning went Mrs. Laura Partridge, key witness for the Government. Her purpose: to testify against directors of the mammoth General Products Corporation, charged with violation of the Smith-Wadsworth Anti-Lobbying Act. With her went businessman Edward L. McKeever, former Washington department head, who, the Government charged, was pressured by General Products directors. . . . A little later Clifford Snell, treasurer of General Products, and one of the accused men gives a statement to our television reporter.

(*We see* SNELL, *in a corner of the building, lighting a cigarette, talking to a reporter, microphone in hand*)

SNELL. Mrs. Partridge's testimony is completely untrue. The decision to seek contracts in Washington was entirely her own. Speaking for the directors of General Products, we did not even know that she had gone to Washington until we read about it in the newspapers.

(*And now we go to* DWIGHT BROOKFIELD *and the second newsroom, used in Act I.*)

BROOKFIELD. A very good evening, ladies and gentlemen. This is Dwight Brookfield bringing the eleven o'clock news right into your own living room. At exactly four-thirty this afternoon, the Government's case against one of the nation's largest corporations came to an abrupt end. A federal jury refused to convict the corporation's directors, and instead severely censured Mrs. Laura Partridge, the Government's chief witness. Subsequently, Federal Judge Manson J. Madison also criticized Mrs. Partridge's action, declaring that as a stockholder in General Products she stood to profit by influencing a government employee in its favor.

(*LAURA and* ED MC KEEVER *are shown coming down the courthouse steps. They have newspapers over their heads to thwart the photographers, and are plainly trying to evade questioning reporters. As the reporters become more importunate they quicken their steps, finally breaking into a run. At the foot of the steps they find a taxi—reporters crowding close.*)

The Narrator: SO CINDERELLA WENT AWAY FROM THERE, CLOSELY FOLLOWED BY

REPRESENTATIVES OF THE TIMES, THE TRIB-UNE, THE NEWS, THE MIRROR, THE POST, THE JOURNAL, THE WORLD-TELEGRAM, AND WOMEN'S WEAR. AND THIS SHOULD TEACH EVERYONE A GREAT LESSON. WHENEVER YOU SEE A LAWYER, ANYWHERE, RUN LIKE HELL.

SCENE FOUR

The big office.
The unholy quartet are ranged behind the desk this time. And it is MRS. PARTRIDGE *who is sitting nervously before them.*

SNELL. So under the circumstances, Mrs. Partridge, I'm afraid that's the way it will have to be.

MRS. PARTRIDGE. You're angry because I testified for the other side. That's why you're discharging me.

BLESSINGTON (*not very convincing*). Why, not at all, Mrs. Partridge!

GILLIE. Not at all!

SNELL (*unctuous*). Nothing could be further from our minds.

MRS. PARTRIDGE. Hasn't my work been satisfactory?

BLESSINGTON. Yes, indeed. Very much so.

MRS. PARTRIDGE. Letters are coming in every day, hundreds of them.

METCALFE. We know that, Mrs. Partridge.

MRS. PARTRIDGE. If it's another retrenchment move, I'd be willing to take a slight cut.

SNELL. I'm afraid not.

MRS. PARTRIDGE. Say a hundred dollars. Just because I like the work.

SNELL. No, no.

MRS. PARTRIDGE. Eighty-five? That's Equity minimum.

SNELL. The cashier has your check waiting for you, Mrs. Partridge, terminating your employment as of this afternoon. (*Rising*) And now if you will excuse us—

MRS. PARTRIDGE. Of course. . . . No one wants to say anything else? (*There is silence.*) Well, I do. . . . The way you men are running things, I wouldn't be surprised if this company closes on Saturday night. (*And she goes.*)

BLESSINGTON. What did she mean by that?

SNELL. What's the difference what she says? There's nothing she can do any more.

GILLIE. I'm kind of worried about it.

BLESSINGTON. She might still show up at the meeting—queer everything.

SNELL. Not a chance! After the way the judge laced into her? Nobody would listen to a word she said. . . . No, sir, we're in the clear. Forget about that grouse woman —we're going to have our biggest year.

METCALFE. We are?

SNELL. You bet we are! With McKeever out of Washington we're starting to get Government contracts again.

BLESSINGTON. And *are* we soaking them! You know those ten million filing cabinets we got stuck with last year?

GILLIE. Yes?

BLESSINGTON. Well, we pressed them down flat and sold 'em to the Government for fences.

METCALFE. What's the Government want with all those fences?

BLESSINGTON. Indians. You can't let 'em run around, can you?

SNELL. Yes, sir, our biggest year! And, gentlemen, *no excess profits tax.*

GILLIE. Why not?

SNELL. Because there isn't any any more.

GILLIE. Oh, I thought maybe we just weren't going to pay it.

SNELL. Anybody want a drink?

BLESSINGTON. I wish you fellows would bring a bottle of your own in here some day. My expense account is beginning to look outrageous.

SNELL. $1155 last month. I checked it myself.

BLESSINGTON. Who told you to stick your nose into my business?

SNELL. I'm Treasurer, you know. . . . Say, *we* didn't drink all that whiskey, did we?

BLESSINGTON. It wasn't just whiskey—there were other things. (*His watch*) Four-thirty. . . . Would you fellows mind taking your drinks and drifting into one of the other offices?

METCALFE. Not going to work, are you, Jack?

BLESSINGTON (*the phone*). Miss Condon. I forgot. Get my home—tell Mrs. Blessington I've got to stay in town tonight.

SNELL (*raising his glass*). Well, boys! Here's to General Products! And to us!

GILLIE. You're sure nothing can happen? I'm still a little nervous.

SNELL. Relax, Warren—She's probably got her check and is out of the building by this time. (*His glass on high again*) To General Products!

BLESSINGTON. General Products!

GILLIE. General Products!

(*And* MC KEEVER *stalks in. There is a chorus of greeting: "How do you do, Mr. McKeever." "Ed!" "Hello, Ed!"*)

MC KEEVER (*not even a curt nod. Takes off his coat and throws it onto a chair*). On your feet, goddam it! All of you!

GILLIE (*placatingly*). Now look here, Mr. McKeever—

METCALFE. What the hell's the matter with you, Ed?

SNELL. Take it easy, McKeever. You'll get ulcers.

MC KEEVER. I don't *get* ulcers. I *give* 'em.

SNELL. What kind of grandstand play is this?

MC KEEVER. I want you to give that woman her job back.

BLESSINGTON. My dear fellow!

METCALFE. Is *that* all?

BLESSINGTON. The way you steamed in here, one would have thought it was something important.

MC KEEVER. It's important to *me*.

SNELL. May I ask why?

MC KEEVER. Because she loves that job, and I want her to have it back.

GILLIE. Of course, Mr. McKeever.

SNELL. Well! We'd like to help you, Mc-Keever. But it puts us in rather an untenable position. She's been dismissed—severance papers sent through half an hour ago. You know your own policy—never rescind an order.

MC KEEVER. I don't give a damn about details. I want her back.

SNELL. You don't mean to say that the great Ed McKeever came in here just to ask for an old lady's job?

MC KEEVER. I know what's eating you. The trial. That wasn't her doing. It was mine.

SNELL. Then how do you have the gall to come here and ask a favor!

BLESSINGTON. Something in what he says, Ed—when you come to think of it.

GILLIE. Fair's fair, you know, Mr. Mc-Keever.

MC KEEVER. I'm just telling you to give that woman her job back.

SNELL (*entirely too quietly*). You're not telling us anything.

MC KEEVER. Yes, yes. These are your offices now, aren't they? Not mine. You're

running the company, not me.

SNELL. And don't get the idea you can do anything about it.

BLESSINGTON. He's right, Ed. Be sensible. We've got control, the four of us.

METCALFE. For old times' sake, Ed, I don't like to see you make a fool of yourself.

BLESSINGTON. Take my advice, Ed—don't make an issue of it.

MC KEEVER. Are you boys trying to tell me the financial setup of my own company?

SNELL. Our company.

MC KEEVER. My mistake.

SNELL. Times have changed, McKeever. And you're getting a little old.

MC KEEVER. Why, you miserable—

BLESSINGTON. Now hold on, Ed! Clifford's worked extremely hard for this company. We all have. It's all we've had our minds on, day and night.

(*And right on cue* MISS L'ARRIERE *enters. Mink coat, everything.*)

MISS L'ARRIERE. Honest to God, Jack, aren't you ever coming?—Oh, I didn't know you had a meeting, Mr. Blessington. Excuse me. (*And she tiptoes out.*)

MC KEEVER (*enjoying himself hugely*). Day and night, eh?

BLESSINGTON. I don't know what you're talking about.

MC KEEVER. I'll tell you what I'm talking about. Ruthie. The girl downstairs in the cafeteria that made the chicken croquettes. And the girl in the shipping department who had to come up here to keep you informed about what kind of twine we were using. And the receptionist who got pains from sitting so long, you had to let her rest on your couch.

BLESSINGTON. Really! (*As* SNELL *laughs*) Clifford!

MC KEEVER. Yes, I don't know what Snell's laughing about. Did I ever tell you boys about the night he got stuck in the transom, trying to sneak into my office? I never did find out what you were after that night, Snell. What was it?

SNELL (*pretty mean, by this time*). There's nothing here for you any more, McKeever. You're through. So why don't you get the hell out?

MC KEEVER (*looks at each one in turn. They fail to meet his eye. He takes the gold key from his pocket*). Thirty-nine years. Well, I don't need a key to get out. (*Tosses

the key onto the desk, turns and goes.)
(*Pretty tense, we can tell you.*)

The Narrator: WELL! THINGS LOOKED
PRETTY BLACK FOR CINDERELLA AND PRINCE
CHARMING, I CAN TELL YOU THAT. NOT ONLY
WAS THE GLASS SLIPPER LOST, IT WAS BROKEN
IN A THOUSAND PIECES. YOU PROBABLY THINK
THAT VIRTUE IS NOT GOING TO BE REWARDED.
BUT DON'T GIVE UP YET, BECAUSE IF CIN-
DERELLA DOES NOT WIND UP HAPPY, WE WILL
GIVE ALL YOU YOUR MONEY BACK. AND THERE
IS A FAT CHANCE OF THAT.

SCENE FIVE

LAURA PARTRIDGE's *office.*
MRS. PARTRIDGE, *having been fired, is
cleaning out her desk.*
*This is equivalent to a woman emptying
out her handbag, but on a large scale. The
things that come out of* MRS. PARTRIDGE's
*desk are quaint indeed, and yet rather to
be expected:*
    A sheaf of papers
    *A red galosh. But no second one, though
    she searches high and low*
    A coffee pot
    A cup and saucer
    A piggy bank
    A box of Lux
    A fan
    A mirror
    An umbrella
    An empty milk bottle
    A pair of nylons
    A raincoat
    A hot-water bottle
    *The second galosh, at last. From some-
    where in the bookcase*
    A girdle, from the filing cabinet
*She busily stows all these things into a
great brief case, then fishes up an old Variety from a bottom drawer and settles
down happily to read. At which point* MR.
MC KEEVER *strides in.*
MRS. PARTRIDGE. Oh, Mr. McKeever!
. . . Goodness. Imagine your walking in
on me like this. This place must look a
mess. I'm packing.
MC KEEVER. Yes, I know. And I'm burning mad.
MRS. PARTRIDGE. Nonsense. You mustn't
feel that way. I'm glad.
MC KEEVER. Glad that I didn't get you
your job back?

MRS. PARTRIDGE. Glad that I was here. Because if I hadn't been I never would have
learned about second breakfasts and things
like that. Oh, well. There's no business
like business.
(GILLIE *and* SNELL *stroll in.*)
SNELL. Now, my idea, Gillie . . . (*He
sees* MC KEEVER.) Oh, still here? . . . My
idea is to put shelves in here—wall to wall.
Floor to ceiling.
GILLIE. Floor to ceiling. Very good.
SNELL. We're going to use this room for
dead storage. You see, we're putting in a
whole new system. Modern. (*To*
MC KEEVER. *Right to* MC KEEVER) Because
once something is over and finished with,
McKeever, it's better to get it out of the
way. (*He turns back to* GILLIE.) And say
listen, why don't we go down to the cellar?
I'll bet we can find a spot down there for
that bust. (*A nasty look at* MC KEEVER, *and
they go.*)
MC KEEVER. I wish I knew about seven
new words.
MRS. PARTRIDGE. You'll beat them, Mr.
McKeever. You're Aries the Ram. You're
strong, forceful, determined.
MC KEEVER. Y'know, these past few
weeks, Mrs. Partridge, I've got to know
you pretty well. I hope you won't laugh at
what I'm going to say.
MRS. PARTRIDGE. I never laugh at you,
Mr. McKeever. Oh, you mean that recitation. That was the material, not you.
MC KEEVER. Anyhow, dropping in here
every few days the way I've been doing,
I've read some of those letters you've been
sending out. And I read some of the answers you got from the stockholders, too.
. . . Mrs. Partridge, I'll come right to the
point. I'm going back into business. What
would you think of joining me?
MRS. PARTRIDGE. Oh, I'm not a business
woman. Anyhow, not a real one. I haven't
done so well here at General Products.
MC KEEVER. Forget about General Prod-
ucts. It's big, but there's room for more
than one big show in this town.
MRS. PARTRIDGE. Oh, there certainly is!
Why, when the Hippodrome opened . . .
MC KEEVER. Yes. . . . Then what do you
say? We could sound a whole new note in
industry.
MRS. PARTRIDGE. Well, I don't know.
MC KEEVER. Edward L. McKeever &
Company.
MRS. PARTRIDGE. What?

MC KEEVER. Edward L. McKeever & Company.

MRS. PARTRIDGE. Well, I never was a star, but in my last three plays . . . Couldn't it be Edward L. McKeever *with* Laura Partridge?

MC KEEVER. Anything you say. McKeever & Partridge.

MRS. PARTRIDGE. Equal billing. That's very generous . . . but I don't know. . . .

MC KEEVER. Only before we go any further, there's something I've got to tell you.

MRS. PARTRIDGE. Yes?

MC KEEVER. I never would have mentioned it if this hadn't come up.

MRS. PARTRIDGE. What is it, Mr. McKeever?

MC KEEVER. It's something you ought to know. I hope it won't disturb you too much.

MRS. PARTRIDGE. You can tell me anything, Mr. McKeever. Anything.

MC KEEVER (*hangs his head*). I've only got fifteen million dollars. (*Looks up with a brave smile.*) But I've got a group of men behind me who'll come in on anything if I give the word.

MRS. PARTRIDGE (*she can understand this*). You mean you've got backers, too?

MC KEEVER. I guess that's what you call them.

MRS. PARTRIDGE. Well, with all that money, what would you think of starting a little repertory theatre?

MC KEEVER. Theatre?

MRS. PARTRIDGE. Repertory. That means doing a different play every night. Just good plays, you understand. I think it's the very thing New York wants.

MC KEEVER. A theatre, eh? Might be something in *that,* too. Would you act in it?

MRS. PARTRIDGE. Well, I could. Maybe some of the old Sarah Bernhardt plays. They had wonderful women's parts in them.

MC KEEVER. Ye-es. . . . What are the men's parts like in those shows?

MRS. PARTRIDGE (*Oh, no!*). On second thought, Mr. McKeever, I don't think New York is ready for repertory.

MC KEEVER. I wouldn't expect to play big parts—at least not right away.

MRS. PARTRIDGE (*firmly*). No, Mr. McKeever. I'm afraid we'd better forget that kind of partnership.

MC KEEVER. And you're sure you don't want to go into business with me?

MRS. PARTRIDGE. You're being very kind, Mr. McKeever, but it's a little late for me to start studying new lines.

MC KEEVER. Is there anything I can do for you? Anything at all? (MRS. PARTRIDGE *shakes her head, smiles.*) Well—what are you going to do?

MRS. PARTRIDGE. Oh, I've made arrangements. I'm going into the Actor's Fund Home.

MCKEEVER. Actors' Home? I couldn't let you do that.

MRS. PARTRIDGE. Oh, it's not like it sounds. You're perfectly independent there, and there are other actors and actresses, and lots of talk about show business. I'm signing over my ten shares of stock to them, but the dividends will be mine, as long as I live.

MC KEEVER. I see.

MRS. PARTRIDGE. If you'd like to, you can visit me sometimes. Englewood isn't a very long drive—with that big car of yours and the chauffeur. You will drive out, won't you, Mr. McKeever? My, that will impress those old character women, all right. . . . Well, I've got to be getting these things together. (*Picks up letters.*) All of these people that have been writing to me. I'm taking some of their letters home to answer—I really feel that they've sort of become friends.

MC KEEVER. Where'd you get this? (*Picking up a little green slip of paper*)

MRS. PARTRIDGE. It must have been in this letter. (*Looks at it.*) Yes. . . . Mrs. Weaver. (*She reads.*) "Enclosed please find photograph of Harold. It was taken last summer in the back yard next to the garage. Am also inclosing my proxy for the next stockholders' meeting." . . . Is that a proxy?

MC KEEVER. Yes, it is.

MRS. PARTRIDGE (*continues to read*). "I generally don't bother sending them back, but since you and I have been corresponding I feel much closer to the company. So I wrote your name in the blank space, because you are the only one at General Products I'm acquainted with. I hope it arrives in time." (*She looks again at the proxy.*) Thirty shares.

MC KEEVER (*delving into her pile of papers.*) Here's another one. Fifty shares. (*Reads from the accompanying letter*) "I am sending this to you because I feel that you have my interests at heart. I know that you will cast my vote for the best man there."

MRS. PARTRIDGE. My goodness, I don't know what to do with these. Do you, Mr. McKeever?

(MC KEEVER *nods sagely. At which point* MARK JENKINS *enters, pushing a small truck loaded to the gills with mail.* JENKINS *is pretty well mussed up—collar open, shirt torn. He is followed by an agitated* MISS SHOTGRAVEN.)

JENKINS. Well, I made it.

MRS. PARTRIDGE. Mark Jenkins! What's happened to you?

MISS SHOTGRAVEN. He's been fired! That's what's happened. A fist fight with Mr. Snell.

JENKINS. Laid him out cold, if you must know.

MC KEEVER. You did? Oh, that's too bad.

MRS. PARTRIDGE. But why?

JENKINS. He didn't want me to make this delivery.

MISS SHOTGRAVEN. Oh, Mark! *Now* what are we going to do?

JENKINS. I tell you, Mrs. Partridge, ever since I've been in the mail room, we've never had a flood like this.

MRS. PARTRIDGE (*picking up a letter*) It's another one of those proxy papers. Mercy! Two hundred shares.

MISS SHOTGRAVEN. Fifty-five shares!

MC KEEVER. A hundred and sixty!

MISS SHOTGRAVEN. Mark, close the door!

MC KEEVER. Three hundred shares! Mark, lock the door!

(*But* SNELL *and* BLESSINGTON *have entered, full steam ahead.*)

SNELL (*to* BLESSINGTON). Here you are! See for yourself! You and that damned letter writing you put her up to!

BLESSINGTON. Just a moment, Mrs. Partridge! What is the meaning of this! (*To* SNELL) You're sure these are all proxies?

SNELL. Of course, I'm sure! (*To* MRS. PARTRIDGE) You're not working for General Products any more, Mrs. Partridge! These are company property!

MRS. PARTRIDGE. Goodness! Well, I don't want any trouble.

MC KEEVER. Pardon me, gentlemen! These belong to Mrs. Partridge, all of them. Her name is on every one.

SNELL. That doesn't matter! A mere handful! We've got more than that up in the office.

JENKINS. No, you haven't, Mr. Snell!

There are five thousand letters here, and twice as many down in the mail room. All you've got is about three hundred.

(MC KEEVER *starts digging in the cart.*)

SNELL. Shut up, Jenkins! You've been discharged too!

(METCALFE *and* GILLIE *come hurrying in.*)

METCALFE. So this is where you are!

GILLIE. Why weren't we told about this?

SNELL. Oh, shut up, Gillie. I can lick *you!*

MC KEEVER. Five thousand letters! And they average about two hundred shares.

MRS. PARTRIDGE (*beaming*). Aren't they the darlingest people?

MC KEEVER. You don't realize it, Mrs. Partridge, but you're in control of this entire company.

MRS. PARTRIDGE. I am?

MC KEEVER. You certainly are!

SNELL. But that's purely technical, you understand, Mrs. Partridge.

MRS. PARTRIDGE. Goodness, I understand! I've learned about business. Well—This means just one thing. Gentlemen, you're all fired.

(*Everyone enjoys it except our four villains.*)

The Narrator: AND SO, A FEW DAYS LATER, ARM IN ARM WITH PRINCE CHARMING, CINDERELLA MADE ANOTHER TRIP DOWNTOWN. ONLY THIS TIME, NOT IN THE SUBWAY, NOT IN A COACH DRAWN BY SIX WHITE HORSES, BUT IN A SOLID GOLD CADILLAC, DRIVEN BY A SOLID GOLD CHAUFFEUR.

SCENE SIX

The stockholders' meeting.

ED MC KEEVER *and* LAURA *behind the big table*—MISS SHOTGRAVEN *at the side, busily taking notes. And no one else.*

MRS. PARTRIDGE (*on her feet, and obviously just finishing her contribution to the proceedings*). Respectfully submitted, at this, the sixtieth annual meeting of General Products, Incorporated. . . . Signed, Laura Partridge, Vice-President, Secretary and Treasurer.

MC KEEVER. You have heard the report of the Vice-President, Secretary and Treasurer. Those in favor say aye.

(JENKINS *brings on a great wire basket, filled with proxies.*)

MRS. PARTRIDGE (*blandly*). Voting 17 million shares by proxy, I say Aye. (*The old lucky number*)

MC KEEVER. All opposed? . . . Motion carried! (*But a little old lady gets to her feet.*) Yes, Madam?

OLD LADY. Excuse me. May I ask a question?

MRS. PARTRIDGE. Oh, no! That's how I got *my* start! (*She grabs the gavel and starts banging.*) The meeting is adjourned! The meeting is adjourned!

AND THE FINAL CURTAIN FALLS

ALBRIGHT, H. D.; HALSTEAD, WILLIAM P.; and MITCHELL, LEE. *Principles of Theatre Art*. Boston: Houghton Mifflin Co., 1955.

ALDRICH, RICHARD S. *Gertrude Lawrence as Mrs. A*. New York: Greystone Press, 1954.

ANGOFF, CHARLES. *The World of George Jean Nathan*. New York: Alfred A. Knopf, 1952.

BAILEY, MABEL DRISCOLL. *Maxwell Anderson: The Playwright as Prophet*. New York: Abelard-Schuman, 1957.

BARNES, ERIC W. *The Lady of Fashion*. New York: Charles Scribner's Sons, 1954. (The theatrical career of Anna Cora Mowatt, author of *Fashion*.)

———. *The Man Who Lived Twice*. New York: Charles Scribner's Sons, 1956. (The life of Edward Sheldon.)

BENTLEY, ERIC. *In Search of Theatre*. New York: Alfred A. Knopf, 1953.

———. *The Dramatic Event: An American Chronicle*. New York: Horizon Press, 1954.

———. *From the American Drama*. (*The Modern Theatre*, Vol. 4.) New York: Doubleday & Co., 1957. (A collection of 5 plays from *Captain Jinks* to *Guys and Dolls*.)

———. *What Is Theatre?* New York: Horizon Press, 1957.

BINNS, ARCHIE and KOOKEN, OLIVE. *Mrs. Fiske and the American Theatre*. New York: Crown Publishers, 1955.

BLUM, DANIEL. *A Pictorial History of the American Theatre, 1900-1956*. Revised Edition. New York: Greenberg, 1956.

BROWN, JOHN MASON. *As They Appear*. New York: Whittlesey House, 1952. (Contains play reviews by this brilliant writer.)

BOYLE, WALDEN P. *Central and Flexible Staging*. Berkeley: University of California Press, 1956.

CHAPMAN, JOHN. *The Best Plays of 1951-52*. New York: Dodd, Mead & Co., 1952.

———. *Theatre '53* (*Theatre '54, Theatre '55, Theatre '56*). New York: Random House, 1953 (1954, 1955, 1956).

CHEKHOV, MICHAEL. *To the Actor, on the Technique of Acting*. New York: Harper & Bros., 1953.

CHORPENING, CHARLOTTE. *Twenty-One Years with Children's Theatre*. Anchorage (Ky.): Children's Theatre Press, 1954.

CLURMAN, HAROLD. *The Fervent Years*. Revised Edition, with a chapter on the theatre from 1945 to 1955. New York: Hill & Wang, 1957.

COLE, TOBY and CHINOY, HELEN KRICH. *Directing the Play*. Indianapolis: Bobbs-Merrill Co., 1953.

COSGRAVE, LUKE. *Theatre Tonight*. Hollywood: House-Warren, 1955. (Theatre in the Southwest and West.)

COURTNEY, MARGUERITE. *Laurette*. New York: Rinehart & Co., 1955. (The life of Laurette Taylor.)

DERWENT, CLARENCE. *The Derwent Story*. New York: Henry Schuman, 1953.

DIETRICH, JOHN. *Play Direction*. New York: Prentice-Hall, 1953.

DOWNER, ALAN S. *Fifty Years of American Drama: 1900-1950*. Chicago: Henry Regnery Co., 1951.

ENGEL, EDWIN A. *The Haunted Heroes of Eugene O'Neill*. Cambridge: Harvard University Press, 1953.

ENGEL, LEHMAN. *Planning and Producing the Musical Show*. New York: Crown Publishers, 1957.

EWEN, DAVID. *Richard Rodgers*. New York: Henry Holt & Co., 1957.

FARNSWORTH, MARJORIE. *The Ziegfeld Follies*. New York: G. P. Putnam's Sons, 1956.

FELHEIM, MARVIN. *The Theatre of Augustin Daly*. Cambridge: Harvard University Press, 1956.

FORD, GEORGE D. *These Were Actors*. New York: Library Publishers, 1955. (The story of the Chapman-Drake family of actors who performed on the showboats and in the frontier theatres in the 19th century.)

FREEDLEY, GEORGE, and REEVES, JOHN A. *A History of the Theatre.* Revised Edition. New York: Crown Publishers, 1955.

GAGEY, EDMOND M. *The San Francisco Stage: A History.* New York: Columbia University, 1950.

GARD, ROBERT. *Grassroots Theatre: A Search for Regional Arts in America.* Madison: University of Wisconsin Press, 1955. (A discussion of rural theatre.)

GASSNER, JOHN. *Form and Idea in the Modern Theatre.* New York: Dryden Press, 1956.

———. *The Theatre in Our Times.* New York: Crown Publishers, 1954.

———. *Best American Plays: Third Series, 1945-1951.* New York: Crown Publishers, 1952.

———. *Twenty Best European Plays on the American Stage.* New York: Crown Publishers, 1957.

———. *Masters of the Drama.* New York: Random House, 1940. Third Revised and Enlarged Edition. New York: Dover Publications, 1954.

———. *Producing the Play.* Third Edition. New York: Dryden Press, 1953.

GAVER, JACK. *Critics' Choice: New York Drama Critics' Circle Prize Plays, 1935-1955.* New York: Hawthorn Books, 1955.

GREEN, ABEL. *Show Biz from Vaude to Video.* New York: Henry Holt & Co., 1951.

HEWITT, BARNARD; FOSTER, J. F.; and WOLLE, MURIEL SIBELL. *Play Production.* Philadelphia: J. B. Lippincott, 1952.

HUGHES, GLENN. *A History of the American Theatre, 1700-1950.* New York: Samuel French, 1951.

JONES, MARGO. *Theatre-in-the-Round.* New York: Rinehart & Co., 1951. (A history of the author's Dallas arena theatre.)

KAHN, E. J. *The Merry Partners.* New York: Random House, 1955. (The life and stage careers of Harrigan and Hart.)

KENDALL, JOHN S. *The Golden Age of New Orleans Theatre.* Baton Rouge: Louisiana State University Press, 1952.

KERR, WALTER F. *How Not to Write a Play.* New York: Simon & Schuster, 1955.

———. *Pieces at Eight.* New York: Simon & Schuster, 1957.

KINNE, WISNER PAYNE. *George Pierce Baker and the American Theatre.* Cambridge: Harvard University Press, 1954.

KRONENBERGER, LOUIS. *The Best Plays* (annually since 1952-53). New York: Dodd, Mead & Co., 1953, 1954, 1955, 1956, 1957.

KRUTCH, JOSEPH WOOD. *"Modernism" in Modern Drama.* Ithaca: Cornell University Press, 1953.

———. *American Drama Since 1918.* Amplified Edition. New York: George Braziller, 1957.

LANGNER, LAWRENCE. *The Magic Curtain.* New York: E. P. Dutton, 1951. (History of the Theatre Guild, its antecedents, and related enterprises.)

LAURIE, JOE. *Vaudeville.* New York: Henry Holt & Co., 1954.

LE GALLIENNE, EVA. *With a Quiet Heart.* New York: Viking Press, 1953. (An autobiography.)

McCLINTIC, GUTHRIE. *Me and Kit.* Boston: Little, Brown & Co., 1955. (The stage career of Katharine Cornell and the producer-director who is her husband.)

McGAW, CHARLES J. *Acting Is Believing.* New York: Rinehart & Co., 1955.

MacGOWAN, KENNETH. *A Primer of Playwriting.* New York: Random House, 1951.

MacGOWAN, KENNETH, and MELNITZ, WILLIAM. *The Living Stage: A History of the World Theatre.* New York: Prentice-Hall, 1955.

MANEY, RICHARD. *Fanfare: The Confessions of a Press Agent.* New York: Harper & Bros., 1957.

MAYORGA, MARGARET. *Best Short Plays of 1953-1954.* New York: Dodd, Mead & Co., 1954.

———. *Best Short Plays of 1955-1956.* Boston: Beacon Press, 1956.

———. *Best Short Plays.* 20th anniversary edition. Boston: Beacon Press, 1957.

MILLER, ARTHUR. *Collected Plays.* New York: Viking Press, 1957. (This volume contains much prefatory comment by the playwright.)

Moody, Richard. *The Astor Place Riot*. Bloomington: Indiana University Press, 1958.
———. *America Takes the Stage (Romanticism in American Drama and Theatre, 1750-1900)*. Bloomington: Indiana University Press, 1955.
Morris, Lloyd. *Curtain Time: The Story of the American Theatre*. New York: Random House, 1953.
Nathan, George Jean. *Theatre in the Fifties*. New York: Alfred A. Knopf, 1953.
Patrick, J. Max. *Savannah's Pioneer Theatre from Its Origins to 1910*. Athens: University of Georgia Press, 1953.
Playbook: Five Plays for a New Theatre. New York: New Directions, 1956. (American poetic plays including James Merrill's *The Immortal Husband*.)
Robbins, Phyllis. *Maude Adams—An Intimate Study*. New York: G. P. Putnam's Sons, 1956.
Ruggles, Eleanor. *Prince of Players*. New York: W. W. Norton & Co., 1953. (The life and stage career of Edwin Booth.)
Selden, Samuel. *Man in His Theatre*. Chapel Hill: University of North Carolina Press, 1957.
Shipley, Joseph T. *Guide to Great Plays*. Washington: Public Affairs Press, 1956.
Sievers, W. David. *Freud on Broadway*. New York: Hermitage House, 1955.
Sobel, Bernard. *Broadway Heartbeat*. New York: Hermitage House, 1953.
———. *A Pictorial History of Burlesque*. New York: G. P. Putnam's Sons, 1956.
Sothern, E. H. *Julia Marlowe's Story*, ed. Fairfax Downey. New York: Rinehart & Co., 1954.
Stevens, David H. *Ten Talents in the American Theatre*. Norman: University of Oklahoma Press, 1957.
Strickland, F. Cowles. *The Technique of Acting*. New York: McGraw-Hill, 1956.
Timerlake, Craig. *The Bishop of Broadway: The Life and Work of David Belasco*. New York: Library Publishers, 1954.
Van Druten, John. *Playwright at Work*. New York: Harper & Bros., 1953.
———. *The Widening Circle*. New York: Charles Scribner's Sons, 1957. (Van Druten's autobiography.)
Wilder, Thornton. *Three Plays*. New York: Harper & Bros., 1957. (*Our Town, The Skin of Our Teeth, The Matchmaker,* with a Preface.)
Wodehouse, P. G., and Bolton, Guy. *Bring on the Girls*. New York: Simon & Schuster, 1953. (A story of American musical comedy.)
Wright, Edward A. *A Primer for Playgoers*. New York: Prentice-Hall, 1958.
Young, John Wray. *The Community Theatre*. New York: Harper & Bros., 1957.
Zolotow, Maurice. *No People Like Show People*. New York: Random House, 1951.

A SUPPLEMENTARY LIST OF PLAYS

From the 1951-52 to the 1956-57 season*

A CLEARING IN THE WOODS. By Arthur Laurents. January 10, 1957. An imaginative psychological drama concerning a woman's traumatic experiences as recollected by her in an expressionistic manner of presentation.

A HOLE IN THE HEAD. By Arnold Shulman. February 28, 1957. An affectionate comedy of a romantic Miami hotel-keeper's difficulties with relatives who try to stabilize his life and that of his little orphaned son.

ALL SUMMER LONG. By Robert Anderson, based on the novel *A Wreath and a Curse* by Donald Wetzel. September 23, 1954. A reflective, somewhat symbolic drama of a family's chronic failure of understanding and deficient sense of reality which costs the life of a spirited lad who puts his elders to shame with his energy and courage.

A VERY SPECIAL BABY. By Robert Alan Aurthur. November 14, 1956. A short-lived but authentic study of a family dominated by a strong-willed father.

BAREFOOT IN ATHENS. By Maxwell Anderson. October 31, 1951. An historical drama, of contemporary suggestiveness concerning the struggle for freedom of thought, dealing with the martyrdom of Socrates.

BERNARDINE. By Mary Chase. October 16, 1952. A comedy of gauche adolescence and of the relations between youth and middle-age.

BULLFIGHT. By Leslie Stevens. January, 1954. An exciting dramatization of the emotions engendered by bullfighting, given an exciting off-Broadway production at the Theatre de Lys.

CAMINO REAL. By Tennessee Williams. March 19, 1953. A poetic fantasy "concerning the world's dispossessed," as the author put it, and symbolic of the struggle with a corrupt world and a tyrannical society.

CAN-CAN. A musical comedy, with book by Abe Burrows and music and lyrics by Cole Porter. May 7, 1953.

CANDIDE. A musical version of Voltaire's classic, with book by Lillian Hellman; lyrics by Richard Wilbur, John Latouche, and Dorothy Parker; music by Leonard Bernstein. December 1, 1956.

CAREER. By James Lee. April 30, 1957. An incisive treatment of an acting career; first produced by Nina Vance at the Alley Theatre in Houston, Texas, on August 28, 1956, and subsequently given an off-Broadway production in Greenwich Village.

DAMN YANKEES. A musical comedy by George Abbott and Douglass Wallop, based on Wallop's novel *The Year the Yankees Lost the Pennant*. Music and lyrics by Richard Adler and Jerry Ross. May 5, 1955.

END AS A MAN. By Calder Willingham. September 15, 1953. A drama of hazing and sadism in a Southern military school; an adaptation of the author's novel of the same name.

GIGI. By Anita Loos, based on the novel by Colette. November 24, 1957. A comedy of a girl's coming-of-age in a family of fashionable French courtesans.

HIGH NAMED TODAY. By David Z. Goodman. December, 1954. A study of the tensions of an American family with a long military tradition, produced off-Broadway at the Theatre de Lys in Greenwich Village.

* The date given next to each play is the date of the New York opening. Revivals are not listed.

IN THE SUMMER HOUSE. By Jane Bowles. December 29, 1953. The drama of a domineering woman and the timid daughter who ultimately rejects her.

JANE. By S. N. Behrman, based on a story by Somerset Maugham. February 1, 1952. A comedy of manners revolving around the theme of tolerance and the maneuvers of a clever middle-aged woman.

JANUS. By Carolyn Green. November 24, 1955. A triangle in which a common literary interest produces domestic complications.

JOHN BROWN'S BODY. Poem by Stephen Vincent Benét, produced as a "reading" by Paul Gregory (with Judith Anderson, Tyrone Power, and Raymond Massey). February 14, 1953.

KING OF HEARTS. By Jean Kerr and Eleanore Brooke. April 1, 1954. A comedy of an insufferably egotistic comic-strip artist who is deflated in the eyes of his adopted son and his secretary.

LADIES OF THE CORRIDOR. By Dorothy Parker and Arnaud D'Usseau. October 21, 1953. Scenes of failure and frustration in a residential hotel occupied by widows, divorcées, and spinsters.

LONG DAY'S JOURNEY INTO NIGHT. By Eugene O'Neill. November 7, 1956. O'Neill's autobiographical masterpiece, written about 1939.

MADAM, WILL YOU WALK? By Sidney Howard. December 1, 1952. A fantastic comedy about the Devil's benign influence on the frustrated daughter of a discredited political boss.

MIDDLE OF THE NIGHT. By Paddy Chayefsky. February 8, 1956. The romance of a middle-aged widower and an unhappily married young woman; noteworthy for the author's re-creation of ordinary life and, especially, for Edward G. Robinson's playing of the leading role.

MISTER JOHNSON. By Norman Rosten, based on the novel by Joyce Cary. March 29, 1956. A tragic picture of the conflict of white and Negro cultural patterns in South Africa, revolving around an impulsive young African clerk caught between two worlds.

MRS. McTHING. By Mary Chase. February 20, 1952. A fantastic comedy about a genteel woman's troubles with fractious children, mobsters, and a witch.

MRS. PATTERSON. By Charles Sebree and Greer Johnson, with songs and incidental music by James Shelton. December 1, 1954. A romantic semi-musical comedy about an overimaginative Negro girl and her fancies and dreams, a showpiece for Eartha Kitt.

MY 3 ANGELS. By Sam and Bella Spewack, a free adaptation of the French play *La Cuisine des Anges* by Albert Husson. March 11, 1953. A comedy about three convicts in the penal colony of French Guiana who rally to the defense of a family that has befriended them.

MY FAIR LADY. Musical adaptation of Bernard Shaw's *Pygmalion,* by Alan Jay Lerner (book and lyrics) and Frederick Loewe (music). March 15, 1956.

NEW GIRL IN TOWN. Musical version of O'Neill's *Anna Christie,* by George Abbott (book) and Bob Merrill (music and lyrics). May 14, 1957.

OH, MEN! OH, WOMEN! By Edward Chodorov. December 17, 1953. A comic romance between a psychoanalyst and his fiancée.

ORPHEUS DESCENDING. By Tennessee Williams. March 21, 1957. A revision of the author's *Battle of Angels,* produced by the Theatre Guild in 1940 but withdrawn in Boston. A naturalistic yet also symbolic drama of frustrations and violence in small-town Southern life.

POINT OF NO RETURN. By Paul Osborn, based on the novel by John P. Marquand. December 13, 1951. A rising young executive's evaluation of his situation and motivations.

SABRINA FAIR. By Samuel Taylor. November 11, 1953. A glossy comedy of a wealthy Long Island family and of its relations with a servant and his adventurous, cultivated daughter.

SILK STOCKINGS. A musical adaptation of the film *Ninotchka;* by George S. Kaufman, Leween McGrath and Abe Burrows (book); and Cole Porter (music and lyrics). February 24, 1955.

TAKE A GIANT STEP. By Louis Peterson. September 24, 1953. The drama of a Negro boy's growing pains in the North.

THE BAD SEED. By Maxwell Anderson, based on the novel by William March. December 8, 1954. A psychological drama dealing with a mother's discovery her little daughter is homicidal.

THE CLIMATE OF EDEN. By Moss Hart. November 6, 1952. A drama of psychological tensions in a missionary's home in the British Guiana jungle; based on Edgar Mittelhölzer's novel *Shadows Move Among Them.*

THE CRETAN WOMAN. By Robinson Jeffers. 1954-55. A free version of Euripides' *Hippolytus,* first produced at the Arena Theatre, Washington, D.C., and then at the Provincetown Playhouse, New York.

THE DESK SET. By William Marchant. October 24, 1955. A comedy about automation, revolving around a fabulously well-informed spinster, played by Shirley Booth, who is a match for almost any machine.

THE DESPERATE HOURS. By Joseph Hayes. February 10, 1955. A melodrama about a family man's struggle to save his wife and children from escaped convicts who have invaded his home; based on the novel of the same name by the same author.

THE DIARY OF ANNE FRANK. By Albert Hackett and Frances Goodrich, based on Anne Frank's famous *Diary of a Young Girl.* October 5, 1955.

THE EMPEROR'S CLOTHES. By George Tabori. February 9, 1953. A tense political drama set in Hungary in 1930, dealing with the troubles of a schoolteacher in a totalitarian state.

THE FIFTH SEASON. By Sylvia Regan. January 26, 1953. A comedy of harassed and antic business life in New York's garment center.

THE FLOWERING PEACH. By Clifford Odets. December 28, 1954. A philosophical folk-play about the Deluge, in which Noah appears as a Bronx patriarch in speech and manner.

THE GIRL ON THE VIA FLAMINIA. By Alfred Hayes. February 9, 1954. A drama of tragic misunderstanding between an American soldier and a spirited Italian girl after the liberation of Rome from the Germans; based on the novel of the same name by the same author.

THE GOLDEN APPLE. Musical play by John Latouche (book and lyrics) and Jerome Moross (music). March 11, 1954. An extravagant American folkplay, reworking the Homeric epics.

THE GRASS HARP. By Truman Capote. March 27, 1952. A poetic comedy about a meek spinster's revolt against a domineering sister.

THE GREAT SEBASTIANS. By Howard Lindsay and Russel Crouse. January 4, 1956. A comedy with a political background in communist Czechoslovakia, notable as a vehicle for the Lunts as a pair of professional mind-readers.

THE HAPPIEST MILLIONAIRE. By Kyle Crichton, based on *My Philadelphia Father* by Cordelia Drexel Biddle and Kyle Crichton. November 20, 1956. A comedy about brilliant eccentricity based on the life of Anthony J. Drexel Biddle.

THE IMMORALIST. By Ruth and Arthur Goetz, based on the novel by André Gide. February 1, 1954. A study of a young husband's losing struggle against homosexuality in French North Africa.

THE KING AND I. By Richard Rodgers and Oscar Hammerstein II. March 29, 1951.

THE MOST HAPPY FELLA. A musical adaptation of the late Sidney Howard's *They Knew What They Wanted,* by Frank Loesser. May 3, 1956.

THE PAJAMA GAME. Musical comedy by George Abbott and Richard Bissell (book) and Richard Adler and Jerry Ross (lyrics and music); based on Bissell's novel *7½ Cents.* May 13, 1954.

THE PONDER HEART. By Joseph Fields and Jerome Chodorov, based on a novel by Eudora Welty. February 16, 1956. A comedy of misunderstandings among extravagantly naïve persons in a deep-South hinterland.

647

THE RAINMAKER. By N. Richard Nash. October 28, 1954. A bizarre comedy about a lovable charlatan who promises to produce rain—and does, also managing to liberate a shy girl from her inhibitions.

THE REMARKABLE MR. PENNY-PACKER. By Liam O'Brien. December 30, 1953. A period comedy about an eccentric Philadelphia rebel against Victorianism who rears two families simultaneously.

THE SAINT OF BLEECKER STREET. By Gian-Carlo Menotti. December 27, 1954. An opera about a sickly girl and her unworldly aspirations in New York's Little Italy.

THE SHRIKE. By Joseph Kramm. January 15, 1952. A psychological drama about a ruthless woman and the sensitive husband she drives to desperation and institutionalizes as a mental case after his attempt at suicide.

THE TEAHOUSE OF THE AUGUST MOON. By John Patrick, based on the novel by Vern Sneider. October 15, 1953. An imaginative comedy about the American occupation of Okinawa.

THE TIME OF THE CUCKOO. By Arthur Laurents. October 15, 1952. A touching comedy about an American spinster's search for romance in Venice.

THE TRIP TO BOUNTIFUL. By Horton Foote. November 3, 1953. The comedy of an unhappy old woman's disillusioning attempt to return to the long-abandoned scene of her happy girlhood.

THE WISTERIA TREES. By Joshua Logan. February 2, 1955. A Southern transplantation of Chekhov's *The Cherry Orchard*.

TIME LIMIT! By Henry Denker and Ralph Berkey. January 24, 1956. A compassionate drama about the brain-washing of American captives in the Korean War.

TIME OUT FOR GINGER. By Ronald Alexander. November 26, 1952. A comedy about a girl who is infatuated with playing football but reassuringly settles for more feminine occupations.

VISIT TO A SMALL PLANET. By Gore Vidal. February 7, 1957. A fantastic farce about a visitor to earth from interstellar space, spiced with satire of human folly in peace and war.

WONDERFUL TOWN. Musical adaptation of the play *My Sister Eileen,* by Joseph Fields and Jerome Chodorov (book), with lyrics by Betty Comden and Adolph Green, and music by Leonard Bernstein. February 25, 1953.